ELVIS

HIS LIFE FROM A TO Z

FRED L. WORTH AND STEVE D. TAMERIUS

CB
CONTEMPORARY
BOOKS
CHICAGO · NEW YORK

Library of Congress Cataloging-in-Publication Data

Worth, Fred L.
    Elvis : his life from A to Z / Fred L. Worth and Steve D.
Tamerius.
        p.   cm.
    ISBN 0-8092-4528-0
    1. Presley, Elvis, 1935–1977—Miscellanea.   2. Presley, Elvis,
1935–1977—Dictionaries, indexes, etc.   I. Tamerius, Steve D.
II. Title.
ML420.P96W73   1988
784.5′4′00924—dc19
[B]   88-20332
                                                               CIP
                                                               MN

Published by Contemporary Books, Inc.
180 North Michigan Avenue, Chicago, Illinois 60601
Manufactured in the United States of America
Library of Congress Catalog Card Number: 88-20332
International Standard Book Number: 0-8092-4528-0

Published simultaneously in Canada by Beaverbooks, Ltd.
195 Allstate Parkway, Valleywood Business Park
Markham, Ontario L3R 4T8 Canada

To Kelli McWilliams
—F. L. W.

To my father and mother,
and Bonnie Tamerius,
and to my sister, Jeannie Cully
—S. D. T.

Contents

PART III: HIS MUSIC

Acknowledgments

First of all, we thank our photographers: Don Fink and his assistant Bonnie Redelings, Jeff Wheatcraft, John Dawson, and Mike Boyd.

Special mention should also go to Gary F. Patrick of Gary's Record Service, P.O. Box 5811, Colorado Springs, Colorado 80391. Gary provided most of the material in the novelty and tributes sections and was a tremendous help in some of the other musical entries as well. Howard DeWitt should also be singled out for his valuable assistance on the list of personal appearances made by Elvis.

Dozens of people have been supportive and helpful over the past several years, including (in alphabetical order) James Ahles, Alan's Custom Lab, Ben Armstrong Jr., John Beach, William T. Booth, Ernest Bowen, Bill Bram, Fred Burgess Jr., Bonnie Burnette, Kathy Burnette, Jim Carbonetti, Columbia Pictures, Fran Colvin, Dick Dekker, Dave Eckstrom of Forever Young Records (1221 W. Airport Freeway, #205, Irving, Texas 75062), Jimmy Ellis, Randy Erdman, Vivian Evans, Marty Fitzgerald, Marie Fletcher, Mrs. Tina Goffin, LeRoy Green Jr., Elvis D. Griffiths, S. K. Harvey, Brehon Herlihy, George Janssens, Mr. and Mrs. Robert Job, Glen Johnson, Stan Kesler, Tom Kirby, Pamela Larm, Gregory Larsen, Frank Leaver, Larry Lewis, Robert Lubowitz, Sandra Luther, Steve Matthes, Basil S. Mills, Mary Cannedy Missildine, Keith Mitchell, Todd Morgan of the *Graceland Express*, Bob and Kathy Nicholas (Elvis Video Club), Marge Nichols, Ilsa Ouellette, Miss Terry Owen, Darrell Parkinson, Beth Pease and Josh Cooke of the *Graceland News* (P.O. Box 161431, Memphis, Tennessee 38116), Barbara Reed, Bob Reed, Tandy Rice, Eddie Romberg, William Shutts, Mary K. Schneider, Herb Webber, Burbank Public Library, Lee County Library (Tupelo, Mississippi), Margaret Herrick Library at the Academy of Motion Picture Arts and Sciences, Memphis Public Library, Cinema Collectors, Eddie Brandt's Saturday Matinee, 20th Century–Fox, Paramount Pictures, MGM/UA, Universal Pictures, Warner Bros., Columbia Pictures Television, New World Television, Dick Clark Productions, and RCA Records.

We'd be remiss if we didn't mention our agent, Peri Winkler, and the wonderful staff at Contemporary Books: Nancy Crossman, Kathy Willhoite, Ilyce Glink, Lisa Waitrovich, and Al Simonaitis.

Preface

When *Variety* first tabbed Elvis Presley as the "King of Rock 'n' Roll" in October 1956, no one realized how enduring and appropriate that title would be. Elvis became a show business phenomenon without parallel. Because the music market is so fragmented today, it's unlikely that any performer will dominate the record charts the way Elvis did in the 1950s and early 1960s or sell as many records—now estimated to be over *one billion!*—as he did during his twenty-three-year career. The sales of his records have never stopped. Elvis is still big business eleven years after his untimely death.

More books have been published on Elvis (including one written by us a few years ago) than on probably any performer in history. Why so many books? Because the average Elvis fan has a voracious appetite for any morsel on the King. Never before, however, has any one book contained as much information as the one you are now holding in your hands.

Elvis: His Life from A to Z is separated into three parts to facilitate the location of facts. The portion devoted to Elvis's films is quite comprehensive—more so than entire books devoted to the subject. The cast lists are longer, the background information more detailed. And we doubt that the reader will ever find a more useful guide to Elvis's music career than that presented in Part III.

Our goal in writing *Elvis: His Life from A to Z* was to provide a one-stop reference guide to the King of Rock & Roll. We believe we've succeeded. Of course, we'll never be completely satisfied. There's so much to learn. In a book of this nature, there is bound to be an occasional mistake or omission, although we've made every effort to eliminate such problems. If you spot a mistake or omission, or just want to enlighten us with new or updated material, please write to us. We'd be particularly interested in rare, one-of-a-kind photos. Every song has a story behind its composition, and that information would be useful to us. We could also use biographical material on all the composers. If you know of any other songs sung by Elvis in concert, but never recorded, send the information to us, documenting the place and date. Precise dates on concert appearances in 1954 and 1955 are especially welcome. Complete foreign discographies from any country, especially Great Britain, France, West Germany, Japan, and Australia, would also be appreciated. We hope we'll have the opportunity to update this book sometime in the future. With your support, we will. Please send all correspondence to:

Steve Tamerius
Box 1275
Burbank, California 91507

A word about the Elvis Presley fan clubs. As far as we're concerned, the fan clubs are the glue that binds this Elvis phenomenon together. Elvis appreciated his fans and we do, too. We'd love to hear from the clubs. If feasible, we'd like to be added to your mailing list. Obviously, to subscribe to the hundreds of fan club newsletters—as we'd like to do—would be a financial impossibility.

Elvis had a number one record album in 1961 that sums up this book—*Something for Everybody*. We put a lot of time and effort into this book. We hope you enjoy it.

Quotations

THE PROS:

"The things that he did during his career, the things that he created, are really something important."
—*Bing Crosby*

"Without Elvis none of us could have made it."
—*Buddy Holly*

"Nothing really affected me until Elvis."
—*John Lennon*

"If I could find a white man who had the Negro sound and the Negro feel, I could make a million dollars."
—*Sam Phillips*

"To command such a large following, he must be a great performer." —*Paul Anka*

"He taught white America to get down."
—*James Brown*

"Elvis is the greatest blues singer in the world today."
—*Joe Cocker*

"Elvis Presley was a symbol of the country's vitality, rebelliousness, and good humor."
—*President Jimmy Carter*

"When I met him, he only had a million dollars worth of talent. Now he's got a million dollars!"
—*Colonel Tom Parker*

"Elvis is my man." —*Janis Joplin*

"There have been contenders, but there is only one King." —*Bruce Springsteen*

"The only possibility in the United States for a humane society would be a revolution with Elvis Presley as leader." —*Phil Ochs*

"There's no way to measure his impact on society or the void that he leaves. He will always be the King of Rock & Roll." —*Pat Boone*

"That boy can charm the birds right out of the trees."
—*Richard Egan (1956)*

"It was Elvis who really got me hooked on beat music. When I heard 'Heartbreak Hotel' I thought, This is it!"
—*Paul McCartney*

THE CONS:

"He can't last. I tell you flatly, he can't last."
—*Jackie Gleason*

"He can't sing a lick." —*Jack O'Brien*

"I wouldn't have Presley on my show at any time."
—*Ed Sullivan*

"I wouldn't let my daughter walk across the street to see Elvis Presley perform." —*Billy Graham*

"I want to count Elvis's hound dogs twenty years from now. Only time will tell if Elvis is collecting Cadillacs in 1976." —*Spike Jones in 1956*

"Mr. Presley has no discernible singing ability."
—*Jack Gould (New York Times)*

"Where do you go from Elvis Presley—short of obscenity, which is against the law." —*John Crosby*
(New York Herald Tribune in 1956)

"He [Elvis] never contributed a damn thing to music."
—*Bing Crosby*

"Elvis Presley was a weapon of the American psychological war aimed at inflicting a part of the population with a new philosophical outlook of inhumanity . . . to destroy anything that is beautiful in order to prepare for war." —*Youth World*
(East German Communist newspaper)

"The fact that someone with so little ability became the most popular singer in history says something significant about our cultural standards." —*Steve Allen*

"Extraordinarily untalented." —*John L. Wasserman*
(San Francisco Chronicle)

Chronology

June 17, 1893—Elvis's paternal grandmother, Minnie Mae Hood Presley, born.

June 26, 1909—Colonel Thomas Andrew Parker born.

April 25, 1912—Elvis's mother, Gladys Love Smith Presley, born.

April 19, 1916—Elvis's father, Vernon Presley, born.

June 17, 1933—Vernon Presley and Gladys Love Smith married in Pontotoc, Mississippi.

January 8, 1935—Elvis Presley born at 4:35 A.M. in East Tupelo, Mississippi. A twin brother, Jesse Garon Presley, was stillborn.

January 9, 1935—Jesse Garon Presley buried in the Priceville Cemetery northeast of Tupelo, Mississippi.

June 1, 1938–February 6, 1939—Vernon Presley served a term of imprisonment for forgery in the Parchman Mississippi Penitentiary.

May 25, 1945—Priscilla Ann Wagner (Beaulieu) born.

October 3, 1945—Elvis won second place in the talent show of the Mississippi-Alabama Fair and Dairy Show.

January 8, 1946—Elvis received a $7.75 guitar—his first—for his eleventh birthday.

September 12, 1948—The Presleys moved from Tupelo, Mississippi, to Memphis, Tennessee, and obtained a one-bedroom apartment at 572 Poplar Avenue.

September 13, 1948—Elvis enrolled at the Christine School.

February 1949—Vernon Presley began work for the United Paint Company.

June 17, 1949—Mrs. Jane Richardson, an advisor from the Memphis Housing Authority, interviewed the Presleys to see if they qualified for financial assistance. They did.

September 20, 1949—The Presleys moved from 572 Poplar Avenue to a two-bedroom apartment in the Lauderdale Courts at 185 Winchester Street.

1950—Memphis Recording Service founded by Sam Phillips.

June 3, 1951—Elvis began working at Precision Tool, lasting just one month.

September 1951—Elvis attended a few football practices at Humes High.

March 1, 1952—Sun 174 ("Blues in My Condition"/"Sellin' My Whiskey" by Jackie Boy and Little Walter) became the first release for Sun Records.

April 17, 1952—Elvis obtained a part-time job at Loew's State Theater. He was fired when he punched a fellow usher for telling the manager that Elvis was getting free candy from the girl at the concession stand.

August 6, 1952—Elvis began working at Upholsteries Specialties Company.

September 1952—Elvis began working for MARL Metal Products next door, but soon had to quit when his mother discovered he was falling asleep in school.

January 7, 1953—The Presleys were evicted from 185 Winchester and moved into an apartment house at 398 Cypress Street.

April 9, 1953—Elvis appeared in the Humes High Talent Show.

April 1953—The Presleys moved from 398 Cypress Street to a two-story apartment house at 462 Alabama Street.

June 3, 1953—Elvis graduated from L. C. Humes High School. He took the General Aptitude Test Battery at the Tennessee Employment Security in Memphis.

July 1953—Elvis began working for Crown Electric Company.

Summer 1953—On a Saturday afternoon, Elvis recorded "My Happiness" and "That's When Your Heartaches Begin" on a ten-inch acetate record at the Memphis Recording Service. He left with the original.

January 4, 1954—Elvis recorded "Casual Love Affair" and "I'll Never Stand in Your Way" on a ten-inch acetate at the Memphis Recording Service. He met Sam Phillips.

Early June 1954—Sam Phillips had Elvis try to record "Without You." It wasn't the sound Phillips was looking for, so he had Elvis sing several other songs that Elvis knew. None of them suited Phillips.

June 27, 1954—Elvis first met Scotty Moore and Bill Black at Moore's house. They rehearsed several songs before recording the following week at Sun Records.

July 5, 1954—Elvis's first commercial recording session at Sun Records. The first song put on tape was "Harbor Lights" followed by "I Love You Because." "That's All Right (Mama)" was recorded that evening.

July 6, 1954—Elvis recorded "Blue Moon of Kentucky."

July 7, 1954—Disc jockey Dewey Phillips of Memphis radio station WHBQ became the first person to play an Elvis Presley record on the air when he played "That's All Right (Mama)." It was played on his program, "Red Hot and Blue," shortly after 9:30 P.M. Later that night, Elvis gave his first media interview on Phillips's program.

July 12, 1954—Scotty Moore became Elvis's first manager when Elvis and his parents signed a one-year contract with Moore.

July 19, 1954—Sun 209 (That's All Right (Mama)"/"Blue Moon of Kentucky") became Elvis's first commercial record release.

July 28, 1954—Elvis's first newspaper interview (by Edwin Howard) appeared in the Memphis *Press-Scimitar*.

July 30, 1954—Elvis made his first concert appearance at the Overton Park Shell in Memphis. The appearance was advertised in both Memphis newspapers. Slim Whitman was the featured performer.

September 9, 1954—Elvis, Scotty, and Bill played for the grand opening of the Katz Drug Store in Memphis.

September 25, 1954—Sun 210 ("Good Rockin' Tonight"/"I Don't Care if the Sun Don't Shine") was released.

October 2, 1954—Elvis made his first and only appearance on the Grand Ole Opry, singing "Blue Moon of Kentucky."

October 16, 1954—Elvis made his first appearance on the "Louisiana Hayride," singing "That's All Right (Mama)" and "Blue Moon of Kentucky."

Late 1954—The Presleys moved from 462 Alabama Street to a house at 2414 Lamar Avenue.

January 1955—Bill Randle of WERE in Cleveland became the first disc jockey in the North to play an Elvis Presley record.

January 1, 1955—Scotty Moore let Elvis out of his managerial contract. Bob Neal became Elvis's new manager.

January 8, 1955—Sun 215 ("Milkcow Blues Boogie"/"You're a Heartbreaker") was released.

February 14, 1955—Colonel Thomas Parker first became involved with Elvis's career. He helped Bob Neal book Elvis into Carlsbad, New Mexico.

March 1955—Elvis auditioned for "Arthur Godfrey's Talent Scouts" TV program in New York City and was rejected. It was Elvis's first trip to New York and his first airplane flight.

March 5, 1955— Elvis made television debut by appearing on the regionally telecast "Louisiana Hayride."

April 1, 1955—Sun 217 ("Baby Let's Play House"/"I'm Left, You're Right, She's Gone") was released.

May 13, 1955—Elvis made a concert appearance in Jacksonville, Florida. It was the first Presley concert to cause a riot. Future singer Johnny Tillotson was in the audience.

May 25, 1955—Elvis made a concert appearance at the two-day Jimmie Rodgers Memorial Day Celebration in Meridian, Mississippi.

Mid-1955—The Presleys moved from 2414 Lamar Avenue to 1414 Getwell Street.

June 1955—*Cowboy Songs* magazine became the first magazine to feature an article on Elvis Presley.

August 6, 1955—Sun 223 ("Mystery Train"/"I Forgot to Remember to Forget") was released.

October 15, 1955—Elvis played the Cotton Club in Lubbock, Texas. The warm-up act was Buddy and Bob—Buddy Holly and Bob Montgomery. Fourteen-year-old future songwriter Mac Davis was in the audience.

November 20, 1955—RCA purchased Elvis's contract from Sun Records for $25,000, and Hill and Range Music purchased Sam Phillips's Hi-Lo Music pub-

lishing company for $15,000. In addition, Elvis received a $5,000 bonus from RCA to cover the future royalties he would have gotten from Sun Records.

December 16, 1955—Elvis made his last regular appearance on the "Louisiana Hayride" doing a benefit for the YMCA in Shreveport.

January 10, 1956—Elvis's first RCA recording session took place in Nashville. The first song taped was "I Got a Woman."

January 27, 1956—RCA 20/47-6420 ("Heartbreak Hotel"/"I Was the One") was released—Elvis's first RCA release of new material.

January 28, 1956—Elvis made his national television debut on the Dorsey Brothers' "Stage Show" on CBS.

February 4, 1956—Elvis's second appearance on "Stage Show."

February 11, 1956—Elvis's third appearance on "Stage Show."

February 15, 1956—Both sides of Sun 223 ("Mystery Train"/"I Forgot to Remember to Forget") reached number one on *Billboard*'s country chart, Elvis's first number one record.

February 18, 1956—Elvis's fourth appearance on "Stage Show."

March 15, 1956—Colonel Thomas A. Parker officially became Elvis's manager.

March 17, 1956—Elvis's fifth appearance on "Stage Show."

March 24, 1956—Elvis's sixth and last appearance on "Stage Show."

April 1, 1956—Elvis made his screen test, performing a scene from *The Rainmaker*.

April 3, 1956—Elvis's first appearance on "The Milton Berle Show."

April 11, 1956—While flying to Nashville for a recording session, Elvis's plane experienced trouble and almost crashed. Later that day, Elvis recorded "I Want You, I Need You, I Love You."

April 23, 1956—Elvis's first appearance in Las Vegas at the New Frontier Hotel. His scheduled four-week engagement was canceled after the second week because of the poor reception.

May 11, 1956—The Presleys moved from 1414 Getwell Street to a house on 1034 Audubon Drive.

June 5, 1956—Elvis's second appearance on "The Milton Berle Show," introducing the song "Hound Dog."

June 20, 1956—Elvis was interviewed by Wink Martindale on KLAC-TV's "Dance Party" in Memphis.

July 1, 1956—Elvis made an appearance on "The Steve Allen Show."

July 2, 1956—First Presley recording session to include the Jordanaires (RCA studios in New York City). "Hound Dog," "Don't Be Cruel," and "Any Way You Want Me" were recorded at the session.

August 23, 1956—Elvis began filming *Love Me Tender*.

September 3, 1956—Elvis bought his mother a pink Cadillac.

September 8–14, 1956—*TV Guide* featured Elvis on the cover and contained an article by Paul Wilder.

September 9, 1956—Elvis's first appearance on "The Ed Sullivan Show".

September 26, 1956—Elvis Presley Day in Tupelo, Mississippi.

October 18, 1956—Ed Hopper incident in Memphis.

October 28, 1956—Elvis's second appearance on "The Ed Sullivan Show."

November 15, 1956—*Love Me Tender* released.

November 23, 1956—Louis Balint incident in Toledo.

December 4, 1956—Million-Dollar Quartet session at the Sun studios. Participants included Elvis, Johnny Cash, Jerry Lee Lewis, and Carl Perkins.

January 4, 1957—Elvis took his pre-induction Army physical at the Kennedy Veterans Hospital in Memphis.

January 6, 1957—Elvis's third and last appearance on "The Ed Sullivan Show." This was the only television performance by Elvis during which he was shown only from the waist up.

January 30, 1957—The NBC-TV program, "Kraft Television Theatre," presented "The Singing Idol," starring Tommy Sands. The main character, Ewell Walker, was modeled after Elvis.

March 1957—Elvis purchased Graceland from Mrs. Ruth Brown Moore.

April 2, 1957—Elvis made a concert appearance in Toronto, Ontario.

April 3, 1957—Elvis made a concert appearance in Ottawa, Ontario.

April 10–June 5, 1957—"All Shook Up" was number one on *Billboard*'s Top 100 chart for eight weeks—the longest of any Presley song.

July 9, 1957—"Loving You" premiered in Memphis.

August 31, 1957—Elvis made a concert appearance in Vancouver, British Columbia.

October 17, 1957—"Jailhouse Rock" premiered in Memphis.

December 19, 1957—Memphis draft-board chairman Milton Bowers hand-delivered Elvis's draft notice to Graceland.

December 21, 1957—Frank Freeman, Paramount Studios' production chief, sent Elvis's draft board a letter asking for a sixty-day deferment so Elvis could complete filming *King Creole*. Freeman was told that Elvis would have to ask for the deferment himself.

December 26, 1957—Elvis donated a truckload of teddy bears to the National Foundation for Infantile Paralysis.

January 20, 1958—Original date Elvis was to have entered the U.S. Army. He received a deferment to March 24.

March 24, 1958—Elvis inducted into the U.S. Army.

March 25, 1958—Elvis received his Army haircut from James Peterson at Fort Chaffee, Arkansas.

March 27, 1958—Elvis given medical inoculations at Fort Chaffee (typhoid, tetanus, and Asian flu).

March 28, 1958—"The Phil Silvers Show" repeated an episode titled "Rock and Roll Rookie," which was a parody of Elvis. Elvis, along with the other recruits, was bused to Fort Hood, Texas, for basic training.

July 2, 1958—*King Creole* released.

August 11, 1958—Elvis's first Gold Disc Award from the Recording Industry Association of America was certified for "Hard Headed Woman."

August 14, 1958—Gladys Presley died in Memphis of a heart attack brought on by hepatitis.

August 16, 1958—Gladys Presley buried in Forest Hill Cemetery in Memphis.

September 19, 1958—Elvis and his Army unit began a train trip from Fort Hood to Brooklyn.

September 22, 1958—Elvis and his Army unit left the Military Ocean Terminal in Brooklyn aboard the USS *General Randall* for Bremerhaven, West Germany.

October 1, 1958—Elvis, aboard the USS *General Randall*, arrived in Bremerhaven.

November 27, 1958—Elvis promoted to private first class.

January 8, 1959—Elvis's twenty-fourth birthday. Dick Clark's "American Bandstand" dedicated its program to Elvis. Clark spoke with Elvis by telephone.

June 1, 1959—Elvis was promoted to specialist fourth class.

June 21, 1959—Elvis sang impromptu at the Lido nightclub in Paris while on leave.

January 20, 1960—Elvis was promoted to sergeant.

March 2, 1960—Elvis left West Germany by plane for the United States, stopping briefly at Prestwick Airport in Scotland. The next day, he arrived at McGuire Air Force Base in New Jersey.

March 5, 1960—Elvis discharged from the U.S. Army.

March 26, 1960—Elvis taped the Frank Sinatra–Timex Special "Welcome Home Elvis," at the Fontainebleau Hotel in Miami.

May 12, 1960—"The Frank Sinatra–Timex Special" aired on ABC-TV at 9:30 P.M. EST.

July 3, 1960—Vernon Presley and Davada (Dee) Stanley were married in Huntsville, Alabama.

October 30–December 25, 1960—"It's Now or Never" was number one in the United Kingdom for eight weeks—the longest of any Presley single in the U.K.

November 23, 1960—*G.I. Blues* released.

December 21, 1960—*Flaming Star* released.

December 25, 1960—Priscilla Beaulieu spent Christmas with Elvis at Graceland.

February 25, 1961—Elvis gave a live concert in the Ellis Auditorium in Memphis—his last live performance (except for the USS *Arizona* benefit) until 1968.

March 25, 1961—Elvis gave a benefit concert for the USS *Arizona* Memorial Fund. The concert was to have been on March 26, Palm Sunday, but Elvis thought that would be in bad taste.

June 22, 1961—*Wild in the Country* released.

November 22, 1961—*Blue Hawaii* released.

January 8, 1962—Elvis's twenty-seventh birthday. Dick Clark's "American Bandstand" dedicated its program to Elvis.

May 23, 1962—*Follow That Dream* released.

August 29, 1962—*Kid Galahad* released.

November 21, 1962—*Girls! Girls! Girls!* released.

April 3, 1963—*It Happened at the World's Fair* released.

June 14, 1963—Priscilla Beaulieu graduated from Immaculate Conception High School in Memphis.

November 27, 1963—*Fun in Acapulco* opened nationally.

December 11, 1963—*Love Me Tender* became the first Elvis Presley film to be shown on television.

January 30, 1964—Elvis purchased Franklin D. Roosevelt's former presidential yacht, *Potomac*. He then gave it to the St. Jude's Children's Hospital.

March 6, 1964—*Kissin' Cousins* premiered in Phoenix, Arizona.

April 20, 1964—*Viva Las Vegas* premiered in New York City.

November 11, 1964—*Roustabout* released.

April 14, 1965—*Girl Happy* released.

May 28, 1965—*Tickle Me* premiered in Atlanta.

August 27, 1965—Elvis met the Beatles at his Perugia Way mansion in Bel Air.

October 21, 1965—Bill Black, Elvis's former bass player, died during surgery.

November 24, 1965—*Harum Scarum* released.

Late 1965—Elvis moved from his house at 565 Perugia Way in Bel Air to 10550 Rocca Place.

March 31, 1966—*Frankie and Johnny* premiered in Baton Rouge, Louisiana.

May 25-28, 1966—In Nashville, Felton Jarvis produced his first Elvis Presley recording session.

June 9, 1966—*Paradise, Hawaiian Style* premiered in Memphis.

November 23, 1966—*Spinout* released.

February 9, 1967—Elvis purchased the Circle G Ranch near Walls, Mississippi.

March 22, 1967—*Easy Come, Easy Go* released.

April 5, 1967—*Double Trouble* released.

May 1, 1967—Elvis and Priscilla Beaulieu are married at the Aladdin Hotel in Las Vegas.

May 7, 1967—Elvis moved from 10550 Rocca Place in Bel Air to 1174 Hillcrest.

May 29, 1967—Elvis held a second wedding reception at Graceland for his friends and employees.

September 29, 1967—Elvis Presley Day is celebrated in Tennessee.

November 22, 1967—*Clambake* released.

Late 1967—Elvis moved from his home at 1174 Hillcrest to 144 Monovale.

February 1, 1968—Lisa Marie Presley is born.

March 8, 1968—*Stay Away, Joe* released.

June 12, 1968—*Speedway* released.

June 27-30, 1968—Elvis taped his NBC-TV special at the Burbank, California, studios. These sessions became known later as the "Burbank Sessions." The TV special aired on December 3, 1968.

October 23, 1968—*Live a Little, Love a Little* released.

December 3, 1968—Elvis appeared on his own TV special on NBC-TV. Sponsored by the Singer Company, it was Elvis's first appearance before an audience since 1961.

January 13-23, 1969—Elvis's first recording session at American Sound Studios in Memphis.

February 17-22, 1969—Elvis's second and last recording session at American Sound Studios.

March 13, 1969—*Charro!* released.

May 21, 1969—Elvis sold the Circle G Ranch to Lou McClellan.

July 31-August 31, 1969—Elvis's first Las Vegas appearance since 1956. He began his comeback at the International Hotel. This was the opening event in the 1979 TV movie, *Elvis*.

September 3, 1969—*The Trouble with Girls (and How to Get into It)* released.

November 10, 1969—*Change of Habit* released.

November 11, 1970—*Elvis—That's the Way It Is* released. Elvis Presley Day in Portland, Oregon.

January 9, 1971—U.S. Jaycees presented an award to Elvis for being one of the "Ten Outstanding Young Men of America."

May 4, 1971—Elvis appeared on the cover of *Look* magazine.

June 1, 1971—Elvis's birthplace in Tupelo, Mississippi, was opened to the public.

September 8, 1971—Elvis received the Bing Crosby Award.

January 19, 1972—Southern portion of Bellevue Boulevard (Highway 51 South) in Memphis renamed Elvis Presley Boulevard.

February 23, 1972—Elvis and Priscilla separated.

August 18, 1972—Elvis sued Priscilla for divorce.

November 1, 1972—*Elvis on Tour* released.

January 14, 1973—TV special, "Elvis: Aloha from Hawaii" was broadcast worldwide.

April 4, 1973—NBC-TV broadcast an expanded version of the "Elvis: Aloha from Hawaii" TV special to the United States.

October 9, 1973—Elvis and Priscilla's divorce is final.

January 8, 1974—Elvis Presley Day in Georgia, by proclamation of Governor Jimmy Carter.

June 18, 1975—Elvis underwent a face-lift at Mid-South Hospital in Memphis.

July 19, 1975—Elvis played the piano in public for the first time at a concert in Uniondale, New York.

December 31, 1975—Elvis broke the record for a single performance at a concert in Pontiac, Michigan. The gate receipts totaled $816,000.

January 14, 1976—While vacationing in Vail, Colorado, Elvis gave away five automobiles.

April 20, 1976—Presley Center Courts, Inc., established to build and manage racquetball courts.

December 2-12, 1976—Elvis's last Las Vegas appearance (at the Las Vegas Hilton).

January 26, 1977—According to Ginger Alden, she accepted Elvis's marriage proposal.

March 3, 1977—Elvis's last will and testament filed.

April 1, 1977—Elvis entered Baptist Memorial Hospital in Memphis. He left on April 5.

May 29, 1977—Elvis walked off the stage at a concert in Baltimore—the first time he had ever stopped in the middle of a concert for health reasons. He returned 30 minutes later.

May 30, 1977—Psychic Gloria James predicted on a talk show on radio station WMEX in Boston that Elvis would soon die.

June 18, 1977—Elvis received two Photoplay Gold Medal Awards as Favorite Variety Star and Favorite Rock Music Star. These were the last awards presented to Elvis before he died.

June 26, 1977—Elvis gave his last public performance at the Market Square Arena in Indianapolis.

July 19, 1977—Psychic Jacqueline Eastland predicted, on the "Nine in the Morning Show" in Los Angeles (KHJ-TV), that Elvis would soon die.

August 1, 1977—The book *Elvis—What Happened?* released. Philadelphia psychic Marc Salem predicted Elvis's death, including the headlines in the Philadelphia newspapers.

August 15, 1977—Elvis had a cavity filled during the evening at the office of dentist Lester Hoffman.

August 16, 1977—Elvis found dead by Ginger Alden at approximately 2:30 P.M. in a bathroom on the second floor of Graceland mansion.

August 17, 1977—Elvis was to have begun another tour, starting with a concert in Portland, Maine.

August 18, 1977—Elvis's funeral at Graceland. He was buried next to his mother at Forest Hill Cemetery. In the early morning hours, Tammy Baiter was injured and Alice Hovatar and Juanita Johnson were killed in front of Graceland by a car driven by Treatise Wheeler III.

August 27, 1977—According to Ginger Alden, Elvis was going to announce his engagement to her.

August 29, 1977—Ronnie Lee Adkins, Raymond M. Green, and Bruce Eugene Nelson arrested for trespassing at Forest Hill Cemetery. Speculation was that they were going to steal Elvis's body and hold it for ransom.

September 6, 1977—*National Enquirer* ran cover photo of Elvis lying in his open coffin.

October 2, 1977—The bodies of Elvis and Gladys Presley were moved from Forest Hill Cemetery to Graceland.

October 3, 1977—The CBS-TV special "Elvis in Concert," was telecast at 8:00 P.M. EST.

October 5, 1977—Charges against Ronnie Lee Adkins, Raymond M. Green, and Bruce Eugene Nelson were dismissed.

October 21, 1977—Dr. Jerry Francisco stated at a press conference that Elvis died of a heart attack—not from drugs.

November 15, 1977—Dee Stanley obtained a Dominican Republic divorce from Vernon Presley.

December 25, 1977—According to Ginger Alden, Elvis and she were to have been married on Christmas Day.

February 1, 1978—Elvis inducted into *Playboy* magazine's Musical Hall of Fame.

September 8, 1978—Bronze, 400-pound statue of Elvis dedicated in the lobby of the Barron Hilton Hotel.

October 18, 1978—"The Gong Show" on NBC-TV aired an entire show of Elvis impersonators.

February 11, 1979—ABC-TV movie *Elvis*, telecast, beating *Gone with the Wind* and *One Flew over the Cuckoo's Nest* in the ratings.

June 26, 1979—Vernon Presley died at the age of sixty-three.

June 28, 1979—Vernon Presley buried next to Elvis and Gladys.

August 19, 1979—The Elvis Presley Chapel in Tupelo, Mississippi, was dedicated.

September 13, 1979—The ABC-TV series "20/20" telecast an episode titled "The Elvis Cover-Up," concerning Elvis's drug problems and the probable cause of his death.

October 31, 1979—Priscilla Presley made her national TV commercial debut appearing for the Wella Corporation.

May 8, 1980—Minnie Mae Presley, Elvis's paternal grandmother, died at the age of eighty-six.

ELVIS

HIS LIFE FROM A TO Z

PART I
THE MAN

A COMPANY
Elvis's assignment at Fort Hood, Texas, while taking Army basic training in 1958. A Company was a part of the Second Medium Tank Battalion, Second Armored Division.

A SCIENTIFIC SEARCH FOR THE FACE OF JESUS
Book by Frank Adams about the Shroud of Turin, which some sources have stated was the book Elvis was reading when he died. The book had been given to him by his friend Larry Geller.

AARON
Correct spelling of Elvis's middle name, although originally it was misspelled as Aron on his birth certificate. As an adult, Elvis legally changed his name to Aaron, and that is how it appears on his gravestone. Elvis was named after Aaron Kennedy, a good friend of Vernon Presley.

In the late 1950s, a rockabilly record label was begun in West Memphis, Arkansas, called Aaron Records, after Elvis's middle name. Before the label folded they released "Oakie Boogie" (Aaron 101), by Hank Swatley. (See *Aron*, *Dr. William R. Hunt*, and *Aaron Kennedy*)

ACADEMY AWARDS
Annual awards presented by the Academy of Motion Pictures Arts and Sciences since 1927. At the presentations for the year 1980, Elvis was shown singing a portion of "Love Me Tender." Televised on March 31, 1981, the show was delayed one day because of the attempted assassination of President Ronald Reagan, who had taped a message for the show.

ACE, JOHNNY
(1929–1954) Rhythm & blues singer, born John Marshall Alexander Jr., in Memphis on June 9, 1929. Johnny Ace's biggest hit was "Pledging My Love" (Duke 136). He was once singer B. B. King's piano player. Ace also sang with a group called the Beale Streeters, which included members B. B. King, Bobby Bland, and Earl Forrest. Sam Phillips had recorded the group. In 1952 Ace recorded two unissued songs for Sun Records, "Remember I Love You," and "I Cried That Night." On Christmas Eve 1954, Ace shot himself while playing Russian roulette before going on stage at the Houston Civic Auditorium, and died the next day. A witness to the tragedy was singer Willie Mae (Big Mama) Thornton. At the time, "Pledging My Love" had just entered the charts.

Elvis's recording of "Pledging My Love" was number one on the country charts at the time of his death in 1977.

ACKERMAN, PAUL
(–1977) Music editor for *Billboard* magazine in the mid-1950s, he was one of the first to recognize the special sound of Elvis. Ackerman was the first national magazine editor to interview Elvis, which had been arranged by Sam Phillips in July of 1954. It was Ackerman who convinced Arnold Shaw to have R&B singer Solomon Burke record the country song, "Just Out of Reach" (Atlantic 2114), in 1960. When Ackerman died in 1977, his friend Sam Phillips delivered the eulogy.

ADAMS, NICK
(1931–1968) Hollywood actor who was born in Nanticoke, Pennsylvania, on July 10, 1931. Adams debuted in a Pepsi-Cola TV commercial with James Dean in 1951. He was a good friend of Dean's and appeared with him in the 1955 movie *Rebel Without a Cause*. (Ironically, Dean was selected to play a character named Nick Adams in the television presentation of Ernest Hemingway's "The Battler" on October 18, 1955, but after Dean died, the part went to Paul Newman.) Adams had a starring role as Johnny Yuma (a part that he created) in the TV series "The Rebel."[1]

Elvis and Adams became good friends, with Adams traveling with Elvis on tours, sometimes trading off the driving with Red West. The pair would sometimes ride their Harley-Davidson motorcycles while dressed in the traditional black leather jacket, motorcycle boots, and cap. Adams was with Elvis at the Mississippi-Alabama Fair and Dairy Show on September 26, 1956, where Elvis performed before his hometown audience in Tupelo on "Elvis Presley Day." At the afternoon show, Elvis introduced Adams to the fans. Elvis also enjoyed visiting with Adams, his wife, Carol Nugent, and their two children, Jeb and Allyson. Elvis tried to get him the role of one of the Reno brothers in the 1956 movie *Love Me Tender*, but he was rejected for the part because he was considered "too young." (Adams was twenty-six.) On February 7, 1968, the day after Lisa Marie Presley was taken home from Baptist Memorial Hospital, Adams committed suicide by taking an overdose of pills. (See *Sing, Boy, Sing* in Part II)

ADKINS, RONNIE LEE
(1951–) Twenty-five-year-old police informant who was one of three men—the other two were Raymond Green (age twenty-five) and Bruce Nelson (age thirty)—who were arrested for trespassing at Forest Hill Cemetery on August 29, 1977. Each man wore a dark jumpsuit over a bulletproof vest and carried an M-1 carbine, a handgun, and hand grenades. The charges were later dismissed on October 5, 1977. Ac-

---

[1]The series theme song, "The Ballad of Johnny Yuma," was sung by Johnny Cash.

cording to speculation, the men were going to steal Elvis's body from his 900-pound casket and hold it for a one-million-dollar ransom. That has never been proved.

Persons who knew Adkins, Green, and Nelson said that the men believed that Elvis wasn't dead and that they wanted to prove to the world that his crypt was empty. This theory made a good defense.

ADLER, RICHARD
(1921–   ) Composer born in New York City on August 3, 1921. He composed such songs as "Hey There," "Everybody Loves a Lover," and "Hernando's Hideaway." With Jerry Ross, Adler composed the song "Rags to Riches," which Elvis recorded in 1970.

AGNEW, SPIRO T.
(1918–   ) Vice President of the United States who resigned in 1973 when faced with a charge of federal income-tax evasion.

Elvis once tried personally to present the vice president with a .357 Magnum revolver worth $2,000, but Agnew refused the gift, as it would have been "illegal" to accept it.

AIRCRAFT
Means of transportation that became necessary for Elvis to complete his concert tours in privacy. At first, Elvis was afraid of flying. He was once a passenger aboard an aircraft that experienced engine trouble on a flight from Nashville to Memphis. In 1962 Elvis became interested in model aircraft, once buying a model airplane for $1,000. Eventually moving up to the real thing, he bought a Convair 880 jet airliner, a Falcon DH-125 aircraft for $600,000, a Jet Commander, and a nine-passenger Lockheed Jetstar. Eddie Fadal, in an interview in *Elvis World* magazine, claimed that just after Gladys's death in 1958, Elvis was given a thirty-minute helicopter ride by the State of Tennessee Highway Patrol, and on their return to Graceland, it was Elvis who was piloting the craft. Fadal further stated that Elvis flew helicopters a number of times.

Elvis's first trip in an airplane was in 1955, when he, Bob Neal, Bill Black, and Scotty Moore flew to New York City to audition for the "Arthur Godfrey's Talent Scouts" television program.

AIRWAY'S USED CARS
Car lot in Memphis that sponsored a Saturday radio show on KWEM on which brothers Johnny and Dorsey Burnette and Paul Burlison performed as a trio in late 1953. One of those in the audience watching was a young country singer named Johnny Cash. The car lot was only a short walking distance from Elvis's future home (1954–55) at 2414 Lamar Avenue. Elvis supposedly asked to sing a few songs with the group on this occasion, as well as on other occasions.

AKERS, DORIS
(1922–   ) Gospel singer and composer born in Brookfield, Missouri, on May 21, 1922. Akers, who is a past winner of the "Female Gospel Singer of the Year"

Award, composed the song "Lead Me, Guide Me," which Elvis recorded in 1971.

ALADDIN HOTEL
Las Vegas hotel where Elvis Presley and Priscilla Beaulieu were married in a double-ring ceremony on May 1, 1967, at approximately 9:41 A.M. The ceremony, which lasted just eight minutes, took place in the private suite

Priscilla and Elvis on their wedding day. (Photo courtesy Wide World Photos)

of Milton Prell, the hotel's owner. Priscilla wore a white chiffon gown with a six-foot train, while Elvis wore a black tuxedo.

In 1980 singer Wayne Newton and Ed Torres bought the Aladdin Hotel, which had cost $85 million to build.

ALAN
One of Elvis's code names at Graceland. Actress Ursula Andress used the name when she telephoned Elvis.

ALBERTA
Black maid at Graceland whom Elvis nicknamed "Alberta VO-5." Alberta, who had been with the Presleys since they lived on Audubon Drive in 1956, looked after the Stanley boys when they lived at Graceland.

ALDEN, GINGER
(1954–   ) Girlfriend of Elvis and the sister of Terry Alden and Rosemary Alden. Terry was Miss Tennessee in 1976. Elvis first saw Terry on local television and wished to meet her, so a meeting was set up by Memphis disc jockey, George Klein. Ginger accompanied Terry to the meeting, but Elvis became fascinated with Ginger rather than Terry.

Ginger was Memphis's "Miss Traffic Safety" and "Miss Mid-South" (both in 1976), as well as first runner-up for the title of "Miss Tennessee University" in 1976. Ginger, who was 19 years younger than Elvis, was his fiancée at the time of his death. Elvis bought her many presents, including a $12,000 white Lincoln Continental Mark V. Ginger claims that Elvis proposed to her on January 26, 1977, in the bathroom adjacent to his bedroom, and bought her an eleven-and-a-half-carat diamond engagement ring valued at $60,000 (some sources say $70,000). It was Ginger who discovered Elvis's body on the day of his death. The two were to have been married on Christmas Day 1977 at the Memphis Greek Orthodox Church, although some doubt that Elvis had even proposed to Ginger.

Ginger recorded her first record, "I'd Rather Have a Memory Than a Dream" (Monument 45295), in 1980, and appeared in the 1980 fictionalized bio-pic *The Living Legend*, which was produced by Earl Owensby. It was her film debut. Her next movie, *Lady Grey*, was also produced by Owensby, who at the time became romantically involved with Ginger.

Since 1980 Ginger has made more than twenty TV commercials in the United States and in Germany, including those for Wella Balsam Shampoo, Avon, and Jordache jeans. In May 1982 Ginger was honored by the Association of Southern Theater Owners as "The Star of Tomorrow."

Ginger wrote an article for the *National Enquirer* (September 6, 1977) describing her last day with Elvis. It appeared in the same issue as the one in which the photo of Elvis in his coffin appeared on the cover. In another *National Enquirer* article (May 16, 1978), it was claimed that Ginger Alden could still communicate with Elvis at will in psychic dreams. In that same article Ginger's mother, Jo, also claimed to have seen Elvis's ghost. Ginger was quoted as saying that Elvis told her to accept the role in *The Living Legend*.

Ginger was portrayed by Andrea Cyrill in the 1981 movie *This Is Elvis*.

ALDEN, JO LAVERNE
Mother of Ginger Alden, who filed a $40,000 claim in 1978 against the Elvis Presley estate, stating that Elvis had promised to pay the remainder of her home mortgage. In addition, Mrs. Alden said that Elvis had also agreed to pay for some home improvements and legal fees in a divorce. Charles Glascock served as Alden's attorney, while Henry Beaty represented the Presley estate. Judge Will Doran dismissed her suit.

ALDEN, ROSEMARY
(1951–   ) Sister of Ginger and Terry Alden, who in an article in the *National Enquirer* (May 16, 1978) claimed to have seen Elvis's ghost in their home, as had Ginger and their mother, Jo.

ALDEN, TERRY
Older sister of Ginger Alden who was Miss Tennessee in 1976. Elvis became intrigued with Terry after seeing her on television. This led to Elvis meeting Terry's sister, Ginger. At his concert appearance in Charlotte, North Carolina, on February 20, 1977, Elvis introduced Terry from the audience as the reigning Miss Tennessee, after which she came up on stage and played a classical selection on the piano.

ALDEN, WALTER
U.S. Army officer who inducted Elvis into the Army on March 24, 1958. Ironically, Walter Alden was the father of Ginger Alden, Elvis's fiancée at the time of his death.

ALI, MUHAMMAD
(1942–   ) Olympic light heavyweight Gold Medal winner (1960) and three-time heavyweight boxing champion (only man to accomplish this feat), Ali was born Cassius Marcellus Clay Jr. on January 17, 1942. In 1964 he recorded "Stand by Me," backed with "I Am the Greatest" on Columbia Records (Columbia 43007).

Elvis once gave Ali a robe valued at $10,000, with Ali's name and the phrase "The People's Champion" embossed on the back. Ali wore the robe when he lost to Ken Norton on March 31, 1973. Ali considered it bad luck and never wore it again.

ALL ABOUT ELVIS
Book written by Fred L. Worth and Steve D. Tamerius and first published by Bantam Books in August 1981. *All About Elvis* was chosen by *USA Today* in August 1987 as one of the five best books on Elvis.

ALL SHOOK UP
A book written by Lee Cotten and published by Pierian Press in 1985. The book is a chronology of Elvis's life from 1935 to 1977.

ALL-STAR SHOWS
Colonel Tom Parker's variety shows in the late 1940s. He used a covered wagon on his letterhead. Parker was still using the All-Star Shows name during the 1960s and 1970s.

ALLEN, PATRICIA
Musician who played piano on Elvis's June 1966 recording session for the film *Double Trouble*. She is the only female pianist to have backed Elvis on record.

ALLEN, REX
(1924–   ) Actor and singer who was born on December 31, 1924, in Willcox, Arizona. Allen was the last of the singing cowboys in the movies while under contract with Republic Pictures. Nicknamed "Mr. Cowboy" and "The Arizona Cowboy," he was voted into the top ten Money Making Western Stars of 1951, '52, '53, and '54 by *Motion Picture Herald-Fame* polls. Allen is perhaps best known as the narrator of most of Walt Disney's nature films.

In 1953 Allen had a million-seller with "Crying in the Chapel" (Decca 9-28758), which Elvis recorded in 1960. Elvis's version was released in 1965 and it, too, became a million-seller.

It was just after playing the song "Don't Say Goodbye," by Rex Allen Jr. (1947–   ), the son of Rex Allen, that disc jockey Asa Thompson of WELO radio in Tupelo, Mississippi, announced at 4:26 P.M., August 16, 1977, that Elvis had died in Memphis.

ALLISON, AUDREY AND JOE
Wife and husband composers of the country song "He'll Have to Go," which Elvis recorded in 1976.

ALPERT, HERB
(1937–   ) Musician born in Los Angeles on March 31, 1937. The trumpet-playing Alpert and his Tijuana

Brass first reached the Top 40 in 1962 with "Lonely Bull" (A&M 703), which reached number six. With Jerry Moss he founded A & M Records in Hollywood in early 1962. Alpert is the only artist in *Billboard* history to have both a number one vocal—"This Guy's in Love with You" (A&M 929) in 1968—and a number one instrumental—"Rise" (A&M 2151)—in 1979. Alpert was in the audience at the International Hotel in Las Vegas on July 31, 1969, for Elvis's first concert in many years.

ALVIS PRESLEY
Spelling of Elvis's name on the tickets for the June 8, 1956, Shrine Auditorium concert in Los Angeles.

ALWAYS ELVIS
Ten-day convention for Elvis fans held at the Las Vegas Hilton, September 1–10, 1978. Carl Romanelli was the show's master of ceremonies. The four special guests were Vernon Presley, Priscilla Presley, Henri Lewin (president of the Hilton Hotel chain), and Conrad Hilton (the owner of the hotel chain). There were no Elvis imitators present. The event, which had been promoted by Colonel Tom Parker, charged fans $15 a day, or a total of $150 for the entire ten-day event.

AMERICAN GUILD OF VARIETY ARTISTS
Union to which Elvis belonged. His membership number was 165890.

AMERICAN MUSIC
One of a number of music publishing companies owned by Elvis. American Music owned the publishing rights to numerous country classics, including "Sixteen Tons," "A Dear-John Letter," and "Smoke, Smoke, Smoke (That Cigarette)."

AMERICAN SOUND STUDIOS
Memphis recording studio, located at 827 Danny Thomas Street, founded by Chips Moman and Bob Crewe[1] in 1964. Singer Sandy Posey was once employed as a secretary at the studio. The Box Tops and Dusty Springfield recorded there in the late 1960s.
In 1969 Elvis held two recording sessions at American Sound Studios: January 13–23 and February 17–

(Photo courtesy Don Fink)

22. When Elvis first walked into the building, he remarked, "What a funky, funky place." It was the first time since his Sun Records days that Elvis had recorded in Memphis. Country singer Ronnie Milsap was one of the session men in January. Singer Neil Diamond had just recorded there earlier that month.
Some of the thirty-five songs Elvis recorded at American Sound Studios included "Kentucky Rain," "In the Ghetto," "Suspicious Minds," and "Don't Cry Daddy." Many consider the thirty-five songs he recorded there to be among his best.
The studio musicians who performed at the Elvis sessions were: Bobby Wood, Tommy Cogbill, Mike Leech, Reggie Young, John Hughey, Gene Chrisman, Ed Kollis, and Bobby Emmons. Those same musicians backed various artists at the studio, placing 125 recordings on the record charts over a five-year period.

AMIGOS
Vocal group consisting of Jose Vadiz, German Vega, Miguel Alcaide, and Pedro Berrios who, with the Jordanaires, sang backup at Elvis's recording session at Radio Recorders in Hollywood on January 22–23, 1963, for the soundtrack of the movie, *Fun in Acapulco*.

Ampex tape recorder used at Sun Studios in the 1950s. It was this tape recorder that Marion Keisker used to record a portion of "My Happiness" and all of "That's When Your Heartaches Begin" in the summer of 1953 when Elvis came into the Memphis Recording Service to cut his first four-dollar acetate.

AMPEX 350 C
Tape recorder used to record the sessions at Sun Records. It was on this machine (serial number 54L-220) that Elvis was first taped. Marion Keisker used the Ampex 350 C (made in Redwood City, California) to tape the last third of "My Happiness" and all of "That's When Your Heartaches Begin." The control panel connected to the tape recorder was made by RCA. (See *Memphis Recording Service, RCA Consolette*)

ANAGRAM
Elvis = Lives
Presley = R Sleepy

---

[1]Bob Crewe was the producer of the Rays' 1957 hit "Silhouettes" and cowriter of many of the Four Seasons' hits. In 1966 he had the hit "Music to Watch Girls By" (Dyno Voice 229), which Pepsi-Cola used as its theme song.

ANDERSON, ELLEN
Member of the Norwegian Consulate in Los Angeles who presented Elvis with three Norwegian Silver Records in 1962 for "Good Luck Charm." Elvis was the first artist to receive three Norwegian Silver Records.

ANDREOLI, PETER
Composer, with Vince Poncia Jr., of the song "Harem Holiday," which Elvis sang in the 1965 movie *Harum Scarum*.

ANITA KERR SINGERS
Vocal group that backed Elvis on the song "Tomorrow Night." Elvis recorded the song in 1955 while he was at Sun Records. On March 18, 1965, the Anita Kerr Singers, who backed numerous artists on RCA Records, recorded the overdubbed vocal backing to "Tomorrow Night."

Under the name the Little Dippers, the Anita Kerr Singers had a number nine hit in 1961 with "Forever" (University 210).

ANKA, PAUL
(1941–   ) Singer-songwriter born July 30, 1941, in Ottawa, Ontario. Anka made his first public appearance at the age of twelve as an impersonator. His first chart hit was "Diana"[1] (ABC Paramount 9831) in 1957. "Diana," which has sold over nine million copies through the years, was written about Diana Ayoub, the twenty-year-old babysitter of Anka's younger brother. Anka had a crush on Ayoub at the time.

Anka was the first Canadian solo artist to have a million-selling record, and through the years he has done just about everything in the entertainment world. He has written more than 225 songs, including four movie themes and the theme for "The Tonight Show Starring Johnny Carson." One of the movie themes Anka composed was for *The Longest Day*,[2] a movie in which he also had an acting role.

At the Elvis concert at Lake Tahoe on August 1, 1971, Elvis and Anka exchanged friendly quips. After singing "One Night," Elvis remarked to Anka: "Look, Anka! When I'm singing and you're in the audience, you listen to me! I go to hear you sing—I listen! You don't talk when I sing!" Elvis reached over the stage and gave Anka a gentle nudge. Later in the show he introduced Anka as "Paul Anchor."

Anka wrote the English lyrics to "My Way" in 1969 for Frank Sinatra. In concert, Elvis sang Anka's number one hit, "Diana." Elvis recorded "My Way" his way in concert in 1973. In 1967 Anka recorded "Until It's Time for You to Go" (RCA 9128), which Elvis later recorded. In August 1959, Elvis's "A Big Hunk o' Love" knocked Paul Anka's "Lonely Boy" (ABC Paramount 10022) out of the number one spot on *Billboard*'s Hot 100 chart.

ANN-MARGRET
(1941–   ) Singer, dancer, and actress born on April 28, 1941, in Sweden. Ann-Margret (real name: Ann-Margret Olsson) was discovered by comedian George Burns while she performed with a combo named the Shuttletones at the Dunes Hotel in Las Vegas in 1960. She made her national TV debut on "The Jack Benny Program." She made her movie debut in *Pocketful of Miracles* (1961) and then starred in the 1963 movie *Bye Bye Birdie*. Elvis and Ann-Margret had a close relation-

Ann-Margret. (Photo courtesy Eddie Brandt's Saturday Matinee)

ship while filming *Viva Las Vegas*. As Rusty Martin in the 1964 film, she sang "The Lady Loves Me" in duet with Elvis. "The Lady Loves Me" was finally released officially on the album *Elvis—A Legendary Performer, Vol. 4*. She also sang "My Rival" and "Appreciation" in the film. Ann-Margaret lunched with Elvis each day while he was filming the 1965 movie *Girl Happy*. He sent a large flower arrangement in the shape of a guitar whenever she opened an engagement. When Ann-Margret telephoned Elvis at Graceland, she used the code name "Bunny" (later changed to "Thumper" after the rabbit in the 1942 Walt Disney animated movie *Bambi*).

---

[1] Paul Anka's first record was "I Confess" (RPM 499), which he recorded in Los Angeles in 1956. The vocal backup was provided by the Jacks.
[2] *The Longest Day* was the most expensive movie ever filmed in black and white.

It has been reported that Elvis finally broke with Ann-Margret after she had announced to the press that she and Elvis were engaged to be married.

In 1972 Ann-Margret was nominated for an Oscar for *Carnal Knowledge*. In September 1972 she fell twenty-two feet off the stage at the Sahara Tahoe Hotel, breaking her jaw, fracturing her left arm, and suffering a concussion. After her recovery, she underwent plastic surgery.[1]

Ann-Margret and her husband, actor Roger Smith, attended Elvis's funeral. Early in her career, Ann-Margret was referred to as the "female Elvis," but that waned when she failed to pursue a career as a rock & roll singer. Ann-Margret certainly had both the looks and the talent to become a superstar. Had her career been handled differently, she could have become one of the most successful female rockers in music history. Today, Ann-Margret won't talk about Elvis and their relationship. All she'll say is, "He was a wonderful man."

APOLLO THEATER

Largest theater in New York City's Harlem section, located at 125th Street and Eighth Avenue. For years, "Amateur Night" was broadcast at eleven on Wednesday nights over WMCA radio. The theater, which has a seating capacity of 1,800, is owned by Frank Schiffman. Prior to his purchase it was called Hurtig and Seamon's Theater. The first white performers to appear at the Apollo were Buddy Holly and the Crickets[2] in 1957.

While singing "Body and Soul" on an "Amateur Night" show at the Apollo in 1940, Sarah Vaughan was discovered by Billy Eckstine.

While in New York City in 1956 to appear on the Dorsey Brothers' "Stage Show," Elvis spent time at the Apollo. One of the entertainers Elvis enjoyed watching was Bo Diddley, whom he met there. (See *Bo Diddley*)

APOLZON, GEORGE

Texas millionaire and antique collector who, in 1982, bought a 1975 Plymouth Fury that was used to transport Elvis on August 2, 1976, for a concert appearance in Roanoke. Apolzon paid $2,632 for the car with two checks: $1,819.35 (the day Elvis was born) and $816.77 (the day Elvis died). The market value of the car was only $1,000.

ARDEN, TONI

Singer, born Antoinette Aroizzone, who recorded the first cover of an Elvis record at RCA Victor before RCA rereleased Elvis's Sun recordings. Arden's version of "I Forgot to Remember to Forget" (RCA Victor 6346) was released shortly before Elvis's reissue in November 1955. (The next RCA cover of Elvis was the Turtles' unsoulful version of "Mystery Train.") Elvis later returned the favor when he recorded a version of Arden's 1958 hit song "Padre" (Decca 30628).

In 1955 sheet music for Hi-Lo Music's song "I Forgot to Remember to Forget" was published with both Toni Arden from RCA Records and Elvis Presley from Sun Records on the cover.

ARE YOU LONESOME TONIGHT?

Book written by Lucy de Barbin and Dary Matera that was published by Villard Books of New York City in 1987. The book, which spans a period of twenty-five years, was advertised as "The Untold Story of Elvis Presley's One True Love and the Child He Never Knew." The book was immediately serialized in the *National Enquirer*. *Us* magazine called the book "long on details of their meeting and short on evidence." In the book, Lucy de Barbin claimed to have met Elvis in 1953 when she was sixteen years old and that the relationship resulted in the birth of their daughter, Desiree. Supposedly, Desiree was Elvis's pet name for Lucy. (The two had seen the 1954 Marlon Brando film *Desiree*.) Upon publication of the book, Lucy and Desiree undertook an intense publicity campaign, appearing on numerous radio and television talk shows. Most of the hosts asked for more proof of her allegations. Lucy made two claims: Elvis had given her a poem and he had sent her tapes. The poem was authenticated in August 1987 by New York handwriting expert Charles Hamilton, who stated that the handwriting was that of Elvis Presley. Hamilton had earned a reputation as the man who exposed the famous "Hitler Diaries" in 1983, proving they were fakes. Even though she continued to refer to the tapes in interviews, Lucy de Barbin never produced them.

For TV's "Entertainment Tonight," Geraldo Rivera conducted one of his "investigative reports" into the authenticity of the de Barbin claims, and concluded that he was still an unbeliever.

There is too little evidence in *Are You Lonesome Tonight?* to make the book credible. Members of the Memphis Mafia have said that if Elvis was carrying on an affair for that length of time, one of them would have known about it, and none did.

ARIZONA, USS

United States battleship sunk by Japanese fighter-bombers at Pearl Harbor on December 7, 1941, "The Day of Infamy." The ship's skipper, Captain Frank van Valkenburg, was posthumously awarded the Congressional Medal of Honor. The USS *Arizona* is still a commissioned ship in the U.S. Navy, although it lies with its 1,102 crew members at the bottom of Pearl Harbor. In 1958 Congress authorized building the USS *Arizona*

---

[1]Several other artists have also fallen off a stage, including singer Bing Crosby. In 1977 punk rocker Patti Smith fell off a fifteen-foot stage in Tampa, suffering a broken neck.

[2]The person who booked Buddy Holly and the Crickets thought they were a black group. In 1954 there was a black rhythm & blues group called Dean Barlow and the Crickets.

Memorial as a national shrine. On March 25, 1961, Elvis performed at a benefit concert for the USS *Arizona* Memorial Fund, helping to raise $62,000. With the state of Hawaii contributing $100,000, congress authorizing $150,000, and the public giving $250,000, the USS *Arizona* Memorial was finally dedicated on Memorial Day, May 30, 1962. On August 17, 1977, the day after Elvis died, the Navy laid a wreath at the memorial in his honor.

Pearl Harbor is mentioned by Elvis in the lyrics of the song "He's Your Uncle, Not Your Dad," which was sung in the 1968 movie *Speedway*. (See *Bloch Arena*)

ARMY LIFE

Elvis was drafted into the U.S. Army on December 19, 1957, by Memphis Draft Board #86. He asked for and received a sixty-day deferment to finish the movie *King Creole*. Elvis, who reported for duty on March 24, 1958, traveled from Memphis to Fort Chaffee, Arkansas, on a Greyhound bus with twelve other recruits. The thirteen recruits were: Alex E. Moore (US 53310760), Elvis A. Presley (US 53310761), Louis C. Hern (US 53310761), Farley R. Guy (US 53310763), Nathanial Wiggison (US 53310764), Robert T. Maharrey (US 53310765), James Payne Jr. (US 53310766), William C. Montague (US 53310767), Timothy Christopher Jr. (US 53310768), Gilmore Daniel (US 53319768), Donald R. Mansfield (US 25255673), Wallace J. Hoover (US 24887433), and William R. Norvell (US 25347005). After just four days at Fort Chaffee, Elvis and the other recruits were bused to Fort Hood, Texas, to begin basic training.

There had been pressure on Elvis to become a part of Special Services, but Colonel Tom Parker was not going to let the Army have his client perform for them for two years free of charge; so he flew to Washington, D.C., to visit Lt. General William H. Arnold, the commander of the Fifth Army. He explained that Elvis wanted no special treatment and just wanted to be an average soldier.

At Fort Hood, Elvis was assigned to A Company, Second Medium Tank Battalion, Second Armored Division. He earned $78 a month, down from the $400,000 a month he had been making as a civilian.

On September 22, 1958, Elvis and his fellow soldiers left Brooklyn aboard the USS *General Randall* for a trip to Bremerhaven, West Germany. Elvis was stationed in West Germany for the remainder of his time in the service. During November 1958, Elvis and other members of the 32nd Tank Battalion took part in maneuvers close to the Czechoslovakian border.

It was in the Army that one of Elvis's sergeants gave him and the other soldiers Dexedrine pills to stay awake at night while on guard duty. This was Elvis's first exposure to drugs.

Elvis achieved the rank of private first class on November 27, 1958, and the rank of specialist fourth class on June 1, 1959. He was discharged on March 5, 1960, holding the rank of buck sergeant, but he wore an extra stripe on his custom-made uniform giving himself the rank of staff sergeant.

Elvis weighed 185 pounds when he was inducted into the Army and 170 pounds upon discharge two years later.

ARNOFF, CAROL

Young woman who lived with her parents on Audubon Drive in Memphis as neighbors of the Presleys. Carol and a girlfriend visited Elvis in his home one day, inspiring her to author the article "Elvis Was My Neighbor" for *Modern Screen* magazine.

ARNOLD, CHRIS

Composer with Geoffrey Morrow and David Martin of the songs "A Little Bit of Green," "Let's Be Friends," "This Is the Story," and "Sweet Angeline," all of which Elvis recorded.

ARNOLD, EDDY

(1918–   ) Country singer born in Henderson, Tennessee, on May 15, 1918. Arnold, a member of the Country Music Hall of Fame (1966), was managed by Colonel Tom Parker from 1942 to 1951. Arnold's first big professional break came when he appeared with Pee Wee King's Golden West Cowboys on the Grand Ole Opry. It was the show's host, George C. Hay, who gave Arnold his nickname, "The Tennessee Plowboy."

Through the years Eddy Arnold has charted more than seventy songs in the top ten of *Billboard*'s country chart—the most of any performer. In 1948 he had nine records in the top ten and four number one hits.

Hunk Houghton (Mickey Shaughnessy) in the 1957 movie *Jailhouse Rock* claimed to have performed on the same bill with Eddy Arnold and Roy Acuff. With Hal Horton and Tommy Dilbeck, Eddy Arnold composed the song "I'll Hold You in My Heart."

Elvis recorded the following Eddy Arnold hits:

"I Really Don't Want to Know" (RCA Victor 5525)
"I'll Hold You in My Heart" (RCA Victor 2332)
"It's a Sin" (RCA Victor 2241)
"Just Call Me Lonesome" (RCA Victor 6198)
"Make the World Go Away" (RCA Victor 8679)
"Welcome to My World" (RCA Victor 6502)
"You Don't Know Me" (RCA Victor 6502)

Elvis sang Arnold's 1955 hit, "Cattle Call" (RCA Victor 6139) in concert.

ARNOLD, JAMES (KOKOMO)

(1901–1968) Chicago blues singer who was born in Lovejoy, Georgia, on February 15, 1901. Arnold composed "Milk Cow Blues," which Elvis recorded in 1955 as "Milkcow Blues Boogie." The name "Kokomo" was taken from the title of Arnold's 1934 blues song "Old Original Kokomo Blues."

ARON

Spelling of Elvis's middle name on his birth certificate. It was the result of Vernon Presley's misspelling of the biblical name Aaron. Vernon and Gladys had intentionally given their sons rhyming middle names.

RCA used the spelling Aron for their 1980 album set, *Elvis Aron Presley*. (See *Dr. William R. Hunt* and *Aaron Kennedy*)

ARTHUR GODFREY'S TALENT SCOUTS

CBS-TV series (1948–58) hosted by Arthur Godfrey, which had been created by Irving Mansfield, the onetime husband of author Jacqueline Susann. Elvis and the Blue Moon Boys (Scotty Moore and Bill Black) went to New York City in March 1955 to audition for "Arthur Godfrey's Talent Scouts."[1] They were turned down.[2] At nearly the same time, Pat Boone auditioned for the show and won first place. He later became a regular on Godfrey's other TV series, "Arthur Godfrey and His Friends."

Buddy Holly and the Crickets also failed an audition for "Arthur Godfrey's Talent Scouts" in 1957. In the same week that George Hamilton IV failed to win first place on the show in 1956, his recording of "A Rose and a Baby Ruth"[3] (Colonial 420 and ABC Paramount 9725) was released. The song reached #6 on the charts. Other artists who made their TV debuts on "Arthur Godfrey's Talent Scouts" include Steve Lawrence, Connie Francis, Jimmie Rodgers, Tony Bennett, Guy Mitchell, Rosemary Clooney, the Chordettes,[4] Carmel Quinn, and Patsy Cline, who made her debut in 1957 singing "Walkin' After Midnight."[5]

Gordon Stoker of the Jordanaires won first place on the show in 1957 singing "Dig a Little Deeper." In 1954 the Foggy River Boys, with lead singer Charlie Hodge, also won on the program. Elvis recalled watching that particular episode.

ASHLEY, EDWARD L.

California man who filed a $6.3 million lawsuit against Elvis, claiming that Elvis's bodyguards beat him up at the Sahara Tahoe Hotel on May 20, 1974, after Ashley had admitted turning off the circuit-breaker switches on the floor on which Elvis was staying. He had been refused admittance to Elvis's party. The suit, which was filed on October 11, 1974, was later dismissed by the courts.

ATKINS, CHET

(1924–   ) Guitarist, born Chester Burton Atkins in Luttrell, Tennessee, on June 20, 1924, the same day as World War II hero and actor Audie Murphy. Atkins, who recorded a number of instrumental albums and played guitar behind Hank Williams, the Everly Brothers, and numerous other artists, later produced many recording sessions for RCA artists. Chet's brother, Jimmy Atkins, was once a member of the Les Paul Trio. Chet Atkins came to Nashville in 1948. He had been hired by Steve Sholes by mail that year after Sholes heard his 1947 recording of "Canned Heat" (RCA 20-2472). Chet Atkins[6] was inducted into the Country Music Hall of Fame in 1973. For fourteen consecutive years he won the Best Instrumentalist Award in the *Cashbox* magazine poll.

Chet Atkins. (Photo courtesy Jeff Wheatcraft)

Atkins played at Elvis's Nashville recording sessions of January 10–11, 1956; April 11, 1956; and June 10–11, 1958. He and Boudleaux Bryant composed "How's the World Treating You," which Elvis recorded in September 1956. Atkins had borrowed the title from the first line of the popular song "What's New." In 1960 Chet Atkins became the A&R manager of RCA and in 1968 he became RCA's vice president.

After Elvis's death in 1977, Atkins said of Elvis: "When he came along, he was so different in everything that he did. And I think that was one of the big reasons he had such great impact on the business. He was the first to start the thing about rhythm. He dressed differently and moved differently from anybody we had ever seen. He was electrifying. I don't think anything like this will ever happen again, at least not in my lifetime. And I don't think there will ever be another like him."

ATLANTIC RECORDS

The most successful independent record label of the 1950s. New York City-based Atlantic Records was founded in October 1947 by Ahmet Ertegun (the son of

---

[1]Godfrey's orchestra leader (1948–54) Archie Bleyer founded Cadence Records in 1952 (originally called Bleyer Records) and signed Julius LaRosa as his first artist. Bleyer and LaRosa were both fired by Godfrey on October 19, 1953. LaRosa was fired on the air just after singing "I'll Take Manhattan." Godfrey later said he fired him because "he lacked humility."

[2]Had the trio decided to sing "I Believe" they might have appeared on the show, since no one who sang "I Believe" on the show ever lost.

[3]The rockabilly song on the flip side, "If You Don't Know," mentioned Elvis by name in the lyrics.

[4]The Chordettes were Dick Clark's first live guests on "American Bandstand" (August 5, 1957).

[5]That same year Patsy also made an appearance as a contestant on the Groucho Marx TV game show, "You Bet Your Life."

[6]In 1974 Atkins and Floyd Cramer, with a group called the Country Hams, made a record titled "Walking in the Park with Eloise" (Apple 3977). The Country Hams was an assumed name used by Paul McCartney and Wings. Paul McCartney's father, James McCartney, had written the song.

a Turkish ambassador to the United States) and Herb Abramson.

Atlantic recorded mostly rhythm & blues artists such as the Clovers, Chuck Willis, the Drifters, LaVern Baker, Joe Turner, Ruth Brown, and many other artists who influenced Elvis. In 1952 Atlantic paid Los Angeles's Swingtime Records $2,500 for Ray Charles's contract. Atco Records (Atlantic Company), which was founded in 1955 and was the label on which the Coasters, Young Jessie, and Bobby Darin recorded, was a subsidiary of Atlantic.

Atlantic unsuccessfully bid $25,000 for Elvis in 1955.[1] (Had they been successful, Atlantic would have had both Elvis Presley and Ray Charles on the same label.)

Elvis had been listening to Atlantic artists for years. For example, Atlantic released the following songs with label numbers 1047, 1048, 1050, and 1053: "Tweedlee Dee"/"Tomorrow Night" by LaVern Baker, "White Christmas" by the Drifters, "I've Got a Woman" by Ray Charles, and "Flip, Flop and Fly" by Joe Turner, all of which Elvis covered. Founder Ahmet Ertegun[2] is the present owner of the New York Cosmos soccer team. Jerry Wexler, who joined Atlantic in 1953, is credited with coining the phrase "rhythm & blues."

ATOMIC POWERED SINGER, THE

Billing for Elvis at Las Vegas's New Frontier Hotel in April 1956. In California he was billed as "The Nation's Only Atomic Powered Singer."

AUBERBACK, LARRY

Elvis's agent with the William Morris Agency.

AUSBORN, CARBEL LEE

(See *Mississippi Slim*)

AUSTIN, GENE

(1900–1972) Crooner and composer born in Gainesville, Texas, on June 24, 1900. In 1927 Gene Austin recorded "My Blue Heaven," which became a multimillion-seller. It was the best-selling record of all time until it was surpassed by Bing Crosby's "White Christmas" in 1942. Colonel Tom Parker was once Austin's booking agent. Contrary to what has been printed, Parker never managed Austin, but obtained some bookings for him in Tampa, Florida. It was from this experience that Parker convinced other artists, such as Eddy Arnold, to let him become their manager. Country artist Tommy Overstreet is a nephew of the late Gene Austin.

AUTRY, GENE

(1907–   ) Cowboy actor, singer, composer (over 275 songs), and successful investor who was born Orvon Gene Autry in Tioga, Texas, on September 29, 1907. Early in his career, Autry was known as "Oklahoma's Singing Cowboy." He made his film debut in the 1934 movie *In Old Santa Fe*. Autry was the first cowboy to make recordings, the first to make singing Western movies, and the first to head a rodeo in New York. A successful investor, he has owned Challenge Records,[2] Republic Records (with which Pat Boone began his recording career), the California Angels baseball team, and the Golden West radio network.

Gene Autry's biggest record was 1949's "Rudolph, the Red-Nosed Reindeer" (Columbia 38610), which is Columbia Records' all-time biggest seller (over eight million sold). Autry recorded a number of songs that Elvis later recorded. They include "Frankie and Johnny" (1929), "The Yellow Rose of Texas" (1933), "Blue Hawaii" (1937), "Blueberry Hill" (1941), "I'll Never Let You Go (Little Darlin')" (1941), and a song which Autry cowrote, "Here Comes Santa Claus" (1947).

AVON THEATER

West Memphis theater located at 124 West Broadway. It was one of the theaters that Elvis rented for his private movie showings.

AXTON, HOYT WAYNE

(1938–   ) Singer and composer born in Comanche, Oklahoma, on March 25, 1938. Axton is the son of Mae Axton, cocomposer of "Heartbreak Hotel." He played the inventive father in the 1984 Steven Spielberg–produced movie *Gremlins*. In the 1986 TV movie *Dallas: the Early Years*, Axton played Aaron Southworth, Miss Ellie's father. He composed "Greenback Dollar," which the Kingston Trio recorded in 1963 (Capitol 4898). Three Dog Night recorded two Axton compositions, "Joy to the World" (Dunhill 4272) and "Never Been to Spain" (Dunhill 4299), both in 1971. Elvis recorded "Never Been to Spain" in February 1972; thus he recorded songs written by both a mother and her son.

AXTON, MAE BOREN

Cowriter, with Tommy Durden, of "Heartbreak Hotel." Mae Axton, who is the mother of singer/songwriter and actor Hoyt Axton, once worked as a publicist for country singer Hank Snow. Mae Axton, who is the sister of Senator David Boren of Oklahoma, also worked for the Grand Ole Opry for a time. She first saw

---

[1] It is interesting to speculate how Elvis would have been handled on Atlantic. Would he have been given country songs, as Atlantic had no country-music artists; would he have been given rhythm & blues songs, their main releases; or would he have recorded on the Atco label singing many of the same Leiber and Stoller compositions that he did on RCA? He certainly would not have had the Jordanaires, Chet Atkins, or Floyd Cramer.

[2] Frank Zappa named his son Ahmet Rodan Zappa, after Ertegun.

[2] The Champs recorded "Tequila" on Challenge Records (Challenge 1016) in 1958. Glen Campbell, Jimmy Seals, and Dash Crofts joined the group a short time after. Autry named the Champs after Champion, his Wonder Horse.

Elvis when he appeared in Jacksonville on May 13, 1955, as a member of the Hank Snow All-Star Jamboree, which she had helped promote. In November 1955, at the Disc Jockey Convention in Nashville, she played for Elvis a demo with Glenn Reeves singing "Heartbreak Hotel" in her suite at the Andrew Jackson Hotel.

In 1977 Axton wrote some of the liner notes for Ronnie McDowell's album *The King Is Gone.* (See *Jimmy Velvet*)

AYERS, RICK
(1955–　　) One of Elvis's Memphis hairdressers in the 1970s. Ayers was a second cousin of Elvis's and he often worked out with him when Elvis was practicing martial arts at Graceland.

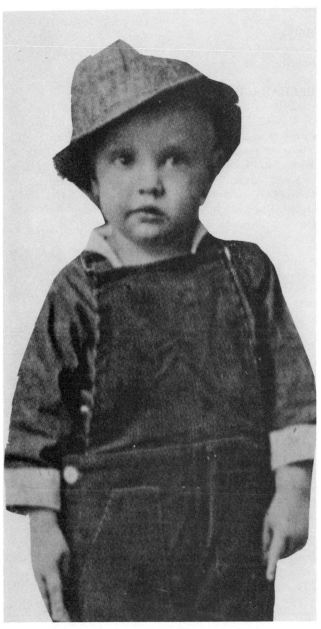

Elvis at the age of two. (Photo courtesy Cinema Collectors)

BABA
Collie dog owned by Elvis at Graceland. Baba was one of his favorite pets, and Elvis took him along to Beverly Hills in the 1960s. Baba made a cameo appearance in the 1966 movie *Paradise, Hawaiian Style.*

BABCOCK, JOE
Composer of the country song "I Washed My Hands in Muddy Water," which Elvis recorded in 1970. Babcock sang background vocals at Elvis's recording sessions at the RCA Studios in Nashville on May 26–27, 1963, and at the American Sound Studio on February 17–22, 1969.

BABY
Name that Elvis called his mother, Gladys, from childhood.

BACHARACH, BURT F.
(1928–   ) Composer born in Kansas City, Missouri, on May 12, 1928. Bacharach is the composer of numerous movie themes and musical director for Dionne Warwick (later spelled Warwicke and back again to Warwick). A former husband of actress Angie Dickinson and current husband of Carole Bayer Sager, he composed a number of hit songs with lyricist Hal David. Bacharach, with Bob Hilliard, composed "Any Day Now," which Elvis recorded in 1969.

Elvis was a recipient of many police badges, including this one from the Monroe, Louisiana, Police Department. (Photo courtesy John Dawson)

BADGES
One of Elvis's hobbies was collecting badges. President Richard M. Nixon personally saw to it that Elvis received a Narcotics Bureau badge that had previously been denied by Deputy Director John Finlator.

BAER, HERBERT
Foundry worker in Manitowoc, Wisconsin, who, on December 18, 1978, legally changed his name to Elvis Presley. Previously, Elvis impersonators had been re-fused the name change because it would have allowed them to make financial gains. Herbert Baer's wife and children retained the Baer name.

BAER JR., MAX
(1937–   ) Actor-director born Maximilian Adelbert Baer Jr. in Oakland, California, on December 4, 1937. Max Baer Jr. is the son of heavyweight boxing champion Max Baer (June 14, 1934–June 13, 1935). As an actor, Max Baer Jr. played Jethro Bodine on the TV series "The Beverly Hillbillies" (1962–71). He directed the 1967 movie *Ode to Billie Joe.* Baer was a close personal friend of Elvis's, and sometimes played on Elvis's Bel Air football team.

BAITER, TAMMY
St. Clair, Missouri, girl who was seriously injured by a car driven by Treatise Wheeler III on August 18, 1977, in front of Graceland. Two other girls (Alice Hovatar and Juanita Johnson) were killed in the accident. Baiter's pelvis was shattered in four places.

Baiter was born on Elvis's birthday in 1960. (See *Alice Hovatar*; *Juanita Johnson*; *Treatise Wheeler III*)

BAIZE, BILL
Tenor singer with J. D. Sumner and the Stamps. Elvis considered Baize to have one of the finest voices in the world. At Elvis's funeral in 1977, Baize sang "When It's My Turn."

BAKER, LAVERN
(1929–   ) Rhythm & blues artist of the 1950s and early '60s who was born in Chicago on November 11, 1929. Nicknamed "Little Miss Sharecropper,"[1] Baker had three million-sellers: "Tweedlee Dee"[2] (Atlantic 1047) in 1955, "Jim Dandy" (Atlantic 1116) in 1957, and "I Cried a Tear" (Atlantic 2007) in 1958. In the early 1950s she and singer Johnnie Ray appeared together at Detroit's Flame Club.

Elvis recorded three songs that were consecutive hits for Baker: "Shake a Hand" (Atlantic 2048), "Saved" (Atlantic 2099), and "See See Rider" (Atlantic 2167). He also sang "Tweedlee Dee" on the "Louisiana Hayride" in 1955. Baker recorded "Hey Memphis" (Atlantic 2119) as an answer to Elvis's "Little Sister."

BALINT, LOUIS JOHN
Unemployed Toledo, Ohio, sheetmetal worker who took a swing at Elvis on November 23, 1956, at Toledo's Commodore Perry Hotel. Balint claimed that his wife's love for Elvis broke up their marriage. He was fined $19.60 for assault and was jailed because he didn't

[1]Baker chose the nickname "Little Miss Sharecropper" because another popular singer had the nickname "Little Miss Cornshucks."
[2]"Tomorrow Night," a song recorded by Elvis, was on the flip side.

have the money to pay the fine. Later Balint claimed that a Presley aide had paid him $200 plus payment of any fine to pull the stunt. His story was considered phony.

BALLARD, CAROLINE
Elvis's first girlfriend (he was nine). Her father was the Reverend James Ballard, who at that time, was the Presley family's pastor in East Tupelo. Elvis loved the sound of Caroline's voice.

BALLARD, REVEREND JAMES
Pastor in the mid-1940s of the East Tupelo First Assembly of God Church, the church attended by the Presleys. (See *First Assembly of God Church*)

BALTIMORE, MARYLAND
Site of a May 29, 1977, Elvis concert. During this performance at the Civic Center, Elvis walked off the stage, the first time he had ever stopped in the middle of a concert. After being attended to by a physician, he reappeared on stage thirty minutes later.

BAPTIST MEMORIAL HOSPITAL
Memphis, Tennessee, medical facility, at 899 Madison Avenue, that Elvis entered on April 1, 1977, suffering from both fatigue and intestinal flu. He left on April 6.

(Photo courtesy Don Fink)

His previous visits were in March 1970 (three days, for an eye infection that was discovered to be glaucoma of the left eye); October 1973 (two weeks, for pneumonia); January–February 1975 (two weeks, for an impacted colon and hypertension); August–September 1975 (two weeks, for exhaustion). While Elvis was in the hospital in January 1975, Vernon Presley was brought in after suffering a heart attack.

Baptist Memorial is also the facility where Lisa Marie Presley was born on February 1, 1968. Musician Bill Black died there on October 21, 1965, a victim of a heart attack. Elvis's body was brought to the facility's Trauma Room #2 on the day of his death, August 16, 1977. Vernon Presley died there of a heart attack on June 26, 1979.

BARBEE, SAM
Disc jockey with whom Elvis talked in a telephone interview while he was stationed in West Germany.

BARBIN, LUCY DE
(1934/1936–   ) Clothing designer and mother of six children who gave birth to Desiree Presley in Alexandria, Louisiana, on August 23, 1968, claiming that Elvis was the father. In her 1987 book, *Are You Lonesome Tonight?*, cowritten with Dary Matera, de Barbin claims to have carried on a twenty-four-year relationship with Elvis, never telling him that he was the father of one of her children. Coauthor Matera has claimed that Elvis's last girlfriend, Ginger Alden, was a dead ringer for Lucy. If having an affair with the world's number one singer wasn't enough for de Barbin, she also claimed in her book to have had a relationship with the world's number one actor, John Wayne.

On TV's "Entertainment Tonight" in 1987, Geraldo Rivera stated that he uncovered facts that contradicted de Barbin's story. He referred to her book as "Elvisgate." De Barbin claimed to have married 25-year-old Dick D. Ware in Mississippi, but Rivera produced a marriage certificate from Monroe, Louisiana. That certificate was dated January 28, 1946. De Barbin has claimed that she was born in 1936 and married at age eleven (even though she wrote seventeen on her marriage certificate). But according to Rivera, had she been born in 1936, she would have been nine years old when she married. If indeed she was eleven when she married, she would have had to be born in 1934.

Coincidentally, in a 1978 magazine, *Elvis One Year Later*, there was an article titled "The Girl Elvis's Mother Wanted Him to Marry," which had been written by a woman who claimed to have been Elvis's love interest over a long period of time. It was stated that the story had been given to a reporter in 1969 by a woman who didn't want to reveal her identity. The story made some of the same claims that Lucy de Barbin later did. But in the article the woman stated that Elvis had been an interstate truck driver for Main-Line, which he never was. She claimed, as has de Barbin, that Elvis sent her secret messages with his hand gestures while he was performing on television.

BARBIN, MARY DE
Sister of Lucy de Barbin, coauthor of *Are You Lonesome Tonight?* Mary lived on Lauderdale Street in Memphis and, according to the book, Elvis mowed her lawn several times, which is quite a coincidence. It is true, however, that Elvis's father had bought Elvis a push mower so that he could mow lawns after school.

BARDOT, BRIGITTE
(1934–   ) French actress and ballerina who was born in Paris on September 28, 1934. Bardot was nicknamed "The Sex Kitten." Elvis wanted to meet her while in the

Army. In 1958, as Private Presley, Elvis said, "The first place I want to go is to Paris and look up Brigitte Bardot." Bardot didn't wish to meet Elvis at the time. Interestingly, Bardot had also been John Lennon's favorite actress.

Ironically, on December 3, 1968, Brigitte Bardot's TV special immediately followed the NBC-TV special, "Elvis."

BARKAN, MARK
Composer with Dolores Fuller of "I'll Take Love" and "How Would You Like to Be" with Ben Raleigh, both of which Elvis recorded.

BARNES, HOWARD LEE
(1918–   ) Composer born in Hobart, Oklahoma, on September 9, 1918. Barnes composed with Don Robertson the song, "I Really Don't Want to Know," which Elvis recorded.

BARRETT, RONA
(1936–   ) Hollywood gossip columnist who was born Rona Burstein on October 8, 1936, in New York City. Barrett announced on her radio program in 1967 that Elvis and Priscilla were to be married in Palm Springs, California. In reality they were married in Las Vegas. In the 1950s, as a teenager, Barrett was the president of Eddie Fisher's National Fan Club.

Barrett was seen in the 1970 movie, *Elvis: That's the Way It Is* attending Elvis's concert in Las Vegas.

BARRIS, GEORGE
(1925–   ) One of the country's leading automobile customizers, owner of Kustom City at 10811 Riverside Drive in North Hollywood. Barris customized Elvis's forty-foot-long Greyhound touring bus in 1962, which took four months to complete. Elvis later gave the bus to country singer T. G. Sheppard. Barris also customized the 1960 "Solid Gold Cadillac" 75 Limousine, which is now on display at the Country Music Hall of Fame in Nashville.

When Elvis brought Priscilla to Beverly Hills in the summer of 1962, she stayed with Barris and his wife, Shirley.

Barris was mentioned by name in the 1988 TV miniseries "Elvis and Me."

BARTHOLOMEW, DAVE
(1920–   ) New Orleans bandleader who backed Fats Domino[1] beginning in 1948. Bartholomew also cowrote with Fats a number of hit records. Previously, Bartholomew had been a trumpet player with Duke Ellington's band. He ranks third (tied with Fats Domino) behind Paul McCartney and John Lennon for composing the most million-selling songs. Bartholomew wrote and originally recorded in 1952 "My Ding-a-Ling" (King 4544), which in 1972 became Chuck Berry's only number one hit record (Chess 2131). Bartho-

---

[1]Actually, Domino began as a member of Bartholomew's band.

lomew, with Pearl King, composed "One Night," which Elvis recorded in 1957, and "Witchcraft," which Elvis recorded in 1963.

BARTON MEMORIAL HOSPITAL
Recipient of the proceeds of Elvis's special Mother's Day concert at Lake Tahoe, Nevada, on May 13, 1973. The concert was held in memory of Elvis's mother, Gladys.

BASS, RALPH
Composer, with John Thornton, Piney Brown, and Earl Washington, of the song "Just a Little Bit," which Elvis recorded in 1973.

BATCHELOR, RUTH
(1934–   ) Journalist for the *Sunday Times* in London and a Los Angeles film critic who was born in New York City on February 12, 1934. Batchelor became a songwriter, composing with Bob Roberts five songs that Elvis sang in films: "Because of Love," "Cotton Candy Land," "King of the Whole Wide World," "Thanks to the Rolling Sea," and "Where Do You Come From." Another song, "Love is for Lovers," was never used.

In 1962 she recorded "Mr. Principal"/"Lemon Drops, Lolly Pops" (Parkway 852). In 1988 Batchelor was the entertainment editor of "Good Morning America" and wrote under the name Ruth Batchelor Kory.

BATTERSBY, C. M.
Composer, with Charles H. Gabriel, of the religious song "An Evening Prayer," which Elvis recorded in 1971.

BATY, TIM
Composer of the song "Thinking About You," which Elvis recorded in 1973 and a member of Elvis's vocal backing group, Voice.

BAUGH, GEORGE
Security guard at Graceland who coauthored, with Harold Loyd, the book *The Gates of Graceland*.

BAUM, BERNIE
(1929–   ) Composer born in New York City on October 13, 1929. Baum has produced for the Chantels and the Crystals. From 1962 to 1969, he served as a staff writer for Hill and Range Music. Baum is the composer, with Bill Giant and Florence Kaye, of forty-one songs that Elvis recorded, most of them for his films. The songs are:

"Animal Instinct"	"El Toro"
"Ask Me"	"Everybody Come Aboard
"Beach Shack"	"Go East, Young Man"
"Catchin' on Fast"	"Golden Coins"
"City by Night"	"House of Sand"
"(You're the) Devil in Disguise"	"I Don't Wanna Be Tied"
"Do Not Disturb"	"Kissin' Cousins (#2)"
"Do the Vega"	"Mirage"
"Edge of Reality"	"Night Life"

"One Boy, Two Little Girls"
"One-Track Heart"
"Paradise, Hawaiian Style"
"Plantation Rock"
"Poison Ivy League"
"Power of My Love"
"Queenie Wahine's Papaya"
"Roustabout"
"Scratch My Back"
"Shake That Tambourine"
"Shout It Out"
"Sound Advice"

"The Sound of Your Cry"
"Spring Fever"
"Stop Where You Are"
"Tender Feeling"
"There's Gold in the Mountains"
"This Is My Heaven"
"Today, Tomorrow and Forever"
"Wisdom of the Ages"
"Wolf Call"
"A World of Our Own"
"You Gotta Stop"

BAXTER, LOU

Composer, with Johnny Moore, of the song "Merry Christmas Baby," which Elvis recorded in 1971.

BAXTER, SIR MALCOLM

Former life lived by Elvis in Sussex, England, in the eighteenth century, according to a theory by Drs. Barbara Williams and Carl Giles in an article in *Weekly World News* dated April 22, 1980. Baxter's wife, Madelaine, became his mother, Gladys, in his most recent incarnation. Sir Malcolm was a heavy drug user, according to Williams and Giles. According to the article, other previous lives of Elvis included a citizen of ancient Greece, a citizen of the lost continent of Atlantis, and an Irish sheep farmer.

BEAN, ORVILLE S.

Dairy farmer on Saltillo Road in Tupelo, Mississippi, for whom Vernon Presley worked before Elvis's birth. Bean bought $180 worth of lumber for Vernon so that Vernon could build a house for his family. After completion of the house on Old Saltillo Road, Bean rented it to the Presleys. It was in this house that Elvis was born. Bean's daughter, Oleta, taught Elvis in the fifth grade at East Tupelo Consolidated School (also known as Lawhon Grammar School) in 1945 and 1946. Bean was financially well-to-do, owning several lots and houses in Tupelo. Although difficult to believe, Vernon Presley later bought a new house on Berry Street from Orville Bean in August 1945, only to sell it a year later. (See *Parchman Penitentiary*)

BEARD, ELDENE

Fifteen-year-old Memphis girl who may have been the first person to buy an Elvis Presley record. Eldene bought a copy of "That's All Right (Mama)"/"Blue Moon of Kentucky" (Sun 209) at 9:00 A.M. on July 19, 1954, at Charles Records on Main Street. The store was located across from the Suzore Theater. Eldene first heard the record on WHBQ and was the first in line when the store opened on the day of the record's release.

BEATLES

Most successful musical group in the history of show business. Members of the group were John Winston Lennon, James Paul McCartney, George Harrison, and Ringo Starr (Richard Starkey). John Lennon once noted that, "Nothing really affected me until I heard Elvis. If there hadn't been Elvis, there would not have been the Beatles."[1]

The Fab Four visited Elvis at his home in Bel Air (565 Perugia Way) on Friday night, August 27, 1965, during their second U.S. tour. They arrived at Elvis's home at 10:00 P.M. and stayed until 2:00 A.M., during which time they told stories, joked, and listened to records. Elvis drank Seven-Up while the Beatles drank either scotch or bourbon. The five of them even had an impromptu vocal jam session, with Elvis playing drums, the piano, and showing Paul how he could play the intro to "I Feel Fine" on bass guitar. One of the songs they tinkered with was Cilla Black's hit song, "You're My World." According to one story, a tape recorder was turned on while the supergroup jammed (although in a 1987 interview in *Creem* magazine George Harrison denied that they were being taped). After the meeting, Ringo said, "Fantastic, he was just like one of us, none of the old Hollywood show-off thing." The group jokingly invited Elvis to become the fifth Beatle. Colonel Tom Parker and Brian Epstein were also present, the two keeping themselves busy playing roulette in another room. Elvis had previously invited the Beatles to stay at Graceland while they were in Memphis in 1964, but Brian Epstein had declined for security reasons.

Elvis sent the Beatles a telegram congratulating them on their first "Ed Sullivan Show" appearance of February 9, 1964. The Beatles sent Elvis a toy water pistol during their first American tour.

Elvis mentioned the Beatles by name in the altered lyrics of the song "I've Never Been to Spain," which he sang in the 1972 documentary *Elvis on Tour*. The Beatles can be seen in the 1981 movie *This Is Elvis*.

Elvis and the Beatles appeared on the same album in 1964. It was a U.S. Marines release for military radio stations. The LP, which was titled *Sounds of Solid Gold*, included "Kissin' Cousins" by Elvis and "I Want to Hold Your Hand" by the Beatles.

In a sad note, Elvis would later denounce the Beatles as a subversive group. On the British TV show "Juke Box Jury," the Beatles once remarked that Elvis "had gone down the nick," in reviewing one of his latest songs.

An interesting story has it that the Beatles asked Colonel Tom Parker to be their manager after the death of Brian Epstein. Parker said he would, but that Elvis would still be number one. The group declined. (See *John Lennon, Paul McCartney, George Harrison, Ringo Starr*)

BEAULIEU, ANN

(1927–   ) Mother of Priscilla Beaulieu and wife of Joseph Paul Beaulieu, whom she married after the death of her husband, James Wagner, in 1945. Ann met

---

[1]Elvis and the Beatles, although reaching the top in two different decades, the 1950s and 1960s, actually started out within a few years of each other. Elvis began playing professionally in 1954, while the Beatles began (as the Quarrymen) in 1956.

James Wagner when she was fifteen years old, marrying him two years later.

BEAULIEU, DONALD

(1950–   ) Brother of Priscilla Beaulieu. Upon his return from Vietnam, where he had served as a helicopter pilot, he was met at McGuire Air Force Base in April 1971 by Elvis and Priscilla. Elvis once gave Donald a new Mustang automobile.

BEAULIEU, JEFFREY

(1954–   ) Brother of Priscilla Beaulieu. He was listed as the Presley home-movie researcher in the credits of the 1988 TV mini–series "Elvis and Me."

BEAULIEU, JOSEPH PAUL

Priscilla Beaulieu's stepfather, who adopted her when she was a child. (Her father, James Wagner, died when she was six months old.) Captain Beaulieu was attached to the 1405 Support Squadron at the Wiesbaden Air Force Base in West Germany when Priscilla first met Elvis at a party in 1959. He was later transferred to Travis Air Force Base in California and held the rank of colonel upon his retirement from the Air Force.

BEAULIEU, MICHELLE

(1954–   ) Younger sister of Priscilla Beaulieu. Michelle served as the maid of honor at Priscilla's wedding to Elvis on May 1, 1967.

BEAULIEU, PRISCILLA ANN

(1945–   ) Onetime wife of Elvis Presley. Priscilla, the five-foot-three-inch gray-eyed daughter of Ann Beaulieu and Navy Lieutenant James Wagner, was born on May 25, 1945. Wagner died in a 1945 plane crash when Priscilla was six months old. She was later adopted by Joseph Beaulieu. Priscilla has one younger halfsister, Michelle (1954–   ), and four younger halfbrothers, Donald (1950–   ), Jeffrey (1954–   ), and twins, Tim and Tom (1962–   ). Joseph Beaulieu, her stepfather, was a captain in the U.S. Air Force stationed with his family in Germany at the same time that Elvis was in the Army. In 1959, at the age of fourteen, Priscilla was introduced to Elvis by U.S. Airman Currie Grant at a party. She wore a blue and white sailor-suit dress with white socks. Elvis started to see Priscilla shortly afterward and soon the two fell in love. Elvis called her "Cilla." He convinced her to dye her hair black because he liked actress Debra Paget's black hair from the 1956 movie *Love Me Tender*. With the help of Elvis's grandmother and stepmother, Priscilla was invited to spend Christmas with Elvis at Graceland in 1960. After the stay, Priscilla returned to Germany on January 2. It was then that Elvis realized how much he missed her. In January 1961 Elvis called Priscilla's father, Captain Beaulieu, and asked if Priscilla could finish her schooling in Memphis under the watchful guardianship of Elvis's family. Captain Beaulieu finally agreed more than a year later, and Priscilla moved into Graceland in October of 1962. She was

Priscilla Presley today. (Photo courtesy Eddie Brandt's Saturday Matinee)

enrolled at Immaculate Conception High School. On June 14, 1963, Priscilla graduated and enrolled at the Patricia Stevens Finishing School. As a graduation gift, Elvis bought her a Corvair, which over the years was followed by a Chevrolet Sports Coupe, an Oldsmobile Toronado, a Cadillac El Dorado, and a Mercedes. After Priscilla turned twenty-one years old, and at Colonel Tom Parker's insistence, Elvis proposed on Christmas Eve 1966, and on May 1, 1967, Elvis and Priscilla were married in a private ceremony held in Milton Prell's suite at the Aladdin Hotel in Las Vegas. The couple then honeymooned in Palm Springs, California. After the honeymoon the couple moved into a mansion at 1174 Hillcrest Road in Beverly Hills, California. On February 1, 1968, nine months after the marriage, Lisa Marie Presley was born to the Presleys. Lisa would be the couple's only child.

Priscilla left Elvis on February 23, 1972, becoming

romantically involved with karate instructor Mike Stone, who himself was obtaining a divorce from his wife. It had been Elvis who, after meeting Stone, suggested that Stone teach Priscilla karate. Elvis sued Priscilla for divorce on August 18, 1972, in Santa Monica, California. On October 9, 1973, the divorce was granted. The divorce settlement made Priscilla economically secure. She soon entered into several business ventures, including the Bis and Beau's boutique in Los Angeles, which was sold in 1976. In 1979, both Priscilla Presley and Persis Khambatta turned down the new role of Tiffany Welles on TV's "Charlie's Angels." Shelly Hack got the part. Priscilla made her TV debut as a guest on Tony Orlando's NBC special in 1979. She then went on to become a cohost of the TV series "Those Amazing Animals," and in 1983 became a regular on the prime-time TV soap "Dallas," playing the role of Jenna Wade. Priscilla was involved in an affair with actor and model Michael Edwards from 1978 to 1985, and was then linked with hairdresser Ellie Ezerzer. On March 1, 1987, Priscilla gave birth to Navarone, the son of Brazilian writer-director Marco Garibaldi.

Priscilla was portrayed by Season Hubley in the 1979 TV movie *Elvis*; by Rhonda Lyn and Lisha Sweetnam (narration) in the 1981 movie *This Is Elvis*; and by Susan Walters in the 1988 TV miniseries "Elvis and Me" (which was based on her autobiography).

BECAUD, GILBERT
Composer, with Mann Curtis and Pierre Delanoe, of "Je T'Appartiens," which Elvis recorded as "Let It Be Me." He was also the composer, with Pierre Delanoe, of "Et Maintenant," which Elvis recorded as "What Now My Love."

BEDFORD, ELOISE
Girl whom Elvis liked in the fifth grade at the East Tupelo Consolidated School.

BEE GEES
Australian vocal group (the members were born in England) composed of brother Barry (1946–   ) and twins Robin and Maurice (1949–   ). The Bee Gees were once managed by Robert Stigwood. Scottish singer LuLu (real name: Marie McDonald McLaughlin Lawrie), who costarred with Sidney Poitier in the 1967 movie *To Sir, with Love*, was once married to Maurice Gibb. The Bee Gees' album *Saturday Night Fever* has become the all-time best-selling soundtrack album.

In 1969 Elvis recorded the Bee Gees' 1967 composition "Words."

BEENE, WALLY
Staff writer for the U.S. Armed Forces newspaper *Stars and Stripes.*[1] In late February 1960, Beene became the only reporter to obtain an exclusive interview with Elvis while Elvis was in the Army.

BEHR, DAVID
Psychic who claimed to have made contact with Elvis on the evening of December 1, 1978, in a seance that was recorded on tape. The two-way conversation, in which Elvis supposedly answered sixty-five questions, was later sold on records and cassettes for $9.95 via advertisements in magazines.

BEL AIR CLUB
Memphis lounge at the Bel Air Motel, located at 1850 S. Bellevue, in which Elvis appeared as a guest artist with Doug Poindexter and the Starlight Wranglers in mid-1954. Jack Clement and his band once backed Elvis at the club.

BELEW, BILL
Tailor who designed Elvis's jumpsuits and capes beginning in 1968. Belew was the one who designed Elvis's black leather costume for the 1968 TV special. Belew's outfits cost Elvis several thousand dollars apiece.

BELLEVUE BOULEVARD
Main north-south street in Memphis. The southern portion of Bellevue Boulevard (Highway 51 South) was renamed Elvis Presley Boulevard on January 18, 1972. The reason the entire boulevard wasn't renamed was because of the protests of the Bellevue Baptist Church (70 Bellevue), whose members said they did not wish their church's name to be affiliated with that of a rock & roll singer and did not want to be known as Elvis Presley Baptist Church.

BELLEVUE-STRATFORD HOTEL
Hotel in Philadelphia where Elvis stayed while appearing at the Spectrum on November 8, 1971. In 1976 the hotel became the site of the famous Legionnaires' disease outbreak in which twenty-nine people died.

BELL, FREDDIE, AND THE BELLBOYS
Obscure mid-1950s rock & roll band that became the first American rock act to tour Britain when they toured with Tommy Steele in 1956. The band appeared in the 1956 movie *Rock Around the Clock*, and in the 1964 movie *Get Yourself a College Girl* (British title: *The Swingin' Set*). Roberta Linn sang with the band in the latter film. Elvis, Scotty Moore, Bill Black, and D. J. Fontana heard Freddie Bell and the Bellboys singing "Hound Dog" while in Las Vegas in April 1956. Elvis liked the song and recorded it on July 2, 1956, exactly as Freddie Bell and the Bellboys had sung it. One year earlier, Freddie Bell had made a recording of "Hound Dog"/"Move Me Baby" (Teen 101).

BENEVOLENT CON MAN, THE
Title of the autobiography (subtitled: *How Much Does It Cost If It's Free?*) that Colonel Tom Parker was writing in 1956. He turned down a $100,000 advance from a publisher with this reply: "Well, I guess I could let you

---

[1]The father of singer Jackson Browne was also a reporter for *Stars and Stripes* in West Germany.

have the back cover for that!" Parker planned to run full-page advertisements between chapters in his book, selling each ad for $25,000. The book was never completed.

BENJAMIN, BENNIE
(1907–   ) Composer born in Christiansted, St. Croix, Virgin Islands, on November 4, 1907. Benjamin composed many songs, including "I Don't Want to Set the World on Fire" in 1941 and "Wheel of Fortune" in 1952. He wrote "Anyone (Could Fall in Love with You)" with Sol Marcus and Louis A. DeJesus; "Lonely Man" with Sol Marcus; and "I Will Be Home Again" with Raymond Leveen and Lou Singer, all of which Elvis recorded.

BENNETT, ROY C.
(1918–   ) Composer born in Brooklyn on August 12, 1918. With Sid Tepper, Bennett composed forty-three songs that Elvis sang in his motion pictures. The songs were:

"A Boy Like Me, a Girl Like You"
"A House That Has Everything"
"All That I Am"
"Am I Ready"
"Angel"
"Beach Boy Blues"
"Beginner's Luck"
"Cane and a High Starched Collar"
"Confidence"
"Drums of the Islands"
"Earth Boy"
"Five Sleepy Heads"
"For the Millionth and Last Time"
"Fort Lauderdale Chamber of Commerce"
"G.I. Blues"
"Hawaiian Sunset"
"I Love Only One Girl"
"Island of Love (Kauai)"
"Ito Eats"
"It's a Wonderful World"
"Just for Old Time Sake"
"Kismet"
"Lonesome Cowboy"
"Mexico"
"Mine"
"New Orleans"
"Once Is Enough"
"Petunia, the Gardener's Daughter"
"Puppet on a String"
"Relax"
"Shoppin' Around"
"Slicin' Sand"
"Smorgasbord"
"Song of the Shrimp"
"Stay Away"
"Take Me to the Fair"
"The Bullfighter Was a Lady"
"The Lady Loves Me"
"The Walls Have Ears"
"There Is So Much World to See"
"Vino, Dinero y Amor"
"Western Union"
"Wheels on My Heels"

BENNETT, TONY
(1926–   ) Singer born Anthony Dominick Benedetto in New York City on August 3, 1926. In 1953 Bennett charted a number one hit with "Rags to Riches" (Columbia 40048), a song Elvis would later record. Bennett's sister, Carole, was the wife of Currie Grant, the airman who introduced Priscilla Beaulieu to Elvis in 1959.

BERGEN, EDGAR
(1903–1978) Ventriloquist who featured dummies Charlie McCarthy, Mortimer Snerd, Effie Klinker, and Podine Puffington. Like anyone else in the United States who had a radio, Elvis listened to the antics of Edgar Bergen and Charlie McCarthy each week. Bergen's daughter is actress Candice Bergen (1946–   ).

Elvis took New York model Sandy Preston to see Bergen at the Sahara Hotel in 1956. Also featured on the bill was the Mary Kaye Trio.

BERGSTROM AIR FORCE BASE
Military installation in Austin, Texas, where Captain Joseph Beaulieu, his wife, and adopted daughter, Priscilla, lived in 1956. Priscilla bought her first Elvis album, *Elvis Presley*, at the base PX.

BERLE, MILTON
(1908–   ) Television comedian of the 1950s who was born in New York City's Harlem on July 12, 1908. Berle was nicknamed "Uncle Miltie" and "The Thief of Bad Gags." He hosted his own TV variety show, "The Texaco Star Theater," beginning on September 21, 1948. Berle made his screen debut as a young child being thrown from a train in an episode of the 1914 silent serial *Perils of Pauline*.

Elvis appeared twice on Berle's series: April 3 (San Diego) and June 5 (Hollywood), 1956 . On the April 3 program, Berle played Elvis's twin brother, Melvin Presley, in a comedy skit. (See *The Milton Berle Show* in Part II)

BERLIN, IRVING
(1888–   ) American composer who was born Israel Baline in Russia on May 11, 1888. Berlin composed many classic songs, including "Alexander's Ragtime Band," "Cheek to Cheek," "Easter Parade," and "What'll I Do?" Chances are that, sometime in his life, Elvis sang another one of Berlin's songs, "God Bless America," which was introduced by Kate Smith. Berlin appeared in the 1943 movie *This Is the Army*, in which he sang his own composition "Oh, How I Hate to Get Up in the Morning." At the 1942 Academy Awards, Berlin became the first and only person to present himself an Oscar when he opened the envelope for Best Song and discovered that he had won for "White Christmas." Bing Crosby, of course, sang it in the movie *Holiday Inn* and the 1954 remake, *White Christmas*. Elvis recorded Berlin's "White Christmas" in 1957.

BERNARD, FELIX
Composer, with Dick Smith, of the song "Winter Wonderland," which Elvis recorded in 1971.

BERNERO, JOHNNY

Drummer for the Dean Beard Band who played drums on several of Elvis's Sun recordings, although he was never credited. Bernero played drums on "I Forgot to Remember to Forget," "Tryin' to Get to You," "You're a Heartbreaker," "I'm Left, You're Right, She's Gone," and "When It Rains It Really Pours."

For many years listeners wondered who the uncredited drummer was on some of Elvis's Sun recordings, falsely believing that it was D. J. Fontana. But Fontana has stated that he never played on any Sun record.

BERRY, CHUCK

(1926–) Highly imaginative and talented composer and singer who was born Charles Edward Anderson Berry in St. Louis on October 18, 1926. Berry recorded for Chicago's Chess Record label. His first hit record, "Maybellene" (Chess 1604), was actually written in 1955 by Berry as a country song and sounds almost identical to Bob Wills's song "Ida Red" (Columbia 20312). Berry's songs have been recorded by the Beatles, the Rolling Stones, and Elvis Presley, among thousands of other artists. Elvis covered these original Berry recordings: "Memphis, Tennessee" (Chess 1729), "Johnny B. Goode" (Chess 1691), "Too Much Monkey Business" (Chess 1635), "Merry Christmas Baby" (Chess 1714), and "Promised Land" (Chess 1916). The Beatles covered two Berry recordings: "Rock and Roll Music" (Chess 1671) and "Roll Over Beethoven" (Chess 1612). The Rolling Stones recorded eight of his songs: "Carol" (Chess 1691), "Don't Lie to Me" (Chess 1700), "Around and Around" (Chess 1691), "You Can't Catch Me" (Chess 1645), "I'm Talking About You" (Chess 1779), "Little Queenie" (Chess 1722), "Bye Bye Johnnie" (Chess 1754), and "Come On" (Chess 1799). Although Elvis, the Beatles, and the Rolling Stones recorded a total of fifteen Chuck Berry compositions, none recorded the same song. Berry's first number one record on *Billboard*'s Hot 100 chart was his risque "My Ding-a-Ling" (Chess 2131) in 1972. Berry once played the lounge while Elvis was in the main room at the Hilton Hotel in Las Vegas. As a joke, Elvis and Sammy Davis Jr. danced across the stage during one of Berry's performances.

Elvis sang Berry's "Brown-Eyed Handsome Man" with the Million-Dollar Quartet on December 4, 1956, and "School Day" in concert in the 1970s. He also sang "Rock and Roll Music" in concert.

In Chuck Berry's 1987 autobiography, *Chuck Berry: an Autobiography*, Elvis's name is mentioned only one time, and that was in a list of people, which says something about Berry's ego.

BEVERLY WILSHIRE HOTEL

Beverly Hills hotel at which Elvis and his parents stayed while he was making the 1958 movie *King Creole*. Elvis made the hotel his home until he leased the house at 565 Perugia Way in Bel Air. Actually, he and his friends were asked to leave the hotel because of their rowdiness.

B.F. WOOD MUSIC COMPANY

Music publishing firm that owns the British rights to Elvis's songs.

BIBLE, THE

Elvis kept a copy of the Good Book by his bedside and read from it often. During the 1960s, after his mother's death, Elvis held Bible readings in his Bel Air home. Elvis's favorite passage was from *I Corinthians* 10:13. He once claimed to have a Bible in every room of his houses in Memphis and California. At a Nashville auction in late 1977, a Bible owned by Elvis with his name embossed in gold letters sold for $1,375.

BIBLE, THE (IN THE BEGINNING)

A 1966 movie directed by John Huston.[1] Elvis, Priscilla, and some of the Memphis Mafia attended a Hollywood premiere showing of the film. (The world premiere of *The Bible* was in Rome.)

Elvis didn't care for the movie and wanted to leave at intermission. Although Priscilla tried to persuade him to stay, he and the boys left the theater.

BIENSTOCK, FREDDIE

Manager of Hill and Range Music Publishers (including Elvis Presley Music and Gladys Music) who collected all the material from which Elvis would select songs for his recording sessions. This arrangement eventually led to the deterioration in quality of the material offered to Elvis. Bienstock later succeeded Steve Sholes as A&R man at RCA Victor.

BIG BUNNY

Hugh Hefner's all-black DC-9 jet (N950PB). Elvis used the aircraft during his 1974 concert tour.

BIG D JAMBOREE

Saturday night country music radio show broadcast on Dallas station KRLD. Elvis first appeared on the broadcast on April 16, 1955. Also appearing on the same bill were Sonny James, Hank Locklin, and the Maddox Brothers and Rose. Roy Orbison was a staff member at the time Elvis played the Big D. It was at the "Big D Jamboree" on June 18 that Bob Neal and Colonel Tom Parker first met. In addition to the above two dates, Elvis also appeared on the broadcasts of May 28, July 23, and September 3, all in 1955.

BIGGS, PATRICK (PAT)

(–1966) Husband of Delta Mae Presley (sister of Vernon Presley). Pat Biggs was one of Elvis's favorite uncles. Elvis once helped him buy a nightclub. (See *Delta Mae Presley*)

---

[1]John Huston was the son of actor Walter Huston (who was the first person to record the classic "September Song," from the 1938 musical play *Knickerbocker Holiday*). John Huston's first directorial attempt was *The Maltese Falcon* (1941), which starred Humphrey Bogart, with a cameo by his father.

BIGGS, HOWARD

Composer, with Joe Thomas, of the song "I'm Gonna Sit Right Down and Cry (Over You)," which Elvis recorded in 1956.

BILLBOARD MAGAZINE

Publication dealing with current musical trends, founded in 1894. *Billboard* first reviewed "That's All Right (Mama)" on August 7, 1954. Later that year the magazine voted Elvis Presley the eighth Most Promising Artist of the Year.

BING CROSBY AWARD

Award presented by the National Academy of Recording Arts and Sciences to Elvis on September 8, 1971, by Bing's son Chris Crosby. The award was previously called the Golden Achievement Award. Earlier recipients were Irving Berlin, Frank Sinatra, and Edward Kennedy (Duke) Ellington.

BIO SCIENCE LABORATORIES

Los Angeles medical research facility headed by Dr. Raymond Kelly that analyzed the tissue from Elvis's body. Bio Science concluded that the following depressant drugs were present in Elvis's body at the time of his death: butabarbital, codeine, morphine, pentobarbital, Placidyl, Quaalude, Valium, and Valmid.

BIONDI, RICHARD (DICK)

Disc jockey for Buffalo radio station WKBW who was fired on the air in 1956 for playing an Elvis record. Today Dick Biondi is a Chicago disc jockey.

BIS AND BEAU'S

Beverly Hills boutique opened by Priscilla Presley and professional dress designer Olivia Bis in 1974. The shop, which was located at 9650 Santa Monica Boulevard, was sold on April 1, 1976. Some of their customers included Suzanne Pleshette, Lana Turner, Cher, Barbara Eden, Eva Gabor, Julie Christie, Joanne Woodward, and two former love interests of Elvis's, Natalie Wood and Cybill Shepherd.

BLACK AND WHITE JAMBOREE

Tupelo radio program on WELO sponsored by the Black and White hardware store, a business located on the main floor of WELO's building on Spring Street. Reportedly, Elvis appeared on the program in the fall of 1944 singing "Old Shep" with Mississippi Slim accompanying on guitar. Elvis also appeared on this program at other times. In 1955 Elvis, Johnny Cash, and Carl Perkins appeared together on the program.

BLACK BELT

Ranking designation used in karate. Elvis earned an eighth-degree black belt.

BLACK, BILL

(1926–1965) Bass player, nicknamed "Blackie," who backed Elvis on many of his early recordings. William P. Black was born in Memphis on September 17, 1926, to a poor family. He had two brothers, Johnny ("Jack"), a musician, and Kenny. At one time, he and his brothers and mother, Ruth Black, lived in the same Memphis apartment complex as the Presley family. Prior to joining Elvis, Black played with the Starlight Wranglers, a Doug Poindexter group that included Scotty Moore on guitar. It has often been said that Sam Phillips introduced Elvis to Scotty Moore and Bill Black. But Elvis may have already known Bill and "jammed" with him and his brother Johnny, since they were neighbors at the Lauderdale Courts and their mothers were friends. (In an interview with Jay Thompson in 1956, Elvis stated that he never knew Scotty or Bill before they recorded together; however, Elvis unintentionally gave misinformation in some of his interviews.)

Bill Black, Scotty Moore, and Elvis were briefly known as the Blue Moon Boys in 1955. They performed together on the "Louisiana Hayride" show and in many one-night stands throughout the South. Black added some fun to the performances when he would ride his big bass across the stage. Black played Eddy the bass player in the 1957 movie *Loving You*. After Black and Moore left Elvis on September 21, 1957, because of a salary dispute (Elvis was making millions, while Moore and Black were making paltry $100-a-week salaries), Black formed the Bill Black Combo. Black did play on three more recording session with Elvis (January 15–16, January 23, and February 1, 1958). He was replaced by Bob Moore.

The Bill Black Combo recorded a number of hit records for another Memphis record company, Hi Records. Their hits included the instrumental "Smokie–Part 2" (Hi 2018), and "White Silver Sands" (Hi 2021), both released in 1960. Black also recorded a version of "Don't Be Cruel" (Hi 2026). The Bill Black Combo appeared in the 1961 movie *Teen-Age Millionaire*. Carl McAvoy, an original member of Bill Black's Combo, is a cousin of Jerry Lee Lewis, Mickey Gilley, and evangelist Jimmy Swaggart. Black once owned a recording studio across the street from American Sound Studios in Memphis.

In 1965 Black was hospitalized at the Baptist Memorial Hospital three times, from June to October 8 (when he went into a coma). On October 21, 1965, Bill Black died of a brain tumor during surgery. Vernon Presley attended the funeral, but Elvis did not. Black was survived by his wife, Evelyn, and three daughters.

The stand-up bass that Black used on his recordings with Elvis is today owned by Paul McCartney, a bass player himself[1].

---

[1] On Wings' 1979 album *Back to the Egg*, McCartney played the bass, which still had the name Bill on the lower left, on the song "Baby's Request," which Paul had originally composed for the Mills Brothers.

BLACK ELVIS, THE
Name conferred upon singer Jackie Wilson, a good friend of Elvis's. The late singer-guitarist James Marshal (Jimi) Hendrix (1942–70) was also called "The Black Elvis."

BLACK, JOHNNY
Brother of musician Bill Black who also played stand-up bass. According to several sources, Elvis and Johnny buddied around together in the early 1950s and appeared with Johnny and Dorsey Burnette at various places in Memphis, usually on Saturday nights. According to Paul Burlison in an article in *Goldmine* magazine, it was Johnny Black whom Sam Phillips wanted to play bass behind Elvis in 1954, but Bill volunteered because his brother was away in Texas.

Johnny Black can be seen playing bass for the Johnny Burnette Trio in the 1957 movie *Rock, Rock, Rock.* (The Burnette Trio disbanded soon after the movie, and brothers Johnny and Dorsey Burnette each had successful solo careers.) Johnny Black played bass for Dean Bernard at Sun Records in 1956.

BLACK, LOUIS
Father of musicians Bill Black and Johnny Black and husband of Ruth Black. In Elaine Dundy's book *Elvis and Gladys*, the author states that as early as 1952 Louis was encouraging Elvis to go to the Memphis Recording Service (Sun Records) and record an acetate of his singing.

BLACK MONDAY
Name given by the press to March 24, 1958, the day Elvis was inducted into the U.S. Army.

BLACKWELL, OTIS
(1932–) Prolific black songwriter who was born in Brooklyn on February 16, 1932. Blackwell grew up with singer-actor Tex Ritter as his idol. Under the pseudonym John Davenport, he cowrote "Fever" in 1956, which was recorded by Little Willie John. In 1977 Stevie Wonder presented Blackwell with a rock-music award in recognition of his accomplishments. Some of Blackwell's compositions include: "Great Balls of Fire," "Priscilla," "Just Keep It Up," "Hey Little Girl," and "Breathless."

Elvis recorded a number of Blackwell songs: "Fever" (written with Eddie Cooley), "Don't Be Cruel," "All Shook Up," "Make Me Know It," "Paralyzed," and, the following cowritten with Winfield Scott: "Return to Sender," "(Such an) Easy Question," "One Broken Heart for Sale," "Please Don't Drag That String Around," and "We're Coming in Loaded." On "Don't Be Cruel," "All Shook Up," and "Paralyzed," Elvis is listed as the cowriter through arrangements with Hill and Range Music, even though Otis Blackwell and Elvis had never met. Colonel Tom Parker had a rule (he had a lot of rules) that Elvis should never meet any of his songwriters so as not to interfere with Elvis's publishing rights. Blackwell gave up part of his composer credit to Elvis on those three songs in order to get Elvis to record them. Elvis had nothing to do with the writing of any of Blackwell's songs. Blackwell sang on all of the demos of his own compositions for both Elvis and Jerry Lee Lewis, since he could perform the songs in their respective styles. The demos were recorded at the Allegro Studios in New York City.

In 1977 Otis Blackwell recorded the album *These Are My Songs* (Inner City 1032), which included "Fever," "All Shook Up," "Return to Sender," and "Don't Be Cruel."

BLACKWELL, ROBERT (BUMPS)
(1918–1985) Composer born in Seattle on May 23, 1918. With John Marascalco, Blackwell composed the songs "Ready Teddy" and "Rip It Up." With Enotris Johnson and Richard Penniman (Little Richard), he composed "Long Tall Sally." All three songs were recorded by both Little Richard and Elvis in 1956. Bumps Blackwell died of pneumonia on March 9, 1985.

BLACKWOOD BROTHERS
Gospel quartet from Ackerman, Mississippi. They formed their group in 1934, moving to Memphis in 1950. The original members were R. W. Blackwood,

A high school snapshot of Elvis. (Photo courtesy Jeff Wheatcraft)

James Blackwood (nicknamed "Mr. Gospel Music"), Bill Lyles, and Bill Shaw. Other members have included Cecil Blackwood, Pat Hoffmaster, Ken Turner, and Tommy Fairchild. R. W. Blackwood was killed when his twin-engine Beech aircraft crashed during a landing. The crash also killed Bill Lyles. Cecil Blackwood then became the group's lead singer. A few weeks later, Elvis was asked to join the Blackwoods' younger group, the Songfellows, replacing Cecil Blackwood. Elvis wanted to join the Songfellows but couldn't because he had just begun recording for Sun Records. James and R. W. Blackwood, with Jack Marshall and Bill Lyles, had recorded four songs for Sun Records in 1952, all unreleased. On July 24, 1957, Elvis attended a concert featuring the Blackwood Brothers. They were Gladys Presley's favorite gospel group, and they sang "Rock of Ages" and "Precious Memories" at her August 15, 1958, funeral. Elvis had them flown in by chartered plane for the services.

BLACKWOOD, MALESSA
Nineteen-year-old beauty whom Elvis dated in 1976. Miss Blackwood once held the title "Miss Memphis Southmen." The Memphis Southmen was a franchise in the World Football League.

BLAGMAN, NORMAN
(1926–   ) Musician and composer born in New York City on August 18, 1926. Blagman composed "Give Me the Right" with Fred Wise and "Put the Blame on Me" with Fred Wise and Kay Twomey, both songs recorded by Elvis.

BLAIKLEY, ALAN
Composer with Geoff Stephens and Ken Howard of the songs "Heart of Rome" and "I've Lost You," both of which were recorded by Elvis.

BLAINE, HAL
(1929–   ) Session musician who has played drums on 189 Gold Records, more than any other drummer, including seven Grammy winners and three Academy Award–winning records. Blaine played for Jan and Dean, Frank Sinatra, John Denver, the Carpenters, Johnny Cash, Simon and Garfunkel, and many others. His drums can be heard on the following hit records: "I Got You Babe" (Atco 6359) and "The Beat Goes On" (Atco 6461) by Sonny and Cher; "Be My Baby" (Philles 116) by the Ronettes; "Mr. Tambourine Man" (Columbia 43271) by the Byrds; "California Dreamin' " (Dunhill 4020) by the Mamas and the Papas; "He's a Rebel" (Philles 106) by the Crystals; "I Get Around" (Capitol 5118) and "Good Vibrations" (Capitol 5676) by the Beach Boys; and "Windy" (Warner 7041) by the Association, just to mention a few. Blaine was a member of Johnny Rivers's band and played on his hit recordings "Memphis" (Imperial 66032) and "Secret Agent Man" (Imperial 66159).

Blaine, who had recorded in the 1960s as Hal Blaine and the Young Cougars, played drums behind Elvis beginning with the *Blue Hawaii* session of March 1961, and continuing through the 1968 NBC-TV special.

BLAIR, HAL KELLER
(1915–   ) Composer born in Kansas City, Missouri, on November 26, 1915. Blair was a member of the Jazz String Quartet and the Rhythm Rangers western band, and appeared in several films. He composed, with Don Robertson, the following songs that Elvis recorded: "I Met Her Today," "I'm Yours," "I Think I'm Gonna Like It Here," "What Now, What Next, Where To," and "No More." With Aaron Schroeder, Claude DeMetrius, and Bill Pepper, Blair composed "I Was the One" for Elvis in 1956 .

BLANTON, RAYMOND
(1930–   ) Former governor of Tennessee born on April 10, 1930. On the day of Elvis's funeral, Governor Blanton ordered all flags in the state flown at half-mast. He also attended the funeral services.

Governor Blanton once said of Elvis: "He was the greatest talent this country, maybe the world, has ever produced."

BLOCH ARENA
Four-thousand-seat facility at Pearl Harbor, Hawaii, where Elvis performed a benefit concert for the *USS Arizona* Memorial Fund on March 25, 1961. The concert, sponsored by the Pacific War Memorial Commission, was originally scheduled for Palm Sunday, March 26, but Elvis didn't think that date was appropriate. Elvis and Colonel Parker purchased the first two tickets (at $100 each). (See *Arizona, USS*)

BLOOM, RUBE
(1902–1976) Musician and composer born in New York City on April 24, 1902. Bloom played in the bands of Bix Beiderbecke and the Dorsey Brothers. With Johnny Mercer he composed the 1940 song "Fools Rush In (Where Angels Fear to Tread)," which Elvis recorded in 1971.

BLOSSOMS, THE
Female vocal trio that backed Elvis on the 1968 NBC-TV special "Elvis." The members of the Blossoms were Darlene Love, Jean King, and Fanita James, who later became a member of the oldies act, the Shirelles. The Blossoms were regulars on the ABC-TV series "Shindig." Elvis requested that the Blossoms sing backup for him during his concert tours, but the girls had to bow out because of a prior commitment. Elvis then hired the Sweet Inspirations. They briefly appeared in Elvis's 1969 movie *Change of Habit*. The Blossoms did back up Tom Jones in Las Vegas for a while. (See *Darlene Love*)

BLUE(S)
Word that appeared in the titles of eighteen songs Elvis recorded: "Beach Boy Blues," "Blueberry Hill," "Blue Christmas," "Blue Eyes Crying in the Rain," "Blue Hawaii," "Blue Moon," "Blue Moon of Kentucky," "Blue River," "Blue Suede Shoes," "G.I. Blues," "Indescribably Blue," "Mean Woman Blues," "A Mess of Blues," "Milkcow Blues Boogie," "Moody Blue," "Something Blue," "Steamroller Blues," and "When My Blue Moon Turns to Gold Again."

BLUE CROSS
Medical insurance company that insured Elvis's employees. The employees paid the premiums themselves, and there were no retirement benefits, although they got time off for Elvis's movie openings. In earlier years Elvis had paid for his employees' insurance.

BLUE MOON BOYS
Trio consisting of Elvis, Scotty Moore, and Bill Black. The name was coined by their manager, Bob Neal. The Blue Moon Boys used the name briefly in 1954, but because of Elvis's growing popularity, it was soon dropped.

BMI (BROADCAST MUSIC INC.)
One of two major music publishing unions. BMI was founded on October 14, 1939. The other music publishing union is ASCAP (American Society of Composers, Authors and Publishers), which was founded in 1914 by copyright attorney Nathan Burkan. After Elvis's death, it was discovered that he had been deprived of a great deal of money because he had never registered with BMI. As a result, he never collected royalties on the songs on which he was listed as co-composer. Ironically, it was the popularity of rock & roll that built BMI into such a successful union.

After Elvis's death, BMI attempted to restrict Elvis imitators by limiting them to performing only three Elvis songs during a single performance.

BMW (BAYERISCHE MOTOR WERKE)
One of several cars Elvis owned while stationed in Germany. The German press referred to the sports car, a BMW 507 upholstered in black and white leather and valued at $7,160, as the "Presley Wagen." Elvis bought the car, a used demonstration model, on December 20, 1958, for $3,750, in Frankfurt.

Ursula Siebert and Elvis. (Photo courtesy Wide World Photos)

BOBO, FORREST L.
Proprietor of the Tupelo Hardware Company store on Main Street in Tupelo, Mississippi, who in January 1946, sold Gladys Presley a $7.75 guitar as a birthday present for Elvis. (The total cost of the purchase, including 2 percent sales tax, was $7.91.) Elvis had wanted a .22-caliber rifle and threw a temper tantrum when his mother told him that he couldn't have the rifle.[1] After several minutes of discussion, Mrs. Presley and Bobo persuaded Elvis to get a guitar that was in a glass showcase on the other side of the store.[2] The Tupelo Hardware Company had three different prices of guitars: $3.50, $7.75, and $12.75.

According to Forrest L. Bobo, this was the glass showcase in which Elvis's first guitar was sitting when purchased by Gladys Presley in 1946. (Photo courtesy Don Fink)

BOLAN, MARC
(1948–1977) Rock singer who was born Mark Feld in Hackney, East London. Bolan died in an automobile accident in London on September 16, 1977, four weeks to the day after Elvis died.

Marc Bolan once said of Elvis, "He was the greatest living pop idol in the whole world."

BOLER, RHONDA
(1970–   ) Five-year-old daughter of Mrs. Glenda Boler, to whom Elvis gave his famous Diamond Medallion Cross during a concert in 1975 while singing "Can't Help Falling in Love." Elvis gave her the medallion, which had "R.G. 9th Month '69" engraved on the back, because she reminded him of his daughter, Lisa Marie. The scene was reenacted in the 1979 TV movie *Elvis.*

BOLT, JESSE
Man who underwent plastic surgery in 1978 in order to resemble the late Elvis.

[1]In Jerry Hopkins's book *Elvis: A Biography,* he states that Elvis wanted a bicycle. Interviews with Bobo, however, indicate that it was a rifle.
[2]When this book's authors visited the store in 1980, the same glass case was still being used.

BON AIR CLUB

Memphis nightclub at Summer Avenue and Mendenhall Road, where, in July 1954, Elvis made his first public appearance after the release of his first record ("That's All Right (Mama)"/"Blue Moon of Kentucky"). Elvis was backed by Doug Poindexter and his Starlight Wranglers.

BOND, EDDIE

(1933–   ) Rockabilly artist who was born Eddie James Bond at the Methodist Hospital in Memphis on July 1, 1933. Eddie Bond had a band called the Stompers for which Harold Jenkins (Conway Twitty) once sang. According to some stories, Elvis played some one-night stands with Eddie Bond and the Stompers in 1953 in the Memphis area. Bond toured with Elvis Presley September 5–9, 1955.

In an interview in *Goldmine* magazine, Bond claimed that Elvis sang with his band at the Hi Hat Club in Memphis before Elvis recorded for Sun Records in 1954. Bond said he fired Elvis from the act after one of the female owners told him to do so, or she would fire the entire band.

BOND, JOHNNY

(1915–1978) Singer and composer who was born Cyrus Whitfield Bond on June 1, 1915. In the mid-1940s, Bond cowrote, with Ernest Tubb, "Tomorrow Never Comes," which Elvis recorded in 1970. Bond, who was discovered by Gene Autry, appeared in movies with Roy Rogers, Gene Autry, Tex Ritter, and William Boyd (Hopalong Cassidy). In 1960 he reached the pop charts with "Hot Rod Lincoln" (Republic 2005) on Gene Autry's record label.

BONFA, RICK

Composer, with Randy Starr, of the song "Almost in Love," which Elvis recorded in 1968.

BOOKS

Elvis had a library of approximately 250 books at Graceland, most pertaining to religion or to the occult. Some of the books were:

The Bible
The Face of Jesus by Frank O. Adams
The Prophet by Kahlil Gibran
Autobiography of a Yogi by Paramahansa Yogananda
The Secret Teachings of All Ages by Manly P. Hall
Sun Signs by Linda Goodman
Cheiro's Book of Numbers
The Masters by Anne Besant
Only Love by Sri Daya Mata
The Infinite Way by Joel Goldsmith
The Secret Doctrine by Helena P. Blavatsky
The Impersonal Life by Joseph Berner

Elvis carried two trunks full of books whenever he traveled. Many of the titles were suggested to Elvis by Larry Geller. After Colonel Tom Parker finally broke Geller's influence on Elvis, those two trunks and their contents were burned.

Some of those who encouraged Elvis to read were actress Donna Douglas, martial-arts instructor Ed Parker, columnist May Mann, and mentor Larry Geller. Martial-arts instructor Kang Rhee encouraged Elvis to read books on the martial arts.

BOONE, PAT

(1934–   ) Popular clean-cut singer of the 1950s and 1960s who was born Eugene Charles Patrick Boone in Jacksonville, Florida, on June 1, 1934. While performing he always wore his trademark white buck shoes. Boone was president of his David Lipcomb High School senior class in Nashville. Shirley Foley, his future wife and the daughter of Country Music Hall of Fame singer Red Foley, was voted the school's homecoming queen. Pat is the great-great-great-grandson of frontiersman Daniel Boone.

Elvis and Boone first crossed paths when Pat won first place on the "Arthur Godfrey's Talent Scouts" TV show. Elvis was turned down at the show's rehearsal. Boone and Elvis, who appeared together in a show at the Circle Theatre in Cleveland in October 1955, were also good friends, despite the competition they supposedly had in the 1950s. In Red Robinson's August 31, 1957, interview with Elvis in Vancouver, B.C., Elvis stated that Pat Boone was "undoubtedly the finest voice out now, especially on slow songs" and that he had been a collector of Boone's records.

During the 1960s, Boone sometimes joined the Sunday touch football games at De Neve Park in Bel Air with Elvis and other celebrities. His wife, Shirley, would sometimes have to come and drag him home.

In 1964 Boone recorded an Elvis tribute album titled *Pat Boone Sings . . . Guess Who?* (Dot 25501). In 1977 his daughter, Debby Boone,[1] recorded the best-selling song in two decades (and best ever by a female) with "You Light Up My Life" (Warner Bros 0345).

Pat Boone has for years been accused of recording white covers of black records for Dot Records. These included such songs as "Two Hearts" by the Charms (Deluxe 6065), "At My Front Door" by the El Dorados (Vee Jay 147), "Gee Whittakers" by the Five Keys (Capitol 3267), "Tutti Frutti" by Little Richard (Specialty 561), "I'll Be Home" by the Flamingos (Checker 830), "Long Tall Sally" by Little Richard (Specialty 572), "Chains of Love" by Joe Turner (Atlantic 939), "I Almost Lost My Mind" by Ivory Joe Hunter (MGM 10578), and "Tra La La" by LaVern Baker (Atlantic 1116).

Elvis covered a few more tunes than Pat Boone. The reason he was never accused of covering other people's songs was that he generally recorded obscure songs the public never knew existed or had never heard the original black version. For example, checking the top ten rhythm & blues charts from January to July 1955, these songs appeared: "Reconsider Baby" by Lowell

---

[1]Debby Boone's father-in-law and mother-in-law are actor Jose Ferrer and singer Rosemary Clooney.

(Photo courtesy Jeff Wheatcraft)

Fulson, "Pledging My Love" by Johnny Ace, "I've Got a Woman" by Ray Charles, "My Babe" by Little Walter, "Flip, Flop and Fly" by Joe Turner, and "Unchained Melody" by Roy Hamilton, all of which Elvis covered. There are at least fifty more rhythm & blues songs from 1935 to 1964 that Elvis either "covered" or recorded, whichever way one may wish to look at it.

On December 4, 1956, Elvis sang Boone's "Don't Forbid Me" (Dot 15521) during the famous Million-Dollar Quartet session at Sun Studios. In June 1957, Pat Boone's "Love Letters in the Sand" (Dot 15570) (Boone did his own whistling on the tune) knocked Elvis's "All Shook Up" off the top spot of *Billboard*'s Hot 100 chart. In turn, Elvis's "Let Me Be Your Teddy Bear" replaced "Love Letters in the Sand" at number one.

BOURKE, RORY MICHAEL
(1942–   ) Composer born in Cleveland. Bourke won the ASCAP Writer of the Year Award in 1976 and 1979. Bourke was the composer of "Your Love's Been a Long Time Coming" and "Patch It Up" (with Eddie Rabbitt), both of which were recorded by Elvis.

BOUTAYRE, JEAN-PIERRE
Composer, with J. Claude Francois, of the song, "My Boy," which Elvis recorded in 1973.

BOWDER, BILL
Man to whom Elvis gave his $60,000 touring bus in 1976. Elvis traveled mostly by aircraft in the 1970s.

BOWERS, MILTON
Chairman of Memphis Draft Board #86 who personally delivered Elvis's draft notice to Graceland on De-

cember 20, 1957. The draft board gave Elvis a deferment to March 24, 1958 (from the original January 20), so that he could finish filming *King Creole* (1958).

BOXCAR ENTERPRISES
Elvis and Colonel Tom Parker's management company, established in 1974, that oversaw the merchandising of Elvis-related products, not including films or records. Two days after Elvis's death, Parker had Vernon Presley sign a contract in which the merchandising rights were signed over to Factors Etc, Inc., of New Jersey. The distribution of the profits of Boxcar Enterprises were: Tom Parker (40 percent), Tom Diskin (15 percent), George Parkhill (15 percent), Freddy Bienstock (15 percent), Elvis Presley (15 percent).

In 1974 Parker was paid $27,650, while Elvis was paid $2,750.

In 1975 Parker was paid $24,000, while Elvis was paid $6,000.

In 1976 Parker was paid $36,000, while Elvis was paid $10,500.

BOXCAR RECORDS
Record label based in Madison, Tennessee, begun by Elvis and Colonel Tom Parker as part of Boxcar Enterprises (named for double sixes in dice). It was on this label that the 1974 album *Having Fun with Elvis on Stage* was first released. RCA later distributed the album. The profits of Boxcar Records were distributed this way: Colonel Tom Parker (56 percent), Tom Diskin (22 percent), Elvis (22 percent).

BOY
Elvis's pet dog in the 1950s.

BOYD, MRS. BILLIE (VIRGINIA)
Custodian of Elvis's birthplace in Tupelo, Mississippi, and owner of the Elvis–Tupelo's Favorite Son Gift Shop on Elvis Presley Highway. In 1971 Boyd created the idea of the Elvis museum. Janelle McCombe became head of the organization and, with $80,000, built a chapel on the grounds next to Elvis's house of birth. (See *Elvis Presley Chapel*)

BOYD, PATRICIA
Elvis's secretary at Graceland who married Red West in 1961. Boyd quit as secretary in 1963 to have a baby. She was replaced by Patsy Presley. Elvis and Anita Wood attended Boyd's wedding to Red West on July 1, 1961.

BOYERS, DR. SIDNEY
Physician who treated Elvis on February 13, 1973, when Elvis became ill during his concert appearance in Las Vegas. Elvis gave the doctor a new white Lincoln Continental.

BOYLE INVESTMENT COMPANY
Memphis firm that bought the Circle G Ranch from Elvis in 1969 after Elvis had bought it back from Lou McClellan. (See *Lou McClellan*)

BRADLEY, ARLENE

(1942–   ) Woman who claimed to have been roman-tically involved with Elvis from 1957 to 1963. In 1964 Bradley married, but was divorced five years later.[1] She claimed to have first met Elvis while with her girlfriends—Darlene, Frances, and Heidi. Arlene's story was published in the *National Enquirer* on March 24, 1981.

BRADLEY, OMAR NELSON

(1893–1981) Professional soldier born in Clark, Mis-souri, on February 12, 1893. Bradley served as a gen-eral in the U.S. Army and Chairman of the Joint Chiefs of Staff in 1949 and 1950. General Bradley was one of Elvis's heroes. Elvis once visited Bradley at his home and presented him with a gold TCB chain.

BRADLEY, OWEN

(1915–   ) Decca (MCA) record producer who opened the first recording studio in Nashville. In 1955 Bradley turned down a chance to buy Elvis's contract from Sam Phillips for $5,000. Bradley, who was strictly a country music producer, was not keen on rockabilly or rock & roll music when it first appeared in 1954. As Decca Records' A&R man in Nashville, he once told Buddy Holly and the Crickets that their country-styled original version of "That'll Be the Day" was the worst song he had ever heard. At the time, he was trying to make Holly into a country singer.

BRADLEY, REVEREND C. W.

Pastor of the Memphis Woodvale Church of Christ who conducted Elvis's funeral ceremony at Graceland on August 18, 1977 at 2:00 P.M. Elvis's stepbrother David Stanley, who later became a minister, was influenced by Reverend Bradley.

BRADSHAW, JOAN

Woman whom Elvis dated in Hollywood in 1957.

BRANDO, MARLON

(1924–   ) Academy Award–winning method actor who was born in Omaha, Nebraska, on April 3, 1924. Brando's mother, an acting coach, gave Henry Fonda one of his early breaks in acting. Along with James Dean, Brando was one of Elvis's rebellious teenage heroes in the mid-1950s and was the unsmiling, rugged individual type Elvis longed to play on the silver screen. Brando's second wife, Movita, played opposite Clark Gable in the 1935 movie *Mutiny on the Bounty*. Ironically, Brando played the same role in the 1962 remake and became romantically involved with actress Tarita, who played the same role as had Movita. Brando has been nominated for Best Actor seven times, winning two Oscars: in 1954 for *On the Waterfront* and in 1972 for *The Godfather*. Marlon Brando, James Dean, and Elvis Presley were three of the young men who personified the young rebel in the 1950s.

The role of Pacer Burton in the 1960 movie *Flaming Star* was originally written for Marlon Brando, but Elvis eventually got the part. Elvis once said that his favorite actors were Marlon Brando and Spencer Tracy, and he referred to James Dean as a genius.

Jack Philbin, the executive producer of the Dorsey Brothers' "Stage Show," called Elvis "the guitar-play-ing Marlon Brando." This was one reason Elvis was booked for the show in 1956. Milton Berle once intro-duced Elvis as "the Marlon Brando of Rock."

Additionally, it was after seeing Brando's 1954 movie *Desiree* that Lucy de Barbin named her daughter Desi-ree. She claims Desiree is the daughter of Elvis.

BREMERHAVEN, WEST GERMANY

Port city where Elvis arrived on the troop ship *General Randall* on October 1, 1958. Elvis then traveled by train to Frieburg, his permanent post in West Germany.

BREWER, TERESA

(1931–   ) Cute and perky singer of the 1950s who was born Theresa Breuer in Toledo, Ohio, on May 7, 1931. In early 1950, at the age of eighteen, Brewer had her first and biggest-selling record with "Music, Music, Music" (Coral 65520). In February 1955, she recorded a version of "Pledging My Love" (Coral 61361), which Elvis later recorded.

Elvis met Brewer for the first time when he and some friends attended one of her Las Vegas shows in 1972. Elvis spent an hour backstage talking with her. Accord-ing to some sources Elvis sang one of her hit songs, "Till I Waltz Again with You," at the L. C. Humes An-nual Minstrel Show in April 1953.

BRIGGS, DAVID

Onetime boyfriend of Linda Thompson. Briggs played piano and organ at eight of Elvis's recording sessions, as well as at some of his live concerts (at $3,000 a week). He later became a member of the country-rock band Area Code 615, as did Charlie McCoy and Nor-bert Putnam. In 1966 Briggs recorded "I've Been Look-ing Everywhere for You" (Dot 16929).

BROCK, ROBERT

Los Angeles attorney picked by E. Gregory Hookstrat-ten (Elvis's attorney) to represent Priscilla during the divorce proceedings in 1973.

BROKAW, NORMAN

Priscilla Presley's agent.

BROOKS, DUDLEY ALONZO

(1913–   ) Musician born in Los Angeles, on De-cember 22, 1913. Brooks, who arranged for both Benny Goodman and Count Basie, played piano at many of Elvis's recording sessions from 1956 to 1964. Some of the cuts Brooks appeared on include "(Let Me Be Your) Teddy Bear," "Treat Me Nice," and "Jailhouse Rock." Brooks composed, with Charles O'Curran, two songs that Elvis recorded for the 1962 movie *Girls! Girls! Girls!*: "Mama" and "We'll Be Together."

---

[1]A reappearing theme with many of the women who claim to have had a secret love affair with Elvis is that they eventually marry and then divorce their husbands after only a few years.

BROOKS, TED
Composer, with William Johnson and George McFadden, of two gospel songs recorded by Elvis: "Bosom of Abraham" and "I, John."

BROWN, AUBREY
Six-foot-four-inch Memphis gas station attendant Elvis punched on October 18, 1956, in the Ed Hopper incident. (See *Ed Hopper*)

BROWN, JAMES
(1928–   ) Black singer and entertainer born in Pulaski, Tennessee, on June 17, 1928. Brown has been called "The King of Soul Music," "Soul Brother Number One," and "The Grandfather of Soul." In his youth, he spent three years in a Georgia reform school. He once shined shoes outside an Augusta, Georgia, radio station. Today, Brown owns the station. As a professional boxer, Brown won sixteen of his seventeen bantamweight bouts.

Both Elvis and James Brown were referred to as "Mr. Dynamite." Brown, Richard Penniman (Little Richard), and Otis Redding, three respected soul singers, all came from Macon, Georgia.

Elvis and Brown first met at a party at the Hyatt Continental Hotel in Hollywood. They sang several gospel tunes at the piano, including "Blind Barnabas" and "Old Jonah." They became lifelong friends. Elvis wanted to record with Brown's band, the Famous Flames, but it was nixed by Colonel Tom Parker. Brown was one of several celebrities who attended Elvis's private funeral in 1977. Upon hearing of Elvis's death, Brown immediately flew to Memphis, where he visited with Priscilla and Lisa Marie Presley. One of the best imitations of James Brown is performed by Eddie Murphy, a devoted Elvis fan.

BROWN, MARSHALL
Friend of Vernon Presley's in Tupelo, Mississippi. On June 17, 1933, Brown loaned Vernon three dollars so that he and Gladys Smith could buy a marriage license. Brown himself was married to a Presley, Vona Mae Presley.

BROWN, PINEY
Blues singer who once owned his own club, the "Sunset Crystal Palace," in the 1930s. Singer Joe Turner was his bartender. In 1949 Turner recorded "Old Piney Brown Is Gone" (Swing Time 154). Brown was the composer with John Thornton, Ralph Bass, and Earl Washington of "Just a Little Bit," which Elvis recorded in 1973.

BROWN, ROBERT CARLTON
Reporter who interviewed Elvis at the Warwick Hotel in New York City on March 24, 1956. The twenty-minute interview appeared on the album *Personally Elvis* (Silhouette Music).

BROWN, ROY
(1925–1981) Rhythm & blues singer born in New Orleans on September 10, 1925. Brown composed and originally recorded "Good Rockin' Tonight" (Deluxe 1093), the first release on Jules Braun's Deluxe label, performing it with his band the Mighty Men in 1948. Elvis recorded the song in 1954, much in the style of Brown. Roy Brown was an unusual rhythm & blues singer in that, while Elvis was a white singer with a black sound, Brown was a black singer with a white sound. Brown, who died of a heart attack in 1981, considered Bing Crosby his favorite singer.

According to one story, Elvis invited Brown to Graceland, where he gave him a check for a few thousand dollars when Brown fell behind in paying his federal income tax.

According to another story, Brown claims that Elvis tried to sneak onto the stage during one of his performances in Tupelo in 1954. However, Elvis lived in Memphis in 1954, having left Tupelo in 1948.

Roy Brown's mother True Love Brown had the same middle name as Elvis's mother, Gladys Love Smith.

BROWN, SYLVIA
Medium with the Nirvana Foundation for Psychic Research in Campbell, California, who, in an article in *The Star*, claimed to have contacted Elvis's spirit shortly after his death in 1977.

BROWN, TONY
Piano player with Elvis's touring TCB Band from 1974 to 1977. He replaced Glen D. Hardin.

BROWN, W. EARL
(1928–   ) Composer and musician born Walter Earl Brown in Salt Lake City on December 25, 1928. He has been nominated for five Emmies and was the vocal arranger for "New York, New York." Brown was the conductor of the NBC Orchestra during Elvis's NBC-TV special, recorded June 27–29, 1968. Brown composed the songs "If I Can Dream" and "Up Above My Head," both of which Elvis recorded.

BRUMLEY, A. E.
Composer of the gospel song "If We Never Meet Again," which Elvis recorded in 1960.

BRUNSWICK
Sports equipment manufacturer. Brunswick manufactured Elvis's pool table at Graceland.

BRYANT, BOUDLEAUX
(1920–   ) Songwriter and violinist born in Shellman, Georgia, on February 13, 1920. In 1938 Bryant played violin for the Atlanta Philharmonic Orchestra. Bryant, along with his wife, Felice, (born August 7, 1927, in Milwaukee), are best known as writers of country/pop songs: "Bye Bye Love," "Wake Up Little Susie," "All I Have to Do Is Dream," and "Bird Dog," which they wrote for the Everly Brothers, and "Raining in My Heart" (Coral 62074) for Buddy Holly. In 1961 Bryant wrote the instrumental "Mexico," which Bob Moore successfully recorded (Monument 446).

Bryant cowrote, with Chet Atkins, "How's the World Treating You," which Elvis recorded in 1956. In 1973

Elvis recorded the Boudleaux–Felice Bryant composition "She Wears My Ring."

BUBBLE-GUM CARDS

Set of sixty-six cards relating to Elvis's career, which were first sold in stores in 1956. On one side was a photograph of Elvis. Most cards asked Elvis a specific question (most were rather insipid):

1. How did you get your first start?
2. A list of his first sixteen records.
3. Do you get much fan mail?
4. Who is your favorite actor? (answer: Jimmy Dean)
5. Should people go into show business?
6. What kind of girl do you like best?
7. Do you like to travel?
8. Do you smoke? (answer: No)
9. Would you rather drive a cycle or car?
10. How does it feel to be a celebrity?
11. Would your own TV show be popular?
12. What is your greatest ambition?
13. Do you ever get homesick?
14. When did you realize you could sing?
15. Are you a good guitar player?
16. Are you nervous with audiences?
17. What is your favorite food?
18. What size cities do you like best?
19. Do you move when you make a record? (answer: Yes)
20. Do you like being left alone?
21. Do you object to jokes about you?
22. What's your favorite way of dressing?
23. Do you plan your song movements? (answer: No)
24. Are you religious? (answer: Yes)
25. Why do you wear sideburns?
26. Do you like playing in the movies?
27. Are people in Hollywood nice to you?
28. Are you bothered by big crowds?
29. Is rock & roll here to stay?
30. How many miles did you travel last year?
31. Who's your best girl? (answer: Mom)
32. Is it easy to act in movies?
33. What will you do with your earnings?
34. How did you like being on a TV show?
35. Why do you wiggle?
36. Are there problems being so popular?
37. Would you like a large family? (answer: Yes)
38. Do you plan to continue making movies? (answer: Yes)
39. How many hours do you sleep at night? (answer: Eight)
40. Would you like to perform in Europe? (answer: Yes)
41. Would marriage hurt your career?
42. Has success changed you much?
43. How do folks feel about your fame?
44. What do you do on a typical date?
45. Do you think school helped you?
46. Do you enjoy singing?

(The next 20 cards were scenes from the movie *Love Me Tender*)

47. Clint and Cathy Reno
48. Farm chores
49. New member of the family
50. Hard work
51. Happy homecoming
52. Porch performance
53. "I want an honest answer"
54. Heading for the farm
55. Singing up a storm
56. Bad news
57. I'm going to Vance
58. Rescue ride
59. Clint's plan
60. "Don't try to stop me"
61. Fighting mad
62. Two against one
63. Setting the trap
64. "Let him have it, Clint"
65. Clint takes aim
66. "Go back to Vance"

Elvis and Margrit Buergin. (Photo courtesy Jeff Wheatcraft)

BUERGIN, MARGRIT

(1942–   ) Sixteen-year old German stenographer Elvis dated while he was stationed in West Germany. Elvis, who called her "Little Puppy," had met Margarite in a park in Bad Nauheim while she was with a German photographer. She spoke only a few words of English. Margarite had been dubbed the "German Junior Edition of Brigitte Bardot" by the press.

BULLOCK, JAMES

City policeman in Marion, Arkansas, who lost his leg in an automobile accident while in the line of duty. Elvis heard about the incident over the radio and sent Bullock and his wife, Karen, a check for $1,000.

BURCH, FRED

Composer, with Gerald Nelson, of the songs "Yoga Is as Yoga Does" and "Sing, You Children," and composer, with Gerald Nelson and Chuck Taylor, of the song "The Love Machine," all of which Elvis recorded.

BURDINE, NANCY J.

Wife of Abner Tacket. They were the parents of six children, including twins Jerome and Martha Tacket. Nancy was the grandmother of Octavia (Doll) Mansell, the great-grandmother of Gladys Smith, and the great-great-grandmother of Elvis Presley.

BURKE, JOSEPH FRANCIS (SONNY)

(1914–   ) Conductor and composer born in Scranton, Pennsylvania, on March 22, 1914. With Johnny Lange and Walter Heath, Burke composed the song "Somebody Bigger Than You and I," which Elvis recorded in 1966.

BURKE'S FLORIST
Memphis florist, located at 1609 Elvis Presley Boulevard, where Elvis and Priscilla bought their flowers.

BURNETTE, JOHNNY
(1934–1964) Popular country rockabilly recording artist of the 1950s and 1960s born in Memphis, on March 24, 1934. He was the brother of country singer Dorsey Burnette (1932–1979). In his youth Johnny Burnette won a Golden Gloves boxing championship[1]. While playing football for Catholic High School in Memphis he played against Red West, who knocked him out of the game. (Red West would later compose Johnny Burnette's 1961 hit song "Big Big World".) Both Johnny and Dorsey Burnette also attended L. C. Humes High School, along with Elvis and Red West.

Johnny Burnette sang and played in a rockabilly trio consisting of Dorsey Burnette and Paul Burlison. Some sources say that he also played in a trio with Bill Black and Scotty Moore, before the two backed Elvis. Johnny and Dorsey Burnette both worked as electricians at Crown Electric in Memphis in 1952, a year before Elvis was employed there as a truck driver. Johnny also worked for the Merrimac Dish company in Memphis, selling dishes. Johnny Cash was a fellow employee there. In 1953 Johnny Burnette formed the Johnny Burnette Trio (a.k.a. the Rock and Roll Trio), consisting of Johnny, Dorsey, and Paul Burlison.[2] All three band members were once Golden Gloves fighters. The trio disbanded in 1958, but not before recording for Coral Records some of the best rocking rockabilly songs of the time and all in the style of Elvis's Sun sessions such as "Tear It Up" and "The Train Kept a Rollin'."

Elvis sang and played with the Johnny Burnette Trio, backing Johnny on one occasion in 1954 at Airways Used Cars. (Paul Burlison has said that in the early 1950s Elvis sang two noncountry songs, "Take Your Finger Out of It, It Don't Belong to You" and "Talkin' 'bout Your Birthday Cake" with Burlison and Shelby Fowler during a radio broadcast over KWEM, which didn't please disc jockey Joe Shaefter.) Elvis called the Burnette Trio "The Dalton Gang" because of all the trouble they could get themselves into. The Johnny Burnette Trio made some recordings for Sun Records, but none of them has ever been released. In 1955 the trio won three weeks in a row on the "Ted Mack's Original Amateur Hour," making it to the finals, which were telecast at 9:00 P.M., September 9, 1956, on ABC-TV. (This was the same night that Elvis made his first appearance on "The Ed Sullivan Show" one hour earlier on CBS. Earlier Johnny Burnette had made his national TV debut on "The Steve Allen Show.") The trio made their movie debut in the 1957 movie *Rock, Rock, Rock*, singing "Lonesome Train." Carl Perkins's cousin, Tony Austin, later became a drummer for the trio. When Dorsey left the trio to become a solo artist in

1960, charting hits with "Tall Oak Tree" (Era 3012) and "Hey Little One" (Era 3019), he was replaced by Johnny Black, the brother of Bill Black.

Johnny and Dorsey Burnette composed "It's Late," "Just a Little Too Much," and "Believe What You Say" for a West Coast rockabilly singer named Ricky Nelson. (Dorsey had recorded a number of demo records for both Ricky and Elvis.)

Johnny Burnette reached his peak as a successful solo artist with such hits as "Dreamin'" (Liberty 55258) and "You're Sixteen" (Liberty 55285).[3] Brothers Johnny and Dorsey placed the song "Green Grass of Texas" (Infinity 001) at number 100 on *Billboard*'s Hot 100 chart in 1961, recording under the name the Texans. Johnny Burnette drowned on August 1, 1964, in a fishing accident at Clear Lake,[4] California. Dorsey died of a heart attack on August 19, 1979.

When Johnny Burnette died he left behind his eleven-year-old son, Rocky. In 1980 Rocky Burnette had his first hit record with "Tired of Toein' the Line" (EMI America 8043), a song that took him only eighteen minutes to compose. Dorsey Burnette's son, Billy Burnette, born in 1953, just three weeks after Rocky Burnette was born, also became a rockabilly singer. (The first song that Billy ever sang on stage was an Elvis impersonation of "Hound Dog." He was three and a half years old.) Billy recorded two tribute records "Welcome Home Elvis" (Gusto-Starday 167) in 1977 and "The Colonel and the King" (Gusto-Starday 4-9009) in 1978. He has also recorded two tribute albums to Elvis. In 1983 Rocky Burnette recorded the album *Get Hot or Go Home* with the Rock and Roll Trio—Paul Burlison, Johnny Black, and Tony Austin, at Sam Phillips's studio in Memphis. In 1987 Billy became a member of Fleetwood Mac, replacing Lindsey Buckingham.

Sources have credited both the Dorsey Brothers and disc jockey Dewey Phillips with coining the name *rockabilly music*, which appears to have been born in Memphis in the early 1950s. If there seem to be a tremendous number of coincidences occurring in Memphis in the 1950s in the lives of Elvis, Johnny Burnette, Johnny Cash, Bill Black, Scotty Moore, and the others on the scene at the time, it is because there was. When this book's authors walked around Memphis visiting all of the places mentioned here they were surprised by how close many of these places were to one another. People who have the same interests do tend to seek out others of their own kind. Memphis in the early 1950s was indeed a small world.

BURNS, SAM
Composer, with Joe Hill Louis, of the song "Tiger Man," which Elvis recorded.

---

[1]Other Golden Gloves boxers were: Jackie Wilson, Screamin' Jay Hawkins, Billy Ward, Willie Dixon, and Elvis's close friend Red West.
[2]Paul Burlison, who hailed from Walls, Mississippi, was the spitting image of Carl Perkins.
[3]Later covered by Ringo Starr in 1973 (Apple 1870).
[4]Ironically, it was at Clear Lake, Iowa, on February 3, 1959, that Buddy Holly, Ritchie Valens, and Jiles Perry Richardson (The Big Bopper) died in a plane crash during a snowstorm.

BURSE, CHARLIE

(1901–1965) Blues singer born in Decatur, Alabama, on August 25, 1901. Burse and blues singer Will Shade (1898–1966) lived and performed in Memphis on Beale Street during the 1950s. Burse, nicknamed "The Ukulele Kid," moved his body a great deal while he sang and played the guitar on such songs as "Everybody Got a Mojo" and "My Baby Got Another Man." In the early 1950s Robert Henry took Elvis to the Gray Mule Club on Beale Street to watch Burse perform. Henry claims that Elvis "borrowed" some of Burse's movements, saying, "He got that shaking, that wiggle, from Charlie Burse, Ukulele Ike [sic] we called him."

BURTON, JAMES

(1939–   ) Lead guitarist born in Shreveport, Louisiana, on August 21, 1939, who performed in Elvis's TCB touring band of the 1970s, as well as on some of Elvis's later recording sessions. Burton's first recording session was with Dale Hawkins, playing on his 1957 hit "Susie-Q" (Checker 863). Burton then played lead guitar for Ricky Nelson from 1957 to 1968, performing on such hits as "Believe What You Say," "It's Late," "Lonesome Town," "Poor Little Fool," "I Got a Feeling," "Hello Mary Lou," and "Travelin' Man" before joining Elvis's band as lead guitarist from 1969 to 1977 at a salary of $5,000 a week. Elvis paid $6,000 in production costs for an album of instrumental music that Burton recorded at Hollywood's A&M Records. The album, however, was not successful. Elvis mentions Burton by name on the studio jam version of "Merry Christmas Baby."

In 1969 Buddy Cagle recorded the song "Guitar Player (Ballad of James Burton)" (Imperial 55407).

BUTCH

Word that Elvis used for "milk" from childhood until his death.

BUTLER, JERRY

(1939–   ) Singer born in Sunflower, Mississippi, on December 8, 1939. Butler recorded a number of hits, including "He Will Break Your Heart" (Vee Jay 354). In August 1964 Butler and Betty Everett recorded "Let It Be Me" (Vee Jay 613), which Elvis recorded in 1970. Butler composed, with Kenny Gamble and Leon Huff, the song "Only the Strong Survive," which Butler recorded in 1969 (Mercury 72898) and which Elvis recorded later that same year.

BYERS, JOY

(1937–   ) Composer (a.k.a. Joy Johnson) born in Springtown, Texas, on May 19, 1937. Byers composed the following songs, all of which Elvis sang in his motion pictures, except for the song "It Hurts Me." which was cowritten with Charlie Daniels. "There Ain't Nothing Like a Song" was cowritten with William Johnston.

"Baby, If You'll Give Me All of Your Love"
"C'mon Everybody"
"Goin' Home"
"Hard Knocks"
"Hey, Hey, Hey"
"Hey, Little Girl"
"It Hurts Me"
"I've Got to Find My Baby"
"There's a Brand New Day on the Horizon"
"Let Yourself Go"
"The Meanest Girl in Town"
"Please Don't Stop Loving Me"
"She's a Machine"
"So Close, Yet So Far"
"Stop, Look, and Listen"
"There Ain't Nothing Like a Song"

BYRON, AL

(1932–   ) Composer and onetime teacher born in Brooklyn on September 16, 1932. Byron composed, with Paul Evans, the song "Something Blue," which Elvis recorded in 1962.

Publicity still from the 1950s. (Photo courtesy Eddie Brandt's Saturday Matinee)

CABOT, SEBASTIAN

(1918–1977) Actor born in London on July 6, 1918, best known for his role as Giles French, the manservant on the TV series "Family Affair." Cabot's other TV series include "Checkmate," "Ghost Story" (host), and "Suspense." Cabot was one of several celebrities who died (August 23, 1977) within a short time of Elvis's death. (See *Groucho Marx* and *Zero Mostel*)

CADETS

Los Angeles rhythm & blues vocal group who in 1956 recorded a cover version of "Heartbreak Hotel" on the flip side of "Church Bells May Ring" (Modern 985), the latter having been a hit for the Willows[1] (Melba 102) and the Diamonds (Mercury 70835), both in 1956. The Cadets, whose biggest hit was "Stranded in the Jungle" (Modern 994) in 1956, also recorded ballads such as "Why Don't You Write Me?" (RPM 428) under the name the Jacks. Their cover of "Heartbreak Hotel" was the first cover of an original Elvis song by black artists. (See *Paul Anka*)

CADILLAC

Favorite automobile of Elvis. A black Cadillac is mentioned in the lyrics of the song "Santa Claus Is Back in Town," while a pink Cadillac is mentioned in "Baby Let's Play House."

CADILLAC CLUB

New Orleans nightclub on St. Claude Avenue, where Elvis was turned down as a performer by owner Lois Brown in 1954 when agent Keith Lowry Jr. offered him for $150 a night. Brown turned him down because he was an unknown.

CALHOUN, CHARLES E.

Composer of many rhythm & blues songs of the early 1950s, including "Shake, Rattle and Roll" and, with Lou Willie Turner, "Flip, Flop and Fly." Calhoun is a pen name used by composer Jesse Stone (it was actually the name of the man who built his house). Elvis recorded "Shake, Rattle and Roll" in February 1956, and "Flip, Flop and Fly" in 1974.

CALL, ROBERT

Fan who, on the morning of August 16, 1977, while standing outside the gates of Graceland at 12:28 A.M., took a photograph of Elvis as he drove his car into Graceland. Call was with his wife, Nancy, and four-year-old daughter, Abby. Call's photograph, which he took with a twenty-dollar Kodak Instamatic Camera, appeared on the cover of the September 20, 1977, issue of the *National Enquirer* as "The Last Photo of Elvis Alive."

CAMDEN RECORDS

Record label on which Elvis's discount albums were released. Camden was a subsidiary of RCA, named after Camden, New Jersey, the site of the RCA pressing plant (and the location of the first drive-in movie theater in 1932, created by chemical manufacturer Richard Hollingshead Jr.). Camden albums usually featured just ten songs, five on each side. The 1972 album *Burning Love and Hits from His Movies, Volume 2* is the only Gold album that Camden ever produced. (See *Pickwick*)

CAMPBELL, BILL

Composer of the song "One-Sided Love Affair," which Elvis recorded in 1956.

CAMPBELL, GLEN

(1938–   ) Singer, composer, and musician born in Delight, Arkansas, on April 10, 1938. Campbell began his musical career as a studio musician. He played guitar for both the Champs and the Beach Boys, playing lead on "Good Vibrations" (Capitol 5676). Campbell also played behind Frank Sinatra, the Everly Brothers, and on many sessions for other artists. In 1967 Campbell recorded "Gentle on My Mind" (Capitol 5939), which Elvis covered in 1969. In 1962 he recorded an early version of "Long Black Limousine" (Capitol 4856), which Elvis would record in 1969. Campbell played guitar and sang backup on the soundtrack of Elvis's movie *Viva Las Vegas*. Campbell's former wife, Sarah, had previously been married to singer Mac Davis.

In concert, Elvis sang Campbell's 1961 hit "Turn Around, Look at Me" (Crest 1087) and his 1967 hit "By the Time I Get to Phoenix" (Capitol 2015). Campbell does an excellent imitation of Elvis in his nightclub act. At some of Elvis's concerts, Elvis did a brief imitation of Campbell. In 1970 a single issue magazine titled *Glen Campbell/Elvis Presley* was published.

CANADA

Country in which Elvis made only three appearances: April 2, 1957, in Toronto; April 3, 1957, in Ottawa; and August 31, 1957, in Vancouver.

CAPES

Item of clothing that Elvis used in his live concert performances. It was Priscilla who first suggested to Elvis that he should wear capes. (See *Bill Belew*)

CAPRICORN

Astrological sign of Elvis, who was born on January 8, 1935.

---

[1]On the Willows's original version the chimes were dubbed by Neil Sedaka.

**CAPTAIN OF THE
LOUISIANA STATE HIGHWAY PATROL**
Honorary award, with badge, conferred upon Elvis in
1956.

CARDIAC ARRYTHMIA
Irregular and ineffective heartbeat due to hypertensive
heart disease or myocardial infarction. Cardiac arrhythmia was the official cause of Elvis's death.
  Charlie Hodge, Kathy Westmoreland, and Larry
Geller were all told by Dr. George Nichopoulos that
prior to Elvis's fatal heart attack of August 1977, he
had suffered three previous attacks.

CARLSBAD, NEW MEXICO
Town where Elvis performed on February 14, 1955.
The concert appearance was reportedly Colonel Tom
Parker's first involvement with Elvis. He assisted Bob
Neal in getting Elvis booked in Carlsbad.

CARMICHAEL, RALPH R.
(1927–   ) Composer born on May 27, 1927, in
Quincy, Illinois. He wrote the gospel song "Reach Out
to Jesus," which Elvis recorded in 1971.

CAROLE LOMBARD TRIO
Vocal group that, along with the Jordanaires and the
Jubilee Four, sang backup on some songs at Elvis's
recording session for *Girl Happy* in Hollywood in July
1964. The group, as the Carole Lombard Quartet, had
earlier sung backup on the song "What'd I Say" with
the Jubilee Four on Elvis's *Viva Las Vegas* soundtrack
recording session in July 1963. The group got its name
from Carole Lombard the actress wife of actor Clark
Gable, "The King of Hollywood."

CARPENTER, JOHN
(1948–   ) Director-husband of actress Adrienne Bar-
beau who has directed many successful horror movies.
Carpenter directed the 1979 TV movie *Elvis*, produced
by Dick Clark. (Elvis's character name in the 1969
movie *Change of Habit* was Dr. John Carpenter.)

CARR, VICKI
(1941–   ) Singer born Florencia Bisenta de Casillas
Martinez Cardona in El Paso, Texas, on July 19, 1941.
Carr charted her first hit in 1967 with "It Must Be
Him" (Liberty 55986). Elvis once gave her a diamond
ring just for introducing him to a diet doctor in Los
Angeles.
  Elvis and Sheila Ryan attended Carr's opening at the
Tropicana Hotel in Las Vegas on September 4, 1974.

CARROLL, BERT
Composer, with Russell Moody, of the song "Wear My
Ring Around Your Neck," which Elvis recorded in
1958.

CARROLL, JOHNNY
(1937–   ) Rockabilly singer born in Cleburne, Texas,
on October 23, 1937. Carroll appeared on the same bill

with Elvis and Hank Snow in Fort Worth, Waco, and at
the Big D Jamboree in 1955. In 1956 he recorded Elvis's
"Tryin' to Get to You" (Decca 29940), which featured
Owen Bradley on piano, Owen's brother Harold on
rhythm guitar, and Elvis's future guitar player, Grady
Martin, on lead guitar.

CARSON, MARTHA
(1921–   ) Singer born Martha Amburgay in Neon,
Kentucky, and nicknamed "The Queen of Country Music." Martha is the sister of Sun artist Jean Chapel, and
their brother, Don Chapel, was the second husband of
singer Tammy Wynette (who also married singer
George Jones). In the 1940s Martha was married to
singer James Carson, the son of Fiddling John Carson.
Martha Carson toured with Elvis in the South in 1955.
In 1951 she recorded the gospel song "Satisfied" (Capitol 1900), which Elvis would record at Sun in 1954.
(See *Jean Chapel*)

CARSON, WAYNE
Composer, with Mark James and Johnny Christopher,
of the song "Always on My Mind," which Elvis recorded
in 1972.

CARTER, ANITA
(1933–   ) Daughter of Maybelle Carter and sister of
June Carter, born on March 31, 1933. Elvis and Anita
became a love interest while they toured together in
1955 (Anita with her mother and sister). Elvis once
feigned getting sick and being taken to a hospital just
to get Anita's attention.

CARTER, BILLY
(1937–   ) Brother of former president Jimmy Carter
and onetime proponent of Billy Beer, born William
Alton Carter III on March 29, 1937. Billy Carter once
handled the Carter family's peanut business in Plains,
Georgia. He and his wife once visited Elvis in Memphis. Billy commented, "My gosh, you're guarded better than the president!"

CARTER, JIMMY
(1924–   ) Thirty-ninth president of the United States,
born James Earl Carter Jr. on October 1, 1924. President Carter gave, upon Elvis's death, the following
tribute: "Elvis Presley's death deprives our country of a
part of itself. His music and his personality, fusing the
styles of white country and black rhythm and blues,
permanently changed the face of American popular
culture. His following was immense and he was a symbol to people the world over of the vitality, rebelliousness, and good humor of this country."

CARTER, JUNE
(1929–   ) Country singer, born Valerie June Carter
on June 23, 1929. June is one of the three daughters
(including Anita and Helen) of mother Maybelle Addington Carter (1909–1979). June Carter's great-great-
great-grandfather was Henry Addington Sidmouth,
prime minister of England (1801–1804). She is also

related to former president Jimmy Carter (as claimed by the former chief executive himself). June has been married to two country artists: Carl Smith and Johnny Cash. Elvis first met June at the Grand Ole Opry in 1954. The two toured together in 1955, with Colonel Tom Parker serving as her manager. June first became a Johnny Cash fan when Elvis would play Johnny Cash songs on jukeboxes. Elvis then introduced June to Johnny at a North Carolina concert in 1955. During that year Red West and Elvis broke into Carl Smith and June Carter's Nashville house, forcing open a window. They ate and then went to bed, only to be discovered by Carl and June, who surprisingly were not mad at them but actually glad to see them. Red and Elvis decided to stay there since they had little money and thought that Carl and June wouldn't mind.

CARUSO, ENRICO
(1873–1921) Italian opera singer born in Naples on February 27, 1873, who became the first person to sell a million records (collectively). In 1916 Caruso recorded a version of "O Sole Mio" (Victor 87243) on which "It's Now or Never" was based. The 1951 movie *The Great Caruso*, which Elvis saw a half-dozen times, was directed by Richard Thorpe, one of Elvis's future directors. In the film, Mario Lanzo, from South Philadelphia High School, portrayed Caruso. Breese Westmoreland, the father of Kathy Westmoreland, appeared and sang in the 1951 movie.

Elvis, who collected Caruso recordings, surpassed Caruso as RCA's biggest-selling artist.

CARUSO, PAUL
Attorney for Patricia Parker in her paternity suit against Elvis. (See *Patricia Parker*)

CARWILE, BILL
Memphis dry cleaner who in 1979 bought the two tons of gray marble that had been Elvis's first tomb. He carved the marble into 44,000 chunks, each measuring two-by-one inches, and asked $80 for each chunk. He also bought Gladys Presley's tomb at Forest Hill Cemetery after her remains had been moved to Graceland.

CASH, JOHNNY
(1932–   ) Country singer, guitarist, and songwriter born in Kingsland, Arkansas, on February 26, 1932. Cash is the father of singer Rosanne Cash (1955–   ), as well as the father-in-law of singer Rodney Crowell.

Cash was born J. R. Cash, and it was only when he joined the U.S. Air Force that he was given the name Johnny. After his discharge Cash began recording for Sun Records in 1955 with the Tennessee Two (Luther Perkins and Marshall Grant). He recorded a number of hit records for Sun, including: "I Walk the Line" (Sun 241), "Folsom Prison Blues" (Sun 232), and "Ballad of a Teenage Queen" (Sun 283). His first major public appearance after signing with Sun Records was at the Overton Park Shell in Memphis on August 5, 1955. Elvis was also on the bill. Cash, Carl Perkins, and Elvis toured together on the Jamboree tour from Abilene,

Texas, to St. Louis, for two weeks in October 1955. On December 4, 1956, Cash became one of the participants in the famed Million-Dollar Quartet session (although the songs on which he appeared have never been released.) Years later he filed a lawsuit to try to prohibit the session's release on record. Cash left Sun Records in 1958 to record for Columbia Records.

At a live concert at the International Hotel in Las Vegas in August 1969, Elvis jokingly introduced himself by saying, "Hello, I'm Johnny Cash," before singing "Folsom Prison Blues" and "I Walk the Line." (See *Million-Dollar Quartet, Luther Perkins*)

CASSIN, JIMMY
(1926–   ) Composer born James Joseph Cassini Jr. in St. Louis on November 2, 1926. Cassin, with Jim Morehead, composed the song "Sentimental Me," recorded by Elvis in 1961.

CAUGHLEY, HAMBURGER JAMES
Valet of Elvis at Graceland.

CBS-FM REMEMBERS ELVIS
CBS radio program produced and narrated by Jack Miller in 1979. *Billboard* magazine named the program the Top Special Program in a Major Market for 1979.

CEDARS OF LEBANON HOSPITAL
Los Angeles hospital to which Elvis was rushed on May 14, 1957, after experiencing chest pains. Elvis had inhaled a porcelain cap from one of his front teeth while working on a dance number in *Jailhouse Rock*. It had become lodged in a lung and was removed on May 15. Singer Bobby Darin died at Cedars of Lebanon on December 18, 1973.

Elvis helping to launch the March of Dimes campaign in January 1957. (Photo courtesy the Mike Boyd collection)

CHAMPAGNE

French poodle Elvis owned while living in West Germany.

CHAPEL, JEAN

Sun recording artist, born Jean Amburgay in Neon, Kentucky, who, like Elvis, switched to RCA Records in 1956. Chapel recorded an answer to Elvis's "Good Rockin' Tonight" (Sun 244) titled "I Won't Be Rockin' Tonight" (RCA 6681). Chapel composed songs that have been recorded by Roy Rogers and Eddy Arnold. She also recorded under the names Opal Jean, Jean Amber, and Mattie O'Neal. Chapel and her sister Martha Carson recorded as the Amburgay Sisters. Jean's brother, Don Chapel, was the second husband of singer Tammy Wynette, actor Burt Reynolds's former girlfriend. (See *Martha Carson*)

CHARITIES

Elvis was an extremely generous man, who not only gave presents to his family, to his close friends, and to complete strangers, but to many organized charities.

Some of the charities to which Elvis donated money included: Boys Town, Tom's Indian School, Salvation Army, Girls Clubs, Boys Clubs, YMCA, YWCA, Jewish Community Centers, St. Jude Hospital Foundation Muscular Dystrophy Foundation, Cerebral Palsy, March of Dimes, and the Motion Picture Relief Fund. Between 1957 and 1967 Elvis gave more than $1 million to charities. Elvis's favorite gifts were brand-new automobiles—Cadillacs, Lincoln Continentals, Grand Prixes, Corvettes, Porsches, Mercedes Benzes—so many that no exact count can be made. Elvis also gave away jewelry, rings, chains, and bracelets to friends, fans, and complete strangers. He also gave away cash. According to Marty Lacker, Elvis contributed $100,000 to charities every Christmas.

CHARLES, RAY

(1930–   ) Blind rhythm & blues/jazz/country/pop musician, born Ray Charles Robinson on September 23, 1930, in Albany, Georgia. Charles began recording for the Swing time label in Los Angeles in the early 1950s in the style of his idol, Nat (King) Cole. In 1952 he recorded for Atlantic Records, producing such hits as "I've Got a Woman" and "The Right Time." In 1961 Charles joined the ABC Paramount label, where he recorded a number of million-sellers, including two albums of country music. Elvis recorded two Ray Charles hits, which Charles had written, "I've Got a Woman" (Atlantic 1950) (which was retitled "I Got a Woman"), and "What'd I Say" (Atlantic 2031). Elvis also recorded other songs that Ray Charles also recorded: "I Can't Stop Loving You" (ABC Paramount 10330), "You Don't Know Me" (ABC Paramount 10345), "Your Cheatin' Heart" (ABC Paramount 10375), "I'm Movin' On" (Atlantic 2043), "Blue Moon of Kentucky," "Without Love" (ABC Paramount 10453), and "Yesterday" (ABC Paramount 11009). Elvis may have recorded Charles's "This Little Girl of Mine" (Atlantic 1063), but it has never been released. It is believed that Elvis may also have recorded Charles's "Lonely Avenue" (Atlantic 1108).

CHARLES, SONNY

Lead singer of the rock group the Checkmates, Ltd., which charted two 1969 hits, "Black Pearl" (A&M 1053) and a song that Elvis would later record, "Proud Mary" (A&M 1127). Charles was the composer, with Michael Jarrett, of the song "I'm Leavin'," which Elvis recorded in 1971.

CHASE, LINCOLN

Composer of the songs "Tweedlee Dee" and "Such a Night," which Elvis recorded. In 1957 Chase composed and recorded "Save the Last Dance for Me" (Liberty 55080), which the Drifters recorded in 1959. He was the husband of singer Shirley Ellis, for whom he composed her hit novelty songs "The Nitty Gritty" (Congress 202) and "The Name Game" (Congress 230).

CHECKER, CHUBBY

(1941–   ) Popular rock singer and dance-craze innovator (the twist, the pony, the fly, the hucklebuck, the limbo, the Popeye, etc.). Born Ernest Evans in Philadelphia on October 3, 1941, Chubby got his stage name from Dick Clark's wife, Bobbie, as a parody on Fats Domino's name. As a teenager he attended South Philadelphia High School with Frankie Avalon and Fabian. He married Catherine Lodders, Miss World of 1962.

Chubby Checker's version of "The Twist" (Parkway 811), which was an exact copy of Hank Ballard and the Midnighters' version (King 5171), both based on the Drifters' 1955 Hucklebuck song "What 'cha Gonna Do" (Atlantic 1055), reached number one in 1960 and again in 1962. It was "The Twist" that replaced Elvis's "It's Now or Never" as number one on *Billboard*'s Hot 100 chart in September 1960.

Chubby Checker's first record for Philadelphia's Parkway Records was titled "The Class" (Parkway 804), featuring him doing imitations of Elvis, Fats Domino, the Chipmunks, and the Coasters.

In March of 1961 Elvis's "Surrender" knocked Chubby Checker's "Pony Time" (Parkway 818) out of first place on *Billboard*'s Hot 100 chart.

CHENAULT'S

Memphis restaurant, located at 1402 Bellevue Boulevard South, where Elvis threw parties, especially on New Year's Eve. Singer Tommy Sands was once given a birthday party at Chenault's by Colonel Tom Parker, his manager.

CHER

(1946–   ) Popular singer of the 1960s and 1970s and successful actress of the 1980s. Cher, born Cherilyn Sarkisian in El Centro, California, on May 20, 1946, began singing with her husband, Sonny Bono, as session vocalists. They originally recorded under the names Caesar and Cleo. Cher sang backup on the Ronettes' "Be My Baby" and on the Righteous Brothers' "You've Lost That Lovin' Feelin'." Sonny and Cher had a number of hit records, and Cher herself has had a number of hits. They divorced in 1975, after which Cher married guitarist Greg Allman of the Allman Brothers Band.

The first concert that Cher ever attended featured Elvis; she was eleven years old at the time.

CHESS RECORDS
Chicago rhythm & blues record company founded in 1947 by Polish immigrant brothers Leonard and Phil Chess. It was located at 2120 South Michigan Avenue.[1] The label was originally called Aristocrat Records and recorded such artists as Muddy Waters and Chuck Berry, and on their subsidiary label, Chubby Checker, Bo Diddley, Lowell Fulsom, and Dale Hawkins.

Sam Phillips recorded many blues artists at Sun Records, among them Rufus Thomas, Howlin' Wolf, and Ike Turner, selling the tapes to the Chess label, which distributed the songs.

At one time Sam Phillips attempted to sell to Chess his entire catalog of Sun artists, including Elvis, but the Chess brothers turned him down.

Chess Records was located directly across the street from another successful rhythm & blues label, Vee Jay Records (the second label[2] that released the Beatles in the United States).

CHESNUT, JERRY
Composer of "Love Coming Down," "T-R-O-U-B-L-E," and "Woman Without Love," and, with Billy Edd Wheeler, "It's Midnight" and "Never Again," all of which Elvis recorded. Chesnut also composed "The Wonders You Perform," which Elvis sang in concert.

CHI
Jewish symbol of life, which Elvis wore around his neck.

CHILDRESS, HUBERT
U.S. Army captain from Coleman, Texas, who was Elvis's company commander in West Germany.

CHRISSIE AND MIDNIGHT
Pet cats of Colonel Thomas Parker and his wife, Marie.

CHRISTIAN, CHRIS
Composer of the song "Love Song of the Year," which Elvis recorded in 1973.

CHRISTINA
Singer Frank Sinatra's private Lear Jet that brought Elvis and his bride Priscilla from Las Vegas to Palm Springs for their honeymoon in May 1967. It was in this same aircraft that Sinatra's mother, Dolly, was killed when the plane crashed into a mountain on January 6, 1976, while she was en route to Las Vegas to see her son open at Caesar's Palace.

CHRISTINE SCHOOL
School on Third Street in Memphis where Elvis first enrolled to complete the eighth grade after he and his family had moved to Memphis from Tupelo in 1948. The next year, Elvis transferred to the larger L.C. Humes High School.

CHRISTOPHER, JOHNNY
Composer of the song "Mama Liked the Roses," which Elvis recorded in 1969. With Mark James and Wayne Carson, Christopher wrote "Always on My Mind," which Elvis recorded in 1972. With Red West he composed "If You Talk in Your Sleep," which Elvis recorded in 1974.

CHU-BOPS
Bubble gum packaged in a three-by-three-inch replica of a record album. Numbers forty-one through forty-eight were of Elvis's albums: *Blue Hawaii, Elvis, Elvis Presley, G.I. Blues, From Elvis Presley Boulevard, Memphis Tennessee, Aloha from Hawaii Via Satellite, Something for Everybody,* and *Loving You.* The flip side of each featured a concert photo of Elvis.

CHUCK NORRIS STUDIOS
Los Angeles martial-arts studio established by stuntman and actor Chuck Norris. It was where Mike Stone taught Priscilla Presley karate in 1972. After Chuck's school went out of business he took the advice of his friend, actor Steve McQueen, and went into acting, today he's a major star of action films. See *Chuck Norris.*

CHURCH, CHARLES R.
Memphis businessman who installed the closed-circuit TV system (with the master controls in Elvis's bedroom) in Graceland. RCA television sets were used. Church owned an indoor shooting range (Memphis Indoor Shooting Center) and police-accessories store in Whitehaven, a suburb of Memphis.

CIRCLE G RANCH
Name of Elvis's 163-acre cattle ranch (later to be renamed the Flying Circle G because there was already a Circle G in Texas), located at the corner of Horn Lake and Goodman roads in De Soto County near Walls, Mississippi, just ten miles south of Graceland. Elvis had discovered the ranch one day while driving along Horn Lake Road. A fifty-foot-high white cross on the property had caught his eye. Elvis bought the ranch on

---

[1]"2120 South Michigan Avenue" became the title of a song recorded by the Rolling Stones, who in October 1964 cut four songs at the Chess Studios, including their hit "It's All Over Now."

[2]Swan Records released the third Beatles record in the U.S., "She Loves You" (Swan 4152)), but the first was early in 1962 when Decca Records released "My Bonnie" by Tony Sheridan and the Beat Brothers (Decca 31382), who were actually Tony Sheridan and the Beatles. The first Beatles release on Vee Jay was "Please, Please Me" (Vee Jay 498) in early 1963. Tony Sheridan had said that the first rock album he ever owned in England was *Elvis Presley's Greatest Hits Volume I.*

February 9, 1967, from airplane salesman Jack Adams, with Vernon paying the $300,000[1] and putting up Graceland as collateral. The ranch, which had previously been named Twinkletown Farm, was renamed by Elvis as the Circle G, with the "G" standing for Graceland.

A staff, including Ralph Boucher (who had worked for the previous owner), Uncle Earl Pritchett, and Alan Fortas looked after the eighteen head of Santa Gertrudis cattle. Elvis had eight new trailers moved onto the site for him and his entourage to stay in. Although the ranch featured a single-bedroom brick house, he and Priscilla shared the three-bedroom trailer. Elvis bought an inventory of twenty-five Ford Ranchero trucks for the ranch at a cost of $100,000[2] from a Hernando, Mississippi, Ford dealer, trucks he gave to his friends and anyone present at the time. He also stocked the ranch's small lake with fish and erected a ten-foot-high fence to conceal his estate from the public road. The ranch proved expensive to operate and began to drain Elvis's savings, since it didn't generate any income. It was sold on May 21, 1969, to Lou McClellan for $440,100. (Apparently the deal fell through, as it was later reported in May 1973 that Elvis had sold the Flying Circle G to the Boyle Investment Company.) After selling the Flying Circle G, Elvis moved all of his horses back to Graceland (the whole expensive ranching venture had all started after Elvis bought Priscilla the horse Domino.) Soon after Elvis's death, the new owner of the ranch, P. Montes, Jr., began charging two dollars a person for tourists to visit the Circle G.

In the book *Elvis—What Happened?* the ranch is referred to as Rising Sun (which was actually the name of Elvis's favorite horse).

CIRCLE THEATER
Cleveland theater at which Elvis and Pat Boone performed in a concert on October 19, 1955. That was the first time the two singers, who were considered rivals at the time, had met. They soon became friends. Elvis had performed at the Circle Theater on three earlier occasions.

CLARK JR., ALBERT
One of Elvis's groundskeepers and handymen at Graceland. Clark worked for Elvis for twelve years.

CLARK, DICK
(1929–   ) Philadelphia disc jockey born Richard Wagstaff Clark in Mt. Vernon, New York, on November 30, 1929. In the mid-1950s and 1960s Clark hosted the TV series "American Bandstand." During Elvis's Army career, Clark interviewed him via telephone on January 8, 1959. In 1979 Clark produced the TV movie *Elvis*.

Clark was among the many celebrities who attended the premiere Las Vegas concert show at the International Hotel on July 31, 1969, for Elvis's live-performance return.

CLARKE, JANE
Dancer who claimed to have been Elvis's secret lover in a story published in the *National Examiner*, stating that she first met him at the Lido Club in Paris while Elvis was on leave in 1959. She further claimed to have seen him again in 1963 while she was performing at the Tropicana Hotel.

CLASS PROPHECIES
Item in the 1953 L. C. Humes High School yearbook, *The Herald*: "Donald Williams, Raymond McCraig, and Elvis Presley leave, hoping there will be someone to take their places as teacher's pet."

CLASS 202
Elvis's 1953 graduating class at L. C. Humes High School in Memphis. Elvis is the seventh known person from that class to have died.

CLAYTON, MERRY
Solo artist who was a former member of Ray Charles's Raelettes vocal group. Clayton sang duet with Bobby Darin on his 1963 hit "You're the Reason I'm Living" (Capitol 4896) and on the Rolling Stones' *Let It Bleed* album. She has sung backup for such artists as the Supremes, Pearl Bailey, and Joe Cocker. Clayton also sang backup for Elvis at a few of his sessions. In 1987 she joined the cast of the TV series "Cagney & Lacey," on which she played a cop.

CLEMENT, FRANK GOAD
(1920–   ) Politician born on July 2, 1920. As the governor of Tennessee, Clement, in 1953, conferred upon Thomas Andrew Parker the honorary title of Colonel. On July 2, 1954, Governor Clement gave the eulogy at the funeral of R. W. Blackwood and Bill Lyles of the Blackwood Brothers gospel group, who had been killed in an airplane crash. Interestingly, Sun Records artists the Prisonaires recorded an unreleased song tribute to Clement titled "What About Frank Clement (a Mighty, Mighty Man)."

CLEMENT, JACK
(1931–   ) Memphis bandleader, composer, and vocalist, nicknamed "Cowboy Jack," with whom Elvis appeared in late 1954 at the Eagle's Nest, a Memphis ballroom on Lamar Avenue. Elvis sang between sets, earning ten dollars a night.

Clement, who was once the brother-in-law of country singer Waylon Jennings (Clement's wife, Sharon, is the sister of singer Jessi Colter), was the producer of many recordings by Johnny Cash, Carl Perkins, Roy Orbison, Jerry Lee Lewis, and Charlie Rich.

In 1973 Clement was inducted into the Country Music Songwriters Hall of Fame. Five years later, in 1978, Clement finally recorded his first record album, *All I Want to Do in Life*.

[1]The figure $500,000 has also been mentioned in print.
[2]Again, the figures vary from source to source.

CLEOPATRA
Thirty-million-dollar movie spectacular starring Elizabeth Taylor and Richard Burton. Elvis attended the Memphis premiere on December 13, 1964, buying fifty $12.50 seats for him and his friends. It was this film that promted Sonny and Cher to call themselves Caesar and Cleo. Priscilla Presley confessed in 1978 that when she first began using makeup to please Elvis, she tended to overdo it, usually ending up looking like Cleopatra.

CLOVERS
Nineteen-fifties rhythm & blues group that recorded for Atlantic Records and charted a number of hits, such as the original versions of "One Mint Julep" (Atlantic 963) in 1952, "Devil or Angel" (Atlantic 1052) in 1954, and "Love Potion No. 9" (United Artists 180) in 1959. In 1957 the group recorded the soulful "Down in the Alley" (Atlantic 1152), which Elvis covered in 1966. In 1963 Tippie and the Clovers recorded "Bossa Nova Baby" (Tiger 201), which Elvis would record that same year.

It is believed that Elvis recorded the Clovers' 1951 hit "Fool, Fool, Fool" (Atlantic 944) at Sun Records, but it has never been released.

COASTERS
Popular novelty group of the 1950s–'60s. Beginning as the Robins in 1951, they recorded for Jerry Leiber and Mike Stoller's Spark Records. In 1951 they recorded Leiber and Stoller's first published song, "That's What the Good Book Says" (Modern 807). In 1953 the group billed as Bobby Nunn and the Robins recorded "A Fool Such as I" (RCA Victor 47-5175), which Elvis would later record. They spawned a chain of hits for Atco Records beginning in 1956, most of which were Leiber-Stoller compositions. In 1960 the Beatles included their version of the Coasters' "Three Cool Cats" (Atco 6132) on their demo tape. In 1961 the Coasters recorded "Little Egypt" (Atco 6192) and "Girls! Girls! Girls!" (Atco 6704), both of which were also recorded by Elvis. The Coasters also recorded "The Climb" (Atco 6234), which was sung by the Forte Four (Decca 32029) in the 1964 movie *Viva Las Vegas.*

COATS, J. B.
(1901–   ) School teacher and Baptist church pastor born James B. Coats in Summerland, Mississippi. He is the composer of the gospel song "Where Could I Go but to the Lord," which Elvis recorded.

COCHRAN, HANK
(1935–   ) Composer born Garland Perry in Greenville, Mississippi, on August 2, 1935. Cochran wrote a number of hit songs, including "Make the World Go Away," which was recorded by Elvis in June 1970. In his youth Cochran teamed up musically with a young man named Eddie Cochran. Although they billed themselves as the Cochran Brothers, they were unrelated. (Eddie Cochran, who was a clone of Elvis, was killed in a London taxicab accident on April 17, 1960, in which Gene Vincent and Sharon Sheeley were injured.)

COCKE, MARION J.
(1926?–   ) Administration supervisor of nursing services who first met Elvis at the Baptist Memorial Hospital in 1975, after which she became his personal nurse until the following year. Elvis and Marion were good friends, with Elvis calling her "his security blanket." Elvis gave her jewelry, a silver fox stole, and a new Pontiac Grand Prix, among other gifts. Cocke was the first person Elvis told about his engagement to Ginger Alden. Cocke is the author of the 1979 book *I Called Him Babe,* published by Memphis State University Press. Cocke, who appeared on TV's "Good Morning America," to promote the book, gave all of her royalties to charity.

COCOANUT GROVE
Hollywood nightclub located at the Ambassador Hotel where Elvis once watched comedian Milton Berle perform.

CODY, PHIL
(1945–   ) Composer born in Westchester, New York, on June 6, 1945. He composed, with Neil Sedaka, the song "Solitaire," which Sedaka and later Elvis would record.

COFFEE CUP
Restaurant in West Memphis, Arkansas, where Elvis and other Army recruits stopped to eat on March 24, 1958, with Elvis ordering spaghetti. The meal was cut short when fans converged on the restaurant and the recruits had to get back on the bus. The chartered Greyhound bus was en route to Fort Chaffee, where Elvis was to receive his Army indoctrination. Elvis was familiar with the diner, having eaten there many times before.

COFFMAN, RICHARD L.
U.S. Army first lieutenant from Nevada, Missouri, who served as Elvis's platoon leader in West Germany.

COLE, J. D.
Principal of the Lawhon Grammar School in Tupelo, Mississippi, which Elvis attended as a child. Cole entered Elvis in the annual talent show at the 1945 Mississippi-Alabama Fair and Dairy Show. Singing "Old Shep," Elvis won second prize. (See *Mississippi-Alabama Fair and Dairy Show*)

COLEMAN, GEORGE
Electrician who worked at Graceland.

COLEY, HENRY
Elvis's six-foot-three-inch, 230-pound master sergeant at Fort Hood, Texas. Coley hailed from Temple, Texas.

COLGATE
Brand of toothpaste preferred and used by Elvis.

COLONEL
Honorary title conferred on Elvis by Tennessee gover-

nor Buford Ellington in 1961. In actuality, both Elvis and Thomas Parker could be referred to as "Colonel."

COLONEL MIDNIGHT
Vernon Presley's horse at Graceland, bought for him by Elvis.

COLONEL SNOW
Code name that Colonel Tom Parker used to identify himself when calling Vernon Presley at Graceland.

COLT .45
World War II gold-plated commemorative pistol that Elvis gave to President Richard Nixon as a gift when the two met for the first time in the Oval Office on December 21, 1970. The gun had originally been a gift to Elvis.

COLUMBIA RECORDS
Record label that bid $15,000 for Elvis in 1955, but was turned down because Colonel Tom Parker wanted more. One can only speculate what A&R man Mitch Miller would have done with Elvis, since Miller was strongly against rock & roll music. The label, however, was a strong country music contender. It wasn't until the 1960s that Columbia signed its first rock group, Paul Revere and the Raiders.

Columbia Records, which had an excellent country music catalog, bought the contracts of both Johnny Cash and Carl Perkins from Sun Records in 1958.

COMO, PERRY
(1912–   ) Singer born in Canonsburg, Pennsylvania, on May 18, 1912. In 1950 Como had a hit with "Bibbidi-Bobbidi-Boo" (RCA Victor 3113) from the 1950 Walt Disney animated movie *Cinderella*. The song was written by Mack David, who also composed another song for the film, "I Don't Care If the Sun Don't Shine," which was cut. Elvis later recorded the song.

On April 13, 1957, Elvis's "All Shook Up" knocked Como's "Round and Round" (RCA Victor 6815) out of first place on *Billboard*'s Hot 100 chart. Como recorded "Winter Wonderland" (RCA 1968), "Jingle Bells" (RCA EP620), "And I Love Her So" (RCA 0906), and "It's Impossible" (RCA 0387), all of which Elvis later recorded.

COMPLETE ELVIS, THE
Book edited by Martin Torgoff and published by Delilah Books in 1982.

CONCERTO FOR ELVIS
Ballet set to composer Ben Weisman's thirty-minute piano concerto based on three of his songs that Elvis recorded, "As Long as I Have You," "I Slipped, I

Stumbled, I Fell," and "Crawfish." The ballet was directed by choreographer Ann Marie de Angelo, a former Joffrey Ballet dancer. The ballet made its debut in February 1988 at the Terrace Theatre in Long Beach, California.

CONCERT JUMPSUITS
Custom-made jumpsuits worn by Elvis included: Peacock, American Eagle, Indian, Sundial, Burning Love, Red Lion, Nail Studded Suit, White Prehistoric Bird, Flame, Blue Prehistoric Bird, White Eagle, Tiffany, Black Eagle, Blue Aztec, Red Eagle, Blue Rainbow, Sleak, Inca Gold Leaf, Gypsy, Mexican Sundial, Blue Braid, Blue Swirl, Flower, Blue Rainbow, Mad Tiger, and King of Spades.

CONCERTS WEST
Booking organization headed by Jerry Weintraub and Tom Hulett[1] that arranged Elvis's concert bookings. They also took care of the bookings for Neil Diamond, John Denver,[2] and others.

CONNORS, CAROL
(1940–   ) Four-foot-eleven-inch studio musician born Annette Kleinbard in New Brunswick, New Jersey. Connors, who played guitar on many hit records, was the lead singer on the Teddy Bears' 1958 hit "To Know Him Is to Love Him" (Dore 503), recording under her real name. After hearing the song for the first time, Elvis wanted to meet the girl who sang the lead. After the two met they dated during the next ten months. Connors has been quoted in *People* magazine as saying that Elvis was the first man who ever made love to her. Carol cowrote the song "The Rocky Theme (Gonna Fly Now)" and other hit songs, including "Little Cobra."

Another singer on the song "To Know Him Is to Love Him" was Phil Spector, who had written the song based on a saying on his father's gravestone. (See *Phil Spector*)

CONRAD, ROBERT
(1935–   ) Macho television actor born in Chicago on March 1, 1935, who befriended both Elvis and Red West, playing touch football with them on Sundays in Bel Air. Red West played Marine Corps maintenance man Sergeant Andy Micklin on Conrad's 1976–78 TV series "Baa Baa Black Sheep" (a.k.a. "Black Sheep Squadron").[3]

COOLEY, EDDIE
Composer, with John Davenport (Otis Blackwell), of the song "Fever," which Elvis recorded in 1960.

COOPER, JOE
Composer, with Red West, of the song "If You Think I

---

[1]Tom Hulett was a high school quarterback at Garfield High School in Seattle, the alma mater of Quincy Jones, Ron Holden, Jimi Hendrix, and Dave Lewis (Little Green Things).

[2]In 1961 John Denver's father, Henry Deutschendorf Sr., set a world's speed record in a B-58 Hustler bomber, traveling at 1,200 MPH.

[3]That particular show had several actors who would go on to other TV series, such as Larry Manetti ("Magnum, P.I.") and John Larroquette ("Night Court"). Several sons of actors appeared: James Whitmore Jr., Dirk Blocker, and Jeb Adams. Conrad's daughter, Nancy Conrad, played a nurse.

Don't Need You," which Elvis sang in the 1964 movie *Viva Las Vegas*.

COPAS, LLOYD (COWBOY)
(1913–1963) Popular country artist born in Muskogee, Oklahoma, on July 15, 1913, with whom Elvis toured in mid-September 1955. Elvis headlined the tour, which covered North Carolina and Virginia. Cowboy Copas died in a private-plane crash on March 5, 1963, with Patsy Cline and Harold (Hawkshaw) Hawkins. Singer Roger Miller, who was among the search party looking for the plane, was the one who first spotted the crash scene. The trio was returning from Kansas City, Kansas, where they had given a benefit performance for disc jockey Cactus Jack Call, who had been killed in an automobile accident. On March 8, 1963, while en route to the funerals of Copas, Cline, and Hawkins, Jack Anglin, singing partner of Johnny Wright[1] (Johnny and Jack), was killed in an automobile accident.

CORVAIR
First automobile (of many) that Elvis bought for Priscilla. He gave it to her as a present upon her graduation from high school on June 14, 1963.

COSLOW, SAM
(1902–   ) Composer born in New York City on December 27, 1902. With Will Grosz, Coslow, in 1939, composed the song "Tomorrow Night," which Elvis recorded in 1955. Coslow himself has recorded for Vocalion and Victor Records and wrote other classic songs such as "My Old Flame" and "Cocktails for Two." In 1974 Coslow was inducted into the Songwriters Hall of Fame.

COTTRELL, SANDRA
(1945–   ) Woman who started the first Elvis fan club in her hometown of Tupelo, Mississippi. Cottrell named it The Elvis Presley Home Town Fan Club. Cottrell's brother had been in the same Boy Scout troop as Elvis.

COULTER, PHIL
Writer, with Bill Martin, of the English lyrics for the French song "My Boy," written by J. Claude Francois and Jean-Pierre Boutayre, which Elvis recorded in 1975.

COUNTRY AND WESTERN DISC JOCKEY ASSOCIATION
On November 10–13, 1955, the association held its annual convention at the Andrew Jackson Hotel in Nashville. Elvis was named the thirteenth Most-Played Singer on Radio, was sixteenth on the disc jockeys' favorite-singer list ("Baby Let's Play House" was also number sixteen for the year on the country charts), and he was named the Most Promising Country Artist of 1955. An agreement was reached for Elvis to sign with RCA Victor Records, although the actual signing wouldn't take place until November 20, while Elvis was on the road. RCA's decision to purchase Elvis's contract was heavily influenced when Hill and Range Music, at the suggestion of Colonel Tom Parker, agreed to add $15,000 to the pot. RCA had planned to announce the signing in January, but the Colonel insisted that they announce it immediately, which they did.

COUNTRY SONG ROUNDUP
Second magazine to feature an article about nineteen-year-old Elvis, titled "Folk Music Fireball," in their September 1955 issue. Previously, *Country Song Roundup* had been the first magazine to feature an article on Hank Williams, for which he dedicated to the magazine a new song that he had just written, "Moanin' Blues."

Country Song Roundup held a contest to win a date with Elvis in their August 1956 issue. Both Elvis and Carl Perkins were shown on the cover of that edition.

COVINGTON, PAPPY
Booking agent for the "Louisiana Hayride's" artist service bureau who set up the early 1955 tour for Elvis to play in Arkansas, Louisiana, and Texas (Ark-La-Tex) during the weekdays when Elvis wasn't performing on the Hayride. It was during this tour that Elvis was billed as "The Hillbilly Cat," nicknamed "The King of Western Bop," and Bill Black and Scotty Moore were called the "Blue Moon Boys."

COWBOY SONGS
First national magazine to carry an article on Elvis in their June 1955 issue. The article, which had no byline, was titled "Sun's Newest Star."

CRAINE, JIMMIE
Composer, with Al Jacobs, of the song "Hurt," which Elvis recorded in 1976.

CRAMER, FLOYD
(1933–   ) Nashville piano player born in Shreveport, Louisiana, on October 17, 1933, who became well known for his slip-note style of playing, which was taught to him by Don Robertson. Cramer played as a session musician for numerous RCA artists including Elvis, whom he had met on the "Louisiana Hayride." For two weeks in October 1955 Cramer appeared on the same bill as Elvis on the Jamboree tour from Abilene, Texas, to St. Louis. Cramer backed Elvis on Nashville recording sessions from January 1956 to January 1968.

CREATORE, LUIGI
(1920–   ) Producer and composer born in New York City on December 21, 1920. Creatore composed, with Hugo Peretti and George Weiss, three songs that Elvis sang in films, "Can't Help Falling in Love," "Ku-u-i-po," and "Wild in the Country." (See *Hugo Peretti*)

[1]The son of Johnny Wright and singer Kitty Wells, John Wright, played seaman Willy Moss on the TV series "McHale's Navy."

CREEDENCE CLEARWATER REVIVAL
Popular rock group of the late 1960s and early 1970s. CCR[1] recorded one of Elvis's hits, "My Baby Left Me," and Elvis in turn recorded one of their hits, "Proud Mary" (Fantasy 619). The group also recorded Roy Orbison's "Ooby Dooby." If it can be said that any band of the 1960s captured the early Sun sound, it was John Fogerty and Creedence. In concert Elvis sang Creedence's "Bad Moon Rising" and "Lodi."

CREEL, TOM W.
Elvis's double in some films. He resembled Elvis, and had been stationed with him in the Army in Germany.

CROOK, MAX T.
Composer, with Del Shannon, of the song "Runaway," which Elvis recorded in 1969. Crook played musitron on Del Shannon's original recording of the song, playing one of the most identifiable instrumental solos in the history of rock music.

CROSBY, BING
(1903–1977) Crooner, born Harry Lillis Crosby on May 3, 1903, in Tacoma, Washington. Like Elvis, Crosby started out as a member of a three-man group. One of the members of Crosby's group, the Rhythm Boys, was Harry Barris, the father of TV host Chuck Barris. Crosby won an Oscar for Best Actor for the 1944 movie *Going My Way*. He recorded the best-selling record of all time, "White Christmas" (Decca 18429A). Crosby was second only to Elvis for most records sold (as a solo artist). Crosby's son, Gary Crosby, appeared as a guitarist in the 1965 Elvis movie *Girl Happy*.[2]

Both Crosby and Elvis recorded versions of "White Christmas," "The Whiffenpoof Song," "Harbor Lights" "Silver Bells," "Silent Night," "Blue Hawaii," and "Hey Jude," among other songs. Crosby died on October 14, 1977, fifty-nine days after the death of Elvis. The year 1977 robbed the world of two of the top singers of all time.

CROSBY, CHARLES
Paramedic for the Memphis Fire Department (unit 6) who along with paramedic Ulysses S. Jones, Jr., arrived at Graceland on August 16, 1977, in response to an emergency call. The pair attempted to revive Elvis, but he was already dead.

CROSSTOWN THEATER
Memphis movie theater, located at 400 North Cleveland, which Elvis rented for his private showings. Other theaters he used were the Avon Theater and the Memphian Theater.

CROUCH, ANDRAE E.
(1942–   ) Singer and composer of religious songs, born in Los Angeles on July 1, 1942. Crouch composed the gospel song "I've Got Confidence," which Elvis recorded.

CROWN ELECTRIC COMPANY
Memphis electrical contracting firm, located at 353 Poplar Avenue, for which Elvis worked beginning in July 1953. Before Crown, Elvis held various other jobs, including a one-month position with the Precision Tool Company in the summer of 1951. Crown Electric was owned by Jim and Gladys Tipler. In early 1954 the firm moved from 475 North Dunlap to its Poplar Avenue location. Elvis made a little over $1.25 an hour, (clearing $42.51 per week), which he gave to his mother. His job consisted of driving either the company's Ford F-100 pickup truck or their blue panel truck and delivering supplies to the men on the job. In addition, Elvis worked in the warehouse. Elvis claimed to have studied electricity in the evenings to learn more about his job, but where he attended classes has not yet been determined.

The building that formerly housed Crown Electric in the 1950s. (Photo courtesy Don Fink)

Yellow pages advertisement for Crown Electric in 1954. (Photo courtesy (Don Fink)

---

[1]Creedence Clearwater Revival, originally named Tommy Fogerty and the Blue Velvets, then the Golliwogs, chose part of their name from a line in a popular beer commercial.

[2]It is interesting that Elvis appeared in films with the offspring of two of America's most popular singers, Bing Crosby and Frank Sinatra.

Ironically, a few years before, singer Dorsey Burnette had driven a truck for Crown Electric, with brother Johnny Burnette and Paul Burlison also working there.[1] Coincidentally, two other rock superstars worked for electrical firms before they became musicians: George Harrison was employed by Blackers in Liverpool, England, while Paul McCartney was employed by the Liverpool firm of Massey and Coggins.)

While he was with Crown Electric, Elvis began recording for Sun Records. In the fall of 1954 he left Crown Electric to pursue his singing career full time.

Today B&H Hardware stands at 353 Poplar Avenue, where Crown Electric once stood. (See *Johnny Burnette, Gladys Tipler*)

CRUDUP, ARTHUR (BIG BOY)
(1905–1974) Rhythm & blues singer born illegitimate in Virginia on August 24, 1905. Crudup wrote and recorded three songs, which Elvis later recorded, for Victor Records' Bluebird label in Chicago: "So Glad You're Mine" (Victor 20-1949, February 22, 1946), "That's All Right (Mama)" (Victor 20-2205), on September 6, 1946) and "My Baby Left Me" (Victor 130-284, on November 8, 1950). Leonard Chess of Chess Records discovered Crudup in Forest, Mississippi. In addition to his real name, Crudup recorded under the names Perry Lee Crudup and Elmer James. Elvis credited Crudup with influencing his style. In later years Elvis financed Crudup's recording sessions with Fire Records, though the two never did meet. In 1973 a TV special called "Arthur Crudup: Born in the Blues" aired. Crudup died of a stroke at the North Hampton–Accomac Memorial Hospital in Nassawadox, Virginia, on March 28, 1974. (See *Fire Records*)

CRUTCHFIELD, JERRY
Composer of the song "Find Out What's Happening," which Elvis recorded in 1973.

CULTURAL PHENOMENON OF ELVIS PRESLEY: THE MAKING OF A FOLK HERO
Four-unit credit course offered by the University of Tennessee in 1979. The class, which was open only to honor students, was taught by English professor Patsy Guy Hammontree. It was the first accredited university-level course on Elvis. Professor Hammontree authored the article "Audience Amplitude: The Cultural Phenomenon of Elvis Presley," which was published in the 1979 book *Elvis: Images and Fancies*, edited by Jac L. Tharpe.

CULVER CITY
California town in which Colonel Tom Parker's West Coast headquarters is located. Culver City is the home of MGM/UA. (See *Madison, Tennessee*)

CUNNINGHAM, BUDDY BLAKE
Musician born in Jackson, Mississippi, who could be heard on Elvis's Sun recording of "I Don't Care If the Sun Don't Shine," playing what sounded like bongos but was actually a cardboard record box. Cunningham also played on Elvis's "Blue Moon." He has never been credited for those recording sessions. Cunningham, who began recording for Sun Records in 1953, was the first artist released on the Phillips International Record label in 1957. He has recorded under the names Buddy Blake and B. B. Cunningham.

Cunningham's release of "Right or Wrong"/"Why Do I Cry?" (Sun 208) was recorded immediately before Elvis's debut disc, "That's All Right (Mama)"/"Blue Moon of Kentucky" (Sun 209). (See *Holiday Inn Records*)

CURRIE, JIM
Composer, with Lonnie Donegan, of the song "I'll Never Fall in Love Again," which Elvis recorded in 1976.

CURTIS, MANN
(1911–   ) Composer, born Emanuel Kurtz in Brooklyn on November 15, 1911. Mann Curtis composed, with Pierre Delanoe and Gilbert Becaud, the French song "Je T'Appartiens," which Elvis recorded as "Let It Be Me" in 1970.

CURTIS, TONY
(1925–   ) Actor, born Bernard Schwartz in the Bronx on June 3, 1925. Curtis made his screen debut in the 1949 movie *Criss Cross*. Curtis was Elvis's favorite actor in the early 1950s. Elvis even copied Curtis's ducktail hairstyle. Curtis's first wife, actress Janet Leigh, played in the 1963 movie *Bye Bye Birdie*. It has been mentioned in some sources that Elvis was originally offered Tony Curtis's role in Stanley Kramer's 1958 movie *The Defiant Ones*, opposite Sidney Poitier.

CYMBAL, JOHNNY
Singer and producer born in Cleveland. Cymbal charted five songs, beginning with "Mr. Bass Man" (Kapp 503)[2] in 1963. Also in 1963, Cymbal recorded the novelty song "Teenage Heaven" (Knapp 524), in which Elvis's name was mentioned. Under the name Derek, he recorded "Cinnamon" (Bang 558) in 1968. Cymbal co-composed the song "Mary in the Morning," which Elvis recorded in 1970.

---

[1]The odds of two future rock stars working for the same firm at the same time are not as remote as one would think. Michael Zager and Barry Manilow were fellow employees in the CBS-TV mailroom in Los Angeles, while Kris Kristofferson and Billy Swan were both janitors at the Columbia Studios in Nashville.

[2]Ronnie Bright of the Coasters sang bass on the song.

DALLAS

CBS-TV prime-time dramatic series that debuted on April 2, 1978, starring Larry Hagman as John Ross Ewing Jr. and Barbara Bel Geddes as Eleanor Southworth Ewing. Beginning in 1983, Priscilla Presley joined the cast as Jenna Wade, a role previously played by Morgan Fairchild in 1978 and Francine Tacker in 1980. Dale Midkiff, who portrayed Elvis in the 1988 TV miniseries "Elvis and Me," played the young Jock Ewing in the 1986 TV movie *Dallas: The Early Years*, in which Hoyt Axton played Aaron Southworth.

DANIELS, CHARLIE

·(1943–   ) Singer and fiddler, born in Wilmington, North Carolina, on October 28, 1943. Daniels headed a six-piece band called the Charlie Daniels Band. Daniels, who often closes his eyes when he sings, grew up listening to the music of Elvis and Bill Monroe. He played on Bob Dylan's *Nashville Skyline, Self Portrait,* and *New Morning* albums. In 1963 Daniels cowrote the song "It Hurts Me," which Elvis recorded.

DANZIG, FRED

Reporter who interviewed Elvis on January 31, 1956, during Elvis's recording session at RCA Victor's New York City studio.

DARBY, KEN

(1909–   ) Singer, Academy Award–winning composer, and musical conductor, born Kenneth Lorin Darby in Hebron, Nebraska, on May 13, 1909. In 1939, Darby invented the Munchkin voices heard in the film *The Wizard of Oz.* In 1942 the Ken Darby singers, along with John Scott Trotter's orchestra, backed Bing Crosby on the now-famous Decca Records release of "White Christmas." Darby later served as Marilyn Monroe's voice coach. In the 1950s the Ken Darby Singers sang the theme song for the TV Western series "The Life and Legend of Wyatt Earp." Douglas Fowley, the father of musician Kim Fowley, portrayed Doc Holliday on the series.

Darby was the musical director of Elvis's first movie, *Love Me Tender.* Asked to pen four songs for the film, he wrote "Love Me Tender," "We're Gonna Move," "Let Me," and "Poor Boy." The Ken Darby Trio provided the backup vocals for Elvis on those recordings.

Darby's wife, Vera Matson, and Elvis are officially credited with composing the four songs for *Love Me Tender* because of copyright problems. Darby was a writer affiliated with ASCAP (American Society of Composers, Authors, and Publishers) and Elvis's publishing company was affiliated with BMI (Broadcast Music, Inc.).[1] (See *BMI*)

DARIN, BOBBY

(1936–1973) Popular rock & roll singer of the 1950s and 1960s, born Walden Robert Cassotto in the Bronx on May 14, 1936. Darin's recording career began in 1956 with his first two releases, "Rock Island Line"/"Timber" (Decca 29883) and "Silly Willy"/"Blue-Eyed Mermaid" (Decca 29922). In March of the same year he made his national TV debut on "Stage Show," billed as the nineteen-year-old singing sensation (just as Elvis had been, two months earlier).

Darin's first big hit was "Splish Splash" (Atco 6117) in 1958.

The idea for the song came from New York City disc jockey Murray the K's mother. "Splish Splash" reached number three on the charts and became a million-seller. Darin's biggest hit was "Mack the Knife" in 1959, going to number one for nine weeks and selling more than two million copies. The song became the Record of the Year and Darin's trademark.

In 1963, Darin was nominated for Best Supporting Actor for his role in the movie *Captain Newman, M.D.,* becoming the first rock & roller to be nominated for an Oscar. He died on December 20, 1973, at 12:15 A.M., during heart surgery.

Darin, who was one of Elvis's favorite singers, was introduced as a guest at one of Elvis's Las Vegas concerts at the International Hotel. The introduction appeared in the bootleg album *To Know Him is to Love Him* (Black Belt Records).

Darin recorded "Until It's Time for You to Go," which Elvis later sang. Darin also composed "I'll Be There," which Elvis recorded in February 1969. Darin played the role of John Wakefield in the 1962 movie *Too Late Blues,* only after Elvis turned it down. Elvis always liked Darin as a person and a performer and attended several of his performances.

Darin said of Elvis in 1960, "If you put Elvis Presley on one side of the street, and all us Johnny-Come-Latelys on the other, the kids would be mobbing Elvis. The Big El is still the most."

DARION, JOSEPH

(1917–   ) Tony Award–winning composer, born in New York City on January 30, 1917. Darion has written popular songs, musicals, operas, and film scores. He is the composer, with Mitch Leigh, of "The Impossible Dream," which Elvis recorded in 1972.

DAVENPORT, JOHN

Cowriter (with Eddie Cooley) of the song "Fever" in 1956. Davenport was a pseudonym of composer Otis Blackwell. (See *Otis Blackwell*)

---

[1] Singer Gene Pitney used his mother's maiden name, Ann Orlowski, when he cowrote the ASCAP song "Rubber Ball," since he himself was a member of BMI.

DAVID, ELWOOD
Pilot of Elvis's Convair 880 jet, the *Lisa Marie*. David reportedly earned $43,000 a year.

DAVID, HAL
(1921–   ) Academy Award–winning lyricist born in New York City on May 25, 1921, the younger brother of composer Mack David. Hal David has been the lyricist, with Burt Bacharach, on dozens of hit songs, beginning with those of Dionne Warwick. David composed, with Sherman Edwards, the songs "A Whistling Tune" and "Home Is Where the Heart Is," which Elvis sang in the 1962 movie *Kid Galahad*.

DAVID, MACK
(1912–   ) Lyricist born in New York City on July 5, 1912. He is the older brother of lyricist Hal David. Mack David composed the song "I Don't Care If the Sun Don't Shine" for Walt Disney's 1950 animated film *Cinderella*. David, who is a member of the Songwriters Hall of Fame, also composed the theme song for the TV series "77 Sunset Strip," "Hawaiian Eye," "Lawman," and "Surfside 6." Elvis recorded David's "I Don't Care If the Sun Don't Shine" in 1954. He also wrote, with Sherman Edwards, "I'm Not the Marrying Kind," which Elvis sang in his 1962 movie *Follow That Dream*.

DAVIES, RAY
(1944–   ) Lead singer of the British group the Kinks, born in London on June 21, 1944. He authored the rock opera *Tommy*. In 1966 Elvis asked him to write a title song for one of his movies, but it never materialized.

DAVIS, GOVERNOR JIMMY (PAPPY)
(1902–   ) Singer and songwriter born in Quitman, Louisiana, on September 11, 1902. His most famous composition is "You Are My Sunshine." Over the years he recorded about a dozen gospel albums. From 1945 to 1948 Davis served as governor of Louisiana. In 1948 Davis bestowed the honorary title of Colonel upon Tom Parker, who had a friend, Bob Greer, on the governor's staff. It was the first of two honorary colonel titles that Parker would receive. Davis is a member of the Country Music Hall of Fame.

DAVIS, (SCOTT) MAC
(1941–   ) Country-oriented singer and composer born in Lubbock, Texas, on January 21, 1941. On October 15, 1955, in Lubbock, fourteen-year-old Mac Davis attended a show at the Cotton Club that featured Elvis and Buddy Holly on the same bill. In the late 1960s and early 1970s, many Mac Davis compositions were recorded by major artists, including Lou Rawls ("You're Good for Me"), Bobby Goldsboro ("Watching Scotty Grow," about Mac Davis's real-life son), and Glen Campbell ("Within My Memory"). Davis tells his story in his 1980 recording of "Texas in My Rear View

Mirror" (Casablanca NB 2305), in which he talks about Buddy Holly and leaving Lubbock, Texas.

Glen Campbell, who married Davis's former wife, Sarah, gave Davis the nickname "The Song Painter."

Elvis recorded several Mac Davis–Billy Strange compositions, "Clean Up Your Own Back Yard," "Charro," "A Little Less Conversation," "Nothingville," "Memories," and two which Davis had written alone, "In the Ghetto" and "Don't Cry, Daddy."

The $40,000 royalty check that Davis received for "In the Ghetto" helped bail him out of financial problems. On the jacket of Davis's 1980 *Greatest Hits* album he gave special thanks to Billy Strange, Elvis Presley, Clive Davis, and Sandy Gallin.

DAVIS, OSCAR
Agent, nicknamed "The Baron," who worked for Colonel Tom Parker. Davis performed in vaudeville between 1910 and 1917. He once managed country artist Hank Williams, as well as worked with artists such as Eddy Arnold, Hank Snow, Ernest Tubb, Roy Acuff, and others. Davis first heard of Elvis in October 1954, when he watched him perform at the Eagle's Nest in Memphis. It was Davis who told Colonel Parker about Elvis. He then helped Parker promote Elvis. Davis was also singer Jerry Lee Lewis's manager.

DAVIS, RICHARD
One of the men who played touch football with Elvis in Memphis. Davis became a member of the Memphis Mafia in 1962 and served as Elvis's valet for the next seven years, taking care of Elvis's wardrobe during the concert tours. In 1969 he was replaced by Rick Stanley. Elvis once bought Davis a new white Cadillac convertible. Davis was fired from Elvis's employ by Vernon Presley.

DAVIS JR., SAMMY
(1925–   ) Black entertainer, singer, musician, dancer, mimic, and actor born in New York City on December 8, 1925. Davis attended Elvis's private funeral on August 18, 1977. Davis, who made his professional debut at the age of two, was a member of Frank Sinatra's "Rat Pack."[1] In 1954 he had his first chart record, "Hey There" (Decca 29199). He lost an eye that year in an automobile accident. Davis added Broadway to his career when he starred in *Mr. Wonderful* in 1956. Although he has been recording for over a quarter of a century, Davis has had only one number one record— "Candy Man" (from the 1971 movie *Willie Wonka and the Chocolate Factory*).

Davis appeared with Elvis on the 1960 "Frank Sinatra–Timex Special" on ABC-TV. He sang "It's Nice to Go Traveling" with Elvis, Frank Sinatra, Joey Bishop, and Nancy Sinatra. Davis can be seen as a member of the audience in the 1970 documentary *Elvis—That's the Way It Is*. It has been reported that Davis and Elvis once danced down an aisle together at a Chuck Berry

---

[1] Members of the group included, from time to time, Frank Sinatra, Sammy Davis Jr., Peter Lawford, Dean Martin, Joey Bishop, Shirley MacLaine, Tony Curtis, Jimmy Van Heusen, Sammy Cahn, and others.

performance. Elvis enjoyed watching Sammy perform live, which he did at least three times, feeling that he could learn something by watching him perform on stage. Davis sometimes impersonated Elvis as part of his act. Elvis once gave him a $30,000, 157-carat black sapphire ring, taking it off his own finger and handing it over.

Before Elvis recorded "In the Ghetto" the song was offered to Davis, who failed to project it with proper feeling.

DAY ELVIS DIED, THE
Feature article in *TV Guide* magazine in the August 15–21, 1981, issue, showing a portrait of Elvis on the cover that had been painted by Bob Peak.

DAY, JAMES CLAYTON
Steel guitarist with Ray Price's Cherokee Cowboys. Day and the band backed up Elvis on the "Louisiana Hayride" in 1954 and can be heard on "Tweedlee Dee," which they performed in Gladewater, Texas, on December 18, 1954. One story has it that Day and the Cherokee Cowboys backed Elvis during a performance for which Bill Black and Scotty Moore failed to show up because of car trouble. Day also played guitar on the Everly Brothers' 1957 hit "Bye Bye Love" (Cadence 1315).

DEAN, DIZZY
(1911–1974) Baseball pitcher, born Jay Hanna Dean on January 16, 1911, who played for the St. Louis Cardinals (1930–37) and later became a TV baseball announcer. In the 1952 movie *The Pride of St. Louis*, the six-foot-four-inch Dean was portrayed by the six-foot-four-inch Dan Dailey. (It was Dizzy Dean who gave Roy Acuff the nickname "The King of Country Music.")

Dizzy Dean, a member of the Baseball Hall of Fame, was one of the featured performers, along with Elvis, at the Jimmie Rodgers Memorial Day Celebration, May 26, 1955. (See *Jimmie Rodgers Memorial Day Celebration*)

DEAN, JAMES BYRON
(1931–1955) Actor born in Marion, Indiana, on February 8, 1931. After a short, but successful, movie career during which he became a cult figure, Dean was killed in an automobile accident while driving his 550 Porsche Spyder. He crashed into a Ford sedan driven by Donald Turnupseed near Salinas, California.

During the years 1954 to 1956, Elvis was one of the three rebels on the scene. The other two were James Dean and Marlon Brando. Elvis once remarked to producer Hall Wallis about an observation he had made, that successful actors in films never smiled, e.g., James Dean, Marlon Brando, and Humphrey Bogart.

There have been a number of comparisons made between Elvis and Dean. Elvis took over where Dean left off; he was referred to as "the musical James Dean." Actor Nick Adams was a close friend of Dean's (he even dubbed a part of Dean's dialogue in the 1956 movie *Giant*), later becoming a good friend of Elvis's.

James Dean. (Photo courtesy Eddie Brandt's Saturday Matinee)

Actress Ursula Andress had been romantically involved with both Dean and Elvis. Elvis's favorite movie was Dean's 1955 film *Rebel Without a Cause*, from which Elvis had memorized every line. Dean's love interest in the film became Elvis's real-life love interest, actress Natalie Wood. Both Elvis and Dean have been the subject of many books, magazine articles, and songs. Country singer Jimmy Wakely recorded four songs in tribute to Dean, "Giant"/"His Name Was Dean" (Coral 61706) and "James Dean"/"Jimmy, Jimmy" (Coral 61722). Both men (Elvis as "the King") were mentioned in Don McLean's 1971 hit song "American Pie." In 1956 a single issue magazine titled *Elvis and Jimmy* was published. After Dean's death on September 30, 1955, Elvis reportedly wanted to star in the film *The James Dean Story*. Produced by David Weisbart, who had produced *Rebel Without a Cause*, the film ended up as a documentary. In a scene in the 1958 movie *King Creole*, jacket-wearing Elvis holds a knife in one scene in which he resembles James Dean in *Rebel Without a Cause*.

A modest Elvis once said of James Dean: "I would never compare myself in any way to James Dean because James Dean was a genius. I sure would like to, I mean, I guess a lot of actors in Hollywood would like to have had the ability that James Dean had, but I would never compare myself to James Dean in any way."

DEAR ELVIS
Column in *TV & Movie Screen* magazine (January 1963) in which Elvis answered questions from readers.

DEARY, JOAN
Executive in charge of the Elvis catalog for RCA Records. Deary joined RCA in 1954 as Steve Sholes's secretary. In 1972 she became assistant to RCA vice president Harry Jenkins, whose job it was to handle the Elvis Presley material. She produced many albums for RCA, including the *Elvis Aron Presley 25th Anniversary* album set. Deary worked out of the RCA building in Hollywood until her retirement in 1987. Her duties were taken over by Gregg Geller.

DECCA RECORDING STUDIOS
Recording studio at Universal City, California, where Elvis recorded the soundtrack for the 1969 movie *Change of Habit.*

DEE, SYLVIA
(1914–1967) Composer born Josephine Proffitt Faison in Little Rock, Arkansas, on October 22, 1914. Dee was the composer, with Ben Weisman, of the song "Moonlight Swim," which Elvis sang in the 1961 movie *Blue Hawaii.* She also composed, with George Goehring, the song "Suppose," which was cut from the 1968 movie *Speedway.*

DEES, RICK
(1950–   ) Risqué Los Angeles disc jockey (KISS-FM) born Rigdon Osmond Dees III. While living in Memphis, Dees worked as a DJ and program director at Memphis's WMPS radio. Dees and His Cast of Idiots recorded two Elvis novelty records, "I Wanna Be Elvis" (Atlantic 89481) and "He Ate Too Many Jelly Donuts" (RSO 870).

DELANOE, PIERRE
Composer, with Gilbert Becaud of the song "Et Maintenant," which Elvis recorded in 1973 as "What Now My Love." Delanoe was the composer, with Gilbert Becaud and Mann Curtis, of the song "Je T'Appartiens," which Elvis recorded in 1970 as "Let It Be Me."

DE LOUISE, JOSEPH
Chicago psychic who, according to an article in *The Star,* contacted Elvis's spirit in 1977 after his death.

DEL VALLEY JUNIOR HIGH SCHOOL
School attended by Priscilla Beaulieu in Austin, Texas. She defeated her best friend, Pamela Rutherford, to win the title of "Queen of Del Valley Junior High."

DEMETRIUS, CLAUDE
(1917–   ) Composer born in Bath, Maine, on August 3, 1917. DeMetrius composed several songs recorded by Elvis, among them "Hard Headed Woman" and "Mean Woman Blues." With Aaron Schroeder he composed "Santa Bring My Baby Back (to Me)," and with Aaron Schroeder, Hal Blair, and Bill Pepper he composed "I Was the One."

DE MILLE, CECIL B. (BLOUNT)
(1881–1959) Longtime Hollywood director born in De Mille Corners, Ashfield, Massachusetts, on August 12, 1881. De Mille became famous for his religious spectaculars (his father was a minister). De Mille was the only man to successfully film the same movie three times—*The Squaw Man* (1913, 1918, 1931). He filmed his favorite *The Ten Commandments*[1] twice (1923 and 1956).

When Elvis met De Mille in 1956, De Mille asked him if he had seen his film *The Ten Commandments.*[2] Elvis is said to have replied, "Crazy, man, real crazy."

DENE, TERRY
First British Elvis imitator. He began copying Elvis in the mid-1950s. Dene's backup was the Dene-Agers. Dene lived in London, packing records at HMV Records on Oxford Street. One night he jumped up on stage during a Tony Sheridan appearance (on break) and began singing. His bravado brought him to the attention of Decca Records, who signed him to a contract.

DENNIS ROBERT OPTICAL BOUTIQUE
Los Angeles firm from which Elvis bought his prescription sunglasses, which cost approximately $200 each. Elvis also bought his bodyguards sunglasses with "TCB" engraved on them.

DENNY, JAMES R.
(1911–1963) Talent coordinator for the Grand Ole Opry from 1951 to 1954, born in Buffalo Valley, Tennessee, on February 28, 1911. Denny booked the stars through the Artists Service Bureau. After Elvis performed on the Grand Ole Opry on October 2, 1954, Denny told him he should return to driving a truck.[3] According to Jerry Hopkins's book *Elvis,* at a social function a few years later, Denny put his arm around Elvis's shoulder and said, "I always knew this boy had it in him to make it." Needless to say, Elvis was not amused. Previously, on August 11, 1952, Denny had fired singer Hank Williams from the Grand Ole Opry for missing some performances.

In 1955 Denny was selected *Billboard's* "Man of the Year." He was voted into the Country Music Hall of Fame in 1966.

DENSON, LEE
Composer of the religious song "Miracle of the Rosary," which Elvis recorded in 1971.

---

[1]The movie is mentioned in the 1957 Elvis movie *Loving You.*
[2]In the 1956 version (the 1923 version was silent) a young Herb Alpert can be seen with his back to the audience playing a drum as Moses descends from Mount Sinai. Others who claim to have appeared in the film in bit parts are Joan Rivers and Jon Peters.
[3]Ironically, it was Jim Denny who, in 1956, took great interest in the career of another rock & roller, Buddy Holly. He helped Holly sign a contract with Decca Records.

DEPUTY SHERIFF

Honorary law-enforcement designation given to Elvis by the Shelby County, Tennessee, Sheriff's Department. Because he was a deputy sheriff, Elvis was allowed to carry a loaded pistol.

DESHANNON, JACKIE

(1944–   ) Singer-composer born Sharon Myers in Hazel, Kentucky, on August 21, 1944. She has written more than 600 songs, including "Put a Little Love in Your Heart" and "What the World Needs Now Is Love." DeShannon dated Elvis over a six-month period in the mid-1960s. (See *Jimmy O'Neill*)

DEVITA, A.

Composer, with G. Calabrese and Hal Shaper, of the song "Softly, as I Leave You," which Elvis recorded from an Elvis concert.

DEVORE, SY

Fashion designer who created a new wardrobe for Elvis in 1962 at a cost of $9,000.

DIAMOND, NEIL

(1941–   ) Popular singer-songwriter, born in Brooklyn on January 24, 1941, who originally recorded for Columbia Records, then Bang Records,[1] Uni Records, and finally back to Columbia. Diamond's first record release was "Clown Town"/"At Night" (Columbia 42809) in 1963, which failed to reach the charts. His next release, "Solitary Man" (Bang 519) in 1966, did make the charts, reaching #55. When reissued in 1970 (Bang 578), the song peaked at #21.

While at Erasmus High School in Brooklyn, Diamond and Barbra Streisand sang in the same choral group. In 1978 Diamond and Streisand would record "You Don't Bring Me Flowers" (Columbia 10840), which became the biggest-selling single in Columbia Records history. In 1973 Diamond added to his many achievements by scoring the soundtrack of the motion picture *Jonathan Livingston Seagull*.

Elvis recorded Diamond's 1969 hit "Sweet Caroline" (Uni 55136) in 1970 at the International Hotel in Las Vegas. Elvis also recorded the Diamond composition "And the Grass Won't Pay No Mind." Diamond recorded at the American Sound Studio in Memphis in January 1969, immediately before Elvis arrived to record.

DIDDLEY, BO

(1928–   ) Rhythm & blues singer born Ellas McDaniels on December 30, 1928, in McComb, Mississippi. He got his nickname in grade school in Chicago. He was so mischievous that he was called "Bo" for bad boy. He used the nickname when he boxed in the Golden Gloves. In 1955 Bo Diddley walked into Chess Records and auditioned for the owners, Phil and Leonard Chess. He performed a song he wrote called "Uncle John" (the catchy tune was based on the Old English lullaby "Hush Little Baby"). The Chess brothers signed Bo to a contract after which he recorded "Uncle John," changing the title to "Bo Diddley" (Checker 814), as well as cleaning up the rather risqué lyrics.

While Elvis was in New York City in 1956 appearing on the "Stage Show" TV program, he went to the Apollo Theater to see Bo Diddley perform. Many people, including Bo Diddley himself, believe that Elvis copied Diddley's style of performing, since Bo Diddley was one of the first artists to wiggle his hips while singing. Bo Diddley once said: "If he copied me, I don't care. More power to him. I'm not starving." However, Elvis had been gyrating since the Overton Park Shell performance in 1954, a year before he ever saw Bo Diddley perform in New York City.

DILBECK, TOMMY

Composer, with Eddy Arnold and Hal Horton, of the song "I'll Hold You in My Heart," which Elvis recorded in 1969.

DISKIN, TOM

One of Colonel Tom Parker's assistants, nicknamed "The Penguin." Diskin is also Parker's brother-in-law. They first met in 1953 after Parker had booked the Dicken Sisters on several of his shows with Eddy Arnold. The Dicken Sisters were actually named Diskin, and were the sisters of Tom Diskin. According to legend and Jerry Hopkins's book *Elvis: A Biography*, Diskin turned down a request to manage Elvis after Scotty Moore sent him a copy of Elvis's first release. At the time, Diskin was in Chicago working for Jamboree Attractions.

DIVORCE

After six years of marriage, Elvis and Priscilla decided to divorce. Elvis filed for divorce on August 18, 1972 as a favor to Priscilla so that her name would be kept out of print. (Had she filed, her address would have been listed on the public document.) Elvis first agreed to pay Priscilla $1,000 a month, plus $5,000 in child support and a lump sum of $100,000. However, on May 29, 1973, a suit of extrinsic fraud was filed for Priscilla by her attorney, Arthur Toll of Tanker, Toll and Leavitt. Priscilla requested a great deal more per month:

Rent	$700
Property insurance and taxes	$100
Maintenance and residence	$500
Food and household supplies	$1,000
Utilities	$150
Telephone	$400
Laundry and cleaning	$300
Clothing	$2,500
Medical	$200
Insurance	$500
Child care	$300
School	$300
Entertainment	$500
Incidentals	$1,500
Transportation	$1,000
Auto expenses	$500
Installment payments	$1,350
Total	$11,800

---

[1] Bang Records was founded by Bert Berns, Ahmet Ertegun, Nesuhi Ertegun, and Jerry Wexler.

Their divorce was finalized on October 9, 1973. The couple walked out of the Santa Monica court arm-in-arm. Priscilla was given a lump sum of $2 million, $6,000 a month for ten years, $4,200 a month alimony for one year, $4,000 a month child support, $250,000 from the sale of their Los Angeles home and 5 percent of two of Elvis's music publishing companies.

DIXON, EWEL
Resident of Tupelo, Mississippi, who claimed to have let ten-year-old Elvis play the guitar he had in his shop. Dixon also claimed to have given Elvis his first $12.95 guitar in an article "I Gave Elvis His First Guitar" in *Modern Screen* magazine.

DIXON, LUTHER
Composer, with Al Smith of the song "Big Boss Man," which Elvis recorded in 1967.

DIXON, TINY
Country singer who with his own band played in many Memphis clubs including the Eagle's Nest, where, according to some sources, he backed Elvis in September–October 1954.

DIXON, WILLIE
(1915–   ) Blues artist and Golden Gloves boxing champion in Chicago in 1936. Dixon, who was born in Vicksburg, Mississippi, on April 1, 1915, composed two songs that Elvis recorded, "Doncha Think It's Time" and "My Babe," which Dixon originally recorded (Checker 811).

Dixon composed the classic rhythm & blues song "Little Red Rooster," which was recorded by both Sam Cooke and the Rolling Stones.

DOC HAYES–VERNON PRESLEY MOTOR SALES
Memphis used-car dealership with which Vernon Presley was affiliated for a brief time in the 1960s.

DR. STRANGELOVE
1964 British-made film (Subtitle: *Or How I Learned to Stop Worrying and Love the Bomb*) which was one of Elvis's favorite movies. It starred one of his favorite actors, Peter Sellers, in three different roles. Marty Lacker claims that Elvis saw the movie at least fifty times.

DOLAN, KITTY
Brunette singer whom Elvis dated in 1956, having met her in Las Vegas while she was performing at the Tropicana. Dolan sometimes traveled to Memphis and later to Killeen, Texas, to visit with Elvis. In 1958 Dolan wrote an article titled "How Elvis Made Love to Me" for *Movie Mirror* magazine.

DOMINO
Priscilla Presley's favorite horse, given to her by Elvis

and kept at Graceland. Priscilla rode Domino into her eighth month of pregnancy with Lisa Marie. After her divorce from Elvis, she transported Domino to southern California.

DOMINO, FATS
(1928–   ) Rhythm & blues piano player and singer born Antoine Domino in New Orleans on February 26, 1928. Domino's first million-seller (and the derivation of his nickname) was "The Fat Man" (Imperial 59058),[1] which was released in 1949. Most of his tunes have been written by him, in collaboration with Dave Bartholomew. Although he has had twenty-three million-sellers, Domino has never had a number one record.

Domino's biggest hit (and only million-seller not written by him and Dave Bartholomew) was "Blueberry Hill" (Imperial 5407) in 1956. Elvis recorded "Blueberry Hill" in 1957. At one of his concerts Elvis announced, "Hello, I'm Fats Domino."

DONAGGIO, P.
Composer, with V. Pallavicini, of the song "You Don't Have to Say You Love Me," which Elvis recorded.

DONEGAN, LONNIE
(1931–   ) Scottish skiffle singer born Anthony James Donegan in Glasgow, Scotland, on April 29, 1931. In 1956 Donegan recorded the hit folk song "Rock Island Line" (London 1650). In 1961 he had a hit with "Does Your Chewing Gum Lose It's Flavor (On the Bedpost Overnight)" (Dot 15911), which had been based on Billy Rose's "Does Your Spearmint Lose Its Flavor on the Bedpost Overnight," written in 1924 and considered to have been the first commercial jingle. Donegan cowrote, with Jim Currie, "I'll Never Fall in Love Again," which Elvis recorded in 1976.

DONNA REED SHOW, THE
ABC-TV series from 1958 to 1966, featuring Donna Reed, Carl Betz, Shelly Fabares, Paul Petersen,[2] and Jimmy Hawkins. Three of the stars appeared in Elvis movies. Betz, Fabares, and Hawkins appeared in the 1966 movie *Spinout*, while Fabares and Hawkins were in *Girl Happy* (1965). Fabares also appeared in the 1967 movie *Clambake*. Paul Petersen had a 1962 hit record, "She Can't Find Her Keys" (Colpix 620), which made reference to Elvis. Together, in 1962, Petersen and Fabares recorded "What Did They Do Before Rock & Roll" (Colpix 631), which also mentioned Elvis's name.

DONNER, RAL
(1943–1984) One of the more successful Elvis sound-alikes. Donner was born Ralph Stuart Emanuel Donner in Chicago on February 10, 1943. His 1961 version of "The Girl of My Best Friend" (Gone 5102) is almost identical to Elvis's version. Donner's backup group was

---

[1]Many rock historians consider this to be the first rock & roll record.
[2]Paul Petersen's real-life sister, Patty, played Trisha Stone, his stage sister, on "The Donna Reed Show."

called the Starfires.[1] In 1964 Donner also covered Elvis's "Poison Ivy League" (Fontana 1502).

Donner first saw Elvis perform at Chicago's International Amphitheater in 1957. In 1978 Donner recorded
the Elvis tribute record "The Day the Beat Stopped"
(Thunder 7801). A portion of the record's royalties was
donated to the Elvis Presley Memorial in Memphis. On
his recording of "Rip It Up"/"Don't Leave Me Now"
(Starfire 114), Donner was backed by Scotty Moore, D.
J. Fontana, and the Jordanaires, who had backed Elvis
on his versions of the two songs. Donner also narrated
the 1981 movie *This Is Elvis*. Donner died of cancer in
April 1984.

During one of Elvis's Las Vegas shows in 1975, a
member of the audience asked Elvis to sing "If I Can
Dream." Elvis jokingly answered, " 'If I Can
Dream?', I can't sing that. That's by Ral Donner."

DOORS INCORPORATED
Memphis firm, located at 911 Rayner Street, that built
the Music Gates at Graceland in 1957. (See *Music
Gates*)

DORSEY, THOMAS A.
(1899–   ) Chicago bluesman, songwriter, and onetime bandleader for Gertrude (Ma) Rainey, born outside of Atlanta on July 1, 1899. Before 1932 Dorsey
composed mostly blues and jazz tunes.[2] After 1932 he
became America's foremost writer of gospel songs.
Dorsey composed "Peace in the Valley" and "Take My
Hand, Precious Lord," both of which Elvis recorded.
Dorsey has been credited with coining the term "gospel song."

DORS, DIANA
(1931–   ) Actress known as the "Blond Bombshell,"
born in Swindon, England, on October 23, 1931, who
was married to Dennis Hamilton and, later, to TV
game-show host Richard Dawson. According to an article in the *Midnight Globe* (September 20, 1977), which
Dors authored, she carried on a secret love affair with
Elvis while married to Dennis Hamilton. She and Elvis
met at a Hollywood party in 1956. She also claimed
that Elvis bought her a new pink Cadillac and that they
traveled to Mexico one weekend where she watched
Elvis smoke a marijuana cigarette. Dors also wrote an
article for London's *Sunday Mirror* titled "Elvis Was
My Love."

When Dewey Phillips was fired from Memphis's TV
program "Dance Party" on WHBQ in 1967, it was
supposedly because he performed pushups over a life-
size poster of Diana Dors on one program.

DOUGHERTY, PATRICK AND VELMA
Couple who in the 1940s operated a farm in East
Tupelo, Mississippi, near the Presley home on Old Saltillo Road. They were quoted in a newspaper article as
saying they employed Vester Presley, and that Elvis
would often come by their farm during the summers of
1946 and 1947 to look at and sometimes to ride their
two horses.

DRAKE, ERVIN
(1919–   ) Composer born in New York City on April
3, 1919. Drake composed music for more than 700 TV
program episodes from 1948 to 1962. He composed,
with Irvin Graham, Jimmy Shirl, and Al Stillman, the
song "I Believe," which Elvis recorded in 1957.

DRAKE, PETER
(1932–   ) Steel guitarist, born in Atlanta on October
8, 1932, known as the "Talking Steel Guitar Man."
Drake achieved national notoriety in 1964 with the
million-selling record "Forever" (Smash 1867). Drake
played steel guitar on many Elvis recordings, beginning in May 1966, including such songs as "Guitar
Man," "Big Boss Man," and "You'll Never Walk Alone."
In 1968 Drake founded Stop Records. His brother, Jack
Drake, was an original member of Ernest Tubb's Trou-
badours.

DRIFTERS
Popular rhythm & blues vocal group of the 1950s and
1960s. Among the Drifters' lead singers were Clyde
McPhatter, David Baughan, Johnny Moore, Bobby
Hendricks, Ben E. King, Rudy Lewis, and Charlie Tho-
mas.

There were actually two different groups called the
Drifters. The original Drifters disbanded[3] in 1958. The
group's manager, George Treadwell, wanted the name
to continue, so in late 1958 he signed the group the Five
Crowns, who then began recording under the name the
Drifters. The new Drifters' first hit was "There Goes
My Baby" (Atlantic 2025), the first rhythm & blues
recording to incorporate strings, with Ben E. King as
the lead singer. Dionne Warwick was "discovered" by
Burt Bacharach while she was singing backup for the
Drifters.

Elvis recorded four songs that the Drifters had recorded: "Money Honey" (Atlantic 1006), "Fools Fall in
Love" (Atlantic 1123), "Such a Night" (Atlantic 1019),
and "White Christmas" (Atlantic 1048). Elvis also recorded "Without Love (There Is Nothing)" in 1969, a hit
for Clyde McPhatter in 1957.

DUKE
Name of Gladys Presley's French poodle. Duke was
named for actor John Wayne.[4]

---

[1]Originally called the Gents.

[2]Many of his early tunes were rather risqué in their suggestive lyrics. That all ended when he discovered God and dedicated his life to
writing religious songs.

[3]Actually they were fired en masse by George Treadwell, the husband of singer Sarah Vaughan.

[4]John Wayne, whose real name was Marion Michael Morrison, got his nickname "Duke" after his pet airedale. Firemen called him "Big
Duke" and the dog "Little Duke." Wayne's horse in six films, beginning in 1932, was also named "Duke." Before John Wayne, Tom Mix
had ridden the same horse.

DUNAVANT, ROBERT
Probate court clerk who handled Elvis Presley's will.

DUNCAN, SANDRA
Dancer whom Elvis would marry, it was announced in the November 1972 issue of *TV Radio Show* magazine. The magazine was in error.

DUNLEAVY, STEVE
National Star gossip columnist who cowrote with Red West, Sonny West, and Dave Hebler, the 1977 book *Elvis—What Happened?* Dunleavy appeared on TV's "Good Morning America" on August 17, 1977, the day after Elvis's death, on which he and Geraldo Rivera exchanged words. Dunleavy infuriated fans on another interview program when he referred to Elvis as "poor white trash."

DUNN, DONALD (DUCK)
(1941–) Bass guitarist born on November 24, 1941. A resident of Memphis, Dunn began as a member of the Mar-Keys, whose first hit was the instrumental "Last Night" (Satellite 107), and played on many of Otis Redding's hits. He then became a member of Booker T. and the M.G.'s, who charted "Green Onions" (Stax 127) and other instrumentals. Dunn made his movie debut as a member of the Blues Brothers Band in the 1980 John Landis movie *The Blues Brothers*, starring John Belushi and Dan Ackroyd. In the film the band played "Jailhouse Rock."

From 1964 to 1966 Dunn performed as a session musician for Sun Records. At the Stax Studios on July 21–25, 1973, Dunn played bass on Elvis's recording session.

DURDEN, TOMMY
Composer, with Mae Boren Axton, of the song "Heartbreak Hotel." Durden was the steel guitar player in Johnny Tillotson's band. In 1977 he recorded a tribute record titled "Elvis" (Westbound 55405).

While reading the *Miami Herald* one day in 1955 Durden ran across the photograph of a suicide victim whose identity was a mystery. The headline asked, "Do you know this man?" In the dead man's left hand was a note that read, "I walk a lonely street," which inspired Durden and Axton to compose "Heartbreak Hotel." There was a real historic hotel in Florida named the Heartbreak Hotel, which also may have inspired Durden to compose the song.

DVORIN, AL
Producer of Elvis's 1961 Hawaii benefit concert for the USS *Arizona*. He was the show's master of ceremonies. Dvorin was the leader of a twenty-piece orchestra that provided the music for some of Elvis's concerts. He was the announcer on the 1974 album *Elvis Recorded Live on Stage in Memphis*. Dvorin's business association with Colonel Tom Parker goes back a number of years.

DWYER, RONALD
Elvis's attorney who successfully defended him in the lawsuit brought by Kenneth MacKenzie, Jr., Mario Martinez, Roberto MacKenzie, and Marcello Jose Filas. They had claimed that Elvis and his friends attacked them at the Las Vegas Hilton on February 19, 1973. Los Angeles Superior Court judge Robert Weil dismissed the $4 million suit.

DYLAN, BOB
(1941–) Popular poet and folk-rock artist known for his songs of social consciousness and protest. Born Robert Allen Zimmerman in Duluth, Minnesota, on May 24, 1941, he named himself after poet Dylan Thomas, and Bob Dylan is his legal name today. He was once a member of Bobby Vee's touring band, the Strangers. Vee fired Dylan because he believed music was not the field Dylan should pursue. Dylan's first record was "Mixed Up Confusion" (Columbia 4-42656), released in December 1962. Immediately after its release, Columbia took the record off the market because it didn't fit the image of their new "folk" artist.

Elvis recorded two Dylan tunes: "Don't Think Twice, It's All Right" (in 1971) and "Tomorrow Is a Long Time" (in 1966).

Both artists recorded: "Blue Moon," "Early Morning Rain," "Let It Be Me," "I Can't Stop Loving You," "A Fool Such As I" (Dylan charted the song in 1974), and "Can't Help Falling in Love."

Though never officially released on record, Elvis sang the following Dylan songs in concert: "Blowin' in the Wind," "She Belongs to Me",[1] "Mr. Tambourine Man," and "It Ain't Me Babe."

Bob Dylan, a fan of Elvis's, once said, "Elvis recorded a song of mine; that's the recording I treasure most."

[1]The song, which became a hit for Ricky Nelson in 1970 (Decca 32550), never mentions the title words within its lyrics.

8
Elvis's "number" (born January 8), as it was that of one of his favorite singers, Dean Martin (born February 8), and one of his favorite actors, Peter Sellers (born September 8). It is also Colonel Parker's number (born June 26).

11D
Elvis's boot size in the U.S. Army.

$83.20 TO $122.31
Range of Elvis's monthly pay from the time he was inducted into the U.S. Army until his discharge (March 24, 1958–March 5, 1960).

86
Local board number of Elvis's Memphis draft board, where, on Monday morning, March 24, 1958, Elvis was sworn into the U.S. Army.

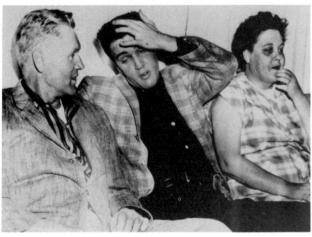

Vernon, Elvis, and Gladys—the day before Elvis was inducted into the Army. (Photo courtesy Jeff Wheatcraft)

EAGLE'S CLUB
U.S. servicemen's club located at Paulinenstrasse 7 in Wiesbaden, West Germany, where in September 1959 fourteen-year-old Priscilla Beaulieu walked two blocks from her family's residence with the sole intention of meeting Airman Currie Grant, who worked there. (See *Currie Grant*)

EAGLE'S NEST
Memphis ballroom owned by Joe Pieraccini, located on Highway 78 at Lamar Avenue and Clearpool, where early in 1954 Elvis made one of his first professional appearances. The facility, which was also called "Clearpool," featured a swimming pool and a twenty-four-hour restaurant. Elvis earned $10 a night singing there. Elvis, Scotty Moore, and Bill Black played there a number of times after their first record was released. In October 1954 Elvis appeared at the Eagle's Nest along with Tiny Dixon and the Eagles (if this was the same group that recorded the song "Tryin' to Get to You," this may be where Elvis first heard it). Elvis appeared at the Eagle's Nest at least ten times between August 7 and October 30, 1954, to sing, with Scotty and Bill, his hit songs "That's All Right (Mama)" and "Blue Moon of Kentucky," and possibly other songs they were working on. John Bruce was quoted in Vince Staten's 1978 book, *The Real Elvis: Good Old Boy*, as saying that he saw Elvis perform there in October 1953,[1] at which time Elvis was introduced by WHBQ disc jockey Dewey Phillips. Phillips introduced him as the "Poor Man's Liberace." The featured group was the Johnny Long Orchestra. In her book *Are You Lonesome Tonight?* Lucy de Barbin claimed that she first saw Elvis perform at the Eagle's Nest in the fall of 1953.

EARNEST, WAYNE
Elvis's elementary-school friend in Tupelo with whom he collected and swapped comic books.[2]

EAST HEIGHTS GARDEN CLUB
Organization that restored Elvis's birthplace in Tupelo, Mississippi. The house is now a monument and was opened to the public for the first time on June 1, 1971.

EAST TUPELO, MISSISSIPPI
Town of Elvis's birth. East Tupelo had a population of a little less than 6,000 in 1935. It merged with Tupelo in 1948. In September 1941 Elvis was enrolled at East Tupelo Consolidated School on Lake Street.

EASTLAND, JACQUELINE, AND JAMES, GLORIA
Two psychics who predicted Elvis's death. Eastland made her prediction on the "Nine in the Morning" show on KHJ-TV in Los Angeles on July 19, 1977, while James made her prediction on a radio talk show on WMEX in Boston on May 30, 1977.

ECKSTINE, BILLY
(1914–) Black singer born William Clarence Eckstein in Pittsburgh on July 8, 1914. Nicknamed "Mr. B," Eckstine was the first black singer to become a national sex symbol. He formed a band in the 1940s that at times included Dizzy Gillespie, Charlie Parker, Miles Davis, Dexter Gordon, and Gene Ammons. One of his female vocalists was Sarah Vaughan. Eckstine and Dean Martin seemed to have been Elvis's two biggest influences in the pop-ballad field in the early 1950s.

---

[1]Some sources claimed that he sang Dean Martin's hit song "That's Amore," but that song wasn't released by Capitol Records until a few weeks later.

[2]Elaine Dundy points out in her excellent book *Elvis and Gladys* that Elvis often fantasized that he was Captain Marvel.

When Scotty Moore first auditioned him, Elvis sang some Billy Eckstine songs that he knew, including "I Apologize." In 1943 Eckstine recorded, with Earl Hines and His Orchestra, "Stormy Monday Blues" (Bluebird 11567), a song that Elvis is believed to have recorded. Eckstine recorded "I Apologize" (MGM 10903) in 1951, another song it is believed Elvis recorded. In addition, Eckstine recorded "Fools Rush In"/"Blue Moon" (MGM 10311), "Blue Christmas" (MGM 10796), and "Love Me" (MGM 0982), all of which Elvis recorded and released. Eckstine also recorded "Only You" (MGM 11984), a song Elvis sang in concert.

EDMUND
One of Elvis's pet dogs.

EDWARDS, MICHAEL
(1945–   ) Model and actor with whom Priscilla Presley became romantically involved for seven years, beginning in 1978, after she broke with Mike Stone. Edwards, who had a daughter by a previous marriage, first met Priscilla at a Beverly Hills party in June 1978 and later introduced Priscilla to Scientology. In the February 1980 issue of *Cosmopolitan* magazine Priscilla and Edwards posed for a photo layout titled "Love in the Afternoon." Edwards was paid a reported $150,000 advance in 1987 for his book *Priscilla, Elvis and Me*, which will be published in 1988.

EDWARDS, SHERMAN
(1919–   ) Composer and arranger born in New York City on April 3, 1919.[1] Edwards cowrote with Sid Wayne, eight songs that Elvis sang in films: "Big Boots," "Britches," "Didja Ever," "Flaming Star," and "Frankfort Special." He wrote "Home Is Where the Heart Is" and "A Whistling Tune" with Hal David and "I'm Not the Marrying Kind" with Mack David.

EDWARDS, TOM
Artist who recorded the spoken record "The Story of Elvis Presley" (Coral 61826). (This was not black singer Tommy Edwards of "It's All in the Game" [MGM 12688] fame.)

EDWARDS, TOMMY
Photographer who took the photo of Elvis and Bill Haley shaking hands at Cleveland's Brooklyn High School auditorium on October 20, 1955. He had hired Elvis, Scotty Moore, and Bill Black for $350 in February 1955 for a program that feature Roy Acuff at Cleveland's Circle Theater.

In August 1977, at the time of Elvis's death, Edwards was the owner of the Record Haven in Cleveland, which within days sold out its entire stock of more than 300 Elvis records.

ELIOT, MAURICE
Vice president of, and spokesman for, the Baptist Memorial Hospital in Memphis. He conducted the August 17, 1977, news conference after Elvis's death.

ELLINGTON, BUFORD
Governor of Tennessee who, on March 8, 1961, conferred upon Elvis the honorary title of colonel, before the General Assembly of the state's legislature. On September 29, 1967, Ellington declared "Elvis Presley Day" throughout the state of Tennessee.

ELLIS AUDITORIUM
Memphis site of Elvis's live concert of February 25, 1961. Except for a benefit in March 1961, it was to be Elvis's last live performance until 1968.

ELLIS, JIMMY
(1945–   ) Singer who for a time sang under the alter ego Orion (Orion Eckley Darnell). Ellis was born in Washington, D.C., on February 26, 1945. He has an excellent voice and as Orion recorded a number of records that sounded very much like Elvis.

Shelby Singleton of Sun International decided to disguise Ellis's identity on his first Sun single, "That's All Right (Mama)"/"Blue Moon of Kentucky" (Sun 1129), leaving listeners to speculate that the songs might be alternate takes of Elvis's first two songs. Instead of listing Ellis on the label, Singleton printed a question mark. Ellis's first album appearance for Sun was as an unidentified singer singing duet with Jerry Lee Lewis on ten tracks of the 1978 album *Duets* (Sun 1011). Charlie Rich sang along with Lewis on two other

(Photo courtesy Jimmy Ellis)

---

[1]Same birthdate as Ervin Drake, who cowrote "I Believe."

(Photo courtesy Jimmy Ellis)

songs. Again, the speculation was that Elvis had sung on the songs, particularly "Save the Last Dance for Me." In 1979 Jimmy Ellis finally emerged with an identity, but it still wasn't himself. He appeared as Orion Eckley Darnell, the character created on August 16, 1977, by Marietta, Georgia, housewife Gail Brewer-Giorgio. Her 1978 novel *Orion* told the story of a rock & roll singer, very much like Elvis, who faked his own death. On Orion's 1979 debut album, *Reborn* (Sun 1912), Ellis appeared on the album cover wearing a mask over his eyes. The album featured some excellent songs, including "Ebony Eyes," "Honey," and "Washing Machine." They were sung in the style in which Elvis would have sung them.

Ellis's Orion character claimed to have been managed by one Colonel Mac Weiman, and to have been born in Ribbonsville, Tennessee on December 31, 1931. Listeners of Orion were initially split into two camps: those who knew that Orion was Jimmy Ellis just having some fun sounding like Elvis, and others who sincerely believed—or wanted to believe—that he was truly Elvis coming back on the scene after faking his own death. As Orion, Ellis reached *Billboard*'s country chart with nine singles. For those who still insist that Jimmy Ellis is not Orion, Ellis has publically admitted to being Orion. Ellis left Sun Records in 1983, never again appearing as Orion.

A fine talent in his own right, Ellis in 1978 recorded the song "I'm Not Trying to Be Like Elvis" (Boblo 536) and the album *By Request—Ellis Sings Elvis* (Boblo 78-829).

EL RANCHO CLUB
Nightclub in Jackson, Mississippi, where in 1954 Elvis first saw Carl Perkins perform.

ELVIS
Name derived from the Norse word *alviss*, meaning "all wise."

ELVIS
Title of a 1977 religious book written by Richard Mann and published by Bible Voice, Inc., of Van Nuys, California.

ELVIS
A book written by Richard Wootton and published in 1985 by Random House.

ELVIS
Subject title of a painting by pop-culture artist Andy Warhol.

ELVIS
Miami police detective Sonny Crockett's (Don Johnson) pet alligator that lives on his boat on the TV series "Miami Vice." (See *Don Johnson*)

ELVIS
Identification name of the middle marker on the ILS (Instrument Landing System) to runway 36R at Memphis Airport.

ELVIS
The Hole-in-the-Wall Gang's pet dog on the 1973–74 animated TV series "Butch Cassidy and the Sundance Kids."

ELVIS
Middle name of Alonzo Elvis (Tony) Alderman, an original member of the string band The Hill Billies of the mid 1920s. It was The Hill Billies name that was the origin of the term *hillbilly* for the type of music that they and others played. The word *hillbilly* was still being used on some of Sam Phillips's country releases into the mid-1950s.

ELVIS
Name of a small red rose hybridized in 1981 by W. W. (Whit) Wells, a member of the American Rose Society.

ELVIS
London play in which three artists impersonated Elvis. Timothy Whitnall (as a teenager), Shakin' Stevens (as a young man), and James (P. J.) Proby (as an adult). Later Proby was replaced by Shawn Simon, who in turn was replaced by Bogdan Kominowsky.

ELVIS
Trade paperback book written by J. Robert Gibson and Sid Shaw, and published in 1985 by McGraw-Hill Book Company of New York.

ELVIS
The 1981 book written by Albert Goldman, who received a $400,000 advance from McGraw-Hill for his

three and a half years of research. Avon Books (which had been founded by William Randolph Hearst) bought the paperback book rights for $1 million. Although long-awaited by Elvis fans, the book turned out to be a disappointment because of Goldman's apparent contempt for his subject. Goldman had previously written the biography of comedian Lenny Bruce, *Ladies and Gentlemen—Lenny Bruce!!!*.[1] The copyright to the book *Elvis* is owned by Albert Goldman, Kevin Eggers, and Lamar Fike.

Author and critic Jeff Tamarkin said it best in his review of the book: "Perhaps no book about rock 'n' roll has been as maligned as Goldman's exhaustive *Elvis* bio, and deservedly so."

ELVIS: A BIOGRAPHY
Book written by *Rolling Stone* magazine writer Jerry Hopkins and first published by Simon[2] and Schuster in 1971. This unauthorized biography of Elvis rates as the standard biography on Elvis and one of the best books compiled about the man. It was serialized in a two-part excerpt in *Look* magazine on May 4 and 11, 1971 and published in paperback by Warner Books in 1972. It was singer Jim Morrison (1943–1971) who had suggested to Hopkins that he write a book about Elvis. Hopkins dedicated the book to Morrison.

ELVIS: A GOLDEN TRIBUTE
Book written by Jordanaires member Neal Matthews and published in 1985.

ELVIS: A GOLDEN TRIBUTE
Book written by Emory Glade and published by Robus Books in 1984.

ELVIS: A 30 YEAR CHRONICLE
Book written by Bill E. Burk and first published in 1985.

ELVIS ARON PRESLEY MEMORIAL HIGHWAY
Name given to that 104-mile portion of Highway 78 that runs between Tupelo, Mississippi, and Memphis, Tennessee. The name change was dedicated in December 1977. It was on this same highway that Vernon Presley took his family to Memphis in 1948. The construction of Highway 78 had been helped by the efforts of Alabama senator William Bankhead, the father of actress Tallulah Bankhead.

ELVIS, AN AMERICAN MUSICAL
Las Vegas stage show performed at the Las Vegas Hilton Hotel from July 1 through August 28, 1981. The production was budgeted at $3 million and had been in the planning for three and a half years.

ELVIS AND GLADYS
Excellent book written by Elaine Dundy. *Elvis and Gladys*, first published in 1985, is the best-researched book covering Elvis's early years in Tupelo, Mississippi. A former actress, Elaine Dundy is the ex-wife of author and critic Kenneth Tynan.

ELVIS AND HIS FANS
Book written by Elvis's uncle Harold Loyd and Lisa De Angel.

ELVIS AND KATHY
Book written by singer Kathy Westmoreland with William G. Quinn and published in 1987 by Glendale House publishers. Westmoreland's editor was Betty Jane Baker, a former Miss Alabama and the second wife of actor Mickey Rooney. It was Mickey Rooney Jr. to whom Kathy gave special thanks for encouraging her to write the book.

ELVIS AND ME
Best-selling book written by Priscilla Beaulieu Presley with Sandra Harmon and published in hardcover in 1985 by P. G. Putnam Publishing Group of New York and in paperback in 1986 by Berkley Books of New York. The book, which was dedicated to her daughter ("For Lisa Marie") was excerpted in *People* magazine. In 1988 the book was made into a TV miniseries.

ELVIS AND THE COLONEL
The 1975 book written by columnist May Mann and published by Drake Books in hard cover and Pocket Books in paperback. It had been called the only "authorized" Elvis biography.

ELVIS AND THE COLONEL
The 1988 book written by Dick Vellenga with Mike Farren and published by Dell Publishers of New York.

ELVIS AT GRACELAND
Book of photographs by William Eggleston of Elvis at Graceland, which was first sold in 1983 by mail by a Memphis publisher. The text is by Ken Brixley and Twyla Dixon.

ELVIS COLLECTIBLES
Book written by Rosalind Cranor and published by Overmountain Press of Johnson City, Texas.

ELVIS COVER-UP, THE
Special "20/20" program hosted by Geraldo Rivera that discussed Elvis's death and the connection to Dr. George Nichopoulos. It was first aired on September 13, 1979, on ABC-TV.

ELVIS ELVIS ELVIS 100 GREATEST HITS
Oversize music book of songs recorded by Elvis, published by the Big 3 Music Corporation.

ELVIS FACE TO FACE
Book written by Wanda June Hill and published in 1985.

---

[1]Ironically, both of Goldman's subjects died while in the bathroom.

[2]Richard Simon, the cofounder of Simon and Schuster, is the father of singer Carly Simon.

ELVIS FOR BEGINNERS
Book written by Jill Pearlman, illustrated by Wayne White, and published in 1986 by Writers and Readers.

ELVIS: IMAGES AND FANCIES
Book edited by Jac L. Tharpe and published in 1981 by the University of Mississippi. The book is an academic analysis of Elvis.

ELVIS IN CONCERT
Book of colored photographs by John Reggero and published by Dell (Delta Special/Lorelei) Books in 1979. David Stanley wrote the introduction.

ELVIS IN HIS OWN WORDS
Book compiled by Mick Farren and Pearce Marchbank and published in 1977 by Omnibus Press of New York City.

In the book, Elvis recounted many of his own experiences—a number of them inaccurately. Elvis claimed that Pat Boone was chosen over him to appear on the Grand Ole Opry. In reality, it was on "Arthur Godfrey's Talent Scouts." Another inaccuracy occurred when Elvis mentioned that the composer of "Bear Cat" had sued the composer of "Hound Dog." Actually it was the reverse.

ELVIS IN PRIVATE
A 1987 paperback book, edited by Peter Haining and published by St. Martin's Press of New York City. The book included 29 articles about Elvis that had been previously published in magazines over the years. The articles were taken from the personal collection of British author Todd Slaughter.

"My Nephew—Elvis Presley"—By Vester Presley
"A Kid from the Northside"—by Bill Leaptrott
"The Guitar-Picker of Beale Street"—By Johnny Burnette
"Just a Long-Haired Country Boy"—by Judd Phillips
"Knocking on the Door of Success"—by Scotty Moore
"Elvis and the Singing Indian"—by Rufus Thomas
"The Girl He Called Annie"—by Anita Wood
"Elvis the Firecracker Kid"—by D. J. Fontana
"The Heartaches of the Record Maker"—by Steve Sholes
"A Recording Session with Sivle Yelserp"—by Chet Atkins
"Jamming the Days Away"—by Gordon Stoker
"Flying in the Face of Danger"—by Roy Orbison
"On Parade with Pfc. Presley"—By Robert R. Fuller
"Freedom in the Army"—By Elvis Presley
"Making Magic at the Lido"—by George Bernard
"The Prince of Hollywood and the King of Rock"—by Hal B. Wallis
"Peter Pan—The Sportsman"—by Norman Taurog
"On the Soundtrack with Elvis"—by Charles O'Curran
"Hounded by the Scandal Sheets"—by Juliet Prowse
"Easy Ridin' with Elvis"—by Ann-Margret
"The Gentle Art of Killing"—by Gary Lockwood
"Ze King and I"—by John Lennon
"The Song Lives On"—by Jimmy Savile
"The Gentleman Rancher"—by Billy Smith
"The Man with the Golden Handshake"—by J. D. Sumner

"Flying High and Low with Elvis"—by Linda Thompson
"The Day We All Died a Little"—by Charlie Hodge
"The Last Word on Elvis"—by Priscilla Presley

ELVIS—IS THAT YOU?
Paperback book written by Harley Hatcher, who claims that, during Elvis's two years in the U.S. Army Hatcher befriended a man named John Crow who was in reality Elvis. Hatcher further claims that Elvis recorded nineteen songs on tape during jam sessions, using the name John Crow.

ELVIS LIVES
Broadway show that starred Elvis look-alike impersonator Larry Seth. The show won the Evening Standard Award for Best Musical[1] for 1977.

ELVIS: LONELY STAR AT THE TOP
A 1977 paperback book written by Hollywood biographer David Hanna. It was published by Leisure Books of New York City.

ELVIS PRESLEY CHAPEL
Twelve-pew, redwood-sided, twelve-hundred-square-foot chapel and meditation center built on the grounds of Elvis Presley Park in Tupelo, created through the efforts of Janelle McComb. The ground-breaking ceremonies for the $800,000 building took place on January 8, 1979 (Elvis Presley's birthday) and the chapel was dedicated on August 17, 1979. Vernon Presley dedicated the family Bible and Mrs. R. L. Laukoff of Memphis dedicated the large stained-glass window. In attendance were Colonel Tom Parker (who arranged the purchase of an organ), singer Kathy Westmoreland, Mississippi governor Cliff Finch, and approximately 4,000 other people.

ELVIS PRESLEY COMPANY
Navy boot camp company that was promised to Elvis by Chief Petty Officer D. U. Stanley if he would enlist in the Navy. Elvis Presley Company was to consist of Memphis enlistees.

ELVIS PRESLEY CONVENTION
Annual worldwide convention, first held at the Las Vegas Hilton, September 1–10, 1978.

ELVIS: MEMORIES . . .
ABC Radio's three-hour special first broadcast in 1978. It was the first network musical show presented on ABC Radio in more than ten years.

ELVIS'S MIDGET FAN CLUB
Publicity stunt created by Colonel Tom Parker for one of Elvis's concerts in 1957. Parker hired a group of midgets to parade through Memphis advertising the fan club and the concert.

---

[1] *A Chorus Line* had won in 1976 and *Annie* in 1978.

Publicity still from the 1950s. (Photo courtesy Eddie Brandt's Saturday Matinee)

ELVIS MONTHLY, THE
Popular British Elvis Presley fan magazine first published in 1959 by Albert Hand. It is distributed by the Official Elvis Presley Fan Club, Worldwide, which was founded in 1956.

ELVIS MYSTIQUE
Article written by Alice Anne Conner that was reprinted in *Reader's Digest* magazine in 1977 from an article in *The Milwaukee Journal* of December 26, 1976. The article again appeared in the paperback book *Unforgettable Characters*, published in 1980 by Berkley/Reader's Digest Books.

ELVIS: NEWLY DISCOVERED DRAWINGS OF ELVIS PRESLEY
Book of illustrations of Elvis by Betty Harper and published by Bantam Books in 1979.

ELVIS: PORTRAIT OF A FRIEND
A 1979 book written by Marty Lacker (a friend and aide to Elvis), Patsy Lacker, and Leslie S. Smith. The book was published by Wimmer Brothers Books, and in paperback by Bantam Books.

ELVIS PRESLEY
Book written by Roger Tomlinson and published in Great Britain in 1973.

ELVIS PRESLEY ALBUM OF JUKEBOX FAVORITES, THE
Folio of fifteen Hill and Range songs, sold in 1955 for one dollar. The four Elvis songs were: "That's All Right (Mama)," "You're a Heartbreaker," "I Forgot to Remember to Forget," and "I'm Left, You're Right, She's Gone." Hill and Range had no idea what frustration they would create over the years when they decided to "fill out" the book with eleven of their non-Elvis songs, leading to speculation that Elvis recorded them at Sun but they were never released (and are now lost). The filler songs were: "Rag Mop," "I Almost Lost My Mind," "Cryin' Heart Blues," "Blue Guitar," "Always Late (with Your Kisses)," "Tennessee Saturday Night," "Gone," "I Need You So," "Give Me More, More, More (of Your Kisses)," "Oakie Boogie," and "That's the Stuff You Gotta Watch." Elvis did attempt to perform "Rag Mop" at Sun, and would later record "I Need You So." The rest are still a mystery, but Elvis may not have recorded them at all. Not everyone will agree that Elvis did not record these songs, and for that reason we have included entries on them in the song section of this book.

ELVIS PRESLEY: A BIO-BIBLIOGRAPHY
Book written by Patsy Guy Hammontree and published by Greenwood Press in 1985.

ELVIS PRESLEY BOULEVARD
Name given to a ten-mile section of U.S. Highway 51 South in Memphis and dedicated on January 19, 1972, by Vernon Presley, Mayor Wyeth Chandler, and Sheriff Roy Nixon. Elvis Presley Boulevard extends through Memphis past Graceland. The north section of U.S. Highway 51 is known as Bellevue Boulevard. Marty Lacker claims to have first made the suggestion to rename the street to Lyman Aldrich, a friend of Mayor Chandler's, who introduced the idea at the next meeting of the city council.

Billy Joel recorded the tribute song "Elvis Presley Boulevard" on Columbia Records.

ELVIS PRESLEY DAY
Official day of recognition proclaimed in many cities and states:

September 26, 1956—Elvis appeared at the Mississippi-Alabama Fair and Dairy Show in Tupelo. He gave back to the city the check for $10,000 that he had received for his performance.
February 25, 1961—By proclamation of Tennessee governor Buford Ellington.
September 29, 1967—By proclamation of Tennessee governor Buford Ellington.
November 11, 1970—By proclamation of the mayor of Portland, Oregon.
January 13, 1973—Celebrated in Honolulu, Hawaii, by the city's mayor.
January 8, 1974—By proclamation of the governor of Georgia, Jimmy Carter.
October 19, 1976—By proclamation of Madison, Wisconsin, mayor Paul Soglin.
January 8, 1981—By proclamation of South Carolina governor Richard W. Riley.
January 8, 1981—By proclamation of Alabama governor Forrest James.
January 8, 1981—By proclamation of Florida governor Bob Graham.
January 8, 1981—By proclamation of Illinois governor James R. Thompson.
January 8, 1981—By proclamation of Georgia governor George Busbee.
January 8, 1981—By proclamation of Kansas governor John Carlin.
January 8, 1981—By proclamation of North Carolina governor James B. Hunt.
January 8, 1981—By proclamation of Pennsylvania governor Richard Thornburgh (letter of recognition).
January 8, 1981—By proclamation of Virginia governor John N. Dalton (a recognition certificate).
January 8, 1982—By proclamation of Tennessee governor Lamar Alexander.
During March 1974, Alabama governor George Wallace declared an Elvis Presley Week.

ELVIS PRESLEY DRIVE
Present name, since August 17, 1979, of the Tupelo, Mississippi, street on which Elvis's birth house is located. The street was previously called Old Saltillo Road.

ELVIS PRESLEY ENCYCLOPEDIA, THE
Small-size, 64-page paperback book compiled and edited by Lawrence Collins and published by Globe Communications Corp. in 1981.

ELVIS PRESLEY ENTERPRISES
Company formed in conjunction with Special Products, Inc., to market more than 180 Elvis-related items in 1956, located at 160 Union Avenue in Memphis. The items included statues, wastebaskets, bookends, dolls, mittens, lipstick, scarves, sneakers, record cases, shirts, jeans, bracelets, photo wallets, polo shirts, pajamas, belts, belt buckles, handkerchiefs, billfolds, handbags, medallions, necklaces, charm bracelets, perfume, wristwatches, and hats. The company was formed by Elvis and Bob Neal when Neal managed Elvis. It was dissolved when Colonel Tom Parker became Elvis's manager.

ELVIS PRESLEY ENTERPRISES
Memphis football team that Elvis sponsored and occasionally played on in the fall of 1963. Elvis also sponsored a baseball team in the city.

ELVIS PRESLEY FOUNDATION FOR UNDERPRIVILEGED CHILDREN
Charity project in Tupelo, Mississippi, begun by Elvis in 1956. He dedicated the proceeds from some of his shows (September 1956 in Tupelo) to the project. Eventually a clubhouse, swimming pool, and baseball field were constructed with Elvis's help.

ELVIS PRESLEY GAME
Board game marketed in 1957. ("A Party Game for the Tender of Heart. See what the Elvis Presley game predicts for you . . . Love, Romance, Marriage.") The five levels for both players are: Getting to Know Him, Learning to Like Him, Can't Do Without Him, Let's Go Steady, Get the Preacher.

ELVIS PRESLEY HEIGHTS
Name, since August 17, 1979, of the area where Elvis was born in East Tupelo, Mississippi. The area had previously been known as East Heights.

ELVIS PRESLEY MUSEUM
Museum founded by singer Jimmy Velvet in June 1979 at 3350 Elvis Presley Boulevard, across the street from Graceland in Memphis. Velvet started out with 270 items, including six Elvis-related automobiles. Some of the items advertised are: Elvis's Mercedes 600 limousine, his Harley-Davidson motorcycle, his wedding album, his family Bible, some of his wardrobe, numerous rings and watches that Elvis wore, some of his movie costumes, and some of his original acetate recordings.

It was reported that on the eve of an auction at the museum, one hundred pieces of jewelry that belonged to Elvis were stolen. Velvet estimated that uninsured loss at $1 million.

ELVIS PRESLEY MUSEUM
"The World's Largest Private Collection of Elvis Memorabilia." The museum is located in Pigeon Forge, Tennessee, and was founded by Mike L. Moon. On display are several automobiles, some jewelry (the original TCB ring), and a souvenir shop.

ELVIS PRESLEY MUSIC, INC.
One of several publishing companies owned by Elvis and Colonel Tom Parker. Together, they received half of its royalties. It was a subsidiary of Hill and Range Music, Inc., which had established it at the request of Colonel Parker. Affiliated with BMI, Elvis Presley Music and Gladys Music, another subsidiary of Hill and Range, were set up in order to receive partial royalties from the composers of Elvis's songs who wrote for Hill and Range. It was Parker's idea that the composer's should pay part of their royalties to Elvis Presley Music, Inc., for the privilege of having Elvis record one of their songs. Elvis sold part of Elvis Presley Music in the late 1960s back to Hill and Range because he needed the money. After Elvis's divorce, Priscilla ended up with 5 percent of the publishing company. (See *Hill and Range*)

ELVIS PRESLEY PARK
Thirteen-and-a-half-acre park created by the Tupelo Park and Recreational Department. Tupelo passed a bond issue to buy the land. Elvis Presley Park encompasses Elvis's birthplace. The park contains a swimming pool, a community building, and a chapel.

ELVIS PRESLEY PLAZA
Area set aside as a tribute to Elvis, located south of downtown Memphis. A statue of Elvis, sculpted by Eric Parks, was unveiled on August 14, 1980.

ELVIS PRESLEY SPEAKS
Book written by psychic researcher Hans Holzer, who claims that contact was made with Elvis beyond the grave. The book was published by Manor books in 1978.

ELVIS PRESLEY STORY, THE
Paperback book, edited by James Gregory, that was published by Hillman Books of New York City in 1960. Dick Clark wrote the introduction to the thirty-five-cent book, which was available through magazines. Today the book is valued at at least $25.

ELVIS PRESLEY STORY, THE
Twelve-hour radio program written by Jerry Hopkins, produced by Ron Jacobs, and narrated by Wink Martindale, which first aired on October 24, 1971. The program consisted of Elvis music and interviews with Elvis's friends and admirers. When Elvis heard about the show, he asked, "Why do they want to do twelve hours on me for?"

ELVIS PRESLEY: THE KING IS HOME
Title of the home movies that Priscilla Presley released in 1980. The movie debuted at the Westworld Casino in Henderson, Nevada.

ELVIS PRESLEY YOUTH FOUNDATION
Tupelo-based charity created by Elvis, to which he donated $100,000 annually. Elvis performed twice in Tupelo, in 1956 and 1957, with the proceeds going to

the foundation. Elvis had the city of Tupelo buy four-teen acres of land, owned by Orville Bean and located behind his birthplace, for the Youth Center, which consisted of a building and a swimming pool. The building was remodeled in 1978.

ELVIS RECORDING SESSIONS
The definitive Elvis sessionography, 1954–1977, written by Ernst Jorgensen, Erik Rasmussen, and Johnny Mikkelson, and published by Jee Productions in Denmark in 1984. It was reprinted in 1986 by Pierian Press under the title *Reconsider Baby*. The foreword to the latter edition was written by Lee Cotten.

ELVIS ROOM
Name given to a special room in the houses of Elvis fans where Elvis memorabilia, photographs, collectibles, and other Elvis-related items are put on display as a testimonial to the singer.

ELVIS SHOWCASE
Special set of prizes offered on an episode of the television game show "The Price Is Right," hosted by Bob Barker. The items offered were: "A white Cadillac fit for any Elvis fan, a stereo to play Elvis albums, a 'Blue Hawaii' album with a trip to Hawaii, and a trip to Elvis Country, Las Vegas."

ELVIS TEN YEARS AFTER
Book written by Anne E. Nixon and Todd Slaughter and first published in Great Britain in 1987.

ELVIS: THE ARMY YEARS, 1958–1960
A 1978 book written by Nick Corvino as a fictionalized re-creation of Elvis's experiences during his Army years.

ELVIS: THE FINAL YEARS
Book written by Jerry Hopkins and published by St. Martin's Press in 1980 and by Berkley Books in 1983. It was originally going to be titled *Elvis: The Final Years—A Nice Abnormal Life*, the latter being from a quote by Linda Thompson in *People* magazine in 1975 (see the introduction to the book for the full quote).

ELVIS: THE GOLDEN ANNIVERSARY TRIBUTE
Book written by Richard Peters with the Official Elvis Presley Fan Club of Great Britain, and published in 1984 by Pop Universal/Souvenir Press and in the United States in 1985 by Salem House.

ELVIS: THE KING LIVES ON
World's best-selling poster in 1978. The year before, the poster didn't even make the top twenty.

ELVIS—THE LEGEND LIVES
A 1978 book written by *Hollywood Reporter* columnist Martin A. Grove and published by Manor Books of New York City.

ELVIS: THE LEGEND OF THE MUSIC
Book written by Richard Woott and John Tobler and published in hard cover in Great Britain by Crescent Books.

ELVIS THE MAN
Article written by Jon Bradshaw that was reprinted in *Reader's Digest* magazine in 1977 from an article in *Esquire* magazine. The article again appeared in the paperback book *Unforgettable Characters*, published in 1980 by Berkley/Reader's Digest Books.

ELVIS—THE PAPERDOLL BOOK
Book by Jim Fitzgerald with artwork by Al Kilgore, published by St. Martin's Press in 1982.

ELVIS THE PELVIS
Nickname conferred on Elvis early in his career. Of all of the nicknames given to him by the media, this one upset him most. In an interview with Hy Gardner, Elvis responded to the nickname: "I don't like being called Elvis the Pelvis—I mean it's one of the most childish expressions I ever heard coming from an adult. But if they want to call me that, I mean there is nothing I can do about it." Elvis's feelings were also expressed in the 1979 TV movie *Elvis*. According to Elaine Dundy in her book *Elvis and Gladys*, it was in Texas that Elvis first got the nickname.

ELVIS THE PRETZEL
Nickname of Elvis that has been credited by some sources to actor Humphrey Bogart, but is doubted by this book's authors.

ELVIS THE RECORD
Magazine produced by Smith-Lacker-Davis, Inc., beginning in 1980. Billy Smith served as the editor-in-chief while Marty Lacker served as the assistant editor.

ELVIS THE SOLDIER
Book written by Rex and Elisabeth Mansfield and published in West Germany in 1983.

ELVIS THE SWINGIN' KID
A 1962 British paperback book written by Charles Hamblett and published by Mayfair Books.

ELVIS, THIS ONE'S FOR YOU
Book written by Arlene Cogan and Charles Goodman, and published in hardcover by Castle Books in 1985.

ELVIS THROUGH THE YEARS
JANUARY 8, 1935–AUGUST 16, 1977
Deluxe souvenir song album published by Shaltinger-International Music Corp. in 1977.

ELVIS UNIQUE RECORD CLUB
Once the largest supplier of rare Elvis records and memorabilia in the United States. The record club was owned and operated by Paul Lichter of Huntingdon Valley, Pennsylvania.

ELVIS, WE LOVED YOU TENDER

Book written by Davada (Dee) Presley, who was Elvis's stepmother until she divorced Vernon Presley in 1977. She wrote the book, published by Delacorte Press, with her sons Rick, David, and Billy (as well as with ghost-writer Martin Torgoff).

ELVIS—WHAT HAPPENED?

Paperback book written by Red West, Sonny West, and Dave Hebler, with Australian columnist Steve Dunleavy. The book made its first appearance in bookstores on August 1, 1977, just fifteen days before Elvis's death. The three former bodyguards and friends of Elvis had written the book as a frustrated appeal to Elvis to change his way of living.

The book's initial print run was 400,000 copies, but on the day of Elvis's death an additional 250,000 copies were printed. By the end of the week after Elvis's death, the K Mart department store chain ordered two million copies of the Ballantine book, the largest book order in history. The book, which referred to drugs in nine of its twenty-two chapters, and had become known as "the bodyguard book," was serialized in *The Star*. When he learned that the trio was working on a book about him, Elvis tried to win them back by offering them $50,000 each if they would give up the book and return to his employ. The three turned the offer down. Many Elvis fans have condemned the book because it revealed so much of Elvis's private life.

ELVIS WHY WON'T THEY LEAVE YOU ALONE?

A 1982 book written by columnist May Mann and published by Signet Books. Mann dedicated the book to Lisa Marie Presley and to her own father, Oscar Perry Randall. The book attacked those who wrote books about Elvis, journalists, and Elvis imitators—everyone except herself.

ELVIS WORLD

Beautiful but expensive book written by Jane and Michael Stern and published by Alfred A. Knopf, Inc., in 1987.

EMANUELE, PATRICIA ANN

Spotswood, New Jersey, woman and mother of three teenagers who, with Maryland congresswoman Barbara Mikulski, introduced a bill in Congress to have Elvis Presley's birthday declared a national holiday. Emanuele began her "National Campaign for Elvis Presley Day" in 1977, after Elvis's death. Emanuele had made a number of TV appearances to talk about her project.

On September 13, 1977, Emanuele and her organization marched in Washington, D.C., in a peaceful demonstration for their cause.

EMERSON, BILLY (THE KID)

(1929–   ) Singer born William Robert Emerson in Tarpon Springs, Florida, on December 21, 1929. He was discovered by singer Ike Turner, who was acting as a talent scout for Sam Phillips. "Billy the Kid" Emerson recorded his first record for Sun in 1954, cutting the original version of "Red Hot" (Sun 219) in 1955. His recording of "When It Rains, It Pours" (Sun 214), with Billy Love on piano, was released on January 8, 1955, on the same day as Elvis's "Milkcow Blues Boogie." Elvis would also record Emerson's song. Strangely, Emerson's tenure at Sun began in 1954 and covered sixteen months, the exact same period as Elvis. Emerson and Elvis once went to the Flamingo Club in Memphis to hear Pee Wee Clayton perform.

ENGINE HOUSE NO. 29

Memphis Fire Department engine house located at 2147 Elvis Presley Boulevard. Engine House No. 29 received Joe Esposito's call for help at 2:33 P.M., August 16, 1977.

ENGLISH ELVIS PRESLEY, THE

Popular nickname conferred in 1957 on British rock & roller Tommy Steele (real name: Tommy Hicks).

ENTERTAINER OF THE YEAR

Award presented to Elvis in 1964 by Tennessee state senator LeRoy Johnson.

E.P. CONTINENTALS

Early Elvis fan club. The E. P. Continentals was named by Elvis himself after his automobile.

EPSTEIN, BRIAN

(1935–1967) Manager (25 percent) of the Beatles, Gerry and the Pacemakers, Billy J. Kramer and the Dakotas, Cilla Black, and other performers. Epstein was born in Liverpool on September 19, 1935, and became the Beatles' manager in 1961, remaining their manager until his death on August 27, 1967, from an accidental overdose of drugs and alcohol. Epstein accompanied the Beatles on the evening of August 27, 1965, when they visited Elvis in Bel Air. Upon Epstein's death, Elvis sent the following telegram:

"Deepest regrets and condolences on the loss of a good friend to you and to all of us."

ESPOSITO, JOE

(1938–   ) Elvis's number one aide, nicknamed "Diamond Joe." Esposito and Elvis first met while both were in the military. They had gone through basic training together at Fort Hood, Texas, but Elvis didn't meet Esposito until they were stationed together in West Germany. "Diamond Joe" (Elvis also gave him the martial-arts nickname "the Lion") served as Elvis's road manager and bodyguard beginning in 1960, and also helped Marty Lacker with the bookkeeping. It was Esposito who arranged females for Elvis to date.

Esposito and Marty Lacker served as best men at Elvis and Priscilla's wedding on May 1, 1967, while Esposito's wife, Joan, served as matron of honor. Joan, a former showgirl, and Priscilla Presley became close friends and spent much time together. As a member of the Memphis Mafia, he drove the backup car to the hospital the day Lisa Marie was born (in case the car taking Elvis and Priscilla broke down).Esposito, who was Elvis's highest-paid employee, played guitar on Elvis's Nashville recording session of May 15–21 and June 8–9, 1971, and percussion at the Las Vegas Hilton Hotel on February 14–17, 1972, and again at Stax Studios in July 1973. Over the years Elvis bought Esposito a new Cadillac convertible, as well as one for his wife.

Though Joe Esposito, Dr. Nichopoulos, and Michael McMahon sued Elvis on May 19, 1977, for $150,000 when Presley Courts fell on financial hard times, Esposito continued to work for him. It was Esposito who told Priscilla over the telephone in Los Angeles that Elvis had died. After Elvis's death Esposito began the Sterling Coach Company, a Los Angeles limousine business. He later became the road manager for the Bee Gees and sang duet with Donna Summer on the recording "Heaven Knows."

Esposito, who appeared in several of Elvis's movies including: *Kissin' Cousins* (1968), *Clambake* (1967), and *Stay Away, Joe* (1968), portrayed himself in the 1981 movie *This Is Elvis* and was portrayed by Wayne Powers in the 1988 TV miniseries "Elvis and Me."

EVANS, JOSEPH
Memphis probate judge who handled Elvis's estate after his death.

EVANS, MARILYN
(1937–   ) Woman whom Elvis accompanied to Sun Records on December 4, 1956, the day of the famous Million-Dollar Quartet session. Evans, a dancer whom Elvis met at the New Frontier in Las Vegas when he appeared there earlier that year, made up, with Cliff Gleaves, the two-person audience to the session, besides the singers and musicians involved and Sam Phillips and Jack Clement.

EVANS, PAUL
(1938–   ) Singer,composer born in Queens, New York, on March 5, 1938, who had two hit records: "Seven Little Girls Sitting in the Back Seat" (Guaranteed 200) in 1959 and "Midnite Special" (Guaranteed 205) in 1960. Evans composed the songs "When" for the Kalin Twins (Herbie and Hal) (Decca 30642) in 1958, "Roses Are Red" for Bobby Vinton (Epic 9509) in 1962, and has written several TV commercial jingles, including Kent Cigarettes' "Happiness Is."

Evans co-composed four songs that Elvis recorded: "I Gotta Know," "Something Blue," "Blue River," and "The Next Step I Love."

EVANS, RAYMOND BERNARD
(1915–) Lyricist member of the Songwriters Hall of Fame, born in Salamanca, New York, on February 4, 1915. Evans wrote such songs as "Tammy," "To Each His Own," and "Mona Lisa." He also wrote with Jay Livingston the theme songs for the TV series "Mr. Ed" and "Bonanza." They both composed, "Silver Bells," which Elvis recorded in 1971.

EVEN ELVIS
A religious book written by Mary Ann Thornton (her first) and published by New Leaf Press, Inc., in 1979.

EVERETT, VINCE
(1941–   ) Pseudonym used by Elvis sound-alike Marvin Benefield (born June 21, 1941) to record several records, including "Baby Let's Play House"/"Livin' High" (ABC Paramount 10472) in 1963. The three musicians on the session were Bill Black, Scotty Moore, and D. J. Fontana. Everett's first record, "Love Me," was produced by singer Ray Stevens.

In 1978 Everett recorded the tribute album *Elvis on My Mind—The Legend Lives On* (States of America 231).

Benefield chose the name Vince Everett from the name of the character Elvis played in the 1957 movie *Jailhouse Rock*. Benefield later became the owner of a nostalgic-record store in London. He opened the Elvis Presley Museum on January 8, 1983, in London.

EVERLE, MARIE
German Red Cross nurse who took Elvis's blood on January 3, 1959, in West Germany. Elvis was one of 180 G.I.s of the Second Armored Division who donated blood that day.

EVERLY BROTHERS
A popular 1950s and 1960s country and pop duo that made a comeback in 1985. Don (born February 1, 1937, in Brownie, Kentucky) and Phil (born January 19, 1939, in Chicago) first appeared on radio (KMA in Shenandoah, Iowa) when they were eight and six, respectively. Don Everly's first song composition, "Thou Shalt Not Steal," was recorded by Kitty Wells in 1954. The Everly Brothers' manager was Elaine Tubb, the daughter of country singer Ernest Tubb. The Everlys were the first act to feature drums on stage at the Grand Ole Opry.[1] Their first hit record came in 1957 with "Bye Bye Love" (Cadence 1315). In 1960 the Everly Brothers recorded "Let It Be Me" (Cadence 1376), which Elvis recorded in February 1970. Don Everly's wife, Venetia, had dated Elvis in 1958. Phil Everly met Elvis on only one occasion.

In October 1957 Elvis's "Jailhouse Rock" replaced the Everly Brothers' "Wake Up Little Susie" (Cadence 1337) at number one on *Billboard*'s Hot 100 chart. In turn, their biggest hit, "Cathy's Clown" (Warner Bros. 5151), replaced Elvis's "Stuck on You" at number one in May of 1960. (See *Cadillac Club, Venetia Stevenson*)

EVIGAN, GREG
(1953–   ) Actor born in South Amboy, New Jersey, on October 14, 1953, who starred in the 1979–81 TV series "B. J. and the Bear" as B. J. McKay. In 1981 Elvis's former press agent, Earl Greenwood, gave Evigan one of Elvis's guitars.

---

[1] Previous bands had to hide their drummers behind the curtain because some country-music fans believed that drums belonged in parades, not in a country song.

EXPO '67
World's fair held in Montreal in 1967. At the American Spirit Pavilion the guitar that Elvis used to record "Heartbreak Hotel" and "Hound Dog" was put on display.

EZERZER, ELLIE
(1943–   ) Beverly Hills hairdresser and boyfriend of Priscilla after she broke up with Mike Stone. Ezerzer had plans to marry Priscilla, but it never came about.

Elvis and admiring West German fans in 1959. (Photo courtesy the Mike Boyd Collection)

5 POUNDS
Elvis's weight at birth,[1] the same as that of singer Hank Williams.

$15
Cost of Elvis and Priscilla's marriage license.

42
Age at which Elvis died, on August 16, 1977.

46
Age at which Gladys Love Smith Presley died (April 25, 1912–August 14, 1958). Gladys always told reporters that she was the same age as her husband, Vernon, although she was actually four years older. On the day they were married she listed her age as nineteen instead of her actual age of twenty-one. Many sources wrongly state that Elvis and his mother both died at the age of forty-two. Gladys's brother John also died at the age of forty-six.

49
Number of cars in Elvis's funeral procession on Thursday, August 18, 1977. It was led by eleven white Cadillacs.

50 PERCENT
Colonel Parker's share of Elvis's income from January 2, 1967, onward. Before 1967 Parker's share had been 25 percent. In the 1963 movie *Fun in Acapulco*, Elvis says to Larry Domasin, after Larry tells Elvis that he wants half of his earnings, "That's pretty much for an agent's commission." Truer words were never spoken, as that is exactly the percentage Elvis was going to pay the Colonel four years later. And since Parker was also paid for being a technical adviser on Elvis's films, he actually made more money from the films than Elvis did.

$450
Price paid for the Presleys' 1942 Lincoln Coupe, which Elvis drove in high school.

40-86-35-16
Elvis Presley's Selective Service number when he registered for the draft.

53310761
Elvis's Army serial number from 1958 to 1960. The number is probably the most well-known service number of all time. Other famous Army serial numbers are: Major Glenn Miller (0505273) and Major Clark Gable (19125047) [enlisted] and 0565390 [officer].

In 1958 the Threeteens recorded the novelty song "Dear 53310761" (Rev 3516), on which both Duane Eddy and Al Casey played guitar.

425-26-8732
Social Security number of Vernon Elvis Presley (sic). When issued to him, he was living at 510½ Maple Street in Tupelo and was listed as unemployed.

$43,000,000,000
Amount mentioned in several sources as the money that Elvis made in his entertainment activities over twenty-three years. Breaking down to a little more than $5,120,000 a day, this amount is exaggerated. There is no way Elvis could have made this much money. Even a figure of $4.3 billion, which RCA has stated that Elvis earned, is too large, as that breaks down to approximately $512,000 each day.

On April 2, 1965, Colonel Tom Parker told the press that to date Elvis's movies had grossed $125 million, while his records had grossed about $150 million. Elvis only received a percentage of those amounts.

FABARES, SHELLEY
(1944–   ) Actress and singer born Michele Fabares in Santa Monica, California, on January 19, 1944. She is the niece of actress Nanette Fabray. Fabares played Valerie in the 1965 movie *Girl Happy*, Cynthia Foxhugh in the 1966 movie *Spinout*, and Dianne Carter in the 1967 movie *Clambake*. On television, Fabares[2] starred in "The Donna Reed Show," "The Brian Keith Show," and "The Practice." In 1962 she had a number one hit record and a million-seller with "Johnny Angel" (Colpix 621). Elvis once said that Fabares was his favorite actress of those with whom he had worked.

In April 1962 Elvis's "Good Luck Charm" knocked Fabares's "Johnny Angel" out of first place on *Billboard*'s Hot 100 chart.

FABIAN
(1942–   ) Singer and actor, born Fabiano Forte in Philadelphia on February 6, 1943. Fabian who resembled Elvis and was a teen idol of the late 1950s and early 1960s. Although many in the music business said he couldn't sing,[3] Fabian had a number of records on the charts, including his biggest hit—"Tiger" (Chancellor 1037), which reached #3 and became a million seller.

In 1959 Fabian made his movie debut in the film *Hound-Dog Man*, starring Carol Lynley and Arthur O'Connell. Dodie Stevens, who had recorded the hit

---

[1] In comparison, singer Frank Sinatra weighed fourteen pounds at birth.

[2] Fabares later became the wife of record producer Lou Adler and the then wife of actor Mike Farrell.

[3] Many of his songs were made by splicing various notes that he sang several times over.

"Pink Shoe Laces" (Crystalette 724),[1] also appeared in the film. Fabian played a western character named Clint who not only had the same name Elvis had in *Love Me Tender* but who resembled his character in dress and manner, including singing some songs. Don Siegel, who had directed Elvis, was the film's director.

Fabian first met Elvis on the lot of 20th Century Fox, where Fabian was just finishing up the movie *North to Alaska*. Elvis approached Fabian and the two hit it off. On December 8, 1960, Elvis and Fabian had a friendly chat when Fabian stopped by Graceland for a visit. While demonstrating karate, Elvis tore his pants. Fabian gave Elvis his pair and kept Elvis's as a souvenir.

Fabian was first considered for the role of Glenn Tyler in the 1961 movie *Wild in the Country*, but Elvis eventually got the part.

In 1986 Fabian, Bobby Rydell, and Chubby Checker went on tour singing their hit records, with Fabian adding some Elvis material to his repertoire.

FACTORS ETC., INC.
Firm in Bear, Delaware, founded by Harry Geissler that once had the exclusive global rights to all Elvis merchandising. It's the largest mass-merchandising company in the world. The company also handles other accounts, such as *Rocky* and *Star Wars*. Within forty-eight hours after Elvis's death, Colonel Tom Parker had Vernon Presley sign an agreement that made Factors the distributor of all authorized Elvis-related products (except for music and films). Half of their share was to go to the Colonel and the other half to be split 25 percent to Boxcar Enterprises (of which Parker owned 40 percent) and the other 25 percent to the Presley estate. Thus, Parker received a much larger share than did the Presley estate. Factors gave Boxcar an advance of $15,000 plus 5 percent of their total sales. A July 1981 court decision gave Factors no rights to merchandise the Presley name. (See *Harry Geissler*)

FADAL, EDWARD (EDDIE) W.
Friend of Elvis's who lived in Waco, Texas, and who was a onetime radio announcer, disc jockey for KRLD in Dallas, and theater manager. Elvis first met Fadal at the Heart O' Texas Coliseum in Waco when Elvis performed there on October 12, 1956. While stationed at Fort Hood in 1958, Elvis sometimes traveled the forty-five miles on weekends to visit with Fadal, his wife, La Nelle, and children, Janice Lyn and Dana, at their home in Waco. Elvis visited the Fadals so often that Eddie had an extra room built onto his house in which he put a piano for Elvis to play. Elvis sang a number of songs that Fadal taped. The songs were released by Paul Lichter in August 1977 on a bootleg album, *Forever Young, Forever Beautiful* (Memphis Flash Records). Fadal was a pallbearer at the funeral of Elvis's cousin Junior Smith, who died in 1958. Fadal is the president

of the Elvis Memorial Club of Texas. On April 12, 1980, his daughter Janice married Lamar Fike (the pair have since divorced). Fadal is in the process of authoring his own book about Elvis to be titled *Deep in the Heart of Texas*. (See *Forever Young, Forever Beautiful* in Part III)

FAIN, HARRY M.
Attorney for Elvis who handled the paternity suit brought against Elvis on August 21, 1970, by Patricia Parker. (See *Patricia Parker*)

FAIRGROUNDS AMUSEMENT PARK
Memphis amusement park located at the Mid-South Fairgrounds that Elvis occasionally rented during the early-morning hours. The park is now called Libertyland. The different rides were: the Pipin roller coaster, the Rocket, the Tumblebug, and the Whip; but Elvis's favorite ride was the Dodgem cars (bumper cars). The rental of the park cost Elvis $2,500.

FALCON JET
Business jet that Elvis gave Colonel Tom Parker as a Christmas present in 1975. Parker gave back the airplane because of the cost of its upkeep.

FAMILY TREE
(See pages 64–66.)

FARRELL, ANN
Woman who, in an article in the *National Examiner*, claimed to have been married to Elvis. She said she met Elvis in Russellville, Alabama, in 1957, and that they were married because she refused to sleep with him unless they were man and wife.

Like other women who have claimed to have been married to Elvis, she said the documents of the marriage had been destroyed (again forgetting that official documents are registered).

FASHION CURTAINS
Memphis business where Gladys Presley and her sister-in-law, Lorene Presley, worked as seamstresses after they both arrived in Memphis in 1948.

FEATHERS, CHARLES
(1932–   ) Country singer born Charles Arthur Lindberg in Holly Springs, Mississippi, on June 12, 1932. Feathers became a Sun recording artist after Elvis had left the label in 1955. He was the cowriter (with Stanley Kesler) of "I Forgot to Remember to Forget," which Elvis recorded. Feathers, a good friend of guitarist Chet Atkins, claimed to have produced some Elvis's early recordings, including "Good Rockin' Tonight," which he says was borrowed from him.[2] Feathers has stated in interviews that he taught Elvis his style: "I

---

[1]Stevens in 1960 recorded "Yes, I'm Lonesome Tonight" (Dot 16167) as an answer to Elvis's "Are You Lonesome Tonight?" Stevens recorded "Merry Christmas Baby" (Dot 16166) prior to Elvis's version.

[2]There are two schools of thought with respect to Feathers's claims. Some researchers give no credence to them whatsoever, while others claim there is more to the Sun story than the legend has revealed. Sam Phillips often utilized producers and session musicians who were never credited on songs. At present the authors of this book don't know what Feathers's contributions were, if any.

ELVIS'S MATERNAL FAMILY TREE

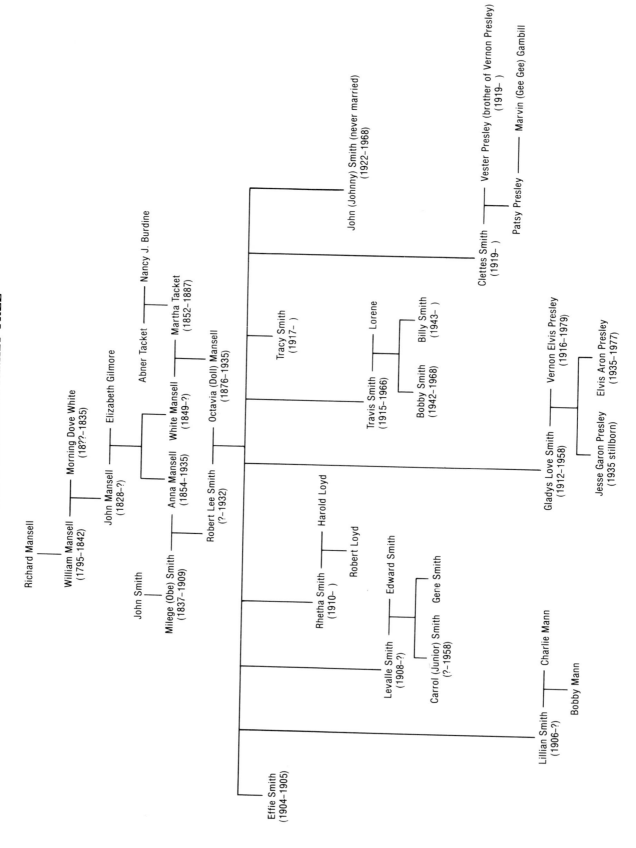

ELVIS'S PATERNAL FAMILY TREE

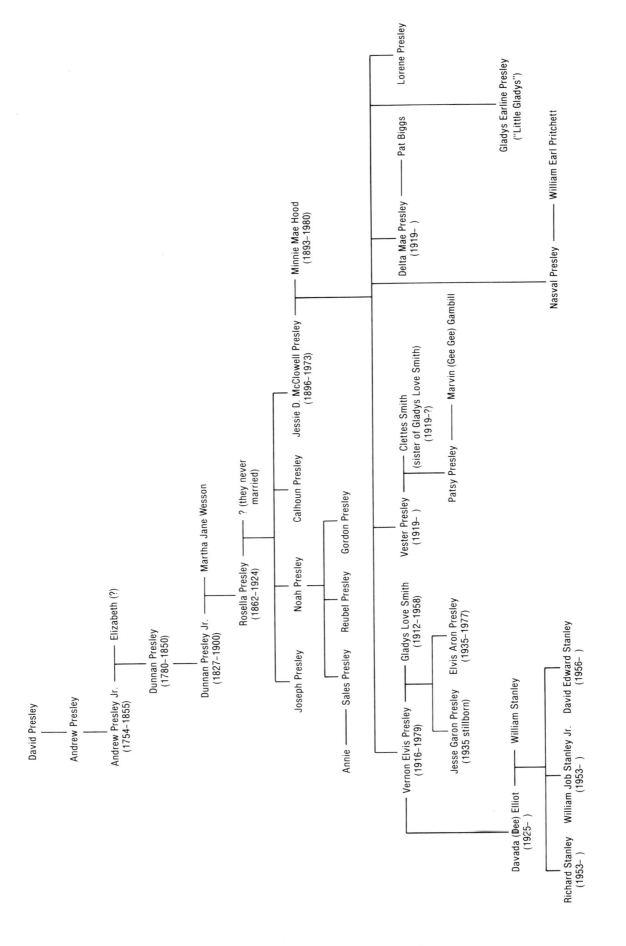

ELVIS'S IMMEDIATE FAMILY TREE

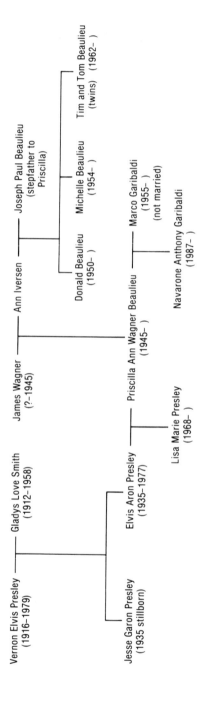

arranged all of Elvis's stuff, definitely, sure did." Feathers claims that not only did he arrange "Blue Moon of Kentucky" but he had recorded the demo for the song, which Scotty Moore denies. Feathers said he once recorded Elvis at a West Helena radio station in 1955. One has to wonder if Feathers is just having fun with the interviewer, since he further claimed to have given Jerry Lee Lewis the idea for his pumping piano. Feathers, who may have been suffering from professional jealousy, did record demos and records for Sun Records, Meteor Records, and for Sam Phillips's Holiday Inn Records in Memphis, as well as having recorded under the names Jess Hooper and Charlie Morgan.

Feathers appeared on the same bill with Elvis at the Overton Park Shell on August 5, 1955 for Bob Neal's 8th Anniversary Jubilee.

FEDERAL NARCOTICS BUREAU BADGE
Badge received by Elvis from President Richard M. Nixon. (See *Badges*)

FELLER, SID
Composer, with Dolores Fuller and Lee Morris, of the song "You Can't Say No in Acapulco," which Elvis sang in the 1963 movie *Fun in Acapulco*.

FERNWOOD RECORDS
Memphis record label located on Fernwood Drive, founded by Slim Wallace (who previously fronted a hillbilly band in Memphis called Slim Wallace's Dixie Ramblers). Scotty Moore was production chief, with the studio located in the Wallace garage. It was Moore who selected the song "Tragedy" for Thomas Wayne to record. The tape was brought over to Sun Records, where Moore added an echo on Sun's tape recorder. Jack Clement also produced some records at Fernwood.

WHBQ disc jockey Dewey Phillips even recorded for Fernwood, cutting "Beg Your Pardon"/"If It Had to Be You" (Fernwood 115).

FETCHIT, STEPIN
(1902–1985) Black character actor born Lincoln Theodore Monroe Andrew Perry (after four U.S. presidents) on May 30, 1902, in Key West, Florida. He chose the name Stepin Fetchit from the name of a racehorse that once won him some money. Reportedly, Fetchit wrote some songs for Elvis, but Colonel Parker wouldn't let Elvis use them.

FIEDLER, ARTHUR
(1894–1979) Conductor of the Boston Pops Orchestra from 1929 until his death in 1979, Fiedler was born in Boston on December 17, 1894. He studied at the Royal Academy of Music in Berlin, Germany. In 1915 he joined the Boston Symphony as a violinist. Fiedler had a million-seller in 1938 with "Jealousy."

Fiedler and Elvis, who both recorded for RCA Records, had planned, shortly before Elvis's death, to make an album together. (Had this been accomplished, it would have been nothing less than sensational.) Elvis was once invited by Fiedler to appear with the Boston Pops, but was turned down when the orchestra could not afford to pay the fee requested by Colonel Tom Parker.

FIELD, EUNICE
Last reporter to interview Elvis. Field was also the first person to interview Elvis in Hollywood.

FIKE, LAMAR
Member of the Memphis Mafia. At 270 pounds (some claim 300-plus; 350 pounds estimated by Patsy Lacker), Fike was the heaviest member of Elvis's entourage. He operated Elvis's lighting system when Elvis appeared in Las Vegas, and sometimes took care of transportation in Memphis and Los Angeles. The German news media dubbed Fike the "Wrestler," but Elvis liked to call him "Buddah" and the "Great Speckled Bird." Fike met Elvis by just hanging around the front of his house at 1034 Audubon Drive in Memphis, until he was finally invited in. Fike, the butt of many jokes, served as the court jester, whom Elvis could kid without Lamar ever getting upset. Elvis bought Fike a number of automobiles, including a brand-new Corvette. When Elvis was drafted in 1958, Fike tried to enlist but was turned down because he was overweight (the same fate that Jackie Gleason encountered during World War II). He left Elvis in 1962 to become the manager for singer Brenda Lee, but returned after a few years. Living with his wife, Nora, Fike lost a lot of weight after he experienced a heart attack. Today he weighs in at around 150 pounds. Fike assisted Albert Goldman in compiling the information for Goldman's book *Elvis*, and was thanked by Goldman in the acknowledgements. Fike is one of three people in whose name the book's copyright is registered. He was portrayed by Neham Ewing in the 1981 movie *This Is Elvis*.

In Goldman's *Elvis* there are thirty-five page references to Fike, the same number as for Gladys Presley. The only people who have more page references are Priscilla Presley, Vernon Presley, Colonel Tom Parker, and Joe Esposito.

FILMS INCORPORATED
Company that handled the distribution of the Elvis movies in 16 millimeter.

FINLATOR, JOHN
Narcotics Bureau deputy director whom Elvis visited in Washington, D.C., on December 21, 1970, through the help of Detective John O'Grady, to obtain a narcotics-agent badge. Elvis offered a contribution of $50,000 to the antidrug campaign, but Finlator declined to give him a badge. Elvis's next step was to go above his head to President Richard M. Nixon.

FIRE RECORDS
New York–based record label for which Arthur (Big Boy) Crudup recorded while being financed by Elvis in the 1960s. Elvis had always been a Crudup fan and was

aware that Crudup received little of the royalties that were rightfully due him as both a composer and recording artist. The two records that Crudup recorded for the label were "Rock Me Mama"/"Mean Ole Frisco Blues" (Fire 1501) and "Katie Mae"/"Dig Myself a Hole" (Fire 1502). Crudup also rerecorded his classics "So Glad You're Mine" and "That's All Right (Mama)" (Fire 103).

Fire Records was one of several labels (Fury, Holiday, Everest, Red Robin, Fling, Vest, and Enjoy) founded by Bobby and Danny Robinson. Buster Brown and Bobby Marchan (previously a member of Huey [Piano] Smith's Clowns) recorded for the label. Don Gardner and Dee Dee Ford recorded "TCB (Taking Care of Business)" on the Fire label (Fire 517).

FIRST ASSEMBLY OF GOD CHURCH
Pentecostal church that Elvis attended as a child in East Tupelo, Mississippi. The church was located at 206 Adams Street, a block and a half from the Presleys' house. While the Presleys lived in Tupelo, pastors of the First Assembly of God Church[1] included Rev. Edward D. Parks, Rev. James F. Ballard, and Rev. Frank Smith. Reverend Smith, who became the pastor in 1944, often played his guitar during the services. Elvis was baptized in the church that same year. Gladys, Vernon, and Elvis all joined in the singing during the services, which usually consisted of only about two dozen people. Vernon was a deacon in the church. The actual church building that Elvis attended still stands, but was moved several years ago to nearby 909 Berry Street. The building now serves as the parsonage.

The Presleys would later attend the First Assembly of God Church at 1085 McLemore in Memphis, where Elvis attended Sunday School, as did Cecil Blackwood, the younger brother of R. W. Blackwood of the Blackwood Brothers gospel group. Elvis's girlfriend Dixie Locke also attended services there.

Gladys Presley once remarked, "When Elvis was just a little fellow, he would slide off my lap, run down the aisle, and scramble up to the front of the church. He would stand looking up at the choir and try to sing with them."

FISHER, EDDIE
(1928–   ) Popular ballad singer born in Philadelphia on August 10, 1928. He recorded for RCA Records during the late 1940s and 1950s. Fisher was married to actress Debbie Reynolds (1955–59), to actress Elizabeth Taylor (1959–64), and actress Connie Stevens (1968–69). Like Elvis, Fisher was drafted into the U. S. Army, but he served in Special Services. When Elvis was drafted, the public thought he would do the same as Fisher had—go into the Special Services—but Elvis's manager, Colonel Tom Parker, talked him out of it. Fisher and Debbie Reynolds (her brother Bill Reynolds was Elvis's makeup man in some films) are the parents of actress Carrie Fisher, who played Princess Leia Organa in the *Star Wars* movie series.

In 1951 Fisher recorded "I'll Hold You in My Heart," which Elvis recorded in 1969.

FISHER, FRED
(1875–1942) Tin Pan Alley composer and lyricist. Fisher, who was born of American parents in Cologne, Germany, on September 30, 1875, composed such songs as "Peg o' My Heart" and "Chicago (That Toddlin' Town)."

Elvis recorded, in 1957, "That's When Your Heartaches Begin," which Fisher, William Raskin, and Billy Hill had composed.

FLAGSTAD, KIRSTEN
Classical singer whose records Elvis collected.

FLAMINGO
Memphis nightclub frequented by Elvis in 1955, according to blues singer Rufus Thomas, who recalled seeing Elvis there.

FLATT, LESTER
(1914–1979) Bluegrass singer and musician born in Overton County, Tennessee, on June 19, 1914. Flatt joined the Grand Ole Opry in 1944 as a member of Bill Monroe's Bluegrass Boys. The following year, Earl Scruggs joined Monroe, and in 1948, Flatt and Scruggs formed their own group. For the next twenty-one years, Flatt and Scruggs were the most popular bluegrass group in the country.

Lester Flatt, with Bill Monroe, composed "Little Cabin on the Hill," which Elvis recorded in 1970.

FLETT, DOUG AND FLETCHER, GUY
British composers of the songs "The Fair Is Moving On," "Just Pretend," and "Wonderful World," all of which were recorded by Elvis.

FLINT, ELMER AND DEBRA
Couple from Dwight, Illinois, who, on June 1, 1978, became the first pair to be married inside the house in which Elvis was born on Old Saltillo Road in East Tupelo, Mississippi. Mr. and Mrs. J. C. Grimes served as the Flints' witnesses.

FLOOR
Code word used to inform Elvis and others at concerts that someone was advancing on Elvis in a threatening manner. After hearing the word Elvis was to throw himself onto the floor while his bodyguards took care of the perpetrators.

FLORENDO, DR. NOEL
Assistant to Dr. E. E. Muirhead at Elvis's autopsy. He believed that the autopsy revealed "no gross evidence of a heart attack."

FLORIDA CLOSE UP
Book by Ger Rijff and Jan Van Gestel, with photo-

---

[1]Country-rock singer Jerry Lee Lewis's parents were members of the First Assembly of God Church in Ferriday, Louisiana.

graphs by Jay B. Leviton. Leviton had been assigned by *Collier's* magazine to photograph Elvis in Jacksonville, Florida, in and out of concert on August 10–12, 1956. The book, which included photos from the concert, was published by Ger Rijff's Tutti Frutti Productions of Amsterdam, Holland.

FLYING CIRCLE G
Second name of Elvis's ranch, the Circle G. It was renamed the Flying Circle G when Elvis discovered that there already existed a ranch in Texas called the Circle G.

FLYNT, LARRY C.
(1942–) Publisher of *Hustler* magazine born in Slayersville, Kentucky, on November 1, 1942. Flynt once claimed to have become a born-again Christian under the guidance of Rev. Ruth Carter Stapleton (sister of President Jimmy Carter). Flynt bought Elvis's Tri-Star jet from the Presley estate for $1.1 million in 1978.

FOLEY, CLYDE JULIAN (RED)
(1910–1968) One of the founding fathers of country music, he was elected to the Country Music Hall of Fame in 1967. Born in Bluelick, Kentucky, on June 17, 1910, Foley was the first major country star to actually record in Nashville[1] (March 1945 in studio B at radio station WSM).

Foley was a veteran of the Grand Ole Opry. In 1955 he moved to network television with "Ozark Jubilee"— a show that he hosted. It was on his program in 1956 that Elvis and Charlie Hodge, lead singer of the Foggy River Boys, first met. One of Foley's daughters, Shirley Lee, is married to Pat Boone and is the mother of singer Debby Boone, Foley's granddaughter.

Elvis recorded a number of songs that Red Foley had previously recorded: "Shake a Hand" (Decca 28839), "Peace in the Valley" (Decca 14573) (the Jordanaires backed both Elvis and Red Foley), "Old Shep" (Decca 46052) (which Foley cowrote), "I Believe" (Decca 28694), "It Is No Secret" (Decca 14566), and "Just Call Me Lonesome" (Decca 29626). Elvis is believed (by some) to have recorded two other Foley songs at Sun Records: "Tennessee Saturday Night" (Decca 46136) and "Blue Guitar" (Decca 29626). Elvis sang Foley's "Just a Closer Walk with Thee" (Decca 14505) at Eddie Fadal's house in 1958.

There is a photo of Red Foley in Vince Everett's (Elvis) cell in the 1957 movie *Jailhouse Rock*. In the 1975 movie *Nashville*, Henry Gibson portrayed Haven Hamilton, a character loosely based on Red Foley.

FONTAINEBLEAU HOTEL
Hotel in Miami Beach where Elvis taped The Frank Sinatra–Timex Special "Welcome Home Elvis" in the Grand Ballroom on March 26, 1960, which aired on May 12. Comedian Jerry Lewis filmed his 1969 movie *The Bellboy* at the Fontainebleau. It is also the hotel where agent James Bond (Sean Connery) first met Auric Goldfinger (Gert Frobe) in the 1964 movie *Goldfinger*.

FONTANA, D. J.
(1934–) Elvis's drummer from 1955 to 1969, born Dominic Joseph Fontana. Elvis first met Fontana while appearing at the "Louisiana Hayride" on October 16, 1954. Fontana, the staff drummer, became the first person to play drums on the "Louisiana Hayride," doing so behind a curtain.[2] Previously he had played his Gretsch drums for radio station KWKH's (Shreveport, Louisiana) studio band.

Popular opinion has it that Fontana was first heard on "I'm Left, You're Right, She's Gone," and then on other Sun recordings by Elvis. However, Fontana has stated that he did not play on any of Elvis's Sun recordings. The drummer at Sun Records was Johnny Bernero.

Fontana, who played behind Elvis on about forty-six recording sessions between 1956 and 1968, left Elvis's band in 1969 to become a session musician in Nashville. He played drums on Ringo Starr's *Beaucoups of Blues* album (the Jordanaires also appeared on the album). Fontana appeared in the 1957 movies *Loving You* and *Jailhouse Rock*. He also played drums for a stripper in the 1975 movie *Nashville*.

Fontana authored the book *D. J. Fontana Remembers Elvis*. (See *Johnny Bernero*)

FOOTBALL
Elvis's favorite sport, as revealed by him in an interview with Red Robinson on August 31, 1957. In a 1962 interview Elvis claimed to know all the NFL players and enjoyed being quizzed on football facts. His favorite pro team was the Cleveland Browns. In addition to having gone out for the school football team at L. C. Humes High School[3], he organized his friends into teams and often played games at Graceland, with hired referees. He and his friends also played football during breaks in the filming of his movies. While in West Germany, Elvis and Red West organized football games with American G.I.s. During one of those touch games, Elvis broke a finger.

Those who played on Elvis's "Elvis Presley Enterprises" football team in Memphis were: Elvis, Dell Dean, James Elam, Charles McSwain, Gene Smith, Freddie Vincent, Delbert West, Jim Kingskey, Billy Dodds, Larry Bell, Jack Counce, Red West, Alan Fortas, Pretty Boy Moore, Wilroy McElhaney, Jerry Baxter, Jerry Ellis, and many others.

---

[1] DeFord Bailey, the first black performer in country music, was probably the first artist ever to record in Nashville (October 2, 1928).

[2] Bob Wills's band had the first drummer to appear on the Grand Ole Opry. He also played behind a curtain so that the audience wouldn't know he was there. Drums were not a welcome instrument to country music fans.

[3] Sources vary as to whether Elvis played football at Humes High. Some claim that he played during his junior year, some say during his sophomore year, some say that he quit after several tryouts because the coach didn't like the length of his hair. In an interview in Jerry Hopkins's book *Elvis: A Biography*, Elvis says he played end in several games.

Elvis sponsored a football team called the E. P. Enterprises. (Photo courtesy Jeff Wheatcraft)

Some of the celebrities who played football with Elvis on Sundays at De Neve Park in Bel Air were: Ricky Nelson, Gary Lockwood, Max Baer Jr., Dean Torrence, Ty Hardin, Lee Majors, Pat Boone, Michael Parks, and Robert Conrad.

When the Memphis Southmen of the World Football League[1] played in 1974, Elvis attended all of their home games. (See *Whitehaven High School*)

FOOTE, MRS. SOPHIE
Neighbor of the Presley family at the Lauderdale Courts in Memphis.

FOR ELVIS FANS ONLY
Column written by Jim Van Hollebeke that appeared in *Goldmine* magazine for several years.

FORBES, EVAN
One of Elvis's close friends at Humes High School. Forbes, who went to work for the Memphis City Works, was nicknamed "Buzzie." Jerry Hopkins interviewed him for his book *Elvis: A Biography.*

FORD, BENJAMIN FRANCIS (WHITEY)
(1901–   ) Grand Ole Opry comedian, born in De Soto, Missouri, on May 12, 1901, who was nicknamed "the Duke of Paducah." Ford served as a scout for Colonel Tom Parker, persuading him to sign Elvis. In 1955 he convinced Vernon and Gladys Presley, who were leery of Parker, how much good Parker could do for their son.

FORD, NAOMI
Wife of guitarist-composer Lee Hazelwood, who is credited with having composed the song "The Fool," which Elvis recorded in 1970. In 1958 a singer named Ann Ford recorded a version of "The Fool" (Apollo 402). (See *Lee Hazelwood*.)

FOREST HILL CEMETERY
Memphis cemetery, located at 1661 Elvis Presley Boulevard, where Elvis and his mother, Gladys Presley, were buried until October 2, 1977, when their bodies were moved to Graceland. Visitors were ruining the grounds at Forest Hill, and there were rumors that Elvis's body might be stolen and held for ransom.

FORT CHAFFEE
U.S. Army post in Arkansas where Elvis received his Army indoctrination in March 1958. He got his medical shots and Army fatigues, and took an aptitude test. After only a few days Elvis was transferred to Fort Hood in Texas.

FORT DIX
U.S. Army post in New Jersey where Elvis was discharged on March 5, 1960. Elvis and the Memphis Mafia left Fort Dix in a private railroad car, the *Tennesseean,* bound for Memphis. (See *McGuire Air Force Base*)

FORT HOOD
U.S. Army post in Texas where Elvis received his basic training. He was assigned to A Company, Second Medium. Tank Battalion, Second Armored Division. His drill instructor was Sgt. William Fraley. Elvis was stationed at Fort Hood from March 28 to September 19, 1958, living with his parents off base, first in a trailer, then in a rented house.

FORTAS, ALAN
(1937–   ) Muscular, five-foot-eleven-inch All-Memphis football halfback in high school and member of the Memphis Mafia beginning in 1958, after having served as a bodyguard while Elvis filmed *King Creole.* Fortas's uncle was U.S. Supreme Court Justice Abe Fortas, who was portrayed in the 1980 TV movie *Gideon's Trumpet* by Jose Ferrer. Alan, whom Elvis had nicknamed "Hog Ears," served as manager of Elvis's Circle G Ranch. Before that he served as Elvis's bodyguard and took care of travel arrangements. Fortas played tambourine on some of the songs in the session for Elvis's NBC-TV Special June 1968. Over the years Elvis bought Fortas a new white Cadillac convertible, a motorcycle, and a pickup truck.

Fortas wrote the 1987 book *My Friend Elvis.*

FOWLER, NORA
Composer, with Shirl Milete, of the song "It's Your Baby, You Rock It," which Elvis recorded in 1970.

FOXHUGH
White Maltese dog that Elvis gave to his girlfriend Linda Thompson in 1973.

---

[1]The WFL lasted only one season with the Birmingham Americans winning the league championship.

FOXX, REDD

(1922–   ) Black comedian, born John Elroy Sanford in St. Louis on December 9, 1922, who starred in the TV series "Sanford and Son." Before the TV series Foxx was known primarily for his off-color nightclub act and comedy record albums. He was the only entertainer invited to Elvis and Priscilla's wedding breakfast at the Aladdin Hotel on May 1, 1967.

FRANCIS, CLAUDE

Composer, with Jean-Pierre Boutayre, of the song "My Boy," which Elvis recorded in 1975.

FRANCISCO, DR. JERRY

Chief Medical Examiner of Shelby County, Tennessee, who was in charge of the three-hour autopsy on Elvis, on August 16, 1977. Dr. Eric Muirhead, department head, performed the autopsy. Dr. Francisco ruled that Elvis's death was the result of coronary arrhythmia—an irregular beating of the heart resulting from hypertensive heart disease.

Because of the controversy surrounding the cause of Elvis's death, in 1979 Dr. Francisco called a press conference in which he stated: "I am not involved and never have been involved in a cover-up."

FRANCOIS, CLYDE

Composer, with Gilles Thibault and Jacques Revaux, of the song "Comme d'Habitude," which Elvis recorded as "My Way" in 1971.

FRANKFURT MILITARY HOSPITAL

Medical facility where Elvis was hospitalized with tonsillitis June 3–9, 1959.

FRAZIER, DALLAS

(1939–   )Country singer and composer born in Spiro, Oklahoma, on October 27, 1939. When he was twelve years old, Frazier won a talent contest sponsored by Ferlin Husky. Shortly after, he began touring with Husky.

In 1957 Frazier composed "Alley Oop," which the Hollywood Argyles (Lute 5905) turned into a number one hit and million-seller in 1960. Elvis recorded four Dallas Frazier songs: "There Goes My Everything" (also "He Is My Everything"), "Wearin' That Loved on Look," "Where Did They Go, Lord," and "True Love Travels on a Gravel Road."

FREBERG, STAN

(1926–   ) Humorist and recording artist born in Los Angeles on August 7, 1926. Freberg has provided the voices for many cartoon characters for Walt Disney, Warner Bros., Columbia, and Paramount Studios. He also dubbed the voices on the TV puppet show "Time for Beany."

In 1950 Freberg signed with Capitol Records and began releasing successful satirical records. In 1953 he had a number one hit and a million-seller with "St. George and the Dragonet" (Capitol 2596)—a parody on the popular TV series "Dragnet." Freberg recorded a satirical version of "Heartbreak Hotel" (Capitol 3480) in 1956, poking fun at the amount of echo used in the song.

FREED, ALAN

(1922–1965) Popular New York City disc jockey for radio station WINS who is often credited with coining the phrase "rock & roll." Freed, who was born in Johnstown, Pennsylvania, on December 15, 1922, was one of the most successful disc jockeys in the country until his career was ruined by the payola scandals of the 1950s. One of the things that got Freed into trouble was his co-composer credits on several songs, including "Sincerely" (Chess 1581) by the Moonglows and "Maybellene" (Chess 1604) by Chuck Berry. Freed was the first DJ in New York City to play Elvis's "Heartbreak Hotel."

FREEMAN, FRANK Y.

(1890–   ) Paramount Studios production chief who sent Elvis's draft board a letter (December 21, 1957) asking for a sixty-day deferment so that Elvis could complete production of *King Creole*. The draft board replied that Elvis would have to ask for the deferment. Elvis did ask for and got the delay.

FRIEDBERG, WEST GERMANY

Town north of Frankfurt, West Germany, where Elvis was stationed. Elvis was assigned to Ray Barracks.

FRIEDMAN, SAM

Acting city judge in Memphis who presided over the court case involving Elvis and Ed Hopper, a gas station manager. Hopper had charged that Elvis assaulted him on October 18, 1956. Elvis was acquitted and Hopper was fined $25. (See *Ed Hopper*)

FRISCH, ALBERT T.

(1916–1976) Composer born in New York City on March 17, 1916. Frisch composed, with Charles Tobias, the song "The Wonderful World of Christmas," which Elvis recorded in 1971.

FRUCHTER, ALF AND JEANETTE

Jewish family who lived upstairs at 464 Alabama Street at the time the Presleys lived in the lower unit at 452 Alabama Street. Fruchter was a rabbi for the Congregation Beth El-Emeth. The Fruchters were good friends of the Presleys, and Elvis sometimes used their telephone. Supposedly, it was the Fruchters' telephone number that Marion Keisker wrote down after Elvis recorded "My Happiness"/"That's When Your Heartaches Begin" in the summer of 1953. However, the Presleys did have a telephone at the time so that story seems unlikely. In Vince Staten's book *The Real Elvis: Good Old Boy*, Elvis was said to have borrowed the Fruchters' phonograph to play his first Sun recordings. Friends of Elvis, however, recall that Elvis did have a phonograph. (See *Marion Keisker*)

FULLER, CANDY JO

(1957–   ) Grand Island, Nebraska, woman born December 22, 1957, who claims to be Elvis's illegitimate daughter. Her mother, Terri Taylor, originated the claim. Fuller is a country singer with her husband's band, Dalton Fuller and the Nebraska Playboys. Occasionally she has been billed as "Elvis Presley's secret daughter." Her son Michael is claimed to be Elvis's grandson. (See *Terri Taylor, Michael Fuller*)

FULLER, DOLORES

Co-composer of a dozen songs that Elvis recorded for his films:

"Barefoot Ballad" (with Lee Morris)
"Beyond the Bend" (with Fred Wise and Ben Weisman)
"Big Love, Big Heartache" (with Lee Morris and Sonny Hendrix)
"Cindy, Cindy" (with Buddy Kaye and Ben Weisman)
"Do the Clam" (with Sid Wayne and Ben Weisman)
"Have a Happy" (with Florence Kaye and Ben Weisman)
"I Got Lucky" (with Fred Wise and Ben Weisman)
"I'll Take Love" (with Mark Barkan)
"Rock-a-Hula Baby" (with Fred Wise and Ben Weisman)
"Spinout" (with Sid Wayne and Ben Weisman)
"Steppin' Out of Line" (with Fred Wise and Ben Weisman)
"You Can't Say No in Acapulco" (with Sid Feller and Lee Morris)

FULLER, MICHAEL

(1976–   ) Candy Jo Fuller's son, who, it is claimed, is Elvis's grandson. Fuller was born on October 4, 1976.

FULSON, LOWELL

(1921–   ) Blues singer born in Tulsa, Oklahoma, the son of a Cherokee Indian father and a black mother. He originally used the spelling *Fulsom*, a name his grandfather had used. Fulson composed "Reconsider Baby," which he recorded (Checker 804) in 1954, and which Elvis recorded in 1960. Fulson, Jimmy McCracklin, and Ray Charles played in the same combo in the early 1960s.

G

GABRIEL, CHARLES H.
(1892–1934) Composer of religious songs born in San Francisco on March 2, 1892. Gabriel composed, with C. M. Battersby, "An Evening Prayer," which Elvis recorded in 1971.

GABRIEL, KATHY
Las Vegas showgirl whom Elvis dated briefly in 1956.

GAITHER, WILLIAM JAMES
(1936–   ) Composer of religious songs born in Alexandria, Indiana, on March 28, 1936. Gaither composed the song "He Touched Me," which Elvis recorded in 1972.

GALLENTINE, SHIRLEY JONES
Winner of the talent contest at the Mississippi-Alabama Fair and Dairy Show in 1945 in which Elvis finished second with his version of "Old Shep." Gallentine sang "My Dreams Are Getting Better All the Time," winning first prize, a $25 war bond. In her book *Elvis and Gladys*, Elaine Dundy mentions that Shirley and Elvis sang duets at school assemblies at East Tupelo Consolidated, performing such songs as "My Blue Heaven," "Deep in the Heart of Texas," and "Blue Moon Over My Shoulder."

Previous sources, including the *Tupelo Daily Journal* in 1977 and *All About Elvis*, have erroneously credited Becky Harris as the girl who beat out Elvis that year, but she won in 1946, not 1945. Ironically, in the 1977 *Tupelo Daily Journal* article, Harris herself tells about the day she beat Elvis.

GAMBILL JR., MARVIN (GEE GEE)
Member of the Memphis Mafia who served as Elvis's valet and chauffeur, beginning in February 1967. Gambill married Elvis's cousin, Patsy Presley. Elvis mentioned how he missed Gee Gee in his 1970 movie *Elvis—That's the Way It Is.*

GAMBILL, PATSY PRESLEY
Elvis's double first cousin (Patsy's mother Clettes was the sister of Elvis's mother, Gladys, and her father, Vester, was the brother of Elvis's father, Vernon. Patsy became one of Elvis's secretaries in 1963 when Pat West, the wife of Red West, quit to have a baby (a son born May 31, 1964). Patsy, whom Elvis nicknamed "Muffin," married Marvin (Gee Gee) Gambill, Elvis's chauffeur and valet. They both attended Elvis's wedding in 1967. Elvis bought Patsy a 1975 blue Pontiac Grand Prix and both her and her husband a 1975 Cadillac. Elvis also bought Patsy a horse, which was kept at Graceland.

Patsy, who had been close to Elvis in Tupelo, later became a close friend of Priscilla's at Graceland, with the two women often going shopping together, or out to the movies.

GAMBLE, KENNY
Composer, with Jerry Butler and Leon Huff, of the song "Only the Strong Survive," which Elvis recorded in 1969.

GANNON, KIM
(1900–1974) Composer born James Kimball Gannon in Brooklyn on November 18, 1900. Gannon, with Walter Kent and Buck Ram, composed the song "I'll Be Home for Christmas," which Elvis recorded in 1957.

GARDNER, BROTHER DAVE
Comedian and friend of Elvis's who performed as the opening act at some of Elvis's Las Vegas concerts.

GARFINKEL, CAROL JO
Longwood, Florida, woman who in an article in *The Examiner* claimed to have spoken to Elvis's spirit during séances. Garfinkel further claimed that Elvis had picked an impersonator named Orion to finish what he could not finish during his lifetime.

GARIBALDI, MARCO
(1955–   ) Writer-director-producer and owner of DeSiny Productions, who fathered Priscilla Presley's son Navarone, born March 1, 1987. Garibaldi, who is ten years Priscilla's junior, is an Italian who was raised in Brazil before moving to the United States, where he became a resident in 1976.

Priscilla, who authored a book about her former husband, Elvis, has made Garibaldi sign a promissory agreement that if they should break up, he will not write a book about her. This was prompted when Priscilla learned that her former boyfriend, Mike Edwards, was reported to be in the process of writing a book about Priscilla, Elvis, and himself. (See *Mike Edwards*)

GARIBALDI, NAVARONE
(1987–   ) Son born on March 1, 1987, at 10:20 A.M. to Priscilla Presley and film producer Marco Garibaldi at St. John's Hospital in Santa Monica, California. Navarone's father affectionately calls him "Ugly Face." As of the publication of this book, Navarone's parents have yet to marry.

GARLAND, HANK (SUGARFOOT)
(1930–   ) Guitarist born Walter Louis Garland on November 11, 1930, in Cowpens, South Carolina. Garland is one of the finest guitarists to play in Nashville. He has played on recording sessions with Eddy Arnold, Jim Reeves, Patsy Cline, Brenda Lee, Cowboy Copas, Red Foley, Patti Page, Webb Pierce, Don Gibson, Jerry Lee Lewis, Charlie Rich, and Elvis, replacing Scotty Moore on lead guitar. Garland backed Elvis from 1958 to 1961 and appeared at Elvis's Pearl Harbor benefit concert on March 25, 1961.

GATES, DAVID

(1940–   ) Singer and composer born in Tulsa, Oklahoma, on December 11, 1940. Gates played on sessions with the Ventures, Duane Eddy, Bobby Darin, Merle Haggard, and Elvis before becoming the lead singer of the group Bread, which later featured another Elvis session musician, Larry Knechtel. Gates and Hugo Montenegro were the musical directors for Elvis's 1969 movie *Charro*. Gates composed the song "Aubrey," which Bread recorded and which Elvis sang in concert in the mid-1970s.

GATHERING OF EAGLES, A

A 1963 movie, starring Rock Hudson and Rod Taylor, about the United States Air Force Strategic Air Command. It was one of Elvis's favorite movies.

GATLIN, LARRY

(1948–   ) Lead singer of the Gatlin Brothers, including Steve (1951–   ) and Rudy (1952–   ). Born in Seminole, Texas, on May 2, 1948. Larry Gatlin composed the song "Help Me," which Elvis recorded in 1973, and composed and originally recorded "Bitter They Are, Harder They Fall" (Monument 8602), which Elvis recorded in 1976. Gatlin appeared in the 1978 TV special "Nashville Remembers Elvis on His Birthday."

GAUTIER, DICK

(1939–   ) Actor born in Los Angeles on October 30, 1939. Gautier played the role of the Elvis-like character Conrad Birdie in the Broadway musical *Bye Bye Birdie*. Gautier is a veteran of four TV series: "Get Smart" (on which he played Hymie, the robot), "Mr. Terrific," "Here We Go Again," and "When Things Were Rotten." (See *Bye Bye Birdie*)

GEISSLER, HARRY

(1930–   ) Board chairman of Factors Etc., Inc., and self-proclaimed "King of the Merchandisers." In August 1977, shortly after Elvis's death, Harry (The Bear) Geissler bought from Vernon Presley and Colonel Tom Parker the merchandising rights to all Elvis products. After Elvis's death Geissler was quoted as saying, "I don't even like Elvis's music, but I was always a fan of Colonel Parker's." He also said, "We are aggressive in protecting the rights of the Presley organization. The pirates are literally stealing money from Elvis's family, and remember it's a family affair, from the grandmother all the way down to little Lisa Marie." What Geissler didn't say was that the Colonel had a bigger share of the profits than did Elvis's family, from the grandmother all the way down to little Lisa Marie. (See *Factors Etc., Inc.*)

GELBER, STANLEY JAY

(1936–   ) Composer born in Brooklyn on June 2, 1936. Gelber composed the songs "On a Snowy Christ-

mas Eve" and "My Desert Serenade," both of which Elvis recorded.

GELLER, GREGG

A&R director for RCA Records who became the head of the Elvis catalog after Joan Deary retired in 1987. Geller is presently trying to locate any of Elvis's missing recordings, as well as accumulating any illegally recorded Elvis concert music, so that it can be released legally.

GELLER, LARRY

(1940–   ) Hairstylist born on August 8, 1940. While cutting singer Johnny Rivers's hair at Jay Sebring's Beverly Hills Salon on April 30, 1964, he got a telephone call requesting that he go to Elvis's Bel Air house to cut and style Elvis's hair. He was then hired as Elvis's personal hairstylist, replacing Sal Orfice. Geller became more than Elvis's friend and employee after he introduced Elvis to the occult, teaching Elvis about parapsychology, religion, the supernatural, and the mystical world. Geller instilled an interest in reading in Elvis, after which Elvis began building a library of books on the occult. Elvis called Larry his "guru," and bought him a new white Cadillac convertible.

Colonel Tom Parker disliked Geller's influence on Elvis and eventually broke the two apart. Parker made sure that someone else was present whenever Geller cut Elvis's hair. After Parker succeeded in breaking Geller's influence, Elvis's collection of occult-related books were taken out and burned. Geller cowrote, with Jess Stearn, the 1980 book *The Truth About Elvis*, and in 1983 Geller authored *Elvis's Spiritual Journey*. Geller portrayed himself in the 1979 TV movie *Elvis*.

GEMINI

Astrological sign of Priscilla Presley, Linda Thompson, Minnie Mae Presley, and Dee Stanley Presley.

GENERAL RANDALL

(See *Randall*, USS *General*)

GENTRY, BOBBIE

(1944–   ) Singer-songwriter born Roberta Streeter in Chickasaw County, Mississippi, on July 27, 1944. Her 1967 record "Ode to Billy Joe," her first, was number one for four weeks, selling three million copies. Gentry[1] received four Grammy Awards in 1967: Best Solo (Female) Performance, Best Arrangement, Best Contemporary Vocal Performance, and Best New Artist. In 1976 "Ode to Billy Joe"[2] was made into a novel and then a feature movie, directed by Elvis's friend Max Baer Jr. Gentry, after an unsuccessful marriage to millionaire Bill Harrah, married singer-songwriter Jim Stafford[3] in 1978.

Gentry, who had dated Elvis, was once under consideration to costar with Elvis in the 1969 movie *The*

---

[1]Gentry chose her last name after seeing the 1952 movie *Ruby Gentry*, starring Charlton Heston and Jennifer Jones.
[2]In the song Bobbie mentions Tupelo, Mississippi, Elvis's birthplace.
[3]Stafford was the cohost with Priscilla Presley and Burgess Meredith on the TV series "Those Amazing Animals."

Trouble with Girls (and How to Get Into It); instead, Marlyn Mason got the part.

In January 1969 Gentry and Glen Campbell recorded "Let It Be" (Capitol 2387), which Elvis would record one year and one month later.

GEORGE, BOBBY
Composer, with Vern Stovall, of the song "Long Black Limousine," which Elvis recorded in 1969.

GERSON, PAT PARRY
Beverly Hills beautician who often styled Elvis's hair. She was married to Dr. Jerry Gerson, with whom she once traveled to Graceland to visit Elvis.

GETLO
Pet chow chow dog of Elvis, which he bought in 1957. On August 1, 1975, Elvis brought Getlo out on stage at the Las Vegas Hilton. That same year Elvis flew the dog to Boston, taking him to the New England Institute of Comparative Medicine in West Boylston, Massachusetts, where Getlo was put under the care of Dr. S. Lynn Kittleson for a kidney ailment. But Getlo died in Memphis only a few months after the rather costly operation. Becky Yancey, one of Elvis's secretaries at Graceland, tells the story in her 1977 book *My Life with Elvis*.

GHANEM, DR. ELIAS
Lebanese-born Las Vegas physician who treated Elvis when the singer appeared in Las Vegas. According to Dr. Ghanem on ABC-TV's "20/20," he "never knew Elvis to take drugs of any kind—only sleeping pills."

GIANT, BILL
Composer, with Jeff Lewis, of the song "Fountain of Love," which Elvis recorded in 1962. With Bernie Baum and Florence Kaye, Giant composed forty-one other songs that Elvis recorded. (See *Bernie Baum* for a list of the songs)

GIBSON, DON
(1928–) Prolific country-music composer and singer born in Shelby, North Carolina, on April 3, 1928. Gibson turned professional at the age of fourteen. In 1958 he recorded a two-sided, million-selling hit record for RCA, "Oh Lonesome Me"/"I Can't Stop Lovin' You" (RCA 7133). He wrote both songs. Ray Charles recorded "I Can't Stop Lovin' You" in 1962 and it became the number one song of the year. Elvis recorded the song on six different occasions, the first being in 1969. In 1959 Gibson recorded "I'm Movin' On" (RCA 47-7629), a song that Elvis would record in 1969.

GIBSON, HENRIETTA
Lisa Marie Presley's nursemaid at Graceland.

GILLILAND, HOMER (GIL)
Elvis's personal Memphis hairdresser for many years, beginning in 1967 after he replaced Larry Geller. He kept Elvis's hair dyed black. Elvis gave Gilliland his $10,000 gold lamé suit.

GILMORE, ELIZABETH (BETSY)
Wife of John Mansell (they married in 1840). They were the parents of ten children, including Ann Mansell and White Mansell. Elizabeth was the grandmother of cousins Robert Lee Smith and Octavia (Doll) Mansell, who would later marry each other. Elizabeth was the great-grandmother of Gladys Smith and the great-great grandmother of Elvis Presley. (See *John Mansell*)

GLADYS
Name that Colonel Tom Parker gave to his twenty-six-foot plastic rowboat, which Elvis had given him for his birthday.

GLADYS MUSIC, INC.
One of three music publishing companies owned by Elvis (the others were Elvis Presley Music, Inc., and Whitehaven Music). Named for Elvis's mother, Gladys Music, was a subsidiary of Hill and Range Music Company. Elvis received 50 percent of the profits. When Elvis needed money in the late 1960s he sold part of Gladys Music back to Hill and Range. (See *Elvis Presley Music, Hill and Range*)

GLAUCOMA
Disorder of the eye that Elvis suffered from and was treated for in his later years. It was a severe case of glaucoma that caused singer Ray Charles to go completely blind at the age of seven.

GLAZER, MELVIN JACOB
(1931–) Composer born in Jersey City, New Jersey, on February 25, 1931. Glazer composed, with Steven Schlaks, the song "Speedway," which Elvis sang in the 1968 movie of the same name.

GLEASON, JACKIE
(1916–1987) Comedian born Herbert John Clarence Gleason in Brooklyn on February 26, 1916. Gleason appeared in films, on television, and led his own orchestra on albums. His best-known comedy TV series was "The Honeymooners." In 1986 Gleason, who was nicknamed "The Great One" by actor-director Orson Welles, was inducted into the TV Academy Hall of Fame.

It was Gleason who decided to have Elvis make his first national TV appearance on the Dorsey Brothers' "Stage Show" on January 28, 1956, followed by five more appearances on the show, which Gleason supervised. His decision to break Elvis nationally followed his infamous statement: "He can't last. I tell you flatly, he can't last."

Linda Miller, Gleason's daughter and the wife of Pulitzer Prize and Tony Award–winning playwright Jason Miller, portrayed Ann Beaulieu, the mother of Priscilla Presley, in the 1988 TV miniseries "Elvis and Me."

GLEAVES, CLIFF

Salaried friend of Elvis's who first introduced him to Anita Wood and who accompanied Elvis to Hollywood in 1956 to film *Love Me Tender*. Gleaves was a rocka-billy singer who cut three unreleased songs for Sun Records, "Your Cheatin' Heart," "As Long As I Have You," and "Love Is My Business" (with Charlie Rich on the piano). He was present at the Million-Dollar Quartet session on December 4, 1956. Gleaves drove Elvis and Dotty Harmon to Kennedy Veterans Hospital in Memphis for Elvis's preinduction physical on January 4, 1957. Later, in 1958, at Elvis's request, Gleaves traveled to West Germany to stay with Elvis and to accompany Elvis to Paris while he was on leave in 1959.

GLENN, DARRELL

Singer who composed the song "Indescribably Blue," which Elvis recorded in 1966. His father, Artie Glenn, had composed "Crying in the Chapel," which his son introduced (Valley 105). Elvis recorded "Crying in the Chapel" in 1960. Elvis thus recorded songs written by a father and by his son, as he did with songs written by a mother and her son when he recorded "Heartbreak Hotel" (co-composed by Mae Axton) and "Never Been to Spain" (composed by Hoyt Axton).

GLICK, CAPT. LEONARD

Army doctor who gave Elvis his preinduction physical in Memphis on January 4, 1957.

GOEHRING, GEORGE ANDREW

(1933–   ) Singer and composer born in Philadelphia on July 16, 1933. He wrote "Lipstick on Your Collar" (MGM 12793) for Connie Francis in 1958. Goehring and Sylvia Dee composed the song "Suppose," which Elvis recorded in 1967.

GOLD, WALTER (WALLY)

(1928–   ) Composer born in Brooklyn on May 15, 1928. Gold, who was once a member of the Four Esquires, composed with Aaron Schroeder three songs that were recorded by Elvis: "Good Luck Charm," "It's Now or Never," and "In Your Arms." The first two reached number one on *Billboard*'s Hot 100 chart.

GOLD CADILLAC

Elvis's favorite custom automobile. The car started as a 1960 Cadillac Series 75 Sedan Limousine, before being converted by famed automobile customizer George Barris. It was painted with diamond-dust gold pearl paint. The Gold Cadillac, valued at $100,000, is on display at the Country Music Hall of Fame in Nashville, Tennessee.

GOLD LAMÉ TUXEDO

Suit designed for Elvis in 1957 by Nudie's of Hollywood at the request of Colonel Tom Parker. Parker loved the suit, while Elvis, who thought it too heavy, hated it. A photograph of Elvis wearing the gold lamé

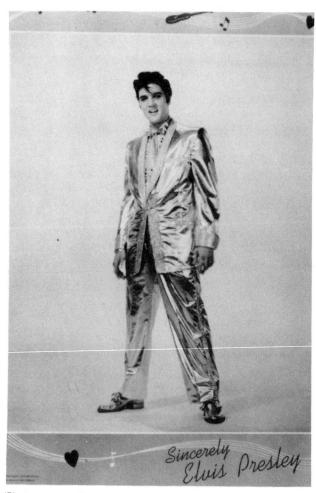

(Photo courtesy Eddie Brandt's Saturday Matinee)

tuxedo appeared on the cover of the 1959 LP *50,000,000 Elvis Fans Can't Be Wrong—Elvis' Gold Records, Volume 2*. The suit was reported to have been valued at $10,000, though Nudie's revealed in 1980 that they "made a profit of $9,950 on the suit."

GOLDBERG, HERB

Composer, with David Hess, of the song "Sand Castles," which Elvis recorded for the 1966 movie *Paradise, Hawaiian Style*. The song was later cut.

GOLDEN, GEORGE

Memphis decorator who decorated the interior of Graceland to Elvis's taste after Elvis bought the mansion in 1957.

GOLDEN GATE QUARTET

Black gospel group headed by Bill Johnson. Both the Jordanaires and Elvis were greatly influenced by this group. Elvis recorded his own versions of a number of their songs, covering most of the songs from the group's 1953 Columbia extended-play album on his own gospel album, *His Hand in Mine*. The quartet also recorded "White Christmas"/"Silent Night" for Apollo Records (Apollo 194), both songs that Elvis would later record.

GOLDMAN, ALBERT
New York English professor who in 1981 authored the book *Elvis*, which was published by McGraw-Hill and in paperback by Avon Books. Goldman previously authored *Ladies and Gentlemen—Lenny Bruce!!!* About writing the book *Elvis*, Goldman said, "One of the greatest problems was trying to find something positive to say about the man." This is probably how Elvis fans now feel about Albert Goldman. (See *Elvis*)

GOLDSMITH'S DEPARTMENT STORE
Memphis establishment, at 4545 Poplar Avenue, that provided the material for the interior decorating at Graceland.

GONE BUT NOT FORGOTTEN
Phrase on one of the two wreaths that Elvis and Colonel Tom Parker placed at the USS *Arizona* Memorial at Pearl Harbor, Hawaii, on August 15, 1965. The bell-shaped wreath was made of 1,177 carnations, in honor of each man who perished aboard the *Arizona* on December 7, 1941.

GONE WITH THE WIND
A 1939 movie starring Clark Gable, Vivien Leigh, Olivia de Havilland, and Leslie Howard. *Gone with the Wind* won ten Oscars, including Best Picture, Best Actress (Vivien Leigh), and Best Supporting Actress (Hattie McDaniel).

In 1977 a survey of 35,000 members of the American Film Institute selected *Gone with the Wind* as the top movie of all time.

Gone with the Wind was shown on television (CBS-TV) for the second time on the evening of February 11, 1979—opposite the ABC-TV movie *Elvis*, and losing out to *Elvis* in the ratings.

Ironically, *Gone with the Wind* played at Loew's State Theater the same week in July that Elvis's first record was played on the radio. Producer Mike Frankovich once said of Elvis, "If I were doing a remake of *Gone with the Wind*, I'd cast Elvis in the Rhett Butler role, and it wouldn't be a musical." (See *Elvis* in Part II)

GONG SHOW, THE
TV variety series hosted by Chuck Barris.[1] On October 18, 1978, "The Gong Show" dedicated the program to Elvis by having Elvis impersonators perform.

GOODING, JUDGE MARION W.
Juvenile Court judge in Jacksonville, Florida, who threatened to have Elvis arrested if he, in the judge's opinion, made any wrong moves when he performed at the Florida Theatre on August 10–11, 1956. Elvis made no wrong moves and wasn't arrested.

GOODMAN, CHARLES (RUSTY)
Composer of the song "Who Am I," which Elvis recorded in 1969.

GOODMAN, DIANA
Woman who won title Miss Georgia and was a contestant in the 1975 Miss USA Pageant. Elvis dated Goodman for a time in the 1970s.

GORDON, JIMMY
Musician who played acoustic guitar on Elvis's 1975 recording of "Bringing It Back," which Gordon had composed.

GORDON, ROSCO
Rhythm & blues singer, born in West Memphis, Arkansas, who recorded for Sun Records. Gordon once performed in a group called the Beale Street Boys, which also featured B. B. King on guitar, Johnny Ace on piano, and Earl Forrest on drums. On October 25, 1956, he recorded the song "Hard Headed Woman"[2] for Sun Records, but it was not released. Gordon appeared in the 1957 movie *Rock Baby Rock It*.[3] He recorded "Just a Little Bit" (Vee Jay 332) in February 1960 (his only charted *Billboard* Hot 100 record). Elvis recorded the song in 1973.

GOTTLIEB, ALEX
Composer, who with Fred Karger and Ben Weisman, arranged the song "Frankie and Johnny," which Elvis sang in the 1966 movie of the same name.

GOULET, ROBERT
(1933–) Singer born in Lawrence, Massachusetts, on November 26, 1933, but who lived in Canada for many years. Goulet, who is a former disc jockey and singer, was for some reason disliked by Elvis. In 1974 Elvis fired a .357 Magnum pistol at a television set because Goulet was on the screen.

GRACELAND
Elvis's Memphis home for the last twenty years of his life. The address was 3764 Elvis Presley Boulevard, Memphis, Tennessee, 38116 (telephone: EX 7-4427.[4] Located in the Memphis suburb of Whitehaven (which was annexed by Memphis in 1969), Graceland had previously been used as a church by the Graceland Christian Church. Its 13¾ acres of land was purchased by Elvis in March 1957 from Ruth Brown Moore for $102,500 ($40,000 in cash, $55,000 for the Presleys' house on Audubon Drive, and a $37,000 note carried by Equitable Life at 4 percent interest), beating out the Memphis YMCA's bid of just $35,000.

Graceland was established as a farm during the American Civil War (1861–1865) by publisher S. E.

---

[1]Barris is the son of piano player Harris Barris, who was a member of Bing Crosby's Rhythm Boys. Chuck Barris composed Freddy Cannon's 1962 hit song "Palisades Park" (Swan 4106).
[2]It is not yet known whether this is the same song that Elvis recorded in 1958, but it's doubtful!
[3]The film starred Johnny Carroll (see entry) and Kay Wheeler. Kay had been one of the founders of the International Elvis Presley Fan Club and was billed in the movie as the "Queen of Rock 'n' Roll."
[4]This was one of Elvis's unlisted telephone numbers. He had given it to the FBI under the name of Col. Jon Burrows of 3764 Highway 51 South, Memphis, Tennessee.

Graceland. (Photo courtesy Don Fink)

The pool room at Graceland. (Photo courtesy John Dawson)

Elvis's karate uniform and some of his jumpsuits. (Photo courtesy John Dawson)

Toof of the *Memphis Daily Appeal*, on land that originally covered 500 acres in Whitehaven. Toof named his estate Graceland after his daughter, Grace Toof. The present estate house was constructed in the late 1930s by Dr. Thomas and Ruth Moore. Ruth was the niece of Grace Toof. It was the couple's daughter, Ruth Marie, a professional musician, who sold Graceland to another professional musician, Elvis Presley.

The two-story mansion was constructed of tan Tennessee limestone and originally contained twenty-three rooms, including five bedrooms. Elvis painted the mansion blue and gold, which glowed at night. The front room featured a white marble fireplace and Louis XIV furniture. Elvis added several rooms, in-

cluding a trophy room. The trophy room, a forty-foot-long room built over the back patio, began as a playroom where Elvis and the boys raced slot cars after Priscilla had given him a small set for Christmas in 1965. The room now displays Elvis's sixty-three gold singles, twenty-six platinum albums, and thirty-seven gold albums. At the time of Elvis's death there were sixteen TV sets at Graceland. On the grounds, Elvis built a barn and a racquetball court. The wall surrounding the estate was constructed in 1957 of Alabama fieldstone.

Elvis added on a $200,000 private recording studio at Graceland. A portable mobile recording studio was brought to Graceland by RCA on two occasions in

1976, February 2–8 and October 29–31. Some of the songs Elvis recorded at Graceland include "Way Down," "Pledging My Love," "Moody Blue," and "Solitaire."

After Elvis's death, Graceland was valued at $500,000, but its annual upkeep was running a reported $500,000, with a $12,000 yearly utility bill. Rather than sell the estate, Priscilla, acting for Lisa Marie, decided to open it to the public, charging $5 a visitor. The doors were first opened on June 7, 1982, in a ceremony. On the tour, visitors can see the living room, dining room, music room, TV room, pool room, jungle den, and automobile collection. The upstairs is closed to the public. Over the years, Graceland has been averaging about 2,500 visitors each day.

In 1986 singer Paul Simon recorded the album *Graceland*, in which he sings about Graceland as a symbol of redemption. The album won the Grammy Award for Album of the Year in 1987. In 1988 the song "Graceland" won a Grammy for Record of the Year.

According to Lucy de Barbin in her book *Are You Lonesome Tonight?*, Elvis was inspired to buy Graceland because it was located on Bellevue Road, Bellevue being Lucy's middle name.

GRAHAM, IRVIN
(1909–) Composer, born in Philadelphia on September 18, 1909, who with Ervin Drake, Jimmy Shirl, and Al Stillman, wrote the song "I Believe," which Elvis recorded in 1957.

GRAND OLE OPRY
Country music show founded by the "Solemn Ol' Judge," George Hay. It originated on radio station WSM on November 28, 1925, and was located at Nashville's Ryman Auditorium from 1942 to 1974. Colonel Tom Parker made his bookings from the free hallway telephones at the theater.

The last song sung at the Ryman Auditorium was "Will the Circle Be Unbroken" on March 15, 1974; after that the show moved to the new Opryland Auditorium. It was for this radio program on October 2, 1954, that Elvis, Bill Black, Scotty Moore, Sam Phillips. and Marion Keisker drove to Nashville from Memphis in two cars. The Hillbilly Cat and the Blue Moon Boys sang "Blue Moon of Kentucky" and "That's All Right (Mama)." In one of the biggest bloopers in music history, Jim Denny suggested to Elvis that he go back to driving a truck. After the performance Elvis was upset by the lack of audience response. Backstage, singer Ernest Tubb told the young singer "not to worry, you have done a fine job and the audience just doesn't know." Tubb, who was known as the "King of Country Music," thus consoled the future "King of Rock & Roll."

Years later, Elvis told Hank Williams Jr. that when he walked out on stage all he could think about was that this was where Hank Williams had once played. Singer Patsy Cline once failed an audition for the Opry. (See *Jim Denny, Ryman Auditorium*)

GRANT, CURRIE
United States Air Force airman first class,[1] based in Wiesbaden, West Germany, who in November 1959 first introduced twenty-four-year-old Elvis to fourteen-year-old Priscilla Beaulieu. Grant introduced her and Elvis reached out his right hand and jokingly said, "Hi, I'm Elvis Pretzel." Grant and his wife, Carole, who is the sister of singer Tony Bennett, had escorted Priscilla to the party. Elvis walked Priscilla out to Grant's car and asked him to please bring her back.

Grant worked as a clerk for Air Force intelligence at the 497th Reconnaissance Technical Squadron at Schierstein near Wiesbaden. He also ran a weekly variety show for the Air Force as well as being involved in the Eagle's Club, a military club in downtown Wiesbaden. It was announced that Grant was writing a book to be titled *Elvis and Priscilla*, and according to his version of the story, Priscilla had sought him out at the Eagle's Club and said, "Hi, I understand you know Elvis Presley." If this is true, another legend dies. Their meeting was not kismet but the result of a scheme set up by Priscilla. However, in Priscilla's autobiography and subsequent TV miniseries, "Elvis and Me," Grant is said to have approached Priscilla and asked her if she wanted to meet Elvis.

GRANT, MARSHALL
Bass-playing member of Johnny Cash's band the Tennessee Two (later Three, with guitarist Luther Perkins). When Elvis and Cash toured together in 1955, both Grant and Perkins sometimes played backup for Elvis on stage.

GRAY, DOBIE
(1942–) Singer born Leonard Victor Ainsworth Jr. in Brookshire, Texas, on July 26, 1942. In 1973 Gray recorded "Lovin' Arms" (MCA 40100), which Elvis would record in 1974. At a Stax Studios recording session in 1973, Elvis seriously considered recording Gray's "We Had It All," until Elvis decided he couldn't top Gray's version.

GRAY, GILDA
(1901–1959) Polish dancer born Marianna Michalska. She is credited with having invented the shimmy. Gray appeared in several movies, including *Lawful Larceny* (1923), *Aloma of the South Seas* (1926), *Cabaret* (1926), *The Devil Dancer* (1928), *Piccadilly* (1929), and *Rose Marie* (1936). Early in Elvis's career when Colonel Tom Parker realized that Elvis danced on stage while singing, he suggested to him that he watch one of Gilda Gray's movies so he could learn how to dance like her. Elvis did and picked up some moves.

GREAT BRITAIN
Country that, contrary to popular opinion, Elvis did

---

[1]In the 1988 TV miniseries "Elvis and Me" Currie was erroneously portrayed as a member of the U.S. Army.

visit, but the visit was short. While en route to the States from West Germany on March 3, 1960, Elvis's C-118 transport plane landed at Prestwick Airport in Scotland to refuel. Elvis briefly stepped off the plane and onto British soil.

Some of Elvis's most devoted fans have been his British fans. The fan clubs in Britain were publishing magazines, newsletters, and books about Elvis years before many were published in the United States. At Elvis's July 31, 1969, news conference he said that he wanted to play all over the world, including Great Britain.

Although British fans always hoped that Elvis would perform in their country, he never did, causing speculation that perhaps Colonel Tom Parker had no intentions of leaving the States because, as later discovered, he was an illegal alien.

GREEK ORTHODOX CHURCH ANNUNCIATION
Memphis church where, it was rumored, Elvis and Ginger Alden were planning to marry on December 25, 1977.

GREEN JR., LEROY
Schoolmate and friend of Elvis's at Milam Junior High School in Tupelo, Mississippi. Elvis and Leroy were two of the poorest children attending the school. Today Green is a disc jockey at Tupelo radio station WELO.

GREEN, LONZO
Man who claimed to have tuned a guitar for young Elvis at the Lauderdale Courts in Memphis while he and his family were there visiting relatives. Green says that he sat with Elvis, tuned his guitar, and then sang several songs and taught him several chords. Green's story is told in the 1980 book *More of Paul Harvey's the Rest of the Story*, which was written by Harvey's son Paul Aurandt.

GREENAWAY, ROGER
Composer, with Tony Macaulay, of the song "Love Me, Love the Life I Lead," which Elvis recorded in 1971.

GREENE, SHECKY
(1925–   ) Comedian born in Chicago on April 8, 1925. Greene was billed below Elvis at the New Frontier Hotel in Las Vegas (April 23–May 6, 1956). Within a few days, however, Greene, who has been called "The King of Las Vegas," was billed above Elvis as Elvis's popularity dwindled. Greene turned down Colonel Tom Parker's request that he tour with Elvis, something he would later regret. One story has it that one night at the New Frontier Hotel, Greene was sitting with singer Bing Crosby watching Elvis perform, when Crosby said to him, "Shecky, he's gonna be the biggest star in show business."

GREENWOOD, EARL
One of Elvis's buddies while he was in the Army at Fort Hood, Texas. The two had grown up together in Tupelo. Greenwood later served as Elvis's publicist. In August 1959 Greenwood wrote the article "Elvis Telephones a Message to His Friends" for *Movie Mirror* magazine, and in May 1960 wrote an article titled "Elvis Presley's Secret Gift" for *Movie Screen* magazine. Greenwood's mother, Nora, went to visit Vernon Presley at the hospital in Memphis during his last days.

GRENADA
Caribbean island country that in 1979 was the first nation to honor Elvis on a postage stamp. At the request of several Caribbean nations, the United States invaded Grenada in 1983, freeing the country from its dictatorship.

GRIFFIN, REX
Composer of the song "Just Call Me Lonesome," which Elvis recorded in 1967.

GRIMES, OLETA BEAN
Daughter of Orville Bean. Oleta was Elvis's teacher in the fifth grade at East Tupelo Consolidated School (Lawhon Grammar School) in Tupelo, Mississippi (1945–46). She and her family lived just two houses away from Elvis on Old Saltillo Road, having moved there about 1936, so she already knew Elvis before he attended her school. After Gladys Presley's death in 1958 Elvis returned to Tupelo to visit Oleta. She once said of Elvis, "People have asked me what kind of boy Elvis was and I couldn't say enough about him, and that was coming from the heart." (See *Orville Bean*)

GROB, DICK
Security chief at Graceland for seven years and member of the Memphis Mafia beginning in 1969. Elvis nicknamed him "Grob the Fox." Grob, who had been a member of the Air Force Academy's first graduating class, served as a fighter pilot in the U.S. Air Force (he flew F-101 McDonnell Voodoos) and a sergeant in the Palm Springs (California) Police Department. Elvis paid for his wedding to his wife, Marilyn, also buying the couple an automobile. After Elvis's death, Grob became Charlie Hodge's manager. It is Grob's theory that Elvis was dying of bone cancer at the time of his death from a heart attack, a belief shared by Dr. George Nichopoulos, Kathy Westmoreland, Larry Geller, and Charlie Hodge. Grob is working on a book with Dan Mingori to be titled *The Elvis Conspiracy*, in which he discusses his theory of the cause of Elvis's death.

GROOM, ARTHUR
Manager of Loew's State Theater in Memphis who fired Elvis on May 28, 1952. The girl who ran the concession stand gave Elvis free candy samples, and another usher reported him. Elvis punched the usher, after which both men were fired.

GROSZ, WILL
(1894–1939) Composer and concert pianist born Wilhelm Grosz in Vienna, Austria, on August 11, 1894. Will Grosz (a.k.a. Hugh Williams) composed the first

radio opera, "Kleine Melodie." He composed, with Jimmy Kennedy in 1937, the song "Harbor Lights" and, with Sam Coslow in 1939, the song "Tomorrow Night," both of which Elvis recorded.

GRUBER, FRANZ
(1787–1863) German organist and choir director. In 1818 he and Josef Mohr composed the classic Christmas song "Stille Nacht, Heilige Nacht," ("Silent Night, Holy Night"). Elvis recorded "Silent Night" in 1957.

GRUENWALD HOTEL
West German hotel in Bad Nauheim where Elvis, Vernon Presley, Minnie Mae Presley, Red West, and Lamar Fike lived before they moved to Goethestrasse 14. Herr Schmidt, the hotel's manager, finally had to ask Elvis and company to leave because of their rowdiness. The majority of the hotel's residents were elderly people who were annoyed when Elvis and Red often got into shaving cream or water pistol fights. They once started a small fire during one of their games. It was at the Gruenwald Hotel that Davada (Dee) Stanley first met Vernon Presley in 1959. (They were married on July 3, 1960). Lamar Fike and Red West often spent time at the nearby Beck's Beer Bar, where West got into a number of fistfights with the locals.

GUERCIO, JOE
Orchestra leader whose twenty-eight-member band backed Elvis in Las Vegas. Guercio served as Elvis's musical arranger in Las Vegas from 1969 to 1976.

GUINNESS BOOK OF WORLD RECORDS
Book of various records first compiled by Norris and Ross McWhirter[1] in 1956 under the title of the *Guinness Book of Superlatives*. After the *Bible*, the *Guinness Book of World Records* is the best-selling book in history.

Elvis often read the Guinness book and is listed in it as having the most Gold Disc Awards for an individual—fifty-one (1958–1986)—but globally he is approaching 80 gold singles. Elvis recorded 170 major hit singles and over 80 hit albums. Guinness also mentions that Elvis probably has surpassed Bing Crosby as the most successful recording artist of all time.

GUIZAR, PEPE
Mexican musician and composer who wrote the song "Guadalajara," which Elvis sang in the 1963 movie *Fun in Acapulco.*

GUNS
Elvis enjoyed owning, collecting, and carrying guns of all types, from derringers to M-16s to Thompson sub-machine guns. From the time he was a small boy Elvis wanted to own guns. While performing on stage in the 1970s he wore a two-shot derringer attached to his left leg.

There are a number of stories of Elvis firing one of his guns at various objects. Elvis once shot his favorite pistol, a .22, at a television set in a motel. The bullet ricocheted and hit Dr. George Nichopoulos just under the heart after barely missing Vernon Presley's head. Fortunately, the bullet was spent by the time it reached the doctor. In February 1974 Elvis fired his .22 pistol at a light switch in his Las Vegas hotel room. The bullet went through the wall and barely missed Linda Thompson. He once fired two pistol loads of bullets into his Ferrari when a dead battery failed to start the car's engine. Elvis shot out a chandelier in the Imperial Suite at the Las Vegas Hilton, and he had been known to shoot a TV set if either singer Robert Goulet or Mel Torme appeared on the screen. Elvis once shot a pistol into the ceiling at a restaurant when the service wasn't fast enough.

According to Elvis's bodyguards Red West, Sonny West, and Dave Hebler in their book *Elvis—What Happened?*, Elvis once threatened to kill martial-arts instructor Mike Stone because Stone had taken his wife and daughter.

According to Elvis's bodyguard and step-brother David Stanley in his autobiography *Life with Elvis*, Elvis threatened to kill both Red West and Sonny West after learning about their upcoming book *Elvis—What Happened?* Elvis and Stanley had flown to Los Angeles to find the pair, but Stanley finally talked him out of it as they drove 120 miles per hour down Santa Monica Boulevard in Elvis's black Ferrari.

Whenever Elvis went to see a private showing of the latest James Bond film, he took along his PK Walther pistol because that was the gun that Q Branch had issued to their agent 007.

At the time of Elvis's death in 1977, he owned thirty-seven guns, rifles, and machine guns, and one sawed-off shotgun. (See *Kerr's*)

GUNTER, ARTHUR
(1926–1976) Blues singer and son of a preacher, born in Nashville on May 23, 1926, who was taught to play the guitar by his older brother Larry. He hung around Ernie Young's small record shop in Nashville in 1954 and would bring Young songs he had written. In 1955 Young finally recorded Gunter singing one of his own songs, "Baby, Let's Play House" (Excello 2047). Elvis covered the record, for which both Gunter and Young received composer royalties.

In 1973, while working for the U.S. Post Office, Gunter won $50,000 in the Michigan State Lottery.

[1]The McWhirters were twins born in London in 1925. Both joined the British navy in World War II. That was the first time they had ever been separated. They were reunited when the two ships on which they served collided in the Malta Harbor. Ross McWhirter was killed by terrorists on November 22, 1975.

HAIR

Elvis was born with blondish-brown hair. As a teenager he was inspired to copy actor Tony Curtis's ducktail hairstyle after seeing him in the 1949 movie *City Across the River*. He was later inspired to dye it black (including his eyebrows) because he liked singer Roy Orbison's jet-black hair. Elvis even convinced his mother Gladys to dye her hair black. In the 1964 movie *Kissin' Cousins*, Elvis is shown with blond hair, but it was a wig.

Elvis was often given extra duty in high school ROTC because his hair was too long. He was asked to shave his sideburns for his 1957 movie *Jailhouse Rock*, and when he refused they had to be somehow covered over.

Charlie Hodge dyed Elvis's hair for him approximately every three to four weeks and washed and styled it before every show. Elvis once told Hodge that if he ever went bald, Charlie would be fired. It was Larry Geller who fixed Elvis's hair for his funeral in 1977.

HALDEMAN, OAKLEY

(1909–) Composer born in Alhambra, California, on July 17, 1909. Haldeman composed, with Gene Autry, the song "Here Comes Santa Claus (Right Down Santa Claus Lane)," which Elvis recorded in 1957.

HALEY, BILL

(1925–1981) Country singer turned rock & roll star of the mid-1950s, born William John Clifton Haley Jr. in Highland Park, Michigan, on July 6, 1925. Haley performed many rhythm & blues hits with an uptempo country beat. Before he became one of the first rock & roll performers, Haley headed a country band called the Saddlemen,[1] which played boogie-type country music. In 1951 Haley covered his first noncountry tune when he recorded the rhythm & blues song "Rocket '88' " (Holiday 105), which was originally recorded by Jackie Brenston[2] at Sun Records and released on Chess Records (Chess 1458). Haley's version is considered by some music historians as the first rock & roll recording by a white artist.

In June of 1953 history was made when Bill Haley and His Comets placed the first rock & roll record on the *Billboard* charts with "Crazy Man, Crazy" (Essex 321) on Philadelphia's small Essex label,[3] reaching number twelve. Haley's style and sound were far ahead of anything any other white artists were doing at the time, although his biggest hits, "(We're Gonna) Rock Around the Clock" (Decca 29124), "See You Later,

Alligator" (Decca 29791), and "Shake, Rattle and Roll" (Decca 29204), were all covers of other artists, Sonny Dae and His Knights (Arcade 123), Robert Charles (Chess 1609), and Big Joe Turner (Atlantic 1026), respectively. Haley and Elvis first met on October 20, 1955, at Cleveland's Brooklyn High School auditorium, and again when Haley was touring Europe. Elvis, Red West, and Lamar Fike went to see him and his Comets perform in Stuttgart, West Germany, on October 29, 1958. Haley died on February 9, 1981.

Bill Haley & His Comets recorded a version of Little Richard's "Rip It Up" (Decca 30028) in July 1956, while Elvis recorded it in September 1956. When Elvis recorded "Shake, Rattle and Roll" in 1956, he sang the less suggestive lyrics that Haley had used in his version (Decca 29204), rather than those of Big Joe Turner's sexy release. It is Bill Haley and His Comets' 1955 hit "(We're Gonna) Rock Around the Clock" that is considered to have been the first record of the "Rock Era," which began on July 9, 1955, when the song went to number one on *Billboard*'s Hot 100 chart. Elvis's "Heartbreak Hotel" would be the tenth number-one song of the rock era.

HALL, ROY

(1922–1984) Rockabilly piano player and singer born James Faye Hall in Big Stone Gap, Virginia, on May 7, 1922. With his band the Jumpin' Cats, Hall, formerly a piano player for singer Webb Pierce, was playing rockabilly music on the scene in 1955. In that year, using the pseudonym Sonny David, Hall, with David Williams, composed one of the greatest songs in rock history, "Whole Lotta Shakin' Goin' On," which he would record with his band plus Hank Garland on guitar (Decca 29697). That same year Hall and his Jumpin' Cats recorded a cover of Robert Charles's "See You Later, Alligator" (Decca 29786).[4] Hall also recorded a cover version of Carl Perkins's "Blue Suede Shoes" (Decca 29880), before cutting two unreleased sides at Perkins's label, Sun Records, on December 12, 1957, "Christine" and "I Lost My Baby," with Stan Kesler on bass. Hall was very much on the scene at the birth or rock & roll, but few people knew of him or have heard of him through the years.

In Nick Tosches's 1984 book *Unsung Heroes of Rock 'n' Roll*, Roy Hall claims that in the summer of 1954 Elvis entered his club, the Music Box on Commerce Street in Nashville, looking for a job. Hall told Tosches in 1981: "I was drunk that night, I didn't feel like playing piano, so I told him to get up there and start doing

---

[1]The name of Haley's group was first the Downhomers, then the Four Aces of Western Swing, then the Saddlemen, and finally the Comets.
[2]Ike Turner (future husband of Tina Turner) played piano on the song. In actuality it was Turner's band on the record, but Brenston got the credit because he was the singer.
[3]It was on the Essex label that Bunny Paul recorded a cover of Clyde McPhatter's "Such a Night" (Essex 352) in 1954, a song that Elvis would also record.
[4]Just five records later Decca would release the song's third version by Billy Haley and His Comets (Decca 29791).

whatever in hell it was that he did. I fired him after just one song that night. He wasn't no damn good." It is an interesting story but highly doubtful, since Elvis was living and working in Memphis at the time. It seems to be popular among rockers who didn't make it big to claim they fired Elvis from their acts or clubs. Singer Eddie Dean also claimed to have fired Elvis. There is one segment of Hall's story that might be credible—that he gave Jerry Lee Lewis a job at his club in 1956, and it was there that Lewis first learned Hall's song "Whole Lotta Shakin' Goin' On."

HAMBLEN, STUART

(1908–   ) Singer and composer of country and gospel songs born in Kellyville, Texas, on October 20, 1908. He appeared on radio and in a number of Western movies. In 1952 Hamblen ran for president of the United States on the Prohibition Party ticket. In 1954 he composed the Rosemary Clooney hit "This Ole House" (Columbia 40266), which was also recorded by the Jordanaires that same year (Columbia 2915). Hamblen became inspired to compose gospel songs after he attended a Billy Graham crusade. Hamblen, who has a star on the Hollywood Walk of Fame, is the composer of the songs "Known Only to Him" and "It Is No Secret," both of which were recorded by Elvis.

HAMILL, REV. JAMES E.

Pastor of the First Assembly of God Church at 1885 McLemore, Memphis, which the Presleys attended. In the fall of 1953 Reverend Hamill held an audition at the church to form a gospel quartet. Elvis auditioned and after he sang, Hamill told him, "Give it up." Reverend Hamill gave the eulogy at Gladys Presley's funeral in August 1958.

HAMILTON, GEORGE

(1939–   ) Actor born in Memphis on August 12, 1939. Hamilton is the son of bandleader George Hamilton Sr. (1901–1957), who recorded for Victor Records. His theme song was "That's Because I Love You." Hamilton portrayed country singer Hank Williams in the 1964 movie *Your Cheatin' Heart*, a role for which Elvis was considered. When Hamilton married Alana Collins in 1972, Colonel Tom Parker served as his best man, while his dog, Georgia, gave the bride away.

HAMILTON, ROY

(1929–1969) Popular black singer during the 1950s and 1960s born in Leesburg, Georgia, on April 16, 1929. He died of a stroke at the age of forty on July 20, 1969. Elvis greatly admired Hamilton's singing ability and style and performed a number of his ballads in Hamilton's style. The two met at the American Sound Studios in January 1969, just months before Hamilton's death. While Elvis recorded there during the night, Hamilton recorded during the day. Elvis would sometimes show up early just so he could hear Hamilton sing. From the many demos that were offered to Elvis, he gave Hamil-

ton the Barry Mann–Cynthia Weill song "Angelica" for him to record.

Hamilton recorded several songs that Elvis also recorded: "You'll Never Walk Alone" (Epic 9015) in 1954,[1] "Hurt" (Epic 9086) in 1954, "Without a Song" (Epic 9125) in 1955, and "Pledging My Love" (Epic 9294) in 1958. Elvis also sang Hamilton's 1961 hit "You Can Have Her" (Epic 9434) in concert.

HAMILTON, WILLIAM

Brother of actor George Hamilton, who was a fellow student of Elvis's at Humes High School in Memphis.

HAMMERSTEIN II, OSCAR

(1895–1960) Pulitzer Prize-winning lyricist (*Oklahoma!* and *South Pacific*), born Oscar Greeley Clendening Hammerstein in New York City on July 12, 1895. Hammerstein wrote numerous songs for musicals and films from 1920 until his death, including such classics as "Ol' Man River," "The Sound of Music," and "Indian Love Call." In 1945 he wrote, with Richard Rodgers, "You'll Never Walk Alone," which Elvis recorded in 1968.

HANCOCK, USS

U.S. Navy aircraft carrier moored in San Diego on which comedian Milton Berle's TV show was aired on April 3, 1956. Elvis was the featured guest on the show, and sang "Shake, Rattle and Roll," "Heartbreak Hotel," and "Blue Suede Shoes." During World War II, actor Richard Boone saw action in the South Pacific aboard the *Hancock*. Elvis's sound-alike, Ronnie McDowell, served aboard the vessel while he was in the Navy.

HAND, ALBERT

(–1972) Founder in 1959 of the newsletter *Elvis Monthly*, which originated in Great Britain. Hand met Elvis in Hollywood in August 1964 on the Paramount Pictures lot, where Elvis was filming *Roustabout*. After Hand's death on April 18, 1972, Todd Slaughter took over as the publisher of *Elvis Monthly*.

HANDMAN, LOU

(1894–1956) Composer and pianist born in New York City on September 10, 1894. Handman composed, with Roy Turk, the song "Are You Lonesome Tonight?", which Elvis recorded in 1960.

HANDY THEATER

Memphis theater named for the "Father of the Blues," W. C. Handy on Park Street, where the local Memphis rhythm & blues artists often put on live shows. Elvis sometimes went there in the 1950s to watch them perform.

HANK SNOW JAMBOREE ATTRACTIONS

Management firm operated by Colonel Tom Parker in the mid-1950s. Hank Snow was his featured star. Elvis

---

[1]The flip side of "You'll Never Walk Alone" was "I'm Gonna Sit Right Down and Cry (over You)," which Elvis also recorded. This single, which was released in November 1953, was Hamilton's first record.

toured with the Hank Snow Jamboree in 1955, with Bob Neal as his manager. For a brief time in 1955 Parker directed Elvis's career while Elvis was still under contract to Bob Neal. Parker made the bookings for Neal.

HANKS, AILEENE
Composer of the gospel song "In My Father's House (Are Many Mansions)," which Elvis recorded in 1960.

HARDIN, GLEN D.
Elvis's piano player from 1970 to 1976. Hardin played on Elvis's recording sessions and appears on many of Elvis's live recordings. Hardin left Elvis to become a member of country singer Emmylou Harris's Fallen Angel Band.

In the 1960s Hardin had been a member of Buddy Holly's former band, the Crickets. He never played behind Holly, who ironically had composed some songs under the pen name Charles Hardin. With Jerry Allison and Sonny Curtis, Hardin re-formed the Crickets after Holly's death. They had two recordings, "I'm Not a Bad Guy" (Liberty 55441) and "My Little Girl" (Liberty 55540). They also backed the Everly Brothers on their hit " ('Til) I Kissed You" (Cadence 1369). In 1976 and 1977 Hardin served as the keyboard player for Jonathan Edwards.

Hardin wrote the arrangement for Elvis's version of "Bridge Over Troubled Water" and a number of other songs, as well as performing on them.

HARDY SHOES
Memphis store on Main Street where Elvis bought his boots. When the manufacturer ceased production of his particular pair, Elvis bought the pattern.

HARMON, MURRAY (BUDDY)
Studio musician who played percussion on Elvis's recording sessions from 1958 to 1968, including nine movie soundtracks. Harmon played bongos at Elvis's June 10–11, 1958, recording session, and was the second drummer, with D. J. Fontana, on "It's Now or Never" and "The Girl Next Door Went A'Walkin." He played drums on the Everly Brothers' 1960 hit song "Cathy's Clown" (Warner Bros. 5151). He played on the Johnny Burnette Trio's session in Nashville on July 4, 1956, which included the song "The Train Kept a Rollin' " (Coral 61758).

Harmon once said, "Between them, the Everlys and Elvis played the biggest part in the development of country music to what we have today."

HARMONY, DOROTHY (DOTTIE)
Blond Las Vegas dancer and singer who accompanied Elvis to his preinduction Army physical at Kennedy Veterans Hospital in Memphis on January 4, 1957. She had been visiting Elvis at Graceland.

HARMS, VALERIE
Woman who claims to have organized and founded the first Elvis fan club in 1955. She first saw Elvis perform at a school auditorium in Stamford, Texas, on June 17, 1955.

HARRIS, BECKY
(See *Shirley Jones Gallentine*)

HARRIS, MRS. FAYE
Friend of Gladys Presley's in Tupelo, Mississippi, who lived with her sister, Mrs. Tressie Miller, on Adams Street, only a couple of blocks from Old Saltillo Road. Both ladies were widowed. Mrs. Harris worked with Gladys at the Tupelo Garment Company.

HARRIS, MRS. WEIR
Employee of the Tennessee Employment Security at 122 Union Avenue in Memphis who administered to Elvis the GATB tests (General Aptitude Test Battery) on June 3, 1953. She recommended Elvis when Gladys Tipler of Crown Electric called her looking for a truck driver that same year.

HARRIS, WOODY
(1911–   ) Composer born in New York City on November 1, 1911. Harris composed the lyrics to two Bobby Darin hits, "Splish Splash" (Atco 6117) and "Queen of the Hop" (Atco 6127). He composed the song "I Want You with Me," which Elvis recorded in 1961.

HARRIS, WYNONIE
(1915–1969) Singer and dancer born in Omaha, Nebraska, on August 14, 1915, and nicknamed "Mr. Blues." In 1948 Harris recorded the song "Good Rockin' Tonight" (King 4210), a song that Elvis would record in 1954. It is believed that Elvis may have sung on the "Louisiana Hayride," as well as recorded on Sun Records, "That's the Stuff You Gotta Watch," a song that Harris had previously recorded on New York City's Apollo label (Apollo 361).

Henry Glover, A&R man at King/Federal Records of Cincinnati and producer of Harris's "Good Rockin' Tonight," told Nick Tosches, "When you saw Elvis, you were seeing a mild version of Wynonie."

HARRIS, ZELDA
Woman who, in an article in the *National Examiner*, claimed to have been married to Elvis. She said she first met him at a concert in Mobile, Alabama, and that within twenty-four hours they were married.

HARRISON, GEORGE
(1943–   ) Lead guitarist for the Beatles until the group's demise in 1970. Harrison was born in Liverpool, England, on February 25, 1943. After the Beatles split up, Harrison became a solo performer and movie producer. He was once sued for allegedly plagiarizing the 1963 Ronald Mack composition "He's So Fine" for his 1970 hit "My Sweet Lord." As a Beatle, Harrison composed "Something," a song Elvis recorded in 1973. Harrison visited with Elvis backstage in Las Vegas several times.

HART, CHERYL

Eleven-year-old Schenectady, New York, girl who was dying of aplastic anemia. She requested an auto-graphed photo of Elvis. When Elvis heard about the girl, he airmailed a photo to her in the hospital at Albany, signing it, "To Cheryl, God Bless You, Elvis." Upon receiving the photo, Cheryl rallied for a short time, but died two weeks later.

HART, DOLORES

(1938–) Actress born Dolores Hicks, who played Elvis's romantic lead, Susan Jessup, in the 1957 movie *Loving You* and the romantic lead, Nellie, in the 1958 movie *King Creole*. Elvis dated Hart for a brief time, nicknaming her "Whistle Britches." In 1959 *Photoplay* magazine printed her article "What It's Like to Kiss Elvis." In another magazine article, Dolores Hart claimed that her parents both died of alcoholism and drugs (sleeping pills). Her godmother had been Maria Cooper Janis, the daughter of actor Gary Cooper.

In 1963 Hart retired from acting and finally became a Catholic nun, taking her vows in 1970. Today, she is Mother Superior at the Convent of Regina Laudis in Bethlehem, Connecticut. Speculation by some writers is that Hart may have become a nun[1] because of her love for Elvis.

Hart said of Elvis in 1959, "Elvis is a young man with an enormous capacity of love . . . but I don't think he has found his happiness. I think he is terribly lonely."

HART, LORENZ

(1895–1943) Lyricist, born in New York City on May 2, 1895, who, with Richard Rodgers, wrote the song "Blue Moon," which Elvis recorded in 1956.

HARTFORD, JOHN

(1937–) Singer and composer born in New York City on December 30, 1937. He composed and recorded the song "Gentle on My Mind" (RCA 9175) in 1967, which Elvis recorded in 1969.

HATHCOCK, JOHN

Composer, with Ray Winkler, of the song "Welcome to My World," which Elvis recorded in 1973.

HAWKINS, DALE

(1938–) Singer born Delmar Allen Hawkins in Bossier, Louisiana, on August 22, 1938. Hawkins charted his first song in 1957 with "Suzie-Q" (Checker 863), with a young James Burton playing lead guitar. Hawkins, like Elvis, performed on records with both Burton and Scotty Moore. Hawkins recorded "My Babe" (Checker 906) in 1958, and "Ain't That Lovin' You Baby" (Checker 923) in 1959, both of which Elvis recorded. In the 1960s, after Scotty Moore and Elvis had a falling out, Moore recorded some tracks for Hawkins.

HAYES, BILLY

(1906–) Composer and guitarist born in New York City on February 17, 1906. Hayes composed, with Jay Johnson, the song "Blue Christmas," which Elvis recorded in 1957.

HAYS, LOWELL

Elvis's Memphis jeweler, from whom he bought much of his jewelry (an estimated $800,000 worth). Hays designed Elvis's most expensive ring (11½ carats), which took three months to complete at a cost of $55,000. As a sign of gratitude, Elvis bought him a new Lincoln Continental Mark V automobile. Hays even traveled with Elvis on some concert tours so that he could always be available for Elvis to buy jewelry.

In 1987 the *National Enquirer* gave away the ring Elvis had worn in his final concert. The ring, made by Hays and valued at $13,000, featured forty-seven dia-monds and four sapphires. Hays somehow obtained the ring after Elvis's death.

HAZELWOOD, LEE

(1929–) Guitarist, born on July 9, 1929, who com-posed the song "The Fool," originally recorded by San-ford Clark (Dot 15481) in 1956 and recorded by Elvis in 1970. The writing credit on the record is actually that of Hazelwood's wife, Naomi Ford. Hazelwood also wrote "Your Groovy Self," which Nancy Sinatra sang in the 1968 movie *Speedway*.

HEARD, DICK

(1936–) Composer born Richard Deveaux in Little Rock, Arkansas, on December 15, 1936. Heard, with Eddie Rabbitt, composed the song "Kentucky Rain," which Elvis recorded in 1969.

HEARN, BARBARA

(1937–) Memphis girl Elvis dated off and on for years in the 1950s and 1960s, beginning in high school. Hearn played a bit part in the 1957 movie *Loving You*. While at Elvis's house on Audubon Drive in Memphis, Hearn got the opportunity to hear the acetate for "Any Way You Want Me" before RCA released the song.

HEATH, WALTER HENRY (HY)

(1890–1965) Composer born in Oakville, Tennessee. Heath composed, with Johnny Lange and Joseph Burke, the gospel song "Somebody Bigger Than You and I," which Elvis recorded in 1966. Heath also com-posed such classics as "Mule Train," "Take These Chains from My Heart," and "I'll Never Stand In Your Way."

HEBLER, DAVE

(1937–) Karate champion born in Pittsfield, Massa-chusetts, and bodyguard of Elvis beginning in 1974. Hebler first met Elvis in 1972 as the owner, with Jim Thompson, of a martial-arts studio on Alsta Avenue in

---

[1]Another Hollywood actress, Juanita Quigley, also gave up her acting career to become a nun, in 1951.

Glendora, California. Hebler was blinded in his right eye during childhood by a BB shot. Elvis once gave Hebler a $10,000 Mercedes-Benz 280SL, which had previously been owned by Charlie Hodge, for whom Elvis bought a new Mercedes 450SL. Hebler was fired by Vernon from Elvis's employ on July 13, 1976. He is the coauthor of the 1977 book *Elvis—What Happened?*

HEFFERMAN, DR. ALBERT
Parapsychologist in Lowell, Michigan, who claimed in an article in the *Sun* that Elvis's spirit appeared before him in a séance held in September 1977.

HEIDT, HORACE
(1901–   ) Big-band leader from the 1920s to the 1940s. In 1939 Horace Heidt and His Musical Knights recorded the original version of the song "Tomorrow Night" (Columbia 35203), with vocals by the Heidt Lights. Elvis recorded the song in 1955. Two vocalists with Heidt's band were future actor Art Carney (who sang with Donna and the Don Juans) and Gordon Mac-Rae. Heidt hosted his own radio program, "Pot of Gold," which the Presleys may have listened to in Tupelo. It was one of radio's first giveaway programs. Heidt featured an electric guitar player (a rarity back then) named Alvino Rey, who would in 1961 play ukulele on the soundtrack of Elvis's movie *Blue Hawaii.*

HELDEN
World War I Memorial in Steinfurth, West Germany, that Elvis helped to move to another location while he was a soldier in the U.S. Army.

HELL ON WHEELS
Motto of the U.S. Army Second Armored Tank Division with which Elvis served in Germany.

HELLER, RON
Former University of Southern California football player who was one of the more experienced men to play on Elvis's football team in Bel Air.

HELM, LEVON
(1943–   ) Musician born in Marvell, Arkansas, on May 26, 1943. Helm was the drummer on Ronnie Hawkins and the Hawks' two 1959 hit songs, "Forty Days" (Roulette 4154) (a cover of Chuck Berry's "Thirty Days" [Chess 1610]) and "Mary Lou" (Roulette 4177) (a cover of Young Jessie's 1955 version [Modern 961]). In the 1960s the Hawks evolved into the Band, which backed Bob Dylan. Helm portrayed singer Loretta Lynn's coal-miner father in the 1980 movie *Coal Miner's Daughter.* In 1987 Helm narrated the Cinemax cable TV special "Elvis '56."

Helm first saw Elvis, Scotty Moore, Bill Black, and drummer D. J. Fontana in a high school gymnasium in Marianna, Arkansas, in June of 1955.

HENDRIX, SONNY
Composer, with Dolores Fuller and Lee Morris, of the song "Big Love, Big Heartache," which Elvis sang in the 1964 movie *Roustabout.*

HENLEY, TISH
Dr. George Nichopoulos's nurse who served as Elvis's private nurse during his concert tours. She and her husband, Tom, a deputy sheriff, lived in a trailer behind the main house at Graceland.

(Photo courtesy Don Fink)

HERALD, THE
L. C. Humes High School yearbook. The 1953 edition of the yearbook included Elvis's picture along with the following entry: Presley, Elvis Aron. Major: Shop, History, English. Activities: ROTC, Biology Club, English Club, History Club, Speech Club.

HERNON, PAT
Reporter who interviewed Elvis in the library of the troopship USS *General Randall* on September 22, 1958, at the Military Terminal in Brooklyn. Hernon's interview was included in the EP *Elvis Sails,* released in December 1958.

HESS, DAVID
(1936–   ) Composer born in New York City on September 19, 1936. He attended the Julliard School of Music from 1956 to 1961. Hess composed the song "Come Along," which Elvis sang in the 1966 movie *Frankie and Johnny,* and composed, with Herb Goldberg, the song "Sand Castles," which Elvis recorded for the 1966 movie *Paradise, Hawaiian Style* and which was later cut in the final print. Hess has also composed and recorded under the name David Hill. (See *David Hill*)

HESS, JAKE
Member of the Statesmen Quartet gospel group. James Blackwood, leader of another gospel group, the Blackwood Brothers, believes that Elvis borrowed his ballad/gospel singing style from Hess. Elvis's style of singing "He Knows Just What I Need" is similar to a version once recorded by Hess and the Statesmen.

At Elvis's funeral Hess and two members of the Statesmen sang "Known Only to Him."

HEYMAN, EDWARD

(1907–   ) Composer born in New York City on March 4, 1907. Heyman composed such evergreens as "Body and Soul," "When I Fall in Love," and "I Wanna Be Loved." He composed, with Victor Young, the song "Love Letters," which Elvis recorded in 1966.

HI HAT CLUB

Memphis nightclub of the 1950s, since torn down. In an interview in *Goldmine* magazine, singer Eddie Bond claimed that Elvis sang with his band there in early 1954, before Elvis recorded for Sun Records. Bond also said that one of the songs they performed was "Tryin' to Get to You," which Elvis would later record.

HI-LO MUSIC

Sam Phillips's BMI publishing company, which he established in February 1954 and which owned the publishing rights to such songs as "Blue Suede Shoes" and "Mystery Train," among many other Sun songs. On November 20, 1955, Hill and Range Music bought Hi-Lo Music from Sam Phillips for $15,000. "I Forgot to Remember to Forget" was the only Hi-Lo song for which Hill and Range did not acquire full ownership, as Arnold Shaw had previously bought half of the song's publishing rights.

The first Elvis-recorded song published by Hi-Lo was "You're a Heartbreaker." (See *Arnold Shaw*)

HI RECORDS

Memphis record label founded by record-store owner Joe Coughi, on which Bill Black recorded. Willie Mitchell was the label's producer. Recording for Hi was done at the Royal Recording Studios at 1320 S. Lauderdale in Memphis. Hi's offices were located at Poplar Tunes, Coughi's record store. The label became a subsidiary of British-owned London Records. Coughi had originally formed Hi Records to record Carl Glasscock, a distant cousin of Jerry Lee Lewis. Hi artist Willie Mitchell performed at some of Elvis's New Year's Eve parties in Memphis. (See *Bill Black*)

HICKOCK, AL

Disc jockey for radio station KEYS in Corpus Christi, Texas, who interviewed Elvis at the County Coliseum in San Antonio on October 13, 1956. His interview was offered on a 78 RPM record on the KEYS record label in 1956. It now appears on several bootleg albums.

HILL, BILLY

(1899–1940) Composer born in Boston on July 14, 1899. He composed such standards as "The Last Round-Up," "Wagon Wheels," and "The Glory of Love." Hill composed, with William J. Raskin and Fred Fisher, the song "That's When Your Heartaches Begin," which Elvis recorded in 1957.

HILL, DAVID

(1936–   ) New York City–born singer-composer who made many Elvis demonstration records for various composers because he sounded like Elvis. In 1956 Hill recorded the original version of "All Shook Up" (Aladdin 3359). He composed, with Aaron Schroeder, "I Got Stung," which Elvis recorded in 1958. In 1959 Hill charted two songs of his own, "Two Brothers"(Kapp 266) and "Living Doll" (Kapp 293), the latter an American cover of the British hit "Livin' Lovin' Doll" by Cliff Richard (Columbia DB 4249).[1] He recorded the demo for Elvis's version of the song "It's Now or Never."

Hill, born David Hess, also composed two songs for Elvis under his real name. (See *David Hess*)

HILL, ED

(1935–   ) Singer born February 23, 1935, just forty-six days after Elvis. Hill was a baritone member of the Prophets Quintet, and from 1973 to 1978, he sang with the Stamps Quartet, backing up Elvis. In 1979 Hill authored the book *Where Is Elvis?*

HILL, WANDA JUNE

Secretary who claimed to have been a close friend and confidante of Elvis's for fifteen years, as well as having talked to him on the telephone just hours before his death on August 16, 1977. Hill authored the 1981 book *We Remember Elvis*. She claimed that Elvis paid her way to Graceland, and once offered to buy her and her daughter Julie a house.

HILL AND RANGE MUSIC COMPANY

New York City–based publishing company located at 1650 Broadway, founded by brothers Jean and Julian Aberbach. The Aberbachs bought Sam Phillips's Hi-Lo Music for $15,000. Elvis and Red West later met with the Aberbachs at the Brown Derby restaurant in New York City so that the brothers could explain to Elvis their plans for Elvis's publicity campaign. Colonel Tom Parker, who for a number of years had had a working relationship with Hill and Range through his RCA Victor clients, Eddy Arnold and Hank Snow, directed Hill and Range to set up two subsidiary companies, Elvis Presley Music and Gladys Music, in order to filter partial royalties to Elvis and the Colonel from the royalties the songwriters made when Elvis recorded one of their songs. The arrangement scared away many talented composers, not to mention those who were already writing for him who didn't wish to share their royalties with anyone. Some of those who did write for Hill and Range included composers of the worst songs that Elvis ever recorded, especially for his movies. Among the songwriters employed by Hill and Range were: Bernie Baum, Roy C. Bennett, Dolores Fuller, Bill Giant, Florence Kaye, Don Robertson, Randy Starr, Sid Tepper, and Sid Wayne.

HILLBILLY CAT

Book written in Holland in 1970 by Hans Langbroek.

---

[1] This may have been the first American cover of a British rock & roll hit record.

HILLIARD, BOB

(1918–1971) Composer born in New York City on January 28, 1918. Hilliard composed, with Burt Bacharach, the song "Any Day Now," which Elvis recorded in 1969.

HINE, STUART K.

English missionary and composer, with Rev. Carl Boberg, of the 1886 gospel song "How Great Thou Art," which Elvis recorded in 1969.

HIRSCHHORN, JOEL

Composer, with Al Kasha, of the song "Your Time Hasn't Come Yet, Baby," which Elvis sang in the 1968 movie *Speedway*. He and Kasha have won two Academy Awards for Best Song. (See *Al Kasha*)

HIT PARADER

Popular magazine of the 1950s that included the lyrics to all of the latest hit songs. Elvis first appeared in the July 1956 issue. In a 1957 British edition of the magazine, the following interview with Elvis was published, which if true, changes the "That's All Right (Mama)" story.

" 'You want to make some blues?' He [Phillips] suggested over the phone, knowing I'd always been a sucker for that kind of jive. He mentioned Big Boy Crudup's name and maybe others too, I don't remember. All I know is, I hung up and ran fifteen blocks to Mr. Phillips's office before he'd gotten off the line—or so he tells me. We talked about the Crudup records I knew, 'Cool Disposition,' 'Rock Me Mama,' 'Hey Mama,' 'Everything's All Right,' and others, but settled for 'That's All Right,' one of my top favorites."

HMV

British record label that released Elvis's records in the United Kingdom until September 30, 1958, after which RCA established its own label. HMV ("His Master's Voice") was a subsidiary of British Decca Records. Elvis had fourteen singles, two EPs, one ten-inch LP, and two twelve-inch LPs released by HMV.

HODGE, CHARLES (CHARLIE) FRANKLIN

(1935–) Rhythm guitarist, singer, and aide to Elvis born just a few days before Elvis. Before joining Elvis, Hodge was a member of the Foggy River Boys[1] on Red Foley's TV show "Ozark Jubilee," and sang on songs by Roy Rogers and Gene Autry, often standing on a Coca-Cola box to reach the microphone.

He first met Elvis in 1956 during a Red Foley show. The two became good friends while both were in the Army at Fort Hood and while stationed together in West Germany. They were both aboard the USS *General Randall* en route to Germany. Aboard ship they sang "I Will Be Home Again," which Elvis would record in October 1960 with Hodge singing duet. Hodge, who lived at Graceland for seventeen years, supervised many musical and personal aspects of Elvis's life, and

during his concerts played guitar—and handed Elvis scarves, water, and anything else he needed on stage. Hodge played guitar on several of Elvis's recording sessions. Hodge was one of the three witnesses to Elvis's will. He drove Elvis and Priscilla to Baptist Memorial Hospital the day Lisa Marie was born. As he did with the other members of the Memphis Mafia, Elvis gave Hodge nicknames, "Slewfoot" and "Waterhead."

Hodge claims in his autobiography that he could sing like Elvis, and at times in concert he would complete some of the fadeouts of Elvis's singing. Charlie sang duet with Elvis on the songs "I Will Be Home Again" and "Could I Fall in Love," and at concerts on the gospel song "You Better Run." Elvis, Hodge, and Red West composed the 1965 song "You'll Be Gone." It was Hodge who first suggested to Elvis that he should hire guitarist James Burton for his TCB Band.

Hodge lived in a converted apartment behind the main house at Graceland for many years, and stayed on at Graceland for five months after Elvis's death. He played bit roles in Elvis's films, including a barber in the 1967 movie *Clambake* and a Mexican peon in 1969's *Charro*. Hodge authored the 1985 autobiography *Me 'n Elvis* with Memphis *Press-Scimitar* reporter Charles Goodman, and contributed to Sean Shaver and Hal Noland's book *The Life of Elvis*. Hodge, at five feet, three inches tall, relates in his autobiography that he, Elvis, and some of the other Memphis Mafia members wore lifts in their shoes.

Hodge portrayed himself in the 1979 TV movie *Elvis*, and his character was featured in the 1988 TV miniseries "Elvis and Me." (See *Last Will and Testament*)

HOFFMAN, AL

(1902–1960) Lyricist who was born in Minsk, Russia, on September 22, 1902. With Dick Manning, Hoffman wrote the English lyrics to Charles E. King's "Hawaiian Wedding Song," a song that Elvis recorded in 1961.

HOFFMAN, DR. LESTER

Dentist whose office is located at 920 Estate Street in Memphis. Elvis, with Ginger Alden, went to Hoffman's office to get a cavity filled on the last night of his life, August 15–16, 1977.

HOLDRIDGE, CHERYL

Child actress who played Julie Foster, Wally's girlfriend, on TV's "Leave It to Beaver." She was a former Mickey Mouse Club Mouseketeer. In 1962 she dated Elvis. Miss Holdridge was once the daughter-in-law of Barbara Hutton.

HOLIDAY INN RECORDS

Memphis record label started in 1968 by Sam Phillips and Buddy Cunningham (former Sun artist who played bongos on recordings by Elvis). Phillips named the label after the hotel chain that was founded by Kemmons Wilson in Memphis in 1952, which in turn was

---

[1]The group recorded several songs in 1956, including "The Devil in His Suitcase"/"Inside the Gate" (Decca 29796).

named after the 1942 Bing Crosby/Fred Astaire movie *Holiday Inn*.[1] Phillips had invested some of the money he had received from selling Elvis's contract to RCA Victor into the Holiday Inn hotel chain. Former Sun artist Charlie Feathers recorded for the label.

HOLLADAYS
Sisters Mary and Ginger Holladay and Jeannie Green, who sang backup on six of Elvis's recording sessions in Nashville, Memphis, and Hollywood from 1969 to 1975. Elvis once said about the girls, "They're white chicks, but they sound black."

Buddy Holly. (Photo courtesy Eddie Brandt's Saturday Matinee)

HOLLY, BUDDY
(1936–1959) Popular rock & roll singer born Charles Hardin Holley in Lubbock, Texas, on September 7, 1936. Holly first met Elvis when Elvis played in Lubbock at the Cotton Club on October 15, 1955. Holly and his friend Bob Montgomery opened the show. The pair hosted "The Buddy and Bob Show" on KDAV radio.[2] According to legend, Elvis told Holly and Montgomery that if they came down to the "Louisiana Hayride" he'd get them on the show, but when they did show up, Horace Logan turned them away, and Elvis wasn't there.

Buddy Holly was killed in a private plane crash on February 3, 1959 ("the day the music died"), in which Ritchie Valens (often billed as "the next Elvis"), and Jiles Perry Richardson (the "Big Bopper"), were also killed. Waylon Jennings, a member of Holly's Crickets, gave up his seat to Richardson before the flight. Dion, who was offered a ride, decided to take the bus. In Fargo, North Dakota, a local talent named Robert Vel-

line filled in for the then-missing artists. Velline would soon find success as Bobby Vee. Upon hearing of the tragedy, Elvis sent a telegram to the Hollys' home in Lubbock.

Both Buddy and Elvis recorded the following songs: "(You're So Square) Baby I Don't Care," "Good Rockin' Tonight," "Blue Suede Shoes," "Ready Teddy," "Shake, Rattle and Roll," and "Rip It Up." In 1956 Holly recorded a demo of "I Forgot to Remember to Forget" for KDAV radio. On February 25, 1958, in Fort Lauderdale, Florida, Holly was recorded playing the guitar and singing the Ray Charles blues ballad "Drown in My Own Tears," while being backed by Jerry Lee Lewis on piano.

Buddy Holly said of Elvis, "Without Elvis, none of us could have made it."

HOLLYWOOD PALLADIUM
Site of an auction of items from Elvis's Beverly Hills mansion held on September 15, 1981. The auction brought in only $50,000. The auctioneer was Don B. Smith of Nashville.

HOLLYWOOD WALK OF FAME
Plaques set in cement in Hollywood (cost: $3,000 each) to commemorate the actors, directors, and pioneers of the entertainment world who made a contribution to the arts of motion pictures, television, radio, recordings, and live theater. The first stars were dedicated in 1958. Elvis Presley's star is located at 6777 Hollywood Boulevard, near Highland Avenue.

HOLZER, DR. HANS
Psychic researcher who authored the book *Elvis Presley Speaks*, which claims that Elvis has spoken to two mediums from beyond the grave.

HOME MOVIES
Elvis made many home movies at Graceland and in Bel Air. He had many developed at a Beverly Hills camera shop, but later developed his own film in a darkroom at home when it was discovered that prints of his movies were suddenly surfacing in southern California. Twenty minutes of Priscilla's private movies appeared in the 1981 movie *This Is Elvis*.

HOME OF THE BLUES
Ruben Cherry's record store on Beale Street at Main Street in Memphis where, in the early 1950s, Elvis bought many 78 RPM records by rhythm & blues artists. Future rocker Johnny Burnette also hung out there. The name of the store may have inspired Johnny Cash, Lily McAlpin, and Glen Douglas to compose the 1957 Johnny Cash recording of "Home of the Blues" (Sun 279).

---

[1] It was in *Holiday Inn* that Bing Crosby first sang Irving Berlin's "White Christmas," the biggest-selling song of all time and a song that Elvis would later record.

[2] KDAV (580KC) in 1953 became the first radio station to broadcast nothing but country music. In 1958 Waylon Jennings became a DJ for KDAV before joining Buddy Holly's Crickets.

HONEY
Poodle that Elvis had given Priscilla for a Christmas present.

HOOKSTRATTEN, E. GREGORY
The Presleys' family lawyer who represented Elvis during his divorce proceedings in Los Angeles. It was Hookstratten who chose Priscilla's attorney. Hookstratten has also represented Dan Rowan, Dick Martin, and Vince Scully.

HOOTEN, ARTHUR
Friend of Elvis's in Memphis in the 1950s. He worked for Elvis at Graceland for a short time.

HOPE, BOB
(1903–   ) Actor and comedian born Leslie Townes Hope in London on May 29, 1903. Elvis was requested to perform at the World's Fair in Seattle, but Colonel Tom Parker wanted $250,000. The fair then settled on comedian Bob Hope, who broke an attendance record and was paid $203,000.

HOPKINS, JERRY
Rolling Stone writer and editor who authored the 1971 book *Elvis: A Biography*, possibly the best biography on Elvis yet written, and the 1981 book *Elvis: The Final Years*. He has also written about other rock artists, such as singer Jim Morrison in *No One Here Gets Out Alive*, with Danny Sugarman. Hopkins wrote the thirteen-part radio program "The Elvis Presley Story," which first aired in 1971 and was repeated in October 1977, after Elvis's death. He authored an article on Colonel Tom Parker for the September 22, 1977, edition of *Rolling Stone* magazine.

What made Hopkins's work so great was that he had to conduct all of his research around the subject without ever obtaining permission to interview Elvis or Colonel Tom Parker, since Parker, who loved to shroud his life in mystery, wanted Elvis to do the same.

HOPPER, ED
Memphis filling-station manager whom Elvis was accused of assaulting on October 18, 1956. Elvis had stopped at the station, a crowd gathered, and Hopper told Elvis to move. Witnesses said Hopper then hit Elvis on the back of the head. A fight ensued and six-foot-four-inch tall Aubrey Brown, an attendant, joined the fight. Elvis was cleared of the charge and both men were fired.

HOPPER, HEDDA
(1890–1966) Hollywood gossip columnist born Elda Furry in Hollidaysburg, Pennsylvania, on May 2, 1890. She was known for her exotic hats, and once wrote in her syndicated column that Elvis was a menace to society and a threat to innocent children. She treated him in her columns as if he were Satan himself, writing, "I don't like Elvis Presley because I consider him a

menace to young girls!" Another time she wrote that "he is the most obscene, vulgar influence on young America today."

Hopper's son, William Hopper, played Detective Paul Drake on the TV series "Perry Mason." He also appeared in the 1955 movie *Rebel Without a Cause*, which was one of Elvis's favorite movies.

But like a good gossip columnist, Hedda Hopper eventually became an Elvis fan and couldn't say enough good things about him after she realized her audience loved the singer and that she was in the minority.

HORSES
Animals that Elvis loved and enjoyed riding after he rode his first horse during the making of the 1956 movie *Love Me Tender*. It is thought, however, that Elvis may have ridden horses as a boy in Tupelo. The first horse kept at Graceland was the four-year-old black quarterhorse, Domino, which Elvis had acquired for Priscilla. Elvis then bought the palomino, Rising Sun, for himself, a horse Jerry Schilling had located for him. Many of Elvis's horses were boarded in a barn called the "House of the Rising Sun" (named after Elvis's favorite horse) at Graceland, and at the Circle G Ranch. At one time or another the following horses were owned by Elvis: Rising Sun, Colonel Midnight (Vernon Presley's horse), Lady, Golden Sun, Scout (same name as Tonto's horse), Flaming Star (named after Elvis's movie), Sheba, Thundercloud, El Poco, Beauty (same name as the horse in the movies *Johnny Guitar* and *Giant*), Traveler (same name as Gen. Robert E. Lee's horse), Bear (Tennessee Walker), Keno, Buckshot (same name as Wild Bill Hickock's horse on the TV series of the same name), Sundown, Star Trek (for the TV series), Big Red (Red West's horse), and Mare Ingram (named for the Memphis mayor). Elvis bought horses for everyone at Graceland to ride. After Elvis and Priscilla's divorce in 1973, Priscilla had her horse, Domino, transported to California.

HORTON, HAL
Composer, with Eddy Arnold and Tommy Dilbeck, of the song "I'll Hold You in My Heart (Till I Can Hold You in My Arms)," which Elvis recorded in 1969.

HOUND DOG AFTERSHAVE
One of the hundreds of Elvis-related products manufactured by Factors Etc., Inc.

HOUND DOG ONE
Call sign of the Convair 880 jet aircraft *Lisa Marie*.

HOUND DOG TWO
Call sign of Elvis's Jetstar aircraft.

HOUSES
Chronological order of the houses in which Elvis and his family have lived.[1]

---

[1]The authors are not certain of the chronological order of the houses in Tupelo, because the Presleys seem to have moved around quite a lot, living with many of their relatives over the years until they moved to Memphis.

Tupelo:

- *Berry Street*—Gladys Smith's family house. She and Vernon lived there with her parents just after their marriage in 1933. The couple then rented two other houses on the same street over the years.
- *Old Saltillo Road*—East Tupelo two-room wood frame house where Elvis was born. The house had been built by Vernon Presley with $180 worth of lumber. It was raised off the ground because of flood waters that sometimes hit the town. (It was later given the address of 306 Old Saltillo Road and is presently 306 Elvis Presley Drive). The Presleys had a cow and some chickens out back. When the family traveled to

Elvis's birthplace on Old Saltillo Road. (Photo courtesy Don Fink)

Pascagoula in 1940, while Vernon worked for the WPA, Vernon's father, J. D. Presley, sold the house. On October 1, 1977, the house was painted and given a new roof and wiring, and on January 8, 1978, it was designated as a state historical site by the Mississippi Department of Archives and History. A plaque was erected next to the house. (See *Old Saltillo Road*)
- *Reese Street*—House in which Vernon, Gladys, and Elvis stayed with Vester and Clettes Presley and their baby Patsy.
- *Kelly Street*—The Presleys lived in this house in 1942.
- *Berry Street*—On August 8, 1945, Vernon put $200 down on the $2,000 house built and owned by Orville Bean. Vernon was forced to sell the house on July 18, 1946, to his friend Aaron Kennedy (after whom Elvis was given his middle name) for $3,000, or lose it for back payment of the $30 monthly payments. It was while the family lived on Berry Street that Minnie Mae Presley moved in with them, staying with them for the rest of her life.
- *Commerce Street*—A shopping mall stands on the site today.
- *510½ Maple Street*—South Tupelo house where Vernon, Gladys, and Elvis lived with her cousin Frank Richards, his wife Leona, and their children.
- *Mulberry Alley*—House located by the railroad tracks, city dump, and near the fairgrounds.
- *1010 North Green Street*—Four-room house in the Shakerag section of Tupelo, near the slaughterhouse, which was owned by Dr. Jim Green. That was the last house in Tupelo in which the Presleys lived. After they left Tupelo for Memphis, Gladys's sister, Lillian, and her family moved into the house.

Memphis:

- *572 Poplar Avenue*—First Memphis address of the Presleys after moving from Tupelo. They lived in the crowded boarding house from September 12, 1948, to September 20, 1949, with fifteen other families, all sharing the same kitchen and single lavatory facility. The Presleys paid $35 a month rent for one room on the ground floor. The sixteen-unit building, which was owned by Clifton and Mallie Johnson, had previously been a large single-family house.
- *185 Winchester Street*, Apartment 328—Memphis address of the Lauderdale Courts, where the Presleys lived from Septem-

Lauderdale Courts at 185 Winchester Street. (Photo courtesy Don Fink)

ber 20, 1949, to January 7, 1953, in a two-bedroom, ground-floor apartment. Their telephone number was 37-4185. The rent in the federally funded, 433-unit housing project was $35 a month. Bill Black's mother, Mrs. Ruth Black, also lived in the housing complex. The previous tenant of the Presleys' apartment had been Joseph P. Massey and his family. A fellow tenant, Mrs. Mary Guy, sometimes complained that Elvis played his guitar at night.
- *398 Cypress Street*—Memphis apartment house where the Presleys lived from January 7, 1953, to April 1953, after being evicted from 185 Winchester Street. The monthly rent here was $52.
- *462 Alabama Street*—Memphis address of the two-story brick apartment building where the Presleys lived from April 1953 to late 1954, after leaving their apartment at 398 Cypress Street. They paid $50 a month rent, plus electricity and water. The Presleys' telephone number was 37-4138. Minnie Mae

462 Alabama Street. (Photo courtesy Don Fink)

Presley slept on a cot in the dining room. Elvis lived at 462 Alabama when he recorded "My Happiness"/"That's When Your Heartaches Begin" at the Memphis Recording Service in the summer of 1953. Ruth Black, the mother of Bill Black, lived in apartment B at nearby 465 Alabama Street. The landlady was named Mrs. Dubrovner.
- *2414 Lamar Avenue*—Memphis brick house rented by the Presleys from late 1954 to mid-1955. Their telephone number was 37-4185, as it had been several months earlier. It was within walking distance of Airway's Used Cars (see entry). In 1968 the two-story house was converted into the Tiny Tot Nursery School.

1414 Getwell Street. (Photo courtesy Don Fink)

- *1414 Getwell Street*—Rented Memphis house in which the Presleys resided from mid-1955 to May 11, 1956. Their telephone number was 48-4921.
- *1034 Audubon Drive*—Single-story, three-bedroom residence of the Presleys in the fashionable section of Memphis from May 11, 1956, to March 1957. This was the first house that Elvis bought after becoming a professional singer. Elvis bought the green and white house for $40,000 in April 1956.

1034 Audubon Drive. (Photo courtesy Don Fink)

He added a swimming pool to the backyard. Elvis used one of the bedrooms to keep his vast collection of stuffed animals. One story has it that a neighbor became upset because Gladys hung her wash outside. The Presleys' telephone number was unlisted. The ranch-style house sold for $55,000 in March 1957, when Elvis and his parents moved to Graceland.
- *3764 Elvis Presley Boulevard (Graceland)*—Memphis residence of Elvis Presley from March 1957 to August 16, 1977 (day of Elvis's death) (See *Graceland*)

Southern California:
- *565 Perugia Way*—Address in Bel Air of the Oriental-style house Elvis rented in 1960, after moving from the Beverly

565 Perugia Way. (Photo courtesy Jeff Wheatcraft)

Wilshire Hotel. The house, which had been designed by Frank Lloyd Wright, and once owned by the Shah of Iran, was the first house that Elvis rented in Hollywood. The Bel Air home had also previously been owned by Ali Khan and his wife, actress Rita Hayworth. Elvis lived there until 1963, when he moved to 1059 Bellagio Road; he moved back in late 1963, staying there until late 1965. Some sources state that Elvis installed a two-way mirror in one of the bedrooms, as well as another in the pool house. The actual house appeared in the 1988 TV miniseries "Elvis and Me."
- *1059 Bellagio Road*—Mediterranean-style house in Bel Air that Elvis rented after moving from the house at 565 Perugia Way. The house had a huge marble entrance and a bowling alley in the basement. It was in this house that the incident occurred in which Elvis supposedly hit a girl with a pool cue after she had called him a "son of a bitch," as told in the book *Elvis— What Happened?*

10550 Rocco Place. (Photo courtesy Jeff Wheatcraft)

- *10550 Rocco Place*—Bel Air house in Stone Canyon, near the Bel Air Hotel, in which Elvis lived from late 1965 until May 7, 1967. Elvis rented this modern ranch-style house.
- *1174 Hillcrest*—Multilevel, three-bedroom French Regency house located in the exclusive Trousdale Estates near Los Angeles. It was built in 1961 with an Olympic-sized swimming pool and bought by Elvis for $400,000 on May 7, 1967. Richard Davis and Joe Esposito stayed there with Elvis and Priscilla, as did Charlie Hodge and Patsy and Gee Gee Gambill at times, living in the guest cottage. The Presleys then moved to 144 Monovale in late 1967.
- *144 Monovale*—Two-story house in the Holmby Hills area of Los Angeles, surrounded by two acres of lawns and orange groves, all enclosed by a high fence, where Elvis and Priscilla lived from late 1967 (when he left is unknown). The house, which was once owned by actor Robert Montgomery, the father of actress Elizabeth Montgomery (former wife of actor Gig Young, who appeared with Elvis in the 1962 movie *Kid Galahad*), had a pool table, a projection room, and a soda fountain. Sonny and Judy West, with their son, stayed in a loft above the den, which had previously been a gym. Elvis paid $400,000 for the house. After Elvis and Priscilla's divorce, Priscilla stayed there until she moved to a two-bedroom apartment near the beach. In 1975 Elvis sold the house to actor Telly Savalas for $650,000.
- *825 Chino Canyon Road*—Palm Springs single-story, white stucco, Spanish-style house Elvis had built in 1965 for $85,000, located on two acres and surrounded by a fence. The fifteen-room house also featured a swimming pool. Elvis, who recorded two songs there, "I Miss You" and "Are You Sincere," with the vocal group Voice, willed the house to Lisa Marie. In 1979 singer Frankie Valli bought the house for $385,000.
- *1350 Leadera Circle*—5,000-square-foot house on a Palm Springs estate leased by Elvis in April 1970. The previous

owner was Marjorie McDonald, an heir to the McDonald Hamburger empire.

Other Houses:

- *906 Oak Hill Drive*—Killeen, Texas, house that Elvis rented from Judge Crawford for $1,400 a month for himself, Gladys, Vernon, and Minnie Mae beginning in May 1958, while he was stationed at Fort Hood, Texas. Previously they lived in a trailer. The house was a four-bedroom bungalow.
- *Goethestrasse 14*—Five-bedroom, white stucco house in Bad Nauheim, West Germany, where Elvis, Vernon, and Minnie Mae lived for fifteen months from 1958 to 1959 during Elvis's stay in the Army. The rent was $800 a month. The landlady, Frau Pieper, lived in a room off the kitchen.
- *4152 Royal Crest Place*—Memphis address of the ranch-style house that Elvis bought for his girlfriend Ginger Alden. The house is one block from Graceland.
- *1167 Summit Avenue*—Priscilla Presley's Beverly Hills, California, house address.
- *1850 Dolan Road*—Memphis address of Vernon Presley's ranch-style house, situated adjacent to Graceland. The house, which had been built in 1961 at a cost of $25,000, was bought in 1978 by Hobart and Bonnie Burnette, the owners of the Hickory Log restaurant. David Stanley married his wife, Annie, in the house.

HOVATAR, ALICE

Nineteen-year-old Monroe, Louisiana, girl who was killed during an all-night vigil at the gates of Graceland on August 18, 1977—the day of Elvis's funeral. A car driven by Treatise Wheeler III, of Memphis, drove through the crowd, killing Hovatar and Juanita Johnson. Wheeler was charged with drunk driving and second-degree murder. (See *Tammy Baiter*)

HOWARD, EDWIN

Reporter with the Memphis *Press-Scimitar*. On July 27, 1954, at Marion Keisker's suggestion, Howard became the first reporter to interview Elvis for his column, "The Front Row."

HOWARD, KEN

Composer, with Alan Blaikley, of the song "I've Lost You," which Elvis recorded in 1970; and, with Geoff Stephens and Alan Blaikley, of the song "Heart of Rome," which Elvis recorded in 1971.

HOWARD, RICHARD

Composer of the religious song "I Believe in the Man in the Sky," which Elvis recorded in 1965.

HOWE, BONES

Record producer who produced and engineered Elvis's recording sessions for the 1968 NBC-TV special "Elvis."

HUFF, LEON

Composer, with Jerry Butler and Kenny Gamble, of the song "Only the Strong Survive," which Elvis recorded in 1969.

HUGO AND SAMSON

Elvis's two poodles.

HUGUENY, SHARON

Actress whom Elvis dated in 1963. Hugueny had previously been married (1961–1962) to Robert Evans, the head of Paramount Studios. Evans, previously an actor, had played a bit role in the original 1937 film version of *Kid Galahad*.

HULETT, THOMAS

President of Concerts West, which booked the many cities where Elvis performed from 1970 to 1976.

HUMBARD, REVEREND REX

(1919–) Evangelist born Alpha Rex Emanuel Humbard in Akron, Ohio, on August 13, 1919. Humbard, who was the host of the "Cathedral of Tomorrow" TV series broadcast on 543 stations), spoke briefly at Elvis's funeral on August 18, 1977. On September 25, 1977, Humbard told his congregation about his meeting with Elvis at the Hilton Hotel in Las Vegas in December 1976. It was the first time that Elvis had met Humbard. He greeted him and his wife, Maude Aimee, backstage. Humbard believed that Elvis sensed his life was coming to an end when he last talked to him, that Elvis had felt that "time was short."

Humbard and the Cathedral Singers recorded "Put Your Hand in the Hand" (RCA 9995) in 1971, a song Elvis would record that same year.

HUMES HIGH SCHOOL
(L. C. HUMES HIGH SCHOOL)

All-white, 1,700-student Memphis high school, located in a three-story red brick building at 659 North Manassas Street, which Elvis attended from 1949 to 1953, while Thomas C. Brindley served as the principal. In 1950 Elvis worked in the library. Singer Johnny

L. C. Humes High School in 1953. (Photo courtesy Jeff Wheatcraft)

Burnette was also a student there. Elvis graduated from Humes High[1] on June 3, 1953, in Class 202. The school, which was named for Laurence Carl Humes, a past president of the Memphis Board of Education (1918–1925), is presently used as a junior high, but back then it served grades seven through twelve. The school had previously been named the North Side High School. Humes High fielded the Tigers football team, which Elvis attempted to join. He went out for a few practices, but quit because the coach, Rube Boyce Jr., gave him a hard time about his hair. On April 9, 1953, Elvis performed at the school's annual Minstrel show. He had been encouraged by teacher Mildred Scrivener. Singing John Lair's "Keep Them Cold Icy Fingers Off of Me," he got the loudest applause from the student audience, which allowed him to sing an encore, his version of Teresa Brewer's "Till I Waltz Again With You."[2] The school program, which also featured Red West playing trumpet, misspelled Elvis's name as Elvis *Prestly*.

In 1955 Elvis would give a benefit show at Humes High. In January 1973 the L. C. Humes High School Marching Band played "Happy Birthday to You" in front of Graceland in honor of Elvis's thirty-eighth birthday.

HUNT, DR. WILLIAM R.

Physician who began practicing medicine in 1913. On January 8, 1935, he delivered at 4:00 A.M. the stillborn Jesse Garon and at 4:35 A.M. Elvis Aaron. Dr. Hunt's fee was $15, which the family didn't pay. The birth took place at the Presleys' home on Old Saltillo Road. His office was located above Riley's Jewelry Store in downtown Tupelo.

The authors of this book have obtained photocopies of the Standard Certificate of Birth for both Elvis and Jesse Presley from the Mississippi State Board of Health. These birth certificates were filled out and signed by Dr. William R. Hunt on January 10, 1935. Interestingly, Jesse Garon's middle name was misspelled "Garion." Dr. Hunt correctly spelled Elvis's middle name "Aaron." We also have a copy of a birth certificate filled out by Vernon Presley in which he misspelled Aaron as "Aron" and incorrectly listed his age as twenty (he was eighteen) and Gladys's as twenty-one (she was twenty-two). Dr. Hunt correctly listed Vernon's age but listed Gladys as being twenty-one. The question we pose is this: Which birth certificate is the official one? No matter how you look at it, one of the twins had his middle name misspelled on his birth certificate!

HUNTER, IVORY JOE

(1922–1974) Blues singer and composer born in Kirbyville, Texas, on October 10, 1922. Hunter was the seventh of thirteen children. His biggest hits were "I Almost Lost My Mind" (MGM 10578) and "Since I Met You Baby" (Atlantic 1111). Elvis recorded five of Hunter's estimated 7,000 lifetime compositions: "My Wish Came True," "I Need You So," "I Will Be True," "It's Still Here," and "Ain't That Lovin' You Baby" (with Clyde Otis), which Elvis recorded in 1958. Hunter also recorded several demo records for Elvis.

HURRICANE CAMILLE

Hurricane that hit the Gulf Coast. Elvis gave a concert in Jackson, Mississippi, on May 5, 1975, for the benefit of the victims of the hurricane in McComb. Elvis's concert raised $108,000.

HYLAND, BRIAN

(1943–   ) Singer, born in Queens, New York, on November 12, 1943, who made many demonstration records for composers because he could sound like Elvis. Hyland's hits included "Sealed with a Kiss" (ABC Paramount 10336) in 1962 and "Gypsy Woman" (UNI 55240) in 1970.

In August 1960, Elvis's "It's Now or Never" knocked Hyland's "Itsy Bitsy Teenie Weenie Yellow Polka Dot Bikini" (Kapp 342) out of first place on *Billboard*'s Hot 100 chart.

HYMAN, B. D.

(1948–   ) Daughter of actress Bette Davis and William Sherry, born Barbara Sherry. Hyman made her movie debut at age three in her mother's 1951 movie *Payment on Demand*. She and her mother have had an ongoing feud, which culminated when Hyman wrote her autobiography *My Mother's Keeper* in 1985, infuriating Davis. In Hyman's book she tells how she met Elvis on the Paramount Pictures lot in 1961 while her mother was filming *Pocketful of Miracles* and Elvis was filming *Blue Hawaii*. Hyman stopped going to Elvis's set when she thought her mother was making too much of her friendship with Elvis, even speculating what it would be like to be Elvis's mother-in-law. Hyman was in constant fear that her mother would approach Elvis and introduce herself to him as Hyman's mother.

---

[1]Over on the other side of Memphis, Booker T. Jones and Maurice White, future drummer for Ramsey Lewis and leader of Earth, Wind and Fire, respectively, were classmates in the same grade school. Booker T. would later attend Booker T. Washington High, where his father taught math and science. Both Johnny Ace and Rufus Thomas had also previously attended Booker T. Washington High.
[2]Some sources indicate the encore was "Old Shep."

I.C. COSTUME COMPANY

Firm from which Elvis purchased the jumpsuits and costumes for his Las Vegas appearances.

"I LOVE YOU, ELVIS"

Words yelled out by John Lennon while he sang "Hound Dog" at the One to One Benefit Concert at Madison Square Garden on August 30, 1972. The charity concert had been organized by journalist Geraldo Rivera.

"I NEVER KNEW A GUITAR PLAYER THAT WAS WORTH A DAMN!"

Statement made by Vernon Presley when Elvis was a young lad. Elvis never let Vernon forget his words, as Elvis had them inscribed on a plaque he displayed at Graceland.

I'VE GOT A SECRET

Television game show hosted by Garry Moore. One of the girls who worked at the Methodist Publishing Company got hold of the pair of pink trousers that Elvis had split at his first recording session in Nashville in 1956. She appeared on the show with that fact as her secret.

ILLIKAI HOTEL

Hotel in Waikiki in Honolulu shown behind actor Jack Lord during the opening credits of the 1969–1980 TV series "Hawaii Five-O."[1] Elvis stayed in room 2225 for six weeks during the filming of the 1966 movie *Paradise, Hawaiian Style.*

IMMACULATE CONCEPTION

Catholic all-girls high school located at 1725 Central Avenue in Memphis attended by Priscilla Beaulieu while she was living with Vernon and Dee Presley at Graceland. Priscilla enrolled at the school, which had been nicknamed "Virginity Row" by the boys in Memphis, in January 1962, at the age of seventeen, and graduated on June 14, 1963. The principal was Sister Mary Adrian Mully.[2] When she graduated, Elvis gave Priscilla her first car, a red Corvair. Priscilla was an

(Photo courtesy Don Fink)

average student, who some felt never applied herself. In her autobiography, Priscilla admits cheating on her algebra final. Elvis did not attend her graduation in order not to cause a disturbance, so he waited outside the cathedral in his car until the ceremony was concluded.

IMPERIAL QUARTET

One of several vocal groups that, beginning in 1969, backed Elvis in concert. In 1969 the Imperial Quartet consisted of Jake Hess, Jim Murray, Gary McSpadden, and Armand Morales. The group later consisted of Terry Blackwood, Joe Moscheo, Armond Morales, and Jim Murray. Other members included Roger Wiles and Greg Gordon. The group won a number of Grammy Awards for their gospel music: "No Shortage" (1975), "Sail On" (1977), and "Heed the Call" (1979).

In August 1971 the Imperials left Elvis to perform with singer Jimmy Dean. The members of the group were unhappy with the salary that Colonel Tom Parker was paying them. They were replaced by J. D. Sumner and the Stamps.

IMPERSONATORS AND IMITATORS

It has been suggested that 5,000 different entertainers made a living impersonating Elvis after his death. This figure seems too high; perhaps several hundred is a more reasonable estimate. There have always been Elvis imitators, but after Elvis's death many became popular because the real Elvis was no longer available. Some imitators are very good and some are very bad. The imitators can be divided into two classes, the look-alikes and the sound-alikes. Elvis enjoyed his imitators, but after his death his estate attempted to bring legal action against them, so that an "official" Elvis impersonator could be authorized. Many of the Elvis fan clubs have wisely adopted the policy of not endorsing any particular Elvis imitator. Listed are some (but not all) of the Elvis imitators (if we have omitted anyone we apologize):

Dave Carlson of Chicago
David Carrol of Minneapolis
Bubba Cauldron
Frankee Cee of San Jose, California
Andy Childs of Memphis
Johnny Cramier (Johnny C) of Knoxville, Tennessee
Terry Dene of Great Britain
El-Ray-Vis of Valparaiso, Indiana ("The Prince of Elvis Magic")
Lee Elvis of Brooklyn
Roger Franke of Blue Springs, Missouri
Ron Furrer of St. Louis
Kenny G. From of Hampshire, England
Tony Galvan of San Francisco
Jim Gutierrez of Vacaville, California
Bill Haney of West Memphis, Arkansas
Johnny Harra
Connie Hartman of Warren, Ohio
Tim Hilliard of Chicago

[1] It was the longest-running TV cop show in prime time history.
[2] Some sources give her name as Sister Adrienne.

Ron Hutchinson of Cheshire, England
Kiyoshi Ito of Tokyo
Richard Larsen of Noah, Utah
Little El (Marcel Forestieri) of Newcastle, Delaware
Rich Locknane of Carlsbad, New Mexico
Steve Long
Mike Malone of Parin, New Jersey
Alan Meyer
Dena Kay Patterson of Edgerton, Kansas (female imitator)
Nick Paulichenko of Hamilton, Ontario
Richard Presley
Terry and Jerry Presley (twin brothers)
Tony Presley
Charles Randall of Fort Worth, Texas
Gil Rogers of Gloucester, Massachusetts
Johnny Rusk of Seattle
Rick Saladan of Philadelphia
Bud Sanders of El Paso, Texas
Rick Saucedo of Chicago
Larry Seth (Big El) of Blackwood, New Jersey
Jonathan Von Brana of Honolulu
Elvis Wade (Wade Cummings)
Dennis Wayne of San Jose, California
Steve Wayne of Springfield, Illinois
Julian Whitaker of Beltsville, Maryland (as Jesse Aaron)
Jim White of Manchester, England
Pete Wilcox of Laurel Canyon, California
John Wilson of Nashville
Dennis Wise of Joplin, Missouri (See entry)

Canadian Elvis imitator Douglas Roy is the only imitator to have actually shared the stage with Elvis. On May 6, 1976, at Lake Tahoe, Nevada, Elvis invited Roy on stage from the audience. Roy then sang "Hound Dog." Terry Dene is considered to be the first British Elvis impersonator. He began copying Elvis in the mid-1950s, heading his band the Dene-Agers. Female Elvis impersonator Tessie Blue had been married to Elvis impersonator Johnny Harra before she married pro wrestler Pat O'Connor, the onetime world heavyweight wrestling champion. Jimmy Breedlove is one of only a few black Elvis imitators. Imitator Bruce Borders is the mayor of Jacksonville, Indiana.

Three of Elvis's imitators have named themselves after Elvis film characters: Marvin Benefield became Vince Everett from *Jailhouse Rock*, Les Grey became Tulsa McLean from *G.I. Blues*, and Deke Rivers took his name from Elvis's character in *Loving You*.

INFLUENCES ON ELVIS
Sideburns (Rudolph Valentino, truck drivers)
Hair color (Roy Orbison)
Hairstyle (Tony Curtis)
Movements (Preachers,[1] various rhythm & blues artists)
Gospel music (Jake Hess, Golden Gate Quartet, the Blackwoods)
Pop music (Dean Martin, Billy Eckstine, Roy Hamilton)
Rhythm & blues music (Rufus Thomas, Arthur Crudup, Roy Brown)

Country music (Jimmie Rodgers, Hank Williams, Jim Reeves, Tennessee Ernie Ford, Red Foley, Hank Snow, Jimmy Wakely, Bill Monroe)
Acting (James Dean, Marlon Brando)

INGRAM, WILLIAM B.
Mayor of Memphis, who on January 4, 1967, proposed naming the new $4.3 million Mid-South Coliseum the Elvis Presley Coliseum, only to have his suggestion objected to by several commissioners. The name change never took effect.

INK SPOTS
Easy-listening black quartet from the 1930s and 40s. The group's theme song was "If I Didn't Care." The members were Orville (Hoppy) Jones, Ivory (Deek) Watson, Charlie Fuqua,[2] and Bill Kenny (there were others). The group split into two factions in 1952. Elvis enjoyed listening to the Ink Spots. When he recorded the acetate "My Happiness" and "That's When Your Heartaches Begin," he was recording two Ink Spot songs. Bill Kenny, who served as the group's lead singer for years, composed "There Is No God but God," which Elvis recorded in 1971.

In 1951 Kenny and the Song Spinners recorded "It Is No Secret (What God Can Do)" (Decca 27326), which Elvis would record in 1957.

Elvis's grave site at Graceland. (Photo courtesy Don Fink)

[1]Many small-town preachers were dynamic speakers and singers who moved around quite a bit while they sang. Elvis once recalled seeing a preacher jump on top of a piano. Although Elvis never went to this extreme, another church-raised rocker, Jerry Lee Lewis, did.

[2]Charlie was the uncle of Harvey Fuqua, producer and onetime lead singer of the 1950s vocal group, the Moonglows.

INSCRIPTION ON ELVIS'S GRAVE BY VERNON PRESLEY

He was a precious gift from God
We cherished and loved dearly.

He had a God-given talent that he shared
with the world. And without a doubt,
He became most widely acclaimed;
capturing the hearts of young and old alike.

He was admired not only as an entertainer,
But as the great humanitarian that he was;
For his generosity, and his kind feelings
For his fellow man.

He revolutionized the field of music and
Received it's highest awards.

He became a living legend in his own time,
Earning the respect and love of millions.

God saw that he needed some rest and
Called him home to be with Him.

We miss you, Son and Daddy. I thank God
that he gave us you as our son.

INSIDE ELVIS

Book written by martial-arts instructor Ed Parker, and published in 1978 by Rampart House, Ltd.

INTERNAL REVENUE SERVICE (IRS)

After Elvis's death the IRS claimed that the Presley estate owed $10 million in back taxes. During his lifetime Elvis had no tax shelters and no financial adviser to help him with his large income. Vernon Presley, who had a poor education, was perplexed by the complicated tax forms involved in handling Elvis's finances, so he turned it over each year to the IRS, allowing them to make out Elvis's return. Although Vernon tried his best to curb Elvis's spending habits, he just didn't have a head for money management.

Colonel Tom Parker once remarked in 1958, "I consider it my solemn duty to put Elvis in the 90 percent tax bracket." This is interesting because Parker himself no doubt used tax shelters and investments to keep himself out of any high tax bracket, as most people normally did.

Elvis even battled the IRS in his 1968 movie *Speedway*.

INTERNATIONAL HOTEL
(See *Las Vegas Hilton*)

INTERNATIONAL KEMPO KARATE ASSOCIATION (IKKA)
Emblem that Elvis had affixed to his guitar. The emblem was on the guitar he used in the 1973 TV special "Elvis: Aloha from Hawaii."

IS ELVIS ALIVE?
A 1981 book written by Steven C. Chanzes which claims that Elvis is not dead and that the body at Graceland is that of a man who had been a terminally ill Elvis look-alike. He further claims that the fake death was set up by Charlie Hodge. After the book's publication, Hodge filed a lawsuit in Fort Lauderdale, Florida, demanding $1 million for libel. *The Globe* serialized part of the book in 1982.

IVY, TROY
(1929–   ) Gardener employed as a temporary worker at Graceland with whom Elvis had an altercation on September 19, 1967. The verbal argument ended when Elvis decked Ivy.

J

JACKSON, AL
(1935–1975) Musician born on November 27, 1935, the same year as Elvis. As a drummer he replaced Willie Hall with Booker T. & the M.G.s. Jackson played drums at Elvis's recording session at Stax Studios on July 21–25, 1973. Previously, Jackson played drums for Jerry Lee Lewis on a session in 1962 that produced "Good Rockin' Tonight." On October 1, 1975, during a robbery, Jackson was shot to death.

JACKSON, PEE WEE
Black man who was employed as one of the many gardeners at Graceland. Jackson died one day after working past quitting time in order to get the yards looking good for Elvis, who was returning to Graceland the next day.

JACKSON, WANDA
(1937–   ) Female rockabilly singer of the 1950s, born Wanda Lavonne Jackson in Maud, Oklahoma, on October 20, 1937. Jackson appeared on the same bill with Elvis on the "Hank Snow Jamboree" in July and August 1955, and a two-week tour that traveled from Abilene, Texas, to St. Louis in October 1955 and again in early 1956.

JACKSONVILLE, FLORIDA
Birthplace of singer Pat Boone in 1934 and the site of a Hank Snow All-Star Jamboree concert on May 13, 1955. It was the first Elvis Presley performance at which the crowd caused a riot. There was so much excitement that Elvis had his clothes torn off by some of the more emotional females in the audience.[1] A local Jacksonville disc jockey named Johnny Tillotson (the future singing star) was in the audience. Other performers on stage included Hank Snow, Slim Whitman, Faron Young, the Davis Sisters (Skeeter and Georgia),[2] the Carter Sisters, and the Wilburn Brothers.

JACOBS, AL
(1903–   ) Composer born Mercedes Gabail in San Francisco on January 22, 1903. Jacobs worked at KSFO radio as a disc jockey. He composed, with Jimmy Craine, the song "Hurt," which Elvis recorded in 1976.

JACOBS, LITTLE WALTER
(1930–1968) Chess Records artist born Marlon Walter Jacobs in Marksville, Louisiana, on May 1, 1930. He performed as Little Walter (and His Jukes).[3] He originally recorded the song "My Babe" in 1955 (Checker 811). Elvis recorded "My Babe" in August 1969.

JAILHOUSE ROCK
Title of a book about the bootleg records of Elvis Presley from 1970 through 1983, written by Lee Cotten and Howard A. DeWitt and published by Pierian Press in 1983.

JAMBOREE ATTRACTIONS
Colonel Thomas Parker's organization that during the early 1950s booked artists throughout the South, including Hank Snow, the Carter Family, and Minnie Pearl.

JAMES, MARK
Composer of the songs "Moody Blue," "Raised on Rock," and "Suspicious Minds," and co-composer, with Wayne Carson and Johnny Christopher, of "Always on My Mind," and, with Steve Tyrell, "It's Only Love," all of which Elvis recorded. James, born Francis Rodney Zambon, who originally recorded with his group the Mark James Trio for Jamie Records, recorded the original versions of "Suspicious Minds" (Scepter 12221) and "Moody Blue" (Mercury 73718). He also recorded the tribute song "Blue Suede Heaven" (CBS Records).

JANS, TOM
Composer of the song "Lovin' Arms," which Elvis recorded in 1973.

JANUARY 8, 1935
Birthday of Elvis Aaron Presley. Others who were born on January 8 include actor Jose Ferrer (1909), singer Shirley Bassey (1937), actress Yvette Mimieux (1939), singer Little Anthony Gourdine (1941), singer David Bowie (1941),[4] guitarist Jimmy Page (1944), Robbie Krieger of the Doors (1946), and Terry Sylvester of the Hollies (1947).

JARRETT, MICHAEL
Composer of the song "I'll Be Home on Christmas Day" and with Sonny Charles, of the song "I'm Leavin'," both of which Elvis recorded in 1971.

JARVIS, FELTON
(1936–1981) Music producer born Charles Felton Jarvis. Jarvis served as Elvis's producer at RCA beginning in 1966, taking over for Chet Atkins. In addition to Elvis, Jarvis had previously produced such artists as Lloyd Price, Fats Domino, Tommy Roe, and Gladys Knight and the Pips for ABC Paramount Records in Atlanta. In 1962 he produced Tommy Roe and the Satins' hit single "Sheila" (ABC Paramount 10329),

---

[1]In 1981, singer Johnny Tillotson said there was no riot, and that the story was created by Colonel Parker for publicity.
[2]In reality, the Davis Sisters were not related. Skeeter's real name is Mary Frances Pencik and her first partner, Bee Jay, who was killed in an automobile accident on August 2, 1953, was named Betty Jack Davis. Betty's sister, Georgia, filled in for her after her death.
[3]Originally named the Night Cats. Little Walter took the name Juke from his number one rhythm & blues hit record in 1952, "Juke."
[4]David Bowie, born David Robert Jones, had to change his name since there was already another singer named David Jones, a member of the Monkees.

which had originally been recorded on Memphis's Judd Records (Judd 1022), the label owned by Judd Phillips, the brother of Sam Phillips.

Jarvis, who kept a pet boa constrictor in a sack in his office, left RCA in 1970 to devote full time to Elvis's recordings and live performances, remaining with Elvis until the singer's death. Jarvis accepted the Hall of Fame Award on behalf of Elvis at Don Kirshner's Third Annual Rock Music Awards in 1977 (the two previous winners were the Beatles and Chuck Berry).

Thanks to Jarvis, Elvis again began to record some good material. Elvis's career had been neglected for many years, with no one overseeing the quality of material he recorded. Colonel Parker was too busy thinking up ways to make more money, Chet Atkins had become too involved in RCA management, and Hill and Range Music was still trying to find composers who were willing to write songs for Elvis at a reduced royalty, regardless of the material's quality. Jarvis definitely saved Elvis's sagging career in the early 1970s. Elvis appreciated what Jarvis was trying to do, and in 1970 financed an operation in which Jarvis was given a new kidney. Elvis once confided in Jarvis after a recording session, saying to him rather downheartedly, "I'm just so tired of being Elvis Presley."

After Elvis's death in 1977, Jarvis produced several sessions for Carl Perkins. With James Fitz, Jarvis produced Ronnie McDowell's songs used in the 1979 TV movie *Elvis*. In 1959 Jarvis himself had recorded the song "Don't Knock Elvis" (Viva 1001), proving that he had always been an Elvis fan. In 1977, after Elvis's death, RCA released the limited production album *Felton Jarvis Talks About Elvis*, which included a Guitar Man belt buckle. Jarvis died of a stroke in January 1981, at the age of forty-six.

JASMINE

Elvis's favorite flower. Jasmine is the main ingredient of many perfumes and the essence sells for $4,090 a pound.

JAYCEES AWARD

(See *Ten Outstanding Young Men of America*)

JEANS

Pants that Elvis wore throughout most of his childhood, as did other boys of his era. As an adult, Elvis preferred to wear slacks and clothing that was entirely different from what he had worn during his early days in Tupelo.

JEFFRIES, AL

(1940–   ) Researcher who wrote an article in *The Globe* (August 10, 1982) claiming that Elvis faked his death and is alive and living in hiding until the day he is ready to face his adoring fans again.

JEFFRIES, ALAN

Composer, with Doc Pomus, of the song "I Feel That I've Known You Forever," which Elvis sang in the 1965 movie *Tickle Me*.

JENKINS, MARY

Black cook (a.k.a. Mary Fleming) at Graceland for fourteen years beginning in 1963. Jenkins worked from 7:00 A.M. to 2:00 P.M. each day, fixing Elvis meals upon request, including one of his favorites, her home-made vegetable soup. Elvis bought Jenkins a house, a new Cadillac, and six other vehicles over the years.

Jenkins portrayed herself in the 1981 movie *This Is Elvis*. In 1984 Jenkins wrote the book *Elvis, The Way I Knew Him*, as told to Beth Pease.

JENNER, BRUCE

(1949–   ) Athlete born in Mt. Kisco, New York, on October 28, 1949. Jenner was called "The World's Greatest Athlete" after he won the decathlon at the 1976 Olympic Games in Montreal at the age of 26. He totaled a record 8,618 points (8618 is the name of his production company). A descendant of Edward Jenner, the British physician who developed the vaccine for smallpox, he made his movie debut in the 1980 film *Can't Stop the Music*, which was directed by actress Nancy Walker (her debut as a director). In late 1979 and 1980, Jenner became the steady boyfriend of Elvis's former girlfriend Linda Thompson. Thirty-one-year-old Jenner and 30-year-old Thompson were married on January 5, 1981. Jenner had previously been married to Chrystie Jenner and had a two-year-old son, Burt, who served as the best man in his wedding to Linda.

After Jenner's split with Linda Thompson in 1987, he became involved with Donna Rice, Gary Hart's "Monkey Business" former acquaintance.

JENNINGS, WAYLON

(1937–   ) Country singer born in Littlefield, Texas, on June 15, 1937. Jennings started out as a disc jockey at Lubbock, Texas, radio station KDAV, and joined Buddy Holly's touring Crickets after Holly bought him his first bass guitar. In the late 1960s Jennings became a successful country singer. In the 1970s he and veteran musician Willie Nelson teamed up to become known as the Outlaws. In 1973 Jennings and Billy Joe Shaver composed "You Asked Me To," which Elvis recorded that year.

After Elvis's death in 1977, Jennings was one of many people who suggested that Elvis probably faked his own death in order to return to a quiet, secluded life. (See *Buddy Holly*)

JERRY LEWIS TELETHON

Annual (since 1966) Labor Day telethon hosted by comedian Jerry Lewis to raise money for the Muscular Dystrophy Association. Elvis donated $5,000 on August 31, 1975, while he was in the hospital. The pledge was announced on the air by Frank Sinatra.

JEWISH COMMUNITY CENTER

Memphis recreation center, located at 6560 Poplar Avenue, where Elvis played racquetball before he built his own court.

JIMMIE RODGERS'S "THE FATHER OF COUNTRY MUSIC" FESTIVAL

Annual musical event held in Meridian, Mississippi. To get to the first festival, held on May 26, 1953, Elvis hitchhiked 240 miles from Memphis with his guitar and entered the talent contest, in which he finished second. He again played the festival in 1955, this time as a professional singer.

JO HAYNES SCHOOL OF DANCING

Memphis dancing school, located 4679 Highway 51 South, where Priscilla Beaulieu studied ballet. While learning to dance, Priscilla got an opportunity to appear in several recitals, under an assumed name.

JOHN CARPENTER

Role played by Elvis (as a ghetto doctor) in the 1969 movie *Change of Habit*. Elvis used the name Dr. John Carpenter when making airline reservations.

By a strange coincidence, John Carpenter is the name of the man who directed the 1979 TV movie *Elvis*.

JOHN, ELTON HERCULES

(1947–   ) Popular British piano player and singer of the 1970s, born Reginald Dwight in Middlesex, England, on March 25, 1947. He chose the name Elton from Elton Dean, a member of his early band, Bluesology, and the name John from six-foot-seven-inch tall Long John Baldry, the leader of a soul band for which he had played. He later legally added the middle name of Hercules.

Elton John was the first white performer to appear on the TV music show "Soul Train," hosted by Don Cornelius. Singer Neil Sedaka[1] made his successful recording comeback in the 1970s on John's Rocket Records label. In 1975, after learning that Elton John had bought his manager, John Reid, a $40,000 Rolls-Royce, Elvis bought his manager, Colonel Tom Parker, an airplane (which Parker smartly turned down because of the maintenance cost of such a luxury).

Elton John was Lisa Marie Presley's favorite rock singer. Elvis arranged for the two to meet on Lisa Marie's birthday on February 1, 1975. In July 1976 John sent a note to Elvis after John's appearance in Washington, D.C., offering to write a song for him, but Elvis never took Elton up on the offer.

JOHN JONES

Code name used by Elvis when he called Lucy de Barbin at her home, according to her autobiography *Are You Lonesome Tonight?* He would ask for Lucy Ware, her code name.

JOHNNY

Phillip Morris cigarette bellboy played by Johnny Roventini, a forty-nine-pound, forty-seven-inch tall midget (sometimes the part was played by Freddy Douglas). Johnny would yell, "Call for Phillip Mor-rees" in the radio and TV commercials.

Johnny and Elvis appeared on the same bill at the Jimmie Rodgers Memorial Day Celebration in Meridian, Mississippi, on May 25, 1955. (See *Jimmie Rodgers Memorial Day Celebration*)

JOHNSON, BLAKE

Hairdresser who owned Blake's Coiffure in Memphis. Elvis had his hair trimmed on several occasions at Blake's at the suggestion of Gladys Tipler, the wife of James Tipler, who owned Crown Electric, where Elvis was working at the time (1953–54).

JOHNSON, DON

(1950–   ) Film and television actor born in Galena, Missouri, on December 15, 1950. He was once married to actress Melanie Griffith, the daughter of actress Tippi Hedren. Johnson played Detective James (Sonny) Crocket (a.k.a. Sonny Burnette), who owned a crocodile named Elvis on the TV series "Miami Vice." In the 1981 TV movie *Elvis and the Beauty Queen*, Johnson portrayed Elvis from 1972 until his death in 1977, putting on forty pounds in order to play the role.

JOHNSON, ENOTRIS

Composer, with Robert (Bumps) Blackwell and Richard Penniman (Little Richard), of the song "Long Tall Sally," which both Little Richard and Elvis recorded in 1956. Johnson rewrote Little Richard's risqué lyrics. He contributed the idea for the song—consisting of only a few lines of lyrics that she had written on a piece of paper.

JOHNSON, FRANCIS

Elvis's first sergeant at Fort Chaffe, Arkansas, during Army indoctrination. (See *Fort Chaffee, Arkansas*)

JOHNSON, JAY W.

(1903–   ) Composer born in Ellis, Kansas, on March 23, 1903. Johnson composed, with Bill Hayes, the song "Blue Christmas," which Elvis recorded in 1957.

JOHNSON, JUANITA JOAN

Monroe, Louisiana, girl who was killed during an all-night vigil at the gates of Graceland on August 18, 1977, the day of Elvis's funeral. A car driven by Treatise Wheeler III of Memphis swung through the crowd, instantly killing her and Alice Hovatar. Wheeler was charged with drunk driving and second-degree murder. (See *Tammy Baiter*)

JOHNSON, LYNDON BAINES

(1908–1973) Thirty-sixth president of the United States, born in Gillespie County, Texas, on August 27, 1908. He served as president from November 22, 1963, to January 20, 1969. All members of President Johnson's immediate family shared the initials LBJ (Lady Bird Johnson, Lucy Baines Johnson, Lynda Bird Johnson). President Lyndon Johnson visited Elvis on the set of the 1966 movie *Spinout*.

---

[1]Elton John sang duet with Sedaka on Sedaka's 1975 hit "Bad Blood," which was released on Elton's own Rocket Records (Rocket 40460).

JOHNSON, NICK
Kentucky state representative from Harlan, Kentucky, who resigned from his draft board because Elvis received a sixty-day deferment in January 1958 in order to finish the movie *King Creole*. Johnson was quoted as saying, "I cannot conscientiously ask any mountain boy to serve the same country unless afforded the same treatment as Presley."

JOHNSON, SUSAN
One of Elvis's teachers at Humes High School in Memphis, who taught Elvis in the ninth grade. She once said of Elvis, "When one of our boys or girls does something special, like Elvis Presley, they should put an extra gold star after his name, because our children have farther to go than most." She also said of Elvis at Humes: "Elvis liked to sing songs to a few friends during lunch or at assembly."

JOHNSON, VAN
(1916–   ) Hollywood actor born in Newport, Rhode Island, on August 25, 1916. Johnson was offered the role of Vernon Presley in the film *The King of Rock and Roll*, which was never completed. According to sources, Elvis supposedly had said that if there ever was a movie about him, he wanted Van Johnson to portray his daddy.

JOHNSON, WILLIAM
Composer, with George McFadden and Ted Brooks, of the gospel songs "Bosom of Abraham" and "I, John," both of which Elvis recorded in 1972.

JOHNSTON, WILLIAM
Composer, with Joy Byers, of the songs "There Ain't Nothing Like a Song," which Elvis sang in the 1968 movie *Speedway*.

JON BURROWS
Code name (sometimes given in sources incorrectly as John Burroughs) used by Elvis for receiving personal mail or telephone calls. Elvis used the name Jon Burrows when he traveled to Washington, D.C., to visit President Richard Nixon. Sometimes he used the name Col. Jon Burrows Jr. or Dr. John Carpenter.

On American Airlines stationery, Elvis wrote President Nixon a letter in 1970, telling him that he used the code name Jon Burrows. (See *John Carpenter*)

JONES, DAVID
Composer, with Larry Banks, of the song "Soldier Boy," which Elvis recorded in 1960. The song, however, is credited to David Jones and Teddy Williams.

JONES, DORY
Composer, with Ollie Jones, of the song "Finders Keepers, Losers Weepers," which Elvis recorded in 1963; and composer, with Bunny Warren, of the song "Rubberneckin'," which Elvis sang in the 1969 movie *Change of Habit*.

JONES, IRA
Army master sergeant who served as Elvis's platoon sergeant in Freidburg, West Germany. Elvis chauffeured Jones in a jeep.

JONES, OLLIE
Composer, with Dory Jones, of the song "Finders Keepers, Losers Weepers," which Elvis recorded in 1963.

JONES, THOMAS S.
Army lieutenant colonel who gave Elvis his orders promoting him to sergeant in January 1960. Elvis got a $22.94 a month raise.

(Photo courtesy Eddie Brandt's Saturday Matinee)

JONES, TOM
(1940–   ) Singer, born Thomas Jones Woodward in Pontypridd, South Wales, on June 7, 1940, whose powerful voice and vitality remind one of Elvis.

When Jones appeared at the Flamingo Hotel in Las Vegas in 1968, Elvis and Priscilla drove there to see his act. Elvis visited him backstage—their first meeting. The two entertainers hit it off and became lifelong friends, with Elvis giving Jones a TCB medallion, which Jones now wears. In the 1970 documentary *Elvis—That's the Way It Is*, Jones sent Elvis a note, which Elvis read: "Here's hoping you have a very successful opening and break both legs—Tom Jones."[1] In 1971 it was announced that managers Colonel Tom Parker and Gordon Mills were making plans for Elvis and Jones to costar in a movie together, but nothing came of the proposal. One story has it that when Jones was appearing in Las Vegas in 1969, Elvis booked the room next to Jones's and paid all of his bills.

Tom Jones was probably the only singer who Elvis thought threatened him, because he had both the voice and the sex appeal, which had always been Elvis's strong points. Both envying and admiring Jones, Elvis "borrowed" some of Jones's stage mannerisms and movements for his act.

Elvis recorded two Tom Jones hits, "I'll Never Fall in Love Again" (Parrot 40018) in 1976 and "Without Love" (Parrot 40045) in 1969. Both artists recorded versions of "Green Green Grass of Home," "Any Day Now," "Yesterday," "Hey Jude," "Polk Salad Annie," "Proud Mary," "You've Lost That Lovin' Feelin'," and "The Impossible Dream."

JORDAN, WILL
Comedian who portrayed TV host Ed Sullivan in the Broadway musical *Bye Bye Birdie* and in the 1979 TV movie *Elvis*. Jordan also portrayed Sullivan in the Broadway play *Elvis—The Legend Lives* and in the movies *The Buddy Holly Story* (1978) and *I Wanna Hold Your Hand* (1978).

JORDANAIRES
Gospel and country vocal group with whom Elvis recorded. The Jordanaires have been called "The Sound Behind the King." Formed in Springfield, Missouri, in 1948, the Jordanaires originally included Bill Matthews, Monty Matthews, Cully Holt, and Bob Hubbard. The members who backed Elvis were: Gordon Stoker (first tenor), Neal Matthews[2] (second tenor), Hoyt Hawkins (baritone), and Hugh Jarrett (bass).[3] The Jordanaires first began singing backup for such artists as Red Foley and Hank Snow. They sang on the Grand Ole Opry for thirteen years.

At the Cotton Carnival in Memphis in early 1954, featuring Eddy Arnold, Elvis came backstage to meet the Jordanaires, remarking, "If I ever cut a record, I want to use you guys singing background with me." Elvis again met the Jordanaires when he appeared at the Grand Ole Opry. Their first recording session with

Elvis occurred on July 2, 1956, producing the hit songs "Hound Dog," "Don't Be Cruel," and "Any Way You Want Me." Beginning with the New York City recording session of June 10–11, 1958, Ray Walker replaced Hugh Jarrett. Songs produced during that session include: "I Need Your Love Tonight," "A Big Hunk o' Love," "Ain't That Loving You, Baby," "A Fool Such As I," and "I Got Stung." Contrary to the popular version of the Elvis legend, the Jordanaires did not sing backup on Elvis's first RCA recording session in Nashville when he recorded "Heartbreak Hotel." Gordon Stoker, Brock Speer, and Ben Speer provided the vocal backup.[4] Although Stoker was a member of the Jordanaires, he was the only one present. While attending David Lipscomb High School in Nashville, Ray Walker sang in a quartet with fellow student Pat Boone. In 1956 the Jordanaires won first place on "Arthur Godfrey's Talent Scouts" TV series.

Through the years, the Jordanaires have backed a number of performers, among them: Ricky Nelson,[5] Marty Robbins, Kitty Wells, Jim Reeves, Tennessee Ernie Ford, Don Gibson, Connie Francis, and Johnny Horton. Specifically, they provided vocal accompaniment on Jimmy Dean's 1961 hit "Big Bad John" (Columbia 42175); Marie Osmond's 1973 hit "Paper Roses" (MGM 14609), which was produced by Sonny James; Merle Haggard's 1977 album *From Graceland to the Promised Land*; and on Tom Jones's 1981 album *Darlin'*. Neal Matthews authored the 1985 book *Elvis: A Golden Tribute*.

The Jordanaires also provided backup to Ronnie McDowell's singing in the 1979 TV movie *Elvis*[6]. The group recorded the album *The Jordanaires Sing Elvis's Gospel Favorites*. They appeared in several Elvis movies, including *Loving You* (1957), *King Creole* (1958), and *G.I. Blues* (1960).

Elvis once told the Jordanaires, "Let's face it, if it hadn't been for you guys, there might not have been a me." It was a kind compliment, although not a bit true.

JOSEPH, CAROLYN
Stephens College (Columbia, Missouri) student whom Elvis dated in the late 1950s.

JUANICO, JUNE
Auburn-haired, blue-eyed receptionist from Biloxi, Mississippi, whom Elvis dated in 1955–56. Juanico first met Elvis backstage after a concert in Biloxi on June 26, 1955. They went swimming, waterskiing, and horseback riding together.

---

[1] In the theater, it is bad luck to wish another performer "good luck" prior to a performance. The phrase "break a leg" is used instead.
[2] Neal Matthews taught Ricky Nelson to play the guitar.
[3] In 1960 Hugh Jarrett, James (Buzz) Cason, and Richard Williams recorded "Blue Velvet" as the Statues on Liberty Records.
[4] The fact that the Jordanaires were not present at the January 1956 recording session has caused confusion for writers, researchers, and for Elvis himself. At the Mississippi-Alabama Fair and Dairy Show in 1956, Elvis even introduced the group as the one that sang backup when he recorded "Heartbreak Hotel." Also contrary to legend, the Jordanaires did not sing backup on "I Was the One" and "I Want You, I Need You, I Love You."
[5] The Jordanaires can be heard on some of Nelson's biggest hits: "Believe What You Say," "Lonesome Town," and "Poor Little Fool." Their backing on Nelson's "Have I Told You Lately That I Love You" was identical to the version that they had performed on Elvis's recording.
[6] On the soundtrack record album The Jordanaires' name was misspelled "Jordanairs." In the movie they appeared at Gladys's funeral portraying the Blackwood Brothers. A younger group portrayed them in the movie.

JUDD RECORDS
Sheffield, Alabama, record company begun by Judd Phillips in the summer of 1958. He and his brother, Sam Phillips, had previously dissolved their partnership. Judd's biggest hit was "Rockin' Little Angel" by Elvis sound-alike Ray Smith in 1960 (Judd 1016). Judd Records was the original label on which Tommy Roe and the Satins recorded "Sheila" in 1960. Judd was sold to NRC Records in 1960. (See *Sam Phillips, Sun Records*)

JUBILEE FOUR, THE
Vocal group who sang, with the Carole Lombard Trio, backup on Elvis's "What'd I Say" at the *Viva Las Vegas* soundtrack recording session in July 1963 and on the *Girl Happy* soundtrack session in June–July 1964.

JUKE BOX JURY
British TV series that reviews the latest record releases. On July 29, 1967, Elvis's "Long Legged Girl" was reviewed by panelists Englebert Humperdinck, Lulu, Ted Ray, and Beverley Adams. They voted it a hit.

JUSTIS, BILL
(1926–1982) Musician born in Birmingham, Alabama, on October 14, 1926. In 1957 Justis recorded his biggest instrumental hit, "Raunchy" (Philips 3519), which added a new slang word to the American vocabulary. Justis, who had been a musical director at Sun Records in the 1950s, played sax on Elvis's *Kissin' Cousins* soundtrack recording session in October 1963.

KAEMPFERT, BERT

(1923–1980) Music producer, composer, and arranger born in Hamburg, Germany, on October 16, 1923. In 1961 Kaempfert charted the number one record and million-seller "Wonderland By Night" (Decca 31141). His instrumental knocked Elvis's "Are You Lonesome Tonight?" out of first place on *Billboard*'s Hot 100 chart. As the producer for Polydor Records of West Germany, he was the first man to record the Beatles when in 1961 he hired them to back singer Tony Sheridan on Sheridan's recording of "My Bonnie"/"When the Saints Go Marching In" (Polydor 24 673).[1] Kaempfert, with Ben Weisman and Kay Twomey, composed "Wooden Heart," which Elvis sang in the 1960 movie *G.I. Blues*. In 1965 Kaempfert, Charles Singleton, and Eddie Snyder composed "Spanish Eyes," which Elvis recorded in December 1973.

KAHANE, JACKIE

Comedian who was the opening act for many of Elvis's live performances. Kahane, who had previously worked with singer Wayne Newton, was selected by Colonel Tom Parker because of his clever jokes. He often told the audience at the end of Elvis concerts, "Ladies and gentlemen, Elvis has left the building." Kahane was once booed off the stage at Madison Square Garden by an audience that became impatient to see and hear Elvis. Kahane, who delivered the eulogy at Elvis's funeral on August 18, 1977, recorded the tribute record "Requiem for Elvis" (Raintree 2206).

KALMANOFF, MARTIN

Composer, with Aaron Schroeder, of the song "Young Dreams," which Elvis sang in the 1958 movie *King Creole*.

KANABE

Piano at the Ellis Civic Auditorium in Memphis on which Elvis first learned to play in the 1950s. He later bought the center a new piano and had this instrument moved to Graceland.

KANTOR, DR. EDWARD

Beverly Hills ear, nose, and throat specialist who tended to Elvis for fifteen years.

KARATE

Elvis's martial-arts hobby for over eighteen years, which he first became interested in while in the Army in Germany. Elvis, whose karate name was Tiger, held an eighth-degree black belt. He studied tae kwon do with Kang Rhee and kempo with Ed Parker. While practicing on September 16, 1974, Elvis broke his wrist—his only serious injury.

Elvis received his black belt in 1960 and his second degree in 1963. He skipped the third degree, and over the years earned his fifth (professor of the art), sixth (senior professor), and seventh degree (associate master), promoted by Kang Rhee. For the eighth degree (master of the art), he was promoted by Ed Parker.

The TV series "Kung Fu," starring David Carradine, was one of Elvis's favorites because of his interest in the martial arts. Elvis used karate in several of his films, including: *G.I. Blues* (1960), *Wild In the Country* (1961), *Blue Hawaii* (1961), *Follow That Dream* (1962), *Kid Galahad* (1962), *Roustabout* (1964), and *Harum Scarum* (1965).

Priscilla Presley, who was taught karate by Mike Stone, attained a green belt.

KARATE

Name of Elvis's speedboat that he sometimes took out on McKeller Lake, just outside of Memphis. *Karate* had a hull designed by Gaspar, and a 50 HP Johnson outboard motor.

KAREN

(1953–1963) Victim of cerebral palsy who was befriended by nurse Lena Canada. Nurse Canada wrote the book *To Elvis, With Love* about Karen. Karen and Elvis were pen pals until she died in 1963 at the age of ten. She died after writing a letter to Elvis, with her last words being the title of Canada's book, *To Elvis, With Love*. *McCall's* magazine first carried the story.

KARGER, FRED

(–1979) Musical director of the 1964 movie *Kissin' Cousins* and of the 1966 movie *Frankie and Johnny*. Karger composed, with Sid Wayne and Ben Weisman, the songs "Chesay" and "We Call on Him," which Elvis recorded. With Alex Gottlieb and Ben Weisman, he arranged "Frankie and Johnny." He was the son of Maxwell Karger, one of the founders of MGM. Fred Karger, the third husband of Jane Wyman (Ronald Reagan was her second), was Marilyn Monroe's voice coach at Columbia Pictures. Karger died seventeen years to the day after Monroe.

KASHA, AL

(1937–   ) Singer and Academy Award–winning composer born in Brooklyn on January 22, 1937. Kasha composed, with Joel Hirschhorn, the song "Your Time Hasn't Come Yet, Baby," which Elvis sang in the 1968 movie *Speedway*.

---

[1] When record dealer Brian Epstein began getting requests for the German record in his store in Liverpool (the first was from eighteen-year-old Raymond Jones at 3:00 P.M. Saturday, October 28, 1961) he sought out the Beatles. After seeing them perform at the Cavern, Epstein became convinced they had tremendous potential. He soon became their manager and persuaded Polydor to release "My Bonnie" in England.

Kasha and Hirschhorn won their Oscars for "The Morning After" (from *The Poseidon Adventure*) and "We May Never Love Like This Again" (from *The Towering Inferno*). Maureen McGovern, who sang the songs on screen, took "The Morning After" to number one on the charts. Both men were also nominated twice for Tony Awards. In 1986 they authored the autobiography *Reading the Morning After*.

KATZ DRUG STORE
Memphis store, located in the Airways Shopping Center at 2256 Lamar Avenue, where on September 9, 1954, Elvis, Scotty Moore, and Bill Black performed for the store's grand opening. They played from the back of a flatbed truck[1] that store manager Peter Morton had rented from Leonard McTyier for $10. One of those in the audience watching and listening was Johnny Cash, and another was Elvis's future secretary Becky Yancey. Elvis, Scotty, and Bill received $65 for their performance. Katz Drug Store is now known as Scagg's.

KAYE, BUDDY
(1918–) Musician and composer born in New York City on January 3, 1918. Kaye composed, with Phil Springer, the song "Never Ending," which Elvis recorded in 1964. He also composed, with Ben Weisman, "Almost," "Change of Habit," and "Let Us Pray." With Ben Weisman and Delores Fuller, Buddy Kaye composed "Cindy, Cindy" and "Have A Happy."

KAYE, FLORENCE
New York City–born composer of forty-one songs sung by Elvis in films. (For a list of her forty-one compositions, see *Bernie Baum*)

KAY'S DRIVE-IN
Memphis restaurant where Elvis and his friends sometimes went to eat and hang out in the early 1950s.

KEATON, MIKE
Man who worked for Elvis at Graceland for a short time in 1964.

KEESLER AIR FORCE BASE
Mississippi training base where Elvis performed in the NCO club on June 27–28 and November 6 and 8, 1955. In September and October 1950, Airman Johnny Cash was stationed at Keesler, where he learned communications.

KEFAUVER, ESTES
(1903–) Politician born Carey Estes Kefauver in Monroe County, Tennessee, on July 26, 1903. Kefauver was the Democratic vice presidential nominee in 1956. As a U.S. senator from Tennessee, Kefauver, on March 5, 1960, placed a tribute to Elvis into the Congressional Record.

KEISKER, MARION
College-educated secretary to Sam Phillips at the Memphis Recording Service and Sun Records during the 1950s. Keisker, who had held the title of "Miss Radio of Memphis," and had been an announcer with WREC Radio, joined Phillips at Sun in early 1953, Phillips's only full-time nonfamily employee. She was present when Elvis entered the Memphis Recording Service to cut "My Happiness" and "That's When Your Heartaches Begin" in the summer of 1953. On that occasion, Keisker asked Elvis who he sounded like. "I don't sound like nobody," Elvis said. It was Keisker's foresight that made her turn on the master Ampex tape recorder while Elvis was singing and then to ask him for his address and telephone number, writing on the note: "Good ballad singer, hold." Most of the books written about Elvis, as well as the 1979 movie *Elvis*, have repeated her famous exchange with Elvis.
"What kind of singer are you?"
"I sing all kinds."
"Who do you sound like?"
"I don't sound like nobody."
"Hillbilly?"
"Yeah, I sing hillbilly."
"Who do you sound like in hillbilly?"
"I don't sound like nobody."
Keisker should rightfully be given credit for discovering Elvis. (This does not in the least take away from Sam Phillips's foresight and patience in developing Elvis. Surely, Sam Phillips can be considered a genius in the history of rock music.)

Keisker even contributed a verse to the song "I Don't Care If the Sun Don't Shine," which Elvis recorded in September 1954. In September 1957 Keisker quit Sun Records to join the Air Force, where she received a commission. Keisker, who had just been promoted to the rank of captain at the time that Elvis was in the service, met with Elvis in West Germany, where she was working with the Armed Forces Television Network as an assistant manager.

In the 1979 TV movie *Elvis*, Keisker was portrayed by Ellen Travolta, the elder sister of actor John Travolta. (See *Memphis Recording Service*)

KENNEDY, AARON
Tupelo, Mississippi, friend of Vernon Presley's. Kennedy and his wife, Mattie Sue, were living at the home of J. D. Presley, Vernon's father, at the time of Elvis's birth on January 8, 1935, so Vernon gave his son, Elvis Aaron, Kennedy's name, misspelling it on the birth certificate as Aron. In 1946 J. D. Presley sold Kennedy the house on Berry Street in Tupelo. (See *Houses*)

KENNEDY, CAROLINE BOUVIER
(1957–) Daughter of the thirty-fifth president of the United States, John Fitzgerald Kennedy, and Jacqueline Kennedy Onassis. Caroline, who was born in

---

[1]John Lennon and his group, the Quarrymen, made their professional debut in 1957 playing from the back of a flatbed lorrie (truck) in Liverpool.

New York City on November 27, 1957, was one of the photo journalists for *Rolling Stone* magazine who covered Elvis's funeral in August 1977. Her article, "Graceland: A Family Mourns," appeared in the September 22, 1977, edition (#248) of *Rolling Stone*.

Like Lisa Marie, Caroline had an aircraft named after her—*Caroline* (Air Force One, a Boeing 707)—while her father was president.

KENNEDY, JERRY
Denver police captain and head of the vice squad to whom Elvis gave a new 1976 Lincoln Continental Mark IV, valued at $13,000 on January 14, 1976. Kennedy was given the car because of his previous assistance to Elvis as a security guard. In addition, Elvis gave Kennedy's wife a new Lincoln of her own. Elvis was vacationing in Vail, Colorado, at the time. (See *Dr. Gerald Starkey, Kumpf Lincoln-Mercury*)

KENNEDY, JIMMY
British composer of many show tunes, including in 1937, with Will Grosz (a.k.a. Hugh Williams), "Harbor Lights," which Elvis recorded in 1954.

KENNEDY VETERANS HOSPITAL
Memphis medical facility located at 1030 Jefferson Avenue where Elvis underwent his preinduction physical on January 4, 1957. When he was inducted into the Army on March 24, 1958, Elvis signed his loyalty oath and took his mental examinations and blood tests at the Kennedy Veterans Hospital. In August of 1954, shortly after recording "That's All Right (Mama)" and "Blue Moon of Kentucky," Elvis performed at the hospital's benefit show.

KENNY, BILL
(See *The Ink Spots*)

KENT, ARTHUR
(1920–   ) Composer born in New York City on July 12, 1920. Kent composed, with Ed Warren, the song "Take Good Care of Her," which Elvis recorded in 1973.

KENT, WALTER
(1911–   ) Composer born in New York City on November 29, 1911. Kent composed such songs as "White Cliffs of Dover" and "Come Rain or Come Shine." He composed, with Kim Gannon and Buck Ram, the song "I'll Be Home for Christmas," which Elvis recorded in 1957.

KERBY, RAYMOND
Guitar player with the hillbilly band the Ripley Cotton Choppers, who in 1953 became the first white artists to record for Sun Records. Producer Sam Phillips was so impressed with Kerby that he asked him if he and his band would back a new young singer that Phillips had met. In what is perhaps the biggest mistake of Kerby's

life, he and his band turned down the chance to back the new singer, Elvis Presley, because they already had a lead singer. Phillips then made the offer to Bill Black and Scotty Moore, and the rest is history.

KERKORIAN, KIRK
Owner of the International Hotel and an associate of Colonel Tom Parker's, who signed Elvis to play at his hotel in Las Vegas beginning in 1969. Kerkorian also loaned Elvis his private DC-9 jet aircraft to use for his concert tours.

KERR'S
Sporting goods store in Beverly Hills where Elvis purchased, in December 1970, $38,000 worth of guns, including a $1,900 .357 Colt Python revolver and a $1,800 .44 Roger Black Hawk revolver. Elvis bought more guns, such as a Colt Detective Special revolver, on November 28, 1972.

KESLER, STANLEY A.
Steel guitarist and bass player on many Sun recordings in the 1950s. Kesler toured with Elvis in 1954 and 1955.

Stan Kesler. (Photo courtesy Don Fink)

He composed five songs that Elvis recorded: "I'm Left, You're Right, She's Gone" (cowritten with Bill Taylor),[1] "I Forgot to Remember to Forget" (cowritten with Charlie Feathers), "Playing for Keeps," "Thrill of Your Love," and "If I'm a Fool (for Loving You)."

KESSEL, BARNEY
(1923–   ) Musician born in Muskogee, Oklahoma, on October 17, 1923. Kessel played as a member of Artie

---

[1]Kesler and Taylor both played at the Cotton Club in West Memphis in the early 1950s with Clyde Leoppard's Snearly Ranch Boys.

Shaw's and Chico Marx's dance bands, and was once a member of the Oscar Peterson Trio. Kessel was a session musician who played guitar on Elvis's recording session at Radio Recorders in Hollywood for the *Girls, Girls, Girls* soundtrack in March 1962; for the *Fun In Acapulco* soundtrack on January 22–23, 1963; and again on sessions on July 26–27 and August 4–5, 1965.

KILLEEN, TEXAS
Town near Fort Hood, Texas, where Gladys, Vernon, and Elvis lived while Elvis got his Army basic training during the summer of 1958. Soon after arriving at Fort Hood, Elvis moved off base to Killeen—first renting a three-bedroom trailer and then a three-bedroom house. Elvis's girlfriend, Anita Wood, would sometimes stay in Killeen while Elvis was there.

KING, B. B.
(1925–   ) Blues singer, nicknamed "King of the Blues," who was born Riley B. King, on September 16, 1925, in Indianola, Mississippi. King was a disc jockey at Memphis radio station WDIA when he got his nickname "Blues Boy," given to him by station manager Don Kern. King recorded for Sun Records before Elvis. He claims to have known Elvis before Elvis became a successful singer. Elvis, who had seen King play at a club on Beale Street, appeared with King at the WDIA Goodwill Review in December 1956.

King lends credence to the belief that Elvis hung around several nightclubs in Memphis while still in school. "He used to come around and be around us a lot," King said. "There was a place we used to go and hang out at on Beale Street. People had little pawn shops there and a lot of us used to hang around in certain of these places, and this was where I met him."

KING, PEARL
Composer, with Dave Bartholomew, of the songs "One Night," which Elvis recorded in 1958 and "Witchcraft," which Elvis recorded in 1963.

KING, WARREN
Police chief of Burbank, California, who administered the lie detector test to both Elvis and Patricia Parker to determine if Elvis was the father of her son in a suit brought by Parker. After the polygraph and blood tests, the case was thrown out of court. (See *Patricia Parker*)

KING: WHEN ELVIS ROCKED THE WORLD
Book written by Peter Nelson and published by Proteus Books in 1985.

KING, THE
Title conferred upon two entertainers—actor Clark Gable and singer Elvis Presley. When both men died, the news media headlined "The King is Dead." Columnist May Mann claims to have been the first to dub Elvis "The King."

On Sunday, February 11, 1979, the TV movie *Elvis*, on ABC, got a higher rating than *Gone with the Wind*, on CBS. One "King" beat out the other.

KING COTTON
West Coast brand of bacon that Elvis especially preferred.

KING IS DEAD—ELVIS PRESLEY, THE
A 1977 book written by *Hollywood Reporter* columnist Martin A. Grove and published by Manor Books of New York.

KING IS HOME, THE
Title of Priscilla Presley's home movies, which were shown publicly.

KING OF HEARTS
Award presented to Elvis by the March of Dimes on April 28, 1956.

KING'S COURT
Name given to the social gatherings of Elvis and his friends, especially those held at Graceland.

KINGSLEY, JAMES
Staff reporter for the Memphis *Commercial Appeal*. Kingsley is said to have been the reporter closest to Elvis. James, himself, had a twin brother named John.

KINGSLEY, JAMES
Hollywood stuntman who, before going into films, was employed by Elvis as a bodyguard.

KIRKHAM, MILDRED (MILLIE)
Backup singer for Elvis on many recordings and in live performances for a period of fifteen years from the 1950s to the 1970s. On occasion, Kirkham and Dolores Dinning sang with the Jordanaires. She first sang on the *Elvis Christmas Album* session of September 5–7, 1957. When Millie left, she was replaced by Kathy Westmoreland.

KIRSCH, JACK
Pharmacist at the Prescription House, at 1247 Madison Avenue in Memphis, who filled Dr. George Nichopoulos's prescriptions for Elvis. Over a seven-month period Kirsch prepared 5,684 pills for Elvis. In April 1980 he lost his pharmacist's license for life.

KLEIN, GEORGE
Disc jockey and later program director for Memphis radio station WHBQ. Elvis met Klein while they attended Humes High School, and they soon became close friends. Klein was president of Elvis's senior class. In a magazine article it was written that while Elvis was in high school in 1953, his schoolmate George Klein, an announcer at a local radio station, WKEM, convinced Elvis to appear at the station and sing "Keep Them Cold Icy Fingers Off of Me." Listeners responded by demanding to hear more from Elvis in the future. Years later Elvis paid for Klein to have plastic surgery done on his nose to improve his appearance.

On March 10, 1961, Klein cut one record for Sun, titled "U.T. Party" (Sun 358). The title refers to the University of Tennessee. Charlie Rich played piano on the recording. Klein had bit parts in the Elvis movies *Frankie and Johnny* (1966) and *Double Trouble* (1967). His disc jockey voice is heard in the 1972 documentary *Elvis on Tour*.

When Klein married Barbara Little, who had once worked for Dr. George Nichopoulos, Elvis served as his best man, staging the wedding in his Imperial Suite at the Las Vegas Hilton. George and Barbara would also attend Elvis's marriage to Priscilla. It was through Klein that Elvis first met Dr. Nichopoulos. Later, Klein introduced Elvis to Linda Thompson, inviting her to a movie theater that Elvis had rented.

In December 1977 a Memphis jury found George Klein guilty of mail fraud, after which he served sixty days in the Shelby County Jail. Earlier in the trial, Elvis had called President Jimmy Carter, hoping the president would intercede on Klein's behalf in the federal case. The president wisely stayed out of it. Klein wrote the screenplay for the uncompleted 1979 movie *The King of Rock 'n' Roll*. Klein appeared as the interviewer in the novelty song "The Return of Jerry Lee Lewis" (Sun 301) by Klein and Lewis (flip side of "Lewis Boogie," which mentioned Elvis in the lyrics).

KNECHTEL, LARRY
Session musician who played bass guitar on sessions with Elvis, beginning on Elvis's soundtrack recording session for *Speedway* in June 1967, and his NBC-TV special June 27–29, 1968. Knechtel, who had once been a member of Duane Eddy's Rebels, had played on sessions for Neil Diamond, Simon and Garfunkel, and Johnny Webb, and from 1971 to 1977 was a member of the group Bread, replacing Robb Royer.

KNIGHT, BAKER
(1933–   ) Singer and composer of more than eight hundred songs, born Thomas Baker Knight Jr. in Birmingham, Alabama. Knight has written songs for Hank Snow, Mickey Gilley, Hank Williams, Jr., and about a dozen tunes for Dean Martin. In 1958 he composed "I Got a Feeling" and "Lonesome Town" for Ricky Nelson. In 1959 he wrote "The Wonder of You" for Perry Como, but RCA Records gave it to Ray Peterson. Elvis recorded Knight's "The Wonder of You" in 1970.

KOSLOFF, IRA
Composer, with Maurice Mysels, of the song "I Want You, I Need You, I Love You," which Elvis recorded in 1956.

KOSLOSKI, MARY
March of Dimes poster girl in 1960, who posed with Elvis.

KRISTOFFERSON, KRIS
(1937–   ) Singer-songwriter-actor born in Brownsville, Texas, on June 22, 1936. After serving as a helicopter pilot in the Army in Vietnam, Kristofferson's first paid job with Columbia Records was as a janitor, cleaning their Nashville studios.

Kristofferson wrote "Me and Bobby McGee," which Roger Miller (Smash 2230) and Janis Joplin (Columbia 45314) recorded. Soon after, he signed a recording contract with Monument Records. In addition to his music career, Kristofferson began a movie career in the early 1970s. In 1976 he costarred with Barbra Streisand in *A Star Is Born*, a movie for which he wrote many of the songs, and a role for which Elvis had been considered. Elvis recorded three Kris Kristofferson songs: "Help Me Make It Through the Night," "Why Me Lord," and "For the Good Times."

KUI LEE CANCER FUND
Charity named for Hawaiian composer Kuiokalani Lee, who died of cancer in 1966. Elvis's TV special "Elvis: Aloha from Hawaii" was a benefit for the cancer fund, raising $75,000, with Elvis and Colonel Tom Parker each paying $100 for their tickets. Kuiokalani Lee composed "I'll Remember You," which Elvis sang during the benefit concert. Earlier in 1966, Elvis recorded the song.

KUMPF LINCOLN-MERCURY
Denver car dealership from which Elvis bought five cars (totaling $70,000) for friends on January 14, 1976. Elvis was vacationing in Vail, Colorado, at the time. (See *Jerry Kennedy, Gerald Starkey*)

KUZMA, LEROY
(1960–   ) Son of Frankfurt, West Germany, nightclub singer Margot Heine Kuzma, born December 23, 1960. In an article in the *The Globe* dated June 24, 1980, Kuzma's mother claimed that Leroy was the son of Elvis, with whom she had had an affair while he was living in Germany, first meeting him in August 1959. Leroy's birth certificate, issued in Germany, listed no father's name.

LABOSTRIE, DOROTHY
Composer, with Robert Blackwell and Richard Penniman (Little Richard), of the song "Tutti Frutti," which both Little Richard and Elvis recorded in 1956. LaBostrie had rewritten the suggestive lyrics to make them more acceptable.

LACKER, MARTY
(1937–   ) Member of the Memphis Mafia from 1960 to 1967 who first met Elvis at Humes High, where Lacker played football. Lacker and his wife, Patsy, lived with their daughters, Sheri and Angie, and their son, Marc, in an apartment that had once been a garage at Graceland. Beginning in 1964 Lacker served as Elvis's personal bookkeeper and secretary. He and Joe Esposito served as Elvis's best men at his wedding in 1967, with both men signing the marriage certificate. Elvis once bought Lacker a new Cadillac sedan. In 1979 Lacker coauthored, with his wife and Leslie S. Smith, the book *Elvis: Portrait of a Friend*.

Marge Crumbaker and Gabe Tucker, in their book *Up and Down With Elvis: The Inside Story*, relate how Lacker's mother, Rose, and his sister, Anne Grenadien, sometimes visited both Lacker and Minnie Mae Hood Presley at Graceland. During one visit in April 1967, Vernon and Elvis got into a heated shouting match with Lacker and his family.

LACKER, PATSY
Wife of Memphis Mafia member Marty Lacker. She and the Lacker children moved to Graceland in 1960. Patsy claims in her book, *Elvis: Portrait of a Friend*, that she and Elvis built up a tolerance for each other, but that she blames Elvis for introducing her husband to drugs. She also told of her jealousy toward Priscilla and her resentment of her husband's dedicated relationship with Elvis. Patsy is honest and candid in revealing that she had difficulty getting along with many of the people who lived and worked at Graceland.

LAMB, CHARLES
Publisher of *Music Reporter* magazine, who claims to have been the president of the very first Elvis fan club.

LANGE, JOHNNY
(1909–   ) Composer born in Philadelphia on August 15, 1909. Lange composed, with Walter Heath and Joseph Burke, the gospel song "Somebody Bigger Than You and I," which Elvis recorded in 1966.

LANSKY BROTHERS
Memphis men's clothing store, officially named Lansky's Clothing Emporium, located at 126 Beale Street, established in 1949 by Bernard and Guy Lansky as an Army surplus store. Lansky's specialized in loud clothing, i.e., yellow suits, pink sport coats, and white shoes. The store catered mainly to black patrons, including Rufus Thomas and Junior Parker. Elvis first shopped there in 1952, and afterward bought clothing from Lansky's for many years. Many of the Sun recording artists—Sonny Burgess, Billy Lee Riley, Charlie Feathers, Roy Orbison, Bill Justis, and brothers Johnny and Dorsey Burnette—also bought their clothes at Lansky's. Lansky Brothers provided the suits for both Elvis's and Vernon Presley's pallbearers at each one's funeral. Among other things, the Lansky brothers owned their own Memphis record label for a while, Peak Records. In 1956 Elvis traded Bernard Lansky his Messerschmidt automobile for new clothing. (See *Messerschmidt*)

(Photo courtesy Don Fink)

LANTZ, JOHNNY
Composer, with Eddie Miller, of the song "After Loving You," which Elvis recorded in 1969.

LARUE, JACQUES
Composer, with Alain Romans, of the song "Padre," which Elvis recorded in 1971.

LAST, JAMES
(1929–   ) Musician born in Bremen, Germany, on April 17, 1929, who, with American-born Carl Sigman, composed the song "Fool," which Elvis recorded in 1973.

LASTFOGEL, ABE
President of the William Morris Agency who served as Elvis's personal agent and who was nicknamed "The Little Square Man." Lastfogel and Colonel Tom Parker were good friends.

LAST PHOTOGRAPH
Rare photograph of Elvis lying in his open coffin, taken

by Elvis's cousin Bobby Mann. The *National Enquirer*, which owns the exclusive rights to the photograph, ran it on the cover of its September 6, 1977, issue, selling out in record time.

Because of Elvis's hairstyle[1] in the picture, members of the Jordanaires, friends of Elvis, and many fans believed the photo to be phony.

LAST WILL AND TESTAMENT
Elvis's thirteen-page will, dated March 3, 1977, and witnessed by Charles Hodge, Ginger Alden, and Ann Dewey Smith (wife of the attorney). Copies of Elvis's will were being hawked in Memphis for four dollars each, after the singer's death. (See pages 111–114.)

LAS VEGAS HILTON
New name (since March 1971) of the International Hotel in Las Vegas, after Barron Hilton bought it. Elvis had four lengthy engagements at the hotel from 1969 to 1971, under the hotel's original name. He also appeared there on thirteen occasions under the new name, from 1971 through 1976. Suites 446–447 were reserved as Colonel Tom Parker's private rooms. Parker gambled heavily at the casino on blackjack and roulette. It has been estimated that he lost $1 million a year there. For Parker to gamble at the casino where his client signed a contract with the owner was a conflict of interest. Today the fifteen-hundred-room Las Vegas Hilton rents out, at a cost of $2,000 a night, the same suite in which Elvis slept and which he helped design.

During Elvis's first four-week engagement at the hotel in 1969 (July 31 to August 28), his first live concert performances in eight years, he set a Las Vegas record of 101,509 paid customers and produced a gross take of $1.5 million.

LAUDERDALE COURTS
Federally funded housing project at 185 Winchester Street in Memphis where the Presleys resided for $35 a month in one of 433 units. In the project was a recreation hall where Elvis and some of the local young people sometimes sang. (See *Houses*)

LAW ENFORCEMENT
Police-accessories store in Memphis, owned by Charles Church, where Elvis bought his guns.

LAWHON ELEMENTARY SCHOOL
East Tupelo, Mississippi, grammar school on Lake Street attended by Elvis as a boy. Gladys Presley enrolled him there from the first grade in September 1941. At the time, the school, which had been built in 1926, was named the East Tupelo Consolidated School. It was renamed in honor of school Superintendent Ross Lawhon. The school's principal, J. D. Cole, entered Elvis in the talent contest at the Mississippi-Alabama Fair and Dairy Show on October 3, 1945. (See *East Tupelo Consolidated School*)

LEAKE AND GODLETT LUMBER COMPANY
Tupelo company located on East Main Street where Vernon Presley worked for $18 a week after he got out of Parchman Penitentiary in 1939.

LEAPTROT, BILL
Classmate and friend of Elvis's at L. C. Humes High School in Memphis. He and Elvis were members of Class 202, the graduating class of 1953. Leaptrot, a photographer for the *Press-Scimitar*, accompanied Elvis after his discharge from the Army. He wrote the article "A Kid from the Northside," which appears in the 1987 book *Elvis in Private*.

LEE COUNTY JAIL
Facility where Vernon and Vester Presley were incarcerated after they were convicted of check forgery in 1937. The brothers were then transferred to Parchman Penitentiary for a three-year term, but only served nine months.

LEE, DICKEY
(1943–) Singer born Richard Lipscomb in Memphis on September 21, 1943. Lee recorded the hit song "Patches" (Smash 1958), produced by Jack Clement in 1962. Lee, a former Golden Gloves champion, composed "She Thinks I Still Care," which Elvis recorded in 1976. Lee was a friend of Elvis's and visited Graceland on a number of occasions. Lee's band was called the Collegiates, and his first Sun release, "Good Lovin'" (Sun 280) in 1957, closely resembled Elvis's version of "Too Much."

Lee's first record in 1957, "Dream Boy"/"Stay True Baby" (Tampa 131), was produced by disc jockey Dewey Phillips, after which Sam Phillips signed Lee to his Sun label, where he recorded several songs.

LEE, KUIOKALANI
(–1966) Singer and composer of several songs, including "I'll Remember You" (Columbia 43776) in 1966, which Elvis would record the same year. Lee died of cancer in 1966. (See *Kui Lee Cancer Fund*)

LEE, PEGGY
(1920–) Singer of the 1940s and 1950s, born Norma Egstrom on May 26, 1920, in Jamestown, North Dakota. Lee composed the theme music for the 1954 movie *Johnny Guitar* and for the 1960 movie *The Time Machine*. Lee replaced Elvis as headliner at the Las Vegas Hilton on August 23, 1976, after Elvis became ill (Elvis returned to Memphis where he was hospitalized at the Baptist Memorial Hospital). Bill Cosby and Roy Clark were signed for the remainder of the Presley engagement. Lee recorded a hit version of "Fever" (Capitol 3998) in 1958. Elvis recorded "Fever" in 1960.

[1]The style was similar to the one he had worn when he got out of the Army in 1960.

LAST WILL AND TESTAMENT
OF
ELVIS A. PRESLEY

I, ELVIS A. PRESLEY, a resident and citizen of Shelby County, Tennessee, being of sound mind and disposing memory, do hereby make, publish and declare this instrument to be my last will and testament, hereby revoking any and all wills and codicils by me at any time heretofore made.

ITEM I
Debts, Expenses and Taxes

I direct my Executor, hereinafter named, to pay all of my matured debts and my funeral expenses, as well as the costs and expenses of the administration of my estate, as soon after my death as practicable. I further direct that all estate, inheritance, transfer and succession taxes which are payable by reason of my death, whether or not with respect to property passing under this will, be paid out of my residuary estate; and I hereby waive on behalf of my estate any right to recover from any person any part of such taxes so paid. My Executor, in his sole discretion, may pay from my domiciliary estate all or any portion of the costs of ancillary administration and similar proceedings in other jurisdictions.

ITEM II
Instructions Concerning Personal
Property: Enjoyment in Specie

I anticipate that included as a part of my property and estate at the time of my death will be tangible personal property of various kinds, characters and values, including trophies and other items accumulated by me during my professional career. I hereby specifically instruct all concerned that my Executor, herein appointed, shall have complete freedom and discretion as to disposal of any and all such property so long as he shall act in good faith and in the best interest of my estate and my beneficiaries, and his discretion so exercised shall not be subject to question by anyone whomsoever.

I hereby expressly authorize my Executor and my Trustee, respectively and successively, to permit any beneficiary of any and all trusts created hereunder to enjoy in specie the use or benefit of any household goods, chattels, or other tangible personal property (exclusive of choses in action, cash, stocks, bonds or other securities) which either my Executor or my Trustee may receive in kind, and my Executor and my Trustee shall not be liable for any consumption, damage, injury to or loss of any tangible property so used, nor shall the beneficiaries of any trusts hereunder or their executors or administrators be liable for any consumption, damage, injury to or loss of any tangible personal property so used.

ITEM III
Real Estate

If I am the owner of any real estate at the time of my death, I instruct and empower my Executor and my Trustee (as the case may be) to hold such real estate for investment, or to sell same, or any portion thereof, as my Executor or my Trustee (as the case may be) shall in his sole judgment determine to be for the best interest of my estate and the beneficiaries thereof.

ITEM IV
Residuary Trust

After payment of all debts, expenses and taxes as directed under ITEM I hereof, I give, devise, and bequeath all the rest, residue, and remainder of my estate, including all lapsed legacies and devises, and any property over which I have a power of appointment, to my Trustee, hereinafter named, in trust for the following purposes:

(a) The Trustee is directed to take, hold, manage, invest and reinvest the corpus of the trust and to collect the income therefrom in accordance with the rights, powers, duties, authority and discretion hereinafter set forth. The Trustee is directed to pay all the expenses, taxes and costs incurred in the management of the trust estate out of the income thereof.

(b) After payment of all expenses, taxes and costs incurred in the management of the trust estate, the Trustee is authorized to accumulate the net income or to pay or apply so much of the net income and such portion of the principal at any time and from time to time for the health, education, support, comfortable maintenance and welfare of: (1) my daughter, Lisa Marie Presley, and any other lawful issue I might have, (2) my grandmother, Minnie Mae Presley, (3) my father, Vernon E. Presley, and (4) such other relatives of mine living at the time of my death who in the absolute discretion of my Trustee are in need of emergency assistance for any of the above mentioned purposes and the Trustee is able to make such distribution without affecting the ability of the trust to meet the present needs of the first three numbered categories of beneficiaries herein mentioned or to meet the reasonably expected future needs of the first three classes of beneficiaries herein mentioned. Any decision of the Trustee as to whether or not distribution shall be made, and also as to the amount of such distribution, to any of the persons described hereunder shall be final and conclusive and not subject to question by any legatee or beneficiary hereunder.

(c) Upon the death of my father, Vernon E. Presley, the Trustee is instructed to make no further distributions to the fourth category of beneficiaries and such beneficiaries shall cease to have any interest whatsoever in this trust.

(d) Upon the death of both my said father and my said grandmother, the Trustee is directed to divide the Residuary Trust into separate and equal trusts, creating one such equal trust for each of my lawful children then surviving and one such equal trust for the living issue collectively, if any, of any deceased child of mine. The share, if any, for the issue of any such deceased child, shall immediately vest in such issue in equal shares but shall be subject to the provisions of ITEM V herein. Separate books and records shall be kept for each trust, but it shall not be necessary that a physical division of the assets be made as to each trust.

The Trustee may from time to time distribute the whole or any part of the net income or principal from each of the aforesaid trusts as the Trustee, in its uncontrolled discretion, considers necessary or desirable to provide for the comfortable support, education, maintenance, benefit and general welfare of each of my children. Such distributions may be made directly to such beneficiary or to any person standing in the place of a parent or to the guardian of the person of such beneficiary and without responsibility on my Trustee to see to the application of any such distributions and in making such distributions, the Trustee shall take into account all other sources of funds known by the Trustee to be available for each respective beneficiary for such purpose.

e) As each of my respective children attains the age of twenty-five (25) years and provided that both my father and grandmother then be deceased, the trust created hereunder for such child shall terminate, and all the remainder of the assets then contained in said trust shall be distributed to such child so attaining the age of twenty-five (25) years outright and free of further trust.

(f) If any of my children for whose benefit a trust has been created hereunder should die before attaining the age of twenty-five (25) years, then the trust created for such child shall terminate on his death, and all remaining assets then contained in said trust shall be distributed outright and free of further trust and in equal shares to the surviving issue of such deceased child but subject to the provisions of ITEM V herein; but if there be no such surviving issue, then to the brothers and sisters of such deceased child in equal shares, the issue of any other deceased child being entitled collectively to their deceased parent's share. Nevertheless, if any distribution otherwise becomes payable outright and free of trust under the provisions of this paragraph (f) of this ITEM IV of my will to a beneficiary for whom the Trustee is then administering a trust for the benefit of such beneficiary under the provisions of this last will and testament, such distribution shall not be paid outright to such beneficiary but shall be added to and become a part of the trust so being administered for such beneficiary by the Trustee.

ITEM V
Distribution to Minor Children

If any share of corpus of any trust established under this will becomes distributable outright and free of trust to any beneficiary before said beneficiary has attained the age of eighteen (18) years, then said share shall immediately vest in said beneficiary, but the Trustee shall retain possession of such share during the period in which such beneficiary is under the age of eighteen (18) years, and, in the meantime, shall use and expend so much of the income and principal of each share as the Trustee deems necessary and desirable for the care, support and education of such beneficiary, and any income not so expended shall be added to the principal. The Trustee shall have with respect to each share so retained all the power and discretion had with respect to such trust generally.

ITEM VI
Alternate Distributees
In the event that all of my descendants should be deceased at any time prior to the time for the termination of the trusts provided for herein, then in such event all of my estate and all the assets of every trust to be created hereunder (as the case may be) shall then be distributed outright in equal shares to my heirs at law per stirpes.

ITEM VII
Unenforceable Provisions
If any provisions of this will are unenforceable, the remaining provisions shall, nevertheless, be carried into effect.

ITEM VIII
Life Insurance
If my estate is the beneficiary of any life insurance on my life at the time of my death, I direct that the proceeds therefrom will be used by my Executor in payment of the debts, expenses and taxes listed in ITEM I of this will, to the extent deemed advisable by the Executor. All such proceeds not so used are to be used by my Executor for the purpose of satisfying the devises and bequests contained in ITEM IV herein.

ITEM IX
Spendthrift Provision
I direct that the interest of any beneficiary in principal or income of any trust created hereunder shall not be subject to claims of creditors or others, nor to legal process, and may not be voluntarily or involuntarily alienated or encumbered except as herein provided. Any bequests contained herein for any female shall be for her sole and separate use, free from the debts, contracts and control of any husband she may ever have.

ITEM X
Proceeds From Personal Services
All sums paid after my death (either to my estate or to any of the trusts created hereunder) and resulting from personal services rendered by me during my lifetime, including, but not limited to, royalties of all nature, concerts, motion picture contracts, and personal appearances shall be considered to be income, notwithstanding the provisions of estate and trust law to the contrary.

ITEM XI
Executor and Trustee
I appoint as Executor of this, my last will and testament, and as Trustee of every trust required to be created hereunder, my said father.

I hereby direct that my said father shall be entitled by his last will and testament, duly probated, to appoint a successor Executor of my estate, as well as a successor Trustee or successor Trustees of all the trusts to be created under my last will and testament.

If, for any reason, my said father be unable to serve or to continue to serve as Executor and/or as Trustee, or if he be deceased and shall not have appointed a successor Executor or Trustee, by virtue of his last will and testament as stated above then I appoint National Bank of Commerce, Memphis, Tennessee, or its successor or the institution with which it may merge, as successor Executor and/or as successor Trustee of all trusts required to be established hereunder.

None of the appointees named hereunder, including any appointment made by virtue of the last will and testament of my said father, shall be required to furnish any bond or security for performance of the respective fiduciary duties required hereunder, notwithstanding any rule of law to the contrary.

ITEM XII
Powers, Duties, Privileges and
Immunities of the Trustee
Except as otherwise stated expressly to the contrary herein, I give and grant to the said Trustee (and to the duly appointed successor Trustee when acting as such) the power to do everything he deems advisable with respect to the administration of each trust required to be established under this, my last will and testament, even though such powers would not be authorized or appropriate for the Trustee under statutory or other rules of law. By way of illustration and not in limitation of the generality of the foregoing grant of power and authority of the Trustee, I give and grant to him plenary power as follows:

(a) To exercise all those powers authorized to fiduciaries under the provisions of the Tennessee Code Annotated, Sections 35-616 to 35-618, inclusive, including any amendments thereto in effect at the time of my death, and the same are expressly referred to and incorporated herein by reference;

(b) Plenary power is granted to the Trustee, not only to relieve him from seeking judicial instruction, but to the extent that the Trustee deems it to be prudent, to encourage determinations freely to be made in favor of persons who are the current income beneficiaries. In such instances the rights of all subsequent beneficiaries are subordinate, and the Trustee shall not be answerable to any subsequent beneficiary for anything done or omitted in favor of a current income beneficiary, but no current income beneficiary may compel any such favorable or preferential treatment. Without in anywise minimizing or impairing the scope of this declaration of intent, it includes investment policy, exercise of discretionary power to pay or apply principal and income, and determination of principal and income questions;

(c) It shall be lawful for the Trustee to apply any sum that is payable to or for the benefit of a minor (or any other person who in the judgment of the Trustee, is incapable of making proper disposition thereof) by payments in discharge of the costs and expenses of educating, maintaining and supporting said beneficiary, or to make payment to anyone with whom said beneficiary resides or who has the care or custody of the beneficiary, temporarily or permanently, all without intervention of any guardian or like fiduciary. The receipt of anyone to whom payment is so authorized to be made shall be a complete discharge of the Trustee without obligation on his part to see to the further application thereof, and without regard to other resources that the beneficiary may have, or the duty of any other person to support the beneficiary;

(d) In dealing with the Trustee, no grantee, pledgee, vendee, mortgagee, lessee or other transferee of the trust properties, or any part thereof, shall be bound to inquire with respect to the purpose or necessity of any such disposition or to see to the application of any consideration therefor paid to the Trustee.

ITEM XIII
Concerning the Trustee
And the Executor
(a) If at any time the Trustee shall have reasonable doubt as to his power, authority or duty in the administration of any trust herein created, it shall be lawful for the Trustee to obtain the advice and counsel of reputable legal counsel without resorting to the courts for instructions; and the Trustee shall be fully absolved from all liability and damage or detriment to the various trust estates or any beneficiary thereunder by reason of anything done, suffered or omitted pursuant to advice of said counsel given and obtained in good faith, provided that nothing contained herein shall be construed to prohibit or prevent the Trustee in all proper cases from applying to a court of competent jurisdiction for instructions in the administration of the trust assets in lieu of obtaining advice of counsel.

(b) In managing, investing, and controlling the various trust estates, the Trustee shall exercise the judgment and care under the circumstances then prevailing, which men of prudence, discretion and judgment exercise in the management of their own affairs, not in regard to speculation, but in regard to the permanent disposition of their funds, considering the probable income as well as the probable safety of their capital, and, in addition, the purchasing power of income distribution to beneficiaries.

(c) My Trustee (as well as my Executor) shall be entitled to reasonable and adequate compensation for the fiduciary services rendered by him.

(d) My Executor and his successor Executor shall have the same rights, privileges, powers and immunities herein granted to my Trustee wherever appropriate.

(e) In referring to any fiduciary hereunder, for purposes of construction, masculine pronouns may include a corporate fiduciary and neutral pronouns may include an individual fiduciary.

ITEM XIV
Law Against Perpetuities

(a) Having in mind the rule against perpetuities, I direct that (notwithstanding anything contained to the contrary in this last will and testament) each trust created under this will (except such trusts as have heretofore vested in compliance with such rule or law) shall end, unless sooner terminated under other provisions of this will, twenty-one (21) years after the death of the last survivor of such of the beneficiaries hereunder as are living at the time of my death; and thereupon that the property held in trust shall be distributed free of all trust to the persons then entitled to receive the income and/or principal therefrom, in the proportion in which they are then entitled to receive such income.

(b) Notwithstanding anything else contained in this will to the contrary, I direct that if any distribution under this will becomes payable to a person for whom the Trustee is then administering a trust created hereunder for the benefit of such person, such distribution shall be made to such trust and not to the beneficiary outright, and the funds so passing to such trust shall become a part thereof as corpus and be administered and distributed to the same extent and purpose as if such funds had been a part of such trust at its inception.

ITEM XV
Payment of Estate and
Inheritance Taxes

Notwithstanding the provisions of ITEM X herein, I authorize my Executor to use such sums received by my estate after my death and resulting from my personal services as identified in ITEM X as he deems necessary and advisable in order to pay the taxes referred to in ITEM I of my said will.

IN WITNESS WHEREOF, I, the said ELVIS A. PRESLEY, do hereunto set my hand and seal in the presence of two (2) competent

witnesses, and in their presence do publish and declare this instrument to be my Last Will and Testament, this ___3___ day of

_____MARCH_____, 1976.

Elvis A. Presley
ELVIS A. PRESLEY

The foregoing instrument, consisting of this and eleven (11) preceding typewritten pages, was signed, sealed, published and declared by ELVIS A. PRESLEY, the Testator, to be his Last Will and Testament, in our presence,

and we, at his request and in his presence and in the presence of each other, have hereunto subscribed our names as witnesses, this ___3___

day of ___MARCH___, 1976, at Memphis, Tennessee.

Ginger Alden residing at ___4152 Royal Crest Place___

Charles F. Hodge residing at ___3764 Elvis Presley Blvd___

Ann Dewey Smith ___2237 Court Avenue___

STATE OF TENNESSEE)
COUNTY OF SHELBY)

___GINGER ALDEN, CHARLES F. HODGE___ and ___ANN DEWEY SMITH___, after being first duly sworn, make oath or affirm that the foregoing Last Will and Testament was signed by ELVIS A. PRESLEY and for and at that time acknowledged, published and declared by him to be his Last Will and Testament, in the sight and presence of us, the undersigned, who at his request and in his sight and presence, and in the sight

and presence of each other, have subscribed our names as attesting witnesses on the ___3___ day of ___MARCH___, 1976, and we further make oath or affirm that the Testator was of sound mind and disposing memory and not acting under fraud, menace or undue influence of any person, and was more than eighteen (18) years of age; and that each of the attesting witnesses is more than eighteen (18) years of age.

Ginger Alden
Charles F. Hodge
Ann Dewey Smith

SWORN TO AND SUBSCRIBED before me this ___3___ day of ___MARCH___, 1976.

Drayton Beecher Smith II
NOTARY PUBLIC

My commission expires:
___Aug. 8, 1979___

Admitted to Probate and Ordered Recorded August 22, 1977
JOSEPH W. EVANS, JUDGE

Recorded August 22, 1977
B. J. Dunavant, Clerk
By: Jan Scott, D. C.

State of Tennessee,

SHELBY COUNTY

ss.

I, B. J. DUNAVANT, Clerk of the Probate Court of this County, do hereby certify that the foregoing

Thirteen (13) - - - - - - - - - - - - - pages contain a full, true and exact copy of the

Last Will and Testament of Elvis A. Presley, Deceased:

as the same appears of record or on file in Will Book 209, Page 266

of this office.

IN TESTIMONY WHEREOF, I have hereunto set my hand and affixed the seal of said Court, at office.

in the City of Memphis this 24th day of August 19 77.

B. J. DUNAVANT, Clerk

By Margaret Klare D. C.

LEECH, MIKE

Session musician who played bass guitar on a number of Elvis songs, including the Memphis sessions at American Sound Studios in January–February 1969, which produced thirty-six songs. He later provided overdub bass guitar on Elvis's March 10–13, 1975, session. Leech authored an article for *US* magazine on August 24, 1987, titled "He Was Like One of the Guys."

LEFEVRE, MYRON R.

Composer of the gospel song "Without Him," which Elvis recorded in 1966.

LE GAULT, LANCE

Louisiana blues singer and double for Elvis in his movies from 1960 to 1968. Le Gault was also assistant choreographer on some films. A blooper occurred in the 1963 movie *Kissin' Cousins*, in which Elvis played lookalike cousins. When both the cousins were on the screen, Le Gault would be the cousin with his back to the camera. In one of the film's scenes, Le Gault could be seen looking straight into the camera, but it was left in because director Sam Katzman didn't think anyone would notice.

Among his many talents, Le Gault was also a Jerry Lee Lewis imitator. He starred as Iago in the 1974 movie *Catch My Soul*, the role previously turned down by Lewis. Season Hubley and Tony Joe White also appeared in the film. In the 1980s Le Gault has made appearances as an actor on a number of TV series, including "The A Team," on which he played Col. Roderick Decker, and on "Magnum, P. I."

LEGEND OF A KING, THE

Three-hour radio program about the life of Elvis produced by Associated Broadcasters, Inc., in 1980.

LEIBER, JERRY AND MIKE STOLLER

Prolific songwriting team. Jerry Leiber was born in Baltimore on April 25, 1933, and Mike Stoller was born on Long Island on March 13, 1933. The pair has com-posed hit songs for many artists, beginning in 1952. Leiber and Stoller composed "Jailhouse Rock," "Treat Me Nice," "I Want to Be Free," and "Baby I Don't Care" in a period of only four hours one afternoon. Among the songs they have composed are: "Kansas City," "Down in Mexico," "Searchin'," "Yakety Yak," "Poison Ivy," "Charlie Brown," "Black Denim Trousers," "Love Potion #9," "On Broadway," "Ruby Baby," "I Am Woman," and many more.

Those compositions of Leiber and Stoller that Elvis recorded are:

"(You're So Square) Baby, I Don't Care"
"Bossa Nova Baby"
"Dirty, Dirty Feeling"
"Don't"
"Fools Fall in Love"
"Girls! Girls! Girls!"
"Hot Dog"
"Hound Dog"
"I Want to Be Free"
"If You Don't Come Back"
"Jailhouse Rock"
"Just Tell Her Jim Said Hello"
"King Creole"
"Little Egypt"
"Love Me"
"Loving You"
"Santa Claus Is Back in Town"
"Saved"
"She's Not You" (with Doc Pomus)
"Steadfast, Loyal, and True"
"Three Corn Patches"
"Treat Me Nice"
"Trouble"

Stoller appeared with Elvis in the 1957 movie *Jailhouse Rock*, playing piano for Vince Everett's (Elvis) band. On July 26, 1956, Stoller, along with actress Betsy Drake, were aboard the Italian liner *Andrea Doria* when it was rammed by the Swedish liner *Stockholm* off Nantucket, causing the *Andrea Doria* to sink.

In 1980 a British album was released titled *Elvis Presley Sings Leiber & Stoller*, on which the pair appeared on the cover with Elvis and for which they wrote the liner notes.

LEIGH, MITCH

(1928–   ) Composer born in Brooklyn on January 30, 1928. Leigh composed, with Joe Darion, the song "The Impossible Dream," which Elvis recorded in 1972.

LEKTRONIC

Electric razor used by Elvis. It is on display at the Elvis Presley Museum in Memphis.

LENNON, JOHN

(1940–1980) Musician born John Winston Lennon in Liverpool, England, on October 9, 1940. Lennon played rhythm guitar with the Beatles, who visited Elvis at his Bel Air home on August 27, 1965. Lennon and Paul McCartney composed the songs "Hey Jude" and "Yesterday," which Elvis recorded.

Mike Stoller, Elvis, and Jerry Leiber. (Photo courtesy Eddie Brandt's Saturday Matinee)

Lennon said: "Before Elvis there was nothing," and "If there hadn't been Elvis, there would not have been the Beatles." (See *The Beatles*)

LEPLEY, SLEEPY-EYED JOHN

Memphis disc jockey at WHHM radio who booked the Eagle's Nest ballroom, where Elvis made some of his first professional appearances in early 1954, earning $10 a night. In many ads the club is called "Sleepy-Eyed John's Eagle's Nest." According to legend, Lepley tried to become Elvis's manager, but Scotty Moore beat him to it.[1] Lepley was one of the first disc jockeys to play "Blue Moon of Kentucky," the country side of "That's All Right (Mama)," in July 1954 on WHHM. Lepley recorded several songs at Sun Records in April 1952. Singer Johnny Horton charted a song in 1961 called "Sleepy-Eyed John" (Columbia 41963). (See *Scotty Moore, WHHM*)

LEVEEN, RAYMOND

Composer, with Bennie Benjamin and Lou Singer, of "I Will Be Home Again," which Elvis recorded in 1960.

LEVITCH, HARRY

Memphis jeweler who owned Harry Levitch Jewelers, at 159 Union Avenue, from whom Elvis bought Priscilla's wedding ring in 1967. It was a $4,000 three-carat diamond ring surrounded by twenty smaller diamonds. Harry and his wife, Frances, flew to Las Vegas to deliver the ring to Elvis and to take part in his wedding.

LEWIS, AL

(1901–1967) Composer born in New York City on April 18, 1901. In 1940, along with Larry Stock and Vincent Rose, Lewis composed the song "Blueberry Hill," which Elvis recorded in 1957.

LEWIS, BARBARA JEAN

Woman who claimed to have met Elvis in North Carolina in 1954 and, after a sexual encounter, to have become pregnant in 1955 with her daughter Deborah (Presley).

LEWIS, GEORGE

One of the guards employed to protect Graceland.

LEWIS, JEFF

Composer, with Bill Giant, of the song "Fountain of Love," which Elvis recorded in 1962.

LEWIS, JERRY LEE

(1935–   ) Country/rock singer born in Ferriday, Louisiana, on September 29, 1935 (the same year as Elvis). In his youth, Lewis listened to many Al Jolson records (he still has a large collection). On November 2, 1954, he cut an acetate disc in the studio of KWKH radio in Shreveport, "I Don't Hurt Anymore"/"I Need You Now."

Lewis traveled to Memphis in 1956 to record for the Sun label, where he would one day become the label's most recorded artist. His first release was "Crazy Arms"/"End of the Road" (Sun 259) in December 1956. Lewis's biggest hit record was "Whole Lotta Shakin' Goin' On"[2] (Sun 267). On the label he was billed as Jerry Lee Lewis and his Pumping Piano. Nicknamed "The Killer," he was the only guest to appear on "American Bandstand" who sang live rather than lip-synch to his record. Jerry made his national debut on "The Steve Allen Show," later naming one of his sons Steve Allen Lewis (the boy drowned in the family pool in 1962). Lewis's career in rock & roll was ruined when in 1958 he married his thirteen-year-old cousin, Myra Gale Brown.[3] In 1960 he cut an instrumental on the Phillips International label, "In the Mood"/"I Get the Blues When It Rains" (Phillips 3559), under the name Hawk.

Lewis was one of the participants in the famed Million-Dollar Quartet session on December 4, 1956, in which Elvis relinquished playing the piano so Lewis could play. In a session at Sun on February 14, 1958, Lewis tried his hand at performing a number of Elvis's hits, "Good Rockin' Tonight," "Jailhouse Rock," "Hound Dog," and "Don't Be Cruel," perhaps just to see how he would have done on the songs. He left Sun Records on September 29, 1963, to record for Mercury's subsidiary label Smash, then run by Shelby Singleton. In November 1976 Lewis was arrested for shooting a gun outside the gates of Graceland in the early morning hours, when he was refused permission to see Elvis. Lewis was a patient of Dr. George Nichopoulos, from whom he could obtain prescriptions for vast amounts of legal pills. Lewis has been successful in both the rock and country fields. In 1958 country artist Mickey Gilley recorded an unreleased version of "Whole Lotta Shakin' Goin' On" at Sun Records. Gilley, who was once the co-owner of Gilley's, the largest nightclub in the world, is Lewis's first cousin, and both Lewis and Gilley are cousins of evangelist Jimmy Swaggart. Lewis's father, Elmo Lewis, like Vernon Presley, had spent time in prison—in Lewis's case for making moonshine. In 1962 Elmo Lewis recorded eight unreleased songs for Sun Records.

There was always great mutual respect between Elvis and Jerry Lee Lewis. In Germany, at the party where he first met Priscilla, Elvis did an impersonation of Lewis playing the piano and singing.

Elvis recorded several Lewis hits, "Whole Lotta Shakin' Goin' On" (Sun 267) and "What'd I Say" (Sun 356). In concert, Elvis performed Lewis's "Breathless" (Sun 288) and "It'll Be Me" (Sun 267). In the 1988 TV

---

[1]There is a little confusion as to whether Lepley once served as Elvis's manager. In several sources it has been alleged that in the early 1950s Lepley booked Elvis into some clubs in Memphis. Jerry Hopkins also makes mention of this in his first book on Elvis. The authors of this book would love to see a copy of any contract signed between Elvis and John Lepley.

[2]John Lennon called it "the greatest rock 'n' roll song ever written."

[3]As if that wasn't bad enough, Lewis was two weeks short of his final divorce decree from his previous (and second) wife, Jane. He had married his first wife, Dorothy, when he was only fourteen years old.

miniseries "Elvis and Me," Elvis (Dale Midkiff) was shown singing "Great Balls of Fire." Both Elvis and Lewis recorded "High Heel Sneakers" and "Tomorrow Night," among other songs.

Lewis mentions Elvis in two songs, "Lewis Boogie" (Sun 301) in 1958 and "It Won't Happen with Me" (Sun 364) in 1961.

LEWIS, PAULETTE SHAFER
One of a number of secretaries who worked at Graceland. Lewis's father, Paul Shafer, was the president of the Malco movie chain in Memphis, and he would reserve a theater for Elvis so that he could watch the latest films in privacy.

LEWIS, SAMMY
Producer at the New Frontier Hotel in Las Vegas who signed Elvis for his first Las Vegas performance, April 23 through May 6, 1956.

LEWIS, SMILEY
(1920–1965) Rhythm & blues artist of the early 1950s, born Overton Amos Lemon in Union, Louisiana, on July 5, 1920. Fats Domino covered Smiley's 1954 hit "Blue Monday"; Gale Storm covered his 1955 hit "I Hear You Knocking"; and Elvis covered his 1956 hit "One Night." (Lewis's version was originally titled "One Night of Sin.")

LIBERACE
(1919–1987) Legal name of pianist born Wladziu Valentino Liberace on May 16, 1919, in West Allis, Wisconsin (Lee was his nickname). Elvis visited Liberace and his brother, George, in Las Vegas at the Riviera Hotel on November 16, 1956, and got Liberace's autograph to give to his mother. Photos of the two meeting were published in many magazines. While Liberace "played" a guitar, Elvis held Liberace's candelabra and sang "Blue Suede Shoes." Legend has it that when Dewey Phillips introduced Elvis at the Eagle's Nest in October 1953, he called him "the poor man's Liberace."

LIBERTYLAND
Memphis amusement park, on East Parkway, previously called Fairgrounds Amusement Park and rented by Elvis for $2,500 on August 8, 1977, from 1:15 A.M. until dawn, as a present for his daughter Lisa Marie. Elvis, Lisa Marie, Ginger Alden, and about a dozen friends rode the park's fourteen rides, including the Fender Bender and the Little Dipper.

LICHTER, PAUL
(1944–   ) President of the Elvis Unique Record Club, the *Memphis Flash* bi-monthly magazine, and owner of the Memphis Flash record label in Huntingdon, Pennsylvania. Lichter, who began collecting Elvis memorabilia in 1970, walked a fine line after Elvis's death. He spoke of his devotion to Elvis while at the same time making a lot of money ($30,000 a month) selling Elvis-related products, including bootleg material. It has

been suggested that Lichter's interest in Elvis has made him a millionaire. He acquired Elvis's "Burning Love" jumpsuit by donating $5,000 and a rare Sun recording by Elvis to a cerebral palsy telethon in March 1974. Lichter is the author of several books on Elvis, such as *Elvis in Hollywood* (1975) and *The Boy Who Dared to Rock: The Definitive Elvis* (1978). There have been a number of newspaper articles about Lichter's success, as well as an interview by Geraldo Rivera. It appears that perhaps Lichter began believing his own publicity when he himself wrote in *The Boy Who Dared to Rock*: "Over the past years Lichter's name has been linked with Elvis's as much as Colonel Tom Parker."

LIDO, THE
Paris nightclub where in June 1959 Elvis appeared on stage as an unplanned act after he, Charlie Hodge, Rex Mansfield, and Lamar Fike traveled to the "City of Light" on leave. The brothers George and Bert Bernard were the featured singers. Elvis played "Willow Weep for Me" on the piano. The four men stayed at the Hotel de Galles on Avenue George V (some sources say that the group stayed at the Prince of Wales Hotel). They also visited other clubs, such as the Folies-Bergere, the Cafe de Paris, the Carousel, the Moulin Rouge, and the 4 O'Clock Club.

After Elvis and the boys had arrived at Paris's Orly Airport in a chartered plane, Elvis discovered that he had left his Army hat back in Germany. He asked Lamar Fike to fly back and get it for him, which Fike did. Elvis and the boys were joined by publishers Jean Aberbach and attorney Ben Starr, who were sent over to keep an eye on the gang of four. At the 4 O'Clock Club the boys picked up the entire Blue Bell chorus line and took them back to their hotel. For the return trip back to his base, Elvis hired a Cadillac limousine at a cost of $800, so that he could be back on the last night of the leave. It has been estimated that the two-week vacation cost Elvis $10,000.

LIFE MAGAZINE
First national magazine to publish a feature story on Elvis. They interviewed him in Amarillo, Texas, in 1956. Upon Elvis's return from the Army in 1960, *Life* wanted to put his photo on the cover of the next edition, with a feature story on the singer. But Colonel Tom Parker wanted *Life*, which rarely paid for a cover photo, to pay him $25,000. *Life* then canceled the request and passed on the feature story. This was just another example of how Parker mishandled portions of Elvis's career. Later in 1960, however, *Life* did print a story on the making of *G.I. Blues*.

LIFE OF ELVIS PRESLEY, THE
A 1979 book by Hal Noland and Elvis's photographer Sean Shaver, published by Timur Publishing Inc. The beautiful book, with hundreds of color photographs and text by Hal Noland, Charlie Hodge, Dick Grob, and Billy Smith, was dedicated to Elvis Presley, "Thanks for Living in Our Lifetime."

LIFE WITH ELVIS
The 1986 autobiography written by Elvis's step-brother and bodyguard David Stanley, with David Wimbish, and published by the Fleming H. Reveld Company.

LIGHTFOOT, GORDON
(1938–   ) Singer and composer born in Orillia, Ontario, on November 17, 1938. He wrote "Early Morning Rain" and "For Lovin' Me," both of which were originally recorded by Peter, Paul and Mary. Elvis recorded both songs on March 15, 1971.

LILLEY, JOSEPH J.
(1914–   ) Composer and conductor born in Providence, Rhode Island, on August 16, 1914. Lilley, who attended the Julliard School of Music, composed, with Abner Silver and Sid Wayne, the song "Tonight's All Right for Love," which Elvis recorded for the 1960 movie *G.I. Blues.* Lilley was the musical director for *G.I. Blues* and *Blue Hawaii.*

LINDE, DENNIS
(1943–   ) Composer born in Abilene, Texas, on March 13, 1943. He occasionally served as the bass guitarist in Elvis's recording band in the 1970s. He composed "For the Heart," "Burning Love," and "I Got a Feelin' in My Body," which were recorded by Elvis. Linde provided the overdubbing for Elvis's recording session at Graceland on February 2–8, 1976, and concert recordings from April 24–25, 1977. He played guitar on Elvis's version of "Burning Love."

Linde has been a member of Kris Kristofferson's band, and has recorded several records for Monument Records, including "Under the Fire" (Monument 8681).

LIPSTICK
Elvis-related product sold in the 1950s, each tube costing a dollar. The colors were: Tender Pink, Heartbreak Pink, Love-ya Fuchsia, Hound Dog Orange, Tutti Frutti Red, and Cruel Red.

LIPTON, PEGGY
(1948–   ) Actress born in Lawrence, New York, in 1948. She played Joanna on the TV series "The John Forsythe Show" and Julie Barnes on TV's "The Mod Squad." Lipton composed the song "L.A. Is My Lady," which Frank Sinatra recorded. From 1972 to 1986 she was married to singer Michael Jackson's producer, Quincy Jones. Lipton claims to have dated both Elvis and Paul McCartney, referring to each in a 1988 *People* magazine article as "very sweet," and "very savvy," respectively.

LISA MARIE
Elvis's custom blue-and-white Convair 880 jet (N880EP), bought for $1.2 million in November 1975 and requiring an additional $750,000 for remodeling, which was done in Fort Worth, Texas. Named for his daughter, the jet required a crew of four, including the stewardess, Carol Bouchere. Its emblem was the letters TCB (Taking Care of Business) and a lightning bolt in gold on the tail section, under an American flag. Members of the crew were Elwood David (captain), Ron Strauss (copilot), and Jim Manning (flight engineer). The *Lisa Marie* was equipped with a $14,000 queen-size bed, a conference room, four TV sets, a bar, leather swivel chairs, and a pair of couches.

LISBONA, EDWARD
(1915–   ) Pianist and composer born in Manchester, England, on July 16, 1915. Also known as Eddie (Piano) Miller, he composed, with Murray Wizell, the song "Gently," which Elvis recorded in 1961.

LISTER, MOSIE
Composer of the religious songs "His Hand in Mine," "Jesus Knows What I Need" (a.k.a. "He Knows Just What I Need"), and "Where No One Stands Alone," all of which Elvis recorded. Mosie Lister was the leader of the Statesmen Quartet.

LITTLE, RICH
(1938–   ) Comedian and impressionist born in Ottawa, Canada, on November 26, 1938. During one of Elvis's Las Vegas concerts, he kidded Little from the stage, telling him he couldn't learn to imitate Elvis unless he sat closer to the stage.

LITTLEBIT
Name of the toy French poodle that Elvis gave Anita Wood for Christmas in 1958.

LITTLE LISA MARIE
Nickname of Elvis's Jetstar aircraft, which was smaller than the Convair 880, *Lisa Marie.*

LITTLE RICHARD
(1932–   ) Rock & roll singer born Richard Wayne Penniman in Macon, Georgia, on December 5, 1932. Originally a rhythm & blues singer, he was known as Little Richard because of his height. After little success for RCA Victor and Duke Records, he recorded a number of hits on the Specialty label in Los Angeles. In 1957 Little Richard quit recording to become a minister, only to return in 1959 on George Goldner's End label. Elvis recorded the following songs previously recorded by Little Richard: "Tutti Frutti" (Specialty 561) in 1955, "Long Tall Sally" (Specialty 572) in 1956 (both Elvis and the Beatles covered this song), "Ready Teddy" (Specialty 579) in 1956, "Shake a Hand" (Specialty 670) in 1957, and "Crying in the Chapel" (Atlantic 2181) in 1963. Little Richard cowrote "Tutti Frutti" and "Long Tall Sally." Interestingly, Elvis covered both sides of the single "Rip It Up"/"Ready Teddy." Although Elvis has been called the "King of Rock & Roll," Little Richard always felt that he should own the title, and at times has referred to himself as such.

In a *Rolling Stone* magazine interview, Little Richard said, "I thank God for Elvis Presley. I thank the Lord for sending Elvis to open the doors so I could walk down the road."

In 1969 Elvis said of Little Richard, "Your music has inspired me—you are the greatest."

LIVINGSTON, JAY
(1915–   ) Composer born in McDonald, Pennsylvania, on March 28, 1915. Livingston wrote many popular songs with Ray Evans ("To Each His Own," "Tammy," "Mona Lisa," etc.). He also wrote the theme songs for the TV series "Mr. Lucky" and "Mr. Ed," among others. Livingston is the coauthor (with lyricist Ray Evans) of "Silver Bells," which Elvis recorded in 1971. Livingston composed, with Sid Wayne, the song "What a Wonderful Life," which Elvis sang in the 1962 movie *Follow That Dream*.

LLOYD, JACK
(1922–1976) Composer and television writer born in Duisburg, Germany, on December 23, 1922. Lloyd composed, with Fred Wise and Ben Weisman, the song "Summer Kisses, Winter Tears," which Elvis sang in the 1960 movie *Flaming Star*.

LLOYD WEBBER, ANDREW
Composer of Broadway musicals, including *Jesus Christ Superstar*, *Evita*, *Cats*, and *Phantom of the Opera*. Lloyd Webber and Tim Rice composed the song "It's Easy for You," which Elvis recorded in 1976.

LOCKE, DIXIE
(1938?–   ) Girlfriend of Elvis during his high school days. They both attended the First Assembly of God Church at 1885 McLemore in Memphis. Locke first met Elvis at the Rainbow Rollerdome in the winter of 1953 and dated him steadily until late 1955. The two went to the Southside High School prom together, double-dating with Gene Smith and his date, Betty. Locke became

On Dixie Locke's prom night. Elvis and Dixie Locke, Gene Smith and his date, Betty. (Photo courtesy Cinema Collectors)

president of the first Elvis Presley fan club. The popular photograph of Elvis's prom night is actually Dixie's prom in 1954.

Some believe that Elvis wanted to marry Dixie, but before he could, she decided to break off their relationship because he was on the road too often. She married, becoming Mrs. Dixie Semmons. Locke was loosely portrayed by Melody Anderson as a girl named Bonnie in the 1979 TV movie *Elvis*.

LOCKLIN, HANK
(1918–   ) Country singer born in McLellen, Florida, on February 15, 1918. In his youth Locklin leaned toward becoming an Irish tenor. He appeared on the same bill with Elvis at the "Big D Jamboree" in Dallas on April 16, 1955.

LOEW'S PALACE THEATER
Memphis theater that is incorrectly pointed out by some tours as the theater where Elvis once worked as an usher. Elvis actually worked at Loew's State Theater, which no longer exists. In 1951 blues singer Bobby (Blue) Bland won first prize at Loew's Palace in an amateur show.

LOEW'S STATE THEATER
Memphis movie theater (152 S. Main) where, from April 17 to May 28, 1952, Elvis worked as an usher after high school at $12.75 a week, which he turned over to his mother. His hours were five to ten weeknights. Elvis, who had previously worked at Precision Tool, was fired by theater manager Arthur Groom after Elvis got into a fistfight with a fellow usher who had told Groom that the female candy concessionaire was giving Elvis free candy samples.

On December 4, 1956, on the day of the Million-Dollar Quartet at Sun Studios, the movie *Love Me Tender* was being shown at Loew's State. Elvis's 1957 MGM movie *Jailhouse Rock* had its premiere on October 17, 1957, at the Loew's State Theater.

The late comedian Freddie Prinze was himself an usher at New York City's Loew's Theater (it no longer exists). Other celebrities who have been employed as ushers: Frances Farmer, Carol Burnett (who was fired), Sylvester Stallone (who was fired), Linda Evans, and Johnny Carson.

LOGAN, HORACE
Director of the "Louisiana Hayride." Singer Slim Whitman first told Logan about Elvis after Whitman appeared with Elvis at the Overton Park Shell in Memphis, but he couldn't remember his name. In 1981 *The Globe* ran an article by Logan titled, "I Made Elvis a Star," which claimed that Logan signed Elvis to the Hayride twelve months before Elvis had signed with Colonel Tom Parker.

LOGGINS, KENNY
(1948–   ) Singer and composer born in Everett, Washington, on January 7, 1948 (one day before Elvis's

thirteenth birthday). Loggins and Jim Messina recorded as a duet from 1972 to 1976. They composed and recorded, in 1972, the song "Your Mama Don't Dance" (Columbia 45719), which Elvis recorded in 1974. Kenny Loggins is a cousin of singer Dave Loggins.

LONDON RECORDS
British record company founded in 1947 as an American label for British Decca artists. The label was later licensed to release American recordings in Britain, including those of Sun Records.

LONG, SHORTY
Musician who played piano on a number of Elvis's songs, including "One-Sided Love Affair," "My Baby Left Me," "Hound Dog," "Don't Be Cruel," "Any Way You Want Me," "Tutti Frutti," and "Blue Suede Shoes."

Long, who had cut several records for RCA, played on three of Elvis's recording sessions, January 30–31, February 3, 1956, and again on July 2, 1956.

LONG LONELY HIGHWAY
Book compiled by Ger Rijff and first published in Great Britain in 1985. It was reprinted with additions by Pierian Press in the United States in 1987 with a foreword by Lee Cotten. *Long Lonely Highway* was a scrapbook of Elvis in the 1950s.

LOOK MAGAZINE
Popular weekly magazine on whose cover Elvis appeared on May 4, 1971.

LORD, JACK
(1930–   ) Television actor born in New York City on December 30, 1938. He starred in two successful TV series, "Stoney Burke" and "Hawaii Five-O" (the longest-running police show in TV history, running from 1968 to 1980). Lord and Elvis became good friends. Lord and his wife, Marie, traveled to Las Vegas to watch Elvis perform on six occasions. Elvis gave Lord the belt to his costume before taping one of his concerts. He also gave Lord a solid gold gun, a jeweled belt, and to Marie he gave an emerald ring.

LOS ANGELES INDIAN TRIBAL COUNCIL
In December 1960 Elvis was inducted into the council by Chief Wah-Nee-Ota. This was in recognition of his "constructive portrayal of a man of Indian blood" in the 1960 movie *Flaming Star*.

LOUIS, JOE HILL
(1921–1957) Blues singer born in Raines, Tennessee, on September 23, 1921. Louis had been a boxer before becoming a singer. In 1950 he recorded for Modern Records, and in 1951 for Sun Records. He was the first artist recorded on Sam and Dewey Phillips's Phillips

Record label, with "Gotta Let You Go" (Phillips 9001). On November 17, 1952, Louis recorded the original version of "Tiger Man," which he and Sam Burns had written and which Elvis would record in 1969. Louis's version was unreleased. In June 1953 Rufus Thomas recorded his version of "Tiger Man (King of the Jungle)" (Sun 188) with Louis playing guitar.

LOUISE, TINA
(1934–   ) Actress born in New York City on February 11, 1934. She is best known for playing the role of Ginger Grant on the TV series "Gilligan's Island." Louise covered Elvis's Army homecoming on radio, on March 3, 1960, for the Mutual Broadcasting Network.

LOVE, DARLENE
(1938–   ) Member of the Blossoms vocal group, born Darlene Wright in Los Angeles. The Blossoms sang backup for Elvis on some of his recordings. Love sang lead[1] for the Crystals on their number one hit "He's a Rebel" (Philles 106) in 1962 and joined Bob B. Soxx and the Blue Jeans a few days later to record "Zip-A-Dee Doo-Dah" (Philles 107). Love is the sister of Edna Wright of Honey Cone. Love and the other Blossoms played neighbors in Elvis's 1970 movie *Change of Habit*. (See *The Blossoms*)

LOVE, LEILA
(1870–   ) Neighbor of the Mansells in Saltillo, Mississippi. It was after Leila Love that Gladys Love Smith Presley was given her middle name.

LOVE IS FOREVER
TV movie (a.k.a. *Comeback*) first aired in April 1983, produced by and starring Michael Landon. Priscilla Presley made her movie debut, playing the female lead, a scuba teacher, while soft-core pornography actress Laura Gemser played a role under the pseudonym Moira Chen. It was while watching the film that producer Philip Capice decided to offer Priscilla a part on his TV series "Dallas."

LOVE LETTERS TO ELVIS
Book of letters written to Elvis by his fans, compiled by Bill Adler, who also compiled the book *Love Letters to the Monkees*.

LOVE ME TENDER
Name of a candy created in 1956. One unwrapped bar is worth up to $75 today.

LOVE ME TENDER PERFUME
One of the hundreds of Elvis-related products manufactured by Factors Etc., Inc.

---

[1]It was one of Phil Spector's strange arrangements. Love was not a member of the Crystals, nor did she get any credit on the record label; she was only the lead singer.

LOYD, HAROLD

(1931–   ) Son of Rhetha Smith Loyd (sister of Gladys Smith Presley), who died while Harold was growing up in Tupelo. Loyd then lived with different relatives in Tupelo, moving from one home to another. He was employed by his first cousin, Elvis, as a nightshift gate guard at Graceland. After Elvis's death, Loyd recorded a tribute record titled "A Prayer for Elvis" on the Modern Age Enterprises label in Memphis. He also founded the Graceland Fan Club of Memphis. Loyd cowrote, with George Baugh, the 1978 book *The Gates of Graceland*.

LOYD, ROBERT

Security guard at Graceland who is the son of Harold Loyd. It was Robert who called Memphis police at 3:07 A.M. on November 23, 1976, when Jerry Lee Lewis was making threats with his .38 derringer outside Graceland. Patrolman B. J. Kirkpatrick arrested Lewis, after which Memphis judge Albert Boyd found Lewis not guilty.

LUBBOCK, TEXAS

Hometown of Buddy Holly, Mac Davis, and Waylon Jennings. It was the site of the October 15, 1955, concert headlined by Elvis in the Cotton Club dance hall. Two local musicians named Buddy and Bob (Buddy Holly and Bob Montgomery) started the show. Thus, two legendary performers played on the same stage that night, Buddy Holly and Elvis Presley. After the performance, Jim Denny of Decca Records approached Holly with an offer to record for his label. One of the enthused spectators watching the show was a young lad named Scott (Mac) Davis, who would one day compose songs for Elvis.

LULU BELLE

(1913–   ) Singer and guitarist born Myrtle Eleanor Cooper on December 24, 1913. Lulu Belle performed with her husband, Scott Wiseman, as Lulu Belle and Scotty. In 1945 the couple composed and recorded the song "Have I Told You Lately That I Love You," which Elvis recorded in 1957.

LYRIC THEATER

Movie house in Tupelo, Mississippi, managed by John Grower in the mid-1940s. Elvis attended movies at the Strand and the Lyric theaters while living in Tupelo. One story has it that Elvis performed on stage there at several Saturday morning talent contests. (This may have occurred after his second place finish at the Mississippi-Alabama Fair and Dairy Show in 1945, and if true, establishes that Elvis performed on stage starting in boyhood.)

Publicity photo, 1956. (Photo courtesy Eddie Brandt's Saturday Matinee)

MacCOLL, EWAN
Composer of the song "The First Time Ever I Saw Your Face," which Elvis recorded in 1971.

MacLELLAN, GENE
Composer of the songs "Snowbird" and "Put Your Hand in the Hand," both of which Elvis recorded. In 1971 MacLellan himself recorded "Snowbird" (Capitol 2959).

MACAULAY, TONY
Composer, with John McCloud, of "If I Get Home on Christmas Day," and with Roger Greenaway of "Love Me, Love the Life I Lead." Both songs were recorded by Elvis in 1971.

MADISON CADILLAC
Memphis automobile dealership, located on Union Avenue, where Elvis bought many of his Cadillacs beginning in 1957. After 1967 Elvis bought his Cadillacs through salesman Howard Massey. On July 27, 1975, Elvis bought fourteen Cadillac Eldorados, which he gave away to friends.

MADISON, TENNESSEE
Town, north of Memphis, where Colonel Tom Parker made his home on Gallatin Road. It was also the headquarters of Parker's national business operations. In 1955 he used the address: Box 417, Madison, Tennessee. Parker and his wife, Marie, moved there after he became singer Eddy Arnold's manager because that is where Arnold made his home.

The Colonel and his wife later moved to a house at 1166 Vista Vespero Drive in Palm Springs, California.

MAID, THE MAN, AND THE FANS: ELVIS IS THE MAN, THE
Book written by Elvis's cook Nancy Rooks with Mae Gutter and published by Vantage Press.

MAINEGRA, RICHARD
Composer, with Red West, of the song "Separate Ways," which Elvis recorded in 1972.

MAJORS, LEE
(1939–   ) Hollywood actor born Harvey Lee Yeary in Wyandotte, Michigan, on April 23, 1939, the same day as actor David Birney. Majors, who was once married to actress Farrah Fawcett, has starred in such TV programs as "The Big Valley," "The Six Million Dollar Man" and "The Fall Guy." Majors and Elvis, who resembled each other to a certain degree, became friends, with Elvis once bringing him out on stage with him. For a time, Elvis appeared to be a little jealous of Majors's attentions toward singer Kathy Westmoreland and kidded him about it.

MALCO THEATRES, INC.
Memphis theater corporation located at 89 Beale Street. Paul Shafer, a Malco executive, supplied Elvis with movies for his private parties. *Let's Rock* (also known under the title *Keep It Cool*), the movie featuring Memphis disc jockey Wink Martindale, had its world premiere at the Malco Theatre in 1958.

MANHATTAN CLUB
Memphis nightclub, located on Bellevue Boulevard, that Elvis rented for New Year's Eve parties in 1962 and 1963. Rufus Thomas was the house performer at the time. One year, George Klein drove Priscilla back to Graceland, while Elvis stayed at the party. In 1967 Elvis again rented the club, inviting five hundred guests, but failed to show up because he was too tired from horseback riding all day.

MANN, BARRY AND CYNTHIA WEIL
Songwriting team originally with Aldon Music (Al Nevins and Don Kirshner). They composed hit records for Paul Petersen, the Crystals, Paul Revere and the Raiders, and the Righteous Brothers. The pair composed two songs Elvis recorded, "You've Lost That Lovin' Feelin'" (with Phil Spector) and "I Just Can't Help Believin'." In 1961 Mann recorded the hit "Who Put the Bomp" (ABC Paramount 10237). In 1968 he recorded the original version of "I Just Can't Help Believin'" (Capital 2217).

MANN, BOBBY
Hairdresser son of Charles Mann and Lillian Smith Mann, the older sister of Gladys Smith Presley. Mann, who was Elvis's cousin, photographed Elvis in his coffin for the *National Enquirer*, using a Minox camera. With the photograph on its cover, the *Enquirer* sold a record 6.5 million copies. The *Enquirer* supposedly paid $78,000 for the single photo.

A member of the Jordanaires commented about the photo in an interview in the *New Musical Express*: "Elvis hadn't looked like that in twenty years. I think that was the cruelest thing that's been done to him, that they superimposed an older picture of him in his coffin for the front of their newspaper. Everyone who was at the funeral knows that it was a one hundred percent fake photo."

MANN, CARL
(1941–   ) Singer and composer born in Jackson, Tennessee. Mann recorded the first rock version of "Mona Lisa" (Phillips International 3539), which Conway Twitty later copied in 1959. He also recorded the original version of "I'm Comin' Home" (Phillips International 3555), which Elvis recorded in 1961.

MANN, KAL AND BERNIE LOWE

Composers who founded Cameo-Parkway Records in Philadelphia in 1956. They composed the Elvis hit "Teddy Bear." Previously they wrote Pat Boone's 1956 hit "Remember You're Mine" (Dot 15602). The two men composed "Butterfly" for Charlie Gracie (Cameo 105) in 1956 under the pseudonym Anthony September.

MANN, MAY

Former Miss Utah and writer of the syndicated column "Going Hollywood with May Mann." Mann has authored a number of magazine articles, such as "I Want to Get Married by Elvis Presley, As Told to May Mann" for *Movieland* magazine; and several books about Elvis, such as *Elvis and the Colonel* (1975), *The Private Elvis* (1977), and *Elvis Why Won't They Leave You Alone?* (1982), in addition to books on other celebrities, including actress Jayne Mansfield (1973). Mann was one of only a few reporters to obtain access to Elvis, authorized by Colonel Tom Parker. In 1957 Mann was also the only person to have interviewed Parker. Mann, who was a protégé of actor Clark Gable (who was called "The King"), claims to have given Elvis the title "The King" in her syndicated column in *Fabulous Las Vegas* magazine.

MANNING, DICK

(1912–) Lyricist born in Gomel, Russia, on June 12, 1912. With Al Hoffman, Dick Manning cowrote the English lyrics to Charles E. King's "Hawaiian Wedding Song," which Elvis recorded in 1961. Manning wrote, with Fred Wise, the song "(There's) No Room to Rumba in a Sports Car," which Elvis sang in his 1963 movie *Fun in Acapulco*.

MANNING, JAMES

Flight engineer of Elvis's Convair 880 jet. He reportedly earned $39,000 a year in that capacity.

MANSELL, ANNA

(1854–1935) Daughter of John Mansell and Elizabeth Gilmore Mansell. Anna was the sister of White Mansell, who married Martha Tacket and parented Octavia (Doll) Mansell. Anna married Milege Obedia (Obe) Smith on December 13, 1874, and parented seven children: Jim, William, Hal, John, Tabby, Bell, and Robert Lee Smith, who married Octavia (Doll) Mansell, his cousin. Anna was the grandmother of Gladys Love Smith and the great-grandmother of Elvis Presley.

MANSELL, JOHN

(1828– ?) Son of William Mansell and Morning Dove White Mansell. John Mansell was the brother of Morning Dizenie Mansell and James J. Mansell. John married Elizabeth Gilmore in 1850 and they parented ten children, including Anna Mansell and White Mansell. Anna was the mother of Robert Lee Smith and White Mansell was the father of Octavia (Doll) Mansell (Robert married his first cousin, Octavia). John Mansell was the grandfather of both Robert Lee Smith and Octavia (Doll) Mansell, the great-grandfather of Gladys Love Smith and the great-great-grandfather of Elvis Presley.

MANSELL, MELLISA

Sister of Doll Mansell Smith (mother of Gladys Smith Presley). While Vernon was serving time in Parchman Penitentiary in 1938–39, Gladys and Elvis moved in with Frank and Leona Richards and their family. Frank Richards was the son of Mellisa Mansell.

MANSELL, OCTAVIA LAVENIA (DOLL)

(1876–1935) Daughter of White Mansell and Martha Tacket and the wife of her first cousin Robert Lee Smith. Doll Mansell was born in Spring Hill, Missouri, during America's Centennial year. She and Robert were the parents of Gladys Love Smith, as well as John, Clettes, Tracy, Travis, Rhetha, Levalle, Lillian, and Effie (who died at one year and two months of age). Octavia (Doll) Mansell was the grandmother of Elvis Presley.

MANSELL, RICHARD

Revolutionary War soldier who was the father of William Mansell, the grandfather of John Mansell, the great-grandfather of Anna Mansell and White Mansell, the great-great-grandfather of Robert Lee Smith and Octavia (Doll) Mansell, the great-great-great-grandfather of Gladys Love Smith, and the great-great-great-great-grandfather of Elvis Presley.

MANSELL, WHITE

(1849–) Son of John Mansell and Elizabeth Gilmore Mansell. White was the brother of Anna Mansell, who married Milege (Obe) Smith and parented Robert Lee Smith. White married Martha Tacket on January 22, 1870, and parented Octavia (Doll) Mansell, who would marry Robert Lee Smith. After Martha's death, White married Sarah (Dealy) Kemp. White Mansell was the grandfather of Gladys Love Smith and the great-grandfather of Elvis Presley.

MANSELL, WILLIAM

(1795–1842) Son of Richard Mansell, the husband of Morning Dove White, and the father of John Mansell (1828–), Morning Dizenie Mansell (1832–), and James J. Mansell (1835–). William was the grandfather of Anna Mansell and White Mansell. He was the great-grandfather of Robert Lee Smith and Octavia (Doll) Mansell, the great-great-grandfather of Gladys Love Smith, and the great-great-great-grandfather of Elvis Presley. William was a soldier who fought the Indians under General Andrew Jackson. In November 1955, at the Andrew Jackson Hotel in Nashville, RCA Victor agreed to sign Elvis to their label.

MANSFIELD, DONALD (REX)

(1936–) Friend of Elvis's in the Army in West Germany. Mansfield, who was born in Dresden, Tennessee, was nicknamed "Rexadus" by Elvis. Elvis practiced his karate with Mansfield, who had been one of the twelve soldiers to travel with Elvis from Memphis to Fort Chaffee, Arkansas, aboard a Greyhound bus on the day of his induction. Mansfield, who was promoted to sergeant before Elvis, was with Elvis through boot camp, as well as being stationed with him in West Germany, and was discharged at the same time. Mansfield married Elvis's secretary in West Germany, Elisabeth Stefaniak, having had a secret affair with her while she lived in Elvis's house. In 1981 the Mansfields authored the book *Elvis in Deutschland*; in 1983 they wrote *Elvis the Soldier*; and in 1985 they authored *Elvis the Private Soldier*, all of which were published in West Germany.

In the book *Elvis the Soldier*, Mansfield claims that Elvis gave him amphetamine pills at Goethestrasse 14 in Bad Nauheim in January 1959, and that Elvis was buying pills from a soldier who worked in the dispensary.

MANZANERO, ARMANDO
Composer, with Sid Wayne, of the song "It's Impossible," which Elvis recorded in concert in 1972.

MARASCALCO, JOHN
Composer, with Robert (Bumps) Blackwell, of the songs "Ready Teddy" and "Rip It Up," both of which Elvis recorded in 1956.

MARCUS, SOL
Composer, with Bennie Benjamin and Louis A. DeJesus, of the song "Anyone (Could Fall in Love with You)," which Elvis sang in the 1964 movie *Kissin' Cousins*; and, with Bennie Benjamin, of the song "Lonely Man," which Elvis sang in the 1961 movie *Wild in the Country*.

MARE INGRAM
One of the horses Elvis boarded at the Circle G Ranch. The horse was named for William Ingram, who was the mayor of Memphis at the time.

MARG, HAL
Vice president of RCA Victor Records who, in 1956, presented Elvis with his Gold Record for "Heartbreak Hotel."

MARKET SQUARE ARENA
Indianapolis auditorium where, on June 26, 1977, Elvis gave his last live concert.

MARL METAL MANUFACTURING COMPANY
Memphis firm located at 208 Georgia Avenue where Elvis worked for a dollar an hour for two months, starting in September 1952. The company manufactured dinette sets. He worked a full shift from 3:00 P.M. to 11:30 P.M. When he began to fall asleep in his high school classes, his parents made him quit his job at Marl Metal.

Marl stood for *Morris*, *Albert*, *Robert*, and *Louis* Bozoff, the brothers who owned the company. Elvis was hired by Robert Bozoff to work in the fabricating division.

MARMANN, ELSIE
Elvis's music teacher at L. C. Humes High School in Memphis. Marmann told Elvis that he couldn't sing, when on one occasion Elvis sang off key in class. Marmann is quoted in Jerry Hopkins's book *Elvis: A Biography* as having said, "He wasn't in my glee club. He didn't have the kind of voice I could use in a glee club."

MARQUETT, ROBERT STEPHEN
(1952–   ) Young polio victim son of an Army master sergeant with whom Elvis posed in 1959, as a private in the Army, to launch the March of Dimes drive. Marquett was one of a number of children with whom Elvis posed.

The March of Dimes was a campaign of the National Foundation of Infantile Paralysis to raise money for polio victims. The foundation was founded on January 3, 1938, by President Franklin D. Roosevelt, himself a victim. The phrase "March of Dimes" was coined by comedian Eddie Cantor. In 1964 Elvis tried to present his yacht the *Potomac* to the March of Dimes, but the organization turned it down.

MARTIN, BECKY
Schoolmate of Elvis's at Lawhon School in Tupelo, Mississippi. As an adult, Martin once visited Elvis at Graceland. She remembered Elvis singing the song "God Bless My Daddy" while in chapel one day.

MARTIN, BILL
Composer, with Phil Coulter, of the English lyrics of the song "My Boy," which was composed by J. Claude Francois and Jean-Pierre Boutayre, and recorded by Elvis in 1975.

MARTIN D-28 AND GIBSON J-200
Brands of acoustic guitars played by Elvis during the 1950s.

MARTIN, DAVID
Composer, with Chris Arnold and Geoffrey Morrow, of the songs "A Little Bit of Green," "Let's Be Friends," "This Is the Story," and "Sweet Angeline," all of which Elvis recorded.

MARTIN, DEAN
(1917–   ) Singer and actor born Dino Crocetti Jr. in Steubenville, Ohio, on June 7, 1917. Martin worked as the straight man of the comedy team Martin and Lewis (Jerry Lewis), until they split up in 1956. After the comedians split, they did not see each other again for twenty years, until Frank Sinatra surprised Lewis on September 5, 1976, at one of his telethons in Las Vegas by bringing Martin on stage. There, the twenty-year-old feud died.

Martin became a successful recording artist and actor. He was one of Elvis's singing idols in the early 1950s, perhaps his favorite. Martin's daughter Gina married Carl Wilson of the Beach Boys in 1987. In the 1953 movie *Scared Stiff*, Martin sang "I Don't Care If the Sun Don't Shine," which Elvis would record the following year. Elvis sang Martin's 1964 number one hit song "Everybody Loves Somebody" (Reprise 0281) in concert at the International Hotel on January 26,

1970, with Martin in the audience. It is believed that Elvis sang Martin's 1953 hit "That's Amore" (Capitol 2589) in Memphis clubs in early 1954.

MARTIN, DINO
(1951–1987) Son of singer and actor Dean Martin, born Dean Paul Anthony Martin Jr. in Los Angeles on November 12, 1951. In 1987 Dino was killed when his Air National Guard F-4 Phantom jet crashed into a California mountain. In 1965 Dino formed the rock band Dino, Desi and Billy (Desi Arnaz Jr. and Billy Hinsche, brother of Carl Wilson's former wife). The trio was discovered by Frank Sinatra, who signed them to his record label, Reprise Records. Martin was once ranked #250 in World Tennis. He was also drafted by the Portland Storm of the World Football League, but he never played. He was married to Olympic skater Dorothy Hamill and to actress Olivia Hussey.

In 1957 Martin convinced his father to take him to Paramount Studios to meet Elvis. In 1977, in their last concert together, Elvis told John O'Grady that he'd do just about anything legal to date ice skater Dorothy Hamill, who was Martin's former wife.

MARTIN, FREDDY
(1906–) Popular bandleader of the 1940s, born in Cleveland on December 9, 1906. Martin's theme song, "Tonight We Love" (Bluebird 11211), based on "Tchaikovsky's Piano Concerto No. 1," became a huge hit in 1941. Singer and TV producer Merv Griffin was once a vocalist for the band. Martin was the featured performer at the New Frontier Hotel in Las Vegas when Elvis appeared there in 1956.

MARTIN, GRADY
(1929–) Musician born Thomas Grady Martin in Chapel Hill, Tennessee, on January 17, 1929. A guitarist, Martin has played on recordings by Buddy Holly, Brenda Lee, and Marty Robbins. He and Chet Atkins are the only musicians to have played behind both Hank Williams and Elvis. Martin played lead guitar on Marty Robbins's number one hit "El Paso" (Columbia 41511), and later recorded his own version (Decca 31619). Martin played on Elvis's recording sessions from March 1962 to February 1965. He can be seen in the 1980 Willie Nelson movie *Honeysuckle Rose.*

MARTIN, JANIS DARLENE
(1940–) Singer, born on March 27, 1940, in Sutherlin, Virginia, who was billed by RCA Victor Records as "The Female Elvis," an idea created by Steve Sholes. Martin was also called "the girl with the Elvis Presley voice." She appeared with Dave Garroway on the "Today Show" in 1957, singing "My Boy Elvis." RCA Victor released "My Boy Elvis" (RCA 6652) and "Ooby Dooby" (RCA 6560) in 1957. In 1958 a ten-inch album titled *Janis and Elvis* was issued in South Africa on the Teal Record label. Both Janis and Elvis were featured, singing six songs each. When Colonel Tom Parker found out about the release and what RCA was doing, he protested loudly, and within days the albums were withdrawn from stores. In 1985 that same album was legally released in France by RCA. Martin had been married since the age of fifteen, but the fact was kept secret by RCA.

MARTIN, ROY
Grocer whose store was located on Lake Street at the intersection of Highway 78 and North Saltillo Road in Tupelo, Mississippi. Vernon Presley worked for Martin in the late 1940s, delivering groceries in his truck, especially into Shakerag, a black section of Tupelo. It was at Martin's that Gladys shopped for her groceries.

MARTINDALE, SANDY FERRA
Wife of singer and TV host Wink Martindale. As a teenager Ferra dated Elvis in 1960 while he was filming *G.I. Blues.*

MARTINDALE, WINK
(1934–) Country singer born Winston Conrad Martindale in Bells, Tennessee, on December 4, 1934. Martindale has also been called Win Martindale. He has hosted the TV game shows "Gambit," "How's Your Mother-in-Law?" "Can You Top This," "What's This Song," "Words and Music," and "Tic Tac Dough," among others.

Martindale worked at WHBQ in Memphis beginning on April 20, 1953, and was there when Dewey Phillips first played an Elvis record. Martindale met Elvis for the first time that evening.

On Memphis's KLAC-TV's "Dance Party," Martindale interviewed Elvis in 1956. Martindale, like almost everyone else in Memphis, cut an unreleased song at Sun Records, "Bug a Bop," backed by Bill Justis's orchestra. He made his movie debut in the 1958 rock & roll movie *Keep It Cool.* In 1959 Martindale recorded a hit record titled "Deck of Cards" (Dot 15968).

MARTINE JR., LAYNG
Singer and composer of the song "Way Down," which Elvis recorded in 1976. In 1971 Martine charted the song "Rub It In" (Barnaby 2041).

MARX, GROUCHO
(1890–1977) Member of the famed Marx Brothers comedy team. Born Julius Marx, on October 2, 1890, he died on August 19, 1977, just three days after Elvis's death. Groucho, as host of the TV quiz show "You Bet Your Life" (Elvis's hero, General Omar Bradley, and a young singer named Patsy Cline were two of his contestants), once interviewed the president of the Elvis Presley Fan Club. (It was shown in the 1981 movie *This Is Elvis.*) He was one of several celebrities to die shortly after Elvis. (See *Zero Mostel, Sebastian Cabot*)

MASON, BARRY
Composer, with Les Reed, of the song "Girl of Mine," which Elvis recorded in 1973.

MATSON, VERA
Listed composer of Elvis's "Love Me Tender," "Let Me,"

"We're Gonna Move," and "Poor Boy." Matson is the wife of singer Ken Darby, who was the actual composer of the songs.[1]

MAWN, CAPT. JOHN

Public information director at Fort Chaffee, Arkansas, when Elvis was indoctrinated in March 1958.

MAYFIELD, CURTIS

(1942–   ) Singer and composer born in Chicago on June 3, 1942. He sang as a member of the Impressions, who backed Jerry Butler on his hit song "For Your Precious Love" (Abner 1013), and also played guitar. Mayfield wrote the number one hit song "Hit the Road Jack" (ABC Paramount 10244) for Ray Charles. Mayfield composed new lyrics to the gospel song "Amen" with John W. Pate Sr. Elvis frequently sang "Amen" in concert.

MAYFIELD, PERCY

Composer of "Stranger in My Own Home Town" (which he recorded in 1963). Elvis recorded this song in 1969.

M. B. PARKER MACHINISTS SHOP

Memphis tool company owned by M. B. Parker and David Parker. Elvis worked there in 1953, quitting in September.

McCARTY, L. P.

Vegetable wholesaler for whom Vernon Presley worked in Tupelo, Mississippi, from 1946 to 1948 for $22 a week. Elvis often liked to ride in the truck his dad used for deliveries. After Vernon lost his job there in September 1948, the family packed up and moved to Memphis. One story has it that Vernon was fired because he used McCarty's truck to distribute moonshine.

In 1979 the Elvis Memorial Chapel in Tupelo was unveiled. It was designed by L. P. McCarty's son, L. P. (Buddy) McCarty Jr.

McCARTNEY, PAUL

(1942–   ) Musician born James Paul McCartney in Liverpool, England, on June 19, 1942. As members of the Beatles, he and John Lennon composed "Hey Jude" and "Yesterday," both of which Elvis recorded.

McCartney once noted, "Every time I felt low, I just put on an Elvis record and I'd feel great, beautiful." (See *The Beatles*)

McCLELLAN, LOU

Purchaser of Elvis's Circle G Ranch in May 1969 for a $440,100 note carried by Elvis, with plans to turn it into a gun club. Because of problems in getting a permit for a gun club, McClellan had to put the ranch up for auction and Elvis bought it back.

McCOMBE, JANELLE

Tupelo, Mississippi, bookkeeper who was the force behind the construction of the Elvis Memorial Chapel. McCombe once asked Elvis at Graceland how he would like to be honored in Tupelo, to which he replied, "Why not build a chapel to God in my name."

McCORD, KENT

(1942–   ) Television actor born in Los Angeles on September 26, 1942. McCord played Los Angeles police officer Jim Reed on the TV series "Adam-12." McCord first began to appear on television after a friend of his, actor and singer Ricky Nelson, recruited him for a football team that was to play against Elvis's undefeated Bel Air team.

McCOY, CHARLIE

(1941–   ) Musician born in Oak Hill, West Virginia, on March 28, 1941. McCoy played harmonica on several of Elvis's sessions, beginning in 1965. He played on the soundtrack sessions for the films *Harum Scarum*, *Frankie and Johnny*, *Easy Come, Easy Go*, and *Paradise, Hawaiian Style*. McCoy has also backed other artists, such as Bob Dylan and Ringo Starr. He played in the house band at the Grand Ole Opry.

McCOY, ROSE MARIE

Composer, with Kelly Owens, of the song "I Beg of You," which Elvis recorded in 1957; and, with Margie Singleton, of the song "Tryin' to Get to You," which Elvis recorded in 1955. McCoy recorded a song in 1972 titled "I Do the Best I Can with What I Got" (Brunswick 55541).

Ronnie McDowell. (Photo courtesy Tandy Rice)

---

[1] Composers sometimes list wives, mothers, or other relatives as a song's composer when they are writing a song for one union while they are a member of another, such as BMI or ASCAP.

McDOWELL, RONNIE

(1950–) Country artist and Elvis sound-alike born in Portland, Tennessee, on March 26, 1950. McDowell recorded the tribute record "The King Is Gone" (Scorpion 135), which peaked at number thirteen on *Billboard*'s Hot 100 singles chart in 1977. McDowell recorded the vocals used in the 1979 TV movie *Elvis*. He actually recorded thirty-six songs, but not all of them were used in the film. McDowell also sang the Elvis vocals for the 1981 TV movie *Elvis and the Beauty Queen* and for the 1988 TV miniseries "Elvis and Me." As a boy of eight, McDowell first saw Elvis in the 1958 movie *King Creole*.

McFADDEN, GEORGE

Composer, with William Johnson and Ted Brooks, of the religious songs "Bosom of Abraham" and "I, John," both of which Elvis recorded.

McFARLAND, J. LESLIE

Composer, with Winfield Scott, of the song "Long Legged Girl (with the Short Dress On)," which Elvis recorded in 1967, and "Stuck on You," with Aaron Schroeder.

McGARRITY, BONYA

One of Elvis's personal secretaries at Graceland, along with Pat Boyd and Becky Yancey. McGarrity was hired through the Tennessee State Employment Agency. She left Graceland in mid-1962.

McGREGOR, MIKE

One of Elvis's groundskeepers and handymen at Graceland. McGregor also attended to Elvis's horses.

McGUIRE AIR FORCE BASE

U.S. Air Force facility located next to the U.S. Army's Fort Dix in New Jersey, where the MATS C-118 transport aircraft, carrying Elvis and seventy-four other G.I.s returning home from their European assignment, landed in a snowstorm on March 3, 1960. Elvis, Alex Moore, and Rex Mansfield, who had been inducted together, were now discharged together, receiving $147 in mustering out pay. One of the people present to meet Elvis was singer Nancy Sinatra, who was romantically linked with Elvis at the time. Elvis left McGuire AFB and traveled the short distance to Fort Dix, where he was discharged.

McINTYRE, SGT. ROBERT

ROTC instructor at L. C. Humes High School in Memphis while Elvis was a student there and a member of the ROTC.

McKELLER LAKE

Lake outside of Memphis where Elvis went boat racing and water skiing in one of several boats he owned. Vernon Presley owned a cabin on the lake.

McLEAN, DON

(1945–) Singer and composer born in New Rochelle, New York, on October 2, 1945. McLean composed and recorded the song "And I Love You So," which Elvis recorded in 1975. In 1971 McLean recorded the hit song "American Pie" (United Artists 50856), which referred to Elvis as "The King." In the song McLean also refers to "The Queen," who it is speculated is singer Connie Francis.

McMAHON, MIKE

Business associate of Elvis's who played racquetball with him at Graceland. It was McMahon who in 1975 first suggested that Elvis lend his name and invest in the Presley Center Courts, Inc.

McMAINS, PADDY

Composer, with Bob Roberts, of the song "Echoes of Love," which Elvis recorded in 1963.

McMANN, BETTY

Memphis girl with whom Elvis went steady when he was fifteen years old. Betty, who was Elvis's first girlfriend, taught him to dance.

McNULTY, DONALD LESLIE

Australian who legally changed his name to Elvis Presley. McNulty decided to change his name after seeing Elvis in the 1960 movie *G.I. Blues*; he further decided that he looked like Elvis. Don (Elvis Presley) McNulty also named his son Elvis.

McPHATTER, CLYDE

(1931–1972) Singer born in Durham, North Carolina, on November 15, 1931. Like Elvis, McPhatter served in the U.S. Army in Germany. He began as the lead singer of Billy Ward and His Dominoes from 1950 to 1953, leaving to join the Drifters. He was replaced by the equally talented Jackie Wilson. Elvis recorded several songs recorded by the Drifters on which McPhatter sang lead vocal, "Money Honey" (Atlantic 1006), "Such a Night" (Atlantic 1019), and "White Christmas" (Atlantic 1048), as well as McPhatter's solo effort "Without Love (I Have Nothing)" (Atlantic 1117). Billy Swan, who had once worked as a gate guard at Graceland, wrote McPhatter's 1962 hit "Lover Please" (Mercury 71941).

Elvis once said to Sam Phillips after hearing McPhatter sing over the car radio, "You know, if I had a voice like that man, I'd never want for another thing." (See *The Drifters*)

ME 'N ELVIS

Autobiography of Charlie Hodge written in 1985 by Hodge with Memphis *Press-Scimitar* reporter Charles Goodman, and published by Castle Books.

MEADE, NORMAN

Composer, with Doc Pomus, of the song "Girl Happy," which Elvis sang in the 1965 movie of the same name.

MEDALS

During Elvis's Army career he was awarded two medals for expert marksmanship—one for rifle and pistol, the other for sharpshooting with a carbine.

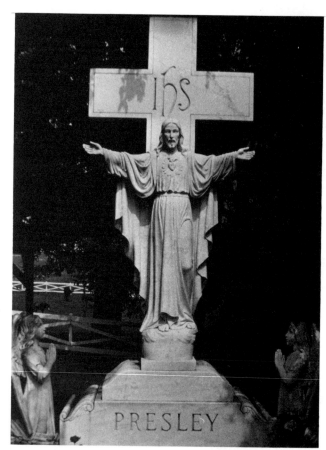

Statue dedicated to Gladys Presley in the Meditation Gardens. (Photo courtesy Don Fink)

MEDITATION GARDENS

Gravesite at Graceland of Elvis Presley, Gladys Presley, Vernon Presley, and Minnie Mae Presley, as well as the location of a plaque to Jesse Garon Presley (spelled Jessie). The Gardens were designed and built in 1963 by Marty Lacker's sister Anne and her husband Bernie Granadier. The bodies of both Elvis and Gladys were moved from Forest Hill Cemetery to the Meditation Gardens on Sunday night, October 2, 1977. On November 27, 1977, the Gardens were opened to the public, but the remainder of Graceland remained off limits. Vernon Presley's body was laid to rest there on June 28, 1979, with his mother, Minnie Mae, following the next year. At Vernon's funeral, songs sung by Elvis were played over a loudspeaker, including "Peace in the Valley." Vernon's funeral was officiated by the Reverends C. W. Buddy and M. H. Kennedy.

One story has it that on the night of Elvis's death the lights illuminating the Gardens went out for an unknown reason.

MEDLEY, BILL

(1940–   ) Former member of the Righteous Brothers, born in Santa Ana, California, on September 19, 1940, who along with Sammy Davis Jr. was offered the song "In the Ghetto" before Elvis recorded it. Unlike Davis, Medley turned it down.

Elvis once interrupted a Bill Medley performance in Las Vegas by walking across the stage as a joke. Elvis repeated the prank the next night. Medley recorded the tribute song to Elvis titled "Old Friend" on his album *Still Hung Up on You.*

MEET ELVIS PRESLEY

A 1971 trade paperback book written by F. Louis Friedman and published by Scholastic Books. The book was written for school children.

MELLO MEN

Vocal group that backed Elvis on the 1963 song "One Broken Heart for Sale," and the flip side "They Remind Me Too Much of You." This was the only single on which the group performed. The Mello Men appeared in the 1963 movie *It Happened at the World's Fair,* having sung backup on the soundtrack session at Radio Recorders in Hollywood in October 1962.

MEMPHIAN THEATRE

One of the Memphis theaters, located at 51 South Cooper, which was rented by Elvis for his private movie showings. It was there that he first met Linda Thompson in 1972. In 1981 the movie *This Is Elvis* made its world premiere at the Memphian.

MEMPHIS FUNERAL HOME

Mortuary, at 1177 Union Avenue in Memphis, that handled the funerals of Elvis, Vernon Presley, and Bill Black. (See *National Funeral Home*)

MEMPHIS MAFIA

Close friends, associates, and employees of Elvis, as labeled by the news media about 1960, much like Frank Sinatra's Clan or Rat Pack of the 1960s and Humphrey Bogart's Holmby Hills Rat Pack of the 1950s. Since there were so many people with whom Elvis came in contact, a precise list would be impossible. Here is a partial list of the members: Alan Fortas, Sonny West, Charlie Hodge, Red West, Gene Smith, Billy Smith, Marty Lacker, Joe Esposito, Lamar Fike, Ray Sitton, Marvin Gamble, Patsy Gamble, Bitsy Mott, Louis Harris, George Klein, Jimmy Kingsley, Cliff Gleaves, Larry Geller, and Jerry Schilling.

Before being named the Memphis Mafia, they were called El's Angels and Elvis Presley's boys. The members who worked for Elvis made approximately $250 a week each in the 1960s, which rose to $425 a week in the 1970s, but Elvis often loaned or gave them the money needed for down payments on houses. He also gave them automobiles, bonuses, and money whenever he felt the urge. However, even with all the gifts, the money wasn't that much, so many of them worked for Elvis for a personal reason. Many acted as bodyguards, carrying .38 pistols to protect Elvis. It has been suggested that in order to become a member of Elvis's inner circle, each member went through an initiation ceremony; but if true, little is known of this.

MEMPHIS POOL AND LANDSCAPING COMPANY

Memphis firm, at 6620 Highway 70, that took care of the Graceland swimming pool.

MEMPHIS RECORDING SERVICE
Recording studio, located at 706 Union Avenue in Memphis (telephone: JAckson 7-7197), begun by Sam Phillips in 1950 in what had previously been a radiator shop. For four dollars, a person could record a two-sided acetate at the studio. The motto of the firm was "We Record Anything—Anywhere—Anytime." Elvis came to the Memphis Recording Service in the summer of 1953 (the exact date is unknown) and, after talking to secretary Marion Keisker, recorded two songs: "My Happiness" and "That's When Your Heartaches Begin." In interviews (by May Mann) Elvis repeated the story that he decided to cut a record as a birthday present for his mother, even though Gladys's birthday had already passed by several months. Elvis returned to the Memphis Recording Service on January 4, 1954, to record two more songs: "I'll Never Stand in Your Way" and "Casual Love Affair." Sam Phillips was there on that occasion, but Marion Keisker was not. The Memphis Recording Service was also the home of Sun Records. (See *Sun Records, Sam Phillips, Marion Keisker*)

MEMPHIS STATE UNIVERSITY
School where Elvis sometimes played racquetball.

MERCEDES-BENZ
Four-door black sedan automobile owned by Elvis while he was stationed in Germany. The car was involved in an accident when another car pulled in front of Vernon Presley on the Autobahn. He and his passenger, Elisabeth Stefaniak, were shaken up but not injured.

MERCER, JOHNNY
(1909–1976) Songwriter born in Savannah, Georgia, on November 18, 1909. Mercer composed dozens of classic songs, including "That Old Black Magic" (with Jerome Kern), "Satin Doll" (with Duke Ellington), and "Moon River" (with Henry Mancini). In 1942 Mercer and Buddy de Sylva, with the administration of Glenn E. Wallichs, founded Capitol Records. (It was Capitol that first turned down the U.S. distribution rights to the Beatles.) Mercer composed, with Rube Bloom, "Fools Rush In (Where Angels Fear to Tread)," which Elvis recorded in 1971.

MERCURY RECORDS
Chicago-based record label founded in 1946 that unsuccessfully bid $10,000 for Elvis in October 1955. Dee Kilpatrick made the company's offer. In 1951 Scotty Moore played guitar on Eddie Hill's "Hot Guitar," which was released on Mercury.

MESSERSCHMIDT
Red and black German car (I.D. #56007) bought by Elvis in March 1956. In August of that year Elvis gave the three-wheeled car to clothing store owner Bernard Lansky in exchange for selecting a wardrobe from his store. Elvis spent two and a half hours picking out the clothing.

MESSINA, JIM
(1947–) Singer and composer born in Maywood, California, on December 5, 1947. Messina was a member of the band Poco before he joined Kenny Loggins. Messina and Loggins composed and recorded "Your Mama Don't Dance" (Columbia 45719) in 1972, which Elvis recorded in 1974.

METHODIST CHURCH
Nashville church facility owned by the Methodist TV, Radio and Film Commission, located at 1525 McGavock Street, where, on January 10, 1956, Elvis recorded "Heartbreak Hotel." RCA Victor used the converted facility as a recording studio that day. Ironically, the first song recorded at the session was "I Got a Woman," a cover of the song by Ray Charles that he had based on the gospel tune "My Jesus Is All the World I Need."

METHODIST HOSPITAL
Memphis medical facility at 1265 Union Avenue, where Gladys Love Presley died of a heart attack on August 14, 1958. She had been sequestered in room 688. (See *Gladys Presley*)

MEYER, ALAN
Elvis sound-alike entertainer, billed as "Alan," who provided the Elvis songs "Love Me Tender," "Teddy Bear," and "I Was the One" for the 1980 movie *Touched by Love*. This former NASA engineer is the highest paid of all Elvis imitators, earning $50,000 a week in Las Vegas. Alan, who is managed by Chet Actis, began impersonating Elvis in 1974 and sounds like Elvis in his early years. Alan has been featured in the Las Vegas show "Elvis Forever." He told *Hollywood Reporter* columnist Martin A. Grove in June 1978: "I do not consider it flattering to be considered the best imitator. That just puts me at the top of the garbage heap. As a matter of fact, I'm the best Elvis imitator because I don't imitate him at all. I happen to sound like him—I can't control that. But I don't want to be categorized with the imitators. I like to think I pay tributes."

MEYER, DR. DAVID
Elvis's eye doctor, whose Memphis offices are located at 909 Ridgeway Loop Road.

MGM
Metro-Goldwyn-Mayer studios in Culver City, California, where Elvis became the first person to be given two dressing rooms. One of those rooms had been used previously by another "king," actor Clark Gable. The dressing room had also been used by actor Robert Taylor.

The MGM studios were featured prominently in the 1970 documentary *Elvis—That's the Way It Is*.

MID-SOUTH HOSPITAL
Memphis medical facility where, on June 18, 1975, Elvis underwent a face-lift.

MID-SOUTH LAUNDRY
Tupelo cleaning establishment where Gladys Presley worked in 1947.

MILAM JUNIOR HIGH SCHOOL
Junior high school located at the corner of Gloser and Jefferson streets in Tupelo, Mississippi. Elvis entered

Milam Junior High School class photo. Elvis is in the upper righthand corner wearing overalls. (Photo courtesy Jeff Wheatcraft)

the school in the fall of 1946, attending the sixth, seventh, and part of the eighth grade. He left when he and his family moved to Memphis in 1948. Two of Elvis's teachers there were Mrs. Quay Web Camp and Virginia Plumb.

MILES, C. AUSTIN
(1868–1946) Composer born in Lakehurst, New Jersey, on January 7, 1868. Miles composed the religious song "In the Garden," which Elvis recorded in 1966.

MILETE, SHIRL
Singer and composer of the songs "Life," "My Little Friend," "When I'm over You," and, with Nora Fowler, "It's Your Baby, You Rock It," all of which Elvis recorded. In 1964 Milete recorded "God Bless My Woman" (Capitol 3750).

MILITARY OCEAN TERMINAL
Elvis's port of embarkation, located in Brooklyn, from which he left the United States on September 22, 1958. The Army band played "All Shook Up," "Hound Dog," "Don't Be Cruel," "Tutti Frutti," "Dixie," and "Sentimental Journey" in military fashion.

MILLER, EDDIE
Composer, with W. S. Stevenson (Dub Williams), of the song "Release Me (and Let Me Love Again)," which Elvis recorded in 1970. Miller composed, with Johnny Lantz, the song "After Loving You," which Elvis recorded in 1969.

MILLER, LOU ANN
Only female who worked with Colonel Tom Parker in his organization.

MILLER, MINDY
Woman whom Elvis dated after his breakup with Linda Thompson in 1976.

MILLER, MITCH
(1911–   ) Head A&R man for Columbia Records during the 1950s, born William Mitchell Miller in Rochester, New York, on July 4, 1911. Miller was once the Amateur Athletic Union wrestling champion of New York (at 105 pounds). He did not like rock & roll music, once saying, "It's not music, it's a disease." Because of this, Columbia Records was the last major label to record rock artists (the same was not true of Columbia [EMI] Records of Britain, which signed the first British rock star, Cliff Richard, in 1958). Columbia's first rock group was Paul Revere and the Raiders, who joined the label in 1965. In 1950 Frank Sinatra left Columbia because Miller gave him such poor material to record. The song that broke the camel's back was a duet with the sexy Dagmar titled "Mama Barks." Sinatra went to the Capitol label.

After being told about Elvis by Gene Weiss, Miller showed interest in obtaining Elvis for the Columbia label, but when Bob Neal told Miller that the bid was up to $18,000, Miller said, "Oh, forget it, nobody's worth that much." With Miller's attitude toward rock music and his refusal to envision the future of music, it is just as well that he did not bid on Elvis. Miller had also turned down Connie Francis for Columbia Records. He did sign singer Anita Bryant, whom he met when he was a judge at one of her beauty contests.

Miller and Elvis both recorded the song "Yellow Rose of Texas." Miller's album *Sing Along with Mitch* (Columbia 1160) in 1958 prevented Elvis's *King Creole* album from going to number one on *Billboard*'s album chart.

MILLER, NED
(1925–   ) Singer and songwriter born in Rains, Utah, on April 12, 1925. Miller wrote and recorded "From a Jack to a King" (Fabor 114) in 1957, which became a hit in 1963. Elvis recorded the song in 1969. Miller also composed the song "Dark Moon," which became a hit for Gale Storm (Dot 15558) and for Bonnie Guitar (Dot 15550) in 1957. Miller later recorded his own version of "Dark Moon" (Capitol 4652). Elvis recorded "Dark Moon" in a private home session.

MILLER, SANDY
(1941–   ) Denver woman who was Vernon Presley's nurse and girlfriend. Miller attended to him at the time of his heart attack in 1979, and Vernon left her most of his estate. Vernon was seeing Miller while he was still married to Dee Stanley, who filed for divorce when she learned of their relationship. Stanley once confronted Miller about her affair with her husband.

MILLION-DOLLAR QUARTET
(See entry in Part III)

MILLROSE, VICTOR D.

(1935–   ) Composer and record producer born in Boston on May 25, 1935. Millrose composed, with Lenore Rosenblatt, the song "Smokey Mountain Boy," which Elvis sang in the 1964 movie *Kissin' Cousins*, and the song "Startin' Tonight," which Elvis sang in the 1965 movie *Girl Happy*.

MILSAP, RONNIE

(1944–   ) Blind country singer born in Robbinsville, North Carolina, on January 16, 1944. Ronnie Milsap and the Short Kids were the featured performers at Elvis's 1969 New Year's Eve party at T.J.'s in Memphis, where Milsap played regularly. Milsap, who was also an RCA Victor artist, sang backup and played piano on Elvis's recording session at American Sound Studio in Memphis in January 1969. He sang duet with Elvis on "Don't Cry Daddy." George Klein has said that Milsap sang the high parts on Elvis's "Kentucky Rain," which were later overdubbed onto the song.

Milsap was born on the same day as director John Carpenter, who directed the 1979 TV movie *Elvis*.

MINOR, WILMA

Los Angeles nutritionist whom vegetarian Larry Geller talked Elvis into visiting in 1966 to straighten out his diet. Minor warned Elvis that he would have to change his eating habits or his health would deteriorate.

MINSTREL, THE

White leather-bound book written by Bernard Benson in December 1976. The 1,600-word text, with stick figures as illustrations, originally sold for $250 a copy. The book, which was published by Minstrel Publishing Company in Memphis, was personally delivered by Benson in his white Cadillac. Benson, born in 1922, had flown with Great Britain's Royal Air Force during World War II. Afterward he turned to inventing, reportedly helping develop such weapons as the air-to-air missile and working on the Concorde.

Elvis owned a copy of *The Minstrel*, which Benson had sent to Elvis on his forty-second birthday. In publicity ads for the book, Charlie Hodge was quoted as saying, "The truest story about Elvis ever written. Understanding *The Minstrel* is understanding the true Elvis." And Dick Grob was quoted as saying, "The book is probably the truest story of Elvis that could have been written, especially from a spiritual standpoint."

MISSISSIPPI-ALABAMA FAIR AND DAIRY SHOW

Annual fair in Tupelo, Mississippi, launched in 1904 as the Lee County Fair. On October 3, 1945, J. D. Cole, principal of the Lawhon Grammar School, entered Elvis in the annual talent contest sponsored by WELO radio. Elvis won second prize ($5 and free admission to all the amusement rides that day), singing "Old Shep." Shirley Jones Gallentine won first prize. This was Elvis's first public appearance, and since the talent show was broadcast over WELO, also his first radio performance. The two featured performers at the fair that year were Minnie Pearl and Pee Wee King.

(Photo courtesy Don Fink)

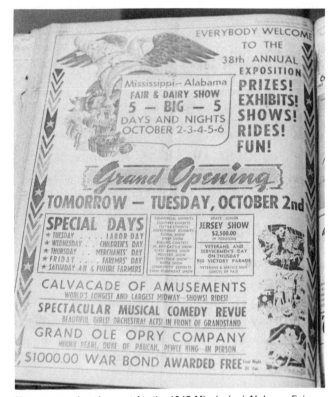

Newspaper advertisement for the 1945 Mississippi-Alabama Fair and Dairy Show. (Photo courtesy Don Fink)

On September 26, 1956, Tupelo celebrated "Elvis Presley Day," featuring a parade and a concert at the fairgrounds. Elvis performed two shows. In the afternoon show he sang "Heartbreak Hotel," "Long Tall Sally," "I Was the One," "I Want You, I Need You, I Love You," "I Got a Woman," "Don't Be Cruel," "Ready Teddy," "Love Me Tender," and "Hound Dog." In the evening show he sang "Love Me Tender," "I Was the One," "I Got a Woman," "Don't Be Cruel," "Blue Suede Shoes," "Baby Let's Play House," and "Hound Dog." The Jordanaires sang backup. RCA Victor released the concert on record/tape in 1984 in the *Golden Celebration* set.

Elvis returned on September 27, 1957, to perform before the hometown people, donating his $10,000 fee to the town of Tupelo. (See *Shirley Jones Gallentine, J. D. Cole, WELO*)

MISSISSIPPI SLIM
Country singer born Carvel Lee Ausborn. Mississippi Slim was the brother of James Ausborn, a friend of Elvis's in junior high school. According to Vince Staten in his book *The Real Elvis: Good Old Boy*, Elvis made his first radio appearance on Tupelo radio station WELO's Black and White Jamboree from the Lee County Courthouse (sponsored by the Black and White Store, above which the station was located) on May 15, 1944. Mississippi Slim accompanied on guitar while Elvis sang "Old Shep." Mississippi Slim had his own show on Saturdays on WELO and may have had Elvis on the program several other times.

Mississippi Slim has recorded such songs as "I'm Through Crying Over You" and "Tired of Your Eyes."

MODUGNO, DOMENICO
(1928–   ) Italian singer born in Polignano Mare, Italy, on January 9, 1928. In 1958 he had a worldwide hit with "Nel Blu Dipinto Di Blu (Volare)" (Decca 30677), which went to number one on the American charts. Modugno composed the song "Ask Me," with Bill Giant, Bernie Baum, and Florence Kaye writing the English lyrics. Elvis recorded "Ask Me" in 1964.

MOHR, JOSEPH
(1792–1848) Austrian theologian and poet who composed, with Franz Gruber, "Stille Nacht, Heilige Nacht" ("Silent Night, Holy Night") in 1818. Elvis recorded the song more than a century later, in 1957.

MOMAN, CHIPS
Producer at the American Sound Studios in Memphis, where Elvis recorded in 1969.

MONOPOLY AND SCRABBLE
Elvis's favorite board games. Monopoly was created in 1933 by Charles Darrow. Parker Brothers, the manufacturer of Monopoly, prints more money annually than the United States mint. When Elvis and the Beatles got together on the evening of August 27, 1965, they played a game of Monopoly.

Scrabble is produced by Sel Right. The name *Elvis Presley* totals twenty points in Scrabble, although it can't be used because it's a proper noun.

MONROE, BILL
(1911–1984) Country bluegrass fiddler and singer called the "Father of Bluegrass," who was born William Smith Monroe in Rosine, Kentucky, on September 13, 1911. Monroe is a direct descendant of President James Monroe.[1] In 1970 Monroe was elected to the Country Music Hall of Fame. Elvis recorded two songs that Monroe composed and recorded, "Blue Moon of Kentucky" (Columbia 20370) and "Little Cabin on the Hill" (Columbia 20459). Elvis performed an imitation of Monroe on the song "Little Cabin on the Hill" at the Million-Dollar Quartet session on December 4, 1956, before recording the song in 1970.

MONTE'S CATERING SERVICE
Memphis firm, located at 3788 Summer Avenue, that provided the food for Elvis and Priscilla's Memphis wedding reception in Graceland's Blue Room, on May 29, 1967.

MONTGOMERY, LARRY
Tupelo police officer who sang "The Star-Spangled Banner," "Love Me Tender," and "Precious Moments" at the dedication of the Elvis Presley Memorial Chapel in Tupelo, Mississippi, on August 17, 1979.

MONTREAL
Canadian city that Elvis was banned from playing by the Catholic Church in 1957.

MONTY PYTHON AND THE HOLY GRAIL
A 1974 British film directed by Terry Gilliam, which Elvis watched five times.

MONUMENT RECORDS
Hendersonville, Tennessee, record label founded by Fred Foster in 1958 on which Boots Randolph, Roy Orbison, Bob Moore, and Bill Justis all recorded. Ginger Alden made her debut record on Monument with "I'd Rather Have a Memory Than a Dream"/"Boogie on Down" (Monument 4595), released in 1980.

MOODY, RUSSELL
Composer, with Bert Carroll, of the song "Wear My Ring Around Your Neck," which Elvis recorded in 1958.

MOORE, BOB
(1933–   ) Bass guitarist and popular Nashville session musician who played on 28 of Elvis's recording sessions from 1958 to 1966, after Bill Black had departed because of a salary dispute. Moore was born in Nashville on November 30, 1932. In 1961 Moore had a hit instrumental titled "Mexico" (Monument 446), and also composed the theme song for the TV series "My Three Sons."

MOORE, JOHNNY
Singer who composed, with Lou Baxter, "Merry Christmas Baby," which was recorded in 1950 by Johnny Moore's Three Blazers (Swingtime 328) with Charles Brown on vocal, and which was rereleased in 1954 (Hollywood 1921). Elvis recorded "Merry Christmas Baby" in 1971. In 1955 Moore joined the Drifters, singing lead on "Fools Fall in Love" (Atlantic 1123), a song that Elvis recorded.

MOORE, ROBBIE
(1936–   ) Woman who sued Elvis because she objected to having her picture taken with him in September 1956. Elvis gave Moore $5,500 in an out-of-court settlement in October 1956.

[1]Actress Marilyn Monroe's mother also claimed to be descended from President Monroe.

MOORE, SCOTTY
(1931–   ) Musician born Winfield Scott Moore III on December 27, 1931. Moore played lead guitar for Elvis from his first recording sessions in July 1954, through June 1968. Moore first formed a band while he was in the U.S. Navy.

Moore was a member in 1954, along with Bill Black, of Doug Poindexter's Starlight Wranglers, a band that performed in the Memphis area. While with that group, Moore was asked by Sam Phillips to invite Elvis over to Moore's apartment to rehearse a few songs. On Sunday, June 27, 1954, Elvis went to Moore's apartment, with Bill Black arriving later that afternoon. Some of the songs the three rehearsed were: "I Don't Hurt Anymore," "I Apologize," and "I Really Don't Want to Know."

A week later, on July 5, Elvis, Scotty, and Bill recorded "That's All Right (Mama)" at the Sun Studios. The full sound they created was so good that Sam Phillips didn't bother to add any additional instrumentation.

On July 12, 1954, a week after the first Sun recording session, Moore became Elvis's first manager. He and Elvis signed a one-page contract giving Moore a ten percent commission on all of the bookings he made. Elvis's parents also signed the document because their son was not yet twenty-one. When Moore discovered that he could not be both musician and manager, he allowed Elvis to void the contract, thus allowing him to sign with Bob Neal.

For a brief time, on the "Louisiana Hayride" and while touring in the South in 1955, Elvis, Scotty, and Bill were known as the Blue Moon Boys.

In September 1957 Moore and Black split with Elvis because they didn't like the salary they were receiving (they got a flat fee—no royalties). Both came back to record with Elvis until he went into the Army. Bill Black never recorded with Elvis again. Moore did go back to Elvis in 1960, staying with him until 1968. During his two-year hiatus, Moore produced and played on some Jerry Lee Lewis recording sessions, with songs that included: "Sweet Little Sixteen," "Good Rockin' Tonight," "Hello, Josephine," and "Be-Bop-a-Lula." He recorded the 1973 album *The Guitar That Changed the World* on Epic Records. Moore's last work with Elvis was for the 1968 NBC-TV special, on which Elvis asked him to appear. It was also the last time that Moore would see Elvis.

Although Sam Phillips is given credit for developing Elvis's talents in the early years (and rightly so!), Moore hasn't gotten much acknowledgment. Moore, perhaps more than anyone, must be given credit for creating the driving guitar sound on his Gibson guitar that became known as the "Elvis Presley sound." Singer Elton John once said of Moore, "It was Scotty Moore's guitar riff when he was doing "The Steve Allen Show" that got me into rock music."

Moore was portrayed by Emory Smith in the 1981 movie *This Is Elvis*.

MOREHEAD, JIM
Composer, with Jimmy Cassin, of the song "Sentimental Me," which Elvis recorded in 1961.

MORENO, RITA
(1931–   ) Academy Award–winning actress born Rosita Dolores Alverio in Humacao, Puerto Rico, on December 11, 1931, and nicknamed the "Puerto Rican Bombshell." Moreno won her Oscar in 1961 for her role as Anita in *West Side Story*. Moreno has won an Oscar, a Tony, a Grammy, and an Emmy.

Elvis dated Moreno in 1957 while he was filming *Loving You*. He once took her to the Moulin Rouge in Los Angeles, where they watched Dean Martin perform.

MORRIS, BOBBY
Musical conductor for Elvis at the International Hotel in Las Vegas in 1969, and for his concert tour. It was Morris who convinced Elvis to record the song "Suspicious Minds."

MORRIS, JOE
Rhythm & blues singer who composed the song "Shake a Hand," which Elvis recorded in 1975.

MORRIS, LEE
(1912–1978) History teacher and composer born in Boston on March 12, 1912. Morris composed, with Sid Feller and Dolores Fuller, the song "You Can't Say No in Acapulco," which Elvis sang in the 1963 movie *Fun in Acapulco*; and, with Dolores Fuller, the song "Barefoot Ballad," which Elvis sang in the 1964 movie *Kissin' Cousins*. With Dolores Fuller and Sonny Hendrix, Morris composed the song "Big Love, Big Heartache," which Elvis sang in the 1964 movie *Roustabout*.

MORRIS, WILLIAM L.
Shelby County, Tennessee, sheriff to whom Elvis gave a $9,000 Mercedes-Benz automobile on December 25, 1970. Sheriff Morris traveled with Elvis to Washington, D.C., on December 30, 1970, so that Elvis could tour FBI headquarters. Morris issued Elvis a permit that allowed him to carry firearms in Memphis.

MORROW, GEOFFREY
Composer, with Chris Arnold and David Martin, of the songs "A Little Bit of Green," "Let's Be Friends," "This Is the Story," and "Sweet Angeline," all of which Elvis recorded.

MOSCHEO, JOE
(1937–   ) Member of the Imperials Quartet and piano player for Elvis's recording sessions at the RCA Studios in Nashville on May 15–21, 1971. Moscheo also played piano at Elvis's funeral in 1977.

MOST, DAVID
Composer, with Clive Westlake, of the song "How the Web Was Woven," which Elvis recorded in 1970.

MOSTEL, ZERO
(1915–1977) Comedian who died on September 8, 1977, three weeks after Elvis died. Mostel, who was born Samuel Joel Mostel in Brooklyn on February 28, 1915, acquired his nickname in elementary school, because his shyness prevented him from answering many of the teacher's questions. He was one of several celebrities who died around the time of Elvis's death. (See *Groucho Marx, Sebastian Cabot*)

MOTION PICTURE RELIEF FUND
Organization to help retired actors and actresses, founded in 1923 by actor Jean Hersholt, with producer Joseph Schenck serving as its first president. Elvis once contributed $50,000 to the MPRF. The check, given to President George L. Bagnell, was the largest contribution ever given to the fund by an individual. Actress Barbra Streisand was present at the ceremonies.

MOTT, ELISHA MATTHEW (BITSY)
(1920–   ) Brother of Marie Mott Ross Parker and the brother-in-law of Colonel Tom Parker. Bitsy Mott, who traveled with Elvis for a short time in 1955 and 1956, has been considered a member of the Memphis Mafia. Mott played professional baseball for the Philadelphia Phillies in ninety games in 1945, hitting .222 and playing shortstop and second base. Mott appeared as a soldier in the 1960 movie *G.I. Blues* and as a state trooper in the 1961 movie *Wild in the Country*.

MOULIN ROUGE
West German nightclub managed by a Mr. Schumann, who with Elvis sang, in jest, "O Sole Mio"—until Elvis was advised that he wasn't supposed to sing in public while he was in the military. Many photographs of Elvis with a number of German girls were published in Diego Cortez's 1978 book *Private Elvis*, which was originally published in West Germany.

MOUNTAIN VALLEY
Brand of mineral water preferred by Elvis.

MUDD, ROGER
(1928–   ) CBS Evening News anchorman, born in Washington, D.C., on February 9, 1928 (and descendant of Dr. Samuel Mudd), who on August 16, 1977, was filling in for Walter Cronkite, who was on vacation. That evening Mudd announced the death of Elvis, but six minutes into the program. The lead story was the Panama Canal. The other two networks, NBC and ABC, announced Elvis's death as the lead story. CBS only allotted one minute and ten seconds of the news to Elvis, the least of the three networks. That error in judgment earned CBS the lowest rating of the three.

MUFFIN
White-haired Great Pyrenees dog that Elvis owned as a pet at Graceland. Muffin was injured at obedience school and had to be put to sleep.

MURPHY, EDDIE
(1961–   ) Black comedian born in Brooklyn on April 3, 1961. Murphy, who is one of the most popular actors in America, has an obsession with Elvis. In 1985 he charted the number two hit song "Party All the Time (Columbia 05609), which was written and produced by Rick James. Murphy is a fan who reads everything he can about Elvis. He even bought his 22-room estate in New Jersey because it resembled Graceland. He owns several oil portraits of Elvis. In Murphy's 1987 movie *The Golden Child*, a portrait of Elvis hung on his apartment wall. In 1987 Murphy dated Elvis's daughter, Lisa Marie Presley. Like Elvis, Murphy also enjoys giving away expensive automobiles.

Murphy has said of Elvis, "Elvis was the greatest entertainer who ever lived."

MURPHY, GEORGE
(1902–   ) Actor, dancer, and U.S. senator, born in New Haven, Connecticut, on July 4, 1902. Murphy is the son of Michael Charles Murphy, who coached Jim Thorpe at the 1912 Olympic Games in Stockholm, Sweden. Murphy served as president of the Screen Actors Guild until replaced by Ronald Reagan in 1947.

Some sources say that Murphy accompanied Elvis from Los Angeles to Washington, D.C., on an airline flight. Upon arriving in Washington, Murphy set up an appointment for Elvis to meet the deputy director of the Narcotics Bureau, John Finlator. Other sources credit the meeting as being set up by Detective John O'Grady.

MUSIC GATES
Name given to the wrought-iron front gates at Graceland. They were built in 1957 by Doors Inc. of Memphis. Country singer Hank Williams previously had a musical gate at his estate, with notes from his hit song "Lovesick Blues."

MUSIC SALES
Memphis firm, located at 117 Union Avenue, that distributed Sun records locally in the 1950s.

MYSELS, MAURICE
Cowriter, with Ira Kosloff, of the 1956 Elvis hit song "I Want You, I Need You, I Love You." On the 78 RPM record pressing and first 45 RPM pressing of the song his name was incorrectly credited as Maurice Myself.

91 PERCENT

Elvis's peak tax bracket. He allowed the IRS to figure out his taxes, failing to have enough investments to create any shelters.

97TH GENERAL HOSPITAL

U.S. Army hospital in West Germany where Elvis was hospitalized for tonsillitis in late October 1959.

1935

Birth year of Elvis and the following celebrities: Woody Allen (December 1), Carol Burnett (April 26), Steve Lawrence (July 8), Johnny Mathis (September 30), and Lee Remick (December 14).

1939 PLYMOUTH

Green automobile that Vernon Presley owned when he, Gladys, and Elvis moved to Memphis from Tupelo, Mississippi, on September 12, 1948.

1942 LINCOLN COUPE

Automobile that Elvis drove during his high school days. The car cost $450.

1954 CADILLAC

Automobile that Elvis bought in 1955 to transport himself and his group to their various one-night appearances throughout the South. The car, which accumulated a great many miles, burned up near Texarkana, Arkansas, the same night that Gladys Presley had a premonition that Elvis was involved in a fire. In the 1979 TV movie *Elvis*, the car is shown as a Ford instead of a Cadillac. This 1954 Caddy was the first of many he'd own during his lifetime.

1954 CHEVROLET BEL AIR

Automobile that Scotty Moore bought on his, and his wife's, credit (she worked at Sears) so that he, Elvis, and Bill Black would have a car to take them to their appearances throughout the South in 1955. Elvis's 1942 Lincoln wasn't in good shape, so Moore bought the Chevy. After the Chevrolet finally gave out, Elvis bought a 1951 Lincoln Continental, only to have Bill Black destroy it in a collision with a truck. Elvis then bought his 1954 Cadillac. (See *1954 Cadillac*)

1954 FORD

Automobile that Elvis bought for his parents in 1955, and then had it painted pink and white. It was the first car he ever bought for them. Elvis had to use the Ford for a short time during his touring in 1955 after his 1954 Cadillac caught fire.

1975 CADILLAC COUPE DeVILLE

Gold-colored Cadillac that Elvis gave to Vester Presley in 1975.

1976 CADILLAC ELDORADO

Elvis's last car. It included gold-plated hubcaps, a bar, telephone, CB radio, television, and sun roof.

N777EP

U.S. registration number of Elvis's Jet Commander aircraft.

N880EP

U.S. registration number of Elvis's Convair 880 jet aircraft. N = November (U.S. registration), 880 = Convair 880, EP = Elvis Presley.

NAPIER-BELL, SIMON

Composer, with Vicki Wickham, of the English lyrics to the song "You Don't Have to Say You Love Me," written by V. Pallavicini and P. Donaggio, which Elvis recorded in 1970.

NASH, W. S.

Pharmacist at Baptist Memorial Hospital in Memphis who made out Dr. George Nichopoulos's last prescription for Elvis, the day before Elvis's death.

NASHVILLE EDITION

Vocal group that sang backup for Elvis on the Nashville recording sessions at the RCA studio on March 15 and June 4–8, 1970, and again on March 15, 1971.

NASSAU COLISEUM

Uniondale, New York, concert site where, on July 19, 1975, Elvis played the piano in public for the first time. He accompanied himself as he sang "You'll Never Walk Alone."

Elvis was to have appeared at the Nassau Coliseum on August 22, 1977, but death took him first. Those who held tickets to that concert had until 1983 to redeem them. Today those souvenirs of the concert "that never was" are valuable as collector's items.

NATHAN NOVICK'S PAWN SHOP

Establishment at 142 Beale Street in Memphis that has been erroneously pointed out on Memphis tours for years as the place where Elvis bought his first guitar. In reality Elvis bought his first guitar at the Tupelo Hardware Store in Tupelo, Mississippi, in 1946. How this misconception got started is hard to say, but it hasn't hurt Nathan Novick's business.

NATIONAL BANK OF COMMERCE

Memphis banking institution where Elvis banked. Elvis had a checking account (# 011-143875) with the bank. He signed all his checks as E. A. Presley. Sam Phillips (at least in the 1950s) also banked at the National Bank of Commerce. At the time of his death in 1977, Elvis had $1,055,173.69 in his interest-free checking account.

On February 18, 1978, the National Bank of Commerce filed a claim of $1,434,536.69 against the Presley estate, stating that it was the balance owed them on three notes signed by Elvis, one for the purchase of his Convair 880 aircraft.

NATIONAL FUNERAL HOME

Memphis mortuary, located at 1177 Union Avenue, that handled the funeral services of Gladys Presley in August 1958. The facility was then affiliated with National Life and Burial Insurance. In 1962 National changed its name to the Memphis Funeral Home. (See *Memphis Funeral Home*)

NEAL, BOB

(1917–   ) Music agent born Robert Neal Hopgood in the Belgian Congo in 1917. His family moved to the United States in 1930. Neal became a disc jockey for WMPS in Memphis during the 1940s. He had his own program called "The Bob Neal Farm Show," on which he played the ukulele and told jokes. Neal was also the owner of the Bob Neal Record Shop on Main Street in Memphis. In addition, he hosted a fifteen minute afternoon radio show called "The High Noon Roundup" before a studio audience of which Elvis was sometimes a member, especially when Neal featured the local Blackwood Brothers.

In 1952 Neal became a promoter, establishing the Memphis Promotions Agency at 160 Union Avenue. From January 1, 1955, to March 15, 1956, he served as Elvis's manager, collecting 15 percent of Elvis's earnings off the top, after which Colonel Tom Parker sneaked into the picture, taking over from Neal. Even after Elvis signed his first contract with Colonel Parker on August 15, 1955, he was still contracted to Neal. Elvis in essence agreed to pay Neal his 15 percent in addition to 25 percent to Parker. In 1956, with the partnership of Sam Phillips, Neal founded Stars Incorporated (Suite 1916 in Memphis's Sterick Building), to handle recording artists. In 1958 Neal became Johnny Cash's first manager. Neal also has handled Jerry Lee Lewis, Carl Perkins, Roy Orbison, Conway Twitty, Warren Smith, Sonny James, Lynn Anderson, Stonewall Jackson, Bobby Helms, Nat Stuckey, and others. Unfortunately, Neal let his most promising artist, Elvis, slip through his fingers in 1956 because he lacked the connections that Colonel Tom Parker could provide.

When Neal's wife, Helen, first saw Elvis perform at the Overton Park Shell, she remarked to Bob, "This isn't just another singer, this boy's different."

In the book *The Maid, the Man and the Fans: Elvis Is the Man*, by Nancy Rooks and Mae Gutter, they erroneously claimed that Elvis's first public appearance was for his friend Sonny Neal, the son of Bob Neal. Sonny was running for class president at the time.

NEELY, RICHARD

Davada (Dee) Stanley's brother. Neely was Vernon Presley's best man when Vernon married Dee. The wedding took place at Neely's Huntsville, Alabama, home on July 3, 1960. Elvis did not attend.

NELSON, GERALD

Composer of the song "If I Were You," and co-composer with Fred Burch of "Sing, You Children" and "Yoga Is as Yoga Does." With Fred Burch and Chuck Taylor, Nelson wrote "The Love Machine." Elvis recorded all four songs.

(Photo courtesy Eddie Brandt's Saturday Matinee)

NELSON, RICKY

(1940–1985) Youngest son of Ozzie[1] and Harriet Nelson. Ricky Nelson was born Eric Hilliard Nelson in Teaneck, New Jersey, on May 8, 1940. Nelson ranks ninth on the list of all-time recording artists. He became popular by appearing on the TV series "The Adventures of Ozzie and Harriet."[2] He and his brother, David, first sang in public when they performed "The Lord's Prayer" for a Sunday School program. Ricky made his movie debut in the 1952 film *Here Come the Nelsons*.[3] As a teenager, in early 1957, Ricky began singing on his parents' TV show. One night while out

---

[1]Ozzie (Oswald) Nelson, at the age of thirteen, was the youngest Eagle Scout in America. He was also a Rutgers honor student before becoming a bandleader with whose orchestra his wife, Harriet Hilliard, sang.
[2]Ozzie and Harriet were the first married couple on television to sleep together in a double bed.
[3]He is often credited with having debuted in the 1959 John Wayne movie *Rio Bravo*, but that was his third movie appearance. His second movie was *The Story of Three Loves* in 1953.

driving with his girlfriend Arlene, they heard an Elvis song on the car radio. The praise that Arlene gave Elvis inspired Ricky to tell her that he, too, was going to make a record. She laughed, so the next day he recorded the Fats Domino hit "I'm Walkin' " at Wallach's Music Store, at the cost of a quarter. After his father heard the song, he set up a professional recording session in which Ricky rerecorded the song.

It was both his respect for, and envy of, Elvis that prompted Ricky to sing on the TV series. He first sang "I'm Walkin' " on an episode titled "Ricky the Drummer," telecast April 10, 1957. On another episode, Ricky attended a costume party dressed like Elvis, while his brother David dressed like Yul Brynner in *The King and I.* On that show Ricky sang a few lines of "Love Me Tender." More than 10,000 letters poured in from television viewers asking to hear more of Ricky singing. Ozzie then set him up with his first recording company, Verve Records. Ricky recorded his first hit, "A Teenager's Romance," backed with "I'm Walkin' " (Verve 10047). By mid-1957 Ricky Nelson was established as a recording artist, with Johnny Burnette, Dorsey Burnette, and Gene Pitney writing his hit songs. Nelson's style was heavily influenced by the rockabilly sound of the South, with a heavy dose of Sun Records music, especially from Elvis. James Burton was the guitar player whose licks gave Nelson's songs their distinctive style, and the Jordanaires provided the vocal backup. Burton would later become a session musician for Elvis, as did Jimmie Haskell on guitar, James Kirkland on bass, and Richie Frost on drums.

Nelson finally got an opportunity to meet Elvis in person at a Hollywood party. Nelson, who was nervous on meeting his idol, was surprised when Elvis approached him in a friendly manner, after which Elvis asked Ricky a number of questions about "The Adventures of Ozzie and Harriet,"[1] recalling a number of episodes he had seen on TV in Memphis.

In 1970 Nelson formed the Stone Canyon Band[2] and had a hit record with "Garden Party" (Decca 32980), which was an account of a real incident that happened to him at Madison Square Garden in 1972, where he was booed off the stage for not singing some of his old hits. On December 31, 1985, Nelson and his band were killed when their chartered DC-3 aircraft crashed in Texas.

NELSON, WILLIE

(1933–   ) Country composer and singer born in Fort Worth, Texas, on April 30, 1933, and nicknamed the "Red Headed Stranger." Nelson composed a number of classic country hits, including "Crazy," "Hello Walls" (cowriter), and "Touch Me." Nelson also composed "Funny How Time Slips Away," which Elvis recorded. In 1975 Nelson recorded a version of "Blue Eyes Crying in the Rain" (Columbia 10176), which Elvis recorded

the following year. Nelson and Leon Russell had a top country hit in 1979 with "Heartbreak Hotel."

As a disc jockey in Pleasanton, Texas, in 1954, Nelson often played Elvis's "Blue Moon of Kentucky."

NESBITT'S

Brand of orange juice soda preferred by Elvis.

NEUTROGENA

Brand of soap that Elvis preferred.

NEW CITY AUDITORIUM

Fort Myers, Florida, concert site where, according to legend, Colonel Tom Parker first watched Elvis perform, on May 9, 1955.

NEW FRONTIER HOTEL

Hotel where Elvis made his first Las Vegas appearance, April 23 to May 6, 1956. The New Frontier's manager, Sammy Lewis, signed Elvis for four weeks at $12,500 a week. Elvis was advertised as the "Atomic Powered Singer." The featured act on the bill was the Freddy Martin Orchestra. Also on the bill were comedian Shecky Greene; Johnny Cochrane; Dave Leonard and Bob Hunter; the Venus Starlets, who danced behind Elvis; Jack Teigen; and Marge Baker and the Martin-Men. In the Venus Room, Elvis performed all his hits plus "Long Tall Sally," "I Got a Woman," and "Money Honey." On May 6, his last day, Elvis sang "Heartbreak Hotel," "Long Tall Sally," "Blue Suede Shoes," and "Money Honey." Because of the poor reception by the middle-aged audience, Colonel Parker and the New Frontier ended Elvis's engagement after only two weeks. He was replaced by Jana Martin. Before Elvis departed, Colonel Parker took some film of Elvis performing on stage. Elvis would not play Las Vegas again until 1969, thirteen years later. An excerpt from Elvis's performance at the New Frontier Hotel can be heard on the 1980 RCA boxed set, *Elvis Aron Presley.*

NEW ORTHOPHONIC

High fidelity recording process first introduced by RCA Records in the mid-1950s. Elvis's first albums were produced using this process.

NEWBURY, MICKEY

(1940–   ) Songwriter born in Houston on May 19, 1940. Newbury wrote such hits as "Just Dropped In (to See What Condition My Condition Was In)," "Sweet Memories," and "Time Is a Thief." Newbury is married to former New Christy Minstrels singer Susan Pack. Newbury arranged and orignally recorded "An American Trilogy" (Elektra 45750), which Elvis recorded and frequently sang in concert.

---

[1]Elvis's sidekick in the 1957 movie *Loving You* was played by Skip Young, who appeared as a friend of David Nelson on the series from 1957 to 1966.
[2]Member Randy Meisner later left to help form the Eagles.

NEWTON, BILLIE JOE

(1941–   ) Woman who claimed to have been Elvis's first wife and the mother of his three children, the first when she was just nine years old. She said she and Elvis were married when she turned fourteen. Newton further claimed that Elvis divorced her in 1956 at Colonel Tom Parker's suggestion. Newton stated that her marriage certificate and birth certificate have both been destroyed.[1] This story was published in *The Globe* on March 17, 1981. The article also stated that two other women claimed to have married Elvis, Ann Farrell in Russellville, Alabama, in 1957 and Zelda Harris in 1960, who after meeting him at a Mobile, Alabama, concert, married him within twenty-four hours.

NEWTON, WAYNE

(1942–   ) Popular singer born in Norfolk, Virginia, on April 3, 1942. Newton is the highest-paid performer in Las Vegas. Newton made his TV debut on "The Jackie Gleason Show" in September 1962. Shortly after, Bobby Darin signed him to Capitol Records and produced Newton's first hit, "Heart" (Capitol 4920). In 1972 Newton was the first artist signed by the Chelsea label. His first million-seller, "Daddy, Don't You Walk So Fast" (Chelsea 0100), was also Chelsea Records' first million-seller. In 1961 a young Newton recorded the song "Little Jukebox" (George 7778), which mentioned Elvis's name in the lyrics. As part of his stage show, Newton does an Elvis impersonation. On the album *Elvis in Concert*, Elvis introduced himself to his audience in Rapid City, South Dakota, as "Wayne Newton." Newton is part owner of Las Vegas's Aladdin Hotel, where Elvis married Priscilla on May 1, 1967. Newton bought Elvis's Jet Commander aircraft for $300,000.

The August 4, 1987, edition of the *National Enquirer* featured an article titled "Wayne Newton Exclusive Interview: Elvis's Ghost Talks to Me." In the article Newton claimed that Elvis's spirit spoke to him and that he has also seen the singer's image. Newton, who greatly admired Elvis, said in the article that when Elvis died he lost a member of his family.

NEWTON-JOHN, OLIVIA

(1948–   ) Popular Australian singer born in Cambridge, England, on September 26, 1948. Newton-John has gained fame in both rock and country music. She is the granddaughter of Cambridge University professor Max Born, who won the Nobel Prize in 1954. Newton-John had a hit in late 1973 with "Let Me Be There" (MCA 40101), which Elvis recorded in 1974, and a hit in April 1974 with "If You Love Me (Let Me Know)" (MCA 40209), which Elvis recorded in 1977.

While Elvis holds the record for charting the most movie songs, in *Billboard*'s Top 40 with twenty-three, Olivia Newton-John holds the record for a female, with seven.

NICHOLSON, PAULINE

(1929–   ) Cook and maid at Graceland for fifteen years, beginning in 1963. Elvis gave her a new 1964 Buick LeSabre. Nicholson portrayed herself in the 1981 movie *This Is Elvis*.

NICHOPOULOS, DEAN

(1955–   ) Son of Dr. George and Edna S. Nichopoulos, who often played racquetball with Elvis. He sometimes worked for Elvis on his concert tours, taking care of his wardrobe. Elvis once bought him a brand-new automobile. David Stanley tells a story in his autobiography about Elvis laying hands on Nichopoulos's injured leg after a skiing accident. Elvis placed his hand on Dean's leg, closed his eyes, and concentrated. Nichopoulos suddenly got up and the pain was gone.

NICHOPOULOS, DR. GEORGE C.

(1927–   ) Personal physician of Elvis and his family, born George Constantine Nichopoulos in Ridgway, Pennsylvania. Nichopoulos's offices were located at

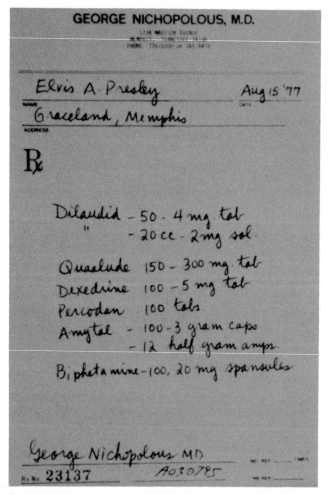

Dr. Nick's last prescription for Elvis. (Photo courtesy John Dawson)

---

[1]Many other women who have claimed either to have married Elvis or had his child also claim that their marriage or birth certificate had been lost or destroyed, forgetting that these official documents are on file, usually in the town or county where the event took place. The authors have no way of determining the authenticity of stories printed in the *Globe, Star, National Enquirer,* or other weekly tabloids; the stories are related here because they have appeared in print, and it is up to readers to use their own discretion as to determining their validity.

1734 Madison Avenue in downtown Memphis. Nichopoulos, nicknamed "Doctor Nick," was attending to Elvis at the time of the star's death. For years he and his wife, Edna, were close friends of both the Presleys and members of the Memphis Mafia. Elvis once gave him a new yellow Cadillac. Dr. Nichopoulos introduced Elvis to the sport of racquetball. Dr. Nichopoulos invested in a number of projects in the Memphis area, one of which was a medical building at 1750 Madison Avenue. He and his wife were heavily indebted to Elvis for loans (estimated at over $300,000). Dr. Nichopoulos prescribed large amounts of drugs to sixteen of his patients, including Marty Lacker and Jerry Lee Lewis. Between January 20 and August 16, 1977, he prescribed to Elvis 5,684 narcotic and amphetamine pills (an average of 25 a day). Elvis filled eight different prescriptions the day before he died.[1]

In September 1979, Dr. Nichopoulos, who was a pallbearer at Elvis's funeral, was charged by the Tennessee Board of Medical Examiners with "indiscriminately prescribing 5,300 pills and vials for Elvis in the seven months before his death." In January 1980 the Tennessee Board of Medical Examiners suspended Nichopoulos's license to practice medicine for three months for overprescribing addictive drugs to ten patients, including Elvis and Jerry Lee Lewis. Nichopoulos was finally acquitted by a jury of eight blacks and four whites, who found him not guilty of malpractice or unethical conduct.

During a football game in Memphis in 1979 someone took a shot at Nichopoulos, but the bullet missed its target.

NICKNAMES

Elvis was given a number of nicknames, some by his friends, some by his enemies, and some by the press:

Big E
Big El
The Bopping Hillbilly
The Cat
The Chief
The Country Cat
Crazy
E
Elvis the Pelvis
Elvis Pretzel
E.P.
The Hillbilly Cat
The Hillbilly Bopper
The King
The King of Rock & Roll
The King of Swoon
The King of Western Bop
Memphis Flash
Mr. Dynamite
Mr. Rhythm
Mr. Wiggle and Shake
Sir Swivel Hips
Tiger Man
Wiggle Hips

In his youth Elvis had been nicknamed "Elvy," which he hated, and "Mama's Boy" by his fellow students because his mother would walk him to school each day (singer Frank Sinatra had been given the same nickname when he was growing up). At L. C. Humes High School, Elvis was called "Teacher's Pet" by some of the students. The press called Elvis the "Hillbilly Frank Sinatra" when he appeared on the Grand Ole Opry. It has been alleged that actor Humphrey Bogart gave Elvis the nickname "Elvis Pretzel." Elvis accepted most nicknames in stride, but the one nickname he hated was "Elvis the Pelvis," about which he said, "That's about the most stupid thing I have heard from a so-called intelligent adult." (The line is slightly different in the 1979 TV movie *Elvis*.) Even Colonel Tom Parker got into the act when, in 1956, he nicknamed Elvis "The Nation's First Atomic Powered Singer." Although Elvis has been called "The King of Rock & Roll" since October 1956, when *Variety* first used the nickname, columnist May Mann claims to have conferred the nickname "The King" on Elvis via her column a few years later.

Actress Judy Spreckles began calling Elvis "El," a nickname he disliked. Yet that is what Lucy de Barbin, in her autobiography *Are You Lonesome Tonight?*, claimed to have called him, in addition to "El Lancelot." Priscilla called Elvis "Fire Eyes" when he got mad. Linda Thompson called Elvis "Buttons" and "Bunting."

Elvis called his mother "Sattnin." He also had nicknames for such items as milk, "butch"; feet, "sooties"; water, "duckling"; etc. Elvis called his grandmother Minnie Mae Presley "Dodger" because she dodged out of the way of a flying object a young Elvis had once thrown. Elvis called Priscilla "Cilla," "Baby," "Little Girl," "Little One," and "Sattnin." Priscilla called herself "Beau" when she was young. Elvis called Linda Thompson "Precious" and "Ariadne" (after the three-year-old girl in *Follow That Dream*). Elvis called Ginger Alden "Gingerbread" and "Chicken Neck."

Elvis enjoyed giving nicknames to people who were close to him and to people he liked. Some of the karate nicknames that he gave at Kang Rhee's karate school were: Elvis, "Tiger"; Red West, "Mr. Dragon"; Sonny West, "Mr. Eagle" (the Eagle); Charlie Hodge, "Mr. Cobra"; Lamar Fike, "Mr. Bull." (Other nicknames can be found throughout this book.)

NIELSEN, SHERRILL

Irish tenor, former member of the Speer Family, and member of the vocal group Voice, who sang backup for Elvis at many of his live performances. Nielsen met Elvis on May 25, 1966, at RCA's recording studio in Nashville, where, as a member of the Imperial Quintet, he sang backup on Elvis's album *How Great Thou Art*. Elvis loved to hear him sing "Walk with Me." He sang duet with Elvis on "Spanish Eyes" and "Softly as I Leave You" at his concerts. Nielson also sang a solo

---

[1]Singer Hank Williams also had a physician who prescribed too many pills, one Dr. Toby Marshall, who served several prison terms, one for armed robbery.

version of "O Sole Mio" before Elvis sang "It's Now or Never" at concerts. Today he performs by the name Shaun Nielsen. In 1981 he recorded an album titled *The Songs I Sang for Elvis* on Adonda Records.

NIPPER
RCA Victor dog in the trademark "His Master's Voice." Nipper was born in Bristol, England, in 1884, and raised by his first master John Daggett. Nipper died in 1895, after which he was stuffed. The original painting of Nipper was made by his second master, Francis Barroud. Nipper was at first the symbol of the Gramophone Company, then of the Victor Talking Company, and finally of RCA Victor in 1929. The phonograph player shown in the trademark painting is a 1905 Victor Gold Medal.

Elvis wrestled with a papier-mâché Nipper at the Pan Pacific concerts, October 28–29, 1957. At the USS *Arizona* benefit concert in Honolulu on March 25, 1961, Elvis sang to a statue of Nipper. A picture of the white dog has appeared on the label of Elvis's RCA Victor recordings for many years. In his Graceland bedroom, Elvis kept a small model of Nipper.

NIXON, RICHARD MILHOUS
(1913–   ) Thirty-seventh president of the United States, born in Yorba Linda, California, on January 9, 1913. Elvis visited President Nixon at 12:30 P.M. on December 21, 1970, after showing up at the White House gate unannounced. It was aide H. R. Haldeman who granted permission. Elvis talked President Nixon into getting him a Narcotics Bureau badge. During the meeting Elvis gave the president a commemorative World War II Colt .45 pistol encased in a wooden box.[1] Elvis asked the president if he could invite into the Oval Office his two friends, Jerry Schilling and Sonny West, who had accompanied him. The bodyguards shook hands with Nixon. Elvis then convinced the president to give both men and their wives a souvenir. The meeting was first reported by columnist Jack Anderson in his column "Washington Merry-Go-Round."

During his campaign, President Nixon used the same F-28 jet aircraft that Elvis used on his 1971 tour. When Nixon was hospitalized in 1975, Elvis called to wish him well. President Nixon called Elvis at the Baptist Memorial Hospital when Elvis was there in 1975.

In 1975 President Nixon requested that Elvis perform at the White House, only to have Colonel Tom Parker request a payment of $25,000 for Elvis and an orchestra. The White House informed Colonel Parker that performers were never paid to perform at the White House. Parker, who never gave away what he could sell, informed the White House that no one asks Elvis to play for free. So yet another historic opportunity for Elvis was destroyed by Parker's greed. (See pages 141–143.)

NIXON, ROY
County sheriff, and later mayor of Memphis, who gave Elvis his badge for his collection, and later his blue flashing light for Elvis's car.

NO HALL OF FAME
Fictitious seventy-two-page book written by Cleo C. Baker in 1961 about Elvis playing football. It was published in 1978.

NO TIME FOR SERGEANTS
A 1958 movie, starring Andy Griffith as Pvt. Will Stockdale, which was the movie debut of actor Don Knotts. Elvis saw the film in 1958 at the Waco Theater in Waco, Texas, attending with Anita Wood and Eddie Fadal. Elvis's friend Nick Adams appeared in the movie as Will Stockdale's friend, Ben. At the same time, *King Creole* was playing at the Orpheum Theater in Waco.

NOGUCHI, THOMAS T.
Former chief medical examiner of Los Angeles County who was the inspiration of the coroner Quincy on the TV series "Quincy, M.E.," starring Jack Klugman. Noguchi, who has been nicknamed "Coroner to the Stars," was in charge of the autopsies of such celebrities as Robert Kennedy, Marilyn Monroe, Natalie Wood, Sharon Tate, William Holden, and John Belushi. Noguchi is the author of two biographies, *Coroner* and *Coroner at Large*. In the latter book, written with Joseph DiMona and published in 1985, Noguchi relates the story of Dr. Jerry Francisco, the chief examiner of Shelby County, Tennessee, who called Noguchi after the death of Elvis to seek advise on how to handle Elvis's autopsy and the publicity surrounding his death. Noguchi suggested that Francisco appoint a panel of pathologists to assist him with the autopsy. Francisco followed Noguchi's advice.

NORRIS, CHUCK
(1939–   ) Martial-arts champion turned Hollywood actor, born in Ryan, Oklahoma. Norris and Bruce Lee made their movie debuts in the same film, playing bit roles in 1969's *The Wrecking Crew*, which starred Dean Martin as Matt Helm.

It was at Chuck Norris's martial-arts studio in Sherman Oaks, California, where Priscilla met instructor Mike Stone on August 5, 1973. Priscilla would earn a green belt in karate before giving up the sport. It was Ed Parker who first introduced Priscilla to Norris. Norris, his wife, Diane, and Mike Stone once traveled together to Las Vegas to watch Elvis's show at Elvis's request and expense.

NORTH, ALEX
(1910–   ) Composer-singer born in Chester, Pennsylvania, on December 4, 1910. North composed the music for a number of movies, including the 1956 film *The*

---

[1] It is shocking to think that someone could show up at the White House unannounced and obtain permission to see the president while carrying a gun. Only Elvis could have pulled this off.

Rainmaker, for which Elvis made his first screen test. He also composed the music for the 1954 movie *Desiree*, which Lucy de Barbin claims is the source of her (and Elvis's) daughter's name. North, with Hy Zaret, composed the song "Unchained Melody," which Elvis recorded in 1977.

NORVELL, WILLIAM R.
Army soldier stationed at Fort Hood whom Elvis befriended and nicknamed "Nervous Norvell." Norvell was among the thirteen soldiers who traveled on the Greyhound bus from Memphis to Fort Chaffee, Arkansas, in March 1958.

NUDIE'S RODEO TAILORS
North Hollywood clothes-designing firm founded by Nudie Cohen. Nudie's created Elvis's $10,000 gold lamé tuxedo. The firm also designed gaudy automobiles. Singer Hank Williams was a Nudie's buff. Nudie's created a $7,500 suit for Elvis imitator Alan Meyer.

Dear Mr. President:

First I would like to introduce myself. I am Elvis Presley and admire you and Have Great Respect for your office. I talked to Vice President Agnew in Palm Springs 3 weeks and expressed my concern for our country. The Drug Culture, the Hippie Elements, the SDS, Black Panthers, etc. do not consider me as their enemy or as they call it the Establishment. I call it America and I Love it. Sir I can and will be of any service that I can to help the country out. I have no concern or motives other than helping the country out. So I wish not to be given a title or an appointed position. I can and will do more good if I were made a Federal agent at Large, and I will help best by doing it my way through my communications with people of all ages. First and Foremost I am an

entertainer but all I need is the Federal
credentials. I am on the Phone with
Sen. George Murphy and We
have been discussing the problems
that our Country is faced with.
So I am Staying at the Washington
hotel Room 505-506-507~ I have
2 men who work with me by the
name of Jerry Schilling and Sonny
West. I am registered under the name
of Jon Burrows. I will be here
for as long as it takes to get
the credentials of a Federal agent.
I have done an in depth study of
Drug abuse and Communist Brainwashing
Techniques and I am right in the
middle of the whole thing. where
I can and will do the most good
I am Glad to help just so long
as it is kept very Private. you can
have your staff or whomever call
me anytime today tonight or Tomorrow
I was nominated the coming year
one of America's Ten most outstanding
young men. that will be in January
18 in my Home Town of Memphis Tenn.
I am sending you the short autobiography
about myself so you can better understand this

approach. I would love to
meet you just to say hello if
you're not to Busy.

        Respectfully

        Elvis Presley

P.S. I believe that you Sir
were one of the Top Ten outstanding Men
of America also.

I have a personal gift for you also
which I would like to present to you
and you can accept it or I will keep it
for you until you can take it.

Mr. President

PHONE NUMBERS	
These are all my PVT numbers	
Beverly Hills	278-3496
	278-5935
Palm Springs PVT #	325-3241
Memphis	392-4427
	398-4882
	398-9722
PVT. #	
Col. P.S. #	325-4781
Col. B.H. #	274-8498
Col. OFF. Mem	870-0370

WASHINGTON HOTEL) PHONE ME 85900
        RM 505-506-
        UNDER THE NAME
        OF JON BURROWS

PRIVATE
AND CONFIDENTIAL

    Attn. President Nixon
    Via Sen George Murphy
from
Elvis Presley

1-CF652

Tennessee license plate number of the white Cadillac hearse that carried Elvis's body from Graceland to Forest Hill Cemetery on August 18, 1977.

(Photo courtesy Don Fink)

1,087

Number of photographs of Elvis that sisters Graylee and Sharyn Davolt had hanging on their bedroom wall in their Memphis home in 1957. A photograph of their bedroom has appeared in most Elvis fan magazines.

165890

Elvis's membership number in the American Guild of Variety Artists.

$1,040,000

Income guaranteed by RCA Victor for a twenty-year contract specifying $1,000 a week for twenty years. This was a contract proposed by RCA but never accepted by Elvis. Had Elvis accepted this contract he would have lost millions of dollars in royalties over the years.

$150,000,000

Reportedly, the amount grossed at the box office by Elvis's thirty-one movies and two documentaries.

O

Elvis's blood type.

OBEY

Word intentionally left out of Elvis and Priscilla's wedding vows.

O'BRIEN, CARL (CUBBY)

Onetime member of TV's "Mickey Mouse Club." He and Karen Pendleton were the two cute "Meeseketeers" on the program. Cubby O'Brien, who in the 1960s became a drummer for the Carpenters, played drums for Elvis's *Charro!* soundtrack recording session on October 15, 1968, and for the *Change of Habit* soundtrack recording session on March 5–6, 1969.

O'BRIEN, JIM

Colonel Tom Parker's personal secretary, who has been with him since 1956. O'Brien previously worked for Hill and Range Music.

O'CURRAN, CHARLES

Musical director on the 1957 movie *Loving You* and the 1961 movie *Blue Hawaii*. O'Curran composed two songs that Elvis recorded, "Mama" and "We'll Be Together." O'Curran was married to singer Patti Page. (See *Patti Page*)

"ODD"

One-word reply by Beatle Paul McCartney when asked by reporters his impression of Elvis. (The Fab Four had just finished visiting Elvis at his Bel Air home on August 27, 1965.)

ODD FELLOWS

Independent Order of Odd Fellows, a society, founded in 1795, with lodges throughout the world. Elvis belonged to an Odd Fellows group while attending L. C. Humes High School.

OFFICIAL ELVIS PRESLEY FAN CLUB OF GREAT BRITAIN, WORLDWIDE

The world's oldest established Elvis fan club. It was founded in 1956 by Jeannie Seward. The club's address is P.O. Box 4, Leicester, England. The 1988 album *Essential Elvis: The First Movies*, was dedicated to all members of the Official Elvis Presley Fan Club of Great Britain.

O'GRADY, JOHN

Private investigator who, along with his wife, Genevieve, was befriended by Elvis after Elvis hired him to investigate charges against him in a paternity suit. O'Grady had once been in charge of the Narcotics Division of the L.A.P.D. It was after he showed Elvis his narcotics badge that Elvis became intrigued by obtaining a collection of badges. O'Grady, whom Elvis nicknamed "Reverend" because he seldom swore, helped Elvis obtain a U.S. Narcotics Bureau badge. In 1973 Elvis's lawyer Ed Hookstratten hired O'Grady and another private eye, Jack Kelly, to investigate who was supplying Elvis with his drugs. Elvis wasn't aware of these investigations. The pair did their job and uncovered Elvis's three "feelgood" doctors and one dentist. It was supposedly O'Grady who suggested to Elvis that he fire Red West, Sonny West, and Dave Hebler.

During a performance in Las Vegas in 1974, Elvis introduced O'Grady on stage, telling the audience about the rumors that O'Grady was writing an autobiography which included information about a recent paternity suit filed against Elvis. O'Grady's autobiography, written with Nolan Davis, is titled *O'Grady: The Life and Times of Hollywood's No. 1 Private Eye.*

"OK, I WON'T"
Last words spoken by Elvis before he died, on August 16, 1977. They were spoken in response to Ginger Alden's admonition (as Elvis was going into the bathroom with a book): "Don't fall asleep."

O'KEEFE, DANNY
Composer of and original performer of the song "Good Time Charlie's Got the Blues," which Elvis recorded in 1973.

O'NEAL, DORIS
One of the secretaries employed at Graceland to answer fan mail.

ONE FLEW OVER THE CUCKOO'S NEST
A 1975 Oscar-winning movie based on Ken Kesey's novel about patients in a mental hospital. Produced by Michael Douglas (son of actor Kirk Douglas and the first member of his family to win an Academy Award, as producer of the film), *One Flew over the Cuckoo's Nest* is one of only two movies to win the top five Academy Awards: Best Picture, Best Actor (Jack Nicholson), Best Actress (Louise Fletcher), Best Director (Milos Forman), and Best Screenplay (Lawrence Hauben and Bo Goldman). The other movie to accomplish the feat was *It Happened One Night*, in 1934.

On February 11, 1979, *One Flew Over the Cuckoo's Nest* aired on NBC-TV opposite the ABC-TV telecast of *Elvis* and CBS-TV's telecast of *Gone with the Wind. Elvis* beat out both feature films in the ratings. (See *Elvis, Gone with the Wind*)

O'NEILL, JIMMY
Host of the ABC-TV show "Shindig" in the mid-1960s. O'Neill was a friend of Elvis's and double-dated with him a few times. Elvis was dating Jackie DeShannon at the time. O'Neill's first wife was songwriter Sharon Sheeley,[1] a close friend of DeShannon's. (See *Shindig, Jackie DeShannon*)

OPERATION ELVIS
The U.S. Army's official program for handling Elvis while he was in the Armed Forces (March 24, 1958, to March 5, 1960).

OPERATION ELVIS
A 1960 book written by Louisville, Kentucky, reporter Alan Levy about Elvis's military career. In 1962 a paperback edition was published.

ORBISON, ROY K.
(1936–   ) Popular country/rock singer and contemporary of Elvis's. Orbison, who was born in Wink, Texas, on April 23, 1936, began his recording career while a student at North Texas State University. After school, Orbison and his band played locally in Texas, where he was given his own local TV show in Odessa. Elvis and Johnny Cash were guests on the program on May 31, 1955. It was Elvis's sound that finally inspired Orbison to contact Sun Records. In 1956 Orbison and his band the Teen Kings[2] (originally named the Wink Westerners), recorded "Ooby Dooby" at their own expense at Norman Petty's studio in Clovis, New Mexico. It was the first record ever cut at the now famous studios. The release, on JEW-EL Records (JEW-EL 101)[3] was not successful. But on the insistence of Johnny Cash, Orbison sent Sam Phillips a copy of "Ooby Dooby." Phillips liked the record and had Orbison re-record a slightly different version on his Sun label (Sun 242), with Carl Perkins on lead guitar. The flip side of "Ooby Dooby" on the JEW-EL label was "Tryin' to Get to You,"[4] which Elvis recorded in 1955.

In 1958 the Everly Brothers recorded an Orbison composition titled "Claudette," named after Orbison's wife. (Claudette was killed in a motorcycle accident in 1965.)

Like Elvis, Orbison went to RCA after leaving Sun, but he stayed with RCA for only one year (1958). Orbison departed Sun Records because Sam Phillips wouldn't let him record any ballads. He came into national prominence in 1960 with his first million-seller, "Only the Lonely," on Monument Records (Monument 421). Orbison was Elvis's chief rival from 1960 to 1964, charting a number of hits. Singer Bobby Goldsboro was once a member of Orbison's backup band, the Candymen. (Several members of the Candymen became the Atlanta Rhythm Section in the 1970s, while others joined B.J. Thomas's band Beverteeth.)

In May and June 1963, Orbison toured England with an up-and-coming British group called the Beatles,

---

[1] Sharon Sheeley was the composer of Ricky Nelson's 1958 hit "Poor Little Fool" (Imperial 5528). She was the fiancée of singer Eddie Cochran when he was killed in a London taxicab accident on April 17, 1960. Singer Gene Vincent was injured in the accident. Sheeley escaped injury.

[2] The members of the Teen Kings were: Billy Ellis, Jack Kennelly, James Morrow, and Johnny (Peanuts) Wilson. Peanuts Wilson, in 1957, cut a record for Brunswick called "Cast Iron Arms." He composed the Kenny Rogers hit "Love the World Away," before he died in 1981.

[3] Today the record is a collector's item and a single copy may sell for $200.

[4] When Imperial Records bought the master of "Ooby Dooby" and "Tryin' to Get to You" from JEW-EL, they did an unexplained thing with the B side. Imperial released "Tryin' to Get to You" on the flip side of "So Long, Good Luck, and Goodbye" by Weldon Rogers (Imperial 5457), and credited both sides of the records to Rogers. The reason was that Rogers was the owner of JEW-EL Records and this was his way of getting back at Roy Orbison for leaving his label.

making Orbison the only artist to have toured with both Elvis and the Beatles.

Elvis greatly admired Orbison's singing. Even Elvis's hairstyle was much like Orbison's—to the point of being dyed black. During one of his Las Vegas concerts, Elvis introduced Orbison in the audience and then sang a segment of Orbison's 1964 hit song "It's Over" (Monument 837).

Like Elvis, Orbison was also ignored by the Grammy Awards. He had to wait until 1981 before he received his first Grammy and that was for a duet with Emmylou Harris, "That Lovin' You Feelin' Again."

Orbison composed and recorded several songs for the 1980 Elvis-related movie *The Living Legend.* (See *The Living Legend*, Part II)

ORION
(See *Jimmy Ellis*)

ORJUELLA, MARIO
Colombian-born chef who was Elvis's favorite at the Las Vegas Riviera Hotel.

OTIS, CLYDE
First black A&R executive for a major record company, Mercury Records of Chicago, in the 1950s. Otis cowrote (with Willie Dixon) "Doncha' Think It's Time," which Elvis recorded in 1958 and released as a single in 1964. Otis wrote, with Ivory Joe Hunter, "Ain't That Loving You Baby," which Elvis recorded in 1958. Timi Yuro's original version of "Hurt" (Liberty 55343) in 1961 was produced by Otis. "Hurt" was recorded by Elvis in February 1976.

OUACHITA VALLEY JAMBOREE
Country music show originating from the Ouachita Valley Fairgrounds in Monroe, Louisiana, where, according to Richard Wilcox in an interview in the book *Are You Lonesome Tonight?*, Elvis unsuccessfully attempted to get onto the show in both 1952 and 1953.

"OVERNIGHT SENSATION"
Headline of Edwin Howard's "Front Row" newspaper column for the Memphis *Press–Scimitar*, published on Wednesday, July 28, 1954. The column featured a photo of Elvis. This was the first newspaper article written about Elvis's singing career.

OVERTON PARK SHELL
Memphis outdoor stage where, on July 30, 1954, Elvis made his first appearance before a concert audience. Bob Neal promoted the concert. Elvis sang "That's All Right (Mama)" and "Blue Moon of Kentucky." Headlining the show were Slim Whitman and Billy Walker and the Louvin Brothers (Ira and Charlie).

On August 10, 1954, Elvis made an unbilled appearance at the Overton Park Shell. Slim Whitman and Carl

Elvis at his August 5, 1955, appearance at the Overton Park Shell. (Photo courtesy the *Graceland News*)

Smith were the headliners for the two shows—one in the afternoon and one in the evening. In the afternoon, Elvis sang "Old Shep" and "That's When Your Heartaches Begin," receiving little response from the audience. His reception in the evening, when he sang "Good Rockin' Tonight" and "That's All Right (Mama)," was overwhelming—so much so that Webb Pierce declined to perform.

On August 5, 1955, Elvis was the featured artist at the Overton Park Shell. At that concert, Johnny Cash and the Tennessee Two made their first concert appearance, singing "Cry, Cry, Cry" and "Hey Porter."

OWENS, AL L. (DOODLE)
Singer and composer who wrote the song "Let's Forget About the Stars" and, with Dallas Frazier, the songs "True Love Travels on a Gravel Road," "Wearin' That Loved On Look," and "Where Did They Go, Lord," all of which Elvis recorded. In 1966 Owens recorded the song "Ninety Days" (Dot 16928).

OWENS, CLIFF
Composer, with Aaron Schroeder, of the song "Any Way You Want Me (That's How I Will Be)," which Elvis recorded in 1956.

OWENS, KELLY
Composer, with Rose Marie McCoy, of the song "I Beg of You" which Elvis recorded in 1957.

PAGE PATTI

(1927–   ) Singer born Clara Ann Fowler in Clare-
more, Oklahoma, on November 8, 1927.[1] Page was one
of Elvis's two favorite female vocalists (the other was
Kay Starr), as revealed by him in Red Robinson's Vancouver, British Columbia, interview on August 31,
1957. Patti Page got her stage name from her radio
sponsor, the Page Milk Company. Her biggest hit, "The
Tennessee Waltz" (Mercury 5534), came in 1950; it
became the biggest-selling song of all time by a female
singer, with more than ten million copies sold. Frank
Sinatra was offered the song but turned it down.

Page's husband, Charles O'Curran,[2] was the musical
director on the 1961 movie *Blue Hawaii*. One night
Elvis and Patti had a chance to meet for the first time,
and spent the evening together on the terrace of the
Coco Palms Hotel, talking and singing.

Elvis covered Page's 1950 recording of "I Don't Care
If the Sun Don't Shine" (Mercury 5396), which he
recorded at Sun in September 1954. Page also recorded
a version of "Love Letters" (Columbia 42902) in 1964,
before Elvis did.

PAGET, DEBRA

(1933–   ) Hollywood actress born Debralee Griffin
on August 19, 1933, in Denver. Paget was Elvis's female
costar in the 1956 movie *Love Me Tender*, playing
Cathy Reno, Elvis's wife. She was first introduced to
Elvis by Milton Berle when they both appeared on
Berle's television show on June 5, 1956, in a skit in
which Berle asked Elvis what actress he liked. Elvis
said, "Debra Paget," to which Berle replied: "She's not
in your league, stick to Heartbreak Hotel and stay away
from the Waldorf. She'd never go out with a singer like
you, she's much too sophisticated." Paget then came
out on stage, screamed, and kissed Elvis. In 1957 Paget
wrote an article for *TV & Movie Screen* magazine titled
"What I Found Out About Elvis!" One of the reasons
that Paget and Elvis did not become romantically involved was producer Howard Hughes, whom Paget
was seeing at the time.

PAINTERS UNION LOCAL 49

Memphis AFL-CIO union that picketed Graceland in
May 1957 because a nonunion painting contractor,
C. W. Nichols, had been hired to paint the mansion.

PAJAMAS

Elvis owned twenty pairs of pajamas at the time of his
death. When he died, he was wearing pajamas with a
blue top and yellow bottom.

PALLAVICINI, V.

Composer, with P. Donaggio, of the song "You Don't
Have to Say You Love Me," which Elvis recorded in
1970.

PALLBEARERS

The five pallbearers at Elvis's funeral on August 18,
1977, were: Joe Esposito, Dr. George Nichopoulos,
Lamar Fike, Charlie Hodge, and Billy Smith. Producer
Felton Jarvis was to have been the sixth member, but
he couldn't attend the funeral.

PALM SPRINGS

California resort town where Elvis and Priscilla spent
their honeymoon in May 1967. Elvis later bought a
house at 825 Chino Canyon Road in Palm Springs.
Colonel Tom Parker's California home is located in
Palm Springs. (See *Houses*)

PALMS CLUB

Memphis nightclub located on Summer Avenue where,
it is believed by some sources, Elvis performed sometime around 1951 or 1952. The appearance had been
set up by disc jockey Sleepy Eyed John.

PARAMOUNT THEATER

New York City's flagship movie theater where, on November 16, 1956, *Love Me Tender* premiered.

PARCHMAN PENITENTIARY

Mississippi state prison where Vernon Presley and his
brother-in-law, Travis Smith, both served nine months
(June 1, 1938, to February 6, 1939) of a three-year
prison term for forgery. Vernon and Travis were transferred there from the Lee County Jail. Presley was
convicted of forging the check of a local farmer, Orville Bean. He sold Bean a calf for $4[3] and altered the
check to read $40. Friends of the Presleys—Forrest L.
Bobo and his wife, Flora—took Gladys and Elvis to
Parchman to visit Vernon on one occasion. According
to some sources, both Vernon and Travis were bull-
whipped, both carrying the scars on their backs to
their graves. For that reason, Vernon never went shirt-
less at Graceland.

Also convicted of forgery with Vernon and Travis
was Luther Gable. All three men originally pleaded not
guilty, only to change their plea to guilty at the trial.
On May 23, 1938, the three were sentenced by Circuit
Court Judge Thomas H. Johnston, who that day handed
out sentences totaling thirty-two years to nine different people. Of the three, Vernon was the only one who

[1]As a young girl, Clara Ann Fowler baby-sat for Mark Dinning. In 1960 Dinning recorded the number one hit and million-seller "Teen
Angel" (MGM 12845), which was banned from British radio as too morbid.
[2]Ironically, O'Curran is connected to Elvis's other favorite female singer, Kay Starr. He had been married to actress Betty Hutton, whose
sister, singer Marion Hutton, had been married to Victor Schoen, the former husband of singer Kay Starr.
[3]Sources vary on the amount of the check. Some say as high as $200; another says that the men filled out a blank check.

had not been released on bail, as no one put up the money. Vernon's own father and J. G. Brown bailed out Travis, not Vernon, while J. H. Gable and C. E. Biggerstaff bailed out Luther Gable.

In 1928 and 1929 blues singer Eddie House spent time at Parchman, as did blind blues singer Booker (Bukka) Washington. White blues singer Mose Allison recorded the song "Parchman Farm" (Prestige 130) in 1959, as did the Kingston Trio, as "Parchman Farm Blues" (Decca 31806), in 1965.

PARIS
(See *The Lido*)

PARKER, ED
College-educated (B.A. degree in sociology from Brigham Young University) bodyguard and personal karate instructor for Elvis. Parker, who was born Edmund K. Parker in Honolulu, was nicknamed "Kahuna" (Kahuna is Hawaiian for "high priest") by Elvis. Parker is a cousin of Hawaiian singer Don Ho. He specializes in kempo karate, which consists of chopping and jabbing blows with the hands. Parker appeared in a bit role in the 1978 Peter Sellers comedy *The Revenge of the Pink Panther*. He also appeared in an episode of TV's "The Lucy Show," teaching Lucille Ball how to use karate against a burglar. Parker first began instructing Elvis in karate in 1972 in his own Santa Monica studio. In 1973 Elvis flew up to San Francisco to attend the California State Karate Championships organized by Parker. On his way from the airport Elvis saw a sign promoting the event that read "Elvis Presley in Person." Elvis turned around, flew back to Los Angeles, and didn't speak to Parker for a long time afterward.

As a young boy Parker, along with the author Edgar Rice Burroughs and eleven-year-old future boxer Carl (Bobo) Olson, witnessed the Japanese bombing of Pearl Harbor on December 7, 1941.

Parker is the author of the 1978 book *Inside Elvis*, published by Rampart House, Ltd.

PARKER, LITTLE JUNIOR
(1932–1971) Rhythm & blues singer, born Herman Parker Jr. in West Memphis, Arkansas.[1] Parker was nicknamed "Junior" by blues singer Sonny Boy Williamson. Parker recorded for various small labels in the South, such as Duke, Peacock, and Sun. It was on Sun that Little Junior Parker and the Blue Flames[2] first recorded "Mystery Train" (Sun 192), which Parker cowrote with Sam Phillips. The record's label listed the performers as Little Junior's Blue Flames. Elvis also recorded "Mystery Train" for Sun Records, but sang it at a faster pace. Parker charted several hit records during the 1960s. He died during an operation to correct an eye problem.

PARKER, MARIE MOTT ROSS
Wife of Colonel Tom Parker, born Marie Mott, who kept a low profile during her husband's busy career as Elvis's manager. Colonel Parker met Marie, whom he calls "Miz' Rie," in Tampa, Florida, in the winter of 1932. Marie had previously been married, but widowed. Her son, by her first marriage, died in 1977 of multiple sclerosis. Marie Parker lent her name for that of Elvis's daughter, Lisa Marie Presley.

PARKER, PAMELA
One of Elvis's secretaries at Graceland whose job was answering fan mail. Parker had previously worked for evangelist Oral Roberts.

PARKER, PATRICIA ANN
(1949–   ) Hollywood waitress who, on August 21, 1970, brought a paternity suit against Elvis in Los Angeles, claiming that her child, Jason, born in Presbyterian Hospital in Hollywood on October 19, 1970, was fathered by Elvis, after Elvis had posed with her for a photograph in Las Vegas. She requested $1,000-a-month child support. Her lawyer handed Elvis the court papers while Elvis was performing at the Forum in Inglewood on November 14, 1970. On January 6, 1971, Judge William Hogoboom ordered Elvis to take a lie detector test and a blood test, which proved negative. After nine months of litigation, Parker's lawyer, Paul Caruso, dropped the suit.

PARKER, COLONEL THOMAS ANDREW
(1909–   ) A 300-pound promoter and agent, born Andreas Cornelius van Kuijk in Breda, Holland, on June 26, 1909. Parker immigrated into the United States illegally in 1929, after which he claimed Huntington, West Virginia, as his place of birth. He served in the U.S. Army with the 64th Coast Artillery from 1929 to 1932, having enlisted at Fort McPherson in Atlanta. When he joined he swore allegiance to the United States, thus renouncing his Dutch citizenship. Since Parker isn't a citizen of the United States, it has been suggested that he is technically a "man without a country." In 1932 he married Marie Mott Ross, whom he had met in Tampa, Florida.

Parker began his hawking career in carnivals and fairs, pushing anything he thought he could sell. He founded the Great Parker Pony Circus and, later, Colonel Tom Parker and His Dancing Chickens, in which Parker placed live chickens on a hot plate covered with sawdust, accompanied by a record player as the chickens "danced" to the music. At the age of thirty-two Parker was elected dogcatcher of Tampa. In the 1950s Parker became the promoter of singer Gene Austin and manager of country singers Eddy Arnold (from 1942 to 1951) and Hank Snow (from 1954 to 1956). He also managed singer Tommy Sands. On March 15, 1956, Parker officially became the manager

---

[1]Another sun artist, Rosco Gordon, was also born in West Memphis.
[2]British rocker Georgie Fame in the 1960s also fronted a band called the Blues Flames.

Elvis and the Colonel, 1956. (Photo courtesy Wide World Photos)

of Elvis Presley, for a 25 percent fee. Parker, an honorary colonel since 1953, was Elvis's manager until Elvis's death, never taking on another client.

Parker is a shrewd, hard-working, and demanding individual who worked for the financial betterment of both Elvis and himself, especially himself. For this reason Parker has become controversial. By establishing two publishing companies for Elvis in the early 1960s, the quality of the songs offered to Elvis greatly deteriorated, because the industry's talented composers refused to forfeit a share of their legitimate royalties to anyone. Parker espoused the philosophy of never giving away anything you can sell, i.e., interviews, photograph sessions, advice, even a *Life* magazine cover. Parker's asking price for an interview was $25,000 for the short version and $100,000 for the long version. Though Parker wasn't his agent at the time, Elvis signed his first contract, with Parker, for some appearances in the South, on August 15, 1955. On January 2, 1967, Parker renegotiated his managerial/agent contract with Elvis, somehow persuading Elvis to increase Parker's share from 25 percent to 50 percent of every cent Elvis made. Parker used the argument that Elvis

was his only client, and probably mentioned heaven knows what other facts to convince Elvis to sign. That contract ran until January 22, 1976.

On one occasion during the 1970s, Vernon Presley attempted to tell Parker that Elvis was going to fire him as his manager and continue to work without him. The quick-witted Parker stopped the slower-thinking Vernon in his tracks when he produced an itemized bill for $5 million, claiming that it was what Elvis owed him if he was indeed fired. Intimidated by Parker, Vernon blinked and dropped the idea. He had to inform his son that Parker was once again his financial guru.

Everyone, including Elvis and Parker, were aware that Elvis's movies deteriorated to Grade C formula films. Parker even admitted to not bothering to read the scripts, once saying, "Anybody who'll pay my boy a million dollars can make any kind of picture he wants." The quality control in Elvis's career sank rapidly. Felton Jarvis rescued Elvis's recording career in the late 1960s, but no one came along in time to rescue his film career. A number of times Elvis was offered decent roles, e.g., *Thunder Road* (1958) and *A Star Is Born*

(1976)—only to have Parker ruin the deal by asking for too much money. Elvis had an opportunity to perform with Arthur Fielder and the Boston Pops, perform before royalty in London, tour Europe, Australia, Japan, even perform for President Richard Nixon at the White House, all of which Parker nixed one way or another. It's a shame that so many millions of Elvis's fans in Great Britain and other countries never got the opportunity to see Elvis live in concert, only because Parker couldn't leave the United States. If he had applied for a passport, his alien status might have been discovered. Many believe that Parker was more interested in quantity (money) than quality (establishing Elvis as a respectable actor).

In 1976 Parker convinced Elvis to sell his entire catalog of singles and albums to RCA Records for a mere $6 million, with, of course, Parker getting half. Since Elvis had no investments, as Parker did, he was in such a high income-tax bracket that his share of the deal, the $3 million, was greatly reduced. It was a shrewd deal for RCA, but a terrible deal for Elvis. Elvis had no financial adviser outside of his father, so no one could tell him it was a bad transaction. Parker also created a conflict of interest in Elvis's concert appearances in Las Vegas, by gambling heavily in the same casinos that hired Elvis to perform. It has been estimated that Parker lost about a million dollars a year in Las Vegas casinos. It was reported that in November 1980 Parker sold to Warner Bros., for $750,000, the rights to film a movie about Elvis's life. Parker's share was $200,000, the Presley estate received $200,000, and Parker's associates and employees received $350,000.

Few people, however, can argue with Parker's success in guiding Elvis's career.[1] For most of their relationship, there were few accounts of Elvis (who affectionately called him "Admiral") ever disagreeing with Parker's decisions, and few accounts of the two ever having anything but a good working relationship and friendship—although that relationship seriously deteriorated in Elvis's later years. Parker has also been criticized for his nonchalant attitude, especially as reflected by his attire at the funerals of both Elvis and Vernon Presley—he wore shorts, a colorful shirt, and a baseball cap, while all of the other guests were suitably attired. The day after Elvis's death, Parker had Vernon sign papers allowing Factors Etc., Inc., to handle all of the merchandising Elvis-related products.

After Elvis's death the courts ruled that Parker had no legal rights or interest to the Presley estate, and he was forced to relinquish any connection to the Elvis Presley name. During some of the litigation against Parker, he used the defense that he was not an American citizen and therefore could not be sued in an American court. In the book *Elvis: Portrait of a Friend*, Ed Parker is quoted as saying about Tom Parker: "Parker is a rude, crude, son of a bitch, and you can quote me."

In the 1981 movie *This Is Elvis*, Colonel Tom Parker remarked, "I own 25 percent of Elvis alive [ed. note: he owned 50 percent at the time] and I own 25 percent of him dead [ed note: he still owned 50 percent]."

PARNES, PAUL
(1925–   ) Composer born in New York City on January 25, 1925. Parnes has written music for a number of children's television programs. He composed, with Paul Evans, the song "The Next Step Is Love," which Elvis recorded in 1970.

PASCAGOULA, MISSISSIPPI
Location of the shipyards built by the WPA, where in 1940, after getting out of prison, Vernon worked for eight months and took Gladys and Elvis with him. They lived next door to Sales and Annie Presley. When Sales and his wife decided to leave and return to Tupelo, Vernon and his family were right behind them.

PATE SR., JOHN W.
Composer, with Curtis Mayfield, of the new lyrics to the gospel song "Amen," which Elvis sang in concert.

PATRICIA STEVENS FINISHING AND CAREER SCHOOL
Memphis school, located at 111 Monroe Avenue, that Priscilla Beaulieu attended after graduating from high school in June 1963, to study dancing and modeling.

PATTERSON, AARON ELVIS PRESLEY
(1978–   ) Son of Elbert and Deborah Patterson of Asheboro, North Carolina, who was publicized by his parents as the "reincarnation of Elvis." "For $20 people will be given a membership card to the Baby Elvis Fan Club, an Elvis 'Living Tribute to the King' T-shirt and a Baby Elvis newsletter." Aaron's mother launched the advertising campaign.

PAYNE, LEON
(1917–1969) Blind musician and composer who played in Bob Wills's band, the Texas Playboys. In 1949 Payne composed "I Love You Because," which Elvis recorded in July 1954.

PAYNE, SILAS
Black plantation worker, employed by Sam Phillips's father, who taught young Sam many of the blues songs of the day. Payne is reminiscent of another black singer, Tee-Tot, who taught another young Southern boy how to play the guitar and sing the blues. That boy's name was Hank Williams. Carl Perkins was also influenced by a black blues guitarist, John Westbrook, and Jerry Lee Lewis and his cousins Mickey Gilley and Jimmy Swaggart were inspired in their youth by a black piano player named Old Sam.

---

[1]Although we, the authors, personally feel that Elvis's career could have been even more spectacular than it was, how does one argue with success? How does one tell Parker that he was wrong, when he has solid proof of his success with Elvis, while all we have is a theory. Although it's a tough argument to make, we still believe in our theory.

PEANUT BUTTER AND MASHED BANANA SANDWICHES
Reportedly one of Elvis's favorite snacks.

PEARL, MINNIE
(1912–) Country comedian born Sarah Ophellia Colley, in Centerville, Tennessee, on October 25, 1912, and nicknamed "The Queen of Country Comedy." College-educated ("Howw-dee") Minnie Pearl appeared regularly at the Grand Ole Opry and on TV's "Hee Haw" series. A member of the Country Music Hall of Fame, Pearl wears a hat with a $1.98 price tag on it. She made her debut at the Grand Ole Opry in 1940.

Pearl and Pee Wee King were the two featured performers at the Mississippi-Alabama Fair and Dairy Show in Tupelo in 1945, when Elvis won the second-place prize in the talent contest. Pearl performed with Elvis in March 1961 at a benefit for the USS *Arizona* Memorial Fund.

PENNIMAN, RICHARD WAYNE
(See *Little Richard*)

PENNINGTON, ANN
Elvis's girlfriend for a short time, after his breakup with Linda Thompson.

PEPPER, GARY
(1932–1980) Memphis cerebral palsy victim to whom Vernon Presley sent $400 a month at Elvis's request. Two months after Elvis's death in 1977, Vernon ceased the payments. Pepper was on Elvis's payroll, employed to handle mail from fans and fan clubs.

As president of the Elvis Presley Tankers Fan Club, Pepper regularly placed flowers on Gladys Presley's grave on the anniversary of her death. He wrote the article "Elvis's Last Days," which was published in *Elvis Monthly* magazine in 1977.

Pepper, whose idea it was in 1966 to rename Memphis's Mid-South Coliseum as the Elvis Presley Coliseum, only to have the idea rejected, died in Long Beach, California, on March 29, 1980.

PEPPER, STERLING
One of a number of men employed as gate guards at Graceland. Pepper obtained the job through his son, Gary Pepper.

PEPSI-COLA
Elvis's favorite soft drink. Also that of Hugh Hefner. Elvis's grandfather, Jessie D. Presley, was a night watchman for a Pepsi-Cola plant in 1947.

Actors James Dean and Nick Adams made their screen debuts in a Pepsi-Cola commercial in 1951. Elvis fan Bruce Springsteen is also a lover of Pepsi.

Pepsi-Cola was the inspiration for Elvis's song "All Shook Up." Al Stanton, one of the owners of Shalimar Music, an employee of the music-publishing company Hill and Range, was talking to composer Otis Blackwell one day as he was drinking a bottle of Pepsi. As he shook the bottle, Stanton said to Blackwell: "Otis, I've got an idea. Why don't you write a song called 'All Shook Up'?" Blackwell accepted the challenge and wrote the song.

PERETTI, HUGO
(1918–1986) Songwriter and producer at RCA Victor Records who worked together with composer Luigi Creatore. The pair charted three songs before buying Roulette Records in 1956 and later founding Avco Embassy Records. They had written songs under the pseudonym Mark Markwell, and produced records for RCA Victor, including the classic Isley Brothers hit "Shout" (RCA Victor 7588) and Sam Cooke's records. In 1957 Peretti and Creatore recorded the song "Rockabilly Party" (Roulette 4012), which mentioned Elvis in the lyrics. Peretti, with George Weiss and Creatore, composed "Can't Help Falling in Love," "Ku-u-i-po," and "Wild in the Country," all of which Elvis recorded.

PERKINS, CARL LEE
(1932–) Rockabilly singer born in Tipton County, Tennessee, on April 9, 1932. Perkins began as a disc jockey (WTJS radio in Jackson, Tennessee) before he turned recording artist in the mid-1950s. At the age of thirteen Perkins won a talent show on WTJS when he sang "Home on the Range," winning twenty-five dollars. Perkins first recorded for Flip Records, a non-union subsidiary label of Sun Records. His first release was "Movie Magg" (Flip 501), recorded on January 22, 1955. Perkins first met Elvis in Bethel Springs, Tennessee, in 1954, where Perkins was playing a club. Perkins and Elvis appeared together in Memphis on November 13, 1955. Perkins recorded his composition "Blue Suede Shoes" (Sun 234) on December 19, 1955. On March 27, 1956, Perkins was injured in an automobile accident that took the life of his brother and manager, Jay. Disc jockey David Stewart fell asleep at the wheel while the band was en route to New York City to appear on TV's "Ed Sullivan Show" and "The Perry Como Show," which would have given them national exposure. At the time of the accident, Perkins's version of "Blue Suede Shoes" had reached number two on the charts. After the accident he was taken to the General Hospital in Dover, Delaware, where he received a Western Union telegram from Elvis on March 28, 1956, that read: "We were all shocked and very sorry to hear of the accident. I know what it is for I had a few bad ones myself. If I can help you in any way please call me. I will be at the Warwick Hotel in New York City. Our wishes are for a speedy recovery for you and the other boys. Sincerely Elvis Presley, Bill Black, Scotty Moore and D. J. Fontana."

Elvis, who recorded a faster version of Perkins's "Blue Suede Shoes" in 1956, was present at Perkins's recording session on December 4, 1956, when he recorded "Matchbox" and other songs. (Ironically, Perkins himself would be present at the Beatles' recording session in 1964 when they recorded their version of

"Matchbox," with George Martin on piano.[1]) That impromptu get-together was later dubbed the Million-Dollar Quartet. Elvis last played with Perkins on July 4, 1976, for a Bicentennial concert in Memphis. After Elvis's death, Perkins recorded the tribute record "The Whole World Misses You" (Jet 117). (In 1974 he recorded the novelty record "The E.P. Express" [Mercury 73609].) Perkins, Jerry Lee Lewis, Johnny Cash, and Roy Orbison recorded "We Remember the King" (American Smash 88142-7).

RCA's Chet Atkins once remarked to Sam Phillips, when Perkins had the number two record in the country with "Blue Suede Shoes," "We thought for a while we bought the wrong Sun artist."

The Beatles recorded the following Carl Perkins compositions: "Honey Don't" (flip side of "Blue Suede Shoes"), "Everybody's Trying to Be My Baby," and "Matchbox."

Jackson, Mississippi, celebrated Carl Perkins Day on February 4, 1969.

Perkins once said of Elvis, "This boy had everything. He had the looks, the moves, the manager, and the talent. And he didn't look like Mr. Ed, like a lot of us did. In the way he looked, way he talked, way he acted—he really was different."

PERKINS, LUTHER

(1928–1968) Member of Johnny Cash's Tennessee Two and the brother of singer Thomas Wayne. Perkins was born on January 8, 1928, seven years to the day before Elvis's birthday. Perkins died on August 5, 1968 (Elvis also died in August). The Bill Black Combo once recorded a tribute record to Perkins titled "Cashin' In (a Tribute to Luther Perkins)" on Hi Records (Hi 78508). Perkins and Marshall Grant had played live behind Elvis on one occasion during their 1955 tour of the South.

PETERS, GERALD

Elvis's Beverly Hills chauffeur, who had previously served in the same capacity for British Prime Minister Sir Winston Churchill (so the story goes). Peters, whom Elvis called "Sir Gerald," ran the London Towne Livery Service in Beverly Hills.

PETERS, VICKI

Woman who dated Elvis in 1971. In an October 24, 1971, article in the *National Insider*, Peters stated that Elvis had a drug problem.

PETERSON, JAMES B.

Civilian barber from Gans, Oklahoma, who gave Elvis his first Army haircut at Fort Chaffee, Arkansas, on March 25, 1958. Elvis paid sixty-five cents for his three-minute haircut, but initially forgot to pay Peterson. After the haircut Elvis remarked, "Hair today, gone

tomorrow," while Colonel Tom Parker, looking down at the floor, gave one of his typical observations: "That hair is worth a fortune."

PETTIT, DONALD

Soldier friend of Elvis's at Fort Hood and in West Germany until a magazine called *Elvis in the Army* published an article written by Pettit, after which Elvis shunned him.

PHILLIPS, DEWEY MILLS

(1926–1968) Memphis disc jockey for WHBQ radio who on his program "Red Hot and Blue," on July 7, 1954, first played an Elvis song on radio.[2] Phillips was so taken by the record that he played "That's All Right (Mama)" fourteen times during the show. According to fellow WHBQ disc jockey, Wink Martindale, Phillips played both sides of the 78 RPM acetate, flipping it over the entire evening. Later that night, after receiving fourteen telegrams and forty-seven phone calls, Phillips interviewed Elvis, Elvis's first media interview.

It was Dewey Phillips who often "broke" Sam Phillips's latest releases over the air in Memphis. Dewey and Sam's friendship went back to 1950, when the two men launched their own record label, Phillips Records, billed as "The Hottest Thing in the Country." Singer Carl Perkins has said that Dewey may have been the first to use the term *rockabilly*, when on his program he would use the expression, "Man, they're rockin' country music, they're rockabillys."

It was Dewey Phillips who played the first Jerry Lee Lewis record over the air on WHBQ in 1956, when he played "Crazy Arms" (Sun 259).

Phillips died of pneumonia on September 28, 1968, at the age of forty-two (the same age Elvis would be at the time of his death), while working at a small radio station in Millington, Tennessee. Elvis attended Phillips's funeral, where he embarrassingly broke into a fit of nervous giggles.

PHILLIPS, JERRY

Musician son of producer Sam Phillips. Jerry played acoustic guitar on John Prine's version of "Baby Let's Play House," which was produced by Jerry and his brother Knox. Phillips portrayed Bill Black in the 1981 movie *This Is Elvis*.

PHILLIPS, JUDD

Brother of producer Sam Phillips. Judd, a former Army chaplain who fought in both World War II and Korea, once helped to promote singer Roy Acuff and comedian Jimmy Durante, and worked for Colonel Tom Parker for a time. In July 1953 Judd joined Sam Phillips at Sun Records as a co-owner, until Sam bought him out in October 1955. Judd worked for Sam on the Phillips International record label in 1957. In

---

[1]It has been speculated that Perkins actually played guitar on the Beatles' versions of "Matchbox" and "Honey Don't." If so, Perkins is the only musician to have played on a recorded song with both Elvis (Million-Dollar Quartet session) and the Beatles.

[2]Dewey Phillips was not only the first DJ to play an Elvis record, he was the first DJ to play a Sun Record, when on March 1, 1952, he aired the first record released commercially by Sun Records. The record was "Blues in My Condition"/"Sellin' My Whiskey" (Sun 174) by Jackie Boy and Little Walter.

1959 Judd Phillips launched Judd Records of Sheffield, Alabama, on which Sun artist Ray Smith recorded his 1960 hit "Rockin' Little Angel" (Judd 1016). Judd sold the label to NRC Records in 1960.

One story has it that Judd was standing in front of the Memphis Recording Service while Elvis was pacing the sidewalk one day in the summer of 1953. Judd supposedly encouraged Elvis to go inside and record his first record, a four-dollar acetate. Judd Phillips's son, Judd Jr., became an executive for Mercury Records.

PHILLIPS, KNOX
Son of record producer Sam Phillips, who has become a record producer himself. Knox portrayed his father in the 1979 TV movie *Elvis.*

PHILLIPS, SAM CORNELIUS
(1923–   ) Record producer born in Florence, Alabama, on January 5, 1923. Phillips began in music as a radio station engineer and later worked as a disc jockey. He worked for the following radio stations: 1942—WLAY, Muscle Shoals, Alabama; 1943—WHSL, Decatur, Alabama; 1945—WLAC, Nashville; 1946–49—WREC, Memphis.

In 1950 Phillips became a record producer when he cut two songs for his newly founded record label, Phillips Records ("The Hottest Thing in the Country"), with Joe Hill Louis singing "Gotta Let You Go"/"Boogie in the Park," but the record only sold 350 copies. Later that year Phillips founded the Memphis Recording Service.

Phillips began recording rhythm & blues demo records, which he sold to other independent record companies, such as Chess and Modern Records. Among the artists he recorded were Jackie Brenston, Rosco Gordon, B. B. King, and Ike Turner. Phillips's most successful record was Brenston's "Rocket 88"[1] (Chess 1438), which oddly enough was recorded with a broken amplifier, giving it a fuzz sound.

In February 1952 Phillips started Sun Records so that he could record both rhythm & blues singers and country & western artists (then known as hillbilly music). It was located in the same building, 706 Union Avenue, that housed the Memphis Recording Service. Phillips's first release was on March 1, 1952, with "Blues in My Condition"/"Sellin' My Whiskey" by Jackie Boy and Little Walter (Sun 174). Phillips is listed as the composer of Rufus (Hound Dog) Thomas's "Bear Cat" (Sun 181) and the cowriter of the song "Mystery Train." Among the Sun artists Phillips recorded were Rufus Thomas, the Prisonaires, Junior Parker, Little Milton, Doug Poindexter, and the Johnny Burnette Trio, before recording Elvis's first record, "That's All Right (Mama)" in 1954.

Secretary Marion Keisker always remembered Phillips telling her, "If I could find a white man who had the Negro sound and the Negro feel, I could make a billion dollars."[2] When Keisker first heard Elvis sing, she heard that "Negro sound." When Elvis became popular in the South, Phillips often repeated to disc jockeys, reporters, etc., "the story of Elvis's success at Sun." However, he related the falsehood that Elvis had recorded his first acetate that summer as a birthday present for his mother, whose birthday was actually in April. After the success of Elvis on Sun, other rockabilly and country singers came to Phillips's label. Some of these were: Johnny Cash, Carl Perkins, Charlie Feathers, Jerry Lee Lewis, Roy Orbison, Billy Lee Riley, Sonny Burgess, Ray Harris, Dickie Lee, Conway Twitty, Charlie Rich, Harold Dorman, Bill Justis, Carl Mann, David Houston, Thomas Wayne, and dozens of lesser-known performers. In 1955 Phillips sold Elvis's contract to RCA Victor in order to obtain the needed capital to help groom an up-and-coming artist named Carl Perkins. From 1957 to 1966 Sam Phillips owned Phillips International, a subsidiary label of Sun Records.

In 1969 Phillips sold Sun records, including all stock, records, and tapes to Shelby Singleton. Among the items that changed hands was a boxful of Elvis's Sun 45s and the Million-Dollar Quartet session tapes.

The influence of Phillips's small Sun label was major to the field of rock & roll music of the 1950s. Aside from the talented artists he recorded, many other singers copied, to some extent, the "Sun sound," such as Ricky Nelson, Buddy Holly, and John Fogerty. At present Phillips is the owner of the Memphis radio station WLVS, having selected the call letters in honor of his most famous recording artist, Elvis.

Phillips can be called nothing less than a genius, because he possessed that rare talent of being able to recognize talent.

Sam Phillips has been quoted as saying, "I knew Elvis was going to be big, but I never knew he'd be that big!"

PHILLIPS, THOMAS
Older brother of Sam and Judd Phillips, who ran the Sun warehouse in Memphis and took care of shipments, returns, and the inventory of 45 and 78 RPM records.

PHIL SILVERS SHOW, THE
Popular situation-comedy TV series of the late 1950s, focusing on Army life. It starred Phil Silvers as Sgt. Ernie G. Bilko, head of the motor pool at Fort Baxter in Roseville, Kansas (later Camp Fremont in Grove City, California).

For the first six episodes "The Phil Silvers Show" was known as "You'll Never Get Rich" (September 20–October 25, 1955), but the title was changed to capitalize on the popularity of its star. The producers hired an

---

[1]It was the debut of Ike Turner and his band on record. Phillips calls it the first rock & roll record.

[2]In a *Goldmine* interview, Phillips said that although Jerry Hopkins has quoted him as saying it in his book, he never uttered those now famous words.

Army officer as the show's technical adviser. The adviser, George Kennedy, played bit roles at times and finally got the acting bug, becoming a major star in the late 1960s.

"The Phil Silvers Show" did a parody on Elvis in 1957 with a character called Elvin Pelvin, whose big hit was "You're Nothin' But a Raccoon." Pelvin was played by Tom Gilson. The scheming Sgt. Bilko attempted to become Pelvin's manager. The episode titled "Rock and Roll Rookie" was repeated on Friday, March 28, 1958, at 9:00 P.M., four days after Elvis was inducted into the Army.

PHOTOPLAY GOLD MEDAL AWARD
Two awards presented to Elvis by *Photoplay* magazine on June 18, 1977, for Favorite Variety Star and Favorite Rock Music Star. These were the last awards presented to Elvis before his death.

PIANO
Musical instrument played by Elvis in addition to the guitar. On "Lawdy Miss Clawdy," "Wear My Ring Around Your Neck," "I'll Hold You in My Heart," and "One-Sided Love Affair," Elvis played the piano. At his concerts, he accompanied himself on piano when he sang "Unchained Melody." On his *How Great Thou Art* album, Elvis played piano on some of the cuts. Elvis also played piano during part of the Million-Dollar Quartet session, but after a while gave up his seat to Jerry Lee Lewis. Kathy Westmoreland has said she heard Elvis play Beethoven's "Moonlight Sonata" on the piano, while composer Ben Weisman has said that Elvis loved the classics and that he could play Debussy's "Claire de Lune."

PICCADILLY CAFETERIA
Memphis restaurant at 123 Madison Avenue where Priscilla modeled for a brief time in the mid-1960s, after she had attended the Patricia Stevens Finishing School.

PIERCE, WEBB
(1926–   ) Singer and composer born near West Monroe, Louisiana, on August 8, 1926. Pierce has had a number of successful country records, beginning in 1952. Faron Young and Floyd Cramer were once members of Pierce's band. Pierce composed, with Wayne Walker, "How Do You Think I Feel," which Elvis recorded in September 1956. Some accounts say that in 1954 Pierce called Elvis a "son of a bitch" when Elvis had finished performing at the Overton Park Shell just before Pierce went on to perform. He actually said the words tongue-in-cheek to Dewey Phillips, knowing that he could never top Elvis. Pierce has said that Elvis told him he created his wiggle on stage to prevent himself from fainting. Pierce said of Elvis in 1955, "That boy could put us all out of business."

PINK AND BLACK
Elvis's favorite colors in the early 1950s. He sometimes wore black pants with a pink shirt, which he bought at Lansky Brothers.

The pink Cadillac Elvis bought for his mother on September 3, 1956. (Photo courtesy John Dawson)

PINK CADILLAC
1957 automobile that Elvis bought for his mother, Gladys, on September 3, 1956, although she didn't drive. Elvis still had the car at Graceland on the day he died. In the song "Baby Let's Play House," Elvis changed the lyric from "You may get religion" to "You may get a pink Cadillac." Elvis had promised to give the car to his daughter, Lisa Marie, when she turned eighteen in 1986.

PITTMAN, BARBARA
Singer, originally with Clyde Leoppard's Snearly Ranch Boys, whom Elvis dated in the mid-1950s. Pittman, who also recorded for Sun Records and Phillips International, recorded the demo for Elvis's "Playing for Keeps." In an article in *Mean Mountain Music* magazine, Pittman claimed to have been dating Elvis at the time and recorded the demo in his style and key.

Drummer Johnny Bernero, who played on a few Sun recordings with Elvis, also played drums for Pittman on her April 1956 recording of "I Need a Man"/"No Matter Who's to Blame" (Sun 253).

PLASTIC PRODUCTS
Memphis firm, located at 1746 Chelsea Avenue, that pressed the 45 RPM and 78 RPM records for Sun Records. It was one of several pressing plants employed by Sun.

PLATTERS, THE
Vocal group founded in Los Angeles in 1953, consisting of Tony Williams, Zola Taylor, Herb Reed, Paul Robi, and David Lynch. The Platters were managed by Buck Ram, who wrote their hit songs "Only You" and "The Great Pretender." It is believed that Elvis recorded the Platters' "Only You" (Mercury 70753), which he sang in concert in La Crosse, Wisconsin, on May 14, 1956, as well as having sung "The Great Pretender" (Mercury 70753) in concert. Both Elvis and the Platters recorded the song "Harbor Lights." The Platters also recorded "Love Me Tender" (Mercury 72359).

In August 1956, the Platters' "My Prayer" (Mercury 70893) knocked Elvis's "I Want You, I Need You, I Love You" out of first place on *Billboard*'s Hot 100 chart. Elvis then knocked "My Prayer" out of first place with "Don't Be Cruel"/"Hound Dog." (See *Buck Ram*)

PLAYBOY MAGAZINE HALL OF FAME
Annual feature in *Playboy* magazine in which various musical artists are honored. Elvis was inducted on February 8, 1968. When *Playboy* was first published in 1954, it was to have been known as *Stag Party*.

POEMS THAT TOUCH THE HEART
Book that Elvis read on the troopship USS *General Randall* during his voyage to Bremerhaven, West Germany (September 22–October 1, 1958).

POINDEXTER, DOUG
Country & western singer who headed his own hillbilly band in Memphis in the 1950s called the Starlight Wranglers. Two of the members were Scotty Moore on lead guitar and Bill Black on stand-up bass. According to Colin Escott and Martin Hawkins in their book *Catalyst: The Sun Records Story*, Elvis played with the band for a short time at the Bel Air Club in Memphis in July 1954.

On May 25, 1954, Poindexter recorded his only record for Sun, "Now She Cares No More for Me"/"My Kind of Carryin' On" (Sun 202), with Scotty Moore on guitar, Bill Black on bass, Millard Yeow on steel guitar, Tommy Seals on fiddle, and Clyde Rush on guitar. Scotty Moore composed "My Kind of Carryin' On."

POINTER SISTERS
Popular female vocal group made up of sisters Ruth, Anita, Bonnie, and June, the daughters of preacher parents. In 1979 the Pointer Sisters recorded their biggest hit, "Fire" (Planet 45901), composed by Bruce Springsteen. Bonnie had left the group to go solo in 1978.

Anita and Bonnie were the composers of "Fairytale," which the group recorded (Blue Thumb 254) in 1974, becoming the first song recorded by a black female group to reach the country charts (#37). Elvis recorded "Fairytale" in March 1975.

POMUS, DOC
(1925–   ) Wheelchair-bound songwriter born Jerome Pomus in Brooklyn on June 27, 1925. Pomus, in the early 1950s, recorded "No Home Blues"/"Send for the Doctor" (Chess 1440). Because of Colonel Tom Parker's protective shell around Elvis, Pomus never got the opportunity to meet Elvis.

As a team, Pomus and Mort Shuman composed the following Elvis songs:

"Doin the Best I Can"
"Double Trouble"
"Gonna Get Back Home Somehow"
"His Latest Flame"
"I Need Somebody to Lean On"
"Kiss Me Quick"
"Little Sister"
"Long Lonely Highway"
"A Mess of Blues"
"Never Say Yes"

"Night Rider"
"Surrender"
"Suspicion"
"Viva Las Vegas"
"What Every Woman Lives For"

He also wrote the songs "Girl Happy" (with Norman Meade), "I Feel That I've Know You Forever" (with Alan Jeffries), and "She's Not You" (with Jerry Leiber and Mike Stoller).

In 1985, RCA of France released the album *Elvis Sings Mort Shuman and Doc Pomus*.

PONCIA JR., VINCE
Composer, with Peter Andreoli, of the song "Harem Holiday," which Elvis sang in the 1965 movie *Harum Scarum*.

PONTIAC, MICHIGAN
Site of a December 31, 1975, Elvis concert at which he broke the record for a solo artist when the concert grossed $816,000 for a single performance.

POPLAR TUNES RECORD SHOP
Record store, located at 308 Poplar Avenue, that became a hangout for Elvis when he was in high school. The store was founded by Joe Coughi, who also launched Hi Records.[1]

POPS-RITE POPSTAR AWARD
Award presented to Elvis for helping to sell more popcorn in movie theaters from 1956 to 1957. The award was presented by Judy Powell Spreckels and Jim Blevins, the mayor of Popcorn Village (which is close to Nashville).

PORKCHOPS
Elvis's favorite food, served with brown gravy and apple pie for dessert.

PORTER, COLE
(1892–1964) Composer born in Peru, Indiana, on June 9, 1892. Porter composed such classic tunes as "Night and Day," "Begin the Beguine," and "I Got You Under My Skin." Porter was portrayed by Cary Grant in the 1946 movie *Night and Day*. In 1957 Elvis recorded the Cole Porter song "True Love."

PORTNOY, LILLIAN
Model who gave Elvis a box of cheesecake and kissed him goodbye as he boarded the USS *Randall* on September 22, 1958. Portnoy was the last girl to kiss Elvis goodbye as he sailed for Europe.

POTOMAC
Former presidential yacht (used by President Franklin D. Roosevelt) that Elvis gave to actor Danny Thomas in care of St. Jude's Children Hospital in Memphis, in a presentation at Long Beach, California. Originally

[1]In the late 1940s and early 1950s a number of independent record labels were begun as a sideline by record-store owners, such as Randy Wood's Dot Records in Gallatin, Tennessee, in 1951.

built in 1934 as the Coast Guard cutter *Electra*, the 135-foot yacht was bought by Elvis for $55,000 at an auction on January 30, 1964, from the marketing firm of Hydro-Capital Inc. The March of Dimes and the Coast Guard Auxiliary had previously rejected the vessel as unsafe.

In March 1981 the *Potomac* sprang a leak and sank at Treasure Island in San Francisco Bay, where she had been towed after a raid in 1980 that netted twenty tons of marijuana.

PRECIOUS MEMORIES
Gladys Presley's favorite hymn. It was sung at her funeral by the Blackwood Brothers Quartet. "Precious Memories" was composed in 1925 by J. B. F. Wright of Tennessee.

PRECISION TOOL
Memphis company located at 1132 Kansas that manufactured ordnance shells for the U.S. Army. Elvis had a brief factory job at Precision Tool from June 3, 1951, to July 1, 1951. He earned $30 a week, working from 7:00 A.M. to 3:20 P.M., five days a week. A story has it that Elvis was fired because of a fight with the foreman over the length of his hair, but he was actually fired by management for being underage, a fact that Elvis revealed on his next job application. Brothers Travis and John Smith worked there, and it was through them that both Elvis and his cousin Gene Smith got jobs at Precision Tool.

PRELL, MILTON
Principal owner of the Aladdin Hotel in Las Vegas. It was in Prell's private suite that Elvis and Priscilla were married, on May 1, 1967.

PRESCRIPTION HOUSE
Memphis drugstore, located at 1737 Madison Avenue, where Elvis's prescriptions were filled.

PRESLEY, ANDREW
Immigrant from Scotland to America in 1745. Andrew Presley settled in Anson County, North Carolina. Andrew was the father of Andrew Presley Jr., the grandfather of Dunnan Presley, the great-grandfather of Dunnan Presley Jr., the great-great-grandfather of Rosella Presley, the great-great-great-grandfather of Jessie D. Presley, the great-great-great-great-grandfather of Vernon Presley, and the great-great-great-great-great-grandfather of Elvis Presley.

PRESLEY JR., ANDREW
(1754–1855) Son of Andrew Presley and a soldier in the Continental Army who fought in the American Revolutionary War. Andrew Presley Jr. was the husband of Elizabeth, the father of Dunnan Presley, the grandfather of Dunnan Presley Jr., the great-grandfather of Rosella Presley, the great-great-grandfather of Jessie D. Presley, the great-great-great-grandfather of Vernon Presley and the great-great-great-great-grandfather of Elvis Presley.

PRESLEY, ANNIE
Wife of Sales Presley, the son of Noah Presley (brother of Jessie D. Presley). Annie Presley worked at the Tupelo Garment Factory with her close friend Gladys Presley. Sales had a twin brother named Gordon Presley. Sales and Annie would become the grandparents of twins.

PRESLEY CENTER COURTS, INC.
Corporation headquartered on Poplar Avenue in Memphis that had been founded in 1975 as Racquet Ball of Memphis, Inc., by Dr. George Nichopoulos (as president), Joe Esposito (as vice president) and real-estate developer Michael McMahon, to build and manage ten racquetball-court facilities costing approximately $700,000 each, but which eventually cost $1.3 million. Elvis had to borrow the money from the National Bank of Commerce. Joe Esposito's mother mortgaged her house to raise money for the initial investment. This was the first commercial venture for which Elvis authorized the use of his name. Elvis served as chairman of the board and became liable for 25 percent of the company, which was later renamed Elvis Presley Center Courts, Inc. Elvis left the company before the end of the year in 1976, after the investment turned out to be a financial disaster, and with the company wanting Elvis to invest still more money. Dr. Nichopoulos and Joe Esposito later sued Elvis for $150,000 in damages, claiming that Elvis reneged on his agreement to lend money to the company. Mike McMahon was general manager of the company, which was formed on April 20, 1976.

PRESLEY, DAVADA (DEE)
Second wife of Vernon Presley and Elvis's stepmother. (See *Davada [Dee] Stanley*)

PRESLEY, DELTA MAE
(1919–   ) Daughter of Jessie D. Presley and Minnie Mae Hood Presley. Delta Mae, who called herself "Peggy," was married to Patrick Biggs, who died in 1966. Delta then moved, in 1967, in with her brother Vernon at Graceland, where she worked as a housekeeper. Delta shared a room with her mother, Minnie Mae, who had moved in with the family years before. After the death of Gladys, both women moved into Vernon Presley's old room.

PRESLEY, DUNNAN
(1780–1850) Son of Andrew Presley Jr. and the father of Dunnan Presley Jr., the grandfather of Rosella Presley, the great-grandfather of Jessie D. Presley, the great-great-grandfather of Vernon Presley, and the great-great-great-grandfather of Elvis Presley. Dunnan Presley Sr. was a North Carolina farmer.

PRESLEY JR., DUNNAN
(1827–1900) Son of Dunnan Presley, Sr., and father of Rosella Presley, the grandfather of Jessie D. Presley, the great-grandfather of Vernon Presley, and the great-great-grandfather of Elvis Presley. Born in Madison-

ville, Tennessee, Dunnan was married four times and twice deserted during the Civil War. Dunnan married Elvis's great-great-grandmother Martha Jane Wesson in 1861.

PRESLEY, ELVIS AARON
Vital Statistics
Birthplace: Tupelo, Mississippi
Birthdate: January 8, 1935
Death: August 16, 1977
Height: Six feet tall
Weight: (Adult) 170 to 260 pounds
Eyes: Blue
Hair: Dishwater blond, dyed black
Neck size: 15½"–16"
Chest size: 39"
Scar: Under left eye

PRESLEY, ELVIS AARON
(1935–1977) At 4:35 A.M. on January 8, 1935, in East Tupelo, Mississippi, Elvis Aaron Presley was born. The son of Vernon Elvis and Gladys Love Smith Presley, Elvis was a twin. His twin brother, Jesse Garon, was stillborn and buried in an unmarked grave in the Priceville Cemetery the next day.

In his early childhood, Elvis loved to sing the gospel songs that were sung in the First Assembly of God Church just one block from his family's home. Elvis attended the church with his parents, who also enjoyed joining in on the musical praises.

While in the fifth grade at Lawhon Elementary School, Elvis's teacher, Mrs. J. C. (Oleta) Grimes, discovered that Elvis had an unusual singing talent when he extemporaneously sang "Old Shep" in class one day. Grimes informed the school's principal, J. D. Cole, of Elvis's talent and, on October 3, 1945, he entered Elvis in the annual talent contest at the Mississippi-Alabama Fair and Dairy Show. The talent contest was sponsored and broadcast live by Tupelo radio station WELO. Singing "Old Shep," Elvis garnered second place, winning five dollars and free admission to all of the amusement rides.

On Elvis's next birthday, January 8, 1946, he received his first guitar—a $7.75 model purchased by his mother at the Tupelo Hardware Store. According to the proprietor, Forrest L. Bobo, Elvis wanted a rifle and raised quite a ruckus in the store when it became evident that Gladys was not about to buy him the gun. Gladys finally persuaded Elvis to accept the guitar.

Late in the summer of 1948 the Presleys moved to Memphis. Though the circumstances remain clouded, it appears that Vernon Presley was in trouble with the law. Apparently he had been selling moonshine whiskey. (Earlier, in 1938 and 1939, Vernon Presley served an eight-month sentence in Parchman Penitentiary for forgery.) Reportedly, Tupelo authorities gave Vernon two weeks to leave town. In any case, the Presleys moved from Tupelo to Memphis in September 1948, and Elvis was enrolled at the Christine School. The following year he entered Humes High School.

Elvis's years at Humes High were uneventful, except for his senior year. During that year (1952–1953), Elvis was persuaded by his history and homeroom teacher, Mrs. Mildred Scrivener, to perform in the annual Humes High Minstrel show, which she produced. He got more applause than any of the other contestants and was asked to do an encore.

While attending Humes High School, Elvis went to work for the Precision Tool Company on June 3, 1951. He was employed there only a month. (Reportedly Elvis was fired when the owners discovered he was underage.) After graduating from high school in 1953, Elvis was hired by the Crown Electric Company as a truck driver. His job consisted primarily of delivering supplies to the men on construction sites.

During a lunch break on a Saturday afternoon in the summer of 1953 (the exact date is unknown, but it was probably in August or September), Elvis stopped his Crown Electric pickup in front of the Memphis Recording Service at 706 Union Avenue. The Memphis Recording Service was a lucrative sideline for Sam Phillips, the owner of Sun Records. While there were several similar companies in Memphis, Elvis chose the Memphis Recording Service because it was owned by Phillips. Elvis knew he had a good voice, and his sole purpose for stopping at 706 Union Avenue was to be "discovered" by Phillips. Legend has it that Elvis wanted to make a record for his mother's birthday; however, Gladys Presley's birthday was on April 25, so that story can be discounted.

Marion Keisker, a former "Miss Radio of Memphis" and then Sam Phillips's secretary, was in the studio when Elvis arrived. Phillips was not there. Elvis proceeded to record two songs—"My Happiness," and "That's When Your Heartaches Begin." Midway through "My Happiness," Keisker recognized in Elvis the quality that Phillips was looking for: "A white singer with a Negro voice." She immediately threaded a piece of discarded recording tape onto the Ampex tape recorder used in the studio and succeeded in recording the last third of "My Happiness" and all of "That's When Your Heartaches Begin." Before Elvis left the studio with his record, Keisker asked for his address and telephone number.

When Sam Phillips returned to the studio, Keisker played Elvis's tape for him. He was impressed, but not overly so.

A few months later, on Monday, January 4, 1954, Elvis again returned to the Memphis Recording Service to make another four-dollar record. Since Phillips had not been there the previous time, a Saturday, Elvis figured he had a better chance of meeting Phillips if he stopped by during the week. He was right. Phillips was in and Elvis recorded two songs—"Casual Love Affair" and "I'll Never Stand in Your Way." Though Phillips was impressed with Elvis's talent, he concluded that Elvis needed a lot of work.

In early June of 1954, Phillips couldn't locate the black singer of a demo record of "Without You" that he had brought back from Peer Music in Nashville. He decided to record it with someone else, and Marion Keisker suggested he try Elvis. A recording session was

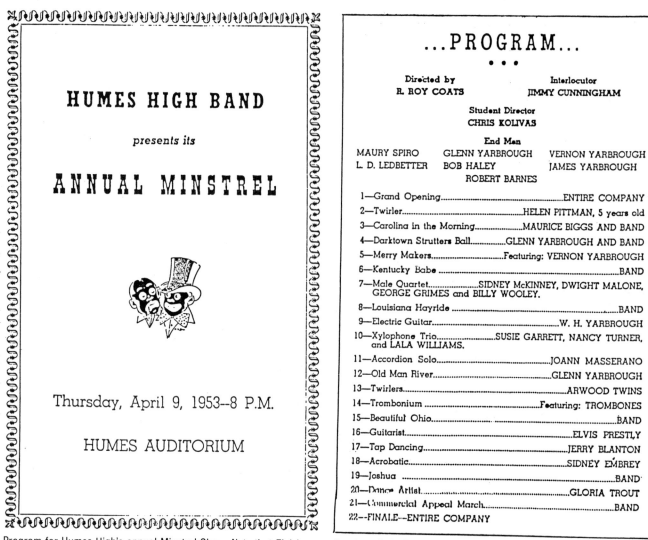

Program for Humes High's annual Minstrel Show. Note that Elvis's name is misspelled. (Photo courtesy Keith Mitchell)

booked, but Elvis didn't project the sound that Phillips was looking for. Elvis was then asked to sing several songs he knew. He sang "Rag Mop" and several Dean Martin hits. None of them was satisfactory to Phillips.

Phillips later asked Scotty Moore to invite Elvis over to his apartment to rehearse some numbers—which he did. On Sunday, June 27, Elvis and Moore got together to rehearse. Later that afternoon Bill Black stopped by. Neither Moore nor Black was greatly impressed with Elvis's talent.

The following week, on Monday, July 5, 1954, Elvis had his first commercial recording session at Sun Records. The first song put on tape was "Harbor Lights." During a refreshment break, Elvis began cutting up and singing an upbeat version of Arthur (Big Boy) Crudup's blues standard "That's All Right (Mama)." Moore and Black joined in. Phillips was so impressed with the sound that he immediately had them put it on tape. The next evening they decided on an up-tempo version of Bill Moore's "Blue Moon of Kentucky" for the flip side of the record.

Phillips took acetates of Elvis's first record to many of the local disc jockeys. On the evening of July 7, on

his WHBQ radio program, "Red Hot and Blue," disc jockey Dewey Phillips (no relation to Sam) played "That's All Right (Mama)." The response was so terrific that Dewey Phillips called Elvis at home to arrange an interview. Elvis wasn't home—he was at the Suzore Theater watching a movie. Vernon Presley went to the theater to tell Elvis about Phillips's call. Later that night, Elvis gave his first media interview. The interview and record made him an overnight celebrity in Memphis.

Elvis signed a managerial contract with Scotty Moore on July 12, and later that week signed a recording contract with Sun Records. The following week, on July 19, "That's All Right (Mama)"/"Blue Moon of Kentucky" (Sun 209) was released. Eventual sales totaled less than twenty thousand, but it was the beginning of a career that would be unmatched by anyone in the history of the entertainment industry.

Elvis's first professional appearance after signing with Sun Records was at the Overton Park Shell on July 30. Slim Whitman was the featured performer that day. Elvis soon began making many professional appearances, among them the grand opening of the

Katz Drug Store in September. On October 2, he made his first and only appearance at the Grand Ole Opry, singing "Blue Moon of Kentucky." The audience response was lukewarm and Jim Denny, the talent coordinator for the Opry, suggested that Elvis go back to truck driving. Two weeks later, however, Elvis performed on the "Louisiana Hayride," and the response was so good that he was asked to become a regular.

On January 1, 1955, Scotty Moore, no longer able to fully devote his time to the management of Elvis's career, relinquished his managerial duties to WMPS disc jockey Bob Neal.

Elvis, Scotty, and Bill auditioned for "Arthur Godfrey's Talent Scouts" in New York City in April 1955, failing to make the show.

In the fall of 1955, Sam Phillips was faced with a problem: should he continue to devote his energies to promoting Elvis, or should he sell Elvis's contract to the highest bidder and use the money to develop several of the potential stars he had at Sun Records? He chose the latter. At the Warwick Hotel in New York City, on November 20, Phillips sold Elvis's Sun contract to RCA Victor for the total sum of $40,000 ($25,000 from RCA and $15,000 from the Hill and Range Music Company), plus a $5,000 bonus to Elvis to cover the amount he would have received in royalties from Sun Records. With part of the $5,000 bonus, Elvis bought his mother a Cadillac.

Though he was with Sun for only sixteen months, Elvis recorded five records: Sun 209 ("That's All Right [Mama]"/"Blue Moon of Kentucky"); Sun 210 ("Good Rockin' Tonight"/"I Don't Care If the Sun Don't Shine"); Sun 215 ("Milkcow Blues Boogie"/"You're a Heartbreaker"); Sun 217 ("Baby, Let's Play House"/"I'm Left, You're Right, She's Gone"); and Sun 223 ("Mystery Train"/"I Forgot to Remember to Forget").

In late 1954, Colonel Thomas Andrew Parker, a former carnival worker, began taking an interest in Elvis's career, and it was he who helped to secure the RCA Victor contract. In 1955, Parker assisted Bob Neal in booking several performances for Elvis. Although Bob Neal was Elvis's legal manager, Parker began to guide his career in mid-1955. On March 15, 1956, Parker officially took over the managerial duties.

After signing with RCA Victor, all of Elvis's Sun singles were re-released on RCA's label, and on January 10, 1956, Elvis had his first recording session for RCA in Nashville. The first song put on tape was "I Got a Woman," but the big hit from the session was "Heartbreak Hotel," a tune written by Tommy Durden and Mae Boren Axton (country singer Hoyt Axton's mother). "Heartbreak Hotel," backed with "I Was the One," was released on January 27, and the following evening, Elvis, Scotty, and Bill made their national television debut on the Dorsey Brothers' "Stage Show." Five more appearances followed. By the time of the last appearance, on March 24, "Heartbreak Hotel" was the number one song on *Billboard* magazine's popularity chart, and Elvis was on his way to becoming a millionaire.

Elvis made a screen test for Hal Wallis of Paramount Studios on April 1. He did a scene from *The Rainmaker* with veteran actor Frank Faylen and sang "Blue Suede Shoes." Two days later, Elvis made the first of two appearances on "The Milton Berle Show." A disastrous two-week stand at the New Frontier Hotel in Las Vegas followed later in April and early May. Originally scheduled for four weeks, Elvis's Las Vegas debut was cut short after the second week because of poor audience response. On June 5, Elvis made his second appearance on "The Milton Berle Show," and "The Steve Allen Show" followed on July 1. Elvis's big break came when he performed on "The Ed Sullivan Show" on September 9. After that he was truly a national phenomenon. His performance was viewed by an estimated 54 million people.

Elvis's first movie, *Love Me Tender*, premiered in November, and he was on his way to becoming a successful movie star. Three other films were made in the 1950s: *Loving You*, *Jailhouse Rock*, and *King Creole*.

Before filming *King Creole*, Elvis received his draft notice. Originally scheduled to report for duty on January 20, 1958, Elvis requested and received a deferment to March 24 so that he could finish filming *King Creole*.

On Monday morning, March 24, Elvis was inducted into the U.S. Army. He received his indoctrination at Fort Chaffee, Arkansas, and was then sent to Fort Hood, Texas, for boot camp. Though Elvis's Army career was primarily uneventful, two events did occur that were to change his life.

While Elvis was stationed at Fort Hood, his mother became ill. She died on August 14, 1958, at the Methodist Hospital in Memphis. Gladys Presley was forty-six, though it was erroneously believed she was forty-two.

In September, Elvis was assigned to the Second Armored Division in West Germany. During his stay in Germany, Airman Currie Grant introduced Elvis to his future wife, Priscilla Beaulieu.

Vernon Presley also met his future wife in West Germany. Davada (Dee) Stanley was in the process of divorcing her husband, an Army sergeant, when Vernon met her. On July 3, 1960, Vernon and Dee Stanley were married in a private ceremony in Huntsville, Alabama. Elvis did not attend.

Soon after Elvis's discharge on March 5, 1960, he traveled to Miami to film the Frank Sinatra–Timex Special "Welcome Home, Elvis" for ABC-TV. Just before Christmas, Elvis placed a call to Col. Joseph Beaulieu (Priscilla's father) to ask for permission for Priscilla to spend the holiday at Graceland. After talking with Vernon Presley, Colonel Beaulieu agreed. More than a year later, Elvis arranged for Priscilla to live at Graceland, enrolling her in Immaculate Conception High School.

Elvis gave a benefit concert for the USS *Arizona* Memorial Fund in Honolulu on March 25, 1961. It was to be his last live performance for eight years. "Good Luck Charm," Elvis's last number one single until 1969, was released the following year.

During the 1960s, Elvis busied himself with making movies, filming twenty-seven of them during the decade. His most successful film was *Blue Hawaii* in

1961. None of the movies received rave reviews from the critics, but Elvis's legion of fans made certain that they all showed a profit at the box office.

Musically, the mid-1960s was a period of decline for Elvis. None of his singles released reached number one and almost all of them were from his movies. His records weren't the giant hits they were in his golden years of the 1950s and early 1960s. Elvis's decline can be attributed to several factors. Foremost among them is the advent of the British invasion and, specifically, the Beatles. The sheer number of instrumental and vocal groups and single performers on the music charts simply diluted the market. There was more competition for the public's record-buying dollar, and it took a much stronger record to reach number one or to become a million-seller.

On May 1, 1967, Elvis and Priscilla were married at the Aladdin Hotel in Las Vegas. Nine months later, on February 1, 1968, their child, Lisa Marie, was born. Elvis's marriage and the birth of Lisa Marie seemed to give him a new drive for success and the urge to perform before a live audience again.

After seven years of concert inactivity, Elvis decided the time was ripe to start performing before the public once again. The first step on his comeback trail was an NBC television special titled "Elvis." He filmed the special in June of 1968 at NBC's Burbank, California, studios. The special, which aired on December 3, received critical acclaim and good ratings. Elvis was truly back.

If there were any doubts as to Elvis's comeback, they were quickly dispelled the next year. In January 1969 Elvis had his first Memphis recording sessions since his days with Sun Records. His recordings at the American Sound Studios were among the most dynamic of his career. On July 31, Elvis began a spectacular one-month engagement at the International Hotel in Las Vegas—his first appearance in Las Vegas since the disastrous booking at the New Frontier Hotel thirteen years earlier. In November 1969 Elvis once again reached the top of the music charts with "Suspicious Minds," his first number one song since 1962. At the same time, *Change of Habit*, his last movie (except for two documentaries), was released.

Elvis was presented an award by the U.S. Jaycees for being one of the "Ten Outstanding Young Men of America" in 1971. Two years later one of the crowning achievements of Elvis's career occurred. On January 14, 1973, he performed before a worldwide television audience in a special called "Elvis: Aloha from Hawaii." A taped and expanded version of the special was televised by NBC-TV in the United States on April 4.

Everything seemed to be coming up roses for Elvis in the early 1970s—at least professionally. But the constant touring, filming, and long periods of separation from Priscilla put a strain on their marriage. In addition, Priscilla had to compete with Elvis's entourage, the Memphis Mafia, for his attention. So, in 1972, Priscilla left Elvis for Mike Stone, her karate instructor. Elvis and Priscilla were divorced in October 1973.

Even before his divorce, and shortly after his separation, Elvis began dating other women. Although he dated Sheila Ryan, Malessa Blackwood, and several others, Linda Thompson was foremost in Elvis's life and was his steady companion from 1972 to 1976. Linda had been a Miss Tennessee.

Toward the end of 1976, Elvis had a new steady girlfriend—Ginger Alden, a first runner-up in the 1976 Miss Tennessee beauty pageant. According to Alden, Elvis proposed to her on January 26, 1977, and they were to be married on Christmas Day of that year. That day never came.

Elvis made several concert appearances in 1977, the last in Indianapolis on June 26. After that tour, Elvis retired to Graceland for rest and recuperation before embarking on his next tour. In August, Lisa Marie came to visit for a few days.

On the night of August 15–16, just one day before leaving on yet another tour, Elvis visited the office of dentist Lester Hoffman to get a cavity filled. A few hours later, he played racquetball with Billy Smith (a cousin) and his wife, Jo. After playing racquetball, Elvis went to bed. He awoke late in the morning to go to the bathroom, taking a book, *The Scientific Search for the Face of Jesus*, with him to read. Ginger said, "Don't fall asleep," and Elvis replied, "OK, I won't." Those were the last words ever spoken by Elvis Presley.

Shortly after 2:00 P.M., Ginger awoke and noticed that Elvis was not in the bedroom. She became worried and entered the bathroom, where she found him slumped on the floor. She called for Joe Esposito, who tried to revive Elvis. At approximately 2:30, paramedics Charlie Crosby and Ulysses S. Jones Jr. arrived at Graceland to render assistance and to take Elvis to Baptist Memorial Hospital. All attempts at resuscitation by the doctors failed, and Elvis Presley was pronounced dead at 3:30.

Throughout the world, Elvis's fans went into mourning, and many booked flights to Memphis. Reverend C. W. Bradley officiated at the private funeral services at Graceland on Thursday, August 18, and Elvis's body was later entombed at Forest Hill Cemetery next to that of his mother. Because of an attempted body snatching on August 29, and the tremendous crowds at Forest Hill Cemetery, the bodies of Elvis and Gladys Presley were moved to the grounds of Graceland on the night of October 2.

Much speculation surrounds the death of Elvis Presley. He did have a history of health problems (some claim that he had had three previous heart attacks), and drugs did contribute to his death (some claim he had been taking prescription drugs because he was slowly dying of bone cancer). No matter what the cause of death, the world lost a great entertainer and the King of Rock & Roll—Elvis Aaron Presley.

PRESLEY, ELVIS, AS COMPOSER, ARRANGER, AND ADAPTER

Elvis has been credited with composing, arranging, or adapting the following songs:

"All Shook Up"—Cowriter with Otis Blackwell
"Aloha Oe"—Adapted and arranged
"Amazing Grace"—Adapted
"America, the Beautiful"—Adapted
"By and By"—Adapted
"Don't Be Cruel"—Cowriter with Otis Blackwell
"Farther Along"—Adapted and arranged
"The First Noel"—Adapted and arranged
"I Was Born About Ten Thousand Years Ago"—Adapted
"I'll Take You Home Again Kathleen"—Adapted
"I'm Gonna Walk Dem Golden Stairs"—Adapted
"Joshua Fit the Battle"—Adapted and arranged
"Let Me"—Cowriter with Vera Matson
"Love Me Tender"—Cowriter with Vera Matson
"Milky White Way"—Adapted and arranged
"O Come All Ye Faithful"—Adapted and arranged
"Oh Little Town of Bethlehem"—Arranged
"Paralyzed"—Cowriter with Otis Blackwell
"Poor Boy"—Cowriter with Vera Matson
"Run On"—Adapted and arranged
"Santa Lucia"—Arranged
"So High"—Arranged
"Stand by Me"—Arranged
"Swing Down, Sweet Chariot"—Arranged
"That's Someone You Never Forget"—Cowriter with Red West
"We're Gonna Move"—Cowriter with Vera Matson
"You'll Be Gone"—Cowriter with Charlie Hodge and Red West

PRESLEY FAMILY COOKBOOK, THE

A book written by Vester Presley and Nancy Rooks, who was the cook at Graceland beginning in 1967. The 192-page book includes recipes for Mashed Sweet Turnips, Fried Squash, and Ham Hocks with Pinto Beans.

PRESLEY, GLADYS EARLINE

Daughter of Jessie D. Presley and Minnie Mae Hood Presley and sister of Vernon Presley, Vester Presley, Delta Mae Presley, Nasval Presley, and Lorene Presley. After Vernon married Gladys Love Smith, Gladys Earline Presley was nicknamed "Little Gladys," so as not to be confused with Vernon's wife. When Gladys married, she became Mrs. Gladys Earline Dowling.

PRESLEY, GLADYS LOVE SMITH

(1912–1958) Daughter of Robert Lee Smith and Doll Mansell Smith, born in Pontotoc County, Mississippi, on April 25, 1912. Gladys Smith was the sister of John Smith, Clettes Smith, Travis Smith, Lillian Smith, Levalle Smith, Rhetha Smith, and Tracy Smith. Twenty-one year-old Gladys Smith married seventeen-year-old Vernon Presley on June 17, 1933, in Pontotoc County, witnessed by Marshall Brown and his wife, Vona Mae Presley Brown. Elvis, born on January 8, 1935, was the couple's only child, as Elvis's twin brother, Jesse Garon, was stillborn. Gladys's last attempt to give Elvis a sibling was in 1942, when she was taken to the hospital where she had a miscarriage.

Gladys worked as a sewing-machine operator in Tupelo, and later in Memphis worked as a nurse's aide at St. Joseph's Hospital and as a seamstress. Mother and son were very close, with Elvis always keeping his mother's needs uppermost in his mind. They called each other affectionate pet names, Elvis calling her "Sattnin." He bought her automobiles and houses and maintained a close relationship with her until her death. Unfortunately, the more popular Elvis became, the more unhappy Gladys became. As Elvis spent more time away from her, Gladys began drinking, usually vodka in her later years. Some sources say that she began taking diet pills to lose weight for her son. Gladys truly missed her son, but felt more and more that she didn't fit into his new world. A country woman, Gladys enjoyed a simple lifestyle, even after her loving son surrounded her with luxury. Gladys enjoyed the basic things that she was used to, such as raising chickens, which she did at Graceland. Few photographs of Gladys before her death show her smiling; most reveal a sad woman. Both Gladys's and Vernon's voice can be heard in an interview at the Mississippi-Alabama Fair and Dairy Show on September 26, 1956. In the interview Gladys mentions "Don't Be Cruel" as one of her favorite songs by her son, while Vernon couldn't seem to remember any of their titles. "He has recorded so many of them," he said.

Gladys Presley died of a heart attack, bought on by acute hepatitis, at the Methodist Hospital in Memphis on August 14, 1958, at 3:00 A.M. She was forty-six years old. (Many books including the 1977 book *Elvis—What Happened?* erroneously stated that she was forty-two, the same age at which Elvis would die.) Her body was buried at Forest Hill Cemetery until after Elvis died, when it was moved next to Elvis in the Meditation Gardens at Graceland. At Gladys's funeral the Blackwood Brothers sang her favorite gospel songs, while such celebrities as Marlon Brando, Dean Martin, Tennessee Ernie Ford, Ricky Nelson, and Sammy Davis Jr. sent remembrances. Although the cause of death was listed as a heart attack, both Elvis and Vernon refused to allow an autopsy to be performed to confirm it. Elvis took Gladys's death hard, and was emotional at her funeral.

Gladys and Vernon Presley were pictured with their son on the cover of the 1971 album *Elvis Country*. Gladys was portrayed by Academy Award–winning actress Shelly Winters in the 1979 TV Movie *Elvis* and by Debbie Edge and Virginia Kiser in the 1981 movie *This Is Elvis*. After Gladys's death, Red River Dave recorded the tribute record "New Angel Tonight (A Tribute to Elvis's Mother)" (Marathon RRD502).

On Gladys's gravestone in Graceland's Meditation Gardens is written:

GLADYS SMITH PRESLEY
APRIL 25, 1912—AUGUST 14, 1958
BELOVED WIFE OF VERNON PRESLEY
AND MOTHER OF ELVIS PRESLEY
SHE WAS THE SUNSHINE OF OUR HOME

PRESLEY, JESSE GARON

(1935) Son of Vernon Presley and Gladys Smith Presley, stillborn on January 8, 1935. Jesse was Elvis's twin brother, delivered dead, thirty-five minutes before Elvis was born. Jesse Garon was laid in a tiny cardboard box in the front room of the Presley home that same day. The next day, Jesse was buried in an unmarked grave,[1] next to a tree in the Priceville Cemetery, northeast of East Tupelo. Jesse Garon was named for his paternal grandfather, Jessie D. McClowell Presley. It has been written often that Jesse was Elvis's identical twin, but there is no medical proof.

In Graceland's Meditation Gardens there is a plaque in the ground to Jesse Garon Presley, but it is spelled *Jessie* Garon Presley.

PRESLEY, JESSIE D. MCCLOWELL

(1896–1973) Illegitimate son of Rosella Presley and the father of Vernon Presley, Gladys Earline Presley, Nasval Presley, Lorene Presley, Delta Mae Presley, and the grandfather of Elvis Presley. Jessie's brothers were Noah Presley, Joseph Presley and Calhoun Presley, among others. J. D. Presley, who was born in Itawamba County, Mississippi, married Elvis's grandmother, Minnie Mae Hood of Fulton, Mississippi, in 1913 (he was seventeen, she was twenty-five), divorcing her thirty-three years later, in 1946. On January 7, 1936, Jessie D. Presley was elected the mayor of East Tupelo. In 1947 he married a schoolteacher named Vera Pruitt, who stayed with him in Tennessee until his death in 1973.

Jessie didn't like his son Vernon. When Vernon was arrested for forgery in 1938, Jessie refused to post his bail, although he bailed out Travis Smith, the brother of his daughter-in-law Gladys. Jessie sold Vernon's house on Old Saltillo Road while Vernon was in prison. Those are probably two good reasons Elvis ignored his grandfather as Elvis grew more popular. Another story has it that it was Jessie who first told Elvis that there was no Santa Claus. After Elvis became a star in 1958, Jessie attempted to cash in by making a record called *The Roots of Elvis*, which included the songs "The Billy Goat Song," "Swinging in the Orchard," and "Who's That Kickin' My Door?" (Legacy Park 2000), billed as Grandpa Jessie Presley. Elvis supposedly spent some time with Jessie in Louisville, Kentucky, on Sunday, November 25, 1956, after which he bought him a new car. Jessie went to see Elvis perform in Louisville on November 7, 1971.

PRESLEY, DR. JOHN

(1932–   ) Physician who, according to an article in the 1981 magazine *Elvis: The Legend Lives On*, claimed to be Elvis's secret brother. Dr. Presley's wife is Mary Beth Presley and his daughter is named Elvia. The article claims that the doctor held a news conference in which he showed a birth certificate indicating that his parents were Gladys and Vernon Presley of Tupelo. He gave his birthdate as January 8, 1932, exactly three years to the day before Elvis's birth. Dr. Presley further claimed that his parents, Vernon and Gladys, had put him in an orphanage.

PRESLEY, JOHN BARON

Name that Elvis and Priscilla would have named their child had it been a boy.

PRESLEY, JOSEPH

Youngest illegitimate son of Rosella Presley and brother of Jessie D. Presley, Calhoun Presley, and Noah Presley, among others. Joseph Presley was one of Elvis's great-uncles.

PRESLEY, LISA MARIE

(1968–   ) Daughter of Elvis and Priscilla Presley, their only child. Lisa Marie was born at 5:01 P.M. on February 1, 1968 (nine months to the day after Elvis and Priscilla were married), on the fifth floor of the east wing of Baptist Memorial Hospital in Memphis, six hours and nineteen minutes after Priscilla entered.

Lisa Marie Presley's first photo—February 5, 1968. (Photo courtesy Wide World Photos)

Lisa Marie, who was delivered by Dr. T. A. Turman, weighed six pounds and fifteen ounces and measured 20 inches long. Her middle name, Marie, was given to her in honor of Colonel Tom Parker's wife, Marie. Lisa had been visiting with her father at Graceland at the time of his death in August 1977. Upon the death of both Vernon Presley and Minnie Mae Presley (Elvis's grandmother), Lisa Marie became the sole heir in Elvis's will and receiver of all assets of the estate, when she reaches the age of twenty-five in 1993. In 1978 it was reported that Priscilla had enrolled ten-year-old Lisa Marie into the Church of Scientology in Los Angeles. Lisa Marie appeared on the front cover of the February 13, 1984, edition of *US* magazine.

PRESLEY, LORENE

Daughter of Jessie D. Presley and Minnie Mae Hood Presley and the sister of Vernon Presley. Lorene Presley was Elvis's aunt.

---

[1]This book's authors have been to the site of Jesse's grave, which was located unmarked under a tree in the Priceville Cemetery. In the 1979 TV movie *Elvis*, Jesse's grave was shown to have a headstone.

Elvis, Grandma Minnie Mae Presley, and Priscilla. (Photo courtesy the *Graceland News*)

PRESLEY, MINNIE MAE HOOD

(1893–1980) Wife of Jessie D. McClowell Presley, born in Fulton, Mississippi, on June 17, 1893 (some members of the family suggest 1888 as her year of birth). Minnie Mae Hood married J. D. Presley in 1913 and divorced him in 1946. She is the mother of Delta Mae Presley Biggs, Nasval Presley Pritchett, Gladys Earline Dowling, and Vernon Presley. Minnie Mae was the paternal grandmother of Elvis Presley. She was nicknamed "Dodger" by Elvis when he was five years old. He had thrown a baseball during a temper tantrum and just missed hitting her head, because she dodged out of the way. Minnie Mae lived with Vernon and Gladys beginning in Tupelo, and lived with them at Graceland, wearing sunglasses both day and night and using snuff, which she kept in a box. On her first airplane flight she traveled to Germany with Vernon to live with Elvis at Goethestrasse 14 in Bad Nauheim, West Germany. She once hit the landlady with a broom. Minnie Mae Presley died on May 8, 1980, at the age of eighty-six, having been bedridden for two months. She was buried in the Meditation Gardens, with Gladys, Vernon, and Elvis. Minnie Mae, Lisa Marie, and Vernon Presley were the only heirs in Elvis's will.

PRESLEY, NASVAL (NASHVILLE)

Daughter of Jessie D. Presley and Minnie Mae Hood, who was nicknamed "Nash" and "Nashville." Nasval was the sister of Vernon Presley, Vester Presley, Delta Mae Presley, Lorene Presley, and Gladys Presley, and wife of minister William Earl Pritchett. Nasval is an ordained minister in the Assembly of God ministry. She served as the pastor of the First Assembly of God

Church in Walls, Mississippi, a church that Elvis help build through his donations. She authored the 1987 book *One Flower While I Live*.

PRESLEY, NOAH

Illegitimate son of Rosella Presley (and an unknown father) and brother of Jessie D. McClowell Presley, Joseph Presley, and Calhoun Presley, among others. Noah Presley was Elvis's great-uncle.

PRESLEY, PATSY

(See *Patsy Gambill*)

PRESLEY, PRISCILLA

(See *Priscilla Beaulieu*)

PRESLEY, RICHARD (DUKE)

An Elvis imitator who claims to be a cousin of Elvis's.

PRESLEY, ROSELLA (ROSIE)

(1862–1924) Daughter of Dunnan Presley Jr. and Martha Jane Wesson Presley. Rosella, who never married, mothered nine or ten illegitimate children, including Jessie D. McClowell Presley, and Joseph Presley, Noah Presley, and Calhoun Presley (their fathers' last names are unknown). Rosella, who was the grandmother of Vernon Presley and the great-grandmother of Elvis, gave her son Jessie the last name of his father, McClowell, as his middle name. Rosella gave all of her children her maiden name as their last name, rather than their fathers' last name. Had she given Jessie the last name McClowell, Vernon and Elvis would have had the last name McClowell, not Presley. Elvis would have been known as Elvis Aron McClowell.

PRESLEY, SALES AND GORDON

Fraternal twin brothers born to the son of Noah Presley, the brother of Jessie D. Presley. There have been several twins born in the Presley family. Sales and his wife, Annie, sometimes sang gospel music with Vernon and Gladys in Tupelo. Sales had worked for the WPA in Pascagoula, Mississippi, along with Vernon. Annie Presley was one of many people interviewed for Elaine Dundy's book *Elvis and Gladys*.

PRESLEY, SAM

First cousin of Vernon Presley. With T. B. Richardson (who with Sammy Lewis would sign Elvis to appear at the New Frontier Hotel in Las Vegas in 1956), Sam Presley ran a gambling club called the Sage Patch on the border between Mississippi and Alabama.

PRESLEY SPEAKS, A

A book by Vester Presley, as told to Deda Bonura, published by Wimmer Brothers Books in 1978.

PRESLEY, VERNON ELVIS

(1916–1979) Six-foot-two-inch tall son of Jessie D. McClowell Presley and the brother of Vester Presley, Delta Mae Presley, Nasval Presley, Lorene Presley, and Gladys Presley, as well as the father of Elvis Presley.

Vernon Presley was born in Fulton, Mississippi, on April 19, 1916, and died in Memphis on June 26, 1979. Vernon married twenty-one-year-old Gladys Love Smith on June 7, 1933, when he was seventeen. He and Gladys worked hard in Tupelo, where they made their home, but money was difficult to come by. Poorly educated (an eighth-grade dropout), Vernon worked at various jobs—farmer, truck driver, and painter. In 1938 and 1939 Vernon spent nine months at the Parchman Penitentiary for forgery. In 1940 he worked for the WPA (Works Progress Administration), a part of FDR's New Deal. He worked in the shipyards at Pascagoula, Mississippi, constructing public outhouses. In 1948 Vernon moved his family from Tupelo to Memphis, as he had obtained a job at the United Paint Company there. His name was misspelled "Preseley" in the Memphis telephone book in the early 1950s.

After the death of his wife, Gladys, in 1958, he devoted himself solely to his successful son's career. On July 3, 1960, Vernon married Davada (Dee) Stanley, becoming the stepfather to her three sons. Elvis did not attend their marriage. Elvis became upset when Dee, who lived in Graceland for a time, began redecorating the house that his mother had decorated. Vernon, Dee, and the boys then moved to a five-bedroom house on Hermitage Street, adjacent to Graceland (their backyard gate opened directly onto the grounds of Graceland). It was in their home that Priscilla lived when she first came to Memphis from Germany. Vernon dressed as Santa Claus for Lisa Marie's first Christmas at Graceland in 1968. Vernon and Dee divorced in November 1977. Vernon's last girlfriend was Sandy Miller (1939–   ), the mother of three children. After Elvis's death, Vernon signed with the William Morris Agency, and for a single interview demanded $25,000. Vernon died of heart failure at 9:20 A.M. on June 26, 1979. He was sixty-three years old. Among those who attended his funeral were: Priscilla, Lisa Marie, Linda Thompson, Joe Esposito, Colonel Tom Parker, Dee Presley, and Sandy Miller.

Elvis always called Vernon "Daddy." At the time of Elvis's death in 1977, he was paying his father a salary of $75,000 a year as his business manager, a job that was over Vernon's head. Elvis should have hired a certified public accountant or a financial adviser instead of putting his financial and tax responsibilities in the hands of a man who had only an eighth-grade education. There is no doubt that Vernon attempted to do a competent job. He often tried to get Elvis to curb his spending. After Elvis's death, Vernon attempted to recover money that Elvis had given or loaned to friends.

A photograph of Vernon Presley and Colonel Tom Parker standing in front of Graceland appeared on the cover of the 1979 Elvis album *Our Memories of Elvis Volume 1.*

Vernon Presley, who had appeared as an extra in two of Elvis's films, *Loving You* (1957) and *Live a Little, Love a Little* (1968), was portrayed by Bing Russell in the 1979 TV movie *Elvis*, by John Crawford in the 1981 TV movie *Elvis and the Beauty Queen*, by Lawrence Koller and Michael Tomack in the 1981 movie *This Is*

Elvis, and by Billy Green Bush in the 1988 TV miniseries "Elvis and Me." (See *Gladys Presley, United Paint Company, Davada [Dee] Stanley, Parchman Penitentiary*)

PRESLEY, VESTER
(1919–   ) Son of Jessie D. McClowell Presley and Minnie Mae Hood and brother of Vernon Presley, Delta Mae Presley, Nasval Presley, Lorene Presley, and Gladys Presley. Vester married Clettes Smith, the younger sister of Gladys Smith, in September 1935, fathering their daughter, Patsy Presley. Vester is Elvis's double uncle. Vester helped Vernon build his house on Old Saltillo Road in East Tupelo, Mississippi. He gave Elvis a few guitar lessons after Elvis received his first guitar on his eleventh birthday. Vester was employed as Elvis's head gate guard at Graceland, usually working from 7:00 A.M. to 6:00 P.M. six days a week, beginning in March 1957. Vester often poses for photographs with Elvis's fans. He even posed with Lucy de Barbin, who included the photograph in her book *Are You Lonesome Tonight?* Vester coauthored, with Deda Bonura, the book *A Presley Speaks.* He also coauthored *The Presley Family Cookbook.* In 1979 Vester recorded the record "A Message to Elvis Fans and Friends" (Ves Pres 1).

Vester Presley is the only surviving member of Elvis's family still working at Graceland. Vester portrayed himself in the 1981 movie *This Is Elvis*.

PRESLEYANA
A price guide compiled by Jerry P. Osborne and Bruce Hamilton, and published in 1980 by O'Sullivan, Woodside & Company.

PRESSLEY
Spelling of Vernon Presley's last name on his Social Security card, in the Memphis telephone directory, and at his trial in Tupelo in 1938. Whether or not this spelling was intentional on Vernon's part, there is no way of knowing.

PRESTON, SANDY
Las Vegas chorus girl whom Elvis dated briefly in 1956.

PRICE IS RIGHT, THE
Long-running CBS-TV daytime game show produced by Mark Goodson Productions that featured an "Elvis Showcase" in September 1974. The showcase consisted of a White Cadillac, a trip to "Blue Hawaii," and a trip to Las Vegas's "Elvis Country."

PRICE, RAY NOBEL
(1926–   ) Popular country singer born in Perryville, Texas, on January 12, 1926, and nicknamed "The Cherokee Cowboy." Price was once a member of Hank Williams's Drifting Cowboys. Years later Willie Nelson, Roger Miller, and Johnny Paycheck would become members of his band, the Cherokee Cowboys. Price's first record label was Bullet Records of Nashville,

founded as the first label in Nashville by Jim Bulleit, who owned an interest in Sun Records from 1952 to 1954. Price recorded versions of "Release Me" (Columbia 21214) in 1954, "For the Good Times" (Columbia 45178) in 1970, "She Wears My Ring" (Columbia 44628), and "Help Me" (Columbia 19503), all of which Elvis recorded. Ray Price appeared on a few bills with Elvis in 1955 and 1956. The Cherokee Cowboys backed Elvis on the "Louisiana Hayride" on April 30, 1955.

PRICEVILLE CEMETERY
Burial spot of Jesse Garon Presley, Elvis's twin brother, who was stillborn on January 8, 1935. He was buried in an unmarked grave the next day. Priceville Cemetry is located three miles northeast of Tupelo on Feemster Lake Road. The exact location of Jesse's grave is known to only a few people. (See *Jesse Garon Presley*)

Priceville Cemetery. (Photo courtesy Don Fink)

PRIDDY, AL
(1911–   ) Disc jockey at KEX radio in Portland, Oregon, who was fired in December 1957 because he played several cuts from *Elvis' Christmas Album*. The station manager, Mel Bailey, thought the album was in "extremely bad taste." The cuts thought most objectionable were: "Oh Little Town of Bethlehem," "White Christmas," and "Silent Night."

PRISCILLA AND ELVIS
An unauthorized biography written by Caroline Latham and published in 1985 by Signet Books.

PRISONAIRES
Early 1950s black vocal group who recorded for Sun Records. The Prisonaires were inmates at the Tennessee State Prison. The Sun label read: "Prisonaires Confined to the Tennessee State Prison, Nashville." The group consisted of Johnny Bragg (lead tenor, who sang with the Marigolds after getting out of prison), John E. Drue (tenor), William Stewart (baritone), Marcell Sanders (bass), and Edward L. Thurman (tenor). The Prisonaires' biggest Sun release came in April 1953 with "Just Walking in the Rain" (Sun 186).[1] Lead singer Johnny Bragg once claimed that Elvis helped him with pronouncing the lyrics of the song (Elvis had been hanging around the Sun studios at about the time he and Scotty Moore were practicing at Scotty's apartment). Other sources claim that the Prisonaires once sang behind Elvis at a charity marathon in Nashville, and that Elvis visited Johnny Bragg in prison.

PRITCHETT, WILLIAM EARL
Husband of Nasval Presley Pritchett and uncle of Elvis. Pritchett was employed at Graceland as the head groundskeeper. (See *Nasval Presley*)

PRIVATE ELVIS, THE
The 1977 book written by columnist May Mann and published by Pocket Books. The book, which was rushed to publication after Elvis's death, with a few additions, was actually a new edition of her 1975 book *Elvis and the Colonel.*

PROBY, P. J.
(1938–   ) Stage name of singer James Marcus Smith, born in Houston on November 6, 1938. Proby was one of several singers who used to cut Elvis sound-alike demo records of material that Elvis would select from to record. Proby wrote the 1961 Johnny Burnette song "Clown Shoes."

Proby, after making several records under the pseudonym Jet Powers and not finding success in the United States, went to England before the Beatles' success. There he became a pop star but also controversial, especially after his pants ripped at a number of live concerts. Because of this, he was eventually forbidden to perform live concerts in Great Britain. Proby charted a number of hit records on the British charts, but could never become the star in America that he was in Europe.

Proby portrayed Elvis in London's West End musical *Elvis*. Throughout his career Proby claimed that Elvis was his close friend.

PROPHET, THE
Religious philosophy book written by Khalil Gibran, which Elvis enjoyed reading after columnist May Mann gave him a copy. In the 1979 TV movie *Elvis*, Elvis (Kurt Russell) read to Priscilla from the book. *The Prophet* was one of actress Carole Lombard's favorite books, as well as one of actress Joan Crawford's.[2]

PUFF
Lisa Marie Presley's pet white cat at Graceland.

PURSUIT OF HAPPINESS, THE
A 1934 movie starring Francis Lederer and Joan Ben-

---

[1]Johnnie Ray had a number two hit and a million-seller in 1956 with his version of "Just Walking in the Rain" (Columbia 40729).
[2]Excerpts from *The Prophet* were read by Robert Limm at the 1978 funeral of Terry Kath, the lead singer of Chicago, who accidentally shot himself while playing Russian Roulette. *The Prophet* had been Kath's favorite book.

nett, which was playing at the Strand Theater in Tupelo, Mississippi, on January 8, 1935, the day Elvis was born.

PUSSER, BUFORD
(1937–1974) Sheriff of McNairy County, Tennessee, who came to national prominence fighting organized crime. Like Elvis, the six-foot-six-inch, 250-pound Pusser, was chosen by the Jaycees as one of the "Ten Outstanding Young Men of America" (1969). Pusser was the subject of three theatrical movies and one made-for-TV movie,[1] as well as the subject of a TV series, "Walking Tall," starring Bo Svenson. Elvis, who greatly admired Pusser, anonymously sent him a check for a substantial amount of money after his house was burned down while he was fighting organized crime. Pusser died in a mysterious car accident on August 24, 1974. His death car is on display at the Police Museum in Pigeon Forge, Tennessee.

PUTNAM JR., CLAUDE (CURLY)
Composer of the song "Green Green Grass of Home," which Elvis recorded in 1975.

[1]The movies were: *Walking Tall* (1973), with Joe Don Baker; *Walking Tall Part II* (1975), with Bo Svenson; *Final Chapter—Walking Tall* (1977), with Bo Svenson; *A Real American Hero* (1978 TV), with Brian Dennehy.

Q

QUATRO, SUSI
(1950–   ) Rocker born in Detroit on June 3, 1950. In 1974 Quatro and her band recorded their version of "All Shook Up" (Bell 45,477). Elvis was so impressed that he telephoned Quatro to praise it, telling her that it was the best version since he recorded it. He even invited her to his house, but her schedule didn't allow her the visiting time. Quatro also recorded a version of "Heartbreak Hotel."

RABBITT, EDDIE

(1944–   ) Country singer and composer, born Edward Thomas Rabbitt in New York City on November 27, 1944. Rabbitt composed the songs "Inherit the Wind," "Patch It Up" (with Rory Bourke), and "Kentucky Rain" (with Dick Heard), all of which Elvis recorded. In 1979 Rabbitt had a hit with the title song of the Clint Eastwood movie *Every Which Way but Loose*, beginning a chain of hit songs for him.

RADER, PAUL

Composer of the song "Only Believe," which Elvis recorded in 1970.

RADIO RECORDERS

Hollywood recording studio where Elvis had his first Hollywood recording session (Studio B), September 1–3, 1956, and numerous other sessions. Elvis recorded the majority of his sessions at Radio Recorders, which was owned by Thorne Nogar. (See *Studio Recording Sessions* in Part II)

RAINBOW ROLLERDOME

Memphis roller-skating rink, located at 2881 Lamar Avenue, which Elvis enjoyed frequenting in the 1950s. The manager was Joe Pieraccini. Elvis sometimes took Dixie Locke there on Friday nights in 1953. It was there in 1958 that Red West first introduced Elvis to his cousin Sonny West. The Rainbow Rollerdome was situated next to the Rainbow Lake swimming pool. In the 1950s it cost fifty cents to get in and twenty-five cents to rent skates. As a celebrity, Elvis rented the rink for the entertainment of him and his friends at about $70 a night. Some of the games they played were "War" and "Crack the Whip," which at times got pretty physical. After a while they began to wear knee and elbow pads. Elvis rented the Rainbow Rollerdome the night before he was inducted into the Army, March 23, 1958.

RAINEY, MA

(1886–1939) Blues singer who first recorded "See See Rider Blues" (Paramount 12252) in 1925, with Fletcher Henderson on piano and Louis Armstrong on cornet. Rainey (real name: Gertrude Pridgett Rainey)[1] was called the "Mother of the Blues." Her trademark, until it was stolen, was a necklace of gold coins. It was Ma Rainey who discovered blues singer Bessie Smith.

On some British releases of "See See Rider," Ma Rainey is listed as the song's composer. (See *See See Rider* in Part II)

RAINGER, RALPH

(1901–1942) Composer born in New York City on October 7, 1901, who, with Leo Robin, wrote the song "Blue Hawaii," which Elvis recorded in 1961.

RALEIGH, BEN

Composer, with Mark Barkan, of the song "How Would You Like to Be," which Elvis sang in the 1963 movie *It Happened at the World's Fair*.

RAM, BUCK

(1908–   ) Manager and songwriter, originally for the Ink Spots then for two 1950s rhythm & blues groups: the Penguins and the Platters. In 1956 Mercury Records of Chicago wanted to sign the Penguins, but Ram insisted they sign both of his groups. Mercury signed the Platters just to get the Penguins. The Penguins rerecorded their classic "Earth Angel" for Mercury (Mercury 70943), but never had another hit, while the Platters had a string of successes, including their 1960 hit "Harbor Lights" (Mercury 71563), a song that Elvis recorded in 1954. Ram was a cowriter, with Walter Kent and Kim Gannon, of "I'll Be Home for Christmas," which Elvis recorded in September 1957. (See *The Platters*)

RAMBO, DOTTIE

(1934–   ) Composer born Joyce Reba Rambo in Madisonville, Kentucky, on March 2, 1934. Dottie Rambo was once a member of the Singing Rambos. She is the composer of the song "If That Isn't Love," which Elvis recorded in 1973.

RAMSEY, JAY

Composer of the song "We Can Make the Morning," which Elvis recorded in 1971.

RANDALL, USS GENERAL

Troopship on which Elvis traveled (with 1,400 other soldiers) to Bremerhaven, West Germany. He left the Military Ocean Terminal in Brooklyn on September 22, 1958, and arrived in West Germany on October 1. Charlie Hodge also sailed on the USS *General Randall*, sharing the same room with Elvis at Elvis's request.

During World War II, comedian Soupy Sales (born Milton Hines, Soupy Sales is now his legal name) served aboard the USS *General Randall*. The ship appeared in the 1956 movie *Away All Boats*.

RANDI, DON

Session keyboard player who played piano and organ on Elvis's 1968 NBC-TV special "Elvis." Randi also played piano on Elvis's *Speedway* soundtrack recording session in June 1967. Randi was previously a session musician for Phil Spector and was a member of his Wrecking Crew band, which created the "Wall of Sound." Other members of the Wrecking Crew who have played for Elvis are: Carole Kaye (guitar), Hal Blaine (drums), Glen Campbell (guitar), Barney Kessel (guitar), and Leon Russell (keyboard).

---

[1]Another Ma Rainey (real name: Lilian Glover) was popular in Memphis in the 1950s–1970s. Also known as Big Memphis Ma Rainey, she had one release on the Sun label in 1953, "Call Me Anything"/"Baby No No" (Sun 184).

RANDLE, BILL

Cleveland disc jockey, on radio station WERE, who was the first disc jockey outside the South to play Elvis records on a regular basis, beginning in late 1954. Randle had a Saturday morning show on CBS in New York City and commuted from Cleveland once a week. In the fall of 1954, Randle was approached by Arnold Shaw, general professional manager of the Edward B. Marks Music Corp., who asked Randle to play some Elvis records on his CBS radio program. Randle thought that Elvis was a bit too much for the New York audience, but he did start playing the records on WERE. The audience response was phenomenal. This was one of the major factors in getting national exposure for Elvis.

Randle introduced Elvis on Elvis's first appearance on TV's "Stage Show," on January 28, 1956.

The Diamonds signed a recording contract with Mercury Records through Randle's influence. He convinced Coral Records (subsidiary label of Decca Records) to sign the Johnny Burnette Trio and told Don George that his adaptation of "The Yellow Rose of Texas" had pop potential.

In 1956 Randle cut the record "Disc Jockey's Love Song" (Coral 61544). (See *The Pied Piper of Cleveland* in Part II)

RANDOLPH, BOOTS

(1927–   ) Popular saxophone player and Nashville session musician born Homer Louis Randolph in Paducah, Kentucky, on June 3, 1927. Randolph played saxophone and vibes on many of Elvis's recordings, beginning on April 3, 1960, for twenty-one sessions through January 15–17, 1968. In 1963 Randolph had a big hit of his own with "Yakety Sax" (Monument 804), a tune that comedian Benny Hill adopted as his theme song.

Randolph is the only musician to have played on record for both Elvis and Buddy Holly.

RASHKOW, MICHAEL

Composer, with Johnny Cymbal, of the song "Mary in the Morning," which Elvis recorded in 1970.

RASKIN, WILLIAM J.

(1896–1942) Composer born in New York City on November 3, 1896. Raskin composed, with Bill Hill and Fred Fisher, the song "That's When Your Heartaches Begin," which Elvis recorded in 1957.

RAY, JOHNNIE

(1927–   ) Ballad singer of the 1950s born John Alvin Ray in Dallas, Oregon, on January 10, 1927. Ray, whom Elvis said he liked, was known as the "Prince of Wails" and the "Nabob of Sob" because of his wailing singing style. (Ray learned his style from rhythm & blues artist Ruth Brown.) Before Elvis, Ray was probably the most popular white artist singing versions of rhythm & blues songs. Ray's biggest hits were "Cry" (Okeh 6840)[1]

(number one for eleven weeks) and the flip side, "Little White Cloud That Cried" (number two), and a cover of the Prisonaires' "Just Walking in the Rain" (Columbia 40729) (number two)—all million-sellers. In 1953 Ray recorded "Satisfied" (Columbia 40006), and in 1954 a cover version of the Drifters' "Such a Night" (Columbia 40200), a version of "Flip, Flop and Fly" (Columbia 40471), and in 1959, "I'll Never Fall in Love Again" (Columbia 41438), all of which Elvis recorded.

Elvis met Ray backstage at the Desert Inn in Las Vegas in 1956. Disc jockey Bill Randle mentioned Johnnie Ray when he introduced Elvis on TV's "Stage Show" on January 28, 1956.

RCA

Radio Corporation of America. Manufacturer of record players, television sets, radios, and records (RCA Victor, X, Groove, and Vik Records), which was one of the sponsors of "The Milton Berle Show" on which Elvis appeared on April 3, 1956.

RCA was the brand of the two color TV sets that Elvis had mounted in the ceiling of his bedroom at Graceland. They were installed by Charles R. Church. (See *Charles R. Church*)

RCA CONSOLETTE

Monaural mixing console, type 76-D, that was used by the Memphis Recording Service and Sun Records in producing Elvis's first recordings ("My Happiness"/ "That's When Your Heartaches Begin"; "Casual Love Affair"/"I'll Never Stand in Your Way"; "That's All Right [Mama]"/"Blue Moon of Kentucky," etc.) The console (serial #1011) was previously used in a Florida radio station. Sam Phillips used the monaural console for several years at Sun Records.

Control console used to record Elvis's first songs at Sun Records. (Photo courtesy Don Fink)

RCA VICTOR

Highly successful record company founded in 1901 as Victor Records. The label then became RCA Victor, and in the 1970s was called simply RCA. In 1948 the company introduced the 45 RPM record to compete with the larger, more breakable, 78 RPM disc. RCA Victor's first rock & roll record was a watered-down version of Gene and Eunice's 1955 rhythm & blues hit "Ko Ko Mo

---

[1]The Four Lads sang backup on "Cry" and "Little White Cloud That Cried."

(I Love You So)" (Combo 64) by crooner Perry Como (RCA Victor 5994), which charted in February 1955.

On November 20, 1955, RCA Victor A&R man Steve Sholes purchased Elvis's contract from Sam Phillips. Sholes offered $25,000 from RCA, while Hill and Range Music offered an additional $15,000 to purchase Hi-Lo Music. Several other record labels were also making bids at the time: Columbia Records dropped out at $15,000 and Atlantic Records at $25,000. Elvis was given a $5,000 advance against his royalties, which he used to buy a new Cadillac for his mother. The purchase of Elvis's contract was a daring feat by Sholes at the time; in 1955, $40,000 was a large sum of money. Steve Sholes's boldness paid off, for Elvis went on to become RCA Victor's greatest asset, with worldwide record sales by 1978 in excess of 500 million units. The signing of Elvis to the RCA Victor label took place at the Warwick Hotel in New York City. Colonel Tom Parker occupied, at no charge, a suite of offices in the RCA Building at 6363 Sunset Boulevard in Hollywood until shortly after Elvis's death in 1977.

When RCA began releasing Elvis's singles, for the most part they assigned an even number to each one, i.e., 6540, 6640, 6800, 7000, 7150, 7240, 7280, etc. They did save the luckiest release number 7777 for one of Elvis's most popular songs, "It's Now or Never." In addition to Elvis's releases, RCA capitalized on his success by releasing several Elvis-related records, including Toni Arden's "I Forgot to Remember to Forget" (RCA 6346), Janis Martin's "My Boy Elvis" (RCA 6652), Lou Monte's "Elvis Presley for President" (RCA 6704), Homer and Jethro's "Houn' Dog" (RCA 6706), and Henri Rene's version of "Love Me Tender" (RCA 6728). (See *Hi-Lo, X Records, Steve Sholes*)

REAL ELVIS: GOOD OLD BOY, THE
Book written by television critic Vince Staten and published in 1978 by Media Ventures, Inc. The book revealed some little-known facts about Elvis in his early years in the 1950s.

REBEL WITHOUT A CAUSE
A 1955 movie starring James Dean, Natalie Wood, Sal Mineo, and Nick Adams. *Rebel Without a Cause* was one of Elvis's favorite films. It was produced by David Weisbart, who the next year would produce Elvis's debut film, *Love Me Tender*. Elvis watched the movie so often that he could recite Jim Stark's (James Dean) dialogue from memory. In the 1979 TV movie *Elvis*, Kurt Russell (as Elvis) watched *Rebel Without a Cause* at Graceland. (See *James Dean*)

RED COACH CLUB
Nightclub in Monroe, Louisiana, 300 miles south of Memphis, where Elvis is said to have performed on a number of occasions in either 1952 or 1953, according to Richard Wilcox in Lucy de Barbin's book *Are You Lonesome Tonight?* Questions such as why Elvis per-

formed there, how he got there, how much he got paid, and how it came about were not addressed.

RED HOT AND BLUE
Radio program on Memphis station WHBQ in the 1950s, hosted by Dewey Phillips. "Red Hot and Blue,"[1] which was on from nine to midnight, aired mostly rhythm & blues and rockabilly music (the same music that Sam Phillips was recording at Sun Records). It was on this program, on July 7, 1954, that an Elvis record was first played by Phillips, who helped introduce many rhythm & blues and rockabilly artists. (See *Dewey Phillips*)

RED SEAL
RCA label used only once on an Elvis record, the 1958 album *Elvis' Golden Records* (RCA RB-16069), released in Great Britain.

RED'S PLACE
Frayser, Tennessee, club where, it has been said by one source, Elvis performed on Friday nights as a solo act during the summer of 1953.

REDELL, TEDDY
Composer and original artist of the song "Judy," which Elvis recorded in 1967.

REED, JERRY
(1937–) Guitarist, singer, composer, session musician, and actor, born in Atlanta on March 20, 1937, whose real name is Jerry Reed Hubbard. Reed wrote two Elvis hit records, "Guitar Man" (1967) and "U.S. Male" (1968), on which he played lead guitar. Elvis invited him to Graceland after hearing his song "Guitar Man" over the car radio. Reed also composed "A Thing Called Love," which Elvis recorded in 1971, and "Talk About the Good Times," which he recorded in 1970 (RCA 9804), and which Elvis recorded in 1973.

In 1967 Reed recorded "Tupelo Mississippi Flash," an Elvis novelty record. He has appeared in four movies with Burt Reynolds: *W. W. and the Dixie Dancekings* (1975), *Gator* (1976), *Smokey and the Bandit* (1977), and *Smokey and the Bandit II* (1980).

Reed's wife, Priscilla, once sang with the Jordanaires. Reed said in a *People* magazine article that when he first went to Graceland to meet Elvis, "I walked in and looked at the dude, and I'm telling you, that was the prettiest man I'd ever seen." In an article in *US* magazine, Reed said, "The day Elvis walked through the studio door, I was so excited that the first thing I blurted out was 'God Almighty, you're the best-looking thing I've ever seen!' "

REED, JIMMY
(1926–1976) Blues singer, born in Leland, Mississippi, who began recording for Chicago's Vee-Jay Records in December 1953. Reed's first major hit was "You Don't

---

[1]*Red Hot and Blue* was also the title of a 1936 musical in which Bob Hope and Ethel Merman introduced the Cole Porter song "It's De-Lovely."

Have to Go" (Vee-Jay 119) in 1955. Elvis recorded "Baby What You Want Me to Do" (Vee-Jay 333), which Reed cowrote.

REED, LES
Composer, with Barry Mason, of the song "Girl of Mine," and, with Geoff Stephens, of the songs "Sylvia" and "This Is Our Dance," all of which Elvis recorded.

REED'S GARMENT COMPANY
Tupelo firm where Gladys Presley worked as a seamstress while Vernon was serving time in Parchman Penitentiary in 1938–39.

REEVES, GLEN
Singer and disc jockey who in 1955 recorded the demo record of "Heartbreak Hotel" for Elvis. Elvis recorded his version almost exactly as Reeves had recorded it, including voice inflections and soul. Reeves recorded several records himself, including a 1957 version of "Drinking Wine Spo-Dee O'Dee" (Atco 6080).

REEVES, JIM
(1924–1964) Country music singer of the 1950s and 1960s, born in Panola County, Texas, on August 20, 1924, who had a velvet voice. Tex Ritter[1] also hailed from Panola County, Texas. "Gentleman" Jim Reeves played minor-league baseball for the St. Louis Cardinals' farm team in Lynchburg, Virginia, until a leg injury ended his career.[2] In the early 1950s he was a staff announcer for radio station KWKH in Shreveport, Louisiana. Reeves and Elvis appeared together on the "Louisiana Hayride" on several occasions.

Reeves had many top ten country hits, ranking number three behind Eddy Arnold and Webb Pierce for the most top ten records. Even after his death in a plane crash on July 31, 1964, Mary Roberts Reeves, Jim's widow, continued to release his recordings.

RCA Victor artists Elvis and Jim Reeves both recorded several of the same songs.

REFLECTIONS
An Elvis newsletter that was begun in April 1979 by Charlie Hodge and Dick Grob.

REICHNER, BIX
(1905–   ) Composer born S. Bickley Reichner in Philadelphia on April 6, 1905. Reichner composed, with Sid Wayne, the song "I Need Your Love Tonight," which Elvis recorded in 1958.

REID, DON S.
(1945–   ) Member of the famed country vocal group the Statler Brothers,[3] who was born in Staunton, Virginia, on June 5, 1945. Though primarily a country

group, the Statler Brothers reached number four on the pop charts in early 1966 with "Flowers on the Wall" (Columbia 43315). In 1973 Reid composed "Susan When She Tried" for the Statler Brothers (Mercury 73625). Elvis recorded the song in 1975.

REVAUX, JACQUES
Composer, with Gilles Thibault and J. Claude Francois, of the song "My Way," which Elvis sang in concert in the 1970s on many occasions.

REYNOLDS, BURT
(1936–   ) Hollywood actor who erroneously was reported to have attended Elvis's private wedding in 1967, and again erroneously reported to have attended Elvis's private funeral in 1977. Reynolds's father was once the chief of police in Riviera Beach, Florida. Reynolds played football at Florida State and was drafted by the Baltimore Colts, but turned down the offer after he was injured in a car accident. Reynolds was the first man to pose nude for the centerfold of *Cosmopolitan* magazine (April 1972). Actress Mamie Van Doren dated both Reynolds and Elvis, and rated them in her 1987 autobiography.

After Elvis's death, Reynolds said of Elvis, "We were both from the South, and one of the things I most respect in Elvis was the fact that he never forgot that he was a man who cared for good and humble people."

Elvis with his karate instructor, Kang Rhee. (Photo courtesy Kang Rhee)

---

[1]Tex Ritter is the father of actor John Ritter and is the only person elected to both the Cowboy Hall of Fame and the Country Music Hall of Fame.

[2]Roy Acuff and Charley Pride also played minor-league baseball. Pride was the first player cut by the California Angels in their first season.

[3]The Statler Brothers were discovered by Johnny Cash. Group members include: Don Reid, Harold Reid (Don's older brother), Lew De Witt, and Phil Balsley.

RHEE, KANG

Korean-born owner of the Kang Rhee Institute of Self Defense, Inc., located at 1911 Poplar Avenue in Memphis. Kang Rhee was a good friend of Elvis's and one of his martial-arts instructors beginning in 1970. Rhee, whom Elvis always addressed as "Master Rhee," specialized in tae kwon do karate, which emphasizes the feet. Elvis gave Kang Rhee a reported $50,000 to build a new karate school, as well as a new 1973 Cadillac Eldorado.

RHOADES, CALVIN

U.S. Army master sergeant who gave Private Elvis his Asiatic flu shot on March 26, 1958.

RIAA

Recording Industry Association of America. The RIAA audits record companies and certifies record sales, presenting a Gold Disc Award for million-sellers. Perry Como[1] received the first RIAA Gold Disc Award for "Catch a Falling Star" (RCA Victor 47-7128) on March 14, 1958. Elvis's first Gold Disc Award was for "Hard Headed Woman" on August 11, 1958.

RICE, BILL

Composer, with Thomas Wayne, of the song "Girl Next Door," which Elvis recorded in 1960 as "The Girl Next Door Went A'Walking."

RICE, DENNY

Composer, with Troy Seals, of the song "There's a Honky Tonk Angel (Who Will Take Me Back In)," which Elvis recorded in 1973.

RICE, TIM

Composer, with Andrew Lloyd Webber, of the song "It's Easy for You," which Elvis recorded in 1976. Tim Rice is coauthor of several books on the British charts, including *The Guinness Book of 500 Number One Hits.*

RICH, CHARLIE

(1932–   ) Country singer born in Colt, Arkansas, on December 14, 1932. Rich, who is nicknamed the "Silver Fox," recorded from the mid-1950s until the early 1970s before he achieved national popularity. While in the U.S. Air Force he formed a group called the Velvetones, with his wife, Margaret, singing lead. Rich recorded for Sam Phillips's Phillips International record label. Phillips thought that Rich came closer to copying Elvis than any of the other Sun artists. In March 1959, Rich and Bill Justis were fired by Phillips for insubordination. Rich composed songs for Johnny Cash, Jerry Lee Lewis, and Elvis. It is Rich's voice that can be heard on Jerry Lee Lewis's "Am I to Be the One" release. Rich last saw Elvis alive in the elevator of the Liberty Bowl Memorial Stadium before a football game in 1976. Rich composed "I'm Comin' Home," which Elvis recorded in 1961.

RICHARD, CLIFF

(1940–   ) British pop-rock singer born Harry Rodger Webb in Lucknow, India, on October 14, 1940. Richard's first demo recording was "Breathless"/ "Lawdy Miss Clawdy" and his first recording was "Move It" (Columbia DB 4178), backed with "School Boy Crush," a remake of the 1958 Bobby Helms release. Richard traveled to Bad Nauheim, West Germany, in 1960 to meet Elvis, only to be turned away at his door. When Elvis learned about this, he sent Richard a telegram of apology. There are also photographs showing Richard standing outside the gates of Graceland. He is second only to Elvis in the number of number one singles by a solo artist in Great Britain with ten.

RICHARDSON, JANE

Home-service adviser for the Memphis Housing Authority of the 1940s and 1950s. Richardson visited the Presleys in early 1949 to determine whether they qualified for financial assistance. The Presleys did qualify and, on September 20, moved into an apartment at the Lauderdale Courts, at 185 Winchester Street. (See *Houses*)

RICKLES, DON

(1926–   ) Comedian born in Queens, New York, on May 8, 1926. Elvis once interrupted Rickles in his act at the Riviera Hotel in Las Vegas. Rickles introduced Elvis to the audience, and Elvis convinced Rickles to read excerpts from the occult book *Voices* to the audience.

RIJFF, GER

(1951–   ) Foremost Elvis fan who lives and writes in Amsterdam, Holland. Rijff has written such Elvis-related books as *Long Lonely Highway* and, with Jan Van Gestel, *Florida Close Up* (published by his own Tutti Frutti Productions).

RILEY, BILLY LEE

(1933–   ) Singer and session musician born in Pocahontas, Arkansas, on October 5, 1933. Riley played guitar on Jerry Lee Lewis's hits "Whole Lotta Shakin' Goin' On" (Sun 267) and "Great Balls of Fire" (Sun 281). In 1972 Riley barely charted (number ninety-three) song "I've Got a Thing About You Baby" (Entrance 7508), which Elvis would record in 1973. Riley played at Elvis's New Year's Eve parties in 1968 and 1969. Riley founded Rita Records, in which Harold Dorman recorded the hit song "Mountain of Love" (Rita 1003) in 1960.

RIPLEY COTTON CHOPPERS

Hillbilly band comprising the following members: Ernest Underwood (vocal and fiddle), Jettie Cox (vocals), Raymond Kerby (guitar), James Kerby (vocals), Jessie Frost (lead vocals), Bill Webb (guitar), James Wiseman

---

[1]Perry Como, like Elvis, had a street named after him—Perry Como Avenue (formerly Third Avenue) in his hometown of Canonsburg, Pennsylvania, which is also the hometown of singer Bobby Vinton. Como was the first vocalist to have two releases each reaching two million in sales at the same time, "Till the End of Time," and "If I Loved You," both in 1945.

(bass), Pete Wiseman (bass), and James Haggard (mandolin). The band recorded one song for Sun Records on July 11, 1953, "Silver Bell" (Sun 190), which Bob Neal adopted as his radio theme song at WMPS Radio.

Guitarist Raymond Kerby was asked by Sam Phillips at a recording session of the Ripley Cotton Choppers if they would be interested in backing a new singer he was considering recording. After a short discussion with the band members, Kerby told Phillips they weren't interested, as they preferred to back their lead singer, Jessie Frost, Kerby's nephew. Phillips never asked the band, who had turned down Elvis, to record for him again.

RISING SUN
Palomino horse born in 1956 and bought by Elvis for $3,500; it was one of his favorites. Rising Sun's stable was called "The House of Rising Sun"—a play on the title of the 1964 hit song by the Animals (which was taken from a version by Bob Dylan based on a traditional black folk song often sung by Josh White).

RITCHIE, MARTIN
Fourteen-year-old Chicago youth who died of electrocution in an attempt to hang an effigy of Elvis in 1956.

RITTENBAND, LAURENCE J.
Santa Monica, California, Superior Court judge who granted Elvis and Priscilla their divorce on October 9, 1973.

RITTER'S PARK HOTEL
Plush hotel in Bad Homberg, West Germany, where Elvis, his father, and his grandmother stayed while looking for a house to rent in October 1958.

RIVERA, GERALDO
(1943–   ) Investigative reporter and attorney born July 4, 1943, in New York City. Rivera was a reporter on the ABC-TV series "20/20," hosted by Hugh Downs. On the September 13, 1979, edition, titled "The Elvis Cover-Up," Rivera made a convincing case for a cover-up of Elvis's death. The report revealed Elvis's drug use before his death, and the number of prescriptions authorized by Dr. George Nichopoulos. Rivera mistakenly credited Elvis with filming twenty-eight movies, instead of thirty-three. Rivera, who emphasized Elvis's drug use on the program, had just two years earlier on "Good Morning America," told Steve Dunleavy that he didn't believe a word Dunleavy was saying about Elvis's drug addiction.

On June 9, 1971, Rivera emceed Elvis's press conference at the Las Vegas Hilton Hotel. Rivera, the former son-in-law of author Kurt Vonnegut Jr. (in December 1971 Rivera had married Edith Vonnegut), quit "20/20" in 1985, when the show's producers suppressed a story on the death of Marilyn Monroe because it implicated President John F. Kennedy. In 1987 Rivera appeared on "Entertainment Tonight" to discuss the authenticity of Lucy de Barbin's book *Are You Lonesome Tonight?*

ROAD-E-O
Memphis automotive contest sponsored by the Jaycees in which Elvis was named "Mr. Safety" in the fall of 1952. Elvis also got his picture in the local newspaper.

ROBBINS, MARTY
(1925–1982) Country music singer and songwriter born Martin Robinson in Glendale, Arizona, on September 26, 1925. Robbins made his Grand Ole Opry debut on January 7, 1953.

Robbins toured with Elvis in June 1955: June 26, in Biloxi, Mississippi; June 27–28, at Keesler AFB, Mississippi; and June 29–30, at the Curtis Gordon Club in Mobile, Alabama. Robbins recorded "That's All Right (Mama)" (Columbia 21351) on December 7, 1954, adding a fiddle on his version. He was one of first to "cover" an Elvis recording. The first person to cover an Elvis recording appears to have been country singer Smiley Maxedon, who recorded a version of "That's All Right (Mama)" (Columbia 21301), exactly fifty Columbia releases before Marty Robbins. Robbins, who was always open to many types of music, was also the first to cover Chuck Berry, when he recorded a version of "Maybellene." And he also was one of the first to cover a Little Richard record, when he recorded "Long Tall Sally" (Columbia 40679) in 1956. Robbins' 1959 hit and million-seller "El Paso" (Columbia 41511), was the first record more than four minutes long to reach number one. Robbins died in 1982; his last movie appearance was in *Honky Tonk Man* (1982), in which he sang for a dying singer, played by Clint Eastwood.

It has been said that while in the Army, Elvis didn't like to sing his own songs but enjoyed singing songs from Marty Robbins's 1959 album *Gunfighter Ballads and Trail Songs* (Columbia 1349), which featured a song that Elvis would sing in concert, "El Paso."

In 1957 Robbins recorded "Aloha Oe" (Columbia 21213), which Elvis recorded in 1961. In 1973 Elvis recorded a Robbins composition, "You Gave Me a Mountain," which was a tremendous hit for Frankie Laine in 1969. (See *Grady Martin*)

ROBERTS, BOB
Composer, with Paddy McMains, of the song "Echoes of Love," and, with Ruth Batchelor, of the following movie songs: "Because of Love," "Cotton Candy Land," "King of the Whole Wide World," "Thanks to the Rolling Sea," and "Where Do You Come From," all of which Elvis recorded.

ROBERTS, DENNIS
Las Vegas optician who created more than 400 pairs of sunglasses for Elvis.

ROBERTS, ORAL
(1918–   ) Evangelist born in Ada, Oklahoma, on January 24, 1918. Roberts once asked Colonel Tom Parker if Elvis would appear on his religious TV program at Oral Roberts University in Tulsa, Oklahoma, but the Colonel turned him down.

ROBERTSON, DON

(1922–) Singer, musician, and composer who was born in Peking, China, on December 5, 1922. Robertson's father was the head of the Department of Medicine at Peking's Union Medical College.

In 1956 Robertson had a number six hit and million-seller with his own composition, "The Happy Whistler" (Capitol 3391). On the recording, he also did the whistling. Robertson once told singer Sheb Wooley a joke that his son had told him. That joke became the inspiration for Wooley's 1958 number one hit song, "The Purple People Eater"(MGM 12651).

Floyd Cramer learned his slip-note style of piano playing from Robertson. Robertson is a prolific songwriter. He composed Lorne Greene's 1960 hit "Ringo" (number one and a million-seller). Other songs include: "I Really Don't Want to Know" (with Howard Barnes), "Please Help Me, I'm Falling," and "I Love You More and More Every Day." Robertson composed nine songs for Elvis on his own:

"Anything That's Part of You"
"I Really Don't Want to Know"
"I'm Counting on You"
"I'm Falling in Love Tonight"
"Love Me Tonight"
"Marguerita"
"Starting Today"
"There's Always Me"
"They Remind Me Too Much of You"

And five more, with Hal Blair:

"I Met Her Today"
"I Think I'm Gonna Like It Here"
"I'm Yours"
"No More"
"What Now, What Next, Where To"

ROBERTSON, JANE

Assumed name of a young woman who in 1971 was taken to the hospital, where her stomach was pumped after she overdosed on prescription Hycadon, which both she and Elvis had been taking, according to the book *Elvis—What Happened?* The incident was kept out of the press. However, in the May 1980 issue of the fan magazine *Teddy Bear*, an article contradicted the report in the book. The article stated that at the time of the incident, neither Red West nor Sonny West were present.

ROBERTSON JR., MARVIN

(1951–) Eighteen-year-old black man, a member of the singing group the Young Americans, who was traveling on the same United Airlines DC-8 as Elvis, from Honolulu to Los Angeles in 1969. Robertson got into a conversation with Elvis and mentioned how much he admired Elvis's $2,500 ring, at which point Elvis removed the ring from his finger and gave it to him.

ROBEY, DON R.

(1904–1975) Founder of Peacock Records of Houston in 1949, and discoverer of Johnny Ace. In July 1952, Peacock bought the Duke label. Robey, with Ferdinand Washington, composed "Pledging My Love," which both Johnny Ace (1954) and Elvis (1976) recorded.

ROBIN, LEO

(1900–) Composer, born in Pittsburgh on April 6, 1900, who, with Ralph Rainger, composed the song "Blue Hawaii," which Elvis recorded in 1961.

ROBIN, SYDNEY (SID)

(1912–) Composer born in New York City on July 12, 1912. Robin composed in 1937, with brothers Bob and Joe Shelton, the song "Just Because," which Elvis recorded in 1954.

ROBINSON, MRS. EDNA

Tupelo woman who served as a midwife to Gladys Presley on January 8, 1935, during the birth of Elvis, until Dr. William R. Hunt could arrive.

ROBINSON, JESSE MAE

Composer of "Party," which Elvis recorded in 1957.

ROBINSON, RED

Canadian disc jockey who interviewed Elvis in Vancouver, British Columbia, on August 31, 1957, at the Empire Stadium. Robinson claims to have been the first Canadian disc jockey to play Elvis records on the air.

Robinson is the narrator of the LP *Elvis—a Canadian Tribute*, for which Robinson received a double Platinum Award (over 100,000 units sold in Canada). In 1977 he released the album *The Elvis Tapes*. (See *Elvis—a Canadian Tribute*, *The Elvis Tapes*, in Part III)

ROCK AND ROLL

Song sung by the Boswell Sisters in the 1934 movie *Transatlantic Merry-Go-Round*. "Rock and Roll" (Brunswick 7302) was the first song to be given that title. The year of the song's debut, 1934, was the same year in which Gladys Presley was pregnant with Elvis.

ROCK AND ROLL HALL OF FAME

Hall of Fame dedicated to the history of rock & roll music in America. In February 1986, the first ten inductees were: Elvis Presley, Chuck Berry, Little Richard, the Everly Brothers, James Brown, Sam Cooke, Buddy Holly, Ray Charles, Fats Domino, and Jerry Lee Lewis.

ROCK 'N' ROLL 'N' DRAG

Short article that Elvis wrote for *Rod Building and Customizer* magazine, which appeared in the September 1956 issue (cost twenty-five cents).

ROCKEFELLER, WINTHROP

(1912–) Politician born on May 1, 1912. Rockefeller is a former Arkansas governor and the brother of onetime U.S. vice president Nelson A. Rockefeller. Winthrop bought Elvis's prize cattle when Elvis sold the Circle G Ranch in 1969.

RODGERS, JIMMIE

(1897–1933) Country singer born James Charles Rodgers in Meridian, Mississippi, on September 8, 1897. Rodgers was called "The Father of Country Music," and "The Singing Brakeman," getting the latter nickname because he once worked for the Mobile and Ohio Railroad. Rodgers's first recording was "The Soldier's Sweetheart," on August 4, 1927.[1] Rodgers, who died of tuberculosis on May 26, 1933, at the age of thirty-six, was one of three persons (with Fred Rose and Hank Williams) to be elected to the Country Music Hall of Fame (November 3, 1961) in its first year of existence.

On May 25, 1955, Elvis performed in a concert at the two-day Jimmie Rodgers Memorial Day Celebration in Meridian, Mississippi.

RODGERS, JIMMIE

(1933–   ) Folk-rock singer born in Camas, Washington, on September 18, 1933. In the 1950s Rodgers charted a number of hits on Hugo Peretti and Luigi Creatore's Roulette label, songs such as "Honeycomb" (Roulette 4015), "Kisses Sweeter Than Wine" (Roulette 4031), and "Oh-Oh I'm Falling in Love Again" (Roulette 4045). In 1966 Rodgers composed and recorded "It's Over" (Dot 16861), which Elvis sang in concert in the 1970s.

RODGERS, RICHARD

(1902–   ) Composer born in New York City on June 28, 1902. Rodgers, with Lorenz Hart, composed the song "Blue Moon," which Elvis recorded in 1954. With Oscar Hammerstein II, in 1945, Rodgers composed "You'll Never Walk Alone," which Elvis recorded in 1968.

ROI-TAN

Brand of blunt-tip cigars smoked by Elvis.

ROLLING STONE

Rock magazine founded by Jann Wenner in 1967, with John Lennon featured on the cover of the first issue. On September 22, 1977, the magazine (issue No. 248) dedicated half of its issue to Elvis, with Elvis's photo featured on the cover. That particular issue was the magazine's first to be produced entirely in New York City, after the magazine moved there from San Francisco. In the issue was an article titled "Graceland: A Family Mourns," written by Caroline Kennedy.

ROLLS-ROYCE PHANTOM V

Prestige British-made automobile (California license plate ULL 501) that Elvis bought on March 18, 1961, from Coventry Motors in Beverly Hills. At times, Sonny West served as his chauffeur. In 1964 the Rolls was auctioned off and the proceeds donated to a Memphis charity.

ROMANELLI, CARL

Sculptor of the six-foot-tall bronze statue of Elvis commissioned by Colonel Tom Parker for $150,000 and placed in the lobby of the Las Vegas Hilton Hotel. The statue was dedicated by Priscilla Presley on September 8, 1978.

ROMANS, ALAIN

Composer, with Jacques Larue, of the song "Padre," which Elvis recorded in 1971.

ROOKS, NANCY W.

(1938–   ) Black cook and maid born in Fayette County, Tennessee, on August 8, 1938. Rooks, who was hired by Dee Stanley Presley, worked at Graceland for eleven years. Elvis once gave her a yellow 1974 Pontiac Ventura—the first new car she had ever owned. Rooks cowrote, with Vester Presley, the 1980 book *The Presley Family Cookbook*. Rooks and Mae Gutter authored the book *The Maid, the Man and the Fans: Elvis Is the Man*. She portrayed herself in the 1981 movie *This Is Elvis*.

ROOSTER

Symbol of Sun Records. The rooster appeared on the labels of the 78 RPM records—but not on the 45 RPM records. Sun discontinued 78s in 1958, as did most other companies. When Elvis switched to RCA Victor, their symbol was a dog—Nipper.

ROSE, FRED

(1897–1954) Songwriter born in Evansville, Indiana, on August 24, 1897. Rose, who founded the Acuff-Rose Music Publishing Company in 1942, played piano on Hank Williams's early recordings. In 1945 Rose was made an honorary colonel of the state of Louisiana by governor Jimmie Davis (composer of "You Are My Sunshine"). Rose died in Nashville on December 1, 1954. In 1961 Rose was elected to the Country Music Hall of Fame. His son, Wesley Rose, is a music publisher today.

Rose composed, with Zeb Turner, "It's a Sin," which Elvis recorded in 1961. He also composed "I'll Never Stand In Your Way" with Walter Heath, which Elvis recorded on a demo in 1954. Rose was portrayed by Henry Arnold in the 1980 TV special "Hank Williams—The Man and His Music."

ROSE, LEON

Composer of "Blue Eyes Crying," which Elvis recorded in 1976.

ROSE, VINCENT

(1880–1944) Bandleader and composer born in Palermo, Italy, on June 13, 1880. Rose composed, with Al Lewis and Larry Stock, the song "Blueberry Hill" in 1940, which Elvis recorded in 1956.

ROSENBERG, LEE

Composer, with Bernard Weinman, of the song "Too Much," which Elvis recorded in 1957.

---

[1]On the same day that Rodgers auditioned for Ralph Peer of Victor Records in Bristol, Virginia, on August 1, 1927, A. P. Carter and Maybelle Carter were also present to audition, an incredible coincidence.

ROSENBLATT, LENORE
Composer, with Victor Millrose, of the song "Smokey Mountain Boy," which Elvis sang in the 1964 movie *Kissin' Cousins*, and the song "Startin' Tonight," which Elvis sang in the 1965 movie *Girl Happy*.

ROSS, BEVERLY
Composer, with Sam Bobrick, of the song "The Girl of My Best Friend," which Elvis recorded in 1960.

ROSS, JERRY
(1926–1955) Child actor and composer born in New York City on March 9, 1926. Ross composed, with Richard Adler, the song "Rags to Riches," which Elvis recorded in 1970.

ROSTILL, JOHN
(1942–1973) Guitarist and composer born in England on June 16, 1942. Rostill played with the instrumental group the Shadows,[1] who backed singer Cliff Richard. Rostill became Olivia Newton-John's record producer, writing two of her hit songs, which Elvis would also record, "If You Love Me (Let Me Know)" (MCA 40209) and "Let Me Be There" (MCA 40101). Rostill died on November 26, 1973.

ROTC
Reserve Officers Training Corps, formed on October 21, 1916. Elvis was a member of ROTC (two-year course) while a sophomore at Humes High School. In later years Elvis bought new uniforms for the school's ROTC drill team.

ROWAN, ELWYN (RIP)
U.S Army captain and Memphis recruiter in the late 1950s. Captain Rowan recruited Elvis in 1958.

ROWLAND, DAVE
A member of the Stamps Quartet in 1973 who sang backup for Elvis. Rowland left to form the successful country-music trio, Dave and Sugar.[2]

ROYAL COMMAND VARIETY PERFORMANCE
Annual presentation for British royalty of some of the world's most talented entertainers. In 1961 Elvis was invited to perform before Queen Elizabeth II in London. For an unstated reason, Elvis refused to be presented to Her Majesty the Queen. One reason Elvis may not have agreed to perform was that Colonel Tom Parker, an illegal alien, never wanted to leave the United States. This was another historic opportunity missed by Elvis.

RUSSELL, BOBBY
Composer husband of actress Vicki Lawrence, who recorded her husband's number one hit song, "The Night the Lights Went Out in Georgia" (Bell 45303).[3] Russell composed the song "Do You Know Who I Am," which Elvis recorded in 1969.

RUSSELL, KURT VOGEL
(1951–   ) Actor born in Springfield, Massachusetts, on March 17, 1951. Russell made his film debut in the 1963 movie *It Happened at the World's Fair* (he played a small boy who kicked Elvis in the leg).

Russell has appeared in three TV series: "The Travels of Jaimie McPheeters," "The New Land," and "The Quest."

In 1978 Russell, who had been known previously for his work in Walt Disney films, was chosen from more than 700 actors to portray Elvis in the TV movie *Elvis* (Colonel Tom Parker had wanted Sylvester Stallone). On March 17, 1979, at a Unitarian church in New York City, Russell married his costar in *Elvis*, Season Hubley, only to divorce her in just a few years. In 1988 Russell married his costar in a number of other films, actress Goldie Hawn.[4]

RUSSELL, LEON
(1942–   ) Multitalented musician born in Lawton, Oklahoma, on April 2, 1942. Russell played piano for the soundtrack recordings of many Elvis movies. Russell was previously a member of the rock group the Hawks (as was Levon Helm [See *Levon Helm*]), who evolved into the Band. He has backed Jerry Lee Lewis, been a studio musician for Phil Spector, played with the Rolling Stones, and produced recordings by Bob Dylan. Russell played piano for both George Harrison and Bob Dylan at the famed "Concert for Bangladesh," on August 1, 1971. David Gates and Russell both attended the same high school in Tulsa, Oklahoma, and played in the same school band.

RUSSELL, NIPSEY
(1920–   ) Black comedian born in Atlanta on October 13, 1920. Russell opened Elvis's concerts in Lake Tahoe, Nevada, from July 20 to August 2, 1971, until replaced by comedian Bob Melvin.

RUSSWOOD PARK
Memphis park where Elvis performed a benefit concert on July 4, 1956. Elvis and his band were backed by the Bobby Morris Orchestra.

RYAN, SHEILA
(1953–   ) *Playboy* playmate whom Elvis dated in 1975. Elvis had been introduced to Ryan by Joe Esposito. They went together after Elvis broke up with Linda Thompson and before he met Ginger Alden. Twenty-three-year-old Ryan married thirty-seven-year-old actor James Caan in January 1976. She graced the cover of the October 1973 issue of *Playboy* magazine.

---

[1] The group originally called themselves the Drifters, until they discovered that the name was already being used by an American group.
[2] Sugar is made up of Vicki Hackeman Baker and Sue Powell. Dave and Sugar's first record, "Queen of the Silver Dollar," became a huge hit. Their second record, "The Door Is Always Open," went to number one.
[3] Years later, Cher found out that her husband Sonny Bono had turned down the song for her to record.
[4] Hawn was previously married to Bill Hudson of the Hudson Brothers. Hudson later married actress Cindy Williams.

RYMAN AUDITORIUM

Nashville building from which WSM radio broadcast the Grand Ole Opry from 1942 until 1974. Ryman Auditorium, which originally served as a tabernacle, was named for riverboat captain Thomas Ryman. During the late 1940s and early 1950s, the Ryman had free telephones in the lobby, which Colonel Tom Parker used to book his next acts. The TV series "The Johnny Cash Show" was telecast from the auditorium from 1969 to 1971.

Elvis performed at the Grand Ole Opry in the Ryman Auditorium on October 2, 1954. (See *Grand Ole Opry*)

Publicity photo, 1956. (Photo courtesy Eddie Brandt's Saturday Matinee)

S

6
Number of tiers on Elvis and Priscilla's five-foot-high wedding cake.

16
Number of coaches in Elvis's 1955 song "Mystery Train." Ironically, there were sixteen limousines in Elvis's funeral procession.

17
Number of portraits of Elvis hanging throughout Graceland at the time of his death.

ST. JOSEPH'S HOSPITAL
Memphis medical facility where Gladys Presley worked as a nurse's aide, making beds, scrubbing floors, and bathing patients, from 1949 to 1952, after Vernon had injured his back.

ST. JUDE'S HOSPITAL
Memphis children's hospital, located at 264 Jackson Avenue, founded by comedian and actor Danny Thomas. It was at the hospital's grand opening that Elvis first met country singer Patsy Cline. In 1964 Elvis gave his yacht, the *Potomac*, to the hospital so that they could raise funds for needy children.

SAINT-MARIE, BUFFY
(1941–) Singer and composer born in San Antonio, Texas, on November 6, 1941. Saint-Marie composed the song "Until It's Time for You to Go," which Elvis recorded in 1971.

SALEM, MARC
Philadelphia man who, on August 12, 1977, predicted Elvis's death. Salem placed his written prediction inside an aspirin box that was baked into a pretzel. This was done under the guidance of Arlen Spector, former Philadelphia district attorney. Salem not only predicted Elvis's death, but also the headlines: *Philadelphia Daily News*—"The King Is Dead"; *Philadelphia Inquirer*—"The King Dies at 42"; *Philadelphia Bulletin*—"Elvis Dies."

SALK VACCINE
Vaccine against polio, developed by Jonas Salk in 1954. In 1968 Elvis posed for photographers as he was being given a Salk vaccine shot in front of his daughter, Lisa Marie.

SALLEE, CHARLES ALVIN (JACK)
Composer of the song "You're a Heartbreaker," which Elvis recorded in 1954.

SANDS, TOMMY
(1937–) Singer, actor, and onetime husband of Nancy Sinatra and son-in-law of Frank Sinatra, born on August 27, 1937, in Chicago. Actress Paula Prentiss and Sands were classmates at Lamar High School in Houston. Sands was discovered by Colonel Tom Parker, who was his manager from the time Sands was twelve years old until he was sixteen. Parker discovered him singing in a tavern in Houston. Sands is one of several people who have claimed to have told the Colonel about Elvis, after he toured with Elvis in Texas and appeared with him on the "Louisiana Hayride." Sands and Elvis first performed together on the same bill on New Year's Day in 1955 in Houston.

Sands played an Elvis-like character in the TV play *The Singing Idol* and in the 1958 movie *Sing, Boy, Sing*.

Elvis once said that Tommy Sands was one of his favorite singers.

SAPERSTEIN, HANK
Associate of Colonel Tom Parker's in 1956 who was the merchandising and exploitation manager for Elvis-related products, establishing Factors Etc., Inc. Saperstein previously merchandised Wyatt Earp, Lone Ranger, and Lassie products.

SCATTER
Elvis's pet forty-pound chimpanzee, which had originally appeared on a local Memphis TV show. Elvis and the boys would often dress Scatter in human clothes. Scatter, who stood three feet tall, developed a taste for straight scotch and bourbon, and eventually died of cirrhosis of the liver. He was caged behind Graceland after he started to become violent, and that's where he died one day. Scatter was with Elvis both at Graceland and in Bel Air.

SCHEFF, JERRY
Session musician who played bass on Elvis's *Easy Come, Easy Go* soundtrack recording session in Hollywood on September 28–29, 1966, as well as on a number of other sessions. Scheff was also a member of Elvis's TCB Band in the years from 1969 to 1976. Scheff was previously a member of the rock group the Doors, headed by the late Jim Morrison. He composed the song "There's a Fire Down Below," which Elvis was to record but never added the vocal track.

SCHILLING, JERRY
(1943–) Elvis's bodyguard and member of the Memphis Mafia from 1964 to 1976. He first met Elvis when Elvis was nineteen years old. The two men became good friends after they played together in a touch football game in Memphis in 1964. Schilling had played football for Arkansas State University and was probably the best educated member of the Memphis Mafia. Elvis gave Schilling the martial-arts nickname "The Cougar." He bought him several automobiles over the years, and paid for his wedding to his first wife,

Sandy. Schilling had met Sandy in 1965 while Elvis was filming *Paradise, Hawaiian Style.* After he and Sandy split, Schilling dated singer Kathy Westmoreland. He eventually quit the Memphis Mafia to try his hand at film editing for Paramount Pictures. Schilling was also the manager of the Sweet Inspirations and later of the Beach Boys. He later formed an entertainment management firm. Schilling married Myrna Smith, a member of the Sweet Inspirations.

SCHLAKS, STEPHEN
(1940–   ) Composer born Stephen David Schlaks in New York City on May 13, 1940. Schlaks composed, with Mel Glazer, the movie title song "Speedway," which Elvis recorded in 1968.

SCHROEDER, AARON
(1926–   ) Composer born Aaron Harold Schroeder in Brooklyn on September 7, 1926. Schroeder was once the manager of singer Gene Pitney and the founder, with Art Talmadge, of Musicor Records in 1961. He co-composed a number of Elvis songs:

"Any Way You Want Me" (with Cliff Owens)
"A Big Hunk o' Love" (with Sid Wyche)
"Dixieland Rock" (with R. Frank)
"Don't Leave Me Now" (with Ben Weisman)
"First in Line" (with Ben Weisman)
"Good Luck Charm" (with Wally Gold)
"Got a Lot o' Livin' to Do" (with Ben Weisman)
"I Got Stung" (with David Hill)
"I Was the One" (with Claude DeMetrius, Hal Blair, Bill Pepper)
"In Your Arms" (with Wally Gold)
"It's Now or Never" (with Wally Gold)
"Santa Bring My Baby Back (to Me)" (with Claude DeMetrius)
"Shoppin' Around" (with Sid Tepper and Roy C. Bennett)
"Stuck on You" (with J. Leslie McFarland)
"Young and Beautiful" (with Abner Silver)
"Young Dreams" (with Martin Kalmanoff)

After Jerry Leiber, Mike Stoller, Doc Pomus, Mort Shuman, Aaron Schroeder, Claude DeMetrius, Abner Silver, Otis Blackwell, and a few others stopped writing songs for Elvis, the quality of his material deteriorated rapidly until about 1969, when Elvis finally learned that these composers had stopped composing for him because they refused to relinquish part of their royalties, an arrangement instituted by Colonel Tom Parker.

SCHWARTZ AND ABLESER
Beverly Hills jeweler from which Elvis purchased many rings that he then gave to his friends.

SCOTCH
Brand of magnetic recording tape used by Sam Phillips to record the Elvis sessions at Sun Records.

SCOTT, WINFIELD
Composer of the song "Stranger in the Crowd." Scott composed, with J. Leslie McFarland, the song "Long Legged Girl (with the Short Dress On)"; and co-composed five songs with Otis Blackwell: "(Such an) Easy Question," "One Broken Heart for Sale," "Return to

Sender," "Please Don't Drag That String Around," and "We're Coming in Loaded," all of which Elvis recorded. Scott also wrote "Jim Dandy" for LaVern Baker.

SCOTTY AND BILL
Billing of guitarist Scotty Moore and bass player Bill Black under Elvis's name on the original Sun records of 1954 and 1955.

SCOUT JEEP DRIVER
Duty that Elvis was assigned to while stationed in Freidburg, West Germany. He had to know everything possible about the condition of the roads. He also chauffeured his platoon sergeant, M. Sgt. Ira Jones.

SCRIVENER, MILDRED
History teacher at L. C. Humes High School and Elvis's homeroom teacher during his senior year. Scrivener took a liking to Elvis and later said that "Elvis always acted like a gentleman." She put Elvis in the annual Minstrel Show on April 9, 1953, which she also produced. After Elvis sang his version of "Keep Them Cold Icy Fingers Off of Me," he received more applause than anyone else and was asked to do an encore. Scrivener told him, "It's you, Elvis, go on out there and sing another song." Elvis went out and sang his version of Teresa Brewer's new hit "Till I Waltz Again with You" (some sources indicate that the encore was "Old Shep"). After he was finished he ran off the stage and said to Scrivener, "They really liked me, Miss Scrivener, they really liked me!"

SEALS, TROY
(1938–   ) Singer and composer born in Big Hill, Kentucky, on November 16, 1938. Seals was married to singer Jo Ann Campbell. He composed the song "Pieces of My Life," which Elvis recorded in 1975 as one of a number of songs that reflected his state of mind at the time. Seals composed, with Denny Rice, "There's a Honky Tonk Angel," which Elvis recorded in 1973. In the 1970s Seals recorded several songs for Columbia.

SEAMON, KATHY
Private nurse who worked at Graceland in September and October 1975. (See *Marion Cocke*)

SEARS, DAN
Newscaster at Memphis radio station WMPS who first announced that Elvis had died. Sears read the news at 2:58 P.M. on August 16, 1977, although Elvis was not officially pronounced dead until 3:30 P.M.

SEDAKA, NEIL
(1939–   ) Singer and composer born in New York City on March 13, 1939. Sedaka charted hit songs spanning the mid-1950s through the 1970s. He and Howard Greenfield scored Connie Francis's debut movie *Where the Boys Are* (1960). He composed the hit "Oh! Carol" (RCA 7595) and dedicated it to composer Carole King. Pianist Arthur Rubenstein selected Sedaka as the best young pianist in New York City in

1956. Sedaka composed, with Phil Cody, "Solitaire," which Sedaka recorded and which Elvis recorded in 1976. It is believed that Elvis also recorded Sedaka's "Love Will Keep Us Together."

SEELIG, JACK
One of Elvis's high school friends at L. C. Humes High.

SELLERS, PETER
(1925–1980) Elvis's favorite comedy actor. Sellers[1] was born on September 8, 1925, the same day as actor Cliff Robertson. In 1963 John Lennon named his favorite actors as Robert Mitchum and Peter Sellers. Sellers was mentioned by name in the 1986 Elvis-related movie *Touched by Love*.

SEYDEL, JURGEN
German black belt martial-arts instructor from Usingen who taught Elvis karate while Elvis was stationed in West Germany.

SHAFER, PAUL
Executive for Malco Theaters, Inc., in Memphis. Shafer and Elvis became good friends after Shafer quit as a disc jockey at Memphis radio station WHHM. Anita Wood, Elvis's girlfriend, went to work as Shafer's secretary. Shafer obtained the feature films for Elvis's private showings. Shafer's daughter, Paulette Shafer Lewis, worked at Graceland as a secretary.

SHAFT
A 1971 movie directed by Gordon Parks that starred Richard Roundtree as private eye John Shaft. The film's theme song became a hit song for Isaac Hayes, who recorded it on Memphis's Enterprise Records label, a subsidiary of Stax. After seeing the film, Elvis went out and paid $55,000 for a stretch Lincoln limo like the one in the film. Elvis was also impressed by the way Shaft dressed.

SHALSKI, LEE MATTHEW McCLOWELL
(1957–) Youth who claimed that he was Elvis's son and that Elvis told him so at a Little Rock, Arkansas, concert in 1972. However, in 1980 *The Globe* revealed that Lee Shalski was actually a she, and that she was born on December 8, 1957, as Lisa Marie Shalski in Fort Smith, Arkansas. Lee's mother denied Lee's assertions that he/she is Elvis's child. Being named Lisa Marie was a coincidence.

SHANE, BOB
(1934–) Folksinger born in Hawaii on February 1, 1934, and onetime member of the Kingston Trio, who, before he became a singer, performed in Hawaii as an Elvis impersonator. (See *John Stewart*)

SHANNON, DEL
(1939–) Rock & roll singer born Charles Westover

on December 30, 1939. He composed (with Max Crook) and recorded "Runaway" (Big Top 3067)[2] in 1961, and it went to number one in both the United States and United Kingdom. Elvis recorded "Runaway" in 1969. Shannon composed Peter and Gordon's 1965 hit "I Go to Pieces" (Capitol 5335). In 1963 he was the first American artist to record a John Lennon–Paul McCartney composition, "From Me to You" (Big Top 3112).

SHAPER, HAL
Composer, with G. Calabrese and A. DeVita, of the song "Softly, as I Leave You," which Elvis recorded in concert December 13, 1975, at the Las Vegas Hilton. It was released in 1978.

SHAPIRO, DR. MAX
Beverly Hills dentist who makes house calls. Dr. Shapiro supplied Elvis with "medication" when Elvis resided in southern California. After Elvis's death in 1977, Dr. Shapiro filed suit to recover $14,000 in dental fees for several of Elvis's friends, Elvis having authorized their treatment by Shapiro. In the book *Elvis: Portrait of a Friend*, it is stated that Dr. Shapiro claimed to have invented an artificial heart.

SHARE
Hollywood women's charity for mentally retarded children, to which Elvis donated the proceeds after auctioning off his $35,000 1964 Rolls-Royce on July 4, 1968.

SHARP, NANCY
College-educated, blond wardrobe assistant whom Elvis dated. Elvis met Sharp in 1960 while filming *Flaming Star*. She was once engaged to singer Tommy Sands.

SHAVER, BILLY JOE
(1941–) Musician and composer born in Corsicana, Texas, who, with Waylon Jennings, composed the song "You Asked Me To," which Elvis recorded.

SHAVER, SEAN
(1943–) Elvis's official photographer in the 1970s. Over the years Shaver accumulated a collection of 80,000 photos of Elvis. One thousand of his favorites were included in his 1980 book *The Life of Elvis Presley*. (See *The Life of Elvis Presley*)

SHAW, ARNOLD
Music publisher (vice president of Hill and Range Music), record producer, and general professional manager in the 1950s for the Edward B. Marks Music Corporation, one of New York City's oldest music publishing companies. Edward B. Marks Music obtained 50 percent of "I Forgot to Remember to Forget" before Sam Phillips sold his other Hi-Lo songs to Hill and Range Music.

---

[1]Sellers, singer Stephen Stills, and Ringo Starr all lived in the same house in Surrey, England, at different times.
[2]Big Top Records of New York City was founded by Jean and Julian Aberbach in 1959, as a part of their Hill and Range publishing empire.

Shaw, who worked in the music business from 1944 to 1966, helped to get Elvis signed by RCA. In late 1954 Elvis was still a regional phenomenon. With a national base, Colonel Parker would get top dollar for Elvis's Sun contract. Parker requested that Shaw get Elvis's records played in the North. Shaw asked disc jockey Bill Randle of WERE in Cleveland to program Elvis. Soon after, Elvis had national notoriety and, on November 20, 1955, RCA bought Elvis's Sun contract. Shaw has authored a number of music-related books, including: *The Rockin' 50's, Sinatra, The World of Soul, The Rock Revolution, Belafonte,* and *Honkers and Shouters.* Shaw is today a professor of music at the University of Nevada at Reno. (See *RCA Victor, Bill Randle*)

SHELBY COUNTY DEPUTY SHERIFF
Honorary nonsalaried law-enforcement position to which Elvis was sworn in on September 1, 1976.

SHELTON, BOB
Composer, with brother Joe Shelton and Sid Robin, of the song "Just Because," which Elvis recorded in 1954. Bob and Joe Shelton sang duet honky tonk as the Shelton Brothers, after starting out in 1933 with Leon Chapplear as the Lone Star Cowboys. They recorded their version of "Just Because" (Decca 5872) as the Shelton Brothers in 1942.

SHELTON, JOE
Composer, with brother Bob Shelton and Sid Robin of the song "Just Because," which Elvis recorded in 1954. In 1935 Shelton recorded "Matchbox Blues," which Carl Perkins would record on December 4, 1956, as "Matchbox," just before the famous Million-Dollar Quartet session.

SHEPHERD, CYBILL
(1949–   ) Model turned actress, born in Memphis on February 18, 1949, who won the title "Miss Teenage Memphis" and was selected Miss Congeniality in the Miss Teenage America pageant. Shepherd costars on the TV series "Moonlighting," and dated Elvis in 1966 when he was thirty-one and she was seventeen.

SHEPPARD, T. G.
(1944–   ) Country singer born Bill Browder in Humboldt, Tennessee, on July 20, 1944. Sheppard and Elvis first met while rollerskating at the Rainbow Rollerdome in Memphis, after two of Elvis's bodyguards knocked him off his feet. Elvis apologized, and the two began to talk and eventually became friends. It was through Sheppard that Elvis met Linda Thompson, after Sheppard had invited her to a private movie showing at the Memphian Theatre. Elvis gave Sheppard a customized GMC bus in 1975. Before his success as a solo artist, Sheppard played backup for the Beach Boys and for Jan and Dean.

SHERRY, DOROTHY
(1946–   ) Thirty-two-year-old housewife who claims to have talked to the dead Elvis in a series of séances, the first being held in a New York City hotel on July 13, 1978. Sherry's story is told in Hans Holzer's book *Elvis Presley Speaks.*

SHINDIG
ABC-TV show (1964–1966), hosted by Jimmy O'Neill. Reportedly, it was one of Elvis's favorite TV programs. The Blossoms, who later backed Elvis on his 1968 recording sessions, appeared as regulars on the show. Some of the musicians who appeared on "Shindig" were: Glen Campbell, David Gates, Leon Russell, Billy Preston, Glen Hardin, Delaney Bramlett, and James Burton. (See *The Blossoms, Jimmy O'Neill*)

SHIRL, JIMMY
(1909–   ) Composer born in New York City on October 7, 1909. Shirl composed, with Ervin Drake, Irvin Graham, and Al Stillman, the song "I Believe," which Elvis recorded in 1957.

SHOLES, STEVE
(1911–1968) Graduate of Rutgers University and a member of the Country Music Hall of Fame (1967), born in Washington, D.C., on February 12, 1911. Sholes was an RCA Victor executive until his death in 1968. He moved to Nashville to record a number of artists, such as Hank Snow, Pee Wee King, and Johnny and Jack, for the RCA Victor label. It was Sholes who signed Elvis to the RCA Victor label in 1955. He had seen Elvis for the first time at the Grand Ole Opry. One of the smartest things Sholes did was to allow Elvis to "run" his own recording sessions, to make his own decisions on what to record and how to record it. It was this freedom that brought out the creativity in Elvis.

SHOOK, JERRY
Bass player in Elvis's TCB Band. Shook previously played with the Association, two of whose biggest hits were "Along Comes Mary" (Valiant 741) and "Cherish" (Valiant 747), both released in 1966.

SHORE, SAMMY
Comedian who opened many of Elvis's live concerts in the 1970s. Shore was replaced by comedian Jackie Kahane.

SHRINERS
During the week of Elvis's death in August 1977, 16,000 members of the Shriners met in Memphis for a convention. When word of Elvis's death hit the news media, thousands of Elvis fans began converging on Memphis, only to find a shortage of hotel rooms because of the Shriners' convention.

THE SHROUD OF TURIN
Book written by Ian Wilson that some sources say Elvis was reading when he died. The book had been given to him by Larry Geller as a present. Other sources have said the book Elvis had been reading was *The Scientific Search for the Face of Jesus* by Frank Adams.

SHUMAN, MORT

(1936–) Composer born in New York City on November 12, 1936. Shuman composed a number of songs recorded by Elvis. He wrote, mostly with Doc Pomus, such rock classics as "This Magic Moment" (Atlantic 2050) and "Save the Last Dance for Me" (Atlantic 2071) for the Drifters, and "A Teenager in Love" (Laurie 3027) for Dion and the Belmonts. Shuman composed Elvis's song "You'll Think of Me" by himself. (See *Doc Pomus* for a list of their compositions for Elvis)

SIDEBURNS

Part of Elvis's hairstyle, along with a ducktail cut first worn by him at age sixteen while a student in high school. Most of his fellow male students wore crew cuts or other short hairstyles at the time. Sideburns were named for General Ambrose Burnside, who served with the Union Army during the Civil War and became the first president of the National Rifle Association in 1871. Elvis was influenced by actor Rudolph Valentino and by the truck drivers he saw in the early 1950s.

SIGMAN, CARL

(1909–) Composer born in Brooklyn on September 24, 1909. With German-born musician James Last, Sigman wrote the song "Fool," which Elvis recorded in 1972. Sigman wrote the English lyrics for the song "What Now My Love," which was composed by Pierre Delanoe and Gilbert Becaud, recorded by Elvis in 1972.

SILVER, ABNER

(1899–1966) Composer born on December 28, 1899. Silver composed with Sid Wayne the following songs that Elvis recorded: "Lover Doll," "Tonight's All Right for Love (with Joe Lilley), "Tonight Is So Right for Love," "What's She Really Like," and "Young and Beautiful" (with Aaron Schroeder). He had also authored the book *All Women Are Wolves*. Abner Silver, who was born in the nineteenth century and wrote some great rock & roll songs for Elvis in the twentieth century, died on November 24, 1966.

SILVER RECORD

Trophy received by Colonel Tom Parker from RCA Victor Records each time Elvis received a Gold Record.

SILVER STALLION

Memphis nightclub, located at 1447 Union Street, where Elvis is believed to have performed at times while he was still a student at L. C. Humes High School. The club was referred to in the school yearbook.

SIMON, PAUL

(1941–) Singer and composer born in Newark, New Jersey, on October 13, 1941. Simon had some of his biggest hits as half of the duo of Simon and Garfunkel. He and Carole King once recorded demo records as the Cosines. Melissa Manchester was one of Simon's students when he taught at New York University. Elvis recorded the Paul Simon composition "Bridge over Troubled Water" in 1970. In 1986 Simon recorded his Grammy Award–winning album *Graceland*.

Simon has said of Elvis: "I grew my hair like him and imitated his stage act. Once I went all over New York looking for a lavender shirt like the one he wore on one of his albums."

SINATRA, FRANK

(1915–) Singer and actor born in Hoboken, New Jersey, on December 12, 1915. Sinatra, whose nickname is "Ol' Blue Eyes," has enjoyed a career spanning five decades, from the 1940s to the present. He began as a member of the Hoboken Four vocal group and later appeared on radio's "Your Hit Parade." He won an Oscar for Best Supporting Actor for the 1953 movie *From Here to Eternity*. It was on Sinatra's May 12, 1960, TV special that Elvis made his first TV appearance after his discharge from the Army. During the filming of *G.I. Blues*, Sinatra visited Elvis in his dressing room. Sinatra's love interest at the time was Elvis's costar, actress Juliet Prowse. Sinatra's eldest daughter, Nancy, costarred with Elvis in the 1968 movie *Speedway*.

Sinatra was performing at the Alpine Valley Music Theater in Wisconsin when he learned of Elvis's death. He told his audience that evening that he had "lost a dear friend and tremendous asset to the business."

Some interesting similarities between Elvis and Sinatra:

1. Both experienced complications in their birth.
2. Both were "mama's boys."
3. Both made a debut at New York's Paramount Theater.
4. Both of their first records sold approximately 8,000 copies.
5. Both played opposite Juliet Prowse in a movie.
6. Both fathered daughters.
7. Both performed with Tommy Dorsey.
8. Both owned publishing companies.
9. Both recorded songs with Nancy Sinatra.
10. Both had hundreds of fan clubs throughout the world.
11. Both were generous to their friends.
12. Both recorded the songs "Blue Hawaii" and "Love Me Tender."
13. Both recorded "My Way," which was considered "their" song.
14. Both had groups of friends with whom they traveled.
15. Both were given a number of nicknames.
16. Both have been the subject of numerous biographies.
17. Both became successful movie actors.
18. Both lost their mothers, with whom they were close.

SINATRA, NANCY

(1940–) Daughter of Frank and Nancy Sinatra. Born Sandra Sinatra on June 8, 1940, Nancy[1] was once married to singer Tommy Sands, one of Colonel Tom

---

[1]Songwriter Jimmy Van Heusen, a descendant of Stephen Foster, wrote (with comedian Phil Silvers) the song "Nancy With the Laughin' Face" for Nancy when she was five years old. A songwriter named Jack Lawrence composed the song "Linda" in 1946 about his attorney's little girl, Linda Eastman. Today, Linda Eastman is Mrs. Paul McCartney.

Parker's clients, with whom Elvis had toured in 1955. She appeared with her father on the "Welcome Home Elvis" TV special, aired May 12, 1960, on which Elvis was featured. Nancy costarred (as Susan Jacks) with Elvis in the 1968 movie *Speedway*. She sang "Your Groovy Self" in the movie. On September 8, 1970, Elvis, Priscilla, and Vernon and Dee Presley all attended Nancy Sinatra's opening at the Las Vegas International Hotel. There had been rumors of Elvis and Nancy having a relationship. It was Nancy who gave Priscilla her baby shower.

SINCE I MET YOU BABY
Elvis and Ginger Alden's "song." It was Ginger's all-time favorite. In an article in the *National Enquirer* (May 16, 1978), it was claimed that after Elvis's death Ginger once saw him above her bed wearing a white jumpsuit and singing "Since I Met You Baby," a song Elvis never recorded.

SINGER
Sewing machine manufacturer that sponsored Elvis's NBC-TV special, "Elvis," broadcast Tuesday, December 3, 1968, at 9:00 P.M. A special album titled *Singer Presents Elvis Singing Flaming Star and Others* was released in 1968 through Singer stores, with Singer's name on the album cover.

SINGER, LOU
(1912–1966) Composer born in New York City on February 26, 1912. Singer was the composer, with Bennie Benjamin and Raymond Leveen, of the song "I Will Be Home Again," which Elvis recorded in 1960.

SINGLETON, CHARLES
Composer, with Eddy Snyder and Bert Kaempfert, of the song "Spanish Eyes," which Elvis recorded in 1973.

SINGLETON, MARGIE
Singer who composed, with Rose Marie McCoy, the song "Tryin' to Get to You," which Elvis recorded in 1955. Singleton recorded a number of songs, several in duet with Faron Young. She appeared on the "Louisiana Hayride" with Elvis and that may have been where Elvis heard her sing "Tryin' to Get to You." In 1962 Singleton recorded "Magic Star" (Mercury 72079), a vocal version of the Tornadoes' instrumental hit "Telstar" (London 9561).

SINGLETON, SHELBY
(1931–   ) Highly successful record producer born on December 16, 1931. Among his many hit records was "Wooden Heart" (Smash 1708) by Joe Dowell, which Singleton produced in 1961. In 1968 he founded Plantation Records, which produced the million-selling single by Jeannie C. Riley, "Harper Valley P.T.A." (Plantation 3). In 1969 Singleton bought Sun Records from Sam Phillips, acquiring four thousand master recordings. Singleton began releasing many of the Johnny Cash, Roy Orbison, Carl Perkins, and Charlie Rich material on Sun International Records. Always an in-novator, Singleton released albums with lifetime guarantees against wearing out (for one dollar, Sun International would replace the record). In 1978 Singleton brought out a series of mysterious duet records, featuring Jerry Lee Lewis and someone sounding like Elvis on "Save the Last Dance for Me" and "Am I to Be the One." One album was titled *Duets* (Sun 1011), but it was not revealed whom Lewis was singing with. Shelby Singleton is also responsible for the several Orion singles and albums featuring the voice of Jimmy Ellis. Singleton today owns the famed "Million-Dollar Quartet" tapes, kept safely in a bank vault. They were included in the tapes that Sam Phillips sold to Singleton. Vivian Keith, Singleton's secretary, wrote the song "Before the Next Teardrop Falls," which became a hit for Freddy Fender.

SITTON, RAYMOND
Two-hundred-eighty-pound member of the Memphis Mafia, nicknamed "Chief." Sitton was present the night the Beatles visited Elvis in Bel Air. He later became a movie character actor.

SIVLE YELSERP
Cover name that producer Chet Atkins used for Elvis's March 1960 recording session to hide Elvis's identity and keep crowds away. The name is Elvis Presley spelled backward. During the session, RCA ordered one hundred hamburgers at the nearby Crystal hamburger stand.

SKIPPY PEANUT BUTTER
Favorite food of Elvis as a young boy in Tupelo. When company arrived, he would often hide the jar for fear it would be eaten.

SKYLAR, ALEXIS
Twenty-four-year-old woman who announced that she was to marry Elvis in 1974. Although some newspapers carried the account, it proved to be a hoax.

SLAUGHTER, HENRY
Session musician who played piano and organ on Elvis's recording sessions at the RCA Studios in Nashville on May 25–28 and June 10, 1966. Slaughter composed the gospel song "If the Lord Wasn't Walking by My Side," which Elvis recorded in 1966.

SLAUGHTER, TODD
Avid British Elvis fan and author of the 1977 book *Elvis Presley*. Slaughter took over the British publication of *Elvis Monthly* magazine after the death of founder Albert Hand. Slaughter wrote the liner notes on a British K-Tel Elvis album and the foreword for the 1987 book *Elvis in Private*. He and Ernst Jorgenson were the project researchers for the 1988 album *Essential Elvis—The First Movies*.

SLEEPY-EYED JOHN
(See *John Lepley*)

SLEMANSKY, HANK
Elvis's original martial-arts instructor, who taught him karate while he was in the Army in Germany in 1959. Slemansky was killed in Vietnam in the 1960s.

SMALL, DANNY
Composer of the song "Without Love (There Is Nothing)," which Elvis recorded in 1969.

SMITH, AL
Composer, with Luther Dixon, of the song "Big Boss Man," which Elvis recorded in 1967.

SMITH, ANN DEWEY
Wife of Vernon Presley's lawyer, Beecher Smith III, and one of the three witnesses to Elvis's will. The other two witnesses were Charlie Hodge and Ginger Alden.

SMITH III, BEECHER
Vernon Presley's lawyer, who drew up Elvis's will and who represented Vernon in his divorce from Dee Stanley Presley.

SMITH, CARROL (JUNIOR)
(–1958) Son of Edward Smith and Levalle Smith Smith and the brother of Gene Smith. Junior Smith was Elvis's cousin and a close friend who accompanied him on trips in the 1950s. Smith was with Elvis when Elvis traveled to New York to appear on "The Steve Allen Show" in 1956. Junior Smith, who had been disabled during the Korean War, died in September 1958, just three weeks after Gladys Presley died.

SMITH, CLETTES
(1919–   ) Daughter of Robert Lee Smith and Octavia (Doll) Mansell Smith, and the younger sister of Gladys Love Smith Presley. In September 1935 Clettes married Vester Presley, the brother of Vernon Presley, making Clettes Elvis's double aunt. Clettes Smith is the mother of Patsy Presley Gambill.

SMITH, EFFIE
(1904–1905) First child (of nine) born to Robert Lee Smith and Octavia (Doll) Mansell Smith. Effie, who was Gladys Smith Presley's sister and Elvis's aunt, died as a baby at one year and two months of age.

SMITH, GENE
Son of Edward Smith and Levalle Smith Smith and the brother of Junior Smith. Elvis's maternal cousin was employed for ten years as a chauffeur. He and Elvis had worked together at Precision Tool Company in Memphis in the 1950s. The two men were close, cutting lawns together, going out on double dates, and just hanging out. Gene was a member of the Memphis Mafia until the late 1960s, after which he left because of a conflict. He lived at Graceland and sometimes slept in the same room with Elvis to prevent him from sleepwalking (a trait that had haunted Elvis since childhood). While Elvis was in Hollywood, it was Gene Smith who looked after Elvis's wardrobe. According to the book *Elvis—What Happened?*, it was Gene who looked after Elvis's "kit bag."

SMITH, GLADYS LOVE
(1912–1958) Maiden name of Elvis's mother. Gladys Smith was also the real name of actresses Mary Pickford and Alexis Smith. (See *Gladys Presley*)

SMITH, JOHN (JOHNNY)
(1922–1968) Son of Robert Lee Smith and Octavia (Doll) Mansell Smith and the brother of Gladys Smith Presley. John Smith was one of Elvis's uncles, and helped teach him to play the guitar. Smith, who never married, was employed as a gate guard at Graceland until his death on October 6, 1968. In her book *Elvis: Portrait of a Friend*, Patsy Lacker states that Smith, who had been drinking, tried to break into her room one night at Graceland and wouldn't go away until she threatened to call the police.

SMITH, LEVALLE
(1908–   ) Daughter of Robert Lee Smith and Octavia (Doll) Mansell Smith and the older sister of Gladys Smith Presley. Levalle married Edward Smith (unrelated), and they were the parents of Junior and Gene Smith. Levalle's mother, Doll Smith, went to live with Levalle after the death of her husband, Robert Lee Smith.

SMITH, LILLIAN
(1906–   ) Eldest daughter of Robert Lee Smith and Octavia (Doll) Smith and the sister of Gladys Smith Presley. Lillian married Charlie Mann and they were the parents of Bobby Mann. Charlie died in 1957, after which Lillian, from 1960 to 1962, was employed at Graceland as a secretary who answered Elvis's fan mail. Lillian, who later became Mrs. Fontenberry, was interviewed by Elaine Dundy for her book *Elvis and Gladys*. (See *Bobby Mann*)

SMITH, MILEGE OBEDIA (OBE)
(1837–1909) Son of John Smith, father of Robert Lee Smith, grandfather of Gladys Smith, and great-grandfather of Elvis Presley. Obe married Gladys's grandmother, Ann Mansell, on December 13, 1874. Obe's brother was Steven S. Smith.

SMITH, RHETHA
(1910–   ) Daughter of Robert Lee Smith and Octavia (Doll) Mansell Smith and the older sister of Gladys Smith Presley. Rhetha married a man named Loyd in 1929 and became the mother of Harold Loyd. Rhetha Smith died in a house fire in Tupelo.

SMITH, RICHARD B.
(1901–1935) Composer born in Hondesdale, Pennsylvania, on September 29, 1901. In 1934 Smith composed, with Felix Bernard, the song "Winter Wonderland," which Elvis recorded in 1971.

SMITH, ROBERT LEE

(–1932) Son of Obe Smith and Ann Mansell Smith, father of Gladys Smith, and grandfather of Elvis Presley. Robert Smith married his older first cousin, Octavia (Doll) Mansell, on September 20, 1903 (Gladys Smith was also older than Vernon Presley).

SMITH, STEVEN S.

Son of John Smith and brother of Milege Obedia (Obe) Smith. Steven Smith and his wife, Mary, were the parents of five children: Elizabeth, Ann, Wesley, Pelham, and Leila Love. Leila's middle name was passed on as the middle name of Gladys Love Smith Presley, Elvis's mother.

SMITH, TONY

Elvis imitator who claims he is a cousin of Elvis, and that his father was Gladys's brother. He performs as Tony Presley.

SMITH, TRACY

(1917–   ) Deaf-mute second son (of three) and seventh child (of nine) born to Robert Lee Smith and Octavia (Doll) Mansell Smith. Tracy Smith was the brother of Gladys Smith and the uncle of Elvis Presley.

SMITH, TRAVIS

(1915–1966) Son of Robert and Octavia Smith and brother of Gladys Smith. Travis and his brother Johnny worked for Precision Tool in Memphis in the 1950s. Travis was employed as a gate guard at Graceland and lived in a three-bedroom wooden house behind Graceland, which Elvis later bulldozed down.

On June 29, 1966, after six weeks of hospitalization, Travis Smith died.

SMITH, WILLIAM (BILLY)

(1943–   ) Son of Travis and Lorene Smith and the brother of Bobby Smith. Billy Smith, who was one of the closest people to his cousin Elvis and about whom Elvis was very protective, was a member of the Memphis Mafia. He took care of Elvis's wardrobe and served as valet. He lived with his wife, Jo, in a trailer behind the main house at Graceland. He once doubled for Annette Day in the 1967 movie *Double Trouble*. Billy and Jo played racquetball with Elvis on the last night of his life on August 16, 1977. After Elvis' death, Smith became the editor of *Elvis the Record* magazine.

SNOOPY

One of the two Great Danes that Elvis bought for Priscilla (the other was Brutus). Snoopy, named for Charles Schulz's cartoon beagle, eventually became Lisa Marie's dog.

SNOW, HANK

(1914–   ) Country singer born Clarence Eugene Snow, in Liverpool, Nova Scotia, on May 9, 1914. In 1954 Snow became a client of Colonel Tom Parker's. On January 7, 1949, Snow debuted on the Grand Ole Opry, with the same lack of audience enthusiasm that Elvis got in 1954. (Snow, like Hank Williams and Elvis, produced a sound that was ahead of its time.) During the 1955 Hank Snow Jamboree tour, Colonel Parker signed a contract with Elvis, creating a conflict in which Snow threatened to sue Parker. Shrewdly, Parker forced Snow out of the picture when he unrealistically suggested they both pool all of their money to buy Elvis's contract from Bob Neal. (In 1961 Snow filed a lawsuit against Parker claiming that he and Parker were once partners and that it was he [Snow] who actually discovered Elvis and brought him to the attention of RCA Victor Records.) Elvis, who was being managed by Bob Neal, had signed an agreement with Snow for the Jamboree tour. In early 1955 Snow unsuccessfully tried to persuade Steve Sholes of RCA Records to buy Elvis's contract from Sam Phillips for $10,000. It was Snow who introduced Elvis during Elvis's appearance on the Grand Ole Opry on October 2, 1954. Snow originally wrote and recorded "I'm Movin' On," (RCA Victor 0328), which Elvis recorded in January 1969.

SNOW, JIMMY RODGERS

Son of singer Hank Snow with whom Elvis toured on the Hank Snow Jamboree in 1955. Years later, Jimmy became a minister who would denounce rock & roll. In some photos, magazines, and books Jimmy Rodgers Snow is misidentified as the son of singer Jimmie Rodgers, after whom Hank Snow named him. Jimmy Snow authored the 1977 autobiography *I Cannot Go Back*.

In November 1954, Snow recorded "How Do You Think I Feel" (RCA Victor 47-5900), which Elvis would record in 1956. In December 1954, Snow recorded "Love Me" (RCA Victor 47-5986), which Elvis would record in 1956. Since the two had toured together, Elvis may have first heard these songs when Snow performed them, and it may have been Snow's versions that influenced Elvis. In 1956 Snow would record a song that Elvis had recorded, "The Milcow Blues Boogie" (RCA 47-6430).

SNYDER, EDDY

Composer, with Charles Singleton, of the song "Spanish Eyes," which Elvis recorded.

SONGFELLOWS

Gospel group for which Elvis auditioned in 1954 at the Memphis auditorium. The Songfellows were a group of young singers associated with the well-known Blackwood Brothers Quartet. Elvis was asked to join because Cecil Blackwood was leaving to join the Blackwood Brothers; however, Elvis couldn't, because he had just signed with Sun Records. (See *J. D. Sumner, Blackwood Brothers*)

SOTHEBY PARK-BERNET

New York City auction house that inventoried Elvis's possessions after his death in 1977.

SOUNDING STORY, THE

First book written about Elvis. It was written in Germany by Peter de Vecchi before 1959.

SOUR APPLE AWARD
Negative honor conferred upon Elvis by the Hollywood Women's Press Club for Least Cooperative Actor of the Year (1967). At the same presentation, Natalie Wood received the Least Cooperative Actress Award.

SOUTH, JOE
(1940–   ) Composer and singer born in Atlanta on February 28, 1940. South made the charts with the songs "Games People Play" (Capitol 2248) and "Walk a Mile in My Shoes" (Capitol 2704). Elvis recorded South's composition "Walk a Mile in My Shoes" in 1970.

SPEARHEAD
The Second Armored Division, to which Elvis was assigned. The division was commanded by General George Smith Patton during World War II. General Patton was the first American to enter the Olympic Pentathlon when it was introduced in 1912; he finished fifth.

SPECIAL PROJECTS, INC.
Beverly Hills firm that handled Elvis products beginning in 1956. Special Projects, Inc., was owned by Hank Saperstein and Howard Bell (Saperstein also took over the administration of the Elvis Presley National Fan Club). The company also handled products for the Lone Ranger and for Ding Dong School.

SPECTOR, PHIL
(1939–   ) Singer and composer born Harvey Phillip Spector in the Bronx, New York, on December 26, 1939. Spector was a teenage millionaire who created the "Wall of Sound" on records for the Righteous Brothers, the Crystals, the Ronettes, Darlene Love, etc. He was once married to Ronnie Bennett Spector, the lead singer of the Ronettes and later was producer for the Beatles on their album *Let It Be*. During the 1960s Spector produced some of the demo records of material sent to Elvis. He cowrote "You've Lost That Lovin' Feelin'," which Elvis recorded. Spector is the only man to produce for both Elvis (indirectly) and the Beatles. It has been said that Spector believed that Colonel Tom Parker hypnotized Elvis. Actually, Parker did have the ability to hypnotize people.

Mike Stone was a bodyguard for Spector. At the Las Vegas Hilton in January 1972, Spector and Stone went backstage to meet Elvis, after which Spector left and Stone stayed on to discuss martial arts with Elvis. That was the first meeting between Elvis and Stone, and Elvis thought Stone could teach Priscilla some karate.

Spector, an ardent fan of Elvis's, said of him: "Gosh, he's so great, you have no idea how great he is, really you don't. You have no comprehension, it's absolutely impossible. I can't tell you why he's so great, but he is. He's sensational. He can do anything with his voice. He can sing anything you want him to, anyway you tell him. The unquestionable King of Rock 'n' Roll."

SPEER, BEN AND BROCK
Members of the Speer Family vocal group (other members are: Faye Speer, Brian Speer, Harold Lane, Diane Mays, John Mays, and Steve Williams). Ben and Brock Speer, along with Gordon Stoker, sang backup on Elvis's "Heartbreak Hotel," "I Want You, I Need You, I Love You," and other songs at Elvis's first four RCA recording sessions.

Chet Atkins had attempted to hire the entire Speer Family to back up Elvis on his first records, but only Ben and Brock were available.

SPEER, WILLIAM
(1917–   ) Professional Memphis photographer who took Elvis's first publicity stills in 1954 and 1955 at his Blue Light studio.

SPIELMAN, FRED
Composer born Fritz Spielmann in Vienna, Austria. Spielman composed, with Janice Torre, the song "I Don't Want To," which Elvis sang in the 1962 movie *Girls! Girls! Girls!*

SPINKS, BRUCE
Sportswriter for the *Honolulu Advisor* who caught Elvis's cape when Elvis threw it into the audience at the "Elvis: Aloha from Hawaii" TV concert on January 14, 1973.

SPRECKLES, JUDY POWELL
(1932–   ) Heiress to the Spreckles sugar fortune who was romantically linked to Elvis in 1958. Spreckles and Jim Blevins presented Elvis the Pops-Rite Popstar Award on March 23, 1958. The following day she accompanied Elvis to his Army induction. In 1964 she became millionaire Adolph Spreckles's[1] sixth wife, a marriage that lasted just thirty-four days. (Another wife of Spreckles's was Kay Williams, who in 1955 became Clark Gable's fifth wife.) Judy gave Elvis a four-star black sapphire ring in Las Vegas.

SPREEN, GLEN
Saxophonist who, as a member of the Memphis Horns, overdubbed *The Trouble with Girls* soundtrack session in 1968 and both sessions at the American Sound Studios in 1969. He cocomposed with Red West the songs "Holly Leaves and Christmas Trees" and "Seeing Is Believing," both of which Elvis recorded in 1971.

SPRINGER, PHIL
New York City–born composer who scored TV series' such as "Gunsmoke" and "Mannix." Springer was the composer, with Buddy Kaye, of the song "Never Ending," which Elvis recorded in 1964.

SPRINGSTEEN, BRUCE
(1949–   ) Singer, born September 23, 1949, in Freehold, New Jersey, nicknamed "The Boss." Springsteen first saw Elvis live at the Philadelphia Spectrum on

---

[1]Actor Errol Flynn once decked Adolph Spreckles in a fistfight in 1941.

May 28, 1977. During his 1976 "Born to Run" tour, Springsteen and Steve Van Zandt went to visit Elvis at Graceland, where Bruce jumped the fence and made it to the front door before he was confronted by the guards and ejected. Elvis wasn't home anyway; he was in Lake Tahoe. Springsteen, a lifelong Elvis fan, first saw him sing on "The Ed Sullivan Show" on TV in 1956, when he was just seven years old. Springsteen's favorite Elvis song is "Follow That Dream," which he sometimes performs at his concerts. Minister and rock singer Little Richard officiated at Springsteen's marriage to Julianne Phillips.

Springsteen said of Elvis: "There have been a lot of tough guys. There have been pretenders, there have been contenders. But there is only one King. Everything starts and ends with him. He wrote the book."

SRI DAYA MATA

Religious leader born Fay Wright. Mata was the head of the Self-Realization Fellowship Center on Mount Washington in the Hollywood Hills. Elvis was introduced to Mata by Larry Geller in the 1960s and for a time followed her teachings. In 1955 Mata, then a secretary, took over the SRF after the death of its founder, Yogi Paramahansa Yogananda. Mata authored the book *Only Love*, which Elvis read and kept in his library.

STAFFORD, TERRY

Singer, born in Amarillo, Texas, who recorded a cover version of Elvis's "Suspicion" (Crusader 101) in 1964, beating Elvis's version as a single by two months. Stafford also recorded "Playing with Fire" (Crusader 105) (the flip side of "I'll Touch a Star," which he charted in 1964), a song that Elvis had recorded for the 1961 movie *Blue Hawaii*, but which was never released.

STAMPS

Vocal group lead by J. D. Sumner that sang backup for Elvis at his concerts from 1972 to 1977. Members have included Ed Enoch, Ed Hill, Larry Strickland, Donnie Sumner, Bill Baize, Buck Buckles, and Richard Sterban, who later joined the Oak Ridge boys. The Stamps recorded a number of albums, including *Elvis's Favorite Gospel Songs* and *Memories of Our Friend Elvis*. In 1979 former member Ed Hill wrote the book *Where Is Elvis?* (See *J. D. Sumner*)

STANLEY, DAVADA (DEE) ELLIOT

(1925–   ) Blond and blue-eyed daughter of James Wright Elliot and Bessie May Heath Elliot and the mother of Billy, David, and Rick Stanley, born in Clarkesville, Tennessee, on January 19, 1925. On July 3, 1960, she became Vernon Presley's second wife and Elvis's stepmother (ten years Elvis's senior). Vernon met Davada Stanley in West Germany in 1959, while Elvis was in the Army. She was at the time in the process of divorcing her husband of ten years, Army sergeant William Stanley, whom she had married in 1949. Vernon Presley and Dee were married in a private ceremony at the Huntsville, Alabama, home of her brother, Richard Neely. Elvis did not attend. After having lived with Dee and her boys at Graceland, and then in their own home on Dolan Drive for seventeen years, where she had one miscarriage with Vernon's baby, Vernon Presley filed for divorce on May 5, 1977, citing irreconcilable differences. It was reported on November 15, 1977, that Dee Stanley had obtained a Dominican Republic divorce. After her divorce from Vernon, Dee married Lewis Tucker, five years her junior. In 1979 Delacorte published her and her sons' biography, *Elvis, We Loved You Tender*.

STANLEY, DAVID EDWARD

(1956–   ) Son of William and Dee Stanley, born in Fort Eustis, Virginia, on August 30, 1956. When his mother married Vernon Presley, David became Elvis's stepbrother. He was employed as a security guard at Graceland at the time of Elvis's death. In his 1986 autobiography, *Life with Elvis*, Stanley admitted he had a serious drug problem and mentioned that Elvis used prescription cocaine, a fact that has been denied by other writers. Stanley, who today is a minister, coauthored the book *Elvis, We Loved You Tender* with his mother and his brothers and later authored *Life with Elvis* with David Wimbish.

STANLEY, RICHARD (RICK) EARL

(1953–   ) Son of William and Dee Stanley born on December 13, 1953. When Vernon Presley married his mother in 1960, Rick became Elvis's stepbrother. He was working at Graceland on the night of Elvis's death. Elvis, who nicknamed him "Reckless Rick," once gave him a new Pontiac Trans Am. Under orders from Elvis, Stanley delivered to Elvis two packets of pills, which may have contributed to Elvis's death. Stanley married his girlfriend, Angela Payne, on November 21, 1971, with Vernon Presley as his best man. The couple sometimes went on tour with Elvis. In 1977 they divorced and in 1981 Stanley married his second wife, Kandis Lanier. In 1975 he was arrested for obtaining drugs from the Methodist Hospital Pharmacy (David Stanley has said that it occurred at the Baptist Hospital) with a forged prescription, but the charges were later reduced to malicious mischief, carrying a fine of just $50 and a six-month suspended sentence. Stanley was finally fired after he bad-mouthed Linda Thompson, which she overheard and told Elvis about, but was rehired later after she left. Stanley is the coauthor of the book *Elvis, We Loved You Tender*, in which he says that Elvis once asked him if he could date his girlfriend Jill. In 1978 Stanley began studying to become a minister at the Christian Center in Destin, Florida. Today he is a practicing minister, and the author, with Michael Hunes, of the 1986 book *The Touch of Two Kings*.

STANLEY, WILLIAM (BILLY)

U.S. Army NCO who was Davada Elliot's first husband (married February 1, 1949) and father of her three sons, Billy, David, and Rick. While with the U.S. Army in Europe during World War II, six-foot-two-inch, 280-pound William Stanley served as General George S.

Patton's bodyguard. After his divorce from Dee Stanley in 1960, he married a woman named Lois.

STANLEY JR., WILLIAM (BILLY) JOB

(1953–   ) Son of William and Dee Stanley born in Fort Monroe, Virginia, on January 18, 1953. Billy became Elvis's stepbrother in 1960 when Vernon Presley married Billy's mother. Billy became an employee on Elvis's payroll. Elvis called Billy "Charles Manson" because his long hair and blue eyes reminded Elvis of the cult leader. Billy was one of the cowriters of the book *Elvis, We Loved You Tender*. In 1977 Star Fleet Publishers released his book *Elvis: His Last Tour*. In the book *Elvis, We Loved You Tender*, Billy claimed that Elvis had a one-month affair with his eighteen-year-old bride, Anne, after which Billy and Anne were divorced. Billy later married a woman named Diana.

STANPHILL, IRA

Composer of the gospel song "Mansion Over the Hilltop," which Elvis recorded in 1960.

STAR WARS

A 1977 movie starring Mark Hamill, Harrison Ford, Carrie Fisher, and Alec Guinness. It has become one of the biggest-grossing films of all time. Elvis tried to obtain a print of *Star Wars* to show to Lisa Marie on the night of August 15, 1977, but was unable to do so. He died the next day.

STARKEY, DR. GERALD

Police doctor to whom Elvis gave a $13,000 Lincoln Continental Mark IV on January 14, 1976. (See *Jerry Kennedy*)

STARLIGHT WRANGLERS

Country band, headed by Doug Poindexter, who appeared in the local clubs in Memphis and who cut a few records for the Sun label. Both Bill Black and Scotty Moore were members of the group. In 1952 Johnny Burnette occasionally sang with the band. Elvis once appeared with the band in the Eagle's Nest club in Memphis in late 1954. Sam Phillips originally considered having the Starlight Wranglers back Elvis, but when two of the band's members, Bill Black and Scotty Moore, first began backing Elvis, the sound they created filled the bill. An agreement was reached among Elvis and Black and Moore that Elvis would get 50 percent of future earnings, with Black and Moore each getting 25 percent. Later, when Colonel Parker entered the picture, they were paid a flat fee. The members of the Starlight Wranglers were: Scotty Moore (guitar); Bill Black (bass); Millard Yeow (fiddler); Clyde Rush (guitar); Tommy Seals (steel guitar). Doug Poindexter made one record for Sun—"Now She Cares No More for Me"/"My Kind of Carryin' On" (Sun 202) in 1954.

STARR, KAY

(1922–   ) Pop singer of the 1950s born Kay Stark in Dougherty, Oklahoma, on July 21, 1922. Starr was one of Elvis's two favorite female singers (the other was Patti Page) as told to interviewer Red Robinson in Vancouver, British Columbia, on August 31, 1957.

It is believed that Elvis recorded two unreleased songs that Kay Starr also recorded, "Fool, Fool, Fool" (Capitol 2151) and "Noah" (Capitol 2334).

STARR, RANDY

(1930–   ) New York City–born composer and singer who in 1957 charted the hit song "After School" (Dale 100).[1] Starr composed the following songs that Elvis recorded:

"Could I Fall in Love"
"The Girl I Never Loved"
"Old MacDonald"
"Who Needs Money"

With Fred Wise, Starr composed the following songs that Elvis recorded:

"Adam and Evil"
"Carny Town"
"Datin' "
"Kissin' Cousins"
"Look Out, Broadway"

Starr and Wise also adapted "The Yellow Rose of Texas"/"The Eyes of Texas," which Elvis recorded.

STARR, RINGO

(1940–   ) Drummer born Richard Starkey on July 7, 1940, in Liverpool, England. Starr is a former member of the most successful musical group of all time, the Beatles. Elvis once gave him a cowboy holster, which Ringo proudly displays in his Weybridge, Surrey, home. (See the *Beatles*)

STATESMEN

Gospel group founded in 1948 by Hovie Lister, with Jake Hess as the lead singer. The Statesmen, who recorded for RCA Victor Records, were made up of Hovie Lister (piano), Tommy Thompson (bass), Ed Hill (baritone), R. D. Rozell (tenor), and Budd Bunton (lead).

At Elvis's funeral in 1977 the Statesmen sang "Sweet, Sweet Spirit" and "Known Only to Him." Hovie Lister played piano for Kathy Westmoreland when she sang "Heavenly Father."

STATUE INSCRIPTION AT THE LAS VEGAS HILTON HOTEL

Elvis Aaron Presley
MEMORIES OF ELVIS WILL ALWAYS BE WITH US. NONE OF US REALLY, TOTALLY, KNOW HOW GREAT A PERFORMER HE WAS. ALL OF US AT THE LAS VEGAS HILTON WERE PROUD TO PRESENT ELVIS IN OUR SHOWROOM. THE DECORATIONS IN THE HOTEL, THE BANNERS, THE STREAMERS, "ELVIS, ELVIS," ALWAYS CREATED GREAT EXCITEMENT WITH HIS LOYAL FANS AND FRIENDS. THE LAS

---

[1] It was bandleader Sammy Kaye who recorded him on his own record label, Dale Records.

VEGAS HILTON WAS ELVIS' HOME AWAY FROM HOME. HIS ATTENDANCE RECORDS ARE A LEGEND. WE WILL MISS HIM. THANKS, ELVIS, FROM ALL OF US.

BARRON HILTON

STAX RECORDING STUDIOS
Memphis recording studio, located at 626 East Mc-Lemore Avenue, founded by Jim Stewart and his sister, Estelle Axton, in 1960, originally as Satellite Records,

(Photo courtesy Don Fink)

on which the Mar-Keys recorded their 1961 hit instrumental "Last Night" (Satellite 107). The studio, where Otis Redding recorded many of his hit songs, was located in the old Capitol Theater. Elvis had two Memphis recording sessions at Stax, on July 21–25 and December 10–16, 1973.

STEFANIAK, ELISABETH CLAUDIA
(1939–   ) Adopted daughter of Army Pfc. Raymond L. McCormick, born in Brandenburg, West Germany. Elisabeth's real father was George Stefaniak. She was employed as Elvis's secretary while Elvis was stationed in Bad Nauheim. Elvis met Elisabeth at the base theater in Grafenwohr, where Elvis's unit had been assigned for a short training mission. After dating Elisabeth, Elvis asked her to become his secretary back at Bad Nauheim. Elisabeth, who was paid just $35 a week, lived with Elvis's family at Goethestrasse 14. One day she and Vernon Presley were involved in a car accident in which another car pulled in front of them on the highway. Although neither one was injured, Elvis's Mercedes was totaled. On June 2, 1960, Elisabeth married Rex Mansfield, a G.I. friend of Elvis's. She and her husband cowrote the book *Elvis the Soldier*, in which she tells about her relationship with Elvis and how Minnie Mae Presley introduced her to Rex and how she dated him, which everybody but Elvis seemed to be aware of. (See *Rex Mansfield*)

STEINMUEHLE ORPHANAGE
Children's home to 1,500 German orphans, in Friedburg, West Germany. Elvis sent an undisclosed donation to the orphanage at Christmas in 1959.

STEPHENS, ANDREA JUNE
Young Atlanta woman who won the "Win a Date with Elvis" contest sponsored by *Hit Parade* magazine in 1956. She was flown to Jacksonville, Florida, on August 11, 1956, where she met Elvis in his room and then went with him to a lunch counter to eat.

STEPHENS, GEOFF
Composer, with Les Reed, of the songs "Sylvia" and "This Is Our Dance"; and, with Alan Blaikley and Ken Howard, of the songs, "Heart of Rome" and "I've Lost You," all of which Elvis recorded.

STEVE GARVEY JUNIOR HIGH SCHOOL
School in Lindsay, California, whose name was changed on February 25, 1978, from Abraham Lincoln Junior High School to Steve Garvey Junior High School, in honor of former Los Angeles Dodgers baseball player Steve Garvey, when the principal let the students choose the school's name. The school's library is named after Tom Lasorda, the Dodgers' manager. The students originally chose the name Elvis Presley Junior High School, but it was vetoed.

STEVENS, CONNIE
(1938–   ) Actress and singer born Concetta Ann Ingolia in Brooklyn on April 8, 1938. Stevens was once married to singer Eddie Fisher, and dated Elvis for a short time in 1961. She became a little miffed one night on a date with Elvis. It started when Joe Esposito, not Elvis, picked her up in a Rolls-Royce. She was taken to Elvis's Bel Air house, where he was surrounded by his male friends and their dates. Stevens, who had been expecting to have dinner with Elvis alone, finally demanded to be taken home.

STEVENSON, VENETIA
Hollywood actress and daughter of movie actress Anna Lee[1] and director Robert Stevenson (*Mary Poppins*, [1964]), whom Elvis dated in 1957 and 1958. While Elvis was in the Army, Venetia once flew to West Germany to spend some time with him. Venetia, who had once been married to actor Russ Tamblyn,[2] married singer Don Everly of the Everly Brothers in 1962.[3]

STEVENSON, W. S.
Composer, with Eddie Miller, of the song "Release Me (and Let Me Love Again)," which Elvis recorded in 1970.

STEWART, JOHN
(1939–   ) Folksinger born in San Diego on September 5, 1939. Stewart, a former member of the Kingston

---

[1]Real name: Joanne Winnifrith.

[2]Russ's brother, Lawrence Tamblyn, played lead guitar for the Standells. Their rhythm guitarist was former Mouseketeer Dick Dodd.

[3]Brother Phil Everly married Jackie Ertel, the daughter of Janet Ertel Blyer, a member of the Chordettes vocal group and wife of Archie Blyer. Both brothers divorced their wives in 1970.

Trio, was the composer of the Monkees' 1967 hit song "Daydream Believer" (Colgems 1012). Stewart began his singing career in high school in Pomona, California, impersonating Elvis.

STILLMAN, AL

(1906–1979) Lyricist born in New York City on June 26, 1906, who composed with Ervin Drake, Irvin Graham, and Jimmy Shirl, the song "I Believe," which Elvis recorded in 1957.

STOCK, LARRY

Composer, with Al Lewis and Vincent Rose, of the song "Blueberry Hill," which Elvis recorded in 1957.

STOKER, GORDON

Singer and piano player born in Gleason, Tennessee, who sang backup to Elvis for thirteen years as a member of the Jordanaires.

STOLL, FRED

Gatekeeper at Graceland for fourteen years.

STOLLER, MIKE

(See *Jerry Leiber and Mike Stoller*)

STONE, FRAN

Former wife of martial-arts instructor Mike Stone. Fran Stone once wrote a magazine article titled "Elvis's Wife Stole My Husband."

STONE, JESSE

(1901–   ) Composer and musical arranger born in Atchison, Kansas, on November 16, 1901. Stone worked as the A&R man for Atlantic Records, starting when it was founded in 1945 as National Records. He arranged and orchestrated Chuck Willis's "C. C. Rider," among other releases. Elvis recorded the following Jesse Stone compositions: "Down in the Alley," "Like a Baby," "Money Honey" (Stone played piano on the Drifters' version), and "Shake, Rattle and Roll" (composed under the pseudonym Charles Calhoun). When Ahmet Ertegun traveled to Memphis in 1955 to meet with Sam Phillips in hopes of buying Elvis's contract, he told Phillips that Stone would be Elvis's producer at Atlantic. He also mentioned that Elvis's first record would be "I Got a Woman," which oddly enough was the first song Elvis would record for RCA Victor.

STONE, MIKE

(1939–   ) Hawaiian-born karate expert who in January 1972 became the bodyguard for producer Phil Spector. It was in Stone's capacity as a bodyguard at the Las Vegas Hilton that Elvis first met him (although he had seen him at the Karate Tournament of Champions in Honolulu on May 25, 1968) and suggested he become Priscilla's karate instructor. On August 5, 1973, Ed Parker, Stone's partner in a Los Angeles martial-arts studio, introduced Stone to Priscilla; the two became good friends and eventually lovers. Stone, who wore an "Afro" hairstyle, was called "Mickey" by Priscilla. It has been estimated that Stone had an annual salary of $20,000, on which he supported a wife and two children. In 1972 Stone's wife of six years, Fran, sued him for divorce. She won the house and custody of their two children, Lorie and Shelley. Stone later moved in with Priscilla in her two-bedroom apartment on the Pacific Ocean at Huntington Beach.

Elvis became suspicious that Priscilla was seeing someone. Red West finally told him Priscilla had been seeing Stone. Stone infuriated Elvis when he overstepped his boundaries and told Priscilla when Elvis could see his own daughter, Lisa Marie. According to Sonny West, in 1973 Elvis wanted him to kill Stone for taking away his wife. On June 3, 1980, *The Star* published the first of a three-part article titled "My Secret Love Affair with Priscilla" by Mike Stone (as told to Al Coombes). Stone claimed in the article that if Elvis had taken his life, a contract would have been put out on Elvis by Stone's underworld connections. After two and a half years, Stone and Priscilla broke up in 1975. Stone moved to Las Vegas, where he was employed as a dealer in one of the clubs.

Elvis hated Stone so much that he wouldn't even watch the ABC-TV series "The Streets of San Francisco" because Karl Malden played Detective Mike Stone.

STORM, TEMPEST

Las Vegas stripper who was romantically involved with Elvis for a week in 1957. One magazine called it a "seven-day whirl." Storm, who was once married to actor Herb Jeffries, onetime member of Duke Ellington's band, tells about her relationship with Elvis in her 1987 autobiography *Tempest Storm: The Lady Is a Vamp*, written with Bill Boyd. In the book Tempest says that she last saw Elvis in 1970, when they both attended a Perry Como concert at the International Hotel in Las Vegas. According to her accounts Elvis visited with her in Las Vegas when she was performing in the Minsky Review. Later at 3:00 A.M. Elvis climbed a fence at her hotel in order to spend the night with her.

STOVALL, VERN

Composer, with Bobby George, of the song "Long Black Limousine," which Elvis recorded in 1969.

STRADA, AL

Elvis's wardrobe man at Graceland beginning in 1972. He was originally hired as a guard. Strada was one of several people Elvis employed over the years to handle his wardrobe. Strada and his wife, Sandy, traveled with Elvis on tour. Elvis once bought him a new Porsche.

STRAND THEATRE

Tupelo, Mississippi, theater attended by Elvis in his youth. The other theater in Tupelo was the Lyric. Elvis and his friend, Charles Farrar, enjoyed going to the Strand on Saturdays.

STRAND THEATRE

Memphis theater where the world premiere of *Loving You* took place on July 9, 1957.

STRANGE, BILLY

Guitarist born William E. Strange, who played with both the Ventures and Duane Eddy. Strange composed, with Mac Davis, the following songs that Elvis recorded, "Charro," "Clean Up Your Own Back Yard," "A Little Less Conversation," "Memories," and "Nothingville." Strange, who was a musical director for the Elvis movies *Roustabout*, *Live a Little, Love a Little*, and *The Trouble with Girls*, played guitar on several of Elvis's recording sessions, including *Viva Las Vegas* in 1963.

STRANGER, THE

Novel by Albert Camus. A copy of the book once owned by Elvis sold at a Nashville auction in late 1977 for $70.

STREISAND, BARBRA

(1942–   ) Singer and actress born Barbara Joan Streisand in Brooklyn on April 24, 1942. Streisand was the first performer to appear at the International Hotel in Las Vegas, opening on July 2, 1969. Elvis was the second performer, opening on July 31, after Streisand's successful four-week appearance. Streisand would have been Elvis's leading lady had Elvis accepted her offer to star in the movie *A Star Is Born*. Streisand and Neil Diamond sang in the same chorus at New York's Erasmus High School. Elvis and Priscilla once visited Streisand backstage at the International Hotel. According to Priscilla's autobiography, *Elvis and Me*, Elvis's first question to Streisand was: "What did you see in Elliot Gould; I never could stand him." Streisand shot back that Gould was the father of her child. In 1978 Streisand broke Elvis's record for the highest-paid entertainer in Las Vegas when she signed for $350,000 a week at the Riviera Hotel.

STURGEIN, DR. PHILLIP

Doctor who gave Elvis his blood-group test in 1971 to prove that he was not the father of Jason Parker, as claimed by Jason's mother, Patricia Parker.

STUTTERING

Speech defect that affects men five times as often as women and which affected Elvis. It occurred whenever Elvis talked rapidly or was nervous. In one scene in the 1964 movie *Kissin' Cousins*, Elvis was seen and heard to stutter slightly. He stuttered even more in a scene in *Wild in the Country*, in which he had been drinking. Country singer Mel Tillis consistently stutters whenever he talks, yet when he sings, the stuttering disappears.

STUTZ BLACKHAWK COUPE

Custom automobile bought by Elvis on September 10, 1971, from dealer Jules Meyers for $38,500. Annual production of the car was a hundred units. It was custom handcrafted in Italy from mostly American parts, and included a General Motors frame, suspension, and 490 h.p. engine. Elvis bought the very first Stutz Blackhawk, and Frank Sinatra bought the next

one. On the way to a car wash Elvis's driver totaled the car. Elvis owned three Stutz Bearcats, giving one to his Las Vegas physician, Dr. Elias Ghanem.

SULLIVAN, ED

(See *Ed Sullivan* in Part II)

SULLIVAN, GENE

Member of the Roy Newman and His Boys Band who recorded duets with Wiley Walker in the late 1930s. Sullivan composed, with Walker, the song "When My Blue Moon Turns to Gold Again," which Elvis recorded in 1956.

SULLIVAN, VIRGINIA

(1940–   ) Laurel, Mississippi, woman who claimed in a story in *The Globe* (March 18, 1980) to have been Elvis's secret lover for fourteen years, from 1963 until his death in 1977. Sullivan, the daughter of a preacher, said she first met Elvis at the Club Creole in Mobile, Alabama, in 1955, and that she visited a six-foot two-inch-tall Elvis (Elvis was actually an even six feet tall) on Audubon Drive (which she spelled Abundun Drive). She also claimed that she and Elvis registered at the Holiday Inn as Mr. and Mrs. Frank Thompson. Like so many other women who have claimed to be Elvis's secret lovers, Sullivan says she married another man but divorced him after just two and a half years.

SUMNER, DONNIE

Stepson of J. D. Sumner and a member of the Stamps Quartet and of Voice, both of which were backup vocal groups for Elvis. In concert, Elvis sometimes let Sumner sing solo, as well as singing duet with him on "Spanish Eyes." Sumner composed the song "I Miss You" and "Mr. Songman," both of which Elvis recorded in 1973.

SUMNER, J. D.

(1925–   ) Bass singer, born John Daniel Sumner and nicknamed "Jim Dandy," who had been a friend of Elvis's since Elvis was sixteen years old. Sumner would often let Elvis in through the back door so that he could attend the gospel group concerts in Memphis. Sumner has sung with the Sunshine Boys and, from 1954 to 1965, with the Blackwood Brothers. His vocal group, the Stamps, backed Elvis in many recording sessions and concerts from 1972 to 1977. Elvis gave Sumner a new white Lincoln automobile in October 1976, a $4,000 silver watch, and a $40,000 diamond ring. Deep voiced, the six-foot-five-inch-tall entertainer often sang along with Elvis on "Why Me Lord" and "Help Me" in concert. In 1977 Sumner recorded the tribute record "Elvis Has Left the Building" (QCA 461), and with the Stamps recorded two tribute albums, *Elvis's Favorite Gospel Songs* (QCA 362) in 1977 and *Memories of Our Friend Elvis* (Blue Mark 373) in 1978.

In 1971 Sumner wrote his autobiography, *Gospel Music Is My Life*.

SUN ELVIS

An extensive book written by Howard DeWitt covering Elvis's life from birth until mid-1956. Published by Pierian Press, it goes into Elvis's early years in great depth. *Sun Elvis* is a good companion to Elaine Dundy's excellent *Elvis and Gladys.*

SUN RECORDS

Memphis record label, located at 706 Union Avenue[1] in a studio measuring just thirty by eighteen feet that leased for $150 a month. It was founded by Sam Phillips in 1952, along with the Memphis Recording Service. Before establishing his own label, Phillips leased his recordings of Howlin' Wolf, B. B. King, Little Walter (Walter Horton), Little Junior Parker, and Bobby (Blue) Bland to various labels, including Chess Records and RPM Records. Phillips produced and recorded Jackie Brenston's "Rocket 88" (Chess 1458).[2] In 1953 Phillips

The Sun Records studio as it appears today. (Photo courtesy Don Fink)

recorded his first country songs and his first white artist when he recorded the hillbilly band the Ripley Cotton Choppers. It was the first Sun release to have the word *hillbilly* on the label. Both the Sun offices and the single recording studio with its one piano were located in the small building that had previously housed a radiator shop. In the late 1950s Sun Records moved to 639 Madison Avenue, the present-day home of Sam Phillips's Recording Service, Inc., and where he launched the Phillips International label.

Shelby Singleton bought Sun Records from Sam Phillips in 1969, and moved the firm to Nashville. The historic original Sun building was sold and became home to a plumbing company and then an auto-parts store. The building was somewhat restored by Grayline Tours after Elvis's death. Today the building has been designated a landmark.

"Blues in My Condition"/"Sellin' My Whiskey" by Jackie Boy and Little Walter (Jack Kelly and Walter Horton) was the first Sun recording (Sun 174). Elvis's Sun record releases were:

Sun 209—"That's All Right (Mama)"/"Blue Moon of Kentucky" (July 1954)
Sun 210—"Good Rockin' Tonight"/"I Don't Care If the Sun Don't Shine" (September 1954)
Sun 215—"Milkcow Blues Boogie"/"You're a Heartbreaker" (January 1955)
Sun 217—"I'm Left, You're Right, She's Gone"/"Baby Let's Play House" (April 1955)
Sun 223—"Mystery Train"/"I Forgot to Remember to Forget" (August 1955)

Other songs recorded for Sun, but which were later released by RCA Victor were: "Blue Moon," "Tomorrow Night," "Harbor Lights," "I'll Never Let You Go (Little Darlin')," "I Love You Because," "Just Because," "When It Rains, It Really Pours," and "Tryin' to Get to You." RCA Victor has also released some alternate takes of the Sun sessions.

Elvis may have recorded the following songs for Sun that were never released (they may have been recorded over, since Sam Phillips reused tapes to save money): "Always Late (with Your Kisses)," "Blue Guitar," "Cryin' Heart Blues," "I Got a Woman," "Maybellene," "Down the Line," "Satisfied," "Give Me More, More, More," "Gone," "Night Train to Memphis," "Tennessee Saturday Night," "That's the Stuff You Gotta Watch," and "Uncle Pen," among others. (See *The Elvis Presley Album of Jukebox Favorites, Sam Phillips, Shelby Singleton, Flip Records, Little Junior Parker, Memphis Recording Service*)

SUNRISE HOSPITAL

Las Vegas medical facility where Elvis went for treatment on several occasions.

SURBER, RAYMOND

Automobile salesman at Memphis's Schilling Lincoln-Mercury, located at 987 Union Avenue, where on September 23, 1974, Elvis bought the dealer's entire stock of five Lincoln Continental Mark IVs, in the colors aqua, red, silver, blue, and black. The total sale was over $60,000. Surber's commission was approximately $4,000.

SURFERS

Group consisting of members Clayton Naluai, Patrick Sylva, Alan Naluai, and Bernard Ching, who sang vocals on Elvis's recording session at Radio Recorders in Hollywood on March 21–23, 1961, for the movie *Blue Hawaii.*

SUZORE NO. 2 THEATER

Neighborhood theater, located at 279 N. Main in Memphis, that Elvis frequented during high school. Elvis and his girlfriend, Dixie Locke, attended movies there

---

[1]Brad Suggs recorded a song on Phillips International Records titled "706 Union Avenue" (Phillips 3545). "706 Union Avenue," composed by Carl Perkins, was sung by the Tennessee Three in the 1970 movie *Little Fauss and Big Halsy.*
[2]"Rocket 88" is one of about a dozen songs in contention by rock music historians as having been the first rock & roll record.

in 1953 and 1954. Sometimes after the show they would get something to eat at Charlie's, right across the street. On July 7, 1954, the night Dewey Phillips first played "That's All Right (Mama)," Elvis went to the Suzore No. 2 to see *The Best Years of Our Lives* because he was too shy to hear his own record on the radio.

SWAN, BILLY

(1942–   ) Singer and composer born in Cape Girardeau, Missouri, on May 12, 1942. Swan was once employed as a gate guard at Graceland and boarded for a time at Travis Smith's house. Before becoming a recording artist and later a producer, he and Kris Kristofferson were employed as janitors at the Columbia Records studios in Nashville. Swan composed and recorded "I Can Help" (Monument 8612) in 1974, which Elvis recorded in 1975. Swan recorded "Don't Be Cruel" (Monument 45275) in 1979.

SWEET INSPIRATIONS

Grammy award–winning female vocal group that sang backup for Elvis in concert dates and on some recording sessions for eight years. The group originally was the backup vocal group for Aretha Franklin. Members were: Emily (Cissy) Houston (the mother of 1980s superstar Whitney Houston),[1] Myrna Smith (wife of Jerry Schilling), Estelle Brown, and Sylvia Shenwell. The group recorded a number of songs for Atlantic Records, the most successful being "Sweet Inspiration" (Atlantic 2476)[2] in 1968. Elvis asked to use the group after he heard them on record. After Elvis's death, the Sweet Inspirations joined Rick Nelson's show and are today a solo act. The group appeared in the 1979 TV movie *Elvis* and in the 1980 movie *The Idolmaker*.

At some Elvis concerts, the Sweet Inspirations started the show off by singing about fifteen minutes worth of Aretha Franklin's biggest hit songs. They sang "Sweet, Sweet Spirit" at the Pontiac, Michigan, concert on December 31, 1975, while Elvis changed his ripped pants.

On July 20, 1975, in Northfolk, Virginia, two of the Sweet Inspirations walked off stage after being in-

sulted by Elvis. Elvis then presented the remaining member, Myrna Smith, with a ring. She later insisted he take it back, after which Elvis apologized to all involved, and presented them rings worth $5,000 apiece.

The Sweet Inspirations recorded "Let It Be Me" (Atlantic 2418) in 1967, and Elvis recorded the song in 1970. They recorded "Unchained Melody" (Atlantic 2551) in 1968, and Elvis recorded the song in 1977. Elvis sang the Sweet Inspirations' hit "Sweet Inspiration" in concert.

SWEETPEA

Gladys Presley's pet dog at the time of her death in 1958. Sweetpea was named for the adopted son of cartoon sailor Popeye.

Elvis and Sweetpea. (Photo courtesy Eddie Brandt's Saturday Matinee)

---

[1] In December 1987 Houston broke a record previously held by Elvis when she charted six consecutive number one songs. Elvis charted five consecutive number one songs.

[2] The group was actually named after the song, which had been written for them. Two of Aretha Franklin's sisters, Carolyn and Erma, were original members of the group.

2D-33501

The 1958 Tennessee license plate number of the Cadillac that Elvis drove to the Army induction center on Monday, March 24, 1958.

2X-139

The 1962 Tennessee license number of Elvis's Gold Cadillac. (See *Gold Cadillac*)

12

Size of Elvis's Army combat boots.

21

Age of Elvis when his character, Clint Reno, died in the 1956 movie *Love Me Tender*, the halfway point of Elvis's life. Twenty-one years later, in 1977, Elvis would die again, but this time for real.

24

Number of teddy bears that Elvis won at a carnival in 1956.

25 PERCENT

Colonel Tom Parker's portion of Elvis's income for his managerial/agent services until 1967, when he escalated it to 50 percent.

282

Number of teddy bears Elvis received for Christmas in 1956. He revealed the fact on "The Ed Sullivan Show" of January 6, 1957.

2001 ENIGMA

Interesting mathematical computation relating to various details of Elvis's life, all of which add up to 2001.

Month Elvis died	8	Day Elvis was born	8
Day Elvis died	16	Day Elvis died	16
Year Elvis died	1977	Age Elvis died	42
	2001	Year Elvis was born	1935
			2001

$2,424.41

Cost of the train trip from Memphis to Hollywood for Elvis and six of his buddies when they rented a private railroad car nicknamed EP1 on the Southern Pacific Sunset Limited in 1960. Elvis was scheduled to begin filming *G.I. Blues*.

$23,789.73

Cost of Elvis's burial at Graceland.

3,166

Number of floral arrangements delivered to Graceland on August 17–18, 1977.

$220,000

Value of jewelry given away by Elvis during his performances in Asheville, North Carolina (July 22–24, 1975).

$250,000

Amount received by Priscilla Presley in 1979 for the rights to Elvis's home movies. They included footage of his wedding and stag parties.

2571459

Elvis's Tennessee driver's license number, issued on September 18, 1975.

TACKET, ABNER

Husband of Nancy J. Burdine and the father of six children, including twins Jerome and Martha Tacket. Abner was the grandfather of Octavia (Doll) Mansell, the great-grandfather of Gladys Smith, and the great-great-grandfather of Elvis Presley.

TACKET, MARTHA

(1852–1887) Daughter of Abner and Nancy J. Burdine Tacket and twin sister of Jerome Tacket. On January 22, 1870, she married White Mansell. White and Martha Tacket Mansell parented Octavia (Doll) Mansell. Martha was the grandmother of Gladys Smith and the great-grandmother of Elvis Presley.

TANKEL, TOLL AND LEAVITT

Los Angeles law firm retained by Priscilla Presley in her divorce proceedings in 1973. They charged that Elvis didn't make a full disclosure of his assets to Priscilla.

TASSEL, LUCILLE VAN

Founder of the spiritualist organization, Luxis Circle, in Sherman Oaks, California, who in an article in *The Star* claimed that after his death, Elvis appeared before her in early July 1978.

TAUROG, NORMAN

(1899–1981) Former child actor turned director, born April 7, 1899. Taurog directed many popular films, including: *The Adventures of Tom Sawyer* (1938), *Boys Town* (1938), and *Young Tom Edison* (1940). He directed the following Elvis movies: *G.I. Blues* (1960), *Blue Hawaii* (1961), *Girls! Girls! Girls!* (1962), *It Happened at the World's Fair* (1963), *Tickle Me* (1965), *Spinout* (1966), *Double Trouble* (1967), *Speedway* (1968), and *Live a Little, Love a Little* (1968). During the production of *Spinout*, Elvis, out of character, lost his temper with Taurog and the film crew. Taurog died on April 7, 1981, at the age of eighty-two, one day before the death of five-star general Omar Bradley, another man Elvis admired.

Elvis enjoyed working with Taurog, who had coincidentally directed many of the comedies of Dean Martin and Jerry Lewis. Martin had been Elvis's singing idol. Elvis bought Taurog a Cadillac, delivering it himself to his Bel Air home, as well as a Sony video recorder, one of the first on the market. Taurog once said of Elvis, "I was always proud of his work, even if I wasn't too proud of the scripts. I always felt that he never reached his peak."

TAYLOR, BILL

(1932–   ) Trumpet player who was a member of Clyde Leoppard's Snearly Ranch Boys. Taylor recorded some rock & roll songs under the name William Tell Taylor. Taylor wrote, with Stan Kesler, the song "I'm Left, You're Right, She's Gone," which Elvis recorded in 1954.

TAYLOR, CHUCK

Composer, with Gerald Nelson and Fred Burch, of the song "The Love Machine," which Elvis sang in the 1967 movie *Easy Come, Easy Go.*

TAYLOR, JAMES

(1948–   ) Singer and composer born on March 12, 1948, in Boston. Taylor has recorded a number of hit songs, including "Fire and Rain," "You've Got a Friend," and "How Sweet It Is." Peter Asher (of Peter and Gordon) is Taylor's manager. Taylor was once married to singer Carly Simon, daughter of Richard Simon, the cofounder of the publishing firm of Simon and Schuster. Taylor's younger sister, Kate, and brother, Livingston, are also recording artists. Elvis's concert version of Taylor's "Steamroller Blues" from the "Elvis: Aloha from Hawaii" TV special was released as a single in 1973.

TAYLOR, RIP

(1934–   ) Comedian born on January 14, 1934. Taylor hosted the 1978 syndicated TV game show "The $1.98 Beauty Contest." Taylor was one of Elvis's favorite comedians. Elvis often went to the Sahara Hotel in Las Vegas to watch him perform. Taylor once remarked to his audience, "I'm the only act in Las Vegas who is *not* doing an Elvis imitation."

TAYLOR, TERRI

(1939–   ) Nebraska woman, born Gloria Lahrs, who it is claimed mothered a child by Elvis. According to Taylor, she first met Elvis in 1955 in Bossier City, Louisiana. She was fifteen years old and traveling and performing as a singer. Taylor (a.k.a. Gloria Stiles) claims that it was while Elvis was performing in Lincoln and Omaha, Nebraska, in February or March of 1957, that she became pregnant with Elvis's child. On December 22, 1957, at St. Elizabeth's Hospital in Lincoln, Nebraska, her child, Candy Jo, was born. Reportedly, Elvis telephoned Taylor and sent her a few checks over the years. She claimed that Elvis remained good friends and that they stayed in touch even through Taylor's two marriages (similar to Lucy de Barbin's claim).

In an interview in the *Midnight Globe* (April 15, 1978) Taylor claimed that Elvis called her one day in 1961 and sang her a "new" song he was recording and asked her what she thought of it. The song was "All Shook Up." Any Elvis fan should know that Elvis recorded "All Shook Up" in 1957, not 1961.

Although several people have substantiated Taylor's story, the records indicate that Elvis did not perform in Nebraska in 1957. (See *Candy Jo Fuller*)

TAYLOR'S RESTAURANT

Memphis restaurant located at 710 Union Avenue, next door to Sun Records. Sun artists, including Elvis, would meet at Taylor's to eat and talk. In the mid-1950s, while recording with Sun, Roy Orbison lived in a two-room apartment above the restaurant, which had been established in 1949. Producer Jack Clement once joked that the secret of Sun Records was the popularity of Taylor's Restaurant.[1]

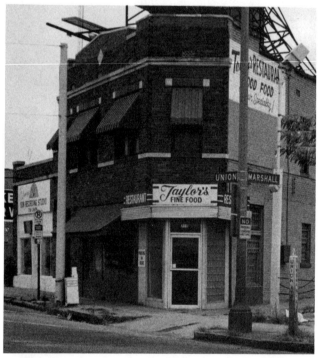

Taylor's Restaurant, next door to Sun Studios. (Photo courtesy Don Fink)

TCB

Taking Care of Business.[2] This was Elvis's business motto and working philosophy. Elvis gave fourteen-carat gold ID bracelets to his male friends, with TCB and their nicknames inscribed on them. Each was worth $175. The letters TCB appeared with lightning bolts through them, which symbolized the Memphis

---

[1]Across the street from the Ryman Auditorium in Nashville was Tootsie's bar and restaurant, where many of the performers would meet and talk.

[2]"Taking Care of Business" was the title of the NBC-TV special broadcast on December 9, 1968, featuring Diana Ross and the Supremes, and the Temptations. The soundtrack album sold over a million copies. The Supremes and the Temptations first appeared together on "The Ed Sullivan Show." "Takin' Care of Business" was a hit record by Bachman-Turner Overdrive (Mercury 73487) in 1974.

Mafia. Elvis was buried with a diamond ring bearing the initials TCB. The emblem was designed by Lee Ableseron, the partner of jeweler Sol Schwartz. A large TCB emblem stands at the head of Elvis's grave at Graceland.

In Kathy Westmoreland's autobiography she states that Elvis once told her about the origin of the insignia. It came about on a dark and stormy night when a lightning bolt struck a marble statue in the Meditation Gardens. The pattern that was left resembled the bolt that had struck it. Elvis interpreted the event as a sign from God. (See *TLC*)

TCB BAND
Band that backed Elvis during his concert appearances in the 1970s. Members included: Hal Blaine (drums), Jerry Scheff (guitar), Ronnie Tutt (drums), James Burton (lead guitar), Joe Osborne (bass), John Wilkinson (rhythm guitar), Marty Harrell (trombone), Pat Houson (trumpet), Glen D. Hardin (piano), and others.

TECHNICAL ADVISOR: TOM PARKER
Credit that appeared in most Elvis films. Beginning in 1967, Parker received 50 percent of Elvis's income, in addition to being paid as the technical advisor on his films. Parker made more money from Elvis's films than Elvis did.

TEDDY BEAR
Cute toy bear created in 1902 by Morris Michton, founder of the Ideal Toy Company. Michton named the toy after President Theodore Roosevelt, who was once photographed with a cute little bear. The original toy bear is on display at the Smithsonian Institution.

Elvis began collecting teddy bears after a rumor was started that he did collect them, prompted by his hit record "Teddy Bear." Fans sent him thousands for his nonexistent collection. On December 26, 1957, Elvis donated a truckload of teddy bears to the National Foundation for Infantile Paralysis. In 1957 he spent $600 at the Memphis Tri-State Fair in order to win teddy bears for his fans.

In Las Vegas, while he sang his hit "Teddy Bear," Elvis would often toss small teddy bears into the audience.

TEDDY BEAR OF ZIZIPOMPOM
French poodle that Elvis obtained in October 1960.

TELEPHONE NUMBERS
Unlisted telephone numbers of Elvis. He had given the numbers to President Richard M. Nixon in a letter he wrote to him.

Beverly Hills	Memphis
278-3496	397-4427
278-5935	398-4882
	398-9722
Palm Springs	
325-3241	

Elvis also included Colonel Tom Parker's telephone numbers.

Beverly Hills: 274-8498
Palm Springs: 325-4781
Memphis: 870-0370

TEN OUTSTANDING YOUNG MEN OF AMERICA
Award presented to Elvis on January 9, 1971, by the U.S. Jaycees. Others selected were: Ron Ziegler (White House aide), Jim Goetz (owner of a chain of radio

Elvis and Priscilla at the U.S. Jaycees prayer breakfast. Elvis was being honored as one of the Ten Outstanding Young Men in America. (Photo courtesy Wide World Photos)

stations), Capt. William Bucha (Medal of Honor winner), Wendell Cherry (part owner of the Kentucky Colonels basketball team), George J. Todaro (cancer scientist), Dr. Mario R. Capecchi (Harvard biophysicist), Thomas Atkins (first black Boston city councilman), Thomas Coll (founder of the Revitalization Corps), and Walter S. Humann (one of the developers of the U.S. Postal System). They received their awards from U.S. Jaycees president Gordon Thomas.

It was the only award that Elvis ever received in person. Upon accepting it, Elvis remarked, "I am very humbled by this award, not so much in receiving it but receiving it in the company of the other nine men honored here today. . . . I learned very early in life that, without a song, the day would never end, without a song, a man ain't got a friend, without a song, the road would never bend, without a song, so I'll keep singing the song. Goodnight."

TEN YEARS AFTER
Successful rock band of the 1960s who gave themselves that name because they formed in 1966, ten years after Elvis began.

TENNESSEE BOARD OF MEDICAL EXAMINERS
Medical governing board that in September 1979 charged Dr. George Nichopoulos with gross negligence in overprescribing drugs for his patient Elvis Presley. Dr. Nichopoulos was accused of prescribing 5,684 pills for Elvis in the seven months before Elvis's death. Among the pills were Quaaludes, Dexedrine, and Demerol, a narcotic painkiller.

TENNESSEE KARATE INSTITUTE
Memphis martial-arts studio, located at 1372 Overton (above a Rexall drugstore), founded by Red West and Elvis's first cousin Bobby Mann. Elvis gave a ninety-minute demonstration and lecture on karate at the studio on July 4, 1974.

TEPPER, SID
(1918–   ) Composer born in New York City on June 25, 1918. Tepper composed, with Ben Weisman, "There Is So Much World to See," which Elvis sang in his 1967 movie *Double Trouble*. (For a list of Sid Tepper's forty-two compositions with Roy C. Bennett, see *Roy C. Bennett*)

THARPE, SISTER ROSETTA
Gospel singer whose recordings were played over Tupelo radio station WELO on Sunday afternoons in the late 1940's. Elvis often listened to her program. She composed "Saved," which Elvis sang in his 1968 TV special "Elvis."

THOMAS, B. J.
(1942–   ) Singer born in Houston on August 7, 1942, as Billy Joe Thomas. B. J. used the first two initials of his name so as not to be confused with singer Billy Joe Royal. He recorded the theme song of the 1969 movie *Butch Cassidy and the Sundance Kid*, a Burt Bacharach–Hal David composition titled "Raindrops Keep Fallin' on My Head." Elvis recorded several of Thomas's hits, "I Just Can't Help Believin'" (Scepter 12283), "It's Only Love" (Scepter 12244), and "Tomorrow Never Comes" (Scepter 12165). Elvis also sang Thomas's "Hooked On a Feeling" (Scepter 12230) in concert. Both Thomas and Elvis recorded Hank Williams's "I'm So Lonesome I Could Cry." In 1978 Thomas, with Jerry B. Jenkins, wrote his autobiography, *Home Where I Belong*, which told about his singing career, his drug problems, and his eventual discovery of God.

Elvis, who was a fan of Thomas's, mentioned him by name during the Las Vegas concert in his 1970 movie *Elvis—That's the Way It Is*.

THOMAS, JOE
Composer of the song "Anyplace Is Paradise," which Elvis recorded in 1956. With Howard Biggs, Joe Thomas composed "I'm Gonna Sit Right Down and Cry (Over You)," which Elvis recorded in 1956.

THOMAS, RUFUS
(1917–   ) Rhythm & blues singer, born in Cayce, Mississippi, on March 26, 1917. Thomas was a disc jockey on Memphis radio station WDIA in the 1950s, and became the first black disc jockey to play Elvis records on a regular basis. He recorded "Tiger Man (King of the Jungle)" for Sun Records on June 30, 1953 (Sun 188). In 1963 Thomas recorded "Walking the Dog" (Stax 140). He recorded several more songs based on the dance called "The Dog," such as "The Dog," "Can Your Monkey Do the Dog," and "Somebody Stole My Dog." Thomas portrayed Tee-Tot, the old black musician who taught Hank Williams to play the guitar, in the 1980 TV special "Hank Williams: the Man and His Music."

Thomas is the father of soul singer Carla Thomas, the "Queen of the Memphis Sound," whose biggest hits were "Gee Whiz (Look at His Eyes)" (Atlantic 2086) (Stax Records' first Gold Record) in 1961 and "B-A-B-Y" (Stax 195) in 1966. Carla has a degree in English literature from Howard University.

Rufus Thomas's "Tiger Man" can be heard playing on the Crown Electric delivery truck's radio in the 1979 TV movie *Elvis*. Elvis recorded "Tiger Man" in 1968. (See *Hound Dog, Bear Cat*)

Thomas once said, "Elvis gave an injection to black music that no black artist had ever done."

THOMPSON, JAY
(1935–   ) Disc jockey who hosted "The Hillbilly Hit Parade" at KSTB radio in Breckenridge, Texas.[1] Thompson interviewed Elvis in Wichita Falls, Texas, on April 10, 1956 according to RCA. (The actual date was probably April 13.) His interview appeared on several albums, including *Elvis—A Legendary Performer, Volume 2* and *The Sun Years*.

THOMPSON, LINDA DIANE
Woman who was romantically involved with Elvis in the 1970s. Thompson was voted the Best Dressed Coed at Memphis State University, where she majored in English. The five-foot-nine-inch-tall Thompson won the titles of Miss Liberty Bowl and Miss Memphis State, in addition to having been the third runner-up in the Miss USA Pageant. She lived with Elvis at Graceland for four and a half years, from 1972 to 1976. When Elvis was admitted to Baptist Memorial Hospital for eighteen days in November 1973, Thompson stayed with him in the same room. The hospital bent its rules and supplied her with a cot. In 1975 Elvis gave her a rag doll that she named Patty Alice. It is estimated that Elvis spent more than a million dollars on jewelry for Linda during their romance. It's been reported that just before breaking up with Elvis she ran up a large number of purchases on his credit cards (estimated at $30,000). She claims she left Elvis because she was

---

[1] Fellow disc jockey Benny Hill composed the song "Blue Days, Black Nights," which Buddy Holly recorded in 1956 (Decca 29854).

Linda Thompson. (Photo courtesy Eddie Brandt's Saturday Matinee)

tired of seeing him self-destruct on drugs. According to the book *Are You Lonesome Tonight?*, in July 1976 Elvis had John O'Grady "throw Linda out [of Graceland]."

Thompson has been a regular on TV's "Hee Haw," and has appeared on episodes of "Starsky and Hutch" and "Bustin' Loose." She made her acting debut in an episode of "The Rookies" titled "Shadow of A Man." She also appeared in Joan Rivers's movie *Rabbit Test (1978)*. Thompson recorded the single "Ooh, What a Night Part 1"/"Ooh, What a Night Part 2" (RCA 19453).

THOMPSON, SAM
Security guard at Graceland and one of Elvis's bodyguards in the 1970s. Thompson was a former police officer and the brother of Linda Thompson. It was Sam who delivered to Elvis Linda's "Dear John" letter after the two had broken up.

THORNTON, JOHN
Composer, with Piney Brown, Ralph Bass, and Earl Washington, of the song "Just a Little Bit," which Elvis recorded in 1973.

THORNTON, MARY ANN
Missouri woman who claims that God told her to seek out Elvis in 1973 to help him find God. In 1979 her book *Even Elvis* was published by New Leaf Press.

THORNTON, WILLIE MAE
(1926–) Blues artist born in Montgomery, Alabama, on December 11, 1926. Thornton is the daughter of a minister. Influenced by Bessie Smith, she in turn influenced Janis Joplin, who recorded Thornton's "Ball and Chain." In August 1952 in Los Angeles, Thornton (backed by Johnny Otis on vibes and Peter [Guitar] Lewis on lead guitar) originally recorded "Hound Dog" (Peacock 1612). In the same session she recorded "They Call Me Big Mama," the origin of her nickname, "Big Mama." She received only $500 for her version of "Hound Dog."

In Thornton's later years she began to tell writers how she had been "ripped off" by Elvis with her song "Hound Dog," creating the false belief that she had written it, whereas the composers were Jerry Leiber and Mike Stoller. Her story became the subject of an unfair book that discussed the exploitation of black artists and how Elvis had exploited Thornton's song "Hound Dog." In reality it was Thornton who was doing the exploiting by convincing people she had written somebody else's song.

THOSE AMAZING ANIMALS
ABC-TV prime-time series that aired from August 24, 1980, to August 23, 1981, cohosted by Burgess Meredith, Priscilla Presley, and Jim Stafford. It was Priscilla's first TV series.

THROUGH MY EYES
Tentative title of Elvis's autobiography, which he had planned to write one day to set the record straight about his life. According to Lucy de Barbin in her book *Are You Lonesome Tonight?*, Elvis wanted her to help him write the book.

THUNDERBIRD LOUNGE
Memphis nightclub owned by Fred Alfans, located at 750 Adams Avenue, where Elvis's New Year's Eve party took place on December 31, 1968. The house band was Flash and the Board of Directors, and guest musicians included B. J. Thomas, Ronnie Milsap, and former Sun artist Billy Lee Riley.

THURSDAY
Day of the week on which both Elvis and Vernon Presley were buried (Elvis on August 18, 1977, and Vernon on June 28, 1979).

TILLOTSON, JOHNNY
(1939–) Popular singer of the 1960s born in Jacksonville, Florida, on April 20, 1939. Tillotson is a former country disc jockey for Palatka, Florida, radio station WWPF. Tillotson, who had been a member of Mae Axton's high school English class in 1954–55, interviewed Elvis in Jacksonville in August 1956. He got Elvis's attention by imitating his singing of "Baby Baby Ba Ba Baby," which Elvis enjoyed. Tillotson became popular in both the country and pop fields ("Poetry in Motion" [Cadence 1384] went to number two on the charts). As a singer and composer he wrote the Hank Locklin hit "Send Me the Pillow You Dream On" (RCA

7127) and sang the theme song of the TV series "Gidget" (starring Sally Field). In 1969 Elvis recorded the Tillotson composition "It Keeps Right on a-Hurtin'," which Tillotson had recorded in 1962 (Cadence 1418). Tillotson and Elvis both recorded versions of "Pledging My Love," "I'm So Lonesome I Could Cry," and "Funny How Time Slips Away." (See *Jacksonville, Florida*)

TIMBRELL, H. J. (TINY)
Session musician who played guitar on Elvis's recording sessions at Radio Recorders in Hollywood from 1957 to 1966, playing on the soundtracks of thirteen Elvis movies from *Loving You* to *Easy Come, Easy Go.*

TIPLEY III, COLEMAN
RCA Victor Records executive who signed the contract that sent Elvis from the Sun label to RCA Victor on November 20, 1955.

T.J.'S
Memphis nightclub managed by former Memphis Mafia member Alan Fortas, in which Elvis held a few New Year's Eve parties. In 1969 country singers Ronnie Milsap and Mark James were the featured entertainers.

TLC
Tender Loving Care.[1] Elvis gave gold necklaces to his girlfriends and to the wives and girlfriends of his male friends. The letters TLC, with a lightning bolt through them, appeared on the necklaces. The lightning bolt symbolized the West Coast Mafia.

TO ELVIS WITH LOVE
A 1979 book by Lena Canada about a young cerebral palsy victim named Karen and her relationship with Elvis as a pen pal. It was made into a 1980 TV movie titled *Touched by Love.* (See *Karen*)

TOBIAS, CHARLES
(1898–1970) Composer born in New York City. Tobias was the brother of composers Harry Tobias and Henry Tobias and the father of composer Fred Tobias, who also composed a song that Elvis recorded. Charles Tobias wrote such standards as "Don't Sit Under the Apple Tree" and "The Old Lamplighter." He composed, with Albert T. Frisch, the song "The Wonderful World of Christmas," which Elvis recorded in 1971. (See *Fred Tobias*)

TOBIAS, FRED
(1928–) Composer born in New York City on March 25, 1928, the son of composer Charles Tobias. Fred Tobias composed, with Paul Evans, the song "Blue River," which Elvis recorded in 1966.

TOMLIN, DON
One of Elvis's bodyguards. Tomlin, a karate black belt, obtained the job through his friend J. D. Sumner.

TOO SOON THE HERO
Article about Elvis written by Abbie Hoffman for *Crawdaddy* magazine.

TORME, MEL
(1925–) Popular jazz singer and crooner born Melvin Howard Torme on September 13, 1925, and nicknamed the "Velvet Fog." Torme, who once sang with the Chico Marx band, was the voice of Joe Corntassel on the radio series "Little Orphan Annie." He authored the 1970 book *The Other Side of the Rainbow*, about the later years of singer Judy Garland.

A prolific songwriter, Torme wrote "The Christmas Song," which was a big hit for Nat (King) Cole (Capitol 3561) in 1946. Torme sang "Blue Moon" in the 1948 movie *Words and Music* and recorded "Comin' Home" (Atlantic 2165) in 1962. "Comin' Home" was used as the instrumental theme for introducing the members of Elvis's TCB Band.[2]

Elvis liked Torme (who hated rock & roll and let it be known) about as much as he liked Robert Goulet. Elvis once shot out a TV set with his .357 Magnum when Torme appeared on the screen.

TORRE, JANICE
New Orleans–born composer who, with Fred Spielman, wrote the song "I Don't Want To," which Elvis sang in the 1962 movie *Girls! Girls! Girls!*

TRADER, BILL
(1922–) Composer born William Marvin Trader in Darlington, South Carolina, on May 11, 1922. Trader composed the song "(Now and Then There's) a Fool Such as I," which Elvis recorded in 1958.

TRAVIS, MERLE ROBERT
(1917–) Singer, songwriter, and cartoonist born in Ebenezer, Kentucky, on November 29, 1917. Travis composed and originally recorded "Sixteen Tons"/ "Dark As a Dungeon" (Capitol 48001) and "Nine Pound Hammer" (Capitol 15124), all of which it is believed Elvis may have recorded. Travis appeared in the 1953 movie *From Here to Eternity*, in which he sang his composition "Re-enlistment Blues."

TREE OF LIFE
Medallion that Marty Lacker and the boys gave Elvis as a birthday present on January 8, 1967. Elvis wore it until his death.

TREE PUBLISHING COMPANY
Nashville music-publishing firm founded in 1956 by Jack Stapp. Tree Publishing obtained the publishing rights to "Heartbreak Hotel" as one of their first songs.

TRIBBLE, ILADEAN
(1932–)Forty-four-year-old widow, with four adult children, who claimed that she and Elvis were to be married at the First Baptist Church in Athens, Ala-

---

[1]In 1960 Jimmie Rodgers recorded a song titled "Tender Love and Care (T.L.C.)" (Roulette 4218).
[2]In 1954 Torme recorded the song "Tutti Fruitti" (Coral 61263), but it was not the same song that Elvis would later record.

bama, on April 17, 1976. Earlier that month Tribble placed the announcement in the local paper. Five hundred people showed up for the wedding. Her mother, Mrs. Homer McLamore, finally realized they had been victims of a hoax.

TRUTH ABOUT ELVIS, THE
A book by Jess Stern and Larry Geller, published in 1980 by Jove Books. (See *Larry Geller*)

TRYIN' TO GET TO YOU
Book written by Valerie Harms and published by Atheneum Press in 1979. Harms, who claims to have started the first Elvis fan club in 1955, made a few mistakes in her book, such as spelling the Jordanaires as the *Jordonnaires*, and anachronisms such as Elvis singing "Blue Suede Shoes" at Humes High in December 1952.

TSCHECHOWA, VERA
Teenage German actress occasionally dated by Elvis while he was stationed in West Germany from 1958 to 1960.

TUAL, BLANCHARD L.
Memphis entertainment attorney who was appointed by a probate court in May 1980 as Lisa Marie's guardian and to investigate Elvis's assets with respect to his business relationship with Colonel Tom Parker. It was Tual's determination that Parker had "violated his duty to Elvis and to the estate." The judge ruled that any payments from Elvis's estate to Parker should cease and instructed Tual to file charges against Parker in order to recover money already paid to him. Parker was no longer entitled to half of Elvis's earnings after Elvis's death. In 1983, in an out-of-court settlement between Parker and RCA, Parker was paid $2 million for his interests in Elvis's recordings. He sold his merchandising rights to Factors Etc., Inc., and he also agreed not to use or mention Elvis's name again.

TUBB, ERNEST
(1914–1984) Singer born in Crisp, Texas, on February 9, 1914. Tubb composed, with Johnny Bond, "Tomorrow Never Comes," which he recorded in 1949 (Decca 46106), and which Elvis recorded in 1970. When he was a lad in 1936, Jimmie Rodgers's widow gave Tubb one of her husband's guitars. In 1940 Tubb began a long association with Decca Records. His record store, the Ernest Tubb Record Store in Nashville, is world famous. It was out of that shop that publicist Gabe Tucker worked. Elvis appeared on Ernest Tubb's radio program, "Midnight Jamboree," the same night he made his only appearance on the Grand Ole Opry, October 2, 1954. Tubb wrote and recorded, "I'm Walking the Floor over You," which has been recorded by several people, including Bing Crosby. Tubb's son, Justin Tubb, toured with Elvis from January to April 1956.

Tubb, who in 1965 was inducted into the Country Music Hall of Fame, was portrayed by Ed Moates in the 1980 TV special "Hank Williams: The Man and His Music."

TUBB, JUSTIN WAYNE
(1935–   ) Singer and songwriter son of Ernest Tubb, born in San Antonio, Texas, on August 20, 1935. As a client of Gabe Tucker's, Tubb joined Elvis's tour in 1956, but complained to Tucker about Elvis getting too much attention from the audience. When Elvis heard about the complaint he became upset.

TUCKER, GABE
Musician, who played bass and fiddle for Eddy Arnold in 1955, after which he became an employee of Colonel Tom Parker. In 1956 Tucker became the manager of singer Justin Tubb who, through Parker, joined Elvis's tour. In the 1960s, through Parker's help, Tucker went to work for the William Morris Agency. Tucker authored, with Marge Crumbaker of the *Houston Post*, the 1981 book *Up and Down with Elvis: The Inside Story*.

Tucker, like Tommy Sands, Oscar Davis, Hank Snow, Horace Logan, and others, has claimed to be the first to suggest to Colonel Tom Parker that Parker should become Elvis's manager.

TUCKER, TOMMY
(1934–1982) Singer born Robert Higgenbotham in Springfield, Ohio, on March 5, 1934. Tucker, who was a Golden Gloves boxer in the early 1950s, composed and recorded his biggest hit, "Hi-Heel Sneakers" (Checker 1067), in 1964. Elvis recorded "High Heel Sneakers" (note the spelling change) in 1967.

TUESDAY
Day of the week on which both Elvis and Vernon Presley died (Elvis on August 16, 1977 and Vernon on June 26, 1979).

TUPELO GARMENT COMPANY
Milltown, Mississippi, firm, located on South Green Street, where Gladys Presley was employed as a sewing-machine operator, beginning in December 1932 at two dollars a day. Gladys quit working there in 1935, after the birth of Elvis.

TUPELO HARDWARE COMPANY
Main Street store in Tupelo, Mississippi, where in January 1946 Gladys Presley bought Elvis his first guitar, a $7.75 model,[1] which was sold to her by Mr. Forrest L. Bobo, the proprietor.[2] Elvis was taught to play the guitar by his two uncles, Johnny Smith and Vester Presley. His father Vernon said that "he never met a guitar player who was worth a damn." (See *Forrest L. Bobo*)

---

[1]Other first guitars include: Chuck Berry's ($4), B. B. King's ($8), Lonnie Mack's ($10), George Benson's ($15), Denny Dia's (of Steely Dan) ($5), Pop Staple's (of the Staple Singers) ($5). Buddy Holly bought Waylon Jennings his first bass guitar. Steve Miller was given his first guitar and lessons by Les Paul (Miller was five years old). Bill Haley made his first guitar out of cardboard.
[2]Likewise, singer Hank Williams's mother also gave her son his first guitar, a $3.50 model, when he was seven years old.

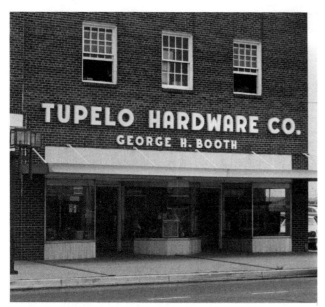

Tupelo Hardware Co. (Photo courtesy Don Fink)

TUPELO, MISSISSIPPI

Lee County town credited as the birthplace of Elvis Presley on January 8, 1935, at 4:35 A.M. The name Tupelo was derived from the Chickasaw Indian word for "lodging place." Actually, Elvis was born in East Tupelo, which wasn't annexed by Tupelo until 1948. The population of Tupelo at the time of Elvis's birth was approximately 6,000 people. Previously the town had been called Gum Pond. In 1936 Tupelo was the first town to be provided electricity by the Tennessee Valley Authority (TVA). George (Machine Gun) Kelly (real name George Barnes) once robbed the Citizens State Bank in Tupelo of $17,000. Blues singer Howlin' Wolf was born in West Point, not far from Tupelo.

"Tupelo" was the title of a 1961 blues song recorded by John Lee Hooker on Vee Jay Records (Vee Jay 366), telling about the great flood of 1936 (through which the Presleys lived). Tupelo is mentioned in the lyrics of Bobbie Gentry's number one hit song "Ode to Billie Joe" (Capitol 5950).

TURK, ROY

(1892–1934) Composer born in New York City on September 20, 1892. Turk composed, with Lou Handman, the song "Are You Lonesome Tonight?", which Elvis recorded in 1960.

TURMAN, T. A.

Doctor who delivered Lisa Marie Presley at the Baptist Memorial Hospital on February 1, 1968.

TURNER, BIG JOE

(1911–1985) Blues singer born Joseph Vernon Turner in Kansas City, Missouri, on May 18, 1911. Turner composed the original version of "Shake, Rattle and Roll" (Atlantic 1026) in 1954, and cowrote with Charles Calhoun (Jesse Stone) the song "Flip, Flop and Fly," which

Turner recorded in 1955 (Atlantic 1053). Elvis recorded both songs. Turner died of a heart attack on November 24, 1985.

TURNER, TITUS

Singer who in 1959 charted the song "We Told You Not to Marry" (Glover 201), and in 1961 charted "Sound-Off" (Jamie 1174). In 1956 Turner composed the song "Tell Me Why," which Elvis recorded in 1957.

TURNER, ZEB

Composer, with Fred Rose, of the song "It's a Sin," which Elvis recorded in 1961.

TURTLES, THE

Vocal group that in 1955 recorded "Mystery Train" (RCA Victor 47-6356) with the Hugo Winterhalter Orchestra. Their version of the Elvis song sounded more like folk than rock & roll. Their record was issued by RCA immediately before the release on RCA of Elvis's Sun version (RCA Victor 47-6357). This group is not the Turtles of the 1960s, which was founded by Howard Kaylan and Marc Volman.

TV GUIDE

Television magazine published by Triangle Publications of Radnor, Pennsylvania, beginning with the April 3–9, 1953 issue. The premiere edition featured a cover photo of Lucille Ball and her three-month-old son, Desiderio Arnaz IV (Desi Arnaz Jr.). Its September 8–14, 1956, issue featured Elvis on the cover and an article, "The Plain Truth About Elvis Presley," by Paul Wilder, on the inside, with two more segments continued in the September 22–28 and September 29–October 4 issues. Elvis was featured on the cover of another edition: May 7–13, 1960 (with Frank Sinatra). The November 10–16, 1973 edition featured Elvis and seven other specials on its cover. (NBC-TV was repeating the April 4, 1973, telecast of Elvis: Aloha From Hawaii special on November 14.) "How TV Reacted the Day Elvis Died" was the lead article in the August 15–21, 1981 *TV Guide*. Again, Elvis was on the magazine's cover. An article by Dave Marsh titled "Elvis, How He Rocked the World," with Elvis's photo on the front cover, was featured in the April 9–15, 1983, issue. The January 5–11, 1985, edition featured an article titled "Why the Elvis Craze Won't Die" by Marshall Frady. In the January 30–February 5, 1988, issue, Priscilla Beaulieu Presley wrote an article about her TV miniseries "Elvis and Me." She and Elvis were shown on the magazine's cover. Priscilla herself appeared on three other covers: September 20–26, 1980; March 17–23, 1984; and December 15–21, 1984.

THE TWILIGHT ZONE

TV series which, on its September 22, 1986, episode (second-season premiere), titled "The Once and Future King," featured a story about an Elvis imitator accidentally killing the real Elvis. Jeff Yagher played the imitator, while Red West played the owner of Crown Electric.

TWITTY, CONWAY

(1933–   ) Tremendously successful country singer born Harold Lloyd Jenkins on September 1, 1935, in Friars Point, Mississippi, who early in his career sounded much like Elvis. Even his speech was similar. According to legend, Twitty was about to sign with the Philadelphia Phillies to play baseball when he heard Elvis singing "Mystery Train" over the radio. When Twitty finally made his first public appearance on the Ozark Jubilee he sang "Mystery Train" and several other Elvis songs.

Twitty recorded eight unreleased songs for Sun Records in 1956 ("Born to Sing the Blues," "Crazy Dreams," "Give Me Some Love," "Rockhouse," "Lawdy Miss Clawdy," "Jim Dandy," "Long Black Train," and "Baby Let's Play House") under his real name, Harold Jenkins. After changing his name (he looked at a map and spotted the towns of Conway, Arkansas, and Twitty, Texas), he composed his first hit, "It's Only Make Believe" (MGM 12677) in seven minutes during an intermission at the Flamingo Club in Hamilton, Ontario, Canada. When the record was first released many people thought it was Elvis singing under a humorous pseudonym. In the song, Twitty borrowed Elvis's deep rolling style, which can be heard on "Lonesome Cowboy." Twitty's recording reached number one on *Billboard*'s Hot 100 chart and sold over a million copies in 1958.

The Elvis-like character in the play and movie *Bye Bye Birdie* had a name that satirized Conway Twitty's— Conrad Birdie.

In 1964 Twitty recorded two Elvis songs, "My Baby Left Me" and "Such a Night" (ABC Paramount 1055). He has recorded a number of duets with Loretta Lynn.

When Elvis learned that Twitty had bought a customized van, Elvis bought himself a $25,000 vehicle from Van Man, Inc. In December 1973 Elvis recorded "There's a Honky Tonk Angel (Who Will Take Me Back In)," but it wasn't released until January 1975, after Twitty's version had made the country charts in 1974 (MCA 40173).

TWOMEY, KAY

(1914–   ) Composer born Kathleen Greeley Twomey in Boston on April 27, 1914. Twomey composed, with Fred Wise and Norman Blagman, the song "Put the Blame on Me," which Elvis sang in the 1965 movie *Tickle Me*. She also composed the English lyrics, with Ben Weisman, Fred Wise, and Bert Kaempfert, to the song "Wooden Heart," which Elvis sang in the 1960 movie *G.I. Blues*.

TYRELL, STEVE

Composer, with Mark James, of the song "It's Only Love," which Elvis recorded in 1971.

UCLA

University of California at Los Angeles. College that Elvis tried to enroll in to take some night courses during his movie-making days in Hollywood. He was just discovering reading and wanted to further his education, but was turned down by school officials, who thought his presence would be disruptive.

UFO

Unidentified Flying Object. Sightings of UFOs are "close encounters of the first kind." On June 24, 1947, while flying near Mount Rainier, in Washington, Kenneth Arnold spotted nine UFOs. He later filed the first official UFO sighting report.

Elvis once watched a UFO execute erratic maneuvers over Memphis. One night in 1966, Elvis, Sonny West, and Jerry Schilling watched what they thought was a UFO from Elvis's house on Perugia Way in Bel Air. Since even President Jimmy Carter once filed a UFO sighting, Elvis was in good company. Others who have reported UFO sightings include: John Lennon (August 23, 1974, in New York City); Academy Award–winning actor Cliff Robertson (in 1965); Jackie Gleason; Senator Barry Goldwater; Shirley MacLaine, and Michelle Phillips. Actor Lee Majors and his former wife, actress Farrah Fawcett, watched a UFO in Philadelphia one evening (the previous night Majors had had a dream about a UFO).

UNCLE RICHARD

Country music disc jockey at Memphis's WMPS radio station who, according to Vince Staten in his book *The Real Elvis: Good Old Boy*, was the first disc jockey (not Dewey Phillips) to play an Elvis song when he spun "Blue Moon of Kentucky." If it was a double-sided 78 RPM acetate that Uncle Richard played, then chances are he was also the first to play "That's All Right (Mama)."

UNIT NO. 6

Memphis Fire Department rescue vehicle that arrived at Graceland shortly after 2:30 P.M. on August 16, 1977, to respond to Elvis's collapse.

UNITED ARTISTS SOUTHBROOK 4

Theater complex rented by Elvis on August 10, 1977, in order to see a midnight showing of Roger Moore as James Bond in the film *The Spy Who Loved Me*. Elvis took his PK Walther pistol with him.

UNITED PAINT COMPANY

Memphis firm, located at 446 Concord Avenue, for which Vernon Presley worked as a packer from 1951 to 1953. His income was $2,000 a year. According to Elaine Dundy, in her book *Elvis and Gladys*, Vernon went to work there as early as 1949 and received a $10-a-week raise in 1951, enough to get him and his family kicked out of the Lauderdale Courts.

UNITED RECORDERS

Los Angeles recording studio where Elvis recorded the soundtrack for MGM's *The Trouble with Girls* on August 23, 1968.

UNIVERSITY PARK CLEANERS

Laundry, located at 613 McLean Boulevard in Memphis, owned by Carney Moore in the 1950s. Moore employed his brother Scotty Moore, who had just gotten out of the Navy. It was while working there that Scotty became a member of the Starlight Wranglers. The mother of singer Tammy Wynette (born Wynette Pugh) once worked for Carney Moore at University Park Cleaners.

UP AND DOWN WITH ELVIS: THE INSIDE STORY

A book written by *Houston Post* columnist Marge Crumbaker and former Colonel Tom Parker employee Gabe Tucker.

UPHOLSTERIES SPECIALTIES COMPANY

Memphis business, located at 210 West Georgia Avenue, where Elvis worked in the table department beginning on August 6, 1952, while in high school. Elvis gave his birthdate as January 8, 1934, to add one year to his age. As job references, he listed his previous jobs with Precision Tool and Loew's State Theater.

V

VAIL, COLORADO
Ski resort where Elvis vacationed in January 1976 to celebrate his forty-first birthday. On January 14 he gave away three new Cadillacs and two new Lincoln Continental Mark IVs. Three police department employees, a doctor, and a TV newsman were the lucky recipients. (See *Kumpf Lincoln-Mercury*)

VALENTINO, RUDOLPH
(1895–1926) Silent movie star and romantic idol of the 1920s, born Rodolfo Alfonzo Raffaele Pierre Filibert Guglielmi in Castellaneta, Italy, on August 23, 1895. He was nicknamed "The Sheik."

In the 1965 movie *Harum Scarum*, Elvis finally played a Valentino role. In 1975 Elvis was offered the lead role as Rudoph Valentino in a musical tribute at the Radio City Music Hall to be called "Ciao Rudy." Colonel Parker nixed the deal when he demanded $2.5 million.

Valentino, like Elvis, had a huge public funeral, in which an estimated crowd of 100,000 showed up outside Campbell's Funeral Home on Broadway in New York City on August 24–25, 1926. Valentino, like Elvis, has been portrayed in a number of motion pictures.

VAN DOREN, MAMIE
(1931–) Sexy blond actress born Joan Lucille Olander on February 6, 1931. Van Doren has been called the "poor man's Marilyn Monroe." In her 1987 autobiography, *Playing the Field*, she claimed that while performing at the Riviera Hotel in Las Vegas in 1957, she went out with Elvis, although she was married to musician Ray Anthony.[1] Elvis, who was four years Van Doren's junior, took her to the New Frontier Hotel where he had appeared the year before, and then to see Louie Prima and Keely Smith at the Desert Inn.

Van Doren imitated Elvis when she danced and sang in the 1957 movie *Untamed Youth*.

VAN MAN, INC.
Elkhart, Indiana, company owned by Luther Roberts that customized a Dodge van for Elvis. Elvis was prompted to buy the van because he liked singer Conway Twitty's so much.

VANDERHOOF, BRUCE
San Francisco disc jockey at radio station KYA who in 1957 played "Love Me Tender" at various speeds fourteen consecutive times to protest his station's policy of banning Elvis songs from the air between 10:00 A.M. and 4:00 P.M. For his actions, Vanderhoof was fired.

VELVET, JIMMY
Recording artist ("It's Almost Tomorrow" [Phillips 40285] and "We Belong Together" [ABC-Paramount 10488]) and good friend of Elvis's. In 1974 Elvis gave Velvet his 1969 Mercedes 600 limo. Velvet claims he toured with Elvis in the mid-1950s, first meeting him in 1955. He has said that he had a premonition of Elvis's death. While attending Paxton High School in Jacksonville, Florida, Velvet's English teacher was Mae Axton.

After Elvis's death, Velvet created an Elvis memorabilia show that went on tour throughout the United States. He also founded the Elvis Presley Museum located across the street from Graceland.

Although a sincere individual and a dedicated Elvis fan, Velvet has a tendency to exaggerate his own recording career. In an interview in *Elvis the Record* in 1980, Velvet claimed to have had a number one hit record with "We Belong Together" in 1963. However, according to *Billboard* magazine, the record never made it higher than number seventy-five in January 1964. Velvet has also claimed that he charted seventeen songs. According to *Billboard*, he charted only two songs in the Hot 100 chart and none on the country chart. Velvet has also laid claim to having hits with the songs "Blue Velvet" and "Teen Angel," which were actually hits for Bobby Vinton and Mark Dinning, respectively. Regardless of his fuzzy past, it is hard not to like Jimmy Velvet.

VESCO, ROBERT L.
Fugitive financier and onetime friend of President Richard M. Nixon who fled the United States in 1972, just before being indicted in connection with a Securities and Exchange Commission fraud investigation. In January 1975, Elvis made a $75,000 deposit on Vesco's Boeing 707 jetliner, nicknamed "Big Bird." Total purchase price was to have been $775,000. The plane was included in a bankruptcy sale by one of Vesco's companies. Its renovated interior housed a gymnasium, a sauna, and a discotheque.

Elvis's offer was withdrawn when he received a telegram from agents of Vesco threatening to seize the plane if it ever landed outside the United States.

Years later, the Boeing 707 ended up as a nightclub named "Club 707," sitting on recovered swamp land in Manila in the Philippines.

VILLIGER KELL
Elvis's favorite brand of cigars. Villiger Kell is a German brand.

VINCENT, GENE
(1935–1971) Rockabilly singer born Vincent Eugene Craddock in Norfolk, Virginia. Vincent was born on February 11, 1935 (just thirty-four days after Elvis).

---

[1]In March 1953, Anthony recorded "You're a Heartbreaker" (Capitol 2349), with Jo Ann Greer on vocal, the song Elvis would record in December 1954.

"Discovered" by disc jockey Bill Randle, Vincent was one of the early rock & roll artists, reaching the charts in 1956 with "Be-Bop-a-Lula" (Capitol 3450). Before 1956 Vincent served in Korea with the Navy. He won an Elvis impersonation contest sponsored in 1956 by Hollywood's Capitol Records, who hoped to find another Elvis. He became the first singer to perform in black leather. Capitol Records signed him to their label, hoping he could compete with Elvis. Vincent's backup group was called the Blue Caps. Tommy Facenda, who had the 1959 hit "High School U.S.A." was once a member of the Blue Caps.[1] The group had named itself after President Dwight D. Eisenhower's favorite blue golf cap. In 1968 Vincent recorded the song "Story of the Rockers" (Playground 100), in which he mentioned Elvis. Vincent died on October 12, 1971.

Elvis's versions of "Frankie and Johnny" and "You'll Never Walk Alone" are similar to those on the 1958 album *Vincent Rocks, Blue Caps Roll* (Capitol T-970).

VIVA LAS VEGAS II
Movie being filmed by an overweight Elvis (John Belushi) as a singing busboy in a comedy skit on the TV series "Saturday Night Live," first telecast in 1977. Belushi sang "Jailhouse Rock," as he would in the 1978 movie *The Blues Brothers*.

VOICE
Vocal group that backed Elvis on some recordings and in live concerts from 1973 to 1975. The members of Voice were Donnie Sumner, Tim Baty, and Sherrill Nielsen (previously with the Statesmen and the Imperials), plus piano player Tony Brown, guitarist John Rich, and bassist Tommy Hensley. Donnie Sumner also sang with his stepfather J. D. Sumner and the Stamps. Elvis himself named the group Voice, and paid them $10,000 a month in salary.

---

[1]Other members of the group were: Galloping Cliff Gallup, Wee Willie Williams, Be-Bop Harrell, and Jumpin' Jack Neal.

WAGNER, JAMES
Biological and legal father of Priscilla Beaulieu Presley. The World War II Navy lieutenant was killed in 1945 when the plane in which he was flying back from leave crashed.

WAKELY, JIMMY
(1914–   ) Popular singer of the 1940s, born in Mineola, Arkansas, who appeared in movies with Roy Rogers and Gene Autry. Merle Travis and Spade Cooley have both played in Wakely's band. Wakely has recorded duets with Margaret Whiting (the daughter of composer Richard Whiting [1891–1938]), and is the composer of "I'll Never Let You Go (Little Darlin')," which he originally recorded in 1943 (Decca 5973) and which Elvis recorded in January 1955. Wakely was a good friend of Charlie Hodge's, having toured with him in the 1950s and 1960s.

Wakely was once asked his opinion of Elvis. His reply was: "Man, he's great! Fifteen years ago I wrote a song called 'I'll Never Let You Go (Little Darlin'),' and nothing happened. Presley put it into one of his albums and so far I've gotten $4,300 in royalties."

WALKER, CHARLIE
Disc jockey with San Antonio, Texas, radio station KMAC who interviewed Elvis in April 1956, introducing him as Elvis (the Cat) Presley. Walker's interview can be heard on the album *The Sun Years*.

WALKER, CINDY
Singer and composer born in Mexia, Texas. With Eddy Arnold, she composed the song "You Don't Know Me," which Elvis recorded in February 1967. Walker's grandfather, F. L. Finland, is the composer of the popular hymn "Hold to God's Unchanging Hands." Cindy Walker recorded for Columbia records.

WALKER, WAYNE P.
(1925–   ) Composer born in Quapaw, Oklahoma, on December 13, 1925. Walker wrote, with Webb Pierce, the song "How Do You Think I Feel," which Elvis recorded in 1956. He also composed the song "Are You Sincere," which Elvis recorded in 1973. (It was released in 1979.) Walker has recorded for such labels as Chess, ABC Paramount, and Columbia Records.

WALKER, WILEY
Composer, with Gene Sullivan, of the song "When My Blue Moon Turns to Gold Again" in 1941, which Elvis recorded in 1956.

WALKING IN HIS FOOTSTEPS
A book about Elvis written by Patricia Thompson and Connie Gerber and published in 1981 by Towery Press.

WALLACE, BILL (SUGARFOOT)
Former world middleweight karate champion who was one of Elvis's martial-arts instructors and bodyguards. Wallace injured his left leg in a match in 1973 and had to drop out of competition. Elvis invited him to Graceland one evening where he had an acupuncturist stick eighteen needles into the injured leg. Wallace has claimed that "fifteen minutes after he stuck those needles in there, you could kick me in the same leg and it wouldn't hurt." Elvis had helped cure Wallace's leg. Wallace began teaching Elvis in August 1974.

WALLACE, GEORGE CORLEY
(1919–   ) Governor of Alabama born in Clio, Alabama, on August 25, 1919. Wallace made Elvis an honorary colonel in Alabama. After Wallace was wounded in an assassination attempt in 1972, Elvis telephoned him to wish him well.

WARD, BILLY (AND THE DOMINOES)
Rhythm and Blues group of the 1950s that featured Clyde McPhatter and later Jackie Wilson as lead vocalists. In 1951 they recorded "Harbor Lights" (Federal 12010), which Elvis would record in 1954. In 1953 the group recorded "Rags to Riches" (King 1280), a song that Elvis would record in 1970. Elvis watched the group perform in Las Vegas, and at the Million-Dollar Quartet session on December 4, 1956, raved about the way the lead singer (Jackie Wilson) sang some of Elvis's songs, especially the slower version of "Don't Be Cruel."

WARD, CHARLES
Policeman who gave Elvis a speeding ticket in Hattiesburg, Mississippi, on July 31, 1956, as Elvis drove to Memphis.

WARDLOW, BILLIE
Memphis girl who became Elvis's girlfriend, after he split with Betty McMann. It is believed that Elvis seriously thought about asking Wardlow to marry him.

WARREN, BUNNY
Composer, with Dory Jones, of the song "Rubberneckin'," which Elvis sang in the 1969 movie *Change of Habit*.

WARREN, ED
(1920–1962) Composer born in Norfolk, Virginia, on June 19, 1920. Warren composed, with Arthur Kent, the song "Take Good Care of Her," which Elvis recorded in 1974.

WARWICK HOTEL
New York City hotel where on November 20, 1955, Colo-

nel Tom Parker and RCA executive Steve Sholes signed the contract that made Elvis an RCA Victor artist. While appearing on the Dorsey Brothers' "Stage Show" from January to March 1956, Elvis, Scotty Moore, and Bill Black stayed at the Warwick Hotel— Elvis in room 527. The trio also stayed at the Warwick while appearing three times on "The Ed Sullivan Show." (See *Arnold Shaw, RCA Records*)

WASHINGTON, EARL
Composer, with John Thornton, Piney Brown, and Ralph Bass, of the song "Just a Little Bit," which Elvis recorded in 1973.

WASHINGTON, FERDINAND
Composer, with Don Robey, of the song "Pledging My Love," which Elvis recorded in 1976.

WASHINGTON HOTEL
Washington, D.C., hotel where Elvis stayed, in room 506, in December 1970 under the name Jon Burrows, after he traveled to Washington on American Airlines from Memphis to visit President Richard M. Nixon so that he could obtain a narcotics agent badge. According to Lucy de Barbin in her book *Are You Lonesome Tonight?*, she met Elvis at the hotel on his first trip there. De Barbin says that Elvis wore his velvet suit and cape, a fact that Albert Goldman mentioned in his biography. Charlie Hodge has said that Elvis actually wore a black suit and cape.

WATERS, DICKIE
Instructor who taught Elvis to water ski on McKeller Lake near Memphis in 1957.

WATERS, MUDDY
(1915–1983) Grammy Award–winning blues singer and rhythm & blues composer born McKinley Morganfield on April 4, 1915, in Rolling Fork, Mississippi. His grandmother gave him the nickname "Muddy" because as a boy he often played in a nearby muddy creek. Waters's 1950 song "Rollin' Stone" (the title of which influenced the naming of a group and a rock magazine) was Chess Records' first hit record (Chess 1426) in 1950. In 1956 Waters wrote and recorded "Got My Mojo Working," which was recorded by Elvis in 1970.

WATTS, DEBBIE
(1956–   ) Twenty-one-year-old girl who claimed in a *Star* article (September 20, 1977) to have been Elvis's secret lover for five years, from 1972 to 1977, going steady with him for six months.

WAYNE, JOHN
(1907–1979) Popular American motion-picture actor born Marion Michael Morrison on May 26, 1907, in Winterset, Iowa. Like Elvis's Graceland, Wayne's place

of birth is now a protected tourist attraction. John Wayne was one of Elvis's heroes. Lucy de Barbin, in her book *Are You Lonesome Tonight?*, claims she became involved with John Wayne in 1958 after she had been involved with Elvis. This was quite a coup for one woman to have had a romance with America's number one singer and then with America's number one actor.

At the International Hotel on August 22, 1969, Elvis introduced John Wayne's son, Patrick Wayne, from the audience.

WAYNE, SID
(1923–   ) Composer born in New York City on January 26, 1923. Wayne wrote, with Ben Weisman, Sherman Edwards, Fred Karger, and others, a number of movie songs that Elvis recorded:

"All I Needed Was the Rain"
"Big Boots"
"Britches"
"Chesay"
"Clambake"
"Cross My Heart and Hope to Die"
"Didja Ever"
"Do the Clam"
"A Dog's Life"
"Easy Come, Easy Go"
"Flaming Star"
"Frankfort Special"
"Fun in Acapulco"
"Happy Ending"
"Hard Luck"
"He's Your Uncle, Not Your Dad"
"How Can You Lose What You Never Had"
"I Need Your Love Tonight"
"I'll Be Back"
"I'll Never Know"
"It Won't Be Long"
"It's Carnival Time"
"It's Impossible"
"Lover Doll"
"Slowly but Surely"
"Spinout"
"Stay Away, Joe"
"Tonight Is So Right for Love"
"We Call on Him"
"What a Wonderful Life"
"What's She Really Like"
"Who Are You (Who Am I)"

WAYNE, THOMAS
(1941–1971) Singer, born in Memphis on July 22, 1941, who in 1959 recorded the hit song "Tragedy" (Fernwood 109), which was produced by Scotty Moore and featured Scotty, Bill Black, and three high school girls named the DeLons singing behind Wayne.[1] The song was rereleased in 1961 on Capehart 5009 with violins added. Wayne, born Thomas Wayne Perkins, was a graduate of Humes High School.[2] His brother Luther Perkins played guitar for Johnny Cash. Wayne and Bill Rice composed the song "The Girl Next Door" (a.k.a.

"The Girl Next Door Went a' Walking"), which Wayne recorded (Fernwood 122) in 1959 and which Elvis recorded in 1960. (See *Luther Perkins*)

WDIA

Memphis rhythm & blues radio station, located at 2074 Union Avenue, which Elvis listened to in the early 1950s. WDIA was founded in 1948 as the first black radio station in the South. It was advertised as "America's Only 50,000-Watt Negro Radio Station." Rufus Thomas, a disc jockey at WDIA, recorded one of the first releases for the Sun label with "Bear Cat" (Sun 181) in 1953. Blues singer B. B. King also served as a disc jockey at WDIA. James Mattis, another disc jockey at the station, founded Duke Records of Houston, on which Johnny Ace and Bobby (Blue) Bland recorded. Joe Hill Louis, another Sun artist, had his own show on WDIA. White blues artist Mike Bloomfield once recorded a song titled "WDIA."

Originally, WDIA's program director David James instructed the station's disc jockeys not to play Elvis records, in a bit of reverse discrimination, but disc jockey Rufus Thomas played him anyway, because he liked Elvis's sound.

WDIA GOODWILL REVIEW

Concert held at the Ellis Auditorium in Memphis on December 22, 1956. The artists were: Little Junior Parker, Earl Malone, B. B. King, and Bobby (Blue) Bland. Although Elvis did not perform, he did appear in a walk-on, visited with the other artists, and appeared in publicity poses. The black audience applauded Elvis, with the girls going wild.

WDIA disc jockey Rufus Thomas has remarked about the show, "Never in my life have you seen such a surge of black faces converging on that stage. In my lifetime, I know of only one other person who could have that kind of magnetism, and that was Dr. Martin Luther King."

WEATHERLY, FRED ERIC EDWARD

Composer in 1913 of the song "Danny Boy," which Elvis recorded in 1976.

WEBB, TRENT

Driver of the hearse that carried Elvis's body to Forest Hill Cemetery on August 18, 1977.

WEBSTER, PAUL FRANCIS

(1907–) Academy Award–winning lyricist born in New York City on December 20, 1907. Webster wrote many songs for motion pictures, as well as TV theme songs such as "Maverick," "Sugarfoot," etc. He wrote the English lyrics of the French song "Padre," written by Jacques Larue and Alain Romans, which Elvis recorded in 1971.

WEBSTER, R. A.

Composer, with Roger Whittaker, of the song "The Last Farewell," which Elvis recorded in 1976.

WEINMAN, BERNARD

Composer, with Lee Rosenberg, of the song "Too Much," which Elvis recorded in 1957.

WEISMAN, BEN

(1921–) Songwriter born in Providence, Rhode Island, on November 16, 1921. Weisman co-composed more than fifty songs for Elvis. The first song Weisman composed for Elvis was "First in Line" and the first movie song was "Got a Lot o' Livin' to Do." Weisman appeared frequently on the CBS-TV daytime serial "The Young and the Restless," as a pianist in the Club Allegro.

Weisman cowrote, with Fred Wise and others, the following songs for Elvis:

"All I Needed Was the Rain"
"Almost"
"Almost Always True"
"As Long As I Have You"
"Beyond the Bend"
"Change of Habit"
"Chesay"
"Cindy, Cindy"
"Clambake"
"Crawfish"
"Cross My Heart and Hope to Die"
"Danny"
"A Dog's Life"
"Do the Clam"
"Don't Ask Me Why"
"Don't Leave Me Now"
"Easy Come, Easy Go"
"Fame and Fortune"
"First In Line"
"Follow That Dream"
"Forget Me Never"
"Frankie and Johnny"
"Fun in Acapulco"
"Got a Lot o' Livin' To Do"
"Happy Ending"
"Hard Luck"
"Have A Happy"
"He's Your Uncle, Not Your Dad"
"How Can You Lose What You Never Had"
"I Got Lucky"
"I Slipped, I Stumbled, I Fell"
"I'll Be Back"
"I'll Never Know"
"In My Way"

---

[1]Scotty Moore had recorded the demo at Sun Records with Al Jackson on bass.
[2]There have been other situations where two future singers attended the same high school at the same time: David Gates and Leon Russell attended the same Tulsa, Oklahoma, high school, where they played in the same band. David Bowie and Peter Frampton attended the same British school. Bowie's art teacher was Frampton's father. Rod Stewart and Raymond Davies played football for the same school team in England. Tommy Sands and actress Paula Prentiss were classmates at Lamar High School in Houston. Kenny Rogers and Mickey Newberry were schoolmates at Jefferson Davis High in Houston. Of course, the most famous combination, Barbra Streisand and Neil Diamond attended Erasmus High in New York City, singing together in the same school choir. Elvis and Johnny Burnette both attended Humes High.

"It Feels So Right"
"It Won't Be Long"
"It's Carnival Time"
"Let Us Pray"
"Moonlight Swim"
"Pocketful of Rainbows"
"Riding the Rainbow"
"Rock-a-Hula Baby"
"Slowly but Surely"
"Spinout"
"Stay Away, Joe"
"Steppin' Out of Line"
"Summer Kisses, Winter Tears"
"There Is So Much World to See"
"This Is Living"
"Twenty Days and Twenty Nights"
"We Call on Him"
"Who Are You (Who Am I?)"
"Wooden Heart"
"Yellow Rose of Texas/The Eyes of Texas" (adaptation)

Weisman and Fred Wise also composed "Playing with Fire," which Elvis recorded but which was not released.

WEISS, GEORGE DAVID
(1921–   ) Composer born in New York City on April 9, 1921. Since 1946, Weiss has written many songs for films. He composed three songs with Hugo Peretti and Luigi Creatore that Elvis recorded, "Ku-u-i-po," "Wild in the Country," and "Can't Help Falling in Love."

WELLA CORPORATION
Hair-care company with which Priscilla Presley signed a three-year contract in 1979. Wella Balsam had already helped launch the careers of Farrah Fawcett, Jaclyn Smith, and Cheryl Ladd. Priscilla's first TV commercial was shown on all three networks on October 31, 1979.

WELO
Tupelo, Mississippi, radio station at 580 KC on the dial, located at 212 South Spring Street, above the Black and White hardware store. WELO, which first went on the air in 1941, holds the distinction of being the first radio station to broadcast Elvis, when they broadcast him live from the annual talent show at the Mississippi-Alabama Fair and Dairy Show on October 3, 1945, with Elvis singing the old Red Foley classic "Old Shep." Station manager Charlie Boren booked Elvis on WELO's "Black and White Saturday Jamboree," which was broadcast from 1:00 P.M. to 4:30 P.M., a number of other times, sometimes accompanied on guitar by Mississippi Slim, who had his own show on WELO. Elvis may even have appeared on the program in the fall of 1944, which would predate his "first" radio broadcast from the fair in 1945. It is not known what songs Elvis performed on the show, but two that have been mentioned in sources are "Old Shep" and "God Bless My Daddy, He's Over There." Another WELO program that Elvis enjoyed listening to was Sister Rosetta Tharpe,

who played black gospel music on her Sunday afternoon show. (See *Mississippi-Alabama Fair and Dairy Show*)

WERTHEIMER, ALFRED
Professional photographer who snapped 3,800 photographs of Elvis during 1956. Some of his best photos appear in his 1979 book *Elvis '56: In the Beginning.* The 1987 Cinemax special "Elvis '56" was based on Wertheimer's book.

WESSON, MARTHA JANE
Wife of Dunnan Presley Jr. She was the mother of Rosalinda and Rosella Presley, the grandmother of Jessie D. McClowell Presley, the great-grandmother of Vernon Presley, and the great-great-grandmother of Elvis Presley.

WEST, DELBERT (SONNY)
(1938–   ) Cousin of Red West. He first saw Elvis at Humes High and later met him at the Rainbow Rollerdome, where he was introduced by Red West. Sonny, who had been working at the Ace Appliance Store in Memphis, quit his job and went to work for Elvis, taking care of Elvis's vehicles and living in a converted apartment at Graceland. "The Eagle" (or Mr. Eagle) was Sonny's karate nickname, which was given to him by Elvis. Elvis served as best man and Priscilla as the maid of honor at Sonny and Judy Morgan's wedding on December 28, 1971, at the Trinity Baptist Church in Memphis, during which Elvis carried a flashlight. West's brother-in-law was Bill Thorpe, who was the all-schools boxing champion in Memphis during the 1950s. Elvis bought West a black Cadillac convertible, in addition to a motorcycle, a pickup truck, and other vehicles. He played small roles in a number of Elvis films, including the 1968 movie *Stay Away, Joe*. In 1958 a Sonny West recorded the single "Rave On!" (Atlantic 1174), but it is not yet known if it is the same person. West was fired by Vernon Presley on July 13, 1976.

WEST, ROBERT (RED) GENE
(1936–   ) Close friend of Elvis's and a member of the Memphis Mafia. Red West is a cousin of Delbert (Sonny) West. West first met Elvis in high school, where he was a year behind him and on at least one occasion broke up a situation in school in which Elvis was about to be beaten up by a group of guys from the football team, the Tigers, a team on which West played center.[1] The six-foot-two-inch tall West was very athletic. He boxed in Golden Gloves and played football for Jones Junior College. Jones won the Tennessee state championship and, with West at center, played in the Junior Rose Bowl in Pasadena, California, where they lost the title by just eight points.

West lived with his mother, Mrs. Lois West, in the Hurt Housing project in Memphis. One time in 1956 he and Elvis sneaked two girls up to West's apartment

[1]In the book *Elvis—What Happened?*, which was cowritten by West, is the sentence: "He is decent and good-natured, and one of the best centers Humes High School had ever produced."

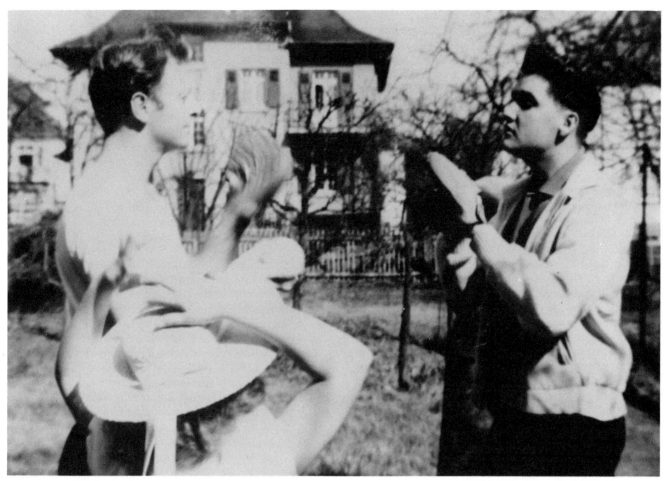

Elvis and Red West preparing to play softball in West Germany in 1959. (Photo courtesy the Mike Boyd Collection)

when his mother wasn't home. Elvis and West became close friends in 1955–56 when Red volunteered to drive Elvis, Scotty Moore, Bill Black, and later D. J. Fontana to different cities in the South for live appearances. West served in the U.S. Marines from 1956 to 1958, stationed in Norfolk, Virginia, which allowed him to stay in contact with Elvis. On August 14, 1958, on the same day as Elvis's mother, Gladys, West's father, Newton Thomas West, died. Funeral services for Newton West took place on the day after Gladys's, in the same funeral home. In December 1958 *Movie Mirror* magazine published an article written by Bobby (Red) West titled "His Best Friend Explodes the Lies About Elvis."

After Elvis's discharge from the U.S. Army in 1960, West was employed as Elvis's bodyguard. His martial-arts nickname was "The Dragon" (or Mr. Dragon), a name given to him by Elvis. Over the years Elvis bought West a number of vehicles, including a new Mercedes-Benz as a wedding present, a new Cadillac Eldorado convertible, a motorcycle, a pickup truck, and other presents. A man of many talents, West became a movie stuntman, appearing in numerous films, including many of Elvis's films, as well as in the 1960 movie *Spartacus.* He married one of Elvis's secretaries, Pat Boyd, on July 1, 1961. In Memphis, West operated the Tennessee Karate Institute. In 1961 a Red West recorded "Unforgiven"/"Midnight Ride" (Dot 16268),

but it is not yet known if this is the same person.

West wrote a number of songs that Pat Boone, Ricky Nelson, and Johnny Rivers recorded. He either wrote or cowrote the songs "If You Think I Don't Need You" (with Joe Cooper), "If Every Day Was Like Christmas" and "Holly Leaves and Christmas Trees" (with Glen Spreen), "If You Talk in Your Sleep" (with Johnny Christopher), "That's Someone You Never Forget" (with Elvis Presley), "Seeing Is Believing" (with Glen Spreen), "Separate Ways" (with Richard Mainegra), and "You'll Be Gone" (with Elvis Presley and Charlie Hodge), all of which Elvis recorded. West, a bodyguard, composed better material for Elvis than some of the professional composers writing songs for Elvis's movies. West appeared in approximately fifteen of Elvis's movies, including *Flaming Star* (1960), as an Indian; *Wild in the Country* (1961), as Hank; *Blue Hawaii* (1961), as a party guest; *Follow That Dream* (1962), as a bank guard; *Girls! Girls! Girls!* (1962), as a sailor who played bongos; *It Happened at the World's Fair* (1963), as Fred; *Roustabout* (1964), as a carnival worker; *Tickle Me* (1965), in a fight scene; *Harum Scarum* (1965), as an assassin; *Clambake* (1967), as an ice cream vendor. He also appeared in three Robert Conrad TV series: "The Wild, Wild West"; "Baa Baa Black Sheep" (as Sgt. Andy Micklin 1977–78); and "The Duke." In 1979 he made a Chevy truck TV commercial.

On July 13, 1976, Vernon Presley fired Red West, Sonny West, and Dave Hebler from Elvis's employ. They collaborated on a book about Elvis, which was published just two weeks before Elvis's death in 1977. Red West and his cousin Sonny West have been condemned for their heavy-handed tactics as Elvis's bodyguards while Elvis performed in concert. Although on occasion Red and Sonny used what may have seemed like too much physical persuasion, they did not have an easy job, considering the logistics involved in moving to a new city almost every day, transportation to and from a new hotel in each city, and the difficult job of keeping the weirdos away from Elvis, who was the target of a number of death threats. Whether one cares to agree or disagree with Red and Sonny's protective style, it can be said that their track record speaks for itself; they did keep Elvis out of harm's way. But what they did to Elvis later is considered by some to have been worse. The Wests and Dave Hebler have been sharply criticized by Elvis fans for writing their "bodyguards book," *Elvis—What Happened?*, in which they relate many personal events in Elvis's life. Although the revelation of many of those events is questionable, to say the least, perhaps it should be noted that many of the fans wanted to "kill" the messengers of the bad news, rather than to condemn the bad news itself, for at the time they wrote their book, something was desperately wrong in Elvis's life.

WESTERN RECORDERS

Los Angeles recording studio where Elvis recorded the soundtrack for MGM's *Live a Little, Love a Little*, on March 7, 1968.

WESTINGHOUSE CREDIT CORPORATION

Memphis lending institution, located at 3003 Airways Boulevard, through whose Mobile Home Division Elvis financed the eight trailers he bought for the men (and their wives and girlfriends) of his Memphis Mafia. The trailer homes were hauled to the Circle G Ranch, where they were set up. This was one of the few times that Elvis bought anything on credit.

WESTLAKE, CLIVE

Composer of the songs "It's a Matter of Time," "How the Web Was Woven" (with David Most), and "Twenty Days and Twenty Nights" (with Ben Weisman), all of which Elvis recorded.

WESTMORELAND, KATHY

(1945–   ) Soprano singer born on August 10, 1945, in Texarkana, Arkansas. Bressee (Breezy) Westmoreland, Kathy's father, sang and appeared in two MGM motion pictures, *The Great Caruso* (1951) and *The Student Prince* (1954). In 1962, seventeen-year-old Kathy was a runner-up in the Miss Teenage America contest. She and comedian Steve Martin were both members of the Class of 1963 at Garden Grove High School (Garden Grove, California), where they were friends. Replacing Millie Kirkham, Westmoreland toured with Elvis in his concert appearances and can be heard on many Elvis

recordings between 1970 and 1977. Elvis, who dated Kathy for a time, often described her at concerts as the "beautiful little girl with the high voice." Over the years, Elvis bought her several automobiles, including a new blue Continental Mark V.

A rather embarrassing incident occurred at the Greensboro, North Carolina, concert on July 20, 1975, when Elvis introduced Westmoreland by saying, "This is Kathy Westmoreland, our soprano singer, who doesn't like the way I introduce her—and if she doesn't like it, she can get the hell off the stage." Embarrassed, Kathy and two members of the Sweet Inspirations walked off the stage in front of the audience. The introduction to which Kathy had previously objected was: "This is Kathy Westmoreland. She will take affection from anybody, anytime, anyplace; in fact, she gets it from the whole band." The little feud lasted over several concert appearances, with Elvis giving her some digs during the introductions. Elvis later apologized to her about the incident and the two were once again friends.

In Westmoreland's revealing autobiography, *Elvis and Kathy*, she admits to falling in love with Elvis and sleeping with him, but with no sex involved. She also said that "Elvis never took street drugs." She further says that she, Larry Geller, and Charlie Hodge were all told in "strict confidence" (by Dr. George Nichopoulos) that Elvis was dying of bone cancer at the time of his death in 1977 and that he had suffered three heart attacks before the one that killed him. Both Geller and Hodge in their autobiographies have said that Elvis was dying of bone cancer (which may help explain some of the prescription drugs that he was taking during the later years of his life).

Like Elvis, Kathy has had her own fan clubs and imitators. In 1978 she recorded the tribute record "You Were the Music" (Age of Woman 5789). A recording of the song "My Father Watches over Me," which she sang at Elvis's funeral in 1977, was released on record in 1978 (Age of Woman 7144). Westmoreland authored the 1987 autobiography *Elvis and Kathy* with William G. Quinn. Westmoreland appeared in the Broadway show *The Legend Lives*, which ran from February to March 1978 and she sang on the soundtrack of the 1979 TV movie *Elvis*.

WHBQ

Memphis radio station (telephone: JAckson 6-5456), located in the Chisca Hotel at 272 South Main, that became the first station to play an Elvis record, on July 7, 1954, when disc jockey Dewey Phillips gave Elvis's "That's All Right (Mama)" a spin. (See *Dewey Phillips, Red Hot and Blue*)

WHBQ-TV

Memphis television station, an ABC affiliate (channel 13), that became the first TV station in the world to break the news of Elvis's death, on August 16, 1977. At 3:32 P.M. news producer Gordon Wilson gave the go-ahead to reporter Jack Chestnut to read an announcement that had been prepared by reporter Kathy Wolfe:

"Ladies and gentlemen, Eyewitness News interrupts regular programming. We have just learned through reliable sources that Elvis Presley has been pronounced dead at Baptist Hospital."

WHEELER, BILLY EDD
(1932–) Singer and composer born in Whitesville, West Virginia, on December 9, 1932. Wheeler composed, with Jerry Chesnut, the songs "It's Midnight" and "Never Again," both of which Elvis recorded.

WHEELER, KATE
Girl whom Elvis occasionally dated in 1956.

WHEELER III, TREATISE
(1959–) Eighteen-year-old Memphis driver who ran into three girls, killing Juanita Joan Johnson and Alice Marie Hovatar of Monroe, Louisiana, at 4:00 A.M. on August 18, 1977. Wheeler drove his 1963 white Ford Fairlane at an estimated speed of 55 MPH in a 40 MPH zone into a crowd of Elvis mourners and, after hitting the three girls drove off, only to be caught by Memphis police. One source has said that he had three female passengers with him at the time of the accident. The police actually rescued Wheeler from the crowd, which began to chant, "Lynch him up," and "Hang him up." The third girl, seventeen-year-old Tammy Baiter of St. Clair, Missouri, was injured. Wheeler was charged with drunk driving, two counts of second-degree murder, leaving the scene of an accident, public drunkenness, and reckless driving. Wheeler was released from prison in 1983, serving only half of his ten-year sentence.

WHEN ELVIS DIED
A 1980 book written by Neal and Janice Gregory and published by Communications Press, Inc.

WHERE IS ELVIS?
A book written by Ed Hill (former member of the Stamps), as told to Don Hill. It was published in 1979 by Cross Road Books of Atlanta.

WHHM
Memphis country-music radio station, located on Sterich Boulevard, on which, according to legend, disc jockey Sleepy-Eyed John Lepley first played Elvis's version of "Blue Moon of Kentucky" in July 1954. "Blue Moon of Kentucky" was the country side of Elvis's debut record, Sun 209. Dewey Phillips of WHBQ had been the first disc jockey to play the rhythm & blues side, "That's All Right (Mama)"[1] (See *John Lepley, Dewey Phillips*)

WHIRLING DERVISH OF SEX
Term applied to Elvis in 1956 by the Rev. Charles Howard Graff of St. John's Episcopal Church in Greenwich Village, New York City.

WHITE
Color of the telephone at Elvis's bedside in Graceland.

WHITE, CARRIE
Beverly Hills hair stylist who occasionally cut Elvis's hair, at $35 a visit, when Elvis was in Hollywood.

WHITE, KITTY
Black singer who sang duet with Elvis on the song "Crawfish" on the soundtrack of the 1958 movie *King Creole*. White, who became the first person to sing duet with Elvis, recorded a number of songs for the Mercury label in the 1950s, including "Cry Me a River" (Mercury 70722) and "A Teen Age Prayer" (Mercury 70750).

WHITE, MORNING DOVE
(1800?–1835) Cherokee Indian wife of William Mansell, who was the mother of John Mansell (1828–?), Morning Dizenie Mansell (1832–?) and James J. Mansell, the great-grandmother of Robert Lee Smith and Octavia (Doll) Mansell, the great-great-grandmother of Gladys Love Smith, and the great-great-great-grandmother of Elvis Presley.

WHITE, TONY JOE
(1943–) Country singer and composer, born in Oak Grove, Louisiana, on July 23, 1943, who recorded for Monument Records. His compositions that were recorded by Elvis are: "Polk Salad Annie," "I've Got a Thing About You, Baby," "For Ol' Times Sake," and "Rainy Night in Georgia" (sung live in the documentary *Elvis on Tour*). White originally charted "Polk Salad Annie" (Monument 1104) in 1969.

WHITEHAVEN
Former suburb of Memphis in which Graceland is located, at 3764 Elvis Presley Boulevard. Annexed by Memphis in 1969, Whitehaven is now in South Memphis.

WHITEHAVEN BOWLING LANES
Memphis bowling alley where Elvis occasionally bowled.

WHITEHAVEN HIGH SCHOOL
School, located at 4851 Elvis Presley Boulevard, where Elvis rented the stadium to play football with his friends. Elvis, who played end, would hire an official to call the game.

WHITEHAVEN MUSIC
Music-publishing company of which Elvis owned part interest.

WHITMAN, SLIM
(1924–) Country singer born Otis Whitman Dewey Jr. in Tampa, Florida, on January 20, 1924. Whitman

---

[1]Although Lepley is credited as being the first to play Elvis's "Blue Moon of Kentucky," it is hard to believe that Dewey Phillips would play the same record over and over, receiving numerous phone calls and telegrams, and not once flip the record over just to hear what was on the other side.

was on the same bill with Elvis in Elvis's first stage appearance, on July 30, 1954, at Memphis's Overton Park Shell, before a crowd of 2,000. Whitman, who was managed for a short time by Colonel Tom Parker, was the first country entertainer to perform at the London Palladium. The Jordanaires, who seem to have backed almost every country singer at one time or another, sang backup on some of Whitman's recordings. In 1957 Whitman recorded "A Fool Such As I" (Imperial 8322), which Elvis would record in 1958. The only song that Whitman ever charted on *Billboard*'s Hot 100 chart was "I'll Take You Home Again, Kathleen" (Imperial 1310) in 1957, a song that Elvis would record in 1971.

In the 1970s Whitman's *The Very Best of Slim Whitman* was sold through TV ads, selling one and a half million copies. The ad used the publicity line: "Slim Whitman has stayed at number one in England for a record nineteen weeks. This is longer than Elvis."

WHITTAKER, ROGER
British ballad singer born in Nairobi, Kenya. Whittaker composed, with R. A. Webster, and originally recorded "The Last Farewell" (RCA 50030) in 1975, which Elvis recorded in 1976.

WICKHAM, VICKI
Writer, with Simon Napier-Bell, of the English lyrics to the song "You Don't Have to Say You Love Me," composed by V. Pallavicini and P. Donaggio, which Elvis recorded in 1970.

WILBANK, JUNE
Girl whom Elvis dated on three occasions in 1958.

WILCOX, PETER
(1951–   ) Elvis imitator whose voice can be heard as that of Elvis sung over a jukebox in the TV series "Happy Days" and "Laverne and Shirley." Wilcox played Officer King, an Elvis imitator, on the short-lived TV series "The Last Precinct." He sang "Blue Suede Shoes" and "Hound Dog" dressed in gold lamé in the movie *Dudes*. He also played an Elvis impersonator who marries couples in a Las Vegas chapel in the September 1987 episode of TV's "L.A. Law."

Wilcox got the opportunity to meet Elvis in person, but it was by accident when he saw Elvis in the now defunct Schwab's Drug Store on Sunset Boulevard in Hollywood.

WILEY, SHARON
Girl whom Elvis seriously dated in the 1950s.

WILLIAM MORRIS AGENCY
Large talent agency through which Colonel Tom Parker booked Elvis's early concerts. The William Morris Agency got a 10 percent commission. In 1977 Priscilla Presley employed the William Morris Agency to represent her blossoming acting career. (See *Abe Lastfogel*)

WILLIAMS, BILLIE JEAN JONES
(1933–   ) Former wife of country singer Hank Williams (who died in 1953) and of country singer Johnny Horton (who died in 1960). Billie Jean Jones had been introduced to Hank Williams by country singer Faron Young and then married him on stage at the New Orleans Municipal Auditorium at 7:00 P.M. on October 20, 1952, before a paid audience of 14,000. The wedding was produced by Colonel Tom Parker's associate Oscar Davis. Billie Jean recorded the song "Oceans of Tears" (Fox 266) under her second married name, Billie Jean Horton.

In Lucy de Barbin's book *Are You Lonesome Tonight?*, Billie Jean recalled that in 1953 Elvis visited Shreveport, Louisiana, where she "remembers giving Elvis money." This story seems hard to accept because there's no evidence that Elvis was in Shreveport prior to his 1954 debut on the "Louisiana Hayride." In 1964, when Elvis was considered for the role of Hank Williams in the movie *Your Cheatin' Heart*, Billie Jean vetoed the idea because she thought that Elvis's personality would have overridden that of her late husband's.

What are the odds that a woman who had already been involved with perhaps the greatest country artist of all time, Hank Williams, would marry another country legend, Johnny Horton, and would take an interest in an unknown eighteen-year-old boy who would become the greatest rock & roll singer of all time. This whole scenario makes one ask: How did they meet? What was their relationship? What was Elvis doing in Shreveport in 1953? And where is Billie Jean's book?

WILLIAMS, BARBARA AND CARL GILES
Black Mountain, North Carolina, psychologists who in an article in the *Weekly World News* (April 22, 1980) claimed that Elvis and Priscilla had been married three other times in previous lives. In the eighteenth century Elvis was Sir Malcolm Baxter of Sussex, England, and in the 1850s he was an American country preacher. Williams and Giles have even said that Elvis was previously someone called JoLeuk on the now sunken island of Atlantis.

WILLIAMS, ERNESTINE
Graceland maid for five years.

WILLIAMS, HANK
(1923–1953) Highly popular and influential singer and composer who wrote and sang country music from his heart. Williams was born in Georgiana, Alabama, on September 17, 1923. His country band was called the Drifting Cowboys. On June 11, 1949, Williams made his debut at the Grand Ole Opry, singing "Lovesick Blues" over and over again at the audience's request. During his short life span of twenty-nine years, Williams wrote a long string of country songs that are classics today. On January 1, 1953, William's chauffeur, Charles Carr, found him dead in the backseat of

his Cadillac. Williams's second wife, Billie Jean, would also be married to singer Johnny Horton when Horton died in a car accident in 1960. In 1961 Williams was elected to the Country Music Hall of Fame. Some of Williams's compositions include: "Cold, Cold Heart"; "Hey, Good Lookin' "; "Half As Much"; "Jambalaya"; "Move It Over"; "Your Cheatin' Heart"; and "I'm So Lonesome I Could Cry." Elvis recorded the last two for his 1977 album *Welcome to My World*. Like Elvis, Williams entered a talent contest (at the age of twelve), singing "WPA Blues" and winning fifteen dollars. A photograph of Williams can be seen in Vince Everett's (Elvis) cell in the 1957 movie *Jailhouse Rock*.

Williams was portrayed by George Hamilton in the 1964 movie *Your Cheatin' Heart* (in which Hank Williams Jr. dubbed in the singing for Hamilton), a role for which Elvis was originally considered.

WILLIAMS, MAURICE

(1938–   ) Singer, born in Lancaster, South Carolina, on April 26, 1938, who sang as the lead for the Gladiolas and later the Zodiacs. Williams's biggest hit with the Zodiacs was "Stay" (Herald 552). At one minute, thirty-seven seconds, it is the shortest song ever to go to number one. Williams composed "Little Darlin'," which the Gladiolas recorded in 1957 (Excello 2101). Elvis recorded "Little Darlin' " in concert in 1977.

In November 1960, Elvis's "Are You Lonesome Tonight?" knocked Maurice Williams and the Zodiacs' "Stay" out of first place on *Billboard*'s Hot 100 chart.

WILLIAMS, PAUL HAMILTON

(1940–   ) Academy and Grammy Award–winning composer born in Bennington, Nebraska, on September 19, 1940. Williams has appeared in a number of movies and TV episodes. His brother, Mentor Williams, wrote the song "Drift Away" for Dobie Gray (Decca 33057). Paul Williams composed the song "Where Do I Go from Here," which Elvis recorded in 1972.

WILLIAMS, TERRY AND JEFF SAMUELS

Two men who attempted to sell illegal copies of a photograph of Elvis in his coffin. They were arrested for theft of the photo, which belonged to the *National Enquirer*. The pair sold a negative for $20,000. (See *Last photograph*)

WILLIAMS JR., THEODORE

Composer, with David Jones, of the song "Soldier Boy," which Elvis recorded in 1960.

WILLIS, CHUCK

(1928–1958) Blues singer born in Atlanta on January 31, 1928. Willis was called "Sheik of the Blues" and "King of the Stroll" when he introduced "C.C. Rider" in 1957. Willis died during an operation on April 10, 1958. His last hit was ironically titled "What Am I Living For"

backed with "Hang Up My Rock and Roll Shoes" (Atlantic 1179). Elvis recorded two Chuck Willis hits, "Feel So Bad" (Okeh 7029) (as "I Feel So Bad") and "C.C. Rider" (Atlantic 1130) (as "See See Rider").

WILLS, BOB

(1905–1975) Member of the Country Music Hall of Fame, born James Wills in Hall County, Texas, on March 6, 1905. Bob Wills and His Texas Playboys were the first country band to include drums, which they kept hidden behind the curtain whenever they played the Grand Ole Opry. Wills, along with his brother John, composed and first recorded "Faded Love," which Elvis recorded in 1970. A member of Wills's band was blind guitar player Leon Payne, to whom Wills would often say, "Take it away, Leon," during a song. Payne composed the song "I Love You Because," which Elvis recorded.

WILLS, JOHNNIE LEE

(1912–   ) Country bandleader and composer, brother of Bob Wills. With Deacon Anderson he composed "Rag Mop" and recorded it in 1950 on Bullet Records (Bullet 696). Elvis may have recorded "Rag Mop" in 1954.

For a number of years Wills's lead guitarist was Tommy Allsup, who later became a member of Buddy Holly's Crickets.

WILSON, JACKIE

(1934–1984) One of Elvis's favorite artists. On occasion, Wilson was referred to as the "Black Elvis." His first hit song, in 1957, titled "Reet Petite" was co-composed by Berry Gordy Jr.,[1] founder of Motown Records. In the 1950s Wilson was a member of Billy Ward and His Dominoes: (their 1951 hit "Sixty Minute Man" [Federal 12022], which was the first rhythm & blues record to chart on *Billboard*'s Hot 100, can be heard in the 1979 movie *Elvis*.) Wilson replaced Clyde McPhatter, who had just departed the group to join the Drifters. In 1975, when Wilson suffered a disabling stroke while singing "Lonely Teardrops" at the Latin Casino nightclub in Cherry Hill, New Jersey, Elvis offered to help pay the hospital bill, sending Wilson's wife a check for $30,000. Elvis said to Wilson, upon meeting him in Las Vegas, "I thought it was about time the white Elvis Presley met the black Elvis Presley."

At the Million-Dollar Quartet session on December 4, 1956, Elvis remarked that in Las Vegas (November 1956) he saw Billy Ward and the Dominoes perform six times and that the lead singer sang a terrific version of "Don't Be Cruel," in a style he wished he had recorded it. Unknown to Elvis at the time, that lead singer was Jackie Wilson. Wilson, who had been in a coma and paralyzed since September 29, 1975, died on January 21, 1984.

---

[1]Berry Gordy Jr., a former Golden Gloves boxer, founded Motown Records in 1959 by first establishing the Tamla label on a borrowed $700. His two sisters, Gwen and Anna (founder of Anna Records, on which Barrett Strong recorded "Money" in 1960) were married to Harvey Fuqua and Marvin Gaye, respectively. Berry Gordy Jr. is also the father-in-law of Jermaine Jackson of the Jacksons.

WILTSHIRE, MICHAEL

Fourteen-year-old boy from Perth, Australia, who won a trip to America by naming all forty-two Elvis songs played during a contest conducted by a radio station a few days after Elvis's death. Wiltshire also wrote a tribute song called "Elvis Aaron Presley," which he performed at the Memphis Motel.

WINFIELD, NIGEL

Miami entrepreneur who located for Elvis the Convair 880 jet and two other planes that Elvis then purchased.

WINKLER, RAY

Disc jockey who wrote, with John Hathcock, the song "Welcome to My World," which Elvis recorded in 1973. As a disc jockey in Amarillo, Texas, in 1955, Winkler became the first DJ in his town to play an Elvis record.

WINNEBAGO

Recreational vehicle (named after an American Indian tribe) that Elvis bought in Los Angeles while filming the 1964 movie *Kissin' Cousins.*

WISE, FRED

(1915–1966) Songwriter born in New York City on May 27, 1915. He composed more than thirty of Elvis's songs, with Ben Weisman, Randy Starr, and others:

"Adam and Evil"
"Almost Always True"
"As Long as I Have You"
"Beyond the Bend"
"Carny Town"
"Crawfish"
"Danny"
"Datin' "
"Don't Ask Me Why"
"Fame and Fortune"
"Follow That Dream"
"Forget Me Never"
"Give Me the Right"
"I Got Lucky"
"I Slipped, I Stumbled, I Fell"
"In My Way"
"It Feels So Right"
"Kissin' Cousins"
"Look Out, Broadway"
"(There's) No Room to Rumba in A Sports Car"
"Pocketful of Rainbows"
"Put the Blame on Me"
"Riding the Rainbow"
"Rock-a-Hula Baby"
"Steppin' Out of Line"
"Summer Kisses, Winter Tears"
"This Is Living"
"Wooden Heart"
"Yellow Rose of Texas"/"The Eyes of Texas" (adaptation)

Fred Wise and Ben Weisman also composed the song "Playing with Fire," which Elvis recorded but which has not been released.

WISEMAN, SCOTT

(1909–1981) Singer born in Spruce Pine, North Caro-lina. Wiseman and his wife, Lulu Belle, performed as "The Sweethearts of Country Music." They composed and recorded the song "Have I Told You Lately That I Love You?," which Elvis recorded in 1957. The year after Elvis's version was released, the pair retired from performing. (See *Lulu Belle*)

WIZELL, MURRAY

Composer, with Edward Lisbona, of the song "Gently," which Elvis recorded in 1961.

WOLFMAN JACK

Popular disc jockey born Robert Westing Smith. Wolfman Jack played Elvis records in the 1950s over radio station XERP in Mexico. He portrayed himself in the 1973 film *American Graffiti.*[1] In Las Vegas in 1969 Elvis talked about his memories of listening to Wolfman Jack, and then he introduced the Wolfman from the audience. After Elvis's death in 1977, Wolfman Jack proclaimed, "Two thousand years from now they'll still be hearing about Elvis Presley."

Elvis and Anita Wood. (Photo courtesy Jeff Wheatcraft)

---

[1] George Lucas attempted to get permission to play an Elvis song or two in the movie, but the cost was prohibitive.

WOOD, ANITA

Memphis disc jockey for WHHM Radio, television personality, and singer who hosted the Memphis TV show "Top Ten Party." After being introduced to Elvis by Cliff Gleaves in 1957, Wood became romantically involved with him. Elvis called her by the pet name "Little Beadie." In 1958 Elvis gave her a toy French poodle for Christmas named Little Bit. Wood and Elvis sometimes went to Eddie Fadal's house in Waco, Texas, while Elvis was stationed at Fort Hood. On one occasion Fadal recorded an impromptu session in which Elvis sang a number of songs and Anita sang "I Can't Help It" and "Who's Sorry Now." Wood, Elvis, and Fadal all sang "Just a Closer Walk with Thee." The session appears on the bootleg album *Forever Young, Forever Beautiful.* A Memphis newspaper revealed that Elvis was to marry Anita on the eve of his departure for West Germany. It is believed that Elvis and Anita wanted to get married, but that it was Colonel Tom Parker who insisted that Elvis remain single. For a number of years Elvis kept a photograph of Wood on his dresser.

Wood later married Johnny Brewer, a former foot-seven-year contract with ABC Paramount Records. In 1961 she recorded two Elvis novelty songs, "Memories of You" (Santo 9008) and "I'll Wait Forever" (Sun 361). In the 1960s she recorded several songs for MGM Records, including "Break My Mind" (MGM 13797) and, in 1964, "Dream Baby"/"This Happened Before" for Sue Records of New York City.

Wood later married . Johnny Brewer, a former football player with the Cleveland Browns. In 1977 it was reported that she had won a $240,000 libel judgment in a suit she filed against a Memphis newspaper that linked her romantically with Elvis after she had married.

WOOD, NATALIE

(1938–1981) Hollywood actress born Natasha Gurdin on July 20, 1938, the same day as actress Diana Rigg. Wood was given her screen name by motion-picture executives William Goetz and Leo Spitz in honor of their late friend, director Sam Wood (director of several Marx Brothers movies). Elvis dated Wood in 1956, after having been introduced to her by his friend Nick Adams. Newspaper stories accused them of having a "motorcycle romance." In October 1956, Elvis, Wood, and his parents spent a week together in Memphis. Wood was married to actor Robert Wagner twice.

On November 28, 1981, Natalie Wood accidentally drowned. In the 1979 TV movie *Elvis*, Wood was portrayed by Abi Young.

Eighteen-year-old Natalie once said of her relationship with Elvis: "We value our friendship. We want to keep on being friends, but I dread the publicity we're getting because I know it can ruin a friendship. We're not in love. We are both eager about our careers, too young."

WOOD, RANDY

Founder of Dot Records in Gallatin, Tennessee, in 1951. In early 1955 Sam Phillips attempted to sell Elvis's contract to Wood for $7,500. Wood declined because he already had an up-and-coming artist, Pat Boone, whom he had just acquired from Gene Autry's Republic Records. (Randy Wood was also the name of the president of Chicago's Vee Jay Records). After Dot Records moved to Los Angeles, the label turned down a local band who later became the Beach Boys.

WRIGHT, LOU

(1937–   ) Psychic who did readings for Elvis (through Charlie Hodge). In an article in *The Star*, Wright claimed to have been Elvis's psychic adviser during the last three years of his life. She further claimed to have contacted Elvis's spirit after his death. In the *Midnight Globe* it was written that she had been Elvis's secret psychic since 1970.

WSM

Nashville radio station that broadcasts the Grand Ole Opry. The National Life and Accident Insurance company originally owned the radio station, and the call letters WSM stood for "We Shield Millions." WSM-FM was the first licensed FM station in the United States. The Presleys, along with most of the people in the South, tuned into WSM on Saturday nights to hear the Opry. (See *Grand Ole Opry*)

WYCHE, SID

Composer, with Aaron Schroeder, of the song "A Big Hunk o' Love," which Elvis recorded in 1958.

X

X RECORDS
Subsidiary label of RCA Victor Records, established in 1952, for which Joe Delaney, the label's manager, attempted to get Elvis to record in 1955. The head of RCA Victor, Mannie Sach, declined Bob Neal's offer.

It was on X Records that eleven-year-old Frankie Avalon made his recording debut as a trumpet player in 1952. He recorded the instrumental "Trumpet Sorrento" (X 0006).

It was on another company record label, also named X Records, that the Beach Boys made their first recording, "Surfin'" (X 301) in 1962. "Surfin'" was later released on the Candix label [Candix 331] in 1962, after RCA objected to the West Coast label using their label name.

RCA eventually discontinued the X label in 1956 in favor of the Vik label. A number of Elvis releases appeared on the Vik label in foreign distribution.

Y

YANCEY, BECKY
(1940–   ) One of the secretaries who worked at Graceland. Yancey was in Elvis's employ from March 1962 to July 1975, joining Bonya McGarrity and Pat Boyd in answering fan mail and other chores. All three women signed Elvis's name to his replies. Yancey's starting salary was $65 a week, rising to $125 a week by the time she departed. While working at Graceland, she befriended Priscilla. Yancey and Cliff Linedecker wrote the 1977 book *My Life with Elvis.*

YELVINGTON, MALCOLM
Country Singer who headed a band called the Star Rhythm Boys (Jake Ryles, Gordon Mashburn, Reece Fleming, and Miles Wimm) in Memphis in the early 1950s, recording for Sun Records. It has been said that in late 1954 Elvis sang with the band at the Eagle's Nest, a performance that had been set up by Sleepy-Eyed John Lepley at the request of Sam Phillips. In an interview with Howard DeWitt for his book *Sun Elvis,* Yelvington denied that Elvis ever sang with his band.

YOGANANDA, YOGI PARAMAHANSA
(–1955) Religious leader and teacher who authored the book *Autobiography of a Yogi.* Yogananda founded the Self-Realization Fellowship in 1955. Sri Daya Mata, the Yogi's secretary, took over leadership of the SRF upon his death. For a time, Elvis was a follower of the Yogi's teachings. (See *Sri Daya Mata*)

YOUNG, BARBARA
(1939–   ) Woman who claimed to have had a two-year relationship with Elvis beginning in 1954, which produced a daughter, Deborah Presley, born on March 4, 1956. Young filed a $125 million lawsuit against the Presley estate in 1987. In an article in the *National Enquirer* (March 8, 1988), Young claimed that she met Elvis in Charlotte, North Carolina, where he was singing in a recording studio. She states that she loved it when Elvis sang for her, especially "Blue Moon over Kentucky" (giving the wrong title and wrong lyrics).[1] Young married at the age of sixteen, divorcing her husband (she told him that he was not the father of Deborah) on the very day that Elvis died, August 16, 1977).

YOUNG, ELAINE
Hollywood real-estate agent who was the onetime wife of actor Gig Young. Among the many celebrities to whom Young leased houses were John F. Kennedy and Elvis Presley.

YOUNG, FARON
(1932–   ) Popular country singer who got his start on the "Louisiana Hayride" radio program in the late 1940s and early 1950s. Young was born on February 25, 1932, in Shreveport, Louisiana, just one day before Johnny Cash. In the 1950s he appeared in the movie

---

[1] It appears that in just about all cases in which women claimed to have been Elvis's secret lover, they always make some blatant mistakes in their story that someone in their position should not make.

The Young Sheriff, and since that time has been called "The Singing Sheriff."

Young had a two-million-seller with "Hello Walls" in 1962 and another hit with "It's Four in the Morning" in 1972. Frieda's cat in the Charles Schulz comic strip Peanuts is named Faron after the singer. Singer Roger Miller was once a member of Young's band.

Young, who appeared with Elvis in concert in the Hank Snow All-Star Jamboree in the spring of 1955, composed "Is It So Strange," which Elvis recorded in 1957.

YOUNG, TAMMY
High school friend of Elvis's with whom he played pool.

YOUNG, VICTOR
(1900–1956) Bandleader and composer born in Chicago on August 8, 1900. Young received an Academy Award, posthumously, for his musical score of the 1956 movie *Around the World in 80 Days*. Young composed (music), with Edward Heyman (lyrics), the song "Love Letters" as the theme of the 1945 movie *Love Letters*. Elvis recorded the song in May 1966.

Z

ZAGER, LT. JACK
U.S. Army lieutenant who administered Elvis's mental examinations on the day of his induction into the Army—March 24, 1958.

ZANCAN, SANDRA
Las Vegas showgirl dated by Elvis in 1972, after he and Priscilla had separated.

ZARET, HY
(1907–   ) Composer born Hyman H. Zaret in New York City on August 21, 1907. Zaret and Alex North composed the song "Unchained Melody," which Elvis recorded in 1977.

ZEHETBAUER, ANJELIKA
Nightclub dancer whom Elvis dated while he was stationed in Germany. Zehetbauer has been called "Elvis's German fraulein."

ZENOFF, JUDGE DAVID
Justice of the Nevada State Supreme Court who performed the wedding ceremony for Elvis and Priscilla on May 1, 1967. (See *Aladdin Hotel*)

ZIEGLER, RONALD L.
Press secretary for President Richard M. Nixon. Ziegler was one of the Ten Outstanding Young Men of America (1971), as selected by the U.S. Jaycees. Elvis was also one of the ten.

ZIMBALIST, STEPHANIE
(1956–   ) Actress born in New York City on October 8, 1956. Zimbalist is the daughter of actor Efrem Zimbalist, Jr. She portrayed Linda Thompson in the 1981 TV movie *Elvis and the Beauty Queen*. Zimbalist's grandmother, Alma Gluck (1884–1938), was the first female singer to record a million-selling record with "Carry Me Back to Old Virginny" (Victor 88481) in 1915.

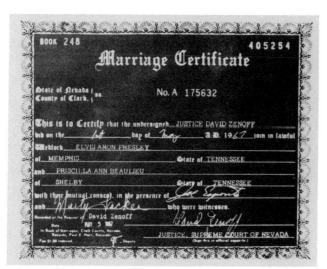

(Photo courtesy Jeff Wheatcraft)

PART II
THE PERFORMER

Elvis had to be in Los Angeles on April 3, 1956, to appear on "The Milton Berle Show." He flew out a week early to meet with producer Hal B. Wallis. After their meeting, it was decided that a screen test would be filmed on the Paramount Studios lot on Sunday, April 1.

For his screen test, Elvis was told to go through a few emotions before the camera. He then sang "Blue Suede Shoes" and performed a scene from *The Rainmaker*, a Paramount film then in the planning stages. Elvis tried out for the role of Jimmy Curry, which Earl Holliman was to later play in the film. *The Rainmaker* starred Burt Lancaster and Katharine Hepburn.

Appearing with Elvis in the screen test was veteran actor Frank Faylen, who was then on the lot making *Gunfight at the O.K. Corral* (in the role of Cotton Wilson) for Hal Wallis. Faylen made his screen debut in the 1936 Warner Bros. film *Bullets or Ballots*. Most movie buffs will recognize him as Bim, the sadistic male nurse in *The Lost Weekend* (1945). Television watchers will remember him as Dobie Gillis's long-suffering father, Herbert T. Gillis, in "The Many Loves of Dobie Gillis."

Apparently Elvis was dissatisfied with his performance and requested to do another screen test, probably the next day. Actress Cynthia Baxter appeared with Elvis in the second screen test. A photograph of Elvis and Baxter appeared in the September 8–14, 1956, issue of *TV Guide*.

Five days after the screen test, on April 6, Elvis signed a seven-year, three-movie contract with Paramount Pictures. His salary for the three films was to escalate: $100,000 for the first, $150,000 for the second, and $200,000 for the third. The contract was later renegotiated.

THE PIED PIPER OF CLEVELAND

Cleveland disc jockey Bill Randle, who was the first radio personality to play an Elvis Presley record outside the South, was quite busy in the mid-1950s. For a while he traveled between Cleveland and New York to host radio shows in both cities. Randle rivaled Alan Freed in popularity.

Universal Pictures took notice of Randle's popularity and decided to make a 15-to-20-minute documentary about a day in his life. The working title was *The Pied Piper of Cleveland: A Day in the Life of a Famous Disc Jockey*. Creative differences caused Universal to pull out of the project, leaving Randle to go it alone. He eventually produced the film with director Arthur Cohen and cinematographer Jack Barnett on a budget of $4,000.

Elvis had appeared in Cleveland three times in 1955 (February 26, March 28, and August 20). During his third trip to the city, Elvis was signed by Randle to appear in his film.

On October 19, 1955, Elvis came back to Cleveland to perform with Roy Acuff and Kitty Wells at the Circle Theatre. He was free to appear in Randle's film the next day. Headliners were the Four Lads, whose current release, "Moments to Remember," was climbing the charts and would eventually reach #2. Bill Haley and His Comets and Pat Boone also appeared. Haley had already had seven top twenty hits, including the classic "Rock Around the Clock," a few weeks earlier. Boone was riding the top of the charts with his first number one record (of an eventual six), "Ain't that a Shame." His next top ten hit, "At My Front Door (Crazy Little Mama)" had just been released and hadn't yet reached the charts.

Elvis, the Four Lads, Bill Haley and His Comets, and Pat Boone sang all of their hits at an afternoon (1:00 P.M.) concert for Brooklyn High School students. An additional show was performed that evening at St. Michael's Hall. Both shows were captured by Jack Barnett's cameras.

For his part, Elvis sang "That's All Right (Mama)," "Blue Moon of Kentucky," "Good Rockin' Tonight," "Mystery Train," and "I Forgot to Remember to Forget."

A few weeks after the concerts, a 48-minute rough cut of *The Pied Piper of Cleveland* was shown at Euclid Shore Junior High School. A clip or two eventually appeared on WEWS-TV, Channel 5, sometime in 1956.

To date, *The Pied Piper of Cleveland*, Elvis's film debut, remains unreleased, probably because of problems involving the legal ownership of the film. Bill Randle owns a copy of the short and Universal apparently has the 35-millimeter original hidden away in some vault. It is *The Pied Piper of Cleveland* that Bill Randle referred to in his introduction of Elvis on "Stage Show" on January 28, 1956.

Feature Films

LOVE ME TENDER

Twentieth Century–Fox, 1956. A David Weisbart production. Running time: 89 minutes. Elvis's first film.

CAST

Vance Reno.....................................RICHARD EGAN
Cathy Reno......................................DEBRA PAGET
Clint Reno....................................ELVIS PRESLEY
Mr. Siringo................................ROBERT MIDDLETON
Brett Reno...............................WILLIAM CAMPBELL
Mike Gavin.....................................NEVILLE BRAND
Martha Reno................................MILDRED DUNNOCK
Major Kincaid................................BRUCE BENNETT
Ray Reno...JAMES DRURY
Ed Galt..RUSS CONWAY
Mr. Kelso..KEN CLARK
Mr. Davis...BARRY COE
Pardee Fleming..................................L. Q. JONES
Jethro..PAUL BURNS
1st Train Conductor.......................JERRY SHELDON
Storekeeper....................................JAMES STONE
Auctioneer...ED MUNDY
1st Soldier......................................JOE DI REDA
Station Agent..................................BOBBY ROSE
Paymaster...................................TOM GREENWAY
Major Harris.....................................JAY JOSTYN
2nd Train Conductor.......................STEVE DARRELL
Bit...RUELL SHAYNE

Wardrobe test for *Love Me Tender*. (Photo courtesy Cinema Collectors)

CREW

Producer.....................................DAVID WEISBART
Director.....................................ROBERT D. WEBB
Screenplay...................................ROBERT BUCKNER
Based on a Story by.....................MAURICE GERAGHTY
Director of Photography..........................LEO TOVER
Art Directors.............................LYLE R. WHEELER
                                       MAURICE RANSFORD
Set Decoration............................WALTER M. SCOTT
                                            FAY BABCOCK
Special Photographic Effects....................RAY KELLOGG
Editor.....................................HUGH S. FOWLER
Makeup..BEN NYE
Hairstyles...................................HELEN TURPIN
Costumes......................................MARY WILLS
Executive Wardrobe Designer..............CHARLES LEMAIRE
Assistant Director..........................STANLEY HOUGH
Technical Advisor.......................COL. TOM PARKER
Sound Recording...........................ALFRED BRUZLIN
                                       HARRY M. LEONARD
Cinemascope Lenses by.......................BAUSCH & LOMB
Music.....................................LIONEL NEWMAN
Vocal Supervision...............................KEN DARBY
Orchestration...........................EDWARD B. POWELL

SONGS

1. "We're Gonna Move"—Sung on the front porch of the Renos' home.
2. "Love Me Tender"—Sung on the front porch of the Renos' home right after "We're Gonna Move" and at the very end of the film.
3. "Let Me"—Sung at a community get-together to build a new schoolhouse.
4. "Poor Boy"—Sung immediately after "Let Me."

"Beautiful Dreamer" was played on the harmonica by a Union soldier at the Greenwood railroad station.

PRODUCTION NOTES

✓ *Love Me Tender* premiered in New York City on November 15, 1956, at the Paramount Theater. A fifty-foot-tall cardboard picture of Elvis stood in front of the theater. On the same bill was *The Girl I Left Behind*, starring Tab Hunter and Natalie Wood. Thirty-five policemen and twenty extra ushers were used for the premiere. Theater patrons began lining up outside the box office as early as 8:00 A.M.

✓ *Love Me Tender* opened nationally on November 21, 1956. It was double-billed with *The Desperados Are in Town* in many areas of the United States. Kathy Nolan and Robert Arthur starred.

✓ The original title of *Love Me Tender* was *The Reno Brothers*. In late August 1956, the title was changed to capitalize on Elvis's singing popularity. *The Reno Brothers* was a novel by Maurice Geraghty.

✓ Robert Wagner and Jeffrey Hunter were considered for the role of Clint Reno, the part played by Elvis.

✓ While filming in Hollywood, Elvis and his parents stayed at the Hollywood Knickerbocker Hotel on Ivar Avenue. Elvis rented the entire eleventh floor.

✓ Debra Paget's younger brother, Ruell Shayne, had a bit role in *Love Me Tender*.

Debra Paget, Mildred Dunnock, Elvis. (Photo courtesy Eddie Brandt's Saturday Matinee)

✓ Twentieth Century–Fox ordered more than 500 prints from De Luxe Laboratories of *Love Me Tender*. The normal print order was about 200 or 300.

✓ Elvis's salary was a flat $100,000.

✓ The production costs were recovered within the first three days of release, while the negative costs were recouped within a couple of weeks.

✓ On opening day in Minneapolis, anti-Presley filmgoers at the RKO Orpheum Theatre interrupted the showing with heckling. Two policemen were put on duty to prevent any further disorder.

✓ Total production costs on *Love Me Tender* were just under $1 million.

✓ The original ending of *Love Me Tender* had Mildred Dunnock ringing the dinner bell for the three brothers working in the field. Pain was shown in the eyes of Dunnock and Debra Paget. The credits followed this scene.

✓ Bruce Bennett, who played Major Kincaid, was the silver medalist in the shot put in the 1928 Olympic Games under his real name, Herman Brix. In 1935 he became the movies' seventh Tarzan, appearing in two of those films. Brix formally changed his name to Bruce Bennett in 1940 and appeared in a number of films, among them *Mildred Pierce* (1945) and *The Treasure of the Sierra Madre* (1948).

✓ Director Robert D. Webb was married to Barbara McLean, the Oscar-winning editor of *Wilson* (1944).

✓ Actor Neville Brand, the man who "killed" Elvis in *Love Me Tender*, was the fourth most-decorated American soldier in World War II. (Audie Murphy was the most decorated.) Brand portrayed Al Capone twice: *The George Raft Story* (1961) and *The Scarface Mob* (1962).

✓ For his performance in *Love Me Tender*, Elvis was given a "Worst Supporting Actor Award" by the *Harvard Lampoon*.

✓ Filming began on August 23, 1956, and was completed on October 8. Exteriors were shot in the San Fernando Valley near Los Angeles. Interiors were filmed at the Twentieth Century–Fox studios.

✓ In early October 1956, an ending was filmed in which Elvis lived, but it was decided not to use it.

✓ Debra Paget first appeared with Elvis on "The Milton Berle Show" on June 5, 1956. She began her film career at the age of fifteen in *Cry of the City* (1948). Her career voluntarily ended with the release of

MR. ROCK 'N' ROLL IN THE STORY HE WAS BORN TO PLAY!

RICHARD EGAN
DEBRA PAGET
and introducing
ELVIS PRESLEY
in
Love Me Tender
from 20th CENTURY-FOX

CINEMASCOPE

co-starring
ROBERT MIDDLETON · WILLIAM CAMPBELL · NEVILLE BRAND
with MILDRED DUNNOCK · BRUCE BENNETT
PRODUCED BY DAVID WEISBART · DIRECTED BY ROBERT D. WEBB · SCREENPLAY BY ROBERT BUCKNER · BASED ON A STORY BY MAURICE GERAGHTY

(Photo courtesy Cinema Collectors)

1963's *The Haunted Palace.* Contrary to popular opinion, Paget did *not* give Elvis his first screen kiss. That honor went to Jana Lund in *Loving You.*

✓ *Love Me Tender* reached #2 in *Variety's* weekly list of top-grossing films. For the year 1956, it ranked #23.

✓ Producer David Weisbart (1915–1967) was nominated for an Oscar for Best Editing for *Johnny Belinda* (1948). His first film as producer was 1952's *Carson City. Rebel Without a Cause* is the film he's most remembered for. Weisbart went on to produce three Elvis films: *Flaming Star* (1960), *Follow That Dream* (1962), and *Kid Galahad* (1962).

✓ *Love Me Tender* was the only film in which Elvis did not receive top billing. Richard Egan and Debra Paget were both billed ahead of Elvis in the credits.

Egan starred in the 1962–63 NBC-TV series "Empire." After one season the series was canceled and a spin-off called "Redigo" (also starring Egan) took its place. The ratings were so bad that NBC canceled "Redigo" after only three months. A few months later, ABC picked up the property and aired new episodes of the original series, "Empire." This was the only time in TV history that a show was canceled, replaced with a spin-off that was also canceled, and then new episodes of the original series reappeared on another network.

At the February 23, 1972, concert at the Las Vegas Hilton, it was Richard Egan who stood up and began an ovation while Elvis was singing his closing number, "Can't Help Falling in Love."

TRIVIA

★ The opening scenes of *Love Me Tender* took place on April 10, 1865, the day after General Robert E. Lee surrendered to General Ulysses S. Grant at the Appomattox Court House in Virginia, thus ending the Civil War.

★ *$12,250*—Amount of the Union payroll taken by the Reno brothers when they robbed a Louisiana & Western train in Greenwood, Louisiana, on April 10, 1865. In actuality, the first train robbery in U.S. history took place on October 6, 1866, when the Ohio & Mississippi Railroad was robbed of $10,000 at Seymour, Indiana. The gang that robbed the train was the Reno brothers.

★ The Union soldiers whose identities Vance Reno and his men assumed were from the 12th Michigan Cavalry.

★ The Reno brothers were from East Texas.

★ *Randall's Raiders*—Band of rebel cutthroats commanded by General Randall. Vance Reno served under General Randall.

★ The Reno brothers' father was John W. Reno (1798–1864).

★ "When Johnny Comes Marching Home" was heard on the soundtrack as the Reno brothers rode into their old homestead after the end of the Civil War.

★ Elvis's first words on screen: "Whoa! . . . Brett . . . Vance . . . They told us you were dead!"

★ *Bedford, Texas*—Town near the Renos' farm.

★ *East Texas Railroad*—Railroad line that was taking the Reno brothers into Tyler, Texas, to stand before their accusers in the Greenwood, Louisiana, train-station robbery. Their former rebel friends helped them escape from the train.

★ *Hannah's Mill*—Site where Vance Reno was to meet his brothers and rebel friends after retrieving the stolen money hidden on the farm.

★ Clint Reno was born in 1843 and died in 1865.

★ Blooper: In a night scene in which Debra Paget is at her window crying, a car can be seen briefly in the background.

★ Clint Reno's dying words: "Everything's gonna be all right."

LOVING YOU

Paramount, 1957. A Hal B. Wallis production. Running time: 101 minutes. Elvis's second film.

CAST

Jimmy Tompkins (Deke Rivers)	ELVIS PRESLEY
Glenda Markle	LIZABETH SCOTT
Walter (Tex) Warner	WENDELL COREY
Susan Jessup	DOLORES HART

Elvis, Lizabeth Scott. (Photo courtesy Eddie Brandt's Saturday Matinee)

Carl Meade	JAMES GLEASON
Jim Tallman	RALPH DUMKE
Skeeter	PAUL SMITH
Wayne	KEN BECKER
Daisy Bricker	JANA LUND
Harry Taylor	VERNON RICH
Mr. Castle	DAVID CAMERON
Mrs. Gunderson	GRACE HAYLE
Mack	DICK RYAN
Mr. O'Shea	STEVE PENDLETON
Ed Grew	SYDNEY CHATTON
TV Announcer	JACK LATHAM
Mr. Jessup	WILLIAM FORREST
Mrs. Jessup	IRENE TEDROW
Lieutenant	HAL K. DAWSON
Bit Woman	HELEN HATCH
Bit Woman	MADGE BLAKE
Editor	JOE FORTE
Sally	YVONNE LIME
Teenagers	DONNA JO GRIBBLE
	VICTORIA KING
Waitress	KAREN SCOTT
Bit Woman	ALMIRA SESSIONS

Bit Girl	STEFFI SIDNEY
Frank, Manager of the Buckhorn Tavern	JULIUS M. TANNEN
1st Girl	FLORINE CARLAN
2nd Girl	NANCY KILGAS
3rd Girl	MYRNA FAHEY
Assistant Director	BUCK YOUNG
Teddy	SKIP YOUNG
Bit Girls	JOAN BRADSHAW
	MELINDA BYRON
Teenagers	LEO GASTILLO
	CAROLE DULAINE
	ELAINE DUPONT
	MICHAEL HADGE
Bit Girl	HEATHER HOPPER
Teenager	JERRY HUNTER
Bit Messenger	MIKE MAHONEY
Bit Girl	CARLA MEREY
Teenager	MICHAEL A. MONAHAN
Bit Girls	JOY REYNOLDS
	JOY A. STONER
Teenager	JEANETTE TAYLOR
Pitchman	DAVE WHITE
Bit Girls	BRENDA LOMAS

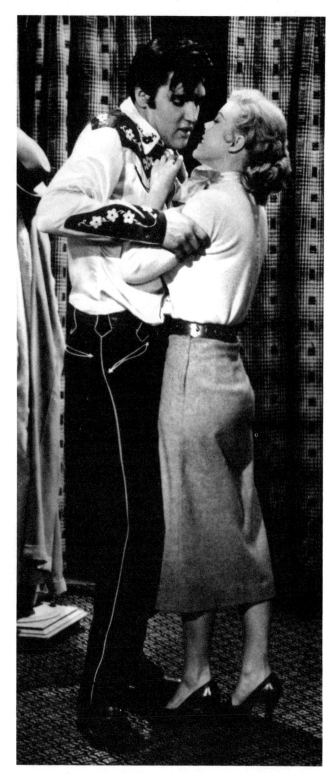

Elvis about to get his first screen kiss from Jana Lund. (Photo courtesy Eddie Brandt's Saturday Matinee)

	AUDREY LOWELL
	LINDA RIVERA
Bunk	DREW CAHILL
Leola	GWEN CALDWELL
Eddie	LES CLARK
Eddie, (Bass Player)	BILL BLACK

Glenn	BEACH DICKERSON
Musician (Drummer)	D. J. FONTANA
Barney	JAMES HORAN
Musician (Guitar Player)	SCOTTY MOORE
Sis Jessup	KATHIE ANDERSON
Buzz Jessup	TIMOTHY BUTLER
Candy	GAIL LUND
Mayor of Freegate	HARRY CHESHIRE
Sorority Girls	SUE ENGLAND
	CECILE ROGERS
Bit Women (in audience at Grand Theater)	MAIDA SEVERN
	TRUDE SEVERN
	ELSIE BAKER
Bit	BARBARA HEARN
Extras in Audience at Grand Theater	VERNON PRESLEY
	GLADYS PRESLEY
The Jordanaires	THE JORDANAIRES

CREW

Producer	HAL B. WALLIS
Director	HAL KANTER
Screenplay	HERBERT BAKER
	HAL KANTER
From a Story by	MARY AGNES THOMPSON
Director of Photography	CHARLES LANG JR.
Technicolor Color Consultant	RICHARD MUELLER
Art Directors	HAL PEREIRA
	ALBERT NOZAKI
Set Decoration	SAM COMER
	RAY MOYER
Special Photographic Effects	JOHN P. FULTON
Process Photography	FARCIOT EDOUART
Assistant Director	JAMES ROSENBERGER
Editor	HOWARD SMITH
Costumes	EDITH HEAD
Makeup Supervision	WALLY WESTMORE
Hairstyle Supervision	NELLIE MANLEY
Sound Recording	HUGO GRENZBACH
	CHARLES GRENZBACH
Associate Producer	PAUL NATHAN
Numbers Staged by	CHARLES O'CURRAN
Music Conducted and Arranged by	WALTER SCHARF
Vocal Accompaniment	THE JORDANAIRES
Technical Advisor	COL. TOM PARKER

SONGS

1. "Got a Lot o' Livin' to Do"—Sung with Tex Warner's band in Delville at the urging of Lizabeth Scott. Later in a medley with "Teddy Bear" and "Hot Dog," on a jukebox during a fight, and on stage in Freegate, Texas.
2. "(Let's Have a) Party"—Sung on stage first in Longhorn, Texas, and then in other towns on the tour.
3. "(Let Me Be Your) Teddy Bear"—Sung in a medley with "Got a Lot o' Livin' to Do" and "Hot Dog." Later, sung on stage at the Grand Theater in Amarillo.
4. "Hot Dog"—Sung in a medley with "Teddy Bear" and "Got a Lot o' Livin' to Do." Sung later on stage in Towanda.
5. "Lonesome Cowboy"—Sung on stage in Rodeo City.
6. "Mean Woman Blues"—Sung in the Buckhorn Tavern. "Accompaniment" was provided by a jukebox.
7. "Loving You"—Sung on the Jessups' farm and later in the Freegate Civic Auditorium.

Dolores Hart sang "Dancing on a Dare," "Detour," and "The Yellow Rose." Tex Warner's Rough Ridin' Ramblers played "Candy Kisses."

PRODUCTION NOTES

✓ *Loving You* premiered in Memphis on July 9, 1957, at the Strand Theater. Elvis, his parents, and Anita Wood attended a midnight showing. The film opened nationally on July 30, double-billed in many areas with the Van Johnson film *Action of the Tiger.* Four days earlier, *Loving You* was sneak-previewed at the Alhambra Theater in Sacramento, California. All moviegoers were given a photo of Elvis.

✓ Production on *Loving You* began on January 21, 1957, and was completed on March 8. Except for the Jessups' farm scenes, the film was shot entirely on the Paramount lot.

✓ *Loving You* was based on the story *A Call From Mitch Miller,* by Mary Agnes Thompson, which appeared in the June 1956 issue of *Good Housekeeping* magazine. The lead character in the story was Lonesome Harris, who sang with Tex Warner and His Red River Ramblers. His girlfriend was Susan Harris, and the setting was Oklahoma. On July 30, 1956, Hal B. Wallis bought the rights to Miss Thompson's story as a vehicle for Elvis.

✓ The original title for *Loving You* was *The Lonesome Cowboy.* That title was changed to *Running Wild* in the fall of 1956. As a matter of fact, on Elvis's last appearance on "The Ed Sullivan Show," Sullivan referred to Elvis going to Hollywood to make his latest film, *Running Wild.* Another title for the film briefly considered was *Something for the Girls.*

✓ While filming *Loving You,* Elvis and his parents stayed at the Hollywood Knickerbocker Hotel.

✓ Actress Dolores Hart made her film debut in *Loving You.* After making only ten films, she retired from acting in 1963 to become a nun. Today, Hart (real name: Dolores Hicks) is known as Mother Dolores at the convent of Regina Laudis in Bethlehem, Connecticut. Her last film was *Come Fly with Me* (1963). In 1959 *Photoplay* magazine published Hart's article "What It's Like to Kiss Elvis."

✓ Joe Gray was Elvis's stand-in on the set of *Loving You.*

✓ Elvis first met actress Yvonne Lime on the set of *Loving You.* The two dated for a time in 1957. Lime was a regular on three TV series: "Father Knows Best" (as Dottie Snow, Betty Anderson's best friend), "The Many Loves of Dobie Gillis" (as Melissa Frame), and "Happy" (as Sally Day).

✓ James Gleason appeared in over 150 films, mostly in character parts. He made five more films after *Loving You,* the last being *The Last Hurrah* (1958).

✓ Like Elvis, actress Lizabeth Scott was signed to a Paramount contract after a screen test for producer Hal Wallis. She was called "The Threat" by studio publicity agents. *Loving You* was Lizabeth Scott's last film, except for a 1972 British release, *Pulp.*

✓ Wendell Corey was elected to the Santa Monica, California, city council in 1965. He was defeated in the 1966 Republican primary race for the House of Representatives. Like Elvis and Lizabeth Scott, Corey was signed by Hal Wallis to a movie contract. He made his debut in *Desert Fury* (1947), which also starred Lizabeth Scott. Elvis had a cat named Wendell.

✓ *Loving You* was Elvis's first color film.

✓ Making their screen debuts in *Loving You* were Scotty Moore, Bill Black, D. J. Fontana, Vernon Presley, Gladys Presley, and the Jordanaires.

✓ Art director Hal Pereira won an Oscar for *The Rose Tattoo* (1955). After 26 years in the film business, he retired. His last film was 1968's *Will Penny.*

✓ Director-writer Hal Kanter was the executive producer of the hit CBS sitcom "All in the Family."

✓ *Loving You* reached #7 on *Variety*'s weekly list of top-grossing films.

✓ In July 1959, *Loving You* was rereleased as a double feature with *King Creole* in selected theaters.

TRIVIA

★ *Jim Tallman*—Politician running for governor for whom Glenda Markle worked as a publicity agent. Tex Warner's band played at rallies for Tallman. To finance Tallman's campaign, Tallman's Terrific Tonic was sold to those in the audience.

★ At the beginning of the film, Tallman was campaigning in the city of Delville.

★ *Highway Beverage*—Delville beverage distributor for which Deke Rivers worked. He earned $18 a week plus tips. In his last week he earned $26.

★ *Art Hawkins*—Bandleader who was breaking all

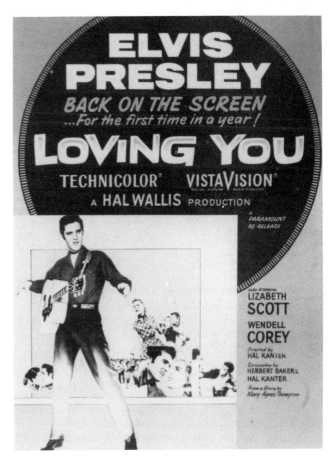

(Photo courtesy Cinema Collectors)

records in Chicago at the State Lake Theater. Tex Warner was jealous of Hawkins because Warner had created the band's sound and written all of its arrangements.

★ Tex Warner's band was known as the Rough Ridin' Ramblers. Scotty Moore, Bill Black, and D. J. Fontana had bit roles in the film as members of the band.

★ The first town in which Deke Rivers sang professionally was Longhorn, where he sang "(Let's Have a) Party." He sang there at the Community Fair Night.

★ Question: At what event did Deke Rivers sing in the town of Harolsville? Answer: The Lions Club Barbecue.

★ *Baker*—One of the towns in which Deke Rivers performed. Baker (population: 1,234) was known as "The Small Town With a Big Welcome." Some of the other towns where he performed included Jordan Crossing, Indian Wells, Big Hill, Alkalai Wells, and Lone Star.

★ Question: How long had Glenda worked for Jim Tallman? Answer: Two years.

★ *Adams High School Hop*—One of the events at which Deke Rivers and Tex Warner's Rough Ridin' Ramblers performed. After the event, Susan presented Deke with a guitar that Tex had bought for him. Tex announced that from that time on, Deke would appear on stage with the band and not just come out of the audience as he had before.

★ *Montgomery Ward*—Rodeo City store where Deke bought a green shirt with Susan's assistance. Deke referred to the store as "Monkey Wards." A pre–movie star Gregory Peck modeled clothes for the 1940 Montgomery Ward catalog.

★ Skeeter's parakeet was named Matilda.

★ Question: Who was the Delville lawyer who prepared Deke's contract for Glenda? Answer: Mike Harris.

★ Bill Black made his screen debut in *Loving You*. His first screen line: "Hey, Deke. See the picture in the paper of the gals fighting over you?" His next line was: "Yeah. From what it says in here, Deke's just about...."

★ *Carl Meade*—Booking agent for Tex Warner.

★ Question: What amount was punched by the cashier on the cash register at the end of "Mean Woman Blues"? Answer: $95.00.

★ *Grand Theatre*—Amarillo theater where Deke and Tex Warner performed. The 1957 Jerry Lewis movie *Sad Sack* was being shown at the Grand Theatre.

★ Question: What did Wayne, the boy Deke fought in the Buckhorn Tavern, say he did for a living? Answer: He worked with his "old man in auto accessories."

★ *Farmingdale*—Town near which the Jessup farm was located.

★ When asked by Susan what he and Deke were going to do during their vacation, Skeeter replied, "Maybe we'll see *The Ten Commandments* twice."

★ Elvis received his first movie kiss from Jana Lund (Daisy Bricker) during the dressing room scene at the Grand Theatre in Amarillo.

★ *That's Kissin', Cousins*— Newspaper photo caption showing Deke Rivers being kissed by Daisy Bricker. The accompanying article was titled "Deke Rivers and Femme Fan Find Fun."

★ The rooster on the Jessups' farm was named Joseph.

★ Deke Rivers's real name was Jimmy Tompkins. His early years were spent in an orphanage run by Miss Whipshaw. When the orphanage burned down eleven years before, Jimmy ran away and happened upon the Woodbine Cemetery near Allen City. In the cemetery he saw a tombstone that read: "R.I.P., Deke Rivers, 1878–1934. He was alone but for his friends who miss him." Jimmy Tompkins assumed the name Deke Rivers on that day.

★ *KTED*—Freegate, Texas, television station that provided the broadcast facilities for the national TV special that starred Deke Rivers. The telecast was aired from the Freegate Civic Center. The Jordanaires were seen in the telecast.

★ Gladys and Vernon Presley were extras in the audience at the Freegate TV broadcast. Gladys could be seen in the fourth row, aisle seat. Vernon was seated next to her.

★ The song "Detour," which Dolores Hart sang in *Loving You*, was a 1951 hit for Patti Page. "Detour" (Mercury 5682) reached #12 on *Billboard*'s pop chart.

JAILHOUSE ROCK

MGM, 1957. An Avon production. Running time: 96 minutes. Elvis's third film.

CAST

Vince Everett	ELVIS PRESLEY
Peggy Van Alden	JUDY TYLER
Hunk Houghton	MICKEY SHAUGHNESSY
Mr. Shores	VAUGHN TAYLOR
Sherry Wilson	JENNIFER HOLDEN
Teddy Talbot	DEAN JONES
Laury Jackson	ANNE NEYLAND
Warden	HUGH SANDERS
Sam Brewster	PERCY HELTON
Jack Lease	PETER ADAMS
Studio Head	WILLIAM FORREST
Paymaster	DAN WHITE
Jake the Bartender	GEORGE CISAR
Dotty	ROBIN RAYMOND
Ken	JOHN DAY
Worker	KEN L. SMITH
Judge	S. JOHN LAUNER
Guard	DICK RICH
Mr. Simpson	GLENN STRANGE
1st Mail Clerk	JOHN DENNIS
2nd Mail Clerk	TOM MAYTON
Orderly	BOB STRATTON
Cleaning Woman	ELIZABETH SLIFER
Stripteaser	GLORIA PALL
Bartender	FRED COBY
Shorty	WALTER JOHNSON
Drunk	FRANK KREIG
August Van Alden	GRANDON RHODES
Mrs. Van Alden	KATHARINE WARREN
Man	RUSSELL WHITNEY

(Photo courtesy Cinema Collectors)

Woman	ALYN LOCKWOOD
2nd Man	CHARLES POSTAL
2nd Woman	JO GILBERT
3rd Woman	PAULA TRENT
Record Shop Girl	JOAN DUPUIS
Record Distributor	WILLIAM TANNEN
Record Engineer	WILSON WOOD
Studio Gate Man	JOE MCGUINN
Announcer	BOB HOPKINS
Director	TOM MCKEE
Mr. Bardeman	ROBERT BICE
Photographer	DONALD KERR
Assistant Director	STEVE WARREN
Mr. Drummond	CARL MILLETAIRE
Mickey Alba	DON BURNETT
Waiter	FRANCOIS ANDRE
Surgeon	FRANCIS DESALES
Ad–Libs	JOHN LOGAN
	JACK YOUNGER
	MATT WINSTON
Guard Who Horse-Whipped Vince Everett	BILL HICKMAN
Piano Player	MIKE STOLLER
Guitar Player	SCOTTY MOORE
Bass Player	BILL BLACK
Drummer	D. J. FONTANA
Hotel Clerk	HARRY HINES
Guard	BILL HALE
Girl in Booth	TRACY MORGAN
Girl in Bathing Suit	LINDA WILLIAMS
Bit Men	ORV MOHLER
	JACK HERRIN
	SID KANE
	JACK SHEA

CREW

Producer	PANDRO S. BERMAN
Director	RICHARD THORPE
Screenplay	GUY TROSPER
Story	NED YOUNG
Director of Photography	ROBERT BRONNER
Art Directors	WILLIAM A. HORNING
	RANDALL DUELL
Set Decoration	HENRY GRACE
	KEOGH GLEASON
Special Effects	A. ARNOLD GILLESPIE
Assistant Director	ROBERT E. RELYEA
Editor	RALPH E. WINTERS

Associate Producer	KATHRYN HEREFORD
Makeup	WILLIAM TUTTLE
Recording Supervisor	DR. WESLEY C. MILLER
Music Supervisor	JEFF ALEXANDER
Technical Advisor	COL. TOM PARKER

SONGS

1. "Young and Beautiful"—Sung in a jail cell right after Mickey Shaughnessy sang "One More Day." It was later sung in the Club La Florita and in a hotel room at the end of the film.
2. "I Want to Be Free"—Sung on the TV show "Breath of a Nation."
3. "Don't Leave Me Now"—Sung in the recording studio twice.
4. "Treat Me Nice"—Sung in the recording studio.
5. "Jailhouse Rock"—Sung in rehearsal for an NBC-TV special.
6. "(You're So Square) Baby, I Don't Care"—Sung at a poolside party.

Mickey Shaughnessy sang "One More Day."

PRODUCTION NOTES

✓ *Jailhouse Rock* premiered in Memphis on October 17, 1957. It opened nationally on November 8. In many areas, *Jailhouse Rock* was double-billed with *The Wayward Girl*, which starred Marcia Henderson, Peter Walker, and Whit Bissell.

✓ Principal photography began on May 13, 1957, at MGM's Culver City studios and was completed on June 14th.

✓ The technical advisor in the fight scenes was Johnny Indrisano, a former welterweight boxer who previously worked on *Somebody Up There Likes Me* (1956).

✓ Crisp bacon, mashed potatoes, and dark brown gravy were added to the menu at MGM's commissary during the filming of *Jailhouse Rock* because of Elvis's affinity for those foods.

✓ Frank Kreig, who played the drunk who harassed Elvis in the first nightclub, played a member of Alcoholics Anonymous two years earlier in *I'll Cry Tomorrow*.

✓ Elvis was paid $250,000 plus 50 percent of the profits for *Jailhouse Rock*.

✓ During production, Elvis swallowed a tooth cap and had to be hospitalized for a day at Cedars of Lebanon Hospital.

✓ *Jailhouse Rock* was Jennifer Holden's film debut. In competition with over a dozen starlets, she walked into MGM in May 1956 and walked out five minutes later with a contract. Her only previous experience was drama study with Lillian Roth and an appearance at the Palace Theatre in New York City. Elvis's love scene with the brown-eyed, blonde beauty (37-21-35) lasted three minutes on the screen, but took about four hours to film. On the last day of filming, a small heater in Holden's dressing room caught fire. As the property man put out the fire, Elvis carried her to safety.

✓ At the age of seventeen, Judy Tyler (1934–1957) began playing Princess Summerfall Winterspring on the "Howdy Doody" TV series. Her real name was Judith Hess. Julian Hess, her father, was a trumpet player with both Benny Goodman and Paul Whiteman.

Bill Black, D. J. Fontana, Judy Tyler, Mike Stoller, Scotty Moore, and Elvis. (Photo courtesy Eddie Brandt's Saturday Matinee)

In the 1955 Broadway play *Pipe Dream*, Tyler and William Johnson introduced the Rodgers and Hammerstein song "All at Once You Love Her." She made her film debut in *Bop Girl Goes Calypso* (1957). In that film Bobby Troup played a psychologist who predicted that calypso music would succeed rock & roll as the nation's most popular music. *Jailhouse Rock* was Tyler's second and last film appearance. She and her husband of four months, George Lafayette, were killed in a car accident near Billy the Kid, Wyoming, on July 3, 1957. The 23-year-old driver of the other vehicle was also killed. After Tyler's death, Kenny Baker recorded a tribute record entitled "Good-bye Little Star."

✓ Shortly after filming *Jailhouse Rock*, Elvis was made an honorary colonel in Louisiana.

✓ "One More Day," which was sung by Mickey Shaughnessy, was written by Sid Tepper and Roy C. Bennett.

✓ Dean Jones, known mostly for his work in Disney films, was once a blues singer. He was coached on his disc jockey role in *Jailhouse Rock* by Ira Cooke of Los Angeles and Dewey Phillips of Memphis.

✓ Elvis briefly dated costar Anne Neyland during filming.

✓ Before being chosen for the role of Hunk Houghton, Mickey Shaughnessy had a nightclub act in which he ridiculed Elvis. In 1971 Shaughnessy costarred with Dean Jones in the CBS-TV series "The Chicago Teddy Bears."

✓ Glenn Strange, who played Mr. Simpson in *Jailhouse Rock*, played the Frankenstein monster in three films: *House of Frankenstein* (1945), *House of Dracula* (1945), and *Abbott and Costello Meet Frankenstein* (1948). Television audiences will remember Glenn Strange as Sam the bartender at the Long Branch Saloon in the TV series "Gunsmoke."

✓ *Jailhouse Rock* reached #3 in *Variety's* weekly list of top-grossing films. For the year 1957 it was ranked #14. Total gross was $4 million.

✓ On March 9, 1960, *Jailhouse Rock* was rereleased to coincide with Elvis's discharge from the Army.

TRIVIA

★ *14 Months*—Time in prison served by Vince Everett for killing a man in a bar. His sentence was one to ten years.

★ Question: What song was playing on the jukebox during a barroom fight in which Vince Everett killed a man? Answer: "Red River Valley." The song, which was originally titled "The Bright Mohawk Valley," served as the theme for *The Grapes of Wrath* (1940) and *The Ox-Bow Incident* (1943).

★ *6239*—Vince Everett's prison number. Hunk Houghton's prison number was 7239.

★ Vince and Hunk were incarcerated in cellblock 21.

★ Hunk had once toured with Eddy Arnold and Roy Acuff.

★ Question: How much was Vince Everett's paycheck that he cashed at the bar? Answer: $108.

★ *Breath of a Nation*—Live coast-to-coast television show on which Vince Everett sang "I Want to Be Free." "Breath of a Nation" was broadcast from the prison.

★ *Pickerel*—Brand of cigarettes that Hunk Houghton showed to Vince Everett as being the rate of exchange in prison.

★ Vince met Peggy Van Alden at the Club La Florita, a nightclub owned by Sam Brewster.

★ Question: How much money did Vince get from the state upon his release from prison? Answer: $54.

★ *Crying to the Stars*—Top record (it got 84 plays) by Mickey Alba on the jukebox in the Club La Florita. It was one of the records being promoted by Peggy Van Alden.

★ *Mary Jane Hamilton*—Fifteen-year-old girl from Riverport who wrote Vince Everett a fan letter that he read in his hotel room. She gave her measurements as 33-25-36, hair as brown, eyes as blue, and telephone number as LOckwood-4357.

★ During the recording session of "Don't Leave Me Now," photos of several RCA artists could be seen, including the Ames Brothers, Tony Martin, Harry Belafonte, Lena Horne, Jaye P. Morgan, Hugo Winterhalter, Eddie Fisher, and Dinah Shore.

★ *Geneva Records*—Record company owned by Jack Lease for which singing star Mickey Alba recorded. Peg took Vince Everett's first recording, "Don't Leave Me Now," to Geneva, but Lease rejected it only to later release the song by Mickey Alba using Vince's style and arrangement.

★ After the rejection by Geneva Records, Peg took Vince's "Don't Leave Me Now" to Deltona Records. They never released the record because Mickey Alba's version was the first on the market.

★ Peggy's father, August Van Alden, was a professor at Bertrand College.

★ A record by jazz musician Stubby Wrightmeyer was played at Peggy's parents' home.

★ *Laurel Records*—Record label founded by Vince and Peggy. He got 51 percent, she got 40 percent, and their lawyer, Mr. Shore, got 9 percent. Laurel Records' first release was "Treat Me Nice" (Laurel 101).

★ *Size Pet Shop*—Business for which disc jockey Teddy Talbot read a commercial during the playing of Vince Everett's "Treat Me Nice." He did it so as to have an excuse to play the record a second time, giving it more airplay. The telephone number of Size Pet Shop was MAmmoth 6-2480.

★ Peggy's hotel room number in Joplin, Missouri, was 421.

★ Question: From what car dealer did Vince Everett buy a new white Cadillac? Answer: World Motors.

★ *Uncle Matthew's Bonded Bourbon*—Twelve-year-old liquor served to Hunk by Vince.

★ To honor the contract he signed with Hunk in prison, Vince gave Hunk 10 percent of his earnings.

★ Blooper: Concerning the Laurel Records partnership, Shores mentioned that the "40 percent participant failed to telephone the 60 percent partner," i.e.,

Judy Tyler, Elvis. (Photo courtesy Cinema Collectors)

Peggy failed to telephone Vince. However, Shores was a 9 percent partner in the firm, which left Vince with 51 percent of the company, not 60 percent.

★ The Capitol Records building in Hollywood could be seen in the film.

★ *Climax Studios*—Hollywood movie studio with which Vince signed a nonexclusive contract to make movies. The actual studio shown was MGM.

★ Question: The house of what comedian was pointed out on a Hollywood tour taken by Vince and starlet Sherry Wilson? Answer: Jack Benny.

★ *314*—Vince Everett's hospital room after he was hit in the throat by Hunk.

★ The song "The Tender Trap" was heard on the soundtrack during the scene in which Vince and Sherry Wilson swam. "The Tender Trap" was the theme for the 1955 movie of the same title, which starred Frank Sinatra and Debbie Reynolds.

★ During the "Jailhouse Rock" production number, Vince wore prison number 6240.

★ *1313*—Number on all the cell doors in the "Jailhouse Rock" production number.

KING CREOLE

Paramount, 1958. A Hal B. Wallis production. Running time: 116 minutes. Elvis's fourth film.

CAST

Danny Fisher	ELVIS PRESLEY
Ronnie	CAROLYN JONES
Maxie Fields	WALTER MATTHAU
Nellie	DOLORES HART
Mr. Fisher	DEAN JAGGER

Jack Grinnage, Elvis, Vic Morrow. (Photo courtesy Eddie Brandt's Saturday Matinee)

Forty Nina........................LILIANE MONTEVECCHI
Shark..VIC MORROW
Charlie LeGrand...........................PAUL STEWART
Mimi Fisher................................JAN SHEPARD
Sal..BRIAN HUTTON
Dummy....................................JACK GRINNAGE
Eddie Burton...............................DICK WINSLOW
Mr. Evans................................RAYMOND BAILEY
Mr. Primont..............................GAVIN GORDON
Ralph...VAL AVERY
Dr. Patrick.........................ALEXANDER LOCKWOOD
Dr. Michael Cabot.......................SAM BUFFINGTON
Hotel Clerk.................................NED GLASS
Mrs. Pearson...............................HELEN HATCH
Mr. Furst...............................CHARLES EVANS
Eddie.......................................RIC ROMAN
Catherine...............................LILYN CHAUVIN
Master of Ceremonies.....................SLICK SLAVEN
Chico, Bartender at the Gilded Cage.........TONY RUSSO
Drug Clerk...................................LEON TYLER
Doorman................................CANDY CANDIDO
Mr. McIntyre.................WALTER ANTHONY MERRILL
Entertainer..................................ZIVA RODANN
Cigarette Girl..............................RITA GREEN
Collector................................JOHN INDRISANO
"B" Girl.....................................KAY HAYDN
Salesgirls................................BARBARA GAYLE
                                        SUSANNE SYDNEY
                                        JACQUELINE PARK
                                        JACKIE JOSEPH
Bit Girl...................................NINA VAUGHN
Woman Who Asks for Water..................HAZEL BOYNE
Woman...................................BLANCHE THOMAS
Street Vendor..............................KITTY WHITE

CREW

Producer...................................HAL B. WALLIS
Director...................................MICHAEL CURTIZ
Screenplay................................HERBERT BAKER
                             MICHAEL VINCENTE GAZZO
Based on a Novel by.......................HAROLD ROBBINS
Director of Photography..................RUSSELL HARLAN
Art Directors................................HAL PEREIRA
                          JOSEPH MACMILLAN JOHNSON
Set Decoration..............................SAM COMER
                                        FRANK MCKELVY

Editorial Supervision............................WARREN LOW
Special Photographic Effects................JOHN P. FULTON
Process Photography......................FARCIOT EDOUART
Makeup..................................WALLY WESTMORE
Hairstyles...............................NELLIE MANLEY
Costumes...................................EDITH HEAD
Assistant Director.......................D. MICHAEL MOORE
Sound Recording...........................HAROLD LEWIS
                                        CHARLES GRENZBACH
Associate Producer...........................PAUL NATHAN
Musical Numbers Staged by................CHARLES O'CURRAN
Music Adapted and Scored by..................WALTER SCHARF
Vocal Accompaniment......................THE JORDANAIRES
Technical Advisor..........................COL. TOM PARKER
Dialogue Coach.............................NORMAN STUART

SONGS

1. "Crawfish"—Sung in duet with Kitty White from an apartment balcony. She was in a horse-drawn cart.
2. "Steadfast, Loyal and True"—Sung in the Gilded Cage.
3. "Lover Doll"—Sung in the department store while Shark, Sal, and Dummy stole merchandise.
4. "Trouble"—Sung on stage at the Gilded Cage at the "prompting" of Walter Matthau.
5. "Dixieland Rock"—Sung in the King Creole nightclub.
6. "Young Dreams"—Sung in the King Creole nightclub.
7. "New Orleans"—Sung in the King Creole nightclub.
8. "Hard Headed Woman"—Sung in the King Creole nightclub.
9. "King Creole"—Sung in the King Creole nightclub right after "Hard Headed Woman."
10. "Don't Ask Me Why"—Sung in the King Creole nightclub.
11. "As Long as I Have You"—Sung in the King Creole nightclub at the end of the film.

"Turtles, Berries and Gumbo" was sung by three black street vendors. Liliane Montevecchi sang "Banana." "Danny" was recorded for *King Creole* as the original song title, but it was not used.

PRODUCTION NOTES

✓ *King Creole* opened nationally on July 2, 1958. In many areas it was double-billed with *Bullwhip*, a western starring Guy Madison and Rhonda Fleming. In other areas, *Summer Love* was the cofeature. *Summer Love* was a sequel to *Rock Pretty Baby* and starred John Saxon and Rod McKuen. In still other areas, the Otto Kruger–Mala Powers horror film *Colossus of New York* was on the same bill.

✓ Production on *King Creole* began on January 20, 1958, and was completed on March 10. In order to be able to do the film, Elvis had to request a deferment from his local draft board. On December 27, 1957, the Memphis Draft Board granted Elvis a 60-day deferment. Paramount production chief Frank Freeman had previously tried to get the deferment for Elvis.

✓ Producer Hal B. Wallis purchased the rights to Harold Robbins's novel *A Stone for Danny Fisher* in February 1955 for $25,000. The intention was for Michael V. Gazzo to write the screenplay and for Ben Gazzara to star. At about that time, *A Stone for Danny Fisher* was playing off-Broadway.

✓ *King Creole* was the first Elvis movie to be filmed on location. Some of the New Orleans locations used in

Elvis, Walter Matthau, Carolyn Jones. (Photo courtesy Eddie Brandt's Saturday Matinee)

the film were the French Quarter, the Vieux Carre Saloon, Lake Pontchartrain, and a local high school.

✓ While filming in New Orleans, Elvis stayed on the tenth floor of the Roosevelt Hotel. He stayed at the Beverly Wilshire Hotel while in Hollywood.

✓ In Harold Robbins's book *A Stone for Danny Fisher*, Fisher was a boxer, not a singer. The book was set in New York City.

✓ The original name of Danny Fisher was Danny Finnell before the filming of *King Creole*. Some reference sources even today use the name Danny Finnell when listing the film's cast of characters.

✓ Two titles first considered for *King Creole* were *Danny* and *Sing, You Sinners*.

✓ Elvis's dressing room at Paramount Pictures had just been used by Anna Magnani, who was filming *Wild Is the Wind* (1957) at the studio.

✓ Hal B. Wallis planned to remake *King Creole* in 1976, but the project never got off the ground.

✓ Actress Carolyn Jones has the distinction of playing the shortest role by a female ever nominated for an Oscar. She received a Best Supporting Actress nomination for her few minutes appearance in 1957's *The Bachelor Party*. Most audiences today know Carolyn

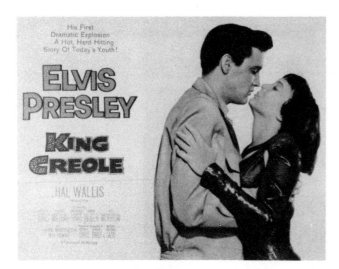

(Photo courtesy Cinema Collectors)

Jones for her role as Morticia Addams in the TV comedy "The Addams Family."

✓ Candy Candido, who played a doorman in *King Creole*, was the cartoon voice of Popeye in the 1930s.

✓ Hungarian-born director Michael Curtiz (real name: Mihaly Kertesz) directed over 100 films during his career, most of them for Warner Bros. in the 1930s and 1940s. He received four Oscar nominations, two of them in the same year: *Angels with Dirty Faces* (1938), *Four Daughters* (1938), *Yankee Doodle Dandy* (1942), and *Casablanca* (1942). He won for *Casablanca*. *King Creole* came at a later stage of his career. He directed just seven more films, his last being *The Comancheros* in 1961.

✓ Walter Matthau's father was a Catholic priest in Czarist Russia before marrying. *King Creole* was Matthau's sixth film. In 1966 he received an Oscar for Best Supporting Actor for his performance in *The Fortune Cookie*. Interestingly, in the 1974 movie *Earthquake*, in which Matthau played a drunk, he was billed under his real name in the credits—Walter Matuschanskayasky.

TRIVIA

★ *Gilded Cage*—Bourbon Street nightclub owned by Maxie Fields at which Danny Fisher worked sweeping the floors before school.

★ *Regal Pharmacy*—Drug store where Mr. Fisher worked as a pharmacist. His boss was Mr. Primont.

★ The five-and-dime store where Shark, Sal, and Dummy shoplifted while Danny sang was located on Charles Street. Nellie worked at the store.

★ *205*—Hotel room to which Danny took Nellie.

★ Question: In the hotel room, what did Danny first tell Nellie his name was? Answer: George.

★ Charlie LeGrand once managed Ronnie when she was a nightclub singer.

★ *King Creole*—Bourbon Street nightclub owned by Charlie LeGrand at which Danny Fisher sang. His beginning salary was $85 a week. Danny was first billed as Danny (Boom Boom) Fisher. The previous headliner at the King Creole was stripper Forty Nina.

★ The apartment where Danny lived with his father and sister, Mimi, was located at 29 Royal Street.

★ "Banana," the song sung by Forty Nina, was written by Sid Tepper and Roy C. Bennett.

★ Ronnie once won a contest called "The Best Legs in the State of Maine."

★ Carolyn Jones sang a few lines of "As Long as I Have You" without musical accompaniment.

★ *Royal High School*—New Orleans high school attended by Danny Fisher. The school song was "Steadfast, Loyal and True."

★ Question: What was the name of the priest to whom Nellie went to discuss her relationship with Danny? Answer: Father Franklin.

★ Note given to Danny by Dummy: "You did me a favor once. Think you should know your father is with Maxie Fields. *Be careful.*"

★ "Turtles, Berries and Gumbo," the song sung by three black street vendors in the film's opening sequence was written by Al Wood and Kay Twomey.

G. I. BLUES

Paramount, 1960. A Hal B. Wallis production. Running time: 104 minutes. Elvis's fifth film.

CAST

Tulsa McLean	ELVIS PRESLEY
Lili	JULIET PROWSE
Cookey	ROBERT IVERS
Tina	LETICIA ROMAN
Rick	JAMES DOUGLAS
Marla	SIGRID MAIER
Sergeant McGraw	ARCH JOHNSON
Jeeter	MICKEY KNOX
Captain Hobart	JOHN HUDSON
Mac	KEN BECKER
Turk	JEREMY SLATE
Warren	BEACH DICKERSON
Mickey	TRENT DOLAN
Walt	CARL CROW
Papa Mueller	FRED ESSLER
Harvey	RONALD STARR
Trudy	ERIKA PETERS
Puppet Show Owner	LUDWIG STOSSEL
German Guitarist Leader	ROBERT BOON
Mrs. Hagermann	EDIT ANGOLD
Orchestra Leader	DICK WINSLOW
Red	ED FAULKNER
Bandleader	EDWARD COCH
Herr Klugmann	FRED KRUGER
Head Waiter	TORBEN MEYER
Businessman	GENE ROTH
Businessman	ROY C. WRIGHT
MP	HARPER CARTER
Chaplain	WALTER CONRAD
Sgt. "Dynamite" Bixby	EDWARD STROLL
Kaffeehaus Manager	WILLIAM KAUFMANN
Waitress	KAREN MANN
MP	TIP MCCLURE
Strolling Girl Singer	HANNERL MELCHER
Bit Sergeant	ELISHA MATTHEW MOTT JR.
Bartender	BLAINE TURNER

Juliet Prowse, Elvis. (Photo courtesy Eddie Brandt's Saturday Matinee)

Fritzie	JUDITH RAWLINS
Britta, the Redhead	BRITTA EKMAN
Rick's Baby	KERRY CHARLES RAY
	TERRY EARL RAY
	DAVID PAUL RANKIN
	DONALD JAMES RANKIN
	DONALD CLARK WISE
	DAVID CLARK WISE
Bargirl	MARIANNE GABA
Bargirl	SALLY TODD
Bit Girl	TRUDE WYLER
MP	MICHAEL SARGENT
Blonde	MARLYN GLADSTONE
Brunette	LIZ DUBROCK
Puppeteers	ROBERT ALLISON BAKER III
	DONALD G. SAHLIN
	F. ALTON WOOD
Musicians	SCOTTY MOORE
	D. J. FONTANA

CREW

Producer	HAL B. WALLIS
Director	NORMAN TAUROG
Screenplay	EDMUND BELOIN
	HENRY GARSON
Director of Photography	LOYAL GRIGGS
Art Directors	HAL PEREIRA
	WALTER TYLER
Set Decoration	SAM COMER
	RAY MOYER
Special Photographic Effects	JOHN P. FULTON JR.
Process Photography	FARCIOT EDOUART
Technical Color Consultant	RICHARD MUELLER
Second Unit Assistant Director	D. MICHAEL MOORE
Makeup	WALLY WESTMORE
Hairstyles	NELLIE MANLEY
Costumes	EDITH HEAD
Dialogue Coach	JACK MINTZ
Editorial Supervision	WARREN LOW

Elvis and the Jordanaires sing "Frankfort Special." (Photo courtesy Cinema Collectors)

Associate Producer.............................PAUL NATHAN
Sound Recording.............................HAROLD LEWIS
                                    CHARLES GRENZBACH
Musical Numbers Staged and Choreographed by.........
                          ....CHARLES O'CURRAN
Music Scored and Conducted by................JOSEPH J. LILLEY
Vocal Accompaniment.......................THE JORDANAIRES
Technical Advisor...........................COL. TOM PARKER
Military Technical Advisor.............CAPT. DAVID S. PARKHURST

SONGS

1. "What's She Really Like"—Sung in the shower with no musical accompaniment. This partial version lasted eighteen seconds.
2. "G. I. Blues"—Sung in the Rathskeller Club.
3. "Doin' the Best I Can"—Sung in the Rathskeller Club. It was interrupted when a patron played "Blue Suede Shoes" on the jukebox.
4. "Blue Suede Shoes"—Played on a jukebox in the Rathskeller Club by a disgruntled patron, interrupting "Doin' the Best I Can."
5. "Frankfort Special"—Sung on the train to Frankfort.
6. "Shoppin' Around"—Sung in the Club Europa after first meeting Juliet Prowse.
7. "Tonight Is So Right for Love"—Sung in a German nightclub, the Bergreller.
8. "Wooden Heart"—Sung at a puppet show.
9. "Pocketful of Rainbows"—Sung to Juliet Prowse while riding up a mountain in a cable car.
10. "Big Boots"—Sung to Rick's baby in Lili's apartment.
11. "Didja Ever"—Sung at an Armed Forces show.

European prints of *G. I. Blues* substituted "Tonight's All Right for Love" for "Tonight Is So Right for Love" because of copyright reasons. Reportedly, "Whistling Blues" was recorded for the movie, but no further information is available on the song.

PRODUCTION NOTES

✓ After a sneak preview at the Majestic Theatre in Dallas on August 18, 1960, *G. I. Blues* opened nationally on November 23. The second feature at many theaters was *Walk Tall*, which starred Willard Parker and Joyce Meadows. Before opening nationally, *G. I. Blues* played several military bases.

✓ Los Angeles TV station KTTV planned to televise the opening at the Fox Wilshire Theatre in the city on November 15, 1960. But the telecast was canceled because of the inability to get a Sherman tank for the premiere. The special showing, which was a benefit for the Hemophilia Foundation, *was* covered on radio. Among the celebrities interviewed were Juliet Prowse, Ronald Reagan, and Cesar Romero.

✓ Production on *G. I. Blues* began on May 2, 1960, and lasted until late June. All of Elvis's scenes were filmed on the Paramount lot. A camera crew was sent to West Germany for several weeks of location shooting to use as atmosphere in the film.

✓ Elvis stayed at the Beverly Wilshire Hotel during filming.

✓ Originally, Elvis's character was called Tulsa McCauley. That was changed to Tulsa McLean before the start of production. However, many reviews of the day, as well as many reference books through the years, incorrectly used the original name.

✓ During filming on the Paramount lot, Elvis played host to the King and Queen of Nepal, the King and Queen of Thailand, and princesses from Sweden, Norway, and Denmark.

✓ In the barracks shower scene, wooden blocks were used in place of soap in long camera shots. The real thing was used for close-ups.

✓ Actresses Leticia Roman (real name: Leticia Novarese) and Sigrid Maier made their screen debuts in *G. I. Blues*. Director Norman Taurog's thirteen-year-old daughter, Priscilla, also made her first movie appearance in the film. She was one of the children in the puppet show scene.

✓ Paramount launched a talent search for three sets of twin boys to play the baby of Rick and Marla in the film. The twins had to be about a year old and have brown hair and brown eyes. Three sets of twins were required because the laws of California prevented any one child from working more than four hours a day or two hours before the cameras. Each boy was issued a Social Security card and received $22.05 for each day of work.

✓ One of the early titles considered for *G. I. Blues* was *Café Europa*.

✓ Arch Johnson was an Associated Press correspondent in Europe before becoming an actor in the 1950s.

✓ *G. I. Blues* was the last film in character actor Ludwig Stossel's career. The Austrian-born actor began his career in Germany in 1930. Perhaps his most remembered roles were in *The Pride of the Yankees* (1942) (as Lou Gehrig's father) and *The Beginning or the End* (1947) (as Albert Einstein).

✓ *G. I. Blues* was the first of nine Elvis movies directed by Norman Taurog. In 1913, at the age of fourteen, Taurog began a short-lived acting career. He began directing at the age of twenty and eventually directed dozens of films, many of them classics. They include *The Adventures of Tom Sawyer* (1938) and *Words and Music* (1948). He won an Oscar for Best Director for *Skippy* (1931), in which he directed his nephew, Jackie Cooper, to a Best Supporting Actor nomination. Taurog received one other Academy Award nomination for *Boys' Town* (1940).

✓ *G. I. Blues* was RCA's first video disc.

✓ Juliet Prowse was born in Bombay, India, and raised in South Africa. Her first film was *Gentlemen Marry Brunettes* (1955), her second was *Can-Can* (1960), and her third was *G. I. Blues*. For a time, Prowse was Frank Sinatra's fiancée. Elvis dated her briefly. In the 1965–66 TV season, Prowse starred in her own series, "Mona McCluskey."

✓ A showing of *G. I. Blues* in Mexico City caused a riot. Theater patrons ripped seats and broke windows.

The Mexican government banned all future Elvis films.

✓ *G. I. Blues* reached #2 on *Variety*'s weekly list of top-grossing films. For the year 1960, it ranked #14, grossing an incredible $4.3 million the last six weeks of the year.

TRIVIA

★ *Pretty Boy II*—Nickname of Tulsa McLean's tank crew.

★ *The Three Blazes*—Combo consisting of Tulsa, Rick, and Cookey. The Three Blazes played in the Rathskeller, a German club owned by Papa Mueller.

★ Scotty Moore and D. J. Fontana could be seen playing in the Rathskeller.

★ Question: How much did Papa Mueller pay Tulsa for singing in the Rathskeller the first night? Answer: 40 marks.

★ *The Chili Parlor*—Former business on the Oklahoma Turnpike that Tulsa, Rick, and Cookey wanted to transform into a hot nightspot after they were discharged from the Army. To get the lease on the building, they needed $600.

★ Before entering the Army, Tulsa worked in a gas station back in his native Oklahoma.

★ Sgt. Dynamite Bixby was shipped to Alaska because of his many extracurricular activities with the West German girls.

★ Tulsa's friend Jeeter had been married six times.

★ Henninger was the brand of beer sold at the Rathskeller.

★ *Café Europa*—Frankfort nightclub where Lili was the featured performer.

★ Tulsa learned to play the guitar from his grandfather, a full-blooded Cherokee Indian. The real name of his Uncle Charlie was Leaping Bear.

★ Tina was from Milan, Italy, where her father was a butcher.

★ *Fritz Liebe Emma, 1959*—Message carved into a table on the boat taken by Tulsa and Lili from Cologne to Dusseldorf. Also seen were "Fritz Liebe Dora" and "Fritz Liebe Hilda." This was a blooper as the correct German usage should have been "Fritz Liebt Emma."

★ *Operation Lili–Europa*—Plan to observe Tulsa to see if he could spend the night with Lili.

★ Question: What was the number on the side of the cable car taken by Tulsa and Lili up to the summit of the mountain? Answer: 76.

★ Question: In what city were Rick and Marla married? Answer: Heidelberg.

★ *Tiger*—Tulsa and Lili's nickname for Rick and Marla's baby boy.

★ *Kaffeehaus*—Restaurant across from Lili's apartment where Cookey, Mac, and Harvey spent the night waiting for Tulsa to leave. They wanted to confirm the fact that he had spent the night in her apartment so they would win a bet.

★ Tulsa McLean was in the 3rd Armored Division.

★ *Didja Ever*—Elvis's last words in *G. I. Blues*. He looked at the viewer, said "Didja ever," and then kissed Juliet Prowse.

FLAMING STAR

Twentieth Century–Fox, 1960. A David Weisbart production. Running time: 101 minutes. Elvis's sixth film.

CAST

Pacer Burton	ELVIS PRESLEY
Clint Burton	STEVE FORREST
Roslyn Pierce	BARBARA EDEN
Neddy Burton	DOLORES DEL RIO
Sam Burton	JOHN MCINTIRE
Buffalo Horn	RUDOLPH ACOSTA
Dred Pierce	KARL SWENSON
Doc Phillips	FORD RAINEY
Angus Pierce	RICHARD JAECKEL
Dorothy Howard	ANNE BENTON
Tom Howard	L. Q. JONES
Will Howard	DOUGLAS DICK
Jute	TOM REESE
Ph'Sha Knay	MARIAN GOLDINA
Ben Ford	MONTE BURKHART
Mr. Hornsby	TED JACQUES
Indian Brave	RODD REDWING
Two Moons	PERRY LOPEZ
Matt Holcom	ROY JENSON
Posseman	BOB FOLKERSON
1st Man at Crossing	TOM FADDEN
2nd Man at Crossing	GRISWOLD GREEN
3rd Man at Crossing	TOM ALLEN
4th Man at Crossing	GUY WAY
5th Man at Crossing	JOE BROOKS
6th Man at Crossing	WILLIAM HERRIN
Dottie Phillips	BARBARA BEAIRD
Mrs. Phillips	VIRGINIA CHRISTINE
Driver	BOB ADLER
1st Brave	LON BALLENTYNE
2nd Brave	PAT HOGAN
3rd Brave	FOSTER HOOD
Bird's Wing	SHARON BERCUTT
Indian Chief	LARRY CHANCE
Brave	HENRY AMARGO
Indian	RAY BELTRAM
Indian	RED WEST
Bit	CHARLES HORVATH

Barbara Eden, Elvis, Steve Forrest. (Photo courtesy Eddie Brandt's Saturday Matinee)

CREW

Producer....................................DAVID WEISBART
Director...DON SIEGEL
Screenplay..................................CLAIR HUFFAKER
NUNNALLY JOHNSON
Based on a Novel by.........................CLAIR HUFFAKER
Director of Photography...................CHARLES G. CLARKE
Art Directors..............................DUNCAN CRAMER
WALTER M. SIMONDS
Set Decoration............................WALTER M. SCOTT
GUSTAV BERNTSEN
Second Unit Director......................RICHARD TALMADGE
Editor.....................................HUGH S. FOWLER
Assistant Director........................JOSEPH E. RICKARDS
Makeup..BEN NYE
Hairstyles...................................HELEN TURPIN
Costumes...................................ADELE BALKEN
Sound Recording..........................E. CLAYTON WARD
WARREN B. DELAPLAIN
Music.....................................CYRIL J. MOCKRIDGE
Music Conducted by.........................LIONEL NEWMAN
Orchestration............................EDWARD B. POWELL
Dances Staged by...........................JOSEPHINE EARL
Technical Adviser..........................COL. TOM PARKER
Vocal Accompaniment.......................THE JORDANAIRES

SONGS

1. "Flaming Star"—Sung over the opening credits.
2. "A Cane and a High Starched Collar"—Sung in the Burtons' cabin during the first few minutes of the film.

"Britches" and "Summer Kisses, Winter Tears" were both cut from the film.

PRODUCTION NOTES

✓ *Flaming Star* premiered in Los Angeles on December 20, 1960, and was released nationally the next day. It was double-billed with *For the Love of Mike* at many theaters. *For the Love of Mike*, which starred Richard Basehart and Stu Erwin, also had an Indian theme. Some theaters featured *Freckles*, starring Martin West and Carol Christensen, on the same bill.

✓ Production on *Flaming Star* began on August 16, 1960, and was completed on October 4. Much of the movie was photographed on three ranches in the San Fernando Valley near Los Angeles, including the 8,000-acre Conejo Movie Ranch outside of Thousand Oaks, California. Interiors were shot on Stage 14 at Twentieth Century–Fox.

✓ *Flaming Star* took two and a half years to get to the screen. Numerous title changes were made. It was originally announced in April 1958 that *The Brothers of Broken Lance* by Clair Huffaker was to be published by Random House. Twentieth Century–Fox bought the movie rights before the book was published. One month later, Random House said that it might change the title of the book to the probable movie title, *The Brothers of Flaming Arrow*. On May 27, 1958, it was announced that Marlon Brando and Frank Sinatra were set to play the roles of the two brothers. Filming was to have begun on June 16, 1958, but negotiations with the two stars broke down. In the meantime, the title was changed to *Flaming Lance*.

Two years later, on June 12, 1960, it was announced that Elvis Presley had been signed to star in *Flaming*

Relaxing on the *Flaming Star* set. (Photo courtesy Eddie Brandt's Saturday Matinee)

Lance. Before the cameras rolled on August 16, 1960, the title was again changed, this time to *Flaming Heart*, and then to *Black Star*. During filming, the title became *Black Heart*. Finally, on September 2, 1960, *Flaming Star* was chosen as the film's title.

✓ After he had thought about the story for several years, Clair Huffaker wrote the book *Flaming Lance* in ten days. It took Huffaker and Nunnally Johnson *30 weeks* of work to turn out an acceptable screenplay!

✓ *Flaming Star* was Clair Huffaker's first movie screenplay. Specializing in Westerns, he later wrote screenplays for *The Comancheros* (1961), *The War Wagon* (1967), and *100 Rifles* (1969).

✓ Nunnally Johnson's writing career dated from the 1920s. Among his numerous credits were *Dimples* (1936), *The Grapes of Wrath* (1940), *Tobacco Road* (1941), *The Three Faces of Eve* (1957), and *The Dirty Dozen* (1967). In 1930 Johnson created the popular cartoon series, *There Ought to Be a Law*.

✓ Tests were made with Elvis wearing brown-tinted contact lenses, but it was decided to discard the idea.

✓ Stuntman Tom Sweet was hired by the producers to double for Elvis in the tough fight scenes, but he was not needed because Elvis did such a good job.

✓ *Flaming Star* was banned in South Africa because of strict racial laws. The film depicted Elvis as the son of a white father and an Indian mother.

✓ Barbara Eden was first offered the role of Roslyn Pierce, but had to turn it down because she was still filming *Double Trouble* (also known as *Swingin' Along*), a Charles Barton–directed movie that starred Tommy Noonan and Peter Marshall. British actress Barbara Steele was given the role, but it became apparent during filming that her accent posed a problem. By that time, Barbara Eden was free. So, Steele was fired and Eden hired.

✓ During a fight with Elvis, Red West, playing an Indian, broke his arm.

✓ Charles Horvath, who had a bit role as one of the men who tried to molest Dolores Del Rio, was a judo

John McIntire, Dolores Del Rio, Elvis. (Photo courtesy Eddie Brandt's Saturday Matinee)

and karate instructor for the FBI and Marine Corps.

✓ During filming, Elvis suffered a fall from a runaway horse, but was not injured.

✓ Director Don Siegel was born in Chicago, but was educated at Cambridge University in England. He studied acting at the Royal Academy of Dramatic Arts. In 1946 Siegel directed his first feature film, *The Verdict.* Other Siegel-directed films include *Invasion of the Body Snatchers* (1956), *Dirty Harry* (1971)—in which he also made a cameo appearance—and *The Shootist* (1976), John Wayne's last film.

✓ Newspaper advertisements for *Flaming Star* in December 1960 incorrectly stated that it had "*four* new songs."

✓ "Britches," one of the songs cut from the film, was originally sung in the scene in which Elvis and Steve Forrest were riding together on horseback talking about Barbara Eden's character, Roslyn Pierce. Elvis referred to her as a gal who wore britches.

✓ Rodd Redwing, a Chickasaw Indian stuntman who played a bit role in *Flaming Star*, taught Elvis how to handle a pistol expertly. Redwing previously worked with Clayton Moore (the Lone Ranger on television) and Gail Davis (TV's Annie Oakley).

✓ On November 23, 1960, *Flaming Star* was sneak-previewed at the Loyola Theatre in Westchester, California, with two songs. Two days later, in Inglewood,

California, a four-song print was shown to an audience at the Academy Theatre. After that showing it was decided to release the two-song version of the film.

✓ Steve Forrest, whose real name is William Forrest Andrews, is the brother of actor Dana Andrews.

✓ Virginia Christine, who played Mrs. Phillips, played Mrs. Olson in the Folgers Coffee commercials for two decades.

✓ *Flaming Star* was Dolores Del Rio's first Hollywood film in 18 years and only her second American release during that period. Del Rio, known as the "First Lady of the Mexican Cinema," was the second cousin of silent-screen star Ramon Novarro.

✓ Barbara Eden was an All-American cheerleader in the early 1950s. She made her film debut in Robert Ryan's 1956 movie *Back from Eternity.* Eden is perhaps best known for her role as Jeannie in the "I Dream of Jeannie" TV series. From 1958 to 1973 she was married to another Elvis costar, Michael Ansara (*Harum Scarum*).

✓ *Flaming Star* reached #12 on *Variety*'s weekly list of top-grossing films.

TRIVIA

★ "Flaming Star" referred to the vision some Indians claimed to see as a sign of impending death.

★ Neddy Burton belonged to the Kiowa Indian tribe.

★ Question: What did Roslyn give Clint for his birthday? Answer: A shaving mirror.

★ Lame Crow, the old man of the Kiowas, was Neddy's uncle.

★ *Flaming Star* took place in Texas in 1878.

★ *The Crossing*—White settlers' village.

★ The Kiowas had a name for Neddy Burton that meant "the thin woman who deserted her own people."

★ Neddy Burton's favorite Bible verse was Genesis 3:20, which reads: "And Adam called his wife's name Eve, because she was the mother of all living."

★ Sam Burton gave Neddy's father a shotgun and a pound of black powder for her.

★ *Pierce's General Store*—Business owned and operated by Dred Pierce and his daughter, Roslyn. Pierce's General Store was located at The Crossing.

WILD IN THE COUNTRY

Twentieth Century–Fox, 1961. A Company of Artists, Inc., production. Running time: 114 minutes. Elvis's seventh film.

CAST

Glenn Tyler	ELVIS PRESLEY
Irene Sperry	HOPE LANGE
Noreen	TUESDAY WELD
Betty Lee Parsons	MILLIE PERKINS
Davis	RAFER JOHNSON
Phil Macy	JOHN IRELAND
Cliff Macy	GARY LOCKWOOD
Rolfe Braxton	WILLIAM MIMS
Dr. Underwood	RAYMOND GREENLEAF
Monica George	CHRISTINA CRAWFORD
Flossie, Phil Macy's Secretary	ROBIN RAYMOND
Mrs. Parsons	DOREEN LANG
Mr. Parsons	CHARLES ARNT
Sarah, Irene Sperry's Maid	RUBY GOODWIN
Willie Dace	WILL CORY
Professor Joe B. Larson	ALAN NAPIER
Judge Parker	JASON ROBARDS SR.
Bartender	HARRY CARTER
Sam Tyler	HARRY SHANNON
Hank Tyler	RED WEST
State Trooper	ELISHA M. MOTT
Mr. Spangler	WALTER BALDWIN
Woman in Booth	FRANKIE SILVER
Huckster	MIKE LALLY
Mr. Dace	JOE BUTHAM
Conductor	HANS MOEBUS
Juror	JAMES HORAN
Doctor	LINDEN CHILES JR.
Dr. Creston, the Coroner	JACK ORRISON
Mr. Longstreet	PAT BUTTRAM

CREW

Producer	JERRY WALD
Director	PHILIP DUNNE
Screenplay	CLIFFORD ODETS
Based on a Novel by	J. R. SALAMANCA
Director of Photography	WILLIAM C. MELLOR
Art Directors	JACK MARTIN SMITH
	PRESTON AMES
Set Decoration	WALTER M. SCOTT
	STUART A. REISS
Assistant Director	JOSEPH E. RICKARDS
Editor	DOROTHY SPENCER
Makeup	BEN NYE
Hairstyles	HELEN TURPIN
Costumes	DON FELD
Sound Recording	ALFRED BRUZLIN
	WARREN B. DELAPLAIN
Associate Producer	PETER NELSON
Music	KENYON HOPKINS
Orchestration	EDWARD B. POWELL

SONGS

1. "Wild in the Country"—Sung over the opening credits.
2. "I Slipped, I Stumbled, I Fell"—Sung to Millie Perkins in a pickup truck. "Instrumentation" was provided by the radio.
3. "In My Way"—Sung to Tuesday Weld on the steps at the back of Rolfe Braxton's store.
4. "Husky Dusky Day"—Sung in duet with Hope Lange in her car while driving back from the university.

"Lonely Man" and "Forget Me Never" were cut from the film.

PRODUCTION NOTES

✓ *Wild in the Country* premiered in Memphis on June 15, 1961, and opened nationally on June 22. The cofeature at many theaters was *The Right Approach*, which starred Frankie Vaughan and Juliet Prowse.

Millie Perkins, Elvis. (Photo courtesy Eddie Brandt's Saturday Matinee)

Tuesday Weld, Elvis. (Photo courtesy Eddie Brandt's Saturday Matinee)

✓ Filming began on November 11, 1960, at the Victorian Ink House in St. Helena, California. Exterior scenes were filmed in and around Napa Valley, including the town of Calistoga. Interiors were shot on the Twentieth Century–Fox lot. Filming was completed on January 18, 1961—two weeks overdue.

✓ *Wild in the Country* was based on *The Lost Country*, J. R. Salamanca's first novel. The second novel of Salamanca, a former actor and graduate of London's Royal Academy of Dramatic Arts, was *Lilith*, which also was made into a movie.

✓ "Wild in the Country" is a phrase from Walt Whitman's *Leaves of Grass*. Producer Jerry Wald said he'd been waiting for years for a film in which he could use that title.

✓ *Wild in the Country* differed from Salamanca's book in that the Glenn Tyler character was a writer, not an artist. Also, Irene Sperry was a psychologist in the film, a schoolteacher in the book.

✓ During shooting of the film, Elvis received a platinum watch from RCA for having sold 75 million records for the company.

✓ Although only a year older than Elvis, Hope Lange played a character who was supposed to be several years older. Lange made her Broadway debut in *The Patriots* in 1943. In 1956 she made her screen debut in *Bus Stop*, as did her future husband, Don Murray. They were divorced during the production of *Wild in the Country*. Lange rewrote some of her dialogue in the film so well that director Philip Dunne gave her his Writers Guild of America membership card.

✓ While in Hollywood, Elvis stayed at the Beverly Wilshire Hotel.

✓ Elvis dated wardrobe girl Nancy Sharp during production. He had met her while making *Flaming Star*.

✓ While slapping Elvis in a scene, Millie Perkins broke her wrist.

✓ The college scenes were filmed at UCLA. About seventy-five extras from the campus were used.

✓ Cinematographer William C. Mellor won Oscars for his work on *A Place in the Sun* (1951) and *The Diary of Anne Frank* (1959). Mellor only worked on two more films after *Wild in the Country*: *State Fair* (1962) and *The Greatest Story Ever Told* (1965). He died during the production of the latter film.

✔ Rosy, Hope Lange's four-year-old Irish setter in the film, was owned by Rudd Weatherwax. *Wild in the Country* was Rosy's debut.

✔ Although Red West had appeared in bit roles in previous films, he had his first speaking part in *Wild in the Country*.

✔ Fabian was first considered for the role of Glenn Tyler.

✔ Rafer Johnson was the Olympic decathlon champion in 1960. *Wild in the Country* was his second film. A few months earlier he had made *The Fiercest Heart* with Stuart Whitman and Juliet Prowse. He and Roosevelt Grier served as bodyguards to Robert F. Kennedy in 1968. When Kennedy was shot on June 5, 1968, at the Ambassador Hotel in Los Angeles, Johnson and Grier disarmed Sirhan Sirhan. Kennedy died early the next day.

✔ Tuesday Weld was born Susan Ker Weld on Thursday, August 27, 1943. She made her movie debut in 1956's *Rock, Rock, Rock*. Her singing voice was dubbed by Connie Francis in that film. For one season (1959–60), Weld played Thalia Menninger, the object of Dobie Gillis's affections, in the TV series "The Many Loves of Dobie Gillis." During the filming of *Wild in the Country*, she started work on *Return to Peyton Place*. Her schedule was juggled for a brief time so that she could do both films. Weld created a minor ruckus on the Twentieth Century-Fox lot when she insisted on having her white Alsatian dog with her on the set, which was against studio regulations.

✔ Except for one experimental film, Christina Crawford made her film debut in *Wild in the Country*. Christina is the adopted daughter of actress Joan Crawford. In 1978 she wrote a bestselling autobiography about her relationship with her mother, titled *Mommie Dearest*.

✔ *Wild in the Country* was Millie Perkins's second film. She won an Oscar for Best Supporting Actress in her debut, *The Diary of Anne Frank*. For a time (1960–64), the former magazine cover model was married to actor Dean Stockwell, who visited her on the set of *Wild in the Country*.

✔ During filming, Elvis was treated for boils on his rear end.

✔ Director Philip Dunne gained fame as a screenwriter. Some of his best-known films include *How Green Was My Valley* (1941), *The Ghost and Mrs. Muir* (1947), and *The Robe* (1953). In 1960 Dunne served as a speechwriter for presidential candidate John F. Kennedy. After *Wild in the Country* he directed only two more films.

✔ Some advertising lines used for the film: "Lonely Man . . . Loving Man . . . Singing Man!"; "Sings of Love to Three Women!"; "Giving His Heart to Three Girls!"

✔ Originally, *Wild in the Country* was to have been filmed without Elvis songs, but that idea was quickly discarded. One of the songs, "Lonely Man," was once under consideration as the film's title. But the song was cut from the final print of *Wild in the Country*.

Hope Lange, Elvis. (Photo courtesy Eddie Brandt's Saturday Matinee)

✔ Jason Robards Sr., who played Judge Parker, was the father of Oscar-winning actor Jason Robards Jr. *Wild in the Country* was the elder Robards's final film. On radio he played Chandu, the magician in that series.

✔ Two endings were filmed for *Wild in the Country*: one in which the Hope Lange character died and one in which she lived. Sneak preview audiences voted for her to live and that was the ending used for general release of the film.

✔ Readers of *Teen* magazine voted Elvis and Tuesday Weld the Damp Raincoat Award for Most Disappointing Performers of 1961.

✔ John Ireland, who played Phil Macy, was nominated for an Oscar for Best Supporting Actor for his role in *All the King's Men* (1949). He was married for seven years (1949–56) to Joanne Dru, sister of the TV game-show host Peter Marshall. Ireland is the brother of comedian Tommy Noonan.

✔ Despite the fact that "Lonely Man" and "Forget Me Never" were cut from *Wild in the Country*, some movie reviews then and several reference books today still list those two songs in the movie's credits.

TRIVIA

★ Glenn Tyler was almost nine years old when his mother died. Before he appeared in court for stealing a car, he had been picked up twice on drunkenness charges.

★ To illustrate that Glenn was basically a good boy, the minister asked him this Biblical question in court: "What was the Master's cry from the cross?" Glenn's answer (from Matthew 27:46 and also from Mark 15:34): "Eli, Eli, lama sabachthani," which means "My God, my God, why hast thou forsaken me?"

★ *Rosy*—Irene Sperry's Irish setter.

★ *Old Seminole Tonic*—Elixir sold by Rolfe Braxton's health-tonic business. Old Seminole Tonic, which was 87 percent water and 13 percent alcohol, was sold in every state in Dixie. Johnson and Perry sold the same formula under their own label, Shenandoah Elixir.

★ Glenn earned $12.50 a week for working for his Uncle Rolfe.

★ *High Tension Grove*—Dance hall to which Glenn took Betty Lee Parsons.

★ At the age of twelve, when she and Glenn were wading at Felcher's Creek, Noreen first knew she wanted Glenn.

★ *Mrs. Noreen Martin*—Name used by Noreen to protect her baby born out of wedlock and her reputation. The baby's father was a New York salesman with a big green Cadillac.

★ Uncle Rolfe was the cousin of Glenn's mother.

★ Noreen was born in July.

★ *Sycamore*—Town in which *Wild in the Country* was set.

★ *Sycamore Hospital Fund Bazaar*—Festival to which Glenn took Noreen for a night of fun and dancing.

★ Irene Sperry's deceased husband was named Paul. He died in a car accident.

★ *Bermuda Bomb*—Elixir sold by Rolfe to a widow who later claimed that her husband died because Rolfe told her it was a cure for cancer. Attorney Phil Macy urged her not to press charges.

★ The state university was located in the city of Radford.

★ *Spangler's Rest Motel*—Motel where Glenn and Irene Sperry spent the night because it was raining too hard to drive back to Sycamore. Glenn stayed in room #15, Irene in #16. Rooms were normally six dollars each, but Glenn persuaded Mr. Spangler to give him both rooms for eight dollars.

★ Question: What flavor of soda pop did Glenn and Irene drink at Spangler's Rest Motel? Answer: Cherry.

★ As the rain was pouring down, Glenn quoted Genesis 7:10 in Irene's motel room: "And it came to pass after seven days, that the waters of the flood were upon the earth."

★ Question: What was the number of the room at Spangler's Rest Motel that Cliff Macy stayed in the same night that Glenn and Irene checked into the motel? Answer: #11.

★ Author Zane Grey once stopped at Spangler's Motel right after World War II and signed two of his books. Glenn took a couple of Zane Grey novels to his room to read.

BLUE HAWAII

Paramount, 1961. A Hal B. Wallis production. Running time: 101 minutes. Elvis's eighth film.

CAST

Chad Gates	ELVIS PRESLEY
Maile Duval	JOAN BLACKMAN
Sarah Lee Gates	ANGELA LANSBURY
Miss Abigail Prentice	NANCY WALTERS
Fred Gates	ROLAND WINTERS
Jack Kelman	JOHN ARCHER
Mr. Chapman	HOWARD MCNEAR
Tucker Garvey	STEVE BRODIE
Enid Garvey	IRIS ADRIAN
Waihila	HILO HATTIE
Ellie Corbett	JENNIE MAXWELL
Selena (Sandy) Emerson	PAMELA KIRK
Patsy Simon	DARLENE TOMPKINS
Beverly Martin	CHRISTIAN KAY
Carl Tanami	LANI KAI
Ernie Gordon	JOSE DEVEGA
Ito O'Hara	FRANK ATIENZA
Wes Moto	RALPH (TIKI) HANALEI
Ping Pong, the Gates' Houseboy	GUY LEE
Paul Duval	GREGORY GAY
Lonnie, the Bartender	CLARENCE EDWARD LUNG
Harmonica-Playing Convict	RICHARD J. REEVES
Lieutenant Gray, the Desk Sergeant	MIKE ROSS
Lawyer	ROGER CLARK
Matron	LILLIAN CULVER
Bits	SHARON LEE CONNORS
	VERONICA REED
Man at Party	THOMAS GLYNN
Woman at Party	KATE-ELLEN MURTAGH
General Anthony	GEORGE DENORMAND
Waitress	IRENE H. MIZUSHIMA
Specialty Dancers	NGARUA
	TANI MARSH
Mrs. Maneka, Maile's Grandmother	FLORA K. HAYES
Party Guest	RED WEST
Bits	GEORGE HALAS
	YOLANDA HUGHES
	DEBRA M. KAWAMURA
	ROBERT M. LUCK
	ROBERT KENUI POPE
	BELLA RICHARDS
	ELSIE RUSSELL
	PAT TACKENTHALL

CREW

Producer	HAL B. WALLIS
Director	NORMAN TAUROG
Screenplay	HAL KANTER
Story	ALLAN WEISS
Director of Photography	CHARLES LANG JR.
Art Directors	HAL PEREIRA
	WALTER TYLER
Set Decoration	SAM COMER
	FRANK MCKELVY
Special Photographic Effects	JOHN P. FULTON
Process Photography	FARCIOT EDOUART
Assistant Director	D. MICHAEL MOORE
Editorial Supervision	WARREN LOW
Editor	TERRY MORSE
Makeup	WALLY WESTMORE
Hairstyles	NELLIE MANLEY
Costumes	EDITH HEAD
Technicolor Color Consultant	RICHARD MUELLER
Second Unit Photography	W. WALLACE
Dialogue Coach	JACK MINTZ
Sound Recording	PHILIP MITCHELL
	CHARLES GRENZBACH
Associate Producer	PAUL NATHAN
Music Scored and Conducted by	JOSEPH J. LILLEY

Elvis, Joan Blackman, Roland Winters, Angela Lansbury. (Photo courtesy Cinema Collectors)

Vocal Accompaniment........................THE JORDANAIRES
Musical Numbers Staged by................CHARLES O'CURRAN
Technical Advisor...........................COL. TOM PARKER

SONGS

1. "Blue Hawaii"—Sung over the opening credits and incorporated instrumentally throughout the film.
2. "Almost Always True"—Sung to Joan Blackman in a car with car radio accompaniment.
3. "Aloha Oe"—Sung in a canoe.
4. "No More"—Sung on the beach with some Hawaiian friends.
5. "Can't Help Falling in Love"—Sung to Maile's grandmother after giving her a music box for her birthday.
6. "Rock-a-Hula Baby"—Sung at a party.
7. "Moonlight Swim"—Sung in a car while escorting Miss Prentice and her four students around Oahu.
8. "Ku-u-i-Po"—Sung at a luau.
9. "Ito Eats"—Sung at a luau right after someone says, "Ito eats like teeth are going out of style!"
10. "Slicin' Sand"—Sung at a luau while putting out the campfire.
11. "Hawaiian Sunset"—Sung at the Island Inn.
12. "Beach Boy Blues"—Sung while in jail after a fight at the Island Inn.
13. "Island of Love (Kauai)"—Sung while guiding Miss Prentice and her four students around Kauai on horseback.
14. "Hawaiian Wedding Song"—Sung during the marriage ceremony at the end of the film.

"Steppin' Out of Line," "La Paloma," and "Playing with Fire" were cut from the film.

PRODUCTION NOTES

✓ *Blue Hawaii* opened nationally on November 22, 1961. In most areas it was double-billed with *Desert Warrior*, a Spanish-Italian film starring Ricardo Montalban.

✓ The first announced title of *Blue Hawaii* in the fall of 1960 was *Hawaii Beach Boy*. In early January 1961 the title was changed to *Blue Hawaii*. Walter Mirisch protested the title because it was too similar to his *Hawaii*, which was then in preproduction for United Artists.

✓ Production began on March 17, 1961, in Hawaii. Some of the locations used on Oahu included Waikiki Beach, the Ala Wai Yacht Harbor, Honolulu International Airport, the jail at Honolulu's Police Department, the Punchbowl, Ala Moana Park, Hanauma Bay, Tantalus, and the Waiola Tea Room. Locations on Kauai included Kauai Airport, Anahola, Coco Palms Resort Hotel, Lydgate Park, and the Wailua River. Location filming ended on April 17. Further filming took place on the Paramount lot.

✓ Flora K. Hayes, who played Mrs. Maneka, Maile's grandmother, was a former Hawaii Territorial Representative to the U.S. Congress.

✓ Elvis signed a five-year contract with Hal B. Wallis just before filming *Blue Hawaii*.

✓ Juliet Prowse was signed on February 7, 1961, to play the role of Maile Duval. She was on loan to Paramount from Twentieth Century–Fox. On March 6, Prowse announced that she was not going to report for filming until three conditions were met: (1) she wanted her Fox makeup man, Roy Stork, to also be loaned out for the film; (2) she wanted Hal Wallis and Paramount to pay the traveling expenses to have her secretary accompany her to Hawaii; and (3) she wanted a change in her billing clause in the contract.

On March 13, Wallis announced that Prowse was going to be replaced. Two days later he named Joan Blackman as Elvis's new costar. Prowse was put on suspension by her own studio, Twentieth Century–Fox.

✓ Before *Blue Hawaii*, Joan Blackman's credits included *Good Day for a Hanging* (1958), *Career* (1959), *Visit to a Small Planet* (1960), and *The Great Imposter* (1960). It's been reported that Elvis disliked working with Blackman, although it's worth noting that a year later she again appeared with him in *Kid Galahad*.

✓ *Blue Hawaii* was the first film for which former Los Angeles newspaperman Allan Weiss provided the story. The film was based on his book *Beach Boy*. Weiss later wrote several screenplays for Elvis.

✓ In late October 1962, Mexico's Office of Public Entertainment banned *Blue Hawaii* because at a previous Elvis film, *G. I. Blues*, fans tore up the seats and broke windows at the Americas Theatre in Mexico City. *Blue Hawaii* had been scheduled to open at the Mexico Theatre.

✓ On September 13, 1966, NBC's "Tuesday Night at the Movies" was scheduled to open its new season with an airing of *Blue Hawaii*, but NBC was forced to pull it from the schedule because of an agreement with Paramount Pictures. The deal stipulated that NBC had to wait until *Paradise, Hawaiian Style*, which had been released only three months earlier, had run its course in the theaters. The studio felt that there would be confusion because of the similarity in film titles. NBC replaced *Blue Hawaii* with *Living It Up*, a Dean Martin–Jerry Lewis film.

✓ Angela Lansbury's grandfather, George Lansbury, was the leader of the British Labour Party from 1931 to 1935. Lansbury, who was only 35 years old, played the mother of 26-year-old Elvis. In 1962's *The Manchurian Candidate* she played Laurence Harvey's mother, although she was only three years older than Harvey. Lansbury was nominated for a Best Supporting Actress Oscar for *Gaslight* (1944), which was her first movie.

✓ Roland Winters was one of six non-Chinese actors to play Charlie Chan in the movies. He starred in six Chan features for Monogram in the late 1940s.

✓ *Blue Hawaii* reached #2 on *Variety*'s weekly list of top-grossing films. Because of a strong showing the last six weeks of 1961, it ranked #18 for the year, with a gross of $2 million. *Blue Hawaii* also ranked high for the year 1962, placing #14 on the list. Its total gross through 1962 was $4.7 million.

TRIVIA

★ *Eddie*—Motorcycle cop who pulled Maile over for speeding at the beginning of the film.

Jennie Maxwell, Elvis. (Photo courtesy Cinema Collectors)

★ Chad Gates had just served a two-year stint in the Army in Italy.

★ Maile Duval was part French (father) and part Hawaiian (mother).

★ *Kahalo*—City in which Chad's parents lived.

★ *Duke*—Chad's dog.

★ Question: What was the name of the woman who gave a lei to Maile to put around Chad's neck when he stepped off the plane? Answer: Waihila.

★ *Captain Matthew Polk*—Great-grandfather of Sarah Gates who fought with the Union Army in the Civil War.

★ Maile's grandmother, Mrs. Maneka, was 78 years old.

★ *Great Southern Hawaiian Fruit Company*—Firm for which Fred Gates worked as a supervisor. The home office of the Great Southern Hawaiian Fruit Company was in Atlanta. The company had 317 salespeople nationwide.

★ Chad gave Maile's grandmother a music box from Austria that played "Can't Help Falling in Love."

★ *Hawaiian Tourist Guide Service*—Firm managed by Mr. Chapman at which Maile worked. Chad later went to work for the company.

★ To see how well Chad knew the Hawaiian Islands, Mr. Chapman quizzed him. His first question: "Where's the 'Crouching Lion'?" Chad's correct answer: "A rock formation on a cliff just north of Cobble Beach. It used to be a native fishing shrine."

★ Chad Gates was born in Atlanta.

★ *Hawaiian Village Hotel*—Hotel where Miss Abigail Prentice and her four students stayed.

★ Blooper: In the scene at the pineapple fields, the car door is open in one camera shot, but closed in the very next shot.

★ Question: From what state did Tucker and Enid Garvey hail? Answer: Oklahoma.

★ In one scene at the Island Inn, Ellie was carrying on with Tucker Garvey. At this point Chad tells her there's "no use steppin' out of line." This is where the song "Steppin' Out of Line" was originally sung before it was cut from the film.

★ The harmonica playing of the convict played by Richard J. Reeves was dubbed by George Fields.

★ The fight between Chad and Tucker Garvey caused $700 worth of damage at the Island Inn.

★ *Duchess*—Chad's nickname for Ellie Corbett.

★ *No-Britches Bardot*—Chad's name for Ellie as he carried her out of his hotel room on Kauai after she had forced herself on him.

★ *Gates of Hawaii*—Travel agency founded by Chad and Maile after their marriage.

FOLLOW THAT DREAM

United Artists, 1962. A Mirisch Company production. Running time: 110 minutes. Elvis's ninth film.

CAST

Toby Kwimper............................ELVIS PRESLEY
Pop Kwimper........................ARTHUR O'CONNELL
Holly Jones.................................ANNE HELM
Alicia Claypoole..........................JOANNA MOORE
H. Arthur King............................ALAN HEWITT
Mr. Endicott...........................HERBERT RUDLEY
Nick...................................SIMON OAKLAND
Carmine...............................JACK KRUSCHEN
Teddy Bascombe...........................ROBIN KOON
Eddy Bascombe............................GAVIN KOON
Ariadne Pennington..........................PAM OGLES
George Binkley........................HOWARD MCNEAR
Judge Wardman.........................ROLAND WINTERS
Jack.................................FRANK DE KOVA
Al..................................ROBERT CARRICART
Blackie..................................JOHN DUKE
Governor.............................HARRY HOLCOMBE
Bank Guard................................RED WEST

CREW

Producer...............................DAVID WEISBART
Director..............................GORDON DOUGLAS
Screenplay............................CHARLES LEDERER
Based on a Novel by.....................RICHARD POWELL
Director of Photography.....................LEO TOVER
Art Director................................MAL BERT
Set Decoration.........................FRED MCCLEAN
                                       GORDON GURNEE
Editor............................WILLIAM B. MURPHY
Assistant Director.......................BERT CHERVIN
Production Supervisor....................ALLEN K. WOOD
Production Manager.................HERBERT E. MENDELSON
Sound Recording........................JACK SOLOMON
                                       BUDDY MYERS
Sound Effects Editor................CHARLES G. SCHELLING
Makeup.................................DAN STRIEPEKE
Hairdresser............................MADINE DANKS

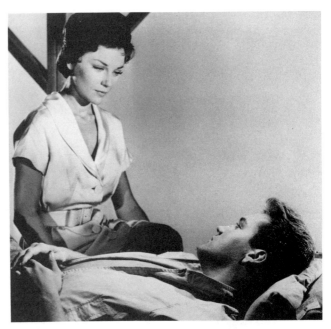

Joanna Moore, Elvis. (Photo courtesy Eddie Brandt's Saturday Matinee)

Wardrobe...................................RUTH HANCOCK
                                          SID MINTZ
Music....................................HANS J. SALTER
Music Editor.............................ROBERT TRACY
Technical Advisor..........................COL. TOM PARKER
Script Supervisor.......................DOLORES RUBIN
Property Manager..........................TOM COLEMAN
Casting............................STALMASTER-LISTER CO.

SONGS

1. "What a Wonderful Life"—Sung over the opening credits.
2. "I'm Not the Marrying Kind"—Sung to Anne Helm on the beach.
3. "Sound Advice"—Sung in the Kwimpers' cabin.
4. "On Top of Old Smokey"—Sung briefly (four lines) to Joanna Moore while lying on the beach. Music was provided by a portable radio.
5. "Follow That Dream"—Sung to Joanna Moore while lying on the beach. Music was provided by a portable radio.
6. "Angel"—Sung on the porch of the Kwimpers' cabin at the end of the film.

"A Whistling Tune" was recorded for *Follow That Dream* but not used. Instead, it was used in *Kid Galahad*.

PRODUCTION NOTES

✓ *Follow That Dream* premiered in Ocala, Florida, on April 11, 1962. It opened nationally on May 23. The cofeature in many areas was *Deadly Duo*, which starred Craig Hill and Marcia Henderson. In a few theaters, Jerry Lewis's *The Errand Boy*, in a second run, was the companion feature.

✓ *Follow That Dream* was based on the 1957 novel *Pioneer, Go Home*, by Richard Powell. The novel appeared in *Reader's Digest* in condensed form.

✓ Filming began in Crystal River, Florida, on July 11, 1961. Elvis didn't arrive until a couple of weeks later. Locations used included Tampa, Ocala, Yankeetown, Inverness, and Bird Creek. Interiors were shot in

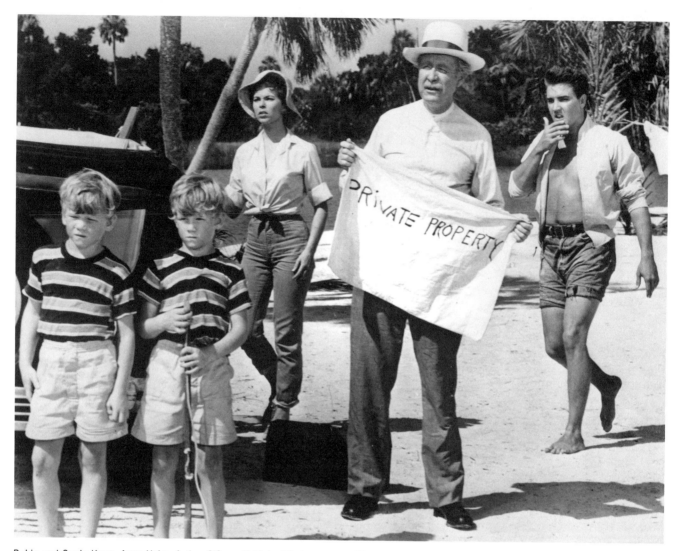

Robin and Gavin Koon, Anne Helm, Arthur O'Connell, Elvis. (Photo courtesy Cinema Collectors)

a bank in Ocala and the courthouse in Inverness. Some shots were done at the studio in Culver City, California. Filming was completed on August 28.

✓ Elvis arrived on location in Florida in a bus. He brought along a twenty-one-foot speedboat and two of his cars.

✓ The original title of *Follow That Dream* was *Pioneer, Go Home*. But because the composers were unable to come up with a rhyme for the word *Pioneer*, for a title tune, the film's title was changed to *What a Wonderful Life* just before the start of location shooting. Other titles considered were *It's a Beautiful Life* and *Here Come the Kwimpers*.

✓ George Marshall was originally slated to direct *Follow That Dream*, but he was replaced by Gordon Douglas in March 1961.

✓ Eight-year-old identical twins Gavin and Robin Koon, who played the roles of Eddy and Teddy Bascombe, made their film debuts in *Follow That Dream*. They were the sons of Charles Koon, the art director on "The Lawrence Welk Show."

✓ Joanna Moore made her screen debut in *Slim*

Carter (1957). For a brief time she was married to Ryan O'Neal (1963–66). She is the mother of Griffin O'Neal and Tatum O'Neal, the youngest person to win an Academy Award (for Best Supporting Actress for *Paper Moon* in 1973).

✓ Gambling was illegal in Florida in 1961. When two large dice tables and other gambling equipment were needed for the film, a member of the Chamber of Commerce of a Florida city and a couple of anonymous gangsters brought the needed items to the location.

✓ Director Gordon Douglas directed several of the *Our Gang* shorts in the 1930s, as well as many Hal Roach features. Some of his best known films are *Young at Heart* (1954), *Rio Conchos* (1964), and *Tony Rome* (1967). Douglas is the only person to have directed both Elvis Presley and Frank Sinatra.

✓ Despite some of the publicity generated by United Artists about Anne Helm being a "screen newcomer," she actually made her movie debut in *Desire in the Dust* (1960).

✓ Howard McNear, who played loan officer George Binkley, is perhaps best known to TV audiences as

Floyd, the barber in "The Andy Griffith Show."

✓ Tough-looking Simon Oakland was actually a violinist at one point early in his career. He's a veteran of hundreds of television guest roles and was a regular in the TV series "Toma" (1973–74), "Kolchak: The Night Stalker" (1974–75), "Baa Baa Black Sheep" (1976–78), and "David Cassidy—Man Undercover" (1978–79).

✓ Jack Kruschen was nominated for an Oscar for Best Supporting Actor for his performance in *The Apartment* (1960).

✓ Arthur O'Connell was a two-time Oscar nominee for Best Supporting Actor: *Picnic* (1956) and *Anatomy of a Murder* (1959). He later gained fame in television commercials as Mr. Goodwin, the friendly druggist in the Crest toothpaste advertisements.

✓ Location shots for *Follow That Dream* were made near the home of eleven-year-old Tom Petty, who in 1976 formed the rock & roll group Tom Petty and the Heartbreakers.

TRIVIA

★ *$63.80*—Amount of the monthly disability check received by Toby Kwimper from the U.S. government. He twisted his back during his first judo lesson in the Army. However, it twisted right back during the second lesson.

★ Question: When Pop Kwimper's automobile gas gauge read "empty," how many gallons of gas did he say he still had in the tank? Answer: Three gallons.

★ Holly Jones was nineteen years old. She had been living with the Kwimpers since she was thirteen, after her parents were killed in an automobile accident. She had been the twins' baby-sitter.

★ *Amy Plotkin*—Girl Toby grabbed during band practice while in school. He was sent home by the band director.

★ Question: What did Toby use to dig for water on the beach? Answer: A fender from his father's car.

★ *Cranberry County*—County just on the other side of the state line, from which the Kwimpers hailed.

★ Pop Kwimper's car cost him $50.

★ *$2,000*—Amount borrowed by Toby from the bank to build a dock and buy some rowboats for his thriving fishing business.

★ Question: How much time was left on the parking meter where Toby parked in front of the bank? Answer: Fifty minutes.

★ Toby's responses to Alicia Claypoole's word-association test: hurt (response: ow!); help (response: help); steal (response: home); girl (response: Dad); love (response: 30); and sex (response: 1 times 1 is 1, 1 times 2 is 2, 1 times 3 is 3).

★ *Westinghouse*—Brand of Alicia's portable radio.

★ Question: What baseball player did Toby mention during Alicia's word-association test? Answer: Willie Mays.

★ The judge's responses to Alicia's word-association test in court: court (response: crime); child (response: labor); and moon (response: shine).

KID GALAHAD

United Artists, 1962. A Mirisch Company production. Running time: 95 minutes. Elvis's tenth film.

CAST

Walter Gulick	ELVIS PRESLEY
Willy Grogan	GIG YOUNG
Dolly Fletcher	LOLA ALBRIGHT
Rose Grogan	JOAN BLACKMAN
Lew Nyack	CHARLES BRONSON
Mr. Lieberman	NED GLASS
Mr. Maynard	ROBERT EMHARDT
Otto Danzig	DAVID LEWIS
Joie Shakes	MICHAEL DANTE
Mr. Zimmerman	JUDSON PRATT
Mr. Sperling	GEORGE MITCHELL
Marvin	RICHARD DEVON
Ralphie	JEFFREY MORRIS
Father Higgins	LIAM REDMOND
Jerry, the Promoter	ROY ROBERTS
Peter J. Prohosko	RALPH MOODY
Ramón (Sugarboy) Romero	ORLANDO DE LA FUENTE
Romero's Manager	FRANK GERSTLE
Romero's Trainer	GEORGE J. LEWIS
Frank Gerson	ED ASNER
Bit	SONNY WEST
Fight Announcer	JIMMY LENNON

CREW

Producer	DAVID WEISBART
Director	PHIL KARLSON
Screenplay	WILLIAM FAY
Based on a Story by	FRANCIS WALLACE
Director of Photography	BURNETT GUFFEY
Art Direction	CARY O'DELL
Set Decoration	EDWARD G. BOYLE
Editor	STUART GILMORE
Property Master	FRANK AGNONE
Sound	LAMBERT DAY
Sound Effects Editor	DEL HARRIS
Dialogue Coach	EUGENE BUSCH
Production Supervisor	ALLEN K. WOOD
Unit Production Manager	ROBERT E. RELYEA
Assistant Director	JEROME M. SIEGEL
Script Supervisor	CHARLSIE BRYANT
Technical Advisor	COL. TOM PARKER
Music	JEFF ALEXANDER

Elvis, Lola Albright, Gig Young. (Photo courtesy Cinema Collectors)

Music Editor...................................ROBERT TRACY
Assistant Film Editor....................MARSHALL M. BORDEN
Makeup.......................................LYNN REYNOLDS
Hairdresser....................................ALICE MONTE
Wardrobe....................................BERT HENRIKSON
                                          IRENE CAINE
Special Effects....................................MILT RICE
Boxing Adviser...........................MUSHY CALLAHAN
Casting...........................STALMASTER-LISTER CO.

SONGS

1. "King of the Whole Wide World"—Sung over the opening credits.
2. "This Is Living"—Sung on the front steps of Grogan's training lodge.
3. "Riding the Rainbow"—Sung in a Model T Ford while driving to Albany.
4. "Home Is Where the Heart Is"—Sung to Joan Blackman while sitting in a sulky.
5. "I Got Lucky"—Sung at a Fourth of July celebration.
6. "A Whistling Tune"—Sung while strolling with Joan Blackman to the Church of St. Stanislaus.

"Love Is for Lovers" was cut from the film.

PRODUCTION NOTES

✓ *Kid Galahad* opened nationally on August 29, 1962. In many areas, the cofeature was *The Nun and the Sergeant*, a film set in the Korean War and starring Robert Webber and Anna Sten.

✓ *Kid Galahad* originated as a story in the *Saturday Evening Post* in the 1930s. The story was first filmed in 1937 by Warner Bros. Stars included Edward G. Robinson, Bette Davis, Humphrey Bogart, and Wayne Morris. During World War II, Morris (who played the same role that Elvis would later play) was one of the most decorated of the U.S. combat pilots. He shot down seven Japanese aircraft and sank two destroyers. Morris was awarded four Distinguished Flying Crosses. In the 1960s, the title of the film was changed to *The Battling Bellhop* so as not to be confused with Elvis's version. Warner Bros. remade *Kid Galahad* in 1941 as *The Wagons Roll at Night*, this time in a circus setting. Humphrey Bogart, Sylvia Sidney, and Eddie Albert starred.

✓ Much of *Kid Galahad* was filmed in Idylwild, California, a popular resort ninety miles east of Los

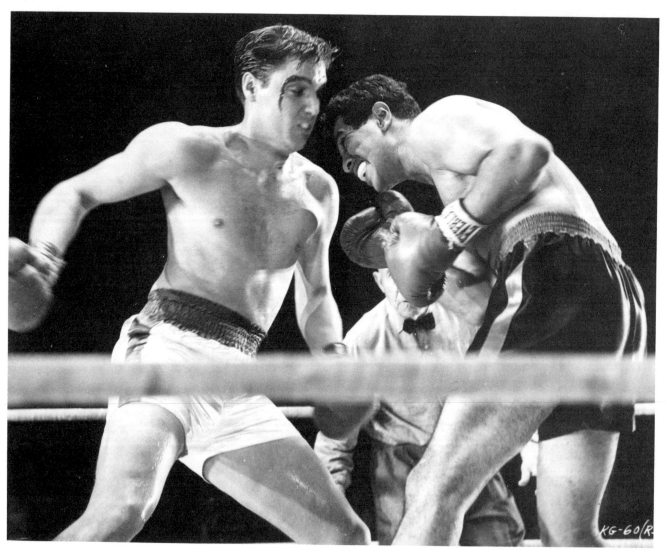

(Photo courtesy Cinema Collectors)

Angeles. Filming began in November 1961, and was completed on December 21. Interiors were shot on MGM/UA's Culver City lot.

✓ Mushy Callahan, a former world junior welterweight boxing champion (1926–1930), coached Elvis for his fight scenes. Callahan was assisted by Al Silvani, trainer and cornerman for Floyd Patterson, Jake LaMotta, Rocky Graziano, and Carmen Basilio, among others.

✓ Director Phil Karlson began in the movie industry as a prop man at Universal. While directing *The Phenix City Story* (1955) in Alabama in the mid-1950s, Karlson uncovered evidence that helped convict the murder suspects in the trial, which was still in progress (*The Phenix City Story* was a dramatization of that case). Other films directed by Phil Karlson include *The Young Doctors* (1961), *The Silencers* (1966), and *Walking Tall* (1973).

✓ Jimmy Lennon, fight announcer at the Olympic Auditorium in Los Angeles, announced two fights in *Kid Galahad*.

✓ Orlando de la Fuente, an undefeated 18-year-old welterweight boxer, played Sugarboy Romero in *Kid Galahad*. It was his film debut.

✓ The Ruth Batchelor–Sharon Silbert song "Love Is for Lovers" was cut from the film. Despite that, several movie reviews in 1962 listed the song as one of those sung in *Kid Galahad*. Even today, some reference books list "Love Is for Lovers" in the movie's credits.

✓ Gig Young, who played Willy Grogan, was nominated for an Oscar three times: *Come Fill the Cup* (1951), *Teacher's Pet* (1958), and *They Shoot Horses, Don't They?* (1969). For his role as Rocky, the master of ceremonies of the dance marathon in the latter film, he won his only Academy Award. Young (real name: Byron Ellsworth Barr) took his stage name from a character he played in the 1942 movie *The Gay Sisters*. On October 19, 1978, he committed suicide.

✓ Ed Asner made his film debut in *Kid Galahad*.

✓ Charles Bronson (Lew Nyack in *Kid Galahad*) went from playing Igor in the 3-D film *House of Wax* (1953) to being one of the highest-paid actors in the world. Bronson (real name: Charles Buchinsky), Clark Gable, and Sabu all served as tail gunners in bombers during World War II.

✓ *Kid Galahad* reached #9 on *Variety*'s list of top-grossing films. For the year 1962, it was ranked #37, grossing $1.75 million.

TRIVIA

★ *Orth Van & Storage*—Company on whose truck Walter Gulick rode into Cream Valley. Orth Van & Storage was affiliated with the Mayflower franchise.

★ *Cream Valley*—Catskills community that was the setting for *Kid Galahad*. The sign on the outskirts of the community ("Welcome to Cream Valley") listed four businesses: Levine's Loch Lovely, Mintz's Mayfair (formerly Mother Mintz's), Shangri-La Lieberman's (The Lieberman Family Welcomes You), and Grogan's Gaelic Garden ("The Cradle of Champions Since 1937").

★ Walter Gulick was born in Cream Valley. Walter was raised by an aunt in Lowbridge, Kentucky, after his parents died when he was fourteen months old.

★ While in the Army, Walter was stationed in Okinawa. He worked in the motor pool.

★ *Prohosko's Repair Shop*—Automotive repair business owned by Peter J. Prohosko. After his last fight, Walter was to become an equal partner in the facility.

★ *$150*—Amount Willy Grogan owed to the company that financed his convertible. Because of his inability to pay the $150, the finance company repossessed the car.

★ Walter was paid five dollars a round to spar with Joie Shakes.

★ *Cream Valley 1732*—Telephone number of Grogan's training camp.

While cleaning out a barn, Walter discovered an old boxing poster advertising the heavyweight championship fight between Jack Dempsey and Georges Carpentier (July 2, 1921).

★ Kid Galahad's first fight was a ten-round bout with Ezzard Bailey at the Capitol Casino in Albany, New York. The purse for the fight was $750. Kid Galahad weighed 180 pounds; Bailey weighed 181 pounds.

★ Walter was baptized on August 14, 1939.

★ Willy Grogan's publicity on Kid Galahad stated that he had won seventeen straight fights in Australia, which was a fabrication.

★ *Milton's Meadows*—Location of Cream Valley's Independence Day Picnic and Jamboree. Walter and Rose attended the event together.

★ Ed Asner (with hair!) played Frank Gerson, an assistant district attorney.

★ *Ramón Romero*—Boxer fought by Kid Galahad on Labor Day weekend. Romero, nicknamed "Sugarboy," was from Tijuana. He weighed in at 181½ pounds for the bout; Kid Galahad weighed in at 178½. The Kid knocked out Romero in the third round. (Willy Grogan had bet $1,800 on the Kid.)

★ *Church of St. Stanislaus*—Church pastored by Father Higgins at which Walter and Rose were to be married.

GIRLS! GIRLS! GIRLS!

Paramount, 1962. A Hal B. Wallis production. Running time: 106 minutes. Elvis's eleventh film.

CAST

Ross Carpenter	ELVIS PRESLEY
Robin Gantner	STELLA STEVENS
Wesley Johnson	JEREMY SLATE
Laurel Dodge	LAUREL GOODWIN
Kin Yung	BENSON FONG
Sam	ROBERT STRAUSS
Chen Yung	GUY LEE
Papa Stavros	FRANK PUGLIA
Mama Stavros	LILI VALENTY
Madam Yung	BEULAH QUO
Mai Ling	GINNY TIU
Tai Ling	ELIZABETH TIU
Mai Ling's Brother	ALEXANDER TIU
Mr. Peabody	GAVIN GORDON

Laurel Goodwin, Elvis. "The Walls Have Ears" number. (Photo courtesy Eddie Brandt's Saturday Matinee)

Drunk	KENNETH BECKER
Clerk	RICHARD COLLIER
Mr. Morgan	NESTOR PAIVA
Mrs. Morgan	ANN MCCREA
Mrs. Figgor	MARY TREEN
Mrs. Dick	MARJORIE BENNETT
Crew Members on Tuna Boat	ALEXANDER T. DIDIO
	WILFRED WATANABE
	STANLEY WHITE
Bongo-Playing Crewman on Tuna Boat	RED WEST
Cigarette Girl	PAMELA DUNCAN
Woman in Hat Shop	JUNE JOCELYN
Leona Stavros	BARBARA BEALL
Linda Stavros	BETTY BEALL
Guest	FRANK ATIENZA
Busboy	ROBERT M. KUPIHEA
Hostess	ANNA WAI HONG LIN
Mr. Dodge	ROLF MACALISTER
Village Woman	LINDA RAND
Man on Dock	EDWARD SHEEHAN
Fluffy Girl	MASAKO YOSHIMOTO
Skipper of Tuna Boat	RICHARD H. FAIRSERVICE

CREW

Producer	HAL B. WALLIS
Director	NORMAN TAUROG
Screenplay	EDWARD ANHALT
	ALLAN WEISS
Story	ALLAN WEISS
Director of Photography	LOYAL GRIGGS
Technicolor Consultant	RICHARD MUELLER
Art Directors	HAL PEREIRA
	WALTER TYLER
Set Decoration	SAM COMER
	FRANK R. MCKELVY
Process Photography	FARCIOT EDOUART
Assistant Director	D. MICHAEL MOORE
Dialogue Coach	JACK MINTZ
Editor	STANLEY JOHNSON
Editorial Supervision	WARREN LOW
Costumes	EDITH HEAD
Second Unit Photography	IRWIN ROBERTS
Makeup Supervision	WALLY WESTMORE
Hairstyle Supervision	NELLIE MANLEY
Sound Recording	HAROLD LEWIS
	CHARLES GRENZBACH
Associate Producer	PAUL NATHAN
Musical Numbers Staged by	CHARLES O'CURRAN
Music Scored and Conducted by	JOSEPH J. LILLEY
Vocal Accompaniment	THE JORDANAIRES
Technical Advisor	COL. TOM PARKER

SONGS

1. "Girls! Girls! Girls!"—Sung over the opening credits and later on a fishing boat.
2. "I Don't Wanna Be Tied"—Sung in the Pirates Den club.
3. "We'll Be Together"—Sung at an anniversary party for Papa and Mama Stavros.
4. "A Boy Like Me, a Girl Like You"—Sung to Laurel Goodwin aboard the *Westwind*.
5. "Earth Boy"—Sung at Kin Yung's home with the Tiu sisters.
6. "Return to Sender"—Sung in the Pirates Den club.
7. "Because of Love"—Sung in the Pirates Den club.
8. "Thanks to the Rolling Sea"—Sung on a tuna boat as the crewmen were pulling in their nets.
9. "Song of the Shrimp"—Sung aboard a tuna boat.
10. "The Walls Have Ears"—Sung in Laurel's apartment.
11. "We're Coming in Loaded"—Sung on a tuna boat.
12. "Dainty Little Moonbeams"—Sung at Paradise Cove while the Tiu sisters danced. The song only lasts fifty seconds and leads into "Girls! Girls! Girls!" (second version).
13. "Girls! Girls! Girls!" (second version)—Sung at Paradise Cove at end of film.

Elvis recorded "Plantation Rock," "Potpourri," "Mama," and "I Don't Want To" for the film, but none were used. Stella Stevens soloed on "Never Let Me Go," "The Nearness of You," and "Baby, Baby, Baby." "Mama" was sung by the Four Amigos.

PRODUCTION NOTES

✓ *Girls! Girls! Girls!* opened nationally on November 21, 1962. The companion feature in most areas of the United States was *It Happened in Athens*, a low-budget film starring Jayne Mansfield and Bob Mathias. The world premiere of *Girls! Girls! Girls!* occurred in Honolulu on October 31.

✓ Two titles originally considered for the film were *A Girl in Every Port* and *Welcome Aboard*. A few

The Four Amigos: Frank Puglia, Laurel Goodwin, Lili Valenty, Elvis. (Photo courtesy Eddie Brandt's Saturday Matinee)

months before filming was to begin *Gumbo Ya-Ya* was selected as the working title, but that was changed in March 1962 to *Girls! Girls! Girls! Gumbo Ya-Ya*, by the way, is a Creole expression meaning "everybody talks at once."

✓ Although "I Don't Want To" was cut from the film, it was heard in the movie trailer.

✓ When Elvis arrived in Hawaii to begin filming, he was mobbed by several thousand fans. He was stripped of his diamond ring, a tie clip, and his watch.

✓ Filming began on April 9, 1962. Most of the month was spent in Hawaii. The crew then moved to Paramount's Hollywood studios for interior shots. Principal photography was completed by mid-May.

✓ The Bumble Bee Tuna Company plant near Waikiki Beach was used as a location for the film. Another location was the Ala Wai Yacht Harbor.

✓ Stella Stevens (real name: Estelle Eggleston) made her film debut in *Say One for Me* (1959). She was *Playboy*'s Playmate of the Month for January 1960. Kate Jackson married Stella's son, Andrew Stevens, on August 23, 1978. *Girls! Girls! Girls!* was the first film in which Stevens sang.

✓ While filming in Hawaii, Elvis stayed at the Hawaiian Village Hotel on Oahu.

✓ According to a 1977 *TV Guide* article, *Girls! Girls! Girls!* was the tenth most-shown film on television.

✓ Actress Laurel Goodwin made her film debut in *Girls! Girls! Girls!*

✓ "Never Let Me Go," sung by Stella Stevens in the film, was written by Jay Livingston and Ray Evans in 1956 and introduced by Nat King Cole that same year in the Paramount movie *The Scarlet Hour*.

✓ *Girls! Girls! Girls!* reached #6 on *Variety*'s list of top-grossing films. Although released in late November, it still grossed $2.6 million by year's end and was ranked #31 of all films released in 1962.

✓ Robert Strauss, who played Sam, received an Oscar nomination for Best Supporting Actor for his role as Animal in *Stalag 17* (1953).

✓ "The Nearness of You," sung by Stella Stevens, was written by Ned Washington and Hoagy Carmichael in 1938 and introduced by Gladys Swarthout in Paramount's *Romance in the Dark* that same year. Composer Carmichael considered "The Nearness of You" to be among his top four songs.

(Photo courtesy Cinema Collectors)

TRIVIA

★ *Kingfisher*—Ross Carpenter's charter fishing boat.

★ *Westwind*—Sailboat built by Ross Carpenter and his father. When his father died, Mr. Stavros bought the *Westwind* and let Ross live on it. Because of health reasons, Stavros had to sell his boats, including the *Westwind*. Wesley Johnson bought it for $6,000.

★ Robin Gantner sang in the Pirates Den, a local nightclub.

★ *Mariners*—Restaurant where Ross and Laurel were to have lunch, but Ross walked away when he saw Laurel with another man.

★ *Sir Galahad*—Robin's pet name for Ross.

★ Kin and Madam Yung lived in Paradise Cove.

★ During a nighttime rainstorm at Kin Yung's house, Ross told Laurel that "it's not a fit night for man nor beast." That line was originally used by W. C. Fields in his 1933 short *The Fatal Glass of Beer*.

★ Question: How much did Laurel Dodge have in her checking account? Answer: Eight thousand dollars.

★ Ross danced the twist once while on stage at the Pirates Den and during the "Girls! Girls! Girls!" number at the end of the film.

★ Laurel hailed from Chicago.

★ *136 Bay Street, Apartment 3*—Laurel Dodge's home address.

★ Red West could be seen playing bongos on the tuna boat during "Song of the Shrimp."

★ During "The Walls Have Ears" number, Ross and Laurel danced the flamenco.

★ *Kapoo*—Kin Yung's weather-forecasting cat. White spots in Kapoo's eyes meant rain.

★ In addition to the *Kingfisher*, Ross Carpenter also skippered the *Kilohana* during some of his tuna runs. Call letters of the *Kilohana* were WY 2768.

★ Ross and his crew brought in one ton, twenty pounds of tuna during their first run, earning a paltry twenty-three dollars from Wesley Johnson.

★ *TR 6-2412*—Telephone number of Wesley Johnson.

★ *New Plaza*—Run-down hotel where Laurel told Ross she lived, although she actually lived in an apartment on Bay Street.

★ Laurel bought the *Westwind* from Wesley Johnson for $10,000. She had planned to give it to Ross, but he made her sell it back to Johnson.

IT HAPPENED AT THE WORLD'S FAIR

MGM, 1963. A Ted Richmond production. Running time: 105 minutes. Elvis's twelfth film.

CAST

Mike Edwards	ELVIS PRESLEY
Diane Warren	JOAN O'BRIEN
Danny Burke	GARY LOCKWOOD
Sue-Lin	VICKY TIU
Vince Bradley	H. M. WYNANT
Miss Steuben, the Head Nurse	EDITH ATWATER
Barney Thatcher	GUY RAYMOND
Miss Ettinger	DOROTHY GREEN
Walter Ling	KAM TONG
Dorothy Johnson	YVONNE CRAIG
Sheriff Garland	RUSSELL THORSON
Mechanic	WILSON WOOD
Mr. Farr, the Foreman at Great Washington Produce	ROBERT B. WILLIAMS
Henry Johnson	OLAN SOULE
Emma Johnson	JACQUELINE DEWIT
Charlie	JOHN DAY
Fred	RED WEST
Poker Players	PAUL GORSS
	JOHN INDRISANO
	TROY MELTON
June	SANDRA GILES
Rita	EVELYN DUTTON
Redhead on Monorail	LINDA HUMBLE
Boy Who Kicks Elvis	KURT RUSSELL
Erna, a Concessionaire	ERNA TANLER
Chinese Attendant	JONG OK KIM
Second Attendant	KATHRYN MACGUINNESS
Crap Shooter	GEORGE CISAR
Dice Players	HAL RIDDLE
	SID KANE
	DON BRODIE
Waitress	PAULA LANE
Guards	DAVID TYRRELL

Joan O'Brien, Elvis. (Photo courtesy Cinema Collectors)

	JOHN FRANCIS
Airport Guard	MIKE MAHONEY
Lieutenant Staffer	TOM GREENWAY
NASA Recruiting Officer	PATRICK WALTZ
Carnival Man	JOSEPH ESPOSITO
Mechanic	J. LEWIS SMITH
Crap Shooters	HERBERT BRESS
	GEORGE MILAN
	JOE QUINN
	CHARLES VICTOR
Policeman	PETE KELLETT
Cab Driver	MAX CUTLER

CREW

Producer	TED RICHMOND
Director	NORMAN TAUROG
Screenplay	SI ROSE
	SEAMAN JACOBS
Director of Photography	JOSEPH RUTTENBERG
Art Directors	GEORGE W. DAVIS
	PRESTON AMES
Set Decoration	HENRY GRACE
	HUGH HUNT
Technical Advisor	COL. TOM PARKER
Editor	FREDRIC STEINKAMP
Assistant Director	AL JENNINGS
Makeup	WILLIAM TUTTLE
Hairstyles	SYDNEY GUILAROFF
Music Score	LEITH STEVENS
Recording Supervisor	FRANKLIN MILTON
Vocal Backgrounds	THE JORDANAIRES
	THE MELLO MEN
Musical Numbers Staged by	JACK BAKER

SONGS

1. "Beyond the Bend"—Sung over the opening credits as Elvis pilots a biplane.
2. "Relax"—Sung at Yvonne Craig's house.
3. "Take Me to the Fair"—Sung to Vicky Tiu on the back of a flatbed truck while playing the ukulele.
4. "They Remind Me Too Much of You"—Sung on the monorail at night while Vicky Tiu slept. The song was sung over the soundtrack—Elvis didn't lip-synch.
5. "One Broken Heart for Sale"—Sung at the Century 21 Estates. The Mello Men sang backup.
6. "I'm Falling in Love Tonight"—Sung to Joan O'Brien in the restaurant at the top of the Space Needle.
7. "Cotton Candy Land"—Sung to Vicky Tiu while trying to get her to fall asleep in the trailer.
8. "A World of Our Own"—Sung to Joan O'Brien outside the trailer.
9. "How Would You Like to Be"—Sung to Vicky Tiu in the trailer. She joins him in a duet.
10. "Happy Ending"—Sung at the conclusion of the film while marching in front of a band. Joan O'Brien joins in a partial duet.

PRODUCTION NOTES

✓ *It Happened at the World's Fair* opened in Los Angeles on April 3, 1963. On April 10, it opened nationally. In some areas, the film was double-billed with *The Slave*, starring Steve Reeves. In all other areas, *No Time to Kill* was the cofeature.

✓ In February 1962 it was announced that the screenplay would be written by William Fay. However, in late March, Si Rose and Seaman Jacobs were signed.

✓ One of the first titles considered for *It Happened at the World's Fair* was *Mister, Will You Marry Me*. In February 1962 the title was changed to *Take Me Out to the Fair*. One month later it became *Take Me to the Fair*.

✓ Filming began on August 27, 1962, in Culver City. On September 5, the production moved to Seattle with the monorail scene being the first put on film.

✓ While in Seattle, Elvis stayed on the fourteenth floor of the New Washington Hotel.

✓ *It Happened at the World's Fair* included the following World's Fair scenes: Monorail Ride, Skyride, Dream Car Exhibit, Bell Telephone Exhibit, Floating City of Tomorrow, Theme Building, Science Exhibit, Filipino Building, Space Needle, and the restaurant in the Space Needle.

✓ MGM arranged for a hundred special policemen to protect Elvis from Fair crowds while filming. Six Pinkerton plainclothes detectives were at his side every second he wasn't in front of the cameras.

✓ Elvis's wardrobe cost $9,300 and included ten suits, four sports jackets, thirty shirts, fifteen pairs of slacks, two cashmere coats, and fifty-five ties.

✓ Gary Lockwood was expelled from UCLA for a year for fighting. He became a movie stuntman during the forced hiatus. Lockwood's first film was *Tall Story* (1960) in which he doubled for Tony Perkins. Playwright Josh Logan changed Gary's name Yusolfsky, to Lockwood because it was Logan's own middle name. He also earned a small role in the film. His second film was Elvis's *Wild in the Country*.

✓ Vicky Tiu made her film debut in *It Happened at the World's Fair*.

✓ Joan O'Brien was once a singer in the country music field. She made her movie debut in *Too Hot to Handle* (1959).

✓ *It Happened at the World's Fair* was ranked #55 in *Variety*'s list of top-grossing films for 1963. It grossed $2.25 million for the year.

✓ During production, Elvis dated Yvonne Craig,

Kurt Russell, Elvis. (Photo courtesy Eddie Brandt's Saturday Matinee)

who played Dorothy Johnson in the film. During the 1967–68 TV season, Craig played Barbara Gordon in the "Batman" series.

TRIVIA

★ *Bessie*—Nickname for Mike Edwards's plane. Its registration number was N6340.

★ *Greater Washington Produce Company*—Company for which Mike and Danny dusted potatoes. Mr. Farr was the foreman.

★ Mike Edwards's hometown was Sherrington, Washington.

★ Dorothy Johnson's home address in Clary, Washington, was 3820 Maple Street.

★ *Charlie's Garage*—Clary, Washington, business where Danny lost $700 in a poker game. The ensuing fight caused Mike and Danny to leave town quickly.

★ *Ling's Produce*—Sherrington, Washington, fruit and vegetable firm owned by Walter Ling.

★ Question: When Elvis bought Vicky Tiu an egg roll at the World's Fair, what did he give the cashier (besides money)? Answer: A sucker.

★ While in Seattle, Mike and Danny stayed in a trailer at the Century 21 Estates on Lakeview Road. Barney Thatcher was the camp's manager. Danny won free use of Barney's station wagon by defeating him in a gin rummy game.

★ About forty-five seconds after singing "One Broken Heart for Sale," Elvis met Kurt Russell. Here's the dialogue:

ELVIS: Hey, kid. How would you like to kick me in the shin?
RUSSELL: How would *I* like to kick you in the shin?
ELVIS: Uh huh.
RUSSELL: Mister, are you drunk?
ELVIS: Nah, nah. No kidding. I'll tell you what—you kick me in the shin real hard and I'll give you a quarter. OK. Go ahead. Play it. [Russell kicked him in the shin.] Aagh! Whew! That's a good one! That's a good one, boy!

RUSSELL: Adults: They're all nuts!

In a later scene, Russell again kicked Elvis.

★ Barney Thatcher's unseen wife was named Thelma.

★ *Tiger*—Nickname for Vicky Tiu's large stuffed dog, which she won at the Fair.

★ During the "How Would You Like to Be" number, Elvis and Vicky Tiu danced the twist and a waltz.

★ *Globe Taxicab*—Cab taken by Mike from the airport to Century 21 Estates. The fare—$5.60.

★ Question: What was hood Vince Bradley trying to get Mike and Danny to smuggle into Canada? Answer: Furs.

FUN IN ACAPULCO

Paramount, 1963. A Hal B. Wallis production. Running time: 97 minutes. Elvis's thirteenth film.

CAST

Mike Windgren	ELVIS PRESLEY
Marguerita Dauphin	URSULA ANDRESS
Dolores Gomez	ELSA CARDENAS
Maximillian Dauphin	PAUL LUKAS
Raoul Almeido	LARRY DOMASIN
Moreno	ALEJANDRO REY
José Garcia	ROBERT CARRICART
Janie Harkins	TERI HOPE
Mariachi Los Vaqueros	THEMSELVES
Mariachi Aguila	THEMSELVES
Dr. John Stevers	HOWARD MCNEAR
Mr. Ramirez, Manager of the Hilton	ALBERTO MORIN
Mrs. Stevers	MARY TREEN
Mr. Perez, Manager of La Perla	SALVADOR BAGUEZ
Mr. Delgado, Manager of the Ambassador	EDWARD COLMANS
Mr. Harkins	CHARLES EVANS
Guard	MIKE DEANDA
Manager of the Tropicana Hotel	MARTIN GARRALAGA
Señorita at Torito's	STELLA GARCIA
Photographer	TOM HERNANDEZ
Desk Clerk	FRANCISCO ORTEGA
Senorita at the Telegraph Desk	LINDA RIVERA
Waiter	DONALD A. DIAMOND
Secretary	ADELE PALACIOS
1st Girl	DARLENE TOMKINS
Bellboy	ROBERT DE ANDA
Maitre D' and Waiter	ROBERT IGLESIAS
Taxi Driver	ROBERT M. ALDERETTE
Bullfighter	MARCO ANTONIO
Master of Ceremonies at the Hilton	LUIS DE URBAN
Bullfighter	GENARO GOMEZ
Bullfighter	CARMELO MANTO
Bullfighter	ALBERTO MONTE
2nd Girl	LINDA RAND
Photographer	DAVID BENARD
Waiter	BOB HARVEY
Guest	JOHN INDRISANO
1st Diver	LOREN BROWN
2nd Diver	ELLY C. ENRIGUEZ
3rd Diver	STUART GRAY
4th Diver	RONALD VETO
5th Diver	RALPH HANALEI
Bartender	ALEX GIANNINI
Castanet Player	RACHEL PARRA
Diver	GEORGE SIMMONS
Poolside Guest	RED WEST

CREW

Producer	HAL B. WALLIS
Director	RICHARD THORPE
Screenplay	ALLAN WEISS
Director of Photography	DANIEL L. FAPP
Art Direction	HAL PEREIRA
	WALTER TYLER
Set Decoration	SAM COMER
	ROBERT BENTON
Makeup Supervision	WALLY WESTMORE
Hairstyle Supervision	NELLIE MANLEY
Sound Recording	HUGO GRENZBACH
	CHARLES GRENZBACH
Assistant Director	D. MICHAEL MOORE
Editorial Supervision	WARREN LOW
Editor	STANLEY E. JOHNSON
Costumes	EDITH HEAD
Second Unit Photography	IRWIN ROBERTS
Technicolor Color Consultant	RICHARD MUELLER
Special Photographic Effects	PAUL K. LERPAE
Process Photography	FARCIOT EDOUART
Associate Producer	PAUL NATHAN
Musical Numbers Staged by	CHARLES O'CURRAN
Music Scored and Conducted by	JOSEPH J. LILLEY
Vocal Accompaniment	THE JORDANAIRES
	THE FOUR AMIGOS
Technical Advisor	COL. TOM PARKER

SONGS

1. "Fun in Acapulco"—Sung over the opening credits.
2. "Vino, Dinero y Amor"—Sung in Torito's with the Four Amigos.
3. "I Think I'm Gonna Like It Here"—Sung in Torito's with the Four Amigos.

Elsa Cardenas, Elvis. (Photo courtesy Cinema Collectors)

Elvis, Ursula Andress. (Photo courtesy Eddie Brandt's Saturday Matinee)

4. "Mexico"—Sung in duet with Larry Domasin while riding on a bicycle.
5. "El Toro"—Sung in the Chapultepec Room of the Acapulco Hilton.
6. "Marguerita"—Sung at La Perla.
7. "The Bullfighter Was a Lady"—Sung in the Chapultepec Room of the Acapulco Hilton.
8. "(There's) No Room to Rhumba in a Sports Car"—Sung in a sports car with Elsa Cardenas.
9. "Bossa Nova Baby"—Sung at the Tropicana Hotel.
10. "You Can't Say No in Acapulco"—Sung at poolside at the Acapulco Hilton.
11. "Guadalajara"—Sung after making the dive at La Perla.

"Malagueña" was scheduled for the film, but not used in the final product.

PRODUCTION NOTES

✓ *Fun in Acapulco* opened nationally on November 27, 1963. The companion feature in most areas was a reissue of the 1959 western, *Last Train from Gun Hill*, which starred Kirk Douglas and Anthony Quinn.

✓ Although several locations were photographed in Acapulco, Elvis did not travel to the city. All of his shots were shot on the Paramount lot in Hollywood.

✓ Production of *Fun in Acapulco* began on January 28, 1963, and lasted to mid-March.

✓ Eight-year-old Larry Domasin had previously appeared in the 1963 film, *Dime with a Halo*.

✓ The soundtrack album of *Fun in Acapulco* had thirteen songs, it was Elvis's thirteenth film, and there are thirteen letters in the film's title.

✓ *Fun in Acapulco* was Ursula Andress's first American film. The Swiss-born actress (daughter of a diplomat) had appeared on screen since 1954, mostly in Italian films. She costarred in two James Bond flicks, *Dr. No* (1962) and *Casino Royale* (1967). Andress married director-actor John Derek in 1957, but the two were divorced in 1966. She was once romantically linked with Elvis.

✓ *Vacation in Acapulco* was first considered as the film's title.

✓ The Beatles went to see *Fun in Acapulco* at a drive-in theater in Miami on February 18, 1964, during their first American tour.

✓ Actor Paul Lukas was born on a train near Budapest, Hungary. After 26 years in films he won an Oscar for Best Actor for *Watch on the Rhine* (1943), a role he had earlier created on Broadway. Lukas made only two additional films after *Fun in Acapulco.*

✓ To promote *Fun in Acapulco,* Paramount printed promotional passports. The movie posters for the film also included a passport (serial no. 483473).

✓ *Fun in Acapulco* reached #5 on *Variety's* weekly top-grossing films list. For the year 1963, it ranked #33, grossing more than $1.5 million for the last six weeks of that year.

TRIVIA

★ *Torito's*—Nightclub where Mike Windgren met Dolores Gomez.

★ The Four Amigos consisted of Armando, Pedro, Pablo, and Sam.

★ *Chapultepec Room*—Cabaret at the Acapulco Hilton where Mike Windgren replaced El Trovador as the featured singer.

★ *136 Feet*—Height of the La Perla cliffs off which Moreno and others dived.

★ During Elvis's singing of "You Can't Say No in Acapulco," Red West could be seen at a poolside table.

★ *Tampa, Florida*—Hometown of Mike Windgren. His parents, Mr. and Mrs. Jack Windgren, lived at 2201 Robert Road.

★ Mike and his parents formed a trapeze act known as the Flying Windgrens. He quit after causing his partner to be seriously injured.

★ *Princess*—Mike's nickname for Marguerita.

★ Question: In addition to the Acapulco Hilton, at what other hotel did Mike Windgren perform? Answer: Ambassador Hotel.

KISSIN' COUSINS

MGM, 1964. A Four Leaf production. Running time: 96 minutes. Elvis's fourteenth film.

CAST

Josh Morgan	ELVIS PRESLEY
Jodie Tatum	ELVIS PRESLEY
Pappy Tatum	ARTHUR O'CONNELL
Ma Tatum	GLENDA FARRELL
Capt. Robert Jason Salbo	JACK ALBERTSON
Selena Tatum	PAM AUSTIN
Cpl. Midge Riley	CYNTHIA PEPPER
Azalea Tatum	YVONNE CRAIG
Gen. Alvin Donford	DONALD WOODS
M. Sgt. William George Bailey	TOMMY FARRELL
Trudy	BEVERLY POWERS
Dixie Cate	HORTENSE PETRA
Gen. Donford's Aide	ROBERT STONE

Yvonne Craig, Elvis as Josh Morgan. (Photo courtesy Cinema Collectors)

Gen. Sam Kruger	ROBERT CARSON
Mike	JOE ESPOSITO
Hairy Willie	W. J. (SAILOR) VINCENT
Lorraine, Leader of the Kittyhawks	MAUREEN REAGAN
Jonesy	JOAN STALEY
Minnie	LONNI LEES

CREW

Producer	SAM KATZMAN
Director	GENE NELSON
Screenplay	GERALD DRAYSON ADAMS
	GENE NELSON
Story	GERALD DRAYSON ADAMS
Director of Photography	ELLIS W. CARTER
Art Directors	GEORGE W. DAVIS
	EDDIE IMAZU
Set Decoration	HENRY GRACE
	BUDD S. FRIEND

Elvis as Jodie Tatum. Note Maureen Reagan to Elvis's immediate right. (Photo courtesy Academy of Motion Picture Arts and Sciences)

Assistant Director....................................ELI DUNN
Editor...BEN LEWIS
Makeup...WILLIAM TUTTLE
Hairstyles................................SYDNEY GUILAROFF
Recording Supervisor.....................FRANKLIN MILTON
Music Scored and Conducted by...................FRED KARGER
Choreography..................................HAL BELFER
Technical Advisor..........................COL. TOM PARKER

SONGS

1. "Kissin' Cousins"—Sung over the opening and closing credits.
2. "Smokey Mountain Boy"—Sung while driving a jeep to the Tatum property.
3. "One Boy, Two Little Girls"—Sung to Pam Austin and Yvonne Craig while walking through the woods.

4. "Catchin' on Fast"—Sung while kissing Yvonne Craig.
5. "Tender Feeling"—Sung (as Jodie Tatum) to Cynthia Pepper.
6. "Barefoot Ballad"—Sung (as Jodie Tatum) during a party to celebrate Pappy Tatum's rescue.
7. "Once Is Enough"—Sung during a party to celebrate Pappy Tatum's rescue.
8. "Kissin' Cousins (No. 2)"—Sung (as both Josh Morgan and Jodie Tatum) at the end of the film.

"Anyone (Could Fall in Love with You)" was cut from the film. Glenda Farrell sang "Pappy, Won't You Please Come Home."

PRODUCTION NOTES

✓ *Kissin' Cousins* was filmed in October 1963. The sixteen-day shoot was budgeted at $800,000.

✓ Exteriors were shot at Big Bear Lake, California. All interiors were filmed at MGM's Culver City studios.

✓ *Kissin' Cousins* premiered in Phoenix on March 6, 1964. A sneak preview was held at the Crest Theatre in North Long Beach, California, on February 21, 1964. National release occurred in April. The cofeature in most areas was *Beauty and the Body*, a sports documentary on surfing and skindiving. (*Beauty and the Body* was made in cooperation with the U.S. government's Physical Fitness Program for Youth.)

✓ MGM recruited thirteen actresses to play the Kittyhawks, the gang of mountain girls who try to capture the soldiers. One of them was Maureen Reagan, eldest daughter of Ronald Reagan and actress Jane Wyman. Maureen Reagan made her film debut at the age of eight in the 1949 Warner Bros. movie *It's a Great Feeling*. She had a cameo role, as did her parents.

✓ The soundtrack LP to *Kissin' Cousins* was recorded in Nashville instead of Hollywood so as to give a "country feel" to the songs.

✓ Some theater owners distributed candy kisses at showings of *Kissin' Cousins*. A few ran "Kisses for Charity" booths in their theater lobbies.

✓ Advertising lines: "Elvis has a Blond-Haired Twin the Gals Swoon Over"; "Just-for-Fun, Song-Filled Comedy with Elvis at His Singin'-est Best"; and "Them Kittyhawks Is Swoopin' Down on Poor, Unsuspecting Soldiers."

✓ As a promotion for *Kissin' Cousins*, Colonel Parker made singer Sergio Franchi an honorary colonel in June 1964, on the set of *Girl Happy*.

✓ Pamela Austin, who made her film debut in *Rome Adventure* (1962), was at one time the "Dodge Girl" in television commercials and print advertising for Dodge automobiles. She later played Pauline in *The Perils of Pauline* (1967). *Kissin' Cousins* was Austin's third film.

✓ During its first six weeks at 125 theaters, *Kissin' Cousins* grossed $1,750,000—the most of any MGM Elvis film to that date. It reached #11 on *Variety*'s weekly list of top-grossing films. For the year 1964, it was ranked #26 with a gross of $2.8 million.

✓ Producer Sam Katzman was known in Hollywood as "King of the Quickies." Among the low-budget features Katzman produced through the years were *Spooks Run Wild* (1941), *Jungle Jim* (1948), and *Rock Around the Clock* (1956). He produced two Elvis films: *Kissin' Cousins* and *Harum Scarum*.

✓ Glenda Farrell had her first big role in *Little Caesar* (1930), playing Olga Strassoff, the girlfriend of gangster Enrico Bandello. Often playing wisecracking best friends of lead characters in films, her career had a resurgence in the 1950s when she began playing character parts. In 1963 Farrell won an Emmy as Best Supporting Actress for an episode of "Ben Casey." After *Kissin' Cousins* she made only two more films. Tommy Farrell, who played Sergeant Bailey in *Kissin' Cousins*, is her son.

✓ Actor Jack Albertson, who appeared in one other Elvis film *Roustabout*, has won both an Oscar and an Emmy. The Best Supporting Actor Oscar came in 1968 for *The Subject Was Roses*. In 1976 Albertson won an Emmy for Outstanding Lead Character in a Comedy Series ("Chico and the Man").

TRIVIA

★ *Big Smokey Mountain*—North Carolina area owned by the Tatum family. The Pentagon wanted to lease the site for an ICBM base.

★ Capt. Robert Salbo (serial no. 97887711) had just completed a tour of duty at Goose Bay, Labrador. Before that he had served in Korea, Okinawa, Formosa, Saigon, and Algeria.

★ *Operation Big Smokey*—Pentagon plan to get a lease to the Tatums' land on Big Smokey Mountain. Previous attempts by Captain North and Lieutenant Roth had failed.

★ *Watz Matta You*—Phrase written on Josh Morgan's F84 jet.

★ Josh Morgan was a member of the Shooting Star aerobatic team. (In reality, the Air Force aerobatic team is called the Thunderbirds.)

★ Josh Morgan was born in Hidden Rock, North Carolina.

★ In 1907 Josh Morgan's great-great-aunt, Euphrasia Morgan, married Jubal Tatum.

★ *Tatum Teritoree, So Git*—Sign seen by Captain Salbo and his men as they entered the Tatum family property.

★ Blooper: The jeep driven by Josh Morgan to Big Smokey Mountain had a serial number of 11A-3142491. In a later scene, that same jeep was used by General Donford to drive to Big Smokey Mountain.

★ Question: For a cease-fire flag, what did Josh tie on the aerial of a walkie-talkie? Answer: A nylon stocking.

★ *Hezekiah*—Hound dog belonging to the Tatum family.

★ *The Kittyhawks*—Band of thirteen love-starved women from the Kittyhawk Valley who were looking for husbands.

★ The Pentagon's code name was Big Blue. Captain Salbo's code name for his camp was Big Smokey.

★ *Porcupine Flats*—Area at the base of Big Smokey Mountain where the Army established its camp.

★ Question: How much money did Selena and Azalea have to go shopping in Knoxville? Answer: $6.87.

★ Reporter Dixie Cate worked for the *Knoxville Evening Courier* newspaper.

★ Question: What was Selena and Azalea's major purchase in Knoxville? Answer: Bikinis.

★ Blooper: On the telephone, reporter Dixie Cate thanked a Mr. Billingsley for the tip that the Army had paid for a large order of bikinis. Yet, a few scenes later, she referred to him as Mr. Billings.

★ *W2349687*—Army serial number of Corporal Midge Riley, the WAC stenographer. According to her, her measurements were 36-22-35.

★ *Blue Quail*—Code name for Josh Morgan's search party in looking for Pappy Tatum. Captain Salbo's code name was Magpie.

★ Ma Tatum's moonshine was called Mountain Maiden's Breath.

★ *Howling Devil's Gorge*—Location where Pappy Tatum was stranded in a tree by a bear.

★ Pappy Tatum agreed to lease his land to the Army on three conditions: (1) he would receive $1,000 a month; (2) the Army would build a private road on the other side of the mountain; and (3) a military patrol would see to it that no government personnel would trespass on his side of the mountain.

VIVA LAS VEGAS

MGM, 1964. A Jack Cummings–George Sidney production. Running time: 86 minutes. Elvis's fifteenth film.

CAST

Lucky Jackson	ELVIS PRESLEY
Rusty Martin	ANN-MARGRET
Count Elmo Mancini	CESARE DANOVA
Mr. Martin	WILLIAM DEMAREST
Shorty Farnsworth	NICKY BLAIR
Jack Carter	HIMSELF
Mr. Swanson	ROBERT B. WILLIAMS
Big Gus Olson	BOB NASH
Mr. Baker	ROY ENGEL
Mechanic	BARNABY HALE
Driver	FORD DUNHILL
Master of Ceremonies	EDDIE QUILLAN
Manager at Swingers	GEORGE CISAR
Delivery Boy	RICK MURRAY
Head Captain	IVAN TRIESAULT
Francois	FRANCIS RAVAL
Sons of the Lone Star State	HARRY FLEER
	LARRY BARTON
	CLAUDE HALL
	RED WEST
	JOHN BURNSIDE
	LANCE LEGAULT
Ad-Libs	MIKE RAGAN
	PETE KELLETT

Elvis, Ann-Margret, Cesare Danova. (Photo courtesy Eddie Brandt's Saturday Matinee)

Race Official	LARRY KENT
Starter	HOWARD CURTIS
Race Announcer	ALAN FORDNEY
Showgirls	ALEANE MAMBI HAMILTON
	BEVERLY POWERS
	KAY SUTTON
	INGEBORG KJELDSEN
	TERI GARR
Jugglers	CARL CARLSON
	RUTH CARLSON
Guards	BRAD LOGAN
	TAGGART CASEY
The Forte Four	THEMSELVES

CREW

Producers	JACK CUMMINGS
	GEORGE SIDNEY
Director	GEORGE SIDNEY
Screenplay	SALLY BENSON
Director of Photography	JOSEPH BIROC
Art Direction	GEORGE W. DAVIS
	EDWARD CARFAGNO
Set Decoration	HENRY GRACE
	GEORGE R. NELSON
Assistant Director	MILTON FELDMAN
Editor	JOHN MCSWEENEY JR.
Makeup Supervision	WILLIAM TUTTLE
Hairstyles	SYDNEY GUILAROFF
Costumes Designed by	DON FELD
Choreography	DAVID WINTERS
Recording Supervision	FRANKLIN MILTON
Music	GEORGE STOLL

SONGS

1. "Viva Las Vegas"—Sung over the opening credits, in the Flamingo Hotel talent show, and at the end of the film.
2. "The Yellow Rose of Texas"/"The Eyes of Texas"—Sung at Swingers Casino while trying to quiet down the Sons of the Lone Star State.
3. "The Lady Loves Me"—Sung to Ann-Margret while she's in the women's dressing room near the Flamingo Hotel pool and as she walks to poolside. She then joins Elvis in a duet.
4. "C'mon Everybody"—Sung in the University of Nevada–Las Vegas gymnasium.
5. "Today, Tomorrow and Forever"—Sung while playing the piano in Rusty's apartment.
6. "What'd I Say"—Sung just after Elvis and Ann-Margret had danced the climb.
7. "Santa Lucia"—Sung to Ann-Margret in Mancini's hotel room.
8. "If You Think I Don't Love You"—Sung to Ann-Margret in Mancini's hotel room.
9. "I Need Somebody to Lean On"—Sung while walking through the Flamingo Hotel lounge after winning the talent contest.

"You're the Boss," "Do the Vega," and "Night Life" were recorded for *Viva Las Vegas*, but not used. Ann-Margret soloed on "My Rival" and "Appreciation." The Forte Four sang "The Climb."

PRODUCTION NOTES

✓ *Viva Las Vegas* premiered in New York City on April 20, 1964. It opened nationally on June 17.

✓ In Great Britain, the film was titled *Love in Las Vegas*.

Elvis, Ann-Margret. (Photo courtesy Eddie Brandt's Saturday Matinee)

✓ The title originally considered for *Viva Las Vegas* was *Only Girl in Town*.

✓ Filming began on July 15, 1963, and was completed on September 16.

✓ Some of the locations used in *Viva Las Vegas* included the drag strip in Henderson, Nevada; the skeet-shooting range at the Tropicana Hotel; the University of Nevada–Las Vegas gymnasium; McCarran Airport; and the swimming pool at the Flamingo Hotel.

✓ While filming in Las Vegas, Elvis stayed at the Sahara Hotel in the Presidential Suite.

✓ It was originally announced in April 1963 that the comedy-writing team of Ray Singer and Dick Chevillet would be doing the screenplay. The story and screenplay were later written by Sally Benson.

✓ *Viva Las Vegas* was released overseas before it was released in the United States. It set box-office records in Tokyo, Manila, and other cities of the Far East.

✓ The western shootout between Elvis and Ann-Margret was filmed at the Old Vegas Amusement Park in Henderson, Nevada. In the scene, Elvis was wearing a special Bianchi holster. His gun was a Ruger Blackhawk .44 Magnum.

✓ *Viva Las Vegas* was paired with *Tamahine*, a Nancy Kwan film, in most theaters.

✓ *Viva Las Vegas* (under the European title, *Love in Las Vegas* was banned in Gozo, the sister island of Malta. Showings at the Aurora Theatre were cancelled after Catholic authorities protested the film. The Gozo College of Parish Priests issued a circular condemning the film as indecent. During Mass, one priest asked his congregation to protest *Viva Las Vegas* and avoid seeing it. Gozo was the only place in the world in which the film was banned. In Malta, *Viva Las Vegas* had a full run.

✓ The entire race sequence was filmed with no sound. A total of forty-three special-effects shots were edited to cover the race. Sound effects were then added to provide the composite (exhaust effects, high-speed whines, tire squeals, etc.). The race itself ranged from the southern branch of Lake Mead to Boulder City to downtown Las Vegas.

✓ Interiors for *Viva Las Vegas* were filmed on the MGM lot in Culver City.

✓ *Viva Las Vegas* reached #14 on *Variety*'s list of top-grossing films. For the year 1964, it was listed in the #11 spot, having grossed $4,675,000.

TRIVIA

★ As the Folies Bergere danced at the Tropicana, the song "Blue Moon" could be heard.

★ *7*—Number on Lucky Jackson's race car.

★ *Sons of the Lone Star State*—Group of rowdy Texans at the Swingers Casino that Elvis quieted by singing "The Yellow Rose of Texas"/"The Eyes of Texas." He then led them outside.

★ While in Swingers Casino, Lucky evoked the names of Sam Houston, Davy Crockett, and John Wayne.

★ *22*—Number on Elmo Mancini's race car.

★ *Thunderbird Gun Club*—Club where Lucky and Rusty went skeet shooting.

★ Rusty Martin was enrolled at the University of Nevada–Las Vegas.

★ Rusty was born in Las Vegas but had lived in Dubuque, Iowa; Chillicothe, Ohio; and Helena, Arkansas. Her father moved to Las Vegas originally to help build the Hoover Dam.

★ *Cal Howard*—Race driver who crashed and was killed. Mancini mentioned Cal Howard's name while talking to Lucky Jackson.

★ Lucky Jackson worked as a waiter at the Flamingo Hotel. Rusty Martin taught swimming there. The Flamingo was the first hotel to appear on the famous Las Vegas Strip. It cost $6 million when built in 1946 by gangster Benjamin (Bugsy) Siegel. He named the hotel, which opened on December 26, 1946, after his girlfriend, Virginia Hill, who was nicknamed "Flamingo."

★ Comedian Jack Carter hosted the Flamingo Hotel employees' talent show. Lucky sang "Viva Las Vegas" in the show, while Rusty sang and danced to "Appreciation." After a tie was declared, Lucky won first place by a flip of a coin—Rusty calling "heads." For winning, Lucky received a silver trophy and an all-expenses paid two-week honeymoon in Las Vegas. Rusty's second prize was a pool table.

★ *Baker's Grand Prix Garage*—Garage where all the race drivers housed their cars in preparation for the Las Vegas Grand Prix.

★ Swanson's Machine Shop was the Los Angeles facility that built Lucky Jackson's racing engine.

★ The Forte Four sang "The Climb" while Lucky and Rusty danced. "The Climb" was written by Jerry Leiber and Mike Stoller and originally recorded by the Coasters (Atco 6234) in 1962. The song was an attempt to capitalize on the various dance crazes of the early 1960s.

★ While preparing a picnic lunch for Lucky and the boys at the garage, Rusty sang "My Rival." The "rival" in the song was a "baby-blue racing car."

★ The Las Vegas Grand Prix, which took place on July 4, 1964, ended in front of the Horseshoe Hotel in Las Vegas.

★ The closing credits featured this credit line: "Folies Bergere" sequence by arrangement with Hotel Tropicana."

ROUSTABOUT

Paramount, 1964. A Hal B. Wallis production. Running time: 101 minutes. Elvis's sixteenth film.

CAST

Charlie Rogers	ELVIS PRESLEY
Maggie Morgan	BARBARA STANWYCK
Cathy Lean	JOAN FREEMAN
Joe Lean	LEIF ERICKSON
Madame Mijanou	SUE ANE LANGDON
Harry Carver	PAT BUTTRAM
Marge	JOAN STALEY
Arthur Nielsen	DABBS GREER
Freddie	STEVE BRODIE
Sam, a College Student	NORMAN GRABOWSKI
Lou	JACK ALBERTSON
Hazel	JANE DULO
Cody Marsh	JOE FLUELLEN
Little Egypt	WILDA TAYLOR
Gus, a Motorcyclist in the Wall of Death	ARTHUR LEVY
Ernie, a Motorcyclist in the Wall of Death	RAY KELLOGG
Dick	TOBY REED
Gregg, Employee at Bill's Motorcycle Repairs	KEN BECKER
Viola	MARIANNA HILL
B. J. Lewis	LESTER MILLER
Cora	BEVERLY ADAMS
Craig	GLENN R. WILDER
Dancer	MERCEDES G. FORD
Barkers	EDDIE MARR
	BOB MATTHEWS
	BUDDY LEWIS
	JACK WHALEN
	LANCE LEGAULT
Sheriff	K. L. SMITH
Deputies	MIKE MAHONEY
	ROGER V. CREED
Billy, the Midget	BILLY BARTY
Stage Manager	JERRY JAMES
Fat Lady	BARBARA HEMINGWAY
Strong Man	RICHARD KIEL
Juggler	MAX MANNING
Elephant Girl	DIANNE SIMPSON
Carnival Worker	RED WEST
Volcano Man	JOHN TURK
Clown	CHESTER HAYES
Concessionaire	JOE FORTE
Candy Concessionaire	HOWARD JOSLIN
College Students	LYNN BORDEN
	LINDA FOSTER
	TERI HOPE
	RAQUEL WELCH
Boys with Balloons	STEVE CONDIT
	DEAN MORAY
Sexy Girl	DIANNE LIBBY
Man	OWEN BUSH
Boy	JIMMY GAINES
1st Farmer	RICHARD DI PAOLO

2nd Farmer	THEODORE E. LEHMANN
Harry Carver's Secretary	MAUGENE H. GANNON
Little Girl	KATIE SWEET

CREW

Producer	HAL B. WALLIS
Director	JOHN RICH
Screenplay	ANTHONY LAWRENCE
	ALLAN WEISS
Story	ALLAN WEISS
Director of Photography	LUCIEN BALLARD
Art Directors	HAL PEREIRA
	WALTER TYLER
Set Decoration	SAM COMER
	ROBERT BENTON
Makeup	WALLY WESTMORE
Hairstyles	NELLIE MANLEY
Sound Recording	JOHN CARTER
	CHARLES GRENZBACH
Assistant Director	D. MICHAEL MOORE
Editorial Supervision	WARREN LOW
Costumes	EDITH HEAD
Technicolor Color Consultant	RICHARD MUELLER
Special Photographic Effects	PAUL K. LERPAE
Process Photography	FARCIOT EDOUART
Associate Producer	PAUL NATHAN
Music Scored and Conducted by	JOSEPH J. LILLEY
Musical Numbers Staged by	EARL BARTON
Vocal Accompaniment	THE JORDANAIRES
Technical Advisor	COL. TOM PARKER

SONGS

1. "Roustabout"—Sung over the opening credits.
2. "Poison Ivy League"—Sung in Mother's Tea House.
3. "Wheels on My Heels"—Sung while riding a motorcycle after being bailed out of jail.
4. "It's a Wonderful World"—Sung while riding on a Ferris wheel with Joan Freeman.
5. "It's Carnival Time"—Sung at the Cat Rack while encouraging people to throw. It was later sung in front of the girlie show.
6. "Carny Town"—Sung in front of the girlie show.
7. "One Track Heart"—Sung on stage at the girlie show.
8. "Hard Knocks"—Sung on stage at the girlie show.
9. "Little Egypt"—Sung at Carver's Combined Shows during Little Egypt's dance.
10. "Big Love, Big Heartache"—Sung at Carver's Combined Shows.

Elvis, Joan Freeman, Barbara Stanwyck, Leif Erickson. (Photo courtesy Cinema Collectors)

11. "There's a Brand New Day on the Horizon"—Sung on the midway at the end of the film.

PRODUCTION NOTES

✓ *Roustabout* opened nationally on November 11, 1964. In most areas the companion feature was *Stage to Thunder Rock*, which starred Barry Sullivan, Scott Brady, and Marilyn Maxwell.

✓ *Roustabout* began filming on March 9, 1964, and was completed on April 20.

✓ The project was first announced in May 1961, but took three years to go before the cameras.

✓ The title originally considered for *Roustabout* was *Right This Way Folks*.

✓ Elvis's character, Charlie Rogers, was originally called Charlie Main. The original name of Maggie Morgan was Maggie Moore.

✓ Exteriors for *Roustabout* were filmed near Thousand Oaks, California. Producer Hal Wallis had one of the large traveling carnivals in the West erect tents and build a midway on some land there. For the big-tent interiors, the giant doors of stages #12, #14, and #15 on the Paramount lot were opened to combine the three stages for the first time in the history of the studio.

✓ Actress Joan Freeman, a Council Bluffs, Iowa, native, first came to the attention of the general public in the 1961–62 ABC-TV series "Bus Stop," in which she played waitress Emma Gahringer. Her grandfather, Daniel Freeman, was the first homesteader in the United States under the Homestead Act of 1863. Freeman homesteaded near Beatrice, Nebraska.

✓ On February 15, 1965, in the New York Supreme Court, professional dancer Little Egypt sued Paramount Pictures, RCA Victor, and Elvis Presley Music, Inc., for $2.5 million in damages. She also sought an injunction restraining exhibitions of *Roustabout* and stopping sales of the *Roustabout* LP, which contained the song "Little Egypt." Her contention was that the tune and the use of the Little Egypt name in the film was done without her authorization, causing her irreparable harm and holding her up to public ridicule. She lost the case. The original Little Egypt, Catherine Devine, caused a sensation when she danced at the Chicago World's Fair in 1893.

✓ Mae West was originally selected for the costarring role of Maggie Morgan, but she decided against playing the part.

✓ Joan Staley, who played Marge, the waitress at Mother's Tea House, was *Playboy* magazine's Miss November in 1958.

✓ *Roustabout* was director John Rich's third feature film. He was previously well established in the television field, directing episodes of such series as "Our Miss Brooks," "I Married Joan," "The Twilight Zone," and "The Dick Van Dyke Show" (for which he won an Emmy for the 1962–63 season).

✓ Fashion stylist Edith Head created a pair of specially fitted blue jeans for Barbara Stanwyck. Head commented, "These blue denims are undoubtedly the most expensive and glamorous blue jeans ever designed." Head was the recipient of numerous Oscars,

Sue Ane Langdon, Elvis. (Photo courtesy Cinema Collectors)

beginning with 1949's *The Heiress*. She played herself in the 1966 film *The Oscar*.

✓ Raquel Welch (born Raquel Tejada in 1940) made her film debut in *Roustabout*. She can be seen in the first few minutes of the film as one of the two college girls who drive up to Mother's Tea House with their boyfriends and go in and sit down at a table. Her first screen line: "Uh, how come they call this place a tea house, dear?"

✓ *Roustabout* was ranked #28 on *Variety*'s list of top-grossing films for the year 1965. By the end of that year, it had grossed $3 million. *Roustabout* reached as high as #8 on *Variety*'s weekly list.

✓ Sue Ane Langdon played Alice Kramden in a few "Honeymooners" sketches on "Jackie Gleason and His American Scene Magazine" in the fall of 1962. She later costarred with Herschel Bernardi in the CBS-TV series "Arnie." For her role as Lillian Nuvo in that series, Langdon won a Golden Globe Award as Best Supporting Actress in a TV series.

✓ Barbara Stanwyck is a member of the National Cowboy Hall of Fame. She made only one more theatrical film (*The Night Walker* in 1964) after *Roustabout*. In 1944 Stanwyck (real name: Ruby Stevens) was the highest-paid woman in the United States. Although nominated for Best Actress four times, she failed to win an Oscar.

✓ Director of photography Lucien Ballard was nominated for an Oscar for *The Caretakers* (1963).

✓ As of *Roustabout*, producer Hal Wallis's films had won a total of 32 Academy Awards and received 121 Oscar nominations in several different categories.

TRIVIA

★ *Mother's Tea House*—Espresso cafe owned by Lou at which Charlie Rogers sang at the beginning of the film.

★ Question: Who was the saxophone player and leader of the house band at Mother's Tea House? Answer: Herbie.

★ *George*—Bartender at Mother's Tea House.

★ Charlie Rogers rode a 1964 Honda 350 motorcycle, California license number 204843.

★ When arrested after the fight at Mother's Tea House, Charlie had only six dollars on him.

★ *Shreveport, Louisiana*—City near which Charlie Rogers lived.

★ Question: Before he was run off the road by Joe Lean, where was Charlie heading? Answer: Phoenix.

★ *Donniker*—Name for restroom in carnival language.

★ Madame Mijanou's real first name was Estelle.

★ *2*—Number of the Ferris wheel seat taken by Charlie and Cathy during the "It's a Wonderful World" number.

★ Billy the Midget was thirty-eight years old.

★ *Topeka, Kansas*—City in which the bank that held the mortgage on Maggie's carnival was located.

★ Question: Who was the leader of the carnival band? Answer: Pete.

★ Harry Carver, the owner of Carver's Combined Shows, was nicknamed "Harry the Undertaker" because he waited for small shows to die and then bought them.

★ Blooper: On a blackboard outside the girlie show, it was indicated that the next show was at 9:30. A few minutes later, the same blackboard had the next show listed for 8:30.

★ *Waterford County Tigers*—Team for which Freddie (Steve Brodie) pitched. Freddie was the man who kept hitting the target in the baseball throw, causing Cathy to be dropped into the tank of water.

★ *Bill's Motorcycle Repairs*—Shop that repaired Charlie's motorcycle. The cost for the repairs was $150 (which Joe paid).

★ For the motorcycles to perform in the "Wall of Death" stunt, a speed of 40 miles per hour had to be attained.

★ *3*—Number of Charlie's dressing room at Carver's Combined Shows.

★ *$1,050*—Salary (three weeks' worth) earned by Charlie while at Carver's Combined Shows. When he left to go back to Morgan's Shows, Charlie gave Carver $50 as partial payment on his contract and $1,000 to Arthur Nielsen as partial payment on Maggie Morgan's overdue loan payment.

GIRL HAPPY

MGM, 1965. A Euterpe production. Running time: 96 minutes. Elvis's seventeenth film.

CAST

Rusty Wells	ELVIS PRESLEY
Valerie Frank	SHELLEY FABARES
Mr. Frank	HAROLD J. STONE
Andy	GARY CROSBY
Wilbur	JOBY BAKER
Sunny Daze	NITA TALBOT
Deena Shepherd	MARY ANN MOBLEY
Romano	FABRIZIO MIONI
Sergeant Benson	JACKIE COOGAN
Doc	JIMMY HAWKINS
Brentwood Von Durgenfeld	PETER BROOKS
Mr. Penchill, Seadrift Motel Manager	JOHN FIEDLER
Betsy	CHRIS NOEL
Laurie	LYN EDGINGTON
Nancy	GALE GILMORE
Bobbie	PAMELA CURRAN
Linda	RUSTY ALLEN
Wolf Call O'Brien	NORMAN GRABOWSKI
Bartender	MIKE DE ANDA
Waiter	ALAN HANLEY
Waiter	OLAN SOULE
Louey	TOMMY FARRELL
Buxom Blonde on Beach	NANCY CZAR
Driver	DARREN DUBLIN
Charlie	DAN HAGGERTY
Officer Wilkins	RICHARD J. REEVES
Officer Jones	RALPH LEE
Boy	HANK JONES
Girl	THERESA COOPER
Police Captain	MILTON FROME
1st Girl	JULIE PAYNE
2nd Girl	BEVERLY ADAMS
3rd Girl	STASSA DAMASCUS
Muscle Boy	JIM DAWSON
Garbageman	TED FISH
Extra in Kit Kat Club	RED WEST

CREW

Producer	JOE PASTERNAK

(Photo courtesy Eddie Brandt's Saturday Matinee)

Jimmy Hawkins, Elvis. (Photo courtesy Eddie Brandt's Saturday Matinee)

Director	BORIS SAGAL
Screenplay	HARVEY BULLOCK
	R. S. ALLEN
Director of Photography	PHILIP H. LATHROP
Art Direction	GEORGE W. DAVIS
	ADDISON HEHR
Set Decoration	HENRY GRACE
	HUGH HUNT
Editor	RITA ROLAND
Assistant Director	JACK ALDWORTH
Technical Advisor	COL. TOM PARKER
Makeup	WILLIAM TUTTLE
Hairstyles	SYDNEY GUILAROFF
Recording Supervisor	FRANKLIN MILTON
Music	GEORGE STOLL
Vocal Accompaniment	THE JORDANAIRES

SONGS

1. "Girl Happy"—Sung over the opening and closing credits.
2. "Spring Fever"—Sung while driving to Fort Lauderdale in a red convertible with Gary Crosby, Jimmy Hawkins, and Joby Baker. They and Shelley Fabares and her friends (in another car) join in the singing.
3. "Fort Lauderdale Chamber of Commerce"—Sung to Shelley Fabares at poolside, and then to other girls at poolside.
4. "Startin' Tonight"—Sung in the Sandbar Club.
5. "Wolf Call"—Sung in the Sandbar Club.
6. "Do Not Disturb"—Sung to Mary Ann Mobley in Elvis's motel room.
7. "Cross My Heart and Hope to Die"—Sung to Mary Ann Mobley in the woods.
8. "The Meanest Girl in Town"—Sung in the Sandbar Club.
9. "Do the Clam"—Sung at a nighttime beach party.
10. "Puppet on a String"—Sung to Shelley Fabares while walking her back to her motel room and later on a sailboat.
11. "I've Got to Find My Baby"—Sung at the Sandbar Club.

"Nita Talbot and Shelley Fabares sang "Read All About It" (also known as "Good News").

PRODUCTION NOTES

✓ *Girl Happy* opened nationally on April 14, 1965. The companion feature at many theaters was *Your Cheatin' Heart,* starring George Hamilton. In other areas, the film was double-billed with *36 Hours,* which starred James Garner and Eva Marie Saint. Both cofeatures had been released the year before.

✓ Filming on *Girl Happy* began on June 22, 1964, and was completed on July 31. Some locations in Fort Lauderdale, Florida, were used. Interiors were shot at MGM's Culver City studios.

✓ During a break in filming on the MGM set, Elvis was awarded a Gold Record from South Africa for "Kiss Me Quick."

✓ By the time *Girl Happy* was filmed, Gary Crosby, Bing's son, was a movie veteran. He made his debut at the age of eight in 1942's wartime extravaganza, *Star-Spangled Rhythm,* which starred his father and Bob Hope, as well as about every other actor on the Paramount lot.

✓ Two ad lines that were used for *Girl Happy:* "What Happens During Easter Vacation at the Beach?" and "See How Youth Reacts When the Gates Are Opened."

✓ Choreographer David Winters created a new dance, the clam, for *Girl Happy.* The dance never caught on with the public.

✓ Actress Mary Ann Mobley was Miss America of 1959 (and Miss Mississippi). The 5'5", 34½-22-35 beauty made her film debut in *Get Yourself a College Girl* (1964). During her first year in the acting business, she served as Hollywood's Lady Ambassador of Goodwill, representing the community at various civic and social functions across the country. In 1965 Mobley was selected as Deb Star ("Newest Motion Picture Star with the Brightest Future"). In addition to *Girl Happy,* she also made *Harum Scarum* with Elvis. Currently, she is married to actor and host of TV's "Hour Magazine," Gary Collins.

✓ Jackie Coogan, who played Sergeant Benson, began his film career at the age of eighteen months when he appeared in the silent movie *Skinner's Baby.* In 1921 comedian Charlie Chaplin selected Coogan to costar with him in *The Kid.* Coogan quickly became one of the highest-paid actors in Hollywood. His struggles to get his childhood earnings from his mother and stepfather when he reached the age of twenty-one led to the passage of the Child Actors Bill (also known as the Coogan Act) in California. Today's audiences know Jackie Coogan best as the eccentric Uncle Fester on TV's "The Addams Family."

✓ *Girl Happy* was the first of three films in which Shelley Fabares costarred with Elvis. (The second and third were *Spinout* and *Clambake.*) Fabares, who starred on TV's "The Donna Reed Show," "The Brian Keith Show," and "The Practice," had a number one record in 1962 with "Johnny Angel" (Colpix 621). Elvis's "Good Luck Charm" replaced "Johnny Angel" at the top in April 1962. Elvis once said that Shelley Fabares was his favorite costar.

✓ Jimmy Hawkins's first regular TV role was as

Shelley Fabares, Elvis. The "Fort Lauderdale Chamber of Commerce" number. (Photo courtesy Academy of Motion Picture Arts and Sciences)

Tagg, Annie Oakley's kid brother, in the syndicated series "Annie Oakley." Shelley Fabares occasionally appeared in guest roles in "Annie Oakley." Hawkins later played Scotty Simpson in "The Donna Reed Show." He appeared in two Elvis films, *Girl Happy* and *Spinout.*

✓ *Girl Happy* was ranked #25 in *Variety*'s list of top-grossing films for the year 1965, earning $3.1 million.

TRIVIA

★ *77 Club*—Chicago nightclub owned by Big Frank, where Rusty Wells and his combo played.

★ Headline on a poster seen in Rusty's 77 Club dressing room: "Fort Lauderdale—Where the Fun Never Sets."

★ *Seadrift Motel*—Fort Lauderdale motel where Rusty Wells and his combo stayed. Valerie Frank and her two friends, Betsy and Laurie, were also registered at the Seadrift Motel.

★ Valerie was a music major in college.

★ *Sandbar Club*—Fort Lauderdale nightclub where Rusty Wells and his combo played.

★ Romano's boat was anchored at the Coral Pier.

★ Whenever Valerie and Romano were together, the song "Santa Lucia" could be heard on the soundtrack.

★ *Drop Dead*—Message Deena wrote in lipstick on Rusty's motel-room mirror.

★ Romano, an Italian exchange student, was a member of royalty, since his grandfather had married a Spanish princess.

★ Question: Valerie's roommates, Betsy and Laurie, were going with guys from what colleges? Answer: Cornell and Purdue, respectively.

★ *5*—Valerie's room number at the Seadrift Motel.

★ Whenever Andy, Wilbur, and Doc were together, the song "Three Blind Mice" could be heard on the soundtrack.

★ *Article 3, Subparagraph B*—Mr. Penchill's rule at the Seadrift Motel: "Thou shalt not have a boy in the room."

★ The nickname of Princeton intellectual Brentwood Von Durgenfeld was "BVD."

★ *J & P Electric Company*—Owner of the searchlight used by Rusty Wells to scout the beach for Valerie.

★ *Kit Kat Club*—Fort Lauderdale nightclub where stripper Sunny Daze performed. It was at the Kit Kat Club that a fight broke out, causing the arrest of forty-six individuals (twenty girls and twenty-six boys).

★ In reference to Rusty's growing attachment to Valerie, Andy (Gary Crosby) said, "The king is dead!"

★ Question: What was the name of the taxi company whose cab transported Mr. Frank to the Seadrift Motel and then to the police station? Answer: City Cab Company.

★ Question: What did Valerie call Andy, Wilbur, and Doc when she saw them after walking out of the police station? Answer: Mouseketeers.

TICKLE ME

Allied Artists, 1965. A Ben Schwalb production. Running time: 90 minutes. Elvis's eighteenth film.

CAST

Lonnie Beale	ELVIS PRESLEY
Vera Radford	JULIE ADAMS
Pam Merritt	JOCELYN LANE
Stanley Potter	JACK MULLANEY
Estelle Penfield	MERRY ANDERS
Deputy Sheriff John Sturdivant	BILL WILLIAMS
Brad Bentley	EDWARD FAULKNER
Hilda	CONNIE GILCHRIST
Barbara	BARBARA WERLE
Adolph, the Chef	JOHN DENNIS
Mr. Dabney	GRADY SUTTON
Mabel	ALLISON HAYES
Ophelia	INEZ PEDROZA
Ronnie	LILYAN CHAUVIN
Donna	ANGELA GREENE
Henry, the Gardener	ROBERT HOY
Janet	LAURIE BURTON
Clair Kinnamon	LINDA ROGERS
Sybil	ANN MORELL
Evelyn	JEAN INGRAM
Mildred	FRANCINE YORK
Pat	EVE BRUCE
Gloria	JACKIE RUSSELL
Dot	PEGGY WARD
Polly	DORIAN BROWN
Mrs. Dabney	DOROTHY CONRAD
Bully in Bar	RED WEST
Jim, the Bartender	RICHARD J. REEVES

CREW

Producer	BEN SCHWALB
Director	NORMAN TAUROG
Screenplay	ELWOOD ULLMAN
	EDWARD BERNDS
Director of Photography	LOYAL GRIGGS
Art Directors	HAL PEREIRA
	ARTHUR LONERGAN
Set Decoration	SAM COMER
	ARTHUR KRAMS
Makeup Supervision	WALLY WESTMORE
Hairstyle Supervision	NELLIE MANLEY
Costumes	LEAH RHODES
Production Manager	FRANK CAFFEY
Assistant Production Manager	CURTIS MICK
Unit Manager	ROBERT GOODSTEIN
Assistant Director	ARTHUR JACOBSON
Technical Advisor	COL. TOM PARKER
Editor	ARCHIE MARSHEK
Dialogue Coach	MIKE HOEY
Choreography	DAVID WINTERS

(Photo courtesy Eddie Brandt's Saturday Matinee)

Sound Recording...........................HUGO GRENZBACH
CHARLES GRENZBACH
Script Supervisor...........................MARVIN WELDON
Special Photographic Effects..................PAUL K. LERPAE
Process Photography.......................FARCIOT EDOUART
Vocal Accompaniment.......................THE JORDANAIRES
Music Scored and Conducted by...............WALTER SCHARF

SONGS

1. "Long, Lonely Highway"—Sung during the opening credits while Elvis is traveling on a Greyhound bus.
2. "It Feels So Right"—Sung in the Corral Bar.
3. "(Such an) Easy Question"—Sung in the yard of the Circle Z guest ranch.
4. "Dirty, Dirty Feeling"—Sung in the stables of the Circle Z.
5. "Put the Blame on Me"—Sung in a saloon in a daydream sequence.
6. "I'm Yours"—Sung at a party for Mr. and Mrs. Dabney.
7. "Night Rider"—Sung in the ranch yard while taking a breather from pitching hay.
8. "I Feel That I've Known You Forever"—Sung to Jocelyn Lane outside of her cabin at the Circle Z. In a later scene, Lane hears the song in her mind while thinking about Elvis's character.
9. "Slowly but Surely"—Sung at the end of the film as Elvis and Jocelyn Lane were driving down the highway on their honeymoon.

PRODUCTION NOTES

✓ *Tickle Me* premiered in Atlanta on May 28, 1965. Fifteen days earlier the movie was previewed at the Hollywood Paramount Theatre.

✓ When *Tickle Me* was first planned in 1958, its working title was *Rodeo*.

✓ Filming began in October 1964.

✓ Actress Jocelyn Lane became a princess in 1971 when she married into British royalty. She first appeared in British films at the age of six. Until *Tickle Me*, she had been billed as Jackie Lane. While Lane was filming *Tickle Me* for Allied Artists, she was under contract to Universal.

✓ *Tickle Me* made its network television premiere on "CBS Friday Night at the Movies" on December 8, 1967. The film was broadcast from 9:00 P.M. to 10:45 P.M. EST.

✓ The print order for *Tickle Me* (over 500) was the largest in the history of Allied Artists up to that point.

✓ *Tickle Me* singlehandedly saved Allied Artists from financial ruin. It became the third highest-grossing film ever released in the company's history. Number one was *55 Days at Peking* (1963), and number two was *El Cid* (1961).

✓ Elvis's salary for the film was $750,000 plus 50 percent of the profits.

✓ *Tickle Me* was filmed entirely on the studio lot, although a few Arizona locations were used for atmosphere.

✓ The budget for the film was $1,480,000 ($4,000 under the original estimate).

✓ The Presidential Suite of the old Pico House in downtown Los Angeles was reproduced for the film for use in the ghost-town sequence. The Pico House was built in the 1860s by Pio Pico, the last Mexican governor of California.

Red West, Elvis. (Photo courtesy Cinema Collectors)

✓ Producer Ben Schwalb spotted Jocelyn Lane in a *Life* magazine layout called the "Great Girl Drought." The hazel-eyed beauty (37-20-36) was one of five girls featured.

✓ *Tickle Me* was double-billed in many areas with *Gunmen of the Rio Grande*, an Italian western that starred Guy Madison as Wyatt Earp.

✓ Although produced by Allied Artists, *Tickle Me* was distributed in the United States by Warner-Pathe. Overseas distribution (except for Great Britain) was handled by Columbia Pictures International.

✓ When the production was first announced in August of 1964, it was stated that twelve songs were earmarked for the film. Nine songs were eventually used, all of which were recorded previously.

TRIVIA

★ *Zuni Wells*—Western town that provided the setting for the film.

★ When Lonnie Beale first arrived in Zuni Wells, Pete Bowman was to give him a job at the Bar B Ranch. Bowman, however, had a run-in with the foreman and quit his job.

★ *The Corral*—Zuni Wells bar at which Lonnie Beale was to have met Pete Bowman.

★ The Jordanaires played the musicians who backed Lonnie on "It Feels So Right" in the Corral Bar.

★ *Circle Z*—Health-oriented guest ranch owned by Vera Radford. Lonnie Beale took care of the horses for Vera at the ranch.

★ *7A*—Cabin at the Circle Z in which Lonnie and Stanley stayed.

★ Stanley referred to the Circle Z as "Yogurt Gulch."

★ Blooper: Although supposedly taking place on a Southwestern guest ranch, palm trees could be seen in some scenes.

★ It cost guests at the Circle Z five hundred dollars a week to stay there.

★ *Silverado*—Ghost town in which Pam Merritt's grandfather once lived and near where his gold mine, the "Dolly D," was located. His fortune consisted of $100,000 in twenty-dollar Double Eagle gold coins. The gold was hidden in Durango's Place.

★ *Panhandle Kid*—Character played by Lonnie in a daydream sequence. The Panhandle Kid drank milk.

★ Mr. and Mrs. Dabney, who were from Houston, financed the Circle Z.

★ *King Canute*—Bull that threw Lonnie at the Phoenix rodeo. No one had ever stayed on King Canute longer than ten and two-fifths seconds. At the same rodeo, Lonnie was thrown by a bucking bronco named Thunderbolt.

★ Some of the cities in which Lonnie participated in rodeos were Elko, Cheyenne, Butte, Calgary, Prescott, Pendleton, and Tucson.

★ In one scene Lonnie mentioned that Pam had sent his letter back marked "return to sender."

★ *26*—Hotel room in Silverado in which Pam stayed the night. Stanley stayed in room 27.

HARUM SCARUM

MGM, 1965. A Four Leaf production. Running time: 95 minutes. Elvis's nineteenth film.

CAST

Johnny Tyronne	ELVIS PRESLEY
Princess Shalimar	MARY ANN MOBLEY
Aishah	FRAN JEFFRIES
Prince Dragna of Lunarkand	MICHAEL ANSARA
Zacha	JAY NOVELLO
King Toranshah, Ruler of Lunarkand	PHILIP REED
Sinan, Lord of the Assassins	THEO MARCUSE
Baba	BILLY BARTY
Mokar	DIRK HARVEY
Julna	JACK COSTANZA
Captain Herat	LARRY CHANCE
Leilah, Aide to Princess Shalimar	BARBARA WERLE

Carolyn Carter, Elvis in *Harum Scarum*'s movie-within-a-movie, *Sands Of The Desert*. (Photo courtesy Cinema Collectors)

Mary Ann Mobley, Elvis. (Photo courtesy Eddie Brandt's Saturday Matinee)

Emerald	BRENDA BENET
Sapphire	GAIL GILMORE
Amethyst	WILDA TAYLOR
Sari	VICKI MALKIN
Mustapha	RYCK RYDON
Scarred Bedouin	RICHARD J. REEVES
Yussef	JOEY RUSSO
Naja	SUZANNA COVINGTON
Heroine of *Sands of the Desert* film	CAROLYN CARTER
Princess	MAJA STEWART
Noble	RALPH LEE
President of Babalstan	ROBERT LAMONT
U.S. Ambassador McCord	HUGH SANDERS
Cashier	JUDY DURELL
Assassin	RED WEST

CREW

Producer	SAM KATZMAN
Director	GENE NELSON
Screenplay	GERALD DRAYSON ADAMS
Director of Photography	FRED H. JACKMAN
Art Directors	GEORGE W. DAVIS
	H. McCLURE CAPPS
Set Decoration	HENRY GRACE
	DON GREENWOOD JR.
Production Coordinator	ROBERT STONE
Editor	BEN LEWIS
Technical Advisor	COL. TOM PARKER
Assistant Director	EDDIE SAETA
Makeup	WILLIAM TUTTLE
Hairstyles	SYDNEY GUILAROFF
Recording Supervisor	FRANKLIN MILTON
Choreography	EARL BARTON
Music Supervised and Conducted by	FRED KARGER
Vocal Accompaniment	THE JORDANAIRES

SONGS

1. "Harem Holiday"—Sung over the opening credits and at the Galaxy Hotel at the end of the film.
2. "My Desert Serenade"—Sung to an Arabian girl within

Johnny Tyronne's movie *Sands of the Desert*, which was screened at the beginning of *Harum Scarum*.

3. "Go East, Young Man"—Sung to the audience immediately after the screening of *Sands of the Desert*.
4. "Mirage"—Sung to Sinan's slave girls in the Garden of Paradise.
5. "Kismet"—Sung to Mary Ann Mobley at the Pool of Omar.
6. "Shake That Tambourine"—Sung in a courtyard while Billy Barty picked the pockets of those in the crowd.
7. "Hey, Little Girl"—Sung to Vicki Malkin while performing a dance number with her in Zacha's palace.
8. "Golden Coins"—Sung to Mary Ann Mobley during her vision of Johnny Tyronne (Elvis) as she gazed into the pool in her palace.
9. "So Close, Yet So Far (from Paradise)"—Sung in a jail cell after being apprehended in King Toranshah's palace.

"Animal Instinct" and "Wisdom of the Ages" were both cut from the film.

PRODUCTION NOTES

✓ *Harum Scarum* premiered on November 24, 1965, in Los Angeles.

✓ *Harum Scarum* went through several title changes and spellings before filming started in early 1965. Titles announced were as follows: January 14—*In My Harem*; February 24—*Harem Holiday*; March 1—*Harem Scarum*; March 8—*Harem Holiday*; March 14—*Harem Scarum*; and, finally, late in the day of March 14—*Harum Scarum*.

✓ The first day of filming was March 15, 1965, on MGM's Culver City lot.

✓ The temple set used in *Harum Scarum* was originally built by Cecil B. De Mille in 1925 at a cost of $3,800, for his film *King of Kings*. It cost MGM more than $40,000 to remodel the set for Elvis's film.

✓ The costumes worn by one hundred extras were originally used in 1944's *Kismet* and later retailored for the 1955 remake.

✓ The dagger Elvis carried in the film was previously used in 1939's *Lady of the Tropics*.

✓ *Harum Scarum* was Mary Ann Mobley's second Elvis film, her first being *Girl Happy* (1965).

✓ During the 1965 Thanksgiving holiday, MGM had more than 550 prints of *Harum Scarum* playing nationwide.

✓ Jack Costanza, who played Julna, was known as "Mr. Bongo." The onetime dancer from Chicago became interested in the bongos during a trip to Africa,

Elvis, Jay Novello, Billy Barty. (Photo courtesy Eddie Brandt's Saturday Matinee)

and in the early 1950s became the first bongo player to work with a jazz band (Stan Kenton's). In 1955 he formed his own band and music publishing company. Costanza provided the rhythmic beat for the lavish production numbers in *Harum Scarum*.

✓ Billy Barty, the three-foot-nine midget who played Baba, won a football letter while attending Los Angeles City College! He was a third-string player. Barty was also sports editor of the school newspaper and public relations director of the athletic department. In addition to his acting career, which began in 1933, Barty is founder and president of the Little People of America organization.

✓ When chickens were needed for one of the film's scenes, producer Sam Katzman contacted one of Hollywood's animal-rental agencies. He became incensed when told the fee and promptly went out and bought twelve chickens, saving several dollars.

✓ *Harum Scarum* was actress Fran Jeffries's third film. Her first two were *The Pink Panther* (1964) and *Sex and the Single Girl* (1964). Jeffries (real name: Frances Makris) married singer Dick Haymes in 1958, divorced him in 1963, and then married director Richard Quine.

✓ Philip Reed made his last movie appearance in *Harum Scarum*.

TRIVIA

★ *Sands of the Desert*—Johnny Tyronne movie that premiered in the Near East country of Babalstan.

★ *Lunarkand*—Arab kingdom to which Johnny Tyronne traveled as a guest of King Toranshah. Its capital city was Taj. Because it was surrounded by the Mountains of the Moon, Lunarkand had been isolated from the rest of the world for 2,000 years.

★ Sinan was known as "Lord of the Assassins." He and his rebel gang took over Sheik El-Hussein's palace fortress.

★ Zacha said he was a member in good standing of the Guild of Marketplace Thieves.

★ *Pool of Omar*—Small body of water near which Johnny Tyronne and Princess Shalimar rendezvoused with Zacha.

★ Upon first meeting Johnny Tyronne, Princess Shalimar told him she was a slave named Yani.

★ Johnny Tyronne offered Zacha $10,000 to get him safely out of Lunarkand.

★ *Palace of the Jackals*—Residence of Zacha and his band of pickpockets.

★ *Bakir Oil Company*—Petroleum corporation that wanted to drill for oil in Lunarkand's Valley of the Moon. When King Toranshah wouldn't allow it, his brother, Prince Dragna, decided to kill the king so that he could profit from the transaction.

★ Prince Dragna offered Sinan 50,000 gold dinars if he would kill King Toranshah.

★ *Galaxy Hotel*—Las Vegas casino at which Johnny Tyronne appeared with his "Harem of Dancing Jewels from the Near East."

FRANKIE AND JOHNNY

United Artists, 1966. An Edward Small production. Running time: 87 minutes. Elvis's twentieth film.

CAST

Johnny	ELVIS PRESLEY
Frankie	DONNA DOUGLAS
Cully	HARRY MORGAN
Mitzi	SUE ANE LANGDON
Nellie Bly	NANCY KOVACK
Peg	AUDREY CHRISTIE
Blackie	ROBERT STRAUSS
Clint Braden	ANTHONY EISLEY
Abigail	JOYCE JAMESON
Joe Wilbur	JEROME COWAN
Proprietor of the New Orleans Costume Shop	JAMES MILHOLLIN
Princess Zolita	NAOMI STEVENS
Gypsy	HENRY CORDEN
Pete, the Bartender	DAVE WILLOCK
Man on the Street	RICHARD J. REEVES
Earl Barton Dancers	WILDA TAYLOR
	LARRI THOMAS
	DEE JAY MATTIS
	JUDY CHAPMAN
Bit	GEORGE KLEIN

CREW

Producer	EDWARD SMALL
Director	FREDERICK DE CORDOVA
Screenplay	ALEX GOTTLIEB
Story	NAT PERRIN
Director of Photography	JACQUES MARQUETTE
Art Director	WALTER M. SIMONDS
Set Decorator	MORRIS HOFFMAN
Associate Producer	ALEX GOTTLIEB
Production Supervisor	COL. HAROLD E. KNOX
Supervising Editor	GRANT WHYTOCK
Costume Designer	GWEN WAKELING
Makeup	DAN GREENWAY
Hairstylist	JOANNE ST. OEGGER
Wardrobe Coordinator	WES JEFFRIES
Property Master	MAX FRANKEL
Assistant Director	HERBERT S. GREENE
Sound	ALFRED J. OVERTON
Rerecording	CLEM PORTMAN
Music Editor	EDNA BULLOCK
Sound Effects Editor	AL BIRD
Casting	HARVEY CLERMONT
Music Scored and Conducted by	FRED KARGER
Musical Numbers Staged by	EARL BARTON
Vocal Accompaniment	THE JORDANAIRES

SONGS

1. "Come Along"—Sung over the opening credits.
2. "Petunia, the Gardener's Daughter"—Sung on the dancehall stage of the *Mississippi Queen* in a duet with Donna Douglas.
3. "Chesay"—Sung at the Gypsy camp. The first four lines were sung by a Gypsy, the rest by Elvis. A few lines were also sung by Harry Morgan and Gypsies.
4. "What Every Woman Lives For"—Sung to Nancy Kovack on the *Mississippi Queen* stage.
5. "Frankie and Johnny"—Sung at a piano after Harry Morgan sang a few lines. This was followed by a production number with a male chorus and Donna Douglas and Sue Ane Langdon. "Frankie and Johnny" was performed twice in the film.

Nancy Kovack, Elvis, Donna Douglas. (Photo courtesy Eddie Brandt's Saturday Matinee)

6. "Look Out, Broadway"—Sung in the dressing room with Harry Morgan at the piano. Elvis, Donna Douglas, Harry Morgan, and Audrey Christie all sang the song.
7. "Beginner's Luck"—Sung in a dream sequence in which Elvis and Donna Douglas were on a picnic.
8. "Down by the Riverside"/"When the Saints Go Marching In"—Medley sung in a New Orleans parade with jazz band accompaniment.
9. "Shout It Out"—Sung at a Mardi Gras costume party.
10. "Hard Luck"—Sung on a New Orleans street after Donna Douglas had thrown Elvis's $10,000 gambling winnings out of a window. A black shoeshine boy accompanied Elvis on the harmonica.
11. "Please Don't Stop Loving Me"—Sung to Donna Douglas on the deck of the *Mississippi Queen*.
12. "Everybody Come Aboard"—Sung in a production number at the end of the film.

PRODUCTION NOTES

✓ The world premiere of *Frankie and Johnny* took place at the Gordon Theatre in Baton Rouge, Louisiana, on March 31, 1966. Stars Donna Douglas, Sue Ane Langdon, and Nancy Kovack were in attendance; Elvis was not.

✓ *Frankie and Johnny* began filming on May 25, 1965.

✓ Although a United Artists release, the film was shot at MGM.

✓ *Frankie and Johnny* was originally filmed in 1934 (but released in 1936) by Republic Pictures, with Helen Morgan and Chester Morris as Frankie and Johnny. It was Morgan's last film appearance.

✓ Donna Douglas's singing in the film was dubbed by Eileen Wilson.

✓ The budget for *Frankie and Johnny* was $4.5 million.

✓ Murals of the legendary Frankie and Johnny by Thomas Hart Benton hang in the Missouri State Capitol Building in Jefferson City. These murals were reproduced by MGM and displayed on the company's Culver City lot during the filming of *Frankie and Johnny.*

✓ Several origins of the "Frankie and Johnny" folk song were discovered when the producers researched the legend. One story placed the song as far back as the War of 1812. When the Tennessee and Kentucky Long Rifles (who served under Andrew Jackson at the Battle of New Orleans) returned home from the war, they sang the song. Supposedly, they heard it in Crescent City, Louisiana, a mostly French-speaking city, under the title "Françoise et Jean."

Another story traced the origin to a hot summer night in St. Louis in 1888. Frankie (a woman) gunned down her boyfriend, Johnny, with a derringer she had hidden in her garter. She had just learned that Johnny had "done her wrong."

✓ *Frankie and Johnny* was actress Donna Douglas's (real name: Doris Smith) first major film appearance. She previously had appeared in small roles in *Career* (1959) and *Lover Come Back* (1961).

✓ Jerome Cowan (who played Joe Wilbur) had earlier acted in a stage presentation of *Frankie and Johnny.*

Naomi Stevens, Elvis, Harry Morgan. (Photo courtesy Cinema Collectors)

✓ Thirty-one costumes were used by the film's leading ladies during the production.

✓ Director Fred de Cordova began his directorial career with *Too Young to Know* in 1945. He later directed Ronald Reagan in *Bedtime for Bonzo* (1951). De Cordova honed his craft by directing several television comedy shows, including "The Jack Benny Program" and "Leave It to Beaver." Currently he directs "The Tonight Show Starring Johnny Carson." *Frankie and Johnny* is his last film to date.

✓ Donna Douglas was a onetime Miss New Orleans.

TRIVIA

★ *SS Mississippi Queen*—Riverboat on which Frankie and Johnny were featured performers.

★ *Princess Zolita*—Gypsy fortune teller to whom Johnny went for advice. In her tea leaves, Zolita saw a new woman—a redhead—coming into Johnny's life.

★ The accordion player in the Gypsy camp was named Laszlo.

★ According to the film the song title "Chesay" meant "Gypsy good luck."

★ During one of his musical numbers, Johnny wore a Yale letter sweater.

★ *Singing Queen of the Riverboats*—Billing of singer Nellie Bly (Nancy Kovack) when she appeared on the Broadway stage (where she bombed). In real life, Nellie Bly was the pseudonym used by 22-year-old reporter Elizabeth Cochrane, who was sent on a trip around the world by Joseph Pulitzer's newspaper *The World*. The idea was to improve upon Jules Verne's fictional story, *Around the World in 80 Days*. The 118-pound Cochrane did it in 72 days, 6 hours, and 11 minutes, finishing on January 21, 1890. She took the pseudonym Nellie Bly from the 1849 Stephen Foster song of the same name.

★ *1*—Number of the roulette wheel bet by Johnny because it was Nellie Bly's favorite number. He won $700.

★ Music publisher Joe Wilbur paid $200 for Cully and Peg's song "Frankie and Johnny."

★ "Beautiful Dreamer" was played in the background as Cully and Johnny waited outside the ladies' lounge for a redhead to walk by.

★ *13*—Number on which Johnny bet and won twice on the roulette wheel at the suggestion of Abigail. He lost all of his money when she suggested that he bet it all on 31. (It again landed on 13.)

★ *Colonial House*—New Orleans hotel-tavern chosen by the crew of the *Mississippi Queen* to stay and enjoy the Mardi Gras. Clint Braden stayed in room 309; Nellie Bly was in 306.

★ At the Mardi Gras costume party, Frankie, Nelly Bly, and Mitzi all wore Madame Pompadour costumes. Peg came dressed as Little Bo Peep and Cully as Father Time. The costume worn by Johnny was exactly like that worn by William Boyd in his Hopalong Cassidy movies. All costumes were rented from the New Orleans Costume Shop.

★ *2 and 5*—Two consecutive numbers played by Johnny on the roulette wheel, winning $10,000. Frankie, wearing her Madame Pompadour costume, stood by for good luck. (Johnny thought she was Nellie Bly. Johnny had won previously on the roulette wheel with Nellie Bly as his good luck charm. He had won with numbers 7 and 1 on that occasion.)

★ *Cricket*—Insect on the medallion that saved Johnny's life. The special medallion was given to him by Frankie. Frankie loaded her gun with a real bullet, which when fired during the musical number, struck the medallion.

PARADISE, HAWAIIAN STYLE

Paramount, 1966. A Hal B. Wallis production. Running time: 91 minutes. Elvis's twenty-first film.

CAST

Greg (Rick) Richards	ELVIS PRESLEY
Judy Hudson (Friday)	SUZANNA LEIGH
Danny Kohana	JAMES SHIGETA
Jan Kohana	DONNA BUTTERWORTH
Lani Kaimana	MARIANNA HILL
Pua	IRENE TSU
Lehua Kawena	LINDA WONG
Joanna	JULIE PARRISH
Betty Kohana	JAN SHEPARD
Donald Belden	JOHN DOUCETTE
Mr. Cubberson	GRADY SUTTON
Andy Lowell	DON COLLIER
Mrs. Daisy Barrington	DORIS PACKER
Moki Kaimana	PHILIP AHN
Mrs. Belden	MARY TREEN

(Photo courtesy Eddie Brandt's Saturday Matinee)

Peggy Holdren...................................GIGI VERONE
Plain Girl..SHANON HALE
First Girl..ANNE MORELL
Next Girl...CHINA LEE
Bit Girl...MIKO MAYAMA
Dancer..EDY WILLIAMS
Chef..LEON LONTOC
Native Dancer...................................LLOYD KINO
Lehua's Escort..................................ROBERT ITO
Pua's Escort........................MAKEE K. BLAISDELL
Joanna's Escort.................................JEFF BROWN
Customer..JERRY JAMES
Makeup Man..................................WILLIAM CORE
Mailman...TIKI SANTOS
Bandleader....................................RALPH HANALEI
Kohana Child..........................JACKIE JODY BROWN
Kohana Child...................................JAMES MILLER
Kohana Child.........................LUKAS T. SHIMATSU
Kohana Child.....................RANDY RICHARD STONE
Stewardess...................................ARLENE CHARLES
Ruggles, the Chauffeur.............VINCENT EDWARD EDER
Nurse...DEANNA LUND
Customer.......................................WALTER DAVIS

Bit Man...HUBIE KERNS
Bit Man...MAX POWERS
Bit Man...JOHN BENSON
Rusty, the Man Who Fights with Elvis..................RED WEST

CREW

Producer.....................................HAL B. WALLIS
Director...................................D. MICHAEL MOORE
Screenplay....................................ALLAN WEISS
                                           ANTHONY LAWRENCE
Story..ALLAN WEISS
Director of Photography...................W. WALLACE KELLEY
Art Directors....................................HAL PEREIRA
                                           WALTER TYLER
Set Decoration...............................ROBERT BENTON
                                           RAY MOYER
Makeup Supervision..........................WALLY WESTMORE
Hairstyle Supervision.........................NELLIE MANLEY
Sound Recording...............................JOHN CARTER
                                           CHARLES GRENZBACH
Editorial Supervision...........................WARREN LOW
Costumes.......................................EDITH HEAD
Aerial Photography............................NELSON TYLER

Pilot for Aerial Photography....................JAMES W. GAVIN
Unit Production Manager...................ROBERT GOODSTEIN
Assistant Director......................JAMES ROSENBERGER
Dialogue Coach...............................EUGENE BUSCH
Special Photographic Effects...............PAUL K. LERPAE
Process Photography........................FARCIOT EDOUART
Associate Producer............................PAUL NATHAN
Musical Numbers Staged by.......................JACK REGAS
Music Scored and Conducted by...............JOSEPH J. LILLEY
Vocal Accompaniment by....................THE JORDANAIRES
Technical Advisor.........................COL. TOM PARKER

SONGS

1. "Paradise, Hawaiian Style"—Sung over the opening credits.
2. "Queenie Wahini's Papaya"—Sung at Danny Kohana's house in a duet with Donna Butterworth.
3. "Scratch My Back (Then I'll Scratch Yours)"—Sung at the Piki Niki Lounge at the Hanalei Plantation in duet with Marianna Hill.
4. "Drums of the Islands"—Sung on a canoe trip with Pua and in a Hawaiian village. Native voices were used on the soundtrack. The song was also sung at the end of the film at the Polynesian Welcoming Festival just after singing "This Is My Heaven."
5. "A Dog's Life"—Sung in a helicopter with Mrs. Barrington's dogs.
6. "Datin' "—Sung in a duet with Donna Butterworth in a helicopter.
7. "House of Sand"—Sung on the beach just after flying to Kauai with Donna Butterworth.
8. "Stop Where You Are"—Sung at the Polynesian Welcoming Festival.
9. "This Is My Heaven"—Sung at the Polynesian Welcoming Festival. "Drums of the Islands" immediately followed.

"Sand Castles" was deleted from the film. Donna Butterworth had a solo effort with "Bill Bailey, Won't You Please Come Home?"

PRODUCTION NOTES

✓ *Paradise, Hawaiian Style* opened nationally on July 6, 1966. In many areas the companion feature was *Get Yourself a College Girl* (1964). The film was sneak-previewed in Memphis on June 9 and opened in New York City on June 15.

✓ Elvis filmed his first scene on August 7, 1965, at Hanauma Bay. It was the helicopter rescue of James Shigeta and Donna Butterworth.

✓ *Paradise, Hawaiian Style* was Michael Moore's first full directing job after having served as a second unit director and first assistant director. He had been a child actor.

✓ During filming in Hawaii, Elvis stayed at the Ilikai Hotel (Suite 2225).

✓ A Bell 47-J-2 helicopter was shipped to Hawaii in four sections aboard a United Airlines cargo plane, to be reassembled upon arrival for use in the film.

✓ *Polynesian Paradise* was the film's first announced title (November 1964). Before filming, the title was changed to *Hawaiian Paradise*. *Hawaiian Paradise* became *Paradise, Hawaiian Style* in September 1965. It's also been reported that *Polynesian Holiday* was once considered for the title.

Elvis, Marianna Hill. The "Scratch My Back" number. (Photo courtesy Eddie Brandt's Saturday Matinee)

✓ Jack Regas, who staged the film's musical numbers, was normally the choreographer at the Polynesian Cultural Center.

✓ *Paradise, Hawaiian Style* was filmed on location in Honolulu, Kauai (Hanalei Plantation Resort), Maui (Maui Sheraton Hotel), and the Kona Coast, as well as the Paramount Studios in Hollywood and the Torrance, California, Airport.

✓ The Polynesian Cultural Center at Laie on the island of Oahu was begun by the Mormon Church. It consists of thirty-six buildings on sixteen acres.

✓ Peter Noone of the British band Herman's Hermits interviewed Elvis at a party at the Polynesian Cultural Center on August 18, 1965. The interview appeared on local radio the following day and has appeared on numerous records through the years.

✓ For the "Drums of the Islands" production number, producer Hal Wallis decided to use a war canoe, and the only one available on the islands was Samoan. Because "Drums of the Islands" was based on a Tongan chant and Tongan rowers were used for the scene, the Samoans took offense and several fights erupted between the two factions.

✓ As a key preselling tool, a 16-millimeter short was made about the filming of *Paradise, Hawaiian Style* and released in May 1966. The featurette, which included a tour of the scenic wonders of Hawaii and a big musical number from the film, was made available to TV stations, schools, church groups, and travel agencies.

✓ *Seventeen* magazine chose *Paradise, Hawaiian Style* as its "Picture of the Month" in June 1966.

✓ In many areas *Paradise, Hawaiian Style* was paired with *Johnny Reno*, a Dana Andrews–Jane Russell western.

✓ For the year 1966, *Paradise, Hawaiian Style* was ranked #40 in the list of top-grossing films. It took in receipts of $2.5 million.

✓ Nine-year-old Donna Butterworth had previously appeared on screen in *The Family Jewels* (1965).

✓ The closing credits of *Paradise, Hawaiian Style* carried the following acknowledgment: "Our gratitude to the peoples of the Pacific at the Polynesian Cultural Center, Laie, Oahu, Hawaii."

✓ British actress Suzanna Leigh made her American film debut in *Boeing Boeing* (1965). *Paradise, Hawaiian Style* was her second American film.

TRIVIA

★ *D. Kohana's Island Charter Service*—Charter airline owned by Danny Kohana. The company's motto was "We Fly You Anywhere."

★ Rick Richards was a commercial airline pilot before being fired from his job.

★ *Johnny*—Driver of the pickup truck owned by the Slim Kidwell Aviation Company who gave Rick a ride from the airport to Danny's place.

★ *Alligator Shoes*—Product sold by Mr. Cubberson.

★ *June 4*—Date Rick and Lehua were to have had dinner. Two years later she was still waiting for that dinner.

★ *Piki Niki*—Lounge at which Lani sang. The Piki Niki was located on the Hanalei Plantation. The cable car that took people downhill from the pool to the lounge was nicknamed "Charlie."

★ Question: Rick and Danny flew Mr. Cubberson to the Maui Sheraton Hotel for his convention of alligator-shoe salesmen, but it was the wrong hotel and convention. What group was holding its convention at the Maui Sheraton? Answer: The Society for the Prevention of Cruelty to Animals.

★ *Danrick Airways*—Helicopter and charter service formed by Rick and Danny Kohana. Their motto was "We Show You the Islands Like Nobody Can." The line "Come Fly with Us" was used in newspaper advertisements.

★ While working as a secretary for Danrick Airways, Judy used the pseudonym Judy Hudson. Danny told Rick that Judy was married and her husband, Roy, was in the Navy. In actuality, Judy was single. Danny was trying to keep Rick and Judy from becoming romantically involved. Rick's nickname for Judy was "Friday."

★ *Bowser Biscuits*—Dog food Rick and Joanna fed to Mrs. Barrington's four dogs aboard the helicopter. Rick picked up the dogs at the Kahala Hilton, where Joanna worked.

★ Rick fought with Judy's date at the Colonel's Plantation Steak House.

★ *MGA 670*—Danny's radio call letters at the office.

★ *Moonlight Beach*—Rick and Lani's favorite romantic spot. It was at Moonlight Beach that Lani playfully threw away the keys to Rick's helicopter, stranding Rick, Lani, and Jan.

★ The registration number of Danny Kohana's helicopter was N5332B. Rick's helicopter was N73202.

SPINOUT
MGM, 1966. A Joe Pasternak production. Running time: 90 minutes. Elvis's twenty-second film.

CAST
Mike McCoy	ELVIS PRESLEY
Cynthia Foxhugh	SHELLEY FABARES
Diana St. Clair	DIANE McBAIN
Les	DEBORAH WALLEY
Susan	DODIE MARSHALL
Curly	JACK MULLANEY
Lt. Tracy Richards	WILL HUTCHINS
Philip Short	WARREN BERLINGER
Larry	JIMMY HAWKINS
Howard Foxhugh	CARL BETZ
Bernard Ranley	CECIL KELLAWAY
Violet Ranley	UNA MERKEL
Blodgett	FREDERIC WORLOCK
Harry	DAVE BARRY
Blonde Beauty	JO ANN MEDLEY
Redhead Beauty	DEANNA LUND
Brunette Beauty	INGA JACKLIN
Blonde Beauty	VIRGINIA WOOD
Platinum Beauty	NANCY CZAR
Race Announcer	JAY JASIN
Award Beauty	VICTORIA CARROLL
Bit Man	JOSH HARDING
Bit Girls	RITA WILSON
	ARLENE CHARLES
	JEANMARIE
	GAY GORDON
	PHYLLIS DAVIS
	THORDIS BRANDY
	FREDDA LEE
	SHERYL ULLMAN

Jack Mullaney, Elvis, Deborah Walley, Jimmy Hawkins. (Photo courtesy Cinema Collectors)

Shorty Bloomquist.............................JAMES MCHALE
Girl...JUDY DURELL
Members of Shorty's Pit Crew.......................RED WEST
                                                JOE ESPOSITO

CREW
Producer.......................................JOE PASTERNAK
Director.......................................NORMAN TAUROG
Screenplay............................THEODORE J. FLICKER
                                                GEORGE KIRGO
Director of Photography.......................DANIEL L. FAPP
Art Direction..............................GEORGE W. DAVIS
                                            EDWARD CARFAGNO
Set Decoration...............................HENRY GRACE
                                                HUGH HUNT
Special Visual Effects..................J. MCMILLAN JOHNSON
                                            CARROLL L. SHEPPIRD
Editor..RITA ROLAND
Dialogue Supervision...........................MICHAEL HOEY
Assistant Director.......................CLAUDE BINYON JR.
Unit Production Manager.........................AL SHENBERG
Technical Advisor.........................COL. TOM PARKER
Recording Supervisor.......................FRANKLIN MILTON
Makeup..WILLIAM TUTTLE
Hairstyles..................................SYDNEY GUILAROFF

Assistant Producer..........................HANK MOONJEAN
Music...GEORGE STOLL
Music Associate..............................ROBERT VAN EPS
Musical Numbers Staged by......................JACK BAKER
Vocal Accompaniment by....................THE JORDANAIRES

SONGS
1. "Spinout"—Sung over opening credits and later at a party.
2. "Stop, Look, and Listen"—Sung at a club in Santa Barbara.
3. "Adam and Evil"—Sung immediately after "Stop, Look, and Listen."
4. "All That I Am"—Sung to Diane McBain at a campsite.
5. "Never Say Yes"—Sung in rehearsal.
6. "Am I Ready"—Sung to Shelley Fabares as a birthday present for her character, Cynthia Foxhugh.
7. "Beach Shack"—Sung at a poolside party.
8. "Smorgasbord"—Sung at a party.
9. "I'll Be Back"—Sung in a club at the end of the film.

PRODUCTION NOTES
✓ *Spinout* opened nationally on November 23, 1966. In many areas the cofeature was *Maya*, a Clint Walker-Jay North jungle tale. A sneak preview of the film

occurred in Memphis at the Malco Theatre on September 13, 1966.

✓ Several titles were originally considered for *Spinout*. Among them were *Jim Dandy, After Midnight,* and *Always at Midnight.* During preproduction, the title was *Never Say No.* That was changed to *Never Say Yes* in November 1965, and finally to *Spinout* in February 1966.

✓ The British title to *Spinout* was *California Holiday.*

✓ Principal photography began in late February 1966, and was completed on April 6.

✓ To film *Spinout*, MGM used seven sound stages and five location sites, including the Ascot Motor Car Racing Ground and Dodger Stadium. For the scene at the beginning of the Sante Fé Road Race (which was filmed at Dodger Stadium), MGM used 200 extras, 28 supporting actors, 50 cars, and 12 custom racing cars.

✓ To salute Elvis's tenth year in films, MGM mounted a massive publicity campaign. Film exhibitors received a *Spinout* press kit that included Elvis photos, posters, flyers, tabloid heralds, and booklets about his gold Cadillac. Also included was a twenty-page anniversary story about Elvis. More than 5,000 radio stations received promo copies of the "Spinout" single release, and MGM prepared open-ended interviews with Shelley Fabares, Deborah Walley, and Diane McBain. Movie and TV trailers were also produced.

Diane McBain, Elvis. (Photo courtesy Jeff Wheatcraft)

Elvis, Shelley Fabares. (Photo courtesy Eddie Brandt's Saturday Matinee)

✓ Carl Betz played the father of Shelley Fabares in *Spinout.* He also played her father on "The Donna Reed Show." Another cast member of that sitcom, Jimmy Hawkins, also appeared in *Spinout.*

✓ Newspaper advertisements for *Spinout* included the catch phrases "Hitting the Curves in His Fastest Adventure Yet" and "With His Foot on the Gas and No Brakes on the Fun."

✓ As a promotion, some theater owners sponsored an essay contest on "The Perfect American Male." Elvis records were given as prizes.

✓ While making *Spinout*, Elvis dated his costar Deborah Walley. Walley had become the second movie Gidget when in 1961 she starred in *Gidget Goes Hawaiian.* (The first Gidget was Sandra Dee, who starred in 1959's *Gidget.*)

✓ *Spinout* was the last film for Carl Betz, Una Merkel, and Frederic Worlock.

✓ Phyllis Davis, who had a bit role in *Spinout,* later became one of the repertory players in the TV series "Love, American Style" (1970–74), and a regular as Beatrice Travis in "Vega$" (1978–81).

TRIVIA

★ *11*—Number on the side of Mike McCoy's 427 Cobra race car. When not racing the car, he towed it behind his antique 1929 Deusenberg (Model J).

★ The three-piece combo that backed Mike was called 1 Plus 2 + ½. The two guitar players were Larry and Curly; the girl drummer was named Les.

★ *Foxhugh Motors*—Automobile manufacturing company owned by Howard Foxhugh. One of his cars was called the Foxhugh Whiplash.

★ Howard Foxhugh paid Mike and his combo $5,000 to sing at his daughter Cynthia's birthday (which was on the 15th).

★ *The Perfect American Male*—New book that was being researched by Diana St. Clair. Her previous two works were *Ten Ways to Trap a Bachelor* and *The Mating Habits of the Single Male.* For the latter book, she dressed like a man and lived with a platoon of Marines to do her research.

★ Les's full name was Lester. Mike called her Buddy.

★ *Fox 5*—New race car built by Howard Foxhugh. He wanted Mike to race the car for him, but eventually drove it himself.

★ The setting for *Spinout* was Santa Barbara, California.

★ *Ranley Manor*—Estate next door to the Foxhugh home. Mike and his combo stayed in the house while the owners, Bernard and Violet Ranley, went on a well-deserved vacation after thirty-seven years of marriage. Their butler was named Blodgett.

★ *Santa Fé Road Race*—A 250-mile race won by Mike McCoy in Shorty Bloomquist's blue SB Special. The car was #9. Red West and Joe Esposito could be seen as members of Shorty's pit crew—the ones who pushed the car to the starting line. Howard Foxhugh offered $50,000 to the winner of the race and $10,000 to each driver who finished ahead of his Fox 5 car.

Elsa Lanchester, Elvis. (Photo courtesy Cinema Collectors)

EASY COME, EASY GO
Paramount, 1967. A Hal B. Wallis production. Running time: 95 minutes. Elvis's twenty-third film.

CAST
Ted Jackson..................................ELVIS PRESLEY
Jo Symington...............................DODIE MARSHALL
Dina Bishop..PAT PRIEST
Judd Whitman.......................PAT HARRINGTON JR.
Gil Carey..SKIP WARD
Madame Neherina......................ELSA LANCHESTER
Captain Jack...................................FRANK MCHUGH
Lt. Marty Schwartz.......................SANDY KENYON
Cooper..ED GRIFFITH
Lieutenant Tompkins......................REED MORGAN
Lieutenant Whitehead....................MICKEY ELLEY
Vicki...ELAINE BECKETT
Mary..SHARI NIMS
Zoltan...DIKI LERNER
Tanya..KAY YORK
Artist......................................ROBERT ISENBERG
Naval Officer.................................TOM HATTEN
Coin Dealer................................JONATHAN HOLE

CREW
Producer..................................HAL B. WALLIS
Director..JOHN RICH
Screenplay..................................ALLAN WEISS
                                        ANTHONY LAWRENCE
Director of Photography.........WILLIAM MARGULIES
Art Directors..............................HAL PEREIRA
                                              WALTER TYLER
Set Decoration..........................ROBERT BENTON
                                              ARTHUR KRAMS
Makeup..................................WALLY WESTMORE
Hairstyles................................NELLIE MANLEY
Sound Recording........................JOHN R. CARTER
                                        CHARLES GRENZBACH
Editor....................................ARCHIE MARSHEK
Costumes..EDITH HEAD
Assistant Director.....................ROBERT GOODSTEIN

Unit Production Manager......................WILLIAM W. GRAY
Special Photographic Effects....................PAUL K. LERPAE
Underwater Photography...................MICHAEL J. DUGAN
Process Photography......................FARCIOT EDOUART
Musical Numbers Staged by....................DAVID WINTERS
Associate Producer............................PAUL NATHAN
Music Scored and Conducted by...............JOSEPH J. LILLEY
Vocal Accompaniment......................THE JORDANAIRES
Technical Advisor............................COL. TOM PARKER

SONGS
1. "Easy Come, Easy Go"—Sung over the opening credits.
2. "The Love Machine"—Sung on stage at the Easy Go-Go.
3. "Yoga Is as Yoga Does"—Sung in a duet with Elsa Lanchester during a yoga class at Jo Symington's house.
4. "You Gotta Stop"—Sung in the Easy Go-Go.
5. "Sing, You Children"—Sung at Jo Symington's party.
6. "I'll Take Love"—Sung in the Easy Go-Go.

"She's a Machine" and "Leave My Woman Alone" were recorded for the film but not used. Two instrumentals "Freak Out" and "Go-Go Jo" were played.

PRODUCTION NOTES
✓ *Easy Come, Easy Go* opened nationally on March 22, 1967. The cofeature in some areas was the Marlon Brando film *The Appaloosa*, which was enjoying a second run after having been originally released several months earlier.

✓ Some of the preliminary titles used for *Easy Come, Easy Go* were *Port of Call*, *A Girl in Every Port*, *Nice and Easy*, and *Easy Does It*.

✓ Production began on September 12, 1966, and lasted through October.

✓ *Easy Come, Easy Go* was the last feature film directed by John Rich. He then gained fame by directing several situation comedies for television including "All in the Family."

✓ Character actor Frank McHugh appeared in more than 150 films, mostly for Warner Bros. *Easy Come, Easy Go* was his last movie.

✓ Pat Priest, who played Dina Bishop, was the second Marilyn Munster in the TV series "The Munsters." (The original girl, Beverly Owen, left in December 1964 to get married.) Priest is the daughter of Ivy Baker Priest, the former treasurer of the United States.

✓ Elsa Lanchester was nominated for an Oscar for Best Supporting Actress twice: *Come to the Stable* (1949) and *Witness for the Prosecution* (1957). In the 1935 horror classic *Bride of Frankenstein*, she played author Mary Shelley and the Frankenstein monster's mate. Lanchester's husband, Charles Laughton, to whom she was married for thirty-three years (1929 to his death in 1962), introduced Elvis in his first appearance on "The Ed Sullivan Show" (September 9, 1956).

✓ *Easy Come, Easy Go* was ranked #50 by *Variety* in its list of top-grossing films for 1967. By year's end, the film had taken in $1.95 million.

TRIVIA

★ *The Love Machine*—Spinning wheel owned by Judd Whitman that contained photos of several girls (as well as their measurements and telephone numbers). Men would spin the wheel and call the girl whose picture came up for a date.

★ Question: What number was on the side of the ship on which Navy Lieutenant Ted Jackson was stationed? Answer: 489.

★ *Rocky Point*—Area near which Lieutenant Jackson defused an old underwater mine.

★ *Captain Jack*—Captain of the Good Ship Lollipop on a Saturday morning children's TV show. (The show was sponsored by Zelda's Cornmeal Mush.) Captain Jack owned Captain Jack's Marine Equipment, from which Ted rented the equipment he used in his salvage operation. The store's motto was "If It's Marine, We Have It."

★ Jo Symington lived in a big house near the end of Silver Canyon.

Dodie Marshall, Elvis. (Photo courtesy Eddie Brandt's Saturday Matinee)

★ *Port of Call*—Ship that sank around 1900 near Rocky Point while carrying a cargo of coffee and a chest of pieces of eight. The *Port of Call* was captained by Jo Symington's grandfather.

★ *Easy Go-Go*—Club owned by Judd Whitman at which Ted Jackson sang.

★ Question: What did Jo serve for lunch on Ted's boat? Answer: Five raw carrots and a jar of prune yogurt.

★ Some of the signs seen at Jo Symington's party: "Conserve Water—Shower Together," "We Protest," and "Narcissism Is the Only Ism for Me."

★ *SIB-912*—License number of Ted Jackson's red convertible. The car was transformed by Zoltan into a pop art piece called "Over the Underpass."

★ *Finders Keepers, Lover*—Note Dina Bishop wrote on a photo of the sunken *Port of Call*. She then left the photo on Ted's boat.

★ After recovering the treasure, Dina and Gil were going to travel to Istanbul, Turkey.

★ *Thirty cents*—Value of each of 13,000 pieces of eight recovered from the *Port of Call*. The coins were made of copper instead of gold.

DOUBLE TROUBLE

MGM, 1967. A B.C.W. production. Running time: 90 minutes. Elvis's twenty-fourth film.

CAST

Guy Lambert	ELVIS PRESLEY
Jillian (Jill) Conway	ANNETTE DAY
Gerald Waverly	JOHN WILLIAMS
Claire Dunham	YVONNE ROMAIN
Harry, a Belgian Detective	HARRY WIERE
Herbert, a Belgian Detective	HERBERT WIERE
Sylvester, a Belgian Detective	SYLVESTER WIERE
Archie Brown	CHIPS RAFFERTY
Arthur Babcock	NORMAN ROSSINGTON
Georgie	MONTY LANDIS
Mr. Morley	MICHAEL MURPHY
Inspector De Groote	LEON ASKIN
Iceman	JOHN ALDERSON
Captain Roach	STANLEY ADAMS
Frenchman	MAURICE MARSAC
Captain Roach's Mate	WALTER BURKE
Gerda	HELENE WINSTON
The G-Men	THEMSELVES
Policemen	MURRAY KAMELHAR
	TED ROTER
	RALPH SMILEY
Flemish Clerk at Hotel Olympia	MONIQUE LEMAIRE
Twins at London Nightclub	MARILYN KEYMER
	MELODY KEYMER
Child	LAURIE LAMBERT
Seaman	JOSH HARDING
Masked Man	HAL BOKAR
Moe	ROBERT HOMEL
Peddler	LUKE GERARD
Customs Officer	FRANK MITCHELL
Discotheque Dancer	JAN REDDIN
Watusi Dancer	MARY HUGHES
Acrobats	RAY SAUNDERS
	TED DEWAYNE
	BILL SNYDER
	RICK TEAGARDEN
	JACK TEAGARDEN
	AUDREY SAUNDERS
Jugglers	BARRY COLE
	DANNY REES
	RODNEY HOELTZEL
Stiltwalker	CHESTER HAYES
Patron	SHERYL ULLMAN
Juggler	BOB JOHNSON
Sleepy Man	GEORGE DEE
Pirate	ROBERT ISENBERG
Chicken Truck Driver	BOB BERGY
Bit	GEORGE KLEIN

CREW

Producers	JUDD BERNARD
	IRWIN WINKLER
Director	NORMAN TAUROG
Screenplay	JO HEIMS
Based on a Story by	MARC BRANDEL
Director of Photography	DANIEL L. FAPP
Art Directors	GEORGE W. DAVIS
	MERRILL PYE
Set Decoration	HENRY GRACE
	HUGH HUNT
Choreography	ALEX ROMERO
Assistant to the Producers	PATRICIA CASEY
Editor	JOHN MCSWEENEY
Assistant Director	CLAUDE BINYON JR.
Unit Production Manager	AL SHENBERG
Technical Advisor	COL. TOM PARKER
Special Visual Effects	J. MCMILLAN JOHNSON
	CARROLL L. SHEPPIRD
Makeup	WILLIAM TUTTLE
Hairstyles	MARY KEATS
Costumes	DON FELD
Recording Supervisor	FRANKLIN MILTON
Music Score	JEFF ALEXANDER

SONGS

1. "Double Trouble"—Sung over the opening credits leading into Elvis's on-stage act in a London nightclub.

Yvonne Romain, Annette Day, Elvis. (Photo courtesy Eddie Brandt's Saturday Matinee)

2. "Baby, If You'll Give Me All Your Love"—Sung in a London nightclub.
3. "Could I Fall in Love"—Sung to Annette Day in Guy Lambert's (Elvis) apartment, in a duet with his own recording.
4. "Long Legged Girl (with the Short Dress On)"—Sung on the deck of the ship Elvis and Annette Day take from London to Belgium.
5. "City by Night"—Sung in a nightclub in Bruges, Belgium.
6. "Old MacDonald"—Sung on the back of a pickup truck loaded with chickens.
7. "I Love Only One Girl"—Sung at a festival on the streets of Antwerp.
8. "There Is So Much World to See"—Sung to Annette Day in an Antwerp hotel room.

"It Won't Be Long" was recorded for *Double Trouble*, but was not used.

PRODUCTION NOTES

✓ Although *Double Trouble* took place in Great Britain and Belgium, all scenes were actually filmed on MGM's Culver City lot.

✓ *Double Trouble* opened nationally on April 5, 1967. The cofeature in most areas was *Three Bites of the Apple*, a comedy starring David McCallum, Tammy Grimes, Harvey Korman, and Italian singer Domenico Modugno ("Volare").

✓ The working title of *Double Trouble* was *You're Killing Me*.

✓ Filming began on June 11, 1966, and was completed in the first week of September.

✓ Actress Annette Day made her film debut in *Double Trouble*. The red-haired, blue-eyed newcomer was discovered by producer Judd Bernard in an antique shop on London's Portobello Road. She was an employee in the shop, which was owned by her father. Day had never acted before this film—not even in local stage productions.

✓ Maltese-born, British-raised Yvonne Romain is married to composer Leslie Bricusse, who won an Oscar for "Talk to the Animals" from 1967's *Doctor Doolittle*. *Double Trouble* was Romain's second U.S. film, the first being *The Swinger* (1966).

Elvis, Marilyn and Melody Keymer. (Photo courtesy Jeff Wheatcraft)

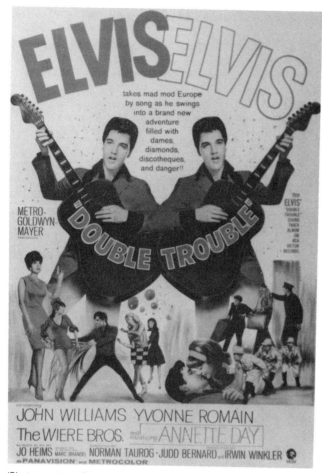

(Photo courtesy Cinema Collectors)

✓ Choreographer Alex Romero used 140 dancers in the film.

✓ While shooting the sequences aboard ship—actually on the MGM lot—sixteen extras got "seasick" and had to be replaced!

✓ Elvis's cousin Billy Smith doubled for Annette Day in a scene.

✓ Both Elvis and Ray Charles made films titled *Double Trouble.* Charles's movie (known as *Swingin' Along* in Great Britain) starred Tommy Noonan and Peter Marshall. Also featured were musical stars Bobby Vee and Roger Williams.

✓ John Williams, who played Uncle Gerald, is best known for his memorable performances as Inspector Hubbard in the stage, screen, and television versions of *Dial M for Murder.*

✓ Although "It Won't Be Long" was cut from the film, some advertisements mentioned that *Double Trouble* had nine songs instead of the eight that were actually sung. The MGM/UA home videocassette box says, "Elvis gets to sing nine great songs along the way."

✓ *Double Trouble* ranked #58 in *Variety's* list of top-grossing films of 1967. The film grossed $1.6 million that year.

TRIVIA

★ *Peca Record Co.*—Record label on which Guy Lambert recorded the song "Could I Fall in Love." When Jill asked Guy to play a record, he put on his own recording and then proceeded to sing a duet with himself. "Could I Fall in Love" was *their* song.

★ *B6*—Guy Lambert's London apartment number.

★ When Jill asked Guy how many lumps he wanted in his tea, he responded, "Four hundred and eighteen—I couldn't care less."

★ *311 Surrey Road*—Home address (in the St. John's Wood section of London) of Jill and her uncle, Gerald.

★ Guy Lambert's backup group was named the G-Men.

★ *204*—Guy Lambert's hotel room number in Bruges, Belgium.

★ In Antwerp, Guy and his group were to perform at the Olympia Theater.

★ *Hotel Victoria*—Antwerp hotel at which Guy and Jill originally registered. They later moved to the Hotel Olympia (room 5) when it became evident they were being followed. The Hotel Olympia was located at 89 Parkstrasse.

★ Just before Guy sang "I Love Only One Girl," "London Bridge" could be heard on the film's soundtrack.

★ *SS Damocles*—Ship Guy and Jill were going to take from Antwerp to Stockholm. They were turned away because they didn't have a boarding pass. Later they took the *SS Damocles* on their honeymoon.

★ Guy Lambert's first engagement in Belgium was in the city of Bruges.

★ Blooper: In one scene, a Volkswagen drove into a Greyhound van. Since the scene took place in Belgium, this would not have been probable.

CLAMBAKE

United Artists, 1967. A Levy-Gardner-Laven production. Running time: 97 minutes. Elvis's twenty-fifth film.

CAST

Scott Hayward	ELVIS PRESLEY
Dianne Carter	SHELLEY FABARES
Tom Wilson	WILL HUTCHINS
James J. Jamison III	BILL BIXBY
Duster Hayward	JAMES GREGORY
Sam Burton	GARY MERRILL
Sally	SUZIE KAYE
Ellie	AMANDA HARLEY
Gloria	ANGELIQUE PETTYJOHN
Gigi	OLGA KAYA
Olive	ARLENE CHARLES
Mr. Hathaway	JACK GOOD
Hal, the Doorman	HAL PEARY
Race Announcer	SAM RIDDLE
Cigarette Girl	SUE ENGLAND
Lisa	LISA SLAGLE
Bartender	LEE KREIGER
Crewman	MELVIN ALLEN

Shelley Fabares, Elvis. (Photo courtesy Academy of Motion Picture Arts and Sciences)

Waiter...................................HERB BARNETT
Bellhop...................................STEVE CORY
Mr. Barasch...............................ROBERT LIEB
Waitress..................................MARJ DUSAY
Ice Cream Vendor..........................RED WEST
Mr. Hayward's Barber.....................CHARLIE HODGE
Bit.....................FRANCES HUMPHREY HOWARD
Bit.....................................JOE ESPOSITO
Bit...................................RICHARD DAVIS

CREW
Producers................................ARNOLD LAVEN
                                        ARTHUR GARDNER
                                        JULES LEVY
Director................................ARTHUR H. NADEL
Screenplay.........................ARTHUR BROWNE JR.
Story................................ARTHUR BROWNE JR.
Director of Photography.............WILLIAM MARGULIES
Art Director............................LLOYD PAPEZ
Set Decoration...........................JAMES REDD
Associate Producer......................ERNST R. ROLF
Production Manager........................BEN BISHOP
Assistant Director....................CLAUDE BINYON JR.
Script Supervisor....................JOSEPH MAZZACA
Editor..................................ERNST R. ROLF
Makeup................................DAN GREENWAY
Hairstyles............................JUDY ALEXANDER
Technical Advisor....................COL. TOM PARKER
Production Assistant.....................B. C. WYLIE
Property Master...........................DOD DONE
Choreography..........................ALEX ROMERO
Assistant to the Choreographer........LANCE LE GAULT
Musical Score........................JEFF ALEXANDER
Music Editor..........................DICK LUCKEY
Vocal Accompaniment................THE JORDANAIRES
Sound...............................WALDEN O. WATSON
                                     FRANK WILKINSON
Casting..............................LYNN STALMASTER

Second Unit Photographer.................IRMIN ROBERTS
Titles Designed by.................FORMAT PRODUCTIONS
Optical Effects...................WESTHEIMS COMPANY
Special Effects..........................BOB WARNER

SONGS
1. "Clambake"—Sung over the opening credits, during a clambake in midfilm, and over the closing credits.
2. "Who Needs Money"—Sung on a motorcycle on the way to Miami Beach. The song was also sung by Will Hutchins while he traveled in a red convertible. (His voice was dubbed by Ray Walker of the Jordanaires.)
3. "A House That Has Everything"—Sung to Shelley Fabares on the beach.
4. "Confidence"—Sung on a playground to a group of children. The children and Will Hutchins join Elvis in singing.
5. "You Don't Know Me"—Sung in the ski shop.
6. "Hey, Hey, Hey"—Sung in the ski shop as Elvis, Will Hutchins, Gary Merrill, and several girls work to coat Burton's boat with protective "goop."
7. "The Girl I Never Loved"—Sung on the beach.

"How Can You Lose What You Never Had" was cut from the final print of the film.

PRODUCTION NOTES
✓ *Clambake* opened nationally on November 22, 1967.

✓ The title originally considered for *Clambake* was *Too Big for Texas*.

✓ Preproduction scenes were filmed in and around Miami.

✓ Major photography was to have begun on March 10, 1967, but was delayed until the last week of March because Elvis fell in the bathroom and hit his head on the bathtub, suffering a minor concussion. Filming was completed on April 27.

✓ Producers Arnold Laven, Arthur Gardner, and Jules Levy had earlier worked on the TV series "The Big Valley" and the Burt Lancaster film *The Scalphunters*.

✓ All of Elvis's scenes were filmed in Los Angeles. A double was used for the Miami Beach scenes.

✓ Frances Humphrey Howard, an extra in *Clambake*, was the sister of Hubert Humphrey, the vice president of the United States at the time of the filming.

✓ Jim David, a local water-ski champion in Miami, was used for the hazardous open-water skiing stunts in the film.

✓ Actual race footage of the Orange Bowl International Power Boat Regatta was incorporated into *Clambake*. The race took place in Miami's Marine Stadium.

✓ Hal Peary, the actor who played Hal the doorman, was the original Throckmorton P. Gildersleeve on radio's "Fibber McGee and Molly" and "The Great Gildersleeve" shows. *Clambake* was Peary's last film. (The producers of "Fibber McGee and Molly" came up with the first name and middle initial for Gildersleeve from Throckmorton Place, a street in New York City.)

✓ Will Hutchins sang a duet with Elvis on "Who Needs Money," but the voice actually heard was that of Ray Walker of the Jordanaires. Hutchins previously

Will Hutchins, Elvis, Red West. The "Confidence" number. (Photo courtesy Eddie Brandt's Saturday Matinee)

starred as Tom (Sugarfoot) Brewster in the 1957–60 TV series "Sugarfoot."

✓ The trained dolphin Flipper made a cameo appearance in *Clambake*. Flipper, whose real name was Susie, was the star of her own NBC-TV series for three seasons (1964–67).

✓ The white suit used by Elvis in *Clambake* reportedly cost $10,000. It was this suit that was cut into small pieces and put into the four-record boxed set *Elvis: The Other Sides— Worldwide Gold Award Hits, Vol. 2.*

TRIVIA

★ *Welcome to Florida—The Happy State*—Road sign seen as Scott Hayward entered Florida.

★ *Heyward Oil Company*—Petroleum firm owed by Scott Hayward's father, Duster. (Note: The producers never seemed to agree on the spelling of Scott's last name. In one of the early scenes, in which Scott and Tom stopped to get a sandwich, a service-station sign clearly said "Heyward Oil Company." At the end of the film, when Scott's driver's license is shown, the spelling is Hayward. Some movie reference sources have the name as Heywood. The authors have chosen to go with the driver's license spelling. After all, Scott wouldn't have lied to the DMV!)

★ Scott and Tom took suites at the Shores Hotel (with Tom staying in the Presidential Suite).

★ *Scarlet Lady*—James Jamison's powerboat. The *Scarlet Lady* had the number D-3 on the side.

★ *J. J. Special*—Special drink ordered by James Jamison III at the Shores Hotel bar. The drink was named after him.

★ Jamison's family manufactured a brand of erotic pajamas in their New York City plant called "Jamison's Jammies."

★ Blooper: Elvis and Shelley Fabares sat around a fire on the beach at sunset in one scene. Since the ocean is east of Miami Beach, the sun would have had to have been rising, not setting.

★ Parts of several songs were used in the "Confidence" production number in *Clambake*. They include "London Bridge Is Falling Down" (instrumental), "Here We Go Around the Mulberry Bush," "Frère

Jacques, Frère Jacques," "Row, Row, Row Your Boat," and "Skip to My Lou." Melodically, "Confidence" sounded like "High Hopes" (the Sinatra song) in some places.

★ Red West played the ice cream vendor in the "Confidence" number. His one line was "Ice cream for everybody!"

★ *Paul and Robbie Are Creeps*—Graffiti seen on the side of a playground building. Also seen was "Jo Carol Loves Danny."

★ *Burton Boat Company*—Firm owned by Sam Burton from which Scott Hayward obtained the boat that he entered in the Orange Bowl International Power Boat Regatta. The company was also known as Burton International.

★ Scott Hayward majored in engineering in college.

★ *Goop*—Protective hard coating developed by Scott Hayward while working at a research lab after graduating from college. "Goop" stood for *g*lycol *oxy*oxynoic *p*hosphate. The original coating deteriorated when it came in contact with water, but Scott refined it and used the substance to coat his race boat.

★ The melody to "Shortnin' Bread" could be briefly heard in the film.

★ *Sultan Suite*—Shores Hotel suite (#26B) taken by James Jamison III.

★ *26D*—Shores Hotel room of Duster Hayward, Scott's father.

★ *Orange Bowl International Power Boat Regatta*—Boat race sponsored by the American Power Boat Association that Scott Hayward won. He received $10,000 plus the Governor's Trophy. James Jamison III had won the race three years in a row.

★ *Raw-Hide*—Name of Sam Burton's boat that Scott Hayward used to win the Orange Bowl Regatta. The boat's number was 99. Other boats in the race included *Vapor Trail* (96), *Bad Boy* (13), and *Terry's Pet* (52).

★ Blooper: Mountains could be seen in the background. Obviously, those shots were taken in California, not Florida.

★ *B351618*—Scott Hayward's Texas driver's license number, as revealed at the end of *Clambake*. The close-up of the license also showed the following information: address (5441 Oak Park Avenue), hair (black), eyes (brown), height (6'2"), weight (175 pounds), and date of birth (February 23, 1940).

★ Elvis didn't kiss Shelley Fabares until the final scene of *Clambake*.

STAY AWAY, JOE

MGM, 1968. A Douglas Laurence production. Running time: 102 minutes. Elvis's twenty-sixth film.

CAST

Joe Lightcloud	ELVIS PRESLEY
Charlie Lightcloud	BURGESS MEREDITH
Glenda Callahan	JOAN BLONDELL
Annie Lightcloud	KATY JURADO

Elvis and Dominick, the bull. (Photo courtesy Cinema Collectors)

Grandpa (Chief Lightcloud)	THOMAS GOMEZ
Hy Slager	HENRY JONES
Bronc Hoverty	L. Q. JONES
Mamie Callahan	QUENTIN DEAN
Mrs. Hawkins	ANNE SEYMOUR
Congressman Morrissey	DOUGLAS HENDERSON
Lorne Hawkins	ANGUS DUNCAN
Frank Hawk	MICHAEL LANE
Mary Lightcloud	SUSAN TRUSTMAN
Hike Bowers	WARREN VANDERS
Bull Shortgun	BUCK KARTALIAN
Connie Shortgun	MAURISHKA
Marlene Standing Rattle	CAITLIN WYLES

Quentin Dean, Elvis. (Photo courtesy Cinema Collectors)

Billie Jo Hump.............................MARYA CHRISTEN
Jackson He-Crow.........................DEL (SONNY) WEST
Little Deer...................................JENNIFER PEAK
Deputy Sheriff Hank Matson....................BRETT PARKER
Orville Witt.................................MICHAEL KELLER
Car Salesman.................................DICK WILSON
Other Indian.................................DAVID CADIENTE
Judge Nibley...............................HARRY HARVEY SR.
Workman......................................JOE ESPOSITO
Announcer at Rodeo...........................ROBERT LIEB

CREW

Producer................................DOUGLAS LAURENCE
Director..................................PETER TEWKSBURY
Screenplay...............................MICHAEL A. HOEY
Based on a Novel by..........................DAN CUSHMAN
Director of Photography.....................FRED KOENEKAMP
Art Directors................................GEORGE W. DAVIS
                                             CARL ANDERSON
Set Decoration................................HENRY GRACE
                                             DON GREENWOOD JR.
Unit Production Manager.................WILLIAM R. FINNEGAN
Editor......................................GEORGE W. BROOKS
Assistant Director..........................DALE HUTCHINSON
Makeup......................................WILLIAM TUTTLE
Hairstyles...............................SYDNEY GUILAROFF

Associate Producer..........................MICHAEL A. HOEY
Recording Supervisor.......................FRANKLIN MILTON
Music Score.................................JACK MARSHALL
Vocal Accompaniment.......................THE JORDANAIRES

SONGS

1. "Stay Away"—Sung over the opening credits.
2. "Stay Away, Joe"—Sung at an all-night party.
3. "Lovely Mamie"—Sung while driving a red convertible. Only one line was sung: "Mamie, Mamie, lovely little Mamie."
4. "Dominick"—Sung to Dominick XII, a bull.
5. "All I Needed Was the Rain"—Sung during a rainstorm while sitting in the completely stripped convertible.

"Goin' Home" was cut from the film.

PRODUCTION NOTES

✓ *Stay Away, Joe* opened nationally on March 8, 1968.

✓ The best-selling novel *Stay Away, Joe* by Dan Cushman was a Book-of-the-Month Club selection.

✓ It was reported in February 1967 that *Stay Away, Joe* would be written and directed by Burt Kennedy and produced by his Brigade Productions. However, it was announced in August that Michael A. Hoey would write the screenplay, Douglas Laurence would produce, and Peter Tewksbury would direct.

✓ Location filming near Sedona, Arizona, began on October 18, 1967. Some principal photography was also done around Cottonwood. Elvis and the crew stayed in Arizona until mid-November.

✓ *Stay Away, Joe* was actress Katy Jurado's first comedy role in more than a hundred films.

✓ Director of photography Fred Koenekamp devised the unique photography used in "The Man from U.N.C.L.E." TV series.

✓ Twenty-five families (139 persons) from the Navajo Indian Reservation near Tuba City, Arizona, appeared as extras in the all-night party scenes.

✓ Katy Jurado gained 22 pounds in 22 days to play the part of Annie Lightcloud.

✓ Actress Susan Trustman, who played Mary Lightcloud, made her movie debut in *Stay Away, Joe*. From 1964 to 1966 she played Pat Matthews in the NBC-TV soap opera "Another World."

✓ For the film, a Navajo Indian reservation was reconstructed in the foothills near Sedona, Arizona.

✓ *Bumblebee, Oh Bumblebee* was one of the titles originally considered for *Stay Away, Joe*. Another title considered was *Born Rich*.

✓ A few days before filming was to begin, Katy Jurado broke some bones in her foot. She removed the cast prematurely to make the film, unbeknownst to producer Douglas Laurence or director Peter Tewksbury. She explained that her limp was part of her characterization!

✓ Joan Blondell wore 18 pieces of jewelry valued at $23,000 in the film.

✓ Some of the ad lines for *Stay Away, Joe* included "Elvis goes West . . . and the West goes wild!"; "Elvis is kissin' cousins again—and also friends, and even some perfect strangers!"; and "He's playing Indian—but he doesn't say 'How' . . . he says 'When!' "

✓ In the film, Katy Jurado wore a turquoise-bead necklace given to her by Spencer Tracy while they made *Broken Lance* (1954), a role for which Jurado received an Oscar nomination as Best Supporting Actress. She also wore a necklace given to her by John Wayne and earrings from Gary Cooper. Helen Hayes gave Jurado the ring she wore.

✓ *Stay Away, Joe* was ranked #65 in *Variety*'s list of top-grossing films of 1968.

✓ Thomas Gomez, who played Grandpa, was nominated for Best Supporting Actor in 1947 for his performance in *Ride a Pink Horse*.

✓ Burgess Meredith was the son-in-law of Antoinette Perry, for whom the Tony Awards were named. A seasoned film veteran by the time he did *Stay Away, Joe* (he debuted in 1936's *Winterset*), Meredith is best known to today's television audiences as the Penguin in the "Batman" series of the mid-1960s.

TRIVIA

★ Joe received twenty heifers and a young bull from Congressman Morrissey to prove that he and his father could successfully raise cattle on the reservation.

★ *Chester Walking Bear*—Indian from Big Springs who sent this message via smoke signals: "Get ready for big hoop-up. Watch squaws. Joe Lightcloud coming home."

★ Mamie Callahan was 19 years old.

★ *Old Gray*—Joe Lightcloud's horse. He traded Old Gray in for a red convertible.

★ To get Glenda Callahan out of the area, Joe agreed to meet her at the Maverick Bar in Flagstaff.

★ *Callahan's*—Grocery store–tavern run by Glenda Callahan.

★ Question: What happened to the young bull Joe received from Congressman Morrissey? Answer: It was barbecued by Bronc Hoverty.

★ *Dominick XII*—Champion bucking bull Joe Lightcloud bought from Hike Bowers.

★ "Brahms' Lullaby" could be heard on the soundtrack several times when the camera was on Dominick, the bull.

★ *JX3-496*—License number of Joe's red convertible.

★ Mary Lightcloud worked at the First National Bank of Arizona. The bank was founded in 1877.

★ "The Man on the Flying Trapeze" could be heard on the soundtrack when the cowboys were being bucked off Dominick.

★ *23rd District*—Congressional district represented by Congressman Morrissey.

★ Joe Lightcloud was called the "Pride of Calgary, Cheyenne, and Madison Square Garden."

SPEEDWAY

MGM, 1968. A Douglas Laurence production. Running time: 94 minutes. Elvis's twenty-seventh film.

CAST

Steve Grayson	ELVIS PRESLEY
Susan Jacks	NANCY SINATRA
Kenny Donford	BILL BIXBY
R. W. Hepworth	GALE GORDON
Abel Esterlake	WILLIAM SCHALLERT
Ellie Esterlake	VICTORIA MEYERINK
Paul Dado	ROSS HAGEN
Birdie Kebner	CARL BALLANTINE
Juan Medala	PONCIE PONCE
The Cook	HARRY HICKOX
Billie Joe	CHRISTOPHER WEST
Miss Charlotte Speedway 100	MISS BEVERLY HILLS (MARY ANN ASHMAN)
Ted Simmons	HARPER CARTER
Lloyd Meadows	BOB HARRIS
Debbie Esterlake	MICHELE NEWMAN
Carrie Esterlake	COURTNEY BROWN
Billie Esterlake	DANA BROWN
Annie Esterlake	PATTI JEAN KEITH
Mike	CARL REINDEL
Dumb Blonde	GARI HARDY
Lori	CHARLOTTE CONSIDINE
Race Announcer	SANDY REED
Mayor Fiergol	S. JOHN LAUNER
1st Waitress	SALLY MILLS
2nd Waitress	BARBRO HEDSTROM

Bill Bixby, Elvis, Nancy Sinatra. (Photo courtesy Eddie Brandt's Saturday Matinee)

3rd Waitress	DIANNE STANLEY
Lori's Bridegroom	JOHN MCDONNELL
Taxpayer	WILLIAM KEENE
Portly, Bald-Headed Man	GEORGE CISAR
Secretary	DEE CARROLL
Mr. Tillman	ROBERT J. STEVENSON
Willa	KAREN HAMILTON
Drunk	CLAUDE STROUD
Janitor at the Coffee Shop	BURT MUSTIN
4th Waitress	KATHY NELSON
5th Waitress	JAMIE MICHAELS
6th Waitress	SHERYL ULLMAN
Bit Girl	RITA ROGERS
Go-Go Dancer	SHARON GARRETT
Dado's Crew Chief	WARD RAMSEY
Dado's Crew	ROBERT JAMES
	RALPH ADANO
	TOM MCCAULEY
	GARY LITTLEJOHN
1st Guitarist's Girlfriend	ARLENE CHARLES
2nd Guitarist's Girlfriend	CASSANDRA LAWTON
3rd Guitarist's Girlfriend	MARILYN JONES
Guitarist	CHARLIE HODGE
1st Assistant	HAL RIDDLE
2nd Assistant	MORGAN HILL
Stock-Car Racers	RICHARD PETTY
	BUDDY BAKER
	CALE YARBOROUGH
	DICK HUTCHERSON
	TINY LUND
	G. C. SPENCER
	ROY MAYNE

CREW

Producer	DOUGLAS LAURENCE
Director	NORMAN TAUROG
Screenplay	PHILLIP SHUKEN
Director of Photography	JOSEPH RUTTENBERG
Art Directors	GEORGE W. DAVIS
	LEROY COLEMAN
Set Decoration	HENRY GRACE
	DON GREENWOOD JR.
Special Visual Effects	CARROLL L. SHEPPIRD

Editor	RICHARD FARRELL
Assistant Director	DALE HUTCHINSON
Unit Production Manager	G. REX BAILEY
Dialogue Coach	MICHAEL A. HOEY
Makeup	WILLIAM TUTTLE
Hairstyles	SYDNEY GUILAROFF
Recording Supervisor	FRANKLIN MILTON
Music Score	JEFF ALEXANDER
Vocal Accompaniment	THE JORDANAIRES

SONGS

1. "Speedway"—Sung over the opening credits.
2. "Let Yourself Go"—Sung in the Hangout club.
3. "Your Time Hasn't Come Yet, Baby"—Sung to Victoria Meyerink near the station wagon.
4. "He's Your Uncle, Not Your Dad"—Sung in the IRS office. Bill Bixby and others joined in.
5. "Who Are You? (Who Am I?)"—Sung to Nancy Sinatra in the hotel coffee shop.
6. "There Ain't Nothing Like a Song"—Sung at the Hangout club after the World 600 race. Nancy Sinatra joined in a duet.

Nancy Sinatra had a solo with "Your Groovy Self" in the Hangout club. "Five Sleepy Heads," "Suppose," and "Western Union" were intended for the film but were cut. Reportedly, Malayan prints of *Speedway* include those three songs.

PRODUCTION NOTES

✓ *Speedway* had its world premiere in Charlotte, North Carolina, on June 12, 1968.

✓ Several titles were considered for *Speedway,* among them *Guitar City, So I'll Go Quietly,* and *Pot Luck.* On May 4, 1967, the title was changed from *Pot Luck* to *Speedway.*

✓ Filming began on June 12, 1967.

✓ Director Norman Taurog's one-and-a-half-year-old granddaughter Patti Jean Keith played Annie, one of the little Esterlake girls. It was her film debut.

✓ Christopher West, who played Billy Joe, was the reigning Queen of the Laguna-Seca Sports Car Races.

✓ *Speedway* was Norman Taurog's eighth Elvis film.

✓ Although a few sources have indicated that *Speedway* was Nancy Sinatra's film debut, she actually had her first movie role in *For Those Who Think Young* (1964). Oscar-winning actress Ellen Burstyn (using the name Ellen McRae) also made her film debut in *For Those Who Think Young.*

✓ Nancy Sinatra was not the first actress offered the costarring role of Susan Jacks. It was first offered to British singing star Petula Clark, who turned it down.

✓ Ross Hagen made his screen debut in *Speedway.*

✓ *Speedway*'s opening credits mentioned seven professional stock-car racers who played themselves: Richard Petty, Buddy Baker, Cale Yarborough, Dick Hutcherson, Tiny Lund, G. C. Spencer, and Roy Mayne.

✓ Producer Douglas Laurence was once director of entertainment for the Flamingo Hotel in Las Vegas.

✓ *Speedway* was filmed on MGM's Culver City lot and on location at North Carolina's Charlotte Speedway. Ten cameras were used to film the Charlotte 500 race.

Christopher West, Bill Bixby, Elvis. (Photo courtesy Eddie Brandt's Saturday Matinee)

✓ Sonny and Cher turned down roles in the film.

✓ The scene in which Victoria Meyerink (as Ellie) stole a dozen hot dogs had to be filmed twice. However, after the first take the property manager could find only ten hot dogs. Meyerink had quickly eaten two!

✓ Eighty-three-year-old actor Burt Mustin played a janitor in the hotel coffee shop. Mustin, who made his film debut in *Detective Story* (1951) at the age of 67, appeared in 54 films and 266 television episodes before his role in *Speedway*. He commented to reporters that *Speedway* was his 154th janitor role.

✓ During the filming, Elvis was given a new office on the MGM lot.

✓ Director of photography Joseph Ruttenberg won four Best Cinematography Oscars out of ten nominations. He won for *The Great Waltz* (1938), *Mrs. Miniver* (1942), *Somebody Up There Likes Me* (1956), and *Gigi* (1959).

✓ Elvis and Nancy Sinatra first met at McGuire Air Force Base on March 3, 1960. She was the official greeter who met Elvis as he stepped off the plane from West Germany.

✓ *Speedway* grossed $3 million in 1968, ranking #40 of all films released that year.

TRIVIA

★ *6*—Number on the side of Steve Grayson's white Dodge Charger race car. His opponent Paul Dado was #43. Both cars were powered by 426 cubic-inch Chrysler Hemi engines.

★ *Charlotte 100*—Race won by Steve Grayson. For winning, he received $7,700 ($7,500 plus $200 lap money). He had finished in the money twenty times.

★ The racing-oriented discotheque where Steve Grayson and Susan Jacks performed was called the Hangout. The house band was Lance and the Spirits. Racing cars sawed in half were used as booths.

★ The mobile home park where Steve and Kenny lived was called The Trailer Trap.

★ Nancy Sinatra sang "Your Groovy Self" in the Hangout. The song, which was written by Lee Hazelwood, is the only solo by an artist other than Elvis to appear on a regular RCA Elvis album.

★ *Drive-In A Go Go*—Restaurant at which Lori worked as a carhop.

★ For winning the Charlotte Speedway 250 race, Steve earned a total of $9,500.

★ *West Hills Community Church*—Church at which Lori married her boyfriend, thanks to the financial assistance of Steve Grayson. The Rev. M. Murdock presided. Murdock's upcoming Sunday sermon was going to be "And He Shall Go Forth."

★ Burt Mustin sang the last line of "Who Are You? (Who Am I?)" to a mop after Steve and Susan left the coffee shop.

★ The song "Five Sleepy Heads" was to have been sung in the scene in which Steve tucks the five Esterlake girls into bed, but it was cut from the film.

★ Paul Dado's qualifying speed for the World 600 was 153.44 MPH. In that race Steve Grayson came in third, earning $7,670 (including lap money).

★ Elvis sang one line of "The Star Spangled Banner" in "He's Your Uncle, Not Your Dad": "O, say can you see."

★ *$4,000*—Amount of Steve Grayson's tax deduction for air, which was disallowed by the IRS.

★ The local IRS office was located in Suites 402–431.

★ After the IRS tax audit, Steve Grayson still owed the government $145,000.

★ Steve was given a $100-a-week allowance by the IRS until his tax obligation was paid. Kenny was put on a $50-a-week allowance.

★ *Mr. Tillman*—Kenny's bookmaker.

★ *1210*—Susan Jacks's room number at the hotel.

★ *$35.50*—Cost of the American Beauty roses Kenny charged to Steve's account and gave to Susan. She, in turn, gave them to Steve and deducted them from his $100 weekly allowance.

LIVE A LITTLE, LOVE A LITTLE

MGM, 1968. A Douglas Laurence production. Running time: 90 minutes. Elvis's twenty-eighth film.

CAST

Greg Nolan	ELVIS PRESLEY
Bernice	MICHELE CAREY
Mike Lansdown	DON PORTER
Louis Penlow	RUDY VALLEE
Harry	DICK SARGENT
Milkman	STERLING HOLLOWAY
Ellen	CELESTE YARNALL
Delivery Boy	EDDIE HODGES
Robbie's Mother	JOAN SHAWLEE
Miss Selfridge	MARY GROVER
Receptionist	EMILY BANKS
Art Director	MICHAEL KELLER
1st Secretary	MERRI ASHLEY
2nd Secretary	PHYLLIS DAVIS
Perfume Model	URSULA MENZEL
1st Model	SUSAN SHUTE
2nd Model	EDIE BASKIN
3rd Model	GABRIELLE
4th Model	GINNY KANEEN
Sally, the Mermaid Model	SUSAN HENNING
1st Motorcycle Cop	MORGAN WINDBEIL
2nd Motorcycle Cop	BENJIE BANCROFT
Editor	RUSS BENDER
Robbie Pussycat	JOHN HEGNER
Landlady	ANN DORAN
Model	HEIDI JENSEN
Workman	JOHN WHEELER
1st Man	JAMES OLIVER
2nd Man	LONNIE BURR
3rd Man	BRITT LOMOND
Female Companion	MYRNA ROSS
1st Woman	MARCIA MAE JONES
2nd Woman	VERONICA ERICKSON
Doctor	BARTLETT ROBINSON
Blonde	THORDIS BRANDT
Man in Elevator	HAL RIDDLE
Lobby Model	BROOKE MILLS
Dancer	BRUCE HOY
Masseuse	HIROKO WATANABE
Workmen	PAUL SORENSON
	JOHN WHEELER
Bystander	MIKE WAGNER
4th Man	MORGAN JONES
Ad-Lib Man	ROBERT ISENBERG
Girl at Party	GAYLE ROGERS
3rd Woman	MARI ALDON
Newspaper Worker	RED WEST
Bits in Newspaper Office	JOE DIANNITO
	RUSS ALEXANDER
	LEON BRUNELLE

CREW

Producer	DOUGLAS LAURENCE
Director	NORMAN TAUROG
Screenplay	MICHAEL A. HOEY
	DAN GREENBURG
Director of Photography	FRED KOENEKAMP
Art Directors	GEORGE W. DAVIS
	PRESTON AMES
Set Decoration	HENRY GRACE
	DON GREENWOOD JR.
Assistant Director	AL SHENBERG
Unit Production Manager	LINDSLEY PARSONS JR.
Editor	JOHN MCSWEENEY
Recording Supervisor	FRANKLIN MILTON
Makeup	WILLIAM TUTTLE

(Photo courtesy Cinema Collectors)

Brutus, Sterling Holloway, Michele Carey, Elvis. (Photo courtesy Eddie Brandt's Saturday Matinee)

Hairstyles...MARY KEATS
Assistant to the Producer....................MICHAEL A. HOEY
Dream Sequence ("Edge of Reality") Choreographer....JACK REGAS
"A Little Less Conversation" Choreographer.........JACK BAKER
Music Score..................................BILLY STRANGE

SONGS
1. "Wonderful World"—Sung over the opening credits.
2. "Edge of Reality"—Sung in a surrealistic dream sequence.
3. "A Little Less Conversation"—Sung to Celeste Yarnall at Don Porter's poolside party.
4. "Almost in Love"—Sung to Michele Carey.

"Let's Live a Little" was cut from the film.

PRODUCTION NOTES
✓ *Live a Little, Love a Little* opened nationally on October 23, 1968.

✓ The screenplay was based on the novel *Kiss My Firm but Pliant Lips*, by Dan Greenburg. It was Greenburg's first novel. Previously, he had written the nonfiction book *How to Be a Jewish Mother*.

✓ Elvis signed to make the movie in December 1967.

✓ The newspaper office scene was filmed at the *Hollywood Citizen–News* in July 1968. Newspaper employees Joe Diannito, Russ Alexander, and Leon Brunelle had bit roles in the film.

✓ During the filming of *Live a Little, Love a Little*, director Norman Taurog and his wife gave Elvis and Priscilla a yellow bassinet for the newly-born Lisa Marie.

✓ Ursula Menzel, who played the perfume model, was a Munich-born beauty making her screen debut in *Live a Little, Love a Little*.

✓ The two-hundred-pound Great Dane dog, Albert, was actually played by Brutus, Elvis's real-life dog.

✓ Two of the advertisement lines for the film were: "Elvis Shoots the Works from Dawn to Darkroom as a Pinup Photographer Who Doesn't Want to Get Pinned Down" and "Watch Elvis Click with All These Chicks."

✓ Susan Henning, who played the mermaid model, was a former Miss USA.

✓ While filming in downtown Los Angeles, a pair of old ladies literally knocked Elvis to the pavement in their haste to get Rudy Vallee's autograph.

✓ Actress Celeste Yarnall was once "Miss Rheingold," and toured the world representing the company. She was later chosen Deb Star of 1967 and the National Association of Theater Owners' "Most Promising Star of 1968." The 36-24-36 blonde was earning a hundred thousand dollars a year as a model at the time of her selection to play Ellen in *Live a Little, Love a Little*. It was her second film. Previously, Yarnall had appeared in *Eve* (1968). In high school her dream was to become an actress and appear with Elvis in a movie.

✓ Mitchell Rhein, special assistant to the producer's unit, worked with director Norman Taurog on 261 previous films in numerous capacities, from April 19, 1919, to April 1968.

✓ Actor Eddie Hodges, who played the delivery boy in *Live a Little, Love a Little*, had two top twenty songs in the early 1960s: "I'm Gonna Knock on Your Door" (Cadence 1397) and "(Girls, Girls, Girls) Made to Love" (Cadence 1421). As a contestant on the quiz show "Name That Tune" in 1958, Hodges won $25,000. His partner was future astronaut and U.S. senator John Glenn. While on the show, Hodges sang a few gospel tunes for the audience. The director of the Broadway play *The Music Man* spotted him and offered him a role in the play. The following year, Hodges made his screen debut as Frank Sinatra's son in *A Hole in the Head*.

✓ *Live a Little, Love a Little* was never released in Great Britain.

✓ *Live a Little, Love a Little* was director Norman Taurog's last film.

✓ Vernon Presley had a role in *Live a Little, Love a Little* as an extra sitting at a table.

✓ Rudy Vallee became the first recipient of a singing telegram when, on July 28, 1933, a delivery boy sang "Happy Birthday" to him. One of the most popular crooners in the pre-Bing Crosby era, Vallee (real name: Hubert Prior Vallee) sang "Empty Saddles" at the funeral of cowboy star Tom Mix in October 1940.

✓ Sterling Holloway, the milkman in *Live a Little, Love a Little*, was the first actor drafted into the U.S. Army during World War II. His voice can be heard in many TV commercials, including those for Puppy Chow and Shout.

✓ In 1979 Michele Carey, a former Powers model in Denver, provided the voice of Effie, the computer in the short-lived Robert Conrad series "A Man Called Sloane."

TRIVIA

★ *Albert*—Bernice's pet Great Dane dog. Albert slept in a baby crib.

★ *Alice*—Name Bernice first gave to Greg. She told the delivery boy her name was Suzy and told the milkman it was Betty.

★ Greg was born in the month of December.

★ Harry's favorite foods were egg rolls and hot dogs.

★ *Purple Valley Dairy*—Dairy that delivered milk to Bernice's house.

★ *Classic Cat Magazine*—Mike Lansdown's girlie magazine. It was located on the eighteenth floor of the office building.

★ Louis Penlow's business was named RKC&P Creative Advertising. It was located on the twenty-first floor of the same office building in which *Classic Cat Magazine* was headquartered.

★ Greg Nolan's home was located at 211 Lookout Mountain Drive.

★ *W67866*—License number of Greg's convertible.

★ Question: What kind of soup did Bernice serve to Greg and Harry? Answer: beef and beer soup.

★ Message left by Bernice in lipstick on Greg's bedroom mirror: "Bernice is very confused. Please don't look for her. Thank you, darling, for making me a woman."

CHARRO!

National General Pictures, 1969. A Harry Caplan production. Running time: 98 minutes. Elvis's twenty-ninth movie.

CAST

Jess Wade	ELVIS PRESLEY
Tracy Winters	INA BALIN
Vince Hackett	VICTOR FRENCH
Marcie	LYNN KELLOGG
Sara Ramsey	BARBARA WERLE
Billy Roy Hackett	SOLOMON STURGES
Opie Keetch	PAUL BRINEGAR
Gunner	JAMES SIKKING
Heff	HARRY LANDERS
Lieutenant Rivera	TONY YOUNG
Sheriff Dan Ramsey	JAMES ALMANZAR
Mody	CHARLES H. GRAY
Lige	RODD REDWING
Martin Tilford	GARRY WALBERG
Gabe	DUANE GREY
Henry Carter	J. EDWARD MCKINLEY
Jerome Selby	JOHN PICKARD
Will Joslyn	ROBERT LUSTER
Christa	CHRISTA LANG
Harvey, the Bartender	ROBERT KARNES
Bit Girls	KATHLEEN DARC
	JACQUI BRANDT
	MEGAN TIMOTHY
Mexican Peon	CHARLIE HODGE

CREW

Executive Producer	HARRY CAPLAN
Producer	CHARLES MARQUIS WARREN
Director	CHARLES MARQUIS WARREN
Screenplay	CHARLES MARQUIS WARREN
Story	FREDERIC LOUIS FOX
Director of Photography	ELLSWORTH FREDERICKS
Art Director	JAMES SULLIVAN

ON HIS NECK HE WORE THE BRAND OF A KILLER.
ON HIS HIP HE WORE VENGEANCE.

A different kind of rôle...

A different kind of man.

National General Pictures

ELVIS PRESLEY as the one called CHARRO!

INA BALIN · VICTOR FRENCH · BARBARA WERLE · SOLOMON STURGES

WINDOW CARD

(Photo courtesy Cinema Collectors)

Set Decoration............................CHARLES THOMPSON
Editor.....................................AL CLARK
Assistant Director.........................DINK TEMPLETON
Special Effects......................GEORGE (BUD) THOMPSON
WOODROW WARD
ROBERT BECK
Unit Production Manager......................MAURIE M. SEUSS
Postproduction Editing Supervisor..............JACK KIRSCHNER
Associate Producer............................DINK TEMPLETON
Sound Recording...............................UREY KAUK
Sound Mixer...................................ROY MEADOWS
Second Assistant Directors.....................W. LES SHELDON
JOE NAYFACK
Makeup...................................WILLIAM REYNOLDS
GENE BARTLETT
Men's Wardrobe................................BOB FUCA
Ladies' Costumes..........................VIOLET B. MARTIN
Script Supervision.........................CHARLSIE BRYANT
Music Composed and Conducted by...........HUGO MONTENEGRO
Music Editor..................................JOHN MICK
Dialogue Director............................ROY LINDEBERG
Casting..................................HARVEY CLERMONT

SONG

1. "Charro"—Sung over the opening credits.

PRODUCTION NOTES

✓ *Charro!* opened nationally on March 13, 1969.

✓ Principal photography began on July 22, 1968, near Apache Junction, Arizona. Most of the filming took place in and around the Superstition Mountains. Interiors were done at MGM's Culver City studios. Filming of *Charro!* continued through August.

✓ Elvis stayed at the Superstition Inn outside of Phoenix while on location.

✓ Costumes for *Charro!* were provided by the Bermans Costume Company.

✓ *Charro!* was previewed in several Southern states before its general release. The states of Oklahoma, Texas, and Louisiana declared Charro! Day. Two groups of actors from the film toured those states in publicity junkets. Solomon Sturges, Kathleen Darc, and Jacqui Brandt comprised one group while James Sikking and Megan Timothy were in the other.

✓ One title originally considered for *Charro!* was *Come Hell, Come Sundown.*

✓ In twenty-five Southwest cities, "Charro Girl" contests were held to publicize the film. Finalists appeared in Dallas and Austin. Texas governor Preston Smith hosted a special *Charro!* salute in Austin in conjunction with the contest.

✓ Solomon Sturges, who played Billy Roy in the film, is the son of writer-director Preston Sturges (*Sullivan's Travels* and *The Miracle of Morgan's Creek* were among his greatest films).

✓ *Charro!* is the only movie in which Elvis wore a beard.

✓ Actress Lynn Kellogg made her movie debut in *Charro!* She had previously appeared in the Broadway production *Hair.*

✓ Ina Balin was the first woman to make a handshake tour of military hospitals in South Vietnam in the 1960s. She made her professional debut on TV's "The Perry Como Show" in the 1950s. The Hollywood Foreign Press Association selected Balin as the International Star of Tomorrow in 1961.

✓ Several actors in *Charro!* had experience as television-series regulars either before or after that film. They include: James Almanzar ("The High Chaparral," and "Here Come the Brides"); Paul Brinegar ("The Life and Legend of Wyatt Earp," "Rawhide," and "Lancer"); Victor French ("The Hero," "Carter Country," "Little House on the Prairie," and "Highway to Heaven"); Robert Karnes ("The Lawless Years"); Harry Landers ("Ben Casey"); James Sikking ("Turnabout" and "Hill Street Blues"); and Tony Young ("Gunslinger").

✓ All music for *Charro!* other than the title tune was scored and conducted by Hugo Montenegro. Previously, Montenegro had a #2 hit (number one in England) with the title tune from Clint Eastwood's 1968 film *The Good, the Bad, and the Ugly.*

✓ Producer-director-screenwriter Charles Marquis Warren was a onetime novelist who specialized in tales of the American West. After World War II he began to write for films, including *Streets of Laredo* (1949) and *Springfield Rifle* (1952). In the 1960s Warren spent much of his time writing, directing, and producing television shows. Those efforts included "Rawhide," "Gunsmoke," and "The Virginian." He was executive producer of "Iron Horse." *Charro!* was Warren's first film in several years and the last in which he served as producer, director, and screenwriter.

(Photo courtesy Eddie Brandt's Saturday Matinee)

TRIVIA

★ Question: What drink did Jess Wade order in the Mexican cantina? Answer: Tequila (cost: two pesos).

★ When frisked by Billy Roy Hackett in front of the cantina, Jess had six dollars in his billfold.

★ *Charro!* was set in 1870.

★ *Rio Seco*—Border town that provided the setting for *Charro!*

★ Question: According to the wanted posters, how tall was Jess Wade? Answer: Six-foot-two.

★ Dan Ramsey had been the sheriff of Rio Seco for twelve years.

★ Vince Hackett's fellow gang member Gunner was a former cannoneer in the Confederate army. According to Gunner, General Stonewall Jackson once said he was "the best—in front of the whole regiment, he said it."

★ In the novel version of *Charro!*, written by Harry Whittington, Jess Wade's horse was named Charlie. The horse was unnamed in the movie.

★ *Victory Gun*—Napoleonic, twelve-pound cannon covered with bronze, silver, and gold. The Victory Gun was the cannon that fired the last shot against Mexican ruler Ferdinand Maximilian, setting the country free

from his rule. Vince Hackett and his boys stole the cannon from the Chapultepec Palace on July 8, 1870.

★ *Norm*—Member of Vince Hackett's gang who suffered a neck wound while escaping from the Chapultepec Palace. Norm later died and was buried in the desert. But Hackett slipped information to the Mexican authorities indicating that it was Jess Wade who was shot stealing the Victory Cannon. To add substance to his false story, Hackett used a red-hot poker to burn a wound into Jess Wade's neck.

★ *$10,000*—Reward offered by the Mexican and American governments for the capture of Jess Wade.

★ Question: What was the name of the man who owned the livery stable in Rio Seco? Answer: Will Joslyn.

★ *Town House*—Rio Seco saloon where Tracy Winters was a dancer.

★ Question: Where did Jess find the key to open Tracy Winters's hotel room? Answer: In a flower pot.

★ *Henry Carter*—Owner of Rio Seco's bank.

★ *$100,000*—Estimated value of the Victory Gun.

THE TROUBLE WITH GIRLS

MGM, 1969. A Lester Welch production. Running time: 97 minutes. Elvis's thirtieth film.

CAST

Walter Hale	ELVIS PRESLEY
Charlene	MARLYN MASON
Betty	NICOLE JAFFE
Nita Bix	SHEREE NORTH
Johnny	EDWARD ANDREWS
Mr. Drewcolt	JOHN CARRADINE
Mr. Jonson (Mr. Morality)	VINCENT PRICE
Carol Bix	ANISSA JONES
Maude	JOYCE VAN PATTEN
Willy	PEPE BROWN
Harrison Wilby	DABNEY COLEMAN
Mayor Gilchrist	BILL ZUCKERT
Mr. Perper	PITT HERBERT
Clarence	ANTHONY TEAGUE
Constable	MED FLORY
Mr. Smith	ROBERT NICHOLS
Olga Prchlik	HELENE WINSTON
Boy with Yale Sweater	KEVIN O'NEAL
Boy with Rutgers Sweater	FRANK WELKER
Boy with Princeton Sweater	JOHN RUBINSTEIN
Boy with Amherst Sweater	CHUCK BRILES
Mrs. Gilchrist	PATSY GARRETT
Lily-Jeanne Gilchrist	LINDA SUE RISK
Cabbie	CHARLES P. THOMPSON
1st Farmhand	LEONARD RUMERY
2nd Farmhand	WILLIAM M. PARIS
3rd Farmhand	KATHLEEN RAINEY
Soda Jerk	HAL JAMES PEDERSON
Chowderhead	MIKE WAGNER
Iceman	BRETT PARKER
The Cranker	DUKE SNIDER
Choral Group	PACIFIC PALISADES HIGH SCHOOL MADRIGALS
Vocal Group	THE JORDANAIRES
Deputy Sheriff	JERRY SCHILLING
Gambler	JOE ESPOSITO

CREW

Producer	LESTER WELCH
Director	PETER TEWKSBURY
Screenplay	ARNOLD PEYSER
	LOIS PEYSER
Based on a Story by	MAURI GRASHIN
Based on a Novel by	DAY KEENE
	DWIGHT BABCOCK
Director of Photography	JACQUES MARQUETTE
Art Directors	GEORGE W. DAVIS
	EDWARD CARFAGNO
Set Decoration	HENRY GRACE
	JACK MILLS
Editor	GEORGE W. BROOKS
Assistant Director	JOHN CLARK BOWMAN
Associate Producer	WILLIAM MCCARTHY
Makeup	WILLIAM TUTTLE
Hairstyles	MARY EVANS
Costumes	BILL THOMAS
Choreography	JONATHAN LUCAS
Recording Supervisor	FRANKLIN MILTON
Music Score	BILLY STRANGE

SONGS

1. "Swing Low, Sweet Chariot"—Sung in a tent at the chautauqua with a vocal group.

(Photo courtesy Cinema Collectors)

2. "The Whiffenpoof Song"—Sung just prior to "Violet (Flower of NYU)" at the chautauqua.
3. "Violet (Flower of NYU)"—Sung with a quartet on stage at the chautauqua.
4. "Clean Up Your Own Backyard"—Sung on stage at the chautauqua.
5. "Sign of the Zodiac"—Sung in a duet with Marlyn Mason on stage at the chautauqua. Mason sang most of the song.
6. "Almost"—Sung with only piano accompaniment in a vacant tent.

A number of songs were heard on the soundtrack to *The Trouble with Girls*, including "America the Beautiful," "Boola Boola," "Greensleeves," "When You Wore a Tulip and I Wore a Big Red Rose," "On Wisconsin," "The Darktown Strutters' Ball," "My Old Kentucky Home," "Mad'moiselle from Armentières," "Rocked in the Cradle of the Deep," "Blow the Man Down," "The Eyes of Texas," "Camptown Races," "Toot Toot Tootsie," "She's Nobody's Baby Now," and the traditional round "Frère Jacques."

PRODUCTION NOTES

✓ *The Trouble with Girls* opened nationally on September 3, 1969. In most areas it was double-billed with *The Green Slime*, a Japanese-American sci-fi flick that starred Robert Horton and Richard Jaeckel.

✓ Production began on October 28, 1968, and was completed on December 16. Filming was done on the MGM lot in Culver City.

✓ *The Trouble with Girls* was subtitled (*And How to Get into It*). It was the only Elvis film with a subtitle.

✓ The origin of *The Trouble with Girls* can be traced back to June 1959. At that time it was announced that Don Mankiewicz was going to write a screenplay based on an unpublished story by Mauri Grashin, Day Keene, and Dwight Babcock. The film was to be titled *Chautauqua*. A year and a half later, in December 1960, MGM announced that Glenn Ford was to star and Edmund Grainger was going to produce *Chautauqua*. The Hollywood trade papers stated that Elvis was slated to costar with Glenn Ford, Hope Lange, and Arthur O'Connell in February 1961. Three months later it was reported that Valentine Davies was writing the screenplay for the film, which was due to begin production in the fall of 1961.

Marlyn Mason, Elvis. (Photo courtesy Eddie Brandt's Saturday Matinee)

In July 1961 it was announced that Elvis was to star in and Edmund Grainger was to produce a film titled *Chautauqua*. William Wister Haines was then writing a screenplay based on a novel by Day Keene and Dwight Babcock. Dell Books was about to release a paperback edition of the novel with a print run of one million copies.

In August 1964, Dick Van Dyke was scheduled to star in *Chautauqua*. Blanche Hanalis was writing the screenplay based on the book *Merrily We Roll Along*, by Gay MacLaren. Three months later it was reported that Richard Morris was writing the screenplay.

MGM sold the property to Columbia Pictures in May 1965. Dick Van Dyke was still the star, but Elliott Arnold was now scripting the film (retitled *Big America*) and Sol C. Siegel was producing.

Finally, MGM got the rights back in April 1968. *Chautauqua* was now an Elvis Presley vehicle.

✓ Singer-songwriter Bobbie Gentry was first considered for the part of Charlene, but the role was eventually given to Marlyn Mason.

✓ Marlyn Mason made her movie debut in *The Trouble with Girls*. Her first paid acting job was in the TV series "Dr. Kildare." From there she went to Broadway. During high school Mason was the athletic team's mascot. She wore a tiger suit for three seasons.

✓ MGM property man Bob Murdock made three crisp one-hundred-dollar bills for the film's final scene. Previously, he had made $10 million for *Where Were You When the Lights Went Out?* (1968) and $2 million for *The Split* (1968).

✓ Dabney Coleman, who's become well known in recent years for his work in *9 to 5* (1980) and TV's "The Slap Maxwell Story," made his film debut in *This Property Is Condemned* (1966). *The Trouble with Girls* was Coleman's second film.

✓ Frank Welker provided the voice for hundreds of cartoon characters through the years, among them Freddy in "Scooby-Doo, Where Are You?" and Wheelie in "Wheelie and the Chopper Bunch." Most of his work has been done for Hanna-Barbera Productions.

✓ John Carradine played Dracula on the screen three times: *House of Frankenstein (1945)*, *House of Dracula* (1945), and *Billy the Kid Vs. Dracula* (1966). Before acting, Carradine earned a living sketching portraits in office buildings.

✓ Vincent Price was once the art-buying consultant to the Sears Roebuck Company. The son of a candy maker, Price made his screen debut in 1938's *Service De Luxe*.

✓ Four hundred and fifty extras were used in the parade sequences (including one hundred children).

Also used were fifty vintage autos, ten vintage trucks, two fire engines, and MGM's steam-driven train.

✓ Nicole Jaffe played Peppermint Patty in a Los Angeles company of *You're a Good Man, Charlie Brown.* She began her career at the age of nineteen when she answered this classified ad in a New York newspaper: "Wanted: A short, chubby blonde with a sense of comedy." The ad was placed by burlesque queen Ann Corio for a part as an out-of-step chorus girl in *This Was Burlesque.* Jaffe got the part. *The Trouble with Girls* was Jaffe's movie debut.

✓ Anissa Jones also made her film debut in *The Trouble with Girls.* Other than her regular role as Buffy in the TV series "Family Affair" (1966–1971), she had acted in only a few TV commercials. During the filming of *The Trouble with Girls,* she knitted three turtleneck sweaters for her pet gopher snakes.

✓ Advertising catchlines used in the promotion of *The Trouble with Girls:* "This Is Elvis '69—His New Look" and "The Chautauqua Circuit and Where It Led."

✓ Director Peter Tewksbury has directed only five feature films to date, two of them starring Elvis (*Stay Away, Joe* and *The Trouble with Girls*). He's been primarily a television director for such hit series as "Father Knows Best" and "My Three Sons."

✓ Chautauqua began in 1873 in Chautauqua, New York, as a broad, twelve-day study program for Sunday School teachers. The two founders were theologian John H. Vincent and Lewis Miller (who was the father-in-law of Thomas Edison). Chautauqua later developed into a loose, rolling canvas college that featured classes, lectures, music, culture, and home reading courses. In the early 1900s, communities looked forward to the arrival of the chautauqua. In her youth, actress Marjorie Main was a lecturer for a chautauqua group, reading from William Shakespeare and Charles Dickens.

✓ Child actor Pepe Brown made his film debut in *The Trouble with Girls.* His previous acting experience had been on the "Daktari" TV series.

✓ Kevin O'Neal, who played the boy with the Yale sweater, is actor Ryan O'Neal's brother.

TRIVIA

★ *Radford Center, Iowa*—Town that provided the setting for the film.

★ Blooper: The narrator of the opening sequence said, "Janet Gaynor just won the first Oscar." The film was set in 1927, but the first Academy Award ceremonies took place on May 19, 1929, in the Blossom Room of the Hollywood Roosevelt Hotel.

★ Question: What popular baseball player was mentioned by the narrator in the opening sequence? Answer: Babe Ruth.

★ *The Student Prince*—Popular 1927 silent movie starring Norma Shearer and Ramon Novarro. *The Student Prince* was advertised on a theater marquee on Main Street in Radford Center.

★ "America the Beautiful" was played by three children on kazoos.

★ "Toot, Toot, Tootsie" was sung by Lily-Jeanne Gilchrist, the mayor's daughter. "Toot, Toot, Tootsie" was written by Gus Kahn, Ernie Erdman, and Dan Russo for the 1922 Broadway musical *Bombo,* starring Al Jolson. Jolson later sang the tune in *The Jazz Singer* (1927), the first talking movie.

★ *The Sun Also Rises*—The 1926 novel by Ernest Hemingway that was mentioned in the film.

★ Question: What was Walter Hale's football uniform number in the football game won by his team 110–97? Answer: 11.

★ *The Darktown Strutters' Ball*—Song performed by Carol and Willy in the auditions for the children's play. "Darktown Strutters' Ball" was written by Shelton Brooks and first recorded by Al Jolson in 1917.

★ The Farmhand Trio sang "Susan Brown" on the street for Walter. The trio consisted of Kathy, Leonard, and Bill.

★ Charlene went to law school for six months.

★ In one scene, Johnny (played by Edward Andrews) sang and whistled one line of "Jeannie with the Light Brown Hair." The song was written by Stephen Foster in 1854 while he was separated from his wife, Jane.

★ Blooper: In one scene, Frank Welker (as the boy with the Rutgers sweater) did a Donald Duck impression. However, Donald Duck wasn't created by Walt Disney until 1936—nine years after the setting for the movie.

★ *36*—Hotel room of Walter and Johnny.

★ The Jordanaires were seen on stage backing Elvis (as Walter Hale) in the "Swing Low, Sweet Chariot" number.

★ Question: Who was the featured singer from the Metropolitan Opera appearing at the chautauqua? Answer: Olga Prchlik.

★ *From Cannibalism to Culture*—One of the featured lectures of the chautauqua on July 14.

★ Betty mentioned the opera *Aida* in one scene. *Aida* was written by Giuseppe Verdi in 1871 to commemorate the opening of the Suez Canal. The opera was first performed in Cairo, Egypt, on December 24, 1871.

★ Maude's time in swimming the English Channel was 14 hours, 21 minutes.

★ Question: What ballet troupe performed at the chautauqua on July 15? Answer: The Imperial Russian Ballet Troupe.

★ *Paragraph 3, Subheading 2*—Portion of Charlene's equity agreement with the chautauqua that she brought up during her contract disputes.

★ The publishing rights to "On Wisconsin," which was sung by a collegiate quartet, are owned by Paul McCartney. "On Wisconsin" is the fight song of the University of Wisconsin, as well as the official state song of the state of Wisconsin.

★ Blooper: Plastic football helmets were used in the football game, but plastic helmets were not used until a number of years later.

★ *Gilroy, Iowa*—Town that was the next scheduled stop for the chautauqua after Radford Center.

★ "Camptown Races" was played by a one-man band.

CHANGE OF HABIT

Universal, 1969. A Universal Pictures and NBC production. Running time: 93 minutes. Elvis's thirty-first film.

CAST

Dr. John Carpenter............................ELVIS PRESLEY
Sister Michelle Gallagher..................MARY TYLER MOORE
Sister Irene Hawkins........................BARBARA MCNAIR
Sister Barbara Bennett..........................JANE ELLIOT
Mother Joseph...................................LEORA DANA
Lieutenant Moretti...........................EDWARD ASNER
The Banker...................................ROBERT EMHARDT
Father Gibbons................................REGIS TOOMEY
Rose...DORO MERANDE
Lily...RUTH MCDEVITT
Bishop Finley.............................RICHARD CARLSON
Julio Hernandez...............................NEFTI MILLET
Desiree....................................LAURA FIGUEROA
Amanda Parker.................................LORENA KIRK
Miss Parker...............................VIRGINIA VINCENT
Colom...DAVID RENARD
Hawk..JI-TU CUMBUKA
Robbie..BILL ELLIOTT
Mr. Hernandez................................RODOLFO HOYOS
1st Stiletto Deb...............................LILITH MILES
2nd Stiletto Deb............................CAITLIN WYLES
Expectant Mother..............................LINDA GARAY
Tomas..ALEX VAL
Tony..ALEX TINNE
Maria..STELLA GARCIA

Fat Man......................................HARRY SWOGER
Chino..TONY DECOSTA
Father Witkowski.................................JIM BEACH
Ajax Market Manager.........................TIMOTHY CAREY
1st Underling.................................JOHN DAHEIM
2nd Underling.................................TROY MELTON
Traffic Cop..............................STANLEY SCHNEIDER
Man in Scene 93................................PEPE HERN
2nd Man...................................FRANK CORSENTINO
3rd Man......................................PAUL FACTOR
Man in Scene 166..............................STEVE CONTE
Teammate....................................ROBERT DEANDA
Cuban Mainliner...........................ROBERTO VARGAS
Woman in Market...............................RITA CONDE
Senora Gavilan................................ARACELI REY
Police Sergeant...............................LEN WAYLAND
Ice Cream Clerk...............................RAY BALLARD
1st Young Man..................................MARIO ANIOV
2nd Young Man.................................A. MARTINEZ
The Blossoms..................................THEMSELVES

CREW

Producer.....................................JOE CONNELLY
Director..................................WILLIAM GRAHAM
Screenplay.....................................JAMES LEE
S. S. SCHWEITZER
ERIC BERCOVICI
Story by......................................JOHN JOSEPH
RICHARD MORRIS
Director of Photography.......................RUSSELL METTY

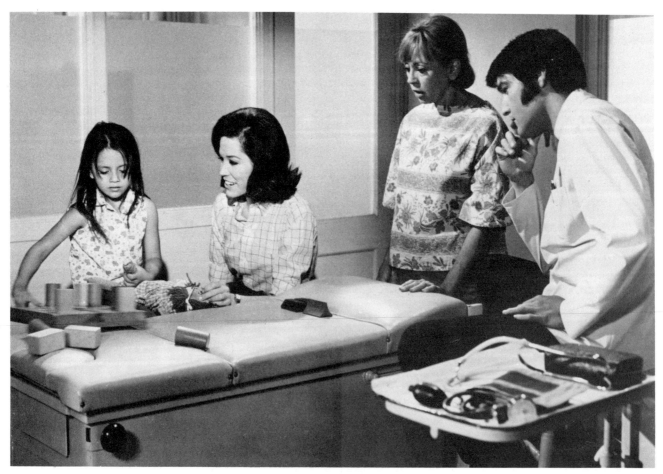

Lorena Kirk, Mary Tyler Moore, Virginia Vincent, Elvis. (Photo courtesy Jeff Wheatcraft)

Art Directors..........................ALEXANDER GOLITZEN
                                                 FRANK ARRIGO
Set Decoration...........................JOHN MCCARTHY
                                                 RUBY LEVITT
Sound.................................WALDEN O. WATSON
                                                 LYLE CAIN
                                                 RONALD PIERCE
Unit Production Manager......................JOSEPH KENNY
Assistant Director.............................PHIL BOWLES
Editor...................................DOUGLAS STEWART
Makeup.....................................BUD WESTMORE
Hairstyles...................................LARRY GERMAIN
Costumes.....................................HELEN COLVIG
Cosmetics.......UNIVERSAL PICTURES PROFESSIONAL COSMETICS
Associate Producer............................IRVING PALEY
Rage Reduction Scene Supervised by......DR. ROBERT W. ZASLOW
Music Supervision..........................STANLEY WILSON
Music................................WILLIAM GOLDENBERG

SONGS

1. "Change of Habit"—Sung over the opening credits.
2. "Rubberneckin' "—Sung in Dr. John Carpenter's apartment above the Washington Street Clinic.
3. "Have a Happy"—Sung on the merry-go-round after a touch football game.
4. "Let Us Pray"—Sung at Father Gibbons's Catholic Church at the end of the film.

"Let's Be Friends" was cut from the film. In the nuns' apartment, Elvis played "Lawdy Miss Clawdy" on the piano with "guitar accompaniment" by Sister Michelle (Mary Tyler Moore). "Let's Forget About the Stars" was recorded for the film but not used.

PRODUCTION NOTES

✓ *Change of Habit* opened nationally on November 10, 1969.

✓ Production began in early March 1969, and principal photography was completed on May 2. Exteriors were shot in downtown Los Angeles, while interiors were photographed on Stage D at Universal Studios.

✓ *Change of Habit* was a fictionalized account of Sister Mary Olivia Gibson's work with handicapped children. Sister Mary was head of the speech clinic at Maria Regina College in Syracuse, New York. In working with children who had speech problems, she used variations of theatrical techniques.

✓ *Change of Habit* was originally announced in the trade papers in November of 1967, but Elvis wasn't signed for the film until January 1969. Mary Tyler Moore had been signed earlier (October 1968).

✓ Singer Mahalia Jackson visited Elvis on the set during filming. A press release later said that Elvis patterned his vocal style after Mahalia Jackson and the Ward Gospel Singers.

✓ Puerto Rican-born actress Laura Figueroa spent years getting rid of her accent. For *Change of Habit* she had to develop a heavy Puerto Rican accent all over again.

✓ Jane Elliot made her film debut in *Change of Habit*. She had previously appeared on the Broadway stage in *The Impossible Years*.

✓ Most of the exterior scenes were filmed in the area of 5th and Main streets in downtown Los Angeles.

✓ During filming, a dozen large rats used in a

Jane Elliot, Elvis, Ed Asner. (Photo courtesy Eddie Brandt's Saturday Matinee)

ghetto apartment scene got loose on Stage D. The crew and actors had to temporarily vacate the premises while animal handlers rounded up the varmints.

✓ A couple of weeks before its national release, *Change of Habit* was screened for psychiatrists, psychologists, and educators from Los Angeles and San José who were involved with autistic children.

✓ Regis Toomey, who played Father Gibbons, first appeared in films in the 1920s. He costarred with Chester Morris in *Alibi* (1929), the first all-talking gangster film.

✓ *Change of Habit* was the last film appearance of Richard Carlson. Carlson and Vincent Price starred in more 3-D movies than anyone else (three each). In 1953 he had his own TV series, the syndicated "I Led Three Lives," in which he portrayed spy Herbert Philbrick.

✓ Character actress Ruth McDevitt and Elvis both made their last acting appearances in *Change of Habit*.

✓ *Change of Habit* reached as high as #17 in *Variety*'s weekly list of top-grossing films.

✓ The network TV debut of *Change of Habit* occurred on NBC's "Friday Night at the Movies" on October 20, 1972.

✓ The book *The Golden Turkey Awards*, listed Mary Tyler Moore as the recipient of the "Ecclesiastical Award for the Worst Performance by an Actor or Actress as a Clergyman or Nun."

TRIVIA

★ *Washington Street Clinic*—New York City clinic run by Dr. John Carpenter. The clinic's address: 934 Washington Street; telephone number: MAdison 6-7234.

★ Blooper: In the film's opening credits, a sign on the side of a bus advertised KDAY Radio, a Los Angeles station. The film, however, was set in New York City.

★ *Gonzales and Green Morticians*—Mortuary next door to the Washington Street Clinic.

★ Sisters Michelle, Barbara, and Irene belonged to the Order of Little Sisters of Mary.

★ Sister Michelle was a psychiatric social worker

with a degree in speech therapy; Sister Barbara was a laboratory technician; and Sister Irene was a registered nurse with a degree in public health.

★ Question: The three nuns' stay at the Washington Street clinic was for how many months? Answer: Two.

★ Dr. John Carpenter was from Shelby County, Tennessee (as was Elvis).

★ The Blossoms could be seen singing backup in the "Rubberneckin' " and "Let Us Pray" numbers.

★ Located across the street from the nuns' apartment was Celestial Gardens, Maria's Café, and a liquor store.

★ *Hamilton Paint*—Brand of paint used to paint the nuns' apartment.

★ Sister Michelle had five brothers.

★ During the touch football game, Sister Michelle wore a sweatshirt from the Notre Dame Athletic Department. Dr. Carpenter's sweatshirt was from the University of Tennessee at Memphis.

★ *Cal Edwards*—Sergeant in Dr. Carpenter's former Army unit. Cal was from Washington Street. Carpenter came to Washington Street because he figured he owed Cal something for his friendship.

★ After the touch football game, Dr. Carpenter and Amanda ordered strawberry ice cream, while Sister Michelle ordered chocolate.

★ *Kool King Auto Refrigeration*—Business in front of which the banker's henchmen beat and kidnapped a man.

★ Question: How much did Sister Irene borrow from the banker? Answer: One hundred dollars.

★ *Ajax Market—Unfair to Consumers*—Words on the picket sign carried by Sister Barbara in front of the Ajax Market. She put the sign on a mop handle she bought from the market for eighty-five cents.

★ *Irene*—Amanda's puppet (named for Sister Irene).

★ *Fiesta of San Juan de Chequez*—August 3rd street festival sponsored by the nuns. The festival was named in honor of the patron saint of Caribbean fishermen.

★ After the closing credits of *Change of Habit*, there was a plug for Universal Studios: "When in Southern California, Visit Universal City Studios."

ELVIS—THAT'S THE WAY IT IS

MGM, 1970. A Herbert F. Soklow production. Running time: 97 minutes. Elvis's thirty-second film.

CREW

Producer	HERBERT F. SOKLOW
Director	DENIS SANDERS
Director of Photography	LUCIEN BALLARD
Editor	HENRY BERMAN
Unit Production Manager	DALE HUTCHINSON
Assistant Director	JOHN WILSON
Sound Recording	LARRY HADSELL
	LYLE BURBRIDGE
Associate Film Editor	GEORGE FOLSEY JR.
Elvis's Wardrobe Designed by	BILL BELEW
Technical Advisor	COL. TOM PARKER

Technical Assistants	RICHARD DAVIS
	TOM DISKIN
	JOE ESPOSITO
	LAMAR FIKE
	FELTON JARVIS
	JIM O'BRIEN
	AL PACHUCKI
	BILL PORTER
	SONNY WEST
Coordinator for RCA Records	GEORGE L. PARKHILL
Musicians with Elvis	JAMES BURTON
	GLEN HARDIN
	CHARLIE HODGE
	JERRY SCHEFF
	RONNIE TUTT
	JOHN WILKINSON
Background Vocalists	MILLIE KIRKHAM
	THE SWEET INSPIRATIONS
	THE IMPERIALS
Orchestra Conductor	JOE GUERCIO

SONGS
Over Opening Credits:
1. "Mystery Train"/"Tiger Man"

In Rehearsal at MGM:
1. "Words"
2. "The Next Step Is Love"
3. "Polk Salad Annie"
4. "Crying Time"
5. "That's All Right (Mama)"
6. "Little Sister"
7. "What'd I Say"
8. "Stranger in the Crowd"
9. "How the Web Was Woven" (Elvis played the piano)
10. "I Just Can't Help Believin' "
11. "You Don't Have to Say You Love Me"

In Rehearsal with Vocal Groups:
1. "You Don't Have to Say You Love Me"
2. "Bridge Over Troubled Water"
3. "Words"

In Rehearsal at the International Hilton:
1. "You've Lost That Lovin' Feelin' "
2. "Mary in the Morning"
3. "Polk Salad Annie"

Performed at the International Hilton:
1. "That's All Right (Mama)"
2. "I've Lost You"
3. "Patch It Up"
4. "Love Me Tender"
5. "You've Lost That Lovin' Feelin' "
6. "Sweet Caroline"
7. "I Just Can't Help Believin' "
8. "Little Sister"/"Get Back"
9. "Bridge Over Troubled Water"
10. "Heartbreak Hotel"
11. "One Night"
12. "Blue Suede Shoes"
13. "All Shook Up"
14. "Polk Salad Annie"
15. "Suspicious Minds"
16. "Can't Help Falling in Love"

PRODUCTION NOTES
✓ *Elvis—That's the Way It Is* opened nationally on November 11, 1970.

(Photo courtesy Cinema Collectors)

✓ Some confusion exists as to the actual title of this documentary. The working title was *Elvis*. MGM's publicity department referred to the film after its release as *Elvis*—"That's the Way It Is." Still others call the film simply *That's the Way It Is*. We've decided to use the title *Elvis—That's the Way It Is*, since that is how most Elvis fans refer to the film.

✓ Principal photography began the second week of July 1970, during rehearsals at MGM. Shows at the International Hotel were filmed in August. Photography was completed on September 9 with the concert in Phoenix at the Veterans Memorial Coliseum.

✓ *Elvis—That's the Way It Is* was rated G by the MPAA.

✓ An advertisement for the 1969 remake of *Good-*

bye, Mr. Chips was seen on the MGM lot. The remake starred Peter O'Toole and Petula Clark.

✓ Recording stages 1 and 1A were used for rehearsals at MGM.

✓ Charlie Hodge's name was spelled "Charley" in the credits.

✓ The following celebrities were greeted as they walked into the International Hotel in the film: Juliet Prowse, Xavier Cugat, Charo, Rona Barrett, Norm Crosby, and Dale Robertson. Seen at tables in the showroom were Cary Grant and Sammy Davis Jr.

✓ An MGM production crew was sent to Luxembourg to film the Fifth Annual Elvis Presley Appreciation Society Convention. Four thousand Elvis fans attended the convention.

✓ Director Denis Sanders wrote the TV special "The Day Lincoln Was Shot," and directed several dramatic series, including "The Defenders," "Route 66," and "Naked City." He has been the recipient of two Oscars for Best Documentary: *A Time Out of War* (1954) and *Czechoslovakia, 1968* (1970).

✓ During the film, one could see a shipment of albums (RCA LSP-4399) being loaded onto a truck. This was not an Elvis album.

✓ The oldest fan waiting in line at the International Hilton was a 100-year-old lady who was ushered in to meet Elvis.

✓ *Elvis—That's the Way It Is* reached #22 on *Variety*'s weekly list of top-grossing films.

ELVIS ON TOUR

MGM, 1972. A Cinema Associates production. Running time: 93 minutes. Elvis's thirty-third film.

CREW

Producers . . . . PIERRE ADIDGE
ROBERT ABEL
Directors . . . . PIERRE ADIDGE
ROBERT ABEL
Director of Photography . . . . ROBERT THOMAS
Associate Producer . . . . SIDNEY LEVIN
Technical Advisor . . . . COL. TOM PARKER
Musicians with Elvis . . . . JAMES BURTON
CHARLIE HODGE
RONNIE TUTT
GLEN HARDIN
JERRY SCHEFF
JOHN WILKINSON
Orchestra Conducted by . . . . JOE GUERCIO
Background Vocalists . . . . KATHY WESTMORELAND
THE SWEET INSPIRATIONS
J. D. SUMNER AND THE STAMPS QUARTET
Onstage Comedian . . . . JACKIE KAHANE
Writers for Jackie Kahane . . . . BARRY ADELMAN
BARRY SILVER
Editor . . . . KEN ZEMKE
Photographed by . . . . DAVID MYERS
ERIK DAARSTAD
MICHAEL LIVESEY
JIM WILSON
DICK PEARCE
FRITZ ROLAND

(Photo courtesy Cinema Collectors)

MIKE BROWN
STEVE LARNER
DAVID STEWART
BERT SPIELVOGEL
Postproduction Coordinators..........................B. LOVITT
GLENN FARR
Additional Editing..............................BUD FRIEDGEN
HYMAN KAUFMAN
B. LOVITT
LEONARD SOUTH
YEU-BUN YEE
Montage Supervisor........................MARTIN SCORSESE
Postproduction Assistants.....................JERRY SCHILLING
PETER ROSTEN
JIM WILSON
YOSSI EICHENBAUM
MIKE HUBBERT
JIM COBLENTZ
PHILLIPPE ADIDGE
TOM WALLS
JERE HUGGINS
RANDY MORGAN

Sound Supervisor...........................JAMES E. WEBB JR.
Documentary Sound............................CAREY LINDLEY
Music Recording.................................AL PACHUCKI
Rerecording Mixers..........................LYLE BURBRIDGE
WILLIAM MCCAUGHEY
Unit Production Manager and Assistant Director.........
..........EPHRAIM (RED) SCHAFFER
Assistants to the Producers................SYLVIA MULCONERY
DAVE DRAPER
DICK ALEXANDER
Research...................................ANDREW W. SOLT
CAROLE KISMARIC
JACK GOELMAN
Assistants to Elvis.........................VERNON PRESLEY
JOE ESPOSITO
JERRY SCHILLING
SONNY WEST
RED WEST
JAMES CAUGHLEY
LAMAR FIKE
MARVIN GAMBILL
Elvis's Wardrobe Designed by......................BILL BELEW

Stage Supervision.............................TOM DISKIN
                                     TOM HENLETT
Tour Coordinators.........................JERRY WEINTRAUB
                                 GEORGE PARKHILL
Titles Designed by............................HARRY MARKS
Animation Designed by.......................CON PEDERSON

Our Special Thanks to:

Sullivan Productions, Inc., and Ed Sullivan for the TV performances of "Ready Teddy" and "Don't Be Cruel."

Scotty Moore, D. J. Fontana, and Bill Black for their instrumental backing.

The Jordanaires for their vocal backing.

Music performed by Elvis in the film may be heard on RCA Records.

SONGS

1. "Johnny B. Goode" (sung over opening credits)
2. "See See Rider"
3. "Polk Salad Annie"
4. "Separate Ways"
5. "Proud Mary"
6. "Never Been to Spain"
7. "Burning Love"
8. "Don't Be Cruel" (clip from "The Ed Sullivan Show")
9. "Ready Teddy" (clip from "The Ed Sullivan Show")
10. "That's All Right (Mama)" (Sun Records release)
11. "Lead Me, Guide Me" (with the Stamps backstage)
12. "Bosom of Abraham" (with the Stamps backstage; Charlie Hodge sang lead, Elvis sang bass)
13. "Love Me Tender"
14. "Until It's Time for You to Go"
15. "Suspicious Minds"
16. "I, John"
17. "Bridge Over Troubled Water"
18. "Funny How Time Slips Away"
19. "An American Trilogy"
20. "Mystery Train" (Sun Records release)
21. "I Got a Woman"/"Amen"
22. "A Big Hunk o' Love"
23. "You Gave Me a Mountain"
24. "Lawdy Miss Clawdy"
25. "Can't Help Falling in Love"
26. "Memories" (sung over closing credits)

Elvis sang the title to "Rainy Night in Georgia," a few lines of "For the Good Times" in a limousine with Red West and Charlie Hodge, and this line backstage: "And I'm never gonna see my wonderland." The Stamps sang "Lighthouse" and "Sweet Sweet Spirit." Joe Guercio's Orchestra played "Also Sprach Zarathustra."

PRODUCTION NOTES

✓ *Elvis on Tour* was released on November 1, 1972. In some areas the companion feature was *Elvis—That's the Way It Is.*

✓ *Elvis on Tour* focused primarily on Elvis's fifteen-city tour in April 1972. The tour began on April 5 in Buffalo, New York, and ended on April 19 in Albuquerque, New Mexico.

✓ *Elvis on Tour* was first known as *Standing Room Only*. The title was then changed during filming to *Elvis on Tour in the USA.*

✓ David Draper, one of the assistants to the producers, was a former Mr. America and Mr. Universe.

✓ The Jackie Kahane monologue at the beginning of the movie was filmed at the T. H. Barton Coliseum in San Antonio, Texas, on April 18, 1972.

✓ In Roanoke, Virginia, Elvis was given the key to the city by mayor Roy Webber (April 11, 1972).

✓ Disc jockey George Klein introduced "Suspicious Minds" while scenes of Graceland were shown.

✓ Pierre Adidge and Robert Abel had previously produced the rock documentary *Joe Cocker: Mad Dogs and Englishmen.*

✓ *Elvis on Tour* grossed $494,270 at 187 theaters in 105 cities in its first weekend of release.

✓ The Hollywood Foreign Press Association (founded in 1940) voted *Elvis on Tour* as the Best Documentary of 1972. It was the only Elvis Presley film to receive such a high honor.

✓ Noted film director Martin Scorsese worked on *Elvis on Tour* as the montage supervisor. This was before he won national acclaim for such films as *Taxi Driver* (1976) and *Raging Bull* (1979). He had previously been a co-supervising editor of *Woodstock* (1970).

✓ *Elvis on Tour* reached #13 on *Variety*'s weekly list of top-grossing films.

✓ Three weeks after Elvis's death, NBC-TV broadcast an abbreviated, sixty-minute version of *Elvis on Tour* (September 7, 1977).

Biographical Films

ELVIS

Dick Clark Motion Pictures, Inc., 1979. A Dick Clark production. Running time: 150 minutes. Air date: February 11, 1979, from 8:00 to 11:00 P.M. on ABC-TV.

CAST

Elvis Presley	KURT RUSSELL
Gladys Presley	SHELLEY WINTERS
Vernon Presley	BING RUSSELL
Red West	ROBERT GRAY
Col. Tom Parker	PAT HINGLE
Priscilla Presley	SEASON HUBLEY
Bonnie	MELODY ANDERSON
D. J. Fontana	ED BEGLEY JR.
Scotty Moore	JAMES CANNING
Sam Phillips	CHARLES CYPHERS
Jim Denny	PETER HOBBS
Sonny West	LES LANNOM
Bill Black	ELLIOTT STREET
Ed Sullivan	WILL JORDAN
Joe Esposito	JOE MANTEGNA
Hank Snow	GALEN THOMPSON
Marion Keisker	ELLEN TRAVOLTA
Natalie Wood	ABI YOUNG
Lisa Marie Presley	FELICIA FENSKE
Elvis as a Boy	RANDY GRAY
Grandma Minnie Mae Presley	MEG WYLIE
Charlie Hodge	CHARLIE HODGE
Teacher	NORA BOLAND
Larry Geller	LARRY GELLER
2nd Reporter	JIM GREENLEAF
Kathy Westmoreland	KATHY WESTMORELAND

And: Christian Berrigan, Robert Christopher, Mark Denis, Mario Gallo, Del Hinkley, Ted Lehman, Jack McCullough, Larry Pennel, Ken Smolka, David Hunt Stafford, Dennis Stewart, and Dick Young.

CREW

Executive Producer	DICK CLARK
Supervising Producer	TONY BISHOP
Producer	ANTHONY LAWRENCE
Director	JOHN CARPENTER
Screenplay	ANTHONY LAWRENCE
Director of Photography	DONALD M. MORGAN
Casting	JOYCE SELZNICK
Associate Producer	JAMES RITZ
Original Score Composed by	JOE RENZETTI
Art Directors	TRACY BOUSMAN
	JAMES NEWPORT
Supervising Editor	TOM WALLS
Editor	RON MOLER
Unit Production Manager	GEORGE SWEENEY
1st Assistant Director	LARRY FRANCO
2nd Assistant Directors	CRAIG BEAUDINE
	GLEN SANFORD
Camera Operator	JAN KIESSER
Assistant Cameramen	RICK MENTION
	ROGER GEBHARD
Assistant Editor	ROBERT D. ISRAEL
Associate Editor	RODGER PARKER
Sound Mixer	WILLIE BURTON
Boom Operators	MARVIN LEWIS
	PHIL BISHOP

Kurt Russell as Elvis. (Photo courtesy Cinema Collectors)

Gaffer	BILL TENNY
Electrical Best Boy	ROBERT FIORE
Key Grip	CAL STERRY
Grip Best Boy	TOM CONLEY
Craft Serviceman	LINN ZUCKERMAN
Set Decorator	BILL HARP
Lead Man	WILLIAM WRIGHT
Property Master	RUSS GOBLE
Assistant Property Master	RICK COWITT
Makeup	MARVIN WESTMORE
Hairstylist	RUBY FORD
Costume Supervisor	TONY FASO
Women's Costumer	SUZANNE GRACE
Men's Costumer	RICHARD MAHONEY

Script Supervisor	CAROLE WESTPHALL
Stunt Coordinator	AARON NORRIS
Location Manager	LYNN KUWAHARA
Production Coordinator	JANET LEE SMITH
Assistant to the Producer	CHERI PALMER KLUBA
Transportation Captain	DON DESMOND
Casting of Extras	EDYE RAMSEY
Auditor	FRAN SWEENEY
Production Assistants	DODY DORN
	JIMMY VAN WYCK
	DAVID BRACCI
Research	LAUREN SAND
	CHARLIE HODGE
Technical Advisors	LARRY GELLER
	BECKY YANCEY
	CLIFF LINEDECKER
Additional Consultants to the Film	DICK GROB
	THE JORDANAIRES
	MARTY LACKER
	SAM PHILLIPS
	BILLY SMITH
	KATHY WESTMORELAND
Music Editors	TED ROBERTS
	JOHN CAPER JR.
Elvis Vocals Sung by	RONNIE MCDOWELL
Elvis Vocals Produced by	FELTON JARVIS
	JAMES RITZ
Music Coordinator	FRANK CAPP
Creative Sound by	NEIMAN-TILLER ASSOCIATES
Opticals by	CINEMA RESEARCH CORP.
Editorial Services Provided by	ASPECT RATIO
Titles by	MICK HAGGERTY
	C. D. TAYLOR
Executive in Charge of Production	FRANCIS C. LA MAINA

SONGS

All songs were sung by Ronnie McDowell.

1. "Mystery Train"
2. "Good Rockin' Tonight"
3. "Old Shep"
4. "My Happiness"
5. "That's All Right (Mama)"
6. "Blue Moon of Kentucky"
7. "Lawdy Miss Clawdy"
8. "Blue Moon"
9. "Tutti Frutti"
10. "Long Tall Sally"
11. "Heartbreak Hotel"
12. "Rip It Up"
13. "Unchained Melody"
14. "(Now and Then There's) A Fool Such as I"
15. "Crying in the Chapel"
16. "Pledging My Love"
17. "Until It's Time for You to Go"
18. "Bosom of Abraham"
19. "Suspicious Minds"
20. "Are You Lonesome Tonight?"
21. "Sweet Caroline"
22. "Blue Suede Shoes"
23. "The Wonder of You"
24. "Burning Love"
25. "An American Trilogy"

PRODUCTION NOTES

✓ *Elvis* was repeated on ABC-TV on February 25, 1980.

✓ The film opened with Elvis at the International Hotel on July 26, 1969. It then flashed back to Tupelo, Mississippi, in 1945.

✓ The movie watched by Elvis on television in the Presidential Suite at the International Hotel was *The Charge at Feather River*, a 1953 3-D flick starring Guy Madison and Vera Miles.

✓ The Century Plaza Hotel in Los Angeles was used to represent the International Hotel in Las Vegas.

✓ The Jordanaires' name was misspelled in the film's credits (Jordinaires).

✓ Ronnie McDowell recorded thirty-six songs for *Elvis*, but only twenty-five were used.

✓ When *Elvis* originally aired, it was opposite two blockbuster movies: *Gone with the Wind* on CBS and *One Flew Over the Cuckoo's Nest* on NBC. Elvis defeated both in the Nielsen ratings. *Elvis* received a Nielsen rating of 27.3, *Gone With The Wind* received a 24.3 rating, and *One Flew Over the Cuckoo's Nest* trailed with a 22.5. *Elvis* was the sixth most-watched program of the week.

✓ Kurt Russell was nominated for an Emmy Award for his performance as Elvis. Also nominated for Emmy Awards were cinematographer Donald M. Morgan and makeup artist Marvin Westmore.

✓ On March 17, 1979, Kurt Russell married costar Season Hubley. They were later divorced.

✓ Ellen Travolta, who played Marion Keisker, is the sister of John Travolta.

✓ Bing Russell, who played Vernon Presley, is the father of Kurt Russell. Thus, father and son played father and son. For several years, Bing Russell played Deputy Clem Poster in the TV series "Bonanza."

✓ *Elvis* was later released theatrically in Europe and did record business at the box office.

✓ It's been reported that Priscilla Presley was paid $50,000 to check the script for accuracy.

✓ *Elvis* was in production from August 4 to December 14, 1978. The total budget was $2.1 million.

✓ Writer Tony Lawrence previously cowrote three Elvis films: *Roustabout, Paradise, Hawaiian Style,* and *Easy Come, Easy Go.*

ELVIS AND THE BEAUTY QUEEN

Columbia Pictures Television, 1981. A David Gerber production. Running time: 100 minutes. Air date: March 1, 1981, from 9:00 to 11:00 P.M. on NBC-TV.

CAST

Linda Thompson	STEPHANIE ZIMBALIST
Elvis Presley	DON JOHNSON
Jeannie LeMay	ANN DUSENBERRY
David Briggs	RICK LENZ
Aunt Betty	ANN WEDGEWORTH
Sanford Thompson	RICHARD HERD
Marge Thompson	JAY W. MCINTOSH
Su-Su	RUTA LEE
Sam Thompson	EDWARD EDWARDS
Vernon Presley	JOHN CRAWFORD
Pete Moore	DARRYL FETTY

Don Johnson as Elvis. (Photo courtesy Eddie Brandt's Saturday Matinee)

Bobby Farr	RICHARD WINTERSTEIN
Ray	GARY LEE DAVIS
Jake	JOHN ASHTON
Pregnant Woman	BOBBI JORDAN
Nurse	SUSAN MULLEN
Doctor	JOHN CHRISTY EWING
Mob Figure	TONY GIORGIO
Redhead	ODETTE MITCHELL
Agent	JOHN BERNABER
Choreographer	ANDRE TAYIR
Boxer	KEN FOREE
Bob	CARY STEIN
Miss Hawaii	CATHY FOY

CREW

Executive Producer	DAVID GERBER
Producer	CHARLES B. FITZSIMONS
Director	GUS TRIKONIS
Teleplay	JULIA CAMERON
Director of Photography	THOMAS DEL RUTH
Editor	FRED A. CHULACK
Sound	RICHARD VAN DYCK
Music	ALLYN FERGUSON
Songs Performed by	RONNIE MCDOWELL
Art Director	MICHAEL BAUGH
Associate Producer	JACK N. REDDISH
Program Consultant	LINDA THOMPSON

SONGS

All songs were sung by Ronnie McDowell.

1. "It's Only Love"
2. "The First Time Ever I Saw Your Face"
3. "A Very Precious Love"
4. "Suspicious Minds"
5. "Amazing Grace"
6. "Silent Night"
7. "Separate Ways"

PRODUCTION NOTES

✓ *Elvis and the Beauty Queen* aired opposite *Miracle on Ice* (ABC-TV) and *The Amityville Horror* (CBS-TV).

✓ The working title of *Elvis and the Beauty Queen* was *Elvis and Me*.

✓ Don Johnson gained forty pounds to portray Elvis in the film.

✓ All scenes were shot in Los Angeles.

✓ Don Johnson, who was once married to Melanie Griffith, the daughter of Tippi Hedren, made his film debut in *The Magic Garden of Stanley Sweetheart* (1970). He later starred in the 1975 cult movie, *A Boy and His Dog*. Johnson wrote two songs that appeared on the Allman Brothers' *Enlightened Rogue* album, and in 1986 reached #5 on the *Billboard* Hot 100 chart with his recording of "Heartbeat."

✓ Director Gus Trikonis was once married to Goldie Hawn. He directed Don Johnson's first film, *The Magic Garden of Stanley Sweetheart*.

✓ Stephanie Zimbalist is the daughter of actor Efrem Zimbalist Jr., and the granddaughter of concert violinist Efrem Zimbalist and singer Alma Gluck. Alma Gluck (1884–1938) was the first female to have a million-selling record—"Carry Me Back to Old Virginny" (Victor 88481) in 1915. Before *Elvis and the Beauty Queen*, Stephanie Zimbalist appeared in the *Centennial* miniseries. From 1982 to 1986 she appeared as Laura Holt in the TV series "Remington Steele."

THIS IS ELVIS

Warner Bros., 1981. A David Wolper production. Running time: 101 minutes. The expanded videotape version runs 144 minutes.

CAST

Elvis Presley	ELVIS PRESLEY
Elvis (at age ten)	PAUL BOENSH III
Elvis (at age eighteen)	DAVID SCOTT

Elvis in the Hospital...........................DANA MACKAY
Elvis (at age forty-two)........................JOHNNY HARRA
Vernon Presley..............................LAWRENCE KOLLER
Gladys Presley..................................DEBBIE EDGE
Priscilla Beaulieu Presley.......................RHONDA LYN
Dewey Phillips.............................LARRY RASPBERRY
Bluesman..FURRY LEWIS
Minnie Mae Presley............................LIZ ROBINSON
Sam Phillips..................................KNOX PHILLIPS
Linda Thompson............................CHERYL NEEDHAM
Ginger Alden..................................ANDREA CYRILL
Bill Black....................................JERRY PHILLIPS
Scotty Moore...................................EMORY SMITH
Vester Presley................................VESTER PRESLEY
Pauline Nicholson.........................PAULINE NICHOLSON
Mary Jenkins...................................MARY JENKINS
Nancy Rooks....................................NANCY ROOKS

NARRATION

Elvis Presley....................................RAL DONNER
Joe Esposito...................................JOE ESPOSITO
Linda Thompson..............................LINDA THOMPSON
Priscilla Beaulieu Presley.....................LISHA SWEETNAM
Gladys Presley................................VIRGINIA KISER
Vernon Presley.............................MICHAEL TOMACK

CREW

Executive Producer..........................DAVID L. WOLPER
Producers, Directors, Writers....................MALCOLM LEO
                                                ANDREW SOLT
Director of Photography (Additional Filming)...........GIL HUBBS
Consultants.................................JERRY SCHILLING
                                                JOE ESPOSITO
Editor..BUD FRIEDGEN
Original Music Score..........................WALTER SCHARF
Technical Advisor............................COL. TOM PARKER
Associate Producer..........................BONNIE PETERSON
Coeditor...GLENN FARR
First Assistant Editor.......................RANDY JON MORGAN
Unit Production Manager.........................LORIN SALOB
Assistant Director................................BOB STEIN
Second Assistant Director.....................JOHN WHITTLE
Postproduction Supervisor......................:BEA DENNIS
Videotape Sequences..........................BUD FRIEDGEN
                                              PHILLIP SAVENICK
Set Decoration.............................CHARLES HUGHES
Makeup...ROD WILSON
Hairstylist..................................BETTY IVERSON
Men's Costumer..................................FRANK TAUSS
Women's Costumer.............................JUDY TRUCHAN
Assistant to the Producers..................SANDRA PERLSTEIN

Paul Boensch III as Elvis, Debbie Edge as Gladys Presley. (Photo courtesy Academy of Motion Picture Arts and Sciences)

Research Coordinator...........................RON FURMANEK
Researchers..................................MICHAEL OCHS
CAROL FLEISCHER
JESSICA BERMAN
JILL HAWKINS
JANET HAYMEN
MARGARET HENRY
HAL POTTER
Production Coordinator.....................AURIEL SANDERSON
Assistant Editors...............................DONALD WYLIE
WILLIAM J. O'SULLIVAN
MARTIN NOVEMBER
PAUL ANDERSON
Negative Cutter...............................MARY NELSON
Sound Mixer.................................MIKE DENECKE
Supervising Sound Effects Mixer.................JIM BESHEARS
Rerecording Mixers............................BILL VARNEY
STEVE MASLOW
GREGG LANDAKER
Production Associates.........................ROBERT ALLEN
DONNA DAVES
IRVING KATONI
PAT O'CONNOR
ROXANNE SMITH
WESLEY VAN EATON
MARK WOLPER
Property Master...............................DON HULETT

SONGS

 1. "(Marie's the Name) His Latest Flame"
 2. "Moody Blue"
 3. "Mystery Train" (sung by David Scott)
 4. "That's All Right (Mama)" (sung by David Scott)
 5. "That's All Right (Mama)"
 6. "Shake, Rattle and Roll"/"Flip, Flop and Fly"
 7. "Heartbreak Hotel"
 8. "I Was the One"
 9. "Hound Dog"
10. "My Baby Left Me"
11. "Love Me Tender"
12. "Merry Christmas Baby"
13. "Mean Woman Blues"
14. "Trouble"
15. "Ready Teddy"
16. "Don't Be Cruel"
17. "(Let Me Be Your) Teddy Bear"
18. "King Creole"
19. "As Long as I Have You"
20. "Jailhouse Rock"
21. "G. I. Blues"
22. "Frankfort Special"
23. "Stuck on You"
24. "Witchcraft"/"Love Me Tender" ending
25. "Blue Hawaii"
26. "Rock-a-Hula Baby"
27. "Too Much Monkey Business"
28. "King of the Whole Wide World"
29. "I've Got a Thing About You, Baby"
30. "I Need Your Love Tonight"
    "Trouble" (second time)
31. "Guitar Man"
32. "Let Yourself Go"
33. "Blue Suede Shoes"
34. "If I Can Dream"
35. "Viva Las Vegas"
36. "Suspicious Minds"
37. "What a Friend We Have in Jesus" (one line)

Mary Jenkins and Johnny Harra as Elvis. (Photo courtesy Eddie Brandt's Saturday Matinee)

38. "Promised Land"
39. "A Big Hunk o' Love"
40. "Can't Help Falling in Love"
41. "Rainy Night in Georgia" (one line)
42. "Always on My Mind"
43. "Are You Lonesome Tonight?"
44. "Love Me"
45. "My Way"
46. "An American Trilogy"
47. "Memories"

Other recordings heard on the soundtrack were "I'll Fly Away" (by Albert Brumley), "Furry Lewis' Blues" (by Furry Lewis), "Sixty Minute Man" (by the Dominoes), "Rocket 88" (by Jackie Brenston), "I Want to Hold Your Hand" (by the Beatles), and "Kung Fu Fighting" (by Carl Douglas).

PRODUCTION NOTES

✓ *This Is Elvis* had a press premiere in Memphis at the Memphian Theater on April 3, 1981. The world premiere was held in Dallas the next day at the USA Film Festival. The film went into general release at 310 theaters in the South on April 10.

✓ Production started on *This Is Elvis* in May 1980. The total budget for the film was just over $5 million.

✓ The working title of *This Is Elvis* was *The Life of Elvis Presley.*

✓ In 1977, at the age of 14, David Scott won an Elvis Presley contest in his native Montreal, singing "Teddy Bear." He did his own singing in *This Is Elvis* on "Mystery Train" and "That's All Right (Mama)."

✓ Before *This Is Elvis*, executive producer David L. Wolper had won 30 Emmy Awards out of 102 nominations and one Oscar out of 11 nominations.

✓ Sam Phillips was played by his son, Knox Phillips. Vester Presley and three Graceland workers, Pauline Nicholson, Mary Jenkins, and Nancy Rooks, played themselves.

✓ The mother of Paul Boensh III, Jean Boyd, was once a nurse-companion to Elvis's grandmother, Minnie Mae Presley. In 1970 she took two-and-a-half year-old Paul to meet Elvis. Elvis remarked how much the boy looked like him. Eleven years later Paul portrayed Elvis as a boy in *This Is Elvis*.

✓ Producers Andrew Solt and Malcolm Leo had previously produced the highly acclaimed ABC-TV special "Heroes of Rock 'n' Roll," which was telecast two days before the Dick Clark production of *Elvis*.

✓ Elvis impersonator Johnny Harra named his daughter Lisa Marie after Elvis's daughter.

✓ The expanded version of *This Is Elvis* (the one that's available on videocassette) incorporated forty-three minutes of unused footage, including Dolores Hart's home movies taken with the movie camera Elvis bought her for her twenty-first birthday and some of Priscilla Presley's home movie footage.

✓ The opening scenes of *This Is Elvis* took place in Portland, Maine, at the Cumberland County Civic Center, on August 16, 1977. Workers were shown preparing for Elvis's next concert, the first on his upcoming tour. It was the day Elvis died.

✓ *This Is Elvis* perpetuated the myth that Elvis's first four-dollar demo record was made for his mother's birthday. Her birthday was on April 25; the record was made sometime in the late summer.

✓ Another blooper (among several) in the film was when the young Elvis (played by David Scott) sang "Mystery Train" in front of his high school class. Narrator Elvis (Ral Donner) said that he "performed an old rhythm and blues song I'd been practicing." Actually, "Mystery Train" wasn't written until a few months after the scene took place in 1953.

ELVIS AND ME
New World Television, 1988. A New World Television production. Air dates: February 7 and 8, 1988, from 9:00 to 11:00 P.M. on ABC-TV.

CAST
Priscilla Beaulieu Presley.....................SUSAN WALTERS
Elvis Presley.....................DALE MIDKIFF
Ann Beaulieu.....................LINDA MILLER
Joseph Paul Beaulieu.....................JON CYPHER
Vernon Presley.....................BILLY GREENBUSH
Grandma Minnie Mae Presley.....................ANNE HANEY
Rick Colton.....................MARSHALL TEAGUE
Col. Tom Parker.....................HUGH GILLIN
Jerry Schilling.....................MARK THOMAS MILLER
Michelle Beaulieu (at age five).....................KRISTIN HOLSTROM
Don Beaulieu (at age ten).....................ELDEN RATLIFF
Don Beaulieu (at age thirteen).....................ERICK RATLIFF
Pam Rutherford.....................MARIA CLAIRE
Lisa Marie Presley (at age four).....................SARAH MARTINECK
Matt.....................CHRIS UFLAND
Currie Grant.....................GREG WEBB
Carole Grant.....................ALICE CADOGAN
Demont.....................KEN GIBBEL
Dee Stanley.....................CYNTHIA HARRISON
Joe Esposito.....................WAYNE POWERS
English Girl.....................LISA STAHL
Linda.....................HOLLY SUSAN DORFF
German Nurse.....................ILONA WILSON
Alberta.....................VIVIAN BONNELL
Tully.....................GRETA BROWN
Director.....................JAY GOLDENBERG
Saleslady.....................DOROTHY GORDON
Hattie.....................LYNN HAMILTON
Principal.....................ALAN BROWN
Woman Reporter.....................DANI NOLAN
German Reporter.....................PETER FRANKLAND
Hotel Stage Manager.....................BRUCE BANKE
Screaming Fan.....................AMY GREENSPUN
Reporters.....................BRIAN GREENSPUN
CHRISTOPHER URSITTI
RAY NADEAU
JEFF LEVINSON
ROGER ROOK
Child.....................JESSICA PUSCAS
Jimmy.....................J. CHRISTOPHER SULLIVAN
Gene.....................CODY HAMPTON
Patsy Gambill.....................LINDA DONA
Mother Superior.....................ELIZABETH HOFFMAN
Billy.....................KIMBERLY MCARTHUR
Assistant Director.....................MICHAEL HERZOG
Stage Manager.....................RENO NICHOLS
Dance Double for Dale Midkiff.....................TONY ROI

CREW
Executive Producers.....................PRISCILLA BEAULIEU PRESLEY
BERNARD SCHWARTZ
JOEL STEVENS
Producer.....................BOB LOVENHEIM
Director.....................LARRY PEERCE
Teleplay.....................JOYCE ELIASON
Director of Photography.....................GIDEON PORATH
Additional Photography.....................PETER STEIN
Technical Adviser.....................JERRY SCHILLING
Supervising Film Editor.....................ERIC SEARS
Film Editors.....................MICHAEL RIPPS
ROBERT F. SHUGRUE
Set Decoration.....................DEBRA COMBS
Art Direction.....................BILL POMEROY
Makeup.....................CLAUDIA THOMPSON
Makeup Assistant.....................ROBIN BEAUCHESNE
Hairstylist.....................RUSSEL L. SMITH
Assistant Hairstylist.....................JASON SICA
Costumes Designed by.....................JUDY TRUCHMAN
Costume Supervisor.....................DON VARGAS
Music Composed by.....................RICHARD STONE
Musical Supervisor.....................STEVE (GOLDE) GOLDSTEIN
Music Coordinator.....................VANESSA HAYES
All Elvis Songs Sung by.....................RONNIE MCDOWELL
All Elvis Songs Produced by.....................STEVE (GOLDE) GOLDSTEIN
Production Manager.....................LYNN GUTHRIE
First Assistant Director.....................JEROME M. SIEGEL
Second Assistant Director.....................JOHN WHITTLE
Second Second Assistant Director.....................BARBARA FARKUS
Documentary Editor.....................SUSAN HEICK
Editor.....................JOHN W. CARR
First Assistant Editor.....................RICHARD C. LEEMAN
Assistant Editors.....................ROBERT HERNANDEZ
URSULA HOELLER
JUDY REIDEL
NICOLE SHUGRUE
Apprentice Editor.....................LUCAS REINER
Film Researcher.....................BENJAMIN RAPOPORT
Set Dresser.....................SUSAN ESCHELBACH
Leadman.....................PAUL FORD
Property Master.....................IAN SCHEIBEL
Assistant Property Master.....................RANDALL WEIGHTMAN

Dale Midkiff as Elvis. (Photo courtesy New World International)

Construction Coordinator	JEFF GARRETT
Script Supervisor	MELANIE MANDER
Production Coordinator	LESLIE CHAPMAN
Assistant Coordinators	JOY EVERY
	NIKA CAVAT
Production Auditor	NANCY RAMEY
Assistant Auditors	BARBARA GUTMAN
	SCOTT SCHIFFMAN
	MARLA BLOOM
Dialogue Coach	J. R. GOLDENBERG
Production Designers	BRYAN RYMAN
	SHAY AUSTIN
Presley Home Movie Research	JEFF BEAULIEU

SONGS

All songs were sung by Ronnie McDowell.

1. "Baby, Let's Play House"
2. "Blue Moon"
3. "Blue Suede Shoes"
   "Blue Moon" (second time)
4. "Great Balls of Fire"
5. "Are You Lonesome Tonight?"
6. "Amazing Grace"
7. "Lawdy, Miss Clawdy"
8. "Love Me"
9. "Don't"

Susan Walters as Priscilla Presley. (Photo courtesy New World International)

"Baby, Let's Play House" (second time)
10. "Stuck on You"
11. "Suspicious Minds"
12. "Return to Sender"
13. "That's All Right (Mama)"
14. "Can't Help Falling in Love"
15. "See See Rider"

"Are You Lonesome Tonight?" (second time)
16. "Always on My Mind"
17. "How Great Thou Art" was used briefly to lead into commercials.

PRODUCTION NOTES

✓ Part I of *Elvis and Me* aired on Sunday night, February 7, 1988, from 9:00 to 11:00 P.M. It won its time slot with a 23.9 rating and a 35 share. Part I of *Sidney Sheldon's "Windmills of the Gods"* on CBS scored a 19.0 rating and a 28 share. *Rambo: First Blood, Part II* on NBC had a rating of 15.5 and a 23 share. Part I of *Elvis and Me* was the fifth most-watched program of the week. Part II did even better in the ratings, receiving a 24.9 rating and 36 share. It was ranked #3 for the week. The competition for Part II was "Designing Women," "Newhart," and "Wiseguy" on CBS. NBC had the made-for-TV movie *Moving Target*, which starred Jason Bateman and Jack Wagner. *Elvis and Me* was the highest-rated TV movie of the 1987–88 television season. Part I was seen by 32,400,000 viewers; Part II by 31,400,000.

✓ The early scenes in West Germany were actually filmed in Quebec City, Quebec. Shooting in Quebec was cut short when the Canadian Forces Army base refused to allow filming in its residential section. Other locations used were Graceland, Las Vegas, and Los Angeles.

✓ The total production budget for *Elvis and Me* was $8 million.

✓ Dale Midkiff's first feature film was *Streetwalkin'* (1984). His other major credit was playing the young Jock Ewing in the 1986 TV movie *Dallas: The Early Years*.

✓ Susan Walters made her film debut in *Russkies* (1987). She has had a recurring role as reservation clerk Ryan Thomas in the ABC-TV series "Hotel," and was a regular in the daytime drama "Loving," as Lorna Forbes.

✓ Director Larry Peerce is the son of tenor Jan Peerce.

✓ Both Dale Midkiff and Susan Walters are from Maryland.

Unrealized Projects

Through the years, Elvis was offered a number of film projects, but for one reason or another the movie didn't get made or someone else got the part. Many times Elvis didn't get the role because of Colonel Parker's uncompromising financial demands. A classic case in point was the 1976 version of *A Star Is Born* for which Barbra Streisand wanted Elvis as her costar. What follows is a list of these unrealized projects. Who knows? If Elvis had had a chance to do some good straight dramatic roles, supported by solid writing, his talent may have blossomed to such an extent that he would have been recognized as an equal among his colleagues in the acting profession.

THE RAINMAKER (1956)
Part of Elvis's screen test for Hal B. Wallis was a scene from the unproduced Paramount film. Elvis played the role of Jimmy Curry in the test. In an interview, he erroneously said that *The Rainmaker* was going to be his movie debut. When the film was eventually made, Burt Lancaster and Katharine Hepburn played the lead roles. The role of Jimmy Curry went to Earl Holliman. Yvonne Lime played Curry's girlfriend, Snooky McGuire. Lime, of course, later appeared with Elvis on the screen.

THE GIRL CAN'T HELP IT (1956)
Little Richard recorded the title song to this film on Specialty Records (Specialty 591). *The Girl Can't Help It* was the first rock & roll movie to be filmed in color. In addition to Little Richard, the other musical stars included Fats Domino, Julie London, Eddie Cochran, Gene Vincent, the Platters, and Ray Anthony. Actors Tom Ewell, Jayne Mansfield, and Edmond O'Brien headed the cast. Twentieth Century–Fox wanted Elvis for the film, but when Colonel Parker asked for $50,000 for Elvis to sing just one song, Fox felt it could do quite well without him.

THE WAY TO THE GOLD (1957)
In late November 1956, Twentieth Century–Fox, based on the response to the just released *Love Me Tender*, offered Elvis $150,000 against 50 percent of the profits to star in *The Way to the Gold*. The start-up date was set for December 17, 1956, and Fox was willing to give Elvis ten days off for Christmas if he'd do the film. Colonel Parker wanted $250,000 against 50 percent of the profits. Fox declined the counteroffer and the film was eventually made with Jeffrey Hunter, Sheree North, and Neville Brand.

THE SINGING IDOL (1957)
NBC-TV's "Kraft Television Theatre" broadcast this play on January 30, 1957, with Tommy Sands playing an Elvis-type character named Ewell Walker. Sands sang "Hep Dee Hootie" and "Teen-Age Crush," which went on to become a million-selling record. "The Singing Idol" was later made into the 1958 movie *Sing, Boy,*

Sing, also starring Tommy Sands. Elvis was originally asked to play the lead in "The Singing Idol," but turned it down. Since the play was telecast in color, it would have been Elvis's first color TV appearance.

THE JAMES DEAN STORY (1957)
Directed by George W. George and Robert Altman, and narrated by Martin Gabel, *The James Dean Story* was a documentary that used readily available film footage of the late movie star. The film was originally to have been a biography, with Elvis wanting desperately to play Dean. However, Warner Bros. decided to make a documentary instead.

THE LOVE MANIAC (1957)
Elvis and Jayne Mansfield were wanted by Twentieth Century–Fox for this project. However, *The Love Maniac*, which was to have been a comedy, was never made.

THE CALLIOPE TRAIL (1957)
It's not known whether *The Calliope Trail* was the working title of a film later made by a studio or a proposed project that was never filmed. In any case, Elvis was under consideration to star in it.

THE DEFIANT ONES (1958)
Reportedly, Elvis was first offered the role of John (Joker) Jackson in this Stanley Kramer–directed film. Tony Curtis, one of Elvis's favorite actors, was later given the role. *The Defiant Ones*, which won an Oscar for Best Screenplay, was the last screen appearance of Our Gang's Carl (Alfalfa) Switzer.

THUNDER ROAD (1958)
Perhaps the definitive film on moonshining, *Thunder Road* starred Robert Mitchum, Gene Barry, and Mitchum's son, James, as the brother of Mitchum's character, in his debut. The film's theme song, "The Ballad of Thunder Road" (Capitol 3986), was composed and recorded by Robert Mitchum. It reached #62 on *Billboard*'s Hot 100 chart. The lead role in *Thunder Road* was first offered to Elvis, according to some reports. Still other accounts have Elvis being offered a supporting role.

WEST SIDE STORY (1961)
United Artists and producer Robert Wise reportedly wanted Elvis, Paul Anka, Fabian, Bobby Darin, and Frankie Avalon to play members of the two gangs, the Jets and the Sharks, in *West Side Story*. One can only imagine what a lead role in the Best Picture of 1961 would have done for Elvis's acting career.

TOO LATE BLUES (1962)
Bobby Darin starred in this John Cassavetes–directed film as a jazz musician in love with a selfish girl, played by Stella Stevens. The lead role of John Wakefield was first offered to Elvis.

SWEET BIRD OF YOUTH (1962)

Elvis was offered the lead role of Chance Wayne in *Sweet Bird of Youth*, which was based on the Tennessee Williams play. But because Elvis would have been playing a "bad guy," Colonel Parker turned down the offer, allowing Paul Newman to win the part. Ed Begley won an Oscar for Best Supporting Actor for his performance as Boss Finley.

BYE BYE BIRDIE (1963)

Jesse Pearson had the title role of Conrad Birdie, an Elvis-like rock & roll idol. Also starring in *Bye Bye Birdie* were Janet Leigh, Dick Van Dyke, and Ann-Margret. Elvis was requested to sing two songs in the film, but Colonel Parker vetoed the idea. *Bye Bye Birdie* was based on the highly successful Broadway play of 1960.

YOUR CHEATIN' HEART (1964)

George Hamilton played country singing legend Hank Williams in this biography of the late singer. Williams's son, Hank Williams Jr., recorded the soundtrack for the film. Elvis was under consideration for the lead role, but Williams's widow, Audrey, was afraid that Elvis, rather than her late husband, would become the focal point of *Your Cheatin' Heart*.

THE FASTEST GUITAR ALIVE (1968)

Elvis was asked to star in *The Fastest Guitar Alive*, but Colonel Parker said no. Instead, Roy Orbison and Sammy Jackson starred in the film, which was about Confederate spies.

MIDNIGHT COWBOY (1969)

Midnight Cowboy is the only X-rated movie ever to win an Oscar for Best Picture. The rating, however, was later reduced to R. The role of Joe Buck, played by Jon Voight, was first offered to Elvis. One can only imagine how Elvis's fans would have reacted to him playing a seedy character in an X-rated film. Bob Dylan originally composed "Lay Lady Lay" for *Midnight Cowboy*, but Harry Nilsson's "Everybody's Talking" was chosen instead.

THE NEW GLADIATORS (1974)

Produced by George Waite, *The New Gladiators* was a karate documentary that was never completed. Elvis provided the financial backing for the film and was its narrator.

CIAO RUDY (1975)

On July 17, 1975, columnist Maggie Daly announced that Elvis was slated to portray silent-screen great Rudolph Valentino in a Broadway play to be titled *Ciao Rudy*. A movie version of the play was supposedly also in the works. For his efforts, Elvis was to have received $2.5 million.

A STAR IS BORN (1976)

A Star Is Born has been filmed on four occasions: *What Price Hollywood?* (1932), with Constance Bennett and Neil Hamilton; *A Star Is Born* (1937), with Janet Gaynor and Fredric March; *A Star Is Born* (1954), with Judy Garland and James Mason; and *A Star Is Born* (1976), with Barbra Streisand and Kris Kristofferson. It was in this last version that Barbra Streisand wanted to costar with Elvis, in what may have been his finest screen role to date. But an agreement couldn't be reached with Colonel Parker, who wanted one million dollars plus top billing for Elvis, rather than to settle for a percentage of the movie's gross. Kenny Loggins also turned down the male role.

The original inspiration for the screenplay for *What Price Hollywood?* was the marriage of actor John McCormick and starlet Colleen Moore.

BILLY EASTER (1977)

At the time of Elvis's death, a screenplay for *Billy Easter* was in preparation. It was to have been financed by Elvis and would have been a nonsinging role.

THE KING OF ROCK 'N' ROLL (1979)

It was rumored in 1979 that Sol Swimmer, Pete Bennett, and Bill Cash were going to produce *The King of Rock 'n' Roll* with a screenplay written by George Klein. To date, the $10 million project has remained unproduced. Reportedly, considered for the role of Elvis were John Travolta, Lee Majors, Kris Kristofferson, and Warren Beatty. Van Johnson was offered the role of Vernon Presley.

Elvis-Related Films

Elvis Presley had some connection with the following films, for one reason or another. His life may have been the inspiration for the screenplay, or a character in the film, or, in some cases, his name was simply mentioned in the dialogue. As this list is by no means exhaustive, the authors would be interested in receiving additional entries from readers.

BABY, THE RAIN MUST FALL (1965)
Movie made in 1965 in which Steve McQueen played ex-con Henry Thomas, who headed a band called the Rockabillies. (Glen Campbell was an uncredited member.) In the film McQueen remarks to his wife, played by Lee Remick, "Maybe I'll be a big movie star like Elvis Presley."

THE BUDDY HOLLY STORY (1978)
Elvis was mentioned in the dialogue of this screen biography of early rock & roller Buddy Holly. Starring Gary Busey as Holly, *The Buddy Holly Story* won an Oscar for Score Adaptation.

BYE BYE BIRDIE (1963)
The lead character in *Bye Bye Birdie* was rock & roll star Conrad Birdie (played by Jesse Pearson). Conrad Birdie (a takeoff on Conway Twitty's name) was based loosely on Elvis. As a matter of fact, the producers wanted Elvis to sing a couple of tunes in the film, but Colonel Parker vetoed the idea. *Bye Bye Birdie* was based on the popular 1960 Broadway play of the same title.

CHEECH & CHONG'S NEXT MOVIE (1980)
Cheech Marin did an impression of Elvis singing "Love Me" in this follow-up to 1978's *Up in Smoke*, the comedy team's film debut.

DINER (1982)
A Baltimore diner provided the setting for this nostalgic look at growing up in the 1950s. A recording of Elvis's "Don't Be Cruel" was played on the film's soundtrack.

ELVIS! ELVIS! (1977)
This Swedish film was based on a series of stories by Maria Gripe about a real Swedish boy named Elvis Karlsson. His mother was a very devoted Presley fan who named her son after the "King of Rock & Roll." The story revolved around Elvis Karlsson's struggles at the age of seven to be understood by his parents. Lele Dorazio played Elvis, Lena-Pia Bernhardsson played his mother, and Fred Gunnarsson played Elvis's father.

THE FAMILY WAY (1966)
Paul McCartney scored this British film that starred Hayley Mills and her father, John Mills. In the movie, the Elvis album *His Hand in Mine* could be seen in Jenny Piper's (Mills) dressing room.

THE GIANT GILA MONSTER (1959)
In this typical 1950s monster flick, disc jockey Steamboat Smith asked the kids at a dance who the singer of a record was. One of the incorrect guesses was "Elvis."

GREASE (1978)
While Stockard Channing was singing "Look at Me, I'm Sandra Dee," Elvis's name was mentioned and his photo was seen. In the same film, the group Sha Na Na (as Johnny Casino and the Gamblers) sang "Hound Dog."

HEAVEN HELP US (1985)
This made-for-cable-TV movie starred Andrew McCarthy, Kevin Dillon, and Donald Sutherland. Elvis's "Blue Suede Shoes" could be heard over the closing credits. *Heaven Help Us* first aired over the Home Box Office cable network.

HOLLYWOOD OR BUST (1956)
This was the last film made by the comedy team of Dean Martin and Jerry Lewis. In one scene, a billboard advertising Elvis's appearances at the New Frontier Hotel could be seen in the background.

THE IDOLMAKER (1980)
Elvis was mentioned in this fictionalized biography of rock producer Bob Marcucci. Marcucci guided the careers of many rock & roll stars in the 1950s, including Fabian and Frankie Avalon.

INTO THE NIGHT (1985)
This John Landis–directed film featured an Elvis impersonator who drove a white 1959 Cadillac with "The King Lives" on the side. Singer Carl Perkins played a hood in the film, and a copy of the book, *Elvis—What Happened?*, could be seen. Don Siegel, who directed Elvis in *Flaming Star*, played a cameo role as did singer David Bowie and a number of Hollywood directors.

LETHAL WEAPON (1987)
Elvis's "I'll Be Home for Christmas" could be heard briefly over the closing credits of this Mel Gibson action film.

LET'S MAKE LOVE (1960)
Marilyn Monroe made her second-to-last film appearance in this George Cukor–directed musical comedy. In the film, Monroe, Yves Montand, and Frankie Vaughan sing "Specialization," which mentions Elvis and Colonel Parker in the lyrics.

LI'L ABNER (1959)
This musical film was based on the successful Broadway play version of Al Capp's comic strip. One of the characters referred to a girl by saying, "She could make Elvis Presley stand still."

LIVING LEGEND (1980)
Producer Earl Owensby played the lead role of Eli Canfield in this loose biography of Elvis Presley. Elvis's last girlfriend, Ginger Alden, played Jeannie Loring, Canfield's female companion. Roy Orbison provided the musical soundtrack for Owensby's lip-syncing. Other roles in the film were played by William T. Hicks

(as Jim Cannon), Jerry Rushing (as Chad), Greg Carswell (as Teddy), Toby Wallace (as Dean), and Kristina Reynolds (as Susan).

MELVIN AND HOWARD (1980)
Based on the story of Melvin Dummar, who produced a will after Howard Hughes's death naming Dummar the recipient of Hughes's wealth. *Melvin and Howard* won Oscars for Best Supporting Actress (Mary Steenburgen) and Best Screenplay (Bo Goldman). In the film, Dummar mentioned "Love Me Tender" and "Don't Be Cruel."

MISCHIEF (1985)
"Don't Be Cruel" could be heard on the film's soundtrack. *Mischief* starred Doug McKeon and Kelly Preston.

ONE TRICK PONY (1980)
Elvis was referred to on three different occasions in this Paul Simon film. Simon scripted the movie and wrote the musical score.

THE PARENT TRAP (1961)
Pictures of Elvis adorned the summer-camp of the twins, played by Hayley Mills.

THE REAL BUDDY HOLLY STORY (1986)
Paul McCartney hosted this BBC-produced documentary on Buddy Holly. Included in the film was color footage of Elvis performing in Lubbock, Texas—possibly on June 3, 1955. The videocassette box claims that this is the earliest-known film footage of Elvis.

ROCK, ROCK, ROCK (1956)
Tuesday Weld made her film debut in this early rock & roll extravaganza. She mentioned Elvis in the dialogue.

ROME ADVENTURE (1962)
Elvis's name was mentioned by Pamela Austin, who two years later appeared with Elvis in *Kissin' Cousins*. Costars Troy Donahue and Suzanne Pleshette married shortly after making *Rome Adventure*.

SAME TIME, NEXT YEAR (1978)
Alan Alda and Ellen Burstyn starred in this drama about a once-a-year weekend romance that spanned a period of twenty-six years. Numerous black and white still photos were shown throughout *Same Time, Next Year* to indicate the passing of time. One photo was of Elvis at a concert performance.

SING, BOY, SING (1958)
Tommy Sands reprised the role he first played in "The Singing Idol," a "Kraft Television Theatre" presentation. The movie, like the teleplay, was loosely based on Elvis. The producers wanted Elvis to sing two songs in *Sing, Boy, Sing*, but Colonel Parker vetoed the idea.

SPACE SHIP SAPPY (1956)
Elvis's name was mentioned in this Three Stooges short. The boys took a spaceship to Venus, where they met three vampiristic Amazons who spoke unintelligible gibberish. Moe said, "Dig that rock and roll dialogue!" Larry replied, "They must have heard Elvis Presley!"

THAT'LL BE THE DAY (1974)
David Essex, Ringo Starr, Billy Fury, and Keith Moon starred in this British production about the early life of a rock & roll star. Elvis's name was mentioned in the dialogue and several photographs of him could be seen.

TIN MEN (1987)
Barry Levinson, who five years earlier directed *Diner*, wrote and directed this Richard Dreyfuss–Danny DeVito comedy. Both films were set in Baltimore diners. Elvis's "(Marie's the Name) His Latest Flame" was heard on the film's soundtrack.

TOUCHED BY LOVE (1980)
Touched by Love was based on Lena Canada's book, *To Elvis, with Love*, which was the working title of the film. Lena Canada was a nurse who befriended a cerebral palsy victim named Karen. To get Karen to come out of her shell, Canada encouraged her to write a letter to her idol, Elvis Presley. Karen and Elvis were pen pals until her death at the age of ten in 1963.

Diane Lane, Deborah Raffin. (Photo courtesy Eddie Brandt's Saturday Matinee)

Deborah Raffin portrayed Lena Canada in *Touched by Love*; Karen was portrayed by Diane Lane. Other cast members included Michael Learned in her feature film debut (as Dr. Bell), John Amos (as Tony), Christina Raines (as Amy), Mary Wickes (as Margaret), Clu Gulager (as Don Fielder), and Twyla Volkins (as Monica). Deborah Raffin received a Golden Globe nomination for her performance.

Clips from "The Ed Sullivan Show" of Elvis singing "Love Me Tender" and "Ready Teddy" were used in the film. Alan, an Elvis impersonator, sang "Don't Be Cruel," "Teddy Bear," "Love Me Tender," "Hound Dog," and "I Was the One."

WILL SUCCESS SPOIL ROCK HUNTER? (1957)
Tony Randall remarked in the dialogue that *Love Me Tender* was going to be remade. *Will Success Spoil Rock Hunter?* was written and directed by Frank Tashlin.

Movie Miscellanea

★ Elvis made three films in black and white:
1. *Love Me Tender*
2. *Jailhouse Rock*
3. *King Creole*

★ Elvis Presley films grossed a reported $150 million at the box office.

★ Colonel Tom Parker, as most Elvis fans know, was listed as the technical advisor in most Elvis films. These are the nine films in which he was not listed in the credits as the technical advisor:
1. *Wild in the Country*
2. *Viva Las Vegas*
3. *Frankie and Johnny*
4. *Stay Away, Joe*
5. *Speedway*
6. *Live a Little, Love a Little*
7. *Charro!*
8. *The Trouble with Girls*
9. *Change of Habit*

★ In two films, Elvis's female costar lost her bikini top while swimming in the ocean: *Blue Hawaii* (Joan Blackman) and *Clambake* (Shelley Fabares).

★ Norman Taurog directed nine Elvis films:
1. *G. I. Blues*
2. *Blue Hawaii*
3. *Girls! Girls! Girls!*
4. *It Happened at the World's Fair*
5. *Tickle Me*
6. *Spinout*
7. *Double Trouble*
8. *Speedway*
9. *Live a Little, Love a Little*

★ Hawaii was the setting for three Elvis films:
1. *Blue Hawaii*
2. *Girls! Girls! Girls!*
3. *Paradise, Hawaiian Style*

★ Elvis wore a beard in only one film: *Charro!*

★ Beginning in 1941, the *Motion Picture Herald-Fame* released a poll of film exhibitors that was called the "Stars of Tomorrow." That first year, Laraine Day barely beat out Rita Hayworth for the top spot. Elvis appeared on the list in 1957 at the #7 spot.
1. Anthony Perkins
2. Sophia Loren
3. Jayne Mansfield
4. Don Murray
5. Carroll Baker
6. Martha Hyer
7. ELVIS PRESLEY
8. Anita Ekberg
9. Paul Newman
10. John Kerr

★ Performers who have appeared in four or more Elvis films:
1. Red West—14 films
2. Joe Esposito—6 films
3. Richard J. Reeves—5 films
4. Ken Becker—4 films
5. George Cisar—4 films

★ Vernon Presley appeared in two of his son's films:
1. *Loving You*
2. *Live a Little, Love a Little*

★ A number of performers made their screen debuts in an Elvis Presley film. Here is the list (movie by movie):
1. Dolores Hart (*Loving You*)
2. Scotty Moore (*Loving You*)
3. Bill Black (*Loving You*)
4. D. J. Fontana (*Loving You*)
5. Vernon Presley (*Loving You*)
6. Gladys Presley (*Loving You*)
7. The Jordanaires (*Loving You*)
8. Jennifer Holden (*Jailhouse Rock*)
9. Leticia Roman (*G. I. Blues*)
10. Sigrid Maier (*G. I. Blues*)
11. Priscilla Taurog (*G. I. Blues*)
12. Kerry Charles and Terry Earl Ray (*G. I. Blues*)
13. David Paul and Donald James Rankin (*G. I. Blues*)
14. Donald Clark and David Clark Wise (*G. I. Blues*)
15. Christina Crawford (*Wild in the Country*)
16. Flora K. Hayes (*Blue Hawaii*)
17. Gavin and Robin Koon (*Follow That Dream*)
18. Orlando de la Fuente (*Kid Galahad*)
19. Ed Asner (*Kid Galahad*)
20. Laurel Goodwin (*Girls! Girls! Girls!*)
21. Vicky Tiu (*It Happened at the World's Fair*)
22. Raquel Welch (*Roustabout*)
23. Annette Day (*Double Trouble*)
24. Susan Trustman (*Stay Away, Joe*)
25. Patti Jean Keith (*Speedway*)
26. Ross Hagen (*Speedway*)
27. Ursula Menzel (*Live a Little, Love a Little*)
28. Lynn Kellogg (*Charro!*)
29. Marlyn Mason (*The Trouble with Girls*)
30. Nicole Jaffe (*The Trouble with Girls*)
31. Anissa Jones (*The Trouble with Girls*)
32. Pepe Brown (*The Trouble with Girls*)
33. Jane Elliot (*Change of Habit*)

★ Conversely, a dozen performers made their last screen appearances in an Elvis film:
1. Judy Tyler (*Jailhouse Rock*)
2. Ludwig Stossel (*G. I. Blues*)
3. Jason Robards Sr. (*Wild in the Country*)
4. Philip Reed (*Harum Scarum*)
5. Carl Betz (*Spinout*)
6. Una Merkel (*Spinout*)
7. Frederic Worlock (*Spinout*)
8. Frank McHugh (*Easy Come, Easy Go*)
9. Hal Peary (*Clambake*)
10. Richard Carlson (*Change of Habit*)
11. Ruth McDevitt (*Change of Habit*)
12. Elvis Presley (*Change of Habit*) (last acting appearance)

★ Elvis twice played characters with the last name Carpenter. In *Girls! Girls! Girls!* he played Ross Carpenter. Dr. John Carpenter was his role in *Change of Habit*.

★ In December 1977, Rob-Rich Films acquired theatrical rights to *Girls! Girls! Girls!*, *G. I. Blues*, *Fun in Acapulco*, *Paradise, Hawaiian Style*, *Roustabout*, *Blue Hawaii*, and *King Creole*. Owner Sidney Ginsberg packaged the films as an Elvis movie festival to be shown one film a day for a week. Ginsberg's festival opened at the Beacon Theatre in New York City on December 26, 1977, and then moved on to Memphis, Dallas, and Oklahoma City.

★ Elvis was listed in the theater owners' Money-Making Stars poll seven times. His highest ranking was #4 in 1957. Here are the complete lists of those seven polls.

1957
1. Rock Hudson
2. John Wayne
3. Pat Boone
4. ELVIS PRESLEY
5. Frank Sinatra
6. Gary Cooper
7. William Holden
8. James Stewart
9. Jerry Lewis
10. Yul Brynner

1961
1. Elizabeth Taylor
2. Rock Hudson
3. Doris Day
4. John Wayne
5. Cary Grant
6. Sandra Dee
7. Jerry Lewis
8. William Holden
9. Tony Curtis
10. ELVIS PRESLEY

1962
1. Doris Day
2. Rock Hudson
3. Cary Grant
4. John Wayne
5. ELVIS PRESLEY
6. Elizabeth Taylor
7. Jerry Lewis
8. Frank Sinatra
9. Sandra Dee
10. Burt Lancaster

1963
1. Doris Day
2. John Wayne
3. Rock Hudson
4. Jack Lemmon
5. Cary Grant

6. Elizabeth Taylor
7. ELVIS PRESLEY
8. Sandra Dee
9. Paul Newman
10. Richard Burton

1964
1. Doris Day
2. Jack Lemmon
3. Rock Hudson
4. John Wayne
5. Cary Grant
6. ELVIS PRESLEY
7. Shirley MacLaine
8. Ann-Margret
9. Paul Newman
10. Richard Burton

1965
1. Sean Connery
2. John Wayne
3. Doris Day
4. Julie Andrews
5. Jack Lemmon
6. ELVIS PRESLEY
7. Cary Grant
8. James Stewart
9. Elizabeth Taylor
10. Richard Burton

1966
1. Julie Andrews
2. Sean Connery
3. Elizabeth Taylor
4. Jack Lemmon
5. Richard Burton
6. Cary Grant
7. John Wayne
8. Doris Day
9. Paul Newman
10. ELVIS PRESLEY

★ Shelley Fabares was the only female to costar with Elvis in three films (*Girl Happy*, *Spinout*, and *Clambake*).

★ To date, only six non-Elvis films have had Elvis recordings on the soundtrack:
1. *Touched by Love* (1980)
   "Love Me Tender"
   "Ready Teddy"
2. *Diner* (1982)
   "Don't Be Cruel"
3. *Heaven Help Us* (1985)
   "Blue Suede Shoes"
4. *Mischief* (1985)
   "Don't be Cruel"
5. *Lethal Weapon* (1987)
   "I'll Be Home For Christmas"
6. *Tin Men* (1987)
   "(Marie's the Name) His Latest Flame"

★ The top ten Elvis films in theatrical rentals:
1. *Viva Las Vegas* ($5.5 million)
2. *Blue Hawaii* ($4.7 million)
3. *Love Me Tender* ($4.5 million)
4. *G. I. Blues* ($4.3 million)
5. *Jailhouse Rock* ($4 million)
6. *Loving You* ($3.7 million)
7. *Girls! Girls! Girls!* ($3.6 million)
8. *Tickle Me* ($3.4 million)
9. *Roustabout* ($3.3 million)
10. *Girl Happy* ($3.25 million)

★ Allan Weiss provided the story for one Elvis film (*Blue Hawaii*) and the screenplay for five other films: *Fun in Acapulco*, *Roustabout*, *Paradise, Hawaiian Style*, *Girls! Girls! Girls!*, and *Easy Come, Easy Go*.

★ Hal B. Wallis produced nine Elvis films:
1. *Loving You*
2. *King Creole*
3. *G. I. Blues*
4. *Blue Hawaii*
5. *Girls! Girls! Girls!*
6. *Fun in Acapulco*
7. *Roustabout*
8. *Paradise, Hawaiian Style*
9. *Easy Come, Easy Go*

Television Appearances

"LOUISIANA HAYRIDE"
(MARCH 5, 1955)
Elvis's television debut occurred on a regional telecast of the "Louisiana Hayride." He was introduced by Horace Logan on the show, which was telecast by Shreveport, Louisiana, station KWKH-TV, the local CBS affiliate.

"TOWN AND COUNTRY JUBILEE"
(MARCH 14, 1955)
While on his way to New York City to audition for the "Arthur Godfrey's Talent Scouts" television show, Elvis stopped at Washington, D.C., TV station WMAL to see country singing star Jimmy Dean. Dean was host of the station's "Town and Country Jubilee" show, a late afternoon variety series featuring any country singing act that happened to be performing in the capital city at the time. Elvis was interviewed by Dean.

"GRAND PRIZE SATURDAY NIGHT JAMBOREE"
(MARCH 19, 1955)
Sponsored by Grand Prize Beer, this series was telecast live from the Eagle's Nest in Houston from 8:00 to 11:00 P.M. by KPRC-TV. Normally a Saturday night radio show on KNUZ, it was occasionally simulcast on television. Appearing with Elvis that night were Tommy Sands, the Dixie Drifters, the Brown Brothers, and Sonny Burns, among others.

"THE ROY ORBISON SHOW"
(MAY 31, 1955)
Before signing with Sun Records in 1956, singer Roy Orbison had his own television show in either Midland or Odessa, Texas. While on tour in 1955, Elvis appeared on Orbison's show. The authors feel that the above date is correct, although it is possible that Elvis's appearance could have been on April 1, July 22, October 12, or October 14.

"STAGE SHOW"
(JANUARY 28, 1956)
Big-band leaders Tommy and Jimmy Dorsey hosted this CBS-TV variety series. "Stage Show" started out as a 1954 summer replacement series for "The Jackie Gleason Show." On October 1, 1955, the series was brought back at 8:00 P.M. as a half-hour lead-in to Gleason's "The Honeymooners." Gleason produced both shows. "Stage Show," which featured the June Taylor Dancers, was telecast from CBS's Studio 50 on Broadway in New York City. Singer Bobby Darin made his television debut on the program in March 1956.

In mid-December 1955 Elvis signed to make four appearances on "Stage Show" at $1,250 a show. Because of the strong audience reaction, the number of appearances was increased to six.

On his first appearance, on January 28, 1956, Elvis was introduced by Cleveland disc jockey Bill Randle. He sang "Shake, Rattle and Roll" (with the "Flip, Flop

Tommy Dorsey, Elvis, Jimmy Dorsey. (Photo courtesy Cinema Collectors)

and Fly" ending) and "I Got a Woman." Also appearing on the show were Sarah Vaughan and Gene Sheldon. The telecast garnered an 18.4 rating versus a 34.6 rating for NBC-TV's "The Perry Como Show."

"STAGE SHOW"
(FEBRUARY 4, 1956)
Elvis sang "Baby, Let's Play House" and "Tutti Frutti." Guest emcee for the evening was comedian Joe E. Brown. Also appearing was the chimpanzee act Tippy and Cobina. The Nielsen rating was 18.2. Again Perry Como reigned supreme with a rating of 38.5.

"STAGE SHOW"
(FEBRUARY 11, 1956)
Elvis sang "Blue Suede Shoes" and his first RCA release, "Heartbreak Hotel." The Dorsey Brothers Orchestra backed Elvis on "Heartbreak Hotel." Jazz singer Ella Fitzgerald was the evening's guest emcee. Comedian Jackie Miles did routines on harassed little people and racetrack touts.

"STAGE SHOW"
(FEBRUARY 18, 1956)
Elvis sang "Tutti Frutti" and "I Was the One." Game show host ("Name That Tune") George De Witt was the evening's guest emcee. The Tokayers, an acrobatic team, also appeared. Previously, "Stage Show" had aired at 8:00 P.M. With this telecast, "Stage Show" flipped time slots with "The Honeymooners" and became an 8:30 P.M. show.

"STAGE SHOW"
(MARCH 17, 1956)
Elvis sang "Blue Suede Shoes" and "Heartbreak Hotel." "King of the One-Liners," comedian Henny Youngman, was guest emcee. Glenn Derringer, an 11-year-old organist, was one of the acts appearing on the

show. Later in the evening NBC telecast the Emmy Awards. Ventriloquist Jimmy Nelson and his dummies, Danny O'Day and Farfel, advertised Nestle's Quik during the commerical breaks.

"STAGE SHOW"
(MARCH 24, 1956)
On his sixth and final "Stage Show" appearance, Elvis sang "Money Honey" and, for the third time, "Heartbreak Hotel." Comedian Jack E. Leonard was the evening's guest emcee. Other guests included Glenn Derringer and Condos & Brandow. The Nielsen rating for the telecast was 20.9. Perry Como got a 31.8 rating. Carl Perkins was scheduled to appear on Como's show that evening, but was seriously injured in a car accident en route to New York City.

"THE MILTON BERLE SHOW"
(APRIL 3, 1956)
Milton Berle, known as "Mr. Television" and the "Thief of Bad Gags," made his TV debut in a closed-circuit experimental telecast in Chicago in 1929. He permanently moved to television in 1948 with "The Texaco Star Theater." For the next eight years he was the king of television comedy. His show underwent two name changes. From 1948 to 1953 it was known as "The Texaco Star Theater." The title was changed to "The Buick-Berle Show" for the next two seasons and finally to "The Milton Berle Show" on September 27, 1955.

Elvis's first of two appearances on "The Milton Berle Show" occurred on April 3, 1956, at 8:00 P.M. The show was broadcast from the deck of the *USS Hancock*, then docked in San Diego. Elvis sang "Shake, Rattle and Roll," "Heartbreak Hotel," and "Blue Suede Shoes." After "Blue Suede Shoes," he and Berle did a brief comedy sketch, with Berle playing his "twin brother," Melvin Presley. During the sketch Berle mistakenly referred to Elvis as "Elvin." After the sketch, Elvis again sang "Blue Suede Shoes" while Uncle Miltie danced. Elvis was paid $5,000 for his performance. Esther Williams was another of Berle's guests that evening.

"THE MILTON BERLE SHOW"
(JUNE 5, 1956)
Elvis sang "Hound Dog" and "I Want You, I Need You, I Love You." After "Hound Dog," Berle came on to dance to a brief rendition of the song. Elvis and Berle did a dialogue about girls. Berle wanted to know Elvis's secret to getting the girls to go crazy over him. Elvis told Berle that he preferred the quiet type. Actress Debra Paget then came on stage and screamed upon meeting Elvis

"I Want You, I Need You, I Love You" was sung in a record-shop setting. This was the first time that the Jordanaires had backed Elvis on television. After the song, Berle presented Elvis with two *Billboard* Triple Crown Awards for "Heartbreak Hotel." The awards signified that the song had topped the disc jockey, jukebox, and sales charts in both the pop and country fields. Elvis received $5,000 for his appearance. Other guests on the show included TV star Irish McCalla ("Sheena, Queen of the Jungle"), seven-year-old singer

Elvis and the Jordanaires singing "I Want You, I Need You, I Love You." (Photo courtesy Jeff Wheatcraft)

Barry Gordon, and comedian Arnold Stang. Music was provided by Les Baxter and his Orchestra.

Milton Berle's eight-year reign on television ended with this June 5, 1956, telecast. It was his last show. He did try a comeback on two other occasions (1958-59 and 1966), but those attempts were unsuccessful.

"DANCE PARTY"
(JUNE 20, 1956)
"Dance Party" was a local Memphis show, à la "American Bandstand," which aired on KLAC-TV. Disc jockey Wink Martindale was the host. Elvis appeared briefly to promote the upcoming (July 4) benefit concert at Russwood Park for the *Memphis Press-Scimitar's* Milk Fund. The concert also aided the Variety Club's Home for Convalescent Children.

"THE STEVE ALLEN SHOW"
(JULY 1, 1956)
Steve Allen is one of the most versatile entertainers in show business. He's been an actor (*The Benny Goodman Story*), composer ("The Start of Something Big" and the lyrics to the Oscar-winning "Picnic"), author (numerous books), and TV host ("Tonight!," the first version of "The Tonight Show").

This second version of "The Steve Allen Show"—the first was on the air from 1950 to 1952—premiered on June 24, 1956, with Kim Novak, Sammy Davis Jr., and Vincent Price as guests. The next week Elvis made his one appearance on the show.

Allen introduced Elvis by saying, "It gives me great pleasure to introduce the *new* Elvis Presley." Elvis came on stage wearing a tuxedo. [Because of the controversy generated on earlier TV appearances, Allen tried to tone Elvis down.] Allen presented Elvis with an

"Range Roundup" skit. (Photo courtesy Cinema Collectors)

18,000-signature petition that Tulsa, Oklahoma, disc jockey Don Wallace had organized requesting Elvis to appear on television again real soon. Elvis then sang "I Want You, I Need You, I Love You."

When the song ended, Allen wheeled in Sherlock, a basset hound, to which Elvis sang "Hound Dog." [Note: Although the Jordanaires backed Elvis on his previous number, they did not back him on "Hound Dog."]

Later in the show, Elvis appeared with Allen, Andy Griffith, and Imogene Coca in a comedy sketch titled "Range Roundup." Elvis's character was called Tumbleweed Presley, Griffith's Rattlesnake Griffith, and Coca's Cactus Coca, the "little flower of the prairie." During the sketch, the performers did a spoof commercial for Tonto Candy Bars, "the candy that comes out of the Old West right into your old mouth." Tonto Candy Bars were made by the Kemo Sabe Candy Company in Ptomaine, Texas. The sketch concluded with the four performers singing "Yippee Yi Yo Yi Yay."

The telecast received a 20.2 Trendex rating, with a 55.3 percent share of the audience. It was the best NBC showing in the 8:00–9:00 Sunday night time slot since May 30, 1954. "The Ed Sullivan Show," which had a 14.8 Trendex rating that evening, featured a tribute to John Huston.

Other guests on "The Steve Allen Show" included Steve Lawrence and Eydie Gormé and Louis Armstrong in a special remote telecast from the Berkshire Music Festival in Lenox, Massachusetts.

"HY GARDNER CALLING"
(JULY 1, 1956)

After appearing on "The Steve Allen Show," Elvis went back to his hotel room and did a remote broadcast on "Hy Gardner Calling." By means of a split-screen technique, Elvis was shown with Gardner, who interviewed him from the studios of WRCA, Channel 4. Gardner asked Elvis about his success and the inane rumor that he once shot his mother. The 11:30 P.M. interview was brief. On March 30, 1958, that episode of "Hy Gardner Calling" was repeated on New York station WABD, Channel 5.

"THE ED SULLIVAN SHOW"
(SEPTEMBER 9, 1956)

"The Ed Sullivan Show" was TV's longest-running variety series. It ran on Sunday nights for twenty-three seasons. Hosted by newspaper columnist Sullivan, whose critics called him the "Great Stone Face," the series began as "Toast of the Town" on June 20, 1948, on the CBS-TV network. That night Dean Martin and Jerry Lewis made their television debuts. Several acts made their TV debuts on "Toast of the Town," including Bob Hope and Jackie Gleason. The series' title was changed to "The Ed Sullivan Show" on September 25, 1955. Many Elvis fans through the years have erroneously referred to Elvis's three appearances on "Toast of the Town," but the title had been changed a year before his first appearance.

Sullivan had said he'd never have Elvis Presley on his show, but the ratings of "The Steve Allen Show" convinced him to sign Elvis for three appearances for a total fee of $50,000.

On August 6, 1956, Sullivan was involved in a head-on automobile accident near Seymour, Connecticut, that put him in the hospital for several weeks. He missed Elvis's first appearance on his show.

Actor Charles Laughton substituted for Sullivan on the night of September 9. Laughton (in New York) introduced Elvis (in Hollywood). Elvis sang "Don't Be Cruel" and "Love Me Tender." Later in the show he sang "Ready Teddy" and "Hound Dog." Trendex ratings for the telecast were 82.6.

Laughton gave a Shakespeare recitation during the show. Other guests included Dorothy Sarnoff (who sang "Something Wonderful"), the Vagabonds, the Amen Brothers (Egyptian tumblers), Conn and Mann (a dance team), and Indian vocal star Amru Sani.

Broadcast opposite "The Ed Sullivan Show" was the National Amateur Talent Championships from Madison Square Garden on "Ted Mack's Original Amateur Hour." Among the seventeen finalists was the Johnny Burnette Trio.

"THE ED SULLIVAN SHOW"
(OCTOBER 28, 1956)

Elvis sang "Don't Be Cruel," " Love Me Tender," "Love Me," and "Hound Dog." During the telecast he was presented with a Gold Record for "Love Me Tender." Guests on the show included ventriloquist Señor Wences, English comedienne Joyce Grenfell, and the Little Gaelic Singers. Live segments from the Broadway play *The Most Happy Fella* were presented. Robert Webb, director of *Love Me Tender*, was spoken to briefly by Ed Sullivan.

"HOLIDAY HOP"
(DECEMBER 31, 1956)

Elvis appeared on this special presentation of KLAC-TV in Memphis. He was interviewed by host Wink Martindale, but did not sing.

"THE ED SULLIVAN SHOW"
(JANUARY 6, 1957)

Only on this telecast, Elvis's third and final appearance on "The Ed Sullivan Show," did the cameras show him from the waist up. Sullivan had gotten some negative feedback on the earlier two appearances.

Elvis sang "Hound Dog," "Love Me Tender," "Heartbreak Hotel," "Don't Be Cruel," "Too Much," "When My Blue Moon Turns to Gold Again," and "Peace in the Valley." After singing "Too Much," Elvis commented that he'd received 282 teddy bears from fans for

Elvis, Leny Eversong, Ed Sullivan. (Photo courtesy Eddie Brandt's Saturday Matinee)

Christmas. Sullivan mentioned Elvis's feelings about the Hungarian relief efforts going on worldwide and his upcoming benefit concert. Sullivan concluded Elvis's appearance by telling the audience that Elvis was a "real decent, fine boy" and that he'd "never had a pleasanter experience on our show with a big name than we've had with you; you're thoroughly all right."

Guests included ventriloquist Arthur Worsley, dancer Nanci Crompton, Brazilian singer Lenny Eversong, comedienne Carol Burnett, singer Lonnie Satin, and Gutis, a European comedy act.

"AMERICAN BANDSTAND"
(JANUARY 8, 1959)

"American Bandstand" was first telecast locally in Philadelphia on WFIL-TV in 1952. The show's original host, Bob Horn, was the first disc jockey to be tried and convicted on charges of payola. Disc jockey Dick Clark took over the show in 1956. On August 5, 1957, "American Bandstand" had its network premiere on ABC-TV, where it remained for twenty years before going into syndication in the fall of 1987. Just about every major rock star appeared on the show through the years except Rick Nelson and Elvis Presley.

Although Elvis never physically appeared on "American Bandstand," Clark had a telephone interview with him on the January 8, 1959, telecast. Elvis was in the Army in West Germany at the time. Clark informed Elvis that he'd been voted Best Singer of the Year and that "King Creole" was Best Song of the Year. The entire program was a celebration of Elvis's twenty-fourth birthday.

"WELCOME HOME, ELVIS"
(MAY 12, 1960)

"Welcome Home, Elvis" was the fourth and final Frank Sinatra–Timex TV special of the 1959–60 season. The special was taped in the Grand Ballroom of Miami Beach's Fontainebleau Hotel on March 26, 1960. Elvis was paid $125,000 for his six-minute appearance on the program. Seven hundred fans (400 of them Elvis Presley fan-club members) crowded the ballroom for

the taping. Elvis sang "Fame and Fortune" and "Stuck on You." In a duet with Sinatra, Elvis sang "Witchcraft" (Sinatra's hit), and Sinatra sang "Love Me Tender." Other guests on the program included Sammy Davis Jr., Peter Lawford, Joey Bishop, and Nancy Sinatra. The Tom Hansen Dancers and Nelson Riddle's Orchestra provided support. To start the show, the entire cast (including Elvis) sang "It's Nice to Go Traveling."

The songs in the telecast included "Witchcraft" (by Sinatra), "There's a Boat That's Leavin' Soon for New York" (by Sammy Davis Jr.)," "Gone with the Wind" (by Sinatra), "All the Way" (by Sammy Davis Jr.), "You Make Me Feel So Young" (by Frank and Nancy Sinatra), "Shall We Dance" (by Sammy Davis Jr. and Peter Lawford), and "It's Nice to Go Traveling" (by Sinatra).

The telecast on ABC-TV got a Nielsen share of 41.5.

"ELVIS"
(DECEMBER 3, 1968)

In January 1968, Colonel Parker announced that Elvis had just signed to do a TV special for NBC. It soon became the most anticipated event of the 1968-69 television season. The Singer Company shelled out $400,000 to sponsor the program and another $275,000 for a later rebroadcast.

On June 17, 18, and 19, Elvis held rehearsals for the "pit" segment of the special. Prerecorded musical tracks were laid at Western Recorders on June 21 and 22. Finally, formal taping of the special began at 6:00 P.M. on June 27 at NBC's Studio 4 in Burbank. It was to be Elvis's first appearance before a live audience in more than seven years. A second show was taped at 8:00 P.M. Two more sessions—again at 6:00 P.M. and 8:00 P.M.—were taped on June 29. Final production taping was done on June 30. Musicians appearing in the "pit" segment were Scotty Moore, Charlie Hodge,

Joey Bishop, Frank Sinatra, Elvis, Nancy Sinatra. (Photo courtesy Jeff Wheatcraft)

(Photo courtesy Eddie Brandt's Saturday Matinee)

D. J. Fontana, and Alan Fortas (on tambourine). The Blossoms and the Claude Thompson Dancers provided support during the production numbers.

Originally, Colonel Parker had wanted the special to end with a Christmas tune. But producer Steve Binder persuaded Elvis to sing a composition Earl Brown had written especially for the occasion—"If I Can Dream." "Let Yourself Go," sung in a bordello scene, was cut from the show, as was "It Hurts Me," "Blue Suede Shoes," and "Don't Be Cruel." Additional songs re-

(Photo courtesy Wide World Photos)

corded for the special but not used were "That's All Right (Mama)," "Love Me," "When My Blue Moon Turns to Gold Again," "Tryin' to Get to You," and "Santa Claus Is Back in Town." An instrumental track for "A Little Less Conversation" was recorded, but Elvis did not provide a vocal track for it.

Production credits for "Elvis" included Bob Finkel (executive producer), Steve Binder (producer and director), Allan Blye and Chris Bearde (writers), Bones Howe (musical producer), and Jaime Rogers and Claude Thompson (choreographers). Elvis's costumes were designed by Bill Belew.

"Elvis" aired on NBC at 9:00 P.M. on December 3, 1968. With a 32 rating and a 42 share, it was the highest-rated program for the week and the most-watched TV special of 1968 by women ages 18 to 49. Executive producer Bob Finkel won a Peabody Award for his work on the show. "Elvis" was rerun on August 22, 1969. "Blue Christmas" was replaced with "Tiger Man" for that telecast. In Great Britain, "Elvis" was shown on BBC-2 on December 31, 1968, without commercials.

Songs
 1. "Trouble"/"Guitar Man"
 2. "Lawdy Miss Clawdy"
 3. "Baby, What You Want Me to Do"
 4. "Heartbreak Hotel"/"Hound Dog"/"All Shook Up"
 5. "Can't Help Falling in Love"
 6. "Jailhouse Rock"
 7. "Love Me Tender"
 8. "Are You Lonesome Tonight?" (a few lines)
 9. "Where Could I Go but to the Lord"
10. "Up Above My Head"
11. "Saved"
    "Baby, What You Want Me to Do" (second time)
12. "Blue Christmas"
13. "One Night"
14. "Memories"
15. "Nothingville"
16. "Big Boss Man"
    "Guitar Man" (second time)
17. "Little Egypt"
    "Trouble" (second time)
    "Guitar Man" (third time)
18. "If I Can Dream"

The Blossoms sang "Sometimes I Feel Like a Motherless Child," "I Found That Light" and "Yes, Yes, Yes".

"ELVIS: ALOHA FROM HAWAII"
(JANUARY 14, 1973)
Approximately one billion people in forty countries watched "Elvis: Aloha from Hawaii"—more than had seen the first moon landing by Apollo 11.

Elvis arrived in Honolulu on January 9, 1973. His arrival at the Hawaiian Village Hotel by helicopter was filmed for the special's opening sequence. After two days of rehearsals, Elvis performed a dress rehearsal concert before 6,000 fans at the Honolulu International Center Arena on January 12. This concert has provided material for numerous bootleg albums over the years, as well as the 1988 RCA LP *The Alternate Aloha*.

On January 14, 1973, "Elvis: Aloha from Hawaii" was beamed by the Intelsat IV communications satellite at 12:30 A.M. (Honolulu time) to Australia, Japan, South

(Photo courtesy Eddie Brandt's Saturday Matinee)

Korea, New Zealand, South Vietnam, Thailand, the Philippines, and other countries in the Far East. Even a few thousand viewers in Communist China saw the telecast. Ratings worldwide were spectacular. In the Philippines, 92 percent of all those watching television watched "Elvis: Aloha from Hawaii." The next day, the special was rebroadcast to twenty-eight nations in Europe.

Produced at a budget of about $2.5 million, "Elvis: Aloha from Hawaii" was a benefit concert for the Kuiokalani Lee Cancer Fund.

After the audience left the building, Elvis recorded five songs for the U.S. edition of the concert, which was broadcast on April 4, 1973, at 8:30 P.M. on NBC. The five songs were "Blue Hawaii," "Ku-u-i-po," "Hawaiian Wedding Song," "Early Morning Rain," and "No More." All but "No More" were used in the telecast. The ninety-minute special, which was sponsored by Chicken of the Sea, was the top-rated show of the week, getting a 33.8 rating and a 51 share. "Elvis: Aloha from Hawaii" was rebroadcast on November 14, 1973, at 8:30 P.M.

Songs in the worldwide telecast were the same (and in the same order) as those sung in the January 12 dress rehearsal, except for the addition of "Johnny B. Goode," "I Can't Stop Loving You," and "Long Tall Sally"/"Whole Lotta Shakin' Goin' On."

Songs

1. "Paradise, Hawaiian Style" (sung over the opening credits)
2. "Also Sprach Zarathustra" (played by the Joe Guercio Orchestra)
3. "See See Rider"
4. "Burning Love"
5. "Something"
6. "You Gave Me a Mountain"
7. "Steamroller Blues"
8. "Early Morning Rain" (U.S. telecast only)
9. "My Way"
10. "Love Me"
11. "Johnny B. Goode"
12. "It's Over"
13. "Blue Suede Shoes"
14. "I'm So Lonesome I Could Cry"
15. "I Can't Stop Loving You"
16. "Hound Dog"
17. "Blue Hawaii" (U.S. telecast only)
18. "What Now My Love"
19. "Fever"
20. "Welcome to My World"
21. "Suspicious Minds"
22. "I'll Remember You"
23. "Hawaiian Wedding Song" (U.S. telecast only)
24. "Long Tall Sally"/"Whole Lotta Shakin' Goin' On"
25. "Ku-u-i-po" (U.S. telecast only)
26. "An American Trilogy"
27. "A Big Hunk o' Love"
28. "Can't Help Falling in Love"
29. Closing Vamp (played by the Joe Guercio Orchestra)

"ELVIS IN CONCERT" (OCTOBER 3, 1977)

After Elvis's death, CBS-TV and RCA rushed to get this one-hour special on the air. "Elvis in Concert" consisted of songs recorded at the Omaha Civic Auditorium in Omaha, Nebraska, on June 19, 1977, and the Rushmore Civic Center in Rapid City, South Dakota, on June 21. The TV special ended with a few words from Vernon Presley.

Songs

1. "Also Sprach Zarathustra" (played by the Joe Guercio Orchestra)
2. "See See Rider"
3. "That's All Right (Mama)"
4. "Are You Lonesome Tonight?"
5. "Teddy Bear"/"Don't Be Cruel"
6. "You Gave Me a Mountain"
7. "Jailhouse Rock"
8. "How Great Thou Art"
9. "I Really Don't Want to Know"
10. "Hurt"
11. "Hound Dog"
12. "My Way"
13. "Early Morning Rain"
14. "Can't Help Falling in Love"

TV Specials Devoted to Elvis

"MEMORIES OF ELVIS"
(NOVEMBER 20, 1977)
Ann-Margret hosted this NBC special composed mainly of footage from the 1968 TV special "Elvis" and the 1973 NBC version of "Elvis: Aloha from Hawaii." "Memories of Elvis" aired from 8:00 to 11:00 P.M. Nine months later, on August 29, 1978, the three-hour special was rebroadcast.

"NASHVILLE REMEMBERS ELVIS ON HIS BIRTHDAY"
(JANUARY 8, 1978)
This NBC-TV tribute was hosted by Jimmy Dean and featured recollections by Jack Albertson, Bill Bixby, Nancy Sinatra, Stella Stevens, and Mary Ann Mobley. Musical highlights included "Love Me Tender" (by Merle Haggard), "The King Is Gone" (by Ronnie McDowell), "An American Trilogy" (by Dottie West), "E. P. Express" (by Carl Perkins), "Lonely Weekends" (by Charlie Rich), "Help Me" (by Larry Gatlin), and "You Win Again" (by Jerry Lee Lewis). "Nashville Remembers Elvis on His Birthday" aired from 9:30 to 11:00 P.M. on January 8, 1978, and was then rerun in a sixty-minute version on February 8, 1980. The latter version was titled "Elvis Remembered: Nashville to Hollywood." Elvis was heard singing "Heartbreak Hotel" and "My Way" during the special.

"ELVIS MEMORIES"
(1981)
Longtime Elvis friend George Klein coproduced this 1981 syndicated special. Interviews and film clips provided the bulk of the footage. One of the highlights was the June 20, 1956, clip of Elvis on Wink Martindale's Memphis TV show, "Dance Party." However, it was annoying to watch clips of Elvis singing with his voice dubbed by a singer named Bill Haney.

"DISCIPLES OF ROCK"
(1984)
Also known as "Mondo Elvis," this syndicated special was a disturbing look at the fringes of Elvis fandom. Included were an Elvis impersonator, various Elvis fans, and two sisters who believed they were Elvis's secret daughters. The sisters were going to name their first-born male child after Elvis, but since they already had a dog named Elvis Presley Jr., the boy would have to be named Elvis Presley III. The soundtrack music consisted of selected Elvis tribute records. "Disciples of Rock" was produced and directed by Thomas Corby and released by Monticello Productions.

"ELVIS: ONE NIGHT WITH YOU"
(JANUARY 5, 1985)
The complete 6:00 P.M. show from the June 27, 1968, taping of the "Elvis" TV special was featured on this Home Box Office cable TV presentation. "Elvis: One Night with You" was first telecast at 8:00 P.M. on January 5, 1985, and was repeated several times during the rest of the month. The show was fifty-three minutes long.

"ELVIS PRESLEY'S GRACELAND"
(JANUARY 8, 1985)
Priscilla Presley served as hostess for this tour of Graceland on the Showtime cable TV network. Produced and directed by Steve Binder, "Elvis Presley's Graceland" was inspired by Jacqueline Kennedy's February 18, 1962, tour of the White House on CBS and NBC. It was filmed in August and November 1984, at a budget of close to $800,000. "Elvis Presley's Graceland" aired on Showtime throughout January 1985.

"ELVIS: THE ECHO WILL NEVER DIE"
(AUGUST 1985)
Interviews with friends and entertainers who knew and worked with Elvis were the focal point of this sixty-minute syndicated special. "Elvis: The Echo Will Never Die" was hosted by Casey Kasem. Some of those interviewed included Sammy Davis Jr., Tom Jones, B. B. King, and Ursula Andress.

"ELVIS '56"
(AUGUST 16, 1987)
"Elvis '56" was a Cinemax cable TV special produced and directed by Alan and Susan Raymond. The production contained vintage clips, stills by Alfred Wertheimer, and home movies documenting Elvis's rise to the top in 1956. Particularly interesting were the recording-session tapes of "Hound Dog" and "Don't Be Cruel." Narrated by Levon Helm, "Elvis '56" was a part of Cinemax's "Crazy About the Movies" series. The special was first telecast at 9:00 P.M. on August 16, 1987, and aired throughout the rest of the month. In 1988, the videocassette release of "Elvis '56" was among the top selling cassettes on *Billboard*'s Top Music Videocassettes.

(Photo courtesy Eddie Brandt's Saturday Matinee)

1940s and 1950s Radio Shows

At the beginning of his career, Elvis made many personal appearances, and in many of those cities he did local radio interviews to promote that evening's concert. On several occasions the performances themselves were aired. What follows is a list of radio shows done by Elvis in the 1940s and 1950s. It is by no means complete. All "Louisiana Hayride" performances are treated separately in the next segment. If any readers can add to this radio list, please send documentation to the authors. It will be included in the next edition of the book.

1944

October or November	WELO; Tupelo, Mississippi ("Black and White Jamboree")

1945

October 3	WELO; Tupelo, Mississippi (Mississippi-Alabama Fair and Dairy Show)

1953

?	WKEM; Memphis (George Klein interview)

1954

July 7	WHBQ; Memphis (Dewey Phillips's "Red Hot and Blue" show)
October 2	WSM; Nashville ("Grand Ole Opry")
October 2	WSM; Nashville ("Ernest Tubbs's Midnight Jamboree")
October ?	KNUZ; Houston ("The Old Texas Corral")
October ?	KSIG; Gladewater, Texas
October 22	?; New Orleans ("The Old Barn Dance")
December 11	KWKH; Shreveport, Louisiana ("Red River Roundup")

1955

January 1	KNUZ; Houston ("Grand Prize Saturday Night Jamboree")
January 16	WBIP; Booneville, Mississippi
January ?	WMPS; Memphis ("Milkman's Jamboree")
January 29	KNUZ; Houston ("Grand Prize Saturday Night Jamboree")
February 26	WERE; Cleveland ("Circle Theatre Jamboree")
March 19	KNUZ; Houston ("Grand Prize Saturday Night Jamboree")
March 28	WERE; Cleveland ("Circle Theatre Jamboree")
April 16	KRLD; Dallas ("Big D Jamboree")
May ?	KOCA; Kilgore, Texas
May 28	KRLD; Dallas ("Big D Jamboree")
June 18	KRLD; Dallas ("Big D Jamboree")
July 2	KEYS; Corpus Christi, Texas
July 23	KRLD; Dallas ("Big D Jamboree")
August 8	KSIG; Gladewater, Texas
August 31	WMPS; Memphis
September 3	KRLD; Dallas ("Big D Jamboree")
September 11	WCMS; Norfolk, Virginia
September 20	WRVA; Richmond, Virginia ("Old Dominion Barn Dance")
December 3	WBAM; Montgomery, Alabama (guest performer on "Talent Search of the Deep South")

1956

April 13	KSTB; Breckinridge, Texas (interview by Jay Thompson in Wichita Falls)
April 15 or 22	WMAC; San Antonio, Texas (interview by Charlie Walker)
July ?	WNOE; New Orleans
July ?	?; New Orleans
October 31	WMPS; Memphis
December 22	WDIA; Memphis ("Goodwill Review")

1957

October 23	WHBQ; Memphis (George Klein interview)

Louisiana Hayride

The "Louisiana Hayride" was a country-music radio show often called the "Junior Grand Ole Opry." The program was broadcast every Saturday night on Shreveport station KWKH from 8:00 to 11:00 P.M., beginning on April 3, 1948. Several country-music greats appeared on the "Louisiana Hayride" over the years, including Jim Reeves, Red Sovine, Jim Ed Brown, Slim Whitman, Johnny Horton, and Hank Williams. Williams was a regular on the show from August 7, 1948, to June 3, 1949, and again from September 4, 1952, until his death on January 1, 1953.

More than 190 CBS radio stations carried the "Hayride" broadcasts in the southern United States. Broadcasts aired from Shreveport's Municipal Auditorium, which was usually packed to the rafters. Adults paid sixty cents and children thirty cents to attend the shows.

Elvis first appeared on the "Louisiana Hayride" on October 16, 1954. He sang both sides of his first Sun Records release, "That's All Right (Mama)" and "Blue Moon of Kentucky." Several bootleg records exist of that first night's performance. Elvis was introduced by emcee Frank Page during the "Lucky Strike Guest Time" segment, which was devoted to new artists.

PAGE: Just a few weeks ago a young man from Memphis,Tennessee, recorded a song on the Sun label and, in just a matter of weeks, that record has sky-rocketed right up the charts. It's really doing well all over the country. He is only nineteen years old. He has a new, distinctive style. Elvis Presley. Let's give him a nice hand. Elvis, how are you this evening?

ELVIS: Just fine. How're you, sir?

PAGE: Are you all geared up with your band—

ELVIS: I'm all geared up.

PAGE: —to let us hear your songs?

ELVIS: Uh, well, I'd just like to say how happy we are to be down here. It's a real honor for us to get a chance to appear on the "Louisiana Hayride." We're gonna do a song for ya—you got anything else to say?

PAGE: No! I'm ready!

ELVIS: We're gonna do a song for ya we got out on Sun Records. It goes something like this." [Elvis sings "That's All Right (Mama).]

Because of audience reaction, Elvis, Scotty Moore, and Bill Black were asked back the following week. On November 6, shortly before their third appearance, Elvis, Scotty, and Bill signed a contract with KWKH station manager Horace L. Logan to appear every Saturday night on the "Hayride" for the next year. The contract was witnessed by Vernon and Gladys Presley. Elvis was paid eighteen dollars for each performance; Scotty Moore and Bill Black were each paid twelve dollars.

On September 8, 1955, Elvis signed a new contract with the "Hayride," to begin on November 12. Again, the contract was for one year. His pay was upgraded to $200 a night.

"Louisiana Hayride." (Photo courtesy Jeff Wheatcraft)

Because of Elvis's growing popularity in early 1956, which caused him to miss many of the "Louisiana Hayride" broadcasts, he entered into an agreement to pay the "Hayride" $400 a night for each missed performance.

Elvis's one and only commercial for any product occurred on the November 6, 1954, broadcast of the "Louisiana Hayride." Elvis plugged a company called Southern Made Doughnuts, singing its jingle: "You can get 'em piping hot after four P.M., you can get 'em piping hot. Southern Made Doughnuts hit the spot, you can get 'em piping hot after four P.M." Reportedly, an acetate of that commercial exists.

Elvis's final appearance on the "Louisiana Hayride" came on December 16, 1956. The performance, at the

Louisiana Fairgrounds, was a benefit concert for the Shreveport YMCA. Close to ten thousand people attended.

The following is a complete list of Elvis's appearances on the "Louisiana Hayride."

1. October 16, 1954
2. October 23, 1954
3. November 6, 1954
4. November 13, 1954
5. November 20, 1954
6. November 27, 1954
7. December 4, 1954
8. December 11, 1954
9. December 18, 1954 (on location in Gladewater, Texas)
10. January 8, 1955
11. January 15, 1955
12. January 22, 1955
13. February 5, 1955
14. February 12, 1955
15. February 19, 1955
16. March 5, 1955 (TV appearance)
17. March 12, 1955
18. March 26, 1955
19. April 2, 1955
20. April 9, 1955
21. April 23, 1955 (on location in Waco, Texas)
22. April 30, 1955 (on location in Gladewater, Texas)
23. May 14, 1955
24. May 21, 1955
25. June 4, 1955
26. June 11, 1955
27. June 25, 1955
28. July 2, 1955
29. August 6, 1955
30. August 27, 1955
31. September 10, 1955
32. September 24, 1955
33. October 1, 1955
34. October 8, 1955
35. October 29, 1955
36. November 5, 1955
37. November 12, 1955
38. November 19, 1955 (on location in Gladewater, Texas)
39. November 26, 1955
40. December 10, 1955
41. December 17, 1955
42. December 31, 1955
43. January 7, 1956
44. January 14, 1956
45. January 21, 1956
46. February 25, 1956
47. March 3, 1956
48. March 10, 1956
49. April 7, 1956
50. December 16, 1956

Concert Appearances

The following is a list of all of Elvis's concert appearances at clubs, concert halls, casinos, stadiums, theaters, fairgrounds, and coliseums—at least as far as is now known. We'll no doubt be adding to the list as the information becomes available. Not included are Elvis's "Louisiana Hayride" performances. Those are covered in their own section.

1954

July ?	Memphis (Bon Air Club)
July 30	Memphis (Overton Park Shell)
August 7	Memphis (Eagle's Nest Club)
August 21	Gladewater, Texas
August 22	Houston
August ?	Memphis (Kennedy Veterans Hospital Benefit Show)
August 27	Memphis (Eagle's Nest Club)
September 9	Memphis (Katz Drug Store opening)
September–November	Memphis (Eagle's Nest Club) (more than ten appearances)
October 2	Nashville (Ryman Auditorium)
October 22	New Orleans
October–November	Sweetwater, Texas
	Boston, Texas
	Lufkin, Texas
	Longview, Texas
	Odessa, Texas
	Memphis (Airport Inn)
December 28	Houston

1955

January 1	Houston (Eagles' Hall)
January 12	Clarksdale, Mississippi
January 13	Helena, Arkansas
January 16	Booneville, Mississippi
January 17	Sheffield, Alabama
January 18	Leachville, Arkansas
January 19	Sikeston, Missouri
January 29	Houston (Eagles' Hall)
February 4	New Orleans (Lake Pontchartrain)
February 6	Memphis (Memphis Auditorium) (two shows)
February 14	Carlsbad, New Mexico
February 15	Albuquerque, New Mexico
February 16	Odessa, Texas
February 18	Monroe, Louisiana
February 22	Hope, Arkansas
February 24	Bastrop, Louisiana
February 26	Cleveland (Circle Theater)
March 6–10	Tennessee, Arkansas, Mississippi, Louisiana, and Missouri
March 19	Houston (Eagles' Hall)
March 28	Cleveland (Circle Theater)
April 1	Odessa, Texas
April 16	Dallas (Sportatorium)
April ?	El Dorado, Arkansas
April ?	Texarkana, Arkansas
April ?	Helena, Arkansas
May 1	New Orleans
May 4–5	Mobile, Alabama
May 6	Birmingham, Alabama
May 7	Daytona Beach, Florida

May 8	Tampa
May 9	Macon, Georgia
May 10	Ocala, Florida
May 13	Jacksonville, Florida
May 16	Richmond, Virginia (Mosque Theater)
May 17	Norfolk, Virginia (two shows)
May 18	Roanoke, Virginia (American Legion Auditorium) (two shows)
May 19	New Bern, North Carolina
May 20	Chattanooga, Tennessee
May 22	Houston (Magnolia Gardens)
May 25	Meridian, Mississippi (Jimmie Rodgers Day)
May 28	Fort Worth, Texas (Northside Coliseum (evening show)
May 29	Dallas (Sportatorium)
May 29	Dallas (Sportatorium) (evening show)
May 30	Abilene, Texas (Fair Park Auditorium)
May 31	Midland, Texas (afternoon show)
May 31	Odessa, Texas (evening show)
May ?	Gainesville, Texas
May ?	Kilgore, Texas
May ?	Breckinridge, Texas
June 1	Guymon, Oklahoma
June 2	Amarillo, Texas (City Auditorium)
June 3	Lubbock, Texas
June 9–10	Lawton, Oklahoma
June 13	Bruce, Mississippi
June 14	Tupelo, Mississippi
June 15	Gobler, Missouri
June 16	El Dorado, Arkansas
June 17	Stamford, Texas
June 18	Dallas (Sportatorium)
June 19	Houston (Magnolia Gardens)
June 20	Beaumont, Texas (two shows)
June 21	Beaumont, Texas (three shows)
June 22	Vernon, Texas
June 23	Lawton, Oklahoma
June 24	Altus, Oklahoma
June 26	Biloxi, Mississippi
June 27–28	Biloxi, Mississippi (NCO club at Keesler Air Force Base)
June 29–30	Mobile, Alabama (Radio Ranch Club)
June ?	Marianna, Arkansas
July 1	Baton Rouge, Louisiana
July 3	Corpus Christi, Texas
July 4	Stephenville, Texas (City Recreational Building)
July 22	Odessa, Texas
July 23	Dallas (Sportatorium)
July 25	Tampa (116th Field Artillery Armory)
July 26–27	Orlando, Florida
July 28–29	Jacksonville, Florida (Gator Bowl)
July 30	Daytona Beach, Florida
July 31	Sheffield, Alabama (Community Center)
August 1–2	Little Rock, Arkansas
August 3	Tupelo, Mississippi
August 4	Camden, Arkansas (two shows)
August 5	Memphis (Overton Park Shell)
August 8–10	Gladewater, Texas, area
August 11	Dallas (Texas State Fairgrounds)

August 12	San Antonio	February 21	Sarasota, Florida (Florida Theater)
August 13	Houston	March 14–15	Atlanta (Fox Theater) (six shows)
August 20	Cleveland (Circle Theater) (two shows)	March 22	Richmond, Virginia (Mosque Theater) (two shows)
September 1	New Orleans	April 4–5	San Diego (San Diego Sports Arena)
September 2	Texarkana, Arkansas (Arkansas Municipal Auditorium) (two shows)	April 13	Wichita Falls, Texas (Municipal Auditorium)
September 3	Dallas (Sportatorium)	April 15	San Antonio (Municipal Auditorium)
September 5	Forrest City, Arkansas	April 16	Corpus Christi, Texas
September 6	Bono, Arkansas	April 17	Waco, Texas
September 7	Sikeston, Missouri	April 18	Tulsa, Oklahoma
September 8	Clarksdale, Mississippi	April 19	Amarillo, Texas
September 9	McComb, Mississippi	April 20	Fort Worth, Texas (Northside Convention Center)
September 11–12	Norfolk, Virginia (City Auditorium)	April 21	Dallas
September 14	Asheville, North Carolina	April 22	San Antonio (Municipal Auditorium) (two shows)
September 15	Roanoke, Virginia (American Legion Auditorium)	April 23–May 6	Las Vegas (New Frontier Hotel)
September 16	New Bern, North Carolina	May 13	St. Paul, Minnesota (two shows)
September 17	Wilson, North Carolina	May 14	LaCrosse, Wisconsin (Mary E. E. Sawyer Auditorium) (two shows)
September 18	Raleigh, North Carolina	May 15	Memphis (Ellis Auditorium)
September 19	Thomasville, North Carolina	May 16	Little Rock, Arkansas (Little Rock Auditorium)
September 20	Richmond, Virginia (two shows)	May 17	Springfield, Missouri (Shrine Mosque)
September 21	Danville, Virginia	May 18	Des Moines
September 22	Kingsport, Tennessee	May 19	Lincoln, Nebraska (University of Nebraska Coliseum)
September 26	Wichita Falls, Texas	May 20	Omaha (two shows)
September 27	Bryan, Texas (Saddle Club)	May 24	Kansas City, Missouri
September 28	Conroe, Texas	May 25	Detroit (Fox Theater) (three shows)
September 29	Austin, Texas (Sports Arena)	May 26	Columbus, Ohio (Veterans Memorial Auditorium) (two shows)
September 30	Gonzales, Texas	May 27	Dayton, Ohio (University of Dayton Fieldhouse) (two shows)
October 9	Lufkin, Texas		
October 10	Brownwood, Texas	June 3	Oakland (Oakland Auditorium) (two shows)
October 11	Abilene, Texas		
October 12	Midland, Texas	June 6	San Diego (San Diego Arena)
October 13	Amarillo, Texas	June 7	Long Beach, California (Long Beach Municipal Auditorium)
October 14	Odessa, Texas	June 8	Los Angeles (Shrine Auditorium)
October 15	Lubbock, Texas (Cotton Club)	June 22	Atlanta (Paramount Theater) (three shows)
October 16	Lubbock, Texas (Hub Motors)		
October 17	El Dorado, Arkansas	June 23	Atlanta (Paramount Theater) (four shows)
October 19	Cleveland (Circle Theater)		
October 20	Cleveland (Brooklyn High School and St. Michael's Hall)	June 24	Atlanta (Paramount Theater) (three shows)
October 21–22	St. Louis	June 25	Savannah, Georgia (Savannah Auditorium) (two shows)
October 26–28	Prichard, Alabama (Fairgrounds)	June 26	Charlotte, North Carolina (Charlotte Coliseum)
November 6	Biloxi, Mississippi		
November 7	Biloxi, Mississippi (NCO club at Keesler Air Force Base)	June 27	Augusta, Georgia (Bell Auditorium)
November 8	Amory, Mississippi	June 28	Charlotte, North Carolina
November 12	Carthage, Texas (afternoon show)	June 30	Richmond, Virginia (Mosque Theater)
November 13	Memphis (Ellis Auditorium) (two shows)	July 4	Memphis (Russwood Park)
November 14	Forrest City, Arkansas	August 3	Miami (Olympic Theater) (three shows)
November 15	Sheffield, Alabama	August 4	Miami (Olympic Theater) (three shows)
November 16	Camden, Arkansas	August 5	Tampa (Ft. Homer Hesterly Armory) (two shows)
November 17	Texarkana, Arkansas		
November 18	Longview, Texas	August 6	Lakeland, Florida (Polk Theater) (three shows)
November 25	Port Arthur, Texas (Woodrow Wilson Jr. High School)	August 7	St. Petersburg, Florida (Florida Theater) (three shows)
December 2	Atlanta (Sports Arena)	August 8	Orlando, Florida (two shows)
December 3	Montgomery, Alabama (State Coliseum)	August 9	Daytona Beach, Florida (Peabody Auditorium) (two shows)
December ?	Memphis (L. C. Humes High School)	August 10	Jacksonville, Florida (Florida Theater) (three shows)

1956

January 29	Richmond, Virginia (Mosque Theater)
February 5	Norfolk, Virginia (Monticello Auditorium)
February 6	Greensboro, North Carolina (National Theater)

Elvis, Scotty, and Bill on tour in 1956. (Photo courtesy Jeff Wheatcraft)

August 11	Jacksonville, Florida (Florida Theater) (three shows)
August 12	New Orleans (Municipal Auditorium)
September 26	Tupelo, Mississippi (Mississippi-Alabama Fair and Dairy Show) (two shows)
October 11	Dallas (Cotton Bowl Stadium)
October 12	Waco, Texas (Heart o' Texas Coliseum)
October 13	San Antonio
October 14	Houston
October 15	Corpus Christi, Texas
November 23	Toledo, Ohio (Sports Arena) (two shows)
November 24	Cleveland
November 25	Louisville, Kentucky (Armory)

1957

March 28	Chicago (International Amphitheatre)
March 29	St. Louis (Kiel Auditorium)
March 30	Fort Wayne, Indiana
March 31	Detroit (Olympia Stadium) (two shows)
April 1	Buffalo
April 2	Toronto (Maple Leaf Garden) (two shows)
April 3	Ottawa (two shows)
April 5	Philadelphia (Sports Arena) (two shows)
April 6	Philadelphia (Sports Arena) (two shows)

April 9	Wichita Falls, Texas (Municipal Auditorium)
August 30	Spokane, Washington (Memorial Stadium)
August 31	Vancouver, British Columbia (Empire Stadium)
September 1	Tacoma, Washington (Tacoma Stadium)
September 2	Seattle (Rainier Ballpark) (two shows)
September 3	Portland, Oregon (Multomah Stadium) (two shows)
September 27	Tupelo, Mississippi (Mississippi-Alabama Fair and Dairy Show) Benefit for the Elvis Presley Youth Recreation Center
October 26	San Francisco (Civic Auditorium) (two shows)
October 27	Oakland (Oakland Auditorium)
October 28–29	Los Angeles (Pan Pacific Auditorium)
November 10	Honolulu (Honolulu Stadium) (two shows)
November 11	Pearl Harbor, Hawaii (Schofield Barracks)
December 31	St. Louis

1958

March 15	Memphis (Russwood Park) (two shows)

1961

| February 25 | Memphis (Ellis Auditorium) (two shows) |
| March 25 | Pearl Harbor, Hawaii (Bloch Arena) |

1969

| July 31–August 28 | Las Vegas (International Hotel) (fifty-seven shows) |

1970

January 26–February 23	Las Vegas (International Hotel) (fifty-seven shows)
February 27	Houston (Astrodome) (two shows)
February 28	Houston (Astrodome) (two shows)
March 1	Houston (Astrodome) (two shows)
August 10–September 7	Las Vegas (International Hotel) (fifty-eight shows)
September 9	Phoenix (Veterans Memorial Coliseum)
September 10	St. Louis (Kiel Auditorium)
September 11	Detroit (Olympia Stadium)
September 12	Miami Beach (Convention Center) (two shows)
September 13	Tampa (Curtis Hixon Hall) (two shows)
September 14	Mobile, Alabama (Municipal Auditorium)
November 10	Oakland (Oakland Coliseum)
November 11	Portland, Oregon (Memorial Coliseum)
November 12	Seattle (Coliseum)
November 13	San Francisco (Cow Palace)
November 14	Los Angeles (Forum) (two shows)
November 15	San Diego (Sports Arena)
November 16	Oklahoma City (State Fairgrounds Arena)
November 17	Denver (Denver Coliseum)

1971

January 26–February 23	Las Vegas (International Hotel) (fifty-seven shows)
July 20–August 2	Stateline, Nevada (Sahara Tahoe Hotel) (twenty-eight shows)
August 9–September 6	Las Vegas (Hilton Hotel) (fifty-seven shows)
November 5	Minneapolis (Metropolitan Sports Center)
November 6	Cleveland (Public Hall Auditorium) (two shows)
November 7	Louisville, Kentucky (Freedom Hall)
November 8	Philadelphia (Spectrum)
November 9	Baltimore (Baltimore Civic Center)
November 10	Boston (Boston Garden)
November 11	Cincinnati (Cincinnati Gardens)
November 12	Houston (The Hofheinz Pavilion)
November 13	Dallas (Memorial Auditorium)
November 14	Tuscaloosa, Alabama (University of Alabama Field House)
November 15	Kansas City, Missouri (Municipal Auditorium)
November 16	Salt Lake City (Salt Palace)

1972

January 26–February 23	Las Vegas (Hilton Hotel) (fifty-seven shows)
April 5	Buffalo (Memorial Auditorium)
April 6	Detroit (Olympia Stadium)
April 7	Dayton, Ohio (University of Dayton Arena)
April 8	Knoxville, Tennessee (Stokely Athletic Center) (two shows)
April 9	Hampton Roads, Virginia (Coliseum) (two shows)
April 10	Richmond, Virginia (Coliseum)
April 11	Roanoke, Virginia (Civic Center Coliseum)
April 12	Indianapolis (Fairgrounds Coliseum)
April 13	Charlotte, North Carolina (Coliseum)
April 14	Greensboro, North Carolina (Coliseum)
April 15	Macon, Georgia (Coliseum) (two shows)

Madison Square Garden. (Photo courtesy Wide World Photos)

April 16	Jacksonville, Florida (Veterans Memorial Coliseum) (two shows)	April 30	Denver (Denver Coliseum)
April 17	Little Rock, Arkansas (Convention Center)	May 4–16	Stateline, Nevada (Sahara Tahoe Hotel) (twenty-five shows) (The engagement was terminated because of Elvis's illness)
April 18	San Antonio (T. H. Barton Coliseum)		
April 19	Albuquerque, New Mexico (Tingley Coliseum)	June 20	Mobile, Alabama (Municipal Auditorium)
June 9	New York City (Madison Square Garden)	June 21	Atlanta (Omni)
June 10	New York City (Madison Square Garden) (two shows)	June 22	Uniondale, New York (Nassau Coliseum)
June 11	New York City (Madison Square Garden)	June 23	Uniondale, New York (Nassau Coliseum) (two shows)
June 12	Fort Wayne, Indiana (Memorial Coliseum)	June 24	Uniondale, New York (Nassau Coliseum)
June 13	Evansville, Indiana (Roberts Memorial Stadium)	June 25	Pittsburgh (Civic Center Arena)
		June 26	Pittsburgh (Civic Center Arena)
June 14	Milwaukee (Milwaukee Arena)	June 27	Cincinnati (Cincinnati Gardens)
June 15	Milwaukee (Milwaukee Arena)	June 28	St. Louis (Kiel Auditorium)
June 16	Chicago (Chicago Stadium)	June 29	Atlanta (Omni)
June 17	Chicago (Chicago Stadium) (two shows)	June 30	Atlanta (Omni) (two shows)
		July 1	Nashville (Municipal Auditorium) (two shows)
June 18	Fort Worth, Texas (Tarrant County Convention Center)	July 2	Oklahoma City (Myriad Convention Center)
June 19	Wichita, Kansas (Henry Levitt Arena)		
June 20	Tulsa, Oklahoma (Civic Assembly Center)	July 3	Atlanta (Omni)
		August 6– September 3	Las Vegas (Hilton Hotel) (fifty-nine shows)
August 4– September 4	Las Vegas (Hilton Hotel) (sixty-three shows)		
November 8	Lubbock, Texas (Municipal Coliseum)	**1974**	
November 9	Tucson, Arizona (Community Center Arena)	January 26– February 9	Las Vegas (Hilton Hotel) (twenty-nine shows)
November 10	El Paso, Texas (Coliseum)	March 1	Tulsa, Oklahoma (Oral Roberts University)
November 11	Oakland (Coliseum)		
November 12	San Bernardino, California (Swing Auditorium)	March 2	Tulsa, Oklahoma (Oral Roberts University)
		March 3	Houston (Astrodome) (two shows)
November 13	San Bernardino, California (Swing Auditorium)	March 4	Monroe, Louisiana (Civic Center)
		March 5	Auburn, Alabama (University Memorial Coliseum)
November 14	Long Beach, California (Long Beach Arena)	March 6	Montgomery, Alabama (Garrett Coliseum)
November 15	Long Beach, California (Long Beach Arena)	March 7	Monroe, Louisiana (Civic Center)
		March 8	Monroe, Louisiana (Civic Center)
November 17	Honolulu (Honolulu International Center)	March 9	Charlotte, North Carolina (Coliseum) (two shows)
November 18	Honolulu (Honolulu International Center) (two shows)	March 10	Roanoke, Virginia (Roanoke Civic Center)
		March 11	Hampton Roads, Virginia (Coliseum)
1973		March 12	Richmond, Virginia (Coliseum)
January 12	Honolulu (Dress rehearsal for the "Elvis: Aloha from Hawaii" TV special performed on January 14)	March 13	Greensboro, North Carolina (Coliseum)
		March 14	Murfreesboro, Tennessee (Murphy Athletic Center)
January 26– February 23	Las Vegas (Hilton Hotel) (fifty-four shows) (He missed three shows due to illness)	March 15	Knoxville, Tennessee (Stokely Athletic Center) (two shows)
		March 16	Memphis (Mid-South Coliseum) (two shows)
April 22	Phoenix (Veteran's Memorial Coliseum)	March 17	Memphis (Mid-South Coliseum) (two shows)
April 23	Anaheim, California (Anaheim Convention Center)	March 18	Richmond, Virginia (Coliseum)
April 24	Anaheim, California (Anaheim Convention Center)	March 19	Murfreesboro, Tennessee (Murphy Athletic Center)
April 25	Fresno, California (Selland Arena) (two shows)	March 20	Memphis (Mid-South Coliseum)
		May 10	San Bernardino, California (Swing Auditorium)
April 26	San Diego (Sports Arena)		
April 27	Portland, Oregon (Memorial Coliseum)	May 11	Los Angeles (Forum) (two shows)
April 28	Spokane, Washington (Coliseum) (two shows)	May 12	Fresno, California (Selland Arena)
April 29	Seattle (Seattle Civic Center) (two shows)		

May 13	San Bernardino, California (Swing Auditorium)		April 29	Murfreesboro, Tennessee (Murphy Athletic Center)
May 16–26	Stateline, Nevada (Sahara Tahoe Hotel) (twenty-two shows)		April 30	Atlanta (Omni)
June 15	Fort Worth, Texas (Tarrant County Convention Center) (two shows)		May 1	Atlanta (Omni)
			May 2	Atlanta (Omni)
June 16	Fort Worth, Texas (Tarrant County Convention Center) (two shows)		May 3	Monroe, Louisiana (Civic Center) (two shows)
June 17	Baton Rouge, Louisiana (University of Louisiana Assembly Center)		May 4	Lake Charles, Louisiana (Civic Center) (two shows)
June 18	Baton Rouge, Louisiana (University of Louisiana Assembly Center)		May 5	Jackson, Mississippi (State Fair Coliseum)
June 19	Amarillo, Texas (Civic Center)		May 6	Murfreesboro, Tennessee (Murphy Athletic Center)
June 20	Des Moines (Veterans Memorial Auditorium)		May 7	Murfreesboro, Tennessee (Murphy Athletic Center)
June 21	Cleveland (Cleveland Convention Center)		May 30	Huntsville, Alabama (Von Braun Civic Center)
June 22	Providence, Rhode Island (Civic Center) (two shows)		May 31	Huntsville, Alabama (Von Braun Civic Center) (two shows)
June 23	Philadelphia (Spectrum) (two shows)		June 1	Huntsville, Alabama (Von Braun Civic Center) (two shows)
June 24	Niagara Falls, New York (International Convention Center) (two shows)		June 2	Mobile, Alabama (Municipal Auditorium) (two shows)
June 25	Columbus, Ohio (St. John's Arena)		June 3	Tuscaloosa, Alabama (University of Alabama Memorial Auditorium)
June 26	Louisville, Kentucky (Freedom Hall)		
June 27	Bloomington, Indiana (Assembly Hall)		June 4	Houston (Hofheinz Pavilion)
June 28	Milwaukee (Milwaukee Arena)		June 5	Houston (Hofheinz Pavilion)
June 29	Kansas City, Missouri (Municipal Auditorium) (two shows)		June 6	Dallas (Dallas Convention Center)
			June 7	Shreveport, Louisiana (Hirsch Coliseum) (two shows)
June 30	Omaha (Civic Auditorium) (two shows)		June 8	Jackson, Mississippi (State Fair Coliseum) (two shows)
July 1	Omaha (Civic Auditorium)		
July 2	Salt Lake City (Salt Palace)		June 9	Jackson, Mississippi (State Fair Coliseum)
August 19– September 2	Las Vegas (Hilton Hotel) (twenty-seven shows) (Elvis missed two additional shows because of illness)		June 10	Memphis (Mid-South Coliseum)
			July 8	Oklahoma City (Myriad Convention Center)
September 27	College Park, Maryland (Maryland Fieldhouse)		July 9	Terre Haute, Indiana (Hulman Civic Center)
September 28	College Park, Maryland (Maryland Fieldhouse)		July 10	Cleveland (Cleveland Coliseum)
September 29	Detroit (Olympia Stadium)		July 11	Charleston, West Virginia (Civic Center)
September 30	South Bend, Indiana (Notre Dame Athletic and Convention Center)		July 12	Charleston, West Virginia (Civic Center) (two shows)
October 1	South Bend, Indiana (Notre Dame Athletic and Convention Center)		July 13	Niagara Falls, New York (International Convention Center) (two shows)
October 2	St. Paul, Minnesota (Civic Center)		July 14	Springfield, Massachusetts (Civic Center)
October 3	St. Paul, Minnesota (Civic Center)		
October 4	Detroit (Olympia Stadium)		July 15	Springfield, Massachusetts (Civic Center)
October 5	Indianapolis (Expo Convention Center) (two shows)		July 16	New Haven, Connecticut (Veterans Memorial Coliseum)
October 6	Dayton, Ohio (University of Dayton Arena) (two shows)		July 17	New Haven, Connecticut (Veterans Memorial Coliseum)
October 7	Wichita, Kansas (Henry Levitt Arena)		July 18	Cleveland (Cleveland Coliseum)
October 8	San Antonio (Convention Center)		July 19	Uniondale, New York (Nassau Coliseum) (two shows)
October 9	Abilene, Texas (Abilene Expo Center)		
October 11–14	Stateline, Nevada (Sahara Tahoe Hotel) (eight shows)		July 20	Norfolk, Virginia (two shows)
			July 21	Greensboro, North Carolina (Coliseum)
1975			July 22	Asheville, North Carolina (Civic Center)
March 18–April 1	Las Vegas (Hilton Hotel) (twenty-nine shows)		July 23	Asheville, North Carolina (Civic Center)
April 24	Macon, Georgia (Coliseum)		July 24	Asheville, North Carolina (Civic Center)
April 25	Jacksonville, Florida (Veterans Memorial Coliseum)		August 18–20	Las Vegas (Hilton Hotel) (five shows) (Elvis canceled because of illness)
April 26	Tampa (Curtis Hixson Hall) (two shows)		
April 27	Lakeland, Florida (Lakeland Civic Center) (two shows)		
April 28	Lakeland, Florida (Lakeland Civic Center)		

| December 2–15 | Las Vegas (Hilton Hotel) (seventeen shows) |
| December 31 | Pontiac, Michigan |

Pontiac, Michigan. Elvis ripped his pants on stage and had to leave to change. (Photo courtesy Eddie Brandt's Saturday Matinee)

1976

March 17	Johnson City, Tennessee (Freedom Hall)
March 18	Johnson City, Tennessee (Freedom Hall)
March 19	Johnson City, Tennessee (Freedom Hall)
March 20	Charlotte, North Carolina (Coliseum) (two shows)
March 21	Cincinnati (Riverfront Stadium) (two shows)
March 22	St. Louis (Kiel Auditorium)
April 21	Kansas City, Missouri (Kemper Arena)
April 22	Omaha (Civic Auditorium)
April 23	Denver (McNichols Arena)
April 24	San Diego (Sports Arena)
April 25	Long Beach, California (Long Beach Arena) (two shows)
April 26	Seattle (Coliseum)
April 27	Spokane, Washington (Coliseum)
April 30–May 9	Stateline, Nevada (Sahara-Tahoe Hotel) (fifteen shows)
May 27	Bloomington, Indiana (Assembly Hall)
May 28	Ames, Iowa (James W. Hilton Coliseum)
May 29	Oklahoma City (Myriad Convention Center)
May 30	Odessa, Texas (Ector County Coliseum) (two shows)
May 31	Lubbock, Texas (Municipal Coliseum)

June 1	Tucson, Arizona (Community Center Arena)
June 2	El Paso, Texas (Civic Center)
June 3	Fort Worth, Texas (Tarrant County Convention Center)
June 4	Atlanta (Omni)
June 5	Atlanta (Omni) (two shows)
June 6	Atlanta (Omni)
June 25	Buffalo (Memorial Auditorium)
June 26	Providence, Rhode Island (Civic Center) (two shows)
June 27	Largo, Maryland (Capital Center) (two shows)
June 28	Philadelphia (Spectrum)
June 29	Richmond, Virginia (Coliseum)
June 30	Greensboro, North Carolina (Coliseum)
July 1	Shreveport, Louisiana (Hirsch Coliseum)
July 2	Baton Rouge, Louisiana (Assembly Center)
July 3	Fort Worth, Texas (Tarrant County Convention Center)
July 4	Tulsa, Oklahoma (Oral Roberts University)
July 5	Memphis (Mid-South Coliseum)
July 23	Louisville, Kentucky (Freedom Hall)
July 24	Charleston, West Virginia (Civic Center) (two shows)
July 25	Syracuse, New York (Onondaga War Memorial Auditorium)
July 26	Rochester, New York (Community War Memorial Auditorium)
July 27	Syracuse, New York (Onondaga War Memorial Auditorium)
July 28	Hartford, Connecticut (Civic Center)
July 29	Springfield, Massachusetts (Civic Center)
July 30	New Haven, Connecticut (Veterans Memorial Coliseum)
July 31	Hampton Roads, Virginia (Coliseum)
August 1	Hampton Roads, Virginia (Coliseum)
August 2	Roanoke, Virginia (Civic Center)
August 3	Fayetteville, North Carolina (Cumberland County Memorial Auditorium)
August 4	Fayetteville, North Carolina (Cumberland County Memorial Auditorium)
August 5	Fayetteville, North Carolina (Cumberland County Memorial Auditorium)
August 27	San Antonio (Convention Center)
August 28	Houston (Hofheinz Pavilion)
August 29	Mobile, Alabama (Municipal Auditorium)
August 30	Tuscaloosa, Alabama (Memorial Coliseum)
August 31	Macon, Georgia (Coliseum)
September 1	Jacksonville, Florida (Veterans Memorial Coliseum)
September 2	Tampa (Curtis Hixson Hall)
September 3	St. Petersburg, Florida (St. Petersburg Bay Front Center)
September 4	Lakeland, Florida (Civic Center) (two shows)
September 5	Jackson, Mississippi (State Fair Civic Center)

September 6	Huntsville, Alabama (Von Braun Civic Center)
September 7	Pine Bluff, Arkansas (Convention Center)
September 8	Pine Bluff, Arkansas (Convention Center)
October 14	Chicago (Chicago Stadium)
October 15	Chicago (Chicago Stadium)
October 16	Duluth, Minnesota
October 17	Minneapolis (Metropolitan Sports Center)
October 18	Sioux Falls, South Dakota (Arena)
October 19	Madison, Wisconsin (Dane County Coliseum)
October 20	South Bend, Indiana (Notre Dame University Athletic and Convention Center)
October 21	Kalamazoo, Michigan (Wings Stadium)
October 22	Champaign, Illinois (Assembly Hall)
October 23	Cleveland (Cleveland Coliseum)
October 24	Evansville, Indiana (Roberts Memorial Stadium)
October 25	Fort Wayne, Indiana (Memorial Coliseum)
October 26	Dayton, Ohio (University of Dayton Arena)
October 27	Carbondale, Illinois (Southern Illinois University Arena)
November 24	Reno, Nevada (Centennial Coliseum)
November 25	Eugene, Oregon (McArthur Court)
November 26	Portland, Oregon (Memorial Coliseum)
November 27	Eugene, Oregon (McArthur Court)
November 28	San Francisco (Cow Palace)
November 29	San Francisco (Cow Palace)
November 30	Anaheim, California (Anaheim Convention Center)
December 2–12	Las Vegas (Hilton Hotel) (fifteen shows)
December 27	Wichita, Kansas (Henry Levitt Arena)
December 28	Dallas (Memorial Auditorium)
December 29	Birmingham, Alabama (Civic Center)
December 30	Atlanta (Omni)
December 31	Pittsburgh (Civic Center Arena)

1977

February 12	Hollywood, Florida (Sportatorium)
February 13	West Palm Beach, Florida (Civic Auditorium)
February 14	St. Petersburg, Florida (St. Petersburg Bay Front Center)
February 15	Orlando, Florida (Sports Stadium)
February 16	Montgomery, Alabama (Garrett Coliseum)
February 17	Savannah, Georgia (Savannah Civic Center)
February 18	Columbia, South Carolina (Carolina Coliseum)
February 19	Johnson City, Tennessee (Freedom Hall)
February 20	Charlotte, North Carolina (Coliseum)
February 21	Charlotte, North Carolina (Coliseum)
March 23	Tempe, Arizona (Arizona State University Activities Center)
March 24	Amarillo, Texas (Civic Center)
March 25	Norman, Oklahoma (Lloyd Noble Center)
March 26	Norman, Oklahoma (Lloyd Noble Center)

March 27	Abilene, Texas (Taylor County Coliseum)
March 28	Austin, Texas (Municipal Auditorium)
March 29	Alexandria, Louisiana (Rapides Parish Coliseum)
March 30	Alexandria, Louisiana (Rapides Parish Coliseum)
April 21	Greensboro, North Carolina (Coliseum)
April 22	Detroit (Olympia Stadium)
April 23	Toledo, Ohio (University of Toledo Centennial Hall)
April 24	Ann Arbor, Michigan (Crisler Arena)
April 25	Saginaw, Michigan (Saginaw Civic Center)
April 26	Kalamazoo, Michigan (Wings Stadium)
April 27	Milwaukee (Milwaukee Arena)
April 28	Green Bay, Wisconsin (Brown County Veterans Memorial Coliseum)
April 29	Duluth, Minnesota (Arena)
April 30	St. Paul, Minnesota (Civic Center)
May 1	Chicago (Chicago Stadium)
May 2	Chicago (Chicago Stadium)
May 3	Saginaw, Michigan (Saginaw Civic Center)
May 20	Knoxville, Tennessee (Stokely Athletic Center)
May 21	Louisville, Kentucky (Freedom Hall)
May 22	Landover, Maryland (Capital Center)
May 23	Providence, Rhode Island (Civic Center)
May 24	Augusta, Maine (Civic Center)
May 25	Rochester, New York (Community War Memorial Auditorium)
May 26	Binghamton, New York
May 27	Binghamton, New York
May 28	Philadelphia (Spectrum)
May 29	Baltimore (Civic Center)
May 30	Jacksonville, Florida (Veterans Memorial Coliseum)
May 31	Baton Rouge, Louisiana
June 1	Macon, Georgia (Coliseum)
June 2	Mobile, Alabama (Municipal Auditorium)
June 17	Springfield, Missouri (Hammons Center)
June 18	Kansas City, Missouri (Kemper Arena)
June 19	Omaha (Civic Auditorium)
June 20	Lincoln, Nebraska (Pershing Municipal Auditorium)
June 21	Rapid City, South Dakota (Rushmore Plaza Civic Center)
June 22	Sioux Falls, South Dakota (Arena)
June 23	Des Moines (Veterans Memorial Auditorium)
June 24	Madison, Wisconsin (Dane County Coliseum)
June 25	Cincinnati (Riverfront Stadium)
June 26	Indianapolis (Market Square Arena) [Elvis's final concert]

1977

Canceled concert shows (before Elvis's death):

March 31	Baton Rouge, Louisiana
April 1	Mobile, Alabama (Municipal Auditorium)
April 2	Macon, Georgia (Coliseum)

Providence, Rhode Island. (Photo courtesy Wide World Photos)

April 3	Jacksonville, Florida (Coliseum)	August 19	Utica, New York
		August 20	Syracuse, New York
(Elvis made up all four of the appearances at a later date.)		August 21	Hartford, Connecticut
		August 22	Uniondale, New York
		August 23	Lexington, Kentucky
1977		August 24	Roanoke, Virginia
Canceled concert shows (after Elvis's death):		August 25	Fayetteville, North Carolina
		August 26	Asheville, North Carolina
August 17–18	Portland, Maine	August 27–28	Memphis (two shows)

PART III
HIS MUSIC

Songs

In this section we've listed every song Elvis is known to have recorded or is thought to have recorded, as well as several songs sung in concert that have not appeared on record.

Each entry contains the composer(s), history of the song (if known), original recordings, any other significant recordings, and the date and place of Elvis's recording session. If a single made any of the *Billboard* charts, we've given the highest position attained. It should be mentioned that *Billboard*'s Hot 100 chart began in August 1958. For the sake of continuity, Elvis's releases before that date are ranked according to *Billboard*'s Top 100 chart, which is the acknowledged predecessor to the Hot 100. This explains why some sources list eighteen number one singles and others only fourteen. "I Want You, I Need You, I Love You," "Hound Dog," "Too Much," and "Hard Headed Woman" never reached number one on the Top 100 chart, although they did reach the top spot on the less prestigious charts, Best Sellers in Stores, Most Played by Jockeys, and Most Played in Juke Boxes. Also included in each entry is every television and movie performance of the song.

Following each song entry, we've listed every Elvis single, EP, and standard RCA album on which the song appears, as well as every bootleg LP listed in this book on which it appears. When the version on the EP, LP, or bootleg is different from the regular RCA release, we've included that information. This includes alternate takes, alternate mixes, and the places and dates of live recordings.

A cutoff date of August 1, 1988, has been used for all musical entries.

ADAM AND EVIL

Elvis sang this Fred Wise–Randy Starr composition in his 1966 film *Spinout*. "Adam and Evil" was recorded in February 1966 at Radio Recorders.

LPs:
• *Spinout*

AFTER LOVING YOU

"After Loving You" was written by Eddie Miller and Johnny Lantz and recorded by Joe Henderson (Todd 1077) in 1962. Elvis recorded the song at American Sound Studios on February 18, 1969. On October 17, 1980, Felton Jarvis laid a new instrumental track for "After Loving You" at Young 'Un Sound in Nashville. The new version was released on the *Guitar Man* album.

LPs:
• *From Elvis in Memphis*
• *Guitar Man* (new instrumental track)
• *The Memphis Record*

AIN'T THAT LOVING YOU BABY

"Ain't That Loving You Baby" was written by Clyde Otis and Ivory Joe Hunter and recorded by Eddie Riff. This song should not be confused with the 1956 Jimmy Reed song "Ain't That Lovin' You Baby." Elvis recorded the song on June 10, 1958, at RCA's Nashville studios, but RCA didn't release it until 1964. That single had a 10-week stay on *Billboard*'s Hot 100 chart, peaking at #16. Sales of over a million copies are claimed for "Ain't That Loving You Baby."

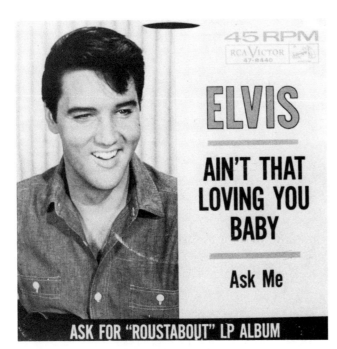

(Photo courtesy Don Fink)

Singles:
• "AIN'T THAT LOVING YOU BABY"/"Ask Me" (RCA 47-8440) September 1964. Standard release. The original picture sleeves read "Coming Soon! ROUSTABOUT Album." In October 1964 the sleeves were changed to read, "Ask for ROUSTABOUT Album."
• "AIN'T THAT LOVING YOU BABY"/"Ask Me" (RCA 447-0649) November 1965. Gold Standard Series reissue.

LPs:
• *Elvis' Gold Records, Volume 4*
• *Elvis: Worldwide 50 Gold Award Hits, Volume 1*
• *Reconsider Baby* (alternate take that has a faster tempo and no Jordanaires)

ALFIE

"Alfie" was written by Hal David and Burt Bacharach for the 1966 film *Alfie*, starring Michael Caine and Shelley Winters. Although Dionne Warwick had the big hit (Scepter 12187), reaching #15 on *Billboard*'s Hot 100 chart, it was Cher's version (Imperial 66192) that was used on the movie soundtrack. "Alfie" was nominated for an Oscar for Best Song, but lost to "Born Free."

Elvis sang one line of "Alfie" before singing "I'll Remember You" at the Las Vegas Hilton on February 20, 1973.

ALL I NEEDED WAS THE RAIN

Elvis sang "All I Needed Was the Rain" in his 1968 film *Stay Away, Joe*. The Sid Wayne–Ben Weisman song was recorded at RCA's Nashville studios on October 2, 1967. The film version had Elvis talking at the end of the song and dogs howling in the background.

LPs:
• *Elvis Sings Flaming Star*
• *Singer Presents Elvis Singing Flaming Star and Others*

ALL I REALLY WANT TO DO

Bob Dylan wrote and recorded "All I Really Want to Do" in 1964. It appeared on his LP *Another Side of Bob Dylan* (Columbia CS 8993). In 1965 both Cher (Imperial 66114) and the Byrds (Columbia 43332) had hit versions, with Cher's release reaching #15 on the Hot 100 chart and the Byrds reaching #40.

Elvis sang "All I Really Want to Do" in concert in the 1970s.

ALL MY TRIALS

(See *An American Trilogy*)

ALL SHOOK UP

While Otis Blackwell was sitting in the office of Shalimar Music in 1956, Al Stanton, one of the owners of Shalimar, came by shaking his bottle of Pepsi-Cola. Stanton said to Blackwell, "Why don't you write a song called 'All Shook Up'?" Blackwell did. At least two artists recorded "All Shook Up" before Elvis. Both David Hill (Aladdin 3359) and Vicki Young (Capitol

3425) recorded the song in 1956. Elvis didn't record "All Shook Up" until January 12, 1957, at Radio Recorders. Featured on piano was Dudley Brooks. Take #10 was chosen for release by RCA. "All Shook Up" entered *Billboard*'s Top 100 chart at #25. By its third week on the chart, it had become number one, replacing Perry Como's "Round and Round." "All Shook Up" spent eight straight weeks at number one before being dethroned by Pat Boone's "Love Letters in the Sand." The total stay on the chart was 30 weeks—the longest of any Presley single. On the country chart, "All Shook Up" peaked at #3, but it topped the rhythm & blues chart for four weeks. In England it became the first Presley single to top the British charts (which it did for seven weeks). Total sales exceeded two million copies. Elvis singing "Yeah, yeah" in the lyrics inspired John Lennon and Paul McCartney to add "Yeah, yeah, yeah" to "She Loves You."

Elvis sang "All Shook Up" in his 1968 TV special, "Elvis," and the 1970 documentary *Elvis—That's the Way It Is*. The latter was from an August 1970 concert at the International Hotel in Las Vegas.

In 1974 Suzi Quatro first reached the charts with her rendition of "All Shook Up" (Bell 45477). The recording peaked at #85 on the Hot 100 chart. After Elvis's death in 1977, Otis Blackwell recorded an album titled *These Are My Songs* (Inner City 1032), which included his version of "All Shook Up."

Singles:
- "ALL SHOOK UP"/"That's When Your Heartaches Begin" (RCA 20-6870) March 1957. Standard 78 RPM release.
- "ALL SHOOK UP"/"That's When Your Heartaches Begin" (RCA 47-6870) March 1957. Standard 45 RPM release.
- "ALL SHOOK UP"/"That's When Your Heartaches Begin" (RCA 447-0618) March 1959. Gold Standard Series reissue.
- "ALL SHOOK UP"/"That's When Your Heartaches Begin" (RCA PB-11106) October 1977. One of 15 singles in the boxed set *15 Golden Records—30 Golden Hits* (RCA PP-11301), and the *20 Hits in Full Color Sleeves* (RCA PP-11340) boxed set released two months later.
- "ALL SHOOK UP"/"Teddy Bear" (RCA PB-13888) October 1984. One of six singles in the boxed set *Elvis' Greatest Hits—Golden Singles, Volume 1* (RCA PP-13897) The record was pressed on gold vinyl and had a special gold "50th" anniversary label.

EPs:
- *A Touch of Gold, Volume 3*
- *Tupperware's Hit Parade*

LPs:
- *Elvis* (RCA DPL2-0056[e])
- *Elvis Aron Presley* (USS *Arizona* Memorial; March 25, 1961) (Dallas; June 6, 1975)
- *Elvis as Recorded at Madison Square Garden* (June 10, 1972)
- *Elvis' Golden Records*
- *Elvis in Person* (Las Vegas; August 22, 1969)
- *Elvis—TV Special* ("Elvis" TV special taping; June 29, 1968, at 6:00 P.M. show)
- *Elvis: Worldwide 50 Gold Award Hits, Volume 1*
- *From Memphis to Vegas/From Vegas to Memphis* (Las Vegas; August 22, 1969)
- *The Number One Hits*
- *Pure Gold*
- *The Top Ten Hits*

Bootleg LPs:
- *America's Own* (Uniondale, N.Y.; July 19, 1975)
- *The Burbank Sessions, Volume 2* ("Elvis" TV special taping; June 29, 1968, at 6:00 P.M. and 8:00 P.M. shows)
- *Cadillac Elvis* (*Elvis—That's the Way It Is* soundtrack)
- *Elvis' 1961 Hawaii Benefit Concert* (USS *Arizona* Memorial; March 25, 1961)
- *From Las Vegas . . . to Niagara Falls* (Niagara Falls, N.Y.; June 24, 1974)
- *The Hillbilly Cat "Live"* (Las Vegas; August 1970)
- *King of Las Vegas Live* (*Elvis—That's the Way It Is* soundtrack)
- *That's the Way It Is* (*Elvis—That's the Way It Is* soundtrack)
- *The Vegas Years, 1972–1975* (Las Vegas; 1972)

ALL THAT I AM

Elvis sang "All That I Am" in his 1966 movie *Spinout*. The recording session took place in February 1966, probably at Radio Recorders. The single release had an eight-week stay on *Billboard*'s Hot 100 chart, peaking at #41. It fared better on the Easy-Listening chart, reaching #9. Sales of over one million copies are claimed for this Sid Tepper–Roy C. Bennett composition.

Singles:
- "Spinout"/"ALL THAT I AM" (RCA 47-8941) September 1966. Standard release. The original picture sleeves read, "Watch for Elvis' SPINOUT LP." In October the sleeves were changed to read, "Ask for Elvis' SPINOUT LP."
- "Spinout"/"ALL THAT I AM" (RCA 447-0658) February 1968. Gold Standard Series reissue.

LPs:
- *Spinout*

ALMOST

"Almost" was written by Buddy Kaye and Ben Weisman and sung by Elvis in his 1969 film *The Trouble with Girls*. He recorded the song on October 14 or 28, 1968, at United Recorders in Hollywood. The film version of "Almost" is a different take than the one on record (which is take #31).

LPs:
- *Let's Be Friends*

Bootleg LPs:
- *Behind Closed Doors* (alternate take, with no string accompaniment)

ALMOST ALWAYS TRUE

Elvis sang "Almost Always True" in his 1961 movie *Blue Hawaii*. The film version had added commentary by Joan Blackman. "Almost Always True" was written by Fred Wise and Ben Weisman, and recorded by Elvis on March 22, 1961, at Radio Recorders.

LPs:
- *Blue Hawaii*

Bootleg LPs:
- *Behind Closed Doors* (take #4 [false start] and take #5)
- *The Blue Hawaii Box* (takes #1–8)
- *The Blue Hawaii Sessions* (takes #1 and #3)
- *Unfinished Business* (alternate take ?)

ALMOST IN LOVE

Written by Rick Bonfa and Randy Starr, "Almost in Love" was sung by Elvis in his 1968 movie *Live a Little, Love a Little*. The instrumental track was recorded on March 7, 1968, at Western Recorders in Hollywood. Elvis's vocal was added at a later date. The album version had a shorter instrumental introduction than the film version. The single release had a short two-week stay on *Billboard*'s Hot 100 chart, reaching #95.

Singles:
- "A Little Less Conversation"/"ALMOST IN LOVE" (RCA 47-9610) September 15, 1968. Standard release.
- "A Little Less Conversation"/"ALMOST IN LOVE" (RCA 447-0667) December 1970. Gold Standard Series reissue.

LPs:
- *Almost in Love*

ALOHA OE

"Aloha Oe" (meaning "Farewell to Thee") was written by Queen Liliuokalani of Hawaii in 1878. A phrase in the song was inspired by "There's Music in the Air" (1854) by Francis Robert Crosby and George Frederick Root. Bing Crosby recorded the song in 1936 (Decca 880). In 1938 Harry Owens had a popular recording of "Aloha Oe" (Decca 1907). The song was heard in the film *Hawaii Calls*.

Elvis recorded "Aloha Oe" on March 21, 1961, at Radio Recorders for his film *Blue Hawaii*. The commercial release was a splice of two different takes.

LPs:
- *Blue Hawaii*

Bootleg LPs:
- *The Blue Hawaii Box* (takes #1–6)
- *Leavin' It Up to You* (alternate take)

ALONG CAME JONES

Jerry Leiber and Mike Stoller wrote "Along Came Jones" in 1959 as a satire on western movies. The title was taken from the 1945 Gary Cooper film *Along Came Jones*. The Coasters recorded "Along Came Jones" (Atco 6141) in 1959, their version reaching #9 on *Billboard*'s Hot 100 chart and #14 on the rhythm & blues chart. In 1969 Ray Stevens's cover recording (Monument 1150) peaked at #27.

Elvis sang one line of "Along Came Jones" to singer Tom Jones at the International Hotel in Las Vegas on August 21, 1970.

ALSO SPRACH ZARATHUSTRA

This classical piece was composed by Richard Strauss (1864–1949) in 1896. "Also Sprach Zarathustra" served as the theme music for Stanley Kubrick's 1968 film, *2001: A Space Odyssey*[1]. Segments of the music also appeared in *Catch-22* (1970) and *The Big Bus* (1976). A rock version of the music was a #2 hit and million-seller for Brazilian-born Deodato[2] (real name: Eumir Deodato Almeida) in 1973 on CTI Records (CTI 12).

Beginning in early 1972, Elvis opened his live concerts with the orchestra playing the distinctive opening portion of "Also Sprach Zarathustra." That opening has appeared on numerous Elvis albums.

ALWAYS LATE (WITH YOUR KISSES)

Written by Lefty Frizzell and Blackie Crawford, "Always Late (with Your Kisses)" was recorded by Frizzell in 1951 (Columbia 20837). It became his greatest hit, topping the country chart. The flip side, "Mom and Dad's Waltz" went to #2. In the spring of 1988 Dwight Yoakam (Reprise 7-27994) had a top 20 country hit with his version of the song.

"Always Late (with Your Kisses)" is one of the songs that appeared in Hill and Range's song folio *The Elvis Presley Album of Juke Box Favorites*. Speculation has it that Elvis recorded the song while at Sun Records, but no tape has ever surfaced. He may, however, have sung "Always Late (with Your Kisses)" on tour in 1954 and 1955 and on the "Louisiana Hayride." But no documentation has been forthcoming.

ALWAYS ON MY MIND

Mark James, Wayne Carson, and Johnny Christopher wrote "Always on My Mind" for Elvis, who recorded the song on March 29, 1972, at RCA's Hollywood studios. Film of the recording session appeared in the 1981 documentary *This Is Elvis*. Although Elvis was the first to record the song, it was Brenda Lee's version (Decca 32975) that was released first. In the summer of 1972 she reached #45 on the country chart. Elvis's single release had a 13-week stay on the country chart, peaking at #16. In 1982 Willie Nelson had an even more successful version of "Always on My Mind" (Columbia 02741), reaching #5 on the Hot 100 chart and topping the country chart. The Country Music Association named "Always on My Mind" the Song of the Year in both 1982 and 1983. The Pet Shop Boys had a top 20 hit with the song in early 1988 (EMI-Manhattan 50123).

Singles:
- "Separate Ways"/"ALWAYS ON MY MIND" (RCA 74-0815) November 1972. Standard release.
- "Separate Ways"/"ALWAYS ON MY MIND" (RCA GB-10486) February 1976. Gold Standard Series reissue.
- "The Elvis Medley"/"ALWAYS ON MY MIND" (RCA PB-13351) November 1982. New release with a different flip side.
- "ALWAYS ON MY MIND"/"My Boy" (RCA PB-14090) July 1985. New release with a different flip side. This record was pressed on purple vinyl and had a special gold "50th" anniversary label.
- "ALWAYS ON MY MIND"/"ALWAYS ON MY MIND" (RCA JK-14090) July 1985. Special disc jockey promotional release pressed on purple vinyl with a special gold "50th" anniversary label.

LPs:
- *Always on My Mind*
- *The Elvis Medley*
- *Separate Ways*
- *This Is Elvis* (alternate take)

---

[1]The movie soundtrack LP (MGM 13) reached #24 on *Billboard*'s top LPs chart. It stayed on the chart for 120 weeks.
[2]Deodato produced Kool and the Gang's records from 1979 to 1982.

AM I READY

Elvis sang "Am I Ready" in his 1966 movie *Spinout*. The recording session took place in February 1966, probably at Radio Recorders. Take #7 was released by RCA. "Am I Ready" was written by Sid Tepper and Roy C. Bennett.

LPs:
* *Burning Love and Hits from His Movies, Volume 2*
* *Spinout*

AMAZING GRACE

This traditional hymn was written by the Rev. John Newton of the Church of England in 1779. "Amazing Grace" uses only six different notes in its sixteen-bar melody. The hymn was first popularized in America by Singin' Billy Walker. In 1971 Judy Collins had a #15 Hot 100 hit and million-seller with "Amazing Grace" (Elektra 45709). The next year, the Royal Scots Dragoon Guards Band (RCA 74-0709) had the only million-seller that ever used bagpipes. The bagpipes solo was performed by Major Tony Crease. Their recording reached #11 on *Billboard*'s Hot 100 chart. A segment of their recording can be heard in the 1978 movie *Invasion of the Body Snatchers*. At the funeral of Ronnie Van Zant, Charlie Daniels and the .38 Special sang "Amazing Grace."

Elvis recorded "Amazing Grace" on March 15, 1971, at RCA's Nashville studios.

LPs:
* *He Touched Me*

AMEN

"Amen" dates back several decades. The composer is unknown. In the 1940 Walter Brennan film *Maryland*, "Amen" was sung by blacks in a church. Sidney Poitier, in his Oscar-winning role of Homer Smith, taught five German nuns to sing "Amen" in *Lilies of the Field* (1963). John W. Pate Sr. and Curtis Mayfield wrote an adaptation of "Amen" for their group, the Impressions, in 1964. That recording, written as a Christmas song, reached #7 on *Billboard*'s Hot 100 chart. Otis Redding charted with still another version of "Amen" (Atco 6592) in 1968.

Elvis sang "Amen" at several of his concerts in the 1970s, always as a tag to "I Got a Woman." An April 9, 1972, performance at Hampton Roads, Virginia, was used in the documentary *Elvis on Tour*. His last concert (at the Market Square Arena in Indianapolis on June 26, 1977) included the "I Got a Woman"/"Amen" medley. "Amen" was uncredited in the LP *Elvis Recorded Live on Stage in Memphis*.

LPs:
* *Elvis Aron Presley* (Dallas; June 6, 1975)
* *Elvis in Concert* (Rapid City, South Dakota; June 21, 1977)
* *Elvis Recorded Live on Stage in Memphis* (Memphis; March 20, 1974)

Bootleg LPs:
* *America's Own* (Uniondale, N.Y.; July 19, 1975)
* *Elvis Presley Is Alive and Well and Singing in Las Vegas, Volume 1* (Las Vegas; August 1975)

* *From Hollywood to Vegas* (*Elvis on Tour* soundtrack)
* *From Las Vegas . . . to Niagara Falls* (Las Vegas; September 3, 1973)
* *The King: From the Dark to the Light* (*Elvis on Tour* soundtrack)
* *The Last Farewell* (Indianapolis; June 26, 1977)
* *Rockin' with Elvis April Fool's Day* (Las Vegas; April 1, 1975)
* *Rockin' with Elvis New Year's Eve Pittsburgh, Pa. Dec. 31, 1976* (Pittsburgh; December 31, 1976)
* *The Vegas Years, 1972–1975* (Las Vegas; August 1975)

AMERICA
(See *America the Beautiful*)

AMERICA THE BEAUTIFUL

Katherine Lee Bates, an English teacher at Wellesley College in Massachusetts, was inspired to write the poem *America the Beautiful* in the summer of 1893 after taking in the view from the summit of Pike's Peak. The poem was first published on July 4, 1895, in *The Congregationalist*, a Boston periodical. It was later set to music (exact date unknown), using the melody of "Materna." "Materna" had been composed by Samuel Augustus Ward and first published on July 12, 1888, in *The Parish Choir* in Boston. It previously had been used as the melody for the hymn "O Mother Dear Jerusalem."

Frank Sinatra had a popular recording of "America the Beautiful" (Columbia 36886) in 1945; it was the flip side of his hit "The House I Live In."

Elvis sang "America the Beautiful" at many of his concerts from 1975 to 1977. The single release was recorded at the midnight show at the Las Vegas Hilton on December 13, 1975. The labels of the promotional copies and some of the commercial releases incorrectly listed the song's title as "America." "America the Beautiful" failed to chart. The song was played by three children on kazoos in Elvis's 1969 movie *The Trouble with Girls*.

Many television stations use Ray Charles's version of "America the Beautiful" to sign off at night.

Singles:
* "My Way"/"AMERICA THE BEAUTIFUL" (RCA PB-11165) November 1977. Standard release.
* "My Way"/"AMERICA" (RCA JH-11165) November 1977. Disc jockey promotional release. The label incorrectly listed "America the Beautiful" as "America."

LPs:
* *Elvis Aron Presley*

AN AMERICAN TRILOGY

"An American Trilogy" is a medley of three songs arranged by Mickey Newbury: "Dixie," "The Battle Hymn of the Republic," and "All My Trials." His recording in 1971 (Elektra 45750) reached #26 on *Billboard*'s Hot 100 chart.

"Dixie" was written on Sunday, April 3, 1859, by Dan Emmett[1] for a minstrel show. The next night, the song was introduced by the Bryant Minstrels in New York City at Mechanics Hall. "Dixie"[2] was first performed in the South in Charleston, South Carolina, in December 1860, by Rumsey and Newcomb. Before General Pickett's charge at Gettysburg, "Dixie" was played to boost the troops' morale. Abraham Lincoln requested that the song be played by the Union band upon hearing the news of General Lee's surrender at the Appomattox Court House on April 9, 1865. "Dixie" was one of several tunes played by the U.S. Army band as Elvis boarded the USS General *Randall* to sail to West Germany in 1958.

The words to "The Battle Hymn of the Republic" were written by Julia Ward Howe in December 1861 at the Willard Hotel in Washington, D.C. A friend of Howe's, the Rev. James Freeman Clarke, had suggested that she write new war lyrics to the melody of "John Brown's Body."[3] In February 1862 the *Atlantic Monthly* published Howe's poem under the title "The Battle Hymn of the Republic." The title was suggested by the editor, who paid Howe five dollars.

Andy Williams sang "The Battle Hymn of the Republic" at the 1968 funeral of Sen. Robert Kennedy. Three years earlier, the Mormon Tabernacle Choir had sung it at the inauguration of President Lyndon Johnson. (Their 1959 recording reached #13 on *Billboard*'s Hot 100 chart [Columbia 41459].)

"All My Trials" is a traditional song whose composer is unknown. In 1959 the Kingston Trio recorded a version of the song titled "All My Sorrows" (Capitol 4221).

Elvis sang "An American Trilogy" in concert on several occasions in the 1970s. It was always a show-stopper. His 1972 single release was recorded from a performance at the Las Vegas Hilton on February 17, 1972. The flute solo on the recording was by Jimmy Mulidore. "An American Trilogy" had a six-week stay on *Billboard*'s Hot 100 chart, peaking at #66. On the Easy-Listening chart the song reached #31. "An American Trilogy" could be heard in the 1972 documentary *Elvis on Tour* (from an April 9, 1972, performance at Hampton Roads, Virginia); in the 1973 TV special "Elvis: Aloha from Hawaii"; and in the 1981 documentary *This Is Elvis* (clip from *Elvis on Tour*).

Wayne Newton sang "An American Trilogy" on July 14, 1980, at the Republican presidential nominating convention.

Singles:
- "AN AMERICAN TRILOGY"/"The First Time Ever I Saw Your Face" (RCA 74-0672) April 1972. Standard release.
- "AN AMERICAN TRILOGY"/"Until It's Time for You to Go" (RCA 447-0685) May 1973. Gold Standard Series original using a different flip side.
- "The Impossible Dream"/"AN AMERICAN TRILOGY" (RCA JH-13302) August 1982. Promotional giveaway for visitors to Tupelo, Mississippi, in August 1982. The picture sleeve read, "Elvis—In Memory—August 16, 1982—Tupelo, Mississippi. You touched all our lives with the heart of your music and the heart of your self. Not one of us is quite the same now that you've come—and gone again. Elvis—we remember you because we can never forget."

LPs:
- *Aloha from Hawaii via Satellite* (Honolulu; January 14, 1973)

- *The Alternate Aloha* (rehearsal concert for "Elvis: Aloha from Hawaii"; January 12, 1973)
- *Elvis Aron Presley* (Las Vegas; February 17, 1972)
- *Elvis as Recorded at Madison Square Garden* (June 10, 1972)
- *Elvis Recorded Live on Stage in Memphis* (March 20, 1974)
- *This Is Elvis* (Hampton Roads, Virginia; April 9, 1972)

Bootleg LPs:
- *Aloha Rehearsal Show—Kui Lee Cancer Benefit* (rehearsal concert for "Elvis: Aloha from Hawaii"; January 12, 1973)
- *A Dog's Life* (rehearsal concert for "Elvis: Aloha from Hawaii"; January 12, 1973)
- *Elvis on Tour* (*Elvis on Tour* soundtrack)
- *From Las Vegas . . . to Niagara Falls* (Niagara Falls, N.Y.; June 24, 1974)
- *Superstar Outtakes, Volume 2* (Las Vegas; 1972)
- *The Vegas Years, 1972–1975* (Las Vegas; 1972)

AN EVENING PRAYER
Elvis recorded this gospel song on May 18, 1971, at RCA's Nashville studios. "An Evening Prayer" was written by C. M. Battersby and Charles H. Gabriel.

LPs:
- *He Touched Me*
- *He Walks Beside Me*

AND I LOVE YOU SO
Don McLean wrote and recorded "And I Love You So" in 1970. It appeared on his debut LP, *Tapestry* (United Artists 5522). Both Bobby Goldsboro (United Artists 50776) in 1971 and Perry Como (RCA 74-0906) in 1973 had hit versions of "And I Love You So," reaching #83 and #29 on the Hot 100 chart, respectively. Como's release reached number one on the Easy-Listening chart, while Goldsboro's peaked at #8.

Elvis recorded "And I Love You So" on March 11, 1975, at RCA's Hollywood studios.

LPs:
- *Elvis Aron Presley—Forever*
- *Elvis in Concert* (Omaha, Nebraska, or Rapid City, South Dakota; June 19 or 21, 1977)
- *Elvis Today*

Bootleg LPs:
- *Elvis Presley Is Alive and Well and Singing in Las Vegas, Volume 1* (Las Vegas; August 1975)
- *Eternal Elvis, Volume 2* (fabricated duet with Shirley Bassey, using Elvis's RCA release)
- *Rockin' with Elvis April Fool's Day* (Las Vegas; April 1, 1975)
- *Standing Room Only, Volume 3* (Omaha, Nebraska, or Rapid City, South Dakota; June 19 or 21, 1977)
- *The Vegas Years, 1972–1975* (Las Vegas; 1975)

AND THE GRASS WON'T PAY NO MIND
Neil Diamond wrote and recorded "And the Grass Won't Pay No Mind" (Uni 55224) in 1970. It was the flip side of "Soolaimon." Later in 1970 Mark Lindsay, lead singer of Paul Revere and the Raiders, had a version

---

[1] Daniel Decatur Emmett was portrayed by Bing Crosby in the 1943 movie *Dixie*.

[2] The term *Dixie*, a synonym for the South, came from a ten-dollar bill that was circulated throughout the South. It was issued by the Citizen's Bank of Louisiana. The New Orleans French population referred to ten as "dix."

[3] "John Brown's Body" was originally titled "Say Brothers, Will You Meet Me." John Brown, the subject of the song, was a descendant of Peter Brown, who came to the New World on the *Mayflower*.

(Columbia 45229) that went to #44 on the Hot 100 chart and #5 on the Easy-Listening chart.

Elvis recorded "And the Grass Won't Pay No Mind" at the American Sound Studios in Memphis on February 18, 1969.

LPs:
- *Back in Memphis*
- *From Memphis to Vegas/From Vegas to Memphis*

ANGEL
Elvis sang "Angel" in his 1962 movie *Follow That Dream*. He recorded the song on July 5, 1961, at RCA's Nashville studios. Sid Tepper and Roy C. Bennett are the composers.

EPs:
- *Follow That Dream*

LPs:
- *C'mon Everybody*
- *Elvis Sings for Children and Grownups Too!*

ANIMAL INSTINCT
"Animal Instinct" had been slated to be sung in Elvis's 1965 film *Harum Scarum*, but was cut from the final print. It's been rumored that some prints of the film with "Animal Extinct" *do* exist, but the authors have never talked with anyone who has seen one. Elvis recorded the song at RCA's Nashville studios in February 1965, probably on the 24th. Bill Giant, Bernie Baum, and Florence Kaye are the composers.

LPs:
- *Harum Scarum*

ANY DAY NOW
Written by Bob Hilliard and Burt Bacharach, "Any Day Now" was recorded by Chuck Jackson (Wand 122) in 1962, the record reaching #23 on *Billboard*'s Hot 100 chart and #2 on the rhythm & blues chart. His version was subtitled "My Wild Beautiful Bird." Percy Sledge had a moderate hit with "Any Day Now" (Atlantic 2616) in 1969, but the biggest hit version has been Ronnie Milsap's 1982 release (RCA PB-13216), which topped the country chart and reached #14 on the Hot 100 chart.

Elvis recorded "Any Day Now" on February 21, 1969, at American Sound Studios. His single release that spring failed to chart.

Singles:
- "In the Ghetto"/"ANY DAY NOW" (RCA 47-9741) April 15, 1969. Standard release. The original picture sleeve read, "Coming Soon—FROM ELVIS IN MEMPHIS Album." One month later, the sleeves were changed to read, "Ask For—FROM ELVIS IN MEMPHIS Album."
- "In the Ghetto"/"ANY DAY NOW" (RCA PB-11100) October 1977. One of 15 singles in the boxed set *15 Golden Records—30 Golden Hits* (RCA PP-11301), and one of 10 singles in the *20 Golden Hits in Full Color Sleeves* (RCA PP-11340) boxed set released two months later.
- "In the Ghetto"/"ANY DAY NOW" (RCA 447-0671) December 1970. Gold Standard Series reissue.

LPs:
- *Elvis: The Other Sides—Worldwide Gold Award Hits, Volume 2*
- *From Elvis in Memphis*
- *The Memphis Record*

Bootleg LPs:
- *Susie Q* (Las Vegas rehearsal; ?)

ANY WAY YOU WANT ME (THAT'S HOW I WILL BE)
Written by Aaron Schroeder and Cliff Owens, "Any Way You Want Me (That's How I Will Be)" was recorded by Elvis on July 2, 1956, at RCA's New York City studios during the first recording session to include all four of the Jordanaires. Take #12 was the one released by RCA. The single release had a 10-week stay on *Billboard*'s Top 100 chart, peaking at #27. Sales of over a million copies were achieved quickly. (Advance orders for the record "Love Me Tender"/"Any Way You Want Me" exceeded one million!)

Singles:
- "Love Me Tender"/"ANY WAY YOU WANT ME" (RCA 20-6643) October 1956. Standard 78 RPM release.
- "Love Me Tender"/"ANY WAY YOU WANT ME" (RCA 47-6643) October 1956. Standard 45 RPM release. Four different color schemes were used for the picture sleeves: black and white, black and green, black and light pink, and black and dark pink.
- "Love Me Tender"/"ANY WAY YOU WANT ME" (RCA 447-0616) March 1959. Gold Standard Series reissue.
- "Love Me Tender"/"ANY WAY YOU WANT ME" (RCA PB-11108) October 1977. One of 15 singles released in the 15-record boxed set *15 Golden Records—30 Golden Hits* (RCA PP-11301). This single was also released two months later in the boxed set *20 Golden Hits in Full Color Sleeves* (RCA PP-11340).

EPs:
- *Any Way You Want Me*
- *DJ-7*

LPs:
- *Elvis' Golden Records*
- *Elvis: Worldwide 50 Gold Award Hits, Volume 1*

ANYONE (COULD FALL IN LOVE WITH YOU)
Elvis recorded "Anyone (Could Fall in Love with You)" on October 3, 1963, at Radio Recorders for his 1964 movie *Kissin' Cousins*, but the song was cut from the final print. Bennie Benjamin, Sol Marcus, and Louis A. DeJesus are the composers.

LPs:
- *Kissin' Cousins*

ANYPLACE IS PARADISE
Elvis recorded "Anyplace Is Paradise," a Joe Thomas tune, at Radio Recorders on September 3, 1956, for his second LP, *Elvis*.

EPs:
- *Elvis, Volume 2*

LPs:
- *Elvis*

ANYTHING THAT'S PART OF YOU

Don Robertson wrote "Anything That's Part of You" for Elvis in early 1961. Elvis recorded the song on October 15, 1961, at RCA's Nashville studios. The single release had an eight-week stay on *Billboard*'s Hot 100 chart, peaking at #31. It did much better on the Easy-Listening chart, reaching a high of #6. Sales of over a million copies are claimed for "Anything That's Part of You."

Singles:
- "Good Luck Charm"/"ANYTHING THAT'S PART OF YOU" (RCA 47-7992) March 1962. Standard release. The picture sleeves came with titles in pink and blue and lavender and rust.
- "Good Luck Charm"/"ANYTHING THAT'S PART OF YOU" (RCA 37-7992) March 1962. Compact 33 Single release.
- "Good Luck Charm"/"ANYTHING THAT'S PART OF YOU" (RCA 447-0636) November 1962. Gold Standard Series reissue.

LPs:
- *Elvis' Golden Records, Volume 3*
- *Elvis: Worldwide 50 Gold Award Hits, Volume 1*

ARE YOU LONESOME TONIGHT?

"Are You Lonesome Tonight?" was written by Roy Turk and Lou Handman in 1926. In 1927 Al Jolson had the first recording of the song, followed closely by popular versions by Vaughn Deleath[1] (Edison 52044) and Henry Burr (Victor 20873). Other recordings of "Are You Lonesome Tonight?" over the years include those by the Blue Barron Orchestra[2] (MGM 10628) in 1950, Jaye P. Morgan (MGM 12752) in 1959, and Donny Osmond (MGM 14677) in 1974. Other than Elvis's recording, Donny Osmond's reached the highest on *Billboard*'s Hot 100 chart—#14.

Elvis recorded "Are You Lonesome Tonight?" on April 4, 1960, at RCA's Nashville studios. Reportedly, it was the only song that Colonel Tom Parker ever urged Elvis to record. Elvis copied his vocal phrasing from the Blue Barron Orchestra's version. The long spoken passage was loosely based on Jacques's speech in Act II, Scene VII of Shakespeare's *As You Like It*. The master is a splice of two or more takes. "Are You Lonesome Tonight?" entered *Billboard*'s Hot 100 chart at #35. The second week, it was #2—the biggest one-week jump within the Top 40 in history. By the third week, "Are You Lonesome Tonight?" had replaced "Stay" by Maurice Williams and the Zodiacs at number one, where it stayed for six weeks. In January 1961, Bert Kaempfert's "Wonderland by Night" took over the top spot. "Are You Lonesome Tonight?" had a total stay in the Hot 100 of 16 weeks. It reached #22 on the country chart and #3 on the rhythm & blues chart. Elvis wouldn't have another song on the country chart until 1968. In England, "Are You Lonesome Tonight?" was number one for four weeks. Worldwide sales have been estimated at four million copies. Elvis received three Grammy Award nominations for "Are You Lonesome Tonight?"—Record of the Year; Best Vocal Performance, Male; and Best Performance by a Pop Singles Artist—but didn't win one.

A July 31, 1969, performance of "Are You Lonesome

(Photo courtesy Don Fink)

Tonight?" at the International Hotel in Las Vegas in which Elvis messed up the lyrics and laughed uncontrollably was released in 1982 in England. That version was released in the United States in 1983 on the *Elvis—A Legendary Performer, Volume 4* LP and on numerous bootlegs.

Singles:
- "ARE YOU LONESOME TONIGHT?"/"I Gotta Know" (RCA 47-7810) November 1960. Standard release.
- "ARE YOU LONESOME TONIGHT?"/"I Gotta Know" (RCA 61-7810) November 1960. "Living Stereo" release.
- "ARE YOU LONESOME TONIGHT?"/"I Gotta Know" (RCA 447-0629) February 1962. Gold Standard Series reissue.
- "ARE YOU LONESOME TONIGHT?"/"I Gotta Know" (RCA PB-11104) October 1977. One of 15 singles in the boxed set *15 Golden Records—30 Golden Hits* (RCA PP-11301), and one of 10 singles in the *20 Golden Hits in Full Color Sleeves* (RCA PP-11340) boxed set released two months later.
- "ARE YOU LONESOME TONIGHT?"/"Can't Help Falling in Love" (RCA PB-13895) October 1984. One of six singles in the boxed set *Elvis' Greatest Hits—Golden Singles, Volume 2* (RCA PP-13898).

EPs:
- *Elvis by Request*

LPs:
- *Elvis—A Legendary Performer, Volume 1* ("Elvis" TV special taping; June 27, 1968, at 8:00 P.M. show)
- *Elvis—A Legendary Performer, Volume 4* (Las Vegas; July 31, 1969) ("Are You Laughing Tonight?" version)
- *Elvis Aron Presley* (USS *Arizona* Memorial; March 25, 1961) (Las Vegas; August 27, 1969)
- *Elvis' Golden Records, Volume 3*
- *Elvis in Concert* (Rapid City, South Dakota; June 21, 1977)
- *Elvis in Person* (Las Vegas; August 22, 1969)
- *Elvis: Worldwide 50 Gold Award Hits, Volume 1*
- *From Memphis to Vegas/From Vegas to Memphis* (Las Vegas; August 22, 1969)

- *A Golden Celebration* ("Elvis" TV special taping; June 27, 1968, at 8:00 P.M. show)
- *The Number One Hits*
- *This Is Elvis*
- *The Top Ten Hits*
- *A Valentine Gift for You*

Bootleg LPs:
- *The Burbank Sessions, Volume 1* ("Elvis" TV special taping; June 27, 1968, at 6:00 P.M. and 8:00 P.M. shows)
- *Elvis' 1961 Hawaii Benefit Concert* (USS *Arizona* Memorial; March 25, 1961)
- *Elvis Rocks and the Girls Roll* (dress rehearsal for the "Elvis" TV special; June 1968)
- *Long Lost Songs* (Las Vegas; 1975)
- *The Monologue L.P.* (Las Vegas; July 31, 1969) ("Are You Laughing Tonight?" version)
- *Rockin' with Elvis New Year's Eve Pittsburgh, Pa. Dec. 31, 1976* (Pittsburgh; December 31, 1976)
- *Standing Room Only, Volume 2* (Pittsburgh; December 31, 1976)
- *Standing Room Only, Volume 3* ("Elvis" TV special taping; June 27, 1968, at 8:00 P.M. show)

ARE YOU SINCERE
"Are You Sincere" was written by Wayne P. Walker in 1957 and first popularized by Andy Williams (Cadence 1340) in 1958. His recording reached #3 on *Billboard*'s Top 100 chart. A 1965 version by Trini Lopez (Reprise 0376) didn't do quite as well, reaching only #85 on the Hot 100 chart and #25 on the Easy-Listening chart.

Elvis recorded "Are You Sincere" on September 24, 1973, at his Palm Springs, California, home. The backing vocals were done by Voice. The original version was released on the LP *Raised on Rock/For Ol' Times Sake*. An alternate version, without the vocal overdubs by Voice, was released on the single and the LP *Our Memories of Elvis, Volume 1*. The single had a 12-week stay on the country chart, peaking at #10.

Singles:
- "ARE YOU SINCERE"/"Solitaire" (RCA PB-11533) May 1979. Standard release.
- "ARE YOU SINCERE"/"Solitaire" (RCA JB-11533) May 1979. Disc jockey promotional release.
- "ARE YOU SINCERE"/"Unchained Melody" (RCA GB-11988) May 1980. Gold Standard Series original with a different flip side.

LPs:
- *Our Memories of Elvis, Volume 1* (alternate take, without overdubbing)
- *Raised on Rock/For Ol' Times Sake*

AS LONG AS I HAVE YOU
Fred Wise and Ben Weisman wrote "As Long as I Have You" for Elvis's 1958 film *King Creole*. Elvis recorded the song at Radio Recorders on January 16, 1958. Two versions were recorded, the one on record and a shorter one that hasn't been officially released, although it has appeared on a few bootlegs. In late 1958 Don Rondo

did a cover version of "As Long as I Have You" (Jubilee 5334) that did not chart.

EPs:
- *King Creole, Volume 1*

LPs:
- *Elvis: The Other Sides—Worldwide Gold Award Hits, Volume 2*
- *King Creole*

Bootleg LPs:
- *From the Beach to the Bayou* (alternate takes #4 and #5, shorter version; Elvis sings with only his piano playing as accompaniment)
- *The Rockin' Rebel* (alternate take ?, shorter version; Elvis sings with only his piano playing as accompaniment)

ASK ME
Originally, "Ask Me" was the Italian song "Io," written by Domenico Modugno. The English lyrics were written by Bill Giant, Bernie Baum, and Florence Kaye. Elvis first recorded "Ask Me" on May 27, 1963, at RCA's Nashville studios. That version has never been released. The released take was recorded at the same studio on January 12, 1964. Elvis's single reached #12 on *Billboard*'s Hot 100 chart during its 12-week stay. An alternate mix was heard on the French single (RCA 45-567): one of the stereo channels was omitted, eliminating the Jordanaires' vocal backing and other instrumentation, and all that was heard was Elvis and Floyd Cramer's organ playing.

Singles:
- "Ain't That Loving You, Baby"/"ASK ME" (RCA 47-8440) September 1964. Standard release. The original picture sleeve read, "Coming Soon! ROUSTABOUT Album." One month later the sleeves were changed to read, "Ask for ROUSTABOUT Album."
- "Ain't That Loving You, Baby"/"ASK ME" (RCA 447-0618) November 1965. Gold Standard Series reissue.

LPs:
- *Elvis' Gold Records, Volume 4*
- *Elvis: The Other Sides—Worldwide Gold Award Hits, Volume 2*

AUBREY
In 1973 Bread had a #15 Hot 100 hit with "Aubrey" (Elektra 45832), which was written by lead singer David Gates. The recording reached #4 on the Easy-Listening chart.

Elvis is known to have sung "Aubrey" in concert in the mid-1970s.

AULD LANG SYNE
This traditional New Year's Eve standard was written by poet Robert Burns in approximately 1789, based on Scottish music published in 1687. Beethoven used variations of "Auld Lang Syne" in his music. In the 1870s a tribute to Ulysses Grant was written based on "Auld Lang Syne"—"Should Brave Ulysses Be Forgot." Guy Lombardo and His Royal Canadians had a 1939 hit

[1]Vaughn Deleath was the first woman to sing on radio.
[2]Trumpet player Danny Davis (later of the Nashville Brass) was a member of the Blue Barron Orchestra.

with the song on Decca Records (Decca 2478). Lombardo became closely identified with "Auld Lang Syne" from then on. Princeton University's school song, "Old Nassau," was inspired by "Auld Lang Syne."

Elvis sang "Auld Lang Syne" at the New Year's Eve concert in Pittsburgh on December 31, 1976. He sang it after "Funny How Time Slips Away."

Bootleg LPs:
- *Rockin' with Elvis New Year's Eve Pittsburgh, Pa. Dec. 31, 1976* (Pittsburgh; December 31, 1976)

AVE MARIA

"Ave Maria" was written in 1859 by Paul Bernard and Charles Gounod. The words were based on Luke 1:28 in the Bible; the music was based on Johann Sebastian Bach's first prelude in "The Well-Tempered Clavichord." In 1949 Perry Como had a #22 hit with "Ave Maria" (RCA 0071). Two years later, Mario Lanza had a popular recording of the song, also on RCA Records (RCA 3228).

Elvis sang "Ave Maria" in a medley with "I Got a Woman" at the International Hotel in Las Vegas in August 1970.

Bootleg LPs:
- *The Hillbilly Cat "Live"* (Las Vegas; August 1970) (in medley with "I Got a Woman")

(YOU'RE SO SQUARE) BABY, I DON'T CARE

Jerry Leiber and Mike Stoller wrote "(You're So Square) Baby, I Don't Care" for Elvis's 1957 movie *Jailhouse Rock*. The instrumental track was recorded on April 30, 1957, at Radio Recorders. Elvis's vocal was recorded sometime in May at MGM. Although the session notes indicate that Dudley Brooks played piano, Mike Stoller has said that he played on the recording. In late 1957 Buddy Holly recorded "(You're So Square) Baby, I Don't Care" for his album *Buddy Holly* (Coral 57210).

EPs:
- *Jailhouse Rock*

LPs:
- *A Date with Elvis* (alternate mix)
- *Elvis: The Other Sides—Worldwide Gold Award Hits, Volume 2*
- *Essential Elvis—The First Movies* (original version, take #16; vocal overdub, take #6)
- *I Was the One* (with overdubbing)

Bootleg LPs:
- *Got a Lot o' Livin' to Do!* (*Jailhouse Rock* soundtrack)

BABY, IF YOU'LL GIVE ME ALL OF YOUR LOVE

Elvis sang "Baby, If You'll Give Me All of Your Love" in his 1967 movie *Double Trouble*. The song, which was written by Joy Byers, was recorded in June 1966 at Radio Recorders.

LPs:
- *Double Trouble*
- *Mahalo from Elvis*

BABY, LET'S PLAY HOUSE

Arthur Gunter wrote and recorded "Baby, Let's Play House" (Excello 2047)[1] in late 1954. Although it got considerable airplay in the South, his recording did not chart nationally. Gunter based the song on Eddy Arnold's number one country hit in 1951, "I Want to Play House with You" (RCA 0476). A number of years later, Gunter's recording inspired John Lennon to write "Run for Your Life."

Elvis recorded "Baby, Let's Play House" on February 5, 1955, at the Sun studios. Instrumental backing was provided by Scotty Moore on lead guitar, Bill Black on bass, and Elvis on rhythm guitar. "Baby, Let's Play House" reached #10 on *Billboard*'s country chart in July 1955—the first Elvis song ever to chart. It remained on the chart for 15 weeks. Elvis sang "Baby, Let's Play House" frequently on tour in 1955 and on his second appearance on "Stage Show" (February 4, 1956).

On May 7, 1956, the Johnny Burnette Trio recorded a song titled "Oh Baby Babe" for Coral Records (Coral 61675) that was an exact copy (even some of the original lyrics are repeated) of Elvis's "Baby, Let's Play

(Photo courtesy Don Fink)

House." Buddy Holly recorded a version of Elvis's recording on his LP *Holly in the Hills* (Coral 57463), calling it "I Wanna Play House with You." In 1963 Elvis sound-alike Vince Everett recorded "Baby, Let's Play House" for ABC-Paramount Records (ABC-Paramount 10472).

Singles:
- "BABY, LET'S PLAY HOUSE"/"I'm Left, You're Right, She's Gone" (Sun 217) April 1, 1955. Standard Sun 78 RPM and 45 RPM release.
- "BABY, LET'S PLAY HOUSE"/"I'm Left, You're Right, She's Gone" (RCA 20-6383) November 1955. Standard RCA 78 RPM reissue of the Sun original.
- "BABY, LET'S PLAY HOUSE"/"I'm Left, You're Right, She's Gone" (RCA 47-6383) November 1955. Standard RCA 45 RPM reissue of the Sun original.
- "BABY LET'S PLAY HOUSE"/"I'm Left, You're Right, She's Gone" (RCA 447-0604) March 1959. Gold Standard Series reissue.
- "BABY, LET'S PLAY HOUSE"/"Hound Dog" (RCA PB-13875) August 1984. Both sides of this record were recorded at the Mississippi-Alabama Fair and Dairy Show in Tupelo, Mississippi, on September 26, 1956. The record was pressed on gold vinyl and was distributed in the Memphis-Tupelo area to kick off the year-long celebration of the 50th anniversary of Elvis's birth.

EPs:
- SPD-15

LPs:
- *The Complete Sun Sessions* (master)
- *A Date with Elvis* (alternate mix, with more reverberation)
- *Elvis: The First Live Recordings* ("Louisiana Hayride"; August 6 or 27, 1955)
- *A Golden Celebration* ("Stage Show"; February 4, 1956) (Tupelo; September 26, 1956)

---

[1]Excello was founded by Ernie Young in 1953. Gunter's "Baby, Let's Play House" was Excello's first hit.

- *I Was the One* (with overdubbing)
- *The Sun Sessions* (alternate mix, with more reverberation)

Bootleg LPs:
- *Dorsey Shows* ("Stage Show"; February 4, 1956)
- *The Entertainer* (Houston; January 29, 1955)
- *The First Year—Recorded Live* (Houston; January 29, 1955)
- *The First Years* (Houston; January 29, 1955)
- *The Rockin' Rebel, Volume 2* (Houston; January 29, 1955)
- *Standing Room Only, Volume 2* (Houston; January 29, 1955)
- *The Sun Years* (studio take)
- *Superstar Outtakes, Volume 2* ("Stage Show"; February 4, 1956)

BABY WHAT YOU WANT ME TO DO
Jimmy Reed wrote and recorded "Baby What You Want Me to Do" in 1960 for Vee Jay Records (Vee Jay 333). His recording was a #10 rhythm & blues hit. Four years later, Etta James (Argo 5459) reached #82 on the Hot 100 chart with her version.

Elvis sang "Baby What You Want Me to Do" in his 1968 TV special, "Elvis." The version that appeared on the air was from the 6:00 P.M. taping on June 27, 1968. "Baby What You Want Me to Do" was one of the songs that Elvis sang in concert infrequently.

LPs:
- *Elvis—A Legendary Performer, Volume 2* ("Elvis" TV special taping; June 27, 1968, at 6:00 P.M. show)
- *Elvis Aron Presley* ("Elvis" TV special taping; June 27, 1968, at 6:00 P.M. show)
- *Elvis—TV Special* ("Elvis" TV special taping; June 27, 1968, at 6:00 P.M. show)
- *A Golden Celebration* ("Elvis" TV special taping; June 27, 1968, at 6:00 P.M. show)

Bootleg LPs:
- *The Burbank Sessions, Volume 1* ("Elvis" TV special taping; June 27, 1968, at 6:00 P.M. and 8:00 P.M. shows)
- *The Burbank Sessions, Volume 2* ("Elvis" TV special taping; June 29, 1968, at 6:00 P.M. show)
- *The Monologue L.P.* (Las Vegas; July 31, 1969)
- *Please Release Me* ("Elvis" TV special taping; June 27, 1968, at 6:00 P.M. show)

BAD MOON RISING
John Fogerty wrote "Bad Moon Rising" for his group, Creedence Clearwater Revival. In 1969 their recording (Fantasy 622) reached #2 on the Hot 100 chart in the United States and number one in England.

Elvis sang "Bad Moon Rising" in some of his 1970s concerts.

BAREFOOT BALLAD
Elvis sang "Barefoot Ballad" in his 1964 movie *Kissin' Cousins*. The song, which was written by Dolores Fuller and Lee Morris, was recorded by Elvis in October 1963 at RCA's Nashville studios.

LPs:
- *Kissin' Cousins*

THE BATTLE HYMN OF THE REPUBLIC
(See *An American Trilogy*)

BEACH BOY BLUES
Sid Tepper and Roy C. Bennett wrote "Beach Boy Blues" for Elvis's 1961 film *Blue Hawaii*. The recording session took place on March 23, 1961, at Radio Recorders in Hollywood. Take #3 was chosen for release.

LPs:
- *Blue Hawaii*

Bootleg LPs:
- *Behind Closed Doors* (take #1 [false start] and #3)
- *The Blue Hawaii Box* (takes 1–3)
- *From the Beach to the Bayou* (take #1 [false start], #2 and #3.

BEACH SHACK
Elvis sang "Beach Shack" in his 1966 film *Spinout*. He recorded the song, which was written by Bill Giant, Bernie Baum, and Florence Kaye, at Radio Recorders on February 15, 16, or 17, 1966.

LPs:
- *Spinout*

BECAUSE OF LOVE
Ruth Batchelor and Bob Roberts wrote "Because of Love" for Elvis's 1962 movie *Girls! Girls! Girls!* Elvis's recording session took place in March 1962 at Radio Recorders. In late 1962 Billy Fury[1] covered Elvis's recording and reached the top 20 on the British charts.

LPs:
- *Girls! Girls! Girls!*

BEGINNER'S LUCK
Sid Tepper and Roy C. Bennett wrote "Beginner's Luck" for Elvis's 1966 movie *Frankie and Johnny*. The recording session took place at RCA's Nashville studios in May 1965.

LPs:
- *Frankie and Johnny*

BEYOND THE BEND
Elvis sang "Beyond the Bend" in *It Happened at the World's Fair*. The song, which was written by Fred Wise, Ben Weisman, and Dolores Fuller, was recorded in September 1962 at Radio Recorders. The backing vocals were performed by the Mello Men.

LPs:
- *It Happened at the World's Fair*

BEYOND THE REEF
"Beyond the Reef" was written by Jack Pittman and recorded in 1950 by Jimmy Wakely and Margaret Whiting (Capitol 1234). That same year, the Blue Barron Orchestra had a popular version for MGM Records (MGM 10766).

On May 27, 1966, Elvis, Red West, and Charlie Hodge recorded "Beyond the Reef" at RCA's Nashville studios. West sang lead, Elvis sang second tenor and played

[1]Billy Fury (real name: Ronald Wyncherley) met Elvis on the set of *Girls! Girls! Girls!* Early in their career, the Beatles *failed* an audition to be the backup band for Fury.

piano, and Charlie Hodge sang first tenor. The recording was unacceptable because of a faulty backing track. On August 9, 1968, a new instrumental track was recorded with personnel consisting of Ray Edenton (guitar), Norbert Putnam (bass), Jerry Byrd (steel guitar), and Buddy Harman (drums). Apparently, the track was recorded right onto the master. "Beyond the Reef" remained unreleased until 1980, when it appeared in the boxed set *Elvis Aron Presley*. In England, "Beyond the Reef" was released as a single with "It's Only Love" (RCA PR-9601).

LPs:
- *Elvis Aron Presley*

BIG BOOTS

"Big Boots" was sung by Elvis in his 1960 film *G. I. Blues*. The song, which was written by Sid Wayne and Sherman Edwards, was first recorded on April 28, 1960, at RCA's Hollywood studios. That version, a slower take, was not released until 1978. The version recorded on May 6, 1960, at Radio Recorders was faster. It was this recording, a splice of two takes, that was used in *G. I. Blues* and the soundtrack album.

LPs:
- *Elvis Sings for Children and Grownups Too!* (April 28, 1960, version)
- *G. I. Blues* (May 6, 1960, version)

BIG BOSS MAN

"Big Boss Man" was written by Al Smith and Luther Dixon and recorded by Jimmy Reed in 1961. His recording (Vee Jay 380) reached #13 on *Billboard*'s rhythm & blues chart and #78 on the Hot 100 chart. In 1964 Gene Chandler recorded the song as "Soul Hootenanny" (Constellation 114).

Elvis recorded "Big Boss Man" on September 10, 1967, at RCA's Nashville studios. His single release had a six-week stay on the Hot 100 chart, reaching #38. Elvis sang "Big Boss Man" in a medley in his 1968 TV special, "Elvis." Both the instumental and vocal tracks were recorded at Western Recorders in Hollywood on June 20 or 21, 1968.

Singles:
- "BIG BOSS MAN"/"You Don't Know Me" (RCA 47-9341) September 1967. Standard release.
- "BIG BOSS MAN"/"You Don't Know Me" (RCA 447-0662) 1970. Gold Standard Series reissue.

EPs:
- *Stay Away*

LPs:
- *Clambake*
- *Double Dynamite*
- *Elvis Sings Hits from His Movies, Volume 1*
- *Elvis—TV Special* ("Elvis" TV special taping; June 27, 1968, at 6:00 P.M. show)

Bootleg LPs:
- *America's Own* (Uniondale, N.Y.; July 19, 1975)
- *Big Boss Man* (Las Vegas; August 19, 1974)

- *Command Performance* (Las Vegas; August 21, 1974)
- *Elvis Presley Is Alive and Well and Singing in Las Vegas Volume 1* (Las Vegas; August 1974)
- *From Las Vegas . . . to Niagara Falls* (Las Vegas; September 3, 1973)
- *Rockin' with Elvis April Fool's Day* (Las Vegas; April 1, 1975)
- *Rockin' with Elvis New Year's Eve Pittsburgh, Pa. Dec. 31, 1976* (Pittsburgh; December 31, 1976)
- *The '68 Comeback* ("Elvis" TV special studio take; June 20 or 21, 1968)
- *Standing Room Only, Volume 3* (Pittsburgh; December 31, 1976)
- *The Vegas Years, 1972–1975* (Las Vegas; 1974)

A BIG HUNK O' LOVE

Elvis recorded "A Big Hunk o' Love" on June 10, 1958, at RCA's Nashville studios. He was on leave from the Army at the time. Take #3 was selected by RCA for release. "A Big Hunk o' Love" reached number one on *Billboard*'s Hot 100 chart for two weeks, and had a 14-week stay on the chart. "A Big Hunk o' Love" was #10 on the rhythm & blues chart. Sales for the record easily exceeded one million copies. An April 9, 1972, performance at Hampton Roads, Virginia, was shown in the documentary *Elvis on Tour*. "A Big Hunk o' Love" was sung in Elvis's 1973 TV special, "Elvis: Aloha from Hawaii." Aaron Schroeder and Sid Wyche are the composers.

Singles:
- "A BIG HUNK O' LOVE"/"My Wish Came True" (RCA 47-7600) July 1959. Standard release.
- "A BIG HUNK O' LOVE"/"My Wish Came True" (RCA 447-0626) February 1962. Gold Standard Series reissue.

LPs:
- *Aloha from Hawaii via Satellite* (Honolulu; January 14, 1973)
- *The Alternate Aloha* (rehearsal concert for "Elvis: Aloha from Hawaii"; January 12, 1973)
- *Elvis* (RCA DPL2-0056[e])
- *Elvis: Worldwide 50 Gold Award Hits, Volume 1*
- *50,000,000 Elvis Fans Can't Be Wrong—Elvis' Gold Records, Volume 2*
- *Greatest Hits, Volume 1* (Las Vegas; February 15, 1972)
- *The Number One Hits*
- *The Top Ten Hits*

Bootleg LPs:
- *Aloha rehearsal Show—Kui Lee Cancer Benefit* (rehearsal concert for "Elvis: Aloha from Hawaii"; January 12, 1973)
- *Elvis on Tour* (*Elvis on Tour* soundtrack)
- *The King: From the Dark to the Light* (*Elvis on Tour* soundtrack)
- *The Legend Lives On* (Las Vegas; February 15, 1972)
- *Superstar Outtakes, Volume 2* (Las Vegas; 1972)
- *The Vegas Years, 1972–1975* (Las Vegas; 1972)

THE BIG HURT

In 1960 Miss Toni Fisher had a #3 Hot 100 hit with "The Big Hurt" (Signet 275), which had been written the previous year by Wayne Shanklin. Del Shannon (Liberty 55866) in 1966 and Vikki Carr (Columbia 45622) in 1972 also recorded "The Big Hurt."

Elvis is reported to have recorded "The Big Hurt" in the 1960s at Graceland, with only guitar accompaniment.

BIG LOVE, BIG HEARTACHE

Elvis sang "Big Love, Big Heartache" in his 1964 movie *Roustabout*. The song, which was written by Dolores Fuller, Lee Morris, and Sonny Hendrix, was recorded in March 1964 at Radio Recorders.

LPs:
• *Roustabout*

BILL BAILEY, WON'T YOU PLEASE COME HOME

This early ragtime classic was written by Hugh Cannon in 1902. Bill Bailey was a real person who died in 1966 in Singapore. He had been a member of the vaudeville team Bailey and Cowan.

Cannon once said that the song was based on fact. He told how Bailey was locked out of his apartment by his wife and that he (Cannon) gave Bailey money to rent a hotel room. Cannon said that he consoled Bailey and told him his wife would forgive him. From that episode, Cannon wrote "Bill Bailey, Won't You Please Come Home." To his dying day Bailey insisted that Cannon's story was a complete fabrication.

Bobby Darin had a 1960 hit with "Bill Bailey, Won't You Please Come Home," but it was titled "Won't You Come Home Bill Bailey" (Atco 6167). A variation of the song was sung by Glenda Farrell as "Pappy, Won't You Please Come Home" in *Kissin' Cousins*. In *Paradise, Hawaiian Style*, Donna Butterworth sang "Bill Bailey, Won't You Please Come Home." Speculation has it that Elvis may have recorded the song in the studio.

BIRDS FLY HIGH

Little is known about this song. Reportedly, Elvis recorded "Birds Fly High" in 1967, but there's been no supporting evidence.

BITTER THEY ARE, HARDER THEY FALL

This song was written and recorded by Larry Gatlin in 1974 as "The Bitter They Are, the Harder They Fall" (Monument 8602). His recording reached #45 on the country chart. Elvis recorded "Bitter They Are, Harder They Fall" (dropping the article *the*) on the night of February 2–3, 1976, at Graceland.

LPs:
• *From Elvis Presley Boulevard, Memphis, Tennessee*
• *Always on My Mind*

BIVOUAC

It's been speculated that Elvis recorded "Bivouac" for his 1966 movie *Spinout*. Nothing else is known about the song.

BLESSED JESUS HOLD MY HAND

(See *Jesus Hold My Hand*)

BLOWIN' IN THE WIND

Bob Dylan wrote[1] and recorded "Blowin' in the Wind" in 1962. In 1963 it was released as a single (Columbia 42856) and on the LP *The Freewheelin' Bob Dylan* (Columbia CS 8786). Peter, Paul and Mary, however, had the big hit that year. Their recording (Warner Bros. 5368) reached #2 on *Billboard*'s Hot 100 chart, number one on the Easy-Listening chart, and sold over a million copies. Stevie Wonder had a number one rhythm & blues hit in 1966 with "Blowin' in the Wind" (Tamla 54136).

Elvis sang "Blowin' in the Wind" in concert on a few occasions in the 1970s.

BLUE CHRISTMAS

"Blue Christmas" was written by Billy Hayes and Jay Johnson. In 1949 there were three big hits with the song. Russ Morgan (Decca 24766) and Hugo Winterhalter (Columbia 38635) had pop hits, reaching #11 and #21 on *Billboard*'s Best-Selling Singles chart, respectively. Ernest Tubb had a #2 country hit with "Blue Christmas" (Decca 46186). In 1950 Billy Eckstine made a popular recording of the song (MGM 10796).

Elvis recorded "Blue Christmas" on September 5, 1957, at Radio Recorders. Take #3 was chosen for release. It wasn't until seven years later that "Blue Christmas" was released as a single, reaching the top of *Billboard*'s special Christmas Singles chart. Elvis sang the song in his 1968 TV special, "Elvis." "Blue Christmas" was replaced in the 1969 repeat of the show with "Tiger Man."

Singles:
• "BLUE CHRISTMAS"/"BLUE CHRISTMAS" (RCA HO7W-0808) November 1957. Disc jockey promotional release. This single was used to promote the LP *Elvis' Christmas Album*.
• "BLUE CHRISTMAS"/"Wooden Heart" (RCA 447-0720) November 1964. Gold Standard Series original release.
• "BLUE CHRISTMAS"/"Santa Claus Is Back in Town" (RCA 447-0647) November 1965. Gold Standard Series original release. This record has been released numerous times over the years.

EPs:
• *Elvis Sings Christmas Songs*

LPs:
• *Elvis—A Legendary Performer, Volume 2*
• *Elvis Aron Presley* ("Elvis" TV special taping; June 27, 1968, at 8:00 P.M. show)
• *Elvis' Christmas Album*
• *Elvis—TV Special* ("Elvis" TV special taping; June 27, 1968, at 8:00 P.M. show)
• *A Golden Celebration* ("Elvis" TV special taping; June 27, 1968, at 8:00 P.M. show)
• *Memories of Christmas*

Bootleg LPs:
• *The Burbank Sessions, Volume 1* ("Elvis" TV special taping; June 27, 1968, at 6:00 P.M. and 8:00 P.M. shows)
• *Elvis Rocks and the Girls Roll* (dress rehearsal for "Elvis"; June 1968)
• *Standing Room Only, Volume 3* ("Elvis" TV special taping; June 27, 1968, at 8:00 P.M. show)
• *Susie Q* (Las Vegas; ?)

---

[1] There's some evidence to indicate that a Millburn, New Jersey, high school student named Lorre Wyatt—not Bob Dylan—wrote "Blowin' in the Wind." In the November 4, 1963, issue of *Newsweek* it was written that several Millburn High students claimed that Wyatt sang the song several months before Dylan's release. It was rumored that Wyatt sold Dylan the rights to the song for $1,000.

BLUE EYES CRYING IN THE RAIN

"Blue Eyes Crying in the Rain" was written by Leon Rose and recorded by Roy Acuff (Columbia 37822) on January 28, 1947. In 1975 Willie Nelson had a big country hit with the song, reaching number one on the country chart. The song peaked at #21 on the Hot 100 chart. Nelson first heard the song when, as a disc jockey, he played an album cut by Arthur (Guitar Boogie) Smith.

Elvis recorded "Blue Eyes Crying in the Rain" on February 8, 1976, at Graceland.

LPs:
• *From Elvis Presley Boulevard, Memphis, Tennessee*

BLUE GUITAR

Burt Bacharach and Hal David wrote "Blue Guitar" in 1955, and it was recorded that year by Red Foley (Decca 29626). In 1964 Sheb Wooley reached #33 on *Billboard*'s country chart with "Blue Guitar."

Reportedly, Elvis sang "Blue Guitar" on the "Louisiana Hayride." It's also been speculated that he recorded the song while at Sun Records, but that's highly unlikely because Foley's version wasn't released until August or September 1955, which was after Elvis's last recording session at Sun Records.

BLUE HAWAII

"Blue Hawaii" was written by Leo Robin and Ralph Rainger in 1937, and introduced in the movie *Waikiki Wedding* by Bing Crosby, who also recorded the song that year. Crosby's recording (Decca 1175) was made with Lani McIntire and His Hawaiians. In 1959 Billy Vaughn reached #37 on the Hot 100 chart with his recording of "Blue Hawaii" (Dot 15879).

Elvis recorded "Blue Hawaii" for his 1961 movie of the same name on March 22, 1961, at Radio Recorders. Take #7 was used for the film and on record. After the worldwide telecast of "Elvis: Aloha from Hawaii," Elvis recorded "Blue Hawaii" for the NBC-TV version of the special, which aired in the United States on April 4, 1973.

LPs:
• *The Alternate Aloha* (Honolulu; January 14, 1973)
• *Blue Hawaii*
• *Elvis—A Legendary Performer, Volume 2* (Honolulu; January 14, 1973)
• *Elvis Aron Presley—Forever*
• *Elvis in Hollywood*
• *Mahalo from Elvis* (Honolulu; January 14, 1973)

Bootleg LPs:
• *The Blue Hawaii Box* (takes #1-7)
• *The Blue Hawaii Sessions* (takes #1-6)

BLUE MOON

"Blue Moon" was composed in 1933 by Richard Rodgers and Lorenz Hart under the title "Make Me a Star." It was to have been sung by Jean Harlow in the film *Hollywood Revue of 1933*, but that project was

scrapped. Hart changed the lyrics and retitled the song "The Bad in Every Man." Shirley Ross sang it in the 1934 film *Manhattan Melodrama*[1]. The lyrics and title were later changed to "Blue Moon." Glen Gray and the Casa Loma Band had a big hit in 1935 with "Blue Moon" (Decca 312), as did Benny Goodman with vocal by Helen Ward (Columbia 3003). Billy Eckstine had a million-seller with the song (MGM 10311) in 1948. Mel Tormé sang "Blue Moon" in the 1948 movie biography of Rodgers and Hart, *Words and Music*. His record (Capitol 15428) was popular that year. The Marcels also had a million-seller with the song (Colpix 186), in 1961. Their recording topped the charts in the United States and England. The Marcels' arrangement was based on "Zoom Zoom Zoom," a 1957 release by the Collegians on the Wimbley label. In 1980 producer John Landis used a version of "Blue Moon" by Bobby Vinton as the opening theme to his film *An American Werewolf in London*. The Marcels' version was heard over the closing credits.

Elvis recorded "Blue Moon" at Sun Records on July 6, 1954. The drummer on the recording was Buddy Cunningham. It was one of several songs he sang on the "Louisiana Hayride" from 1954 to 1956. Elvis's 1956 single release of "Blue Moon" had a 17-week stay on *Billboard*'s Top 100 chart, peaking at #55. A short instrumental rendition of "Blue Moon" was heard in Elvis's 1964 film, *Viva Las Vegas*.

Singles:
• "BLUE MOON"/"Just Because" (RCA 20-6640) September 1956. Standard 78 RPM release.
• "BLUE MOON"/"Just Because" (RCA 47-6640) September 1956. Standard 45 RPM release.
• "BLUE MOON"/"Just Because" (RCA 447-0613) March 1959. Gold Standard Series reissue.

EPs:
• *Elvis Presley* (EPA-830)
• *Elvis Presley—The Most Talked About New Personality in the Past Ten Years of Recorded Music* (RCA EPB-1254)

LPs:
• *The Complete Sun Sessions* (master)
• *Elvis Presley*
• *The Sun Sessions*

Bootleg LPs:
• *Elvis Rocks and the Girls Roll* (dress rehearsals for the "Elvis" TV special; June 1968)

BLUE MOON OF KENTUCKY

Bill Monroe wrote and recorded "Blue Moon of Kentucky" (Columbia 20370) in 1947. His recording could be heard in the 1979 movie *Coal Miner's Daughter*. The Stanley Brothers recorded the song in 1954 (Mercury 70453).

On the evening of July 6, 1954, Elvis, Scotty Moore, and Bill Black were trying to record a flip side to "That's All Right (Mama)," which had been recorded the previous evening. During a break, Black began fooling around with a parody of "Blue Moon of Ken-

[1]*Manhattan Melodrama* was the movie that gangster John Dillinger saw at Chicago's Biograph Theatre just before he was shot and killed by FBI agents led by Melvin Purvis (July 22, 1934).

tucky." Elvis and Scotty joined in. After a few rehearsals, Sam Phillips began taping. Two versions of the song survive from that night: a slow, more traditional version and the uptempo version that was originally released. After the slow version, Phillips could be heard to remark "Fine, man! Hell, that's different. That's a pop song now, nearly 'bout!" After Phillips had both sides of Elvis's first single on tape, he made a few demos and distributed them to Dewey Phillips of WHBQ, Uncle Richard of WMPS, and Sleepy-Eyed John Lepley of WHHM. It's a toss-up as to who first played "Blue Moon of Kentucky" on the air. But it was probably Uncle Richard. In any case, the record was released on July 19. It did not chart nationally, but by September, "Blue Moon of Kentucky" was the number one record in Memphis. Fewer than 20,000 copies were sold. Elvis sang the song on his only appearance on the Grand Ole Opry on October 2, 1956, as well as during his first appearance on the "Louisiana Hayride" on October 16, 1954. Bill Monroe's original version of "Blue Moon of Kentucky" was rereleased after Elvis's release began getting airplay.

Singles:
- "That's All Right (Mama)"/"BLUE MOON OF KENTUCKY" (Sun 209) July 19, 1954. Standard Sun 78 RPM and 45 RPM release.
- "That's All Right (Mama)"/"BLUE MOON OF KENTUCKY" (RCA 20-6380) November 1955. Standard RCA 78 RPM reissue of the Sun original.
- "That's All Right (Mama)"/"BLUE MOON OF KENTUCKY" (RCA 47-6380) November 1955. Standard RCA 45 RPM reissue of the Sun original.
- "That's All Right (Mama)"/"BLUE MOON OF KENTUCKY" (RCA 447-0601) March 1959. Gold Standard Series reissue.
- "That's All Right (Mama)"/"BLUE MOON OF KENTUCKY" (RCA PB-13891) October 1984. One of six singles in the boxed set *Elvis' Greatest Hits—Golden Singles, Volume 2* (RCA PP-13898). The record was pressed on gold vinyl with a special gold "50th" anniversary label.

EPs:
- *Good Rockin' Tonight*
- *Great Country/Western Hits*
- *See the USA, the Elvis Way*
- *A Touch of Gold, Volume 3* (alternate mix, with more reverberation)

LPs:
- *The Complete Sun Sessions* (master and outtake)
- *A Date with Elvis* (alternate mix, with more reverberation)
- *Elvis: The Hillbilly Cat* ("Louisiana Hayride"; October 16, 1954)
- *A Golden Celebration* (slow alternate take)
- *The Sun Sessions* (alternate mix, with more reverberation)

Bootleg LPs:
- *The Entertainer* ("Louisiana Hayride"; October 16, 1954) (Houston; January 29, 1955)
- *The First Year—Recorded Live* (Houston; January 29, 1955) ("Louisiana Hayride"; October 16, 1954)
- *The First Years* (Houston; January 29, 1955)
- *Good Rocking Tonight* (slower alternate take)
- *Loving You* (slower alternate take)
- *The Rockin' Rebel* (slower alternate take)
- *The Rockin' Rebel, Volume 2* (Houston; January 29, 1955) ("Louisiana Hayride"; October 16, 1954)

---

[1]The flip side, "Honey Don't," was later covered by the Beatles.

- *Standing Room Only, Volume 3* ("Louisiana Hayride"; October 16, 1954)
- *The Sun Years* (slower alternate take and released take)

BLUE RIVER
"Blue River" was written by Paul Evans and Fred Tobias and recorded by Elvis on May 27, 1963, at RCA's Nashville studios. The single release of "Blue River" barely made *Billboard*'s Hot 100 chart, peaking at #95 for one week. A version of the song on the French EP *Elvis Presley* (86508) was pressed at a slightly slower speed making it last four seconds longer.

Singles:
- "Tell Me Why"/"BLUE RIVER" (RCA 47-8740) December 1965. Standard release.
- "Tell Me Why"/"BLUE RIVER" (RCA 447-0655) February 1968. Gold Standard Series reissue.

LPs:
- *Double Trouble*

BLUE SUEDE SHOES
"Blue Suede Shoes" was written by Carl Perkins in late 1955. There are two versions of how Perkins came to write the song. Perkins has said that he played for a high school dance in Jackson, Tennessee, on December 4, 1955. During the dance, he spotted a boy with blue suede shoes dancing with a gorgeous girl. The boy told her, "Uh-uh! Don't step on my blue suedes!" Perkins couldn't get the image out of his mind. He awoke at three o'clock the next morning with the lyrics to "Blue Suede Shoes" and wrote them down on a brown paper potato sack. Originally, the first line was "One for the money, two for the show, three to get ready, and go, man, go." But while recording the song at Sun Records, Perkins substituted the word *cat* for *man*. That opening phrase was borrowed from Bill Haley's 1953 recording "What 'Cha Gonna Do" (Essex 321).

Johnny Cash tells a different story about the origin of "Blue Suede Shoes." While Perkins, Elvis, and Cash were performing in Amory, Mississippi, one night in 1955, Cash told Perkins about a black sergeant he had in the Air Force by the name of C. V. White. Sergeant White would frequently step into Cash's room and ask him how he (White) looked and then say, "Just don't step on my blue suede shoes!" (Never mind that Sergeant White was wearing regulation Air Force shoes.) Perkins thought that Cash's story was a good idea for a song. While Elvis was performing on stage, Perkins wrote "Blue Suede Shoes."

Whatever the story, Perkins's "Blue Suede Shoes" (Sun 234)[1] was released on January 1, 1956. By March it was #4 on *Billboard*'s Top 100 chart, #2 on the country chart ("Heartbreak Hotel" kept it from being number one), and #2 on the rhythm & blues chart—the first song in music history to reach all three charts. "Blue Suede Shoes" was a million-seller.

Three versions of "Blue Suede Shoes" charted in 1956: Perkins's, Elvis's, and that by Boyd Bennett and His Rockets (King 4903), who reached #63 on the Top

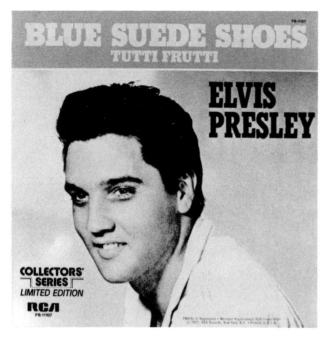

(Photo courtesy Don Fink)

100 chart. In 1973 Johnny Rivers (United Artists 198) peaked at #38 with his recording.

Elvis recorded "Blue Suede Shoes" on January 30, 1956, at RCA's New York City studios. Although the September 1956 single did not chart, earlier in the year "Blue Suede Shoes" had reached #24 on *Billboard's* Top 100 chart as part of the EP *Elvis Presley* (RCA EPA-747). It had a 12-week stay on the chart.

Elvis sang "Blue Suede Shoes" during his screen test for Paramount Pictures on April 1, 1956, and on the following TV programs: "Stage Show" (February 11, 1956; March 17, 1956), "The Milton Berle Show" (April 3, 1956), and "Elvis: Aloha from Hawaii" (January 14, 1973). In addition, a performance of the song at the International Hotel in Las Vegas in August 1970, was used in the documentary *Elvis—That's the Way It Is.* "Blue Suede Shoes" was recorded for the 1968 TV special "Elvis," but was not used. However, a spliced version, using the first portion of the song recorded on June 27, 1968, at the 6:00 P.M. show, and the last portion recorded on June 29, 1968, at the 8:00 P.M. show, was heard in the 1981 documentary *This Is Elvis.* The version of "Blue Suede Shoes" heard on a jukebox in *G. I. Blues* was recorded at RCA's Hollywood studios on April 28, 1960.

In 1985 RCA issued a music video of Elvis's "Blue Suede Shoes" in which Carl Perkins made a cameo appearance.

Singles:
- "BLUE SUEDE SHOES"/"Tutti Frutti" (RCA 20-6636) September 1956. Standard 78 RPM release.
- "BLUE SUEDE SHOES"/"Tutti Frutti" (RCA 47-6636) September 1956. Standard 45 RPM release.
- "BLUE SUEDE SHOES"/"I'm Counting on You" (RCA 47-6492) September 1956. Disc jockey "Record Prevue."
- "BLUE SUEDE SHOES"/"Tutti Frutti" (RCA 447-0609) March 1959. Gold Standard Series reissue.

- "BLUE SUEDE SHOES"/"Tutti Frutti" (RCA PB-11107) October 1977. One of 15 singles in the boxed set *15 Golden Records—30 Golden Hits* (RCA PP-11301), and the *20 Golden Hits in Full Color Sleeves* (RCA PP-11340) boxed set released two months later.
- "BLUE SUEDE SHOES"/"Tutti Frutti" (RCA PB-13885) October 1984. One of six singles in the boxed set *Elvis' Greatest Hits—Golden Singles, Volume 1* (RCA PP-13897). The record was pressed on gold vinyl with a special gold "50th" anniversary label.
- "BLUE SUEDE SHOES"/"Promised Land" (RCA PB-13929) October 1984. New single that was pressed on blue vinyl with a gold "50th" anniversary label.
- "BLUE SUEDE SHOES"/"BLUE SUEDE SHOES" (RCA JK-13929) October 1984. Disc jockey promotional release.

EPs:
- *Elvis Presley* (RCA EPA-747)
- *Elvis Presley* (RCA EPB-1254)
- *Elvis Presley* (RCA SPD-22)
- *Elvis Presley* (RCA SPD-23)
- *Elvis Presley—The Most Talked About New Personality in the Last Ten Years of Recorded Music* (RCA EPB-1254)

LPs:
- *Aloha from Hawaii via Satellite* (Honolulu; January 14, 1973)
- *The Alternate Aloha* (rehearsal concert for "Elvis: Aloha from Hawaii"; January 12, 1973)
- *Elvis—A Legendary Performer, Volume 2* ("Elvis" TV special taping; June 27, 1968, at 8:00 P.M. show)
- *Elvis Aron Presley* (Las Vegas; May 6, 1956)
- *Elvis in Person* (Las Vegas; August 26, 1969)
- *Elvis Presley*
- *From Memphis to Vegas/From Vegas to Memphis* (Las Vegas; August 26, 1969)
- *G. I. Blues* (April 28, 1956, version)
- *A Golden Celebration* ("Stage Show"; February 11, 1956; March 17, 1956) ("The Milton Berle Show"; April 3, 1956) (Tupelo, Mississippi; September 26, 1956, at the evening show) ("Elvis" TV special taping; June 27, 1968, at 6:00 P.M. show)
- *This Is Elvis* ("Elvis TV special taping; first portion from June 27, 1968, at 6:00 P.M. show, and last portion from June 29, 1968, at 8:00 P.M. show)

Bootleg LPs:
- *Aloha Rehearsal Show—Kui Lee Cancer Benefit* (rehearsal concert for "Elvis: Aloha from Hawaii"; January 12, 1973)
- *The Burbank Sessions, Volume 1* ("Elvis" TV special taping; June 27, 1968, at 6:00 P.M. and 8:00 P.M. shows)
- *The Burbank Sessions, Volume 2* ("Elvis" TV special taping; June 29, 1968, at 6:00 P.M. and 8:00 P.M. shows)
- *Cadillac Elvis* (*Elvis—That's the Way It Is* soundtrack)
- *Dorsey Shows* ("Stage Show"; February 11, 1956; March 17, 1956)
- *The Hillbilly Cat "Live"* (Las Vegas; August 1970) (in medley with "Whole Lotta Shakin' Goin' On")
- *The King of Las Vegas Live* (*Elvis—That's the Way It Is* soundtrack)
- *Long Lost Songs* (Las Vegas; 1975)
- *Rockin' with Elvis New Year's Eve Pittsburgh, Pa. Dec. 31, 1976* (Pittsburgh; December 31, 1976)
- *The Sun Years* ("Stage Show"; February 11 or March 17, 1956)
- *Superstar Outtakes, Volume 2* ("Stage Show"; February 11, 1956; March 17, 1956)
- *That's the Way It Is* (*Elvis—That's the Way It Is* soundtrack)

BLUEBERRY HILL
"Blueberry Hill" was written in 1940 by Al Lewis, Larry Stock, and Vincent Rose. Glenn Miller first popularized the song (with vocal by Ray Eberle) in a recording (Bluebird 10768) that reached #2 on *Billboard's*

Best-Selling Singles chart. Gene Autry further popularized "Blueberry Hill" in his 1940 western for Republic Pictures, *The Singing Hill.*

In 1956 Fats Domino had a million-seller with "Blueberry Hill" (Imperial 5407), reaching #4 on the Top 100 chart and number one for eight weeks on the rhythm & blues chart.[1] It was the only million-seller by Domino that was not written by himself or Dave Bartholomew. Louis Armstrong also had a popular version of "Blueberry Hill" (Decca 30091) in 1956, reaching #27 on the Top 100 chart.

Elvis recorded "Blueberry Hill" on January 19, 1957, at Radio Recorders. Take #9 was chosen by RCA for release.

EPs:
• *Just for You*

LPs:
• *Elvis Aron Presley—Forever*
• *Elvis Recorded Live on Stage in Memphis* (Memphis; March 20, 1974) (in medley with "I Can't Stop Loving You")
• *Loving You*

Bootleg LPs:
• *Cadillac Elvis* (alternate take)
• *Susie Q* (Las Vegas; ?)

A BLUES JAM
(See *Reconsider Baby*)

BLUES STAY AWAY FROM ME
"Blues Stay Away from Me" was a #2 country hit in 1949 for the Delmore Brothers (King 803). Later that year, the Owen Bradley Quintet took the song to #9 on the chart (Coral 60107).

In December 1954, Scotty Moore recorded "Blues Stay Away from Me" at Sun Records. His backup musicians were Bill Black on bass and Johnny Bernero on drums. Elvis attended the session and can be heard singing the song off mike. Moore's "Blues Stay Away from Me" remained unreleased until 1987, when it appeared in the boxed set *The Country Years.*

BOOK OF HAPPINESS
"Book of Happiness" is one of several songs that some believe Elvis recorded but for which there is no proof.

BORN TO LOSE
Ted Daffan[2] wrote "Born to Lose" in 1942 using the pseudonym Frank Brown. With his band, the Texans, he recorded the song that following year for Okeh Records (Okeh 6706) and had a million-seller with it. Countless artists have recorded "Born to Lose" over the years. Ray Charles had a 1962 hit (ABC-Paramount 10330) with the song. It was the flip side to his "I Can't Stop Loving You."

Elvis sang "Born to Lose" in concert in the 1970s.

BOSOM OF ABRAHAM
"Bosom of Abraham" was written by William Johnson, George McFaddan, and Ted Brooks in the late 1940s. One of the first recordings was by the Trumpeteers (Score 5031). In 1954 the Jordanaires recorded a version (Decca 29188).

Elvis recorded "Bosom of Abraham" on June 9 or 10, 1971, at RCA's Nashville studios. His single release failed to chart. About ten thousand copies of the record were issued in which both sides played at 33⅓ RPM instead of 45 RPM. RCA quickly recalled the unsold copies and corrected the problem. An April 1972 backstage performance of "Bosom of Abraham" with the Stamps was shown in the documentary *Elvis on Tour.*

Singles:
• "He Touched Me"/"BOSOM OF ABRAHAM" (RCA 74-0651) March 1972. Standard release. The picture sleeves of this record listed the title as "*The* Bosom of Abraham," although the label listed it as "Bosom of Abraham."

LPs:
• *He Touched Me*

Bootleg LPs:
• *America's Own* (Uniondale, N.Y.; July 19, 1975) (Charlie Hodge sang the lead, Elvis the bass line)
• *Elvis on Tour* (*Elvis on Tour* soundtrack) (in medley with "Lighthouse" and "Lead Me, Guide Me")
• *The King: From the Dark to the Light* (*Elvis on Tour* soundtrack) (in medley with "Lead Me, Guide Me" and "I, John")

BOSSA NOVA BABY
"Bossa Nova Baby" was written by Jerry Leiber and Mike Stoller and recorded by Tippy and the Clovers (Tiger 201) in 1962. Their recording did not chart.

Elvis sang "Bossa Nova Baby" in his 1963 film *Fun in Acapulco.* The recording session took place on January 22, 1963, at Radio Recorders. Elvis's single release had a 10-week stay on *Billboard*'s Hot 100 chart, reaching #8. On the rhythm & blues chart, "Bossa Nova Baby" peaked at #20. It was the last Elvis single to appear on the rhythm & blues chart. "Bossa Nova Baby" became a million-seller and is one of only two bossa nova records to make the charts. The other was Eydie Gorme's "Blame It on the Bossa Nova" (Columbia 42661), which reached #7 on the Hot 100 chart in 1963.

Singles:
• "BOSSA NOVA BABY"/"Witchcraft" (RCA 47-8243) October 1963. Standard release. The original picture sleeves read, "Coming Soon! FUN IN ACAPULCO Album." Two months later the sleeves were changed to read, "Ask for FUN IN ACAPULCO Album." In January 1964 the announcement was dropped.
• "BOSSA NOVA BABY"/"Witchcraft" (RCA 447-0642) August 1964. Gold Standard Series reissue.

---

[1] Fats Domino had an unbelievable streak on the R&B chart. "Blueberry Hill" was succeeded by his "Blue Monday," which was at the top for eight weeks. "Blue Monday" was succeeded by "I'm Walkin'," which was number one for six weeks. His total of 22 straight weeks at number one is unsurpassed. Incidentally, the streak began when "Blueberry Hill" succeeded "Hound Dog/"Don't Be Cruel" at the top spot and ended when Elvis's "All Shook Up" dethroned "I'm Walkin'."

[2] In 1939 Daffan wrote the first song about truck drivers titled "Truck Drivers' Blues." It was first recorded by Cliff Bruner with Moon Mullican as vocalist.

LPs:
- *Elvis in Hollywood*
- *Elvis: Worldwide 50 Gold Award Hits, Volume 1*
- *Fun in Acapulco*
- *The Top Ten Hits*

BOURBON STREET

It's been speculated that "Bourbon Street" was recorded for *King Creole* but not used. No other information is available.

A BOY LIKE ME, A GIRL LIKE YOU

Elvis sang "A Boy Like Me, a Girl Like You" in his 1962 movie *Girls! Girls! Girls!* The song, which was written by Sid Tepper and Roy C. Bennett, was recorded in March 1962 at Radio Recorders.

LPs:
- *Girls! Girls! Girls!*

BREAKIN' THE RULES

Hank Thompson had a #10 country hit with "Breakin' the Rules" (Capitol 2758) in mid-1954. Some have suggested that Elvis recorded the song while at Sun Records, but that has not been proved. More than likely, Elvis may have sung "Breakin' the Rules" while on tour in 1954 and 1955.

BREATHLESS

Otis Blackwell wrote "Breathless"[1] for Jerry Lee Lewis, who recorded it in late 1957. Initially his release (Sun 288) didn't sell. But an appearance by Lewis on ABC-TV's "The Dick Clark Show" on Saturday evening, March 18, 1958, gave the record a well-deserved sales boost. Clark's show was sponsored by Beechnut gum. By sending in 50 cents and five Beechnut wrappers, viewers could get a copy of "Breathless." Orders for the record poured in and "Breathless" catapulted to #7 on *Billboard*'s Top 100 chart, #4 on the country chart, and #6 on the rhythm & blues chart. Sales eventually exceeded one million copies.

It's been rumored that Elvis recorded "Breathless" for RCA in the late 1950s or early 1960s, but no tape has ever been found.

BRIDGE OVER TROUBLED WATER

Paul Simon wrote "Bridge over Troubled Water" in his house on Blue Jay Way in Los Angeles—the same house that inspired George Harrison to write "Blue Jay Way." In the studio, Art Garfunkel added a third verse. Simon and Garfunkel's recording of "Bridge over Troubled Water" (Columbia 33187)[2] sold over five million copies and was the number one song of 1970. It reached the top of both the Hot 100 chart and the Easy-Listening chart. Grammys were awarded for Record of the Year, Song of the Year, and Best Contemporary Song. In 1971 Aretha Franklin topped the rhythm & blues chart with her version of the song (Atlantic 2796). That same year, Buck Owens reached #9 on the country chart with his rendition (Capitol 3023).

Elvis recorded "Bridge over Troubled Water" at RCA's Nashville studios on June 5, 1970. The 1970 documentary *Elvis—That's the Way It Is* featured Elvis singing the song in an early August 1970 rehearsal at the International Hotel in Las Vegas and during an August 13 performance in concert. The soundtrack LP for that film, however, used the studio recording with overdubbed applause. An April 14, 1972, performance in Greensboro, North Carolina, was used in the 1972 documentary *Elvis on Tour*.

LPs:
- *That's the Way It Is* (studio recording with overdubbed applause)

Bootleg LPs:
- *Big Boss Man* (Las Vegas; August 19, 1974)
- *Elvis on Tour* (*Elvis on Tour* soundtrack)
- *The Hillbilly Cat "Live"* (Las Vegas; August 1970)
- *The King: From the Dark to the Light* (*Elvis—That's the Way It Is* soundtrack)
- *King of Las Vegas Live* (*Elvis—That's the Way It Is* soundtrack)
- *The Last Farewell* (Indianapolis; June 26, 1977)
- *The Legend Lives On* (studio alternate take)
- *Superstar Outtakes* (studio alternate take)
- *That's the Way It Is* (*Elvis—That's the Way It Is* soundtrack)
- *The Vegas Years, 1972-1975* (Las Vegas; 1972)

BRINGING IT BACK

"Bringing It Back" was written by Jimmy Gordon and recorded by Elvis on March 12, 1975, at RCA's Hollywood studios. Composer Gordon played acoustic guitar on the recording. Elvis's single release had a five-week stay on *Billboard*'s Hot 100 chart, reaching #65. In August 1975, Brenda Lee had a #23 country hit with "Bringing It Back" (MCA 40442). Although her single was released before Elvis's single, Elvis's version was issued first on the *Elvis Today* LP.

Singles:
- "BRINGING IT BACK"/"Pieces of My Life" (RCA PB-10401) October 1975. Standard release.
- "BRINGING IT BACK"/"Pieces of My Life" (RCA JA-10401) October 1975. Disc jockey promotional release.

LPs:
- *Elvis Aron Presley—Forever*
- *Elvis Today*

BRITCHES

Elvis recorded "Britches" on August 8, 1960, at Radio Recorders for his film *Flaming Star*, but it was cut from the final print. "Britches," which was written by Sid Wayne and Sherman Edwards, remained unreleased until 1978, when it appeared on the LP *Elvis—A Legendary Performer, Volume 3*.

LPs:
- *Elvis—A Legendary Performer, Volume 3*

---

[1]French director Jean-Luc Godard named his 1961 film *Breathless* after Lewis's hit record. In the 1983 Richard Gere remake, the song was featured prominently.

[2]A second 45 RPM single was later released, this time titled "Bridge over Troubled Waters" (note the *s*), backed with "Keep the Customer Satisfied" (Columbia 45079).

BROWN-EYED HANDSOME MAN

Chuck Berry wrote and recorded "Brown-Eyed Handsome Man" (Chess 1635) in 1956. It was the flip side to his "Too Much Monkey Business." Both songs reached #7 on *Billboard*'s rhythm & blues chart. In 1969 Waylon Jennings revived the song in a popular country hit (RCA 0281), reaching #3.

Elvis sang "Brown-Eyed Handsome Man" three times during the Million-Dollar-Quartet session of December 4, 1956. Years later, Felton Jarvis recorded a studio jam session in which Elvis sang many Chuck Berry tunes, including "Brown-Eyed Handsome Man." The tape has never been released.

Bootleg LPs:
- *The One Million Dollar Quartet* (Sun Records; December 4, 1956)

THE BULLFIGHTER WAS A LADY

Sid Tepper and Roy C. Bennett wrote "The Bullfighter Was a Lady" for Elvis's 1963 film *Fun in Acapulco*. Elvis recorded the song at Radio Recorders on January 22, 1963.

LPs:
- Fun in Acapulco

BURNING LOVE

Dennis Linde composed "Burning Love" for Elvis, who recorded the song at RCA's Hollywood studios on March 28, 1972. Linde played guitar on the recording. "Burning Love" reached #2 during its 15-week stay on *Billboard*'s Hot 100 chart. Only Chuck Berry's "My Ding-a-Ling" kept Elvis from having yet another number one record. "Burning Love" reached #9 on the Easy-Listening chart. On October 27, 1972, the RIAA certified the record as a million seller. An April 1972 concert performance of "Burning Love" was shown in the documentary *Elvis on Tour*. Elvis also sang it in his 1973 TV special, "Elvis, Aloha from Hawaii." Some have reported that Elvis may have recorded a sequel to "Burning Love" titled "Burning Love No. 2," but no proof has come forward.

Singles:
- "BURNING LOVE"/"It's a Matter of Time" (RCA 74-0769) August 1972. Standard release.
- "BURNING LOVE"/"Steamroller Blues" (RCA GB-10156) March 1975. Gold Standard Series original release.
- "THE ELVIS MEDLEY"/"Always on My Mind" (RCA PB-13351) November 1982. "The Elvis Medley" featured excerpts from "Jailhouse Rock," "Teddy Bear," "Hound Dog," "Don't Be Cruel," "Burning Love," and "Suspicious Minds."
- "THE ELVIS MEDLEY"/"THE ELVIS MEDLEY" (short version) (RCA JB-13351) November 1982. Disc jockey promotional release.
- "Suspicious Minds"/"BURNING LOVE" (RCA PB-13896) October 1984. One of six singles in the boxed set *Elvis' Greatest Hits—Golden Singles, Volume 2* (RCA PP-13898). The record was pressed on gold vinyl with a special gold "50th" anniversary label.

LPs:
- *Aloha from Hawaii via Satellite* (Honolulu; January 14, 1973)
- *The Alternate Aloha* (rehearsal concert for "Elvis: Aloha from Hawaii"; January 12, 1973)
- *Burning Love and Hits from His Movies, Volume 2*
- *Double Dynamite*
- *Elvis Aron Presley* (Dallas; June 6, 1975)
- *Elvis' Gold Records, Volume 5*
- *The Elvis Medley*
- *Greatest Hits, Volume 1*
- *The Top Ten Hits*

Bootleg LPs:
- *Aloha Rehearsal Show—Kui Lee Cancer Benefit* (rehearsal concert for "Elvis: Aloha from Hawaii"; January 12, 1973)
- *America's Own* (Uniondale, N.Y.; July 19, 1975)
- *Elvis on Tour* (*Elvis on Tour* soundtrack)
- *Elvis Presley Is Alive and Well and Singing in Las Vegas Volume 1* (Las Vegas; August 1975)
- *The King: From the Dark to the Light* (*Elvis on Tour* soundtrack)
- *Leavin' It Up to You* (rehearsal concert for "Elvis: Aloha from Hawaii"; January 12, 1973)
- *Rockin' with Elvis April Fool's Day* (Las Vegas; April 1, 1975)
- *Sold Out* (*Elvis on Tour* soundtrack)
- *The Vegas Years, 1972–1975* (Las Vegas; August 1975)

BUTTERFLY

"Butterfly" was written by Bernie Lowe and Kal Mann (who founded the Cameo-Parkway record company) the using pseudonym Anthony September. Both Charlie Gracie (Cameo 105) and Andy Williams (Cadence 1308) had million-sellers in 1957 with the song. Each one had a stay at number one on the various *Billboard* pop charts. In addition, Gracie's version was a #10 rhythm & blues hit. Bob Carroll (Bally 1028) also had a 1957 version of "Butterfly," which reached #61 on the Top 100 chart. Composers Mann and Lowe have said that they loosely based "Butterfly" on "Don't Be Cruel," which they also wrote.

On April 2, 1957, Elvis sang "Butterfly" in a performance at the Maple Leaf Gardens in Toronto.

BY AND BY

This traditional gospel tune was recorded by Elvis on May 27, 1966, at RCA's Nashville studios.

LPs:
- *How Great Thou Art*

BY THE TIME I GET TO PHOENIX

Jimmy Webb wrote "By the Time I Get to Phoenix" in 1967. The first recording of the song was by Johnny Rivers on an LP. Glen Campbell heard the album and decided to record the song himself. "By the Time I Get to Phoenix" (Capitol 2015) peaked at #2 on *Billboard*'s country chart and #26 on the Hot 100 chart. Four years later, Campbell and Anne Murray recorded a medley of "I Say a Little Prayer" and "By the Time I Get to Phoenix" (Capitol 3200). It, too, was a hit. Other hit recordings of the song include those by Wanda Jackson (Capitol 2085), Floyd Cramer (RCA 47-9396), and Harry Belafonte (RCA 47-9542) in 1968, and Isaac Hayes (Enterprise 9003) and the Mad Lads (Volt 4016) in 1969.

Elvis sang "By the Time I Get to Phoenix" in concert in the 1970s.

C

C. C. RIDER
(See *See See Rider*)

CAN YOU FIND IT IN YOUR HEART
Tony Bennett originally recorded this Al Stillman–Robert Allen tune in 1956. His version of "Can You Find It in Your Heart" (Columbia 40667) reached #16 on *Billboard*'s Top 100 chart. The song was first considered to lead into "Memories" in the 1968 TV special "Elvis," but the idea was dropped.

CANDY KISSES
"Candy Kisses" was written by George Morgan in 1948 and first recorded by him that year on Columbia Records (Columbia 20547). Morgan got the idea for the song while driving to work one day, and it took him just ten minutes to write. "Candy Kisses" reached number one on *Billboard's* country chart in 1949 and became a million-seller. One of the first cover versions of "Candy Kisses" was by Bill Haley and the Four Aces of Western Swing (Cowboy 1701) shortly after Morgan's original was released. Red Foley (Decca 46151) and Elton Britt (RCA 0006) also had top recordings of "Candy Kisses" in 1949, with Foley's record reaching #6 on the country chart and Britt's #4. Roy Rogers sang "Candy Kisses" in his 1949 movie *Down Dakota Way*.

Elvis is believed by some to have recorded "Candy Kisses" for his second film, *Loving You*, although it was cut from the final print. Throughout the movie, however, the song can be heard being played by Tex Warner's (Wendell Corey) Rough Ridin' Ramblers.

CANE AND A HIGH STARCHED COLLAR
Elvis recorded "Cane and a High Starched Collar" for his 1960 film *Flaming Star*. The recording session took place in August 1960, probably at Radio Recorders. Jimmie Haskell played accordion. Although sung in the movie, "Cane and a High Starched Collar" remained unreleased until the 1976 LP *Elvis—A Legendary Performer, Volume 2*, arrived in the music stores in January of that year. Sid Tepper and Roy C. Bennett are the composers.

LPs:
- *Elvis—A Legendary Perfomer, Volume 2* (take #2, a false start; and take #3, the film version)

Bootleg LPs:
- *Please Release Me* (*Flaming Star* soundtrack)

CAN'T HELP FALLING IN LOVE
"Can't Help Falling in Love" was written for Elvis's film *Blue Hawaii* by George Weiss, Hugo Peretti, and Luigi Creatore. They based the song on the classical French composition "Plaisir d'Amour," by Giovanni Martini (1741–1816). Elvis recorded "Can't Help Falling in Love" on March 23, 1961, at Radio Recorders. The take released as a single was #29. The single release had a 14-week stay on *Billboard*'s Hot 100 chart,

peaking at #2. ("Peppermint Twist" [Roulette 4401] by Joey Dee and the Starliters was number one at the time.) On the Easy-Listening chart, "Can't Help Falling in Love" replaced "When I Fall in Love" by the Lettermen at the top spot in January 1962. After six weeks at number one, it was replaced by Burl Ives's "A Little Bitty Tear." In England, "Can't Help Falling in Love" was number one for four weeks. A Gold Record was certified by the RIAA on March 30, 1962.

Elvis sang "Can't Help Falling in Love" in the documentaries *Elvis—That's the Way It Is* and *Elvis on Tour*. The former performance was at the International Hilton in August 1970, while the latter took place on April 9, 1972, in Hampton Roads, Virginia. The song was also performed in the TV specials "Elvis," "Elvis: Aloha from Hawaii," and "Elvis in Concert." Elvis ended his concerts in the 1970s with "Can't Help Falling in Love," just as he ended his 1950s concerts with "Hound Dog."

Other popular recordings of "Can't Help Falling in Love" include those by Al Martino (Capitol 2746) and Andy Williams (Columbia 45094), both in 1970.

Singles:
- "CAN'T HELP FALLING IN LOVE"/"Rock-a-Hula Baby" (RCA 47-7968) December 1961. Standard release.
- "CAN'T HELP FALLING IN LOVE"/"Rock-a-Hula Baby" (RCA 37-7968) December 1961. Compact 33 Single release.
- "CAN'T HELP FALLING IN LOVE"/"Rock-a-Hula Baby" (RCA 447-0635) November 1962. Gold Standard Series reissue.
- "CAN'T HELP FALLING IN LOVE"/"Rock-a-Hula Baby" (RCA PB-11102) October 1977. This was included in the boxed sets *15 Golden Records—30 Golden Hits* and *20 Golden Hits in Full Color Sleeves*.
- "Are You Lonesome Tonight?"/"CAN'T HELP FALLING IN LOVE" (RCA PB-13895) October 1984. One of six singles included in the boxed set *Elvis' Greatest Hits—Golden Singles, Volume 2*. The record was pressed on gold vinyl and had a special gold "50th" anniversary label.

LPs:
- *Aloha from Hawaii via Satellite* (Honolulu; January 14, 1973)
- *The Alternate Aloha* (rehearsal concert for "Elvis: Aloha from Hawaii"; January 12, 1973)
- *Blue Hawaii*
- *Elvis* (RCA DPL2-0056[e])
- *Elvis—A Legendary Performer, Volume 1*
- *Elvis Aron Presley* (take #24, alternate film version) (Dallas; June 6, 1975)
- *Elvis as Recorded at Madison Square Garden* (June 10, 1972)
- *Elvis in Concert* (Omaha, Nebraska; June 19, 1977)
- *Elvis in Person* (Las Vegas; August 24, 1969)
- *Elvis Recorded Live on Stage in Memphis* (Memphis; March 20, 1974)
- *Elvis—TV Special* ("Elvis" TV special taping; June 29, 1968, at 6:00 P.M. show)
- *Elvis: Worldwide 50 Gold Award Hits, Volume 1*
- *From Memphis to Vegas/From Vegas to Memphis* (Las Vegas; August 24, 1969)
- *The Top Ten Hits*
- *A Valentine Gift for You*

Bootleg LPs:

- *Aloha Rehearsal Show—Kui Lee Cancer Benefit* (rehearsal concert for "Elvis: Aloha from Hawaii"; January 12, 1973)
- *America's Own* (Uniondale, N.Y.; July 19, 1975)
- *Behind Closed Doors* (takes #20 [false start], #21 [false start], #22 [false start], and #24)
- *Big Boss Man* (Las Vegas; August. 19, 1974)
- *The Blue Hawaii Box* (takes #1–9)
- *The Burbank Sessions, Volume 2* ("Elvis" TV special taping; June 29, 1968, at 6:00 P.M. and 8:00 P.M. shows)
- *A Dog's Life* (rehearsal concert for "Elvis: Aloha from Hawaii"; January 12, 1973)
- *From Las Vegas . . . to Niagara Falls* (Las Vegas; September 3, 1973) (Niagara Falls, N.Y.; June 24, 1974)
- *From the Beach to the Bayou* (takes #13–29)
- *The Hillbilly Cat "Live"* (Las Vegas; August 1970)
- *The Last Farewell* (Indianapolis; June 26, 1977)
- *The Legend Lives On* (Las Vegas; August 1969)
- *Plantation Rock* (takes #7–9)
- *Rockin' with Elvis April Fool's Day* (Las Vegas; April 1, 1975)
- *Rockin' with Elvis New Year's Eve Pittsburgh, Pa. Dec. 31, 1976* (Pittsburgh; December 31, 1976)
- *Special Delivery from Elvis Presley* (alternate take)
- *Standing Room Only, Volume 2* (Indianapolis; June 26, 1977)
- *Superstar Outtakes* (Las Vegas; August 1969)
- *That's the Way It Is* (*Elvis—That's the Way It Is* soundtrack)
- *To Know Him Is to Love Him* (Las Vegas; 1969 or 1970)
- *Unfinished Business* (alternate take)
- *The Vegas Years, 1972–1975* (Las Vegas; 1972)

CARNY TOWN

"Carny Town" was sung by Elvis in his 1964 movie *Roustabout*. Written by Fred Wise and Randy Starr, the song was recorded by Elvis in March 1964 at Radio Recorders.

LPs:

- *Roustabout*

CARRY ME BACK TO OLD VIRGINNY

James Bland was inspired to compose "Carry Me Back to Old Virginny" in 1878 while looking at a plantation in the Tidewater section of Virginia. He remembered a girl in college who remarked that a dream carried her back to "old Virginny." The song was quite popular in the late 1800s and early 1900s. Alma Gluck's 1915 recording of "Carry Me Back to Old Virginny" for Victor Records is credited with being the first record to sell one million copies, which it did by 1918.

Elvis sang one line of "Carry Me Back to Old Virginny" just before singing "Never Been to Spain" in Las Vegas on February 22, 1972.

CASUAL LOVE AFFAIR

"Casual Love Affair" is one of two songs recorded by Elvis on his second trip to the Memphis Recording Service on January 4, 1954. The other song was "I'll Never Stand in Your Way (Little Darlin')." At a cost of four dollars, "Casual Love Affair" was recorded on a 10-inch acetate. Elvis kept the only copy. It was at this time that Elvis first met Sam Phillips. There's no evidence that he ever recorded "Casual Love Affair" again. Reportedly, a tape from Elvis's acetate exists.

CATCHIN' ON FAST

Elvis sang "Catchin' on Fast" in his 1964 movie *Kissin' Cousins*. He recorded the song, which was written by Bill Giant, Bernie Baum, and Florence Kaye, at RCA's Nashville studios in October 1963.

LPs:

- *Kissin' Cousins*

THE CATTLE CALL

In the winter of 1934 Tex Owen was on the eleventh floor of the Pickwick Hotel in Kansas City waiting to do a broadcast for KMBC Radio. He began thinking about all the cattle back on the ranch that were cold and hungry. Within 30 minutes he had written "The Cattle Call." In 1955 Eddy Arnold had a number one country hit and million-seller with "The Cattle Call" (RCA 6139). Slim Whitman also had a hit with the song that year, his version (Imperial 8281) rising to #11 on the country chart.

Elvis sang "The Cattle Call" in concert on at least a couple of occasions in the 1950s.

CHAIN GANG

Sol Quasha and Herb Yakus wrote "Chain Gang" in 1956. Sam Cooke had a tremendous hit with the song (RCA 7783) in 1960. It reached #2 on both the Hot 100 and rhythm & blues charts. Sales easily exceeded one million copies.

Elvis sang "Chain Gang" at several concerts in the 1970s.

CHANGE OF HABIT

Ben Weisman and Buddy Kaye wrote "Change of Habit" for Elvis's 1969 movie of the same name. The instrumental track was recorded on March 5 or 6,

Randy Starr's songwriter's demo for "Change of Habit." (Photo courtesy Don Fink)

1969. Elvis's vocal was recorded later at the Decca Recording Studios in Universal City.

LPs:
- *Let's Be Friends*

CHARRO

"Charro" was the title tune to Elvis's 1969 movie of the same name. The instrumental track was recorded on October 15, 1968, at the Samuel Goldwyn Studios. Elvis's vocal was recorded at a later date. The Jordanaires and Hugo Montenegro's Orchestra backed Elvis on this recording. Former Mouseketeer Carl (Cubby) O'Brien was the drummer on the session. Although released as a single, "Charro" did not chart. Billy Strange and Mac Davis are the composers, although the film credits list Alan and Marilyn Bergman in that capacity.

Singles:
- "Memories"/"CHARRO" (RCA 47-9731) March 1969. Standard release.
- "Memories"/"CHARRO" (RCA 447-0669) December 1970. Gold Standard Series reissue.

LPs
- *Almost in Love*
- *Elvis in Hollywood*

CHAUTAUQUA

Elvis recorded "Chautauqua" for his 1969 film, *The Trouble With Girls*, but it was not used and has never been released. The song, which was written by Ben Weisman and Buddy Kaye, was recorded at United Recorders. The instrumental track was laid on August 23, 1968, and Elvis's vocal was recorded at a later date. "Chautauqua" used the same melody as "Almost," but in a march tempo.

CHESAY

Elvis sang "Chesay" in his 1966 movie *Frankie and Johnny*. In the film version of the song the opening lines were sung by another voice, and Harry Morgan added two lines. "Chesay" was written by Fred Karger, Sid Wayne, and Ben Weisman and recorded by Elvis in May 1965 at Radio Recorders.

LPs:
- *Frankie and Johnny*

CINDY, CINDY

Several versions of "Cindy, Cindy" using different lyrics and sometimes different titles have been recorded through the years. In the 1959 movie *Rio Bravo*, Ricky Nelson sang the song as "Get Along Home, Cindy." A year later Teddy Vann had a release on Triple X Records (Triple X-101) that used the title "Cindy." Florence Kaye, Ben Weisman, and Dolores Fuller adapted the traditional lyrics for Elvis in 1970. Elvis recorded the song as "Cindy, Cindy" in a session at RCA's Nashville studios on June 4, 1970.

LPs:
- *Love Letters from Elvis*

CITY BY NIGHT

Bill Giant, Bernie Baum, and Florence Kaye wrote "City by Night" for Elvis's 1967 movie *Double Trouble*. The film version had added instrumentation. Elvis recorded the tune at Radio Recorders in June 1966. Take #3 was the one used by RCA on record.

LPs:
- *Double Trouble*

CLAMBAKE

This title song to Elvis's 1967 movie *Clambake* was written by Sid Wayne and Ben Weisman. Elvis recorded "Clambake" on February 21, 1967, at RCA's Nashville studios.

EPs:
- *Clambake*

LPs:
- *Clambake*

CLEAN UP YOUR OWN BACK YARD

On August 23, 1968, Elvis recorded "Clean Up Your Own Back Yard" at United Recorders in Los Angeles. It was sung in his 1969 movie *The Trouble with Girls*. The single release reached #35 on the Hot 100 chart (for an eight-week stay), #74 on the country chart, and #37 on the Easy-Listening chart. On October 17, 1980, Felton Jarvis added a completely new instrumental track to Elvis's vocal at Young 'Un Sound in Nashville for the *Guitar Man* LP. "Clean Up Your Own Back Yard" was composed by Billy Strange and Mac Davis.

Singles:
- "CLEAN UP YOUR OWN BACK YARD"/"The Fair Is Moving On" (RCA 47-9747) June 1969. Standard release.
- "CLEAN UP YOUR OWN BACK YARD"/"The Fair Is Moving On" (RCA 447-0672) December 1970. Gold Standard Series reissue.

LPs:
- *Almost in Love*
- *Elvis' Gold Records, Volume 5*
- *Guitar Man* (new instrumental backing)

CLOSE TO YOU

"Close to You" was written by Hal David and Burt Bacharach in 1963 and had appeared on albums by Dionne Warwick and Dusty Springfield before the Carpenters (A&M 1183) took it to number one on both the Hot 100 and Easy-Listening charts in 1970. It was a quick million-seller for the Carpenters. The full title of the song is "(They Long to Be) Close to You."

Elvis sang "Close to You" on September 14, 1970, in a Mobile, Alabama, concert and probably on a few other occasions as well.

C'MON EVERYBODY

Elvis recorded "C'mon Everybody," a Joy Byers song, for his 1964 film *Viva Las Vegas*. The movie version had a heavier beat and extra voices. The recording session took place at Radio Recorders in Hollywood on July 7, 1964. Take #5 is the one used by RCA on record.

In 1958 Eddie Cochran had a hit with a completely

different song called "C'mon Everybody" (Liberty 55166). That recording was the first rock & roll record ever bought by Rod Stewart. It was originally titled "Let's Get Together."

EPs:
- *Viva Las Vegas*

LPs:
- *C'mon Everybody*

Bootleg LPs:
- *Eternal Elvis* (*Viva Las Vegas* soundtrack)
- *Please Release Me* (*Viva Las Vegas* soundtrack)
- *Viva Las Vegas!* (*Viva Las Vegas* soundtrack)

COLD, COLD ICY FINGERS
(See *Keep Them Cold Icy Fingers Off of Me*)

COLOR MY RAINBOW
On July 25, 1973, an instrumental track for "Color My Rainbow" was recorded at Stax Studios in Memphis. Elvis, however, never recorded a vocal track for this song.

COME ALONG
"Come Along" was sung by Elvis in his 1966 movie *Frankie and Johnny*. The song was recorded in May 1965 at Radio Recorders. David Hess is the composer.

LPS:
- *Frankie and Johnny*

COME OUT, COME OUT (WHEREVER YOU ARE)
On January 14, 1969, an instrumental track for "Come Out, Come Out (Wherever You Are)" was recorded at American Sound Studios. There's no record of Elvis ever recording a vocal track. The composers are Don Thomas and Mike Millius.

COME WHAT MAY
"Come What May" was written by Franklin Tableporter in 1958 and recorded that year by Clyde McPhatter (Atlantic 1185). McPhatter's recording reached #43 on *Billboard*'s Hot 100 chart and #20 on the rhythm & blues chart. The full title of the song is "Come What May (You Are Mine)."

Elvis recorded "Come What May" on May 28, 1966, at RCA's Nashville studios. His single release never made the charts, but it *was* listed as "Bubbling Under" at #109. The song has not yet appeared on an RCA album.

Singles:
- "Love Letters"/"COME WHAT MAY" (RCA 47-8870) June 1966. Standard release. The original picture sleeves read, "Coming Soon—PARADISE, HAWAIIAN STYLE." In July 1966, the sleeves were changed to read, "ASK FOR—PARADISE, HAWAIIAN STYLE."
- "Love Letters"/"COME WHAT MAY" (RCA 447-0657) February 1968. Gold Standard Series reissue.

Bootleg LPs:
- *The Hillbilly Cat, 1954–1974, Volume 1* (RCA release)

COMIN' HOME BABY
Whenever Elvis introduced the members of his TCB band to the audience, "Comin' Home, Baby" was played. Both Mel Tormé (Atlantic 2165) in 1962, and Kai Winding (Verve 10295) in 1963 recorded the song.

CONFIDENCE
Elvis sang "Confidence" in his 1967 movie *Clambake*. The film version was longer than that on record and included a children's chorus. "Confidence," which was written by Sid Tepper and Roy C. Bennett, was recorded by Elvis at RCA's Nashville studios on February 22, 1967. The record version had a female chorus, which was overdubbed on September 19, 1967.

LPs:
- *Clambake*
- *Elvis Sings Hits from His Movies, Volume 1*

COTTON CANDY LAND
"Cotton Candy Land" was written by Ruth Batchelor and Bob Roberts for Elvis's 1963 movie *It Happened at the World's Fair*. The film version had added strings and a shorter ending. "Cotton Candy Land" was initially considered for a movie-song medley in the 1968 TV special "Elvis," but the idea was dropped. The song was recorded in September 1962 at Radio Recorders.

LPs:
- *Elvis Sings for Children and Grownups Too!*
- *It Happened at the World's Fair*

COULD I FALL IN LOVE
Elvis sang "Could I Fall in Love" in his 1967 film *Double Trouble*. In the movie, "Could I Fall in Love" was a hit for Guy Lambert (Elvis). Elvis recorded this Randy Starr composition at Radio Recorders in June 1966.

LPs:
- *Double Trouble*

The Stone Crushers' cover version. (Photo courtesy Don Fink)

CRAWFISH

"Crawfish" was sung by Elvis in a duet with Kitty White in the 1958 movie *King Creole*. Written by Fred Wise and Ben Weisman, the song was recorded on January 15, 1958, at Radio Recorders (take #7 is on the record). Later in 1958, the Stone Crushers recorded "Crawfish" on RCA Records (RCA 47-7309).

EPs:
- *King Creole, Volume 2*

LPs:
- *Elvis: The Other Sides—Worldwide Gold Award Hits, Volume 2*
- *King Creole*

Bootleg LPs:
- *From the Beach to the Bayou* (take #7, the complete version, with Kitty White's beginning and ending vocals)
- *Loving You* (*King Creole* soundtrack)

CRAZY ARMS

In 1956 Ray Price had a number one country hit and million-seller with "Crazy Arms" (Columbia 21510). The song, which was written by Ralph Mooney and Chuck Seals, peaked at #27 on the Top 100 chart. Mooney wrote "Crazy Arms" after his wife temporarily left him because of his drinking. In 1963 Marion Worth had a #18 country hit with his rendition (Columbia 42703).

Elvis and Jerry Lee Lewis sang a few lines of "Crazy Arms" during the Million-Dollar-Quartet session on December 4, 1956. Just three days earlier, Sun Records released "Crazy Arms" as Lewis's first record (Sun 259).

Bootleg LPs:
- *The Million Dollar Quartet* (Sun Records; December 4, 1956)
- *The One Million Dollar Quartet* (Sun Records; December 4, 1956)

CROSS MY HEART AND HOPE TO DIE

This tune was sung by Elvis in his 1965 film *Girl Happy*. Written by Sid Wayne and Ben Weisman, "Cross My Heart and Hope to Die" was recorded by Elvis at Radio Recorders in June or July 1964.

LPs:
- *Girl Happy*

CRYIN' HEART BLUES

"Cryin' Heart Blues" was written by J. Brown in 1951 and first recorded by the Hugh Ashley Orchestra that year on RCA Records. The hit, however, was by Johnnie and Jack (RCA 0478), whose recording reached #10 on *Billboard*'s country chart in August 1951.

Elvis sang "Cryin' Heart Blues" on the "Louisiana Hayride." There has been speculation that he recorded the song at Sun Studios, but no tape has surfaced.

CRYING

"Crying" was written by Roy Orbison and Joe Melson and recorded by Orbison in 1961. His recording (Monument 447) reached #2 on *Billboard*'s Hot 100 chart and sold over a million copies. Orbison wrote "Crying" after he spotted a girlfriend with whom he had just broken up. The first words of the song came to him when he began crying after realizing he'd blown the relationship.

Reportedly, Elvis attempted to record "Crying" in 1976, but was dissatisfied with the results. It has never been released.

CRYING IN THE CHAPEL

Artie Glenn wrote "Crying in the Chapel" for his son, Darrell, who recorded it in 1953 (Valley 105). His recording reached #7 on the country chart and #9 on the Best-Selling Singles chart. Other popular recordings of "Crying in the Chapel" in 1953 included those by Rex Allen (Decca 28758), Sonny Til and the Orioles (Jubilee 5122) (a number one rhythm & blues hit), and June Valli (RCA 5368). The releases by Rex Allen and June Valli were million-sellers. In 1957 Elvis's girlfriend, Anita Wood, recorded "Crying in the Chapel" (ABC-Paramount 9747).

Elvis recorded "Crying in the Chapel" on October 31, 1960, at RCA's Nashville studios. It remained unissued for five years. The 1965 single release reached #3 on *Billboard*'s Hot 100 chart, staying on the chart for 14 weeks. In May 1965, on the Easy-Listening chart, "Crying in the Chapel" replaced the instrumental "Cast Your Fate to the Wind," by Sounds Orchestral, at number one. After a seven-week stay at the top, it was replaced by a Horst Jankowski instrumental, "A Walk in the Black Forest." In England, "Crying in the Chapel" was number one for two weeks. It was Elvis's first number one since the advent of the Beatles. Worldwide sales exceeded one million copies.

Singles:
- "CRYING IN THE CHAPEL"/"I Believe in the Man in the Sky" (RCA 447-0643) April 1965. Gold Standard Series original release.
- "CRYING IN THE CHAPEL"/"I Believe in the Man in the Sky" (RCA PB-11113) October 1977. One of 15 singles in the 15-record boxed set *15 Golden Records–30 Golden Hits* (RCA PP-11301).

LPs:
- *Elvis—A Legendary Performer, Volume 3*
- *Elvis: Worldwide 50 Gold Award Hits, Volume 1*
- *How Great Thou Art*
- *The Top Ten Hits*

Bootleg LPs:
- *Long Lost Songs* (Las Vegas; December 1975) (in medley with "Rip It Up")

CRYING TIME

Buck Owens wrote and first recorded "Crying Time" (Capitol 5336) in 1964. It was the flip side of his number one country hit "I've Got a Tiger by the Tail." Two years later Ray Charles took the song to #6 on the Hot 100 chart, #5 on the rhythm & blues chart, and number one on the Easy-Listening chart.

Elvis can be seen singing "Crying Time" in a July 1970 rehearsal at the MGM Studios in the documentary *Elvis—That's the Way It Is*. The song has never been released by RCA.

Bootleg LPs:
- *From Hollywood to Vegas* (*Elvis—That's the Way It Is* soundtrack)
- *Long Lost Songs* (Las Vegas; 1970)
- *That's the Way It Is* (*Elvis—That's the Way It Is* soundtrack)

DAINTY LITTLE MOONBEAMS

Elvis sang a portion of "Dainty Little Moonbeams" (50 seconds) in his 1962 movie *Girls! Girls! Girls!*, leading into the end title version of "Girls! Girls! Girls!" The song was written by Jerry Leiber and Mike Stoller and recorded by Elvis in March 1962 at Radio Recorders. "Danity Little Moonbeams" has never been officially released by RCA.

Bootleg LPs:
- *Elvis Rocks and the Girls Roll* (alternate take)
- *Eternal Elvis* (*Girls! Girls! Girls!* soundtrack)
- *From Hollywood to Vegas* (*Girls! Girls! Girls!* soundtrack)

DANCING ON A DARE

Elvis is believed to have recorded "Dancing on a Dare" for his 1957 movie *Loving You*, but no tape has ever surfaced. Dolores Hart, however, *did* sing the song right after Elvis sang "Got a Lot o' Livin' to Do." Whenever *TV Guide* lists the movie, "Dancing on a Dare" is mentioned as one of Elvis's songs.

DANNY

"Danny" was to have been the title song of *King Creole*, then known as *A Stone for Danny Fisher*. But the song was not used in the film or on the soundtrack album. Elvis recorded "Danny" on January 23, 1958, at Radio Recorders. It remained unreleased until the 1978 LP *Elvis—A Legendary Performer, Volume 3*. In 1959 Gene Bua recorded "Danny" (Warner Bros. 5098). That same year, Cliff Richard included the song on his Columbia LP *Cliff*. Conway Twitty recorded "Danny" under the title "Lonely Blue Boy" (MGM 12857), and had a million-seller with it in 1960. His recording peaked at #6 on *Billboard*'s Hot 100 chart. "Danny" was composed by Fred Wise and Ben Weisman.

(Photo courtesy Don Fink)

LPs:
- *Elvis—A Legendary Performer, Volume 3* (take #8)

DANNY BOY

"Danny Boy" was written in 1913 by Frederic Edward Weatherly, with music adapted from the Irish song "Londonderry Air." The song has been recorded countless times over the years by such artists as Ernestine Shumank-Heink (Victor 88592) in 1918, Gracie Fields (Victor 26377) in 1939, the Glenn Miller Orchestra (Bluebird 10612) in 1940, Bing Crosby (Decca 18570) in 1943 (the flip side of "I'll Be Home for Christmas"), Conway Twitty (MGM 12826) in late 1959 (a #10 hit on the Hot 100 chart), and Ray Price (Columbia 44042) in 1967 (a #9 country hit). "Danny Boy" has served as Danny Thomas's theme song for years and was the theme of the radio series "The O'Neills." It was one of the songs played at Elvis's funeral.

Elvis recorded "Danny Boy" on the night of February 5–6, 1976, at Graceland. Recently, a home recording made while Elvis was in the army was discovered.

LPs:
- *From Elvis Presley Boulevard, Memphis, Tennessee*
- *A Golden Celebration* (West Germany; 1958–1960)

DARK AS A DUNGEON

"Dark as a Dungeon" was written by Merle Travis in 1947 and first appeared on his LP *Folk Songs of the Hills*. The first cover version was by Louis Marshall (Grandpa) Jones in 1950 (King 896). In 1964 Johnny Cash reached #49 on the country chart with "Dark as a Dungeon"; it was the flip side of his number one hit "Understand Your Man" (Columbia 42964).

"Dark as a Dungeon" is one of several songs Elvis may have recorded at Sun Records, although no tape has surfaced.

DARK MOON

Ned Miller wrote "Dark Moon" in 1957. Several recordings of the song were released that year, but it appears that Bonnie Guitar (Dot 15550) had the original version in April. Her recording, which was pressed by Fabor Records (Fabor 1018) and then leased to Dot, reached #6 on *Billboard*'s Top 100 chart. Close on her heels was Gale Storm's cover version (Dot 15558) which did even better, peaking at #4. Hawkshaw Hawkins had a country release of "Dark Moon" (RCA 6910) in June 1957 that did not chart.

Elvis recorded "Dark Moon" at Graceland in the 1960s with his own guitar accompaniment. It surfaced on the *A Golden Celebration* LP in 1984.

LPs:
- *A Golden Celebration* (Graceland; 1960s)

DATIN'

Elvis sang *Datin'* in duet with Donna Butterworth in

his 1966 film *Paradise, Hawaiian Style*. The instrumental track was recorded on July 26, 1965, at Radio Recorders. Elvis recorded his vocal on August 4, 1965. "Datin' " was written by Fred Wise and Randy Starr. Take #14 is the one that appeared in the film and on the *Paradise, Hawaiian Style* album.

LPs:
- *Elvis Aron Presley* (false starts #6, #7, #8, and #11 and complete take #12)
- *Paradise, Hawaiian Style*

DETOUR
"Detour" was popularized in a late 1945 recording by Spade Cooley (Columbia 36935) and became a #12 hit for Patti Page (Mercury 5682) in 1951. Dolores Hart sang the song in Elvis's 1957 film *Loving You*. Some sources have indicated that Elvis may have recorded "Detour" for the movie, but this is unverified.

(YOU'RE THE) DEVIL IN DISGUISE
Elvis recorded "(You're the) Devil in Disguise" on May 26, 1963, at RCA's Nashville studios. His single release reached #3 on *Billboard*'s Hot 100 chart during its 11-week stay on the chart. It peaked at #9 on the rhythm & blues chart. In England, the song topped the charts for one week in August 1963. The recording sold over one million copies worldwide. Bill Giant, Bernie Baum, and Florence Kaye are the composers. In late 1963 Rex Guido recorded a version of "(You're the) Devil in Disguise" in German (Capitol 5076).

Singles:
- "(YOU'RE THE) DEVIL IN DISGUISE"/"Please Don't Drag That String Around" (RCA 47-8188) June 1963. Standard release.
- "(YOU'RE THE) DEVIL IN DISGUISE"/"Please Don't Drag That String Around" (RCA 447-0641) August 1964. Gold Standard Series reissue.

LPs:
- *Elvis' Gold Records, Volume 4*
- *Elvis: Worldwide 50 Gold Award Hits, Volume 1*
- *The Top Ten Hits*

DIANA
Paul Anka wrote "Diana" in 1957 about his younger brother and sister's baby-sitter, Diana Ayoub. Anka, himself only 15 years old, wrote a poem and sent it to the 20-year-old girl after she rejected his romantic advances. He later set the poem to music and had his first number one record and million-seller—the first Canadian solo artist to have a million-seller. In 1963 Anka recorded a follow-up record, "Remember Diana" (RCA 47-8170).

Elvis sang "Diana" in concert on a few occasions.

DIDJA EVER
Elvis sang "Didja Ever" in his 1960 movie *G. I. Blues*. The regular release had the backing of the Jordanaires, while the film version had several voices answering Elvis. "Didja Ever," written by Sid Wayne and Sherman Edwards, was recorded by Elvis on April 27, 1960, at RCA's Hollywood studios.

LPs:
- *G. I. Blues*

DIRTY, DIRTY FEELING
"Dirty, Dirty Feeling" was sung by Elvis in his 1965 movie *Tickle Me*. Written by Jerry Leiber and Mike Stoller, the song had actually been recorded by Elvis five years earlier on April 4, 1960, at RCA's Nashville studios.

EPs:
- *Tickle Me*

LPs:
- *Elvis Is Back*

Bootleg LPs:
- *Elvis Sings Songs from* Tickle Me (alternate take)

DIXIE
(See *An American Trilogy*)

DIXIELAND ROCK
Elvis recorded "Dixieland Rock" on January 16, 1958, at Radio Recorders for his 1958 film *King Creole*. Take #14 is the one that was commercially released by RCA. The version of "Dixieland Rock" on the *King Creole* LP was different in that it had seven downbeats instead of two. Aaron Schroeder and R. Frank are the composers. The EP, *King Creole, Volume 2*, incorrectly listed the composers as Claude DeMetrius and Fred Wise.

EPs:
- *King Creole, Volume 2*

LPs:
- *Elvis: The Other Sides—Worldwide Gold Award Hits, Volume 2*
- *King Creole*

DO NOT DISTURB
Bill Giant, Bernie Baum, and Florence Kaye wrote "Do Not Disturb" for Elvis's 1965 film *Girl Happy*. Elvis recorded the tune in June or July 1964 at Radio Recorders in Hollywood. Take #36 is the one chosen by RCA for commercial release.

LPs:
- *Girl Happy*

DO THE CLAM
"Do the Clam" was sung by Elvis in his 1965 film *Girl Happy*. The single release reached #21 on *Billboard*'s Hot 100 chart during its eight-week stay. It was tremendously successful in Japan for some unknown reason. Elvis recorded the song in June or July 1964 at Radio Recorders. Sid Wayne, Ben Weisman, and Dolores Fuller are the composers.

Singles:
- "DO THE CLAM"/"You'll Be Gone" (RCA 47-8500) February 1965. Standard release.
- "DO THE CLAM"/"You'll Be Gone" (RCA 447-0648) November 1965. Gold Standard Series reissue.

LPs:
- *Girl Happy*

(Photo courtesy Don Fink)

DO THE VEGA

Although Elvis recorded "Do the Vega" (another attempt to create a new dance hit) for his 1964 film *Viva Las Vegas*, the song was cut from the final print of the film. The recording session took place in July 1963 at Radio Recorders. Bill Giant, Bernie Baum, and Florence Kaye are the composers.

LPs:
- *Elvis Sings Flaming Star*
- *Singer Presents Elvis Singing Flaming Star and Others*

DO YOU KNOW WHO I AM

On February 19, 1969, Elvis recorded this Bobby Russell[1]-composed song at American Sound Studios in Memphis.

LPs:
- *From Memphis to Vegas/From Vegas to Memphis*
- *Back in Memphis*

A DOG'S LIFE

"A Dog's Life" was sung by Elvis in his 1966 film *Paradise, Hawaiian Style*. The film version included barking dogs. The instrumental track for "A Dog's Life" was recorded on July 27, 1965, at Radio Recorders. Elvis's vocal track was recorded on August 4. Take #9 is the one released by RCA. Sid Wayne and Ben Weisman are the composers.

LPs:
- *Elvis Aron Presley* (false start #3 and complete take #4)
- *Paradise, Hawaiian Style*

Bootleg LPs:
- *A Dog's Life* (take #8)
- *Hawaii USA* (take #7)

[1]Bobby Russell is the ex-husband of comedienne and singer Vicki Lawrence.

- *Unfinished Business* (take #?)

DOIN' THE BEST I CAN

This Doc Pomus–Mort Shuman tune was sung by Elvis in *G. I. Blues* (1960). The recording session took place on April 27, 1960, at RCA's Hollywood studios.

EPs:
- *The EP Collection, Volume 2* (take #9)

LPs:
- *G. I. Blues*

DOMINICK

Dominick was a bull in Elvis's 1968 movie *Stay Away, Joe*, and "Dominick" was the song Elvis sang to him. RCA has never officially released the tune. The recording took place on October 2, 1967, at RCA's Nashville studios.

Bootleg LPs:
- *Please Release Me* (*Stay Away, Joe* soundtrack)

DONCHA' THINK IT'S TIME

Clyde Otis and Willie Dixon wrote "Doncha' Think It's Time" for Elvis in 1958. Elvis first recorded the song on January 23, 1958, at Radio Recorders, but all takes were deemed unsatisfactory. An acceptable take (#40) was recorded on February 1, 1958. The single release reached #21 on *Billboard*'s Top 100 chart during its six-week stay.

Singles:
- "Wear My Ring Around Your Neck"/"DONCHA' THINK IT'S TIME" (RCA 20-7240) April 1958. Standard 78 RPM release.
- "Wear My Ring Around Your Neck"/"DONCHA' THINK IT'S TIME" (RCA 47-7240) April 1958. Standard 45 RPM release.
- "Wear My Ring Around Your Neck"/"DONCHA' THINK IT'S TIME" (RCA 447-0622) 1961. Gold Standard Series reissue.

LPs:
- *Elvis: The Other Sides—Worldwide Gold Award Hits, Volume 2*
- *50,000,000 Elvis Fans Can't Be Wrong—Elvis' Gold Records, Volume 2* (alternate take)

DON'T

"Don't" was recorded on September 6, 1957, at Radio Recorders, just after Elvis had finished recording "Silent Night." This was the first session that featured a female voice (Millie Kirkham). Twenty-six takes were recorded; take #7 was the one released. Reportedly, the last take was taped with the studio lights turned off and Elvis lying on the floor. Jerry Leiber and Mike Stoller wrote "Don't" at Elvis's request. The single release of "Don't" replaced the Silhouettes' "Get a Job" at number one on the Top 100 chart. After one week at the top, it was replaced by the Champs' "Tequila." "Don't" spent a total of 20 weeks on the Top 100 chart. It peaked at #2 on the country chart and #4 on the rhythm & blues chart. Advance orders for the record were over a million.

Singles:
- "DON'T"/"I Beg of You" (RCA 20-7150) January 1958. Standard 78

RPM release.
- "DON'T"/"I Beg of You" (RCA 47-7150) January 1958. Standard 45 RPM release.
- "Wear My Ring Around Your Neck"/"DON'T" (RCA SP-45-76) January 1960. Disc jockey promotional release that was used to promote the LP *50,000,000 Elvis Fans Can't Be Wrong—Elvis' Gold Records, Volume 2*.
- "DON'T"/"I Beg of You" (RCA 447-0621) 1961. Gold Standard Series reissue.

EPs:
- *A Touch of Gold, Volume 1*

LPs:
- *Elvis: Worldwide 50 Gold Award Hits, Volume 1*
- *50,000,000 Elvis Fans Can't Be Wrong—Elvis' Gold Records, Volume 2*
- *I Was the One* (with overdubbing)
- *The Number One Hits*
- *The Top Ten Hits*

DON'T ASK ME WHY
Elvis recorded "Don't Ask Me Why," a Fred Wise and Ben Weisman tune, at Radio Recorders on January 16, 1958. Take #12 was chosen by RCA for release. The single release peaked at #28 on *Billboard*'s Top 100 chart during its nine-week stay. On the rhythm & blues chart, "Don't Ask Me Why" reached #2.

Singles:
- "Hard Headed Woman"/"DON'T ASK ME WHY" (RCA 20-7280) June 1958. Standard 78 RPM release.
- "Hard Headed Woman"/"DON'T ASK ME WHY" (RCA 47-7280) June 1958. Standard 45 RPM release.
- "Hard Headed Woman"/"DON'T ASK ME WHY" (RCA 447-0623) 1961. Gold Standard Series reissue.

EPs:
- *A Touch of Gold, Volume 3*

LPs:
- *Elvis: The Other Sides—Worldwide Gold Award Hits, Volume 2*
- *King Creole*

DON'T BE CRUEL
Otis Blackwell wrote "Don't Be Cruel" in 1955 and sold the publishing rights to the song on Christmas Eve of that year to Shalimar Music for $25. The song's full title is "Don't Be Cruel (to a Heart That's True)." Reportedly, the song was first offered to the Four Tunes, a rhythm & blues group that recorded for RCA Records, but they turned it down. When Elvis heard Blackwell's demo of "Don't Be Cruel," he fell in love with it. To get Elvis to record the song, Blackwell had to give 50 percent of his writers' royalties rights to Elvis. That's why Elvis is listed as co-composer. The recording session took place at RCA's New York City studios on July 2, 1956—the first session to feature all four of the Jordanaires. To get the interesting drum sound on the recording, D. J. Fontana put Elvis's guitar case on his lap and struck it with mallets. Other musicians included Scotty Moore (guitar), Bill Black (bass), and Shorty Long (piano). Take #28 was the one released. "Don't Be Cruel" entered *Billboard*'s Top 100 chart at #28. By early September 1956 it had ascended to the top of the

chart, replacing the Platters' "My Prayer." It remained at the top for seven straight weeks and was replaced by "The Green Door" by Jim Lowe. "Don't Be Cruel" had a stay of 27 weeks on the chart. The song also reached number one on the country and rhythm & blues charts, for five weeks and one week, respectively. "Don't Be Cruel" was the first of three Presley songs to reach number one on all three charts (the other two were "Teddy Bear" and "Jailhouse Rock"). Total sales of "Don't Be Cruel"/"Hound Dog" have been estimated at over nine million copies.

Elvis sang "Don't Be Cruel" on "The Ed Sullivan Show" (September 9, 1956; October 28, 1956; and January 6, 1957) and on his 1977 TV special "Elvis in Concert" (October 3, 1977). The song was recorded during the tapings for the 1968 TV special, but was not used for the telecast or the subsequent soundtrack album. "The Ed Sullivan Show" appearance of January 6, 1957, was used in the documentary *This Is Elvis*.

"Don't Be Cruel" has been recorded by several other artists over the years, most of them unsuccessfully. Bill Black had a 1960 instrumental version (Hi 2026) that reached #11 on the Hot 100 chart. Scotty Moore played guitar on that recording. In 1963 Barbara Lynn barely made the Hot 100 (#93) with her recording of "Don't Be Cruel" (Jamie 1244).

During the Million-Dollar-Quartet session of December 4, 1956, Elvis commented to Jerry Lee Lewis and Carl Perkins that he'd heard a member of Billy Ward and His Dominoes sing "Don't Be Cruel" in Las Vegas. He enjoyed the slower version so much that he wished he'd recorded it that way. The unnamed member of the Dominoes to whom Elvis was referring was Jackie Wilson. Elvis then demonstrated to Lewis and Perkins how Wilson sang "Don't Be Cruel."

Singles:
- "Hound Dog"/"DON'T BE CRUEL" (RCA 20-6604) July 1956. Standard 78 RPM release.
- "Hound Dog"/"DON'T BE CRUEL" (RCA 47-6604) July 1956. Standard 45 RPM release. Two versions of the picture sleeve were used. One had "Hound Dog" printed above "Don't Be Cruel" in larger letters. The other had the reverse. This was the first sleeve to feature a photograph of Elvis.
- "Hound Dog"/"DON'T BE CRUEL" (RCA 447-0608) March 1959. Gold Standard Series reissue.
- "Hound Dog"/"DON'T BE CRUEL" (RCA PB-11099) October 1977. One of 15 singles in the boxed set *15 Golden Records—30 Golden Hits* (RCA PP-11301) and one of 10 singles in the *20 Golden Hits in Full Color Sleeves* boxed set released two months later.
- "Hound Dog"/"DON'T BE CRUEL" (RCA PB-13886) October 1984. One of six singles in the boxed set *Elvis' Greatest Hits—Golden Singles, Volume 1* (RCA PP-13897). Each record was pressed on gold vinyl and had a special gold "50th" anniversary label.

EPs:
- *Elvis Presley* (RCA SPD-23)
- *The Real Elvis*

LPs:
- *Elvis* (RCA DPL2-0056[e])
- *Elvis—A Legendary Performer, Volume 1*
- *Elvis Aron Presley* (USS *Arizona* Memorial; March 25, 1961)
- *Elvis as Recorded at Madison Square Garden* (June 10, 1972)

- *Elvis' Golden Records*
- *Elvis in Concert* (Omaha, Nebraska; June 19, 1977) (in medley with "Teddy Bear")
- *The Elvis Medley*
- *Elvis: Worldwide 50 Gold Award Hits, Volume 1*
- *A Golden Celebration* (Mississippi-Alabama Fair and Dairy Show; September 26, 1956) ("The Ed Sullivan Show"; September 9, 1956; October 28, 1956; and January 6, 1957)
- *The Number One Hits*
- *Pure Gold*
- *This Is Elvis* ("The Ed Sullivan Show"; January 6, 1957)
- *The Top Ten Hits*

Bootleg LPs:
- *America's Own* (Uniondale, N.Y.; July 19, 1975)
- *The Burbank Sessions, Volume 2* ("Elvis" TV special taping; June 29, at 6:00 P.M. and 8:00 P.M. shows)
- *Elvis' 1961 Hawaii Benefit Concert* (USS *Arizona* Memorial; March 25, 1961)
- *Eternal Elvis, Volume 2* (fabricated duet using Elvis's recording with Jerry Lee Lewis)
- *From Las Vegas . . . to Niagara Falls* (Las Vegas; September 3, 1973) (Niagara Falls, N.Y.; June 24, 1974)
- *From the Waist Up* ("The Ed Sullivan Show"; September 9, 1956; October 28, 1956; and January 6, 1957)
- *The Hillbilly Cat, 1954–1974, Volume 1* ("The Ed Sullivan Show"; September 9, 1956; October 28, 1956)
- *The King Goes Wild* ("The Ed Sullivan Show"; September 9, 1956; October 28, 1956; January 6, 1957)
- *The Last Farewell* (Indianapolis; June 26, 1977)
- *The Monologue L.P.* (Las Vegas; July 31, 1969)
- *The Rockin' Rebel, Volume 3* ("The Ed Sullivan Show"; September 9, 1956)
- *Sold Out* (Las Vegas; September 3, 1973)
- *The Sun Years* ("The Ed Sullivan Show"; September 9, 1956)
- *The Vegas Years, 1972–1975* (Las Vegas; 1972)

DON'T CRY, DADDY
Mac Davis wrote "Don't Cry, Daddy" after his son, Scotty[1], said to him, "Don't cry, daddy," upon seeing his father's tearful reaction to a newsclip of the massacre of a Vietnamese hamlet. Elvis recorded the song at American Sound Studios in Memphis on January 15, 1969. Ronnie Milsap sang harmony and Ed Kollis played harmonica on the recording. The single release had a 13-week stay on *Billboard*'s Hot 100 chart, peaking at #6. It reached #13 on the country chart. Sales of over a million copies were achieved and a Gold Record was certified by the RIAA on January 21, 1970.

Singles:
- "DON'T CRY, DADDY"/"Rubberneckin' " (RCA 47-9768) November 1969. Standard release.
- "DON'T CRY, DADDY"/"Rubberneckin' " (RCA 447-0674) December 1970. Gold Standard Series reissue.

LPs:
- *Always on My Mind*
- *Elvis: Worldwide 50 Gold Award Hits, Volume 1*
- *Greatest Hits, Volume 1* (Las Vegas; February 17, 1970)
- *The Memphis Record*
- *The Top Ten Hits*

Bootleg LPs:
- *Behind Closed Doors* (Las Vegas; February 17, 1970)

- *The Entertainer* (Las Vegas; February 17, 1970)

DON'T FORBID ME
"Don't Forbid Me" was written for Elvis by Charles Singleton in 1956, as Elvis revealed during the Million-Dollar-Quartet session. He said the song was sent to him at the house and stayed there "for ages. I never did see it." After telling the story, Elvis sang "Don't Forbid Me." Pat Boone had a number one hit and million-seller with the song in late 1956 (Dot 15521).

Bootleg LPs:
- *Million Dollar Quartet* (Sun Records; December 4, 1956)
- *The One Million Dollar Quartet* (Sun Records; December 4, 1956)

DON'T LEAVE ME NOW
Elvis sang "Don't Leave Me Now" three times in *Jailhouse Rock*. The version (take #29) that appeared on the *Loving You* album was recorded on February 23, 1957, at Radio Recorders. The version on the *Jailhouse Rock* EP was different; it was recorded on April 30, 1957, at Radio Recorders and was the version used in the film. (The master take was either take #18 or #21.) The South African LP *Jailhouse Rock* contained the EP version. "Don't Leave Me Now" was written by Aaron Schroeder and Ben Weisman.

EPs:
- *Jailhouse Rock*

LPs:
- *Essential Elvis—The First Movies* (take #12 from the February 23, 1957, recording session)
- *Loving You*

Bootleg LPs:
- *Got a Lot o' Livin' to Do!* (*Jailhouse Rock* soundtrack)

DON'T THINK TWICE, IT'S ALL RIGHT
Bob Dylan wrote and recorded "Don't Think Twice, It's All Right" in 1963 for his LP *The Freewheelin' Bob Dylan* (Columbia CL-1986). Later in 1963 the song served as the flip side to his single "Blowin' in the Wind" (Columbia 42856). "Don't Think Twice, It's All Right" was based on the traditional folk tune "Who'll Buy Your Chickens When I'm Gone." Peter, Paul and Mary had a #9 hit with their recording of the song (Warner Bros. 5385) in late 1963. Three years later, the Wonder Who (actually the Four Seasons) reached #12 with their version (Phillips 40324).

Elvis's version of "Don't Think Twice, It's All Right" was the result of a 15-minute jam session at RCA's Nashville studios on May 16, 1971. An edited version (2 minutes, 45 seconds) appeared on the LP *Elvis*. Two other, longer versions have appeared on record, but the entire 15 minutes have not yet been released.

LPs:
- *Elvis* (RCA APL1-0283)
- *Our Memories of Elvis, Volume 2* (8½-minute version without overdubbing)

---

[1]The Mac Davis song "Watching Scotty Grow," which was recorded by Bobby Goldsboro, was written about his son.

Bootleg LPs:
- *Behind Closed Doors* (10-minute, 42-second version)
- *The Entertainer* (2-minute, 45-second version spliced with "It's Your Baby, You Rock It")

DON'T YOU KNOW

"Don't You Know" was written by Fats Domino and Dave Bartholomew. Domino's 1955 recording (Imperial 5340) peaked at #12 on *Billboard*'s rhythm & blues chart.

At disc jockey Eddie Fadal's home in Waco, Texas, in the summer of 1958, Elvis sang along with Fats Domino's recording of "Don't You Know."

Bootleg LPs:
- *Forever Young, Forever Beautiful* (Eddie Fadal's home; summer, 1958)

DOUBLE TROUBLE

This was the title tune of Elvis's 1967 film *Double Trouble*. "Double Trouble," a Doc Pomus–Mort Shuman tune, was recorded in June 1966 at Radio Recorders.

LPs:
- *Double Trouble*
- *Elvis in Hollywood*

DOWN BY THE RIVERSIDE/ WHEN THE SAINTS GO MARCHING IN

"Down by the Riverside" is an old standard that Bill Giant, Bernie Baum, and Florence Kaye adapted for Elvis's 1966 film *Frankie and Johnny*. It was sung in a medley with "When the Saints Go Marching In." The recording session took place at Radio Recorders in May 1965. In 1960 Les Compagnons de la Chanson had a moderate hit (#60 Hot 100) with "Down by the Riverside."

"When the Saints Go Marching In" was an old New Orleans funeral hymn and jazz classic, composer unknown. It gained popularity in 1930 from a Decca recording by Louis Armstrong. In 1956 Bill Haley and His Comets recorded a version titled "The Saints Rock 'n' Roll" (Decca 29870) that went to #18 on the Top 100 chart. Three years later, Fats Domino had a moderate hit with "When the Saints Go Marching In" (Imperial 5569).

Both "Down by the Riverside" and "When the Saints Go Marching In" were sung by Elvis during the Million-Dollar-Quartet session on December 4, 1956. Jerry Lee Lewis and Carl Perkins provided vocal support.

LPs:
- *Elvis Sings Hits from His Movies, Volume 1*
- *Frankie and Johnny*

Bootleg LPs:
- *The Million Dollar Quartet* (Sun Records; December 4, 1956) ("Down by the Riverside")
- *The One Million Dollar Quartet* (Sun Records; December 4, 1956) ("Down by the Riverside" and "When the Saints Go Marching In")

DOWN IN THE ALLEY

"Down in the Alley" was written by Jesse Stone and recorded by the Clovers in 1957 (Atlantic 1152). Elvis recorded the song on May 26, 1966, at RCA's Nashville studios. RCA released "Down in the Alley" as a bonus song on the *Spinout* LP.

LPs:
- *Reconsider Baby*
- *Spinout*

DOWN THE LINE

Buddy Holly and Bob Montgomery wrote "Down the Line" in 1955 and recorded it that same year. Norman Petty also received credit for the composition, although it is doubtful that he had anything to do with the writing of the song. It was ten years before "Down the Line" was released on an LP titled *Holly in the Hills* (Coral 57463). The guitar riff in "Down the Line" was later used by the Champs in "Tequila" in 1958.

Elvis first heard Buddy Holly sing "Down the Line" while the two were performing in Texas. It's been reported that Elvis recorded the song while at Sun Records in 1955, but no tape has yet surfaced. "Down the Line" is not to be confused with "Down the Line" (Sun 288) by Jerry Lee Lewis in 1958 or "Go! Go! Go! (Down the Line)" (Sun 242) by Roy Orbison in 1956.

DRUMS OF THE ISLANDS

Elvis sang "Drums of the Islands" twice during *Paradise, Hawaiian Style*. The film versions were longer and slightly different than those on record. The instrumental track for "Drums of the Islands" was recorded on July 26, 1965, at Radio Recorders. Elvis's vocal was added on August 2. RCA chose take #6 to release on record. "Drums of the Islands" was written by Sid Tepper and Roy C. Bennett, based on an old Tongan chant, "Bula Lai," by Iserati Recula.

LPs:
- *Paradise, Hawaiian Style*

Bootleg LPs:
- *Behind Closed Doors* (false starts #1 and #2 and complete take #3)
- *Hawaii USA* (take #2)

EARLY MORNING RAIN

"Early Morning Rain" was written by Gordon Light-foot and first recorded by Peter, Paul and Mary in 1965 (Warner Bros. 5659). Their recording went to #91 on *Billboard*'s Hot 100 chart and #13 on the Easy-Listening chart. The next year, George Hamilton IV took his version of "Early Morning Rain" (RCA 47-8924) to #9 on the country chart. Also in 1966, Chad and Jeremy had a release of the song (Columbia 43490).

Elvis first recorded "Early Morning Rain" at RCA's Nashville studios on March 15, 1971. It was one of the tracks on the *Elvis Now* album. After the worldwide telecast of "Elvis: Aloha from Hawaii" on January 14, 1973, Elvis again recorded the song, this time for inclusion in the expanded U.S. edition of the TV special that aired on NBC-TV on April 4, 1973. That version appeared on the *Mahalo from Elvis* LP. "Early Morning Rain" was also sung in the 1977 CBS-TV special "Elvis in Concert."

LPs:
- *Elvis—A Canadian Tribute*
- *Elvis in Concert* (Rapid City, South Dakota; June 21, 1977)
- *Elvis Now*
- *Elvis Aron Presley—Forever*
- *Mahalo from Elvis* (Honolulu; January 14, 1973)

Bootleg LPs:
- *Elvis Presley Is Alive and Well and Singing in Las Vegas, Volume 1* (Las Vegas; August 1974)
- *The Last Farewell* (Indianapolis; June 26, 1977)
- *The Vegas Years, 1972–1975* (Las Vegas; August 1974)

EARTH ANGEL

While in the Army in West Germany, Jesse Belvin wrote "Earth Angel." The song was originally recorded by the Penguins in late 1954, with Belvin (using the pseudonym Curtis Williams) as the lead singer. "Earth Angel" (DooTone 348) hit the top of the rhythm & blues chart in early 1955 and #8 on the Best-Selling Singles chart. It was the group's only million-seller. Close on the heels of the Penguins' release was a recording by the Crew-Cuts (Mercury 70529) that peaked at #8. Other charted versions include Gloria Mann (Sound 109) in 1955, Johnny Tillotson (Cadence 1377) in 1960, and the Vogues (Reprise 0820) in 1969.

A private recording of Elvis singing "Earth Angel" in West Germany sometime between 1958 and 1960 surfaced on the 1984 LP *A Golden Celebration*.

LPs:
- *A Golden Celebration* (West Germany; 1958–1960)

EARTH BOY

Elvis sang "Earth Boy" in his 1962 movie *Girls! Girls! Girls!* The film version is different from that on record. In the film, the Tiu sisters sang the first portion in Chinese and Elvis followed with a translation of the lyrics while they continued to sing. Elvis then began singing in Chinese and the girls sang in English. The song ended with Elvis and the girls singing in English. Elvis recorded "Earth Boy" at Radio Recorders in March 1962. The version of the song on record is a splice of takes #2 and #5. "Earth Boy" was written by Sid Tepper and Roy C. Bennett.

LPs:
- *Girls! Girls! Girls!*

Bootleg LPs:
- *Elvis Rocks and the Girls Roll* (alternate take)

EASY COME, EASY GO

The instrumental track for "Easy Come, Easy Go" was recorded at Radio Recorders on September 28, 1966. Elvis's vocal was added later; the exact date is unknown. Written by Sid Wayne and Ben Weisman, the song served as the title tune for Elvis's 1967 movie *Easy Come, Easy Go*. The film version had added instrumentation.

EPs:
- *Easy Come, Easy Go*

LPs:
- *C'mon Everybody*
- *Double Dynamite*

(SUCH AN) EASY QUESTION

Otis Blackwell and Winfield Scott wrote "(Such an) Easy Question" for Elvis in early 1962. He recorded the song on March 18, 1962, at RCA's Nashville studios. Three years later, "(Such an) Easy Question" was released as a single after its inclusion in the film *Tickle Me*. The song had an eight-week stay on *Billboard*'s Hot 100 chart, peaking at #11. On the Easy-Listening chart, "(Such an) Easy Question" replaced Horst Jankowski's "A Walk in the Black Forest" as the number one song in July 1965. After two weeks at number one, it was replaced by Gary Lewis and the Playboys' hit "Save Your Heart for Me." "(Such an) Easy Question" spent a total of seven weeks on the chart.

Singles:
- "(SUCH AN) EASY QUESTION"/"It Feels So Right" (RCA 47-8585) May 1965. Standard release. Two picture sleeves were issued: one that read, "Coming Soon! Special TICKLE ME EP," and one issued a month later that read, "Ask for Special TICKLE ME EP."
- "(SUCH AN) EASY QUESTION"/"It Feels So Right" (RCA 447-0653) November 1966. Gold Standard Series reissue.

LPs:
- *Pot Luck*

Bootleg LPs:
- *Elvis Sings Songs from* Tickle Me (alternate take)

ECHOES OF LOVE

"Echoes of Love" was written by Bob Roberts and Paddy McMains and recorded by Elvis on May 26,

1963, at RCA's Nashville studios. It was a bonus tune on the *Kissin' Cousins* LP.

LPs:
• *Kissin' Cousins*

ECSTASY
Ben E. King, former lead singer of the Drifters, had a moderate hit (#56 Hot 100) with "Ecstasy" (Atco 6215) in 1962. Elvis is believed to have recorded "Ecstasy" in the 1960s, but so far a recording has not surfaced.

EDGE OF REALITY
Elvis sang "Edge of Reality" in his 1968 film *Live a Little, Love a Little*. The song was written by Bill Giant, Bernie Baum, and Florence Kaye, and recorded by Elvis on March 7, 1968, at Western Recorders in Hollywood. Although "Edge of Reality" didn't chart, it was listed as "Bubbling Under" at #112 for one week.

Singles:
• "If I Can Dream"/"EDGE OF REALITY" (RCA 47-9670) November 1968. Standard release. With this release, RCA eliminated its trademark, Nipper, from the label. The color of the label was changed from black to orange. The original picture sleeves read, "As Featured on His NBC-TV Special." Two months later the phrase was dropped. A few picture sleeves were made from cardboard and are extremely rare.
• "If I Can Dream"/"EDGE OF REALITY" (RCA 447-0668) December 1970. Gold Standard Series reissue.

LPs:
• *Almost in Love*

EL PASO
Marty Robbins[1] wrote and recorded "El Paso" in 1959. Featured on the recording was Hank Garland's guitar playing. Because of the song's length (4 minutes, 40 seconds), Columbia Records decided to release it on an LP, *Gunfighter Ballads and Trail Songs* (Columbia 1349), instead of a single. But because of the great response, Columbia changed its mind and released "El Paso" (Columbia 41511) in late 1959. By January it was the nation's number one song on both the Hot 100 and country charts. Sales easily exceeded one million copies. Marty Robbins received a Grammy Award for Best Country and Western Performance of 1960. In 1977 Robbins recorded a sequel titled "El Paso City" (Columbia 10305).

"El Paso" was one of a number of songs of which Elvis sang only a line or two in concert in the 1970s.

EL TORO
Elvis sang "El Toro" in his 1963 movie *Fun in Acapulco*. The song was written by Bill Giant, Bernie Baum, and Florence Kaye and recorded by Elvis on January 23, 1963, at Radio Recorders.

LPs:
• *Fun in Acapulco*

THE ELVIS MEDLEY
This medley consisted of excerpts from "Jailhouse Rock," "Teddy Bear," "Hound Dog," "Don't Be Cruel," "Burning Love," and "Suspicious Minds." "The Elvis Medley" reached #71 on the Hot 100 chart in 1982 (for a seven-week stay) and #31 on the country chart.

Singles:
• "THE ELVIS MEDLEY"/"Always on My Mind" (RCA PB-13351) November 1982. Standard release.
• "THE ELVIS MEDLEY"/"THE ELVIS MEDLEY" (short version) (RCA JB-13351) November 1982. Disc jockey promotional release. This promo came in two versions: one with a light yellow label and one pressed on gold vinyl.

LPs:
• *The Elvis Medley*

END OF THE ROAD
"End of the Road" was the flip side of Jerry Lee Lewis's first record at Sun Records (Sun 259), which was released on December 1, 1956. The A side was "Crazy Arms." Lewis sang "End of the Road" (his own composition) during the Million-Dollar-Quartet session on December 4, 1956, accompanying himself on piano. Elvis and Carl Perkins did not participate in this song.

Bootleg LPs:
• *The One Million Dollar Session* (Sun Records; December 4, 1956)

EVERYBODY COME ABOARD
The songwriting team of Bill Giant, Bernie Baum, and Florence Kaye wrote this song, with which Elvis ended his 1966 movie *Frankie and Johnny*. He recorded "Everybody Come Aboard" at Radio Recorders in May 1965.

LPs:
• *Frankie and Johnny*

EVERYBODY LOVES SOMEBODY
"Everybody Loves Somebody" was written by Irving Taylor and Ken Lane in 1948 and first recorded by Frank Sinatra (Columbia 38225) that same year. It served as the flip side of "Just for Now." Although others recorded the song through the years, no one was successful until Dean Martin's 1964 version. "Everybody Loves Somebody" (Reprise 0281) replaced the Beatles' "A Hard Day's Night" at number one on the *Billboard* Hot 100 chart. Based on the success of this song, NBC offered Dean Martin his own variety series. The series—"The Dean Martin Show"—used "Everybody Loves Somebody" as its theme song.

On January 26, 1970, Martin attended Elvis's concert at the International Hotel in Las Vegas. During the performance, Elvis sang "Everybody Loves Somebody" to Martin.

THE EYES OF TEXAS
(See *The Yellow Rose of Texas/The Eyes of Texas*)

---

[1]Robbins was the last individual to sing at the Grand Ole Opry's Ryman Auditorium and the first to perform at the new Opryland.

F

FABULOUS
Both Charlie Gracie (Cameo 107) and Steve Lawrence (Coral 61834) charted versions of "Fabulous" in 1957, with Gracie's reaching #16 on the Top 100 chart and Lawrence's topping out at #71. Elvis may have recorded "Fabulous" in the 1950s, but no tape has yet surfaced.

FADED LOVE
"Faded Love" was written by brothers Bob and John Wills in 1950 and recorded by Bob Wills and His Texas Playboys that year. In early 1962 Leon McAuliff had a #22 country hit with "Faded Love" (Cimarron 4057), and Patsy Cline's recording for Decca Records (Decca 31522) climbed the chart shortly after her death in 1963, peaking at #17.

Elvis recorded "Faded Love" on June 7, 1970, at RCA's Nashville studios. The original album release was an edited version. An alternate mix appeared on the RCA Record Club album *From Elvis with Love*. On October 15, 1980, Felton Jarvis recorded a new instrumental track for "Faded Love" at Young 'Un Sound in Nashville. The new single release did not chart.

Singles:
- "Guitar Man"/"FADED LOVE" (RCA PB-12158) January 1981. Standard release.
- "Guitar Man"/"FADED LOVE" (RCA JH-12158) January 1981. Disc jockey promotional release.

LPs:
- *Elvis Country*
- *Guitar Man* (new instrumental backing)

Bootleg LPs:
- *Behind Closed Doors* (original unedited version)
- *Sold Out* (Nashville; July 1, 1973)
- *Special Delivery from Elvis Presley* (original unedited version)
- *Susie Q* (Las Vegas; ?)

THE FAIR IS MOVING ON
Doug Flett and Guy Fletcher wrote "The Fair Is Moving On," which Elvis recorded on February 21, 1969, at American Sound Studios. The song has also been called "The Fair's Moving On." The 1969 single release did not chart.

Singles:
- "Clean Up Your Own Back Yard"/"THE FAIR IS MOVING ON" (RCA 47-9747) June 1969. Standard release.
- "Clean Up Your Own Back Yard"/"THE FAIR IS MOVING ON" (RCA 447-0672) December 1970. Gold Standard Series reissue.

LPs:
- *Back in Memphis*
- *From Memphis to Vegas/From Vegas to Memphis*
- *The Memphis Record*

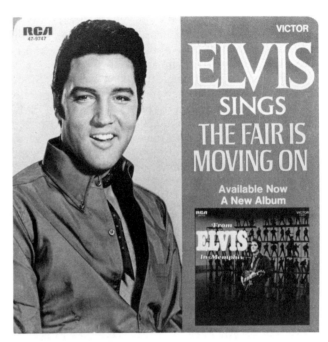

(Photo courtesy Don Fink)

FAIRYTALE
Anita and Bonnie Pointer wrote "Fairytale" for their group, the Pointer Sisters, in 1974. The Pointer Sisters' recording (Blue Thumb 254) reached #13 on *Billboard*'s Hot 100 chart. They were awarded a Grammy in the category Best Vocal Performance by a Duo or Group.

Elvis recorded "Fairytale" on March 10, 1975, at RCA's Hollywood studios. Because of the sad lyrics, Elvis occasionally introduced the song in concert by saying that it was "the story of my life."

LPs:
- *Elvis in Concert* (Omaha, Nebraska or Rapid City, South Dakota; June 19 or 20, 1977)
- *Elvis Today*

Bootleg LPs:
- *Elvis Presley Is Alive and Well and Singing in Las Vegas, Volume 1* (Las Vegas; August 1975)
- *The Last Farewell* (Indianapolis; June 26, 1977)
- *Rockin' with Elvis April Fool's Day* (Las Vegas; April 1, 1975)
- *Rockin' with Elvis New Year's Eve Pittsburgh, Pa. Dec. 31, 1976* (Pittsburgh; December 31, 1976)
- *The Vegas Years, 1972–1975* (Las Vegas; 1975)

FAME AND FORTUNE
"Fame and Fortune" was recorded by Elvis on March 21, 1960, at RCA's Nashville studios during his first recording session after being discharged from the Army. Advance orders for the new single ("Stuck on

You" was on the flip side) were 1,275,077—the biggest advance order in history to that date. Five days after recording "Fame and Fortune," Elvis sang it during the taping of the Frank Sinatra–Timex Special, "Welcome Home, Elvis." That special was telecast on ABC-TV on May 12, 1960. The single release had a 10-week stay on *Billboard*'s Hot 100 chart, peaking at #17. Weeks before Elvis even walked into the recording studio, picture sleeves of his new single had been prepared. Since RCA had no idea what the song titles were going to be, all that was mentioned on the picture sleeve was "Elvis' 1st New Recording for His 50,000,000 Fans All Over the World." A hole was cut in the center of the sleeve so that the label of the record would show through, revealing the song titles. "Fame and Fortune," Elvis's first true stereo release, was written by Fred Wise and Ben Weisman.

Singles:
- "Stuck on You"/"FAME AND FORTUNE" (RCA 47-7740) April 1960. Standard release.
- "Stuck on You"/"FAME AND FORTUNE" (RCA 61-7740) April 1960. "Living Stereo" release.
- "Stuck on You"/"FAME AND FORTUNE" (RCA 447-0627) February 1962. Gold Standard Series reissue.

LPs:
- *Elvis—A Legendary Performer, Volume 3* (alternate take #2)
- *Elvis' Golden Records, Volume 3*
- *Elvis: The Other Sides—Worldwide Gold Award Hits, Volume 2*
- *A Valentine Gift for You*

Bootleg LPs:
- *Eternal Elvis* ("Welcome Home, Elvis" soundtrack)
- *Frank Sinatra—Welcome Home, Elvis* ("Welcome Home, Elvis" soundtrack)
- *Please Release Me* ("Welcome Home, Elvis" soundtrack)

FARTHER ALONG

Reverend W. B. Stone wrote "Farther Along" in 1937. Since that time, the song has served as a standard for gospel groups. In the late 1940s the Stamps Quartet had a popular recording of "Farther Along" on Columbia Records (Columbia 20337). Interestingly, the Stamps had a later release of "Farther Along" on Okeh Records (Okeh 04236) that had the words "Piano Acc. Presley" on the label. The flip side was "A Beautiful Prayer."

Elvis recorded "Farther Along" during the *How Great Thou Art* session on May 27, 1966, at RCA's Nashville studios. During the Million-Dollar-Quartet session on December 4, 1956, Elvis sang "Farther Along" with vocal harmony provided by Carl Perkins and Jerry Lee Lewis.

LPs:
- *How Great Thou Art*

Bootleg LPs:
- *Million Dollar Quartet* (Sun Records; December 4, 1956)
- *The One Million Dollar Quartet* (Sun Records; December 4, 1956)

FEELINGS

Brazilian songwriter Morris Albert wrote and recorded "Feelings" in 1975. It became the number one record in Brazil, Chile, and Mexico before being released in the United States (RCA PB-10937). "Feelings" rose to #6 on *Billboard*'s Hot 100 chart and became a million-seller. Reportedly, "Feelings" was the last song ever recorded by Elvis in a studio session (night of October 31–November 1, 1976, at Graceland). After several takes, the song remained incomplete.

FEVER

Written by John Davenport (a pseudonym for Otis Blackwell[1]) and Eddie Cooley in 1956, "Fever" was a million-seller for both Little Willie John (King 4935) in 1956 and Peggy Lee (Capitol 3998) in 1958. John's recording topped the rhythm & blues chart, while Lee's recording peaked at #8 on the Hot 100 chart. In late 1965 the McCoys did even better, reaching #7 with their version (Bang 511). "Fever" was the song that Juliet Prowse was singing at the Las Vegas Hilton in 1981 when a fire broke out, the resulting inferno killing eight people. She stopped singing and calmed the audience.

Elvis recorded "Fever" on April 4, 1960, at RCA's Nashville studios. He included the song in his 1973 TV special "Elvis: Aloha from Hawaii."

LPs:
- *Aloha from Hawaii via Satellite* (Honolulu; January 14, 1973)
- *The Alternate Aloha* (rehearsal concert for "Elvis: Aloha from Hawaii"; January 12, 1973)
- *Elvis Is Back*
- *Pure Gold*
- *A Valentine Gift for You*

Bootleg LPs:
- *Aloha Rehearsal Show—Kui Lee Cancer Benefit* (rehearsal concert for "Elvis: Aloha from Hawaii"; January 12, 1973)
- *Big Boss Man* (Las Vegas; August 19, 1974)
- *From Las Vegas . . . to Niagara Falls* (Las Vegas; September 3, 1973) (Niagara Falls, N.Y.; June 24, 1974)
- *Leavin' It Up to You* (rehearsal concert for "Elvis: Aloha from Hawaii"; January 12, 1973)
- *Rockin' with Elvis New Year's Eve Pittsburgh, Pa. Dec. 31, 1976* (Pittsburgh; December 31, 1976)
- *To Know Him Is to Love Him* (Las Vegas; 1969 or 1970)

FIND OUT WHAT'S HAPPENING

"Find Out What's Happening" was written by Jerry Crutchfield and recorded by Bobby Bare in 1968. His recording (RCA 47-9450) reached #15 on *Billboard*'s country chart. Barbara Fairchild also had a country release (Columbia 45173) that peaked at #52 in 1970.

Elvis recorded "Find Out What's Happening" on July 22, 1973, at Stax Studios in Memphis.

LPs:
- *Our Memories of Elvis, Volume 2* (without overdubbing)
- *Raised on Rock/For Ol' Times Sake*

[1]Blackwell took the pseudonym from that of his stepfather, John Davenport. Reportedly, Blackwell sold the "Fever" copyright to Henry Glover, Vice President of King Records, for $50.

FINDERS KEEPERS, LOSERS WEEPERS
Dory and Ollie Jones wrote "Finders Keepers, Losers Weepers" for Elvis, who recorded the song on May 26, 1963, at RCA's Nashville studios.

LPs:
• *Elvis for Everyone*

FIRST IN LINE
"First in Line" was the first song Ben Weisman ever wrote for Elvis. He cowrote it with Aaron Schroeder. Elvis recorded "First in Line" for his second LP, *Elvis*, on September 3, 1956, at Radio Recorders in Hollywood. Take #27 was the one released by RCA on record.

EPs:
• *Strictly Elvis*

LPs:
• *Elvis*

THE FIRST NOEL
The composer of this seventeenth century Christmas carol is unknown. "The First Noel"[1] was first published in a collection of carols called *Sandy's Carols* in 1833. "Noel" is a contraction of the phrase "Now all is well."

Elvis recorded "The First Noel" on May 16, 1971, at RCA's Nashville studios.

LPs:
• *Elvis Sings the Wonderful World of Christmas*

THE FIRST TIME EVER I SAW YOUR FACE
Ewan McColl (the brother-in-law of folk singer Pete Seeger) wrote "The First Time Ever I Saw Your Face" in 1965. The first recording of the song was by Peter,

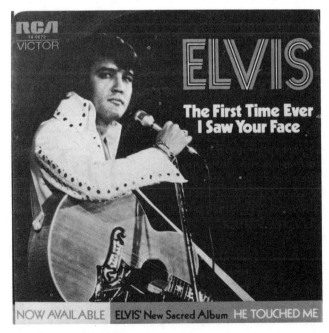

(Photo courtesy Don Fink)

Paul and Mary on their album *See What Tomorrow Brings* (Warner Bros. 1615). Roberta Flack recorded "The First Time Ever I Saw Your Face" in 1969 for her LP *First Take* (Atlanta 8230). When the song was played in the 1971 Clint Eastwood movie *Play Misty for Me*, record dealers were overwhelmed with requests for it. Atlantic Records released a single of Flack's recording (Atlantic 2864) in March 1972. It quickly sold over a million copies and rose to number one on the Hot 100 chart. "The First Time Ever I Saw Your Face" won two Grammy Awards: Record of the Year and Song of the Year.

Elvis recorded "The First Time Ever I Saw Your Face" on March 15, 1971, at RCA's Nashville studios. His single release did not chart. The duet voice on the recording was Temple Riser's. "The First Time Ever I Saw Your Face" did not appear on an album until 1980.

Singles:
• "An American Trilogy"/"THE FIRST TIME EVER I SAW YOUR FACE" (RCA 74-0672) April 1972. Standard release.

LPs:
• *Elvis Aron Presley*

Bootleg LPs:
• *Behind Closed Doors* (alternate take)
• *Command Performance* (Las Vegas; August 21, 1974)
• *From Las Vegas . . . to Niagara Falls* (Las Vegas; September 3, 1973)
• *The Hillbilly Cat, 1954–1974, Volume 1* (RCA release)

FIVE SLEEPY HEADS
Sid Tepper and Roy C. Bennett wrote "Five Sleepy Heads" for Elvis's 1968 film *Speedway*, but it was cut from the final print. Supposedly, "Five Sleepy Heads" *was* included in prints shown in Malaya. Elvis recorded the tune, which was based on "Brahms Lullaby" by Johannes Brahms, in June 1967, at the MGM studios in Culver City, California.

LPs:
• *Elvis Sings for Children and Grownups Too!*
• *Speedway*

FLAMING STAR
This song served as the theme of Elvis's 1960 film *Flaming Star*. Elvis recorded "Flaming Star" in August 1960, probably at Radio Recorders. On the strength of its appearance on the EP *Elvis by Request*, "Flaming Star" spent seven weeks on *Billboard*'s Hot 100 chart, peaking at #14. Sid Wayne and Sherman Edwards are the composers. On the English LP *Flaming Star and Summer Kisses*, a few of the opening notes are missing.

EPs:
• *Elvis by Request*

LPs:
• *Double Dynamite*
• *Elvis in Hollywood*

[1] "The First Noel" was singer Sam Cooke's first solo. He sang it in his Wendall Phillips High School Glee Club in Chicago.

- *Elvis Sings Flaming Star*
- *Singer Presents Elvis Singing Flaming Star and Others*

FLIP, FLOP AND FLY

Charles Calhoun and Lou Willie Turner[1] wrote "Flip, Flop and Fly" in 1955. It was recorded that year by Joe Turner, who had a #3 rhythm & blues hit and million-seller (Atlantic 1053). Soon after Turner's release, Johnnie Ray recorded "Flip, Flop and Fly" (Columbia 40471), but his version did not chart. In 1960 Bill Haley and His Comets also recorded the song (Warner Bros. 5228).

Elvis sang "Flip, Flop and Fly" on his first "Stage Show" appearance (January 28, 1956) as an ending to "Shake, Rattle and Roll." That performance, with a new drum track overdubbed, was used in the 1981 documentary *This Is Elvis.*

LPs:

- *Elvis Recorded Live on Stage in Memphis* (Memphis; March 20, 1974)
- *A Golden Celebration* ("Stage Show"; January 28, 1956—as an ending to "Shake, Rattle and Roll")
- *This Is Elvis* ("Stage Show"; January 28, 1956—as an ending to "Shake, Rattle and Roll," with a new drum track overdubbed)

Bootleg LPs:

- *Dorsey Shows* ("Stage Show"; January 28, 1956—as an ending to "Shake, Rattle and Roll")
- *The Entertainer* ("Stage Show"; January 28, 1956—edited as an ending to "Tweedlee Dee")
- *From Hollywood to Vegas* (Las Vegas; ?—in medley with "Whole Lotta Shakin' Goin' On," "Your Mama Don't Dance," and "Hound Dog")
- *From Las Vegas . . . to Niagara Falls* (Las Vegas; September 3, 1973—in medley with "Long Tall Sally," "Whole Lotta Shakin' Goin' On," "Your Mama Don't Dance," and "Hound Dog")
- *Superstar Outtakes* ("Stage Show"; January 28, 1956—as an ending for "Shake, Rattle and Roll")

FOLLOW THAT DREAM

This title tune to Elvis's 1962 movie *Follow That Dream* was written by Fred Wise and Ben Weisman. Elvis recorded "Follow That Dream" on July 5, 1961, at RCA's Nashville studios.

EPs:

- *Follow That Dream*

LPs:

- *C'mon Everybody*
- *Double Dynamite*
- *Elvis Aron Presley* (alternate take #2)
- *Elvis in Hollywood*

FOLSOM PRISON BLUES

Johnny Cash got the idea for composing "Folsom Prison Blues" after seeing the 1951 movie *Inside the Walls of Folsom.* He recorded the song on July 29, 1955, at Sun Records. "Folsom Prison Blues" (Sun 232) was Cash's second record release. (His first was "Hey Porter"/"Cry, Cry, Cry.") The song reached #5 on *Billboard*'s country chart. In 1968 a rerecording of "Fol-

som Prison Blues" (Columbia 44513) did well on both the Hot 100 and country charts (#32 and number one, respectively), winning Cash a Grammy Award for Best Country and Western Male Vocal in 1969.

Elvis sang "Folsom Prison Blues," paired with "I Walk the Line," at some of his Las Vegas shows.

Bootleg LPs:

- *The Entertainer* (Las Vegas; August 1969)
- *From Hollywood to Vegas* (Las Vegas; August 1969)
- *Long Lost Songs* (Las Vegas; August 14, 1970)
- *To Know Him Is to Love Him* (Las Vegas; August 1969)

FOOL

Elvis recorded "Fool," a Carl Sigman–James Last composition, on March 28, 1972, at RCA's Hollywood studios. His single release reached #17 on *Billboard*'s Hot 100 chart, staying on the chart for 12 weeks. "Fool" peaked at #31 on the country chart and #12 on the Easy-Listening chart. In 1969 Wayne Newton recorded "Fool" (RCA 0126), but it did not chart.

Singles:

- "Steamroller Blues"/"FOOL" (RCA 74-0910) April 1973. Standard release.

LPs:

- *Elvis* (RCA APL1-0283)
- *Elvis Aron Presley*

THE FOOL

Naomi Ford, wife of Lee Hazelwood, wrote "The Fool" in 1955. It was first recorded by Sanford Clark at Audio Recorders in Phoenix. Clark's original release of "The Fool" (MCI 1003) didn't chart, but the rerelease in 1956 (Dot 15481) reached #7 on *Billboard*'s Top 100 chart and sold over a million copies. Al Casey, who recorded an instrumental version of "The Fool" in 1956 called "Fool's Blues" (Dot 15524), played guitar on Clark's recording. The Gallahads also had a hit with "The Fool" (Jubilee 5252) in 1956. In 1963 Jamie Coe had a version of the song on Big Top Records (Big Top 3139). It should be noted that on some records Lee Hazelwood is listed as co-composer.

While in the Army in West Germany, Elvis recorded "The Fool" on a home tape recorder. He played piano and was accompanied by a friend who sang the bass line. That home recording later appeared on the 1984 LP *A Golden Celebration.* On June 4, 1970, Elvis formally recorded "The Fool" at RCA's Nashville studios.

LPs:

- *Elvis Country*
- *A Golden Celebration* (West Germany; 1958–1960)

FOOL, FOOL, FOOL

"Fool, Fool, Fool" was written by Ahmet Ertegun, co-founder of Atlantic Records in 1951. The Cloves had the first recording of the song the same year. "Fool, Fool, Fool" (Atlantic 944) was a number one rhythm & blues hit. Other hit recordings of the song through the years

---

[1]Lou Willie Turner was Joe Turner's wife. Turner actually cowrote the song, but gave his wife the credit.

include those by Kay Starr (Capitol 2151) in 1952, Dickie Lee and the Collegiates (Sun 297) in 1958, and Webb Pierce (Decca 32167), whose 1967 release reached #6 on the country chart.

It's been reported by some that Elvis recorded "Fool, Fool, Fool" while at Sun Records. No proof of that has yet come forth.

A FOOL SUCH AS I

"(Now and Then There's) A Fool Such as I" was written by Bill Trader in 1952 and recorded by Hank Snow late that year. Snow's recording (RCA 5034) rose to #4 on *Billboard*'s country chart. In early 1953 Jo Stafford (Columbia 39930), Tommy Edwards (MGM 11395), and the Robins (RCA 47-5175) had their own versions of the song. Only Stafford's charted (#20, Best-Selling Singles).

Elvis recorded "(Now and Then There's) A Fool Such as I" on June 10, 1958, at RCA's Nashville studios, while on leave from the Army. Take #9 was selected for release. The bass singer on the recording was Ray Walker of the Jordanaires. It was his first session with Elvis. Elvis's single release peaked at #2 on *Billboard*'s Hot 100 chart during its 15 weeks on the chart. Only the Fleetwood's "Come Softly to Me" kept "(Now and Then There's) A Fool Such as I" from reaching the top spot. On the rhythm & blues chart, the song hit #16. It was number one for five weeks in England. The record sold more than a million copies.

Singles:
- "(NOW AND THEN THERE'S) A FOOL SUCH AS I"/"I Need Your Love Tonight" (RCA 47-7506) March 1959. Standard release. The original picture sleeve had an advertisement for the *Elvis Sails* EP. Picture sleeves beginning in April 1959 had lists of Gold Standard singles and EPs.
- "(NOW AND THEN THERE'S) A FOOL SUCH AS I"/"I Need Your Love Tonight" (RCA 447-0625) 1961. Gold Standard Series reissue.

LPs:
- *Elvis—A Legendary Performer, Volume 1*
- *Elvis Aron Presley* (USS *Arizona* Memorial; March 25, 1961)
- *Elvis: Worldwide 50 Gold Award Hits, Volume 1*
- *50,000,000 Elvis Fans Can't Be Wrong—Elvis' Gold Records, Volume 2*
- *The Top Ten Hits*

Bootleg LPs:
- *Elvis' 1961 Hawaii Benefit Concert* (USS *Arizona* Memorial; March 25, 1961)
- *Standing Room Only, Volume 3* (USS *Arizona* Memorial; March 25, 1961)

FOOLS FALL IN LOVE

"Fools Fall in Love" was written by Jerry Leiber and Mike Stoller and recorded by the Drifters in 1957 after 26 takes. Their recording (Atlantic 1123) reached #69 on *Billboard*'s Top 100 chart. Other recordings of "Fools Fall in Love" included those by Sammy Turner (Big Top 3049) in 1960, and Jackie Ward (Mercury 35003) in 1977.

Elvis recorded "Fools Fall in Love" on May 28, 1966,
at RCA's Nashville studios. His single release did not chart, but it was listed as "Bubbling Under" at #102 for five weeks.

Singles:
- "Indescribably Blue"/"FOOLS FALL IN LOVE" (RCA 47-9056) January 6, 1967. Standard Release.
- "Indescribably Blue"/"FOOLS FALL IN LOVE" (RCA 447-0659) 1970. Gold Standard Series reissue.

LPs:
- *Double Dynamite*
- *I Got Lucky*

FOOLS HALL OF FAME

Several artists have recorded "Fools Hall of Fame" over the years, but only Pat Boone's 1959 version (Dot 15982) charted, reaching #29 on *Billboard*'s Hot 100 chart. A year earlier, Jerry Wallace released a recording of "Fools Hall of Fame" on Challenge Records (Challenge 1003). On July 10, 1958, Johnny Cash recorded the song at Sun Records, but it remained unreleased until 1971. Also known to have recorded "Fools Hall of Fame" is Roy Orbison, although his version was never released. Danny Wolf is the composer.

Elvis sang "Fools Hall of Fame" in concert in 1957 in Seattle and other cities on the tour.

FOOLS RUSH IN

Johnny Mercer and Rube Bloom wrote "Fools Rush In" in 1940 based on the melody of Bloom's "Shangri-La." The song was first popularized by Glenn Miller in a recording on the Bluebird label (Bluebird 10728) that reached #3 on the charts in 1940. That same year Frank Sinatra with the Tommy Dorsey Orchestra recorded a version of the song (Victor 26593). Other popular versions include those by Brook Benton (Mercury 71722), whose recording was a #5 rhythm & blues hit in 1960; Ricky Nelson[1] (Decca 31533), who reached #12 on the Hot 100 chart in 1963; and Etta James (Argo 5424) in 1962. The full title of the song is "Fools Rush In (Where Angels Fear to Tread)."

Elvis recorded "Fools Rush In" at RCA's Nashville studios on May 18, 1971. His arrangement was based on Ricky Nelson's arrangement.

LPs:
- *Elvis Now*

FOR LOVIN' ME

Gordon Lightfoot wrote "For Lovin' Me" in 1964. Later that year, Peter, Paul and Mary had the first recording of the song (Warner Bros. 5496). It reached #30 on *Billboard*'s Hot 100 chart. Lightfoot got around to recording his own song in 1965 (Warner Bros. 5621). Waylon Jennings had a country version (RCA 47-8917) in 1966. The song's full title is "(That's What You Get) For Lovin' Me."

Elvis recorded "For Lovin' Me" on March 15, 1971, at RCA's Nashville studios.

---

[1] James Burton played lead guitar on both Ricky Nelson's and Elvis's recordings of "Fools Rush In."

LPs:
- *Elvis* (RCA APL1-0283)
- *Elvis—A Canadian Tribute*

FOR OL' TIMES SAKE

"For Ol' Times Sake" was recorded by Elvis on July 23, 1973, at Stax Studios. The single release spent nine weeks on the Hot 100 chart, peaking at #41 (on the strength of its flip side, "Raised on Rock"). It reached #42 on the country chart. Tony Joe White composed "For Ol' Times Sake."

Singles:
- "Raised on Rock"/"FOR OL' TIMES SAKE" (RCA APBO-0088) September 1973. Standard release.
- "Raised on Rock"/"FOR OL' TIMES SAKE" (RCA DJAO-0088) September 1973. Disc jockey promotional release.

LPs:
- *Raised on Rock/For Ol' Times Sake*

FOR THE GOOD TIMES

Kris Kristofferson wrote "For the Good Times" in 1970. That same year, Ray Price had a number one country hit with the song (Columbia 45178).

Elvis recorded "For the Good Times" on March 27, 1972, at RCA's Hollywood studios. The studio recording has remained unreleased. The version on record was recorded in concert on June 10, 1972, at Madison Square Garden. A backstage rehearsal of "For the Good Times" on April 16, 1972, in Jacksonville, Florida, appeared in the documentary *Elvis on Tour*.

LPs:
- *Elvis as Recorded at Madison Square Garden*
- *Welcome to My World*

FOR THE HEART

"For the Heart" was written by Dennis Linde and recorded by Elvis at Graceland on the night of February 5-6, 1976. Composer Linde played bass on the recording. (It was overdubbed at a later date.) The single release had an 11-week stay on *Billboard*'s Hot 100 chart, peaking at #28 (on the strength of the flip side, "Hurt"). "For the Good Times" reached #6 on the country chart.

Singles:
- "Hurt"/"FOR THE HEART" (RCA PB-10601) March 1976. Standard release.
- "Hurt"/"FOR THE GOOD TIMES" (RCA JB-10601) March 1976. Disc jockey promotional release.
- "Moody Blue"/"FOR THE HEART" (RCA GB-11326) August 1978. Gold Standard Series original release.

LPs:
- *Elvis' Gold Records, Volume 5*
- *From Elvis Presley Boulevard, Memphis, Tennessee*
- *Our Memories of Elvis, Volume 2* (without overdubbing)

FOR THE MILLIONTH AND LAST TIME

Sid Tepper and Roy C. Bennett wrote "For the Millionth and Last Time" for Elvis, who recorded it on October 15, 1961, at RCA's Nashville studios. Gordon Stoker played accordion on the song.

LPs:
- *Elvis for Everyone*

FORGET ME NEVER

Fred Wise and Ben Weisman wrote "Forget Me Never" for Elvis's 1961 movie *Wild in the Country*, but it was cut from the final print of the film. Elvis recorded the song at Radio Recorders on November 7, 1960. RCA chose take #3 for release.

LPs:
- *Elvis for Everyone*
- *Separate Ways*

Bootleg LPs:
- *Behind Closed Doors* (takes #1 and #2 [a false start])
- *The Complete Wild in the Country Sessions* (takes #1-3)
- *Eternal Elvis, Volume 2* (take #?)
- *Unfinished Business* (take #?)

FORT LAUDERDALE CHAMBER OF COMMERCE

"Fort Lauderdale Chamber of Commerce" was written by Sid Tepper and Roy C. Bennett for Elvis's 1965 movie *Girl Happy*. Elvis recorded the song in June or July 1964 at Radio Recorders.

LPs:
- *Girl Happy*

FOUNTAIN OF LOVE

Elvis recorded "Fountain of Love" on March 18, 1962, at Radio Recorders. Bill Giant and Jeff Lewis are the composers.

LPs:
- *Pot Luck*

FRANKFORT SPECIAL

Sid Wayne and Sherman Edwards wrote "Frankfort Special" for Elvis's 1960 movie *G. I. Blues*. The film version had added voices and included horns. Elvis first recorded the song on April 27, 1960, but that version was not released until 1978. The version that was released in the film and on record was recorded on May 6, 1960, at Radio Recorders. Take #10 was edited from 2:55 to 2:29 for release.

LPs:
- *Elvis—A Legendary Performer, Volume 3* (take #2; April 27, 1960)
- *G. I. Blues*

Bootleg LPs:
- *Unfinished Business* (take #2; April 27, 1960)

FRANKIE AND JOHNNY

There are several versions as to the origin of this classic folk song. One story says "Frankie and Johnny" dates back to the War of 1812. When the Tennessee and Kentucky Rifles (who served under Andrew Jackson at the Battle of New Orleans) returned home from the war, they sang the song. Supposedly, they heard it in

Crescent City, Louisiana, a mostly French-speaking city, under the title "Françoise et Jean."

Another story traces the origin to a hot summer night in St. Louis in 1888. Frankie (a woman) gunned down her boyfriend, Johnny, with a derringer she had hidden in her garter. She had just learned that Johnny had "done her wrong."

In 1904 Hughie Cannon had the first published version of the song, using the title "He Done Me Wrong." Several artists have recorded "Frankie and Johnny" over the years, including Ted Lewis (Columbia 1017) in 1927, Gene Autry in 1929, Johnny Cash (using the title "Frankie's Man, Johnny") in 1959 (Columbia 41371), Brook Benton (Mercury 71859) in 1961, and Sam Cooke (RCA 8215) in 1963. Cooke's recording was the highest charted at #14.

Elvis recorded "Frankie and Johnny,"[1] using an arrangement by Alex Gottlieb, Fred Karger, and Ben Weisman, in May 1965 at Radio Recorders. In his film *Frankie and Johnny*, he was backed by a chorus that included Donna Douglas, Sue Ane Langdon, and Harry Morgan. The single release of "Frankie and Johnny" had an eight-week stay on *Billboard*'s Hot 100 chart, peaking at #25.

Singles:
- "FRANKIE AND JOHNNY"/"Please Don't Stop Loving Me" (RCA 47-8780) March 1966. Standard release.
- "FRANKIE AND JOHNNY"/"Please Don't Stop Loving Me" (RCA 447-0656) February 1968. Gold Standard Series reissue.

LPs:
- *Double Dynamite*
- *Elvis in Hollywood*
- *Elvis Sings Hits from His Movies, Volume 1*
- *Frankie and Johnny*

FROM A JACK TO A KING
Ned Miller wrote and recorded "From a Jack to a King" in 1957. Fabor Records (named for its founder, Fabor Robinson) sold the master to Dot Records (Dot 15601) for general release. It did not chart, but the 1962 reissue (Fabor 114) did, reaching #2 on the country chart and #6 on the Hot 100 chart. Sales of a million copies are claimed. Shortly after Miller's 1957 release, Jim Lowe did a rendition on Dot Records (Dot 15611) that did not chart.

Elvis recorded "From a Jack to a King" on January 21, 1969, at American Sound Studios in Memphis.

LPs:
- *Back in Memphis*
- *From Memphis to Vegas/From Vegas to Memphis*

FUN IN ACAPULCO
This title song to Elvis's 1963 movie *Fun in Acapulco* was written by Sid Wayne and Ben Weisman. Additional strings were heard in the film version. Elvis recorded "Fun in Acapulco" on January 23, 1963, at Radio Recorders.

LPs:
- *Elvis in Hollywood*
- *Fun in Acapulco*

FUNKY FINGERS
Elvis is believed by some to have recorded "Funky Fingers" on June 6, 1970, but there is no supporting evidence. According to RCA, the song was recorded by someone else in the studio—not Elvis.

FUNNY HOW TIME SLIPS AWAY
Willie Nelson composed "Funny How Time Slips Away" in 10 minutes on the way to work in 1961. It was recorded that year by Billy Walker (Columbia 42050) and Jimmy Elledge (RCA 47-7946). Walker's version reached #23 on the country chart and Elledge's peaked at #22 on the Hot 100 chart. Sales of over one million copies are claimed for Elledge's release and for one by Joe Hinton (Back Beat 541) in 1964, which was titled "Funny." Hinton's recording reached #13 on the Hot 100 chart. Other renditions of the song included those by Johnny Tillotson (Cadence 1441) in 1963 and Dorothy Moore (Malaco 1033) in 1976.

Elvis recorded "Funny How Time Slips Away" on June 7, 1970, at RCA's Nashville studios. An April 14, 1972, performance of the song in Greensboro, North Carolina, was included in the 1972 documentary *Elvis on Tour*. An alternate mix was used in the RCA Record Club LP *Elvis Memories*.

LPs:
- *Elvis Aron Presley* (Shreveport, Louisiana; June 7, 1975)
- *Elvis as Recorded at Madison Square Garden* (June 10, 1972)
- *Elvis Country*

Bootleg LPs:
- *America's Own* (Uniondale, N.Y.; July 19, 1975)
- *Behind Closed Doors* (alternate take)
- *Elvis on Tour* (*Elvis on Tour* soundtrack)
- *From Las Vegas . . . to Niagara Falls* (Niagara Falls, N.Y.; June 24, 1974)
- *Rockin' with Elvis New Year's Eve Pittsburgh, Pa. Dec. 31, 1976* (Pittsburgh; December 31, 1976)
- *Standing Room Only, Volume 2* (Madison Square Garden; June 10, 1972)

---

[1] He may have patterned his vocal styling from Gene Vincent's version on the 1958 LP *Gene Vincent Rocks and the Blue Caps Roll* (Capitol T-970).

GENTLE ON MY MIND

John Hartford wrote and first recorded "Gentle on My Mind" (RCA 47-9175) in 1967. His record reached #60 on the country chart. He was inspired to compose the song after seeing the movie *Dr. Zhivago*. The traveling scenes and pleasant images left a lasting impression on him. Hartford and music publisher Chuck Glaser had first offered the song to Johnny Cash, who turned it down. A few months after Hartford's release, Glen Campbell recorded "Gentle on My Mind" (Capitol 5939). His recording did slightly better than Hartford's, reaching #30 on the country chart. In 1968 the record was reissued and hit #39 on the Hot 100 chart and #8 on the Easy-Listening chart. "Gentle on My Mind" subsequently became the theme song of Campbell's CBS-TV variety series, "The Glen Campbell Goodtime Hour." The song was awarded four Grammys in 1968; Best Folk Performance, Best Country and Western Recording, Best Country and Western Song, and Best Country and Western Vocal Performance by a Male (Campbell). Other recordings of the song include those by Patti Page (Columbia 44353) in 1968, Boots Randolph (Monument 1081) in 1968, Aretha Franklin (Atlantic 2619) in 1969, and Dean Martin (Reprise 0812) in 1969.

Elvis recorded "Gentle on My Mind" on January 15, 1969, at the American Sound Studios in Memphis. Ronnie Milsap played piano and Ed Kollis played harmonica on the recording.

LPs:
- *From Elvis in Memphis*
- *The Memphis Record*

Bootleg LPs:
- *Behind Closed Doors* (alternate take)
- *Unfinished Business* (alternate take)

GENTLY

Murray Wizell and Edward Lisbona wrote "Gently," which Elvis recorded on March 12, 1961, at RCA's Nashville studios.

LPs:
- *Something for Everybody*

GET BACK

Although credited as a Lennon-McCartney tune, "Get Back" was actually written by Paul McCartney alone. The Beatles with Billy Preston reached number one (for five weeks) on the Hot 100 chart with "Get Back" (Apple 2490) in 1969. It was the first Beatle record to credit another artist on the label. In the 1970 film *Let It Be*, "Get Back" was sung by the Beatles on the roof of the Apple studios in London.

At live appearances in the 1970s, Elvis sometimes sang "Get Back" in a medley with "Little Sister." The performance on the *Elvis Aron Presley* boxed set was recorded at the International Hotel in Las Vegas on August 13, 1970.

LPs:
- *Elvis Aron Presley*

Bootleg LPs:
- *Command Performance* (Las Vegas; August 4, 1972)
- *Sold Out* (Las Vegas; August 16, 1972)
- *Standing Room Only, Volume 2* (Las Vegas; February 21, 1971)

GET RHYTHM

Johnny Cash wrote and recorded "Get Rhythm" (Sun 241) in 1956. It was the flip side of "I Walk the Line." When the song was reissued in 1969 (Sun 1103), it reached #23 on the country chart. Cash wrote "Get Rhythm" for Elvis, but Elvis never recorded it.

G. I. BLUES

This was the title song of Elvis's 1960 movie *G. I. Blues*. "G. I. Blues" was written by Sid Tepper and Roy C. Bennett and recorded by Elvis on April 27, 1960, at RCA's Hollywood studios.

EPs:
- *The EP Collection, Volume 2* (alternate take #7)

LPs:
- *Elvis in Hollywood*
- *G. I. Blues*
- *This Is Elvis*

GIRL HAPPY

"Girl Happy," written by Doc Pomus and Norman Meade, was the title song of Elvis's 1965 film of the same name. The song was recorded in June 1964 at Radio Recorders, and take #13 was the one used on record. For some reason, the speed of the master recording was slightly increased over the other takes.

LPs:
- *Elvis in Hollywood*
- *Girl Happy*

Bootleg LPs:
- *Elvis* (*Girl Happy* soundtrack)

THE GIRL I NEVER LOVED

Elvis sang "The Girl I Never Loved" in his 1967 movie *Clambake*. The film version added string instruments. Elvis recorded "The Girl I Never Loved" on February 21 or 22, 1967, at RCA's Hollywood studios. Randy Starr is the composer.

LPs:
- *Clambake*

THE GIRL NEXT DOOR WENT A'WALKING

"The Girl Next Door Went a'Walking" was written by Bill Rice and Thomas Wayne (real name: Thomas

Wayne Perkins) and originally recorded by Wayne, an L. C. Humes High School graduate, in 1959 (Fernwood 122). On the label of Wayne's record, the title was given as "Girl Next Door." Elvis recorded the song on April 4, 1960, at RCA's Nashville studios. The title appeared as "The Girl Next Door" on the first pressings of the *Elvis Is Back* LP. Later pressings had the title as "The Girl Next Door Went a'Walking."

LPs:
• *Elvis Is Back*

GIRL OF MINE
Elvis recorded "Girl of Mine" on July 24, 1973, at Stax Studios in Memphis. Barry Mason and Les Reed are the composers.

LPs:
• *Raised on Rock/For Ol' Times Sake*
• *Our Memories of Elvis, Volume 1* (without overdubbing)

THE GIRL OF MY BEST FRIEND
This song was written by Beverly Ross and Sam Bobrick and recorded by Elvis on April 4, 1960, at RCA's Nashville studios. The first cover version was by Eddie Wood (Ember 1064) in 1960. Ral Donner, however, had the big hit with the song. He made a demo record with his group, the Gents, in Chicago. It was later rerecorded with vocal backing by the Starfires in Orlando, Florida, in late 1960 and sold to Gone Records. Donner's release of "The Girl of My Best Friend" (Gone 5102) in 1961 reached #19 on the Hot 100 chart. It sounded like Elvis. Los Angeles radio station KRLA held a contest in which they played both Elvis's and Donner's versions, alternating lines. The listeners had to identify who was singing which line. Elvis first heard Ral Donner's release of "The Girl of My Best Friend" on the radio while cruising in his Cadillac.

LPs:
• *Elvis Is Back*

GIRLS! GIRLS! GIRLS!
"Girls! Girls! Girls!" was a Jerry Leiber–Mike Stoller composition originally recorded by the Coasters (Atco 6204) in 1960. Their recording reached #96 on the Hot 100 chart. Elvis recorded "Girls! Girls! Girls!" in March 1962 at Radio Recorders. It was used as the title song to Elvis's 1962 movie *Girls! Girls! Girls!* The main title version (and the one used on record) is take #3. The end title version, with different vocal backing and lyrics, was the result of a splice of three takes.

LPs:
• *Elvis in Hollywood*
• *Girls! Girls! Girls!*

Bootleg LPs:
• *Elvis Rocks and the Girls Roll* (alternate take, end title version)
• *From Hollywood to Vegas* (*Girls! Girls! Girls!* soundtrack)

GIVE ME MORE, MORE, MORE (OF YOUR KISSES)
Lefty Frizzell wrote and recorded "Give Me More, More, More (of Your Kisses)" (Columbia 20885) in late 1951. The song reached #3 on the country chart in early 1952. Elvis is reported to have sung "Give Me More, More, More (of Your Kisses)" on the "Louisiana Hayride" in late 1954 and may have recorded the tune at Sun Records, although no evidence exists for that.

GIVE ME THE RIGHT
Elvis recorded "Give Me the Right" on March 12, 1961, at RCA's Nashville studios. Fred Wise and Norman Blagman are the composers.

LPs:
• *Something for Everybody*
• *A Valentine Gift for You*

GO EAST, YOUNG MAN
Elvis sang this tune in his 1965 film *Harum Scarum*. He recorded "Go East, Young Man" in February (possibly the 24th) 1965 at RCA's Nashville studios. Bill Giant, Bernie Baum, and Florence Kaye are the composers.

LPs:
• *Harum Scarum*

GOD BLESS MY DADDY
Elvis reportedly sang "God Bless My Daddy" at the Lawhon Elementary School in East Tupelo as a young boy.

GOD CALLS ME HOME
This gospel tune was sung in concert by Elvis at least once and probably more times.

Bootleg LPs:
• *Long Lost Songs* (place and date unknown)

GOIN' HOME
Elvis recorded "Goin' Home" for his 1968 film *Stay Away, Joe*, but it was cut from the final print. "Goin' Home" was written by Joy Byers and recorded by Elvis on October 2, 1967, at RCA's Nashville studios.

LPs:
• *Speedway*

GOLDEN COINS
Elvis sang "Golden Coins" in his 1965 film *Harum Scarum*. The song was written by Bill Giant, Bernie Baum, and Florence Kaye and recorded by Elvis in February (probably the 24th) 1965 at RCA's Nashville studios.

LPs:
• *Harum Scarum*

GONE
"Gone" was written in 1952 by Smokey Rogers and first recorded in 1953 by Ferlin Husky (Capitol 2298) using the pseudonym Terry Preston. The full title of the song is "(Since You're) Gone." Gisele MacKenzie also had a 1953 release close on the heels of Husky's. In 1957 Husky recorded a pop remake of "Gone" (Capitol

3628)[1] that reached #4 on the Top 100 chart and number one on the country chart. The record sold well over a million copies.

Elvis is known to have sung "Gone" on the "Louisiana Hayride" and may have recorded it at Sun Records, but no tape has surfaced.

GONNA GET BACK HOME SOMEHOW
Elvis recorded this Doc Pomus–Mort Shuman song on March 18, 1962 at RCA's Nashville studios.

LPs:
• *Pot Luck*

GOOD, BAD, BUT BEAUTIFUL
An instrumental track was recorded for "Good, Bad, but Beautiful" on July 24, 1973, at Stax Studios in Memphis, but Elvis never recorded a vocal track for this Clive Westlake composition.

GOOD LUCK CHARM
Aaron Schroeder and Wally Gold wrote "Good Luck Charm" for Elvis, who recorded the tune on October 15, 1961, at RCA's Nashville studios. In April 1962, "Good Luck Charm" replaced Shelley Fabares's "Johnny Angel" at number one on the Hot 100 chart. After two weeks it was replaced at the top position by the Shirelles' "Soldier Boy." "Good Luck Charm" spent a total of 13 weeks on the chart and became a million-seller. It was Elvis's last number one single until 1969. In England the record was number one for five weeks.

Singles:
• "GOOD LUCK CHARM"/"Anything That's Part of You" (RCA 47-7992) March 1962. Standard release. Two picture sleeves were issued: one with rust and lavender letters and one with blue and pink letters.
• "GOOD LUCK CHARM" "Anything That's Part of You" (RCA 37-7992) March 1962. Compact 33 Single release.
• "GOOD LUCK CHARM"/"Anything That's Part of You" (RCA 447-0636) November 1962. Gold Standard Series reissue.

EPs:
• *The EP Collection, Volume 2* (alternate take #1)
• *RCA Family Record Center*

LPs:
• *Elvis* (RCA DPL2-0056 [e])
• *Elvis' Golden Records, Volume 3*
• *Elvis: Worldwide 50 Gold Award Hits, Volume 1*
• *The Number One Hits*
• *The Top Ten Hits*

GOOD ROCKIN' TONIGHT
Roy Brown wrote and first recorded "Good Rockin' Tonight" (as "Good Rocking Tonight") in 1947 on Deluxe Records (Deluxe 1093). He wrote the song while performing in Galveston, Texas. Originally, Brown didn't sing it, because he did only ballads; the singer in his band sang it. One day his singer was ill and Brown was forced to sing "Good Rockin' Tonight" himself, and the crowd reaction was good. With the lyrics writ-

ten on a paper sack, Brown approached Wynonie Harris to record the song, but Harris wasn't interested. Later, Cecil Gant had Brown sing "Good Rockin' Tonight" over the telephone to the president of Deluxe Records at 3:00 A.M. Brown was soon signed to a recording contract. Ironically, Wynonie Harris covered Brown's version in 1948 and had a more successful hit (King 4210). Pat Boone recorded "Good Rockin' Tonight" in 1959 (Decca 15888) and reached #49 on the Hot 100 chart.

Elvis recorded "Good Rockin' Tonight" on September 10, 1954, at Sun Records with backing by Scotty Moore and Bill Black. The single (Sun 210) was released on September 25, 1954. "Good Rockin' Tonight" was a part of Elvis's concert repertoire for the next few years. It was one of the songs he sang in the unreleased 1955 movie short *The Pied Piper of Cleveland*. The Billy Jack Wills Western Band covered Elvis's recording with their release "There's Good Rockin' Tonight" (MGM 11966), in 1955.

In 1956 Jean Chapel had an answer record titled "I Won't Be Rockin' Tonight" (Sun 244). The 1957 movie *Rock Baby Rock It* featured Johnny Carroll singing "Rockin' Maybelle," which was based on "Good Rockin' Tonight" with a little bit of "Baby, Let's Play House" thrown in ("Have you heard the news, my Maybelle's rockin' tonight").

Singles:
• "GOOD ROCKIN' TONIGHT"/"I Don't Care If the Sun Don't Shine" (Sun 210) September 25, 1954. Standard Sun release in both 78 RPM and 45 RPM versions.
• "GOOD ROCKIN' TONIGHT"/"I Don't Care If the Sun Don't Shine" (RCA 20-6381) November 1955. 78 RPM RCA reissue of the Sun original.
• "GOOD ROCKIN' TONIGHT"/"I Don't Care If the Sun Don't Shine" (RCA 47-6381) November 1955. 45 RPM RCA reissue of the Sun original.
• "GOOD ROCKIN' TONIGHT"/"I Don't Care If the Sun Don't Shine" (RCA 447-0602) March 1959. Gold Standard Series reissue.

EPs:
• *Good Rockin' Tonight*
• *A Touch of Gold, Volume 1*

LPs:
• *The Complete Sun Sessions* (master)
• *A Date with Elvis* (alternate mix)
• *Elvis: The Hillbilly Cat* (Eagle's Hall, Houston; March 19, 1955)
• *The Sun Sessions* (alternate mix)

Bootleg LPs:
• *The Entertainer* (Eagle's Hall, Houston; January 29, 1955)
• *The First Year—Recorded Live* (Eagle's Hall, Houston; January 29, 1955)
• *The First Years* (Eagle's Hall, Houston; January 29, 1955)
• *Good Rocking Tonight* (master)
• *The Rockin' Rebel, Volume 2* (Eagle's Hall, Houston; January 29, 1955)
• *The Sun Years* (master)

GOOD TIME CHARLIE'S GOT THE BLUES
This song was written and recorded by Danny O'Keefe in 1972. "Good Time Charlie's Got the Blues" (Signpost 70006) reached #9 on the Hot 100 chart and #5 on the

---

[1]"Gone" was recorded in the first country session in which a modern vocal group and vibraphone were used.

Easy-Listening chart. Sales exceeded one million copies. Elvis recorded "Good Time Charlie's Got the Blues" on December 13, 1973, at Stax Studios in Memphis. He sang it in concert on a number of occasions, but eliminated the lines "I take the pills to ease my pain, can't find the thing to ease my brain."

LPs:
• *Good Times*

Bootleg LPs:
• *Big Boss Man* (Las Vegas; August 19, 1974)
• *Susie Q* (Las Vegas; ?)

GOODNIGHT MY LOVE
Mack Gordon and Harry Revel wrote this song in 1934. Bing Crosby introduced it in the 1934 Paramount film *We're Not Dressing.* Two years later, "Goodnight My Love" was sung in Shirley Temple's *Stowaway.* Jesse Belvin had a #10 rhythm & blues hit with the tune in 1956 (Modern 1005). Pop recordings of "Goodnight My Love" include those of the McGuire Sisters (Coral 61748) in 1956, the Fleetwoods (Dolton 75) in 1959, and Paul Anka (RCA 47-9648) in 1969. Elvis sang the song in concert in the 1970s.

GOT A LOT O' LIVIN' TO DO
Aaron Schroeder and Ben Weisman wrote "Got a Lot o' Livin' to Do" for Elvis's second film *Loving You.* The song was heard three times during the movie. Elvis recorded the record version on January 12, 1957, at Radio Recorders. The master recording is take #9. In February 1957 he recorded the film versions at the same studio.

EPs:
• *Loving You, Volume 2*

LPs:
• *Elvis: The Other Sides—Worldwide Gold Award Hits, Volume 2*
• *Essential Elvis—The First Movies* (master and unreleased film version)
• *Elvis Aron Presley—Forever*
• *Loving You*

Bootleg LPs:
• *Got a Lot o' Livin' to Do!* (*Loving You* soundtrack)
• *Loving You* (*Loving You* soundtrack)
• *Please Release Me* (*Loving You* soundtrack)

GOT MY MOJO WORKING
Muddy Waters (real name: McKinley Morganfield) wrote and recorded "Got My Mojo Working" (Chess 1652) in 1957. However, his version did not chart. The big hit was Jimmy Smith's 1966 instrumental release on Verve Records (Verve 10393), which peaked at #51 on the Hot 100 chart and #17 on the rhythm & blues chart. A "mojo" is a voodoo charm used to enhance sexual ability. Other mojo-titled recordings by various artists include "Mojo Hand," "Mojo Strut," and "Mojo Blues."

Elvis recorded "Got My Mojo Working" in a studio jam session (paired with "Keep Your Hands Off Her") on June 5, 1970, at RCA's Nashville studios. For some reason, the *Love Letters from Elvis* LP listed Preston Foster as the composer of "Got My Mojo Working."

LPs:
• *Love Letters from Elvis*

THE GREAT PRETENDER
Buck Ram, manager of the Platters, wrote "The Great Pretender" for his group in 1955. The recording became one of their greatest hits. "The Great Pretender" (Mercury 70753) was number one on both the Hot 100 and rhythm & blues charts in early 1956. The record stayed at the top of the rhythm & blues chart for an amazing 10 weeks and quickly became the Platters' second million-seller.

Elvis is known to have sung "The Great Pretender" in concert in the 1950s.

GREEN, GREEN GRASS OF HOME
This classic country song was written by Claude (Curly) Putnam Jr. in 1965 and first recorded by Porter Wagoner (RCA 47-8622) that same year. Wagoner's recording was a #4 country hit.

While watching television one evening in 1965, Curly Putnam saw the 1950 movie *The Asphalt Jungle,* starring Marilyn Monroe[1] and Sterling Hayden. He was impressed by the scene in which criminal Hayden (who had been shot) struggled to go home and see his farm one last time. The house was located on a hill surrounded by "green, green grass." It took Putnam about two hours to write the song, which has become a country standard.

Tom Jones had the biggest hit with "Green, Green Grass of Home" (Parrot 40009). He first sang the song on a TV show in England in 1965. The response was so terrific that he recorded it the following year. "Green, Green Grass of Home" sold over a million copies worldwide and peaked at #11 on the Hot 100 chart. In England, it was number one for six weeks. Bandleader Skitch Henderson recorded an instrumental version in 1968 (Columbia 44333) that went to #30 on the Easy-Listening chart. Most of the top country artists have recorded "Green, Green Grass of Home" at one time or another.

Red West first heard "Green, Green Grass of Home" on a 1966 Jerry Lee Lewis LP, *Country Songs for City Folks* (Smash SRS 67071). At the time, he urged Elvis to record the song, but Elvis decided against it. While traveling back to Memphis in 1970 in his personal Greyhound bus, Elvis heard Tom Jones's recording on the radio. He stopped the bus and had Marty Lacker call disc jockey George Klein. Klein played the record several times on the air for Elvis during the next few hours. On March 11, 1975, at RCA's Hollywood studios, Elvis finally recorded "Green, Green Grass of Home."

---

[1] Marilyn Monroe was given the role over Georgia Holt, Cher's mother.

LPs:
- *Forever—Elvis Aron Presley*
- *Elvis Today*
- *Our Memories of Elvis, Volume 2* (without overdubbing)

Bootleg LPs:
- *Elvis Presley Is Alive and Well and Singing in Las Vegas, Volume 1* (Las Vegas; August 1975)
- *The Vegas Years, 1972–1975* (Las Vegas; 1975)

GREEN ONIONS
Booker T. and the M.G.'s had their first and biggest instrumental hit with "Green Onions" (Stax 127) in 1962. It was a million-seller and reached #3 on the Hot 100 chart and number one on the rhythm & blues chart.

Booker T. and the M.G.'s, the house band at Stax Studios, had just finished a 1962 recording session with Billy Lee Riley when they started jamming. Recording engineer Jim Stewart asked what they were playing. Someone said, "Green Onions." Stewart asked them if they had anything else they'd been working on. The group then played an untitled dance tune. Stewart gave the untitled dance tune the name of "Green Onions" and renamed the blues jam "Behave Yourself." The two songs became the two sides of Booker T. and the M.G.'s first single release.

Elvis's TCB Band played "Green Onions" at a number of concerts while Elvis was rapping with the audience and introducing band members and backup singers. Another song used was "Comin' Home."

GUADALAJARA
"Guadalajara" was written by Pépé Guizar and recorded by Elvis for his 1963 movie *Fun in Acapulco*. The instrumental track was laid on January 23, 1963, at Radio Recorders. Elvis recorded his vocal track on February 27. Both the Jordanaires and the Mello Men sang backup. Guadalajara was popularized by Xavier Cugat in a 1944 recording (Columbia 36694).

LPs:
- *Burning Love and Hits from His Movies, Volume 2*
- *Fun in Acapulco*
- *Elvis—A Legendary Performer, Volume 3* (alternate take #2)

GUILTY
Jim Reeves had a #3 country hit with "Guilty" (RCA 47-8193) in 1963. It's been rumored that Elvis recorded "Guilty" in the 1960s, but no tape has surfaced.

GUITAR MAN
"Guitar Man" was written and first recorded by Jerry Reed (RCA 47-9152) in 1967. His recording reached #53 on *Billboard*'s country chart.

After hearing Reed's record on the radio, Elvis invited him to Graceland. On September 10, 1967, Elvis recorded "Guitar Man" at RCA's Nashville studios, and lead guitar was played by Jerry Reed. Elvis's single release had a six-week stay on the Hot 100 chart, peaking at #43. "Guitar Man" was featured prominently in the 1968 TV special "Elvis." Recordings for the special all took place on June 29 and 30, 1968. After Elvis's death, Felton Jarvis removed the original instrumental backing and recorded a new one on October 16, 1980, at Young' Un Sound in Nashville. Again, Jerry Reed was featured on lead guitar. This new remixed version was released on the *Guitar Man* LP and as a single. "Guitar Man" reached #28 on the Hot 100 chart and had a 14-week stay. On the adult contemporary chart, it had a nine-week stay, peaking at #16. In March 1981, "Guitar Man" replaced the Bellamy Brothers' "Do You Love as Good as You Look" at the number one position on the country chart. A week later, Willie Nelson's "Angel Flying Too Close to the Ground" took over the top spot. "Guitar Man" was Elvis's last number one record on any *Billboard* chart. It had a total stay of 13 weeks on the country chart.

Singles:
- "GUITAR MAN"/"High Heel Sneakers" (RCA 47-9425) January 1968. Standard release. Two picture sleeves were used for this record: one that read, "Coming Soon, ELVIS' GOLD RECORDS, VOLUME 4" and one used in February 1968 that read, "Ask for ELVIS' GOLD RECORDS, VOLUME 4."
- "GUITAR MAN"/"High Heel Sneakers" (RCA 447-0663) 1970. Gold Standard Series reissue.
- "GUITAR MAN"/"Faded Love" (RCA JH-12158) January 1981. Disc jockey promotional release. Some of these promo copies were issued on red vinyl.
- "GUITAR MAN"/"Faded Love" (RCA PB-12158) January 1981. New remixed version.

EPs:
- *Stay Away*

LPs:
- *Clambake*
- *Elvis Sings Hits from His Movies, Volume 1*
- *Elvis—TV Special* (three versions from "Elvis" TV special taping)
- *Guitar Man* (remixed version with longer vocal and "What'd I Say" ending)

Bootleg LPs:
- *The Burbank Sessions, Volume 2* ("Elvis" taping; 8:00 P.M. show on June 29, 1968)
- *The '68 Comeback* ("Elvis" taping; June 30, 1968)
- *The '68 Comeback, Volume 2* ("Elvis" taping; takes #?, #9, and #10; June 30, 1968)
- *Special Delivery from Elvis Presley* ("Elvis" taping; June 30, 1968)

H

HAPPY BIRTHDAY TO YOU

Written by sisters Patty Smith Hill and Mildred J. Hill in 1893, "Happy Birthday to You" is undoubtedly the most sung song in the world. The song was first titled "Good Morning to All" and published in *Song Stories for Children*. Although commonly believed to be in the public domain, "Happy Birthday to You" is copyrighted and has been involved in litigation many times. Perhaps the most celebrated case occurred when Irving Berlin used the song in his musical play *As Thousands Cheer*, in a sketch in which it was sung to John D. Rockefeller. The unauthorized use resulted in a lawsuit won by the Hill sisters' estate.

Marilyn Monroe sang "Happy Birthday to You" to President John F. Kennedy on May 19, 1962, at Madison Square Garden. Film clips of the event turn up frequently on retrospectives of Kennedy and Monroe.

Elvis sang "Happy Birthday to You" on a few occasions in a concert setting.

Bootleg LPs:
- *Cadillac Elvis* (Odessa, Texas; May 30, 1976) (in medley with "Young and Beautiful" and "The Mickey Mouse Club March")
- *Elvis Presley Is Alive and Well and Singing in Las Vegas, Volume 1* (Las Vegas; August 1975) (sung to James Burton)
- *The Legend Lives On* (Las Vegas; August 1969) (sung to James Burton)
- *Superstar Outtakes* (Las Vegas; August 1975) (sung to James Burton)

HAPPY ENDING

Elvis sang "Happy Ending" in his 1963 movie *It Happened at the World's Fair*. The song was recorded in September 1962 at Radio Recorders, with vocal backing by the Jordanaires. In the film, Joan O'Brien also sings with Elvis. "Happy Ending" was written by Ben Weisman and Sid Wayne.

LPs:
- *It Happened at the World's Fair*
- *Mahalo from Elvis*

Bootleg LPs:
- *Elvis* (*It Happened at the World's Fair* soundtrack)

HAPPY, HAPPY BIRTHDAY BABY

Brother and sister team Gilbert J. Lopez and Margo L. Sylvia wrote "Happy, Happy Birthday Baby" in 1952, although it wasn't until five years later that they recorded it with their group, the Tune Weavers.[1] Their release on Checker Records (Checker 872) reached #5 on *Billboard*'s Top 100 chart and #4 on the rhythm & blues chart in October 1957. "Happy, Happy Birthday Baby" was the Tune Weavers' only charted single.

While visiting the Waco, Texas, home of disc jockey

Eddie Fadal in the summer of 1958, Elvis sang along with the Tune Weavers' record a total of seven times. Fadal made a tape of the impromptu performance that later appeared on the bootleg LP *Forever Young, Forever Beautiful*.

Bootleg LPs:
- *Forever Young, Forever Beautiful*

HARBOR LIGHTS

"Harbor Lights" was written by Jimmy Kennedy and Hugh Williams (real name: Will Grosz) in 1937 and popularized in recordings that year by Frances Langford (Decca 1441) and Claude Thornhill and His Orchestra, with vocal by Jimmy Farrell (Vocalion 3595). The song was revived in 1950 by several artists, the most successful being Sammy Kaye, who had a number one recording (Columbia 38963). Other popular versions that year were by Guy Lombardo (Decca 27208), Bing Crosby (Decca 27219), Ray Anthony (Capitol 1190), Ralph Flanagan (RCA 3911), and Ken Griffin (Columbia 38889). Over a million copies of sheet music were sold for "Harbor Lights" in 1950. The song was performed a record 29 times on "Your Hit Parade." In 1960 the Platters' recording of "Harbor Lights" (Mercury 71563) reached #8 on the Hot 100 chart.

"Harbor Lights" was used as the recurring theme song of the 1940 John Ford–directed movie *The Long Voyage Home*, starring John Wayne.

Elvis recorded "Harbor Lights" on July 5, 1954—his first commercial recording session. It was the first song put on tape. Sam Phillips of Sun Records considered the recording to be not worthy of release. In 1976 RCA released the master (take #2) on the LP *Elvis—A Legendary Performer, Volume 2*.

In 1980, the *National Enquirer* sent an unidentified copy of Elvis's "Harbor Lights" to recording studios in Nashville and New York City. The recording was rejected by almost all of the companies.

LPs:
- *The Complete Sun Sessions* (outtake)
- *Elvis—A Legendary Performer, Volume 2* (take #2)
- *A Golden Celebration* (take #2)

HARD HEADED WOMAN

Elvis recorded "Hard Headed Woman" on January 15, 1958, at Radio Recorders for his film *King Creole*. Take #10 was chosen for release. "Hard Headed Woman" entered *Billboard*'s Top 100 chart at #15. The second week, it was #3. Despite this movement, the highest position the record would achieve during its 13 weeks on the chart was #2. Sheb Wooley's "The Purple People Eater"[2] kept "Hard Headed Woman" from ascending

---

[1]The two other members of the Tune Weavers were John Sylvia (husband of Margo Sylvia) and Charlotte Davis (cousin of Gilbert and Margo).

[2]Two number one songs in 1958—"The Purple People Eater" and "Tequila"—ended with the word, "tequila."

to the top spot. The record also reached #2 on both the country and rhythm & blues charts. Sales quickly exceeded one million copies and a Gold Record was certified by the RIAA on August 11, 1958. It was the first of several Gold Records Elvis was to receive during his career. "Hard Headed Woman" was written by Claude DeMetrius.

"Hard Headed Woman" was the first Elvis record to be played on the BBC's Radio One. Disc jockey Emperor Rosk aired the record on his show.

Singles:
- "HARD HEADED WOMAN"/"Don't Ask Me Why" (RCA 20-7280) June 1958. Standard 78 RPM release.
- "HARD HEADED WOMAN"/"Don't Ask Me Why" (RCA 47-7280) June 1958. Standard 45 RPM release.
- "HARD HEADED WOMAN"/"Don't Ask Me Why" (RCA 447-0623) 1961. Gold Standard Series reissue.

EPs:
- *A Touch of Gold, Volume 1*

LPs:
- *Elvis* (RCA DPL2-0056[e])
- *The Elvis Medley*
- *Elvis: Worldwide 50 Gold Award Hits, Volume 1*
- *King Creole*
- *The Number One Hits*
- *The Top Ten Hits*

HARD KNOCKS
Joy Byers wrote "Hard Knocks" for Elvis's 1964 movie *Roustabout*. Elvis recorded the song at Radio Recorders in February 1964.

LPs:
- *Roustabout*

HARD LUCK
Elvis sang "Hard Luck," a Sid Wayne–Ben Weisman composition, in the 1964 film *Frankie and Johnny*. The recording session took place in May 1965 at Radio Recorders.

LPs:
- *Frankie and Johnny*

HAREM HOLIDAY
Peter Andreoli and Vince Poncia Jr. wrote this song for Elvis's 1965 film *Harum Scarum*. Elvis recorded "Harem Holiday" at RCA's Nashville studios in February 1965.

LPs:
- *Harum Scarum*

HAVE A HAPPY
Elvis recorded "Have a Happy" at the Decca Recording Studios in Universal City, California, on March 5 or 6, 1969, for his film *Change of Habit*. The song was composed by Ben Weisman, Buddy Kaye, and Dolores Fuller.

LPs:
- *Elvis Sings for Children and Grownups Too!*
- *Let's Be Friends*

HAVE I TOLD YOU LATELY THAT I LOVE YOU
Songwriter Scott Wiseman was lying in Wesley Memorial Hospital in Chicago in 1944 when his wife, Lulubell, came to visit him. Just before leaving she bent over and whispered, "Have I told you lately that I love you?" The line inspired Wiseman to write the song. He and his wife, as Lulubell and Scotty, introduced "Have I Told You Lately That I Love You" in their nightclub act. Gene Autry became the first to record the song, in 1945 (Columbia 20075). Foy Willing and the Riders of the Purple Sage also recorded it that year (Majestic 6000). Other early versions include those by Bing Crosby and the Andrews Sisters (Decca 24821) in 1950 and Tex Ritter (Capitol 2174) in 1952. In 1957 Ricky Nelson had a #29 hit on the Top 100 chart with his version (Imperial 5463). (It was the flip side of "Be Bop Baby.") Nelson's recording copied Elvis's very closely, even to the extent of using the Jordanaires as vocal backup. A Decca release by Kitty Wells and Red Foley (Decca 32427) reached the country chart.

Elvis recorded "Have I Told You Lately That I Love You" on January 19, 1957, at Radio Recorders. Take #15 was chosen by RCA for release.

Singles:
- "HAVE I TOLD YOU LATELY THAT I LOVE YOU"/"Mean Woman Blues" (RCA 47-7066) October 1957. Disc jockey "Record Prevue."

EPs:
- *Just for You*

LPs:
- *Loving You*

HAWAII USA
(See *Paradise, Hawaiian Style*)

HAWAIIAN SUNRISE
Elvis is believed to have recorded "Hawaiian Sunrise" for his 1961 film *Blue Hawaii*, but so far there's been no supporting evidence.

HAWAIIAN SUNSET
Sid Tepper and Roy C. Bennett wrote "Hawaiian Sunset" for Elvis's 1961 movie *Blue Hawaii*. Elvis recorded the song on March 21, 1961, at Radio Recorders.

LPs:
- *Blue Hawaii*

Bootleg LPs:
- *The Blue Hawaii Box* (takes #1–3)
- *Plantation Rock* (rehearsal concert for "Elvis: Aloha from Hawaii"; January 12, 1973)

HAWAIIAN WEDDING SONG
"Hawaiian Wedding Song" was written in 1926 by Charles E. King under the title "Ke Kali Nei Au." In 1958 Al Hoffman and Dick Manning wrote English lyrics. Andy Williams had the only million-seller of "Hawaiian Wedding Song" (Cadence 1358) in 1959. His recording reached #11 on *Billboard*'s Hot 100 chart. In 1951 Bing Crosby had recorded the song as "Here Ends the Rainbow."

Elvis recorded "Hawaiian Wedding Song" on March 22, 1961, at Radio Recorders for his film *Blue Hawaii*. He later sang it in the U.S. edition of his TV special "Elvis: Aloha from Hawaii" (April 4, 1973). "Hawaiian Wedding Song" did not appear on the soundtrack album of the special, however.

LPs:
- *Blue Hawaii*
- *Elvis Aron Presley—Forever*
- *Elvis in Concert* (Rapid City, South Dakota; June 21, 1977
- *Mahalo from Elvis* (Honolulu; January 14, 1973)

Bootleg LPs:
- *Behind Closed Doors* (take #1)
- *The Blue Hawaii Box* (takes #1-2)
- *Command Performance* (Las Vegas; August 23, 1974)
- *Elvis Presley Is Alive and Well and Singing in Las Vegas, Volume 1*
- *Special Delivery from Elvis Presley* (Sahara Tahoe Hotel; ?)
- *The Vegas Years, 1972–1975* (Las Vegas; August 1974)

HE IS MY EVERYTHING
Dallas Frazier wrote this gospel song based on his hit country tune "There Goes My Everything." Elvis recorded "He Is My Everything" on June 9, 1971, at RCA's Nashville studios.

LPs:
- *He Touched Me*
- *He Walks Beside Me*

HE KNOWS JUST WHAT I NEED
Elvis recorded "He Knows Just What I Need" on October 30, 1960, at RCA's Nashville studios. Take #10 was released by RCA. On the reissue of the *His Hand in Mine* album, the song's title was listed as "Jesus Knows What I Need." Mosie Lister wrote "He Knows Just What I Need" in 1955.

LPs:
- *His Hand in Mine*

HE TOUCHED ME
"He Touched Me," a William J. Gaither gospel song, was recorded by Elvis on May 18, 1971, at RCA's Nashville studios. When first released, the single played at about $33\frac{1}{3}$ RPM, although it had the larger 45 RPM center hole. RCA pressed about 10,000 copies before discovering the error. The single did not chart.

Singles:
- "HE TOUCHED ME"/"Bosom of Abraham" (RCA 74-0651) March 1972. Standard release.

LPs:
- *He Touched Me*

HE'LL HAVE TO GO
One day while talking with his wife on the telephone, songwriter Joe Allison told her to put her mouth closer to the phone because she talked so softly. By the time Allison got home, wife Audrey had written the first line of "He'll Have to Go"—"Put your sweet lips a little closer to the phone." The remainder of the song came quickly for them. "He'll Have to Go" was first recorded by Jim Reeves (RCA 47-7643) in 1959. His recording reached #2 on *Billboard*'s Hot 100 chart, number one on the country chart, and #13 on the rhythm & blues chart. Sales of over three million copies are claimed. In 1960 Jeanne Black recorded a popular answer record, "He'll Have to Stay" (Capitol 4368), which peaked at #4 on the Hot 100 chart and #6 on the country chart. That song was also a Joe Allison–Audrey Allison composition.

Elvis recorded "He'll Have to Go" on the night of October 31–November 1, 1976 at Graceland.

LPs:
- *Moody Blue*

HE'S ONLY A PRAYER AWAY
While in West Germany, Elvis recorded "He's Only a Prayer Away" on a home tape recorder. The recording remained unreleased until 1984.

LPs:
- *A Golden Celebration* (West Germany; 1958–1960)

HE'S YOUR UNCLE, NOT YOUR DAD
Elvis sang "He's Your Uncle, Not Your Dad" in his 1968 movie *Speedway*. The film version had additional voices and instrumentation. The instrumental track was recorded in June 1967 at MGM's Culver City studios. Elvis may have recorded his vocal at a later date. One line of "The Star Spangled Banner" was sung in "He's Your Uncle, Not Your Dad." Sid Wayne and Ben Weisman are the composers.

LPs:
- *Speedway*

HEART OF ROME
Elvis recorded "Heart of Rome" on June 6, 1970, at RCA's Nashville studios. His single release, which did not chart, had additional overdubbing not heard on the album cut. "Heart of Rome" was composed by Geoff Stephens, Alan Blaikley, and Ken Howard.

Singles:
- "I'm Leavin'" /"HEART OF ROME" (RCA 47-9998) July 1971. Standard release.
- "I'm Leavin'" /"HEART OF ROME" (RCA 447-0683) May 1972. Gold Standard Series reissue.

LPs:
- *Love Letters from Elvis*

HEARTBREAK HOTEL
While reading the *Miami Herald* one day in the fall of 1955, songwriter Tommy Durden spotted the headline, "Do You Know This Man?" A photograph of a suicide victim accompanied the article. The man had left no identification, but did leave a note that read, "I walk a lonely street." Miami police were running the article in the hope that the man's next of kin or friends could identify him. Durden thought that the man's suicide note might provide the basis for a great blues song. He excitedly called his collaborator, Mae Axton, and she agreed. The two of them wrote "Heartbreak Hotel" in

about 15 to 20 minutes at Axton's house. Singer Glen Reeves was called in to record a demo. Some reports have indicated that the song was first offered to the Wilburn Brothers, who turned it down. But that has never been substantiated. What did happen was that Mae Axton took her demo to Nashville for the annual disc jockey convention at the Andrew Jackson Hotel on November 10, 1955. After hearing the demo in his hotel room, Elvis was ecstatic. He promised Axton that he would record "Heartbreak Hotel" the next time he was in the recording studio.

Elvis recorded "Heartbreak Hotel" on January 10, 1956, at RCA's Nashville studios. It was the second song he recorded for RCA; the first was "I Got a Woman." Instrumental backing was provided by Scotty Moore (guitar), Chet Atkins (guitar), Floyd Cramer (piano), Bill Black (bass), and D. J. Fontana (drums). Gordon Stoker, Ben Speer, and Brock Speer sang the backing vocals. Elvis's first new RCA single, "Heartbreak Hotel"/"I Was the One" was released on January 27, 1956. In April "Heartbreak Hotel" succeeded Les Baxter's "The Poor People of Paris" as the nation's number one song. After a seven-week stay at the top, it was replaced by Gogi Grant's "The Wayward Wind." "Heartbreak Hotel" was also number one on the country chart and #5 on the rhythm & blues chart—the first Presley record to reach the latter chart. "Heartbreak Hotel" was Elvis's first million-seller and the second record in history to reach all three *Billboard* charts. (The first was Carl Perkins's "Blue Suede Shoes.") Total stay on the Top 100 chart was 27 weeks. Elvis sang "Heartbreak Hotel" on "Stage Show" (February 11, March 17, and March 24), "The Milton Berle Show" (April 3), and "The Ed Sullivan Show" (January 6, 1957). *Billboard* listed it as the number one single of 1956. "Heartbreak Hotel" was sung in the 1968 TV special "Elvis," and in the 1970 documentary *Elvis—That's the Way It Is*.

In 1956 the Cadets recorded a cover version of "Heartbreak Hotel" for Modern Records (Modern 985). It was the first cover of an Elvis record by black performers. Other recordings of "Heartbreak Hotel" through the years include those by Stan Freberg (Capitol 3480), a 1956 parody; Roger Miller (Smash 2066) in 1966, Frijid Pink (Parrot 352) in 1970; and Willie Nelson and Leon Russell (Columbia 3-11023), who had a #1 country duet with the song in 1979.

Singles:
- "HEARTBREAK HOTEL"/"I Was the One" (RCA 20-6420) January 27, 1956. Standard 78 RPM release.
- "HEARTBREAK HOTEL"/"I Was the One" (RCA 47-6420) January 27, 1956. Standard 45 RPM release.
- "HEARTBREAK HOTEL"/"I Was the One" (RCA 447-0605) March 1959. Gold Standard Series reissue.
- "HEARTBREAK HOTEL"/"I Was the One" (RCA PB-11105) October 1977. One of 15 singles in the boxed set *15 Golden Records—30 Golden Hits* (RCA PP-11301), and one of 10 singles in the boxed set *20 Golden Hits in Full Color Sleeves* (RCA PP-11340), released two months later.
- "HEARTBREAK HOTEL"/"Jailhouse Rock" (RCA PB-13892) October 1984. One of six singles in the boxed set *Elvis' Greatest Hits—Golden Singles, Volume 2* (RCA PP-13898). The single was pressed on gold vinyl and had a special gold "50th" anniversary label.

EPs:
- *Heartbreak Hotel*
- *The Sound of Leadership*

LPs:
- *Elvis—A Legendary Performer, Volume 1*
- *Elvis Aron Presley* (Las Vegas; May 6, 1956) (USS *Arizona* Memorial; March 25, 1961)
- *Elvis as Recorded at Madison Square Garden* (June 10, 1972)
- *Elvis' Golden Records*
- *The Elvis Medley*
- *Elvis—TV Special* ("Elvis" TV special taping; June 29, 1968, at 6:00 P.M. show)
- *Elvis: Worldwide 50 Gold Award Hits, Volume 1*
- *A Golden Celebration* ("Stage Show"; February 11, 1956; March 17, 1956; March 24, 1956) ("The Milton Berle Show"; April 3, 1956) (Tupelo, Mississippi; September 26, 1956) ("The Ed Sullivan Show"; January 6, 1957)
- *The Number One Hits*
- *This Is Elvis* ("Stage Show"; March 17, 1956)
- *The Top Ten Hits*

Bootleg LPs:
- *America's Own* (Uniondale, N.Y.; July 19, 1975)
- *The Burbank Sessions, Volume 1* ("Elvis" TV special taping; June 27, 1968, at 6:00 P.M. and 8:00 P.M. shows)
- *The Burbank Sessions, Volume 2* ("Elvis" TV special taping; June 29, 1968, at 6:00 P.M. and 8:00 P.M. shows)
- *Cadillac Elvis* (*Elvis—That's the Way It Is* soundtrack)
- *Dorsey Shows* ("Stage Show"; February 11, 1956; March 17, 1956; March 24, 1956)
- *Elvis' 1961 Hawaii Benefit Concert* (USS *Arizona* Memorial; March 25, 1961)
- *Eternal Elvis, Volume 2* (studio take) ("Elvis" TV special taping; June 27, 1968, at 8:00 P.M. show)
- *From the Waist Up* ("The Ed Sullivan Show"; January 6, 1957)
- *Got a Lot o' Livin' to Do!* (Vancouver, British Columbia; September 1, 1957)
- *The Hillbilly Cat "Live"* (Las Vegas; August 1970)
- *The King Goes Wild* ("The Ed Sullivan Show"; January 6, 1957)
- *King of Las Vegas Live* (*Elvis—That's the Way It Is* soundtrack)
- *Sold Out* (Las Vegas; August 24, 1970)
- *The Sun Years* ("Stage Show"; February 11, 1956)
- *Superstar Outtakes, Volume 2* ("Stage Show"; February 11, 1956; March 17, 1956; March 24, 1956)
- *That's the Way It Is* (*Elvis—That's the Way It Is* soundtrack)

HELP ME
Larry Gatlin wrote "Help Me" for Elvis in 1973. Elvis recorded the tune at Stax Studios in Memphis on December 12, 1973. His single release had a 15-week stay on *Billboard*'s country chart in mid-1974, peaking at #6. In 1977 Ray Price had a successful recording of "Help Me" on Columbia Records (Columbia 10503).

Singles:
- "If You Talk in Your Sleep"/"HELP ME" (RCA APBO-0280) May 1974. Standard release.
- "If You Talk in Your Sleep"/"HELP ME" (RCA DJBO-0280) May 1974. Disc Jockey promotional release.

LPs:
- *Elvis Recorded Live on Stage in Memphis* (Memphis; March 20, 1974)
- *Promised Land*

Bootleg LPs:
- *From Las Vegas . . . to Niagara Falls* (Niagara Falls, N.Y.; June 24, 1974)

• *Standing Room Only, Volume 3* (Memphis; March 20, 1974)

HELP ME MAKE IT THROUGH THE NIGHT

"Help Me Make It Through the Night" was written by Kris Kristofferson and Fred Foster, and first recorded by Sammi Smith (Mega 615-0015)[1] in early 1971. Her recording was a number one country hit and million-seller. It reached #8 on the Hot 100 chart. "Help Me Make It Through the Night" was awarded two Grammys for 1971: Best Country Vocal Performance (Female) and Best Country Song. Other popular recordings of the song include those by Joe Simon (Spring 113), O. C. Smith (Columbia 45435), both in 1971, and Gladys Knight and the Pips (Soul 35094) in 1972. "Help Me Make It Through the Night" served as the theme song to the 1972 John Huston–directed film, *Fat City*, and the short-lived 1987 TV series "Fat City," which was based on the film.

Elvis recorded "Help Me Make It Through the Night" on May 17, 1971, at RCA's Nashville studios. The instrumental track had been recorded the previous day.

LPs:
• *Elvis Now*
• *Welcome to My World*

Bootleg LPs:
• *Sold Out* (Nashville; July 1, 1973)
• *To Know Him Is to Love Him* (Las Vegas; 1969 or 1970)

HERE COMES SANTA CLAUS
(RIGHT DOWN SANTA CLAUS LANE)

Gene Autry served as the grand marshal of the Santa Claus Parade in Hollywood, California, in November 1947. During the parade, he kept hearing kids along the parade route yelling, "Here comes Santa Claus!" Autry and Oakley Haldeman wrote the song based on that line. In December 1947, Autry's recording of "Here Comes Santa Claus (Right Down Santa Claus Lane)" (Columbia 37942) reached #9 on *Billboard*'s Best-Selling Singles chart. The next two years, the record again charted, reaching #8 in 1948 and #24 in 1949.

Elvis recorded "Here Comes Santa Claus (Right Down Santa Claus Lane)" at Radio Recorders in Hollywood on September 6, 1957. RCA chose take #2 for release.

EPs:
• *Christmas with Elvis*

LPs:
• *Elvis' Christmas Album*

HEY, HEY, HEY

Elvis sang "Hey, Hey, Hey" in his 1967 film *Clambake*. The Joy Byers composition was recorded by Elvis on February 21 or 22, 1967, at RCA's Nashville studios.

EPs:
• *Clambake*

LPs:
• *Clambake*

HEY JUDE

John Lennon's 1968 divorce from Cynthia Lennon was a rather messy affair, and their son, Julian, was greatly affected by it. While driving to see Julian, Paul McCartney began improvising a song to console him. Originally, the song began, "Hey, Jules, don't make it bad." He later changed the name to Jude because he thought it sounded better. In a 1980 *Playboy* interview, John Lennon revealed that he believed the song was about *him*.

"Hey Jude" (Apple 2276) was the first release on the Beatles' Apple Records label. It entered *Billboard*'s Hot 100 chart at #10 in September 1968. Two weeks later it was number one, where it stayed for nine weeks—longer than any other Beatle single. "Hey Jude," which had worldwide sales of over six million copies, is the longest record, at 7 minutes, 11 seconds, ever to become number one on the Hot 100 chart. In addition to the Beatles, backing instrumentation included a 40-piece orchestra conducted by George Martin.

An instrumental track for Elvis's version was recorded on January 22, 1969, at American Sound Studios in Memphis. Elvis recorded a vocal track at a later date. He would sometimes sing "Hey Jude" in concert in a medley with "Yesterday."

LPs:
• *Elvis Aron Presley* (Las Vegas; August 1969) (in medley with "Yesterday")
• *Elvis Now*
• *On Stage—February, 1970* (Las Vegas; August 25, 1969) (in medley with "Yesterday")

Bootleg LPs:
• *The Legend Lives On* (Las Vegas; August 1969) (in medley with "Yesterday")
• *The Monologue L.P.* (Las Vegas; July 31, 1969)
• *Superstar Outtakes* (Las Vegas; August, 1969) (in medley with "Yesterday")

HEY, LITTLE GIRL

"Hey, Little Girl" was sung by Elvis in his 1965 movie *Harum Scarum*. The song was recorded in February (probably the 24th) 1965 at RCA's Nashville studios. Joy Byers is the composer.

LPs:
• *Harum Scarum*

HIGH HEEL SNEAKERS

"High Heel Sneakers" was written by Robert Higginbotham and recorded by him under the name Tommy Tucker in 1964. Tucker's recording (Checker 1067), using the title "Hi-Heel Sneakers," reached #11 on *Billboard*'s Hot 100 chart. Other popular recordings of the song include those by Jerry Lee Lewis (Smash 1930) in 1964, Stevie Wonder (Tamla 54119) in 1965, Ramsey Lewis (Cadet 5531) in 1966, and José Feliciano (RCA 47-9641) in 1968.

---

[1]"Help Me Make It Through the Night" was the first release of Mega Records.

∪

Elvis recorded "High Heel Sneakers" on September 11, 1967, at RCA's Nashville studios. Charlie McCoy played harmonica on the recording. It would be 13 years before "High Heel Sneakers" appeared on an album. The single release did not chart.

Singles:
- "Guitar Man"/"HIGH HEEL SNEAKERS" (RCA 47-9425) January 1968. Standard release. The original picture sleeve read, "Coming Soon, ELVIS' GOLD RECORDS, VOLUME 4." A month later, the sleeve was changed to read, "Ask for ELVIS' GOLD RECORDS, VOLUME 4."
- "Guitar Man"/"HIGH HEEL SNEAKERS" (RCA 447-0663) 1970. Gold Standard Series reissue.

LPs:
- *Elvis Aron Presley*
- *Reconsider Baby*

HIS HAND IN MINE
This gospel song was recorded by Elvis on October 30, 1960, at RCA's Nashville studios. His single release did not chart. "His Hand in Mine" was written by Mosie Lister.

Singles:
- "How Great Thou Art"/"HIS HAND IN MINE" (RCA 74-0130) April 1969. Standard release.
- "How Great Thou Art"/"HIS HAND IN MINE" (RCA 447-0670) December 1970. Gold Standard Series reissue.

LPs:
- *His Hand in Mine*

(MARIE'S THE NAME) HIS LATEST FLAME
Elvis recorded "(Marie's the Name) His Latest Flame" on June 26, 1961, at RCA's Nashville studios. At about the same time, Del Shannon recorded the song for his August 1961 album *Runaway* (Big Top 1303). Elvis's single release had an 11-week stay on *Billboard*'s Hot 100 chart, peaking at #4. In England it was number one for four weeks. "(Marie's the Name) His Latest Flame" sold over a million copies. The 1981 documentary *This Is Elvis* used the song to open the film.

Singles:
- "Little Sister"/"(MARIE'S THE NAME) HIS LATEST FLAME" (RCA 47-7908) August 1961. Standard release.
- "Little Sister"/"(MARIE'S THE NAME) HIS LATEST FLAME" (RCA 37-7908) August 1961. Compact 33 Single release.
- "Little Sister"/"(MARIE'S THE NAME) HIS LATEST FLAME" (RCA 447-0634) November 1962. Gold Standard Series reissue.
- "Little Sister"/"(MARIE'S THE NAME) HIS LATEST FLAME")RCA PB-13894) October 1984. One of six singles released in the boxed set *Elvis' Greatest Hits—Golden Singles, Volume 2* (RCA PP-13898). This single was pressed on gold vinyl with a special gold "50th" anniversary label.

EPs:
- *The EP Collection, Volume 2* (takes #1–6)

LPs:
- *Elvis' Golden Records, Volume 3*
- *Elvis: The Other Sides—Worldwide Gold Award Hits, Volume 2*
- *This Is Elvis*
- *The Top Ten Hits*

HOLIDAY INN
Elvis sang "Holiday Inn" as a spoof of "Heartbreak Hotel' on stage at the Nassau Coliseum in Uniondale, Long Island, on June 23, 1973.

HOLLY LEAVES AND CHRISTMAS TREES
Red West and Glen Spreen wrote "Holly Leaves and Christmas Trees" for Elvis, who recorded the song on May 15, 1971, at RCA's Nashville studios.

LPs:
- *Elvis Sings the Wonderful World of Christmas*

HOME IS WHERE THE HEART IS
Elvis sang "Home Is Where the Heart Is" in his 1962 film *Kid Galahad*. The song, written by Sherman Edwards and Hal David, was recorded on October 26, 1961, at Radio Recorders. The film version is mellower than that released on record (take #21).

Singles:
- "King of the Whole Wide World"/"HOME IS WHERE THE HEART IS" (RCA SP-45-118) May 1962. Disc jockey promotional release. This record came in a special sleeve promoting the Elvis EP *Kid Galahad*. No picture of Elvis was used.

EPs:
- *Kid Galahad*

LPs:
- *I Got Lucky*

Bootleg LPs:
- *Behind Closed Doors* (take #7)
- *The Complete Kid Galahad Session, Volume 1* (takes #1–10)
- *The Complete Kid Galahad Session, Volume 2* (takes #11–21)
- *A Dog's Life* (take #4)

HOME, SWEET, HOME
"Home, Sweet, Home" was written by American John Howard Payne[1] and Englishman Sir Henry Bishop in 1823 as the closing number to Act 1 of their opera *Clari*. It was introduced on stage on May 8, 1823, at London's Covent Garden by Maria Tree in the title role. Payne wrote his lyrics based in part on his own homesickness for America. Bishop's melody came from "A Sicilian Air," which he had written one year earlier. "Home, Sweet, Home" gained fame in America primarily through the performance of the renowned Jenny Lind. She used it as the closing number of her act.

In 1842 Henry Bishop was knighted by Queen Victoria for his "Home, Sweet, Home"—the first musician ever knighted.

During the Million-Dollar-Quartet session, Elvis sang "Home, Sweet, Home." While the band was playing the song, Elvis blurted out two lines of "When It Rains, It Really Pours" (You know what it takes, you've got it, baby").

Bootleg LPs:
- *The One Million Dollar Quartet* (Sun Records; December 4, 1956)

---

[1]Payne was a descendant of Robert Treat Paine, one of the signers of the Declaration of Independence.

HOOKED ON A FEELING

Mark James wrote "Hooked on a Feeling" in 1968 and B. J. Thomas recorded the tune at American Sound Studios late that year. His recording (Scepter 12230) reached #5 on the Hot 100 chart in early 1969 and became a million-seller. Five years later, the Swedish group Blue Swede took "Hooked on a Feeling" (EMI 3627) to number one, thus becoming the first Swedish group to top the American charts.

Elvis is thought by some to have recorded "Hooked on a Feeling" in the early 1970s, but no tape has yet surfaced.

HOT DOG

Elvis sang "Hot Dog" three times in his 1957 film *Loving You.* He recorded the song, which was written by Jerry Leiber and Mike Stoller, at Radio Recorders in Hollywood in February 1957.

EPs:
• *Loving You, Volume 2*

LPs:
• *Elvis: The Other Sides—Worldwide Gold Award Hits, Volume 2*
• *Essential Elvis—The First Movies*
• *Loving You*

Bootleg LPs:
• *Got a Lot o' Livin' to Do!* (*Loving You* soundtrack, two versions)
• *Loving You* (*Loving You* soundtrack, three versions)

HOUND DOG

In August 1952 bandleader Johnny Otis called songwriters Jerry Leiber and Mike Stoller and urged them to compose a song for blues singer Willie Mae (Big Mama) Thornton. After meeting with her at Otis's house, they rushed back to Stoller's house and wrote "Hound Dog" in about eight minutes. Originally, the song was about a gigolo.

Big Mama Thornton recorded "Hound Dog" in early 1953. Her version reached number one for six weeks on *Billboard*'s rhythm & blues chart. The record label listed her band as Kansas City Bill's Orchestra, but the group was actually Otis's. Otis, a white musician, played drums on the recording and was credited on the label as the song's composer. Leiber and Stoller had to go to court to get their writers' royalties.

Several cover versions of "Hound Dog" were released in 1953, including those by Tommy Duncan (Intro 6071), former lead singer for the Bob Wills Orchestra, Little Esther Phillips (Federal 12126),[1] Billy Starr (Imperial 8186), and John Brim (Checker 769), who used the title "Rattlesnake."

Almost as soon as Thornton's version of "Hound Dog" was released, Sam Phillips wrote "Bear Cat" as an answer record. Rufus Thomas recorded the song for Phillips's Sun label (Sun 181) on March 8, 1953. Don Robey of Peacock Records in Houston sued Phillips, claiming that "Bear Cat" was a plagiarism of "Hound Dog." After a U.S. District Court ruled in favor of

(Photo courtesy Don Fink)

Robey, an agreement was reached whereby Hi-Lo Music would pay a royalty of two cents to Lion Publishing for every copy of "Bear Cat" sold. Phillips also agreed to change the record label from "Bear Cat (the Answer to Hound Dog)" by Rufus (Hound Dog) Thomas Jr. to "Bear Cat" by Rufus Thomas, Jr. Thomas's band was thereafter known as the Bear Cats.

In 1955 an obscure group named Freddie Bell and the Bellboys recorded a comical version of "Hound Dog" (Teen 101) in which they added the lines: "You ain't never caught a rabbit. You ain't no friend of mine." Although certainly aware of Big Mama Thornton's original version of "Hound Dog," it was the version by Freddie Bell and the Bellboys that Elvis liked and copied. He first heard the group sing the song in Las Vegas while he was appearing at the New Frontier Hotel in late April–early May 1956. When time would allow, Elvis, Scotty Moore, Bill Black, and D. J. Fontanta would catch the Bellboys' act in the lounge. Soon after, Elvis added "Hound Dog" to his repertoire. It was such a crowd favorite that he began using "Hound Dog" as his closing number. D. J. Fontana stole his drum phrasing from Chick Greeney of the Bellboys.

Elvis sang "Hound Dog" during his second appearance on "The Milton Berle Show" (June 5, 1956) and on "The Steve Allen Show" (July 1, 1956). During the latter show he sang it to a basset hound named Sherlock while wearing a tuxedo.

On July 2, 1956, Elvis went into RCA's New York City studios to record "Hound Dog." It was the first song on which the vocal talents of the Jordanaires were used. Take #31 was selected by RCA for release. "Hound Dog" had a 28-week stay on *Billboard*'s Top 100 chart, peaking at #2 for three weeks. The Platters' "My

---

[1]Pete Lewis played guitar on both Big Mama Thornton's version and Little Esther's cover version.

Prayer" and then "Don't Be Cruel" kept "Hound Dog" from the top spot. The song was number one for five weeks on the country chart and number one for one week on the rhythm & blues chart. In England, "Hound Dog" peaked at #2. Sales in 1956 alone exceeded six million copies. To date, total sales have reached nine million copies.

"Hound Dog" was sung on all three "Ed Sullivan Show" appearances (September 9, 1956; October 28, 1956; January 6, 1957), Elvis's last "Louisiana Hayride" appearance (December 16, 1956), the 1968 "Elvis" TV special (December 3, 1968), the "Elvis: Aloha from Hawaii" TV special (January 14, 1973), and "Elvis in Concert" (October 3, 1977). The 1981 documentary *This Is Elvis* used clips from the Milton Berle and Steve Allen shows.

Singles:

- "Don't Be Cruel"/"HOUND DOG" (RCA 20-6604) July 1956. Standard 78 RPM release.
- "Don't Be Cruel"/"HOUND DOG" (RCA 47-6604) July 1956. Standard 45 RPM release. Both song titles are listed on the same side of the picture sleeve. On some sleeves "Don't Be Cruel" is above "Hound Dog"; on others the positions are reversed.
- "Don't Be Cruel"/"HOUND DOG" (RCA 447-0608) March 1959. Gold Standard Series reissue.
- "Don't Be Cruel"/"HOUND DOG" (RCA PB-11099) October 1977. One of 15 singles in the boxed set *15 Golden Records—30 Golden Hits* (RCA PP-11301), and one of 10 singles in the *20 Golden Hits in Full Color Sleeves* (RCA PP-11340) boxed set.
- "The Elvis Medley"/"Always on My Mind" (RCA PB-13351) November 1982. "Hound Dog" is in a medley with "Jailhouse Rock," Teddy Bear," "Don't Be Cruel," "Burning Love," and "Suspicious Minds."
- "The Elvis Medley"/"The Elvis Medley" (short version) (RCA JB-13351) November 1982. Disc jockey promotional release pressed on gold vinyl.
- "HOUND DOG"/"Baby, Let's Play House" (RCA PB-13875) August 1984. This single was released in the Memphis-Tupelo area to begin the yearlong celebration of the 50th anniversary of Elvis's birth. Pressed on gold vinyl, the record had a special gold "50th" anniversary label. Both songs were from performances at the Mississippi-Alabama Fair and Dairy Show on September 26, 1956.
- "HOUND DOG"/"Baby, Let's Play House" (RCA JB-13875) August 1984. Disc jockey promotional release.
- "Don't Be Cruel"/"HOUND DOG" (RCA PB-13886) October 1984. One of six singles in the boxed set *Elvis' Greatest Hits—Golden Singles, Volume 1* (RCA PP-13897). The record was pressed on gold vinyl with a special gold "50th" anniversary label.

EPs:

- *Elvis Presley* (RCA SPD-23)
- *The Real Elvis*

LPs:

- *Aloha from Hawaii via Satellite* (Honolulu; January 14, 1973)
- *Elvis* (RCA DPL2-0056[e])
- *Elvis—A Legendary Performer, Volume 3*
- *Elvis Aron Presley* (USS *Arizona* Memorial; March 25, 1961) (Dallas; June 6, 1975)
- *Elvis as Recorded at Madison Square Garden* (June 10, 1972)
- *Elvis' Golden Records*
- *Elvis in Concert* (Rapid City, South Dakota; June 21, 1977)
- *Elvis in Person* (Las Vegas; August 26, 1969)
- *The Elvis Medley*
- *Elvis Recorded Live on Stage in Memphis* (Memphis; March 20, 1974) (in medley with "Long Tall Sally," "Whole Lotta Shakin' Goin' On," "Your Mama Don't Dance," "Flip, Flop and Fly," and "Jailhouse Rock")
- *Elvis: The First Live Recordings* ("Louisiana Hayride"; December 16, 1956)
- *Elvis—TV Special* ("Elvis" TV special taping; June 29, 1968, at the 6:00 P.M. show)
- *Elvis: Worldwide 50 Gold Award Hits, Volume 1*
- *From Memphis to Vegas/From Vegas to Memphis* (Las Vegas; August 26, 1969)
- *A Golden Celebration* ("The Milton Berle Show"; June 5, 1956) ("The Steve Allen Show"; July 1, 1956) (Tupelo, Mississippi; September 26, 1956, both afternoon and evening shows) ("The Ed Sullivan Show"; September 9, 1956; October 28, 1956; January 6, 1957)
- *The Number One Hits*
- *This Is Elvis* ("The Milton Berle Show"; June 5, 1956) ("The Steve Allen Show"; July 1, 1956)
- *The Top Ten Hits*

Bootleg LPs:

- *Aloha Rehearsal Show—Kui Lee Cancer Benefit* (rehearsal concert for Elvis: Aloha from Hawaii"; June 12, 1973)
- *America's Own* (Uniondale, N.Y.; July 19, 1975)
- *Big Boss Man* (Las Vegas; August 19, 1974)
- *The Burbank Sessions, Volume 2* ("Elvis" TV special taping; June 29, 1968, at 6:00 P.M. and 8:00 P.M. shows)
- *Cadillac Elvis* ("The Steve Allen Show"; July 1, 1956)
- *Elvis' 1961 Hawaii Benefit Concert* (USS *Arizona* Memorial; March 25, 1961)
- *Eternal Elvis, Volume 2* ("The Steve Allen Show"; July 1, 1956)
- *From Hollywood to Vegas* (Las Vegas; ?) (in medley with "Whole Lotta Shakin' Goin' On," "Your Mama Don't Dance," and "Flip, Flop and Fly")
- *From Las Vegas . . . to Niagara Falls* (Las Vegas; September 3, 1973) (in medley with "Long Tall Sally," "Whole Lotta Shakin' Goin' On," "Your Mama Don't Dance," and "Flip, Flop and Fly") (Niagara Falls, N.Y.; June 24, 1974)
- *From the Waist Up* ("The Ed Sullivan Show"; September 9, 1956; October 28, 1956; January 6, 1957)
- *The Hillbilly Cat "Live"* (Las Vegas; August 1970)
- *The Hillbilly Cat, 1954–1974, Volume 1* ("The Ed Sullivan Show"; September 9, 1956; October 28, 1956)
- *The King Goes Wild* ("The Ed Sullivan Show"; September 9, 1956; October 28, 1956; January 6, 1957)
- *The Last Farewell* (Indianapolis; June 26, 1977)
- *The Rockin' Rebel* ("The Milton Berle Show"; June 5, 1956)
- *The Rockin' Rebel, Volume 3* ("The Steve Allen Show"; July 1, 1956) ("The Ed Sullivan Show"; September 9, 1956)
- *Rockin' with Elvis April Fool's Day* (Las Vegas; April 1, 1975)
- *Rockin' with Elvis New Year's Eve Pittsburgh, Pa. Dec. 31, 1976* (Pittsburgh; December 31, 1976)
- *The Sun Years* ("The Ed Sullivan Show"; September 9, 1956)
- *Superstar Outtakes* ("The Steve Allen Show"; July 1, 1956)
- *The Vegas Years, 1972–1975* ("The Ed Sullivan Show"; October 28, 1956) (Las Vegas; 1972)

HOUSE OF SAND

Elvis sang "House of Sand" in his 1966 film *Paradise, Hawaiian Style*. The instrumental track was recorded on July 27, 1965, at Radio Recorders. Elvis's vocal track was done on August 2, 3, or 4. Take #1 was chosen by RCA for release. The film version had a different beginning. "House of Sand" was written by Bill Giant, Bernie Baum, and Florence Kaye.

LPs:

- *Paradise, Hawaiian Style*

HOUSE OF THE RISING SUN

"House of the Rising Sun" is a traditional folk song whose origin is unknown. While growing up in England in the 1950s, Eric Burdon was fascinated by black American music. One of his favorite recordings was "House of the Rising Sun" by Josh White. When Burdon joined the Alan Price Combo in 1962, he urged the group to add the song to its concert repertoire. They based their version of "House of the Rising Sun" on one by Bob Dylan on his 1962 LP *Bob Dylan* (Columbia CS 8579). The Animals (the newly renamed Alan Price Combo) recorded the song in 1964, with Eric Burdon as lead vocalist. "House of the Rising Sun" (MGM 13264), with an arrangement by Alan Price, reached number one in both the United States and England, easily becoming a million-seller.

Elvis sang "House of the Rising Sun" in concert in the 1970s on a few occasions.

A HOUSE THAT HAS EVERYTHING

Elvis sang "A House That Has Everything" in his 1967 film *Clambake*. He recorded the song at RCA's Nashville studios on February 21, 1967. The film version had added instrumentation. " A House That Has Everything" was written by Sid Tepper and Roy C. Bennett.

EPs:
• *Clambake*

LPs:
• *Clambake*

HOW CAN YOU LOSE WHAT YOU NEVER HAD

Although recorded for Elvis's 1967 film *Clambake*, "How Can You Lose What You Never Had" was cut from the final print. The recording session took place on February 22, 1967, at RCA's Nashville studios. Sid Wayne and Ben Weisman are the composers.

LPs:
• *Clambake*

HOW DO YOU THINK I FEEL

Wayne P. Walker and Webb Pierce wrote "How Do You Think I Feel" in 1954. One of the first recordings was by Jimmie Rodgers Snow later that year (RCA 47-5900). In December 1954, Scotty Moore recorded an instrumental version of "How Do You Think I Feel" at Sun Records with Bill Black on bass and Johnny Bernero on drums. The recording was never released.

Elvis recorded "How Do You Think I Feel" on September 1, 1956, at Radio Recorders. Take #7 was chosen by RCA for release.

EPs:
• *Strictly Elvis*

LPs:
• *Elvis* (RCA LPM-1382)

HOW GREAT THOU ART

"How Great Thou Art" was written in 1886 by a Swedish minister, Rev. Carl Boberg, using the title "O Store Gud" ("Oh Great God"). It was translated into German in 1907 under the title "Wie Gross Bist Du" ("How Great Thou Art"). English missionary Rev. Stuart K. Hine found a Russian version of the song while in the Ukraine and translated it into English. Hine added a fourth verse in 1948. George Beverly Shea had a popular recording of "How Great Thou Art" (RCA 47-6068) in 1955, as did the Blackwood Brothers (RCA 47-7130) in late 1957. The Jordanaires sang the hymn at a March 1963 memorial service for Patsy Cline, Hawkshaw Hawkins, and Cowboy Copas at the Grand Ole Opry.

Elvis recorded "How Great Thou Art" on May 25, 1966, at RCA's Nashville studios. His single release three years later did not chart. However, a live version from the 1974 album *Elvis Recorded Live on Stage in Memphis* won Elvis his third and final Grammy Award for Best Inspirational Performance. Another live version, this one from Omaha, Nebraska, on June 19, 1977, was used on the 1977 CBS-TV special "Elvis in Concert."

Singles:
• "HOW GREAT THOU ART"/"So High" (RCA SP-45-162) April 1967. Disc jockey promotional release. This record was used to promote the *How Great Thou Art* LP and the special Palm Sunday radio program.
• "HOW GREAT THOU ART"/"His Hand in Mine" (RCA 74-0130) April 1969. Standard release.
• "HOW GREAT THOU ART"/"His Hand in Mine" (RCA 447-0670) December 1970. Gold Standard Series reissue.

LPs:
• *Elvis—A Legendary Performer, Volume 2*
• *Elvis Aron Presley* (Dallas; June 6, 1975)
• *Elvis in Concert* (Omaha, Nebraska; June 19, 1977)
• *Elvis Recorded Live on Stage in Memphis* (March 20, 1974)
• *He Walks Beside Me*
• *How Great Thou Art*

Bootleg LPs:
• *Elvis Presley Is Alive and Well and Singing in Las Vegas, Volume 1* (Las Vegas; August 1975)
• *Rockin' with Elvis April Fool's Day* (Las Vegas; April 1, 1975)
• *The Vegas Years, 1972–1975* (Las Vegas; August 1975)

HOW THE WEB WAS WOVEN

A July 1970 rehearsal of "How the Web Was Woven" at MGM was shown in the 1970 documentary *Elvis—That's the Way It Is*. The version on the soundtrack album, however, was recorded at RCA's Nashville studios on June 5, 1970. "How the Web Was Woven" was written by Clive Westlake and David Most.

LPs:
• *That's the Way It Is*

Bootleg LPs:
• *The King: From the Dark to the Light* (*Elvis—That's the Way It Is* soundtrack)
• *That's the Way It Is* (*Elvis—That's the Way It Is* soundtrack)

HOW WOULD YOU LIKE TO BE

Elvis sang "How Would You Like to Be" in his 1963 film *It Happened at the World's Fair*. The song was recorded in September 1962 at Radio Recorders in

Hollywood. Originally, the producers of the 1968 TV special "Elvis" planned to use "How Would You Like to Be" in a medley of movie songs, but the idea was scrapped. Ben Raleigh and Mark Barkan composed the song. The 1966 single release of "How Would You Like to Be" did not chart.

Singles:
- "If Every Day Was Like Christmas"/"HOW WOULD YOU LIKE TO BE" (RCA 47-8950) November 25, 1966. Standard release.
- "If Every Day Was Like Christmas"/"HOW WOULD YOU LIKE TO BE" (RCA 447-0681) May 1972. Gold Standard Series reissue.

LPs:
- *Elvis Sings for Children and Grownups Too!*
- *Elvis Sings Hits from His Movies, Volume 1*
- *It Happened at the World's Fair*

HOW'S THE WORLD TREATING YOU

Chet Atkins was inspired to write this song after hearing the 1939 Johnny Burke–Bob Haggard tune "What's New."[1] The song's first line was "What's new, how's the world treating you?" Boudleaux Bryant is co-composer of "How's the World Treating You." The Louvin Brothers had a 1961 country hit with the song (Capitol 4628).

Elvis recorded "How's the World Treating You" on September 1, 1956, at RCA's Nashville studios. Take #7 was released by RCA on record.

EPs:
- *Strictly Elvis*

LPs:
- *Elvis* (RCA LPM-1382)

HURT

"Hurt" was written by Jimmie Craine and Al Jacobs and first recorded by Roy Hamilton (Epic 9086) in 1954. His recording was a #7 rhythm & blues hit. In 1961 Timi Yoro took her version of "Hurt" to #4 on *Billboard*'s Hot 100 chart. Clyde Otis produced her recording. Other popular versions of "Hurt" include those by Little Anthony and the Imperials (DCP 1154) in 1966, a 1967 Italian version ("A Chi") by Fausto Leali on RiFi Records, and by the Manhattans (Columbia 10140) in 1975. Leali's release sold a million copies worldwide.

Elvis recorded "Hurt" on the night of February 5–6, 1976, at Graceland. His single release was a million-seller and had an 11-week stay on *Billboard*'s Hot 100 chart, peaking at #28. It did much better on the country chart, reaching #6. "Hurt" was sung on the 1977 TV special "Elvis in Concert."

Singles:
- "HURT"/"For the Heart" (RCA PB-10601) March 1976. Standard release.
- "HURT"/"For the Heart" (RCA JB-10106) March 1976. Gold Standard Series reissue.

LPs:
- *Always on My Mind*
- *Elvis in Concert* (Rapid City, South Dakota; June 21, 1977)
- *From Elvis Presley Boulevard, Memphis, Tennessee*

Bootleg LPs:
- *The Last Farewell* (Indianapolis; June 26, 1977)
- *Rockin' with Elvis New Year's Eve Pittsburgh, Pa. Dec. 31, 1976* (Pittsburgh; December 31, 1976)

HUSKY DUSKY DAY

Elvis and Hope Lange sang "Husky Dusky Day" briefly as a duet in the 1961 film *Wild in the Country*. The song, which should properly be called "Husky *Dusty* Day," was recorded on the movie set, not in a recording studio. "Husky Dusky Day" has never been released by RCA.

Bootleg LPs:
- *Eternal Elvis* (*Wild in the Country* soundtrack)
- *From Hollywood to Vegas* (*Wild in the Country* soundtrack)

---

[1] In 1983 Linda Ronstadt recorded the album *What's New* (Asylum 60260) with the Nelson Riddle Orchestra. The LP, which was produced by Peter Asher (of Peter and Gordon), reached #3 on *Billboard*'s Top LPs chart.

I APOLOGIZE

"I Apologize" was a pop standard of the 1930s written by Al Hoffman, Al Goodhart, and Ed Nelson. Both Bing Crosby (Brunswick 6179) and Nat Shilkret and the Victor Orchestra (Victor 22781) had hit recordings of the song in 1931. Shilkret's version featured Jimmy Dorsey on clarinet and alto saxophone. In 1951 Billy Eckstine had a #8 pop hit and million-seller with "I Apologize" (MGM 10903). His recording reached #4 on the rhythm & blues chart. Timi Yuro had modest success with a 1961 release (#72 Hot 100 chart) on Liberty Records (Liberty 55343).

Some sources have suggested that Elvis recorded "I Apologize" while at Sun Records, but there is as yet no supporting evidence.

I BEG OF YOU

Elvis first recorded "I Beg of You" on January 13, 1957, at Radio Recorders, but the master (take #12) was not released. The version that *was* released was take #34 from a recording session on February 23, 1957. "I Beg of You" was composed by Rose Marie McCoy and Kelly Owens. Elvis's single release had a 12-week stay on the Top 100 chart, peaking at #8. "I Beg of You" reached #2 on the country chart and #4 on the rhythm & blues chart. Sales of over one million copies were achieved.

Singles:
• "Don't"/"I BEG OF YOU" (RCA 20-7150) January 1958. Standard 78 RPM release.
• "Don't"/"I BEG OF YOU" (RCA 47-7150) January 1958. Standard 45 RPM release.
• "Don't"/"I BEG OF YOU" (RCA 447-0621) 1961. Gold Standard Series reissue.

EPs:
• *A Touch of Gold, Volume 1*

LPs:
• *Elvis: Worldwide 50 Gold Award Hits, Volume 1*
• *50,000,000 Elvis Fans Can't Be Wrong—Elvis' Gold Records, Volume 2*
• *The Top Ten Hits*

I BELIEVE

"I Believe" was written by Ervin Drake, Irvin Graham, Jimmy Shirl, and Al Stillman, and introduced by Jane Froman in her TV series "Jane Froman's U.S.A. Canteen" in late 1952. Her recording of the song (Capitol 2332) in early 1953 reached #11 on *Billboard*'s Best-Selling Singles chart. "I Believe" was the first song in television history to become a hit as a direct result of exposure on the air. Also in 1953, James Elmore had a #9 rhythm & blues hit with the song on Meteor Records (Meteor 5000). Actually, his recording was released a few days before Froman's. The big hit in 1953, however, was by Frankie Laine. His version of "I Believe" (Columbia 39938) reached #2 and sold over a million copies. In England, it set a record that still stands—it was

number one for 18 weeks (nonconsecutive). The Bachelors had a #7 Easy-Listening hit and million-seller in 1964 with their recording (London 9672).

Elvis recorded "I Believe" on January 12, 1957, at Radio Recorders. RCA chose take #9 for release.

EPs:
• *Peace in the Valley*

LPs:
• *Elvis' Christmas Album*
• *You'll Never Walk Alone*

I BELIEVE IN THE MAN IN THE SKY

Elvis recorded "I Believe in the Man in the Sky" on October 30, 1960, at RCA's Nashville studios during the *His Hand in Mine* sessions. Richard Howard is the composer.

Singles:
• "Crying in the Chapel"/"I BELIEVE IN THE MAN IN THE SKY" (RCA 447-0643) April 1965. Gold Standard Series original release.

LPs:
• *Elvis: The Other Sides—Worldwide Gold Award Hits, Volume 2*
• *His Hand in Mine*

I CAN HELP

Billy Swan wrote and recorded "I Can Help" (Monument 8621) in 1974. His recording reached number one on *Billboard*'s Hot 100 chart and became a million-seller. The idea for the song came when Kris Kristofferson and his wife, Rita Coolidge, bought Swan a little RMI organ as a wedding present. Swan was tinkering with the organ one day when he became fascinated with a series of chords. The song was written based on those chords.

Elvis recorded "I Can Help" (copying Billy Swan's arrangement) on March 11, 1975, at RCA's Hollywood studios.

LPs:
• *Elvis Aron Presley—Forever*
• *Elvis Today*
• *Our Memories of Elvis, Volume 2* (without overdubbing)

I CAN SEE CLEARLY NOW

Johnny Nash wrote and recorded "I Can See Clearly Now" (Epic 10902) in 1972 in Jamaica. A few of Bob Marley's Wailers backed Nash instrumentally. "I Can See Clearly Now" reached number one on both the Hot 100 and Easy-Listening charts and soon became a million-seller.

Elvis is known to have sung "I Can See Clearly Now" in concert in the 1970s.

I CAN'T STOP LOVIN' YOU

Don Gibson wrote "I Can't Stop Lovin' You" in 1957 in a mobile home in Knoxville, Tennessee. His recording (RCA 47-7133) hit number one on the country chart in

1958 and sold over a million copies (as did the flip side, "Oh Lonesome Me"). Kitty Wells's version (Decca 30551) also charted in 1958 (#8 on the country chart). In 1962 Ray Charles included "I Can't Stop Loving You" in his best-selling LP *Modern Sounds in Country and Western Music* (ABC-Paramount ABCS-410), the first Gold album for ABC-Paramount Records. His single release from the album reached number one on the Hot 100 chart, rhythm & blues chart, and the Easy-Listening chart. "I Can't Stop Loving You" was the number one song of 1962 and a million-seller. Even Count Basie recorded an instrumental version of the song (Reprise 20170).

Elvis sang "I Can't Stop Loving You" in concert on quite a few occasions, and in his 1973 TV special "Elvis: Aloha from Hawaii." It is these live versions that appear on record.

EPs:
• *Aloha from Hawaii via Satellite*

LPs:
• *Aloha from Hawaii via Satellite* (Honolulu; January 14, 1973)
• *Elvis as Recorded at Madison Square Garden* (June 10, 1972)
• *Elvis in Person* (Las Vegas; August 25, 1969)
• *Elvis Recorded Live on Stage in Memphis* (Memphis; March 20, 1974) (in medley with "Blueberry Hill")
• *From Memphis to Vegas/From Vegas to Memphis* (Las Vegas; August 25, 1969)
• *Welcome to My World* (Madison Square Garden; June 10, 1972, at the afternoon show)

Bootleg LPs:
• *From Las Vegas . . . to Niagara Falls* (Las Vegas; September 3, 1973) (Niagara Falls, N.Y.; June 24, 1974)
• *The Last Farewell* (Indianapolis; June 26, 1977)

I DON'T CARE IF THE SUN DON'T SHINE
"I Don't Care If the Sun Don't Shine" was written by Mack David in 1949 for the Walt Disney animated film *Cinderella.* It was not used, however. In 1950 several versions of the song were released. Perhaps the first was Patti Page's (Mercury 5296). Others soon followed, including those by LeRoy Holmes (MGM 10685) and Dean Martin[1] (Capitol 981). In 1951 Georgia Gibbs had a popular version of "I Don't Care If the Sun Don't Shine" on Coral Records (Coral 60210).

Elvis recorded "I Don't Care If the Sun Don't Shine" on September 10, 1954, at Sun Records. Marion Keisker added a verse to Elvis's version and Buddy Cunningham played drums (actually, an empty record box). He's never been credited on the session.

When Elvis signed with RCA Records in November 1955, RCA reissued all five of his Sun singles. On the strength of its appearance on the EP *Any Way You Want Me*, "I Don't Care If the Sun Don't Shine" reached #74 on *Billboard*'s Top 100 chart in October 1956, staying on the chart for six weeks.

Singles:
• "Good Rockin' Tonight"/"I DON'T CARE IF THE SUN DON'T SHINE" (Sun 210) September 25, 1954. Standard Sun 78 RPM and 45 RPM releases.
• "Good Rockin' Tonight"/"I DON'T CARE IF THE SUN DON'T SHINE" (RCA 20-6381) November 1955. RCA 78 RPM reissue of the Sun original.
• "Good Rockin' Tonight"/"I DON'T CARE IF THE SUN DON'T SHINE" (RCA 47-6381) November 1955. RCA 45 RPM reissue of the Sun original.
• "Good Rockin' Tonight"/"I DON'T CARE IF THE SUN DON'T SHINE" (RCA 447-0602) March 1959. Gold Standard Series reissue.

EPs:
• *Any Way You Want Me*
• *Good Rockin' Tonight*

LPs:
• *The Complete Sun Sessions* (master and outtake)
• *A Golden Celebration* (alternate take)
• *The Sun Sessions* (alternate mix)

Bootleg LPs:
• *Good Rocking Tonight* (alternate take preceded by two false starts)
• *The Rockin' Rebel* (alternate take)
• *The Sun Years* (portions of the commercial release)

I DON'T HURT ANYMORE
Hank Snow had a million-seller with this Don Robertson–Jack Rollins song in 1954. "I Don't Hurt Anymore" (RCA 47-5698) reached number one on the country chart and had an incredible stay of 41 weeks. (In 1988 Curad Bandages used the song in its TV commercials as "*It* Don't Hurt Anymore.")

Elvis is reported to have recorded "I Don't Hurt Anymore" while at Sun Records, but no evidence has surfaced.

I DON'T WANNA BE TIED
Elvis sang "I Don't Wanna Be Tied" in his 1962 film *Girls! Girls! Girls!* He recorded the song in March 1962 at Radio Recorders. As the master, RCA chose a splice of takes #8 and #10. Bill Giant, Bernie Baum, and Florence Kaye are the composers.

LPs:
• *Girls! Girls! Girls!*

Bootleg LPs:
• *Elvis Rocks and the Girls Roll* (alternate take)

I DON'T WANT TO
"I Don't Want To" was written by Janice Torre and Fred Spielman for Elvis's 1962 film *Girls! Girls! Girls!*, but it was cut from the final print. The song does, however, appear in the trailer for the film. Elvis recorded "I Don't Want To" in March 1962 at Radio Recorders.

LPs:
• *Girls! Girls! Girls!*

I FEEL SO BAD
Chuck Willis wrote and recorded "I Feel So Bad" (Okeh 7029) in 1954, using the title "Feel So Bad." The recording reached #8 on the rhythm & blues chart. Other popular versions include those by Little Milton

---

[1]Dean Martin sang this song in the 1951 Martin-Lewis movie *Scared Stiff.*

(Checker 1162) in 1967 and Ray Charles (ABC 11308) in 1971, both using the title "Feel So Bad."

Elvis recorded "I Feel So Bad" on March 12, 1961, at RCA's Nashville studios. He copied Willis's version almost note for note, including a blown line. Both versions featured a piano and saxophone (Floyd Cramer and Boots Randolph played on Elvis's recording). Elvis's single release had a nine-week stay on *Billboard*'s Hot 100 chart, peaking at #5. It reached #15 on the rhythm & blues chart. Sales of over one million copies are claimed.

Singles:
- "I FEEL SO BAD"/"Wild in the Country" (RCA 47-7880) May 1961. Standard release.
- "I FEEL SO BAD"/"Wild in the Country" (RCA 37-7880) May 1961. Compact 33 Single release.
- "I FEEL SO BAD"/"Wild in the Country" (RCA 61-7880) May 1961. "Living Stereo" release.
- "I FEEL SO BAD"/"Wild in the Country" (RCA 447-0631) February 1962. Gold Standard Series reissue.

LPs:
- *Elvis' Golden Records, Volume 3*
- *Elvis: Worldwide 50 Gold Award Hits, Volume 1*
- *Reconsider Baby*
- *The Top Ten Hits*

I FEEL THAT I'VE KNOWN YOU FOREVER
Elvis sang "I Feel That I've Known You Forever" in his 1965 film *Tickle Me*. He actually recorded the song three years earlier, on March 19, 1962, at RCA's Nashville studios. Doc Pomus and Alan Jeffries are the composers.

EPs:
- *Tickle Me*

LPs:
- *Pot Luck*

Bootleg LPs:
- *Elvis Sings Songs from Tickle Me* (alternate take)

I FORGOT TO REMEMBER TO FORGET
"I Forgot to Remember to Forget" was written by Stanley Kesler and Charlie Feathers in 1955, and first recorded by Elvis in July of that year at Sun Records. Instrumentation was provided by Elvis (guitar), Scotty Moore (guitar), Bill Black (bass), and Johnny Bernero (drums). "I Forgot to Remember to Forget" reached number one on *Billboard*'s country chart and remained on the chart for an incredible 40 weeks—the longest of any Elvis single release on any *Billboard* chart. The sheet music from Hi-Lo Music featured the names of Elvis and Toni Arden as performers. While Elvis was at Sun, it was the only sheet music to mention him as the performer. Arden's release (RCA 20-6346) did not chart. Elvis frequently sang "I Forgot to Remember to Forget" on tour in late 1955, including performances on the "Louisiana Hayride."

"I Forgot to Remember to Forget" was one of the most recorded songs at Sun Records. Almost all of the Sun artists recorded it at one time or another, including co-composer Charlie Feathers. On Feathers's re-cording, co-composer Stanley Kesler played the fiddle. Perhaps the definitive version was Johnny Cash's 1958 sun release (Sun 321), which featured Charlie Rich on piano. Jerry Lee Lewis's February 9, 1961, recording of the song featured Hank Garland (guitar), Bob Moore (bass), and Buddy Harman (drums), all three of whom would later play for Elvis.

Singles:
- "Mystery Train"/"I FORGOT TO REMEMBER TO FORGET" (Sun 223) August 1955. Sun 78 RPM and 45 RPM release.
- "Mystery Train"/"I FORGOT TO REMEMBER TO FORGET" (RCA 20-6357) November 1955. RCA reissue of the Sun 78 RPM release.
- "Mystery Train"/"I FORGOT TO REMEMBER TO FORGET" (RCA 47-6357) November 1955. RCA reissue of the Sun 45 RPM release.
- "Mystery Train"/"I FORGOT TO REMEMBER TO FORGET" (RCA 447-0600) March 1959. Gold Standard Series reissue.

EPs:
- *Heartbreak Hotel*
- *SPD-15*

LPs:
- *The Complete Sun Sessions* (master)
- *A Date with Elvis* (alternate mix, with more reverberation)
- *The Sun Sessions* (alternate mix, with more reverberation)

Bootleg LPs:
- *Good Rocking Tonight* (Sun commercial release)
- *The Sun Years* (Sun commercial release)

I GOT A FEELIN' IN MY BODY
"I Got a Feelin' in My Body" was written by Dennis Linde and recorded by Elvis on December 10, 1973, at Stax Studios in Memphis. Composer Linde was overdubbed on guitar at a later date. "I Got a Feelin' in My Body" had a 13-week stay on *Billboard*'s country chart, peaking at #6. The single had no overdubbing.

Singles:
- "There's a Honky Tonk Angel"/"I GOT A FEELIN' IN MY BODY" (RCA PB-11679) August 1979. Standard release.
- "There's a Honky Tonk Angel"/"I GOT A FEELIN' IN MY BODY" (RCA JB-11679) August 1979. Disc jockey promotional release.

LPs:
- *Good Times*
- *Our Memories of Elvis, Volume 2* (without overdubbing)

I GOT A WOMAN
"I Got a Woman" was written and first recorded (using the title "I've Got a Woman") by Ray Charles in 1954 at radio station WGST, on the grounds of Georgia Tech University in Atlanta. Charles based the tune on the gospel song "My Jesus Is All the World I Need." His recording (Atlantic 1050) rose to #2 on *Billboard*'s rhythm & blues chart in early 1955. Other popular versions of "I Got a Woman" include those by Jimmy McGriff (Sue 770), a 1962 instrumental; Ricky Nelson (Decca 31475) in 1963; Freddie Scott (Colpix 709) in 1963; and Bob Luman (Epic 10755) in 1971. Both Charles and McGriff used the title "I've Got a Woman."

Elvis sang "I Got a Woman" on the "Louisiana Hayride" and on tour in 1955. Some speculate that he recorded the song while at Sun Records, but no proof exists.

At 2:00 P.M. on January 10, 1956, Elvis recorded "I Got a Woman" at RCA's Nashville studios. It was his first recording for RCA. Musicians on the session were Elvis, Scotty Moore, Bill Black, D. J. Fontana, and Floyd Cramer. Backing vocals were by Gordon Stoker, Ben Speer, and Brock Speer. "I Got a Woman" appeared on Elvis's first LP, *Elvis Presley*, and later in 1956 was released as a single. It did not chart. In England, "I Got a Woman" was released on albums with the title, "I Got a Sweetie."

Elvis sang "I Got a Woman" on his first appearance on "Stage Show" (January 28, 1956). A performance of the song at Hampton Roads, Virginia, on April 9, 1972, was used in the documentary *Elvis on Tour*. "I Got a Woman" was a staple of Elvis's concert repertoire in the 1970s. He often sang it in a medley with "Amen."

Singles:
- "I GOT A WOMAN"/"I'm Counting on You" (RCA 20-6637) September 1956. Standard 78 RPM release.
- "I GOT A WOMAN"/"I'm Counting on You" (RCA 47-6637) September 1956. Standard 45 RPM release.
- "I GOT A WOMAN"/"Money Honey" (RCA 47-6689) September 1956. Disc jockey "Record Prevue."
- "I GOT A WOMAN"/"I'm Counting on You" (RCA 447-0610) March 1959. Gold Standard Series reissue.

EPs:
- *Elvis Presley* (RCA EPA-747)
- *Elvis Presley* (RCA EPB-1254)
- *Elvis Presley* (RCA SPD-22)
- *Elvis Presley* (RCA SPD-23)
- *Elvis Presley—The Most Talked About New Personality in the Past Ten Years of Recorded Music* (RCA EPB-1254)

LPs:
- *Elvis Aron Presley* (Dallas; June 6, 1975)
- *Elvis in Concert* (Rapid City, South Dakota; June 21, 1977)
- *Elvis Presley*
- *Elvis Recorded Live on Stage in Memphis* (Memphis; March 20, 1974)
- *Elvis: The Hillbilly Cat* (Houston, at the Eagles' Hall; March 19, 1955)
- *A Golden Celebration* (Mississippi-Alabama Fair and Dairy Show; September 26, 1956, both afternoon and evening shows)
- *Pure Gold*

Bootleg LPs:
- *America's Own* (Uniondale, N.Y.; July 19, 1975)
- *Behind Closed Doors* (Las Vegas; August 22, 1969)
- *Dorsey Shows* ("Stage Show"; January 28, 1956)
- *Elvis' 1961 Hawaii Benefit Concert* (USS *Arizona* Memorial; March 25, 1961)
- *Elvis on Tour* (*Elvis on Tour* soundtrack)
- *Elvis Rocks and the Girls Roll* (dress rehearsal for "Elvis" TV special; June 1968)
- *The Entertainer* (Houston; January 29, 1955) (Las Vegas; February 1970)
- *The First Year—Recorded Live* (Houston; January 29, 1955)
- *The First Years* (Houston; January 29, 1955)
- *From Hollywood to Vegas* (*Elvis on Tour* soundtrack)
- *From Las Vegas . . . to Niagara Falls* (Las Vegas; September 3, 1973) Niagara Falls, N.Y.; June 24, 1974)
- *Got a Lot o' Livin' to Do!* (Vancouver, British Columbia; September 1, 1957)
- *The Hillbilly Cat "Live"* (Las Vegas; August 1970)
- *The King: From the Dark to the Light* (*Elvis on Tour* soundtrack)

- *The Last Farewell* (Indianapolis; June 26, 1977)
- *The Rockin' Rebel, Volume 2* (Houston; January 29, 1955)
- *Rockin' with Elvis April Fool's Day* (Las Vegas; April 1, 1975)
- *Rockin' with Elvis New Year's Eve Pittsburgh, Pa. Dec. 31, 1976* (Pittsburgh; December 31, 1976)
- *Sold Out* (Las Vegas; August 24, 1970)
- *Standing Room Only, Volume 3* (Houston; January 29, 1955)
- *Superstar Outtakes, Volume 2* ("Stage Show"; January 28, 1956)

I GOT LUCKY
Elvis sang "I Got Lucky" in his 1962 movie *Kid Galahad*. He recorded two versions of the song on October 27, 1961, at Radio Recorders. The version that was released was take #2 of the second version (2:08 in length). The master of the first version was take #6 (1:30 in length). Dolores Fuller, Fred Wise, and Ben Weisman are the composers.

EPs:
- *Kid Galahad*

LPs:
- *I Got Lucky*

Bootleg LPs:
- *Behind Closed Doors* (take #2 of the second version, with a longer intro)
- *The Complete Kid Galahad Session, Volume 3* (takes #1-6, first version; takes #1 and #2, second version)

I GOT STUNG
"I Got Stung" was written by Aaron Schroeder and David Hill and recorded by Elvis on June 11, 1958, at RCA's Nashville studios. It was the last song Elvis would record until March 20, 1960. RCA chose take #24 for release. The single release of "I Got Stung" had a 16-week stay on *Billboard*'s Hot 100 chart, peaking at #8. In England the song was number one for three weeks. According to RCA, "I Got Stung" was a million-seller.

Singles:
- "I GOT STUNG"/"One Night" (RCA 20-7410) October 1958. Standard 78 RPM release.
- "I GOT STUNG"/"One Night" (RCA 47-7410) October 1958. Standard 45 RPM release.
- "I GOT STUNG"/"One Night" (RCA 447-0624) 1961. Gold Standard Series reissue.
- "I GOT STUNG"/"One Night" (RCA PB-11112) October 1977. One of 15 singles in the boxed set *15 Golden Records—30 Golden Hits* (RCA PP-11301)

LPs:
- *Elvis* (RCA DPL2-0056[e])
- *Elvis: Worldwide 50 Gold Award Hits, Volume 1*
- *50,000,000 Elvis Fans Can't Be Wrong—Elvis' Gold Records, Volume 2*
- *The Top Ten Hits*

I GOTTA KNOW
Elvis recorded "I Gotta Know" on April 4, 1960, at RCA's Nashville studios. The single release reached #20 on *Billboard*'s Hot 100 chart during its 11-week stay and became a million-seller. "I Gotta Know" was written by Paul Evans and Matt Williams.

Singles:
- "Are You Lonesome Tonight?"/"I GOTTA KNOW" (RCA 47-7810) November 1960. Standard release.
- "Are You Lonesome Tonight?"/"I GOTTA KNOW" (RCA 61-7810) November 1960. "Living Stereo" release.
- "Are You Lonesome Tonight?"/"I GOTTA KNOW" (RCA 447-0604) February 1962. Gold Standard Series reissue.
- "Are You Lonesome Tonight?"/"I GOTTA KNOW" (RCA PB-11104) October 1977. One of 15 singles in the boxed set *15 Golden Records—30 Golden Hits* (RCA PP 11301), and one of 10 singles in the *20 Golden Hits in Full Color Sleeves* boxed set.

LPs:
- *Elvis' Golden Records, Volume 3*
- *Elvis: Worldwide 50 Gold Award Hits, Volume 1*

I HEAR A SWEET VOICE CALLING

Two lines of this Bill Monroe tune were sung at the Million-Dollar-Quartet session on December 4, 1956. Elvis sang lead, with harmony by Jerry Lee Lewis and Carl Perkins.

Bootleg LPs:
- *The Million Dollar Quartet* (Sun Records; December 4, 1956)
- *The One Million Dollar Quartet* (Sun Records; December 4, 1956)

I, JOHN

Elvis recorded this gospel song on June 9, 1971, at RCA's Nashville studios. An April 1972 backstage performance of "I, John" with the Stamps was seen in the 1972 documentary *Elvis on Tour*. "I, John" was composed by William Johnson, George McFadden, and Ted Brooks.

LPs:
- *He Touched Me*

Bootleg LPs:
- *Elvis on Tour* (*Elvis on Tour* soundtrack)
- *The King: From the Dark to the Light* (*Elvis on Tour* soundtrack)
- *The Monologue L.P.* (Las Vegas; July 31, 1969)
- *Sold Out* (Sahara Tahoe Hotel; August 1, 1971)
- *To Know Him Is to Love Him* (Las Vegas; 1969 or 1970)

I JUST CAN'T HELP BELIEVIN'

"I Just Can't Help Believin'" was written by Barry Mann and Cynthia Weil and recorded by Mann (Capitol 2217) in 1968. His recording did not chart. The next year, Bob Dileo (Columbia 44858) also had a version that did not chart. B. J. Thomas took "I Just Can't Help Believin'" (Scepter 12283) to #9 on *Billboard*'s Hot 100 chart and number one on the Easy-Listening chart in 1970. David Frizzell (Columbia 45238) had a #36 country hit with the song that same year.

Elvis's rehearsal of "I Just Can't Help Believin'" at the MGM studios in July 1970 was seen in the documentary *Elvis—That's the Way It Is*. Also seen was his performance at the International Hotel on August 13, 1970.

LPs:
- *That's the Way It Is* (Las Vegas; August 13, 1970)

Bootleg LPs:
- *The Hillbilly Cat "Live"* (Las Vegas; August 1970)

- *The King: From the Dark to the Light* (*Elvis—That's the Way It Is* soundtrack)
- *King of Las Vegas Live* (*Elvis—That's the Way It Is* soundtrack)
- *That's the Way It Is* (*Elvis—That's the Way It Is* soundtrack)

I JUST CAN'T MAKE IT BY MYSELF

This gospel song was sung by Elvis during the Million-Dollar-Quartet session on December 4, 1956. Jerry Lee Lewis provided the vocal harmony.

Bootleg LPs:
- *Million Dollar Quartet* (Sun Records; December 4, 1956)
- *The One Million Dollar Quartet* (Sun Records; December 4, 1956)

I LOVE ONLY ONE GIRL

Elvis sang "I Love Only One Girl" in his 1967 movie *Double Trouble*. The first few notes are the same as the beginning of "The Mickey Mouse Club March." Elvis recorded "I Love Only One Girl" in June 1966 at Radio Recorders. The film version had added instrumentation and was longer than that on record. Sid Tepper and Roy C. Bennett are the composers.

LPs:
- *Burning Love and Hits from His Movies, Volume 2*
- *Double Trouble*

I LOVE YOU BECAUSE

"I Love You Because" was written and recorded by blind performer Leon Payne (Capitol 40238) in late 1949. His version reached #4 on *Billboard*'s country chart. In early 1950 Ernest Tubb covered Payne's record, also peaking at #4. Other recordings of "I Love You Because" through the years include those by Jan Garber (Capitol 983) in 1950, Gene Autry (Columbia 20709) in 1950, Eddie Fisher (RCA 20-4619) in 1950, Patti Page (Mercury 5592) in 1951 (the flip side of "Mockingbird Hill"), Johnny Cash (Sun 334) in 1960, and Carl Smith (Columbia 44939) in 1969. The two biggest hit versions were by Al Martino (Capitol 4930), which hit #3 on the Hot 100 chart and number one on the Easy-Listening chart in 1963, and by Jim Reeves, whose 1964 recording (RCA 1385) became the only million-selling single release of "I Love You Because." In England alone, his recording sold almost 900,000 copies. It didn't chart in America until 1976, when it was reissued (RCA PB-10557).

Elvis recorded "I Love You Because" during his first commercial recording session at Sun Records on July 5, 1954. His only instrumental backing was Scotty Moore's guitar, Bill Black's bass, and his own guitar. Apparently, five takes were taped by Sam Phillips, but none deemed worthy of commercial release. However, after Elvis had skyrocketed to fame in 1956, RCA released a single of "I Love You Because" in September 1956, using a splice of takes #3 and #5. That same master had previously appeared on the *Elvis Presley* LP. Take #2 surfaced in 1974 on the LP *Elvis—A Legendary Performer, Volume 1*, and all five takes appeared on the 1987 LP *The Complete Sun Sessions*. Before the release of *The Complete Sun Sessions*, it had been understood that the master was a splice of takes #2 and #4 and that take #1 appeared on *Elvis—A*

Legendary Performer, Volume 1. Elvis is known to have sung "I Love You Because" on the "Louisiana Hayride" in 1954 and 1955.

A historical note: After the five takes of "I Love You Because," Elvis, Scotty and Bill started cutting up with "That's All Right (Mama)" during a break, and the rest, as they say, is history.

Singles:
- "Tryin' to Get to You"/"I LOVE YOU BECAUSE" (RCA 20-6639) September 1956. Standard 78 RPM release.
- "Tryin' to Get to You"/"I LOVE YOU BECAUSE" (RCA 47-6639) September 1956. Standard 45 RPM release.
- "Tryin' to Get to You"/"I LOVE YOU BECAUSE" (RCA 447-0612) March 1959. Gold Standard Series reissue.

EPs:
- *Elvis Presley* (RCA EPA-830)
- *Elvis Presley—The Most Talked About New Personality in the Last Ten Years of Recorded Music* (RCA EPB-1254)

LPs:
- *The Complete Sun Sessions* (master and takes #1–5)
- *Elvis—A Legendary Performer, Volume 1* (take #2)
- *Elvis Presley* (master)
- *The Sun Sessions* (master and take #2)

Bootleg LPs:
- *The Sun Years* (master)

I MET HER TODAY
Don Robertson and Hal Blair wrote "I Met Her Today" for Elvis, who recorded the song on October 16, 1961, at RCA's Nashville studios.

LPs:
- *Elvis for Everyone*
- *Separate Ways*

I MISS YOU
Elvis recorded "I Miss You" at his Palm Springs, California, home on September 24, 1973. Donnie Summer, who wrote the song, provided vocal backing along with Tim Baty and Sherrill Nielsen.

LPs:
- *Always On My Mind*
- *Raised on Rock/For Ol' Times Sake*

I NEED SOMEBODY TO LEAN ON
Doc Pomus and Mort Shuman wrote "I Need Somebody to Lean On" for Elvis's 1964 movie *Viva Las Vegas.* Elvis recorded the tune on July 10, 1963, at Radio Recorders.

EPs:
- *Viva Las Vegas*

LPs:
- *I Got Lucky*
- *A Valentine Gift for You*

Bootleg LPs:
- *Viva Las Vegas* (*Viva Las Vegas* soundtrack)

I NEED YOU SO
Ivory Joe Hunter wrote and recorded "I Need You So" (MGM 10663) in 1950. His recording was a #2 hit on *Billboard*'s rhythm & blues chart.

On February 23, 1957, Elvis recorded "I Need You So" at Radio Recorders. Take #8 was chosen by RCA for release. In 1960 Conway Twitty recorded "I Need You So" (MGM 12943), but it didn't chart.

EPs:
- *Just for You*

LPs:
- *Loving You*

I NEED YOUR LOVE TONIGHT
"I Need Your Love Tonight" was written by Sid Wayne and Bix Reichner for Elvis, who recorded the song on June 10, 1958, at RCA's Nashville studios. Take #18 was used on all RCA releases. "I Need Your Love Tonight" had a 13-week stay on *Billboard*'s Hot 100 chart, peaking at #4. Over one million copies were sold.

Singles:
- "A Fool Such as I"/"I NEED YOUR LOVE TONIGHT" (RCA 47-7506) March 1959. Standard release. The original picture sleeve had an advertisement for the *Elvis Sails* EP on the back. From April onward, various EPs and Gold Standard singles were advertised.
- "A Fool Such as I"/"I NEED YOUR LOVE TONIGHT" (RCA 447-0625) 1961. Gold Standard Series reissue.

LPs:
- *Elvis Aron Presley* (USS *Arizona* Memorial; March 25, 1961)
- *Elvis: The Other Sides—Worldwide Gold Award Hits, Volume 2*
- *50,000,000 Elvis Fans Can't Be Wrong—Elvis' Gold Award Records, Volume 2*
- *The Top Ten Hits*
- *This Is Elvis*

Bootleg LPs:
- *Elvis' 1961 Hawaii Benefit Concert* (USS *Arizona* Memorial; March 25, 1961)

I NEED YOUR LOVING (EVERY DAY)
Don Gardner and Bobby Robinson[1] wrote "I Need Your Loving (Every Day)" in 1962. It was recorded that year by Gardner and Dee Dee Ford on Fire Records (Fire 508). Their recording was a hit on both the Hot 100 (#20) and rhythm & blues (#4) charts.

Elvis sang "I Need Your Loving (Every Day)" at a few of his concert appearances in the 1970s.

Bootleg LPs:
- *From Hollywood to Vegas* (Las Vegas; August 14, 1971)
- *Sold Out* (Las Vegas; August 14, 1971)

I NEVER HAD IT SO GOOD
Elvis may have recorded "I Never Had It So Good" in February or March 1964 at Radio Recorders for his 1964 movie *Roustabout.* It could have been an alternate song for the scene in which "One-Track Heart" was used. Another theory is that "I Never Had It So Good" was the original title of "It's a Wonderful World."

---

[1]Bobby Robinson founded Fire and Fury Records in 1959.

I PLAYED THE FOOL
The Clovers had a #3 rhythm & blues hit with "I Played the Fool" (Atlantic 977) in 1952. Some reports indicate that Elvis may have recorded the song in the 1950s, but no tape has ever surfaced.

I REALLY DON'T WANT TO KNOW
"I Really Don't Want to Know" was written by Don Robertson and Howard Barnes and originally recorded by Eddy Arnold (RCA 47-5525), who had a #2 country hit with the song in 1954. Tommy Edwards had a popular recording of "I Really Don't Want to Know" (MGM 12890) in 1960 that went to #18 on the Hot 100 chart. Other successful versions include those by Solomon Burke (Atlantic 2157) in 1961, Little Esther Phillips (Lenox 5560) in 1963, and Ronnie Dove (Diamond 208) in 1966.

Elvis recorded "I Really Don't Want to Know" on June 7, 1970, at RCA's Nashville studios. His single release had a nine-week stay on *Billboard*'s Hot 100 chart, peaking at #21. It reached #9 on the country chart. "I Really Don't Want to Know"/"There Goes My Everything" was Elvis's first top ten hit on the country chart since 1958, and sales of over one million copies are credited. Elvis sang "I Really Don't Want to Know" in his 1977 TV special, "Elvis in Concert."

Singles:
- "I REALLY DON'T WANT TO KNOW"/"There Goes My Everything" (RCA 47-9960) December 1970. Standard release. The original picture sleeve read "Coming Soon—New Album." One month later the sleeve was changed to read, "Now Available—New Album." Both references were to the *Elvis Country* LP.
- "I REALLY DON'T WANT TO KNOW"/"There Goes My Everything" (RCA 447-0679) February 1972. Gold Standard Series reissue.

LPs:
- *Elvis Country* (alternate mix)
- *Elvis in Concert* (Omaha, Nebraska, or Rapid City, South Dakota; June 19 or 21, 1977)
- *Elvis: The Other Sides—Worldwide Gold Award Hits, Volume 2*
- *Welcome to My World*

Bootleg LPs:
- *The Last Farewell* (Indianapolis; June 26, 1977)

I SHALL NOT BE MOVED
This popular gospel tune was written by John T. Benton in 1949, with an arrangement by Mrs. James A. Pate. Elvis, Jerry Lee Lewis, and Carl Perkins sang "I Shall Not Be Moved" during the Million-Dollar-Quartet session on December 4, 1956.

Bootleg LPs:
- *Million Dollar Quartet* (Sun Records; December 4, 1956)
- *The One Million Dollar Quartet* (Sun Records; December 4, 1956)

I SLIPPED, I STUMBLED, I FELL
Elvis sang "I Slipped, I Stumbled, I Fell" in his 1961 movie *Wild in the Country*. The song was recorded on November 8, 1960, at Radio Recorders. Two versions were recorded: the first was released on record and is in a higher key than the second. RCA chose take #13 for release. Fred Wise and Ben Weisman are the composers.

LPs:
- *Separate Ways*
- *Something for Everybody*

Bootleg LPs:
- *Behind Closed Doors* (takes #14 and #15 [false starts], and #16)
- *The Complete Wild in the Country Sessions* (takes #1–18)
- *Eternal Elvis, Volume 2* (alternate take ?)
- *Leavin' It Up to You* (alternate take ?)
- *Unfinished Business* (alternate take ?)

I THINK I'M GONNA LIKE IT HERE
Elvis sang "I Think I'm Gonna Like It Here" in his 1963 movie *Fun in Acapulco*. The film version differed slightly from that on record because of Elvis's delivery. Elvis recorded the song on January 22, 1963, at Radio Recorders. "I Think I'm Gonna Like It Here" was written by Don Robertson and Hal Blair.

LPs:
- *Fun in Acapulco*

I UNDERSTAND (JUST HOW YOU FEEL)
"I Understand (Just How You Feel)" was written by Pat Best and originally recorded by the Four Tunes (Jubilee 5132) who had a #9 rhythm & blues hit with it in 1954. June Valli also had a popular hit with it in 1954, reaching #13 on *Billboard*'s Best-Selling Singles chart.

While visiting disc jockey Eddie Fadal's home in Waco, Texas, in the summer of 1958, Elvis sang "I Understand (Just How You Feel)," accompanying himself on piano.

LPs:
- *Forever Young, Forever Beautiful* (Waco, Texas; 1958)

I WALK THE LINE
Johnny Cash wrote and recorded "I Walk the Line (Sun 241) in 1956. His version reached #2 on the country chart. Cash had written the song as a ballad, but Sam Phillips thought it sounded better at a faster tempo and released it that way. In 1970 John Frankenheimer directed the Gregory Peck–Tuesday Weld film *I Walk the Line*, which used the title of Cash's song. Cash sang five songs, including the title track, on the film's soundtrack.

Elvis sang "I Walk the Line," paired with "Folsom Prison Blues," at some of his Las Vegas and Lake Tahoe concerts in the 1970s.

LPs:
- *The Entertainer* (Las Vegas; August 1969)
- *From Hollywood to Vegas* (Las Vegas; August 1969)
- *Long Lost Songs* (Las Vegas; August 14, 1970)
- *To Know Him Is to Love Him* (Las Vegas; August 1969)

I WANT IT THAT WAY
Elvis may have recorded "I Want It That Way," but the acetate recordings that are in the hands of collectors are, in the opinion of this book's authors, not by Elvis.

I WANT TO BE FREE
Jerry Leiber and Mike Stoller wrote "I Want to Be Free" for Elvis's 1957 movie *Jailhouse Rock*. Elvis re-

corded the tune on April 30, 1957, at Radio Recorders. The movie version is different from the record version. RCA released take #11.

EPs:
- *Jailhouse Rock*

LPs:
- *A Date with Elvis*
- *Elvis: The Other Sides—Worldwide Gold Award Hits, Volume 2*
- *Essential Elvis—The First Movies*

Bootleg LPs:
- *Got a Lot o' Livin' to Do!* (*Jailhouse Rock* soundtrack)
- *Loving You* (*Jailhouse Rock* soundtrack)

I WANT YOU, I NEED YOU, I LOVE YOU

Elvis recorded "I Want You, I Need You, I Love You," which was written by Maurice Mysels[1] and Ira Kosloff on April 11, 1956, at RCA's Nashville studios. While flying to Nashville, Elvis's plane almost crashed. Reportedly, he was so shook that he could record only the one song and was on his way back to Memphis by noon. Background vocals were provided by Gordon Stoker, Ben Speer, and Brock Speer. Marvin Hughes played piano. "I Want You, I Need You, I Love You" was the only Elvis song on which Hughes played piano. The original release was a splice of takes #14 and #17. "I Want You, I Need You, I Love You" had a 24-week stay on *Billboard*'s Top 100 chart, peaking at #3. It reached number one for one week on the country chart and #10 on the rhythm & blues chart. Sales exceeded one million copies.

Elvis sang "I Want You, I Need You, I Love You" on "The Milton Berle Show" (June 5, 1956) and "The Steve Allen Show" (July 1, 1956). On the Berle show, he once sang the lyrics as "I need you, I miss you, I want you." Both appearances featured the Jordanaires as backup vocalists.

In 1976 an alternate take in which Elvis rearranged the lyrics appeared on the LP *Elvis—A Legendary Performer, Volume 2*

Singles:
- "I WANT YOU, I NEED YOU, I LOVE YOU"/"My Baby Left Me" (RCA 20-6540) May 1956. Standard 78 RPM release.
- "I WANT YOU, I NEED YOU, I LOVE YOU"/"My Baby Left Me" (RCA 47-6540) May 1956. Standard 45 RPM release. For a brief time, a special picture sleeve, "This Is His Life: Elvis Presley," was issued. The sleeve was a cartoon depiction of Elvis's life. Unfortunately, the cartoon gave Elvis's age as 19, whereas he was actually 21 at the time. This, then, was the first Elvis picture sleeve.
- "I WANT YOU, I NEED YOU, I LOVE YOU"/"My Baby Left Me" (RCA 447-0607) March 1959. Gold Standard Series reissue.

EPs:
- *Elvis Presley* (RCA SPD-23)
- *The Real Elvis*

LPs:
- *Elvis* (RCA DPL2-0056[e])
- *Elvis—A Legendary Performer, Volume 2* (alternate take)
- *Elvis' Golden Records*

- *Elvis: Worldwide 50 Gold Award Hits, Volume 1*
- *A Golden Celebration* ("The Milton Berle Show"; June 5, 1956) ("The Steve Allen Show"; July 1, 1965) (Mississippi-Alabama Fair and Dairy Show, afternoon show; September 26, 1956)
- *The Number One Hits*
- *The Top Ten Hits*

Bootleg LPs:
- *Cadillac Elvis* ("The Steve Allen Show"; July 1, 1956)
- *The Rockin' Rebel* ("The Milton Berle Show"; June 5, 1956)
- *The Rockin' Rebel, Volume 3* ("The Steve Allen Show"; July 1, 1956)
- *Standing Room Only, Volume 2* ("The Steve Allen Show"; July 1, 1956)
- *Superstar Outtakes* ("The Steve Allen Show"; July 1, 1956)
- *Unfinished Business* (alternate take—the same as on *Elvis—A Legendary Performer, Volume 2*)

I WANT YOU WITH ME

Elvis recorded this Woody Harris tune on March 12, 1961, at RCA's Nashville studios.

LPs:
- *Something for Everybody*

I WAS BORN ABOUT TEN THOUSAND YEARS AGO

Elvis sang "I Was Born About Ten Thousand Years Ago" in brief snippets to provide continuity between songs on his *Elvis Country* LP. The complete song was later released on the *Elvis Now* album.

LPs:
- *Elvis Country*
- *Elvis Now*

I WAS THE ONE

"I Was the One" was written by Aaron Schroeder, Claude DeMetrius, Hal Blair, and Bill Pepper, and first recorded by Elvis on January 11, 1956, at RCA's Nashville studios. Gorden Stoker, Ben Speer, and Brock Speer provided vocal support. Backed with "Heartbreak Hotel," "I Was the One" was the first RCA release of new material for Elvis. The single had a 16-week stay on *Billboard*'s Top 100 chart, peaking at #23, and topped the country chart for four weeks. Sales of one million copies were achieved. Elvis sang "I Was the One" on his fourth appearance on "Stage Show" (February 18, 1956) and during his last appearance on "Louisiana Hayride" (December 16, 1956).

Singles:
- "Heartbreak Hotel"/"I WAS THE ONE" (RCA 20-6420) January 27, 1956. Standard 78 RPM release.
- "Heartbreak Hotel"/"I WAS THE ONE" (RCA 47-6420) January 27, 1956. Standard 45 RPM release.
- "Heartbreak Hotel"/"I WAS THE ONE" March 1959. Gold Standard Series reissue.
- "Heartbreak Hotel"/"I WAS THE ONE" (RCA PB-11105) October 1977. One of the 15 singles in the boxed set *15 Golden Records—30 Golden Hits* (RCA PP-11301), and one of 10 singles in the boxed set *20 Golden Hits in Full Color Sleeves* (RCA PP-11340)
- "I WAS THE ONE"/"Wear My Ring Around Your Neck" (RCA JB-

---

[1]Maurice Mysels's name was misspelled "Myself" on the 78 RPM release and on the first pressings of the 45 RPM release.

13500) April 1983. New release with a different flip side. This record was pressed on gold vinyl.

EPs:
- *Heartbreak Hotel*

LPs:
- *Elvis: Worldwide 50 Gold Award Hits, Volume 1*
- *For LP Fans Only*
- *A Golden Celebration* ("Stage Show"; February 18, 1956) (Mississippi-Alabama Fair and Dairy Show; September 26, 1956)
- *I Was the One*
- *A Valentine Gift for You*

Bootleg LPs:
- *Dorsey Shows* ("Stage Show"; February 18, 1956)
- *Got a Lot o' Livin to Do!* (Vancouver, British Columbia; September 1, 1957)
- *The Rockin' Rebel, Volume 2* ("Louisiana Hayride"; December 16, 1956)
- *Superstar Outtakes* ("Stage Show"; February 18, 1956)

I WASHED MY HANDS IN MUDDY WATER
Stonewall Jackson had a #8 country hit with "I Washed My Hands in Muddy Water" (Columbia 43197) in 1965. The song had been written a year earlier by Joe Babcock. Other hit versions have included those by Charlie Rich (Smash 1993) in 1965 and Johnny Rivers (Imperial 66175) in 1966.

Elvis recorded "I Washed My Hands in Muddy Water" on June 7, 1970, at RCA's Nashville studios. RCA released a shortened version on record. An alternate mix appeared on the RCA Record Club LP *Country Memories*.

LPs:
- *Elvis Country*

Bootleg LPs:
- *Behind Closed Doors* (longer version of the RCA release that lasts about 4½ minutes without the horn section overdub)
- *Unfinished Business* (alternate take)

I WILL BE HOME AGAIN
Elvis recorded "I Will Be Home Again" on April 4, 1960, at RCA's Nashville studios. It was the first recording on which Charlie Hodge sang duet with Elvis. Bennie Benjamin, Raymond Leveen, and Lou Singer are the composers.

LPs:
- *Elvis Is Back*

I WILL BE TRUE
Ivory Joe Hunter wrote and recorded "I Will Be True" (MGM 11195) in 1952. On May 19, 1971, Elvis recorded the song at RCA's Nashville studios. He played piano on the track.

LPs:
- *Elvis* (RCA APL1-0283)
- *Elvis Aron Presley* (without overdubbing, just Elvis on piano)

I WRITE THE SONGS
Bruce Johnston of the Beach Boys wrote "I Write the Songs." It was first recorded by the Captain and Tennille for their 1975 debut LP, *Love Will Keep Us Together* (A&M SP 4552). In 1975 David Cassidy took the song to #11 in England. Arista Records president Clive Davis heard "I Write the Songs" while in London and decided that it would be a good tune for Barry Manilow. How right he was! Manilow's 1976 single release of "I Write the Songs" (Arista 0157) reached number one on *Billboard*'s Hot 100 chart and became a million-seller.

Elvis sang "I Write the Songs" in concert in 1976 and 1977.

IF EVERY DAY WAS LIKE CHRISTMAS
Red West and Glen Spreen wrote "If Every Day Was Like Christmas" for Elvis, who recorded the song on June 10, 1966, at RCA's Nashville studios. Although the single release did not chart, some sources have credited it with sales of over one million copies. Co-composer Red West later had a recording of his own song on Brent Records (Brent 200).

Singles:
- "IF EVERY DAY WAS LIKE CHRISTMAS"/"How Would You Like to Be" (RCA 47-8950) November 1966. Standard release.
- "IF EVERY DAY WAS LIKE CHRISTMAS"/"How Would You Like to Be" (RCA 447-0681) May 1972. Gold Standard Series reissue.

LPs:
- *Elvis' Christmas Album*
- *Memories of Christmas* (alternate take)

IF I CAN DREAM
Colonel Tom Parker originally wanted the 1968 TV special "Elvis" to end with a Christmas song, but producer Steve Binder had musical director W. Earl Brown write "If I Can Dream" for Elvis's closing number. The instrumental track was recorded on June 20 or 21, 1968, at Western Recorders in Hollywood. Elvis's vocal track was recorded at NBC-TV on June 29. The single was released shortly before the December 3, 1968, telecast of the special. Because of the added exposure on the program, "If I Can Dream" climbed to #12 on *Billboard*'s Hot 100 chart and became a million-seller. It had a total stay on the chart of 13 weeks.

Singles:
- "IF I CAN DREAM"/"Edge of Reality" (RCA 47-9670) November 1968. Standard release. The original picture sleeves read, "As Featured on His NBC-TV Special." In January 1970 the phrase was deleted. A few cardboard picture sleeves were manufactured as an experiment.
- "IF I CAN DREAM"/"Edge of Reality" (RCA 447-0668) December 1970. Gold Standard Series reissue.

LPs:
- *Elvis—A Legendary Performer, Volume 2*
- *Elvis' Gold Records, Volume 2*
- *Elvis—TV Special*
- *Elvis: Worldwide 50 Gold Award Hits, Volume 1*
- *He Walks Beside Me* (alternate take)

Bootleg LPs:
- *The Burbank Sessions, Volume 2* ("Elvis" TV special taping; June 29, 1968, at 6:00 P.M. and 8:00 P.M. shows)

- *Eternal Elvis* ("Elvis" TV special taping; June 29, 1968, at 6:00 P.M. and 8:00 P.M. shows)
- *The '68 Comeback, Volume 2* ("Elvis" TV special taping; June 29, 1968)

IF I GET HOME ON CHRISTMAS DAY
"If I Get Home on Christmas Day" was written by Tony Macaulay and John MacLeod and recorded by Elvis on May 15, 1971, at RCA's Nashville studios.

LPs:
- *Elvis Sings the Wonderful World of Christmas*

IF I WERE YOU
Elvis recorded "If I Were You" at RCA's Nashville studios on June 8, 1970. Gerald Nelson is the composer.

LPs:
- *Love Letters from Elvis*

Bootleg LPs:
- *A Dog's Life* (alternate take)

IF I'M A FOOL (FOR LOVING YOU)
"If I'm a Fool (for Loving You)" was written by Stan Kesler. One of the early recordings was by Jimmy Clanton on Philips Records (Philips 40208) in 1964. Elvis recorded the song at American Sound Studios in Memphis on February 21, 1969.

LPs:
- *Let's Be Friends*

IF THAT ISN'T LOVE
Elvis recorded "If That Isn't Love" at Stax Studios in Memphis on December 16, 1973. Dottie Rambo is the composer.

LPs:
- *Good Times*

IF THE LORD WASN'T WALKING BY MY SIDE
"If the Lord Wasn't Walking by My Side" was written by Henry Slaughter and first recorded by Elvis during the *How Great Thou Art* sessions on May 28, 1966, at RCA's Nashville studios. Composer Slaughter played organ on the recording.

LPs:
- *How Great Thou Art*

IF WE NEVER MEET AGAIN
This gospel song was written by A. E. Brumley and recorded by Elvis at RCA's Nashville studios on October 31, 1960.

LPs:
- *His Hand in Mine*

IF YOU DON'T COME BACK
The Drifters originally recorded this Jerry Leiber–Mike Stoller tune in 1963 (Atlantic 2191). Elvis recorded "If You Don't Come Back" at Stax Studios on July 21, 1973.

LPs:
- *Raised on Rock/For Ol' Times Sake*

IF YOU LOVE ME (LET ME KNOW)
Written by John Rostill, "If You Love Me (Let Me Know)" was first recorded by Olivia Newton-John in 1974 for MCA Records (MCA 40209). Her recording reached #5 on the Hot 100 chart and #2 on the country and Easy-Listening charts. A Gold Record was awarded for sales exceeding one million copies.

Elvis often sang "If You Love Me (Let Me Know)" in concert. It is those live performances that are on record.

LPs:
- *Elvis Aron Presley* (Dallas; June 6, 1975)
- *Elvis in Concert* (Rapid City, South Dakota; June 21, 1977)
- *Moody Blue* (Saginaw, Michigan; April 25, 1977)

Bootleg LPs:
- *America's Own* (Uniondale, N.Y.; July 19, 1975)
- *Big Boss Man* (Las Vegas; August 19, 1974)
- *Elvis Presley Is Alive and Well and Singing in Las Vegas, Volume 1* (Las Vegas; 1974)
- *Long Lost Songs* (Las Vegas; 1975)
- *Rockin' with Elvis April Fool's Day* (Las Vegas; April 1, 1975)
- *The Vegas Years, 1972–1975* (Las Vegas; August 1975)

IF YOU TALK IN YOUR SLEEP
"If You Talk in Your Sleep" was written by Red West and Johnny Christopher and recorded by Elvis on December 11, 1973, at Stax Studios in Memphis. Co-composer Christopher played guitar on the recording. Elvis's single release had a 13-week stay on *Billboard*'s Hot 100 chart, peaking at #17. It did much better on the country and Easy-Listening charts, reaching #6 on both charts.

Singles:
- "IF YOU TALK IN YOUR SLEEP"/"Help Me" (RCA APBO-0280) May 1974. Standard release.
- "IF YOU TALK IN YOUR SLEEP"/"Help Me" (RCA DJBO-0280) May 1974. Disc jockey promotional release.
- "IF YOU TALK IN YOUR SLEEP"/"Raised on Rock" (RCA GB-10157) March 1975. Gold Standard Series original with a different flip side.

LPs:
- *Elvis' Gold Records, Volume 5*
- *Promised Land*

Bootleg LPs:
- *Big Boss Man* (Las Vegas; August 19, 1974)
- *Command Performance* (Las Vegas; August 23, 1974)
- *Elvis Presley Is Alive and Well and Singing in Las Vegas, Volume 1* (Las Vegas; August 1974)
- *The Vegas Years, 1972–1975* (Las Vegas; August 1974)

IF YOU THINK I DON'T NEED YOU
Elvis sang "If You Think I Don't Need You" in his 1964 movie *Viva Las Vegas*. The song was recorded on July 9, 1963, at Radio Recorders. Red West and Joe Cooper are the composers.

EPs:
- *Viva Las Vegas*

LPs:
- *Double Dynamite*
- *I Got Lucky*

Bootleg LPs:
- *Eternal Elvis, Volume 2* (alternate take)
- *Viva Las Vegas!* (three false starts and one short [45 seconds] complete take)

I'LL BE BACK
Sid Wayne and Ben Weisman wrote "I'll Be Back" for Elvis's 1966 movie *Spinout*. Elvis recorded the tune on February 17, 1966, at Radio Recorders. The film ver-

Studio pressing of "I'll Be Back." (Photo courtesy Don Fink)

sion had added instrumentation and was longer than the one on record.

LPs:
- *Spinout*

Bootleg LPs:
- *Elvis Sings Songs from Tickle Me* (alternate take)

I'LL BE HOME FOR CHRISTMAS
"I'll Be Home for Christmas" was written by Walter Kent, Kim Gannon, and Buck Ram in 1943 and first recorded by Bing Crosby (Decca 18570) with the John Scott Trotter Orchestra in that year. Crosby's recording reached #3 on *Billboard*'s Best-Selling Singles chart and sold over a million copies. Several artists have recorded the song over the years, including Joni James (MGM 12368) in December 1956.

Elvis recorded "I'll Be Home for Christmas" on September 7, 1957, at Radio Recorders. Take #15 was used by RCA. Elvis's recording was heard briefly (and uncredited) in the closing credits of the 1987 film *Lethal Weapon*.

EPs:
- *Elvis Sings Christmas Songs*

LPs:
- *Elvis' Christmas Album*
- *Memories of Christmas*

Bootleg LPs:
- *Eternal Elvis* (same as the RCA release)

I'LL BE HOME ON CHRISTMAS DAY
Michael Jarrett wrote "I'll Be Home on Christmas Day," which was first recorded by Elvis at RCA's Nashville studios on May 16, 1971. The song was re-recorded on June 9, 1971, but that version has never been released.

LPs:
- *Elvis Sings the Wonderful World of Christmas*
- *Memories of Christmas* (alternate take)

I'LL BE THERE (IF EVER YOU WANT ME)
Bobby Darin wrote and recorded this tune for Atco Records (Atco 6167) in 1960. His recording reached #79 on *Billboard*'s Hot 100 chart. Tony Orlando recorded "I'll Be There (If Ever You Want Me)" (Epic 9622) in 1963, but it wasn't until 1964 that a successful version was released. Gerry and the Pacemakers reached #14 on the Hot 100 chart with their recording (Laurie 3279).

Elvis recorded "I'll Be There (If Ever You Want Me)" on January 23, 1969, at American Sound Studios. For some reason, Elvis's version incorrectly lists Gabbard and Price as composers.

LPs:
- *Double Dynamite*
- *Let's Be Friends*

Bootleg LPs:
- *Long Lost Songs* (Las Vegas; March 22, 1975) (in medley with "Roses Are Red" and "You're the Reason I'm Living")

I'LL HOLD YOU IN MY HEART (TILL I CAN HOLD YOU IN MY ARMS)
"I'll Hold You in My Heart" was written by Eddy Arnold, Hal Horton, and Tommy Dilbeck, and recorded by Arnold (RCA 2332) in 1947. His recording eventually sold over a million copies. Other popular recordings of "I'll Hold You in My Heart" include those by Eddie Fisher (RCA 4191) in 1951 and Freddie Hart (Kapp 820) in 1967.

Elvis recorded "I'll Hold You in My Heart" on January 23, 1969, at American Sound Studios. He played piano on the recording.

LPs:
- *From Elvis in Memphis*
- *The Memphis Record*

I'LL NEVER FALL IN LOVE AGAIN
Tom Jones recorded "I'll Never Fall in Love Again" (London 59003) in 1967, but the record peaked at only #49 on the Hot 100 chart. When reissued in 1969, it became a million-seller, reaching #6. The song was written by Jim Currie and Lonnie Donegan.

Elvis recorded "I'll Never Fall in Love Again" on the night of February 4–5, 1976, at Graceland.

LPs:
- *From Elvis Presley Boulevard, Memphis, Tennessee*
- *Our Memories of Elvis* (without overdubbing)

I'LL NEVER KNOW
Elvis recorded "I'll Never Know," which was written by Fred Karger, Ben Weisman, and Sid Wayne, on June 5, 1970, at RCA's Nashville studios.

LPs:
- *Love Letters from Elvis*

I'LL NEVER LET YOU GO (LITTLE DARLIN')
Jimmy Wakely wrote and recorded "I'll Never Let You Go (Little Darlin')" (Decca 5973) in 1943. Ten years later, Jimmy Liggins recorded the song on Specialty Records (Specialty 470).

Elvis recorded "I'll Never Let You Go (Little Darlin')" on September 10, 1954, at Sun Records. The original Sun recording was not released until RCA issued it two years later.

Singles:
- "I'LL NEVER LET YOU GO (LITTLE DARLIN')"/"I'm Gonna Sit Right Down and Cry (Over You)" (RCA 20-6638) September 1956. Standard 78 RPM release.
- "I'LL NEVER LET YOU GO (LITTLE DARLIN')"/"I'm Gonna Sit Right Down and Cry (Over You)" (RCA 47-6638) September 1956. Standard 45 RPM release.
- "I'LL NEVER LET YOU GO (LITTLE DARLIN')"/"I'm Gonna Sit Right Down and Cry (Over You)" (RCA 447-0611) March 1959. Gold Standard Series reissue.

EPs:
- *Elvis Presley* (RCA EPB-1254)
- *Elvis Presley* (RCA SPD-22)
- *Elvis Presley* (RCA SPD-23)
- *Elvis Presley—The Most Talked About New Personality in the Last Ten Years of Recorded Music* (RCA EPB-1254)

LPs:
- *The Complete Sun Sessions* (master and outtake)
- *Elvis Presley*
- *A Golden Celebration* (alternate take)
- *The Sun Sessions*

Bootleg LPs:
- *Good Rocking Tonight* (alternate take; first part of the song is missing)
- *The Rockin' Rebel* (alternate take; first part of the song is missing)

I'LL NEVER STAND IN YOUR WAY
Fred Rose and Walter (Hy) Heath wrote this song in 1953. Joni James had the original recording of "I'll Never Stand in Your Way" (MGM 11606) in November 1953. A few days after her record was released, Ernie Lee's version (MGM 11613) hit the record stores.

Elvis recorded "I'll Never Stand in Your Way" on January 4, 1954, at the Memphis Recording Service, along with "Casual Love Affair." The two songs were recorded on a 10-inch acetate at a cost of four dollars. It was at this time that Elvis first met Sam Phillips. Reportedly, a tape of the acetate still exists. Some reports have suggested that Elvis later recorded "I'll Never Stand in Your Way" while under contract to Sun

Records, but there is no evidence to support that contention.

I'LL REMEMBER YOU
"I'll Remember You" was written and recorded by Kui-okalani Lee on Columbia Records (Columbia 43776) in 1966.

Elvis recorded "I'll Remember You" on June 10, 1966, at RCA's Nashville studios. The song was a staple of his live performances in the 1970s. He sang "I'll Remember You" in his 1973 TV special, "Elvis: Aloha from Hawaii."

LPs:
- *Elvis—A Legendary Performer, Volume 4* (Madison Square Garden; June 10, 1972, afternoon show)
- *Aloha from Hawaii via Satellite* (Honolulu; January 14, 1973)
- *The Alternate Aloha* (rehearsal concert for "Elvis: Aloha from Hawaii"; January 12, 1973)
- *Elvis Aron Presley* (Honolulu; January 14, 1973)
- *Spinout*

Bootleg LPs:
- *Aloha Rehearsal Show—Kui Lee Cancer Benefit* (rehearsal concert for "Elvis: Aloha from Hawaii"; January 12, 1973)
- *Plantation Rock* (rehearsal concert for "Elvis: Aloha from Hawaii"; January 12, 1973)
- *Rockin' with Elvis April Fool's Day* (Las Vegas; April 1, 1975)
- *Standing Room Only, Volume 3* ("Elvis: Aloha from Hawaii"; January 14, 1973)

I'LL TAKE LOVE
Elvis sang "I'll Take Love" in his 1967 movie *Easy Come, Easy Go*. The instrumental track was recorded on September 29, 1966, at Radio Recorders. Elvis's vocal track was added at a later date. "I'll Take Love" was written by Dolores Fuller and Mark Barkan.

EPs:
- *Easy Come, Easy Go*

LPs:
- *C'mon Everybody*

I'LL TAKE YOU HOME AGAIN, KATHLEEN
Thomas Westendorf wrote "I'll Take You Home Again, Kathleen" in 1876. He was inspired to write the song while his wife (whose name was Jennie) was away visiting relatives. Westendorf based his tune on "Barney, Take Me Home Again" by Arthur W. French and George W. Brown. "I'll Take You Home Again, Kathleen" was the theme song of the radio series "Orphans of Divorce," and was a particular favorite of Thomas Alva Edison's. As a matter of fact, the song was played at his funeral in 1931. "I'll Take You Home Again, Kathleen" has been recorded by several artists over the years, including Will Oakland (Edison Ambersol 1102) in 1912, Walter Van Brunt (Edison 80160) in 1916, and Slim Whitman (Imperial 8310), whose version went to #93 on *Billboard*'s Hot 100 chart in 1957.

Elvis recorded "I'll Take You Home Again, Kathleen" on May 19, 1971, at RCA's Nashville studios.

LPs:
- *Elvis* (RCA APL1-0283)

- *Elvis Aron Presley* (without overdubbing, just Elvis's vocal and piano playing)

I'M BEGINNING TO FORGET YOU
A home recording of "I'm Beginning to Forget You" surfaced on the *Elvis—A Legendary Performer, Volume 4* LP in 1983. Elvis recorded the song at Graceland sometime in the early 1960s. Jim Reeves had a #17 country hit with "I'm Beginning to Forget You" (RCA 47-7557) in 1959.

I'M COMIN' HOME
Charlie Rich wrote "I'm Comin' Home" for Carl Mann (Phillips International 3555) in 1960. Mann's recording did not chart. However, when Elvis recorded "I'm Comin' Home" on March 12, 1961, at RCA's Nashville studios, he copied Mann's phrasing, and Floyd Cramer copied the piano playing from the record.

LPs:
- *Something for Everybody*

I'M COUNTING ON YOU
"I'm Counting on You" was written by Don Robertson and recorded by Elvis on January 11, 1956, at RCA's Nashville studios. Backing vocals were by Gordon Stoker, Ben Speer, and Brock Speer. Later in 1956, Kitty Wells had a #9 country hit with "I'm Counting on You" (Decca 30094).

Singles:
- "I Got a Woman"/"I'M COUNTING ON YOU" (RCA 20-6637) September 1956. Standard 78 RPM release.
- "I Got a Woman"/"I'M COUNTING ON YOU" (RCA 47-6637) September 1956. Standard 45 RPM release.
- "Blue Suede Shoes"/"I'M COUNTING ON YOU" (RCA 47-6492) September 1956. Disc jockey "Record Prevue."
- "I Got a Woman"/"I'M COUNTING ON YOU" (RCA 447-0610) March 1959. Gold Standard Series reissue.

EPs:
- *Elvis Presley* (RCA EPB-1254)
- *Elvis Presley* (RCA SPD-22)
- *Elvis Presley* (RCA SPD-23)
- *Elvis Presley—The Most Talked About New Personality in the Past Ten Years of Recorded Music* (RCA EPB-1254)

LPs:
- *Elvis Presley*

I'M FALLING IN LOVE TONIGHT
Elvis sang "I'm Falling in Love Tonight" in his 1963 movie *It Happened at the World's Fair*. He recorded the song on September 22, 1962, at Radio Recorders. Backing vocals were by the Mello Men. Don Robertson is the composer.

LPs:
- *Elvis Aron Presley* (false starts #1, #2, #3, and complete take #4)
- *It Happened at the World's Fair*

I'M GONNA BID MY BLUES GOODBYE
Hank Snow recorded "I'm Gonna Bid My Blues Goodbye" (Bluebird 55-3233) in the 1940s. During the Mil-

lion-Dollar-Quartet session on December 4, 1956, Elvis sang a few lines of the song.

Bootleg LPs:
- *The One Million Dollar Quartet* (Sun Records; December 4, 1956)

I'M GONNA SIT RIGHT DOWN AND CRY (OVER YOU)
Joe Thomas recorded "I'm Gonna Sit Right Down and Cry (Over You)" in the early 1950s on King Records. The song was written by Thomas and Howard Biggs.

Elvis recorded "I'm Gonna Sit Right Down and Cry (Over You)" on January 31, 1956, at RCA's New York City studios. His single release did not chart.

Singles:
- "I'll Never Let You Go (Little Darlin')"/"I'M GONNA SIT RIGHT DOWN AND CRY (OVER YOU)" (RCA 20-6638) September 1956. Standard 78 RPM release.
- "I'll Never Let You Go (Little Darlin')"/"I'M GONNA SIT RIGHT DOWN AND CRY (OVER YOU)" (RCA 47-6638) September 1956. Standard 45 RPM release.
- "I'll Never Let You Go (Little Darlin')"/"I'M GONNA SIT RIGHT DOWN AND CRY (OVER YOU)" (RCA 447-0611) March 1959. Gold Standard Series reissue.

EPs:
- *Elvis Presley* (RCA EPB-1254)
- *Elvis Presley* (RCA SPD-22)
- *Elvis Presley* (RCA SPD-23)
- *Elvis Presley—The Most Talked About New Personality in the Last Ten Years of Recorded Music* (RCA EPB-1254)
- *Save-On Records* (RCA SPA-7-27)

LPs:
- *Elvis Presley*

I'M GONNA WALK DEM GOLDEN STAIRS
This spiritual was recorded by Elvis on October 31, 1960, at RCA's Nashville studios.

LPs:
- *His Hand in Mine*

I'M LEAVIN'
Elvis recorded "I'm Leavin'" on May 20, 1971, at RCA's Nashville studios. The single release had a nine-week stay on *Billboard*'s Hot 100 chart, peaking at #36. On the Easy-Listening chart, "I'm Leavin'" reached #2. Only Olivia Newton-John's "If Not for You" kept Elvis's recording from ascending to the top spot. Global sales of over one million copies are claimed for "I'm Leavin'." The composers are Michael Jarrett and Sonny Charles.

Singles:
- "I'M LEAVIN'"/"Heart of Rome" (RCA 47-9998) July 1971. Standard Release.
- "I'M LEAVIN'"/"Heart of Rome" (RCA 447-0683) May 1972. Gold Standard Series reissue.

LPs:
- *Elvis Aron Presley*

Bootleg LPs:
- *The Hillbilly Cat, 1954–1974, Volume 1* (RCA release)

- *The Monologue L.P.* (Las Vegas; 1971?)
- *Sold Out* (Nashville; July 1, 1973)
- *To Know Him Is to Love Him* (Las Vegas; 1971)

I'M LEAVING IT UP TO YOU

"I'm Leaving It Up to You" was written by Don (Sugarcane) Harris and Dewey Terry and first recorded by them on Specialty Records (Specialty 610) in 1957. In 1963 Dale and Grace covered Don and Dewey's recording, reaching number one on both the Hot 100 and Easy-Listening charts. "I'm Leaving It Up to You" (Montel 921) sold over a million copies. Donny and Marie Osmond also had a million-seller with the song, using the title "I'm Leaving It (All) Up to You" (MGM 14735), in 1974. Their recording topped the Easy-Listening chart and reached #4 on the Hot 100 chart.

Elvis never recorded "I'm Leaving It Up to You," but he did sing it in concert on occasion.

Bootleg LPs:
- *Leavin' It Up to You* (Las Vegas rehearsal; 1972?)
- *Sold Out* (Las Vegas; August 1972)

I'M LEFT, YOU'RE RIGHT, SHE'S GONE

Stanley Kesler and Bill Taylor wrote "I'm Left, You're Right, She's Gone" in 1954, based on a Campbell's soup jingle. Elvis first recorded the song on December 18, 1954, at Sun Records. Instrumentation was provided by Elvis (guitar), Scotty Moore (guitar), and Bill Black (bass). The Sun release didn't chart, nor did the RCA reissue in 1956. A slower, bluesier version of "I'm Left, You're Right, She's Gone," called "My Baby's Gone," was recorded during the December 18, 1954, session. Reportedly, Sam Phillips first released that version to

The "My Baby's Gone" acetate given to Dewey Phillips. (Photo courtesy Jeff Wheatcraft)

Memphis disc jockeys, but not to the general public. "My Baby's Gone" has been on numerous bootlegs.

The original copyright title was "You're Right, I'm Left, She's Gone." An advertisement for the Jimmie Rodgers Memorial Day Celebration in Meridian, Mississippi, on May 26, 1955, printed the title that way. It also appeared that way on the LP *The Sun Years.*

Singles:
- "Baby, Let's Play House"/"I'M LEFT, YOU'RE RIGHT, SHE'S GONE" (Sun 217) April 1, 1955. Standard 78 RPM and 45 RPM release.
- "Baby, Let's Play House"/"I'M LEFT, YOU'RE RIGHT, SHE'S GONE" (RCA 20-6383) November 1955. RCA reissue of the Sun 78 RPM release.
- "Baby, Let's Play House"/"I'M LEFT, YOU'RE RIGHT, SHE'S GONE" (RCA 47-6383) November 1955. RCA reissue of the 45 RPM Sun release.
- "Baby, Let's Play House"/"I'M LEFT, YOU'RE RIGHT, SHE'S GONE" (RCA 447-0604) March 1959. Gold Standard Series reissue.

EPs:
- *Any Way You Want Me*

LPs:
- *The Complete Sun Sessions* (master and takes #7–13 ["My Baby's Gone"])
- *For LP Fans Only* (alternate mix, more reverberation)
- *A Golden Celebration* (alternate take)
- *The Sun Sessions* (alternate mix, more reverberation)

Bootleg LPs:
- *Good Rocking Tonight* ("My Baby's Gone" alternate take)
- *The Rockin' Rebel* ("My Baby's Gone" alternate take)
- *The Sun Years* ("My Baby's Gone" alternate take; "You're Right, I'm Left, She's Gone" alternate take)
- *Unfinished Business* ("My Baby's Gone" alternate take)

I'M MOVIN' ON

"I'm Movin' On" was written by Hank Snow in 1945, but not recorded by him until 1950 (RCA 0328). Steve Sholes of RCA didn't want Snow to record the song. "I'm Movin' On" had a total stay of 44 weeks on the country chart, reaching number one. Snow once recorded a follow-up record titled "I'm Still Movin' On" (RCA 1068). In 1959 Ray Charles had a version of "I'm Movin' On" (Atlantic 2043)[1] that reached #11 on the rhythm & blues chart. That same year Don Gibson reached #14 on the country chart with his recording (RCA 47-7629).

Elvis recorded "I'm Movin On" on January 15, 1969, at American Sound Studios in Memphis. On October 14, 1980, Felton Jarvis recorded a new instrumental track at Young'un Sound in Nashville and released the new version on the *Guitar Man* LP.

LPs:
- *Elvis—A Canadian Tribute*
- *From Elvis in Memphis*
- *Guitar Man,* (alternate take, new instrumental track)
- *The Memphis Record*

I'M NOT THE MARRYING KIND

Elvis sang "I'm Not the Marrying Kind" in his 1962

---

[1]The flip side of Ray Charles's record was a blues song titled "I Believe to My Soul," in which Charles dubbed all the voices of a female chorus.

film *Follow That Dream.* The song was recorded on July 5, 1961, at RCA's Nashville studios. Mack David and Sherman Edwards are the composers.

EPs:
• *Follow That Dream*

LPs:
• *C'mon Everybody*

I'M SO LONESOME I COULD CRY

Hank Williams wrote and first recorded "I'm So Lonesome I Could Cry" (MGM 10560) in 1949. The song did not chart, but its flip side, "My Bucket's Got a Hole in It," reached #2 on *Billboard*'s country chart. The record was reissued in 1966 and peaked at #43. Several artists have recorded "I'm So Lonesome I Could Cry" over the years, including Tommy Edwards (MGM 13032) in 1961, Johnny Tillotson (Cadence 1432) in 1962, and the most successful version by B. J. Thomas (Scepter 12129) in 1966. Thomas's recording reached #8 on the Hot 100 chart and became a million-seller. Using the pseudonym Hank Wilson, Leon Russell had a release of "I'm So Lonesome I Could Cry" (Shelter 7336) in 1973.

Elvis never recorded "I'm So Lonesome I Could Cry" in the studio, but he did sing it on occasion in concert. He introduced the song in his 1973 TV special, "Elvis: Aloha from Hawaii," by saying it was the saddest song he ever heard.

EPs:
• *Aloha from Hawaii via Satellite*
• *The Alternate Aloha* (rehearsal concert for "Elvis: Aloha from Hawaii"; January 12, 1973)

LPs:
• *Aloha from Hawaii via Satellite*
• *Welcome to My World*

Bootleg LPs:
• *Aloha Rehearsal Show—Kui Lee Cancer Benefit* (rehearsal concert for "Elvis: Aloha from Hawaii"; January 12, 1973)
• *Plantation Rock* (rehearsal concert for "Elvis: Aloha from Hawaii"; January 12, 1973)

I'M WITH THE CROWD (BUT OH SO LONESOME)

Elvis sang this Ernest Tubb song during the Million-Dollar-Quartet session of December 4, 1956. He imitated Tubb as he sang it.

LPs:
• *The Million Dollar Quartet* (Sun Records; December 4, 1956)
• *The One Million Dollar Quartet* (Sun Records; December 4, 1956)

I'M YOURS

Elvis sang "I'm Yours" in his 1965 movie *Tickle Me.* He recorded the song, however, four years earlier on June 26, 1961, at RCA's Nashville studios. The single release of "I'm Yours" had an 11-week stay on *Billboard*'s Hot 100 chart, reaching #11. On the Easy-Listening chart, it replaced "You Were on My Mind" by We Five at number one in October 1965. After a three-week stay, "I'm Yours" was bounced out of the top spot by Herb Alpert's "Taste of Honey." Sales globally have reportedly exceeded one million copies. "I'm Yours" was composed by Don Robertson and Hal Blair. Eight years after Elvis recorded the song, co-composer Robertson recorded his own composition (RCA 47-9721).

Singles:
• "I'M YOURS"/"(It's a) Long Lonely Highway" (RCA 47-8657) August 1965. Standard release.
• "I'M YOURS"/"(It's a) Long Lonely Highway" (RCA 447-0654) November 1966. Gold Standard Series reissue.

THE IMPOSSIBLE DREAM

Joe Darion and Mitch Leigh wrote "The Impossible Dream" for the 1965 musical play *The Man of La Mancha,* in which it was introduced by Richard Kiley. The next year, Jack Jones had a number one Easy-Listening hit with his recording of the song (Kapp 755). Other versions of "The Impossible Dream" include those by Roy Hamilton (RCA 47-8813) in 1966, Roger Williams (Kapp 907) in 1968, and the Hesitations (Kapp 899), also in 1968. Elvis never recorded "The Impossible Dream" in the studio. Only live concert versions from 1972 exist on record.

Singles:
• "THE IMPOSSIBLE DREAM"/"An American Trilogy" (RCA JH-13302) August 1982. Promotional single sold only in Tupelo, Mississippi, during August 1982.

LPs:
• *Elvis as Recorded at Madison Square Garden* (June 10, 1972)
• *He Walks Beside Me* (Las Vegas; February 16, 1972)

Bootleg LPs:
• *Eternal Elvis, Volume 2* (Madison Square Garden; June 10, 1972)
• *The Legend Lives On* (Las Vegas; February 16, 1972)
• *Superstar Outtakes, Volume 2* (Las Vegas; February 1972)

IN MY FATHER'S HOUSE

This gospel song was written by Aileene Hanks in 1953, based on the biblical verse John 14:2. The complete title is "In My Father's House (Are Many Mansions)." Elvis recorded the song on October 31, 1960, at RCA's Nashville studios.

LPs:
• *His Hand in Mine*

IN MY WAY

Elvis sang "In My Way" in his 1961 movie *Wild in the Country.* The song, written by Fred Wise and Ben Weisman, was recorded on November 7, 1960, at Radio Recorders. Take #8 was released by RCA. In 1965 Dave Kaye recorded "In My Way" (Decca 12073) in England, dedicating it to Elvis. Elvis was also mentioned in the lyrics.

LPs:
• *Elvis for Everyone*
• *Separate Ways*

Bootleg LPs:
• *Behind Closed Doors* (take #1)
• *The Complete Wild in the Country Sessions* (takes #1–8)

IN THE GARDEN

This hymn was written by C. Austin Miles in 1912. The complete title is "(He Walks with Me) In the Garden." According to a poll by *The Christian Herald* in the early 1980s, "In the Garden" was the third most popular hymn among Protestants, following "The Old Rugged Cross" and "What a Friend We Have in Jesus." A version of the hymn was heard in the 1960 movie *Wild River*.

Elvis recorded "In the Garden" at RCA's Nashville studios on May 27, 1966.

LPs:
• *How Great Thou Art*

IN THE GHETTO

"In the Ghetto" was written by Mac Davis and first offered to Bill Medley (of the Righteous Brothers) and then to Sammy Davis Jr., neither of whom decided to record it. Elvis recorded "In the Ghetto" on January 21, 1969, at American Sound Studios. His single release had a 13-week stay on *Billboard*'s Hot 100 chart, reaching #3. On the country chart, "In the Ghetto" peaked at a disappointing #60. It was a #2 hit in England. The RIAA certified the song as a Gold Record on June 25, 1969. The full title of the song is "In the Ghetto (the Vicious Circle)," but RCA was granted permission to release it without the subtitle.

Dolly Parton covered Elvis's recording of "In the Ghetto" later in 1969 (RCA 47-0192). Her version reached #50 on the country chart. In 1972 Candi Staton recorded a version (Fame 91000) that reached #48 on the Hot 100 chart.

Singles:
• "IN THE GHETTO"/"Any Day Now" (RCA 47-9741) April 15, 1969. Standard release. The first 300,000 picture sleeves read, "Coming Soon—FROM ELVIS IN MEMPHIS Album." The sleeves printed from May 1969 on read, "Ask for FROM ELVIS IN MEMPHIS Album."
• "IN THE GHETTO"/"Any Day Now" (RCA 447-0671) December 1970. Gold Standard Series reissue.
• "IN THE GHETTO"/"Any Day Now" (RCA PB-11100) October 1977. One of 15 singles in the boxed set *15 Golden Records—30 Golden Hits* (RCA PP-11301), and in the *20 Golden Hits in Full Color Sleeves* (RCA PP-11340) boxed set that was released two months later.
• "IN THE GHETTO"/"If I Can Dream" (RCA PB-13890) October 1984. One of six singles in the boxed set *Elvis' Greatest Hits—Golden Singles, Volume 1* (RCA PP-13897). The single was pressed on gold vinyl and had a special gold "50th" anniversary label.

LPs:
• *Elvis—A Legendary Performer, Volume 3*
• *Elvis Aron Presley* (Las Vegas; August 1969)
• *Elvis' Gold Records, Volume 5*
• *Elvis in Person* (Las Vegas; August 25, 1969)
• *Elvis: Worldwide 50 Gold Award Hits, Volume 1*
• *From Elvis in Memphis*
• *From Memphis to Vegas/From Vegas to Memphis* (Las Vegas; August 25, 1969)
• *The Memphis Record*
• *Pure Gold*
• *The Top Ten Hits*

Bootleg LPs:
• *The Complete Kid Galahad Session, Volume 3* (alternate take)
• *The Legend Lives On* (Las Vegas; August 1969)

• *Superstar Outtakes* (Las Vegas; August 1969)

IN YOUR ARMS

Aaron Schroeder and Wally Gold wrote "In Your Arms" for Elvis, who recorded it on March 12, 1961, at RCA's Nashville studios.

LPs:
• *Something for Everybody*

INDESCRIBABLY BLUE

"Indescribably Blue" was written by Darrell Glenn and recorded by Elvis on June 10, 1966, at RCA's Nashville studios. The single release had an eight-week stay on *Billboard*'s Hot 100 chart, reaching #33. In the beginning of the third phrase, "I smile and tell them, it's been a day or two," Elvis came in just a fraction of a second too early on the word *I*. Global sales have been estimated at over one million copies.

Singles:
• "INDESCRIBABLY BLUE"/"Fools Fall in Love" (RCA 47-9056) January 6, 1967. Standard release.
• "INDESCRIBABLY BLUE"/"Fools Fall in Love" (RCA 447-0659) 1970. Gold Standard Series reissue.

LPs:
• *Elvis' Gold Records, Volume 4*

INHERIT THE WIND

Eddie Rabbitt wrote "Inherit the Wind," which Elvis recorded at American Sound Studios on January 16, 1969.

LPs:
• *Back in Memphis*
• *From Memphis to Vegas/From Vegas to Memphis*
• *The Memphis Record*

IS IT SO STRANGE

During the Million-Dollar-Quartet session of December 4, 1956, Elvis commented that Faron Young wrote "Is It So Strange" for him. But because Elvis wanted half of the publishing rights, Young recorded the song himself. Elvis sang "Is It So Strange" for Jerry Lee Lewis and Carl Perkins during the Million-Dollar-Quartet session.

On January 19, 1957, Elvis finally got around to recording the song at Radio Recorders. Take #12 was released by RCA.

EPs:
• *Just for You*

LPs:
• *A Date with Elvis*
• *Separate Ways*

Bootleg LPs:
• *The One Million Dollar Quartet* (Sun Records; December 4, 1956)

ISLAND OF LOVE (KAUAI)

Elvis sang "Island of Love (Kauai)" in his 1961 movie *Blue Hawaii*. The song, which was written by Sid Tepper and Roy C. Bennett, was recorded on March 22,

1961, at Radio Recorders. The film version had female vocal backing.

LPs:
- *Blue Hawaii*

Bootleg LPs:
- *Behind Closed Doors* (takes #6 and #7 [false starts], and #8)
- *The Blue Hawaii Box* (takes #1–13)

IT AIN'T ME BABE
Bob Dylan wrote this tune in 1964 for his LP *Another Side of Bob Dylan* (Columbia CS 8993). Later that year, Johnny Cash and his wife, June Carter, had a #4 country hit with "It Ain't Me Babe" (Columbia 43145). The Turtles reached #8 on the Hot 100 chart with their rendition of the song (White Whale 222) in 1965.

Elvis sang "It Ain't Me Babe" in concert in the 1970s.

IT AIN'T NO BIG THING (BUT IT'S GROWING)
Elvis recorded "It Ain't No Big Thing (But It's Growing)" on June 6, 1970, at RCA's Nashville studios. Later that same year, both the Mills Brothers (Dot 17321) and Tex Williams (Monument 1216) made recordings of the song that reached #64 and #50 on the country chart, respectively. "It Ain't No Big Thing (But It's Growing)" was written by Merritt, Joy, and Hall.

LPs:
- *Love Letters from Elvis*

IT FEELS SO RIGHT
Elvis sang "It Feels So Right" in his 1965 movie *Tickle Me*. The song, however, had been recorded five years earlier, on March 21, 1960, at RCA's Nashville studios. Written by Fred Wise and Ben Weisman, "It Feels So Right" had a six-week stay on *Billboard*'s Hot 100 chart, peaking at #55.

Singles:
- "(Such an) Easy Question"/"IT FEELS SO RIGHT" (RCA 47-8585) May 1965. Standard release. The original picture sleeve read, "Coming Soon! Special TICKLE ME EP." One month later the picture sleeve was changed to read, "Ask for Special TICKLE ME EP."
- "(Such an) Easy Question"/"IT FEELS SO RIGHT" (RCA 447-0653) November 1966. Gold Standard Series reissue.

LPs:
- *Elvis Is Back*
- *A Valentine Gift for You*

Bootleg LPs:
- *Elvis Sings Songs from Tickle Me* (alternate take)

IT HURTS ME
"It Hurts Me" was written by Joy Byers and Charlie Daniels, although many record labels credit only Byers. Elvis recorded the song on January 12, 1964, at RCA's Nashville studios. The single release reached #29 on *Billboard*'s Hot 100 chart during its seven-week stay. Elvis again recorded "It Hurts Me" for the "Guitar Man" segment of his 1968 TV special "Elvis," but the song was omitted from the program because of time. The instrumental track for that recording was made at Western Recorders in Hollywood on June 20 or 21,

1968. Elvis's vocal was recorded on June 30 at NBC-TV. An alternate mix of "It Hurts Me" appeared on the bootleg LP *Eternal Elvis*, as well as on an Italian 45 RPM single (N-1410). The orchestration and the Jordanaires' vocal backing from one of the stereo channels was omitted, leaving only Elvis and piano accompaniment (by Floyd Cramer).

Singles:
- "Kissin' Cousins"/"IT HURTS ME" (RCA 47-8307) January 1964. Standard release.
- "Kissin' Cousins"/"IT HURTS ME" (RCA 447-0644) May 1965. Gold Standard Series reissue.

LPs:
- *Elvis—A Legendary Performer, Volume 3* (alternate take without instrumental bridge, from "Elvis" TV special)
- *Elvis' Gold Records, Volume 4*
- *Elvis: The Other Sides—Worldwide Gold Award Hits, Volume 2*

Bootleg LPs:
- *Eternal Elvis* (alternate mix, with one stereo channel missing)
- *The '68 Comeback* (alternate take, with instrumental bridge from "Elvis" TV special)
- *The '68 Comeback, Volume 2* (alternate take, with instrumental bridge from "Elvis" TV special)
- *Superstar Outtakes* (alternate take, with instrumental bridge from "Elvis" TV special)
- *Unfinished Business* (studio alternate take)

IT IS NO SECRET (WHAT GOD CAN DO)
Stuart Hamblen wrote and recorded "It Is No Secret (What God Can Do) (Columbia 20724) in 1950. Once inspired, Hamblen wrote the hymn in 17 minutes. Later in 1950, Red Foley and the Andrews Sisters recorded the song for Decca Records (Decca 14566). Although popular, their version did not chart. It wasn't until 1951 that "It Is No Secret (What God Can Do)" reached the charts. Versions by Jo Stafford (Columbia 39082) and Bill Kenny and the Song Spinners (Decca 27326) both charted, reaching #29 and #18 on the Best-Selling Singles chart, respectively.

Elvis recorded "It Is No Secret (What God Can Do)" on January 19, 1957, at Radio Recorders. Take #13 was chosen by RCA for release.

EPs:
- *Peace in the Valley*

LPs:
- *Elvis' Christmas Album*
- *You'll Never Walk Alone*

IT KEEPS RIGHT ON A-HURTIN'
Johnny Tillotson wrote and recorded "It Keeps Right on a-Hurtin'" (Cadence 1418) in 1962. It reached #3 on *Billboard*'s Hot 100 chart and #4 on the country chart. In 1968 Margaret Whiting (London 119) charted with the song, peaking at #28 on the Easy-Listening chart.

Elvis recorded "It Keeps Right on a-Hurtin'" on February 20, 1969, at American Sound Studios in Memphis.

LPs
- *From Elvis in Memphis*
- *The Memphis Record*

IT WON'T BE LONG
Elvis recorded "It Won't Be Long" in June 1966 at Radio Recorders for his 1967 film *Double Trouble*, but it was cut from the final print. Sid Wayne and Ben Weisman are the composers.

LPs:
• *Double Trouble*

IT WON'T SEEM LIKE CHRISTMAS (WITHOUT YOU)
This Christmas song was written by J. A. Balthrop and recorded by Elvis at RCA's Nashville studios on May 15, 1971. The vocal backing was overdubbed on May 21.

LPs:
• *Elvis Sings the Wonderful World of Christmas*

IT'LL BE ME
"It'll Be Me," written by Jack Clement, was the flip side of Jerry Lee Lewis's 1957 hit "Whole Lotta Shakin' Goin' On" (Sun 267). Elvis may have recorded the song at RCA, but no proof has yet surfaced.

ITO EATS
Elvis sang "Ito Eats" in his 1961 movie *Blue Hawaii*. The song, written by Sid Tepper and Roy C. Bennett, was recorded by Elvis on March 22, 1961, at Radio Recorders.

LPs:
• *Blue Hawaii*

Bootleg LPs:
• *The Blue Hawaii Box* (takes #1-9)
• *The Blue Hawaii Sessions* (takes #1, #2, #5-8)

IT'S A MATTER OF TIME
"It's a Matter of Time" was written by Clive Westlake and recorded by Elvis on March 29, 1972, at RCA's Hollywood studios. The single release had a 13-week stay on *Billboard*'s country chart, peaking at #36. On the Easy-Listening chart, "It's a Matter of Time" reached #9.

Singles:
• "Burning Love"/"IT'S A MATTER OF TIME" (RCA 74-0769) August 1972. Standard release.

LPs:
• *Double Dynamite*
• *Burning Love and Hits from His Movies, Volume 2*

Bootleg LPs:
• *Long Lost Songs* (Las Vegas; August 25, 1973)

IT'S A SIN
Zeb Turner and Fred Rose wrote "It's a Sin" for Eddy Arnold, who recorded it in 1947 (RCA 20-2241). It was Arnold's first successful recording. In 1969 Marty Robbins reached #5 on the country chart with his version (Columbia 44739).

Elvis recorded "It's a Sin" on March 12, 1961, at RCA's Nashville studios.

LPs:
• *Something for Everybody*

IT'S A WONDERFUL WORLD
Elvis sang "It's a Wonderful World" in his 1964 movie *Roustabout*. The original title is believed by some to be "I Never Had It So Good." Although it was not nominated for an Academy Award for Best Song, "It's a Wonderful World" got preliminary consideration. It was the only Elvis song ever to be considered for an Oscar nomination. Elvis recorded "It's a Wonderful World" in March 1964 at Radio Recorders. Sid Tepper and Roy C. Bennett are the composers.

LPs:
• *Roustabout*

IT'S CARNIVAL TIME
"It's Carnival Time" was written by Ben Weisman and Sid Wayne for Elvis's 1964 movie *Roustabout*. The recording session took place at Radio Recorders in March 1964. The phrasing and backing of the film version differ from that on record.

LPs:
• *Roustabout*

IT'S EASY FOR YOU
Lloyd Webber and Tim Rice wrote "It's Easy for You" for Elvis, who recorded the song on the night of October 29-30, 1976, at Graceland. Overdubbing was done at Young 'Un Sound in Nashville on April 6-7, 1977.

LPs:
• *Moody Blue*

IT'S IMPOSSIBLE
"It's Impossible" was written by Sid Wayne and Armando Manzanero[1] and popularized by Perry Como in 1970. His recording (RCA 74-0387) reached #10 on *Billboard*'s Hot 100 chart and number one on the Easy-Listening chart. Sales easily exceeded one million copies. The original title of the song was "Somos Novios." In 1971 New Birth had a #12 rhythm & blues recording of "It's Impossible" (RCA PB-0520).

Elvis sang "It's Impossible" in concert on several occasions in the 1970s.

LPs:
• *Elvis* (RCA APL1-0283)
• *Pure Gold*

Bootleg LPs:
• *The Legend Lives On* (Las Vegas; February 16, 1972)
• *Superstar Outtakes* (Las Vegas; 1972)

---

[1]Manzanero was the first Mexican RCA recording artist to sell over a million dollars' worth of records.

IT'S MIDNIGHT

"It's Midnight" was written by Billy Edd Wheeler and Jerry Chesnut and first recorded by Elvis on December 10, 1973, at Stax Records. His single release had a 14-week stay on *Billboard*'s country chart, reaching #9. On the Easy-Listening chart, the song reached #8.

Singles:
- "Promised Land"/"IT'S MIDNIGHT" (RCA PB-10074) October 1974. Standard release.
- "Promised Land"/"IT'S MIDNIGHT" (RCA JA-10074) October 1974. Disc jockey promotional release.
- "Promised Land"/"IT'S MIDNIGHT" (RCA GB-10488) February 1976. Gold Standard Series reissue.

LPs:
- *Always on My Mind*
- *Our Memories of Elvis* (without overdubbing)
- *Promised Land*

Bootleg LPs:
- *Big Boss Man* (Las Vegas; August 19, 1974)
- *Command Performance* (Las Vegas; August 21, 1974)

IT'S NICE TO GO TRAVELING

Written by Sammy Cahn and Jimmy Van Heusen, "It's Nice to Go Traveling" was sung twice on the 1960 Frank Sinatra–Timex Special "Welcome Home, Elvis." Elvis, Frank Sinatra, Nancy Sinatra, Joey Bishop, and Sammy Davis Jr. sang a few lines to open the show, and Sinatra later concluded the show with the tune. The opening was shown in the 1981 documentary *This Is Elvis*.

Bootleg LPs:
- *Frank Sinatra—Welcome Home, Elvis* ("Welcome Home, Elvis" taping; March 26, 1960)

IT'S NOW OR NEVER

"It's Now or Never" was based on the Italian song "O Sole Mio," written in 1901 by G. Capurro and Eduardo di Capua. ("O Sole Mio" means "My Sunshine.") Over the years, "O Sole Mio" has been recorded by countless singers, including Emilio De Gorgorzo (Victor 74105) in 1908, Enrico Caruso (Victor 87243) in 1916, and Mario Lanza. In 1949 Tony Martin had a #2 hit with "O Sole Mio," using English lyrics and the title "There's No Tomorrow" (RCA 3078). "O Sole Mio" was the first song actor James Stewart learned to play on the accordion. It was also the first song Connie Francis sang at a school recital at the age of 12.

While still in the Army, Elvis decided he wanted to record Tony Martin's "There's No Tomorrow," but he wanted new lyrics and a new arrangement. He told Freddie Bienstock of Hill and Range Music of his interest. Bienstock flew back to his New York office from West Germany. When he arrived, the only songwriters around at the moment were Aaron Schroeder and Wally Gold. They got the job of rewriting "There's No Tomorrow" for Elvis. It didn't take long. The title—"It's Now or Never"—came quickly; the new lyrics took about 30 minutes. A demonstration record for Elvis was recorded by David Hill (real name: David Hess), using an uptempo cha-cha arrangement.

Elvis loved the demo and recorded "It's Now or Never" on April 3, 1960, at RCA's Nashville studios. The single release entered *Billboard*'s Hot 100 chart at #44. Within five weeks "It's Now or Never" was number one, replacing Brian Hyland's "Itsy Bitsy Teenie Weenie Yellow Polkadot Bikini." After five weeks at the top, it was dethroned by Chubby Checker's "The Twist." "It's Now or Never" spent a total of 20 weeks on the chart. It reached #7 on the rhythm & blues chart. In England, "It's Now or Never" *entered* the chart at number one and remained in that position for eight weeks—the longest period for any Presley single in England. Because of copyright reasons, the release of "It's Now or Never" in England was held up for five months. Total global sales of the record exceed 22 million copies—the most for any Presley record. *Billboard* magazine named "It's Now or Never" the Vocal Single of 1960.

Elvis sang "It's Now or Never" in concert on several occasions in the 1970s. Before Elvis's performances, Sherrill Nielsen would sometimes sing a few bars of "O Sole Mio." However, Elvis is known to have sung "O Sole Mio" himself in concert, including a performance at the Las Vegas Hilton on December 13, 1975.

In 1981, John Schneider reached #14 on the Hot 100 chart and #4 on the country chart with his recording of "It's Now or Never" (Scotti Brothers 02105).

Singles:
- "IT'S NOW OR NEVER"/"A Mess of Blues" (RCA 47-7777) July 1960. Standard release.
- "IT'S NOW OR NEVER"/"A Mess of Blues" (RCA 61-7777) July 1960. "Living Stereo" release.
- "IT'S NOW OR NEVER"/"A Mess of Blues" (RCA 447-0628) February 1962. Gold Standard Series reissue.
- "IT'S NOW OR NEVER"/"A Mess of Blues" (RCA PB-11110) October 1977. One of 15 singles in the boxed set *15 Golden Records—30 Golden Hits* (RCA PP-11301).
- "IT'S NOW OR NEVER"/"Surrender" (RCA PB-13889) October 1984. One of six singles in the boxed set *Elvis' Greatest Hits—Golden Singles, Volume 1* (RCA PP-13897). The singles were pressed on gold vinyl with gold "50th" anniversary labels.
- "IT'S NOW OR NEVER"/"I Walk the Line" (by Jaye P. Morgan) (U.S.A.F. Program #125/#126) February 1961. An edited version of the song was contained in this five-minute radio program for the U.S. Air Force.

EPs:
- *Elvis by Request*

LPs:
- *Elvis* (RCA DPL2-0056[e])
- *Elvis—A Legendary Performer, Volume 2*
- *Elvis Aron Presley* (USS *Arizona* Memorial; March 25, 1961)
- *Elvis' Golden Records, Volume 3*
- *Elvis in Concert* (Rapid City, South Dakota; June 21, 1977)
- *Elvis: Worldwide 50 Gold Award Hits, Volume 1*
- *The Number One Hits*
- *The Top Ten Hits*

Bootleg LPs:
- *Command Performance* (Las Vegas; August 21, 1974)
- *Elvis' 1961 Hawaii Benefit Concert* (USS *Arizona* Memorial; March 25, 1961)
- *Elvis Presley Is Alive and Well and Singing in Las Vegas, Volume 1* (Las Vegas; August 1975)
- *Eternal Elvis, Volume 2* (Pittsburgh; December 31, 1976)

- *The Last Farewell* (Indianapolis; June 26, 1977)
- *Rockin' with Elvis New Year's Eve Pittsburgh, Pa. Dec. 31, 1976* (Pittsburgh; December 31, 1976)
- *Sold Out* (Las Vegas; September 3, 1973)
- *Standing Room Only, Volume 2* (Las Vegas; September 21, 1974)
- *Standing Room Only, Volume 3* (Las Vegas; February 1971)
- *The Vegas Years, 1972–1975* (Las Vegas; 1975)

IT'S ONLY LOVE

B. J. Thomas recorded "It's Only Love" in 1969 (Scepter 12244). His recording was a moderate success, peaking at #45 on the Hot 100 chart and #37 on the Easy-Listening chart. Mark James and Steve Tyrell are the composers.

The instrumental track to Elvis's version of "It's Only Love" was recorded on May 20, 1971, at RCA's Nashville studios. Elvis recorded his vocal the next day. The single release had a brief six-week stay on *Billboard*'s Hot 100 chart, reaching a high of #51. It did much better on the Easy-Listening chart, topping out at #19. Reportedly, global sales of "It's Only Love" were over one million copies.

Singles:
- "IT'S ONLY LOVE"/"The Sound of Your Cry" (RCA 48-1017) September 1971. Standard release. This is the only Elvis single to have a "48" prefix.
- "IT'S ONLY LOVE"/"The Sound of Your Cry" (RCA 447-0684) May 1972. Gold Standard Series reissue.

LPs:
- *Elvis Aron Presley*

Bootleg LPs:
- *The Hillbilly Cat, 1954–1974, Volume 1* (same as RCA's commercial release)

IT'S OVER

Jimmie Rodgers wrote and recorded "It's Over" (Dot 16861) in 1966. His version reached #37 on *Billboard*'s Hot 100 chart. Two years later, Eddy Arnold also charted with his rendition of "It's Over" (RCA 47-9525), reaching #74 on the Hot 100 chart and #4 on the country chart.

Elvis occasionally sang "It's Over" in concert in the 1970s. It was one of the songs in his 1973 TV special, "Elvis: Aloha from Hawaii."

LPs:
- *Aloha from Hawaii via Satellite* (Honolulu; January 14, 1973)
- *The Alternate Aloha* (rehearsal concert for "Elvis: Aloha from Hawaii"; January 12, 1973)

Bootleg LPs:
- *Aloha Rehearsal Show—Kui Lee Cancer Benefit* (rehearsal concert for "Elvis: Aloha from Hawaii"; January 12, 1973)
- *A Dog's Life* (rehearsal concert for "Elvis: Aloha from Hawaii"; January 12, 1973)
- *The Legend Lives On* (Las Vegas; February 1972)
- *Superstar Outtakes, Volume 2* (Las Vegas; 1972)

IT'S OVER

This Roy Orbison tune is sometimes confused with Jimmie Rodgers's 1966 song of the same title. Orbison wrote "It's Over" with Bill Dees in 1964. His subse-

quent recording (Monument 837) reached #9 on the Hot 100 chart and number one in England. Total sales exceeded one million copies.

Elvis is known to have sung "It's Over" at least once in concert, but probably did so on other occasions as well.

"IT'S STILL HERE"

Elvis recorded "It's Still Here," an Ivory Joe Hunter tune, on May 19, 1971, at RCA's Nashville studios.

LPs:
- *Elvis* (RCA APL1-0283)
- *Elvis Aron Presley* (without overdubbing, just Elvis singing and playing piano)

Ivory Joe Hunter's demo for Elvis. (Photo courtesy Don Fink)

IT'S YOUR BABY, YOU ROCK IT

On June 5, 1970, Elvis recorded "It's Your Baby, You Rock It" at RCA's Nashville studios. Shirl Milete and Nora Fowler are the composers.

LPs:
- *Elvis Country*

Bootleg LPs:
- *Behind Closed Doors* (edited alternate take)
- *The Entertainer* (edited alternate take spliced with "Don't Think Twice, It's All Right")
- *Unfinished Business* (edited alternate take)

I'VE GOT A THING ABOUT YOU, BABY

"I've Got a Thing About You, Baby" was written by Tony Joe White and first recorded by Billy Lee Riley (Entrance 7508) in 1972. His recording barely made the Hot 100, peaking at #93.

Elvis recorded "I've Got a Thing About You, Baby" on July 22, 1973, at Stax Studios in Memphis. His single release had a 12-week stay on *Billboard*'s Hot 100 chart, peaking at #39. It fared better on the country and Easy-Listening charts, reaching #4 and #27, respectively.

Singles:
- "I'VE GOT A THING ABOUT YOU, BABY"/"Take Good Care of Her" (RCA APBO-0196) January 1974. Standard release.
- "I'VE GOT A THING ABOUT YOU, BABY"/"Take Good Care of Her" (RCA DJBO-0196) January 1974. Disc jockey promotional release.
- "I'VE GOT A THING ABOUT YOU, BABY"/"Take Good Care of Her" (RCA GB-10485) March 1976. Gold Standard Series reissue.

LPs:
- *Good Times*
- *This Is Elvis*

I'VE GOT CONFIDENCE
This gospel song was written by Andrae Crouch and recorded by Elvis on May 18, 1971, at RCA's Nashville studios.

LPs:
- *He Touched Me*

I'VE GOT TO FIND MY BABY
Elvis sang "I've Got to Find My Baby" in his 1965 film *Girl Happy*. The song, which was written by Joy Byers, was recorded in June or July 1964 at Radio Recorders. One verse of the movie version was edited out for release on record.

LPs:
- *Girl Happy*

I'VE LOST YOU
Matthews' Southern Comfort first recorded this Ken Howard–Alan Blaikley song in 1970 on Decca Records.

Elvis recorded "I've Lost You" on June 4, 1970, at RCA's Nashville studios. The single release had a nine-week stay on *Billboard*'s Hot 100 chart, peaking at #32. On the country and Easy-Listening charts "I've Lost You" reached #57 and #5, respectively. Sales reportedly exceeded one million copies. Elvis sang "I've Lost You" in his 1970 documentary *Elvis—That's the Way It Is*. That performance was filmed on August 13, 1970, at the International Hotel in Las Vegas.

Singles:
- "I'VE LOST YOU"/"The Next Step Is Love" (RCA 47-9873) July 1970. Standard release.
- "I'VE LOST YOU"/"The Next Step Is Love" (RCA 447-0677) August 1971. Gold Standard Series reissue.

LPs:
- *Always on My Mind*
- *Elvis: The Other Sides—Worldwide Gold Award Hits, Volume 2*
- *That's the Way It Is* (Las Vegas; August 13, 1970)

Bootleg LPs:
- *The Hillbilly Cat "Live"* (Las Vegas; August 1970)
- *King of Las Vegas Live* (*Elvis—That's the Way It Is* soundtrack)
- *That's the Way It Is* (*Elvis—That's the Way It Is* soundtrack)

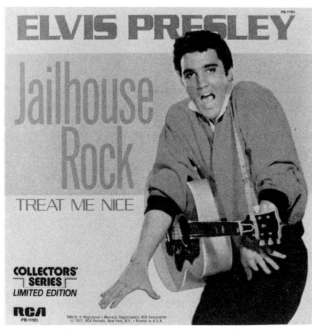

(Photo courtesy Don Fink)

JAILHOUSE ROCK

Jerry Leiber and Mike Stoller wrote "Jailhouse Rock" for the big production number in Elvis's 1957 movie of the same title. Dudley Brooks played piano on the recording, which was made on April 30, 1957, at Radio Recorders. Mike Stoller, however, claims that he played piano on the song. He *did* make a cameo appearance in the film as Vince Everett's (Elvis) piano player. "Jailhouse Rock" entered *Billboard*'s Top 100 chart at #15. Three weeks later it was number one, replacing the Everly Brothers' "Wake Up Little Susie." After seven weeks in the top spot, "Jailhouse Rock" was replaced by Sam Cooke's "You Send Me." Elvis's recording spent a total of 27 weeks on the chart. The record was also number one on the country (for one week) and rhythm & blues (for five weeks) charts. In England, "Jailhouse Rock" *entered* the chart at number one—the first single in the history of the British charts to do so. Worldwide, the record sold several million copies. Take #6 is the one on record.

Elvis sang "Jailhouse Rock" in two of his TV specials, "Elvis" and "Elvis in Concert."

Singles:
- "JAILHOUSE ROCK"/"Treat Me Nice" (RCA 20-7035) September 1957. Standard 78 RPM release.
- "JAILHOUSE ROCK"/"Treat Me Nice" (RCA 47-7035) September 1957. Standard 45 RPM release. For an October 10, 1957, press preview, MGM issued promo copies with special sleeves that wrapped around the standard sleeves.
- "JAILHOUSE ROCK"/"Treat Me Nice" (RCA 447-0619) 1961. Gold Standard Series reissue.
- "The Elvis Medley"/"Always on My Mind" (RCA PB-13351) October 1982. "Jailhouse Rock" is part of a medley with "Teddy Bear,"

"Hound Dog," "Don't Be Cruel," "Burning Love," and "Suspicious Minds."
- "The Elvis Medley"/"The Elvis Medley" (Short Version) (RCA JB-13351) October 1982. Disc jockey promotional release.
- "JAILHOUSE ROCK"/"Treat Me Nice" (RCA PB-11101) October 1977. One of 15 singles released in the boxed set *15 Golden Records—30 Golden Hits* (RCA PP-11301).
- "Heartbreak Hotel"/"JAILHOUSE ROCK" (RCA PB-13892) October 1984. One of six singles released in the boxed set *Elvis' Greatest Hits—Golden Singles, Volume 2*. All singles were pressed on gold vinyl.

EPs:
- *Dealer's Prevue* (RCA SDS-57-39)
- *Extended Play Sampler* (RCA SPA-7-61)
- *Jailhouse Rock*

LPs:
- *Elvis* (RCA DPL2-0056[e])
- *Elvis—A Canadian Tribute*
- *Elvis—A Legendary Performer, Volume 2*
- *Elvis Aron Presley* ("Elvis" TV special taping; June 29, 1968, 8:00 P.M. show)
- *Elvis' Golden Records*
- *Elvis in Concert* (Rapid City, South Dakota; June 21, 1977)
- *Elvis in Hollywood*
- *The Elvis Medley*
- *Elvis Recorded Live on Stage in Memphis* (Memphis; March 20, 1974)
- Elvis—*TV Special* ("Elvis" TV special taping; June 29, 1968, 8:00 P.M. show)
- *Elvis: Worldwide 50 Gold Award Hits, Volume 1*
- *Essential Elvis—The First Movies*
- *The Number One Hits*
- *Pure Gold*
- *This Is Elvis*
- *The Top Ten Hits*

Bootleg LPs:
- *The Burbank Sessions, Volume 2* ("Elvis" TV special taping; June 29, 1968, 6:00 P.M. and 8:00 P.M. shows)
- *Got a Lot o' Livin' to Do!* (*Jailhouse Rock* soundtrack)
- *The Last Farewell* (Indianapolis; June 26, 1977)
- *Loving You Recording Sessions* (alternate take)
- *The Monologue L.P.* (Las Vegas; July 31, 1969 [in medley with "Don't Be Cruel"])
- *Please Release Me* (*Jailhouse Rock* soundtrack)
- *Sold Out* (Las Vegas: September 3, 1973) (Nashville; July 1, 1973 [in medley with "Long Tall Sally," "Whole Lotta Shakin' Goin' On," "Your Mama Don't Dance," and "Shake, Rattle and Roll"])

JAMBALAYA

"Jambalaya" was written and recorded by Hank Williams on MGM Records (MGM 11283) in 1952. His recording hit the top of *Billboard*'s country chart and #23 on the Best-Selling Singles chart. Jo Stafford's recording (Columbia 39838) peaked at #3. Both records sold over a million copies. "Jambalaya" (subtitled "On the Bayou") has been recorded by many artists over the years. Even Fats Domino (Imperial 5796) charted (#30) with the song in 1962.

Elvis sang "Jambalaya" at a concert in Louisiana in

May or June 1975. The city was either Monroe, Lake Charles, or Shreveport.

Bootleg LPs:
• *Eternal Elvis* (Louisiana; May or June 1975)

JERRY'S BOOGIE
"Jerry's Boogie" was a piano solo played by Jerry Lee Lewis during the Million-Dollar-Quartet session on December 4, 1956.

Bootleg LPs:
• *The One Million Dollar Quartet* (Sun Records; December 4, 1956)

JESUS HOLD MY HAND
This gospel song was written by Albert E. Brumley in 1933 and was popular in church services in the 1940s and 1950s. During the Million-Dollar-Quartet session on December 4, 1956, Elvis sang "Jesus Hold My Hand," with Jerry Lee Lewis singing harmony.

Bootleg LPs:
• *The Million Dollar Quartet* (Sun Records; December 4, 1956)
• *The One Million Dollar Quartet* (Sun Records; December 4, 1956)

JESUS KNOWS WHAT I NEED
(See *He Knows Just What I Need*)

JINGLE BELLS
J. S. Pierpont wrote "Jingle Bells" in 1857 as entertainment for a Boston Sunday School class. Since then, this perennial Christmas favorite has been recorded countless times. Perhaps the biggest hit version came in 1943 when Bing Crosby and the Andrews Sisters' recording (Decca 23281) sold over a million copies. The flip side of that disc was another favorite, "Santa Claus Is Coming to Town." Two years earlier, Glenn Miller also had a hit with "Jingle Bells" (Bluebird 11353). One of the most unusual recordings of the song came in 1955, when Don Charles, from Copenhagen, Denmark, spliced a tape of dogs barking at various pitches to the tune of "Jingle Bells." The resultant recording (RCA 6344) eventually sold a million copies.

Elvis sang "Jingle Bells" in concert on a couple of occasions.

JOHNNY B. GOODE
"Johnny B. Goode" is a Chuck Berry hit from 1958 (Chess 1691), which he also composed. Although several sources indicate that the song is autobiographical, Berry has denied it. "Johnny B. Goode" hit #8 on *Billboard*'s Hot 100 chart and #5 on the rhythm & blues chart. It eventually became a million-seller. In 1969 Buck Owens topped the country chart with his rendition (Capitol 2485). Other versions that have charted include those by Dion (Columbia 43096) in 1964 and Johnny Winter (Columbia 45058) in 1970.

Elvis sang "Johnny B. Goode" in concert quiet often, as it was one of his favorites. His performance at the International Hotel in Las Vegas on August 22, 1969, was recorded by RCA for inclusion in the *From Memphis to Vegas/From Vegas to Memphis* LP. *Elvis on Tour* included "Johnny B. Goode" from an April 1972

concert. Two TV specials, "Elvis: Aloha from Hawaii" and "Elvis in Concert," also included the song.

LPs:
• *Aloha from Hawaii via Satellite* (Honolulu; January 14, 1973)
• *Elvis Aron Presley* (Dallas; June 6, 1975)
• *Elvis in Concert* (Omaha, Nebraska, or Rapid City, South Dakota; June 19 or 21, 1977)
• *Elvis in Person* (Las Vegas; August 22, 1969)
• *From Memphis to Vegas/From Vegas to Memphis* (Las Vegas; August 22, 1969)

Bootleg LPs:
• *Elvis on Tour* (*Elvis on Tour* soundtrack)
• *The Hillbilly Cat "Live"* (Las Vegas; August 1970)
• *The Last Farewell* (Indianapolis; June 26, 1977)

JOSHUA FIT THE BATTLE
This traditional black spiritual dates back to about 1865. Marshall Bartholomew made a popular recording of "Joshua Fit the Battle" in 1930, as did Thelma Carpenter in the 1940s (Majestic 1104). The song, also known as "Joshua Fit the Battle of Jericho" and "Joshua Fit de Battle of Jericho," has probably been recorded by every gospel group at one time or another.

Elvis recorded "Joshua Fit the Battle" on October 31, 1960, at RCA's Nashville studios.

Singles:
• "JOSHUA FIT THE BATTLE"/Known Only to Him" (RCA 447-0651) March 1966. Gold Standard Series original.

LPs:
• *His Hand in Mine*

JOY
Mitch Ryder had a moderate hit (#41 Hot 100) with this song (New Voice 824) in 1967. "Joy" was reportedly recorded by Elvis, but no evidence has surfaced.

JUANITA
Rufus Thomas recorded "Juanita" at Sun Records in April 1952. The master was sold to Chess Records, who released it a few months later. "Juanita " (Chess 1517) did not chart.

Some have said that Elvis sang "Juanita" on tour in 1955 and may have recorded it while at Sun Records. While it's doubtful that Elvis recorded the song, he quite possibly sang it on tour, but the authors have yet to see any proof.

JUDY
Teddy Redell wrote and recorded "Judy" (Atco 6162) in 1960. It did not chart. On March 13, 1961, Elvis recorded the song at RCA's Nashville studios. His single release in 1967 had a five-week stay on *Billboard*'s Hot 100 chart, peaking at #78.

Singles:
• "There's Always Me"/"JUDY" (RCA 47-9287) August 1967. Standard release.
• "There's Always Me"/"JUDY" (RCA 447-0661) 1970. Gold Standard Series reissue.

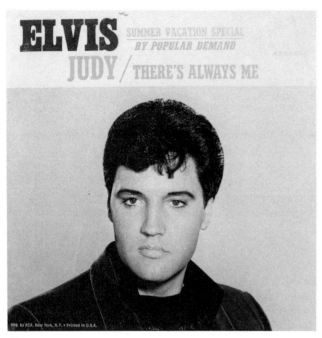

(Photo courtesy Don Fink)

EPs:
• *The EP Collection, Volume 2* (takes #1-4)

LPs:
• *Something for Everybody*

JUST A CLOSER WALK WITH THEE
"Just a Closer Walk with Thee" is a traditional gospel hymn that Red Foley arranged to suit his vocal talents in 1950. His recording (Decca 14505) reached #9 on *Billboard*'s country chart and sold over a million copies. The Jordanaires provided vocal backing. That same year, the Stamps Quartet released "Just a Closer Walk with Thee" (Columbia 20683).

In 1958, at the home of disc jockey Eddie Fadal, Elvis sang "Just a Closer Walk with Thee," accompanying himself on piano. Fadal taped the performance, as well as several other songs that appeared on the bootleg *Forever Young, Forever Beautiful.*

Bootleg LPs:
• *Forever Young, Forever Beautiful* (Waco, Texas; 1958)

JUST A LITTLE BIT
"Just a Little Bit" was recorded by Rosco Gordon (Vee Jay 332) in 1960. The record reached #64 on the Hot 100 chart. A more successful version by Roy Head (Scepter 12116) peaked at #39 in 1965. In England a group called the Undertakers had their only hit with "Just a Little Bit" (Pye 7N15607) in 1964. Elvis recorded "Just a Little Bit" at Stax Studios in Memphis on July 22, 1973. His version lists John Thornton, Piney Brown, Ralph Bass, and Earl Washington as composers, while the earlier recordings by Gordon and Head list the composer as D. Gordon.

LPs:
• *Raised on Rock/For Ol' Times Sake*

JUST A LITTLE TALK WITH JESUS
Cleavant Williams wrote "Just a Little Talk with Jesus" in 1937. It proved to be a popular gospel tune in the 1940s and 1950s. During the Million-Dollar-Quartet session on December 4, 1956, Elvis sang "Just a Little Talk with Jesus" with Jerry Lee Lewis singing harmony.

Bootleg LPs:
• *The Million Dollar Quartet* (Sun Records; December 4, 1956)
• *The One Million Dollar Quartet* (Sun Records; December 4, 1956)

JUST BECAUSE
"Just Because" was composed by Bob Shelton, Joe Shelton, and Sid Robin in 1937 and recorded that year by Dick Stabile (Decca 716). Bunny Berigan played trumpet on Stabile's recording. It wasn't until the early 1940s that the Shelton Brothers recorded their own song (Decca 5872). Frankie Yankovic had a popular version of "Just Because" in 1948.

Elvis recorded "Just Because" at Sun Studios on September 10, 1954. It remained unreleased until his first LP, *Elvis Presley*, reached the stores in March 1956. "Just Because" was one of the songs that Elvis sang on the "Louisiana Hayride."

Singles:
• "Blue Moon"/"JUST BECAUSE" (RCA 20-6640) September 1956. Standard 78 RPM release.
• "Blue Moon"/"JUST BECAUSE" (RCA 47-6640) September 1956. Standard 45 RPM release.
• "Blue Moon"/"JUST BECAUSE" (RCA 447-0613) March 1959. Gold Standard Series reissue.

EPs:
• *Elvis Presley* (RCA EPA-747)
• *Elvis Presley—The Most Talked About New Personality in the Last Ten Years of Recorded Music* (RCA EPB-1254)

LPs:
• *The Complete Sun Sessions*
• *Elvis Presley*
• *The Sun Sessions*

JUST CALL ME LONESOME
Rex Griffin wrote and recorded "Just Call Me Lonesome" in the 1940s. In 1955 Red Foley made a popular recording of the song (Decca 29626), as did Eddy Arnold (RCA 6198). Arnold's release reached as high as #2 on *Billboard*'s country chart.

Elvis recorded "Just Call Me Lonesome" on September 11, 1967, at RCA's Nashville studios.

LPs:
• *Clambake*
• *Guitar Man* (alternate take with new instrumental track overdubbed)

JUST FOR OLD TIME SAKE
Sid Tepper and Roy C. Bennett wrote "Just for Old Time Sake" for Elvis, who recorded the song on March 18, 1962, at RCA's Nashville studios.

LPs:
• *Pot Luck*

JUST PRETEND

On June 6, 1970, Elvis recorded "Just Pretend," a Doug Flett–Guy Fletcher tune, at RCA's Nashville studios. Take #3 is the one released by RCA.

LPs:
* *That's the Way It Is*

Bootleg LPs:
* *Long Lost Songs* (Las Vegas; December 1975)

JUST TELL HER JIM SAID HELLO

"Just Tell Her Jim Said Hello" was written by Jerry Leiber and Mike Stoller and originally recorded by Elvis on March 19, 1962, at RCA's Nashville studios.

Elvis's single release reached #55 on *Billboard*'s Hot 100 chart (for a five-week stay) and #14 on the Easy-Listening chart. Later in 1962, Gerri Granger had an answer record titled "Just Tell Him Jane Said Hello" (Big Top 45-3150).

Singles:
* "She's Not You"/"JUST TELL HER JIM SAID HELLO" (RCA 47-8041) July 1962. Standard release.
* "She's Not You"/"JUST TELL HER JIM SAID HELLO" (RCA 447-0637) June 1963. Gold Standard Series reissue.

LPs:
* *Elvis' Gold Records, Volume 4*
* *Elvis: The Other Sides—Worldwide Gold Award Hits, Volume 2*

KEEP THEM COLD ICY FINGERS OFF OF ME

This traditional country song, written by John Lair, was sung by Elvis at the Humes High School Minstrel Show on April 9, 1953. Another song he sang that day was "Old Shep." Elvis got more applause than any other student and was asked by his teacher, Mildred Scrivener, to do an encore. For years, Elvis fandom has incorrectly called this song "Cold, Cold Icy Fingers."

KEEP YOUR HANDS OFF HER

Elvis recorded "Keep Your Hands Off Her" in a medley with "Got My Mojo Working" on June 5, 1970, at RCA's Nashville studios. It was a studio jam not meant to be recorded, but RCA overdubbed strings, horns, and voices and released it on the *Love Letters from Elvis* LP. "Keep Your Hands Off Her," which was based on the 1961 Damita Jo release (Mercury 71760), "Keep Your Hands Off of Him," does not appear by itself on any RCA releases.

LPs:
• *Love Letters from Elvis*

KEEPER OF THE KEY

At the time of the Million-Dollar-Quartet session on December 4, 1956, country singer Wynn Stewart had just released "Keeper of the Key" (Capitol 3515), which his wife, Beverly, had written with Harlan Howard,[1] Kenny Devine, and Lance Guynes. Although popular in the South, "Keeper of the Key" did not chart nationally. Porter Wagoner later had a version that also did not chart, as did Jimmy Wakely (Shasta 110). At the Million-Dollar-Quartet session, Carl Perkins sang lead, with Elvis and Jerry Lee Lewis singing harmony.

Bootleg LPs:
• *The Million Dollar Quartet* (Sun Records; December 4, 1956)
• *The One Million Dollar Quartet* (Sun Records; December 4, 1956)

KENTUCKY RAIN

Eddie Rabbitt and Dick Heard wrote "Kentucky Rain" for Elvis in 1969. It was recorded at the American Sound Studios in Memphis on February 19, 1969, with Ronnie Milsap providing vocal harmony. The single release in 1970 reached #16 on the Hot 100 chart during its nine-week stay and #31 on the country chart. Sales of "Kentucky Rain" exceeded one million copies.

Singles:
• "KENTUCKY RAIN"/"My Little Friend" (RCA 47-9791) February 1971. Standard release.
• "KENTUCKY RAIN"/"My Little Friend" (RCA 447-0675) August 1971. Gold Standard Series reissue.

LPs:
• *Elvis Aron Presley* (Las Vegas; February 18, 1970)
• *Elvis' Gold Records, Volume 5*
• *Elvis: Worldwide 50 Gold Award Hits, Volume 1*

---

[1]Howard is the husband of singer Jan Howard.

• *The Memphis Record*
• *Pure Gold*

Bootleg LPs:
• *Behind Closed Doors* (Las Vegas; February 18, 1970)
• *The Entertainer* (Las Vegas; February 1970)
• *Standing Room Only, Volume 2* (Las Vegas; February 18, 1970)

KING CREOLE

Jerry Leiber and Mike Stoller wrote this title tune to Elvis's 1958 film *King Creole*. Several attempts were made to record "King Creole." The first session was on January 15, 1958, at Radio Recorders. No takes were deemed worthy of release, although RCA assigned master numbers to takes #3 and #18. Eight days later, on January 23, Elvis finally recorded the version (take #13) that was used on record, but it was much different than the takes from the earlier session. The alternate takes that appear on bootleg albums seem to be from the January 15 session.

EPs:
• *King Creole, Volume 1*

LPs:
• *Elvis in Hollywood*
• *Elvis: The Other Sides—Worldwide Gold Award Hits, Volume 2*
• *King Creole*

Bootleg LPs:
• *From the Beach to the Bayou* (takes #3, #13, #18, and #8 [guitar instrumental])
• *The Rockin' Rebel* (take #18)
• *Special Delivery from Elvis Presley* (take #13)
• *Unfinished Business* (take #?)

KING OF THE WHOLE WIDE WORLD

"King of the Whole Wide World" was written by Ruth Batchelor and Bob Roberts for Elvis's 1962 movie *Kid Galahad*, where it was sung over the opening credits. Elvis first recorded the tune on October 26, 1961, at Radio Recorders. The acceptable master take (#31) was never officially released by RCA, although it has appeared on bootleg LPs. The following day, October 27, Elvis again attempted to record "King of the Whole Wide World," this time with a different arrangement. RCA released take #4 from that session. Boots Randolph's final saxophone solo on that take was deleted before the record's release. Although RCA never issued a single of "King of the Whole Wide World" to the general public, the song reached #30 on *Billboard*'s Hot 100 chart (for a seven-week stay) in 1962, based on the strength of the EP *Kid Galahad*.

Singles:
• "KING OF THE WHOLE WIDE WORLD"/"Home Is Where the Heart Is" (RCA SP-45-118) May 1962. Disc jockey promotional release.

EPs:
• *Kid Galahad*

LPs:
- *C'mon Everybody*

Bootleg LPs:
- *Behind Closed Doors* (take #31 from October 26, 1961)
- *The Complete Kid Galahad Session, Volume I* (takes #16–31 from October 26, 1961)
- *The Complete Kid Galahad Session, Volume 3* (takes #1–4 from October 27, 1961)
- *Leavin' It Up to You* (alternate take #? from October 26, 1961)
- *Unfinished Business* (alternate take #? from October 26, 1961)

KISMET
"Kismet" was written by Sid Tepper and Roy C. Bennett for Elvis's 1965 movie *Harum Scarum*. The song should not be confused with the 1953 Robert Wayne–George Forrest musical play, *Kismet*. Elvis recorded "Kismet" in February (probably the 24th), 1965 at RCA's Nashville studios.

LPs:
- *Harum Scarum*

KISS ME QUICK
"Kiss Me Quick" is a Doc Pomus–Mort Shuman tune written especially for Elvis. The song was recorded by Elvis on June 25, 1961, at RCA's Nashville studios. The single release had a six-week stay on *Billboard*'s Hot 100 chart in 1964, peaking at #34. It was the first original Gold Standard Series issue. An alternate mix of "Kiss Me Quick" appeared on the Spanish EP *Elvis Presley Canta*. One of the stereo channels (with the Jordanaires singing backup) was omitted. The Beatles rated "Kiss Me Quick" when they appeared on the British TV series "Juke Box Jury" in 1964.

Singles:
- "KISS ME QUICK"/"Suspicion" (RCA 447-0639) April 1964. Gold Standard Series original.

LPs:
- *Pot Luck*

Bootleg LPs:
- *Elvis* (RCA single release)

KISSIN' COUSINS
"Kissin' Cousins," written by Fred Wise and Randy Starr, served as the title tune for Elvis's 1964 movie of the same name. Elvis recorded the song in October 1963 at RCA's Nashville studios. "Kissin' Cousins" reached #12 on *Billboard*'s Hot 100 chart, remaining on the chart for nine weeks. It was a million-seller, according to some sources.

Singles:
- "KISSIN' COUSINS"/"It Hurts Me" (RCA 47-8307) January 1964. Standard release.
- "KISSIN' COUSINS"/"It Hurts Me" (RCA 447-0644) May 1965. Gold Standard Series reissue.

LPs:
- *Elvis in Hollywood*
- *Elvis: Worldwide 50 Gold Award Hits, Volume 1*
- *Kissin' Cousins*

KISSIN' COUSINS (NO. 2)
Although Elvis also sang this song in *Kissin' Cousins*, it is a completely different version from the "Kissin' Cousins" that was released as a single. Elvis recorded "Kissin' Cousins (No. 2)" at RCA's Nashville studios in October 1963. It was written by Bill Giant, Bernie Baum, and Florence Kaye.

LPs:
- *Kissin' Cousins*

KNOWN ONLY TO HIM
"Known Only to Him" is a gospel tune written by Stuart Hamblen, the son of a Methodist minister, and originally recorded by him in late 1952 (Columbia 21012). In 1956 George Beverly Shea, Billy Graham's vocalist at his revival meetings for years, recorded the song (RCA 47-6414).

Elvis recorded "Known Only to Him" on October 31, 1960, at RCA's Nashville studios. It is take #5 that is on record.

Singles:
- "Joshua Fit the Battle"/"KNOWN ONLY TO HIM" (RCA 447-0651) March 1966. Gold Standard Series original.

LPs:
- *He Walks Beside Me*
- *His Hand in Mine*

K-U-U-I-PO
Elvis sang "K-u-u-i-po" in his 1961 movie *Blue Hawaii*. The film version had female vocal backup. "K-u-u-i-po," which means "Hawaiian sweetheart," was recorded by Elvis on March 21, 1961, at Radio Recorders. Take #9 is the one released on the *Blue Hawaii* LP. After his January 14, 1973, worldwide TV special "Elvis: Aloha from Hawaii," Elvis recorded a concert version (without an audience) for inclusion in the U.S. edition of the broadcast, which aired on April 4, 1973. The song did not appear on the soundtrack album of the special, but was later included in the *Mahalo from Elvis* LP. "K-u-u-i-po" was written by George Weiss, Hugo Peretti, and Luigi Creatore.[1]

LPs:
- *Blue Hawaii*
- *Mahalo from Elvis* (Honolulu; January 14, 1973)

Bootleg LPs:
- *The Blue Hawaii Box* (takes #1–9)
- *The Blue Hawaii Sessions* (takes #1 and #2)
- *Plantation Rock* (take #1)

[1] In 1957, Peretti and Creatore bought Roulette Records from George Goldner.

LA PALOMA

Elvis reportedly recorded "La Paloma" for his 1961 film *Blue Hawaii*, but it was cut from the final print. Some have suggested that "La Paloma" is another name for "No More," which *was* in the film.

THE LADY LOVES ME

Elvis and Ann-Margret sang "The Lady Loves Me" as a duet in *Viva Las Vegas*. The song was recorded on July 11, 1963, at Radio Recorders. Take #10 was selected by RCA for use in the film. "The Lady Loves Me" remained unreleased by RCA for twenty years until the 1983 LP *Elvis—A Legendary Performer, Volume 4*. Sid Tepper and Roy C. Bennett are the song's composers.

LPs:
• *Elvis—A Legendary Performer, Volume 4*

Bootleg LPs:
• *Cadillac Elvis* (*Viva Las Vegas* soundtrack)
• *Eternal Elvis* (*Viva Las Vegas* soundtrack)
• *Please Release Me* (*Viva Las Vegas* soundtrack)
• *Viva Las Vegas!* (*Viva Las Vegas* soundtrack)

THE LAST FAREWELL

"The Last Farewell" was written by Roger Whittaker and R. A. Webster and recorded by Whittaker in 1975. His recording (RCA PB-50030) reached #19 on the Hot 100 chart.

Reportedly, Barbara Bonner, onetime girlfriend of Elvis's, persuaded him to record "The Last Farewell," which he did on the night of February 2–3, 1976, at Graceland.

LPs:
• *From Elvis Presley Boulevard, Memphis, Tennessee*

LAWDY MISS CLAWDY

"Lawdy Miss Clawdy" was written and recorded by Lloyd Price in 1952. His recording (Specialty 428) was number one on *Billboard*'s rhythm & blues chart for seven weeks in July and August 1952. The piano player on the record was Fats Domino. Although many rock acts over the years have recorded "Lawdy Miss Clawdy," the only other versions to reach the charts were by Gary Stites (Carlton 525) in 1960 and the Buckinghams (U.S.A. 869) in 1967. Cliff Richard's first demo sent to British record companies was "Lawdy Miss Clawdy"/"Breathless."

Elvis recorded "Lawdy Miss Clawdy" on February 3, 1956, at RCA's New York City studios. His single release did not chart in the fall of 1956. On June 27, 1968, Elvis sang "Lawdy Miss Clawdy" on both the 6:00 P.M. and 8:00 P.M. shows for his TV special "Elvis." The 8:00 P.M. performance was used in the special and the soundtrack LP. An April 9, 1972, performance at Hampton Roads, Virginia, was used in the documentary *Elvis on Tour*. Elvis, as Dr. John Carpenter in *Change of Habit*, played a portion of "Lawdy Miss Clawdy" on the piano.

Singles:
• "Shake, Rattle and Roll"/"LAWDY MISS CLAWDY" (RCA 20-6642) September 1956. Standard 78 RPM release.
• "Shake, Rattle and Roll"/"LAWDY MISS CLAWDY" (RCA 47-6642) September 1956. Standard 45 RPM release.
• "Shake, Rattle and Roll"/"LAWDY MISS CLAWDY" (RCA 447-0615) March 1959. Gold Standard Series reissue.

EPs:
• *Elvis Presley* (RCA EPA-830)

LPs:
• *Elvis Aron Presley* ("Elvis" TV special taping; June 27, 1968, at 8:00 P.M. show)
• *Elvis Recorded Live on Stage in Memphis* (Memphis; March 20, 1974)
• *Elvis—TV Special* ("Elvis" TV special taping; June 27, 1968, at 8:00 P.M. show)
• *For Elvis Fans Only*
• *A Golden Celebration* ("Elvis" TV special taping; June 27, 1968, at 8:00 P.M. show)

Bootleg LPs:
• *The Burbank Sessions, Volume 1* ("Elvis" TV special taping; June 27, 1968, at 6:00 P.M. and 8:00 P.M. shows)
• *Cadillac Elvis* (*Elvis on Tour* soundtrack)
• *Elvis on Tour* (*Elvis on Tour* soundtrack)
• *Eternal Elvis, Volume 2* (fabricated duet with Lloyd Price, using Elvis's RCA recording)
• *The King: From the Darkness to the Light* (*Elvis on Tour* soundtrack)
• *The Monologue L.P.* (Las Vegas; July 31, 1969)
• *Sold Out* (*Elvis on Tour* soundtrack)

LEAD ME, GUIDE ME

"Lead Me, Guide Me" was written and recorded by Doris Akers (Imperial 5271) in 1954. In 1955 George Beverly Shea recorded a popular version (RCA 47-6068).

Elvis recorded "Lead Me, Guide Me" at RCA's Nashville studios on May 17, 1971. While on tour in April 1972, he sang it backstage with the Stamps. A clip of that performance appeared in the documentary *Elvis on Tour*.

LPs:
• *He Touched Me*

Bootleg LPs:
• *Elvis on Tour* (*Elvis on Tour* soundtrack)
• *The King: From the Darkness to the Light* (*Elvis on Tour* soundtrack)

LEAF ON A TREE

Elvis sang "Leaf on a Tree" to his class on his last day at Milam Junior High School in Tupelo, the day before the Presleys moved to Memphis in September 1948.

LEAVE MY WOMAN ALONE

Ray Charles wrote and recorded "Leave My Woman Alone" (Atlantic 1108) in 1956.

On September 29, 1966, Elvis recorded the song for his movie *Easy Come, Easy Go*, but it was not used. To this date, the song has not been released in any form.

LET IT BE ME

"Let It Be Me" was written by Pierre Delanoe and Gilbert Becaud in 1955 under the French title "Je T'Appartiens," and was first recorded that year by Becaud. In 1957 Mann Curtis wrote English lyrics and Jill Corey introduced "Let It Be Me" in an episode of the TV series "Climax." Her recording (Columbia 40878) peaked at #57 on *Billboard*'s Top 100 chart. It wasn't until the Everly Brothers recorded the song in 1960, however, that "Let It Be Me" became a hit. Their version (Cadence 1376) reached #7 on the Hot 100 chart. Other popular recordings include those by Betty Everett and Jerry Butler (Vee Jay 613) in 1964, the Sweet Inspirations (Atlantic 2418) in 1967, and Glen Campbell and Bobbie Gentry (Capitol 2387) in 1969.

Elvis sang "Let It Be Me" in concert several times in the 1970s. It is those live versions that are on record.

LPs:
- *Elvis—A Legendary Performer, Volume 3* (Las Vegas; February 1970)
- *On Stage—February, 1970* (Las Vegas; February 17, 1970)

LET ME

Elvis sang "Let Me" in his first movie, *Love Me Tender*. He recorded the song on August 2 or September 24, 1956, at Radio Recorders. The film version had girls screaming and clapping. Although Elvis and Vera Matson are credited with writing "Let Me," Ken Darby is the composer.

EPs:
- *Love Me Tender*

LPs:
- *Elvis: The Other Sides—Worldwide Gold Award Hits, Volume 2*
- *Essential Elvis—The First Movies*

Bootleg LPs:
- *Elvis* (*Love Me Tender* soundtrack)

LET ME BE THERE

"Let Me Be There" was written by John Rostill and recorded by Olivia Newton-John in 1973. Her recording (MCA 40101) sold over a million copies and won a Grammy for Best Female Country Vocal. The song peaked at #6 on *Billboard*'s Hot 100 chart.

Elvis sang "Let Me Be There" quite often in concert in the mid-1970s. The version first released on record was from the March 20, 1974, performance in Memphis.

Singles:
- "LET ME BE THERE"/"LET ME BE THERE" (RCA JH-10951) June 1974. Disc jockey promotional release. Side A was in stereo; side B in mono. This record was released by Al Gallico Music Corp., the song's publisher, in order to force RCA to release the song.

LPs:
- *Elvis Aron Presley* (Dallas; June 6, 1975)
- *Elvis Recorded Live on Stage in Memphis* (Memphis; March 20, 1974)

- *Moody Blue* (Memphis; March 20, 1974)

Bootleg LPs:
- *America's Own* (Uniondale, N.Y.; July 19, 1975)
- *Big Boss Man* (Las Vegas; August 19, 1974)
- *From Las Vegas . . . to Niagara Falls* (Niagara Falls, N.Y.; June 24, 1974)
- *Rockin' with Elvis April Fool's Day* (Las Vegas; April 1, 1975)

LET US PRAY

Elvis sang "Let Us Pray" in his 1969 film *Change of Habit*. The film version of the song was recorded at Decca Recording Studios in Universal City on March 6, 1969. The version on record was recorded at RCA's Nashville studios, probably on September 22, 1969. "Let Us Pray" was written by Ben Weisman and Buddy Kaye.

LPs:
- *You'll Never Walk Alone*

Acetate for "Let Us Pray." (Photo courtesy Don Fink)

LET YOURSELF GO

"Let Yourself Go" was written by Joy Byers for Elvis's 1968 film, *Speedway*. The recording session took place in June 1967 at MGM's Culver City studios. Although "Let Yourself Go" had only a five-week stay on *Billboard*'s Hot 100 chart, peaking at #71, some credit the song with selling over a million copies. "Let Yourself Go" was sung in a bordello scene for the 1968 TV special "Elvis," but was cut from the telecast because it wasn't deemed appropriate. The instrumental track for that version was recorded on June 20 or 21, 1968, at Western Recorders in Hollywood. Elvis's vocal was recorded at NBC-TV on June 30.

Singles:
- "Your Time Hasn't Come Yet, Baby"/"LET YOURSELF GO" (RCA 47-9547) June 1968. Standard release. The original picture sleeves read, "Coming Soon—SPEEDWAY LP." A month later the sleeves

were changed to read, "Ask for SPEEDWAY LP."

- "Your Time Hasn't Come Yet, Baby"/"LET YOURSELF GO" (RCA 447-0666) December 1970. Gold Standard Series reissue.

LPs:
- *Elvis—A Legendary Performer, Volume 3* ("Elvis" TV special taping; June 30, 1968)
- *Speedway*

Bootleg LPs:
- *The '68 Comeback* ("Elvis" TV special taping; June 30, 1968)
- *The '68 Comeback, Volume 2* ("Elvis" TV special taping; June 30, 1968)
- *Superstar Outtakes* ("Elvis" TV special taping; June 30, 1968)

LET'S BE FRIENDS

"Let's Be Friends" was originally scheduled for Elvis's 1969 film *Change of Habit*, but it was cut from the final print. Elvis recorded the song, which was written by Chris Arnold, Geoffrey Morrow, and David Martin, on March 5, 1969, at the Decca Recording Studios at Universal City.

LPs:
- *Let's Be Friends*

LET'S FORGET ABOUT THE STARS

Al Owens wrote "Let's Forget About the Stars" for the film *Charro!*, but it was not used. The instrumental track for the song was recorded on October 15, 1968, at the Samuel Goldwyn Studios. Former Mouseketeer Carl (Cubby) O'Brien played drums on that session. Elvis's vocal was probably added at a later date.

LPs:
- *Let's Be Friends*

LET'S LIVE A LITTLE

Elvis reportedly recorded "Let's Live a Little" for his 1968 film *Live a Little, Love a Little*, but the song does not appear in the sessions files. If he did record the song, it would have been on March 7, 1968, at Western Recorders.

LIFE

Elvis recorded "Life" at RCA's Nashville studios on June 6, 1970. The single release had a seven-week stay on *Billboard*'s Hot 100 chart, peaking at #53. It fared much better on the Easy-Listening chart, making it all the way to #8. On the country chart "Life" reached #34. Marty Robbins recorded "Life" (MCA 40342) in 1975, but it did not chart. The song was composed by Shirl Milete.

Singles:
- "LIFE"/"Only Believe" (RCA 47-9985) May 1971. Standard release.
- "LIFE"/"Only Believe" (RCA 447-0682) May 1972. Gold Standard Series reissue.

LPs:
- *Love Letters from Elvis* (alternate mix; there's more of Elvis's singing at the end)

LIKE A BABY

"Like a Baby" was written by Jesse Stone and recorded by Elvis on April 3, 1960, at RCA's Nashville studios. Three years later, James Brown had a #24 rhythm & blues hit with his recording (King 5710).

LPs:
- *Elvis Is Back*

A LITTLE BIT OF GREEN

Elvis recorded "A Little Bit of Green" at American Sound Studios in Memphis on January 14, 1969. The song was written by Chris Arnold, Geoffrey Morrow, and David Martin.

LPs:
- *Back in Memphis*
- *From Memphis to Vegas/From Vegas to Memphis*

LITTLE CABIN ON THE HILL

Bill Monroe and Lester Flatt wrote "Little Cabin on the Hill" in 1948. Late that year, Bill Monroe's Bluegrass Boys recorded the song (Columbia 20459). The title on the label was "Little Cabin *Home* on the Hill."

Elvis sang "Little Cabin on the Hill," imitating Bill Monroe, during the Million-Dollar-Quartet session on December 4, 1956. Vocal support was provided by Carl Perkins. On June 4, 1970, Elvis formally recorded the song at RCA's Nashville studios.

LPs:
- *Elvis Country*

Bootleg LPs:
- *The Million Dollar Quartet* (Sun Records; December 4, 1956)
- *The One Million Dollar Quartet* (Sun Records; December 4, 1956)

LITTLE DARLIN'

Maurice Williams and his group, the Gladiolas, then known as the Royal Charmers, raised $46 to travel from their home in South Carolina to Nashville in 1956 to meet with Ernie Young. Young had a record store that sponsored "Ernie's Record Hop," a WLAC radio program. In the back of his store he had a makeshift recording studio. After Williams and his group had gone through several songs, Young asked them to sing what they considered to be their *worst* song. They sang "Little Darlin'," which Williams had composed. Young was ecstatic. The Gladiolas recorded the tune with a calypso beat and it was released on the Excello label (Excello 2101) in December 1956. Within a few weeks a copy of the record got into the hands of Nat Goodman, manager of the Diamonds. The Diamonds quickly recorded their version of "Little Darlin'," with Dave Somerville singing lead and Bill Reed performing the spoken interlude. Both records began climbing the charts. When the smoke cleared, the Diamonds' version reached #2 on the Top 100 chart and #3 on the rhythm & blues chart. Sales were well over the million mark. The Gladiolas could only muster a high of #41 on the Top 100 chart and #11 on the rhythm & blues chart. In 1961 Bobby Rydell's moderate hit, "Cherie" (Cameo 186), used the same music as "Little Darlin'," but with different lyrics. At the home of Waco, Texas, disc jockey Eddie Fadal in the summer of 1958, Elvis sang along with the Diamonds' recording.

Elvis's single release was recorded in concert at Saginaw, Michigan, on April 24, 1977. Although it didn't chart, "Little Darlin' " was listed as "Bubbling Under" at #112 for two weeks.

Singles:
- "LITTLE DARLIN' "/"I'm Movin' On" (RCA 50476) October 1978. Standard Canadian single pressed on gold vinyl. Although this book is devoted to American releases, we've chosen to include this single because it received wide distribution in the United States and is the only single appearance of "Little Darlin'."

LPs:
- *Elvis—A Canadian Tribute* (Saginaw, Michigan; April 24, 1977)
- *Elvis Aron Presley* (Shreveport, Louisiana; June 7, 1975)
- *Moody Blue* (Saginaw, Michigan; April 24, 1977)

Bootleg LPs:
- *America's Own* (Uniondale, N.Y.; July 19, 1975)
- *Forever Young, Forever Beautiful* (Waco, Texas; summer 1958)

LITTLE EGYPT
"Little Egypt" was written by Jerry Leiber and Mike Stoller and recorded by the Coasters (Atco 6192) in 1961. Their version reached #23 on *Billboard*'s Hot 100 chart.

Elvis recorded "Little Egypt" in February or March 1964 at Radio Recorders for his film *Roustabout*. Four years later, he sang it in a medley on his TV special "Elvis." The instrumental track for that special was recorded on June 20 or 21, 1968, at Western Recorders. Elvis's vocal was added at NBC's studios on June 30.

LPs:
- *Elvis—TV Special*
- *Roustabout*

Bootleg LPs:
- *The '68 Comeback, Volume 2* ("Elvis" TV special taping; June 30, 1968) (takes #1 and #2)
- *Special Delivery from Elvis Presley* ("Elvis" TV special taping; June 30, 1968) (take #?)

LITTLE GIRL
Ritchie Valens wrote and recorded "Little Girl" in 1958. His posthumous release (Del-Fi 4117) barely made the Hot 100 (#92) in the summer of 1959. Valens wrote the song based on an expression he frequently used.

Elvis is reported to have recorded "Little Girl," but to this date it has not been released.

A LITTLE LESS CONVERSATION
Billy Strange and Mac Davis wrote "A Little Less Conversation" for Elvis's 1968 film *Live a Little, Love a Little*. The instrumental track for the tune was recorded on March 7, 1968, at Western Recorders. Elvis's vocal was probably recorded at a later date. "A Little Less Conversation" had a four-week stay on *Billboard*'s Hot 100 chart, reaching #69. An instrumental track was recorded for the 1968 TV special "Elvis," but it was decided not to use the song in the program. The LP release of "A Little Less Conversation" is an alternate take.

Singles:
- "A LITTLE LESS CONVERSATION"/"Almost in Love" (RCA 47-9610) September 15, 1968. Standard release.
- "A LITTLE LESS CONVERSATION"/"Almost in Love" (RCA 447-0667) December 1970. Gold Standard Series reissue.

LPs:
- *Almost in Love*

LITTLE SISTER
Doc Pomus and Mort Shuman wrote "Little Sister" for Elvis, who recorded it on June 26, 1961, at RCA's Nashville studios. His single release spent a total of 13 weeks on *Billboard*'s Hot 100 chart, reaching #5. Sales exceeded one million copies. In England, "Little Sister" was number one for four weeks. A few months after "Little Sister" was released, LaVern Baker recorded "Hey, Memphis" (Atlantic 2119) as a takeoff on Elvis's recording. "Hey, Memphis," which used the same music as "Little Sister," was also written by Doc Pomus and Mort Shuman. Elvis occasionally sang "Little Sister" in concert in a medley with "Get Back."

A rehearsal of "Little Sister" at MGM Culver City studios in July 1970 was used in the documentary *Elvis—That's the Way It Is*.

In 1988 Dwight Yoakam's music video of "Little Sister" was nominated for Top Country Video at the Country Music Association Awards.

Singles:
- "LITTLE SISTER"/"(Marie's the Name) His Latest Flame" (RCA 47-7908) August 1961. Standard release.
- "LITTLE SISTER"/"(Marie's the Name) His Latest Flame" (RCA 37-7908) August 1961. Compact 33 Single release.
- "LITTLE SISTER"/"(Marie's the Name) His Latest Flame" (RCA 447-0634) November 1962. Gold Standard Series reissue.
- "LITTLE SISTER"/"Paralyzed" (RCA PB-13547) June 1983. New release.
- "LITTLE SISTER"/"Paralyzed" (RCA JB-13547) June 1983. Disc jockey promotional release. Some of the copies were pressed on blue vinyl.
- "LITTLE SISTER"/"Rip It Up" (RCA EP-0517) June 1983. Special 12" single promotional release.
- "LITTLE SISTER"/"(Marie's the Name) His Latest Flame" (RCA PB-13894) October 1984. One of six singles contained in the boxed set *Elvis' Greatest Hits—Golden Singles, Volume 2*. The records were pressed on gold vinyl with a special gold "50th" anniversary label.

EPs:
- *The EP Collection, Volume 2* (alternate take)

LPs:
- *Elvis Aron Presley* (Las Vegas; August 13, 1970) (in medley with "Get Back")
- *Elvis' Golden Records, Volume 3*
- *Elvis in Concert* (Omaha, Nebraska or Rapid City, South Dakota; June 19 or 21, 1977)
- *Elvis: Worldwide 50 Gold Award Hits, Volume 1*
- *I Was the One* (with overdubbing)
- *The Top Ten Hits*

Bootleg LPs:
- *Command Performance* (Las Vegas; August 4, 1972) (in medley with "Get Back")

- *The King: From the Dark to the Light* (*Elvis—That's the Way It Is* soundtrack)
- *The Last Farewell* (Indianapolis; June 26, 1977)
- *Rockin' with Elvis New Year's Eve Pittsburgh, Pa. Dec. 31, 1976* (Pittsburgh; December 31, 1976)
- *Sold Out* (Las Vegas; August 16, 1972) (in medley with "Get Back")
- *Standing Room Only, Volume 2* (Las Vegas; February 21, 1971) (in medley with "Get Back")
- *That's the Way It Is* (*Elvis—That's the Way It Is* soundtrack)

LODI
"Lodi" was written by John Fogerty and first recorded by Creedence Clearwater Revival (Fantasy 622) in 1969. Their version reached #52 on *Billboard*'s Hot 100 chart. That same year, Al Wilson recorded a version of the song (Soul City 775) that peaked at #67.

Elvis is known to have sung "Lodi" in concert in the 1970s.

LONELY AVENUE
Ray Charles had a #8 rhythm & blues hit with this Doc Pomus song in 1956 (Atlantic 1108).

Some have reported that Elvis recorded "Lonely Avenue" for RCA in the 1950s or early 1960s, but to this date no recording has surfaced.

LONELY MAN
Elvis recorded "Lonely Man" on November 7, 1960, for his film *Wild in the Country*, but it was cut from the final print. Two versions of the song were recorded: one for record release and a solo version. "Lonely Man," which was written by Bennie Benjamin and Sol Marcus, reached #32 on *Billboard*'s Hot 100 chart during its five-week stay on the chart.

Singles:
- "Surrender"/"LONELY MAN" (RCA 47-7850) February 1961. Standard release.
- "Surrender"/"LONELY MAN" (RCA 61-7850) February 1961. "Living Stereo" release.
- "Surrender"/"LONELY MAN" (RCA 37-7850) February 1961. Compact 33 Single—the first released by RCA.
- "Surrender"/"LONELY MAN" (RCA 68-7850) February 1961. "Living Stereo" Compact 33 Single—the only one by Elvis released by RCA.
- "Surrender"/"LONELY MAN" (RCA 447-0630) February 1962. Gold Standard Series reissue.

LPs:
- *Elvis' Gold Records, Volume 4*
- *Elvis: The Other Sides—Worldwide Gold Award Hits, Volume 2*

Bootleg LPs:
- *Behind Closed Doors* (take #1, solo version)
- *The Complete Wild in the Country Sessions* (takes #1–4, solo version)
- *Eternal Elvis, Volume 2* (take #?, solo version)

LONESOME COWBOY
Elvis sang "Lonesome Cowboy" in his second film, *Loving You*. The song, which was written by Sid Tepper and Roy C. Bennett, was recorded in February 1957 at Radio Recorders.

EPs:
- *Loving You, Volume 2*

LPs:
- *Elvis: The Other Sides—Worldwide Gold Award Hits, Volume 2*
- *Essential Elvis—The First Movies* (master)
- *Loving You*

Bootleg LPs:
- *Got a Lot o' Livin' to Do!* (*Loving You* soundtrack)
- *Loving You* (*Loving You* soundtrack)

LONG BLACK LIMOUSINE
While Bobby George was stationed in the Air Force in West Germany in 1954, he overheard a wife telling her husband that she wished she was rich so she could ride in a long black limousine. The phrase stayed with him. In 1962 he and Vern Stovall wrote "Long Black Limousine," which was first recorded by Gordon Terry (RCA

A studio pressing from the American Sound Studios sessions. In addition to "Long Black Limousine," songs on this disc include "Suspicious Minds," "I'll Be There," "I'll Hold You in My Heart," and "Without Love." (Photo courtesy Don Fink)

47-7989). Later that year, Glen Campbell also recorded the song (Capitol 4856). Neither version charted. Jody Miller had the first and only chart recording of "Long Black Limousine" (Capitol 2290) in 1968. Her version reached #73 on the country chart.

Elvis recorded "Long Black Limousine" at American Sound Studios on January 13, 1969. It was the first song he recorded there.

LPs:
- *From Elvis in Memphis*
- *The Memphis Record*

LONG JOURNEY
It's been reported that Elvis recorded "Long Journey," but no other information is available.

LONG LEGGED GIRL
(WITH THE SHORT DRESS ON)
J. Leslie McFarland and Winfield Scott wrote "Long Legged Girl (With the Short Dress On)" for Elvis's 1967 film *Double Trouble*. Elvis recorded the song in June 1966 at Radio Recorders. Take #5 was selected by RCA for release. "Long Legged Girl (With the Short Dress On)" had a five-week stay on the Hot 100 chart, reaching #63. At a running time of 1 minute, 26 seconds, it was the shortest Elvis single to make the Hot 100 chart[1].

Singles:
- "LONG LEGGED GIRL (WITH THE SHORT DRESS ON)"/"That's Someone You Never Forget" (RCA 47-9115) May 1967. Standard release. The original picture sleeves read, "Coming Soon—DOUBLE TROUBLE Album." One month later the sleeves were changed to read, "Ask for DOUBLE TROUBLE Album."
- "LONG LEGGED GIRL (WITH THE SHORT DRESS ON)"/"That's Someone You Never Forget" (RCA 447-0660) 1970. Gold Standard Series reissue.

LPs:
- *Almost in Love*
- *Double Trouble* (alternate mix)
- *Elvis Sings Hits from His Movies, Volume 1* (alternate mix)

LONG LIVE ROCK 'N' ROLL
(See *School Day*)

(IT'S A) LONG LONELY HIGHWAY
"(It's a) Long Lonely Highway" was written by Doc Pomus and Mort Shuman and recorded by Elvis on May 27, 1963, at RCA's Nashville studios. The single release, an alternate take from the LP version, did not chart, although it was listed as "Bubbling Under" for two weeks at #112. Elvis sang "(It's a) Long Lonely Highway" in his 1965 film *Tickle Me*.

Singles:
- "I'm Yours"/"(IT'S A) LONG LONELY HIGHWAY" (RCA 47-8657) August 1965. Standard release.
- "I'm Yours"/"(IT'S A) LONG LONELY HIGHWAY" (RCA 447-0654) November 1966. Gold Standard Series reissue.

LPs:
- *Kissin' Cousins*

Bootleg LPs:
- *Elvis Sings Songs from Tickle Me* (alternate take)

LONG TALL SALLY
"Long Tall Sally" was written by Enotris Johnson, Robert (Bumps) Blackwell, and Richard Penniman (Little Richard) in 1956. Little Richard claims to have written the song in a Greyhound bus depot in Macon, Georgia. Titles originally considered for the song were "The Thing" and "Bald-Headed Sally." Little Richard's single release (Specialty 572) topped *Billboard*'s rhythm & blues chart for six weeks and reached #6 on the Top 100 chart. "Long Tall Sally" was Little Richard's second million-seller. Pat Boone had a successful cover

version of "Long Tall Sally" (Dot 15457) in 1956 that reached #8 on the Top 100 chart.

Elvis recorded "Long Tall Sally" on September 2, 1956, at Radio Recorders. Take #4 was selected by RCA for release. Only Enotris Johnson was listed as composer on the *Elvis* LP. Elvis sang "Long Tall Sally" on his 1973 TV special "Elvis: Aloha from Hawaii."

EPs:
- *Strictly Elvis*

LPs:
- *Aloha from Hawaii via Satellite* (Honolulu; January 14, 1973)
- *Elvis*
- *Elvis Aron Presley* (Las Vegas; May 6, 1956)
- *Elvis Recorded Live on Stage in Memphis* (Memphis; March 20, 1974) (in medley with "Whole Lotta Shakin' Goin' On," "Your Mama Don't Dance," "Flip, Flop and Fly," "Jailhouse Rock," and "Hound Dog")
- *A Golden Celebration* (Tupelo, Mississippi; September 26, 1956, at the afternoon show)

Bootleg LPs:
- *From Las Vegas . . . to Niagara Falls* (Las Vegas; September 3, 1973) (in medley with "Whole Lotta Shakin' Goin' On," "Your Mama Don't Dance," "Flip, Flop and Fly," and "Hound Dog")
- *Sold Out* (Nashville; July 1, 1973) (in medley with "Whole Lotta Shakin' Goin' On," "Your Mama Don't Dance," "Shake, Rattle and Roll," and "Jailhouse Rock")

LOOK OUT, BROADWAY
Elvis sang "Look Out, Broadway" in his 1966 movie *Frankie and Johnny*. The film version had additional voices. The song, which was written by Fred Wise and Randy Starr, was recorded by Elvis in May 1965 at Radio Recorders.

LPs:
- *Frankie and Johnny*

LOVE COMING DOWN
"Love Coming Down" was written by Jerry Chesnut and first recorded by Razy Bailey on an album. Elvis recorded the song on the night of February 6–7, 1976, at Graceland.

LPs:
- *From Elvis Presley Boulevard, Memphis, Tennessee*

LOVE IS FOR LOVERS
Elvis recorded "Love Is for Lovers" for his 1962 movie *Kid Galahad*, but it was not used. Supposedly, Elvis sings in a duet with one of the Jordanaires. The recording session took place on October 26 or 27, 1961. "Love Is for Lovers," which is not available on record, was written by Ruth Batchelor and Sharon Silbert.

LOVE LETTERS
Written by Edward Heyman and Victor Young, "Love Letters" served as the theme for the 1945 movie *Love Letters*, starring Joseph Cotten and Jennifer Jones. In 1955 the Paul Weston Orchestra made a popular re-

---

[1]The shortest single ever to make the Hot 100 chart was "Little Boxes" (RCA 47-8301) by Womenfolk in 1964. "Little Boxes" was 1 minute, 2 seconds in length.

cording of the song (Columbia 40385). The big hit with "Love Letters" came in 1962 when Ketty Lester's rendition reached #5 on the Hot 100 chart and #2 on the rhythm & blues chart. It was Lester's only million-seller. The piano player on her recording was Lincoln Mayorga, a former member of the Piltdown Men.

Elvis first recorded "Love Letters" on May 26, 1966, at RCA's Nashville studios. The single release had a seven-week stay on the Hot 100 chart, peaking at #19. It reached #38 on the Easy-Listening chart. "Love Letters" was reportedly a million-seller. Floyd Cramer was pianist on Elvis's recording. On June 7, 1970, Elvis rerecorded "Love Letters" for his album *Love Letters from Elvis*.

Singles:

- "LOVE LETTERS"/"Come What May" (RCA 47-8870) June 1966. Standard release. The original picture sleeves read, "Coming Soon—PARADISE, HAWAIIAN STYLE." One month later the sleeves were changed to read, "Ask for—PARADISE, HAWAIIAN STYLE."
- "LOVE LETTERS"/"Come What May" (RCA 447-0657) February 1968. Gold Standard Series reissue.

LPs:

- *Elvis' Gold Records, Volume 4*
- *Love Letters from Elvis* (June 7, 1970, version)
- *A Valentine Gift for You*

Bootleg LPs:

- *Rockin' with Elvis New Year's Eve Pittsburgh, Pa. Dec. 31, 1976* (Pittsburgh; December 31, 1976)

THE LOVE MACHINE

Elvis sang "The Love Machine" in his 1967 film *Easy Come, Easy Go*. The instrumental track was recorded on September 28, 1966, at Radio Recorders. Elvis's vocal was overdubbed at a later date. "The Love Machine" was written by Gerald Nelson, Fred Burch, and Chuck Taylor.

EPs:

- *Easy Come, Easy Go*

LPs:

- *I Got Lucky*

LOVE ME

Jerry Leiber and Mike Stoller wrote "Love Me" in 1954 as a spoof of country music. They've claimed that it was the worst song they ever wrote. The first recording of "Love Me" was by Willie and Ruth (Spark 105) in 1954. That same year, Georgia Gibbs also recorded the song (Mercury 70473).

Elvis recorded "Love Me" on September 1, 1956, at Radio Recorders. Take #9 was selected for release. Although not released as a single, "Love Me" had a 19-week stay on *Billboard*'s Top 100 chart, reaching #6, based on its appearance in the EP *Elvis, Volume 1*. Sales for the song are claimed to be over one million.

Elvis sang "Love Me" on his second appearance on "The Ed Sullivan Show" (October 28, 1956) and in his 1973 worldwide TV special "Elvis: Aloha from Hawaii." The song was recorded for the 1968 TV special "Elvis," but was not used.

EPs:

- *Elvis, Volume 1*
- *Elvis/Jaye P. Morgan*
- *Perfect for Parties*

LPs:

- *Aloha from Hawaii via Satellite* (Honolulu; January 14, 1973)
- *The Alternate Aloha* (rehearsal concert for "Elvis: Aloha from Hawaii"; January 12, 1973)
- *Elvis* (RCA LPM-1382)
- *Elvis* (RCA DPL2-0056[e])
- *Elvis—A Legendary Performer, Volume 1* ("Elvis" TV special taping; June 27, 1968, at 8:00 P.M. show)
- *Elvis Aron Presley* (USS *Arizona* Memorial; March 25, 1961) (Dallas; June 6, 1975)
- *Elvis as Recorded at Madison Square Garden* (June 10, 1972)
- *Elvis' Golden Records*
- *Elvis in Concert* (Rapid City, South Dakota; June 21, 1977)
- *Elvis Recorded Live on Stage in Memphis* (Memphis; March 20, 1974)
- *Elvis: The Other Sides—Worldwide Gold Award Hits, Volume 2*
- *A Golden Celebration* ("The Ed Sullivan Show"; October 28, 1956) ("Elvis" TV special taping; June 27, 1968, at 8:00 P.M. show)
- *The Top Ten Hits*

Bootleg LPs:

- *Aloha Rehearsal Show—Kui Lee Cancer Benefit* (rehearsal concert for "Elvis: Aloha from Hawaii"; January 12, 1973)
- *America's Own* (Uniondale, N.Y.; July 19, 1975)
- *The Burbank Sessions, Volume 1* ("Elvis" TV special taping; June 27, 1968, at 6:00 P.M. and 8:00 P.M. shows)
- *Elvis' 1961 Hawaii Benefit Concert* (USS *Arizona* Memorial; March 25, 1961)
- *Elvis Rocks and the Girls Roll* (dress rehearsal for the "Elvis" TV special; June 1968)
- *From Las Vegas . . . to Niagara Falls* (Las Vegas; September 3, 1973) (Niagara Falls, N.Y.; June 24, 1974)
- *From the Waist Up* ("The Ed Sullivan Show"; October 28, 1956)
- *The Hillbilly Cat, 1954–1974, Volume 1* ("The Ed Sullivan Show"; October 28, 1956)
- *The King Goes Wild* ("The Ed Sullivan Show"; October 28, 1956)
- *The Last Farewell* (Indianapolis; June 26, 1977)
- *Loving You* (from the EP *Perfect for Parties*)
- *Rockin' with Elvis April Fool's Day* (Las Vegas; April 1, 1975)
- *Rockin' with Elvis New Year's Eve Pittsburgh, Pa. Dec. 31, 1976* (Pittsburgh; December 31, 1976)
- *The Vegas Years, 1972–1975* (Las Vegas; 1972)

LOVE ME, LOVE THE LIFE I LEAD

"Love Me, Love the Life I Lead" was written by Tony Macaulay and Roger Greenaway and recorded by Elvis on May 21, 1971, at RCA's Nashville studios.

LPs:

- *Elvis* (RCA APL1-0283)

LOVE ME TENDER

"Love Me Tender" was composed by Ken Darby, although credited to Elvis and Vera Matson, Darby's wife. It was based on the 1861 ballad "Aura Lee." "Aura Lee," written by W. W. Fosdick and George R. Poulton, was a favorite of the Union Army during the Civil War. With new words and retitled "Army Blue," it was adopted as the class song of West Point graduates in 1865. "Aura Lee" was sung by Frances Farmer in the 1936 movie *Come and Get It*.

Elvis recorded "Love Me Tender" for his first film *The Reno Brothers*. The film's title was later changed to take advantage of the tremendous success of the single. The recording session took place on either August 2 or September 24, 1956, at Radio Recorders in Hollywood. Vita Mumolo was the guitar player heard on the record. Background vocals were provided by Chuck Prescott, John Dodson, and Red Robinson. The film version of "Love Me Tender" had slightly different lyrics and one extra verse. Advanced sales of the single release exceeded one million copies—the first record in history to do so. "Love Me Tender" entered *Billboard*'s Top 100 chart at #12. Over the next nine weeks, it was number one for four weeks, exchanging the top spot with Jim Lowe's "The Green Door." "Singing the Blues" by Guy Mitchell eventually assumed the top position. "Love Me Tender" was #3 on the country chart and #4 on the rhythm & blues chart. Probably the first cover record of "Love Me Tender" was by the Sparrows (Davis 456) in late 1956.

Elvis sang "Love Me Tender" on all three of his appearances on "The Ed Sullivan Show" (September 9, 1956; October 28, 1956; and January 6, 1957) and on his last appearance on the "Louisiana Hayride" (December 16, 1956). One line of the song was sung by Elvis with Frank Sinatra in the Frank Sinatra–Timex Special "Welcome Home, Elvis." Elvis sang "Love Me Tender" in his 1968 TV special "Elvis," and in the documentaries *Elvis—That's the Way It Is* (from an August 13, 1970, appearance at the International Hotel) and *Elvis on Tour* (from a performance in Hampton Roads, Virginia, on April 9, 1972). The film *This Is Elvis* showed a clip of Elvis from "The Ed Sullivan Show" singing "Love Me Tender."

In the fall of 1978 a duet of Elvis and Linda Ronstadt singing "Love Me Tender" gained considerable airplay across the country. Ray Quinn, program manager of radio station WCBM in Baltimore, dubbed together Elvis's 1956 single and Ronstadt's 1978 version from her album *Living in the U.S.A.* Although demand for the tape grew, no copies were made available to the public. A three-dollar bootleg single was made, however, on the Duet label (Duet 101). The duet was inspired by the Barbra Streisand–Neil Diamond duet "You Don't Bring Me Flowers."

"Love Me Tender" was the first song by Elvis that Priscilla Beaulieu ever heard. It became her favorite ballad. For Christmas 1962, Priscilla gave Elvis a musical cigarette case that played "Love Me Tender."

Singles:
- "LOVE ME TENDER"/"Any Way You Want Me" (RCA 20-6643) October 1956. Standard 78 RPM release. The picture sleeves for the record came in black and white, black and green, black and dark pink, and black and light pink.
- "LOVE ME TENDER"/"Any Way You Want Me" (RCA 47-6643) October 1956. Standard 45 RPM release.
- "LOVE ME TENDER"/"Any Way You Want Me" (RCA 447-0616) March 1959. Gold Standard Series reissue.
- "LOVE ME TENDER"/"Any Way You Want Me" (RCA PB-11108) October 1977. One of 15 singles in the boxed set *15 Golden Records—30 Golden Hits* (RCA PP-11301), and the *20 Golden Hits in*

Full Color Sleeves (RCA PP-11340) boxed set that was released two months later.
- "LOVE ME TENDER"/"Loving You" (PB-13893) October 1984. One of six singles in the boxed set *Elvis' Greatest Hits—Golden Singles, Volume 2* (RCA PB-13898). The record was pressed on gold vinyl with a special gold "50th" anniversary label.

EPs:
- *DJ-7*
- *Great Country/Western Hits*
- *Love Me Tender*

LPs:
- *Elvis* (RCA DPL2-0056[e])
- *Elvis—A Legendary Performer, Volume 1*
- *Elvis Aron Presley* (Dallas; June 6, 1975)
- *Elvis as Recorded at Madison Square Garden* (June 10, 1972)
- *Elvis' Golden Records*
- *Elvis—TV Special* (June 29, 1968; 8:00 P.M. show)
- *Elvis: Worldwide 50 Gold Award Hits, Volume 1*
- *Essential Elvis—The First Movies* (master and unreleased version)
- *A Golden Celebration* ("The Ed Sullivan Show"; September 9, 1956; October 28, 1956; January 6, 1957) (Tupelo, Mississippi; September 26, 1956, at afternoon and evening shows)
- *The Number One Hits*
- *Pure Gold*
- *This Is Elvis* ("The Ed Sullivan Show"; September 9, 1956)
- *The Top Ten Hits*

Bootleg LPs:
- *America's Own* (Uniondale, N.Y.; July 19, 1975)
- *The Burbank Sessions, Volume 2* ("Elvis" TV special taping; June 29, 1968, at 6:00 P.M. and 8:00 P.M. shows)
- *Elvis* (*Love Me Tender* soundtrack)
- *Elvis on Tour* (*Elvis on Tour* soundtrack)
- *Eternal Elvis* (*Love Me Tender* soundtrack)
- *From Las Vegas . . . to Niagara Falls* (Las Vegas; September 3, 1973) (Niagara Falls, N.Y.; June 24, 1974)
- *From the Waist Up* ("The Ed Sullivan Show"; September 9, 1956; October 28, 1956; January 6, 1957)
- *The Hillbilly Cat "Live"* (Las Vegas; August 1970)
- *The Hillbilly Cat, 1954–1974, Volume 1* ("The Ed Sullivan Show"; September 9, 1956; October 28, 1956)
- *The King Goes Wild* ("The Ed Sullivan Show"; September 9, 1956; October 28, 1956; January 6, 1957)
- *King of Las Vegas Live* (*Elvis—That's the Way It Is* soundtrack)
- *Loving You* (*Love Me Tender* soundtrack) ("The Ed Sullivan Show"; September 9, 1956)
- *The Rockin' Rebel, Volume 2* ("Louisiana Hayride"; December 16, 1956)
- *The Rockin' Rebel, Volume 3* ("The Ed Sullivan Show"; September 9, 1956) (*March of Dimes Galaxy of Stars* promotional LP)
- *Special Delivery from Elvis Presley* (1978 fabricated duet with Linda Ronstadt)
- *The Sun Years* ("The Ed Sullivan Show"; September 9, 1956)

LOVE ME TONIGHT
Don Robertson wrote "Love Me Tonight" for Elvis, who recorded it on May 26, 1963, at RCA's Nashville studios.

LPs:
- *Fun in Acapulco*

LOVE SONG OF THE YEAR
"Love Song of the Year" was recorded by Elvis at Stax Studios in Memphis on December 12, 1973. Chris Christian is the composer.

LPs:
• *Promised Land*

LOVE WILL KEEP US TOGETHER

Neil Sedaka and Howard Greenfield wrote "Love Will Keep Us Together" in 1974 after deciding to break up their songwriting team. The song was their last collaboration after almost twenty years together. "Love Will Keep Us Together" first appeared on the 1974 LP *Sedaka's Back* (Rocket 463). In early 1975 Toni Tennille and Daryl Dragon were looking for one more song to complete their first album for A&M Records when Kip Cohen, A&R director for the company, played "Love Will Keep Us Together" from Sedaka's LP. They recorded the tune and the single release (A&M 1672) reached number one. "Love Will Keep Us Together" was a million-seller and won a Grammy Award for Record of the Year. (Note: At the end of the song, Toni Tennille says, "Sedaka is back," as a tribute to the composer.) The Spanish version of "Love Will Keep Us Together," called "Por Amor Viviremos" (A&M 1715), was on the Hot 100 chart at the same time as the English version—the only time that two versions of a number one single in two different languages by the same artists were on the Hot 100 chart concurrently.

Elvis is reported to have recorded "Love Will Keep Us Together" in 1975 or 1976, but no tape has yet surfaced.

LOVEBUG ITCH

In 1950, Eddy Arnold had a #2 country hit with "Lovebug Itch" (RCA 0382). Elvis reportedly recorded the song, but there has been no supporting evidence.

LOVELY MAMIE

Elvis sang "Lovely Mamie" in his 1968 film *Stay Away, Joe.* The song lasted just a few seconds and was recorded on the set. Elvis sang, "Mamie, Mamie, lovely little Mamie" to the tune of "Alouette."[1] "Lovely Mamie" has never been released by RCA, but it does appear on bootlegs.

Bootleg LPs:
• *From Hollywood to Vegas* (*Stay Away, Joe* soundtrack)

LOVER DOLL

Sid Wayne and Abner Silver wrote "Lover Doll" for Elvis's 1958 film *King Creole*. In the film, Elvis sang it to divert attention while Vic Morrow and his pals shoplifted at a five-and-dime store. "Lover Doll" was recorded at Radio Recorders on January 16, 1958. Take #7 was selected by RCA for release. The Jordanaires overdubbed their vocal track on June 19, 1958. The *King Creole* LP version of "Lover Doll" is longer than the EP version and includes the Jordanaires, while the EP version doesn't. In West Germany, "Lover Doll" was released as a single twice: "Lover Doll"/"Dixieland Rock" (RCA 47-9200) and "Young and Beautiful"/"Lover Doll" (RCA 47-9224).

EPs:
• *King Creole, Volume 1* (alternate mix; shorter version, no Jordanaires)

LPs:
• *Elvis: The Other Sides—Worldwide Gold Award Hits, Volume 2* (alternate mix; shorter version, no Jordanaires)
• *King Creole*

Bootleg LPs:
• *From the Beach to the Bayou* (take #8; just Elvis and guitar)

LOVIN' ARMS

"Loving Arms" was written by Tom Jans and first recorded by Dobie Gray in 1973. His recording (MCA 40100) reached #61 on *Billboard*'s Hot 100 chart. In 1974 Kris Kristofferson and Rita Coolidge (A&M 1498), and Petula Clark (Dunhill 15019) had recordings of "Loving Arms."

On December 13, 1973, Elvis recorded "Loving Arms" as "Lovin' Arms" at Stax Studios in Memphis. Seven years later, on October 17, 1980, Felton Jarvis directed the recording of a new instrumental track for an alternate take of the song at Young 'Un Sound in Nashville. The resulting single release had a 15-week stay on *Billboard*'s country chart, reaching a high of #8.

Singles:
• "My Boy"/"LOVIN' ARMS" (RCA 2458EX) 1974. Disc jockey promotional release. This rare record was issued to promote the *Good Times* LP. It came with no picture sleeve, just a two-color sleeve with "ELVIS PRESLEY—MY BOY" printed on it.
• "LOVIN' ARMS"/"You Asked Me To" (RCA PB-12205) April 1981. Standard release. This single was the first since 1956 that was not released with a picture sleeve.
• "LOVIN' ARMS"/"You Asked Me To" (RCA JB-12205) April 1981. Disc jockey promotional release. This record was pressed on green vinyl.

LPs:
• *Good Times*
• *Guitar Man* (alternate take; new instrumental track)

LOVING YOU

Jerry Leiber and Mike Stoller wrote "Loving You" for Elvis's 1957 film of the same name. Two versions were recorded for the film: a fast version and a slow, ballad version. The recording session took place on February 14, 1957, at Radio Recorders. Take #12 of the ballad version and take #21 of the fast version were selected as the masters. On February 24, Elvis recorded the rendition that was released on record. Take #4 was chosen as the master. The single release had a 22-week stay on *Billboard*'s Top 100 chart, peaking at #28. Paired with "Teddy Bear," "Loving You" reached number one for one week on the country chart during its eight-week stay. In August 1957, "Teddy Bear"/"Loving You" replaced the Coasters' "Searchin'"/"Young Blood" at the top of the rhythm & blues chart, where it stayed for just one week before being replaced by Jerry Lee Lew-

---

[1] "Alouette" is a traditional French Canadian folk song that was once a standard work song sung by women plucking chickens. The words were first published in 1879.

is's "Whole Lotta Shakin' Goin' On." Sales of "Loving You" were in excess of one million copies.

"Teddy Bear"/"Loving You" (RCA 1013) was the first Elvis single to be released on the RCA label in Great Britain (July 1957).

Singles:
- "Teddy Bear"/"LOVING YOU" (RCA 20-7000) June 1957. Standard 78 RPM release.
- "Teddy Bear"/"LOVING YOU" (RCA 47-7000) June 1957. Standard 45 RPM release.
- "Teddy Bear"/"LOVING YOU" (RCA 447-0620) 1961. Gold Standard Series reissue.
- "Teddy Bear"/"LOVING YOU" (RCA PB-11109) October 1977. One of 15 singles in the boxed set *15 Golden Records—30 Golden Hits* (RCA PP-11301), and the *20 Golden Hits in Full Color Sleeves* (RCA PP-11340) boxed set released two months later.
- "Love Me Tender"/"LOVING YOU" (RCA PB-13893) October 1984. One of six singles in the boxed set *Elvis' Greatest Hits—Golden Singles, Volume 2* (RCA PP-13898). The singles were pressed on gold vinyl and had special gold "50th" anniversary labels.

EPs:
- *Dealer's Prevue*
- *Loving You, Volume 1*

LPs:
- *Elvis* (RCA DPL2-0056[e])
- *Elvis—A Canadian Tribute*
- *Elvis' Golden Records*
- *Elvis: Worldwide 50 Gold Award Hits, Volume 1*
- *Essential Elvis—The First Movies* (unreleased slow version, take #10) (unreleased fast version, takes #20–21) (unreleased fast version, take #1) (unreleased fast version, take #8; Compact Disc release only)
- *Loving You*
- *Pure Gold*

Bootleg LPs:
- *From Hollywood to Vegas* (*Loving You* soundtrack)
- *Got a Lot o' Livin' to Do!* (*Loving You* soundtrack)
- *Long Lost Songs* (Las Vegas; December 1975)
- *Loving You* (*Loving You* soundtrack)
- *Loving You Recording Sessions* (takes #1–6, #9–13, and #15–21; fast version) (takes #2–5, slow version)
- *Loving You Sessions* (takes #1–21, fast version) (takes #1–12, slow version)
- *The Rockin' Rebel, Volume 3* (take #21, fast version) (three false starts and complete take, slow version)
- *Unfinished Business* (alternate take, fast version)

MacARTHUR PARK

Jimmy Webb composed "MacArthur Park" in 1967 as the last movement in a cantata. After the Association turned it down, Richard Harris chose the song for his 1968 LP, *A Tramp Shining* (Dunhill DS 50332). The instrumental track was recorded in Los Angeles with Hal Blaine on drums, Al Casey and Tom Tedesco on guitar, Larry Knechtel and Jimmy Webb on keyboards, and Joe Osborne on bass. The tapes were then flown to England where Harris overdubbed his vocal. Harris's single release of "MacArthur Park" (Dunhill 4134) reached #2 on *Billboard*'s Hot 100 chart and became a million-seller. It received a Grammy Award for Best Arrangement Accompanying Vocalist(s) of 1968. Other recordings of "MacArthur Park" include those by Tony Bennett (Columbia 45032) in 1969, Waylon Jennings and Jessi Colter[1] (RCA 47-0210) in 1969, the Four Tops (Motown 1189) in 1971, Andy Williams (Columbia 45647) in 1972, and Donna Summer's number one disco version (Casablanca 939) in 1978.

Elvis sang a few lines of "MacArthur Park" during the taping of his 1968 TV special "Elvis."

Bootleg LPs:
- *The Burbank Sessions, Volume 2* ("Elvis" TV special taping; June 29, 1968, at 8:00 P.M. show)

MAKE ME KNOW IT

Otis Blackwell wrote "Make Me Know It" for Elvis, who recorded it on March 20, 1960, at RCA's Nashville studios—the first song recorded after his discharge from the Army.

LPs:
- *Elvis Is Back*

MAKE THE WORLD GO AWAY

Hank Cochran wrote "Make the World Go Away" in 1963. The big hits that year were by Ray Price (Columbia 42827), whose version reached #2 on the country chart, and Timi Yuro (Liberty 55587) who peaked at #24 on the Hot 100 chart and #5 on the Easy-Listening chart. Two years later, Eddy Arnold took "Make the World Go Away" (RCA 47-8679) to the top spot on both the country and Easy-Listening charts, and to #6 on the Hot 100 chart. Donny and Marie Osmond also had a moderate hit with the song in 1975 on MGM Records (MGM 14807).

Elvis recorded "Make the World Go Away" at RCA's Nashville studios on June 7, 1970. An alternate mix appeared on the RCA Record Club release *Country Memories*.

LPs:
- *Elvis Country*
- *Welcome to My World* (alternate take)

MALAGUEÑA

"Malagueña" is from the suite "Andalucia," written by Ernesto Lecuona in 1930. English words were written by Marian Banks. An instrumental track for "Malagueña" was recorded on January 23, 1963, at Radio Recorders. Elvis may have recorded a vocal track, but no proof is available. "Malagueña" had been slated for use in *Fun in Acapulco*.

MAMA

Elvis recorded "Mama" in March 1962 at Radio Recorders for use in his film *Girls! Girls! Girls!*, but it was deleted from the final print. The Amigos, however, did sing "Mama" in the film. The song was written by Charles O'Curran and Dudley Brooks.

LPs:
- *Double Dynamite*
- *Let's Be Friends*

Bootleg LPs:
- *Elvis Rocks and the Girls Roll* (alternate take)

MAMA LIKED THE ROSES

Johnny Christopher wrote "Mama Liked the Roses" for Elvis, who recorded it on January 16, 1969, at American Sound Studios. One of the backing vocalists was Sandy Posey. Elvis's single release, paired with "The Wonder of You," reached #9 on *Billboard*'s Hot 100 chart, staying on the chart for 12 weeks.

Singles:
- "The Wonder of You"/"MAMA LIKED THE ROSES" (RCA 47-9835) May 1970. Standard release.
- "The Wonder of You"/"MAMA LIKED THE ROSES" (RCA 447-0676) August 1971. Gold Standard Series reissue.

LPs:
- *Elvis' Christmas Album* (Camden and Pickwick releases)
- *The Memphis Record*

MANSION OVER THE HILLTOP

This gospel song was written by Ira Stanphill in 1949. Red Foley had a popular version of "Mansion over the Hilltop" (Decca 28694) in 1953. It was the flip side of "I Believe."

Elvis recorded "Mansion over the Hilltop" on October 30, 1960, at RCA's Nashville studios. Take #3 was selected by RCA for release.

LPs:
- *His Hand in Mine*

MARGUERITA

Elvis sang "Marguerita" in his 1963 movie *Fun in Acapulco*. The song was written by Don Robertson and

---

[1]For their recording of "MacArthur Park," Jennings and Colter received their first Grammy Award—Best Country and Western Duet, Trio, or Group.

recorded by Elvis on January 22, 1963, at Radio Recorders.

LPs:
• *Fun in Acapulco*

MARY IN THE MORNING

"Mary in the Morning" was written by Johnny Cymbal and Michael Rashkow and recorded by Al Martino (Capitol 5904) in 1967. Martino's recording topped the Easy-Listening chart and peaked at #27 on the Hot 100 chart. Later in 1967 Tommy Hunter had a moderate hit with "Mary in the Morning" (Del-Mar 1013) in the country field.

Elvis recorded "Mary in the Morning" on June 5, 1970, at RCA's Nashville studios. In the documentary *Elvis—That's the Way It Is*, he was filmed singing the song at the International Hotel in Las Vegas in August 1970. The soundtrack LP, however, featured the studio track, not the live version.

LPs:
• *That's the Way It Is* (studio recording)

Bootleg LPs:
• *Leavin' It Up to You* (RCA release with no overdubbing)
• *That's the Way It Is* (*Elvis—That's the Way It Is* soundtrack)

MAYBELLENE

In the early 1950s Chuck Berry performed Bob Wills's song "Ida Red" in his nightclub act, imitating the popular country singers of the day. After signing with Chess records, "Ida Red" was Berry's first recording. He reportedly recorded 36 takes before a version was judged suitable for release. The title was changed to "Maybellene" after Berry remembered a cow named Maybellene in a childhood nursery rhyme. "Maybellene" (Chess 1604) became a number one rhythm & blues hit in 1955. It also did well on the Top 100 chart, peaking at #5. Sales exceeded one million copies. The first cover version of "Maybellene" was by Marty Robbins in late 1955 (Columbia 21446). Johnny Rivers revived the song in 1964 (Imperial 66056), reaching #12 on the Hot 100 chart.

Elvis sang "Maybellene" in concert and on the "Louisiana Hayride" quite often in 1955 and 1956.

LPs:
• *Elvis: The First Live Recordings* ("Louisiana Hayride"; August 6 or 27, 1955)

MEAN WOMAN BLUES

Elvis sang "Mean Woman Blues" in his 1957 movie *Loving You*. The record version was recorded on January 13, 1957, at Radio Recorders. Take #14 was selected for release. The film version was recorded in February 1957. "Mean Woman Blues" was written by Claude DeMetrius. Perhaps the first cover version was by Jerry Lee Lewis on his 1958 EP *The Great Ball of Fire* (Sun EPA-107). In 1963 Roy Orbison had a big hit

with "Mean Woman Blues"[1] (Monument 824), reaching #5 on the Hot 100 chart and #8 on the rhythm & blues chart. Elvis's version of the song was heard in the 1981 documentary *This Is Elvis*.

Singles:
• "Have I Told You Lately That I Love You"/"MEAN WOMAN BLUES" (47-7066) 1957. Disc jockey "Record Prevue."

EPs:
• *Loving You, Volume 2*

LPs:
• *Elvis Aron Presley—Forever*
• *Elvis: The Other Sides—Worldwide Gold Award Hits, Volume 2*
• *Essential Elvis—The First Movies* (alternate film version)
• *Loving You*
• *This Is Elvis* (film version with overdubbing)

Bootleg LPs:
• *Got a Lot o' Livin' to Do!* (*Loving You* soundtrack)
• *Loving You* (*Loving You* soundtrack)

THE MEANEST GIRL IN TOWN

Elvis sang "The Meanest Girl in Town" in his 1965 film *Girl Happy*. The song, which was written by Joy Byers, was recorded by Elvis in June or July 1964 at Radio Recorders.

LPs:
• *Girl Happy*

MEMORIES

Elvis introduced "Memories," which was written by Billy Strange and Mac Davis, in his 1968 TV special, "Elvis." The instrumental track for the recording was made at Western Recorders on June 20 or 21, 1968. Although vocals were recorded at the NBC studios in Burbank on June 27, the vocal on the single release was recorded at a later date. The single had a seven-week stay on *Billboard*'s Hot 100 chart, peaking at #35. It reached #56 on the country chart and #7 on the Easy-Listening chart. "Memories" was sung over the closing credits of *Elvis on Tour* and *This Is Elvis*. In 1970 the Lettermen had a popular version of "Memories" in a medley with "Traces" (Capitol 2697).

Singles:
• "MEMORIES"/"Charro" (RCA 47-9731) March 1969. Standard release.
• "MEMORIES"/Charro" (RCA 447-0669) December 1970. Gold Standard Series reissue.

LPs:
• *Elvis—TV Special*
• *This Is Elvis*

Bootleg LPs:
• *The Burbank Sessions, Volume I* ("Elvis" TV special taping; July 27, 1968, at 6:00 P.M. and 8:00 P.M. shows)
• *The Monologue L.P.* (Las Vegas; July 31, 1969)
• *The '68 Comeback* (same as RCA release)

---

[1]Orbison's version credited Jerry West and Whispering Smith as composers.

MEMORY REVIVAL

An instrumental track for "Memory Revival," which was written by Al Owens and Dallas Frazier, was recorded on February 22, 1969, at American Sound Studios. Elvis may have recorded a vocal track for the song, but no tape has yet surfaced.

MEMPHIS, TENNESSEE

"Memphis, Tennessee" was written and recorded by Chuck Berry in 1959 as the flip side to "Back in the U.S.A." (Chess 1729). He sang it later that year in the movie, *Go, Johnny, Go!*[1] Bo Diddley played rhythm guitar on Berry's recording, which did not chart. Berry's 1964 follow-up to "Memphis, Tennessee," called "Little Marie" (Chess 1912), *did* chart, reaching #54 on the Hot 100 chart. Several artists have recorded "Memphis, Tennessee," including Lonnie Mack (Fraternity 906) in 1963, Johnny Rivers (Imperial 66032) in 1964, and Buck Owens (Capitol 5446) in 1965. All three used the title "Memphis." The biggest hit was Johnny Rivers's recording, which reached #2 on the Hot 100 chart and became a million-seller. "Memphis, Tennessee" was a 1963 hit in England for Dave Berry and the Cruisers. (Berry's real name was David Grundy. He changed his last name to that of his idol, Chuck Berry.)

Elvis first recorded "Memphis, Tennessee" on May 27, 1963, at RCA's Nashville studios, but that version has not been released. The version that appears on record was recorded on January 12, 1964.

EPs:
• *See the USA, the Elvis Way*

LPs:
• *Elvis for Everyone*

Bootleg LPs:
• *To Know Him Is to Love Him* (Las Vegas; 1969 or 1970)

MERRY CHRISTMAS BABY

"Merry Christmas Baby" was written by Lou Baxter and Johnny Moore and first recorded by Johnny Moore's Three Blazers. Featured on the recording were Charles Brown on vocal and piano, Johnny Moore on guitar, and Eddie Wilkins on bass. "Merry Christmas Baby" (Exclusive 63X) reached #9 on *Billboard*'s rhythm & blues chart in December 1949. The record was reissued in 1950, listing Charles Brown with Johnny Moore's Three Blazers as the artists (Swing Time 238). In 1954 the reissue listed the artist as Charles Brown (Hollywood 1021), with no mention of Johnny Moore or the Three Blazers. Other recordings of "Merry Christmas Baby" include those by Chuck Berry (Chess 1714) in 1958 and Dodie Stevens (Dot 16166) in 1960.

Elvis recorded "Merry Christmas Baby" during a jam session at RCA's Nashville studios on May 15, 1971. During the recording, Elvis sang, "Gave me a diamond ring for Christmas, now I'm puttin' it through Al's mike." "Al" was engineer Al Pachucki. Elvis was also heard to say, "Wake up, Puts!" to bass player Norbert

Putnam. James Burton's guitar solo was overdubbed at a later date. The single release of "Merry Christmas Baby" was a minute and a half shorter than on the original album release, *Elvis Sings the Wonderful World of Christmas*. It did not chart.

Singles:
• "MERRY CHRISTMAS BABY"/"O Come, All Ye Faithful" (RCA 74-0572) December 1971. Standard release.
• "MERRY CHRISTMAS BABY"/"Santa Claus Is Back in Town" (RCA PB-14237) November 1985. New single pressed on green vinyl.

LPs:
• *Elvis Sings the Wonderful World of Christmas*
• *Memories of Elvis* (original version without James Burton's guitar solo)
• *Reconsider Baby* (alternate edit)
• *This Is Elvis* (alternate edit with strings overdubbed)

MERRY CHRISTMAS DARLIN'

"Merry Christmas Darlin'" is one of the many songs that Elvis is reported to have recorded while at RCA. No substantiation is available, however. In December 1952, Steve Alamo had a recording of "Merry Christmas Darlin'" on MGM Records (MGM 11380).

A MESS OF BLUES

"A Mess of Blues" was written for Elvis by Doc Pomus and Mort Shuman. Elvis recorded the song on March 21, 1960, at RCA's Nashville studios. The single release had an 11-week stay on *Billboard*'s Hot 100 chart, peaking at #32. "A Mess of Blues" sold over one million copies.

Singles:
• "It's Now or Never"/"A MESS OF BLUES" (RCA 47-7777) July 1960. Standard release.
• "It's Now or Never"/"A MESS OF BLUES" (RCA 61-7777) July 1960. "Living Stereo" release.
• "It's Now or Never"/"A MESS OF BLUES" (RCA 447-0628) February 1962. Gold Standard Series reissue.
• "It's Now or Never"/"A MESS OF BLUES" (RCA PB-11110) October 1977. One of 15 singles in the boxed set *15 Golden Records—30 Golden Hits* (RCA PP-11301).

LPs:
• *Elvis' Gold Records, Volume 4*
• *Elvis: Worldwide 50 Gold Award Hits, Volume 1*

MEXICAN JOE

Jim Reeves had his first number one country hit and million-seller with "Mexican Joe" (Abbott 116) in 1953. The song was written by Mitchell Torok. Some sources indicate that Elvis may have recorded "Mexican Joe" while at Sun Records, but no tape has yet surfaced.

MEXICO

Elvis sang "Mexico" in his 1963 film *Fun in Acapulco*, in a duet with Larry Domasin. The film version had a different background and dialogue that wasn't included in the version on record. "Mexico" was recorded on January 22, 1963, at Radio Recorders. Sid Tepper and Roy C. Bennett are the composers.

---

[1] *Go, Johnny, Go!* was the only film appearance of Ritchie Valens.

LPs:
- *Fun in Acapulco*

THE MICKEY MOUSE CLUB MARCH
This song served as the theme to Walt Disney's "The Mickey Mouse Club" on ABC-TV from 1955 to 1959. "The Mickey Mouse Club March" was written by Jimmy Dodd, host of the TV series. In 1967 singer Julie London had a recording of the song on Liberty Records (Liberty 55966).

Elvis sang "The Mickey Mouse Club March" right after he sang "Young and Beautiful" and "Happy Birthday" to a fan named Karen at a concert appearance in Odessa, Texas, in 1976.

Bootleg LPs:
- *Cadillac Elvis* (Odessa, Texas; May 30, 1976)

MILKCOW BLUES BOOGIE
"Milkcow Blues Boogie" was written and recorded by James (Kokomo) Arnold in 1935 under the title "Milk Cow Blues." The song has been recorded by several artists over the years, including Bob Crosby (Decca 1962) in 1938, Johnny Lee Wills (Decca 5985) in 1941, Moon Mullican as "New Milk Cow Blues" (King 607) in 1946, Bob Wills and His Texas Playboys as "Brain Cloudy Blues" (Columbia 20113) in 1946, and Ricky Nelson (Imperial 5707) in 1961. Nelson's recording reached #79 on the Hot 100 chart.

Elvis recorded "Milkcow Blues Boogie" at Sun records on December 10, 1954. His only instrumental accompaniment was Scotty Moore on guitar, Bill Black on bass, and his own guitar. "Milkcow Blues Boogie" did not chart.

Singles:
- "MILKCOW BLUES BOOGIE"/"You're a Heartbreaker" (Sun 215) January 8, 1955. Standard release in both 78 RPM and 45 RPM.
- "MILKCOW BLUES BOOGIE"/"You're a Heartbreaker" (RCA 20-6540) November 1955. Standard 78 RPM RCA reissue.
- "MILKCOW BLUES BOOGIE"/"You're a Heartbreaker" (RCA 47-6540) November 1955. Standard 45 RPM RCA reissue.
- "MILKCOW BLUES BOOGIE"/"You're a Heartbreaker" (RCA 447-0603) March 1959. Gold Standard Series reissue.

EPs:
- *Great Country/Western Hits*

LPs:
- *The Complete Sun Sessions* (master)
- *A Date with Elvis* (alternate mix with more reverberation)
- *The Sun Sessions* (alternate mix with more reverberation)

Bootleg LPs:
- *The Sun Years* (Sun release)

MILKY WHITE WAY
"Milky White Way" is a gospel standard that Elvis recorded on October 30, 1960, at RCA's Nashville studios. His 1966 single release did not chart.

In 1948 the Trumpeteers had a popular recording of "Milky White Way" (Score 5001).

Singles:
- "MILKY WHITE WAY"/"Swing Down, Sweet Chariot" (RCA 447-0652) March 1966. Gold Standard Series original release.

LPs:
- *His Hand in Mine*

MINE
"Mine" was written by Sid Tepper and Roy C. Bennett and recorded by Elvis at RCA's Nashville studios on September 11, 1967.

LPs:
- *Speedway*

MIRACLE OF THE ROSARY
The instrumental track for "Miracle of the Rosary" was recorded at RCA's Nashville studios on May 15, 1971. Elvis's vocal was recorded on May 19. "Miracle of the Rosary" was written by Lee Denson.

LPs:
- *Elvis Now*
- *He Walks Beside Me*

MIRAGE
Elvis sang "Mirage" in his 1965 film *Harum Scarum*. The recording session took place at RCA's Nashville studios in February (probably the 24th) 1965. "Mirage" was written by Bill Giant, Bernie Baum, and Florence Kaye.

LPs:
- *Harum Scarum*

MR. SONGMAN
"Mr. Songman" was written by Donnie Sumner and recorded by Elvis on December 12, 1973, at Stax Studios in Memphis. He occasionally sang it on tour in 1975 and 1976. The single release of "Mr. Songman" did not chart.

Singles:
- "T-R-O-U-B-L-E"/"MR. SONGMAN" (RCA PB-10278) April 1975. Standard release.
- "T-R-O-U-B-L-E"/"MR. SONGMAN" (RCA GB-10487) February 1976. Gold Standard Series reissue.

LPs:
- *Promised Land*

MR. TAMBOURINE MAN
Often considered to be the first folk-rock song, "Mr. Tambourine Man" was written by Bob Dylan and recorded on a demo by him and Ramblin' Jack Elliott. The demo got into the hands of Jim Dickson, manager of the Byrds, and he persuaded the group to record the song. The only Byrd to actually play on the recording was Roger McGuinn, on a twelve-string guitar. Session musicians Leon Russell, Larry Knechtel, Terry Cole, and Hal Blaine provided additional instrumentation. McGuinn sang lead, with Byrds David Crosby and Gene Clark singing harmony. Terry Melcher, Doris Day's son, produced the record. "Mr. Tambourine Man" (Columbia 43271) reached number one on the Hot 100 chart and became a million-seller. It also topped the British charts.

Elvis is known to have sung "Mr. Tambourine Man" in concert.

MONA LISA

"Mona Lisa" was written by Jay Livingston and Ray Evans for the 1950 movie *Captain Carey, U.S.A.*, in which it was heard in fragments and only in Italian. It won the Oscar for Best Song. Nat King Cole had a number one hit and million-seller with his 1950 recording of "Mona Lisa" (Capitol 1010). Other hits over the years include those by Dennis Day (RCA 20-3753), Art Lund (MGM 10689), Victor Young (Decca 27048), and Moon Mullican (King 886), all in 1950, and Conway Twitty (MGM 12804) and Carl Mann (Philips 3539) in 1959.

A 1960s recording of Elvis singing "Mona Lisa" on a home tape recorder was found at Graceland and issued by RCA in 1983.

LPs:
- *Elvis—A Legendary Performer, Volume 4*

MONEY HONEY

"Money Honey" was written by Jesse Stone and first recorded by the Drifters (Atlantic 1006) in 1953. Their recording was number one on *Billboard*'s rhythm & blues chart for an amazing 11 weeks.[1] The following year, Ella Mae Morse had a popular recording of "Money Honey" (Capitol 2882).

Reportedly, Buddy Holly taught "Money Honey" to Elvis when the two were performing together in Texas in 1955. Elvis recorded the song on January 10, 1956, at RCA's New York City studios—his first commercial session for RCA. Based on the strength of its appearance in the *Heartbreak Hotel* EP, "Money Honey" had a five-week stay on *Billboard*'s Top 100 chart in 1956, peaking at #76. A single release of the song later in 1956 failed to chart.

Singles:
- "MONEY HONEY"/"One-Sided Love Affair" (RCA 20-6641) September 1956. Standard 78 RPM release.
- "MONEY HONEY"/"One-Sided Love Affair" (RCA 47-6641) September 1956. Standard 45 RPM release.
- "MONEY HONEY"/"I Got a Woman" (RCA 47-6689) September 1956. Disc jockey "Record Prevue" with a different flipside.
- "MONEY HONEY"/"One-Sided Love Affair" (RCA 447-0614) March 1959. Gold Standard Series reissue.

EPs:
- *Elvis Presley—The Most Talked About New Personality in the Last Ten Years of Recorded Music* (RCA EPB-1254)
- *Heartbreak Hotel*

LPs:
- *Elvis Aron Presley* (Las Vegas; May 6, 1956)
- *Elvis Presley*
- *A Golden Celebration* ("Stage Show"; March 24, 1956)

Bootleg LPs:
- *Dorsey Shows* ("Stage Show"; March 24, 1956)
- *Superstar Outtakes, Volume 2* ("Stage Show"; March 24, 1956)

MOODY BLUE

Mark James wrote and recorded "Moody Blue" (Mercury 73718) in 1974. His recording did not chart.

Elvis recorded "Moody Blue" on the night of February 4–5, 1976, at Graceland. Strings and horns, which were arranged by Bergen White, were overdubbed later. "Moody Blue" had a 13-week stay on *Billboard*'s Hot 100 chart, peaking at #31. It reached number one for one week on the country chart and #2 on the Easy-Listening chart.

Singles:
- "MOODY BLUE"/"She Thinks I Still Care" (RCA PB-10857) December 1976. Standard release.
- "MOODY BLUE"/"She Thinks I Still Care" (RCA JB-10857) December 1976. Disc jockey promotional release. In May 1977, RCA released this record in five colors (red, blue, white, gold, and green) and an experimental multicolor as an experiment. The multicolor disc is extremely rare.
- "MOODY BLUE"/"For the Heart" (RCA GB-11326) August 1978. Gold Standard Series original release.

LPs:
- *Elvis' Gold Records, Volume 5*
- *Moody Blue*
- *This Is Elvis*

MOONLIGHT SWIM

"Moonlight Swim" was written by Sylvia Dee and Ben Weisman and first recorded by Nick Noble (Mercury 71169) in 1957. Noble's recording reached #37 on *Billboard*'s Top 100 chart. Later that year, actor Tony Perkins had a release of the song (RCA 47-7020) that did even better, reaching #24. The label on his record listed the song as "Moon-Light Swim."

Elvis sang "Moonlight Swim" in his 1962 movie *Blue Hawaii*. The recording session took place on March 22, 1961, at Radio Recorders.

LPs:
- *Blue Hawaii*

Bootleg LPs:
- *Behind Closed Doors* (takes #1 [a false start] and #2)
- *The Blue Hawaii Box* (takes #1–4)

MORE

"More" served as the theme to the 1963 Italian shockumentary *Mondo Cane*. Written by Norman Newell, Riz Ortolani, and N. Oliviero, the song won an Oscar for Best Song. Several artists have recorded "More," including Kai Winding (Verve 10295) and Vic Dana (Dolton 81) in 1963.

Elvis sang a few seconds of "More" in concert on a few occasions.

Bootleg LPs:
- *The Monologue L.P.* (Las Vegas; July 31, 1969)
- *To Know Him Is to Love Him* (Las Vegas; 1969 or 1970)

---

[1]Since "Money Honey," only two songs have exceeded 11 weeks at number one on the rhythm & blues chart: "Honky Tonk" by Bill Doggett in 1956 and "Searchin' "/"Young Blood" by the Coasters in 1957.

THE MOST BEAUTIFUL GIRL

"The Most Beautiful Girl" was written by Norro Wilson, Billy Sherrill, and Rory Bourke, and first recorded by Charlie Rich in 1973. Rich's recording (Epic 11040) reached number one on the Hot 100 chart and became a million-seller. It also hit the top spot on the country chart.

Elvis humorously sang a portion of "The Most Beautiful Girl" to comedian Marty Allen as he (Elvis) knelt before him on the stage ramp at the Las Vegas Hilton on January 27, 1974.

MUSKRAT RAMBLE

"Muskrat Ramble" was written by Ray Gilbert and Edward (Kid) Ory in 1926. The first recording of the song was by Louis Armstrong (Okeh 8300) that same year, with Ory on trombone. In 1954 Armstrong rerecorded "Muskrat Ramble" on Decca Records (Decca 29280). Another popular recording that year was the McGuire Sisters' version (Coral 61278), which reached #10 on *Billboard*'s Top 100 chart. In 1961 Freddy Cannon released a recording of "Muskrat Ramble" (Swan 4066) that was a moderate hit, reaching #54.

An instrumental version of "Muskrat Ramble" was recorded for *King Creole* and used as background music during the film. Some have speculated that Elvis may have recorded a version of the song, but no proof has been forthcoming. The instrumental version, however, can be found on the bootleg LP *From the Beach to the Bayou*.

MY BABE

"My Babe" was written by Willie Dixon and Charles Stone and first recorded by Little Walter Jacobs (Checker 811) in 1955. The song was an adaptation of the gospel tune "This Train," which Sister Rosetta Tharpe wrote in the 1940s. Little Walter's recording topped the rhythm & blues chart for four weeks. In 1960 co-composer Willie Dixon recorded his song under the title "My Baby Don't Stand No Cheating" (Folkways LPF-2386). Roy Head barely made the Hot 100 (#99) in 1966 with his recording of "My Babe" (Back Beat 560).

Elvis sang "My Babe" in concert on a few occasions. Live versions from the International Hotel in August 1969 were released on record by RCA.

LPs:
- *Elvis Aron Presley* (Las Vegas; August 1969)
- *Elvis in Person* (Las Vegas; August 25, 1969)
- *From Memphis to Vegas/From Vegas to Memphis* (Las Vegas; August 24, 1969)

Bootleg LPs:
- *Command Performance* (Las Vegas; August 4, 1972)
- *Sold Out* (Las Vegas; August 4, 1972)
- *Standing Room Only, Volume 2* (Las Vegas; August 24, 1969)

MY BABY LEFT ME

Arthur Crudup wrote and first recorded "My Baby Left Me" on November 8, 1950. His recording (RCA 130-284) did not chart.

Elvis recorded "My Baby Left Me" on January 30, 1956, at RCA's New York City studios. His single release had a 14-week stay on *Billboard*'s Top 100 chart, peaking at #31. On the country chart, "My Baby Left Me" was paired with "I Want You, I Need You, I Love You" and reached the top spot for one week.

Singles:
- "I Want You, I Need You, I Love You"/"MY BABY LEFT ME" (RCA 20-6540) May 1956. Standard 78 RPM release.
- "I Want You, I Need You, I Love You"/"MY BABY LEFT ME" (RCA 47-6540) May 1956. Standard 45 RPM release. For a brief time, a special picture sleeve, "This Is His Life: Elvis Presley," was issued. This sleeve was a cartoon depiction of Elvis's life. Unfortunately, the cartoon had Elvis's age as 19 when he was actually 21 at the time. This, then, was the first Elvis picture sleeve.
- "I Want You, I Need You, I Love You"/"MY BABY LEFT ME" (RCA 447-0607) March 1959. Gold Standard Series reissue.

EPs:
- *Elvis Presley* (RCA SPD-23)
- *The Real Elvis*

LPs:
- *Elvis Recorded Live on Stage in Memphis* (Memphis; March 20, 1974)
- *Elvis: The Other Sides—Worldwide Gold Award Hits, Volume 2*
- *For LP Fans Only*
- *I Was the One* (with overdubbing)
- *Reconsider Baby*
- *This Is Elvis* (with overdubbing)

Bootleg LPs:
- *Big Boss Man* (Las Vegas; August 19, 1974)
- *Standing Room Only, Volume 2* (Memphis; March 20, 1974)

MY BABY'S GONE

(See *I'm Left, You're Right, She's Gone*)

MY BOY

"My Boy" was written by J. Claude Francois and Jean-Pierre Boutayre (English words by Bill Martin and Phil Coulter) and recorded by actor Richard Harris in 1971. His recording (Dunhill 4293) reached #41 on *Billboard*'s Hot 100 chart and #13 on the Easy-Listening chart.

Elvis recorded "My Boy" on December 12, 1973, at Stax Studios in Memphis. His single release in 1975 had an 11-week stay on the Hot 100 chart, peaking at #20. The song reached #14 on the country chart. "My Boy" was sung by Elvis in concert several times before he recorded it.

Singles:
- "MY BOY"/"Thinking About You" (RCA PB-10191) January 1975. Standard release.
- "MY BOY"/"MY BOY" (RCA JH-10191) January 1975. Disc jockey promotional release. The stereo version was on side A; the mono version on side B.
- "MY BOY"/"Loving Arms" (RCA 2458EX) 1974. Disc jockey promotional release. This rare record was issued to promote the *Good Times* LP. It came with no picture sleeve, just a two-color sleeve with "ELVIS PRESLEY—MY BOY" printed on it.
- "MY BOY"/"Thinking About You" (RCA GB-10489) February 1976. Gold Standard Series reissue.

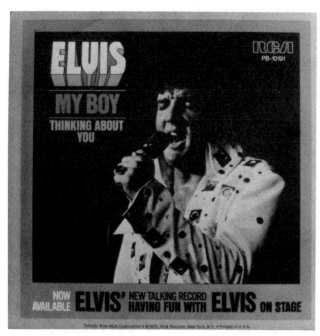

(Photo courtesy Don Fink)

- "Always on My Mind"/"MY BOY" (RCA PB-14090) July 1985. New single release pressed on purple vinyl.

LPs:
- *Always on My Mind*
- *Good Times*
- *Our Memories of Elvis* (without overdubbing)

Bootleg LPs:
- *Command Performance* (Las Vegas; September 2, 1973)
- *From Las Vegas to Hollywood* (Las Vegas; 1973?)
- *From Las Vegas . . . to Niagara Falls* (Las Vegas; September 3, 1973)
- *Rockin' with Elvis April Fool's Day* (Las Vegas; April 1, 1975)

MY DESERT SERENADE

Elvis sang "My Desert Serenade" in his 1965 film *Harum Scarum*. He recorded the song, which was written by Stan Gelber, in February (probably the 24th) 1965, at RCA's Nashville studios.

LPs:
- *Harum Scarum*

MY HAPPINESS

"My Happiness" was written in 1933 by Betty Peterson and Borney Bergantine, but not popularized until 1948 in several best-selling recordings. The first release was by John and Sandra Steele (Damon 11133). Their recording reached #3 on *Billboard*'s Best-Selling Singles chart and became a million-seller. Another million-seller in 1948 was by the Pied Pipers (Capitol 15094) with the Paul Weston Orchestra. Other popular releases in 1948 included those by Ella Fitzgerald (Decca 24446) with the Song Spinners, and the Marlin Sisters (Columbia 38217). An instrumental version of "My Happiness" by the Mulcays, a harmonica group, was popular in 1953. Connie Francis had a million-selling

single of the song in 1959 (MGM 12738), reaching #2 on the Hot 100 chart.

In August or September 1953, Elvis walked into the Memphis Recording Service to record a four-dollar acetate. Elvis knew he had a good voice, and he was hoping to be discovered by Sam Phillips. Phillips was not in that day, but Marion Keisker was. (For the full story, see the *Memphis Recording Service* in Part I.)

The first song that Elvis recorded at the Memphis Recording Service was "My Happiness." The second was "That's When Your Heartaches Begin." Reportedly, a tape of that first acetate exists, but the authors have not heard it.

MY HEART CRIES FOR YOU

"My Heart Cries for You" was written in 1950 by Carl Sigman and Percy Faith, who based the melody on "Chanson de Marie Antoinette." In December 1950, five artists had best-sellers with the song. The first to reach the charts was Guy Mitchell (Columbia 39067). He reached #2 and had his first million-seller with the song. Vic Damone (Mercury 5563), Dinah Shore (RCA 47-3978), and Jimmy Wakely (Capitol 1328) had top 20 hits. In early 1951 Victor Young (Decca 27333) also reached the charts with his recording, peaking at #29.

In the 1960s Elvis made a home recording of "My Heart Cries for You" that was later released on the LP *A Golden Celebration*.

LPs:
- *A Golden Celebration* (Graceland; 1960s)

MY LITTLE FRIEND

Elvis recorded "My Little Friend" on January 16, 1969, at American Sound Studios in Memphis. Shirl Milete is the composer. The single release of "My Little Friend" did not chart.

Singles:
- "Kentucky Rain"/"MY LITTLE FRIEND" (RCA 47-9791) February 1970. Standard release.
- "Kentucky Rain"/"MY LITTLE FRIEND" (RCA 447-0675) August 1971. Gold Standard Series reissue.

LPs:
- *Almost in Love*

MY WAY

"My Way" was written by Gilles Thibault, J. Claude Francois, and Jacques Revaux in 1967, using the French title "Comme d'Habitude." On a rainy day in Las Vegas in 1969, Paul Anka remembered the French melody he had heard while in France. He wrote English lyrics to the melody, with Frank Sinatra in mind. Sinatra recorded "My Way" (Reprise 734) and had a million-seller with it in 1969. The song peaked at #27 on the Hot 100 chart. Sinatra's recording was on the British charts for 122 weeks—a record for that country. The next year, Brook Benton had a rhythm & blues hit with "My Way" (Cotillion 44072), reaching #25.

Elvis sang "My Way" on his 1973 TV special, "Elvis: Aloha from Hawaii," and his 1977 TV special, "Elvis in Concert." A version from the latter special, recorded on

June 21, 1977, at Rapid City, South Dakota, was used for the single release. "My Way" reached #22 during its 12 weeks on the Hot 100 chart. It peaked at #6 on the Easy-Listening chart. Sales of the single exceeded one million copies. The 1981 documentary *This Is Elvis* featured "My Way" on the soundtrack.

Singles:
- "MY WAY"/"America the Beautiful" (RCA PB-11165) November 1977. Standard release. Some of the record labels listed the flip side as "America."
- "MY WAY"/"America the Beautiful" (RCA JH-11165) November 1977. Disc jockey promotional release. All copies of this release had "America the Beautiful" incorrectly listed on the label as "America."
- "Way Down"/"MY WAY" (RCA GB-11504) May 1979. Gold Standard Series original release.

EPs:
- *Aloha from Hawaii via Satellite*

LPs:
- *Aloha from Hawaii via Satellite* (Honolulu; January 14, 1973)
- *The Alternate Aloha* (rehearsal concert for "Elvis: Aloha from Hawaii"; January 12, 1973)
- *Elvis—A Canadian Tribute*
- *Elvis in Concert* (Rapid City, South Dakota; June 21, 1977)
- *This Is Elvis*

Bootleg LPs:
- *Aloha Rehearsal Show—Kui Lee Cancer Benefit* (rehearsal concert for "Elvis: Aloha from Hawaii"; January 12, 1973)
- *A Dog's Life* (rehearsal concert for "Elvis: Aloha from Hawaii"; January 12, 1973
- *Rockin' with Elvis New Year's Eve Pittsburgh, Pa. Dec. 31, 1976* (Pittsburgh; December 31, 1976)
- *Susie Q* (Las Vegas rehearsal; ?)

MY WISH CAME TRUE

Elvis recorded "My Wish Came True" on September 6, 1957, at Radio Recorders. Although he attempted the song on two other occasions (January 23, 1958, and February 1, 1958), it was take #28 from that first session that was released. Elvis's single release of "My Wish Came True" had an 11-week stay on *Billboard*'s Hot 100 chart, reaching a high of #12. It peaked at #15 on the rhythm & blues chart. "My Wish Came True" was written by Ivory Joe Hunter. In 1971 he recorded his song for inclusion on the LP *The Return of Ivory Joe Hunter* (Epic E-30348).

Singles:
- "A Big Hunk o' Love"/"MY WISH CAME TRUE" (RCA 47-7600) July 1959. Standard release.
- "A Big Hunk o' Love"/"MY WISH CAME TRUE" (RCA 447-0626) February 1962. Gold Standard Series reissue.

LPs:
- *Elvis: The Other Sides—Worldwide Gold Award Hits, Volume 2*
- *50,000,000 Elvis Fans Can't Be Wrong—Elvis' Gold Records, Volume 2*

MY WOMAN, MY WOMAN, MY WIFE

Marty Robbins wrote and recorded "My Woman, My Woman, My Wife" in 1970. His single release (Columbia 45091) reached number one on *Billboard*'s country chart and #42 on the Hot 100 chart. Robbins won a Grammy Award for Best Country and Western Song of 1970 for "My Woman, My Woman, My Wife."

Elvis sang "My Woman, My Woman, My Wife" in concert on April 24, 1976, in San Diego.

MYSTERY TRAIN

"Mystery Train" was written by Herman (Little Junior) Parker and Sam Phillips and first recorded by Parker in 1953 (Sun 192). The record label credited "Little Junior's Blue Flames." "Mystery Train" was based on the Carter Family's 1930 song "Worried Man Blues" (Bluebird 6020). The guitar player on Parker's recording was Pat Hare.

Elvis recorded "Mystery Train" at Sun Records on July 11, 1955. Instrumentation was provided by Scotty Moore (guitar), Bill Black (bass), Johnny Bernero (drums), and Elvis (guitar). While Junior Parker's version was more bluesy, Elvis's was faster and more energetic. Scotty Moore's guitar riff was borrowed from Parker's "Love My Baby," which was the flip side of his "Mystery Train" release. Elvis's "Mystery Train" entered *Billboard*'s country chart in September 1955. It took 25 weeks to reach number one. That was the longest climb to the top of any Presley single on any chart. "Mystery Train" spent a total of 31 weeks on the chart.

In late November–early December 1955, when RCA reissued "Mystery Train," the record company simultaneously issued a cover version of the song by the Turtles with Hugo Winterhalter and His Orchestra. Release numbers of the two records were consecutive—the Turtles' was 47-6356 and Elvis's was 47-6357. Why RCA did this is a mystery.

A live performance of "Mystery Train" at the International Hotel in Las Vegas on August 10, 1970, was used in the documentary *Elvis—That's the Way It Is*. The Sun release was heard on the soundtrack of *Elvis on Tour* while various film clips were shown.

Singles:
- "MYSTERY TRAIN"/"I Forgot to Remember to Forget" (Sun 223) August 1955. Standard Sun release in both 78 RPM and 45 RPM versions.
- "MYSTERY TRAIN"/"I Forgot to Remember to Forget" (RCA 20-6357) November 1955. Standard 78 RPM reissue of the Sun original.
- "MYSTERY TRAIN"/"I Forgot to Remember to Forget" (RCA 47-6357) November 1955. Standard 45 RPM reissue of the Sun original.
- "MYSTERY TRAIN"/"I Forgot to Remember to Forget" (RCA 447-0600) March 1959. Gold Standard Series reissue.

EPs:
- *Any Way You Want Me*
- *Great Country/Western Hits*

LPs:
- *The Complete Sun Sessions* (master)
- *Elvis Aron Presley* (Shreveport, Louisiana; June 7, 1975) (in medley with "Tiger Man")
- *Elvis in Person* (Las Vegas; August 26, 1969) (in medley with "Tiger Man")
- *For LP Fans Only* (alternate mix with more reverberation)

- *From Memphis to Vegas/From Vegas to Memphis* (Las Vegas; August 26, 1969) (in medley with "Tiger Man")
- *The Sun Sessions* (alternate mix with more reverberation)

Bootleg LPs:
- *America's Own* (Uniondale, N.Y.; July 19, 1975) (in medley with "Tiger Man")
- *Command Performance* (Las Vegas; August 4, 1972) (in medley with "Tiger Man")
- *Good Rocking Tonight* (Sun Records release)
- *Sold Out* (Las Vegas; September 3, 1973) (in medley with "Tiger Man")
- *The Sun Years* (RCA release)
- *That's the Way It Is* (*Elvis—That's the Way It Is* soundtrack) (in medley with "Tiger Man")

NEVER AGAIN

Written by Billy Edd Wheeler and Jerry Chesnut, "Never Again" was an original recording by Elvis. It was recorded during a session at Graceland on the night of February 6–7, 1976.

LPs:
- *From Elvis Presley Boulevard, Memphis, Tennessee*
- *Our Memories of Elvis, Volume 1* (without overdubbing)

NEVER BEEN TO SPAIN

Three Dog Night originally recorded this Hoyt Axton composition in late 1971. "Never Been to Spain" (Dunhill 4299) rose to #5 on *Billboard*'s Hot 100 chart and #18 on the Easy-Listening chart. Elvis soon incorporated the song into his concert act. During his tour in April 1972, MGM recorded Elvis's performance of "Never Been to Spain" for the documentary *Elvis on Tour*. RCA had intended to include the song in the *Standing Room Only* album, but the LP was never released. A few months later, RCA recorded the evening show at Madison Square Garden on June 10, 1972. It's that version of "Never Been to Spain" that RCA released.

LPs:
- *Elvis as Recorded at Madison Square Garden*

Bootleg LPs:
- *Big Boss Man* (Las Vegas; August 19, 1974)
- *Elvis on Tour* (*Elvis on Tour* soundtrack)
- *Superstar Outtakes, Volume 2* (Las Vegas; 1972)
- *The Vegas Years, 1972–1975* (Las Vegas; 1972)

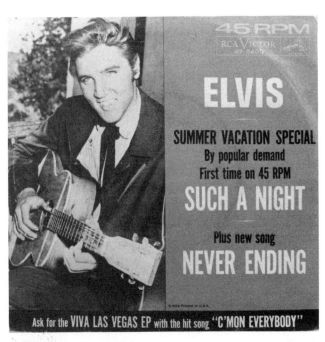

(Photo courtesy Don Fink)

NEVER ENDING

Elvis recorded "Never Ending" on May 26, 1963, at RCA's Nashville studios. Written by Buddy Kaye and Phil Springer, the song never reached *Billboard*'s Hot 100 chart, but it was listed at #111 on the magazine's "Bubbling Under" chart for two weeks.

Singles:
- "Such a Night"/"NEVER ENDING" (RCA 47-8400) July 1964. Standard release.
- "Such a Night"/"NEVER ENDING" (RCA 447-0645) May 1965. Gold Standard Series reissue.

LPs:
- *Double Trouble*

NEVER SAY YES

Doc Pomus and Mort Shuman wrote "Never Say Yes" for Elvis's 1966 film *Spinout*. Elvis recorded the tune on February 16, 1966, at Radio Recorders in Hollywood.

LPs:
- *Spinout*

NEW ORLEANS

Elvis sang "New Orleans," a Sid Tepper–Roy C. Bennett composition, in his 1958 film *King Creole*. He recorded the song at Radio Recorders on January 15, 1958. The version that was released was take #5.

EPs:
- *King Creole, Volume 1*
- *See the U.S.A., The Elvis Way*

LPs:
- *Elvis: The Other Sides—Worldwide Gold Award Hits, Volume 2*
- *King Creole*

THE NEXT STEP IS LOVE

Elvis recorded "The Next Step Is Love" on June 7, 1970, at RCA's Nashville studios. The song was written by Paul Evans and Paul Parnes. In the 1970 documentary *Elvis—That's the Way It Is*, Elvis was seen rehearsing "The Next Step Is Love" at MGM in preparation for his upcoming Las Vegas engagement. The version on the soundtrack album, however, is the studio recording. His single release spent nine weeks on *Billboard*'s Hot 100 chart, peaking at #32. It fared better on the Easy-Listening chart (#5, 10 weeks). A six-week stay on the country chart resulted in a top position of #57.

Singles:
- "I've Lost You"/"THE NEXT STEP IS LOVE" (RCA 47-9873) July 1970. Standard release.
- "I've Lost You"/"THE NEXT STEP IS LOVE" (RCA 447-0677) August 1971. Gold Standard Series reissue.

LPs:
- *Elvis: The Other Sides—Worldwide Gold Award Hits, Volume 2*
- *That's the Way It Is*

Bootleg LPs:
- *Eternal Elvis* (*Elvis—That's the Way It Is* soundtrack)
- *The King: From the Dark to the Light* (*Elvis—That's the Way It Is* soundtrack)
- *Special Delivery from Elvis Presley* (*Elvis: That's the Way It Is* soundtrack)
- *That's the Way It Is* (*Elvis—That's the Way It Is* soundtrack)

NIGHT LIFE

Although written for Elvis's 1964 film *Viva Las Vegas* by Bill Giant, Bernie Baum, and Florence Kaye, "Night Life" was cut from the movie and remained unreleased for five years. Elvis recorded the song at Radio Recorders in July 1963. Take #14 appears on RCA releases.

LPs:
- *Elvis Sings Flaming Star*
- *Singer Presents Elvis Singing Flaming Star and Others*

Bootleg LPs:
- *Elvis Rocks and the Girls Roll* (alternate take)

NIGHT RIDER

"Night Rider" was originally recorded on October 16, 1961, at RCA's Nashville studios, but that version was never released. Five months later, on March 18, 1962, Elvis again attempted the song and recorded a satisfactory take. In 1965, the 1962 recording was used in Elvis's film *Tickle Me*. "Night Rider" was written by Doc Pomus and Mort Shuman.

EPs:
- *Tickle Me*

LPs:
- *Pot Luck*

NIGHT TRAIN TO MEMPHIS

"Night Train to Memphis" was written by Beasley Smith, Owen Bradley, and Marvin Hughes in 1942. The inspiration for the song came from a real night train to Memphis (from Nashville) nicknamed the "Blue Goose." The first recording of "Night Train to Memphis" was by Roy Acuff in 1943 on Okeh Records (Okeh 06693). In 1946 Acuff starred in a movie titled *Night Train to Memphis*. His recording was reissued (Columbia 37029) and became quite popular. Red Foley and Roberta Lee did a version of the song in late 1951 for Decca Records (Decca 27763). Dean Martin also recorded "Night Train to Memphis" (Capitol 1885) in late 1951.

According to some reports, Elvis recorded "Night Train to Memphis" while at Sun Records. So far, those reports have not been confirmed.

NINE POUND HAMMER

"Nine Pound Hammer" was written and recorded in 1947 by Merle Travis for his first LP on Capitol Records, *Folk Songs from the Hills*. A year later, a single release of the song was issued (Capitol 15124). "Nine Pound Hammer" is one of many songs Elvis is reported to have recorded in the 1950s, although no bona fide documentation exists.

NO MORE

"No More" was written by Don Robertson and Hal Blair for Elvis's 1961 movie *Blue Hawaii*. Elvis recorded the song on March 21, 1961, at Radio Recorders. After the January 14, 1973, worldwide telecast of "Elvis: Aloha from Hawaii," Elvis recorded "No More" and four other tunes for inclusion in the expanded U.S. edition of the special, aired on April 4, 1973. "No More" was not used in the telecast, but it was included in the *Mahalo from Elvis* album.

LPs:
- *Blue Hawaii*
- *Burning Love and Hits from His Movies, Volume 2*
- *Elvis Aron Presley—Forever*
- *Mahalo from Elvis* (January 14, 1973, recording)

Bootleg LPs:
- *The Blue Hawaii Box* (takes #1–5, #7–9)
- *The Blue Hawaii Sessions* (takes #1, #3, and #7)
- *Plantation Rock* (takes #2 and #7)

NO PARTICULAR PLACE TO GO

In 1964 Chuck Berry wrote and recorded "No Particular Place to Go" (Chess 1898). It reached #10 on *Billboard*'s Hot 100 Chart. Felton Jarvis once taped a jam session of Elvis singing the tune, and to this day, it has remained unreleased.

(THERE'S) NO ROOM TO RHUMBA IN A SPORTS CAR

Elvis sang "(There's) No Room to Rhumba in a Sports Car," a Fred Wise–Dick Manning composition, in his 1963 film *Fun In Acapulco*. The song was recorded on January 23, 1963, at Radio Recorders.

LPs:
- *Fun in Acapulco*

NOAH

Elvis is rumored to have recorded this gospel tune while at Sun Records. In 1953 "Noah" was the flip side of Kay Starr's popular record "Side by Side" (Capitol 2334). The Jordanaires also recorded a version of the song, the flip side of their 1954 release "Bosom of Abraham" (Decca 29188). If Elvis did sing "Noah" in concert or tried to record it, it probably was the Jordanaires' release that influenced him.

NOTHINGVILLE

Billy Strange and Mac Davis wrote this song for Elvis's 1968 TV special "Elvis." The instrumental track was laid down at Western Recorders in Hollywood on June 20 or 21, 1968. Elvis may have recorded the vocal at that time or possibly at NBC on June 30. During the special, "Nothingville" was sung in a medley with "Guitar Man," "Let Yourself Go," and "Big Boss Man."

LPs:
- *Elvis—TV Special*

Bootleg LPs:
- *The '68 Comeback* (same as commercial release)

NOW IS THE HOUR

Bing Crosby had a #2 hit with "Now Is the Hour" in 1948 (Decca 24279). Other hit versions that year included those by Grace Fields (London 110), Eddy Howard (Majestic 1191), Margaret Whiting (Capitol 15024), and Charlie Spivak (RCA 2704). An instrumental track of "Now Is the Hour" was supposedly laid down at Radio Recorders on July 27, 1965, during the *Paradise, Hawaiian Style* sessions. Elvis may have recorded a vocal track of it in early August.

O COME, ALL YE FAITHFUL

This perennial Christmas favorite was written in France in the mid-1700s under the title "Adeste Fideles." The composers are unknown. "Adeste Fideles" was first published in England in John F. Wade's volume *Cantus Diversi* (1751). In 1841 Frederick Oakeley (1802–1880) translated the Latin words into English.

Bing Crosby recorded "Adeste Fideles" on June 8, 1942. His recording of "Silent Night"/"Adeste Fideles" (Decca 621) has, through the years, sold about 30 million copies. Backing Crosby on both songs was the Max Terr Choir and the John Scott Trotter Orchestra. In 1960 the rerelease of "Adeste Fideles" (Decca 23777) reached #45 on *Billboard*'s Hot 100 chart.

Elvis recorded "O Come, All Ye Faithful" at Radio Recorders on May 16, 1971.

Singles:
- "Merry Christmas, Baby"/"O COME, ALL YE FAITHFUL" (RCA 74-0572) December 1971. Standard release.

LPs:
- *Elvis Sings the Wonderful World of Christmas*
- *Memories of Christmas* (alternate take)

O SOLE MIO

(See *It's Now or Never*)

OAKIE BOOGIE

Johnny Tyler composed "Oakie Boogie" in 1947. Both Ella Mae Morse (Capitol 2072) and Jack Gunthrie (Capitol 2128) recorded the song in 1952. Hank Swatley, a Sun Records artist in the mid-1950s, also recorded "Oakie Boogie." His version was released on a West Memphis, Arkansas, label, Aaron Records (Aaron A101). Aaron Records was named after Elvis's middle name.

It's been reported that Elvis recorded "Oakie Boogie" while at Sun Records, but the authors can find no substantiation. He probably sang the song on the "Louisiana Hayride." Perhaps a transcription of one of those broadcasts will someday surface.

OH HAPPY DAY

"Oh Happy Day" was written by Philip Doddridge in the 1700s and revised by E. F. Rimbault about a hundred years later. The song was popularized in 1969 by the Edwin Hawkins Singers, who featured Dorothy Morrison singing lead. Their recording (Pavilion 20001) reached #4 on *Billboard*'s Hot 100 chart and #2 on the rhythm & blues chart. Sales of over three million copies have been claimed. The Edwin Hawkins Singers' version of "Oh Happy Day" was awarded a Grammy for Best Soul Gospel song of 1969. Glen Campbell made another popular recording of "Oh Happy Day" (Capitol 2787) in 1970.

Elvis never recorded "Oh Happy Day," but he did sing it in concert on occasion and rehearsed it for his 1968 TV special.

Bootleg LPs:
- *Command Performance* (Las Vegas; August 14, 1970)
- *Elvis Rocks and the Girls Roll* (dress rehearsal for the "Elvis" TV special; in medley with "Blue Moon" and "Young Love")
- *From Hollywood to Vegas* (Las Vegas; August 14, 1970)
- *The Monologue L.P.* (Las Vegas; July 31, 1969)

OH LITTLE TOWN OF BETHLEHEM

This popular Christmas carol was written by Phillips Brooks and Lewis H. Redner in 1868. Brooks, pastor of the Holy Trinity Church in Philadelphia, visited Jerusalem and Bethlehem in December 1865. Three years later the impressions of Bethlehem remained clear in his mind. In early December 1868, Brooks wrote a five-stanza poem (modern hymnals omit the third stanza) about Bethlehem. He asked his church organist and Sunday school superintendent, Lewis Redner, to write music to the poem. Redner wrote the music on the night of December 26–27, 1868. That Sunday morning (the 27th), "O Little Town of Bethlehem" was sung for the first time by a chorus composed of six Sunday school teachers and thirty-six children. Originally, Brooks called his Christmas carol "St. Louis"—a different spelling of Lewis Redner's first name.

Elvis recorded "Oh Little Town of Bethlehem" (the *O* was changed to *Oh*) on September 7, 1957, at Radio Recorders. The master take was #4.

EPs:
- *Christmas with Elvis*

LPs:
- *Elvis' Christmas Album*

OLD MACDONALD

Elvis sang this children's song in his 1967 movie *Double Trouble*.[1] Randy Starr provided the arrangement. "Old MacDonald" was recorded in June 1966, probably at Radio Recorders. In 1960 Frank Sinatra reached #25 on *Billboard*'s Hot 100 chart with Ol' MacDonald" (Capitol 4466) and Jesse Belvin and the Chargers barely made the chart (#95) in 1958. The lyrics vary from one version to another.

Several other nursery rhymes have been pop successes over the years. They include "Ten Little Indians" by the Beach Boys, "Little Star" by the Elegants (which was a number one hit), and "Mary Had a Little Lamb" by Paul McCartney.

LPs:
- *Double Trouble*
- *Elvis Sings for Children and Grownups Too!*
- *Elvis Sings Hits from His Movies, Volume 1*

---

[1]William Holden and Susan Strasberg sang "Old MacDonald" in *Picnic* (1955), as did Tony Curtis and the neuropsychiatric ward in *Captain Newman, M.D.* (1963).

OLD SHEP

Red Foley and Willis Arthur wrote "Old Shep" in 1933. The song was about Foley's 19-year-old German shepherd dog, Hoover, who had been poisoned. It wasn't until 1940 that Foley recorded his song. "Old Shep" (Decca 46052) was reissued in 1947.

"Old Shep" was the song Elvis sang to win second prize at the Mississippi-Alabama Fair and Dairy Show in 1945—his first public singing appearance. Later, in 1953, Elvis sang the song at the Humes High School Minstrel Show.

On September 2, 1956, at Radio Recorders, Elvis recorded several takes of "Old Shep," all featuring him on piano. Take #5 was released by RCA on record. An alternate take (#1), however, was used on the first pressing of the British LP, *Elvis Presley No. 2* (HMV-CLP-1105). This alternate take has appeared on numerous bootlegs over the years.

Singles:
• "OLD SHEP"/(blank) (RCA CR-15) December 1956. Disc jockey promotional release used to promote the LP *Elvis*. This record is extremely rare and is much sought by collectors.

EPs:
• *Elvis, Volume 2*
• *Promotion Disc* (RCA PRO-12)

LPs:
• *Double Dynamite*
• *Elvis*
• *Elvis Sings for Children and Grownups Too!*
• *Separate Ways*

Bootleg LPs:
• *Eternal Elvis* (take #1)
• *The Rockin' Rebel, Volume 3* (take #1)

ON A SNOWY CHRISTMAS NIGHT

Elvis recorded this Christmas song on May 16, 1971, at RCA's Nashville studios. "On a Snowy Christmas Night" was written by Stanley A. Gelber.

LPs:
• *Elvis Sings the Wonderful World of Christmas*

ON THE JERICHO ROAD

Donald S. McCrossan wrote "On the Jericho Road" in 1928. The arrangement was by Luther G. Presley, who was not related to Elvis. The Speer Family recorded this traditional gospel tune in early 1951 (Columbia 20762). "On the Jericho Road" was one of the gospel songs that Elvis, Carl Perkins, and Jerry Lee Lewis sang during the Million-Dollar-Quartet session on December 4, 1956.

Bootleg LPs:
• *Million Dollar Quartet* (Sun Records; December 4, 1956)
• *The One Million Dollar Quartet* (Sun Records; December 4, 1956)

ON TOP OF OLD SMOKY

The composer of this American Southern Highlands folk song is unknown. In 1951 the Weavers (with an arrangement by Pete Seeger) had a million-seller on Decca Records (Decca 27515) with "On Top of Old Smoky." Their recording reached #2 on *Billboard*'s Best-Selling Singles chart. That same year, Vaughn Monroe (RCA Victor 4114) and Burl Ives with the Percy Faith Orchestra (Columbia 39328) had top 20 hits with the song, with Monroe reaching #10 and Ives #18. Gene Autry sang "On Top of Old Smoky" in his 1951 movie *Valley of Fire*. John Glazer and the Do-Re-Mi Children's Chorus had a parody called "On Top of Spaghetti" (Kapp 526) in 1963 that peaked at #14 on the Hot 100 chart.

Elvis sang about 10 seconds of "On Top of Old Smoky" in his 1962 film *Follow That Dream*, with accompaniment provided by a radio. The song was recorded on the movie set, not in a recording studio. Because of its short duration, "On Top of Old Smoky" has never been released by RCA.

Bootleg LPs:
• *From Hollywood to Vegas* (*Follow That Dream* soundtrack)

ON WISCONSIN

"On Wisconsin," the University of Wisconsin fight song, was written by Carl Beck and W. T. Purdy in 1909. It later became the official state song of Wisconsin. The publishing rights are now owned by Paul McCartney. "On Wisconsin" was sung by a collegiate quartet in Elvis's 1969 film *The Trouble with Girls*. A few have speculated that Elvis may have recorded a few lines of the song for the film.

Actor Dick Powell made a record of "On Wisconsin" (Decca 2013) in the 1930s. The flip side was "The Eyes of Texas." Both songs were sung in *The Trouble with Girls*.

ONCE IS ENOUGH

Elvis sang "Once Is Enough" in his 1964 film *Kissin' Cousins*. He recorded the tune, which was written by Sid Tepper and Roy C. Bennett, in October 1963 at RCA's Nashville studios.

LPs:
• *Kissin' Cousins*

ONE BOY, TWO LITTLE GIRLS

Bill Giant, Bernie Baum, and Florence Kaye wrote "One Boy, Two Little Girls" for Elvis's 1964 movie *Kissin' Cousins*. The song was recorded at RCA's Nashville studios in October 1963.

LPs:
• *Kissin' Cousins*

ONE BROKEN HEART FOR SALE

Elvis sang "One Broken Heart for Sale" in *It Happened at the World's Fair*. The film version had an extra verse:

Hey cupid, where are you, my heart is growing sadder.
That girl rejected me, just when I thought I had her.

The single release had a nine-week stay on *Billboard*'s Hot 100 chart, peaking at #11. "One Broken Heart for Sale" also appeared on the rhythm & blues chart, peaking at #21. Sales of over one million copies are claimed for the record.

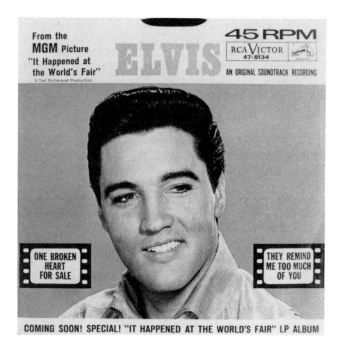

From the MGM Picture "It Happened at the World's Fair"
A Ted Richmond Production

45 RPM
RCA VICTOR
47-8134
AN ORIGINAL SOUNDTRACK RECORDING

ELVIS

ONE BROKEN HEART FOR SALE

THEY REMIND ME TOO MUCH OF YOU

COMING SOON! SPECIAL! "IT HAPPENED AT THE WORLD'S FAIR" LP ALBUM

(Photo courtesy Don Fink)

Elvis recorded "One Broken Heart for Sale" in September 1962 at Radio Recorders. Two versions were taped—one for the film and one for record release. Vocal backing was by the Mello Men. Otis Blackwell and Winfield Scott are the composers.

Singles:
- "ONE BROKEN HEART FOR SALE"/"They Remind Me Too Much of You" (RCA 47-8134) February 1963. Standard release.
- "ONE BROKEN HEART FOR SALE"/"They Remind Me Too Much of You" (RCA 447-0640) August 1964. Gold Standard Series reissue.

LPs:
- *Elvis: Worldwide 50 Gold Award Hits, Volume 1*
- *It Happened at the World's Fair*
- *Mahalo from Elvis*

Bootleg LPs:
- *Eternal Elvis* (*It Happened at the World's Fair* soundtrack)

ONE MORE DAY
"One More Day" was a Sid Tepper–Roy C. Bennett song that Mickey Shaughnessy sang in *Jailhouse Rock*. It's been rumored that Elvis recorded an uptempo version of the song for use in the film but it was not used.

ONE NIGHT
Smiley Lewis first recorded this Dave Bartholomew–Pearl King tune in 1956 as "One Night of Sin" (Imperial 5380). His recording did not chart.

On January 24, 1957, Elvis recorded "One Night of Sin" at Radio Recorders. The risqué version ("One night of sin is what I'm paying for") was not released until 1983, when it appeared on the LP *Elvis—A Legendary Performer, Volume 4*. The cleaned-up version that was first released on singles and LPs ("One night with you is what I'm now praying for") was recorded a month later on February 23, 1957, also at Radio Re-

corders. Take #10 is the master recording. Elvis's single release of "One Night" reached #4 on *Billboard*'s Hot 100 chart during its 17-week stay on the chart, #24 on the country chart, and #10 on the rhythm & blues chart. In England the song went to number one and stayed at the top for three weeks. Worldwide sales have easily exceeded one million copies. In 1976 Roy Head (ABC/Dot 17650) covered Elvis's version. In 1963 Fats Domino (Imperial 5980) had covered Smiley Lewis's original version.

Elvis sang "One Night" in concert countless times. A recording of his performance at the Bloch Arena for the USS *Arizona* Memorial has appeared on several bootlegs. In 1980 RCA finally released the performance on the *Elvis Aron Presley* LP. Elvis came close to the original risqué lyrics in his 1968 TV special "Elvis."

Singles:
- "I Got Stung"/"ONE NIGHT" (RCA 20-7410) October 1958. Standard 78 RPM release.
- "I Got Stung"/"ONE NIGHT" (RCA 47-7410) October 1958. Standard 45 RPM release.
- "I Got Stung"/"ONE NIGHT" (RCA 447-0624) 1961. Gold Standard Series reissue.
- "I Got Stung"/"ONE NIGHT" (RCA PB-11112) October 1977. One of 15 singles in the special boxed set *15 Golden Records—30 Golden Hits* (RCA PP-11301).

EPs:
- *A Touch of Gold, Volume 2*

LPs:
- *Elvis—A Legendary Performer, Volume 4* (alternate take; January 24, 1957 version)
- *Elvis Aron Presley* (USS *Arizona* Memorial; March 25, 1961)
- *Elvis: The Other Sides—Worldwide Gold Award Hits, Volume 2*
- *Elvis—TV Special* ("Elvis" TV special taping; June 27, 1968, at 6:00 P.M. show)
- *50,000,000 Elvis Fans Can't Be Wrong— Elvis' Gold Records, Volume 2*
- *A Golden Celebration* ("Elvis" TV special taping; June 27, 1968)
- *Reconsider Baby* (alternate take; January 24, 1957 version)
- *The Top Ten Hits*

Bootleg LPs:
- *The Burbank Sessions, Volume 1* ("Elvis" TV special taping; June 27, 1968, at 6:00 P.M. and 8:00 P.M. shows)
- *The Burbank Sessions, Volume 2* ("Elvis" TV special taping; June 29, 1968, at 6:00 P.M. show)
- *Elvis' 1961 Hawaii Benefit Concert* (USS *Arizona* Memorial; March 25, 1961)
- *The Hillbilly Cat "Live"* (Las Vegas; August 1970)
- *The King: From the Dark to the Light* (*Elvis—That's the Way It Is* soundtrack)
- *King of Las Vegas Live* (*Elvis—That's the Way It Is* soundtrack)
- *Sold Out* (Las Vegas; August 24, 1970)
- *That's the Way It Is* (*Elvis—That's the Way It Is* soundtrack)

ONE-SIDED LOVE AFFAIR
"One-Sided Love Affair," a country tune written by Bill Campbell, was recorded by Elvis on January 30, 1956, at RCA's New York City studios. Elvis called the song his favorite of those on his first album, *Elvis Presley*.

Singles:
- "Money Honey"/"ONE-SIDED LOVE AFFAIR" (RCA 20-6641) Septem-

ber 1956. Standard 78 RPM release.
- "Money Honey"/"ONE-SIDED LOVE AFFAIR" (RCA 47-6641) September 1956. Standard 45 RPM release.
- "Tutti Frutti"/"ONE-SIDED LOVE AFFAIR" (RCA 47-6466) September 1956. Disc jockey "Record Prevue."
- "Money Honey"/"ONE-SIDED LOVE AFFAIR" (RCA 447-0614) March 1959. Gold Standard Series reissue.

EPs:
- *Elvis Presley* (RCA EPB-1254)
- *Elvis Presley* (RCA SPD-22)
- *Elvis Presley* (RCA SPD-23)
- *Elvis Presley—The Most Talked About New Personality in the Last Ten Years of Recorded Music* (RCA EPB-1254)

LPs:
- *Elvis Presley*

ONE-TRACK HEART

Elvis sang "One-Track Heart" in his 1964 film *Roustabout*. The recording was made in March 1964 at Radio Recorders. "One-Track Heart" was written by Bill Giant, Bernie Baum, and Florence Kaye.

Singles:
- "Roustabout"/"ONE-TRACK HEART" (RCA SP-45-139) November 1964. Disc jockey promotional release.

LPs:
- *Roustabout*

ONLY BELIEVE

Elvis recorded "Only Believe" on June 8, 1970, at RCA's Nashville studios. Paul Rader is the composer. The single release of "Only Believe" had a two-week stay on *Billboard*'s Hot 100 chart, peaking at #95.

Singles:
- "Life"/"ONLY BELIEVE" (RCA 47-9985) May 1971. Standard release.
- "Life"/"ONLY BELIEVE" (RCA 447-0682) May 1972. Gold Standard Series reissue.

LPs:
- *Love Letters from Elvis*

Bootleg LPs:
- *Plantation Rock* (alternate take)

ONLY THE LONELY

Roy Orbison and Joe Melson wrote "Only the Lonely" in 1960. On the way to Nashville to record the song, Orbison stopped by Graceland to see if Elvis wanted to record it. Elvis was asleep when he arrived, so the King lost an opportunity to have yet another million-seller. When Orbison reached Nashville he offered "Only the Lonely" to the Everly Brothers, who declined. So, by default, Orbison recorded the song himself. His release on Monument Records (Monument 421) reached #2 on the Hot 100 chart and became his first million-seller. In 1966 Glen Campbell recorded "Only the Lonely" (Capitol 5773) as the flip side to his hit "Burning Bridges." Sonny James topped the country chart with his version of the song (Capitol 2370) in 1969.

ONLY THE STRONG SURVIVE

"Only the Strong Survive" (Mercury 72898) was a million-seller and number one rhythm & blues hit for Jerry Butler in early 1969. It peaked at #4 on the Hot 100 chart. The song was written by Butler, Kenny Gamble, and Leon Huff.

Elvis recorded "Only the Strong Survive" at American Sound Studios in Memphis on February 20, 1969, just a few weeks after Butler recorded the original version.

LPs:
- *From Elvis in Memphis*
- *The Memphis Record*

ONLY YOU

The Platters had a number one rhythm & blues hit with "Only You" (Mercury 70633) in 1955. The record reached #5 on the Top 100 chart. "Only You" was written by Buck Ram, the Platters' manager, and Ande Rand. Others who have had hits with the song include The Hilltoppers (Dot 15423) in late 1955, Frank Pourcel (Capitol 4165) in 1959, and Ringo Starr (Apple 1876) in late 1974. In the mid-1950s, Elvis occasionally sang "Only You" in concert, including a performance in La Crosse, Wisconsin, on May 14, 1956. The full title of the song is "Only You (and You Alone)."

ONWARD TO VICTORY

Some sources have indicated that Elvis recorded "Onward to Victory" for *The Trouble with Girls*, but that claim is unsubstantiated.

OUT OF LEFT FIELD

"Out of Left Field" is another song that some authorities have listed as being recorded by Elvis, but so far no tape has surfaced.

OUT OF SIGHT, OUT OF MIND

Jimmy Wakely recorded "Out of Sight, Out of Mind" (Capitol 2484) in 1953. His recording didn't chart, nor did one by Porter Wagoner (RCA 47-7457) in 1959. The hit recording was by the Five Keys (Capitol 3502), who reached #23 on the Top 100 chart in 1956. Thirteen years later, Little Anthony and the Imperials had a moderately successful version of the song (United Artists 50552), reaching #52 on the Hot 100 chart and #38 on the rhythm & blues chart.

Elvis sang a few lines of "Out of Sight, Out of Mind" during the Million-Dollar-Quartet session on December 4, 1965. He patterned his styling after the Five Keys' recording.

Bootleg LPs:
- *The One Million Dollar Quartet* (Sun Records; December 4, 1956)

OVER THE LINE

"Over the Line" is one of many songs believed to have been recorded by Elvis. To date, no proof of this recording has surfaced.

PADRE

"Padre" was written by French composers Jacques Larue and Alain Romans, with English lyrics by Paul Francis Webster. The song was first recorded by Lola Dee with Stubby and the Buccaneers (Mercury 70342) in 1954. Toni Arden had a million-seller with "Padre" (Decca 30628) in 1958. Her recording reached #13 on the Hot 100 chart. In 1970 Marty Robbins had a #5 country hit with the song (Columbia 45273).

Elvis recorded "Padre" at RCA's Nashville studios on May 15, 1971.

LPs:
- *Elvis* (RCA APL1-0283)
- *He Walks Beside Me*

PARADISE, HAWAIIAN STYLE

The instrumental track to "Paradise, Hawaiian Style" (the title song of Elvis's 1966 film of the same name) was laid on July 27, 1965, at Radio Recorders. Elvis's vocal was recorded on August 4. The film version had added instrumentation. A splice of takes #3 and #4 was used by RCA on record. "Paradise, Hawaiian Style" was written by Bill Giant, Bernie Baum, and Florence Kaye using the working title of "Hawaii USA." Elvis's 1973 TV special "Elvis: Aloha from Hawaii," began with a few lines from "Paradise, Hawaiian Style," although they aren't on the soundtrack album.

LPs:
- *Paradise, Hawaiian Style*

Bootleg LPs:
- *A Dog's Life* (take #4)
- *Hawaii USA* (takes #3 and #4)

PARALYZED

Otis Blackwell wrote "Paralyzed"[1] for Elvis. It was recorded on September 2, 1956, at Radio Recorders. Take #12 was the one used by RCA. On the strength of its being on the *Elvis* EP, "Paralyzed" had a seven-week stay on the Top 100 chart, peaking at #59. In England, a single release of "Paralyzed" reached #8 on the charts. It wasn't until 1983 that RCA released the song as a single in the United States. During the Million-Dollar-Quartet session on December 4, 1956, Elvis said he wished he'd recorded "Paralyzed" at a slower tempo, similar to the way Jackie Wilson sang "Don't Be Cruel" with Billy Ward and the Dominoes in Las Vegas. Elvis then sang "Paralyzed" at a slower tempo for Carl Perkins and Jerry Lee Lewis.

Singles:
- "Little Sister"/"PARALYZED" (RCA PB-13547) June 1983. Standard release.
- "Little Sister"/"PARALYZED" (RCA JB-13547) June 1983. Disc

jockey promotional release. Two versions were released: one with a light yellow label and one pressed on blue vinyl.

EPs:
- *Elvis, Volume 1*
- *Elvis/Jaye P. Morgan*

LPs:
- *Elvis* (RCA LPM-1382)
- *Elvis: The Other Sides—Worldwide Gold Award Hits, Volume 2*
- *I Was the One* (with overdubbing)

Bootleg LPs:
- *The One Million Dollar Quartet* (Sun Records; December 4, 1956)

PARTY

Jessie Mae Robinson wrote "Party" for Elvis's 1957 movie *Loving You*. In February 1957 Elvis recorded two versions of the song at Radio Recorders—one for the film and one for record release. "Party" was sung several times in *Loving You*. The correct full title is "(Let's Have a) Party." A different version with an added verse can be heard on the bootleg LP *Got a Lot o' Livin' to Do*. Shortly after the release of *Loving You*, the Collins Kids recorded a cover version of "Party" (Columbia 41012), and in 1960, Wanda Jackson released a rendition (Capitol 4397) titled "Let's Have a Party."

EPs:
- *Loving You, Volume 1*

LPs:
- *Essential Elvis—The First Movies* (master take and an unreleased film version)
- *Loving You*

Bootleg LPs:
- *Elvis* (*Loving You* soundtrack)
- *Eternal Elvis* (*Loving You* soundtrack)
- *Got a Lot o' Livin' to Do* (*Loving You* soundtrack, two versions, one with an added verse)
- *Loving You* (*Loving You* soundtrack, two versions, one with an added verse)
- *Special Delivery from Elvis* (*Loving You* soundtrack)

PATCH IT UP

"Patch It Up" was written by Eddie Rabbitt and Rory Bourke and recorded by Elvis on June 8, 1970, at RCA's Nashville studios. The single release had only a three-week stay on *Billboard*'s Hot 100 chart, peaking at #90. Despite the poor performance, some sources have indicated that "Patch It Up" sold over a million copies worldwide. Elvis sang "Patch It Up" in his 1970 documentary *Elvis—That's the Way It Is*. That version was recorded at the International Hotel in Las Vegas on August 13, 1970.

---

[1]"Paralyzed" inspired Terry Noland and Norman Petty to write "Hypnotized," which the Drifters (with Johnny Moore singing lead) recorded in 1957 (Atlantic 1141). Noland recorded his own version of "Paralyzed" (Brunswick 55010) in 1957.

Singles:
- "You Don't Have to Say You Love Me"/"PATCH IT UP" (RCA 47-9916) October 1970. Standard release.
- "You Don't Have to Say You Love Me"/"PATCH IT UP" (RCA 447-0678) February 1972. Gold Standard Series reissue.

LPs:
- *Elvis: The Other Sides—Worldwide Gold Award Hits, Volume 2*
- *Elvis—That's the Way It Is*

Bootleg LPs:
- *King of Las Vegas Live* (*Elvis—That's the Way It Is* soundtrack)
- *Leavin' It Up to You* (alternate take)
- *That's the Way It Is* (*Elvis—That's the Way It Is* soundtrack)
- *Unfinished Business* (alternate take)

PEACE IN THE VALLEY

While Rev. Thomas A. Dorsey was traveling from Indiana to Cincinnati in 1939, the train he was on passed through a valley. Dorsey noticed how peaceful the animals on the farmlands seemed to be. That tranquil scene inspired him to write "Peace in the Valley."[1] The full title of the song is "(There'll Be) Peace in the Valley (for Me)."

In 1951 Red Foley recorded a million-selling rendition of "Peace in the Valley"[2] (Decca 46319) that was a #7 country hit. Decca Records reissued the single in 1957. The Stamps Quartet also recorded the song; their version (Columbia 20836) came out in 1952.

Elvis sang "Peace in the Valley" on his third appearance on "The Ed Sullivan Show" (January 6, 1957). One week later (January 13), he went to Radio Recorders in Hollywood to record the song. Take #9 is the RCA master. Gordon Stoker of the Jordanaires played organ on the track. Based on its appearance in the EP *Peace in the Valley*, "Peace in the Valley" reached #39 on *Billboard*'s Top 100 chart, staying on the chart for ten weeks.

On December 4, 1956, at the Million-Dollar-Quartet session, "Peace in the Valley" was one of the tunes the group sang. Elvis sang lead, with vocal backing by Jerry Lee Lewis.

EPs:
- *Peace in the Valley*

LPs:
- *Double Dynamite*
- *Elvis—A Legendary Performer, Volume 1*
- *Elvis' Christmas Album*
- *A Golden Celebration* ("The Ed Sullivan Show"; January 6, 1957)
- *You'll Never Walk Alone*

Bootleg LPs:
- *From the Waist Up* ("The Ed Sullivan Show"; January 6, 1957)
- *The King Goes Wild* ("The Ed Sullivan Show"; January 6, 1957)
- *The Million Dollar Quartet* (Sun Records; December 4, 1956)
- *The One Million Dollar Quartet* (Sun Records; December 4, 1956)

PETUNIA, THE GARDENER'S DAUGHTER

Elvis and Donna Douglas sang a duet of "Petunia, the Gardener's Daughter" in the 1966 movie *Frankie and Johnny*. Sid Tepper and Roy C. Bennett composed the tune, which Elvis recorded in May 1965 at Radio Recorders.

LPs:
- *Frankie and Johnny*

PIECES OF MY LIFE

"Pieces of My Life" was written by Troy Seals and recorded by Charlie Rich for his 1974 album *The Silver Fox* (Epic 33250). In recent years Rich has concluded his live appearances with the song. Elvis recorded "Pieces of My Life" on March 13, 1975, at RCA's Hollywood studios. The single release had a 10-week stay on *Billboard*'s country chart, peaking at #33.

Singles:
- "Bringing It Back"/"PIECES OF MY LIFE" (RCA PB-10401) October 1975. Standard release.
- "Bringing It Back"/"PIECES OF MY LIFE" (RCA JA-10401) October 1975. Disc jockey promotional release.

LPs:
- *Always on My Mind*
- *Elvis Today*
- *Elvis Aron Presley—Forever*

PINK CADILLAC

"Pink Cadillac" was a regional hit in the South for Sammy Masters in early 1954 (Four Star 1695). Elvis is believed to have sung "Pink Cadillac" while on tour in 1954 and 1955. In 1956, Rusty Draper recorded a version of "Pink Cadillac" (Mercury 70921).

PLANTATION ROCK

Elvis recorded "Plantation Rock" on March 27, 1962, at Radio Recorders for his 1962 film *Girls! Girls! Girls!*, but the song was cut from the final print. This song, written by Bill Giant, Bernie Baum, and Florence Kaye, was available only on the bootleg LP *Plantation Rock* until officially released by RCA in 1983 on the LP *Elvis—A Legendary Performer, Volume 4*.

LPs:
- *Elvis—A Legendary Performer, Volume 4*

Bootleg LPs:
- *Plantation Rock* (a spliced version, making the song longer than it actually is)

PLAYING FOR KEEPS

Stanley A. Kesler wrote "Playing for Keeps" for Elvis. The demo was recorded by Barbara Pittman, a singer at Sun Records who Elvis dated for a brief time. Elvis recorded "Playing for Keeps" at Radio Recorders on September 1, 1956. Take #7 is the one used by RCA. The single release had a nine-week stay on *Billboard*'s Top 100 chart, peaking at #34. Some sources credit "Playing for Keeps" with selling a million copies.

---

[1] While watching gospel singer Clara Ward sing "Peace in the Valley," teenager Aretha Franklin decided she wanted to become a singer.
[2] Red Foley's version of "Peace in the Valley" was heard briefly in the 1971 movie *Two-Lane Blacktop*.

Singles:
- "Too Much"/"PLAYING FOR KEEPS" (RCA 20-6800) January 1957. Standard 78 RPM release.
- "Too Much"/"PLAYING FOR KEEPS" (RCA 47-6800) January 1957. Standard 45 RPM release.
- "Too Much"/"PLAYING FOR KEEPS" (RCA 447-0617) March 1959. Gold Standard Series reissue.

EPs:
- DJ-56

LPs:
- *Elvis: Worldwide 50 Gold Award Hits, Volume 1*
- *For LP Fans Only*
- *A Valentine Gift for You*

PLAY A SIMPLE MELODY

This song dates back to 1914, when it was written by Irving Berlin for the musical play *Watch Your Step*. Bing Crosby and his son Gary had a million-seller with "Play a Simple Melody" (Decca 27112) in 1950. (The record label read "Gary Crosby and Friend.") The song reached #3 on the Best-Selling Singles chart. That same year, Jo Stafford had a version (Capitol 1039) that rose to #27. "Play a Simple Melody" was sung by Ethel Merman and Dan Dailey in the 1954 movie musical *There's No Business Like Show Business*.

An unsubstantiated rumor has it that Elvis recorded "Play a Simple Melody" while at Sun Records.

PLAYING WITH FIRE

Elvis recorded "Playing with Fire" for his 1961 movie *Blue Hawaii*, but it was cut from the final print. The song was recorded on March 21, 22, or 23, 1961, at Radio Recorders. RCA has never released "Playing with Fire" in any form. Written by Fred Wise and Ben Weisman, the song was covered in 1964 by Terry Stafford (Crusader 105).

PLEASE DON'T DRAG THAT STRING AROUND

"Please Don't Drag That String Around" was written by Otis Blackwell and Winfield Scott. Elvis recorded the song on May 26, 1963, at RCA's Nashville studios. Although released as a single, "Please Don't Drag That String Around" did not chart—one of Elvis's few sides in the pre-Beatles era that did not chart. Some sources have credited this song with sales of over a million copies. A few pressings of the single had "Please Don't Drag That String *Along*" on the label instead of *Around*.

Singles:
- "(You're the) Devil in Disguise"/"PLEASE DON'T DRAG THAT STRING AROUND" (RCA 47-8188) June 1963. Standard release.
- "(You're the) Devil in Disguise"/"PLEASE DON'T DRAG THAT STRING AROUND" (RCA 447-0641) August 1964. Gold Standard Series reissue.

LPs:
- *Elvis' Gold Records, Volume 4*
- *Elvis: The Other Sides—Worldwide Gold Award Hits, Volume 2*

PLEASE DON'T STOP LOVING ME

Elvis sang "Please Don't Stop Loving Me" in his 1966 movie *Frankie and Johnny*. It was written for the film by Joy Byers. The tune was recorded by Elvis in August 1965 at Radio Recorders. "Please Don't Stop Loving Me" had an eight-week stay on *Billboard*'s Hot 100 chart, peaking at #45.

Singles:
- "Frankie and Johnny"/"PLEASE DON'T STOP LOVING ME" (RCA 47-8780) March 1966. Standard release.
- "Frankie and Johnny"/"PLEASE DON'T STOP LOVING ME" (RCA 447-0656) February 1968. Gold Standard Series reissue.

LPs:
- *Frankie and Johnny*

PLEDGING MY LOVE

"Pledging My Love" was written by Ferdinand Washington and Don Robey and originally recorded by Johnny Ace (Duke 136) in late 1954. Ace's single release was a number one rhythm & blues hit and a top twenty (#17) hit on the Best-Selling Singles chart. His record[1] had just been released when he committed suicide by playing Russian Roulette on Christmas Eve 1954. Other releases through the years include those by Theresa Brewer (Coral 61362) in 1955, Roy Hamilton (Epic 9294) in 1958, Johnny Tillotson (Cadence 1377) in 1960, Laura and Johnny (Silver Fox 1) in 1969, and Kitty Wells (Decca 32840) in 1971.

Elvis recorded "Pledging My Love" at Graceland on the night of October 29–30, 1976. The instrumental track and overdubbing were done at Creative Workshop in Nashville on January 22 or 23, 1977. Paired with "Way Down," "Pledging My Love" displaced Charlie Rich's "Rolling with the Flow" at number one on the country chart in August 1977. After only one week at the top spot, it was itself replaced by Crystal Gayle's "Don't It Make My Brown Eyes Blue." The total chart stay was 17 weeks.

Singles:
- "Way Down"/"PLEDGING MY LOVE" (RCA PB-10998) July 1977. Standard release.
- "Way Down"/"PLEDGING MY LOVE" (RCA JB-10998) July 1977. Disc jockey promotional release.

LPs:
- *Moody Blue*

POCKETFUL OF RAINBOWS

Elvis sang "Pocketful of Rainbows" in his 1960 movie *G. I. Blues*. Juliet Prowse sang a few lines with him. Elvis first recorded this Fred Wise–Ben Weisman composition on April 28, 1960, at RCA's Hollywood studios. That version was not used by RCA; however, a take (#2) from that session later appeared on the British EP boxed set *The EP Collection, Volume 2*. The version used by RCA was take #2 from the session at Radio Recorders on May 6, 1960.

---

[1]Stevie Wonder recalls Johnny Ace's "Pledging My Love" as the first song he ever heard.

In 1961 Deane Hawley reached #93 on *Billboard*'s Hot 100 chart with his cover recording of "Pocketful of Rainbows."

EPs:
- *The EP Collection, Volume 2* (alternate take #2 from first recording session)

LPs:
- *G. I. Blues*

POISON IVY LEAGUE

Bill Giant, Bernie Baum, and Florence Kaye wrote "Poison Ivy League" for Elvis's 1964 film *Roustabout*. Elvis recorded the song in March 1964 at Radio Recorders.

LPs:
- *Roustabout*

POLK SALAD ANNIE

"Polk Salad Annie"[1] is a Tony Joe White composition. His 1969 recording (Monument 1104) reached #8 on *Billboard*'s Hot 100 chart.

A February 18, 1970, performance of "Polk Salad Annie" by Elvis at the International Hotel in Las Vegas was featured on the album *On Stage—February, 1970*. Rehearsal sessions of "Polk Salad Annie" at the MGM studios and the International Hotel in July and August 1970 were used in the documentary *Elvis—That's the Way It Is*, as was a concert performance. An April 9, 1972, concert rendition at Hampton Roads, Virginia, was used in *Elvis on Tour* (1972).

LPs:
- *Elvis Aron Presley* (Las Vegas; August 1970)
- *Elvis as Recorded at Madison Square Garden* (Madison Square Garden; June 10, 1972)
- *On Stage—February, 1970* (Las Vegas; February 18, 1970)

Bootleg LPs:
- *Behind Closed Doors* (Las Vegas; February 18, 1970)
- *Cadillac Elvis* (*Elvis—That's the Way It Is* soundtrack)
- *Elvis on Tour* (*Elvis on Tour* soundtrack)
- *The Entertainer* (Las Vegas; February 1970)
- *From Las Vegas . . . to Niagara Falls* (Niagara Falls, N.Y.; June 24, 1974)
- *The Hillbilly Cat "Live"* (Las Vegas; August 1970)
- *The King: From the Dark to the Light* (*Elvis—That's the Way It Is* soundtrack)
- *King of Las Vegas Live* (*Elvis—That's the Way It Is* soundtrack)
- *Rockin' with Elvis New Year's Eve Pittsburgh, Pa. Dec. 31, 1976* (Pittsburgh; December 31, 1976)
- *That's the Way It Is* (*Elvis—That's the Way It Is* soundtrack)
- *The Vegas Years, 1972-1975* (Las Vegas; 1972)

POOR BOY

Elvis sang "Poor Boy" in his first film, *Love Me Tender*. Although Elvis and Vera Matson are credited with writing "Poor Boy," it was actually written by Matson's husband, Ken Darby, who was musical director for the film. The song was recorded by Elvis on August 2 or September 24, 1956 at Radio Recorders. The movie version had hand clapping and girls screaming. Based on its appearance in the EP *Love Me Tender*, "Poor Boy" reached #35 on *Billboard*'s Top 100 chart and had an 11-week stay.

EPs:
- *Love Me Tender*

LPs:
- *Elvis: The Other Sides—Worldwide Gold Award Hits, Volume 2*
- *Essential Elvis—The First Movies*
- *For LP Fans Only* (alternate mix)

POOR MAN'S GOLD

On January 15, 1969, an instrumental track for "Poor Man's Gold" was recorded at American Sound Studios. Elvis did not record a vocal track for the song, which was written by Mac Davis.

PORTRAIT OF MY LOVE

Steve Lawrence had a #9 Hot 100 hit with "Portrait of My Love" (United Artists 291) in 1961. Six years later, the Tokens peaked at #36 with their version (Warner Bros. 5900). Elvis sang "Portrait of My Love," which was written by Cyril Ornadel and David West, at a backstage rehearsal in Las Vegas. His only accompaniment was his piano playing.

Bootleg LPs:
- *Special Delivery from Elvis Presley* (Las Vegas rehearsal; ?)
- *Susie Q* (Las Vegas rehearsal; ?)

POTPOURRI

Elvis recorded "Potpourri" for his 1962 movie *Girls! Girls! Girls!*, but it was cut from the final print. "Potpourri" has never been available in any form. The song's composers are probably Sid Tepper and Roy C. Bennett.

POWER OF MY LOVE

Bill Giant, Bernie Baum, and Florence Kaye wrote this song, which Elvis recorded on February 18, 1969, at American Sound Studios in Memphis.

LPs:
- *From Elvis in Memphis*
- *The Memphis Record*

PRIMROSE LANE

Jerry Wallace had his only million-seller with "Primrose Lane" (Challenge 59047) in 1959. The song, which was written by George Callender and Wayne Shanklin, reached #8 on the Hot 100 chart and #12 on the rhythm & blues chart. In 1970 O. C. Smith had a #4 Easy-Listening hit with his version (Columbia 45160). As sung by Mike Minor, the song served as the theme of the 1971–72 Henry Fonda TV series "The Smith Family."

---

[1]On Tony Joe White's version, producer Billy Swan's voice can be heard at the beginning, saying, "Four."

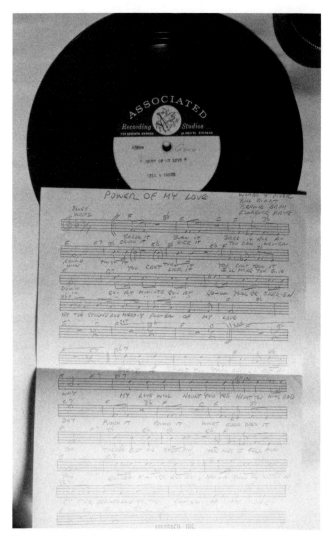

The songwriters' demo and sheet music for Elvis's consideration. (Photo courtesy Don Fink)

Elvis recorded "Primrose Lane" with only guitar accompaniment at Graceland in the 1960s, but the recording has never been released.

PROMISED LAND

Chuck Berry wrote and recorded "Promised Land" (Chess 1916) in 1965. His recording reached #41 on the Hot 100 chart. Freddie Weller had a #3 country hit in early 1971 with "Promised Land" (Columbia 45276), and James Taylor included the song in his popular 1974 LP *Walking Man* (Warner Bros. BS 2794).

Elvis recorded "Promised Land" at Stax Studios in Memphis on December 15, 1973. The tambourine was later overdubbed by David Briggs. Elvis's single release had a 13-week stay on the Hot 100 chart, peaking at #14, and an eight-week stay on the Easy-Listening chart, where it reached #11. "Promised Land" was a mainstay of Elvis's concert repertoire.

Singles:
- "PROMISED LAND"/"It's Midnight" (RCA PB-10074) October 1974. Standard release.

- "PROMISED LAND"/"It's Midnight" (RCA JA-10074) October 1974. Disc jockey promotional release.
- "PROMISED LAND"/"It's Midnight" (RCA GB-10488) February 1976. Gold Standard Series reissue.
- "Blue Suede Shoes"/"PROMISED LAND" (RCA PB-13929) October 1984. Special anniversary reissue of both songs pressed on blue vinyl with a gold "50th" label.

LPs:
- *Promised Land*
- *This Is Elvis*

Bootleg LPs:
- *Big Boss Man* (Las Vegas; August 19, 1974)

PROUD MARY

"Proud Mary" was written by John Fogerty and recorded by Creedence Clearwater Revival (Fantasy 619) in 1969, Their recording sold over a million copies and reached #2 on the Hot 100 chart. Sonny Charles and the Checkmates, Ltd., also had a successful version (A&M 1127) in 1969, as did Solomon Burke (Bell 783). Ike and Tina Turner's 1971 recording of "Proud Mary" (Liberty 52616) reached #4 on the Hot 100 chart and became a million-seller.

Elvis performed a version of "Proud Mary" at the International Hotel in Las Vegas on February 17, 1970, that appeared on the LP *On Stage—February, 1970*. An April 1972 performance was included in the documentary *Elvis on Tour*.

LPs:
- *Elvis as Recorded at Madison Square Garden* (June 10, 1972)
- *On Stage—February 1970* (Las Vegas; February 17, 1970)

Bootleg LPs:
- *Big Boss Man* (Las Vegas; August 19, 1974)
- *Elvis on Tour* (*Elvis on Tour* soundtrack)
- *Standing Room Only, Volume 2* (Madison Square Garden; June 10, 1972)
- *The Vegas Years, 1972–1975* (Las Vegas; 1972)

PUPPET ON A STRING

Sid Tepper and Roy C. Bennett wrote "Puppet on a String" for Elvis's 1965 film *Girl Happy*. Elvis recorded the song at Radio Recorders in June or July 1964. The single release reached #14 on *Billboard*'s Hot 100 chart, remaining on the chart for ten weeks. "Puppet on a String" reached #3 on the Easy-Listening chart. Some sources credit the song with selling over a million copies.

Singles:
- "PUPPET ON A STRING"/"Wooden Heart" (RCA 447-0650) October 1965. Gold Standard Series original release.
- "Teddy Bear"/"PUPPET ON A STRING" (RCA-11320) August 1978. Special reissue of both songs pressed on green vinyl.
- "Teddy Bear"/"PUPPET ON A STRING" (RCA JH-11320) August 1978. Disc jockey promotional release.

LPs:
- *Elvis: The Other Sides—Worldwide Gold Award Hits, Volume 2*
- *Elvis Sings for Children and Grownups Too!*
- *Girl Happy*

PUT THE BLAME ON ME

Elvis sang "Put the Blame on Me" in his 1965 film *Tickle Me*. The song, which was written by Kay Twomey, Fred Wise, and Norman Blagman, was recorded on March 13, 1961, at RCA's Nashville studios.

EPs:
• *Tickle Me*

LPs:
• *Something for Everybody*

Bootleg LPs:
• *Elvis Sings Songs from Tickle Me* (alternate take)

PUT YOUR HAND IN THE HAND

Gene MacLellan wrote "Put Your Hand in the Hand," which was first recorded by Beth Moore (Capitol 3013) in early 1971. The big hit with the song was by Ocean (Kama Sutra 519) later that year. Their recording went to #2 on *Billboard*'s Hot 100 chart and became a million-seller. Anne Murray also had a moderate hit with "Put Your Hand in the Hand" (Capitol 3082) in 1971. Shirley Caesar won a Grammy Award for Best Soul Performance of 1971 for her recording. The full title of the song is "Put Your Hand in the Hand (of the Man from Galilee)."

Elvis recorded "Put Your Hand in the Hand" at RCA's Nashville studios on June 8, 1971.

LPs:
• *Elvis—A Canadian Tribute*
• *Elvis Now*

Q

QUEENIE WAHINE'S PAPAYA

Bill Giant, Bernie Baum, and Florence Kaye wrote "Queenie Wahine's Papaya" for Elvis's 1966 film *Paradise, Hawaiian Style*. In the movie, Elvis sang a duet with Donna Butterworth. The instrumental track for "Queenie Wahine's Papaya" was recorded at Radio Recorders on July 27, 1965. Elvis recorded his vocal on August 4. The official release consisted of a splice of take #2 (two lines) of one version and take #6 of another version.

LPs:
• *Paradise, Hawaiian Style*

Bootleg LPs:
• *Leavin' It Up to You* (long false start)
• *Hawaii USA* (instrumental takes #1, #4,; vocal take #3 of one version and vocal takes #1 and #2 of another version)

RAG MOP

"Rag Mop" was written by Johnny Lee Wills (brother of Bob Wills) and Deacon Anderson (father of Lynn Anderson) in late 1949 and recorded by Johnny Lee Wills (Bullet 696) that same year. In early 1950 several versions were released and made the charts. Wills's original peaked at #10 on *Billboard*'s Best-Selling Singles chart. Lionel Hampton's "Rag Mop" (Decca 24855), featuring Wes Montgomery on guitar, reached #10 on the Best-Selling Singles chart and #4 on the rhythm & blues chart. Ralph Flanagan (RCA 3688) hit #10, and Doc Sausage (Regal 3251) and Joe Liggins and His Honeydrippers (Specialty 350) reached #4 and #10, respectively, on the rhythm & blues chart. The big hit in 1950, however, was the Ames Brothers' release (Coral 60140). It sold over a million copies and topped the Best-Selling Singles chart for one week in February.

In early June 1954, Sam Phillips called Elvis to record "Without You," a song written by an inmate at Nashville's maximum-security prison. None of the takes was acceptable. Phillips asked Elvis what other songs he could sing. Among the several he attempted was "Rag Mop." It's been reported that Elvis recorded "Rag Mop" at Sun Records later in 1954, but no copy of the recording has ever surfaced.

(Photo courtesy Don Fink)

RAGS TO RICHES

Tony Bennett recorded "Rags to Riches," which was written by Richard Adler and Jerry Ross,[1] in 1953. His version (Columbia 40048) reached number one on *Bill-board*'s Best-Selling Singles chart and sold over a million copies. Billy Ward and the Dominoes recorded "Rags to Riches" in 1954 for the King label (King 1280). The record reached #3 on the rhythm & blues chart. A pop version by Sunny and the Sunglows (Tear Drop 3022) charted in 1963 (#45).

Elvis recorded "Rags to Riches" on September 22, 1970, at RCA's Hollywood studios. He later had to dub in the word *kiss*, as it was recorded poorly on the master. The single release peaked at #45 on *Billboard*'s Hot 100 chart, remaining on the chart for five weeks. It's been rumored that Elvis recorded "Rags to Riches" at Sun Records in 1954 or 1955, but that has remained unsubstantiated.

Singles:
- "RAGS TO RICHES"/"Where Did They Go, Lord" RCA 47-9980) February 1971. Standard release.
- "RAGS TO RICHES"/"Where Did They Go, Lord" (RCA 447-0680) February 1972. Gold Standard Series reissue.

LPs:
- *Elvis Aron Presley*

Bootleg LPs:
- *Cadillac Elvis* (RCA release)
- *The Hillbilly Cat, 1954–1974, Volume 1* (RCA release)
- *Rockin' with Elvis New Year's Eve Pittsburgh, Pa, Dec. 31, 1976* (Pittsburgh; December 31, 1976)
- *Special Delivery from Elvis* (alternate take)
- *Superstar Outtakes, Volume 2* (alternate take)

RAINY NIGHT IN GEORGIA

Tony Joe White wrote this song, which Brook Benton recorded in late 1969. By the spring of 1970, "Rainy Night in Georgia" (Cotillion 44057) had become a million-seller and reached number one on *Billboard*'s rhythm & blues chart, #4 on the Hot 100, and #2 on the Easy-Listening chart. In the 1972 documentary *Elvis on Tour*, Elvis sang one line of "Rainy Night in Georgia" (actually, just the title) while traveling in a limousine.

RAISED ON ROCK

Mark James wrote "Raised on Rock" for Elvis, who recorded it on July 23, 1973, at Stax Studios in Memphis. The single release had a nine-week stay on *Billboard*'s Hot 100 chart, peaking at #41. On the Easy-Listening chart it reached #27 and stayed seven weeks. In 1975 Johnny Winter covered Elvis's "Raised on Rock" (Blue Sky 2754), but failed to chart (it was, however, listed as "Bubbling Under" at #108).

Singles:
- "RAISED ON ROCK"/"For Ol' Times Sake" (RCA APBO-0088) September 1973. Standard release.
- "RAISED ON ROCK"/"For Ol' Times Sake" (RCA DJAO-0088) September 1973. Disc jockey promotional release.

[1]Adler and Ross wrote the music for the Broadway plays *Pajama Game* and *Damn Yankees*.

- "If You Talk in Your Sleep"/"RAISED ON ROCK" (RCA GB-10157) March 1975. Gold Standard Series original release.

LPs:
- *Raised on Rock/For Ol' Times Sake*

Bootleg LPs:
- *To Know Him Is to Love Him* (Las Vegas; 1969 or 1970)

REACH OUT TO JESUS
Ralph Carmichael wrote this gospel tune, which Elvis recorded on June 8, 1971, at RCA's Nashville studios. Most of the tracks at the two-day session were gospel songs.

LPs:
- *He Touched Me*

READY FOR LOVE
Not much is known about this song. Elvis is reputed to have recorded "Ready for Love," but no documentation is available.

READY TEDDY
"Ready Teddy" was written by John Marascalco and Robert (Bumps) Blackwell and originally recorded by Little Richard in 1956. His recording (Specialty 579) peaked at #44 on *Billboard*'s Top 100 chart and number one on the rhythm & blues chart.

Elvis recorded "Ready Teddy" on September 3, 1956, at Radio Recorders. Take #27 is the master. "Ready Teddy" was sung on Elvis's first "Ed Sullivan Show" appearance (September 9, 1956), and it proved to be one of his most frequently performed songs in the 1950s.

Singles:
- "READY TEDDY"/blank (no number) 1956. Special one-sided disc jockey promotional release.

EPs:
- *Elvis, Volume 2*

LPs:
- *Elvis* (RCA LPM-1382)
- *A Golden Celebration* ("The Ed Sullivan Show"; September 9, 1956) (Mississippi-Alabama Fair and Dairy Show; September 26, 1956)
- *I Was the One* (with overdubbing)

Bootleg LPs:
- *From the Waist Up* ("The Ed Sullivan Show"; September 9, 1956)
- *The Hillbilly Cat, 1954-1974, Volume 1* ("The Ed Sullivan Show"; September 9, 1956)
- *The King Goes Wild* ("The Ed Sullivan Show"; September 9, 1956)
- *Loving You* ("The Ed Sullivan Show"; September 9, 1956)
- *The Rockin' Rebel, Volume 3* ("The Ed Sullivan Show"; September 9, 1956)
- *Standing Room Only, Volume 3* ("The Ed Sullivan Show"; September 9, 1956)

RECONSIDER BABY
"Reconsider Baby" was written and recorded by Lowell Fulson in late 1953. His recording (Checker 804) reached #3 on *Billboard*'s rhythm & blues chart in 1954.

Elvis recorded "Reconsider Baby" on April 4, 1960, at

RCA's Nashville studios. For years, his performance at the Bloch Arena in Honolulu on March 25, 1961, has appeared on bootleg albums. Finally, in 1980, RCA released the live recording on the *Elvis Aron Presley* boxed set. Originally, a live afternoon performance of the song at Madison Square Garden on June 10, 1972, was scheduled for the 1973 *Elvis* (APL1-0283) LP, but was finally deleted. The performance, which was filed by RCA as "A Blues Jam," later appeared on *Elvis—A Legendary Performer, Volume 4*.

LPs:
- *Elvis Aron Presley* (USS *Arizona* Memorial; March 25, 1961)
- *Elvis—A Legendary Performer, Volume 4* (Madison Square Garden afternoon show; June 10, 1972)
- *Elvis Is Back*
- *Reconsider Baby*

Bootleg LPs:
- *Command Performance* (Madison Square Garden afternoon show; June 10, 1972)
- *Elvis' 1961 Hawaii Benefit Concert* (USS *Arizona* Memorial; March 25, 1961)
- *From Hollywood to Vegas* (Las Vegas; ?)
- *Rockin' with Elvis New Year's Eve Pittsburgh, Pa. Dec. 31, 1976* (Pittsburgh; December 31, 1976)
- *Sold Out* (Madison Square Garden afternoon show; June 10, 1972)
- *Standing Room Only, Volume 2* (USS *Arizona* Memorial; March 25, 1961)

RELAX
"Relax" was recorded by Elvis in September 1962 at Radio Recorders for his film *It Happened at the World's Fair*. Sid Tepper and Roy C. Bennett are the composers.

LPs:
- *It Happened at the World's Fair*
- *Mahalo from Elvis*

RELEASE ME
"Release Me" was written by Eddie Miller and W. S. Stevenson (Dub Williams) in 1953 and recorded by Jimmy Heap (Capital 2518) late that year. His recording reached #5 on *Billboard*'s country chart in early 1954. Just a few weeks later, Kitty Wells (Decca 29023) and Ray Price (Columbia 21214) released their versions, with Price's peaking at #7. In 1962 Little Esther Phillips resurrected the tune as a number one rhythm & blues hit. Her rendition, as well as Englebert Humperdinck's (Parrot 40011) in 1967, were million-sellers. Humperdinck's reached #4 on the Hot 100 chart. The song's full title is "Release Me (and Let Me Love Again)." It is the world's most-performed country song. In 1967 the Music Operators of America called "Release Me" the most popular song of the year in jukebox play. Eddie Miller was inspired to write the song after overhearing a couple arguing in a bar near San Francisco. The wife said, "If you'd release me, we wouldn't have any problems and everything would be all right." Miller thought it was an interesting way to ask for a divorce.

Elvis sang "Release Me" in concert in the 1970s. His performance on February 18, 1970, at the International Hotel in Las Vegas was recorded by RCA for album release.

LPs:
- *On Stage—February, 1970*
- *Welcome to My World*

Bootleg LPs:
- *The Hillbilly Cat "Live"* (Las Vegas; August 1970)
- *The Last Farewell* (Indianapolis; June 26, 1977)
- *Standing Room Only, Volume 3* (Las Vegas; Feburary 18, 1970)
- *To Know Him Is To Love Him* (Las Vegas; 1969 or 1970)

REMEMBERIN'
Elvis is thought to have recorded "Rememberin' " in January 1968 at RCA's Nashville studios. It's not clear whether this was a new song or the 1923 Vivian and Rosetta Duncan tune "Rememb'ring," composed for the Broadway musical, *Topsy and Eva*. Their recording (Victor 19206) was popular in 1924, as were those by Paul Ash (Brunswick 2428), and Ken Griffin (Columbia 39137).

RETURN TO SENDER
"Return to Sender" was featured in Elvis's 1962 film *Girls! Girls! Girls!* The record sold over a million copies and reached #2 on *Billboard*'s Hot 100 chart and stayed on the chart for 16 weeks. It was #2 for five straight weeks. Only the Four Seasons' "Big Girls Don't Cry" prevented "Return to Sender" from reaching the top position. On the rhythm & blues chart, the record peaked at #5 and had a 12-week stay on the chart. In England, "Return to Sender" was number one for three weeks. It was the first number one single in England to feature a saxophone (Boots Randolph). Elvis recorded "Return to Sender" in March 1962 at Radio Recorders. Take #2 is the master recording of this Otis Blackwell–Winfield Scott composition.

Singles:
- "RETURN TO SENDER"/"Where Do You Come From" (RCA 47-8100) October 1962. Standard release.
- "RETURN TO SENDER"/"Where Do You Come From" (RCA 447-0638) June 1963. Gold Standard Series reissue.
- "RETURN TO SENDER"/"Where Do You Come From" (RCA PB-11111) October 1977. Included in the boxed sets *15 Golden Records—30 Golden Hits* and *20 Golden Hits in Full Color Sleeves*

LPs:
- *Elvis* (RCA DPL2-0056[e])
- *Elvis: Worldwide 50 Gold Award Hits, Volume 1*
- *Girls! Girls! Girls!*
- *The Top Ten Hits*

Bootleg LPs:
- *The Entertainer* (Sahara Tahoe Hotel; May 1976)

RIDING THE RAINBOW
Elvis sang "Riding the Rainbow" in his 1962 movie *Kid Galahad*. He recorded the song, which was written by Fred Wise and Ben Weisman, on October 26, 1961, at Radio Recorders. The version that appears on record is a splice of take #1 (first version) and take #7 (second version).

EPs:
- *Kid Galahad*

LPs:
- *I Got Lucky*

Bootleg LPs:
- *The Complete Kid Galahad Session, Volume 2* (takes #1–9, first version; takes #1–7, second version)
- *A Dog's Life* (take #3, a false start, and take #4, a long false start)

RIP IT UP
Composer John Marascalco drove to Los Angeles in 1955 to sell "Ready Teddy" to Specialty Records as a tune for Little Richard to record. After selling the song to Specialty, Robert (Bumps) Blackwell, the label's A&R man, asked Marascalco if he had any other songs. Marascalco told him he had a country tune called "Rip It Up" that he could rework to suit Little Richard. After spending a week rewriting the song at a fleabag motel in Hollywood, Marascalco went back to Specialty and Blackwell bought it, taking partial writing credit, as he had for "Ready Teddy." Little Richard's "Rip It Up" (Specialty 579) sold over a million copies in 1956 and hit number one on *Billboard*'s rhythm & blues chart and #17 on the Top 100 chart. Bill Haley and His Comets' cover version of "Rip It Up" (Decca 30028) peaked at #25, also in 1956.

Elvis recorded "Rip It Up" at Radio Recorders on September 3, 1956. Take #19 is the master. Occasionally over the years, Elvis sang "Rip It Up" in concert. Some of these performances have surfaced on bootleg albums. "Rip It Up" was one of the many songs performed during the Million-Dollar-Quartet session on December 4, 1956.

Singles:
- "Little Sister"/"RIP IT UP" (RCA EP-0517) June 1983, Twelve-inch promotional release.

EPs:
- *Elvis, Volume 1*
- *Elvis/Jaye P. Morgan*

LPs:
- *Elvis* (RCA LPM-1382)
- *Elvis: The Other Sides—Worldwide Gold Award Hits, Volume 2*
- *I Was the One* (overdubbed)

Bootleg LPs:
- *Long Lost Songs* (Las Vegas; December 1975)
- *The One Million Dollar Quartet* (Sun Records; December 4, 1956)

ROCK & ROLL MUSIC
Chuck Berry wrote and recorded "Rock & Roll Music" (Chess 1671) in 1957. His recording reached #8 on the Top 100 chart and #6 on the rhythm & blues chart. It quickly became a million-seller. In 1976 the Beach Boys peaked at #5 on the Hot 100 chart with their rendition of "Rock and Roll Music" (Brother 1354), spelling out the word *and* in the title. During a jam session of several Chuck Berry tunes, Elvis sang "Rock & Roll Music." The session, which was recorded by Felton Jarvis, has never been released.

ROCK AROUND THE CLOCK

"Rock Around the Clock" was written in 1953 by Max C. Freedman and Jimmy De Knight (real name: James E. Myers). At the time, Freedman was 58 years old! The title first considered for the composition was "Dance Around the Clock." Freedman and De Knight reportedly based the tune on an old rhythm & blues song called "My Daddy Rocks Me with a Steady Roll." "Rock Around the Clock" was originally recorded by Sonny Dae and His Knights (Arcade 123) in 1953. The following year, on April 12, 1954, Bill Haley recorded the song in the same session as "Shake, Rattle and Roll." The famous guitar break was played by Danny Cedrone.

When first released, "Rock Around the Clock" (Decca 29124) sold poorly. The label listed the song as a fox-trot! It wasn't until the 1955 movie *Blackboard Jungle* hit the theaters that "Rock Around the Clock" gained popularity. The song served as the film's opening and closing theme. "Rock Around the Clock" reached number one on *Billboard*'s Top 100 chart, where it stayed for eight weeks. Over the years, it has been on the charts for a total of 43 weeks. The song also reached #4 on the rhythm & blues chart. Sales of over 25 million copies worldwide are claimed for Bill Haley's release. It was the first record in England to become a million-seller. Because it was used as the theme song for the TV series "Happy Days," "Rock Around the Clock" reentered the Hot 100 chart in 1974, reaching #39.

Elvis sang "Rock Around the Clock" in concert in 1955 and 1956, including performances on the "Louisiana Hayride" and in Kingsport, Tennessee, on September 22, 1955.

ROCK-A-HULA BABY

"Rock-a-Hula Baby" was recorded by Elvis on March 23, 1961, at Radio Recorders for his movie *Blue Hawaii*." RCA officially released take #5. The single release peaked at #23 on *Billboard*'s Hot 100 chart (for a nine-week stay). In the United Kingdom, "Rock-a-Hula Baby" went to number one and stayed at the top for four weeks. On the label, the song was listed as a "Twist Special." "Rock-a-Hula Baby" was written by Fred Wise, Ben Weisman, and Florence Kay as an attempt to cash in on the Twist craze. Sales of over a million copies are claimed.

Singles:
- "Can't Help Falling in Love"/"ROCK-A-HULA BABY" (RCA 47-7968) December 1961. Standard release.
- "Can't Help Falling In Love"/"ROCK-A-HULA BABY" (RCA 447-0635) November 1962. Gold Standard Series reissue.
- "Can't Help Falling in Love"/"ROCK-A-HULA BABY" (RCA 37-7968) December 1961. Compact 33 Single release. This record, which played at the 33⅓ RPM speed, is extremely valuable.

LPs:
- *Blue Hawaii*
- *Elvis in Hollywood*
- *Elvis: Worldwide 50 Gold Award Hits, Volume 1*

Bootleg LPs:
- *The Blue Hawaii Box* (takes #1–5)
- *The Blue Hawaii Sessions* (take #3)
- *A Dog's Life* (takes #1–3)

ROCKIN' LITTLE SALLY

It's been reported that Elvis recorded this song, but no further information is available.

ROSES ARE RED

Bobby Vinton had his first number one record (on both the Hot 100 and Easy-Listening charts) and million-seller with this song. "Roses Are Red" (Epic 9509) even made the rhythm & blues chart (#5). The song was written in 1961 by Al Byron and Paul Evans. On a few occasions, Elvis sang it in concert. The full title is "Roses Are Red (My Love)."

Bootleg LPs:
- *Long Lost Songs* (Las Vegas; March 22, 1975)

ROUSTABOUT

Elvis recorded "Roustabout," the title song to his 1964 movie of the same name, in March 1964 at Radio Recorders. Even though the Jordanaires are credited with singing backup, it was actually the Mello Men who did the singing. They gave up their claim to credit and were paid by the hour for their services. The film version of "Roustabout" had additional instrumentation. Take #11 is on the standard RCA releases. "Roustabout" was written by Bill Giant, Bernie Baum, and Florence Kaye.

Singles:
- "ROUSTABOUT"/"One-Track Heart" (RCA SP-45-139) November 1964. Promotional release.
- "ROUSTABOUT"/"ROUSTABOUT" (Paramount Pictures SP-2414) November 1964. Promotional release for theater lobbies only. Paramount distributed copies of this single to select theaters. Side 1 was to be used before *Roustabout*'s release. At the end of the song, the announcer said that *Roustabout* was "coming soon." Side 2 was to be used during the film's run. The announcer said that *Roustabout* was "now playing." Both sides featured the same take, but it was an alternate take found on no other release.

LPs:
- *Elvis in Hollywood*
- *Roustabout*

RUBBERNECKIN'

"Rubberneckin'" was written by Dory Jones and Bunny Warren for Elvis's 1969 movie *Change of Habit*. The song was recorded by Elvis on January 20, 1969, at American Sound Studios in Memphis. "Rubberneckin'" had a five-week stay on *Billboard*'s Hot 100 chart, peaking at #69. A performance of the song at the International Hotel in Las Vegas on August 24, 1969, was recorded by RCA but never released.

Singles:
- "Don't Cry Daddy"/"RUBBERNECKIN'" (RCA 47-9768) November 1969. Standard release.
- "Don't Cry Daddy"/"RUBBERNECKIN'" (RCA 447-0674) December 1970. Gold Standard Series reissue.

LPs:
- *Almost in Love*
- *Double Dynamite*
- *The Memphis Record*

Bootleg LPs:
- *Elvis* (*Change of Habit* soundtrack)

RUN ON
This traditional gospel song was arranged and recorded by Elvis at RCA's Nashville studios on May 25, 1966—the first Elvis recording session produced by Felton Jarvis. "Run On" was the first song recorded during the session.

LPs:
- *How Great Thou Art*

RUNAWAY
One night in early 1961 at the Hi-Lo Club in Battle Creek, Michigan, Max T. Crook, musitron player for Del Shannon's band, hit an unusual chord change (A-minor to G). Shannon (real name: Charles Westover) stopped the band and asked Crook to play the chord change again and again. It wasn't too long before Crook and Shannon had written "Runaway." "Runaway" (Big Top 3067) reached number one on *Billboard*'s Hot 100 chart in April 1961, and eventually sold over a million copies. The haunting chord changes by Crook on the musitron (a device put under a piano in which an amplifier is installed) have made "Runaway" one of the rock era's classics. Other recordings include those by Lawrence Welk (Dot 16336) in 1962, Bonnie Raitt (Warner Bros. 8382) in 1977, and Narvel Felts (ABC 12338) in 1978. The 1987–88 NBC-TV series, "Crime Story," used an updated version of "Runaway" recorded by Del Shannon.

RCA recorded Elvis's performance of "Runaway" at the International Hotel in Las Vegas on August 22, 1969. It was one of two songs—the other was "Yesterday"—on the LP *On Stage—February, 1970* not actually recorded in February 1970.

LPs:
- *On Stage—February, 1970*

RUNNING SCARED
After several sessions of tinkering with the song, Roy Orbison and Joe Melson finally wrote "Running Scared" in about five minutes. The recording (Monument 438) reached number one on *Billboard*'s Hot 100 chart in 1961—Orbison's first of two number one records (the other was "Oh, Pretty Woman" in 1964). "Running Scared" quickly became a million-seller. In 1976 Elvis attempted to record the song, but was dissatisfied with the takes. It's never been released.

SAN ANTONIO ROSE

Bob Wills wrote and first recorded this song in 1938. His recording (Okeh 4755) was a hit in both 1938 and 1940. Bing Crosby's recording of "San Antonio Rose" was also popular in 1940. Both recordings eventually became million-sellers. In 1961 Floyd Cramer recorded an instrumental version (RCA 47-7893) that reached #8 on both the Hot 100 and country charts and #3 on the rhythm & blues chart.

Elvis sang "San Antonio Rose" in concert at least once, perhaps more times.

Bootleg LPs:
• *Long Lost Songs* (Las Vegas; September 1, 1970)

SAND CASTLES

"Sand Castles" was originally slated for Elvis's 1966 film *Paradise, Hawaiian Style,* but it was cut from the final print. "Sand Castles," which was written by Herb Goldberg and David Hess, was recorded by Elvis on August 2, 1965, at Radio Recorders. Take #10 was chosen by RCA for release.

LPs:
• *Paradise, Hawaiian Style*

Bootleg LPs:
• *Hawaii USA* (alternate takes #1–4, #6–9, and a vocal overdub by the Jordanaires)
• *Leavin' It Up to You* (takes #5 and #10)

SANDS OF TIME

Reportedly, "Sands of Time" was recorded by Elvis for *Paradise, Hawaiian Style,* but has never been released. Another theory is that "Sands of Time" is an alternate title for "Sand Castles."

SANTA, BRING MY BABY BACK (TO ME)

Aaron Schroeder and Claude DeMetrius wrote this Christmas song for Elvis, who recorded it at Radio Recorders on September 7, 1957. Take #9 was selected by RCA for release.

EPs:
• *Elvis Sings Christmas Songs*

LPs:
• *Elvis' Christmas Album*

SANTA CLAUS IS BACK IN TOWN

"Santa Claus Is Back in Town" was written for Elvis by Jerry Leiber and Mike Stoller. Elvis recorded the song, which is also known as "Christmas Blues," on September 7, 1957, at Radio Recorders. Take #7 was released on record. "Santa Claus Is Back in Town" was recorded for—but not used in—the 1968 TV special "Elvis." The single release did not chart.

Singles:
• "Blue Christmas"/"SANTA CLAUS IS BACK IN TOWN" (RCA 447-0647) November 1965. Gold Standard Series original release.
• "Merry Christmas Baby"/"SANTA CLAUS IS BACK IN TOWN" (RCA PB-14237) November 1985. New release pressed on green vinyl.

EPs:
• *Elvis Sings Christmas Songs*

LPs:
• *Elvis' Christmas Album*
• *Memories of Christmas*

Bootleg LPs:
• *The Burbank Sessions, Volume 1* ("Elvis" TV special taping; June 27, 1968, at 8:00 P.M. show)
• *Elvis Rocks and the Girls Roll* (dress rehearsals for "Elvis" TV special; June 1968)
• *Standing Room Only, Volume 3* ("Elvis" TV special taping; June 27, 1968, at 8:00 P.M. show)

SANTA LUCIA

"Santa Lucia" was written by Italian songwriter Teodoro Cottrau in 1850. English lyrics were by Thomas Oliphant.

Elvis sang "Santa Lucia" in his 1964 movie *Viva Las Vegas.* He recorded the song in July 1963 at Radio Recorders. In the film version, Ann-Margret hummed along with Elvis at the beginning of "Santa Lucia" and then talked with Cesare Danova during the rest of the song.

LPs:
• *Burning Love and Hits from His Movies, Volume 2*
• *Elvis for Everyone*

Bootleg LPs:
• *Viva Las Vegas!* (*Viva Las Vegas* soundtrack)

SATISFIED

"Satisfied" was written and first recorded by Martha Carson (Capitol 1900) in 1952. She sang the song quite often on the Grand Ole Opry. In 1953 Johnnie Ray recorded the song (Columbia 40006).

Elvis undoubtedly heard Martha Carson sing "Satisfied" on the radio, as well as in joint personal appearances the two made on tour. On September 10, 1954, at Sun Studios, Elvis recorded "Satisfied" between takes of "I'll Never Let You Go (Little Darlin')." The one-minute, 15-second song has never been released. Apparently, RCA Records can't find the song among its Sun tapes.

SATISFY ME

Elvis may have recorded "Satisfy Me" in the late 1960s. No further information on the song or date of recording is available.

SAVED

Jerry Leiber and Mike Stoller wrote "Saved," which was recorded by LaVern Baker (Atlantic 2099) in 1960. Her recording was nominated for a Grammy for Best

Rhythm and Blues Recording of 1960.

Elvis sang "Saved" in a gospel medley in his 1968 TV special "Elvis." The song was recorded on June 20 or 21, 1968, at Western Recorders in Hollywood.

LPs:
• *Elvis—TV Special*

Bootleg LPs:
• *The '68 Comeback* ("Elvis" TV special taping; June 20 or 21, 1968)

SCHOOL DAY

Chuck Berry wrote and recorded "School Day" (Chess 1653) in 1957. His recording reached #3 on *Billboard's* Hot 100 chart and number one on the rhythm and blues chart. Sales exceeded one million copies.

Elvis sang "School Day" in a studio jam session that was recorded by Felton Jarvis, but it has never been released. Elvis also sang a couple of lines of "School Day" during his June 6, 1975, concert in Dallas. The performance appeared on the *Elvis Aron Presley* boxed set. For some reason, the song was listed as "Long Live Rock and Roll" and the composer was listed as Colyer, instead of Chuck Berry.

LPs:
• *Elvis Aron Presley* (Dallas; June 6, 1975)

SCRATCH MY BACK
(THEN I'LL SCRATCH YOURS)

Elvis sang "Scratch My Back (Then I'll Scratch Yours)" in a duet with Marianna Hill in his 1966 movie *Paradise, Hawaiian Style*. The instrumental track was recorded on July 26, 1965, at Radio Recorders. Elvis's vocal was recorded on August 3. Take #2 was selected for record release. "Scratch My Back (Then I'll Scratch Yours)" was written by Bill Giant, Bernie Baum, and Florence Kaye.

LPs:
• *Paradise, Hawaiian Style*

Bootleg LPs:
• *A Dog's Life* (take #1)
• *Hawaii USA* (take #2)

SEE SEE RIDER

This traditional blues song was written and originally recorded as "C. C. Rider" by Big Bill Broonzy (real name: William Lee Conley) on Perfect Records (Perfect PE-0313) in the early 1920s. C. C. Rider was a black expression that meant "country circuit preacher." It is perhaps Ma Rainey who is most closely identified with the song. Her "See See Rider Blues" was popular in 1925, as was the 1945 reissue (Paramount 12252). Louis Armstrong (on cornet) and Fletcher Henderson (on piano) played on her recording. Ray Charles recorded "See See Rider" (Swingtime 217) in 1949. Under the title "C. C. Rider" (Atlantic 1130), Chuck Willis (featuring a white female vocal group) had a #3 rhythm & blues hit in 1957. His recordings reached #12 on the Top 100 chart. Other popular recordings have included those by LaVern Baker (Atlantic 2167) in 1962, Bobby

Powell (Whit 714) in 1965, and the Animals (MGM 13582) in 1966. "C. C. Rider" by Mitch Ryder and the Detroit Wheels served as the theme song for the 1970 Joe Namath–Ann-Margret movie, *C. C. and Company*.

Elvis opened many of his concerts in the 1970s with "See See Rider." He based his rendition on LaVern Baker's 1962 hit. All versions of the song on record were sung in concert. An April 9, 1972, performance in Hampton Roads, Virginia, was used in the documentary *Elvis on Tour*. "See See Rider" also appears in the TV specials "Elvis: Aloha from Hawaii" and "Elvis in Concert." Album releases of the song have credited Elvis as the arranger, but no composer is listed. However, the British single listed the title as "C. C. Rider" and Ma Rainey as the composer. Glenn D. Hardin was credited with the arrangement.

LPs:
• *Aloha from Hawaii via Satellite* (Honolulu; January 14, 1973)
• *The Alternate Aloha* (rehearsal concert for "Elvis: Aloha from Hawaii"; January 12, 1973)
• *Elvis Aron Presley* (Shreveport, Louisiana; June 7, 1975)
• *Elvis in Concert* (Rapid City, South Dakota; June 21, 1977)
• *Elvis Recorded Live on Stage in Memphis* (Memphis; March 20, 1974)
• *On Stage—February, 1970* (Las Vegas; February 17, 1970)

Bootleg LPs:
• *Aloha Rehearsal Show—Kui Lee Cancer Benefit* (rehearsal concert for "Elvis: Aloha from Hawaii"; January 12, 1973)
• *America's Own* (Uniondale, N.Y.; July 19, 1975)
• *Command Performance* (Las Vegas; August 4, 1972)
• *Elvis on Tour* (*Elvis on Tour* soundtrack)
• *From Las Vegas . . . to Niagara Falls* (Las Vegas; September 3, 1973) (Niagara Falls, N.Y.; June 24, 1974)
• *The Last Farewell* (Indianapolis; June 26, 1977)
• *Rockin' with Elvis April Fool's Day* (Las Vegas; April 1, 1975)
• *Rockin' with Elvis New Year's Eve Pittsburgh, Pa. Dec. 31, 1976* (Pittsburgh; December 31, 1976)
• *The Vegas Years, 1972-1975* (Las Vegas; 1972)

SEEING IS BELIEVING

Red West and Glen Spreen wrote "Seeing Is Believing" for Elvis, who recorded the song on May 19, 1971, at RCA's Nashville studios.

LPs:
• *He Touched Me*

SENTIMENTAL ME

"Sentimental Me" was written by Jimmy Cassin and Jim Morehead and popularized by the Ames Brothers (Coral 60140) in 1950. Their recording reached #3 on *Billboard's* Best-Selling Singles chart and became a million-seller. The flip side of "Sentimental Me" was the enormously successful "Rag Mop." Other popular recordings of "Sentimental Me" in 1950 included those of Russ Morgan (Decca 24904) and Ray Anthony (Capitol 923).

Elvis recorded "Sentimental Me" on March 13, 1961, at RCA's Nashville studios.

LPs:
• *Double Dynamite*

- *Separate Ways*
- *Something for Everybody*

SEPARATE WAYS

Red West and Richard Mainegra wrote "Separate Ways" for Elvis. It was somewhat biographical in that Elvis and Priscilla had just separated when the song was written. Elvis recorded the song on March 27, 1972, at RCA's Hollywood studios. "Separate Ways" had a 12-week stay on *Billboard*'s Hot 100 chart, peaking at #20. On the country chart, it reached a high of #16; on the Easy-Listening chart, #3. Worldwide sales were well over a million copies. The *Elvis on Tour* documentary used an alternate take of "Separate Ways."

Singles:
- "SEPARATE WAYS"/"Always on My Mind" (RCA 74-0815) November 1972. Standard release.
- "SEPARATE WAYS"/"Always on My Mind" (RCA GB-10486) February 1976. Gold Standard Series reissue.

LPs:
- *Always on My Mind*
- *Double Dynamite*
- *Separate Ways*

Bootleg LPs:
- *Elvis on Tour* (*Elvis on Tour* soundtrack)
- *Special Delivery from Elvis Presley* (*Elvis on Tour* soundtrack)

SHAKE A HAND

"Shake a Hand" was written by Joe Morris and originally recorded by Faye Adams (Herald 416),[1] who had a million-seller with it in 1953. Her recording topped the rhythm & blues chart for nine straight weeks. Other popular recordings of "Shake a Hand" include those by Red Foley (Decca 28839) in 1953, Savannah Churchill (Decca 28836) in 1953, the Mike Pedicin Quintet (Cameo 125) in 1958, LaVern Baker (Atlantic 2048) in 1960, Ruth Brown (Philips 40028) in 1962, and Jackie Wilson and Linda Hopkins (Brunswick 55243) in 1963.

Elvis recorded "Shake a Hand" at RCA's Hollywood studios on March 12, 1975.

LPs:
- *Elvis Aron Presley—Forever*
- *Elvis Today*

Bootleg LPs:
- *Cadillac Elvis* (Asheville, N.C.; July 22, 1975)

SHAKE, RATTLE AND ROLL

"Shake, Rattle and Roll" was written by Jesse Stone using the pseudonym Charles E. Calhoun, and first recorded by Joe Turner (Atlantic 1026) in 1954. Turner's recording was a #2 rhythm & blues hit. Bill Haley and His Comets recorded a version of "Shake, Rattle and Roll" on April 12, 1954—the same day that "Rock Around the Clock" was recorded. Haley's release (Decca 29204), which used less suggestive lyrics,

reached #7 on *Billboard*'s Best-Selling Singles chart and sold over a million copies.

Elvis recorded "Shake, Rattle and Roll" on February 3, 1956, at RCA's New York City studios. His version reverted to Turner's lyrics, although one verse from Haley's recording was used. Elvis's single release did not chart. In late 1956 Buddy Holly recorded "Shake, Rattle and Roll" with virtually the same lyrics as on Elvis's version, but his version was not released until 1964 on the *Showcase* LP.

Elvis sang "Shake, Rattle and Roll" (with a "Flip, Flop and Fly" ending) on his first "Stage Show" appearance on January 28, 1956. He also performed the song on "The Milton Berle Show" on April 3, 1956. A film clip of the "Stage Show" appearance was used in the 1981 documentary *This Is Elvis*. Drums were overdubbed on that clip.

Singles:
- "SHAKE, RATTLE AND ROLL"/"Lawdy Miss Clawdy" (RCA 20-6642) September 1956. Standard 78 RPM release.
- "SHAKE, RATTLE AND ROLL"/"Lawdy Miss Clawdy" (RCA 47-6642) September 1956. Standard 45 RPM release.
- "SHAKE, RATTLE AND ROLL"/"Lawdy Miss Clawdy" (RCA 447-0615) March 1959. Gold Standard Series reissue.

EPs:
- *Elvis Presley* (RCA EPA-830)
- *Good Rockin' Tonight*

LPs:
- *For LP Fans Only*
- *A Golden Celebration* ("Stage Show"; January 28, 1956)
- *This Is Elvis* ("Stage Show"; January 28, 1956) (drums were overdubbed)

Bootleg LPs:
- *Dorsey Shows* ("Stage Show"; January 28, 1956)
- *Elvis* ("Stage Show"; January 28, 1956)
- *Sold Out* (Nashville; July 1, 1973) (in medley with "Long Tall Sally," "Whole Lotta Shakin' Goin' On," "Your Mama Don't Dance," and "Jailhouse Rock")
- *The Sun Years* ("Stage Show"; January 28, 1956)
- *Superstar Outtakes, Volume 2* ("Stage Show"; January 28, 1956)

SHAKE THAT TAMBOURINE

Elvis sang "Shake That Tambourine" in his 1965 film *Harum Scarum*. He recorded the song, which was written by Bill Giant, Bernie Baum, and Florence Kaye, in February 1965, at RCA's Nashville studios.

LPs:
- *Harum Scarum*

SHE BELONGS TO ME

Bob Dylan wrote and recorded "She Belongs to Me" in 1965. It was the flip side of "Subterranean Homesick Blues" (Columbia 43242). In 1969, Rick Nelson reached #33 on *Billboard*'s Hot 100 chart with his recording of the song (Decca 32550).

Elvis reportedly sang "She Belongs to Me" in concert in the 1970s.

---

[1] "Shake a Hand" was the first release for Herald Records, founded by Al Silver in 1953.

SHE THINKS I STILL CARE

"She Thinks I Still Care" was written by Dickie Lee and first recorded by George Jones (United Artists 424), who topped the country chart in 1962. Later that year, Connie Francis recorded the song as "He Thinks I Still Care" (MGM 13096), as did Anne Murray (Capitol 3867) in 1974.

Elvis recorded "She Thinks I Still Care" on the night of February 2–3, 1976, at Graceland. Overdubbing was later done at Young 'Un Sound Studios. Paired with "Moody Blue," "She Thinks I Still Care" had a 13-week stay on *Billboard*'s Hot 100 chart, peaking at #31. On the country charts, the record reached number one for one week.

On October 15, 1980, Felton Jarvis had a new instrumental track recorded at Young 'Un Sound in Nashville, using an alternate take. That recording appeared on the *Guitar Man* LP.

- "Moody Blue"/"SHE THINKS I STILL CARE" (RCA PB-10857) December 1976. Standard release.
- "Moody Blue"/"SHE THINKS I STILL CARE" (RCA JB-10857) December 1976. Disc jockey promotional release. In May 1977, RCA released this record in five colors (red, blue, white, gold, and green) and an experimental multicolor as an experiment. The multicolor disc is extremely rare.

LPs:
- *Guitar Man* (alternate take with a new instrumental backing)
- *Moody Blue*
- *Our Memories of Elvis* (without overdubbing)

SHE WEARS MY RING

"She Wears My Ring" was written by the husband-and-wife songwriting team of Boudleaux and Felice Bryant. The original recording was by Roy Orbison, but his version was not released until his 1964 LP *Early Orbison* (Monument SLP 18023). In 1968 Ray Price had a #6 country hit with "She Wears My Ring" (Columbia 44628).

Elvis recorded "She Wears My Ring" at Stax Studios in Memphis on December 16, 1973.

LPs:
- *Good Times*
- *Our Memories of Elvis, Volume 2* (without overdubbing)

SHE'S A MACHINE

"She's a Machine" was written by Joy Byers for Elvis's 1967 movie *Easy Come, Easy Go*, but it was not used. The instrumental track for the song was recorded at Radio Recorders on September 28 or 29, 1966. Elvis's vocal was done at a later date.

LPs:
- *Elvis Sings Flaming Star*
- *Singer Presents Elvis Singing Flaming Star and Others*

SHE'S NOT YOU

Elvis recorded "She's Not You" on March 19, 1962, at RCA's Nashville studios. His single release had a 10-week stay on *Billboard*'s Hot 100 chart, reaching a high of #5. It was #13 on the rhythm & blues chart and

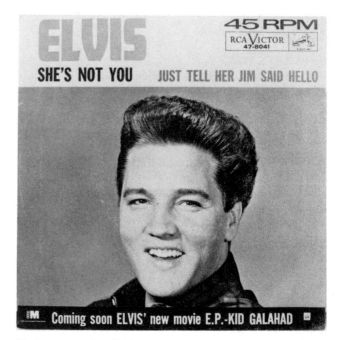

(Photo courtesy Don Fink)

#2 on the Easy-Listening chart. Only Ray Charles's "You Don't Know Me" (which Elvis would later record) kept "She's Not You" from the top position on the latter chart. The record hit number one in England for three weeks. Total worldwide sales exceeded one million copies. "She's Not You" was written by Jerry Leiber, Mike Stoller, and Doc Pomus, and was their first collaboration.

Singles:
- "SHE'S NOT YOU"/"Just Tell Her Jim Said Hello" (RCA 47-8041) July 1962. Standard release.
- "SHE'S NOT YOU"/"Just Tell Her Jim Said Hello" (447-0637) June 1963. Gold Standard Series reissue.

LPs:
- *Elvis' Golden Records, Volume 3*
- *Elvis: Worldwide 50 Gold Award Hits, Volume 1*
- *The Top Ten Hits*

SHOPPIN' AROUND

Elvis sang "Shoppin' Around" in his 1960 film *G. I. Blues*. The song was originally recorded on April 27, 1960, at RCA's Hollywood studios, but that version was not used for the film or on record. It finally appeared on the 1980 LP *Elvis Aron Presley*. The version that *was* used in the film and on record was recorded at Radio Recorders on May 6, 1960. Take #7 was selected by RCA for release. The film version had added horns. "Shoppin' Around" was written by Sid Tepper, Roy C. Bennett, and Aaron Schroeder.

LPs:
- *Elvis Aron Presley* (April 27, 1960, version; two false starts and a complete take)
- *G. I. Blues* (May 6, 1960, version; take #7)

SHOUT IT OUT
"Shout It Out" was written for Elvis's 1966 film *Frankie and Johnny* by Bill Giant, Bernie Baum, and Florence Kaye. Elvis recorded the tune in May 1965 at Radio Recorders.

LPs:
• *Frankie and Johnny*

SIGN OF THE ZODIAC
Elvis sang "Sign of the Zodiac" in a duet with Marlyn Mason in his 1969 film *The Trouble with Girls*. He recorded the song at United Recorders on August 23, 1968. "Sign of the Zodiac" has never been released by RCA, but it does appear on several bootleg albums.

Bootleg LPs:
• *Behind Closed Doors* (studio version without overdubbing)
• *Eternal Elvis* (*The Trouble with Girls* soundtrack)
• *From Hollywood to Vegas* (*The Trouble with Girls* soundtrack)

SILENT NIGHT
Father Joseph Mohr (1792–1848) of the Church of St. Nicholas in Oberndorf, Austria, composed the poem "Stille Nacht, Heilige Nacht" (the original title was "Song from Heaven") after visiting the home of a poor woodcutter. He saw similarities between the birth of the woodcutter's new baby and the birth of Jesus Christ centuries earlier. Mohr had his organist, Franz Gruber (1787–1863), write some music for the poem and they sang it at midnight Mass with guitar accompaniment (the organ had broken down). In the spring of 1819, Karl Mauracher, organ builder and repairman, came to fix Mohr's Grotien pipe organ. Gruber played "Stille Nacht, Heilige Nacht" on the organ and Mauracher fell in love with the tune. He took a copy of it back to his home in the Zillertal.

In 1831, Mauracher arranged the carol for four children's voices and had Joseph, Caroline, Andreas, and Amalie Strasser sing it. After the children sang "Stille Nacht, Heilige Nacht" at the Leipzig Trade Fair in 1832, they were invited to sing for the king and queen in the Royal Saxon Court Chapel in Pleissenburg Castle on Christmas Eve 1832. The carol quickly gained international popularity. "Stille Nacht, Heilige Nacht" was translated into English by the Rev. John Freeman Young (1820–1885) in 1863.

"Silent Night" has been recorded by countless performers over the years. One of the first recordings was by the Haydn Quartet (Victor 4511) in 1905. Bing Crosby recorded "Silent Night" with the John Scott Trotter Orchestra and the Max Terr Choir on June 8, 1942, in Los Angeles. Crosby's "Silent Night" backed with "Adeste Fideles" (Decca 621) has reportedly sold more than 30 million copies over the years, possibly surpassing "White Christmas" as the biggest-selling record of all time. Sister Rosetta Tharpe had a popular rhythm & blues recording of "Silent Night" (Decca 48119) in 1949. In 1962 Mahalia Jackson recorded the song under the title "Silent Night, Holy Night" (Apollo 750).

Elvis recorded "Silent Night" on September 6, 1957, at Radio Recorders. Dudley Brooks (on piano) and Millie Kirkham (backing vocal) were featured on this recording. Take #9 was chosen by RCA for release.

EPs:
• *Christmas with Elvis*

LPs:
• *Elvis' Christmas Album*
• *Memories of Christmas*

SILVER BELLS
Jay Livingston and Ray Evans wrote "Silver Bells" for the 1951 movie *The Lemon Drop Kid*, where it was introduced by Bob Hope and Marilyn Maxwell. Bing Crosby and Carol Richards recorded a popular version of "Silver Bells" (Decca 27229) in 1951.

Elvis recorded "Silver Bells" at RCA's Nashville studios on May 15, 1971.

LPs:
• *Elvis Sings the Wonderful World of Christmas*
• *Memories of Christmas*

SING, YOU CHILDREN
Elvis sang "Sing, You Children" in his 1967 film *Easy Come, Easy Go*. The instrumental track was recorded on September 28 or 29, 1966, at Radio Recorders. Elvis's vocal was added later, with backing by the Mello Men. "Sing, You Children" was written by Gerald Nelson and Fred Burch.

EPs:
• *Easy Come, Easy Go*

LPs:
• *You'll Never Walk Alone*

SINGING TREE
Elvis recorded "Singing Tree," which was written by A. Owens and A. Solberg, on September 12, 1967, at RCA's Nashville studios.

LPs:
• *Clambake*

SIXTEEN TONS
Merle Travis wrote "Sixteen Tons" in 1947 for his LP *Folk Songs of the Hills*. The song was inspired by a line often spoken by Travis's father: "Another day older and deeper in debt." Eight years later, Tennessee Ernie Ford recorded "Sixteen Tons," a song he had previously sung on his NBC-TV daytime series, "The Tennessee Ernie Ford Show." His recording topped both the Top 100 and country charts in November 1955, selling one million copies faster than any record in history up to that time—14 days. (One year later, Elvis's "Love Me Tender" broke that record by selling one million copies *before* release.) Other popular recordings of "Sixteen Tons" include those by Johnny Desmond (Coral 61529) in 1955, Tom Jones (Parrot 40016) in 1967, and the Don Harrison Band (Atlantic 3323) in 1976.

Elvis reportedly recorded "Sixteen Tons" with guitar accompaniment at Graceland in the 1960s.

SLICIN' SAND

Elvis sang "Slicin' Sand" in his 1961 film *Blue Hawaii*. He recorded the song, which was written by Sid Tepper and Roy C. Bennett, on March 21, 1961, at Radio Recorders. Take #19 was chosen for release.

LPs:
• *Blue Hawaii*

Bootleg LPs:
• *The Blue Hawaii Box* (takes #15–19)
• *The Blue Hawaii Sessions* (take #17)
• *Plantation Rock* (take #1 and another take)

SLOWLY BUT SURELY

"Slowly but Surely" was recorded by Elvis on May 27, 1963, at RCA's Nashville studios. Two years later it was used in Elvis's film *Tickle Me*. "Slowly but Surely" was written by Sid Wayne and Ben Weisman.

EPs:
• *Tickle Me*

LPs:
• *Fun in Acapulco*

SMOKEY MOUNTAIN BOY

"Smokey Mountain Boy" was written by Lenore Rosenblatt and Victor Millrose and sung by Elvis in his 1964 film *Kissin' Cousins*. He recorded the song in October 1963 at RCA's Nashville studios.

LPs:
• *Kissin' Cousins*

SMORGASBORD

Elvis sang "Smorgasbord" in his 1966 movie *Spinout*. In the film, he changed the lyrics. Instead of "I'll take the dish I please and please the dish I take," Elvis sang, "I'll take the dish I please and take the please I dish." The instrumental track was recorded at Radio Recorders on February 17, 1966. Elvis's vocal track was recorded at a later date. "Smorgasbord" was written by Sid Tepper and Roy C. Bennett.

LPs:
• *Spinout*

Bootleg LPs:
• *Elvis Sings Songs from Tickle Me* (alternate take)

SNOWBIRD

"Snowbird" was written by Gene MacLellan and recorded by Anne Murray in 1970. Her recording (Capitol 2738) reached #8 on *Billboard*'s Hot 100 chart and sold over a million copies. Murray is the first Canadian female to have a million-seller. Murray's Gold Record was presented to her on November 10, 1970, on "The Merv Griffin Show." In 1971 Chet Atkins won a Grammy Award for his instrumental version of "Snowbird." That same year, composer MacLellan recorded his own song (Capitol 2959).

Elvis recorded "Snowbird" on September 22, 1970, at RCA's Nashville studios. The guitar solo was performed by Harold Bradley.

LPs:
• *Elvis Country*

SO CLOSE, YET SO FAR (FROM PARADISE)

Joy Byers wrote "So Close, Yet So Far (from Paradise)" for Elvis's 1965 movie *Harum Scarum*. Elvis recorded the song in February (probably the 24th) 1965 at RCA's Nashville studios.

LPs:
• *Harum Scarum*
• *Mahalo from Elvis*

SO GLAD YOU'RE MINE

"So Glad You're Mine" was written and recorded by Arthur Crudup (RCA 20-1949) in 1946. Elvis recorded the song at RCA's New York City studios on January 30, 1956. Albert (Sonny) Burgess recorded a cover of Elvis's version of "So Glad You're Mine" at Sun Records in 1957, but it was not released.

EPs:
• *Elvis, Volume 2*

LPs:
• *Elvis* (RCA LPM-1382)
• *Reconsider Baby*

SO HIGH

LaVern Baker recorded "So High" using different lyrics and the title "So High So Low" in 1959. Her recording (Atlantic 2033) was a #12 rhythm & blues hit.

Elvis recorded "So High" at RCA's Nashville studios on May 27, 1966.

Singles:
• "How Great Thou Art"/"SO HIGH" (RCA SP-45-162) March 1967. Disc jockey promotional release. This single was a promotion for the *How Great Thou Art* LP and the special Palm Sunday radio program.

LPs:
• *How Great Thou Art*

SOFTLY AND TENDERLY

This gospel song was written by Will L. Thompson. During the Million-Dollar-Quartet session of December 4, 1956, Elvis sang lead on "Softly and Tenderly" while Jerry Lee Lewis provided harmony.

Bootleg LPs:
• *The One Million Dollar Quartet* (Sun Records; December 4, 1956)

SOFTLY, AS I LEAVE YOU

"Softly, as I Leave You" was written by G. Calabrese, A. DeVita, and Hal Shaper, and first released in the United States by Matt Monroe[1] (Liberty 55449) in 1962. Frank Sinatra recorded a popular version (Reprise

---

[1] Matt Monroe's "Softly, as I Leave You" was playing on the stereo as Elvis and the Beatles said goodbye after spending the evening together at Elvis's Bel Air home on August 27, 1965.

0301) in 1964, reaching #27 on *Billboard*'s Hot 100 chart and #4 on the Easy-Listening chart. In 1967 Eydie Gormé peaked at #30 on the Easy-Listening chart with her version (Columbia 43971).

Elvis sang "Softly, as I Leave You" in concert on a few occasions. Actually, he recited the words while Sherrill Nielsen sang. The midnight show at the Las Vegas Hilton on December 13, 1975, was recorded on a private cassette recorder. It is that version that RCA released as a single in 1978. "Softly, as I Leave You" had an 11-week stay on *Billboard*'s country chart, peaking at #6. It did not reach the Hot 100 chart, but it was listed as "Bubbling Under" at #109. "Softly, as I Leave You" was nominated for a Grammy as Best Country Vocal Performance, Male, but lost to Willie Nelson's "Georgia on My Mind."

Singles:
- "Unchained Melody"/"SOFTLY, AS I LEAVE YOU" (RCA PB-11212) March 1978. Standard release.
- "Unchained Melody"/"SOFTLY, AS I LEAVE YOU" (RCA JH-11212) March 1978. Disc jockey promotional release. Some of the promos had a star on the label of the "Unchained Melody" side.

LPs:
- *Elvis Aron Presley*

Bootleg LPs:
- *Command Performance* (Las Vegas; August 23, 1974)
- *Elvis Presley Is Alive and Well and Singing in Las Vegas, Volume 1* (Las Vegas; August 1974)
- *Sold Out* (Las Vegas; August 24, 1974)
- *The Vegas Years, 1972–1975* (Las Vegas; August 24, 1974)

SOLDIER BOY

"Soldier Boy" was written in Korea in 1951 by David Jones[1] and Larry Banks (although credited to David Jones and Teddy Williams Jr.), and first recorded by the Four Fellows with the Abie Baker Orchestra (Glory 234) in 1955. Other recordings in 1955 included those by Pat O'Day (MGM 12025) and Sunny Gale (47-6227). This is not the same song as the Shirelles' 1962 number one hit.

Elvis recorded "Soldier Boy" at RCA's Nashville studios on March 20, 1960. While stationed in West Germany, Elvis made a home recording of "Soldier Boy" that was released in 1984 on the boxed set *A Golden Celebration*. While he was dating Anita Wood, it was "their song."

LPs:
- *Elvis Is Back*
- *A Golden Celebration* (West Germany; 1958–1960)

SOLITAIRE

Neil Sedaka and Phil Cody wrote "Solitaire" in 1972 for Sedaka's LP *Solitaire* (Kirschner KES-117). The album was recorded in England. Andy Williams had the first single release of "Solitaire" that charted. His 1973 recording (Columbia 45936) peaked at #23 on *Billboard*'s Easy-Listening chart. Two years later, the

Carpenters took "Solitaire" (A&M 1721) to #17 on the Hot 100 chart.

Elvis recorded "Solitaire" at Graceland on the night of February 3–4, 1976. His single release had a 12-week stay on the country chart, reaching a high of #10.

Singles:
- "Are You Sincere"/"SOLITAIRE" (RCA PB-11533) May 1979. Standard release.
- "Are You Sincere"/"SOLITAIRE" (RCA JB-11533) May 1979. Disc jockey promotional release.

LPs:
- *Always on My Mind*
- *From Elvis Presley Boulevard, Memphis, Tennessee*
- *Our Memories of Elvis* (without overdubbing)

SOMEBODY BIGGER THAN YOU AND I

This gospel song was written by Johnny Lange, Walter (Hy) Heath, and Joseph Burke, and recorded by Elvis on May 27, 1966, at RCA's Nashville studios. On the monaural version of the *How Great Thou Art* LP, Johnny Lange was incorrectly listed as Johnny Lane. The Ink Spots had a moderate hit in 1951 with "Somebody Bigger Than You and I" (Decca 27494).

LPs:
- *How Great Thou Art*

SOMETHING

"Something" was written by George Harrison and recorded by the Beatles in 1969. Their recording (Apple 2654) reached #3 on *Billboard*'s Hot 100 chart and became a million-seller. Harrison lifted the song's first line from the title of the James Taylor tune "Something In the Way She Moves." In 1970 both Shirley Bassey (United Artists 50698) and Booker T and the M.G.'s (Stax 0073) had popular versions of "Something."

Elvis sang "Something" in his 1973 TV special "Elvis: Aloha from Hawaii," and in concert on a few occasions.

EPs:
- *Aloha from Hawaii via Satellite*

LPs:
- *Aloha from Hawaii via Satellite*
- *The Alternate Aloha* (rehearsal concert for "Elvis: Aloha from Hawaii"; January 12, 1973)

Bootleg LPs:
- *Aloha Rehearsal Show—Kui Lee Cancer Benefit* (rehearsal concert for "Elvis: Aloha from Hawaii"; January 12, 1973)
- *Plantation Rock* (rehearsal concert for "Elvis: Aloha from Hawaii"; January 12, 1973)

SOMETHING BLUE

"Something Blue" was written by Paul Evans and Al Byron and recorded by Elvis on March 18, 1962, at RCA's Nashville studios.

LPs:
- *Pot Luck*

---

[1]David Jones later founded the Rays, who had a #3 hit in 1957 with "Silhouettes" (Cameo 117).

SONG OF THE SHRIMP

Elvis sang "Song of the Shrimp" in his 1962 movie *Girls! Girls! Girls!* The song, which was written by Sid Tepper and Roy C. Bennett, was recorded in March 1962 at Radio Recorders.

LPs:
- *Girls! Girls! Girls!*

SOUND ADVICE

"Sound Advice" was sung by Elvis in his 1962 movie *Follow That Dream.* The film version had a whistling introduction and was mimed by actor Arthur O'Connell. Elvis recorded "Sound Advice" on July 5, 1961, at RCA's Nashville studios. Bill Giant, Bernie Baum, and Florence Kaye are the composers. (Note: The credits of *Follow That Dream* credit Bill Giant and Anna Shaw as the composers.)

LPs:
- *Elvis for Everyone*

THE SOUND OF YOUR CRY

"The Sound of Your Cry" was recorded by Elvis on June 4, 1970, at RCA's Nashville studios. The single release did not chart. It took ten years for "The Sound of Your Cry" to appear on an American RCA LP. Bill Giant, Bernie Baum, and Florence Kaye are the composers.

Singles:
- "It's Only Love"/"THE SOUND OF YOUR CRY" (RCA 48-1017) September 1971. Standard release. This was the only Elvis single with a "48" prefix.
- "It's Only Love"/"THE SOUND OF YOUR CRY" (RCA 447-0684) May 1972. Gold Standard Series reissue.

(Photo courtesy Don Fink)

LPs:
- *Greatest Hits, Volume 1* (first time in stereo, 50 seconds longer than the single release)

Bootleg LPs:
- *The Hillbilly Cat, 1954–1974, Volume 1* (same as RCA release)
- *Special Delivery from Elvis Presley* (alternate take)
- *Superstar Outtakes, Volume 2* (alternate take)

SPANISH EYES

"Spanish Eyes" was written and recorded by Bert Kaempfert as an instrumental titled "Moon over Naples" (Decca 31812) in 1965. His recording reached #59 on *Billboard*'s Hot 100 chart and #6 on the Easy-Listening chart. Charles Singleton and Eddy Snyder wrote English lyrics to the song and retitled it "Spanish Eyes." Al Martino's recording (Capitol 5542) in 1966 sold over a million copies and reached number one on the Easy-Listening chart and #15 on the Hot 100 chart.

Elvis recorded "Spanish Eyes" on December 16, 1973, at Stax Studios in Memphis. When Elvis sang the song in concert, Sherrill Nielsen sang duet with him.

LPs:
- *Good Times*
- *Our Memories of Elvis* (without overdubbing)

Bootleg LPs:
- *Command Performance* (Las Vegas; February 7, 1974)

SPEEDWAY

The instrumental track to this title song of Elvis's 1968 movie *Speedway* was recorded on June 21, 1967, at the MGM Studios in Culver City. Elvis's vocal was recorded at a later date. "Speedway" was written by Mel Glazer and Stephen Schlaks.

LPs:
- *Speedway*

SPINOUT

"Spinout" was written by Sid Wayne, Ben Weisman, and Dolores Fuller and sung by Elvis in his 1966 film of the same name. The instrumental track was recorded at Radio Recorders in February 1966. Elvis's vocal track was recorded later. The single release of "Spinout" had a seven-week stay on *Billboard*'s Hot 100 chart, peaking at #40. Some sources have indicated that "Spinout" had worldwide sales of over one million copies.

Singles:
- "SPINOUT"/"All That I Am" (RCA 47-8941) September 1966. Standard release. The original picture sleeve read, "Watch for Elvis' SPINOUT LP." One month later the sleeve was changed to read "Ask for Elvis' SPINOUT LP."
- "SPINOUT"/"All That I Am" (RCA 447-0658) February 1968. Gold Standard Series reissue.

LPs:
- *Elvis in Hollywood*
- *Spinout*

SPRING FEVER

Elvis sang "Spring Fever" in his 1965 film *Girl Happy,*

in a duet with Shelley Fabares. The song, which was written by Bill Giant, Bernie Baum, and Florence Kaye, was recorded in July 1964 at Radio Recorders.

LPs:
• *Girl Happy*

Bootleg LPs:
• *Elvis* (*Girl Happy* soundtrack)
• *Special Delivery from Elvis Presley* (*Girl Happy* soundtrack)

STAND BY ME
This gospel song was written by Dr. C. H. Tindley,[1] founder of the Tindley Methodist Church in Philadelphia (where blues singer Bessie Smith was buried on October 4, 1937).

Elvis recorded "Stand by Me" on May 26, 1966, at RCA's Nashville studios.

LPs:
• How Great Thou Art

STARTIN' TONIGHT
Elvis sang "Startin' Tonight" in his 1965 film *Girl Happy*. The song was recorded in July 1964 at Radio Recorders. Lenore Rosenblatt and Victor Millrose are the composers.

LPs:
• *Girl Happy*

STARTING TODAY
Don Robertson wrote "Starting Today" for Elvis, who recorded the song on March 13, 1961, at RCA's Nashville studios.

LPs:
• *Something for Everybody*

STAY AWAY
"Stay Away" was written by Sid Tepper and Roy C. Bennett, who based the song on the melody of "Greensleeves." "Greensleeves" was supposedly written by England's King Henry VIII. In 1952 Mantovani made a successful recording of "Greensleeves" (London 1171), as did the Beverley Sisters (London 1703) in 1957, and Mason Williams (Warner Bros. 7272) in 1969.

Elvis recorded "Stay Away" on October 2, 1967, at RCA's Nashville studios. It was sung over the opening credits of Elvis's 1968 movie *Stay Away, Joe*. His single release had a five-week stay on the Hot 100 chart, peaking at #67. "Stay Away" reportedly sold over a million copies worldwide.

Singles:
• "U.S. Male"/"STAY AWAY" (RCA 47-9465) March 1968. Standard release.
• "U.S. Male"/"STAY AWAY" (RCA 447-0664) 1970. Gold Standard Series reissue.

EPs:
• *Stay Away*

LPs:
• *Almost in Love* (second pressing of the Camden LP and all pressings of the Pickwick reissue)

STAY AWAY, JOE
Sid Wayne and Ben Weisman wrote "Stay Away, Joe" for Elvis's 1968 film of the same name. Elvis recorded the song on October 2, 1967, at RCA's Nashville studios.

LPs:
• *Almost in Love* (first pressing of the Camden LP only)
• *Let's Be Friends*

STEADFAST, LOYAL, AND TRUE
"Steadfast, Loyal, and True" was the school song of Royal High School in Elvis's 1958 film *King Creole*. The film and record versions were recorded on the movie set sometime in January or February 1958. A studio take from the January 16 session at Radio Recorders appears on the bootleg *From the Beach to the Bayou*. Vocal overdubs by the Jordanaires were done on June 19, 1958. "Steadfast, Loyal, and True" was written by Jerry Leiber and Mike Stoller and is the official song of the International Elvis Presley Appreciation Society.

LPs:
• *King Creole*

Bootleg LPs:
• *From the Beach to the Bayou* (alternate studio take #16)

STEAMROLLER BLUES
"Steamroller Blues" was written by James Taylor and first appeared on his 1970 album *Sweet Baby James* (Warner Bros. 1843).

(Photo courtesy Don Fink)

---

[1]Songwriter Thomas A. Dorsey was inspired by Dr. Tindley to move from the blues field to the gospel field, where he became one of the greatest writers of gospel songs.

Elvis sang "Steamroller Blues" in concert several times and in his 1973 TV special "Elvis: Aloha from Hawaii." The concert version was released as a single. "Steamroller Blues" had a 12-week stay on *Billboard*'s Hot 100 chart, peaking at #17. It reached #31 on the country chart.

Singles:
- "STEAMROLLER BLUES"/"Fool" (RCA 74-0910) April 1973. Standard release.
- "Burning Love"/"STEAMROLLER BLUES" (RCA GB-10156) March 1975. Gold Standard Series original release.

LPs:
- *Aloha from Hawaii via Satellite* (Honolulu; January 14, 1973)
- *The Alternate Aloha* (rehearsal concert for "Elvis: Aloha from Hawaii"; January 12, 1973)
- *Greatest Hits, Volume 1* ("Elvis: Aloha from Hawaii" rehearsal concert; January 12, 1973)

Bootleg LPs:
- *Aloha Rehearsal Show—Kui Lee Cancer Benefit* (rehearsal concert for "Elvis: Aloha from Hawaii"; January 12, 1973)
- *From Las Vegas . . . to Niagara Falls* (Las Vegas; September 1973)
- *Sold Out* (Anaheim, California; April 24, 1973)
- *To Know Him Is to Love Him* (Las Vegas; 1969 or 1970)

STEPPIN' OUT OF LINE
Elvis recorded "Steppin' Out of Line" on March 22, 1961, at Radio Recorders for his film *Blue Hawaii*, but it was cut from the final print. The film version was to have been take #8, with #19 added on the ending. Take #17 was released on record. "Steppin' Out of Line" was written by Fred Wise, Ben Weisman, and Dolores Fuller.

LPs:
- *Pot Luck*

Bootleg LPs:
- *Behind Closed Doors* (takes #8 and #19)
- *The Blue Hawaii Box* (takes #1-19)
- *The Blue Hawaii Sessions* (takes #1-16, #18, and #19)
- *Plantation Rock* (take #4 [a false start], #5 [a false start], and #15)
- *Unfinished Business* (alternate take)

STOP, LOOK AND LISTEN
Elvis sang "Stop, Look and Listen," which was written by Joy Byers, in his 1966 film *Spinout*. The instrumental track was recorded at Radio Recorders on February 15, 1966. Elvis's vocal was done at a later date.

LPs:
- *Spinout*

STOP WHERE YOU ARE
Bill Giant, Bernie Baum, and Florence Kaye wrote "Stop Where You Are" for Elvis's 1966 film *Paradise, Hawaiian Style*. The instrumental track was recorded at Radio Recorders on July 27, 1965, and Elvis's vocal on August 3. Take #3 was selected for record release. The instrumental breaks in "Stop Where You Are" were longer in the film version.

LPs:
- *Paradise, Hawaiian Style*

Bootleg LPs:
- *Hawaii USA* (takes #2 and #3, first version; takes #3 and #4, second version)
- *Leavin' It Up to You* (alternate take)

STORMY MONDAY BLUES
"Stormy Monday Blues" was a #5 rhythm & blues hit in 1962 for Bobby Bland (Duke 355). It reached #43 on the Hot 100 chart.

Elvis may have recorded "Stormy Monday Blues" for RCA in the 1960s, but no tape has yet surfaced.

STRANGER IN MY OWN HOME TOWN
"Stranger in My Own Home Town" was written and recorded by Percy Mayfield (Tangerine 941) in 1963.

On February 17, 1969, Elvis recorded "Stranger in My Own Home Town" at American Sound Studios in Memphis. His recording featured an electric sitar played by Reggie Young.

LPs:
- *Back in Memphis*
- *From Memphis to Vegas/From Vegas to Memphis*
- *The Memphis Record*
- *Reconsider Baby* (alternate mix)

STRANGER IN THE CROWD
Winfield Scott wrote "Stranger in the Crowd" for Elvis, who recorded it on June 5, 1970, at RCA's Nashville studios. In the documentary *Elvis—That's the Way It Is*, Elvis was seen rehearsing "Stranger in the Crowd" at MGM's Culver City studios.

LPs:
- *That's the Way It Is*

Bootleg LPs:
- *The King: From the Dark to the Light* (*Elvis—That's the Way It Is* soundtrack)
- *That's the Way It Is* (*Elvis—That's the Way It Is* soundtrack)

STUCK ON YOU
"Stuck on You" was written by Aaron Schroeder and J. Leslie McFarland and recorded by Elvis on March 21, 1960, at RCA's Nashville studios. Take #1 was released on record. Five days later Elvis sang it at the taping for the Frank Sinatra–Timex special, "Welcome Home, Elvis," which aired on ABC-TV on May 12, 1960. The taping took place at the Fountainebleau Hotel in Miami Beach. "Stuck on You" sold over two million copies. Advance orders were 1,275,077—for a record that hadn't yet been recorded. Picture sleeves were prepared for the new single with no song titles—just a die-cut hole in the center of the sleeve so that the record label could be seen to reveal the titles. In May 1960, "Stuck on You" replaced Percy Faith's "Theme from 'A Summer Place'" at the top of *Billboard*'s Hot 100 chart. After a stay of four weeks, "Stuck on You" was replaced at number one by the Everly Brothers' "Cathy's Clown." Total stay on the chart was 16 weeks. On the country chart "Stuck on You" reached #27. It peaked at #6 on the rhythm & blues chart.

Singles:
- "STUCK ON YOU"/"Fame and Fortune" (RCA 47-7740) March 1960. Standard release.
- "STUCK ON YOU"/"Fame and Fortune" (RCA 61-7740) March 1960. "Living Stereo" release. This was Elvis's first stereo release.
- "STUCK ON YOU"/"Fame and Fortune" (RCA 447-0627) February 1962. Gold Standard Series reissue.

LPs:
- *Elvis* (RCA DPL2-0056[e])
- *Elvis' Golden Records, Volume 3*
- *Elvis: Worldwide 50 Gold Award Hits, Volume 1*
- *The Number One Hits*
- *The Top Ten Hits*

Bootleg LPs:
- *Eternal Elvis* ("Welcome Home, Elvis"; March 26, 1960)
- *Frank Sinatra—Welcome Home, Elvis* ("Welcome Home, Elvis"; March 26, 1960)
- *Please Release Me* ("Welcome Home, Elvis"; March 26, 1960)
- *Standing Room Only, Volume 3* ("Welcome Home, Elvis"; March 26, 1960)

SUCH A NIGHT

"Such a Night" was written by Lincoln Chase and recorded by Clyde McPhatter and the Drifters (Atlantic 1019), whose recording reached #5 on the rhythm & blues chart in 1954. Johnnie Ray's recording of "Such a Night" (Columbia 40020) that same year was banned from the air in some areas because of its suggestive lyrics. It reached number one in England, however. Other recordings of "Such a Night" include those by Bonnie Paul with Sy Oliver's Orchestra (Essex 352), Dinah Washington (Mercury 70336), and Jane Turzy (Decca 29087), all in 1954; Vince Everett (ABC Paramount 10313) in 1962, and Conway Twitty (ABC Paramount 10550). Everett's recording was such a close copy of Elvis's that it's sometimes tough to tell them apart.

Elvis recorded "Such a Night" on April 4, 1960, at RCA's Nashville studios. Take #4 was selected for release. The single release had an eight-week stay on *Billboard*'s Hot 100 chart, reaching a high of #16.

Singles:
- "SUCH A NIGHT"/"Never Ending" (RCA 47-8400) July 1964. Standard release.
- "SUCH A NIGHT"/"Never Ending" (RCA 447-0645) May 1965. Gold Standard Series reissue.
- "SUCH A NIGHT"/"SUCH A NIGHT" (RCA JB-50170) 1976. Rare disc jockey promotional release. Side A featured "Such a Night" from the LP *Elvis Is Back*, while the version on side B was from the LP *Elvis—A Legendary Performer, Volume 2*.

LPs:
- *Elvis Aron Presley* (USS *Arizona* Memorial; March 25, 1961)
- *Elvis—A Legendary Performer, Volume 2* (Takes #2 and #3 [false starts], and #4)
- *Elvis Is Back*

Bootleg LPs:
- *Elvis' 1961 Hawaii Benefit Concert* (USS *Arizona* Memorial; March 25, 1961)
- *Long Lost Songs* (Las Vegas; December 12, 1976)

SUMMER KISSES, WINTER TEARS

Elvis recorded "Summer Kisses, Winter Tears" in August 1960 at Radio Recorders. Originally, it was to have been included in the film *Flaming Star*, but was cut from the final print. Fred Wise, Ben Weisman, and Jack Lloyd are the composers.

EPs:
- *Elvis by Request*

LPs:
- *Elvis for Everyone*

SUMMERTIME HAS PASSED AND GONE

Bill Monroe wrote and recorded "Summertime Has Passed and Gone" (Columbia 20503) in late 1948. During the Million-Dollar-Quartet session on December 4, 1956, both Elvis and Carl Perkins sang a line of the song imitating Bill Monroe.

Bootleg LPs:
- *The Million Dollar Quartet* (Sun Records; December 4, 1956)
- *The One Million Dollar Quartet* (Sun Records; December 4, 1956)

SUNSHINE

Elvis reportedly recorded "Sunshine" at Sun Records in 1955, but there is no proof.

SUPPOSE

Elvis first recorded "Suppose" on March 20, 1967, at RCA's Nashville studios, but that version was not released. He again recorded the song on June 21, 1967, this time at MGM's Culver City studios. The second version was originally slated to appear in Elvis's 1968 film *Speedway*, but was cut from the final print. It is believed that the prints shown in Malaya do include "Suppose." Another version of the song, this one a home recording at Graceland from the mid-1960s, surfaced in 1984 in the boxed set *A Golden Celebration*. "Suppose" was written by Sylvia Dee and George Goehring.

LPs:
- *A Golden Celebration* (Graceland; 1960s)
- *Speedway*

SURRENDER

"Surrender" was a contemporary version of the Italian ballad "Torna a Sorrento" ("Come Back to Sorrento"), which was written in 1911 by G. D. de Curtis and Ernesto de Curtis). "Come Back to Sorrento" has been recorded numerous times over the years. Both Toni Arden (Columbia 39348) in 1951 and Dean Martin (Capitol 2140) in 1952 recorded the song.

In 1960 Doc Pomus and Mort Shuman added new English words to the melody and titled the song "Surrender." Elvis recorded "Surrender" on October 30, 1960, at RCA's Nashville studios. It was recorded between the gospel songs "He Knows Just What I Need" and "Mansion over the Hilltop." RCA chose take #4 for release. "Surrender" entered the Hot 100 chart at #24. In five weeks it replaced "Pony Time" by Chubby Checker at number one on *Billboard*'s Hot 100 chart.

At a running time of one minute, 51 seconds, "Surrender" was one of the shortest number one records in history. (The shortest was "Stay" by Maurice Williams and the Zodiacs at 1:36.) After two weeks at the top spot, "Surrender" was replaced by the Marcels' "Blue Moon." "Surrender" spent a total of 12 weeks on the chart. In England, it was number one for four weeks. Sales of over five million copies have been claimed.

Singles:
- "SURRENDER"/"Lonely Man" (RCA 47-7850) February 1961. Standard release.
- "SURRENDER"/"Lonely Man" (RCA 61-7850) February 1961. "Living Stereo" release.
- "SURRENDER"/"Lonely Man" (RCA 37-7850) February 1961. Compact 33 Single release.
- "SURRENDER"/"Lonely Man" (RCA 68-7850) February 1961. "Living Stereo" Compact 33 Single release.
- "SURRENDER"/"Out of a Clear Blue Sky" (by Lawrence Welk) (USAF Program #159/#160) March 1961. An edited version of "Surrender" appeared in this five-minute radio program for the U.S. Air Force.
- "SURRENDER"/"Lonely Man" (RCA 447-0630) February 1962. Gold Standard Series reissue.
- "It's Now or Never"/"SURRENDER" (RCA PB-13889) October 1984. One of six singles in the boxed set *Elvis' Greatest Hits—Golden Singles, Volume 1.* The record was pressed on gold vinyl with a special gold "50th" anniversary label.

LPs:
- *Elvis* (RCA DPL2-0056[e])
- *Elvis—A Legendary Performer, Volume 3*
- *Elvis' Golden Records, Volume 3*
- *Elvis: Worldwide 50 Gold Award Hits, Volume 1*
- *The Number One Hits*
- *The Top Ten Hits*

SUSAN WHEN SHE TRIED
"Susan When She Tried" was a #15 country hit for the Statler Brothers in 1974 (Mercury 73625). Don Reid, a member of the group, is the song's composer.

Elvis recorded "Susan When She Tried" on March 11, 1975, at RCA's Hollywood studios.

LPs:
- *Elvis Today*

SUSIE-Q
Written by Dale Hawkins, Stanley Lewis, and Eleanor Broadwater, "Susie-Q" was a pop hit in 1957 for Dale Hawkins on Checker Records (Checker 863). James Burton played lead guitar on the recording. Other hit recordings of the song include those by Creedence Clearwater Revival (Fantasy 616) in 1968 and José Feliciano (RCA 47-0358) in 1970.

Elvis sang a line or two of "Susie-Q" in one of his Las Vegas concerts.

Bootleg LPs:
- *Susie-Q* (Las Vegas; ?)

SUSPICION
"Suspicion" was written by Doc Pomus and Mort Shuman and recorded by Elvis on March 19, 1962, at RCA's Nashville studios. Elvis's version, however, was not originally released as a single—instead, it was a track on the *Pot Luck* LP. On the Spanish EP *Elvis Presley Canta,* one of the stereo channels was missing, leaving only Elvis and part of the instrumentation, but no Jordanaires. Terry Stafford heard Elvis's version and decided to record a single of "Suspicion" in 1964. All the instruments on Stafford's release were played by producer Bob Simmons, except for bass, which was played by Ron Griffith. "Suspicion" reached #3 on *Billboard*'s Hot 100 chart and became a million-seller. As Stafford's record was climbing the charts, RCA decided to release Elvis's version as a single. It was too late, however; Elvis's release did not chart, although it was listed as "Bubbling Under" briefly at #103.

Singles:
- "Kiss Me Quick"/"SUSPICION" (RCA 447-0639) April 1964. Gold Standard Series original release.

LPs:
- *Pot Luck*

Bootleg LPs:
- *Elvis* (RCA release)

SUSPICIOUS MINDS
"Suspicious Minds" was written by Mark James and recorded by him at American Sound Studios in 1968. His recording (Scepter 12221) did not chart.

On January 23, 1969, Elvis recorded "Suspicious Minds" at American Sound Studios using the same musicians that James had used. Both recordings were produced by Chips Moman. The release of "Suspicious Minds" was a splice of three takes. Horns were overdubbed on August 7, 1969, at United Recording Studios in Las Vegas. In November 1969, "Suspicious Minds" reached the top of *Billboard*'s Hot 100 chart, replacing the Temptations' "I Can't Get Next to You." After only one week at number one, "Suspicious Minds" was replaced by the Fifth Dimension's "Wedding Bell Blues." Elvis would never again have a number one record on the Hot 100 chart. At 4 minutes, 22 seconds, "Suspicious Minds" was Elvis's longest number one record. It spent a total of 15 weeks on the chart. Sales of the record easily exceeded a million copies. On May 21, 1971, "Suspicious Minds" was named the Outstanding Single Recorded in Memphis.

An August 1970 performance of "Suspicious Minds" at the International Hotel in Las Vegas was used in the documentary, *Elvis—That's the Way It Is.* Another performance from his April 1972 tour was used in *Elvis on Tour,* and a performance from the 1973 TV special, "Elvis: Aloha from Hawaii," was used in the 1981 documentary *This Is Elvis.*

For the 1983 film *Breathless,* Orion Pictures wanted to use a portion of "Suspicious Minds" on the soundtrack. The Presley estate and RCA Records wanted $40,000 for the rights. Orion Pictures brought back the original members of Elvis's band to record the song with an Elvis imitator at a cost of only $7,500.

In August 1987, *USA Today* had a telephone call-in

ballot on the callers' favorite Elvis song. "Suspicious Minds" won with a 30.5 percent of the vote. "Love Me Tender" came in second with 24 percent.

Waylon Jennings and Jessi Colter recorded a cover version of "Suspicious Minds" (RCA 47-9920) that made it to #25 on the country chart. A pop version by Dee Dee Warwick (Atco 6810) reached #80 on *Billboard*'s Hot 100 chart in 1971.

Singles:
- "SUSPICIOUS MINDS"/"You'll Think of Me" (RCA 47-9764) September 1969. Standard release.
- "SUSPICIOUS MINDS"/"You'll Think of Me" (RCA 447-0673) December 1970. Gold Standard Series reissue.
- "SUSPICIOUS MINDS"/"You'll Think of Me" (RCA PB-11103) October 1977. One of 15 singles in the boxed set *15 Golden Records—30 Golden Hits* (RCA PP-11301).
- "THE ELVIS MEDLEY"/"Always on My Mind" (RCA PB-13351) November 1982. "The Elvis Medley" featured excerpts from "Suspicious Minds," as well as "Jailhouse Rock," "Teddy Bear," "Hound Dog," "Don't Be Cruel," and "Burning Love."
- "THE ELVIS MEDLEY"/"THE ELVIS MEDLEY" (short version) (RCA JB-13351) November 1982. Disc jockey promotional release.
- "SUSPICIOUS MINDS"/"Burning Love" (RCA PB-13896) October 1984. One of six singles in the boxed set *Elvis' Greatest Hits—Golden Singles, Volume 2*. The record was pressed on gold vinyl with a special gold "50th" anniversary label.

LPs:
- *Aloha from Hawaii via Satellite*
- *The Alternate Aloha* (rehearsal concert for "Elvis: Aloha from Hawaii"; January 12, 1973)
- *Elvis as Recorded at Madison Square Garden* (June 10, 1972)
- *Elvis' Gold Records, Volume 5*
- *Elvis in Person* (Las Vegas; August 22, 1969)
- *The Elvis Medley*
- *Elvis: Worldwide 50 Gold Award Hits, Volume 1*
- *From Memphis to Vegas/From Vegas to Memphis* (Las Vegas; August 22, 1969)
- *Greatest Hits, Volume 1* (first time in true stereo)
- *The Memphis Record*
- *The Number One Hits*
- *This Is Elvis* (shortened version from the TV special "Elvis: Aloha from Hawaii")
- *The Top Ten Hits*

Bootleg LPs:
- *Aloha Rehearsal Show—Kui Lee Cancer Benefit* (rehearsal concert for "Elvis: Aloha from Hawaii"; January 12, 1973)
- *Behind Closed Doors* (Las Vegas; February 16, 1970)
- *The Complete Kid Galahad Session, Volume 3* (alternate take)
- *From Las Vegas . . . to Niagara Falls* (Las Vegas; September 3, 1973) (Niagara Falls, N.Y.; June 24, 1974)
- *The Hillbilly Cat "Live"* (Las Vegas; August 1970)
- *The Legend Lives On* (Las Vegas; August 1969)
- *Superstar Outtakes* (Las Vegas; August 1969)
- *That's the Way It Is* (Elvis—That's the Way It Is soundtrack)
- *To Know Him Is to Love Him* (Las Vegas; 1969 or 1970)

SWEET ANGELINE
"Sweet Angeline" was written by Chris Arnold, Geoffrey Morrow, and David Martin, and recorded by Elvis on September 24, 1973, at his Palm Springs home, with vocal backing by Voice. The instrumental track had been recorded earlier on July 25, 1973, at Stax Studios in Memphis.

LPs:
- *Raised on Rock/For Ol' Times Sake*

SWEET CAROLINE
Neil Diamond wrote and first recorded "Sweet Caroline" (Uni 55136) in 1969. His recording reached #4 on *Billboard*'s Hot 100 chart and became a million-seller. Anthony Armstrong Jones (Chart 5100) in 1970 and Bobby Womack (United Artists 50946) in 1972 also had hits with the song.

Elvis sang "Sweet Caroline" in concert on several occasions. One performance in August 1970 at the International Hotel in Las Vegas was used in the documentary *Elvis—That's the Way It Is*.

LPs:
- *Elvis Aron Presley* (Las Vegas rehearsal; August 1970)
- *On Stage—February, 1970* (Las Vegas; February 18, 1970)

Bootleg LPs:
- *King of Las Vegas Live* (Elvis—That's the Way It Is soundtrack)
- *That's the Way It Is* (Elvis—That's the Way It Is soundtrack)

SWEET INSPIRATION
"Sweet Inspiration" was written by Wallace Pennington and Lindon Dewey Oldham and first recorded by the Sweet Inspirations (Atlantic 2476), who had a #5 rhythm & blues hit with it in 1968. Barbra Streisand reached #37 on the Hot 100 chart in 1972 with her recording of the song (Columbia 45626), which was sung in a medley with "Where You Lead."

Elvis sang a portion of "Sweet Inspiration" in concert on at least a couple of occasions.

Bootleg LPs:
- *The Monologue L.P.* (Las Vegas; July 31, 1969)
- *To Know Him Is to Love Him* (Las Vegas; 1969 or 1970)

SWEETHEART YOU DONE ME WRONG
Bill Monroe wrote and recorded "Sweetheart You Done Me Wrong" (Columbia 20423) in 1948. Lester Flatt played guitar and Earl Scruggs banjo on the recording.

During the Million-Dollar-Quartet session on December 4, 1956, Elvis sang "Sweetheart You Done Me Wrong," with Carl Perkins singing harmony.

Bootleg LPs:
- *The Million Dollar Quartet* (Sun Records; December 4, 1956)
- *The One Million Dollar Quartet* (Sun Records; December 4, 1956)

SWING DOWN, SWEET CHARIOT
"Swing Down, Sweet Chariot" is based on "Swing Low, Sweet Chariot," which was arranged in 1917 by Henry Thacker Burleigh. Burleigh, in turn, based his arrangement on an old black spiritual that dates back to at least 1872. Numerous artists have recorded "Swing Low, Sweet Chariot" over the years, including the Fisk University Jubilee Quartet (Victor 16453) in 1910, Benny Goodman (Victor 25492), the Ink Spots (Decca 1230), and Bing Crosby (Decca 1809). The Champs had an instrumental version in 1958 titled "Chariot Rock" (Challenge 59018).

Elvis recorded "Swing Down, Sweet Chariot" on October 31, 1960, at RCA's Nashville studios. Vocal backing was by the Jordanaires. He recorded another version in 1968 (October 14 or 24) at United Recorders in Hollywood for his film *The Trouble with Girls*. Take #10 was used in the movie. The 1966 single release did not chart.

Singles:

• "Milky White Way"/"SWING DOWN, SWEET CHARIOT" (RCA 447-0652) March 1966. Gold Standard Series original release.

LPs:

• *Elvis Aron Presley* (USS *Arizona* Memorial; March 25, 1961)
• *Elvis—A Legendary Performer, Volume 4* (film version)
• *His Hand in Mine* (October 31, 1960, version)

Bootleg LPs:

• *Behind Closed Doors* (take #10, film version)
• *Elvis' 1961 Hawaii Benefit Concert* (USS *Arizona* Memorial; March 25, 1961)
• *Eternal Elvis* (*The Trouble with Girls* soundtrack)

SYLVIA

Elvis recorded "Sylvia" on June 8, 1970, at RCA's Nashville studios. Geoff Stephens and Les Reed are the composers.

LPs:

• *Elvis Now*

Bootleg LPs:

• *Plantation Rock* (alternate take)

T

TAKE GOOD CARE OF HER

"Take Good Care of Her" was written by Ed Warren and Arthur Kent and first recorded by Adam Wade[1] (Coed 546) in 1961. Wade's recording reached #7 on *Billboard*'s Hot 100 chart and #20 on the rhythm & blues chart. Other popular recordings include those by Mel Carter (Imperial 66208) in 1966; Sonny James (Capitol 5612), whose version was number one on the country chart in 1966; and Johnny Mathis (Columbia 45777) in 1973.

Elvis recorded "Take Good Care of Her" on July 21, 1973, at Stax Studios in Memphis. His single release had a seven-week stay on *Billboard*'s Hot 100 chart, peaking at #39. "Take Good Care of Her" reached #4 on the country chart and #27 on the Easy-Listening chart.

Singles:
- "I've Got a Thing About You, Baby"/"TAKE GOOD CARE OF HER" (RCA APBO-0196) January 1974. Standard release.
- "I've Got a Thing About You, Baby"/"TAKE GOOD CARE OF HER" (RCA DJBO-0196) January 1974. Disc jockey promotional release.
- "I've Got a Thing About You, Baby"/"TAKE GOOD CARE OF HER" (RCA GB-10485) February 1976. Gold Standard Series reissue.

LPs:
- *Good Times*
- *Our Memories of Elvis* (without overdubbing)

TAKE ME TO THE FAIR

Elvis sang "Take Me to the Fair" in his 1963 film *It Happened at the Fair*. The song was recorded in September 1962 at Radio Recorders. Backing vocals were provided by the Mello Men. The film version of "Take Me to the Fair" had only a banjo as instrumental backing. Elvis may have rehearsed "Take Me to the Fair" for his 1968 TV special, although it was not used. Sid Tepper and Roy C. Bennett are the composers.

LPs:
- *It Happened at the World's Fair*

TAKE MY HAND, PRECIOUS LORD

Thomas A. Dorsey was inspired to write "Take My Hand, Precious Lord" in 1939 by the deaths of his first wife and baby daughter in childbirth. From that time forward, he became totally dedicated to writing gospel songs.

Elvis recorded "Take My Hand, Precious Lord" on January 13, 1957, at Radio Recorders. Take #14 was selected by RCA for release.

EPs:
- *Peace in the Valley*

LPs:
- *Elvis' Christmas Album* (not Camden and Pickwick releases)
- *You'll Never Walk Alone*

TAKE THESE CHAINS FROM MY HEART

"Take These Chains from My Heart" was written by Fred Rose and Hy Manning and recorded by Hank Williams in 1953. His recording (MGM 11479) reached number one on *Billboard*'s country chart. In 1963 Ray Charles resurrected the song (ABC-Paramount 10435), and it peaked at #8 on the Hot 100 chart.

Elvis sang one line of "Take These Chains from My Heart" in Las Vegas on August 21, 1974, and may have sung the complete song on a few other occasions.

TAKE YOUR FINGER OUT OF IT, IT DON'T BELONG TO ME

According to Paul Burlison, guitar player with the Johnny Burnette Trio, Elvis was asked to come on stage in a mall in Memphis in 1953 or early 1954 to sing "Take Your Finger Out of It, It Don't Belong to Me" with Shelby Fowler's band.

TALK ABOUT THE GOOD TIMES

Jerry Reed wrote and recorded "Talk About the Good Times" (RCA 47-9804) in 1970. It reached #14 on *Billboard*'s country chart.

Elvis recorded "Talk About the Good Times" on December 14, 1973, at Stax Studios in Memphis.

LPs:
- *Good Times*

TALKIN' 'BOUT YOUR BIRTHDAY CAKE

This was another of the songs that Paul Burlison said Elvis was asked to sing at a mall with Shelby Fowler's band in 1953 or early 1954.

TEARS ON MY PILLOW

Little Anthony and the Imperials had a million-seller with "Tears on My Pillow" (End 1027) in 1958. The song reached #4 on the Hot 100 chart and #2 on the rhythm & blues chart. The piano was played by Dave (Baby) Cortez. The McGuire Sisters revived the song in 1961, reaching #59 (Coral 62276).

In the 1960s Elvis recorded "Tears on My Pillow" at Graceland with his own guitar accompaniment. The recording has never been released.

TEDDY BEAR

Kal Mann and Bernie Lowe composed "Teddy Bear" for Elvis because of his fondness for teddy bears. The song was recorded on January 24, 1957, at Radio Recorders. Elvis sang "Teddy Bear" in his second film *Loving You*, and during the 1977 CBS-TV special "Elvis in Concert." The song's full title is "(Let Me Be Your) Teddy Bear." Elvis's single release succeeded Pat Boone's "Love Letters in the Sand" at number one on *Billboard*'s Top 100 chart in July 1957. After a seven-

---

[1]Adam Wade was the first black to host a network TV game show ("Musical Chairs," 1975)

week stay at the top spot, it was replaced by "Tammy" by Debbie Reynolds. Total stay on the chart was 24 weeks. "Teddy Bear" was also number one (for one week) on the country chart and number one (for one week) on the rhythm & blues chart. It was one of only three Elvis songs to top all three *Billboard* charts. (The other two were "Don't Be Cruel" and "Jailhouse Rock.") Sales easily exceeded one million copies. In 1978, "Teddy Bear" was reissued but did not chart, although it was listed as "Bubbling Under" at #105 for two weeks. "Teddy Bear"/"Loving You" was the first single to be released on the RCA label (RCA 1013) in Great Britain (July 1957).

Singles:
- "TEDDY BEAR"/"Loving You" (RCA 20-7000) June 1957. Standard 78 RPM release.
- "TEDDY BEAR"/"Loving You" (RCA 47-7000) June 1957. Standard 45 RPM release.
- "TEDDY BEAR"/"Loving You" (RCA 447-0620) March 1959. Gold Standard Series reissue.
- "TEDDY BEAR"/"Loving You" (RCA PB-11109) October 1977. One of 15 singles in the boxed set *15 Golden Records—30 Golden Hits* (RCA PP-11301), and the *20 Golden Hits in Full Color Sleeves* (RCA PP-11340) boxed set released two months later.
- "TEDDY BEAR"/"Puppet on a String" (RCA PB-11320) August 1978. New single release, pressed on green vinyl.
- "TEDDY BEAR"/"Loving You" (RCA JH-11320) August 1978. Disc jockey promotional release.
- "The Elvis Medley"/"Always on My Mind" (RCA PB-13351) November 1982. "The Elvis Medley" featured excerpts from "Jailhouse Rock," "Teddy Bear," "Hound Dog," "Don't Be Cruel," "Burning Love," and "Suspicious Minds."
- "The Elvis Medley"/"The Elvis Medley" (short version) (RCA JB-13351) November 1982. Disc jockey promotional release.
- "All Shook Up"/"TEDDY BEAR" (RCA PB-13888) October 1984. One of six singles in the boxed set *Elvis' Greatest Hits—Golden Singles, Volume 1* (RCA PP-13897). The record was pressed on gold vinyl with a special gold "50th" anniversary label.

EPs:
- *Dealers' Prevue* (RCA SDS-7-2)
- *Loving You, Volume 1*

LPs:
- *Elvis* (RCA DPL2-0056[e])
- *Elvis—A Canadian Tribute*
- *Elvis Aron Presley* (Dallas; June 6, 1975)
- *Elvis as Recorded at Madison Square Garden* (June 10, 1972)
- *Elvis' Golden Records*
- *Elvis in Concert* (Omaha, Nebraska; June 19, 1977) (in medley with "Don't Be Cruel")
- *The Elvis Medley*
- *Elvis Sings for Children and Grownups Too!*
- *Elvis: Worldwide 50 Gold Award Hits, Volume 1*
- *Loving You*
- *The Number One Hits*
- *This Is Elvis* (*Loving You* soundtrack)
- *The Top Ten Hits*

Bootleg LPs:
- *America's Own* (Uniondale, N.Y.; July 19, 1975)
- *From Las Vegas . . . to Niagara Falls* (Las Vegas; September 3, 1973) (Niagara Falls, N.Y.; June 24, 1974))
- *Got a Lot o' Livin' to Do!* (*Loving You* soundtrack)
- *The Last Farewell* (Indianapolis; June 26, 1977)
- *Loving You* (*Loving You* soundtrack)

- *Please Release Me* (*Loving You* soundtrack)
- *Sold Out* (Las Vegas; September 3, 1973) (in medley with "Don't Be Cruel")
- *The Vegas Years, 1972–1975* (Las Vegas; 1972)

TELL ME WHY
"Tell Me Why" was written by Titus Turner and first recorded by Marie Knight (Wing 90069) in early 1956. Later that year, both Gale Storm (Dot 15470) and the Crew Cuts (Mercury 70890) recorded the song.

Elvis recorded "Tell Me Why" on January 12, 1957, at Radio Recorders. Take #5 was chosen for release. "Tell Me Why" remained unreleased for nine years. When it was finally released as a single in 1966, it had a seven-week stay on *Billboard*'s Hot 100 chart, peaking at #33. Sales of over a million copies have been claimed for "Tell Me Why."

Singles:
- "TELL ME WHY"/"Blue River" (RCA 47-8740) December 1965. Standard release.
- "TELL ME WHY"/"Blue River" (RCA 447-0655) February 1968. Gold Standard Series reissue.

LPs:
- *Elvis: The Other Sides—Worldwide Gold Award Hits, Volume 2*
- *A Valentine Gift for You*

TENDER FEELING
Elvis sang "Tender Feeling" in his 1964 film *Kissin' Cousins*. The song, which was written by Bill Giant, Bernie Baum, and Florence Kaye, was recorded in October 1963 at RCA's Nashville studios.

LPs:
- *Burning Love and Hits from His Movies, Volume 2*
- *Kissin' Cousins*

TENNESSEE DANCIN' DOLL
According to some, Elvis may have recorded "Tennessee Dancin' Doll," but this has not been substantiated.

TENNESSEE PARTNER
Elvis sang "Tennessee Partner" on tour in 1955, although it is doubtful that he ever recorded it, as some have suggested.

TENNESSEE SATURDAY NIGHT
"Tennessee Saturday Night" was written by Billy Hughes and recorded by Red Foley (Decca 46292) in 1948. His recording reached #3 on the country chart. Other recordings include those by Ella Mae Morse (Capitol 1903) in 1951, Johnny Bond (Columbia 20545) in 1951, and Foley's son-in-law, Pat Boone, in 1954 (Dot 15377).

Elvis sang "Tennessee Saturday Night" on the "Louisiana Hayride" in 1955. Some have indicated that he recorded the song at Sun Records, but that has not yet been proved.

THANKS TO THE ROLLING SEA
Elvis sang "Thanks to the Rolling Sea" in his 1962 film *Girls! Girls! Girls!* The song, which was written by Ruth Batchelor and Bob Roberts, was recorded in March

1962 at Radio Recorders. The original release was a splice of takes #3 and #5.

LPs:
- *Elvis Aron Presley* (take #10, the a cappella version)
- *Girls! Girls! Girls!*

THAT LONESOME VALLEY

This traditional spiritual was arranged by W. Earl Mercer. Both the Carter Family (Vocalion 03112) and Roy Acuff (Vocalion 04730) had popular recordings of "That Lonesome Valley" in the 1940s under the title "Lonesome Valley." Another popular version was Stuart Hamblen's 1955 recording (RCA 47-6152). The Kingston Trio recorded the song as "Reverend Mr. Black" (Capitol 4951) in 1963, reaching #8 on the Hot 100 chart. It was their second most successful recording, after the number one hit "Tom Dooley."

Elvis and Jerry Lee Lewis sang "That Lonesome Valley" during the Million-Dollar-Quartet session, alternating leads.

Bootleg LPs:
- *The Million Dollar Quartet* (Sun Records; December 4, 1956)
- *The One Million Dollar Quartet* (Sun Records; December 4, 1956)

THAT'S ALL RIGHT (MAMA)

Arthur (Big Boy) Crudup wrote and recorded "That's All Right (Mama)" in 1946 under the title "I Don't Know It." In 1949 he again recorded the song—this time as "That's All Right (Mama)" (RCA 50-0000). The flip side was "Crudup's After Hours."

Elvis recorded "That's All Right (Mama)" on the evening of July 5, 1954—his first commercial recording session at Sun Records. As Scotty Moore tells it, he, Elvis, and Bill Black were taking a break in the studio, having already put "Harbor Lights" and "I Love You

The original acetate given to Dewey Phillips on July 7, 1954. (Photo courtesy Jeff Wheatcraft)

Because" on tape, when Elvis began cutting up by singing "That's All Right (Mama)." Moore and Black joined him. Sam Phillips popped out of the control room and asked Elvis what he was doing and would he please do it again. Within a short time, an acceptable take was recorded and Elvis had the A side of his first release. The following evening, "Blue Moon of Kentucky" was recorded as the B side.

Phillips quickly made some acetates of "That's All Right (Mama)"/"Blue Moon of Kentucky" and gave copies to Dewey Phillips of WHBQ, Uncle Richard of WMPS, and Sleepy-Eyed John Lepley of WHHM. On the evening of July 7, 1954, at about nine-thirty, Dewey Phillps played "That's All Right (Mama)" on his radio program "Red, Hot and Blue." When he learned that Phillips was going to play his record, Elvis went to the Suzore No. 2 Theatre to see *The Best Years of Our Lives.* Before leaving home he turned the radio on to WHBQ and told his parents to listen to the program. Legend has it that Phillips played "That's All Right (Mama)" fourteen times and received forty-seven telephone calls from listeners. Wanting to do an interview with Elvis, he called the Presley home. Vernon had to run down to the theatre to get Elvis.

When Elvis arrived at the WHBQ studios, Phillips cautioned him not to say anything dirty. He then cued up a couple of records and began asking Elvis questions. One of the first was where he went to school. When Elvis answered "Humes High," Phillips's audience immediately knew that he was white, since Humes was an all-white school. Many of the listeners had thought the singer was black. After a brief chat, Phillips thanked Elvis. When Elvis asked when he was going to be interviewed, Phillips said that he had just finished interviewing him—the mike had been on all the time. Elvis broke out into a cold sweat.

"That's All Right (Mama)" was officially released on July 19, 1954. Fewer than twenty thousand copies were sold. It did not chart nationally, but reached #4 in Memphis.

Probably the first cover record of Elvis's "That's All Right (Mama)" was by Smiley Maxedon in September 1954 (Columbia 21301). Another cover version was recorded by Marty Robbins (Columbia 21351) in December 1954. Robbins reached #9 on *Billboard*'s country chart and easily outsold Elvis's recording.

Elvis sang "That's All Right (Mama)" on his Grand Ole Opry appearance on October 2, 1954, and during his first appearance on the "Louisiana Hayride" on October 16, 1954. Elvis recorded the song for his 1968 TV special "Elvis," but it was not used. A July 1970 rehearsal of the song at the MGM studios, as well as an August 10, 1970, performance at the International Hotel, were used in the documentary *Elvis—That's the Way It Is.* The Sun recording was heard on the soundtrack of the 1972 documentary *Elvis on Tour.* A June 21, 1977, performance at Rapid City, South Dakota, was used in the TV special "Elvis In Concert," and a remix of the Sun recording was heard in the 1981 documentary *This Is Elvis.*

Singles:
- "THAT'S ALL RIGHT (MAMA)"/"Blue Moon of Kentucky" (Sun 209) July 19, 1954. Standard Sun 78 RPM and 45 RPM release.
- "THAT'S ALL RIGHT (MAMA)"/"Blue Moon of Kentucky" (RCA 20-6380) November 1955. Standard 78 RPM reissue of the Sun original release.
- "THAT'S ALL RIGHT (MAMA)"/"Blue Moon of Kentucky" (RCA 47-6380) November 1955. Standard 45 RPM reissue of the Sun original release.
- "THAT'S ALL RIGHT (MAMA)"/"Blue Moon of Kentucky" (RCA 447-0601) March 1959. Gold Standard Series reissue.
- "THAT'S ALL RIGHT (MAMA)"/"Blue Moon of Kentucky" (RCA PB-13891) October 1984. One of six singles in the boxed set *Elvis' Greatest Hits—Golden Singles, Volume 2* (RCA PP-13898). The record was pressed on gold vinyl with a special gold "50th" anniversary label.

EPs:
- *SPD-15*
- *A Touch of Gold, Volume 2*

LPs:
- *The Complete Sun Sessions* (Sun master and outtake)
- *Elvis—A Legendary Performer, Volume 1*
- *Elvis—A Legendary Performer, Volume 4* ("Elvis" TV special taping; June 27, 1968, at 8:00 P.M. show)
- *Elvis Aron Presley* (USS *Arizona* Memorial; March 25, 1961)
- *Elvis as Recorded Live at Madison Square Garden* (June 10, 1972)
- *Elvis in Concert* (Rapid City, South Dakota; June 21, 1977)
- *Elvis: The First Live Recordings* ("Louisiana Hayride"; August 6 or 27, 1955)
- *Elvis: The Hillbilly Cat* ("Louisiana Hayride"; October 16, 1954)
- *For LP Fans Only* (alternate mix, with more reverberation)
- *The Sun Sessions* (alternate mix, with more reverberation)
- *A Golden Celebration* (alternate take) ("Elvis" TV special taping; June 27, 1968, 8:00 P.M. show)
- *This Is Elvis* (remix)

Bootleg LPs:
- *The Burbank Sessions, Volume 1* ("Elvis" TV special taping; June 27, 1968, at 6:00 P.M. and 8:00 P.M. shows)
- *Cadillac Elvis* ("Elvis" TV special taping; June 27, 1968, at 6:00 P.M. show)
- *Elvis' 1961 Hawaii Benefit Concert* (USS *Arizona* Memorial; March 25, 1961)
- *The Entertainer* ("Louisiana Hayride"; October 16, 1954) (Houston; January 29, 1955)
- *Eternal Elvis, Volume 2* (a portion of the Sun recording)
- *The First Year—Recorded Live* (Houston; January 29, 1955) ("Louisiana Hayride"; October 16, 1954)
- *The First Years* (Houston; January 29, 1955)
- *The Hillbilly Cat "Live"* (Las Vegas; August 1970)
- *The King: From the Dark to the Light* (*Elvis—That's the Way It Is* soundtrack)
- *King of Las Vegas Live* (*Elvis—That's the Way It Is* soundtrack)
- *The Rockin' Rebel, Volume 2* (Houston; January 29, 1955) ("Louisiana Hayride"; October 16, 1954)
- *Special Delivery from Elvis Presley* (*Elvis—That's the Way It Is* soundtrack)
- *Standing Room Only, Volume 3* (Madison Square Garden; June 10, 1972)
- *The Sun Years* (two Sun takes)
- *That's the Way It Is* (*Elvis—That's the Way It Is* soundtrack)

THAT'S AMORE
"That's Amore" was written by Jack Brooks and Harry Warren and introduced by Dean Martin in the 1953 Dean Martin–Jerry Lewis comedy film *The Caddy*. Martin's recording (Capitol 2589) reached #2 on *Billboard*'s Best-Selling Singles chart and became his first million-seller. The Blue Barron Orchestra had a release of "That's Amore" (MGM 11584) at about the same as Martin's, but it did not chart.

Author Vince Staten, in his book *The Real Elvis: Good Old Boy*, said that Elvis sang "That's Amore" on stage at the Eagle's Nest in Memphis in October 1953. Introduced by Dewey Phillips, Elvis was backed by the house band—Johnny Long's Orchestra. If this is true, this would have been Elvis's first professional appearance, before he recorded for Sun Records, and would prove that Elvis had every intention of becoming a professional singer. It's doubtful, however, that Elvis and Dewey Phillips met before July 1954. Another item to consider is that Martin's recording didn't even chart until November 1953.

THAT'S MY DESIRE
Carroll Loveday and Helmy Kresa wrote "That's My Desire" in 1931. Sixteen years later, both Frankie Laine (Mercury 5007) and Sammy Kaye (RCA 2251) had big hits with the song, reaching #7 and #3 respectively on *Billboard*'s Best-Selling Singles chart. Laine's recording was his first million-seller.

"That's My Desire" was sung by Elvis during the Million-Dollar-Quartet session. In 1968 the song was one of many that he rehearsed for the "Elvis" TV special but did not use in the broadcast.

Bootleg LPs:
- *Elvis Rocks and the Girls Roll* (dress rehearsal for "Elvis"; June 1968)
- *The One Million Dollar Quartet* (Sun Records; December 4, 1956)

THAT'S SOMEONE YOU NEVER FORGET
"That's Someone You Never Forget" was written by Red West and recorded by Elvis on June 25, 1961, at RCA's Nashville studios. Six years later, the single release spent one week on the Hot chart at #92.

Singles:
- "Long Legged Girl (with the Short Dress On)"/"THAT'S SOMEONE YOU NEVER FORGET" (RCA 47-9115) May 1967. The original picture sleeve read, "Coming Soon—DOUBLE TROUBLE Album." One month later the sleeve was changed to read, "Ask for—DOUBLE TROUBLE Album."
- "Long Legged Girl (with the Short Dress On)"/"THAT'S SOMEONE YOU NEVER FORGET" (RCA 447-0660) 1970. Gold Standard Series reissue.

LPs:
- *Pot Luck*

THAT'S THE STUFF YOU GOTTA WATCH
"That's the Stuff You Gotta Watch" was written and recorded by Woodrow Wilson (Buddy) Johnnson (Decca 8671) in 1944. The vocalist in his band was Arthur Prysock. Wynonie Harris had a popular recording of the song in 1945 (Apollo 361).

Elvis is reported to have sung "That's the Stuff You Gotta Watch" on the "Louisiana Hayride" in 1955.

Although some have suggested that Elvis recorded the song at Sun Records, that doesn't seem likely, and there is no supporting evidence.

THAT'S WHEN YOUR HEARTACHES BEGIN

"That's When Your Heartaches Begin" was written by William J. Raskin, Billy Hill, and Fred Fisher in 1940. In 1950 the Ink Spots made a successful recording of the song (Decca 25505). The spoken interlude was by Orville (Hoppy) Jones. Bob Lamb (Dot 1050) in 1951 and Billy Bunn and His Buddies (RCA 47-4657) in 1952 also had releases of "That's When Your Heartaches Begin."

Sometime during the summer of 1953 (probably August or September), Elvis walked into the Memphis Recording Service to cut two songs on a four-dollar acetate. The first was "My Happiness," and the second was "That's When Your Heartaches Begin." (For more information of this story, see the *Memphis Recording Service* entry in Part I.) Elvis left the studio with the only copy of the acetate. It's been rumored that "My Happiness"/"That's When Your Heartaches Begin" was transferred onto tape by Elvis at a later date and that the tape has survived.

It appears that, of the four songs Elvis committed to acetate in 1953 and on January 4, 1954, only "That's When Your Heartaches Begin" was ever recorded in the studio at RCA or Sun. The recording session took place on January 13, 1957, at Radio Recorders in Hollywood. Take #7 was selected by RCA for release on record. Elvis's single had a seven-week stay on *Billboard*'s Top 100 chart, peaking at #58.

During the Million-Dollar-Quartet session in 1956, Elvis sang "That's When Your Heartaches Begin" and commented briefly that it was one of the songs he recorded on the first acetate in 1953.

Elvis rehearsed "That's When Your Heartaches Begin" in mid-June 1968 for his TV special "Elvis," but did not record it for the program.

Singles:
- "All Shook Up"/"THAT'S WHEN YOUR HEARTACHES BEGIN" (RCA 20-6870) March 1957. Standard 78 RPM release.
- "All Shook Up"/"THAT'S WHEN YOUR HEARTACHES BEGIN" (RCA 47-6870) March 1957. Standard 45 RPM release.
- "All Shook Up"/"THAT'S WHEN YOUR HEARTACHES BEGIN" (RCA 447-0660) March 1959. Gold Standard Series reissue.
- "All Shook Up"/"THAT'S WHEN YOUR HEARTACHES BEGIN" (RCA PB-11106) October 1977. One of 15 singles in the boxed set, *15 Golden Records—30 Golden Hits* (RCA PP-11301), and the *20 Golden Hits in Full Color Sleeves* (RCA PP-11340) boxed set released two months later.

LPs:
- *Elvis' Golden Records*
- *Elvis: Worldwide 50 Gold Award Hits, Volume 1*

Bootleg LPs:
- *Got A Lot O' Livin' to Do!* (Vancouver, British Columbia; September 1, 1957)
- *Elvis Rocks and the Girls Roll* (dress rehearsals for "Elvis"; June 1968)
- *The One Million Dollar Quartet* (Sun Records; December 4, 1956)

THERE AIN'T NOTHING LIKE A SONG

Elvis sang "There Ain't Nothing Like a Song" in his 1968 film *Speedway*, in a duet with Nancy Sinatra. The song was written by Joy Byers and William Johnston. The instrumental track was recorded in June 1967 at MGM's Culver City studios.

LPs:
- *Speedway*

THERE GOES MY EVERYTHING

Dallas Frazier wrote "There Goes My Everything" in 1965, basing it on the broken marriage of two friends. Jack Greene took the song to the top of the country chart in 1967. His recording (Decca 32023) was named Single of the Year at the annual Country Music Association awards. Composer Frazier received a CMA award for Song of the Year. In 1967 Englebert Humperdinck had a million-seller with "There Goes My Everything" (Parrot 40015), reaching #20 on *Billboard*'s Hot 100 chart. Another popular recording that year was by Sue Raney (Imperial 66222).

Elvis recorded "There Goes My Everything" on June 8, 1970, at RCA's Nashville studios. His single release had a nine-week stay on the Hot 100 chart, peaking at #21. On the country chart, the song, paired with "I Really Don't Want To Know," reached #9—Elvis's first top 10 country record since 1958. "There Goes My Everything" peaked at #2 on the Easy-Listening chart. Only Bobby Goldsboro's "Watching Scotty Grow" kept it from the top spot.

Singles:
- "I Really Don't Want to Know"/"THERE GOES MY EVERYTHING" (RCA 47-9960) December 1970. Standard release. The original picture sleeve read, "Coming Soon—New Album. I'm Ten Thousand Years Old. ELVIS COUNTRY." One month later, the sleeve was changed to read, "Now Available—New Album. I'm Ten Thousand Years Old. ELVIS COUNTRY."
- "I Really Don't Want to Know"/"THERE GOES MY EVERYTHING" (RCA 447-0679) February 1972. Gold Standard Series reissue.
- "You'll Never Walk Alone"/"THERE GOES MY EVERYTHING" (RCA PB-13058) February 1982. New single release.
- "You'll Never Walk Alone"/"THERE GOES MY EVERYTHING" (RCA JB-13058) February 1982. Disc jockey promotional release.

LPs:
- *Elvis Country*
- *Elvis: The Other Sides—Worldwide Gold Award Hits, Volume 2*
- *Greatest Hits, Volume 1*

Bootleg LPs:
- *A Dog's Life* (alternate take)

THERE IS NO GOD BUT GOD

"There Is No God but God" was written by Bill Kenny (former lead singer of the Ink Spots) and undoubtedly recorded by him in the 1950s, but the authors have yet to find his release.

Elvis recorded "There Is No God but God" on June 9, 1971, at RCA's Nashville studios.

LPs:
- *He Touched Me*

THERE IS SO MUCH WORLD TO SEE

Elvis sang "There Is So Much World to See" in his 1967 film *Double Trouble*. The song, which was written by Sid Tepper and Ben Weisman, was recorded by Elvis in June 1966 at Radio Recorders.

LPs:
• *Double Trouble*

THERE'S A BRAND NEW DAY
ON THE HORIZON

Joy Byers wrote "There's a Brand New Day on the Horizon" for Elvis's 1964 film *Roustabout*. Elvis recorded the song in February or March 1964 at Radio Recorders. The film version was slightly different than the one on record.

LPs:
• *Roustabout*

THERE'S A FIRE DOWN BELOW

Elvis's bass player Jerry Scheff wrote "There's a Fire Down Below." The instrumental track was recorded on the night of October 30–31, 1976, at Graceland. Sherrill Nielsen says he provided a vocal track for the band to follow. There's no record of Elvis having ever recorded a vocal track for the song, but Felton Jarvis once said that Elvis did.

THERE'S A HONKY TONK ANGEL
(WHO WILL TAKE ME BACK IN)

"There's a Honky Tonk Angel (Who Will Take Me Back In)" was written by Troy Seals and Denny Rice and first recorded by Conway Twitty in late 1973. In 1974 Twitty's recording (MGM 40173) topped *Billboard*'s country chart.

Shortly after Conway Twitty recorded "There's A Honky Tonk Angel (Who Will Take Me Back In)," Elvis went into Stax Studios in Memphis to record the song. The session took place on December 15, 1973. RCA released the song as a single in 1979. It reached #6 during its 13-week stay on the country chart.

Singles:
• "THERE'S A HONKY TONK ANGEL (WHO WILL TAKE ME BACK IN)"/ "I've Got a Feelin' in My Body" (RCA PB-11679) August 1979. Standard release.
• "THERE'S A HONKY TONK ANGEL (WHO WILL TAKE ME BACK IN)"/ "I've Got a Feelin' in My Body" (RCA JB-11679) August 1979. Disc jockey promotional release.

LPs:
• *Our Memories of Elvis, Volume 2* (without overdubbing)
• *Promised Land*

THERE'S ALWAYS ME

Don Robertson wrote "There's Always Me" for Elvis, who recorded the song on March 13, 1961, at RCA's Nashville studios. The single release six years later had a six-week stay on *Billboard*'s Hot 100 chart, reaching a high of #56.

In 1979 Ray Price had a #30 country hit with "There's Always Me" (Monument 45-277).

Singles:
• "THERE'S ALWAYS ME"/"Judy" (RCA 47-9287) August 1967. Standard release.
• "THERE'S ALWAYS ME"/"Judy" (RCA 447-0661) 1970. Gold Standard Series reissue.

LPs:
• *Something for Everybody*

THERE'S GOLD IN THE MOUNTAINS

Elvis sang "There's Gold in the Mountains" in his 1964 film *Kissin' Cousins*. The song, which was written by Bill Giant, Bernie Baum, and Florence Kaye, was recorded by Elvis in October 1963 at RCA's Nashville studios.

LPs:
• *Kissin' Cousins*

THEY REMIND ME TOO MUCH OF YOU

"They Remind Me Too Much of You" was written by Don Robertson for Elvis's 1963 movie *It Happened at the World's Fair*. Elvis recorded the song on September 22, 1962, at Radio Recorders. The single release had a four-week stay on *Billboard*'s Hot 100 chart, peaking at #53.

Singles:
• "One Broken Heart for Sale"/"THEY REMIND ME TOO MUCH OF YOU" (RCA 47-8134) February 1963. Standard release.
• "One Broken Heart for Sale"/"THEY REMIND ME TOO MUCH OF YOU" (RCA 447-0640) August 1984. Gold Standard Series reissue.

LPs:
• *Elvis Aron Presley* (take #1)
• *Elvis in Hollywood*
• *Elvis Sings Hits from His Movies, Volume 1*
• *Elvis: The Other Sides—Worldwide Gold Award Hits, Volume 2*
• *It Happened at the World's Fair*

A THING CALLED LOVE

"A Thing Called Love" was written by Jerry Reed and first recorded by Jimmy Dean (RCA 47-9454) in 1968. Dean's recording reached #21 on *Billboard*'s country chart. The next year, Reed recorded his own composition, also for RCA Records (RCA 74-0242). Johnny Cash took "A Thing Called Love" (Columbia 45534) to #2 on the country chart in 1972.

Elvis recorded "A Thing Called Love" on May 19, 1971, at RCA's Nashville studios.

LPs:
• *He Touched Me*

THINKING ABOUT YOU

Elvis recorded "Thinking About You" on December 12, 1973, at Stax Studios. His single release did not chart. "Thinking About You" was composed by Tim Baty.

Singles:
• "My Boy"/"THINKING ABOUT YOU" (RCA PB-10191) January 1975. Standard release.
• "My Boy"/"THINKING ABOUT YOU" (RCA GB-10489) February 1976. Gold Standard Series reissue.

LPs:
- *Our Memories of Elvis, Volume 2* (without overdubbing)
- *Promised Land*

THIS IS LIVING

Elvis sang "This Is Living" in his 1962 film *Kid Galahad*. The song, which was written by Fred Wise and Ben Weisman, was recorded on October 27, 1961, at Radio Recorders. Take #10 was selected for release. Reportedly, the original title was "Let's Live a Little."

EPs:
- *Kid Galahad*

LPs:
- *C'mon Everybody*

Bootleg LPs:
- *Behind Closed Doors* (take #3)
- *The Complete Kid Galahad Session, Volume 3* (takes #1–9)

THIS IS MY HEAVEN

Bill Giant, Bernie Baum, and Florence Kaye wrote "This Is My Heaven" for Elvis's 1965 film *Paradise, Hawaiian Style*. The instrumental track was recorded on July 27, 1965, at Radio Recorders. Elvis's vocal was recorded on August 2. The film version had added instrumentation. RCA spliced takes #6 and #8 for release.

LPs:
- *Paradise, Hawaiian Style*

Bootleg LPs:
- *Behind Closed Doors* (take #3)
- *Hawaii USA* (takes #2 and #4)

A studio pressing from the American Sound Studios sessions. Note that the instrumental track "Come Out, Come Out" is on this side, along with "I'm Movin' On," "Wearin' That Loved on Look," "This Is the Story," and "Gentle on My Mind." (Photo courtesy Don Fink)

THIS IS OUR DANCE

"This Is Our Dance" was written by Les Reed and Geoff Stephens and recorded by Elvis on June 6, 1970, at RCA's Nashville studios.

LPs:
- *Love Letters from Elvis*

THIS IS THE STORY

Elvis recorded "This Is the Story" at the American Sound Studios in Memphis on January 13, 1969. The song was composed by Chris Arnold, Geoffrey Morrow, and David Martin.

LPs:
- *Back in Memphis*
- *From Memphis to Vegas/From Vegas to Memphis*

THREE CORN PATCHES

"Three Corn Patches" was written by Jerry Leiber and Mike Stoller and recorded by T-Bone Walker[1] (Reprise 2X56483) in early 1973.

Elvis recorded "Three Corn Patches" on July 21, 1973, at Stax Studios.

LPs:
- *Raised on Rock/For Ol' Times Sake*

THRILL OF YOUR LOVE

Stan Kesler wrote "Thrill of Your Love" for Elvis, who recorded the song on April 4, 1960, at RCA's Nashville studios.

LPs:
- *Elvis Is Back*

TIGER MAN

"Tiger Man" was written by Joe Hill Louis and Sam Burns and recorded by Louis on November 17, 1952. His recording was not released. In 1953 Rufus Thomas recorded "Tiger Man" at Sun Records, with Joe Hill Louis playing guitar. Thomas's recording, which mentioned "hound dog" and "bearcat" in the lyrics, did not chart. Kenneth Banks played bass on both versions.

Some have speculated that Elvis recorded "Tiger Man" at Sun Records, but that has not been substantiated. Elvis *did* sing "Tiger Man" in concert on a number of occasions, usually in medley with "Mystery Train." The August 17, 1969, rebroadcast of the "Elvis" TV special used "Tiger Man" as a replacement for "Blue Christmas," which was sung in the original December 3, 1968, telecast. An August 10, 1970, performance at the International Hotel in Las Vegas was used in the documentary *Elvis—That's the Way It Is*.

LPs:
- *Elvis Aron Presley* (Shreveport, Louisiana; June 7, 1975) (in medley with "Mystery Train")
- *Elvis in Person* (Las Vegas; August 26, 1969) (in medley with "Mystery Train")
- *Elvis Sings Flaming Star* ("Elvis" TV special taping; June 27, 1968, at 8:00 P.M. show)

[1]T-Bone Walker (real name: Aaron Thibeaux Walker) was part Cherokee Indian. As a boy, he served as a guide for blues singer Blind Lemon Jefferson.

- *From Memphis to Vegas/From Vegas to Memphis* (Las Vegas; August 26, 1969) (in medley with "Mystery Train")
- *A Golden Celebration* ("Elvis" TV special taping; June 27, 1968, at 8:00 P.M. show)
- *Singer Presents Flaming Star and Others* ("Elvis" TV special taping; June 27, 1968, at 8:00 P.M. show)

Bootleg LPs:
- *America's Own* (Uniondale, N.Y.; July 19, 1975) (in medley with "Mystery Train")
- *The Burbank Sessions, Volume 1* ("Elvis" TV special taping; June 27, 1968, at 8:00 P.M. show)
- *Command Performance* (Las Vegas; August 4, 1972)
- *The Hillbilly Cat "Live"* (Las Vegas; August 1970)
- *King of Las Vegas Live* (*Elvis—That's the Way It Is* soundtrack, without "Mystery Train")
- *Long Lost Songs* (Las Vegas; 1975)
- *Sold Out* (Las Vegas; September 3, 1973)
- *Standing Room Only, Volume 2* ("Elvis" TV special taping; June 27, 1968, at 8:00 P.M. show)
- *That's the Way It Is* (*Elvis—That's the Way It Is* (in medley with "Mystery Train")

TILL I WALTZ AGAIN WITH YOU
Teresa Brewer had a number one hit and million-seller with "Till I Waltz Again with You" in early 1953. The song was written by Sidney Posen. A cover record by country artist Charlie Gore was recorded in mid-1953 (King 1169). Interestingly, "Till I Waltz Again with You" is not a waltz.

According to some published reports, Elvis sang "Till I Waltz Again with You" at the Humes High School annual Christmas show in December 1952. Since Teresa Brewer's record was released in early December, that is entirely possible. More than likely, however, Elvis sang "Till I Waltz Again with You" at the Humes High School Minstrel Show on April 9, 1953—if at all.

TIP-TOE THROUGH THE TULIPS (WITH ME)
"Tip-Toe Through the Tulips (with me)" was written by Al Dubin and Joseph A. Burke in 1929 for the movie musical *Gold Diggers of Broadway*. In 1968 Tiny Tim (real name: Herbert Khaury) revived the song in a best-selling record (Reprise 0679) that reached #17 on *Billboard*'s Hot 100 chart.

During the 8:00 P.M. taping of the "Elvis" TV special on June 29, 1968, Elvis humorously sang one line of "Tip-Toe Through the Tulips (with me)."

TODAY, TOMORROW AND FOREVER
Elvis sang "Today, Tomorrow and Forever" in his 1964 film *Viva Las Vegas*. He recorded the song on July 11, 1963, at Radio Recorders. Three versions were recorded: The first version (master, take #6) has never been released. The second (master, take #4) was released by RCA on record. A third version (master, take #4) was used in the film, but has been released on bootlegs only. "Today, Tomorrow and Forever" was written by Bill Giant, Bernie Baum, and Florence Kaye

based on "Liebestraume," Franz Liszt's[1] 1850 composition.

EPs:
- *Viva Las Vegas*

LPs:
- *C'mon Everybody*

Bootleg LPs:
- *Viva Las Vegas!* (alternate take, second version)

TOMORROW IS A LONG TIME
Elvis recorded "Tomorrow Is a Long Time," a Bob Dylan–written tune, on May 26, 1966, at RCA's Nashville studios. Dylan's single was not released until five years later (Columbia AE71039).

LPs:
- *Spinout*
- *A Valentine Gift for You*

TOMORROW NEVER COMES
"Tomorrow Never Comes" was written by Ernest Tubb and Johnny Bond and first recorded by Tubb in early 1949 (Decca 46106). In 1966 B. J. Thomas reached #80 on *Billboard*'s Hot 100 chart with his recording of the song (Scepter 12165). Slim Whitman had a popular country version (Imperial 66441) that peaked at #27.

Elvis recorded "Tomorrow Never Comes" on June 7, 1970, at RCA's Nashville studios.

LPs:
- *Elvis Country*

Bootleg LPs:
- *Behind Closed Doors* (alternate mix, without overdubbing)
- *Special Delivery from Elvis Presley* (alternate mix, without overdubbing)

TOMORROW NIGHT
"Tomorrow Night" was written by Sam Coslow and Will Grosz in 1939. One of the first recordings that year was by Horace Heidt and His Orchestra (Columbia 35203), with vocal by the Heidt-Lights. Lonnie Johnson (who played guitar on some of Bessie Smith's recordings) had a million-seller with the song in 1948 (King 4201). Another popular version of "Tomorrow Night" was recorded by LaVern Baker in late 1954. It was the flip side of her hit, "Tweedlee Dee" (Atlantic 1047).

Elvis recorded "Tomorrow Night" at Sun Records on September 10, 1954, with his only accompaniment being Scotty Moore's guitar playing. Since LaVern Baker's recording hadn't yet been released, it was Lonnie Johnson's version that influenced his styling. On March 18, 1965, a new backing track was recorded by RCA with the Anita Kerr Singers, Chet Atkins (guitar), Grady Martin (guitar), Henry Strzelecki (bass), Buddy Harman (drums), and Charlie McCoy (harmonica). The overdubbed version of "Tomorrow Night" was re-

---

[1] Hungarian-born composer Liszt was the father-in-law of composer Richard Wagner. One of Liszt's piano students was Katherine Delaney O'Hara, mother of author John O'Hara.

leased on the *Elvis for Everyone* LP, nine years after Elvis recorded it. For several years it was feared the original master of "Tomorrow Night" was either lost or destroyed. That fear proved to be unfounded, as RCA released the original version in 1985 on the *Reconsider Baby* album.

While visiting the Waco, Texas, home of disc jockey Eddie Fadal in the summer of 1958, Elvis briefly sang the bass line while listening to LaVern Baker's recording of "Tomorrow Night."

LPs:
- *The Complete Sun Sessions* (Sun master)
- *Elvis for Everyone* (Sun master with overdubbing)
- *Reconsider Baby* (Sun master)

Bootleg LPs:
- *Eternal Elvis, Volume 2* (*Elvis for Everyone* version)
- *Forever Young, Forever Beautiful* (Waco, Texas; summer 1958) (Elvis sang bass line to LaVern Baker's recording)

TONIGHT IS SO RIGHT FOR LOVE
Elvis sang "Tonight Is So Right for Love" in his 1960 film *G. I. Blues*. The song was recorded on April 28, 1960, at RCA's Hollywood studios. Composers Sid Wayne and Abner Silver based the melody on "Baca- rolle" by Jacques Offenbach. Because of copyright problems, "Tonight Is So Right for Love" couldn't be released in Europe. Instead, "Tonight's All Right for Love" (similar lyrics, different melody) was recorded for insertion into European releases of *G. I. Blues*. Although the 1980 boxed set *Elvis Aron Presley* listed "Tonight Is So Right for Love" in its contents, the song actually on record was "Tonight's All Right for Love." An alternate take of "Tonight Is So Right for Love" appeared on the 1988 Compact Disc release of *G. I. Blues*. (See *Tonight's All Right for Love*)

LPs:
- *Burning Love and Hits from His Movies, Volume 2*
- *G. I. Blues*

TONIGHT'S ALL RIGHT FOR LOVE
Elvis recorded "Tonight's All Right for Love" for the European editions of *G. I. Blues*. "Tonight Is So Right for Love" couldn't be used because of copyright rea- sons. Sid Wayne, Abner Silver, and Joe Lilley slightly altered the lyrics of "Tonight Is So Right for Love" and used the melody to Johann Strauss's classic "Tales from the Vienna Woods," written in 1868. The title originally considered for this song was "Vienna Woods Rock and Roll." Elvis's recording session for the new song took place at Radio Recorders on May 6, 1960. "Tonight's All Right for Love" was finally released in the United States in 1974 on the LP *Elvis—A Legendary Performer, Volume 1*. The version on the album, how- ever, was edited. The complete recording was released as a single in West Germany, backed with "Wooden Heart," as well as on many foreign LPs. Although the boxed set *Elvis Aron Presley* listed "Tonight Is So Right for Love" in its contents, it was actually "Tonight's All Right for Love."

LPs:
- *Elvis—A Legendary Performer, Volume 1* (edited version)
- *Elvis Aron Presley* (takes #2 [ending], #3 [false start], #4 [false start], #7 [false start], and #8 [complete take])

TOO LATE TO WORRY, TOO BLUE TO CRY
"Too Late to Worry, Too Blue to Cry" was written by Al Dexter in 1944 and recorded that year by his group, the Troopers (Okeh 6718). Glen Campbell recorded the song in 1962 (Capitol 4783), reaching #76 on the Hot 100 chart. In 1969 Little Esther Phillips had the only hit version to date. She reached #35 on *Billboard*'s rhythm & blues chart (Roulette 7031).

Some sources have indicated that Elvis recorded "Too Late to Worry, Too Blue to Cry" in the 1960s or 1970s, but no proof has been forthcoming.

TOO MUCH
"Too Much" was written by Lee Rosenberg and Ber- nard Weinman, and first recorded by Bernard Hardi- son in 1954 (Republic 7111). His version failed to chart. That same year Judy Tremaine (Coral 61150) had a release of "Too Much," as did Frankie Castro (Mercury 70873) in the summer of 1956, both failing to chart.

According to legend, Lee Rosenberg gave "Too Much" to Elvis as the singer was boarding a train for Los Angeles, but Rosenberg has denied the story. Elvis recorded the song on September 2, 1956, at Radio Re- corders. Take #12 was selected by RCA for release. Elvis's single release had a 17-week stay on *Billboard*'s Top 100 chart, peaking at #2 (where it stayed for four weeks). Only Tab Hunter's "Young Love" kept "Too Much" from ascending to the top spot. Sales easily exceeded a million copies. Elvis sang "Too Much" on his third appearance on "The Ed Sullivan Show" (Jan- uary 6, 1957).

In late 1957 Dickey Lee's first Sun release, "Good Lovin' " (Sun 280), closely resembled "Too Much."

Singles:
- "TOO MUCH"/"Playing for Keeps" (RCA 20-6800) January 1957. Standard 78 RPM release.
- "TOO MUCH"/"Playing for Keeps" (RCA 47-6800) January 1957. Standard 45 RPM release.
- "TOO MUCH"/"Playing for Keeps" (RCA 447-0617) March 1959. Gold Standard Series reissue.

EPs:
- *DJ-56*
- *A Touch of Gold, Volume 3*

LPs:
- *Elvis' Golden Records*
- *Elvis: Worldwide 50 Gold Award Hits, Volume 1*
- *A Golden Celebration* ("The Ed Sullivan Show"; January 6, 1957)
- *The Number One Hits*
- *The Top Ten Hits*

Bootleg LPs:
- *From the Waist Up* ("The Ed Sullivan Show"; January 6, 1957)
- *The King Goes Wild* ("The Ed Sullivan Show"; January 6, 1957)

TOO MUCH MONKEY BUSINESS
Chuck Berry wrote and recorded "Too Much Monkey

Business" (Chess 1635) in 1956. His version peaked at #7 on the rhythm & blues chart. Later in 1956, the Gadabouts recorded a cover version of "Too Much Monkey Business" (Mercury 70978) that did not chart. Bob Dylan's 1965 hit "Subterranean Homesick Blues" (Columbia 43242) was based on Berry's recording.

Elvis recorded "Too Much Monkey Business" on January 15, 1968, at RCA's Nashville studios. Jerry Reed played lead guitar. On October 14, 1980, Felton Jarvis produced a new instrumental track at Young 'Un Sound in Nashville for the *Guitar Man* album. Lead guitar was again played by Jerry Reed. "Too Much Monkey Business" could be heard in the 1981 documentary *This Is Elvis*.

LPs:
- *Elvis Sings Flaming Star*
- *Guitar Man* (new instrumental track overdubbed)
- *Singer Presents Elvis Singing Flaming Star and Others*
- *This Is Elvis* (RCA says this is an alternate take, but it's probably an alternate mix with the second verse omitted)

TREAT ME NICE
Jerry Leiber and Mike Stoller wrote "Treat Me Nice" for Elvis's third film, *Jailhouse Rock*. Elvis recorded two versions of the song. The movie version was recorded on April 30, 1957, at Radio Recorders. Take #10 was used on the film soundtrack. This version remained unreleased by RCA until 1988. The record version of "Treat Me Nice" was recorded on September 5, 1957, at Radio Recorders. Take #15 was selected by RCA for release. Elvis's single release had a 10-week stay on *Billboard*'s Top 100 chart, reaching #27. Paired with "Jailhouse Rock," "Treat Me Nice" succeeded Jimmie Rodgers's "Honeycomb" at number one on the rhythm & blues chart. After a five-week stay at the top spot, it was replaced by "You Send Me" by Sam Cooke. "Jailhouse Rock" was on the country chart for 24 weeks. For nine of those weeks, "Treat Me Nice" was also listed, one week at the top. Sales exceeded one million copies.

Singles:
- "Jailhouse Rock"/"TREAT ME NICE" (RCA 20-7035) September 1957. Standard 78 RPM release. In October 1957 MGM prepared a special promotional cover that wrapped around the normal picture sleeve. The promo was used for a special press preview of *Jailhouse Rock* at MGM on October 10.
- "Jailhouse Rock"/"TREAT ME NICE" (RCA 47-7035) September 1957. Standard 45 RPM release.
- "Jailhouse Rock"/"TREAT ME NICE" (RCA 447-0619) 1961. Gold Standard Series reissue.
- "Jailhouse Rock"/"TREAT ME NICE" (RCA PB-11101) October 1977. One of 15 singles released in the boxed set *15 Golden Records—30 Golden Hits* (RCA PP-11301). The single was pressed on gold vinyl with a special gold "50th" anniversary label.

EPs:
- *Dealer's Prevue* (RCA SDS-57-39)
- *A Touch of Gold, Volume 2*

LPs:
- *Elvis' Golden Records*
- *Elvis: Worldwide 50 Gold Award Hits, Volume 1*
- *Essential Elvis* (film version)

Bootleg LPs:
- *Got a Lot o' Livin' to Do!* (*Jailhouse Rock* soundtrack)
- *Loving You Recording Sessions* (alternate take, film version)
- *Please Release Me* (*Jailhouse Rock* soundtrack)

T-R-O-U-B-L-E
"T-R-O-U-B-L-E" was written by Jerry Chesnut and recorded by Elvis on March 12, 1975, at RCA's Nashville studios. The single release had a nine-week stay on *Billboard*'s Hot 100 chart, peaking at #35. On the country chart, "T-R-O-U-B-L-E" reached #11.

Singles:
- "T-R-O-U-B-L-E"/"Mr. Songman" (RCA PB-10278) April 1975. Standard release.
- "T-R-O-U-B-L-E"/"T-R-O-U-B-L-E" (RCA JH-10278) April 1975. Disc jockey promotional release. Side A contained a stereo version of the song, while side B was in mono.
- "T-R-O-U-B-L-E"/"Mr. Songman" (RCA GB-10487) February 1976. Gold Standard Series reissue.

LPs:
- *Elvis Aron Presley* (Dallas; June 6, 1976)
- *Elvis Aron Presley—Forever*
- *Elvis Today*

Bootleg LPs:
- *America's Own* (Uniondale, N.Y.; July 19, 1975)
- *Elvis Presley Is Alive and Well and Singing in Las Vegas, Volume 1* (Las Vegas; August 1975)
- *The Vegas Years, 1972–1975* (Las Vegas; August 1975)

TROUBLE
Elvis sang "Trouble" in his 1958 film *King Creole*. The song, which was written by Jerry Leiber and Mike Stoller, was recorded on January 15, 1958, at Radio Recorders. Take #5 was released. Elvis also sang "Trouble" on his 1968 TV special in a medley with "Guitar Man." The instrumental track for that version was recorded on June 20 or 21, 1968, at Western Recorders in Hollywood. Elvis's vocal was recorded on June 29 and 30.

"Trouble" has been recorded in recent years by the Osmonds, on their 1970 LP *The Osmonds Live* (MGM SE4826).

EPs:
- *King Creole, Volume 2*

LPs:
- *Elvis: The Other Sides—Worldwide Gold Award Hits, Volume 2*
- *Elvis—TV Special* (in medley with "Guitar Man")
- *King Creole*

Bootleg LPs:
- *The Burbank Sessions, Volume 2* ("Elvis" TV special taping; June 29, 1968, at 6:00 P.M. and 8:00 P.M. shows) (sung four times, twice in a medley with "Guitar Man")
- *Command Performance* (Las Vegas; September 2, 1973)
- *From Las Vegas . . . to Niagara Falls* (Las Vegas; September 3, 1973)
- *The '68 Comeback* (studio take; June 30, 1968)
- *The '68 Comeback, Volume 2* (studio takes #1 and #2; disco takes #1 and #2; supper club takes #1, #2, and #3; June 30, 1968)
- *Sold Out* (Las Vegas; September 2, 1973)
- *Special Delivery from Elvis Presley* (studio take)

TRUE LOVE

Cole Porter composed "True Love" for the 1956 movie musical *High Society*, in which it was introduced by Bing Crosby and Grace Kelly.[1] The first record release of "True Love" seems to be the one by Jane Powell (Verve 2018) in 1956. Her version reached #15 on *Billboard*'s Top 100 chart. A few days after Powell's release, the version by Crosby and Kelly began climbing the charts. It peaked at #4 and became a million-seller. The flip side of their record was "Well, Did You Evah," a duet by Crosby and Frank Sinatra.

Elvis recorded "True Love" on February 23, 1957, at Radio Recorders. Take #20 was selected by RCA for release.

EPs:
- *Loving You, Volume 1*

LPs:
- *Loving You*

TRUE LOVE TRAVELS ON A GRAVEL ROAD

"True Love Travels on a Gravel Road" was written by Dallas Frazier and Al Owens and recorded by Duane Dee (Capitol 2332) in late 1968. His recording peaked at #58 on *Billboard*'s country chart.

Elvis recorded "True Love Travels on a Gravel Road" on February 17, 1969, at American Sound Studios in Memphis.

LPs:
- *From Elvis in Memphis*
- *The Memphis Record*

Bootleg LPs:
- *Elvis Rocks and the Girls Roll* (alternate take)
- *Susie Q* (Las Vegas rehearsal; ?)

TRYIN' TO GET TO YOU

"Tryin' to Get to You" was written by Rose Marie McCoy and Margie Singleton, and first recorded by the Eagles (Mercury 70391) in mid-1954.

Elvis attempted to record "Tryin' to Get to You" on February 5, 1955, at Sun Records, but the recording was unsatisfactory. Elvis finally got an acceptable recording on July 11, 1955. That version was released by RCA on the LP *Elvis Presley*. "Tryin' to Get to You" was the only Sun recording by Elvis to use a piano, which was probably played by Elvis himself. Frank Tolley of Malcolm Yelvington's band has also been mentioned as the piano player. Backing Elvis were Scotty Moore (guitar), Bill Black (bass), and Johnny Bernero (drums). Elvis's September 1956 single release of "Tryin' to Get to You" did not chart. On June 27, 1968, Elvis recorded the song for use in his TV special "Elvis," but it was not used.

Singles:
- "TRYIN' TO GET TO YOU"/"I Love You Because" (RCA 20-6639) September 1956. Standard 78 RPM release.
- "TRYIN' TO GET TO YOU"/"I Love You Because" (RCA 47-6639) September 1956. Standard 45 RPM release.
- "TRYIN' TO GET TO YOU"/"I Love You Because" (RCA 447-0612) March 1959. Gold Standard Series reissue.

EPs:
- *Elvis Presley* (RCA SPD-22)
- *Elvis Presley* (RCA SPD-23)
- *Elvis Presley* (RCA EPB-1254)
- *Elvis Presley—The Most Talked About New Personality in the Last Ten Years of Recorded Music* (RCA EPB-1254)

LPs:
- *The Complete Sun Sessions* (master)
- *Elvis—A Legendary Performer, Volume 1* ("Elvis" TV special taping; June 27, 1968, at 8:00 P.M. show)
- *Elvis in Concert* (Rapid City, South Dakota; June 21, 1977)
- *Elvis Presley*
- *Elvis Recorded Live on Stage in Memphis* (Memphis; March 20, 1974)
- *A Golden Celebration* ("Elvis" TV special taping; June 27, 1968, at 8:00 P.M. show)
- *The Sun Sessions* (master)

Bootleg LPs:
- *America's Own* (Uniondale, N.Y.; July 19, 1975)
- *The Burbank Sessions, Volume 1* ("Elvis" TV special taping; June 27, 1968, at 6:00 P.M. and 8:00 P.M. shows)
- *From Las Vegas . . . to Niagara Falls* (Las Vegas; September 3, 1973)
- *Rockin' with Elvis New Year's Eve Pittsburgh, Pa. Dec. 31, 1976* (Pittsburgh; December 31, 1976)

TUMBLING TUMBLEWEEDS

"Tumbling Tumbleweeds" was written by Bob Nolan and recorded by his group, the Sons of the Pioneers, in 1934 (Decca 46027). The original title was "Tumbling Weeds," but Nolan had to add two syllables to make it a better fit in the lyrics. Nolan sang "Tumbling Tumbleweeds" in the 1935 Gene Autry film *Tumbling Tumbleweeds*. Both Roger Williams (Kapp 156) in 1956 and Billy Vaughn (Dot 15710) in 1958 reached *Billboard*'s Top 100 chart, peaking at #60 and #30, respectively.

Before singing "Don't You Know," Elvis sang one line of "Tumbling Tumbleweeds" at the Waco, Texas, home of disc jockey Eddie Fadal in the summer of 1958.

Bootleg LPs:
- *Forever Young, Forever Beautiful* (Waco, Texas; summer 1958)

TUPELO MISSISSIPPI FLASH

Jerry Reed wrote and recorded "Tupelo Mississippi Flash" (RCA 47-9334) in 1967. The song was a novelty tune about Elvis. Reed's recording reached #15 on *Billboard*'s country chart. In 1970 Tom Jones recorded "Tupelo Mississippi Flash" as the flip side to his hit "Daughter of Darkness" (Parrot 40048).

Some sources have suggested that Elvis himself may have recorded "Tupelo Mississippi Flash," but no proof has been offered.

TURN AROUND, LOOK AT ME

Jerry Capehart wrote "Turn Around, Look at Me" in 1961. The first recording of the song was probably by Glen Campbell (Crest 1087) that same year. "Turn

---

[1]Grace Kelly's father, John B. Kelly, won three Olympic Gold Medals for rowing. He won the Sculls in 1920, and Double Sculls in 1920 and 1924. His cousin, Paul V. Costello, won the Double Sculls in 1920, 1924, and 1928.

Around, Look at Me" was Campbell's first chart release, peaking at #62 on the Hot 100 chart. In 1968 the Vogues had a million-seller and #7 hit with "Turn Around, Look at Me" (Reprise 0686).

Elvis sang a line or two of "Turn Around, Look at Me" in a 1970s performance in Las Vegas.

Bootleg LPs:
• *Susie Q* (Las Vegas; ?)

TURN ME LOOSE
"Turn Me Loose" was written for Elvis by Doc Pomus and Mort Shuman in 1959. However, before Elvis could record it (he was in the Army in West Germany at the time), Fabian had a top 10 hit (#9) with "Turn Me Loose" (Chancellor 1033). There's no indication that Elvis ever recorded the song.

TUTTI FRUTTI
In the mid-1950s, Little Richard was singing a song he called "Wop-Bop-a-Loo-Bop" in clubs. The song had suggestive lyrics. During a break in a recording session in New Orleans in late 1955, Little Richard and Bumps Blackwell of Specialty Records went to a nightclub called the Dew Drop Inn. After a while, Little Richard began to sing in an attempt to impress the club's patrons. One of the songs he sang was his "Wop-Bop-a-Loo-Bop." Blackwell flipped over the song. He knew it had the makings of a hit. But first he had to rewrite the risqué lyrics.

Songwriter Dorothy LaBostrie happened to be in the studio watching Little Richard record her song "I'm Just a Lonely Guy," when Blackwell asked her to rewrite the lyrics to "Wop-Bop-a-Loo-Bop." After hearing Little Richard sing the song, she left the studio. Some time later, she came back to the studio with "Tutti Frutti."

It should be mentioned that LaBostrie denies the scenario given by Bumps Blackwell. She says she simply wrote the song after being inspired by a new flavor of ice cream she had eaten, Tutti Frutti. She claims never to have heard Little Richard's "Wop-Bop-a-Loo-Bop."

Little Richard's recording [he played piano] was a #2 rhythm & blues hit in late 1955. "Tutti Frutti" (Specialty 561) reached #17 on the Top 100 chart in early 1956 and sold over three million copies. Pat Boone's cover version (Dot 15443) was actually more successful, reaching #12.

Elvis recorded "Tutti Frutti" on January 31, 1956, at RCA's New York City studios. He sang the tune on "Stage Show" twice (February 4 and 18, 1956). Elvis's September 1956 single release failed to chart.

Singles:
• "Blue Suede Shoes"/"TUTTI FRUTTI" (RCA 20-6636) September 1956. Standard 78 RPM release.
• "Blue Suede Shoes"/"TUTTI FRUTTI" (RCA 47-6636) September 1956. Standard 45 RPM release.
• "TUTTI FRUTTI"/"One-Sided Love Affair" (RCA 47-6466) September 1956. Disc jockey "Record Prevue."

• "Blue Suede Shoes"/"TUTTI FRUTTI" (RCA 447-0609) March 1959. Gold Standard Series reissue.
• "Blue Suede Shoes"/"TUTTI FRUTTI" (RCA PB-13885) October 1984. One of six singles in the boxed set *Elvis' Greatest Hits—Golden Singles, Volume 1* (RCA PP-13897). The record was pressed on gold vinyl with a special gold "50th" anniversary label.

EPs:
• *Elvis Presley* (RCA EPA-747)
• *Elvis Presley* (RCA EPB-1254)
• *Elvis Presley* (RCA SPD-22)
• *Elvis Presley* (RCA SPD-23)
• *Elvis Presley—The Most Talked About New Personality in the Last Ten Years of Recorded Music* (RCA EPB-1254)

LPs:
• *Elvis Presley*
• *A Golden Celebration* ("Stage Show"; February 4, 1956; February 18, 1956)

Bootleg LPs:
• *Dorsey Shows* ("Stage Show"; February 4, 1956; February 18, 1956)
• *Superstar Outtakes* ("Stage Show"; February 4, 1956; February 18, 1956)

TWEEDLEE DEE
"Tweedlee Dee" was written by Winfield Scott and first recorded by LaVern Baker in late 1954. Her recording (Atlantic 1047) reached #4 on the rhythm & blues chart and #14 on the Top 100 chart in January 1955. A cover version by Georgia Gibbs (Mercury 70517) did even better, peaking at #2 on the Top 100 chart. Her version was titled "Tweedle Dee." Both versions became million-sellers. Vicki Young (Capitol 3008) and Pee Wee King (RCA 47-6005) recorded "Tweedleee Dee" in early 1955, but neither recording charted. In 1973 Little Jimmy Osmond recorded a version (MGM 14468) that reached #59 on the Hot 100 chart.

Elvis never recorded "Tweedlee Dee" in the studio, but he did sing it quite frequently on tour in 1955 and 1956. A performance on the "Louisiana Hayride" on December 18, 1954, has appeared on a number of bootlegs and on the LP *Elvis: The First Live Recordings*. In addition to Elvis, Scotty Moore, Bill Black, and D. J. Fontana, Floyd Cramer played piano and Jimmy Day played steel guitar. Although all the sources indicate that December 18, 1954, is the correct date, it's interesting to note that the original recording by LaVern Baker didn't even reach the rhythm & blues chart until January 5, 1955. So, either the "Louisiana Hayride" date is incorrect, or Elvis sang "Tweedlee Dee" almost the same day Baker's recording was released, after hearing it on the radio. Is it possible that the "Louisiana Hayride" date should actually be April 30, 1955?

LPs:
• *Elvis: The First Live Recordings* ("Louisiana Hayride"; December 18, 1954)

Bootleg LPs:
• *The Entertainer* ("Louisiana Hayride"; December 18, 1954)
• *The First Year—Recorded Live* ("Louisiana Hayride"; December 18, 1954)

- *The Rockin' Rebel, Volume 2* ("Louisiana Hayride"; December 18, 1954)
- *Standing Room Only, Volume 2* ("Louisiana Hayride"; December 18, 1954)

THE TWELFTH OF NEVER

"The Twelfth of Never" was written by Paul Francis Webster and Jerry Livingston and recorded by Johnny Mathis (Columbia 40993) in 1956. His recording, backed by the Ray Conniff Orchestra, reached #9 on *Billboard*'s Top 100 chart and became a million-seller. The flip side of the record was "Chances Are," an even bigger hit. Mathis's recording of "The Twelfth of Never" was heard in the 1977 Steven Spielberg movie *Close Encounters of the Third Kind*. In 1973 Donny Osmond (MGM 14503) had a million-seller with his version of the song, reaching #8 on the Hot 100 chart.

Elvis sang "The Twelfth of Never" in concert on a few occasions in the 1970s. One of those performances appeared on the 10-inch bootleg LP *Elvis Special, Volume 2*.

Bootleg LPs:
- *Elvis Special, Volume 2*

TWENTY DAYS AND TWENTY NIGHTS

"Twenty Days and Twenty Nights" was written by Ben Weisman and Clive Westlake, and recorded by Elvis on June 4, 1970, at RCA's Nashville studios.

LPs:
- *That's the Way It Is*

TWENTY FLIGHT ROCK

Eddie Cochran wrote and recorded "Twenty Flight Rock" (Liberty 55112) in 1958. It's been reported over the years that "Twenty Flight Rock" was the song Paul McCartney played on guitar for John Lennon during his audition for the Quarrymen (later to be known as the Beatles). This doesn't seem likely since that Lennon-McCartney meeting occurred before Cochran wrote the song.

Some have reported that Elvis recorded "Twenty Flight Rock" in the 1960s, but no evidence has come forth to prove it.

TWIST ME LOOSE

Elvis recorded "Twist Me Loose" in March 1962 for his film *Girls! Girls! Girls!* The song was not used in the film, nor has it ever been available on record.

UNCHAINED MELODY

"Unchained Melody" was written by Hy Zaret and Alex North for the 1955 movie *Unchained*, starring Elroy (Crazy Legs) Hirsch and Barbara Hale. Todd Duncan, the famous baritone in *Porgy and Bess*, sang it in the film. That same year, Les Baxter's[1] instrumental version (Capitol 3055) reached number one and became a million-seller. Other hit versions in 1955 included those by Al Hibbler (Decca 29441), which reached #5 on the Top 100 and sold over a million copies; Roy Hamilton (Epic 9102) (#6); and June Valli (RCA 6708) (#29). Over the years, "Unchained Melody" has been recorded by numerous artists. The Righteous Brothers (Philles 129) peaked at #4 in 1965, and the Sweet Inspirations (Atlantic 2551), who later backed Elvis, reached #73 in 1968 with the tune.

In the 1970s, Elvis sang "Unchained Melody" in concert. His performance at the Crisler Arena in Ann Arbor, Michigan, on April 24, 1977, was recorded by RCA. Elvis's only accompaniment was his own piano playing. RCA later overdubbed organ, bass, and percussion to the instrumental track and released the song on the *Moody Blue* album. The 1978 single release was recorded at the Rushmore Civic Center in Rapid City, South Dakota, on June 21, 1977. It reached #6 on *Billboard*'s country chart, remaining on the chart for 11 weeks.

Singles:
- "UNCHAINED MELODY"/"Softly as I Leave You" (RCA PB-11212) March 1978. Standard release.
- "UNCHAINED MELODY"/"Softly as I Leave You" (RCA JH-11212) March 1978. Disc jockey promotional release.
- "Are You Sincere"/"UNCHAINED MELODY" (RCA GB-11988) May 1980. Gold Standard Series original release.

LPs:
- *Always on My Mind*
- *Elvis Aron Presley*
- *Moody Blue*

Bootleg LPs:
- *Rockin' with Elvis New Year's Eve Pittsburgh, Pa. Dec. 31, 1976* (Pittsburgh; December 31, 1976)

UNCLE PEN

"Uncle Pen" was written and recorded in 1951 by blue-grass legend Bill Monroe. The song was based on Monroe's real-life uncle, Pendleton Vandiver. Porter Wagoner recorded the song (RCA 6494) in 1956. Elvis sang "Uncle Pen" on tour in 1955 and 1956, including a concert in Richmond, Virginia, on June 30, 1956. It was one of the many songs he sang on the "Louisiana Hayride," including his March 5, 1955, television appearance. Bootlegs of "Uncle Pen" have been rumored to exist for years, probably from a "Hayride" transcription, possibly from a Sun recording session. These bootlegs, however, have failed to surface.

In 1967 an article in the *New Musical Express* in England announced that Pyramid Records was about to release Elvis's "Uncle Pen," with the flip side to be a medley of Elvis hits played by the Anthony Hedley Orchestra. It was later reported that the master was mysteriously damaged and could not be released.

UNTIL IT'S TIME FOR YOU TO GO

Buffy Sainte-Marie, who was born on a Cree Indian Reservation in Saskatchewan, Canada, wrote "Until It's Time for You to Go" in 1965 and recorded it for her album *Many a Mile*. That same year, Monkee member Michael Nesmith, using the pseudonym Michael Blessing, recorded a version of the song on Colpix Records (Colpix 792). In the United Kingdom the Four Pennies reached #19 with their recording. In late 1970 composer Sainte-Marie finally released a single of her song (Vanguard 35116), but it failed to chart. Earlier that year, Neil Diamond (Uni 55204) reached #53 on *Billboard*'s Hot 100 chart. A recording of "Until It's Time for You to Go" by New Birth (RCA 0003) did less well in 1973 (#97).

Elvis often sang "Until It's Time for You to Go" on tour and in Las Vegas in the 1970s. MGM filmed one of his performances in April 1972, for inclusion in the documentary *Elvis on Tour*. It's probable that the single release of the song was recorded at RCA's Nashville studios on May 17, 1971, although RCA claims that it's from the June 8, 1971, session. Elvis's recording reached #40 on *Billboard*'s Hot 100 chart and stayed on the chart for nine weeks. It reached #68 on the country

(Photo courtesy Don Fink)

---

[1]Les Baxter was once a member of Mel Torme's vocal group, the Meltones.

chart (for two weeks), and #9 on the Easy-Listening chart (for seven weeks).

Singles:
- "UNTIL IT'S TIME FOR YOU TO GO"/"We Can Make the Morning" (RCA 74-0619) January 1972. Standard release.
- "An American Trilogy"/"UNTIL IT'S TIME FOR YOU TO GO" (RCA 477-0685) May 1973. Gold Standard Series original release.

LPs:
- *Elvis—A Canadian Tribute*
- *Elvis Now*

Bootleg LPs:
- *Elvis Presley Is Alive and Well and Singing in Las Vegas, Volume 1* (Las Vegas; August 1974)
- *The Monologue L.P.* (Las Vegas; July 31, 1969)
- *To Know Him Is to Love Him* (Las Vegas; 1969 or 1970)
- *The Vegas Years, 1972–1975* (Las Vegas; 1972 and August 1974)

UP ABOVE MY HEAD

Sister Rosetta Tharpe wrote "Up Above My Head" in 1949. Trumpet player Al Hirt had a vocal version in 1964 (RCA 47-8439) that reached #12 on *Billboard's* Easy-Listening chart and #85 on the Hot 100. For Elvis's 1968 TV special, W. Earl Brown adapted the gospel tune for the big production sequence. The instrumental track was recorded on June 20 or 21, 1968, at Western Recorders in Hollywood. Elvis's vocal was either done on the same occasion or on June 30. On the TV special, "Up Above My Head" was sung in a gospel medley that included "Sometimes I Feel Like a Motherless Child," "Where Could I Go but to the Lord," and "Saved."

LPs:
- *Elvis—TV Special*

Bootleg LPs:
- *The '68 Comeback* (studio take)

THE U.S. AIR FORCE SONG

The theme song of the U.S. Air Force was written in 1939 as "The Army Air Corps Song" by Robert Crawford. It has been interpreted in several films over the years, including *Winged Victory* (1944) and *Ice Capades Revue* (1942). Until the establishment of the U.S. Air Force in 1947, the final line of the song had been "Nothing will stop the Army Air Corps."

In the documentary *Elvis on Tour*, Elvis sang one line ("Off we go into the wild blue yonder") of "The U.S. Air Force Song."

U.S. MALE

The original recording of "U.S. Male" was by its composer, Jerry Reed, in early 1967 on his album *The Unbelievable Guitar and Voice of Jerry Reed* (RCA LPM/LSP-3756). Reed later played lead guitar on Elvis's successful single version, which was recorded at RCA's Nashville studios on January 17, 1968. It had a nine-week stay on *Billboard's* Hot 100 chart, peaking at #28. "U.S. Male" reached #55 on the country chart, staying on the chart for six weeks.

Singles:
- "U.S. MALE"/"Stay Away" (RCA 47-9465) March 1968. Standard release.
- "U.S. MALE"/"Stay Away" (RCA 477-0664) 1970. Gold Standard Series reissue.

EPs:
- *Stay Away*

LPs:
- *Almost in Love*
- *Double Dynamite*

VIENNA WOODS ROCK AND ROLL

Original title for "Tonight's All Right for Love." (See *Tonight's All Right for Love*)

VINO, DINERO Y AMOR

Sid Tepper and Roy C. Bennett wrote this song, which means "wine, money, and love," for Elvis's 1963 movie *Fun in Acapulco*. Elvis recorded "Vino, Dinero y Amor" on January 22, 1963, at Radio Recorders in Hollywood.

LPs:
• *Fun in Acapulco*

VIOLET (FLOWER OF NYU)

Elvis sang "Violet (Flower of NYU)" in his 1969 movie *The Trouble with Girls*. The song, which lasted just 15 seconds, was sung to the tune of "Aura Lee." The instrumental track was recorded at United Recorders in Hollywood on August 23, 1968. Elvis's vocal track was laid down later, perhaps on October 14 or 24. RCA has never officially released "Violet (Flower of NYU)," but it has appeared on numerous bootleg albums. On the *Behind Closed Doors* bootleg, the complete lyrics are sung.

Bootleg LPs:
• *Behind Closed Doors* (studio take in medley with "The Whiffenpoof Song")

• *Eternal Elvis* (*The Trouble with Girls* soundtrack)
• *From Hollywood to Vegas* (*The Trouble with Girls* soundtrack)

VIVA LAS VEGAS

Doc Pomus and Mort Shuman wrote this title tune to Elvis's 1964 movie *Viva Las Vegas*. Elvis sang "Viva Las Vegas" three times in the film, once in a duet with Ann-Margret. He recorded the song in July 1963 at Radio Recorders. "Viva Las Vegas" spent seven weeks on *Billboard*'s Hot 100 chart, peaking at #29, and has reportedly sold over a million copies worldwide. All U.S. releases have been in monaural, but true stereo versions have been issued in New Zealand and Japan.

Singles:
• "VIVA LAS VEGAS"/"What'd I Say" (RCA 47-8360) April 1964. Standard release.
• "VIVA LAS VEGAS"/"What'd I Say" (RCA 447-0646) May 1965. Gold Standard Series reissue.

EPs:
• *See the U.S.A., the Elvis Way* (true stereo version)

LPs:
• *Elvis in Hollywood*
• *Elvis: Worldwide 50 Gold Award Hits, Volume 1*
• *This Is Elvis*

Bootleg LPs:
• *Viva Las Vegas!* (*Viva Las Vegas* soundtrack; all three versions)

WABASH CANNONBALL

This traditional song can be traced back to at least 1885 and a real train that ran from Chicago to Kansas City, Missouri, on the Wabash Railroad line. In 1905 William Kindt wrote the first published version of "Wabash Cannonball." He based it on "The Great Rock Island Route," written by J. A. Rolfe in 1882. The earliest recording of "Wabash Cannonball" appears to be that by Hugh Cross in 1929. Roy Acuff, with whom the song is most closely identified, recorded his version on October 21, 1936, in Chicago (Vocalion 4466). Lead vocalist on the recording was Sam (Dynamite) Hatcher. Acuff played guitar and added the train sounds. His is the only million-seller of the song. Viewers of the "Baseball Game of the Week" on CBS-TV back in the 1950s will remember announcer Dizzy Dean singing "Wabash Cannonball" during slow periods in the games. He was joined on occasion by Roy Acuff. In 1970 Danny Davis and the Nashville Brass had a moderate country instrumental hit with "Wabash Cannonball" (RCA 47-9785).

Some have speculated that Elvis recorded "Wabash Cannonball," but as yet there has been no proof.

WALK A MILE IN MY SHOES

Joe South wrote "Walk a Mile in My Shoes" in 1969 and recorded it later that year. His recording (Capitol 2704) peaked at #12 on *Billboard*'s Hot 100 chart and #3 on the Easy-Listening chart in early 1970. Later in 1970, Willie Hightower released a version of "Walk a Mile in My Shoes" (Fame 1465) that was a moderate rhythm & blues hit.

While Joe South's version was riding the charts, Elvis began incorporating "Walk a Mile in My Shoes" into his concert appearances. RCA recorded his February 18, 1970, show at the International Hotel in Las Vegas.

LPs:
• *On Stage—February, 1970*

WALK THAT LONESOME VALLEY

(See *That Lonesome Valley*)

THE WALLS HAVE EARS

Elvis sang "The Walls Have Ears" in his 1962 movie *Girls! Girls! Girls!* He recorded this Sid Tepper–Roy C. Bennett composition in March 1962 at Radio Recorders. The film version had added sound effects simulating crashing walls.

LPs:
• *Girls! Girls! Girls!*

WAY DOWN

Written by Layng Martine Jr., "Way Down" was recorded by Elvis at Graceland on the night of October 29–30, 1976. The bass voice heard on the recording is

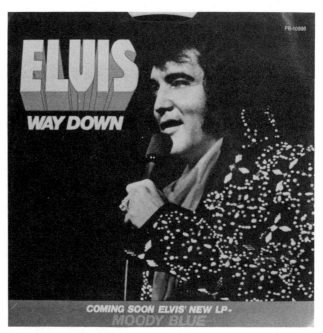

(Photo courtesy Don Fink)

that of J. D. Sumner, who hit a double low C. Paired with "Pledging My Love," "Way Down" replaced Charlie Rich's "Rolling with the Flow" at number one on *Billboard*'s country chart, stayed there for one week, and was replaced at the top spot by Crystal Gayle's "Don't It Make My Brown Eyes Blue." "Way Down" had a 17-week stay on the chart. On the Hot 100 chart, the song peaked at #18 during its 21-week stay. A peak position of #14 was achieved on the Easy-Listening chart. In the United Kingdom, "Way Down" was Elvis's last number one single, with five weeks at the top spot. With "Way Down" Elvis tied the Beatles' British record of 17 number one singles. The RIAA certified the record as a million-seller on September 12, 1977. The following credits were listed on the record label: "Executive Producer: Elvis Presley; Associate Producer: Felton Jarvis."

Singles:
• "WAY DOWN"/"Pledging My Love" (RCA PB-10998) June 1977. Standard release.
• "WAY DOWN"/"Pledging My Love" (RCA JB-10998) June 1977. Disc jockey promotional release.
• "WAY DOWN"/"Pledging My Love" (RCA GB-11504) May 1979. Gold Standard Series reissue.

LPs:
• *Elvis' Gold Records, Volume 5*
• *Moody Blue*
• *Our Memories of Elvis, Volume 2* (without overdubbing)

WE BOTH WENT OUR WAYS

It's been reported that Elvis recorded "We Both Went Our Ways" for his 1969 movie *The Trouble with Girls*, but no tape of the song has yet surfaced.

WE CALL ON HIM

Elvis recorded "We Call on Him," a Fred Karger–Sid Wayne–Ben Weisman composition, on September 11, 1967, at RCA's Nashville studios. The single release never reached the *Billboard* charts, although it was briefly on the "Bubbling Under" list at #106. Despite the poor chart performance, some sources indicate that "We Call on Him" sold over a million copies. Hoyt Hawkins of the Jordanaires played organ on the recording.

Singles:
- "You'll Never Walk Alone"/"WE CALL ON HIM" (RCA 47-9600) April 1968. Standard release.
- "You'll Never Walk Alone"/"WE CALL ON HIM" (RCA 447-0665) December 1970. Gold Standard Series reissue.

LPs:
- *You'll Never Walk Alone*

WE CAN MAKE THE MORNING

"We Can Make the Morning" was written by Jay Ramsey and recorded by Elvis on May 20, 1971, at RCA's Nashville studios. Paired with "Until It's Time for You to Go," the record had a seven-week stay on *Billboard*'s Easy-Listening chart, peaking at #9.

Singles:
- "Until It's Time for You to Go"/"WE CAN MAKE THE MORNING" (RCA 74-0619) January 1972. Standard release.

LPs:
- *Elvis Now*

WEAR MY RING AROUND YOUR NECK

"Wear My Ring Around Your Neck" entered *Billboard*'s Top 100 chart at the #7 position in April 1958—the highest entry position of any Presley single. It eventually peaked at #3 and stayed on the chart for 15 weeks. "All I Have to Do Is Dream" by the Everly Brothers and "Witch Doctor" by David Seville kept "Wear My Ring Around Your Neck" from reaching the top spot. The song also reached #3 on the country chart and #7 on the rhythm & blues chart. Written by Bert Carroll and Russell Moody, "Wear My Ring Around Your Neck" was recorded by Elvis on February 1, 1958, at Radio Recorders. Take #22 was selected by RCA for release. Advance orders for the record exceeded one million. Rock star Bruce Springsteen formerly ended his concerts with "Wear My Ring Around Your Neck."

Singles:
- "WEAR MY RING AROUND YOUR NECK"/"Doncha' Think It's Time" (RCA 20-7240) April 1958. Standard 78 RPM release.
- "WEAR MY RING AROUND YOUR NECK"/"Doncha' Think It's Time" (RCA 47-7240) April 1958. Standard 45 RPM release.
- "WEAR MY RING AROUND YOUR NECK"/"Doncha' Think It's Time" (RCA 447-0622) 1961. Gold Standard Series reissue.
- "Don't"/"WEAR MY RING AROUND YOUR NECK" (RCA SP-45-76) January 1960. Disc jockey promotional release. This single was used to promote the album *50,000,000 Elvis Fans Can't Be Wrong—Elvis' Gold Records, Volume 2*.
- "I Was the One"/"WEAR MY RING AROUND YOUR NECK" (RCA PB-13500) April 1983. New single release.

- "I Was the One"/"WEAR MY RING AROUND YOUR NECK" (RCA JB-13500) April 1983. Disc jockey promotional release. This single was pressed on gold vinyl.

EPs:
- *A Touch of Gold, Volume 2*

LPs:
- *Elvis: Worldwide 50 Gold Award Hits, Volume 1*
- *50,000,000 Elvis Fans Can't Be Wrong—Elvis' Gold Records, Volume 2*
- *I Was the One*
- *The Top Ten Hits*

WEARIN' THAT LOVED ON LOOK

Written by Dallas Frazier and Al Owens, "Wearin' That Loved on Look" was recorded by Elvis on January 14, 1969, at American Sound Studios in Memphis.

LPs:
- *From Elvis in Memphis*
- *The Memphis Record*

WELCOME TO MY WORLD

This country song was written by Ray Winkler and John Hathcock and first recorded by Jim Reeves in 1963. In early 1964, "Welcome to My World" (RCA 47-8289) peaked at #2 on *Billboard*'s country chart. Eddy Arnold had a moderate hit with the song (RCA 47-9993) in 1971.

Elvis sang "Welcome to My World" in his 1973 TV special "Elvis: Aloha from Hawaii." It is this version (January 14, 1973) that RCA recorded.

LPs:
- *Aloha from Hawaii via Satellite*
- *The Alternate Aloha* (rehearsal concert for "Elvis: Aloha from Hawaii"; January 12, 1973)
- *Elvis Aron Presley*
- *Welcome to My World*

Bootleg LPs:
- *Aloha Rehearsal Show—Kui Lee Cancer Benefit* (rehearsal concert for "Elvis: Aloha from Hawaii"; January 12, 1973)

WE'LL BE TOGETHER

Charles O'Curran and Dudley Brooks (who played piano on the recording) wrote "We'll Be Together" for Elvis's 1962 film *Girls! Girls! Girls!* The song was recorded in March 1962 at Radio Recorders. The Amigos provided vocal backing for Elvis. The recorded version of "We'll Be Together" is a splice of takes #9 and #10.

LPs:
- *Burning Love and Hits from His Movies, Volume 2*
- *Girls! Girls! Girls!*

WE'RE COMING IN LOADED

Elvis sang "We're Coming in Loaded" in his 1962 film *Girls! Girls! Girls!* The song, which was written by Otis Blackwell and Winfield Scott, was recorded in March 1962 at Radio Recorders.

LPs:
- *Girls! Girls! Girls!*

WE'RE GONNA LIVE IT UP

Elvis is believed to have recorded "We're Gonna Live It Up" for his 1957 movie *Loving You*, but it is not mentioned in the sessions notes.

WE'RE GONNA MOVE

Elvis sang "We're Gonna Move" in his first film, *Love Me Tender*. It was the first song in the film. Although Elvis and Vera Matson are credited as the song's composers, "We're Gonna Move" was actually written by Matson's husband, Ken Darby. Elvis recorded the song at Radio Recorders on August 2, or September 24, 1956. Vocal backing was by Chuck Prescott, John Dodson, Red Robinson, and others. The guitar player was Vita Mumolo.

EPs:
- *Love Me Tender*

LPs:
- *A Date With Elvis* (alternate mix, more reverberation)
- *Elvis: The Other Sides—Worldwide Gold Award Hits, Volume 2*
- *Essential Elvis—The First Movies*

WESTERN UNION

Elvis recorded "Western Union" on May 27, 1963, at RCA's Nashville studios. Written by Sid Tepper and Roy C. Bennett, the tune turned up as a bonus song on the *Speedway* LP.

LPs:
- *Speedway*

WHAT A FRIEND WE HAVE IN JESUS

Elvis was heard to sing one line (actually just the title) of "What a Friend We Have in Jesus" in the 1981 documentary *This Is Elvis*. The song was written by Joseph Scriven and Charles C. Converse.

WHAT A WONDERFUL LIFE

Sid Wayne and Jay Livingston wrote "What a Wonderful Life" for Elvis's 1962 film *Follow That Dream*. The vocal was recorded by Elvis on July 5, 1961, at RCA's Nashville studios.

EPs:
- *Follow That Dream*

LPs:
- *I Got Lucky*

WHAT EVERY WOMAN LIVES FOR

This Doc Pomus–Mort Shuman composition was written for Elvis's 1966 film *Frankie and Johnny*. Elvis recorded the song in May 1965 at Radio Recorders.

LPs:
- *Frankie and Johnny*

WHAT NOW, MY LOVE

French composers P. Delanoe and Gilbert Becaud wrote "What Now, My Love" in 1962 under the French title "Et Maintenant." Carl Sigman later adapted English lyrics to the song. The first U.S. release of "What Now, My Love" was probably Al Martino's in October 1965 (Capitol 5506). In 1966 Kapp Records released Gilbert Becaud's original version on the LP *What Now, My Love* (Kapp 1353). That same year, Herb Alpert and the Tijuana Brass had a million-selling LP titled *What Now, My Love* (A&M SP4114)[1] that contained the popular song of the same title. The single release (A&M 792) peaked at #2 on *Billboard*'s Easy-Listening chart and #24 on the Hot 100. Other popular versions included those by Sonny and Cher (Atco 6395) in 1966 and Mitch Ryder (DynoVoice 901) in 1967.

Elvis sang "What Now, My Love" in the rehearsal concert (January 12, 1973) for the TV special "Elvis: Aloha from Hawaii," as well as in the special itself on January 14.

EPs:
- *Aloha from Hawaii via Satellite*

LPs:
- *Aloha from Hawaii via Satellite*
- *The Alternate Aloha* (rehearsal concert for "Elvis: Aloha from Hawaii"; January 12, 1973)

Bootleg LPs:
- *Aloha Rehearsal Show—Kui Lee Cancer Benefit* (rehearsal concert for "Elvis: Aloha from Hawaii"; January 12, 1973)
- *The Entertainer* (Las Vegas; February 1973)
- *The Monologue L.P.* (Las Vegas; July 31, 1969)

WHAT NOW, WHAT NEXT, WHERE TO

Don Robertson and Hal Blair wrote "What Now, What Next, Where To" for Elvis, who recorded it on May 26, 1963, at RCA's Nashville studios.

LPs:
- *Double Trouble*
- *Separate Ways*

WHAT'D I SAY

Ray Charles wrote and recorded "What'd I Say" in 1959. His recording (Atlantic 2031) was a number one rhythm & blues hit. On the Hot 100 chart, it peaked at #6. "What'd I Say" was Charles's first million-seller and one of the first recordings to feature an electric piano. Other popular versions of "What'd I Say" include those by Jerry Lee Lewis (Sun 356) in 1961, Bobby Darin (Atco 6221) in 1962, and Rare Earth (Rare Earth 5043) in 1972.

Elvis sang "What'd I Say" in concert frequently. He recorded it in July 1964 at Radio Recorders for his film *Viva Las Vegas*. His single release that year had a six-week stay on *Billboard*'s Hot 100 chart, peaking at #21. Elvis was seen rehearsing "What'd I Say" at MGM in July 1970 in his documentary *Elvis—That's the Way It Is*.

Singles:
- "Viva Las Vegas"/"WHAT'D I SAY" (RCA 47-8360) April 1964. Standard release.

---

[1] *What Now, My Love* was the first eight-track cartridge to be awarded the Gold Cartridge Award for sales exceeding $1 million.

- "Viva Las Vegas"/"WHAT'D I SAY" (RCA 447-0646) May 1965. Gold Standard Series reissue.

LPs:
- *Elvis' Gold Records, Volume 4*
- *Elvis in Concert* (Omaha; June 19, 1977)
- *Greatest Hits, Volume 1* (Las Vegas; August 1969)

Bootleg LPs:
- *The King: From the Dark to the Light* (Elvis—That's the Way It Is soundtrack)
- *The Last Farewell* (Indianapolis; June 26, 1977)
- *The Legend Lives On* (Las Vegas; August 1969)
- *The Monologue L.P.* (Las Vegas; July 31, 1969)
- *Sold Out* (Las Vegas; February 1970)
- *Superstar Outtakes* (Las Vegas; August 1969)
- *That's the Way It Is* (Elvis—That's the Way It Is soundtrack)
- *Viva Las Vegas!* (RCA single release)

WHAT'S SHE REALLY LIKE
Elvis briefly sang "What's She Really Like" in his 1960 film *G. I. Blues*, with no instrumental accompaniment while in the shower. The song lasted just 18 seconds. Written by Sid Wayne and Abner Silver, "What's She Really Like" was recorded by Elvis on April 28, 1960, at RCA's Hollywood studios. The full-length version, with instrumental accompaniment, appeared on the LP *G. I. Blues*.

EPs:
- *The EP Collection, Volume 2* (alternate take #7)

LPs:
- *G. I. Blues*

WHEEL OF FORTUNE
It's been speculated that "Wheel of Fortune" may have been recorded for Elvis's 1967 film *Easy Come, Easy Go*. However, it's more likely that "Wheel of Fortune" was an alternate title for "The Love Machine."

WHEELS ON MY HEELS
Sid Tepper and Roy C. Bennett wrote "Wheels on My Heels" for Elvis's 1964 film *Roustabout*. Elvis recorded the song in March 1964 at Radio Recorders.

LPs:
- *Roustabout*

WHEN GOD CALLS ME HOME
Elvis sang four lines of this gospel tune with the Stamps at the Las Vegas Hilton on December 11, 1976, and may have sung it on other occasions. "When God Calls Me Home" was written by Odis Moore.

WHEN GOD DIPS HIS LOVE IN MY HEART
This gospel song was written by Cleavant Derricks in 1944. A few lines of "When God Dips His Love in My Heart" were sung by Jerry Lee Lewis during the Million-Dollar-Quartet session on December 4, 1956. Elvis and Carl Perkins provided vocal harmony.

Bootleg LPs:
- *The One Million Dollar Quartet* (Sun Records; December 4, 1956)

WHEN I'M OVER YOU
Elvis recorded "When I'm Over You" on June 7, 1970, at RCA's Nashville studios. Shirl Milete is the composer.

LPs:
- *Love Letters from Elvis*

WHEN IT RAINS, IT REALLY POURS
William Robert (Billy the Kid) Emerson wrote and recorded this song as "When It Rains, It Pours" at Sun Records in late 1954. His recording (Sun 214) was released the same day—January 8, 1955—as Elvis's "Milkcow Blues Boogie"/"You're a Heartbreaker" (Sun 215). Later in 1955, probably July 11, Elvis tried to record "When It Rains, It Pours," but no take was deemed acceptable for release. Drummer Johnny Bernero joined Elvis, Scotty Moore, and Bill Black for the session. In 1983, takes #2 (a false start) and #3 surfaced on the LP *Elvis—A Legendary Performer, Volume 4*.

On February 24, 1957, at Radio Recorders in Hollywood, Elvis again attempted to record the song, this time as "When It Rains, It *Really* Pours." The version on the *Elvis for Everyone* LP was take #8 from that session. Elvis sang "When It Rains, It Really Pours" during a dress rehearsal for the 1968 TV special "Elvis," but it was not used in the show.

The 1958 movie *Country Music Holiday* featured an excellent rendition—perhaps the best—of "When It Rains, It Pours" by Faron Young.

LPs:
- *The Complete Sun Sessions* (Sun version, takes #2 [a false start] and #3)
- *Elvis—A Legendary Performer, Volume 4* (Sun version, takes #2 [a false start] and #3)
- *Elvis for Everyone* (RCA version, take #8)
- *A Golden Celebration* (Sun version, takes #2 [a false start] and #3)
- *Reconsider Baby* (RCA version, take #8)

Bootleg LPs:
- *Elvis Rocks and the Girls Roll* (dress rehearsal for "Elvis"; June 1968)
- *The One Million Dollar Quartet* (Sun Records; December 4, 1956)

WHEN MY BLUE MOON TURNS TO GOLD AGAIN
"When My Blue Moon Turns to Gold Again" was written by Wiley Walker and Gene Sullivan in 1941 and recorded by them that same year (Columbia 20264). Walker was inspired to write the song while traveling in West Texas with the full moon in his face. As he drove down the highway, daybreak approached. Walker noted the apparent change of color of the moon from a bluish tint to gold. Other popular versions of "When My Blue Moon Turns to Gold Again" include those by Zeke Manners and his band, the Singing Lariateers, in 1947 (RCA 20-2130) and by Tex Ritter in 1949 (Capitol 1977).

Elvis recorded "When My Blue Moon Turns to Gold Again" on September 2, 1956, at Radio Recorders. Although not released as a single, the song reached #27 on *Billboard*'s Top 100 chart based on the strength of its appearance on the EP *Elvis, Volume 1*. It had a

15-week stay on the chart. Elvis sang "When My Blue Moon Turns to Gold Again" in his third appearance on "The Ed Sullivan Show" (January 6, 1957). It was also sung (in a duet with Charlie Hodge) in the dress rehearsals for the 1968 TV special "Elvis" in mid-June 1968, and the taped studio sessions for the special on June 27. It was not used in the actual broadcast, however.

EPs:
- *Elvis, Volume 1*
- *Elvis/Jaye P. Morgan*

LPs:
- *Elvis* (RCA LPM-1382)
- *Elvis: The Other Sides—Worldwide Gold Award Hits, Volume 2*
- *A Golden Celebration* ("The Ed Sullivan Show"; January 6, 1957)

Bootleg LPs:
- *The Burbank Sessions, Volume 1* ("Elvis" TV special taping; June 27, 1968, at 6:00 P.M. and 8:00 P.M. shows)
- *Elvis Rocks and the Girls Roll* (dress rehearsal for the "Elvis" TV special; June 1968) (in duet with Charlie Hodge)
- *From the Waist Up* ("The Ed Sullivan Show"; January 6, 1957)
- *The King Goes Wild* ("The Ed Sullivan Show"; January 6, 1957)
- *Susie Q* (Las Vegas; ?)

WHEN THE SAINTS GO MARCHING IN
(See *Down by the Riverside/When the Saints Go Marching In*)

WHEN THE SNOW IS ON THE ROSES
"When the Snow Is on the Roses" was written by Bryan Fustukian and first recorded by Ed Ames in 1967. His recording (RCA 47-9319) did poorly on *Billboard*'s Hot 100 chart (#98), but reached number one for four weeks on the Easy-Listening chart. Sonny James recorded (Columbia 45644) the song in 1972.

Elvis sang "When the Snow Is on the Roses" at many of his concerts in 1970, but never recorded it. The song does, however, appear on several bootleg LPs.

Bootleg LPs:
- *From Hollywood to Vegas* (Las Vegas; August 29, 1970)
- *The Hillbilly Cat "Live"* (Las Vegas; August 1970) (Elvis solo with piano accompaniment only)
- *Sold Out* (Las Vegas; August 24, 1970)
- *Special Delivery from Elvis Presley* (Las Vegas; August 19, 1974)

WHEN THE SWALLOWS COME BACK TO CAPISTRANO
This tune was written by Leon Rene in 1940. Both the Ink Spots (Decca 3195) and the Glenn Miller Orchestra (Bluebird 10776) had successful recordings of "When the Swallows Come Back to Capistrano" that same year, reaching #4 and #10 on *Billboard*'s Best-Selling Singles chart, respectively. In 1957 Pat Boone charted (#80, Top 100) with the song, which was the flip side of "April Love" (Dot 15660).

Elvis is known to have sung "When the Swallows Come Back to Capistrano" in concert.

WHERE COULD I GO BUT TO THE LORD
"Where Could I Go but to the Lord" was written by gospel songwriter James B. Coats in 1940 (as "Where Could I Go?") and has been recorded by numerous artists over the years, including Red Foley in 1951 (Decca 14573). It was the flip side of his enormously successful "Peace in the Valley."

Elvis recorded "Where Could I Go but to the Lord" on May 28, 1966, at RCA's Nashville studios. Two years later, he incorporated the song into a gospel medley in his TV special "Elvis." That recording session took place on June 20 or 21, 1968.

LPs:
- *Elvis—TV Special*
- *How Great Thou Art*

Bootleg LPs:
- *The '68 Comeback* (Western Recorders; June 20 or 21, 1968)

WHERE DID THEY GO, LORD
Dallas Frazier and Al Owens wrote "Where Did They Go, Lord" for Elvis, who recorded the song on September 22, 1970, at RCA's Hollywood studios. Elvis's single release had a seven-week stay on *Billboard*'s Hot 100 chart, peaking at #33. It reached #55 on the country chart and #18 on the Easy-Listening chart. Some sources credit "Where Did They Go, Lord" with selling a million copies.

Singles:
- "Rags to Riches"/"WHERE DID THEY GO, LORD" (RCA 47-9980) February 1971. Standard release.
- "Rags to Riches"/"WHERE DID THEY GO, LORD" (RCA 447-0680) February 1972. Gold Standard Series reissue.

LPs:
- *He Walks Beside Me*

Bootleg LPs:
- *The Hillbilly Cat, 1954–1974, Volume 1* (same as RCA release)

WHERE DO I GO FROM HERE
Singer-songwriter Paul Williams wrote and originally recorded "Where Do I Go From Here." On March 27, 1972, Elvis recorded the song at RCA's Hollywood studios.

LPs:
- *Elvis* (RCA APL1-0283)

WHERE DO YOU COME FROM
Ruth Batchelor and Bob Roberts wrote "Where Do You Come From" for Elvis's 1962 movie *Girls! Girls! Girls!* Elvis recorded the tune in March 1962 at Radio Recorders. "Where Do You Come From" spent only one week on *Billboard*'s Hot 100 chart, peaking at #99—the worst performance of any Presley recording to actually reach the chart. Despite its poor showing on the Hot 100, the song is credited with selling over a million copies worldwide.

Singles:
- "Return to Sender"/"WHERE DO YOU COME FROM" (RCA 47-8100) October 1962. Standard release.
- "Return to Sender"/"WHERE DO YOU COME FROM" (RCA 447-0638) June 1963. Gold Standard Series reissue.

- "Return to Sender"/"WHERE DO YOU COME FROM" (RCA PB-11111) October 1977. One of 15 singles released in the boxed set *15 Golden Records—30 Golden Hits* (RCA PP-11301), and one of 10 singles in the *20 Golden Hits in Full Color Sleeves* (RCA PP-11340) boxed set that was released two months later.

LPs:
- *Elvis: Worldwide 50 Gold Award Hits, Volume 1*
- *Girls! Girls! Girls!*

WHERE NO ONE STANDS ALONE
This gospel song was written by Mosie Lister in 1955. Elvis recorded "Where No One Stands Alone" for his *How Great Thou Art* LP on May 26, 1966, at RCA's Nashville studios.

LPs:
- *How Great Thou Art*

Bootleg LPs:
- *Long Lost Songs* (Johnson City, Tennessee; February 19, 1977)

THE WHIFFENPOOF SONG
The music to "The Whiffenpoof Song" was written in 1894 by Guy Sculls, although Tod B. Galloway is sometimes credited. Meade Minnigerode and George S. Pomeroy wrote the lyrics in 1908 based on Rudyard Kipling's poem *Gentleman Rankers*.[1] Minnigerode and Pomeroy were members of the Whiffenpoof[2] Society at Yale University. Their song was adopted as the Society's theme song. Actor James Whitmore and director George Roy Hill were members of the Whiffenpoof Society. Rudy Vallee, a Yale graduate himself, remembered the song from his college days. He featured "The Whiffenpoof Song" in a 1936 broadcast of his radio program and subsequently recorded it in 1937 (Bluebird 7135). Bing Crosby, with Fred Waring's Glee Club, had a #7 pop hit with the song (Decca 23990) in 1947, selling a million copies. Other recordings of "The Whiffenpoof Song" through the years include those by Robert Merrill (RCA 1313) in 1947 and Bob Crewe (Warwick 519) in 1960. The song could be heard in the movies *Winged Victory* (1944) and *Riding High* (1950).

Elvis recorded "The Whiffenpoof Song" in medley with "Violet (Flower of NYU)" at United Recorders in Hollywood on August 23, 1968. It appeared in his 1969 film *The Trouble with Girls*.

Bootleg LPs:
- *Behind Closed Doors* (alternate take) (in medley with "Violet [Flower of NYU]")

WHISTLING BLUES
An instrumental track was recorded for "Whistling Blues" on April 27 or 28, 1960, at RCA's Hollywood studios during the *G. I. Blues* sessions. There's no record of Elvis having recorded a vocal track for the song, although a few people insist that he did.

A WHISTLING TUNE
Elvis first recorded "A Whistling Tune" on July 5, 1961, at RCA's Nashville studios. It was slated for *Follow That Dream*, but was not used. Three and a half months later, on October 26 at Radio Recorders in Hollywood, Elvis again recorded "A Whistling Tune." This time the song was used in *Kid Galahad*. It is that version that appears on record. Sherman Edwards and Hal David are the composers.

EPs:
- *Kid Galahad*

LPs:
- *C'mon Everybody*

Bootleg LPs:
- *Behind Closed Doors* (false starts #3–7)
- *The Complete Kid Galahad Session, Volume 1* (false starts and takes #1–7)

WHITE CHRISTMAS
"White Christmas" is the best-selling song of all time. The song was written by Irving Berlin in 1942 for the film *Holiday Inn*, and recorded for the film by Bing Crosby[3] (Decca 18429A) on May 29 of that year. Crosby was backed by the John Scott Trotter Orchestra and the Ken Darby Singers. Originally, the opening line was "I'm sitting here in Beverly Hills dreaming of a white Christmas." Upon the insistence of Jack Kapp, president of Decca Records, Irving Berlin deleted the line from the song. (The Carpenters' version reinstalled the opening line.) "God Rest Ye Merry Gentlemen" was on the flip side of Crosby's original recording. "White Christmas" won the Oscar for Best Song at the Academy Awards ceremonies. Crosby's version made *Billboard*'s charts every year between 1942 and 1962, except for 1952 and 1953. It was number one in 1942 and #2 in 1946. In the rock era, "White Christmas" cracked the top 10 in 1955 (#7) and almost did it again in 1961 (#12). On the Easy-Listening chart, "White Christmas" was #3 in 1961 and #10 in 1962.

Hundreds of other artists have recorded "White Christmas" since 1942, including Frank Sinatra (Columbia 36756), who reached #7 in 1944 and #8 in 1946; the Drifters (Atlantic 1048), whose recording was a rhythm & blues hit in 1954 and 1955; and Ernest Tubb (Decca 46186), who reached #15 on the country chart in 1949. (The flip side of Tubb's release was "Blue Christmas," which peaked at #2.)

On September 6, 1957, at Radio Recorders in Hollywood, Elvis recorded "White Christmas" based on the Drifters' 1954 recording. Take #9 was chosen by RCA for release. When first released, Elvis's version received much negative publicity, and many disc jockeys refused to play the song or any of the other cuts on the LP *Elvis' Christmas Album*.

---

[1]James Earl Jones got the title for his novel *From Here to Eternity* from a line in *Gentleman Rankers* ("...doomed from here to eternity").
[2]Whiffenpoof was an imaginary character in the operetta *Little Nemo* (1908), by Victor Herbert.
[3]Bing Crosby was the first artist to record for Decca Records (August 8, 1934). Decca was founded by Jack Kapp. Crosby's (and Decca's) first record was "I Love You Truly"/"Just a Wearyin' for You" (Decca DE-100).

EPs:
• *Christmas with Elvis*

LPs:
• *Elvis' Christmas Album*

WHO AM I

"Who Am I" was written by gospel composer-singer Charles (Rusty) Goodman. Elvis recorded the song during his highly productive session at American Sound Studios in Memphis on February 22, 1969. It was the last song recorded by Elvis at the studio.

LPs:
• *He Walks Beside Me*
• *The Memphis Record*
• *You'll Never Walk Alone*

WHO ARE YOU (WHO AM I)

"Who Are You (Who Am I)" was written by Sid Wayne and Ben Weisman for Elvis's 1968 movie *Speedway*. Elvis recorded the tune at Radio Recorders in June 1967.

LPs:
• *Speedway*

WHO NEEDS MONEY

Elvis recorded "Who Needs Money" on February 21, 1967, at RCA's Nashville studios. The film version featured Elvis in a duet with Will Hutchins. (Actually, Hutchins lip-synchs to a vocal recorded by Ray Walker of the Jordanaires.) "Who Needs Money" was written by Randy Starr.

LPs:
• *Clambake*

WHO'S SORRY NOW

"Who's Sorry Now" was written by Bert Kalmar, Harry Ruby, and Ted Snyder in 1923 and introduced by Van and Schenk in vaudeville. Because of their performance of the song, sheet music sales exceeded one million copies. Several recordings of "Who's Sorry Now" were made in 1923, including those by Isham Jones, Marion Harris, Lewis James, Irving Kaufman, and the Original Memphis Five. In 1946 Harry James had a popular recording of the tune. Gloria De Haven sang "Who's Sorry Now" in the 1950 movie biography of Kalmar and Ruby, *Three Little Words*. In 1957 Connie Francis's father remembered the song and urged her to record it at a faster tempo. Her recording (MGM 12588) reached #4 on *Billboard*'s Top 100 chart and became a million-seller. Marie Osmond had a popular country version of "Who's Sorry Now" (MGM 14786) in 1975.

At disc jockey Eddie Fadal's house in Waco, Texas, in the summer of 1958, Elvis's girlfriend, Anita Wood, sang "Who's Sorry Now" twice with Elvis accompanying on piano. Fadal's home recording was later released on the bootleg LP *Forever Young, Forever Beautiful*. Some speculate that Elvis attempted to record "Who's Sorry Now" in the 1950s, but there's been no evidence to support that conjecture.

Bootleg LPs:
• *Forever Young, Forever Beautiful* (Waco, Texas; Summer 1958)

WHOLE LOTTA SHAKIN' GOIN' ON

"Whole Lotta Shakin' Goin' On" was written by Dave (Curly) Williams and Roy Hall (using the pseudonym, Sonny David) while both were in Pahokee, Florida, in 1954. Hall had been Webb Pierce's piano player. The song has been variously copyrighted through the years as "Whole Lot-ta Shakin' Goin' On," "A Whole Lot of Ruckus," and "Whole Lot of Shakin' Going On."

"Whole Lotta Shakin' Goin' On" was first recorded on March 21, 1955, by Big Maybelle (real name: Mabel Smith) in New York City (Okeh 7060). Her band was directed by Quincy Jones. The next documented recording was by co-composer Roy Hall (Decca 29697) on September 15, 1955, in Nashville. Although he was a piano player, no piano was used on the record. Instead, an electric guitar played by Hank (Sugarfoot) Garland was featured. A month later, Dolores Fredericks recorded her version (Decca 29716) in New York City. The Commodores had a release of "Whole Lotta Shakin' Goin' On" (Dot 15431) in December 1955. Finally, after four recordings, we get to Jerry Lee Lewis.

Natchez, Mississippi, disc jockey Johnny Littlefield received Roy Hall's latest Decca Records release, "Whole Lotta Shakin' Goin' On," in the mail in the fall of 1955. He immediately began playing the record on the air. He also began singing the song in his nightclub, the Wagon Wheel (also called the Music Box in some sources). One of the members of his house band was piano player Jerry Lee Lewis. Reportedly, Lewis begged Littlefield to allow him to sing the song in the club. Lewis has said that he first remembers hearing "Big Mama Thornton's" recording of "Whole Lotta Shakin' Goin' On" sometime in 1955. Obviously, Lewis meant Big Maybelle, not Willie Mae Thornton.

In any case, Jerry Lee Lewis incorporated "Whole Lotta Shakin' Goin' On" into his act. In late February or early March 1957, he finally got around to recording the song at Sun Records. Backing Lewis were guitarist Roland Janes and drummer James Van Eaton. The record (Sun 267) was released on April 15, 1957, but it wasn't until Lewis appeared on "The Steve Allen Show" on July 28, 1957, that "Whole Lotta Shakin' Goin' On" got the exposure it needed to finally reach the charts. It peaked at #3 on *Billboard*'s Top 100 chart. "Whole Lotta Shakin' Goin' On" is one of only two records by an artist other than Elvis to reach number one on both the country and rhythm & blues charts. (The other record is "All I Have to Do Is Dream" by the Everly Brothers.) Through the years, Lewis's recording has sold over three million copies.

Although Elvis had sung "Whole Lotta Shakin' Goin' On" in concert on many occasions, it wasn't until September 22, 1970, at RCA's Nashville studios that he first recorded it. In the 1973 TV special "Elvis: Aloha from Hawaii," he sang "Whole Lotta Shakin' Goin' On" in a rock medley. An alternate mix of the song appeared on the RCA Record Club release *Country Memories*.

LPs:
- *Aloha from Hawaii via Satellite* (Honolulu; January 14, 1973) (in medley with "Long Tall Sally")
- *Elvis Country*
- *Elvis Recorded Live on Stage in Memphis* (Memphis; March 20, 1974) (in medley with "Long Tall Sally," "Your Mama Don't Dance," "Flip, Flop and Fly," "Jailhouse Rock," and "Hound Dog")

Bootleg LPs:
- *From Hollywood to Vegas* (Las Vegas; ?) (in medley with "Your Mama Don't Dance," "Flip, Flop and Fly," and "Hound Dog")
- *From Las Vegas . . . to Niagara Falls* (Las Vegas; September 3, 1973) (in medley with "Long Tall Sally," "Your Mama Don't Dance," "Flip, Flop and Fly," and "Hound Dog")
- *The Hillbilly Cat "Live"* (Las Vegas; August 1970) (in medley with "Blue Suede Shoes")
- *Sold Out* (Nashville; July 1, 1973) (in medley with "Long Tall Sally," "Jailhouse Rock," "Your Mama Don't Dance," and "Shake, Rattle and Roll")

WHY ME LORD

Kris Kristofferson wrote and first recorded "Why Me Lord" (as "Why Me") in 1973. His recording (Monument 8571) reached #16 on *Billboard*'s Hot 100 chart and #28 on the Easy-Listening chart. Sales exceeded a million copies.

Elvis performed "Why Me Lord" in concert on March 20, 1974, at the Mid-South Coliseum in Memphis. RCA recorded the concert for release on the *Elvis Recorded Live on Stage in Memphis* LP.

LPs:
- *Elvis Aron Presley* (Shreveport, Louisiana; June 7, 1975)
- *Elvis Recorded Live on Stage in Memphis* (Memphis; March 20, 1974)

WILD IN THE COUNTRY

Elvis recorded "Wild in the Country" on November 7, 1960, at Radio Recorders for his 1961 film of the same title. Take #19 was selected by RCA for release. His single release had a brief five-week stay on *Billboard*'s Hot 100 chart, peaking at #26. On the English LP, *Elvis for Everyone*, maracas were added to the instrumental track. "Wild in the Country" was written by Hugo Peretti, Luigi Creatore, and George Weiss.

Singles:
- "I Feel So Bad"/"WILD IN THE COUNTRY" (RCA 47-7880) May 1961. Standard release.
- "I Feel So Bad"/"WILD IN THE COUNTRY" (RCA 37-7880) May 1961. Compact 33 Single release.
- "I Feel So Bad"/"WILD IN THE COUNTRY" (RCA 61-7880) May 1961. "Living Stereo" release.
- "I Feel So Bad"/"WILD IN THE COUNTRY" (RCA 447-0631) February 1962. Gold Standard Series reissue.

LPs:
- *Elvis Aron Presley* (alternate take #16)
- *Elvis in Hollywood*
- *Elvis: The Other Sides—Worldwide Gold Award Hits, Volume 2*

Bootleg LPs:
- *Behind Closed Doors* (takes #1 [a false start] and #16)
- *The Complete Wild in the Country Sessions* (takes #1–19)
- *From the Beach to the Bayou* (a false start and a complete alternate take)
- *Special Delivery from Elvis Presley* (alternate take)

WILLOW WEEP FOR ME

Ann Ronell composed "Willow Weep for Me" in 1932. Reportedly, it's the only song ever dedicated to George Gershwin. "Willow Weep for Me" was introduced by Irene Bailey with the Paul Whiteman Orchestra and later popularized in a recording by Ruth Etting. In 1964 Chad and Jeremy had a number one Easy-Listening hit with the song (World Artists 1034). It reached #15 on the Hot 100 chart.

"Willow Weep for Me" is believed to be one of the songs Elvis sang at the Lido nightclub in Paris in late June 1959, during an impromptu 30-minute stage show.

WINTER WONDERLAND

This perennial Christmas favorite was written in 1934 by Dick Smith and Felix Bernard. One of the first recordings of "Winter Wonderland" was by Guy Lombardo and His Royal Canadians (Decca 294) in 1934. The next year, Ted Weems and His Orchestra, with vocal by Parker Gibbs, had a popular recording (Columbia 2976). Guy Lombardo with the Andrews Sisters had a million-seller with "Winter Wonderland" (Decca 23722) in 1946, as did Perry Como for RCA Victor (RCA 1968) that same year. Collective sales of "Winter Wonderland" by all artists through the years has exceeded 45 million copies.

Elvis recorded "Winter Wonderland" on May 16, 1971, at RCA's Nashville studios.

LPs:
- *Elvis Sings the Wonderful World of Christmas*

WISDOM OF THE AGES

Elvis recorded "Wisdom of the Ages" in February (probably the 24th) 1965 at RCA's Nashville studios. The song was originally slated to appear in *Harum Scarum*, but was cut from the final print of the film. It's believed that some foreign prints exist with "Wisdom of the Ages" still in the film. Bill Giant, Bernie Baum, and Florence Kaye are the composers.

LPs:
- *Harum Scarum*

WITCHCRAFT

There's some dispute as to who actually wrote this song. Officially, Dave Bartholomew and Pearl King get credit. But Chuck Carbo of the Spiders has said that Bartholomew brought him the lyrics to "Witchcraft," but no music. So, Carbo says he took the music from the Spiders' 1953 release "I Didn't Want to Do It" (Imperial 5265), which was a #2 rhythm & blues hit for them. In any case, the original recording of "Witchcraft" was by the Spiders[1] on Imperial Records (Imperial 5366) in July 1955. Their recording peaked at #7 on *Billboard*'s rhythm & blues chart.

Elvis recorded "Witchcraft" on May 26, 1963, at RCA's Nashville studios. His single release had a seven-week stay on *Billboard*'s Hot 100 chart, peaking at #32. Some sources have credited "Witchcraft" with selling a million copies. This song is not to be confused with Frank Sinatra's "Witchcraft." (Please see next entry.)

Singles:
- "Bossa Nova Baby"/"WITCHCRAFT" (RCA 47-8243) October 1963. Standard release. The original picture sleeve read, "Coming Soon! FUN IN ACAPULCO Album." In December 1963, the sleeve was changed to read, "Ask for FUN IN ACAPULCO Album." One month later, the announcement was omitted.
- "Bossa Nova Baby"/"WITCHCRAFT" (RCA 447-0642) August 1964. Gold Standard Series reissue.

LPs:
- *Elvis' Gold Records, Volume 4*
- *Elvis: The Other Sides—Worldwide Gold Award Hits, Volume 2*

WITCHCRAFT

"Witchcraft" was written by Carolyn Leigh and Cy Coleman in 1957 and introduced by Gerry Matthews in a nightclub show called "Take Five." In 1958 Frank Sinatra had a best-selling record with "Witchcraft" (Capitol 3859), reaching #6 on *Billboard*'s Top 100 chart.

On the Frank Sinatra–Timex Special, "Welcome Home, Elvis," Elvis sang Sinatra's "Witchcraft" in duet with Sinatra singing "Love Me Tender." The program aired on May 12, 1960, on ABC-TV.

The Spiders' original version of "Witchcraft." (Photo courtesy Don Fink)

Bootleg LPs:
- *Frank Sinatra—Welcome Home, Elvis* ("Welcome Home, Elvis" soundtrack)

WITHOUT A SONG

"Without A Song" was composed for the 1929 musical play *Great Day* by Billy Rose, Edward Eliscu, and Vincent Youmans. It was introduced in the play by Lois Deppe and the Jubilee Singers. The first recording was by Paul Whiteman (Columbia 2098) in 1930. It was the flip side of his number one hit "Great Day." Frank Sinatra later recorded "Without a Song" (Victor 36396). In 1955 Roy Hamilton reached #77 on *Billboard*'s Top 100 chart with his recording (Epic 9125).

Elvis read a portion of the lyrics to "Without a Song" when he was presented with an award by the Jaycees as one of the Ten Outstanding Young Men of America on January 9, 1971: "I learned very early in life that without a song the day would never end; without a song a man ain't got a friend; without a song the road would never bend; without a song. So, I'll keep singing the song. Goodnight."

WITHOUT HIM

Elvis recorded "Without Him" on May 27, 1966, at RCA's Nashville studios. The song was written by Myron Lefevre.

LPs:
- *How Great Thou Art*

WITHOUT LOVE (THERE IS NOTHING)

"Without Love (There Is Nothing)" was written by Danny Small and recorded by Clyde McPhatter (Atlantic 1117) in 1957. His recording reached #19 on the Top 100 chart and #6 on the rhythm & blues chart. Other popular recordings of "Without Love (There Is Nothing)" include those by Ray Charles (ABC-Paramount 10453) in 1963, Oscar Toney Jr. (Bell 699) in 1968, and Tom Jones (Parrot 40055), who had a #5 hit and million-seller in 1970.

Elvis recorded "Without Love (There Is Nothing)" in January 23, 1969, at American Sound Studios in Memphis.

LPs:
- *Back in Memphis*
- *From Memphis to Vegas/From Vegas to Memphis*
- *The Memphis Record*

WITHOUT YOU

"Without You" was the first song Elvis recorded for Sam Phillips at Phillips's suggestion. The song was written by a white inmate at Nashville's maximum-security prison. Phillips obtained the song while there recording a session with the Prisonaires. He wanted to record "Without You," but couldn't locate the black singer who had made the demo. Marion Keisker sug-

---

[1]The Spiders, a New Orleans rhythm & blues group, got their name when Chuck Carbo's wife suggested it after spotting a large wood spider on a garage door.

gested he call Elvis, which Phillips did. Elvis ran down to the studio and recorded the song. But no matter how he tried, the song wasn't up to Sam Phillips's standards. At that session, which probably took place in late May or early June 1954, Elvis ran through several other songs he knew. Phillips took note that Elvis had talent and a few weeks later had Scotty Moore and Bill Black meet with him for rehearsals that led to Elvis's first commercial recording session on July 5, 1954.

At Memphis State University on August 16, 1979, Judd Phillips played the Sun tape of Elvis singing "Without You."

WOLF CALL
Elvis sang "Wolf Call" in his 1965 movie *Girl Happy*. The film version had added whistles and wolf howls. "Wolf Call" was written by Bill Giant, Bernie Baum, and Florence Kaye, and recorded by Elvis in July 1964 at Radio Recorders. Take #8 was chosen by RCA for release.

LPs:
• *Girl Happy*

Bootleg LPs:
• *The Complete Kid Galahad Session, Volume 3* (alternate take)

WOMAN WITHOUT LOVE
"Woman Without Love" was written by Jerry Chesnut and originally recorded by Bob Luman (Epic 10416), although his version was released three days after Johnny Darrell's (United Artists 50481) in late 1968. It was Darrell's version that became the hit, peaking at #20 on *Billboard*'s country chart. Luman's release did not chart.

Elvis recorded "Woman Without Love" on March 12, 1975, at RCA's Nashville studios.

LPs:
• *Elvis Aron Presley—Forever*
• *Elvis Today*

THE WONDER OF YOU
"The Wonder of You" was written by Baker Knight for Perry Como, but RCA gave the song to Ray Peterson who recorded it in 1959. His recording (RCA 47-7513) peaked at #25 on *Billboard*'s Hot 100 chart. In 1964 the record was reissued (RCA 47-8333), but could get no higher than #70.

Elvis's single release of "The Wonder of You" was recorded by RCA at the International Hotel in Las Vegas on February 19, 1970. Glen Hardin wrote the arrangement. The record sold over two million copies and had a 12-week stay on *Billboard*'s Hot 100 chart, reaching a high of #9. On the country chart, it peaked at #37. "The Wonder of You" was number one for six weeks in England. It was Elvis's first "live" single release.

Singles:
• "THE WONDER OF YOU"/"Mama Liked the Roses" (RCA 47-9835) May 1970. Standard release.
• "THE WONDER OF YOU"/"Mama Liked the Roses" (RCA 447-0676) August 1971. Gold Standard Series reissue.

LPs:
• *Elvis Aron Presley* (Dallas; June 6, 1975)
• *Elvis: The Other Sides—Worldwide Gold Award Hits, Volume 2*
• *Greatest Hits, Volume 1*
• *On Stage—February, 1970*
• *The Top Ten Hits*

Bootleg LPs:
• *America's Own* (Uniondale, N.Y.; July 19, 1975)
• *The Hillbilly Cat "Live"* (Las Vegas; August 1970)
• *Rockin' with Elvis April Fool's Day* (Las Vegas; April 1, 1975)

WONDERFUL WORLD
Elvis sang "Wonderful World" in his 1968 movie *Live a Little, Love a Little*. The song was written by Guy Fletcher and Doug Flett and recorded by Elvis on March 7, 1968, at Radio Recorders.

LPs:
• *Elvis Sings Flaming Star*
• *Singer Presents Elvis Singing Flaming Star and Others*

THE WONDERFUL WORLD OF CHRISTMAS
Elvis recorded "The Wonderful World of Christmas" on May 16, 1971, at RCA's Nashville studios. The song was written by Charles Tobias and Albert Frisch.

LPs:
• *Elvis Sings the Wonderful World of Christmas*

THE WONDERS YOU PERFORM
Tammy Wynette recorded this Jerry Chesnut composition in 1970. "The Wonders You Perform" (Epic 10687) reached #5 on *Billboard*'s country chart.

On July 25, 1973, an instrumental track was recorded for "The Wonders You Perform" at Stax Studios in Memphis. There's no evidence that Elvis recorded a vocal track.

WOODEN HEART
"Wooden Heart" was recorded by Elvis for his 1960 film *G. I. Blues*. Recorded on April 28, 1960, at RCA's Hollywood studios, it was adapted from the German folk song "Muss I Denn Zum Stadtele Hinaus" by Bert Kaempfert, Kay Twomey, Fred Wise, and Ben Weisman. A few months after the release of the film and the soundtrack album, a single release in the United Kingdom (RCA 1226) reached number one for one week. It remained on the chart for 27 weeks—the longest of any Presley single in that country. The accordion player on Elvis's recording was Jimmie Haskell. A German version by Gus Bacchus (Fono-Graf 1234) was quite successful in Europe and almost cracked the charts in the United States (it reached #102 on the "Bubbling Under" list.)

After watching Elvis in *G. I. Blues*, producer Shelby Singleton Jr. had singer Joe Dowell record a version of "Wooden Heart" in the summer of 1961. Eddie Wilson taught Dowell the German lyrics just three hours before the recording session. Instead of a tuba and accordion as on Elvis's version, a bass guitar (played by Jerry Kennedy) and organ (played by Ray Stevens) were used. The resulting single (Smash 1708) reached number one for one week on *Billboard*'s Hot 100 chart and sold over a million copies.

It wasn't until 1964 that RCA released a single of Elvis's "Wooden Heart" in the United States. That release never charted, although it reached #107 on the "Bubbling Under" list. "Wooden Heart" was reissued the following year, again failing to chart (#110 on the "Bubbling Under" list). Nevertheless, the record was a million-seller for Elvis, easily selling a million in West Germany alone.

In 1975 Bobby Vinton made a successful recording of "Wooden Heart" (ABC 12100). In the 1965 film *Situation Hopeless—But Not Serious*, Robert Redford sang a few lines of the song.

Singles:
- "Blue Christmas"/"WOODEN HEART" (RCA 447-0720) November 1964. Gold Standard Series original.
- "Puppet on a String"/"WOODEN HEART" (RCA 447-0650) October 1965. Gold Standard Series original.

LPs:
- *Elvis—A Legendary Performer, Volume 4* (long false start and a complete take)
- *Elvis Sings for Children and Grownups Too!*
- *Elvis: Worldwide 50 Gold Award Hits, Volume 1*
- *G. I. Blues*

Bootleg LPs:
- *The Entertainer* (Sahara Tahoe Hotel; May 1976) (one line leading into "Young and Beautiful")

WORDS
"Words" was written by the Bee Gees (Barry, Robin, and Maurice Gibb) and recorded by them in 1968. Their version (Atco 6548) reached #15 on the Hot 100 chart and became a million-seller.

Elvis sang "Words" in concert on August 22, 1969, at the International Hotel in Las Vegas. It is that version that is on record. A July 1970 rehearsal of "Words" at the MGM studios was shown in the documentary *Elvis—That's the Way It Is.*

LPs:
- *Elvis in Person*
- *From Memphis to Vegas/From Vegas to Memphis*

Bootleg LPs:
- *The King: From the Dark to the Light* (*Elvis—That's the Way It Is* soundtrack)
- *Special Delivery from Elvis Presley* (*Elvis—That's the Way It Is* soundtrack)

WORKING ON THE BUILDING
This gospel song was written by Hoyle and Bowles and originally recorded by the Blackwood Brothers. In late 1950 the Jordanaires recorded "Working on the Building" (Capitol 1254).

Elvis recorded "Working on the Building," with the Jordanaires on backing vocals, on October 31, 1960, at RCA's Nashville studios.

LPs:
- *His Hand in Mine*

A WORLD OF OUR OWN
"A World of Our Own" was written by Bill Giant, Bernie Baum, and Florence Kaye for Elvis's 1963 movie *It Happened at the World's Fair.* Elvis recorded the song in September 1962 at Radio Recorders. Backing vocals were by the Mello Men. Don Robertson replaced regular session pianist Dudley Brooks for this session.

LPs:
- *It Happened at the World's Fair*

WRITE TO ME FROM NAPLES
Elvis made a home recording of this Alex Alstone–Jimmy Kennedy tune at Graceland in the 1960s. It was included in 1984 boxed set *A Golden Celebration.*

LPs:
- *A Golden Celebration* (Graceland; 1960s)

YEAH, YEAH, YEAH

"Yeah, Yeah, Yeah" is a Jerry Leiber–Mike Stoller song that was recorded by Joe Liggins (Mercury 70440) in 1954. Elvis reportedly recorded the song for *Viva Las Vegas* in July 1963 at Radio Recorders. To date, "Yeah, Yeah, Yeah" has not surfaced.

THE YELLOW ROSE OF TEXAS/
THE EYES OF TEXAS

"The Yellow Rose of Texas" was a marching song written in 1853 by a composer known only as "J. K." It was written for minstrel shows. During the Civil War the song achieved tremendous popularity under the title "The Gallant Hood of Texas"—named for General John B. Hood of the Confederacy. One of the early recordings of "The Yellow Rose of Texas" was made in 1933 by Gene Autry (Perfect 12912). In 1955 Cleveland disc jockey Bill Randle suggested to songwriter Don George that the song had great potential for the pop charts. Mitch Miller had a million-seller—his first—with George's adaptation of "The Yellow Rose of Texas." It was number one for six weeks on *Billboard*'s Top 100 chart. Also in 1955, Johnny Desmond (Coral 61476) peaked at #3 with his recording, Stan Freberg (Capitol 3249) reached #16 with his parody, and Ernest Tubb had a #13 country hit. In the 1956 movie *Giant*, "The Yellow Rose of Texas" was played on a jukebox.

"The Eyes of Texas" was written by John L. Sinclair for a 1903 campus minstrel show based on the melody of "I've Been Working on the Railroad." It serves as the fight song of the University of Texas Longhorns. Also, every time a home run is hit in the Astrodome, the song is played.

Elvis recorded the medley "The Yellow Rose of Texas"/"The Eyes of Texas" in July 1963 at Radio Recorders for his 1964 film *Viva Las Vegas*. Fred Wise and Ben Weisman adapted the tunes for use in the film. "The Eyes of Texas" was sung by itself in the 1969 movie *The Trouble with Girls*.

LPs:
• *Double Dynamite*
• *Elvis Sings Flaming Star*
• *Singer Presents Elvis Singing Flaming Star and Others*

Bootleg LPs:
• *Viva Las Vegas!* (*Viva Las Vegas* soundtrack)

YESTERDAY

Although credited as a John Lennon–Paul McCartney composition, "Yesterday" was actually written by McCartney. The working title was "Scrambled Egg." The other three Beatles were not in the studio when McCartney recorded "Yesterday." The only instrumentation was McCartney's acoustic guitar and a string quartet. "Yesterday" (Capitol 5498) reached number one on *Billboard*'s Hot 100 chart in 1965 and stayed there for four weeks. Sales quickly exceeded one mil-

lion copies. Interestingly, the song was not released as a single in Great Britain until 1976. Matt Monroe had the original hit with "Yesterday" in that country in 1965, reaching #8 on the British chart. In the United States, Ray Charles had a hit rhythm & blues version of the song in 1967 (ABC 11009). "Yesterday" is the most recorded pop song in history, with more than 2,500 cover versions.

Elvis sang "Yesterday" in a medley with "Hey Jude" at many of his concerts in the 1970s. While at the International Hotel in Las Vegas on August 25, 1969, RCA recorded Elvis's medley for inclusion in the *On Stage—February, 1970* LP. Despite the album's title, this song was *not* recorded in February 1970. Vocal overdubs were done on April 1, 1970. A different recording from that of the August 1969 engagement appeared on the *Elvis Aron Presley* boxed set.

LPs:
• *Elvis Aron Presley* (Las Vegas; August 1969)
• *On Stage—February, 1970* (Las Vegas; August 25, 1969)

Bootleg LPs:
• *The Legend Lives On* (Las Vegas; August 1969)
• *Superstar Outtakes* (Las Vegas: August 1969)

YIPPIE YI YO

Elvis sang a few lines of this ditty during a comedy sketch on "The Steve Allen Show" (July 1, 1956). The song was written by Steve Allen. The credits of the documentary *This Is Elvis* list the title as "Yippe Yay Yo Yay Yea" and the publisher as Meadow Lane Music.

Bootleg LPs:
• *The Rockin' Rebel, Volume 3* ("The Steve Allen Show"; July 1, 1956)
• *Superstar Outtakes* ("The Steve Allen Show"; July 1, 1956)

YOGA IS AS YOGA DOES

Elvis sang "Yoga Is as Yoga Does" in a duet with Elsa Lanchester in the 1967 film *Easy Come, Easy Go*. The film version had several backing voices. The instrumental track was recorded on September 28 or 29, 1966, at Radio Recorders. Elvis's vocal was overdubbed at a later date. "Yoga Is as Yoga Does" was written by Gerald Nelson and Fred Burch.

EPs:
• *Easy Come, Easy Go*

LPs:
• *I Got Lucky*

YOU ARE MY SUNSHINE

"You Are My Sunshine" was written by James H. Davis and Charles Mitchell and was first heard in the 1940 film *Take Me Back to Oklahoma*, sung by Tex Ritter. The next year, several popular versions were recorded, including those by Gene Autry (Okeh 6274), Bing Crosby (Decca 39521), and Wayne King (Victor 26767).

In 1944 co-composer James Davis used "You Are My Sunshine" as his campaign song in his successful drive to become governor of Louisiana. Ray Charles had a number one rhythm & blues hit in early 1963 with his rendition of the song (ABC 10375). The flip side was "Your Cheatin' Heart."

"You Are My Sunshine" is one of several songs Elvis is believed to have recorded while at Sun Records, although no tape has ever surfaced.

YOU ASKED ME TO
"You Asked Me To" was written by Billy Joe Shaver and first recorded by Waylon Jennings (RCA APBO-0086) in 1973. His recording reached #8 on *Billboard*'s country chart.

Elvis recorded "You Asked Me To" at Stax Studios in Memphis on December 11, 1973. Felton Jarvis took Elvis's vocal and added a new backing track at Nashville's Young 'Un Sound on October 14, 1980. The recording was then released on the *Guitar Man* LP and as a single. "You Asked Me To" had a 15-week stay on the country chart, peaking at #8, as had Waylon Jennings's version seven years earlier.

Singles:
- "Lovin' Arms"/"YOU ASKED ME TO" (RCA PB-12205) March 1981. Standard release. This was the first Elvis single since 1956 to be released without a picture sleeve.
- "Lovin' Arms"/"YOU ASKED ME TO" (RCA JB-12205) March 1981. Disc jockey promotional release. This record was pressed on green vinyl.

LPs:
- *Guitar Man* (new instrumental track overdubbed)
- *Promised Land*

YOU BELONG TO MY HEART
Written by Ray Gilbert and Augustin Lara, "You Belong to My Heart" was introduced by Dora Luz, who played a live-action bathing beauty in the 1944 full-length animated Disney film *The Three Caballeros*. The song's Spanish title is "Solamente Una Vez." Both Bing Crosby (Decca 23413) and Charlie Spivak (Victor 1663) had hit versions of "You Belong to My Heart" in 1945. Ezio Pinza recorded a version for the 1951 Lana Turner movie *Mr. Imperium*.

"You Belong to My Heart" was one of several tunes sung during the Million-Dollar-Quartet session of December 4, 1956. Elvis sang it primarily by himself, with his own guitar accompaniment.

Bootleg LPs:
- *The One Million Dollar Quartet* (Sun Records; December 4, 1956)

YOU BETTER RUN
This gospel tune was never recorded by Elvis, but he did sing it in concert on a few occasions. Charlie Hodge sang lead, while Elvis sang the bass line. "You Better Run" was sung in a medley with "Bosom of Abraham."

Bootleg LPs:
- *America's Own* (Uniondale, N.Y.; July 19, 1975)

YOU CAN HAVE HER (I DON'T WANT HER)
In 1961 Roy Hamilton had a #6 rhythm & blues hit with "You Can Have Her (I Don't Want Her)," (Epic 9434) which was written by B. Cook. His recording also reached the top 20 of the Hot 100 chart (#12). Other releases of the song include those by the Righteous Brothers (Moonglow 239), Dionne Warwick (Scepter 1294) (as "You Can Have Him"), Timi Yuro (Mercury 72391) (as "You Can Have Him"), all in 1965, and by Sam Neely (A&M 1612) in 1974.

Elvis sang "You Can Have Her (I Don't Want Her)" in concert in the 1970s, basing his performance on that of one of his idols, Roy Hamilton.

Bootleg LPs:
- *Susie Q* (Las Vegas: ?)

YOU CAN'T BLAME A GUY FOR TRYING
Speculation has it that Elvis recorded "You Can't Blame a Guy for Trying" in the 1960s, possibly for a film.

YOU CAN'T SAY NO IN ACAPULCO
Elvis sang "You Can't Say No in Acapulco" in his 1963 movie *Fun in Acapulco*. It was recorded on January 23, 1963, at Radio Recorders. Sid Feller, Dorothy Fuller, and Lee Morris are the composers.

LPs:
- *Fun in Acapulco*

YOU DON'T HAVE TO SAY YOU LOVE ME
Using the title "Io Che Non Vivo (Senza Te)," V. Pallavicini and P. Donaggio wrote "You Don't Have to Say You Love Me" for the San Remo (Italy) song contest in 1965. English lyrics were later written by Vicki Wickham and Simon Napier-Bell. In 1966 Dusty Springfield reached #4 on *Billboard*'s Hot 100 chart and sold a million copies with her recording of the song (Philips 40371). Two years later, the Four Sonics had a mildly successful cover version (Sport 110) that reached #89 on the chart.

Elvis recorded "You Don't Have to Say You Love Me" on June 6, 1970, at RCA's Nashville studios. The brief piano introduction was eliminated from RCA's single release. Elvis can be seen rehearsing the song at MGM in preparation for his upcoming Las Vegas engagement in the 1970 documentary, *Elvis—That's the Way It Is*. Rehearsals at the International Hotel were also seen.

"You Don't Have to Say You Love Me" spent 10 weeks on *Billboard*'s Hot 100 chart, peaking at #11. It replaced the Carpenters' "We've Only Just Begun"[1] at number one on the Easy-Listening chart and was itself replaced after only a week at the top by Perry Como's "It's Impossible." "You Don't Have to Say You Love Me" was on the Easy-Listening chart for 11 weeks. A peak position of #56 was achieved on the country chart. Sales of a million copies were easily attained.

Singles:
- "YOU DON'T HAVE TO SAY YOU LOVE ME"/"Patch It Up" (RCA 47-

---

[1]"We've Only Just Begun" was written by Paul Williams in 1968 as an advertising jingle for the Crocker Bank in California.

9916) October 1970. Standard release.
- "YOU DON'T HAVE TO SAY YOU LOVE ME"/"Patch It Up" (RCA 447-0678) February 1972. Gold Standard Series reissue.

LPs:
- *Elvis as Recorded at Madison Square Garden* (June 10, 1972)
- *Elvis: The Other Sides—Worldwide Gold Award Hits, Volume 2*
- *That's the Way It Is* (*Elvis—That's the Way It Is* soundtrack)

Bootleg LPs:
- *The King: From the Dark to the Light* (*Elvis—That's the Way It Is* soundtrack)
- *Susie Q* (Las Vegas rehearsal; ?)
- *That's the Way It Is* (*Elvis—That's the Way It Is* soundtrack)

YOU DON'T KNOW ME
Eddy Arnold and Cindy Walker wrote "You Don't Know Me" in 1955. Although Arnold probably first recorded the song, it was Jerry Vale's version (Columbia 40710) that was first released in 1956. His record reached #14 on *Billboard*'s Top 100 chart, while Arnold's (RCA 6502) later peaked at #10 on the country chart. Six years later, Ray Charles took "You Don't Know Me" (ABC-Paramount 10345) to #2 on the Hot 100 chart, #5 on the rhythm & blues chart, and number one on the Easy-Listening chart. His is the only recording of the song to become a million-seller.

Elvis sang "You Don't Know Me" in his 1967 movie *Clambake*. The film version, which was backed by a string section, was recorded on February 22, 1967, at RCA's Nashville studios. On September 11, 1967, he recorded the record version. His single release had a six-week stay on the Hot 100 chart, reaching a high of #44. It topped out at #34 on the Easy-Listening chart.

Singles:
- "Big Boss Man"/"YOU DON'T KNOW ME" (RCA 47-9341) September 1967. Standard release.
- "Big Boss Man"/"YOU DON'T KNOW ME" (RCA 447-0662) 1970. Gold Standard Series reissue.

EPs:
- *Clambake* (MTR-244)

LPs:
- *Clambake*
- *Elvis Sings Hits from His Movies, Volume 1*

Bootleg LPs:
- *Eternal Elvis* (*Clambake* soundtrack)
- *Susie Q* (alternate take)

YOU GAVE ME A MOUNTAIN
Although Marty Robbins wrote this song in late 1968, it was Frankie Laine's recording in early 1969 (ABC 11174) that was released first. Laine hit #24 on *Billboard*'s Hot 100 chart and number one on the Easy-Listening chart. Robbins's version was released later in 1969 on his LP *It's a Sin* (Columbia 9811). In the meantime, Johnny Bush (Stop 257) had a #7 country hit with "You Gave Me a Mountain."

Elvis incorporated "You Gave Me a Mountain" into his performances in the 1970s. His performance on April 9, 1972, at Hampton Roads, Virginia, was seen in the documentary *Elvis on Tour*. Elvis also sang "You Gave Me a Mountain" in "Elvis: Aloha from Hawaii" and "Elvis in Concert."

EPs:
- *Aloha from Hawaii via Satellite*

LPs:
- *Always on My Mind* (Honolulu; January 14, 1973)
- *Aloha from Hawaii via Satellite* (Honolulu; January 14, 1973)
- *The Alternate Aloha* (rehearsal concert for "Elvis: Aloha from Hawaii"; January 12, 1973)
- *Elvis Aron Presley* (Honolulu; January 14, 1973)
- *Elvis in Concert* (Rapid City, South Dakota; June 21, 1977)

Bootleg LPs:
- *Aloha Rehearsal Show—Kui Lee Cancer Benefit* (rehearsal concert for "Elvis: Aloha from Hawaii"; January 12, 1973)
- *America's Own* (Uniondale, N.Y.; July 19, 1975)
- *Elvis on Tour* (*Elvis on Tour* soundtrack)
- *From Las Vegas . . . to Niagara Falls* (Las Vegas; September 3, 1973)
- *The Last Farewell* (Indianapolis; June 26, 1977)
- *Leavin' It Up to You* (rehearsal concert for "Elvis: Aloha from Hawaii"; January 12, 1973)
- *Rockin' with Elvis New Year's Eve Pittsburgh, Pa. Dec. 31, 1976* (Pittsburgh; December 31, 1976)
- *Superstar Outtakes, Volume 2* (Las Vegas; 1972)
- *The Vegas Years, 1972–1975* (Las Vegas: 1972)

YOU GOTTA STOP
Elvis sang "You Gotta Stop" in his 1967 movie *Easy Come, Easy Go*. The instrumental track for the song was recorded on September 28 or 29, 1966, at Radio Recorders. Elvis's vocal was done later. "You Gotta Stop" was written by Bill Giant, Bernie Baum, and Florence Kaye.

EPs:
- *Easy Come, Easy Go*

LPs:
- *I Got Lucky*

YOU TURNED THE TABLES ON ME
Alice Faye introduced this song in the 1936 film *Sing, Baby, Sing*. Written by Sidney D. Mitchell and Louis Alter, "You Turned the Tables on Me" became a popular standard with several jazz groups, including Louis Armstrong's and Benny Goodman's. Goodman's recording (Victor 25391) was a big hit in the late 1930s.

"You Turned the Tables on Me" is one of several songs Elvis is believed to have recorded in the studio in the 1950s.

YOU'LL BE GONE
"You'll Be Gone" was recorded by Elvis on March 18, 1962, at RCA's Nashville studios. Elvis, Red West, and Charlie Hodge are credited as the composers. "You'll Be Gone" didn't reach any of the *Billboard* charts, but it was listed as "Bubbling Under" in the #121 position for one week.

Singles:
- "Do the Clam"/"YOU'LL BE GONE" (RCA 47-8500) February 1965. Standard release.
- "Do The Clam"/"YOU'LL BE GONE" (RCA 447-0648) November

1965. Gold Standard Series reissue.

LPs:
• *Girl Happy*

YOU'LL NEVER WALK ALONE

"You'll Never Walk Alone" was written by Oscar Hammerstein II and Richard Rodgers in 1945 for their musical play *Carousel*. It was introduced in that play by Christine Johnson. In the 1956 movie adaptation, Claramae Turner sang it. One of the first recordings of "You'll Never Walk Alone"—if not the first—was by Frank Sinatra (Columbia 36825) in 1945. It was the flip side of "If I Loved You," also from *Carousel*. The next year, Judy Garland released a recording of "You'll Never Walk Alone" (Decca 23539) that was quite popular. Other popular versions of the song over the years include those by Roy Hamilton (Epic 9015), which was a number one rhythm & blues hit in 1954, Patti LaBelle and the Blue Belles (Parkway 896) in 1964, Gerry and the Pacemakers (Laurie 3302) in 1965, and Brooklyn Bridge (Buddah 139) in 1969. The version by Gerry and the Pacemakers topped the British charts for four weeks.

Elvis recorded "You'll Never Walk Alone" on September 11, 1967, at RCA's Nashville studios. His single release reached #90 on *Billboard*'s Hot 100 chart, remaining on the chart for only two weeks. A new release of the song in 1982 had a four-week stay on the country chart, peaking at #73. Elvis copied his vocal styling for "You'll Never Walk Alone" from Roy Hamilton's 1954 recording.

Singles:
• "YOU'LL NEVER WALK ALONE"/"We Call on Him" (RCA 47-9600) April 1968. Standard release.
• "YOU'LL NEVER WALK ALONE"/"We Call on Him" (RCA 447-0665) December 1970. Gold Standard Series reissue.
• "YOU'LL NEVER WALK ALONE"/"There Goes My Everything" (RCA PB-13058) February 1982. New release with a different flip side.
• "YOU'LL NEVER WALK ALONE"/"There Goes My Everything" (RCA JB-13058) February 1982. Disc jockey promotional release.

LPs:
• *Double Dynamite*
• *You'll Never Walk Alone*

YOU'LL THINK OF ME

Written by Mort Shuman, "You'll Think of Me" was recorded by Elvis at the American Sound Studios in Memphis on January 14, 1969. The single release did not chart.

Singles:
• "Suspicious Minds"/"YOU'LL THINK OF ME" (RCA 47-9764) September 1969. Standard release.
• "Suspicious Minds"/"YOU'LL THINK OF ME" (RCA 447-0673) December 1970. Gold Standard Series reissue.
• "Suspicious Minds"/"YOU'LL THINK OF ME" (RCA PB-11103) October 1977. One of 15 singles released in the boxed set *15 Golden Records—30 Golden Hits* (RCA PP-11301).
• "Suspicious Minds"/"YOU'LL THINK OF ME" (RCA GB-13275) January 1983. Gold Standard Series reissue (new number assigned).

LPs:
• *Back in Memphis* (alternate mix)
• *Elvis: The Other Sides—Worldwide Gold Award Hits, Volume 2*
• *From Memphis to Vegas/From Vegas to Memphis* (alternate mix)
• *The Memphis Record*

YOUNG AND BEAUTIFUL

Elvis sang "Young and Beautiful" three times in his 1957 movie *Jailhouse Rock*. He recorded the song on April 30, 1957, at Radio Recorders. It's not apparent exactly which take or takes were used by RCA on record. Possibilities are takes #18 (actually a splice of #12 and #18 and phrases from about three other takes), #19, or #22. Some sources have indicated that take #22 was used on the original release, the *Jailhouse Rock* EP. In West Germany, "Young and Beautiful" was released on a single with "Lover Doll" (RCA 47-9224). Abner Silver and Aaron Schroeder are the composers.

EPs:
• *Jailhouse Rock*

LPs:
• *A Date with Elvis* (alternate mix with more reverberation)
• *Elvis: The Other Sides—Worldwide Gold Award Hits, Volume 2*
• *Essential Elvis—The First Movies* (unreleased version, take #12)
• *I Was the One* (with overdubbing)
• *A Valentine Gift for You*

Bootleg LPs:
• *Cadillac Elvis* (Odessa, Texas; May 30, 1976) (in medley with "Happy Birthday" and "The Mickey Mouse Club March")
• *Elvis Presley Is Alive and Well and Singing in Las Vegas, Volume 1* (Las Vegas; August 1975)
• *The Entertainer* (Lake Tahoe, Nevada; May 1976)
• *Got a Lot o' Livin' to Do!* (three versions from the *Jailhouse Rock* soundtrack)
• *Long Lost Songs* (Las Vegas; 1975)
• *The Vegas Years, 1972–1975* (Las Vegas; 1975)

YOUNG DREAMS

"Young Dreams," an Aaron Schroeder–Martin Kalmanoff composition, was sung by Elvis in his 1958 film *King Creole*. The song was recorded on January 23, 1958, at Radio Recorders. Take #8 is the one that was used on record.

EPs:
• *King Creole, Volume 2*

LPs:
• *Elvis: The Other Sides—Worldwide Gold Award Hits, Volume 2*
• *King Creole*

YOUNG LOVE

Written by Carole Joyner and Ric Cartey, "Young Love" was first recorded by Cartey in 1956 (RCA 47 6751). His version, however, went nowhere. Sonny James then recorded the song (Capitol 3602) later in 1956 and it went to number one on *Billboard*'s country chart. At about the same time, actor Tab Hunter covered James's recording, and the race was on to see who would have the more successful version. When the dust settled, Hunter was atop the Top 100 chart in March 1957, and James was nestled in the #2 spot. "Young Love" was

Tab Hunter's first record. Both versions were million-sellers. The Crew Cuts also had a successful recording of "Young Love" (Mercury 71022) in 1956, which peaked at #17. In 1973 Donny Osmond resurrected the song and had a moderate Hot 100 hit with it (#41).

"Young Love" was one of the songs Elvis rehearsed for his 1968 TV special "Elvis." It was not used for the telecast, however.

Bootleg LPs:
• *Elvis Rocks and the Girls Roll* (dress rehearsal for "Elvis"; June 1968) (sung in medley with "Blue Moon" and "Oh Happy Day")

YOUR CHEATIN' HEART
Hank Williams wrote and recorded "Your Cheatin' Heart" (MGM 11416) in late 1952. The record was issued just after his death on January 1, 1953. It went to #2 on *Billboard*'s country chart and became the top country & western record of the year. The flip side, "Kaw-Liga," reached number one. At about the same time, Joni James recorded a pop version of "Your Cheatin' Heart" (MGM 11426) that rose to #2 on the pop chart. Both recordings were million-sellers. In 1962 Ray Charles (ABC-Paramount 10375) had another popular release of the song.

On February 1, 1958, Elvis recorded "Your Cheatin' Heart" at Radio Recorders. The commercial release was a splice of two or more takes. In 1982 an unspliced alternate take surfaced in the United Kingdom in an eleven-EP boxed set. Earlier, another alternate take was used on a *Reader's Digest* boxed set in that country.

EPs:
• *The EP Collection, Volume 2* (alternate take)

LPs:
• *Elvis for Everyone*
• *Welcome to My World*

YOUR LOVE'S BEEN A LONG TIME COMING
"Your Love's Been a Long Time Coming" was recorded by Elvis at Stax Studios in Memphis on December 15, 1973. The song was written by Rory Bourke.

LPs:
• *Our Memories of Elvis, Volume 1* (without overdubbing)
• *Promised Land*

YOUR MAMA DON'T DANCE
"Your Mama Don't Dance" was composed and recorded by Kenny Loggins and Jim Messina in 1972 (Columbia 45719). They based the tune on the Rooftop Singers' 1963 hit "Mama Don't Allow" (Vanguard 35020). "Your Mama Don't Dance," sometimes referred to as "Mama Don't Dance," reached #4 on *Billboard*'s Hot 100 chart and became a million-seller.

Elvis sang "Your Mama Don't Dance" in a medley with other songs in many of his concerts.

LPs:
• *Elvis Recorded Live on Stage in Memphis* (Memphis; March 20, 1974) (in medley with "Long Tall Sally," "Whole Lotta Shakin' Goin' On," "Flip, Flop and Fly," "Jailhouse Rock," and "Hound Dog")

Bootleg LPs:
• *From Hollywood to Vegas* (Las Vegas; ?) (in medley with "Whole Lotta Shakin' Goin' On," "Flip, Flop and Fly," and "Hound Dog")
• *From Las Vegas . . . to Niagara Falls* (Las Vegas; September 3, 1973) (in medley with "Long Tall Sally," "Whole Lotta Shakin' Goin' On," "Flip, Flop and Fly," and "Hound Dog")
• *Sold Out* (Nashville; July 1, 1973) (in medley with "Long Tall Sally," "Whole Lotta Shakin' Goin' On," "Shake, Rattle and Roll," and "Jailhouse Rock")

YOUR SONG
Some sources have indicated that "Your Song" was recorded by Elvis at RCA's Nashville studios on June 6, 1970. A matrix number has been given—zpa4-1612—but that number was not recorded by Elvis according to the RCA sessions notes. If Elvis *did* record "Your Song," it is certainly not the Elton John tune, because that original release did not chart until later in 1970.

YOUR TIME HASN'T COME YET, BABY
Joel Hirschhorn and Al Kasha wrote "Your Time Hasn't Come Yet, Baby" for Elvis's 1968 film *Speedway*. The recording session took place on June 20, 1967, at MGM's Culver City, California, studios. The single release had a seven-week stay on *Billboard*'s Hot 100 chart, peaking at #72. It reached #50 on the country chart.

Singles:
• "YOUR TIME HASN'T COME YET, BABY"/"Let Yourself Go" (RCA 47-9547) June 1968. Standard release. The picture sleeve read, "Coming Soon—SPEEDWAY LP." In July the picture sleeve was changed to read, "Ask for—SPEEDWAY LP."
• "YOUR TIME HASN'T COME YET, BABY"/"Let Yourself Go" (RCA 447-0666) December 1970. Gold Standard Series reissue.

LPs:
• *Speedway*

YOU'RE A HEARTBREAKER
Contrary to previously published reports, "You're a Heartbreaker" was *not* originally recorded by Elvis. This Charles (Jack) Alvin Sallee tune was written in 1952 and originally recorded by Jimmy Heap (Capitol 2294) late that year. His record was released in January 1953. Two months later, a version by Ray Anthony's orchestra, with vocal by Jo Ann Greer, was issued (Capitol 2349).

Elvis recorded "You're a Heartbreaker" on December 10, 1954, at Sun Records. The single release did not chart nationally, but it was the first Elvis song for which sheet music was issued.

Singles:
• "Milkcow Blues Boogie"/"YOU'RE A HEARTBREAKER" (Sun 215) January 8, 1955. Standard 78 RPM and 45 RPM releases.
• "Milkcow Blues Boogie"/"YOU'RE A HEARTBREAKER" (RCA 20-6382) November 1955. Standard 78 RPM reissue of the Sun original.
• "Milkcow Blues Boogie"/"YOU'RE A HEARTBREAKER" (RCA 47-6382) November 1955. Standard 45 RPM RCA reissue of the Sun original.
• "Milkcow Blues Boogie"/"YOU'RE A HEARTBREAKER" (RCA 447-0669) March 1959. Gold Standard Series reissue.

LPs:
- *The Complete Sun Sessions* (master)
- *For LP Fans Only* (alternate mix with additional overdubbing)
- *The Sun Sessions* (alternate mix with additional overdubbing)

Bootleg LPs:
- *The Sun Years* (alternate mix with additional overdubbing)

YOU'RE RIGHT, I'M LEFT, SHE'S GONE
(See *I'm Left, You're Right, She's Gone*)

YOU'RE THE BOSS
"You're the Boss" is a Jerry Leiber–Mike Stoller song recorded by LaVern Baker and Jimmy Ricks (Atlantic 2090) in 1961. The song peaked at #81 on *Billboard*'s Hot 100 chart. Two years later, in July 1963, Elvis and Ann-Margret recorded "You're the Boss" at Radio Recorders for the film *Viva Las Vegas*. Take #16 was to be used in the film, but the song was cut from the final print. To this date, RCA has not released "You're the Boss," but a poor quality copy can be found on the bootleg album *Elvis Rocks and the Girls Roll*.

Bootleg LPs:
- *Elvis Rocks and the Girls Roll* (dress rehearsal for "Elvis"; June 1968)

YOU'RE THE ONLY STAR
(IN MY BLUE HEAVEN)
Back in the mid-1930s, while Gene Autry was appearing on "The Old Barn Dance" radio show, he began receiving love letters from a woman in Iowa. After several months the woman's doctor wrote to Autry and told him she was mentally disturbed. The physician requested that Autry write to her and tell her that he was not at all interested in her romantic overtures. In the last letter Autry received from the woman, she described being alone. After hearing Autry on the radio she walked outside and stared at the night sky. She wrote: "I looked at the stars in the heavens. I saw millions of them, but you're the only star in my blue heaven." That line inspired Autry to write the song "You're the Only Star (in My Blue Heaven)." His recording (Conqueror 9098) was released in December 1935. Roy Acuff had a popular 1936 recording of the song (ARC 7-04-51). Autry sang the song in his movie *The Old Barn Dance*[1] (1938).

"You're the Only Star (in My Blue Heaven)" was one of the songs sung during the Million-Dollar-Quartet session on December 4, 1956. Jerry Lee Lewis sang a solo with his own piano accompaniment.

Bootleg LPs:
- *The One Million Dollar Quartet* (Sun Records; December 4, 1956)

YOU'RE THE REASON I'M LIVING
"You're the Reason I'm Living" was written by Bobby Darin and recorded by him (Capitol 4897) in 1963. It reached #3 on *Billboard*'s Hot 100 chart and #9 on the rhythm & blues chart.

On a few occasions Elvis sang "You're the Reason I'm Living" in concert, usually in a medley with two or three other songs.

Bootleg LPs:
- *Long Lost Songs* (Las Vegas; March 22, 1975) (in medley with "Roses Are Red" and "I'll Be There")

YOU'VE LOST THAT LOVIN' FEELIN'
Soon after producer Phil Spector bought the Righteous Brothers' contract from Moonglow Records, he flew husband-and-wife songwriters Barry Mann and Cynthia Weil out to California to write a hit song for his new singers. Mann and Weil wrote a tune based on their favorite record at the time, the Four Tops' "Baby I Need Your Loving." Spector helped them write the bridge. "You've Lost That Lovin' Feeling"[2] (Philles 124) was released in late 1964. In February 1965, it hit number one (for two weeks) on *Billboard*'s Hot 100 chart and #3 on the rhythm & blues chart. Sales of over one million copies were quickly achieved. In 1969 Dionne Warwick did a cover version of "You've Lost That Lovin' Feelin' " (Scepter 12262) that did quite well, reaching #16 on the Hot 100 chart. Two years later, Roberta Flack and Donny Hathaway had moderate success with their rendition (Atlantic 2837)

Elvis sang "You've Lost That Lovin' Feelin' " in concert in the 1970s. In the 1970 documentary *Elvis—That's the Way It Is*, Elvis was seen rehearsing the song at the International Hotel in Las Vegas and later singing it in concert on August 14, 1970.

LPs:
- *Elvis Aron Presley* (Las Vegas; August 1970) (rehearsal)
- *Elvis as Recorded at Madison Square Garden* (June 10, 1972)
- *That's the Way It Is* (Las Vegas; August 14, 1970)

Bootleg LPs:
- *The Hillbilly Cat "Live"* (Las Vegas; August 1972)
- *King of Las Vegas Live* (*Elvis—That's the Way It Is* soundtrack)
- *That's the Way It Is* (*Elvis—That's the Way It Is* soundtrack)

---

[1]Roy Rogers, as Dick Weston, appeared in *The Old Barn Dance*.
[2]Cher sang backup on the recording.

Miscellaneous Singles

This section contains medleys, sound sheets, and boxed sets that fit into no other category in this book.

THE AMAZING WORLD OF SHORTWAVE RADIO
(Hallicrafters N2MW-4434)
June 1957. Hallicrafters, a company that manufactured shortwave radios, released this promotional sampler of shortwave radio broadcasts. Elvis's "Loving You," which was played by a French station, was included on the record.

ELVIS LIVE
(Eva-Tone 1037710A&BX)
April 1978. *Elvis Live* was a plastic soundsheet that came with the magazine *Elvis! Collector's Issue!*, which was published by the Green Valley Record Store. The contents was comprised of Elvis's February 25, 1961, press conference at the Claridge Hotel in Memphis.

THE ELVIS MEDLEY/ALWAYS ON MY MIND
(RCA PB-13351)
October 1982. Excerpts from six songs were included in this medley: "Jailhouse Rock," "Teddy Bear," "Hound Dog," "Don't Be Cruel," "Burning Love," and "Suspicious Minds." "The Elvis Medley" reached #71 on *Billboard*'s Hot 100 chart and #31 on both the country and Easy-Listening charts.

THE ELVIS MEDLEY/THE ELVIS MEDLEY (SHORT VERSION)
(RCA JB-13351)
October 1982. Disc jockey promotional release.

ELVIS PRESLEY: "SPEAKS—IN PERSON"
(Rainbo Records)
November 1956. This 78 RPM cardboard soundsheet, manufactured by Rainbo Records of Lawndale, California, was attached to the front cover of the magazine *Elvis Answers Back! Elvis Presley: "Speaks—In Person,"* was perforated so that it could be removed from the magazine's cover. The contents included a brief interview of Elvis in which he talked about his career. The label was dark blue and the cover of the magazine was printed primarily in red ink.

THE ELVIS PRESLEY STORY
(Eva-Tone 726771XS)
July 1977. Eva-Tone produced this 33⅓ RPM sampler soundsheet for the RCA Record Club as a promotion for Candlelite Music's *The Elvis Presley Story* boxed set. It was decided, however, not to follow through with the idea. The soundsheets that had been produced were sold to collectors. Excerpts from eleven songs were featured on *The Elvis Presley Story* sampler: "Don't Be Cruel," "One Night," "Jailhouse Rock," "All Shook Up," "It's Now or Never," "Are You Lonesome Tonight?", "Suspicious Minds," "In the Ghetto," "Burning Love," "Don't Cry, Daddy," and "The Wonder of You."

ELVIS PRESLEY: "THE TRUTH ABOUT ME"
(Rainbo Records)
November 1956. The same material contained on *Elvis Presley: "Speaks—In Person"* was issued on this 78 RPM cardboard soundsheet. Again, the record was attached to the cover of the magazine, *Elvis Answers Back!* The label was light blue, and the magazine printed primarily in green ink.

ELVIS PRESLEY'S GREATEST HITS
(Reader's Digest RDELV-785/86)
197?. To promote the boxed set *Elvis Presley's Greatest Hits, Reader's Digest* issued this plastic 33⅓ RPM sampler. Brian Matthew introduced excerpts from songs and interviews highlighting Elvis's career.

ELVIS: SIX-HOUR SPECIAL
(Eva-Tone 10287733BX)
November 1977. To promote two new radio specials it was offering, the Chicago Radio Syndicate had Eva-Tone produce a 33⅓ RPM plastic soundsheet for insertion in *Billboard* magazine. The two specials offered were "Jamboree USA" and "Elvis: Six-Hour Special." Excerpts from both specials were included on the soundsheet.

ELVIS SPEAKS! "THE TRUTH ABOUT ME"
(Eva-Tone EL-38713T)
1977 or 1978. Eva-Tone reissue of the original 1956 Lynchburg Audio soundsheet. (See the next entry)

ELVIS SPEAKS! "THE TRUTH ABOUT ME"
(Lynchburg Audio 1404-1L)
December 1956. Lynchburg Audio of Lynchburg, Virginia, manufactured this 45 RPM soundsheet for inclusion in *Teen Magazine*. The interview was identical to that previously issued as *Elvis Presley: "Speaks—In Person"* and *Elvis Presley: "The Truth About Me."*

THE GRACELAND TOUR
(Record Digest 25794)
February 1979. Buyers of *Our Best to You*, a book offered to readers of *Record Digest*, received as a bonus this red vinyl 33⅓ RPM soundsheet. *The Graceland Tour* featured Jerry Osborne as Dan Rathernot in a break-in/novelty format. Six hundred soundsheets were manufactured.

THE KING IS DEAD, LONG LIVE THE KING
(Eva-Tone 52578X)
May 1978. Eva-Tone manufactured *The King Is Dead, Long Live the King* for Universal Sounds Unlimited as a

promotion for a proposed syndicated radio special. The soundsheet was pressed on yellow plastic.

THOMPSON VOCAL ELIMINATOR/THOMPSON ANALOG DELAY
(Eva-Tone 12-27785)
December 1978. As a promotion for its electronic products during the Christmas season in 1978, the Thompson Company gave away this eight-inch soundsheet. An excerpt from Elvis's "You Don't Have to Say You Love Me" was included on the record.

WHAT'S IT ALL ABOUT?
(MA-1840; Program #555/556)
December 1980. Songs and interviews were featured on this retrospective of Elvis's life.

Boxed Sets

ELVIS' GREATEST HITS—
GOLDEN SINGLES, VOLUME 1
(RCA PP-13897)

October 1984. To celebrate the 50th anniversary of Elvis's birth, RCA issued this box of six singles. Each record had a new picture sleeve and was pressed on gold vinyl with a special gold "50th" anniversary label.

Contents:
- "Blue Suede Shoes"/"Tutti Frutti" (RCA PB-13885)
- "Don't Be Cruel"/"Hound Dog" (RCA PB-13886)
- "I Want You, I Need You, I Love You"/"Love Me" (RCA PB-13887)
- "All Shook Up"/"Teddy Bear" (RCA PB-13888)
- "It's Now or Never"/"Surrender" (RCA PB-13889)
- "In the Ghetto"/"If I Can Dream" (RCA PB-13890)

ELVIS' GREATEST HITS—
GOLDEN SINGLES, VOLUME 2
(RCA PP-13898)

October 1984. Companion box to Volume 1. Again, each record had a new picture sleeve and was pressed on gold vinyl with a special gold "50th" anniversary label.

Contents:
- "That's All Right (Mama)"/"Blue Moon of Kentucky" (RCA PB-13891)
- "Heartbreak Hotel"/"Jailhouse Rock" (RCA-13892)
- "Love Me Tender"/"Loving You" (RCA PB-13893)
- "Little Sister"/"(Marie's the Name) His Latest Flame" (RCA PB-13894)
- "Are You Lonesome Tonight?"/"Can't Help Falling in Love" (RCA PB-13895)
- "Suspicious Minds"/"Burning Love" (RCA PB-13896)

15 GOLDEN RECORDS—30 GOLDEN HITS
(RCA PP-11301)

October 1977. Shortly after Elvis's death, RCA issued this boxed set of 15 singles, individually packed in full color photo sleeves. A special browser box for record stores was made to hold six complete boxed sets.

Contents:
- "Don't Be Cruel"/"Hound Dog" (RCA PB-11099)
- "In the Ghetto"/"Any Day Now" (RCA PB-11100)
- "Jailhouse Rock"/"Treat Me Nice" (RCA PB-11101)
- "Can't Help Falling in Love"/"Rock-a-Hula Baby" (RCA PB-11102)
- "Suspicious Minds"/"You'll Think of Me" (RCA PB-11103)
- "Are You Lonesome Tonight?"/"I Gotta Know" (RCA PB-11104)
- "Heartbreak Hotel"/"I Was the One" (RCA PB-11105)
- "All Shook Up"/"That's When Your Heartaches Begin" (RCA PB-11106)
- "Blue Suede Shoes"/"Tutti Frutti" (RCA PB-11107)
- "Love Me Tender"/"Any Way You Want Me" (RCA PB-11108)
- "Teddy Bear"/"Loving You" (RCA PB-11109)
- "It's Now or Never"/"A Mess of Blues" (RCA PB-11110)
- "Return to Sender"/"Where Do You Come From" (RCA PB-11111)
- "I Got Stung"/"One Night" (RCA PB-11112)
- "Crying in the Chapel"/"I Believe in the Man in the Sky" (RCA PB-11113)

20 GOLDEN HITS IN FULL COLOR SLEEVES
(RCA PP-11340)

December 1977. All ten of these singles were released two months earlier in the boxed set *15 Golden Records—30 Golden Hits*.

Contents:
- "Don't Be Cruel"/"Hound Dog" (RCA PB-11099)
- "In the Ghetto"/"Any Day Now" (RCA PB-11100)
- "Can't Help Falling in Love"/"Rock-a-Hula Baby" (RCA PB-11102)
- "Are You Lonesome Tonight?"/"I Gotta Know" (RCA PB-11104)
- "Heartbreak Hotel"/"I Was the One" (RCA PB-11105)
- "All Shook Up"/"That's When Your Heartaches Begin" (RCA PB-11106)
- "Blue Suede Shoes"/"Tutti Frutti" (RCA PB-11107)
- "Love Me Tender"/"Any Way You Want Me" (RCA PB-11108)
- "Teddy Bear"/"Loving You" (RCA PB-11109)
- "Return to Sender"/"Where Do You Come From" (RCA PB-11111)

Extended-Play Albums

All known American extended-play albums are included in this list, as well as a couple of significant foreign releases. Every song on these EPs is cross-referenced in the Songs section.

ALOHA FROM HAWAII VIA SATELLITE
(RCA DTFO-2006)
February 1973. This EP was made especially for jukeboxes and contains six tracks from the *Aloha from Hawaii via Satellite* LP. It was released in a 33⅓ Compact Stereo format—the only Elvis EP released in stereo and the second of only two at the 33⅓ speed. The front cover was identical to the LP's, but without the song titles and Quadradisc information. RCA-prepared title strips for jukeboxes were included with the album.

Side 1: "Something," "You Gave Me a Mountain," "I Can't Stop Loving You"
Side 2: "My Way," "What Now My Love," "I'm So Lonesome I Could Cry"

ANY WAY YOU WANT ME
(RCA EPA-965)
October 1956. One of the tracks on this EP—"I Don't Care If the Sun Don't Shine"—reached *Billboard*'s Top 100 chart, peaking at #74. This was almost a year after the song had been released as a single by RCA and more than two years after the Sun Records original. *Any Way You Want Me* came with two covers—one with a song title strip at the top and one without the strip.

Side 1: "Any Way You Want Me," "I'm Left, You're Right, She's Gone"
Side 2: "I Don't Care If the Sun Don't Shine," "Mystery Train"

CHRISTMAS WITH ELVIS
(RCA EPA-4340)
November 1958. *Christmas with Elvis* featured four tracks, two from each side of the 1957 LP *Elvis' Christmas Album*.

Side 1: "White Christmas," "Here Comes Santa Claus"
Side 2: "Oh Little Town of Bethlehem," "Silent Night"

CLAMBAKE
(MTR-244)
1968. This EP is a rare promotional record featuring four tracks from the 1967 film *Clambake*. It used the same cover photo as the *Clambake* LP.

Side 1: "Clambake," "Hey, Hey, Hey"
Side 2: "You Don't Know Me," "A House That Has Everything"

DEALER'S PREVUE
(RCA SDS-7-2)
June 1967. Both sides of Elvis's current RCA single release (47-7000) were featured on this promotional EP issued to record stores. Three other RCA artists were included on the record, each with two songs.

Side 1: "Loving You," "Teddy Bear," "Now Stop" (Martha Carson), "Just Whistle or Call" (Martha Carson)
Side 2: "The Wife" (Lou Monte), "Musica Bella" (Lou Monte), "Mailman, Bring Me No More Blues" (Herb Jeffries), "So Shy" (Herb Jeffries)

DEALER'S PREVUE
(RCA SDS-57-39)
October 1957. This promotional release for record stores contained tracks by six RCA artists. Both sides of their recent singles releases were featured.

Side 1: "The Old Rugged Cross" (Stuart Hamblen), "Old Time Religion" (Stuart Hamblen), "Jailhouse Rock" (Elvis Presley), "Treat Me Nice" (Elvis Presley), "Till the Last Leaf Shall Fall" (Statesmen Quartet), "Every Hour and Every Day" (Statesmen Quartet)
Side 2: "A Slip of the Lip (Kathy Barr), "Welcome Mat" (Kathy Barr), "Just Born" (Perry Como), "Ivy Rose" (Perry Como), "Sayonara" (Eddie Fisher), "That's the Way It Goes" (Eddie Fisher)

EASY COME, EASY GO
(RCA EPA-4387)
March 24, 1967. All six of Elvis's songs from the movie *Easy Come, Easy Go* were included in this EP—in effect, a mini-soundtrack. In addition to being Elvis's last commercially released EP, *Easy Come, Easy Go* was the only EP that included promotional issues as well. One promotional release had "EASY COME, EASY GO—ELVIS PRESLEY" at the top of the label just below RCA VICTOR." Another had in that same position: "RCA Victor Presents ELVIS in the original soundtrack recording from the Paramount Picture EASY COME, EASY GO, a Hal Wallis Production." A strip along the bottom of the cover read, "ASK FOR ELVIS' 1967 COMPLETE COLOR CATALOG."

Side 1: "Easy Come, Easy Go," "The Love Machine," "Yoga Is as Yoga Does"
Side 2: "You Gotta Stop," "Sing You Children," "I'll Take Love"

ELVIS, VOLUME 1
(RCA EPA-992)
October 19, 1956. *Elvis, Volume 1* was basically a mini-version of the *Elvis* LP released on the same day. It featured four songs from side 1 of that album and the same cover photo. Three of the four songs reached *Billboard*'s Top 100 chart, although they have never been released in the United States as singles: "Love Me" (#6), "When My Blue Moon Turns to Gold Again" (#27), and "Paralyzed" (#59). *Elvis, Volume 1* reached number one (for two weeks) on *Billboard*'s EP chart. Within a month it had sold over 500,000 copies and eventually reached the one million mark—the first EP in history to do so. An extremely rare version of this EP was released using the same front cover as the EP *Elvis Presley* (RCA EPA-747). The back cover featured a story about Elvis's first appearance on "Stage Show."

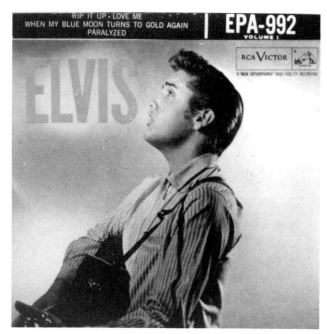

(Photo courtesy Jeff Wheatcraft)

Side 1: "Rip It Up," "Love Me"
Side 2: "When My Blue Moon Turns to Gold Again," "Paralyzed"

ELVIS, VOLUME 2
(RCA EPA-993)
November 1956. Using the same cover photo as the previous *Elvis, Volume 1* EP and *Elvis* LP, *Elvis, Volume 2* featured the first four tracks on side 2 of the LP. One of the songs, "Old Shep," reached #47 on *Billboard*'s Top 100 chart, although it hadn't been commercially released as a single.

Side 1: "So Glad You're Mine," "Old Shep"
Side 2: "Ready Teddy," "Any Place Is Paradise"

ELVIS/JAYE P. MORGAN
(RCA EPA-992/689)
December 1956. *Elvis/Jaye P. Morgan* was a promotional double-pocket, two-record EP set that featured two recent RCA releases: *Elvis, Volume 1* (RCA EPA-992) and *Jaye P. Morgan* (RCA EPA-689). Covers of those two albums adorned the front and back covers of this EP. The two pockets opened up to reveal a center section that contained various facts about the record industry, one of which was that Elvis's EP had outsold Jaye P. Morgan's by about one thousand to one. RCA Victor's sales department sent this promo to its dealers with offers to assist in increasing the stores' future profits.

ELVIS BY REQUEST
(RCA LPC-128)
April 1961. *Elvis by Request* was a 33⅓ RPM EP the size of a 45 RPM single, but with a small spindle hole. Featured were two songs written for the film *Flaming Star*, and two number one hits from the previous year.

One track, "Flaming Star," reached #14 on *Billboard*'s Hot 100 chart. A still photo from the film adorned the EP's cover. Officially called a "Compact 33 Double," *Elvis by Request* was a million-seller and the only 33⅓ Elvis EP released to the public. The "LPC" in the RCA number stood for Long Playing Compact.

Side 1: "Flaming Star," "Summer Kisses, Winter Tears"
Side 2: "Are You Lonesome Tonight?", "It's Now or Never"

ELVIS PRESLEY
(RCA EPA-747)
March 13, 1956. Four songs from Elvis's first LP, *Elvis Presley*, were featured on this EP. One of the tracks, "Blue Suede Shoes," reached #24 on *Billboard*'s Hot 100 singles chart. Two and a half years after its initial release, *Elvis Presley* made a brief (one week) appearance on *Billboard*'s EP chart at the #10 position. A temporary paper sleeve was used for a week or two before the regular album jackets were made available. (The paper sleeve read simply: "Blue Suede Shoes by Elvis Presley; Also Tutti Frutti, I Got a Woman, Just Because; An RCA Extended Play Record.") The regular jacket featured the same cover photo as that used on the *Elvis Presley* LP. Four different back covers are known to exist. One had a story about Elvis and a photo. The other three featured photos of five EPs by various RCA artists. Each one had a different group of albums.

Side 1: "Blue Suede Shoes," "Tutti Frutti"
Side 2: "I Got A Woman," "Just Because"

ELVIS PRESLEY
(RCA EPA-830)
September 1956. The cover featured a photo of Elvis, Scotty Moore, and Bill Black in concert. *Elvis Presley* contained four cuts from three different single releases that were issued the same month. It did not chart.

Side 1: "Shake, Rattle and Roll," "I Love You Because"
Side 2: "Blue Moon," "Lawdy Miss Clawdy"

ELVIS PRESLEY
(RCA EPB-1254)
March 13, 1956. The first four cuts on each side of the *Elvis Presley* LP were presented on this two-record set, which also used the same cover photo as the LP. *Elvis Presley* was the only double EP sold directly to the public. Two years after its release, it appeared on *Billboard*'s EP chart for three weeks, peaking at #9. Three versions of *Elvis Presley* were released. The first had a photo of Elvis on the back cover along with the song titles; in that version, the first record contained sides 1 and 2, the second record sides 3 and 4. Versions two and three had five different photos of recent RCA albums on the back cover along with the song titles; the first record contained sides 1 and 4, the second record sides 2 and 3.

Version #1
Side 1: "Blue Suede Shoes," "I'm Counting on You"

Side 2: "Tutti Frutti," "Tryin' to Get to You"
Side 3: "I Got a Woman," "One-Sided Love Affair"
Side 4: "I'm Gonna Sit Right Down and Cry (over You)," "I'll Never Let You Go (Little Darlin')"

Versions #2 and #3
Side 1: "Blue Suede Shoes," "I'm Counting on You"
Side 2: "I Got a Woman," "One-Sided Love Affair"
Side 3: "Tutti Frutti," "Trying to Get to You"
Side 4: "I'm Gonna Sit Right Down and Cry (over You)," "I'll Never Let You Go (Little Darlin')"

ELVIS PRESLEY
(RCA SPD-22)

October 1956. This two-record, double-pocket EP featured the first four songs from each side of Elvis's first LP, *Elvis Presley*. Both albums used the same cover photograph. The inside pockets of the EP were blank, while the back cover featured the liner notes from the LP. SPD-22 was never released to the general public; however, one could get it free if a four-speed portable Victrola phonograph (Model 7EP2) was purchased at the nationally advertised price of $32.95. If need be, the Victrola could be bought by paying 75 cents down and 75 cents a week. The Victrolas featured "Presley's autograph stamped in gold on the top cover of the extra-strong, scuff-resistant, simulated blue denim cases." To promote the phonographs, print ads were run, and Elvis recorded several radio commercials, which were written by Kenyon and Eckhardt, Inc., of New York City.

Side 1: "Blue Suede Shoes," "I'm Counting on You"
Side 2: "I Got a Woman," "One-Sided Love Affair"
Side 3: "I'm Gonna Sit Right Down and Cry (over You)," "I'll Never Let You Go (Little Darlin')"
Side 4: "Tutti Frutti," "Tryin' to Get to You"

ELVIS PRESLEY
(RCA SPD-23)

October 1956. Four songs from each side of the LP *Elvis Presley* and four hits from both sides of Elvis's second and third RCA singles were included on this special three-record EP. The front cover was the same as the *Elvis Presley* LP, the inside pockets were blank, and the back cover had the same liner notes as the LP. SPD-23 was not sold separately to the general public; one could get it free, however, if an automatic 45 RPM portable Victrola (Model 7EP45) was purchased at the nationally advertised price of $47.95. An easy payment plan of $1.00 down and $1.00 a week was offered. In addition to the Elvis EP, twelve pop records by other RCA artists were included. As with Model 7EP2, Model 7EP45 featured Elvis's autograph stamped in gold.

Side 1: "Blue Suede Shoes," "I'm Counting on You"
Side 2: "I Got a Woman," "One-Sided Love Affair"
Side 3: "I'm Gonna Sit Right Down and Cry (Over You)," "I'll Never Let You Go (Little Darlin')"
Side 4: "Tutti Frutti," "Tryin' to Get to You"
Side 5: "Don't Be Cruel," "I Want You, I Need You, I Love You"
Side 6: "Hound Dog," "My Baby Left Me"

ELVIS PRESLEY—THE MOST TALKED ABOUT NEW PERSONALITY IN THE LAST TEN YEARS OF RECORDED MUSIC
(RCA EPB-1254)

March 1956. All twelve songs from the LP *Elvis Presley* were included on this promotional two-record EP (three songs per side). The EP used the same front cover photo as the LP, but with a green tint. The first record contained sides 1 and 4, the second record sides 2 and 3.

Side 1: "Blue Suede Shoes," "I'm Counting on You," "I Got a Woman"
Side 2: "One-Sided Love Affair," "I Love You Because," "Just Because"
Side 3: "Tutti Frutti," "Tryin' to Get to You," "I'm Gonna Sit Right Down and Cry (over You)"
Side 4: "I'll Never Let You Go (Little Darlin')," "Blue Moon," "Money Honey"

ELVIS SAILS
(RCA EPA-4325)

December 1958. *Elvis Sails* was a songless EP consisting of three interviews with Elvis just before he left for West Germany on September 22, 1958. A newspaper "extra" appeared on the front cover, dated Tuesday, September 22, 1958. Elvis's photo (in his Army uniform) was superimposed on the newspaper. The back cover featured a 1959 calendar with five small photos of Elvis and seven dates circled. (Note: For one of the circled dates—April 10—it said that "Elvis Bought Home for Family in Memphis, April 10, 1956." This was incorrect; it should have been 1957.) A small hole was punched in the top of the *Elvis Sails* cover so that the buyer could hang it on the wall. *Elvis Sails* spent 12 weeks on *Billboard*'s EP chart, eventually rising to #2.

Side 1: Press Interview with Elvis Presley
Side 2: Elvis Presley's Newsreel Interview; Pat Hernon Interviews Elvis in the Library of the USS *Randall* at Sailing

ELVIS SAILS
(RCA EPA-5157)

May 1965. A Gold Standard Series reissue of RCA EPA-4325—this time without the 1959 calendar on the back cover. The front cover was the same, but with the addition of a box reading, "Re-released by Popular Request for Your Collection."

ELVIS SINGS CHRISTMAS SONGS
(RCA EPA-4108)

November 19, 1957. Released on the same day as *Elvis' Christmas Album* (RCA LOC-1035), *Elvis Sings Christmas Songs* featured four songs from side 1 of the LP and a cropped version of its cover photograph. The EP was #2 on *Billboard*'s EP chart for seven weeks. (*Jailhouse Rock* held down the number one position during that stretch.) In 1959 *Elvis Sings Christmas Songs* again surfaced on the EP chart, this time reaching number one for two weeks.

Side 1: "Santa, Bring My Baby Back (to Me)," "Blue Christmas"
Side 2: "Santa Claus Is Back in Town," "I'll Be Home for Christmas"

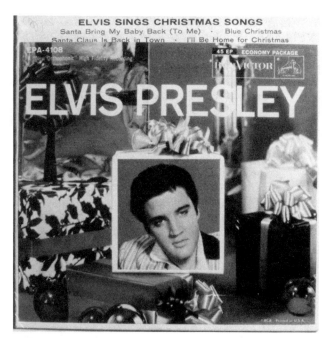

(Photo courtesy Don Fink)

THE EP COLLECTION, VOLUME 2
(RCA EP2)
1982. Eleven extended-play albums were included in this boxed set available only in Great Britain. Three of them [*A Touch of Gold, Volume 2* (RCX-7203), *G. I. Blues—The Alternate Takes, Volume 2* (RCX-2), and *Collectors Gold* (RCX-3)] contained alternate takes not previously released by RCA. RCX-2 and RCX-3 were available only in this boxed set.

A Touch of Gold, Volume 2
Side 1: "Wear My Ring Around Your Neck," "One Night"
Side 2: "Your Cheatin' Heart" (alternate take), "That's All Right (Mama)"

G. I. Blues—The Alternate Takes, Volume 2
Side 1: "What's She Really Like" (alternate take), "G. I. Blues" (alternate take)
Side 2: "Doin' the Best I Can" (alternate take), "Pocketful of Rainbows" (alternate take)

Collectors Gold
Side 1: "(Marie's the Name) His Latest Flame" (alternate take), "Good Luck Charm" (alternate take)
Side 2: "Judy" (alternate take), "Little Sister" (alternate take)

EXTENDED PLAY SAMPLER
(RCA SPA-7-61)
October 1957. This unusual EP sampler was sent to radio stations to promote the latest RCA EPs. The labels did not list song titles—just EP numbers next to the artists' names. The Elvis EP featured was *Jailhouse Rock*, which was represented by the title tune. A total of 12 tunes by 12 artists were sampled on the EP.

FOLLOW THAT DREAM
(RCA EPA-4368)
May 1962. Four of the five songs from the film *Follow That Dream* were featured. The title track reached #5

on *Billboard*'s Easy-Listening chart, and the EP itself peaked at #15 on the Hot 100 chart. The cover of the regular release of *Follow That Dream* read "4 Great Songs from This Great Movie." A special Coin Operator/DJ Prevue cover with no photo proclaimed, "Elvis Sings Four Great Songs from His New Movie, 'Follow That Dream,' Available Now Only on 45 EP."

Side 1: "Follow That Dream," "Angel,"
Side 2: "What a Wonderful Life," "I'm Not the Marrying Kind"

GOOD ROCKIN' TONIGHT
(Motion Picture Service EP-1206)
1956. *Good Rockin' Tonight* was a "Hit of the Month" EP released by the Motion Picture Service.

Side 1: "Good Rockin' Tonight," "I Don't Care If the Sun Don't Shine"
Side 2: "Blue Moon of Kentucky," "Shake, Rattle and Roll"

GREAT COUNTRY/WESTERN HITS
(RCA SPD-26)
November 1956. Four Elvis tunes were included in this special 10-EP boxed set of country songs. It should be noted that on the label of side 15 (record 8) "Milkcow Blues Boogie" is mistakenly printed as "Milkcow Boogie Blues."

Side 1: "Bouquet of Roses," "Molly Darling" (both by Eddy Arnold)
Side 2: "Alabama Jubilee," "Unchained Melody" (both by Chet Atkins)
Side 3: "The Banana Boat Song," "Slow Poison" (both by Johnnie and Jack)
Side 4: "I'm My Own Grandpaw," "Cigareetes, Whuskey and Wild, Wild Women (both by Homer and Jethro)
Side 5: "Looking Back to See," "Draggin' Main Street" (both by Jim Ed and Maxine Brown)
Side 6: "Blue Moon of Kentucky," "Love Me Tender" (both by Elvis Presley)
Side 7: "According to My Heart," "Am I Losing You" (both by Jim Reeves)
Side 8: "I Don't Hurt Anymore," "I'm Movin' On" (both by Hank Snow)
Side 9: "Cool Water," "The Everlasting Hills of Oklahoma" (both by the Sons of the Pioneers)
Side 10: "Company's Coming," "A Satisfied Mind" (both by Porter Wagoner)
Side 11: "Seeing Her Only Reminded Me of You," "Eat, Drink and Be Merry" (both by Porter Wagoner)
Side 12: "I'll Wonder When We'll Ever Know," "Red River Valley" (both by the Sons of the Pioneers)
Side 13: "Old Doc Brown," "Grandfather's Clock" (both by Hank Snow)
Side 14: "Yonder Comes a Sucker," "Waitin' for a Train" (both by Jim Reeves)
Side 15: "Mystery Train," "Milkcow Blues Boogie" (both by Elvis Presley)
Side 16: "Down Yonder," "Aloha Oe" (both by Del Wood)
Side 17: "Slow Poke," "Over the Waves" (both by Homer and Jethro)
Side 18: "Love, Love, Love," "We Live in Two Different Worlds" (both by Johnnie and Jack)
Side 19: "San Antonio Rose," "Arkansas Traveler" (both by Chet Atkins)
Side 20: "The Cattle Call," "I Wouldn't Know Where to Begin" (both by Eddy Arnold)

HEARTBREAK HOTEL
(RCA EPA-821)
April 1956. Both sides of Elvis's first original RCA single were included in this EP, along with two other

songs. "Money Honey" was the only track on *Heart-break Hotel* not to have been previously released. The EP reached #5 on *Billboard*'s EP chart two years after its release, and "Money Honey" peaked at #76 on the Top 100 chart. (When "Money Honey" was released as a single in September 1956, it did not chart.) *Heartbreak Hotel* came with two different covers, each using the same photograph: one had a strip at the top listing the songs and record number, and one didn't.

Side 1: "Heartbreak Hotel," "I Was the One"
Side 2: "Money Honey," "I Forgot to Remember to Forget"

JAILHOUSE ROCK
(RCA EPA-4114)
October 30, 1957. Five of the six songs in Elvis's third film were contained on this EP, including the title track. Three thousand copies of *Jailhouse Rock* were mailed to disc jockeys across the nation for promotional purposes. For the week ending November 2, 1957, *Jailhouse Rock* entered *Billboard*'s EP chart at

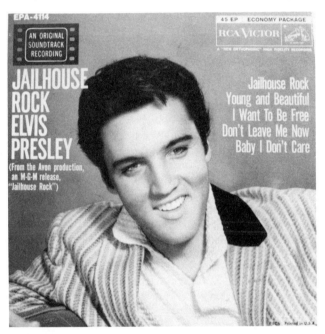

(Photo courtesy Don Fink)

the number one position and stayed there for 22 straight weeks. In the 23rd week, it dipped to #2, but jumped back to number one the following week and stayed there for six more weeks. In all, *Jailhouse Rock* was number one for an amazing 28 weeks and on the chart for 49 weeks. *Billboard* named it 1958's EP of the Year. *Jailhouse Rock* sold well over one million copies and became Elvis's best-selling EP.

Side 1: "Jailhouse Rock," "Young and Beautiful"
Side 2: "I Want to Be Free," "Don't Leave Me Now," "(You're So Square) Baby, I Don't Care"

JUST FOR YOU
(RCA EPA-4041)
September 1957. *Just for You* contained three tracks from the *Loving You* LP, plus "Is It So Strange." In its

one week on *Billboard*'s LP chart, *Just for You* was listed at #16. It peaked at #2 on the EP chart. (Elvis's *Loving You, Volume 1* was number one that week.) At the time of this EP's release, Ricky Nelson's version of "Have I Told You Lately That I Love You" was climbing the singles chart. To promote Elvis's recording of the song on *Just for You*, RCA bought a full-page advertisement in *Billboard* saying that the "Big Version Is by Elvis." Two covers were issued, each with the same photograph: one with the title of the EP and its RCA number, and one without.

Side 1: "I Need You So," "Have I Told You Lately That I Love You"
Side 2: "Blueberry Hill," "Is It So Strange"

KID GALAHAD
(RCA EPA-4371)
September 1962. All six songs from the 1962 movie *Kid Galahad* were featured on this EP. One of the tracks—"King of the Whole Wide World"—made *Billboard*'s Hot 100 chart, peaking at #30. A still photo from the movie adorned the cover of *Kid Galahad*.

Side 1: "King of the Whole Wide World," "This is Living," "Riding the Rainbow"
Side 2: "Home Is Where the Heart Is," "I Got Lucky," "A Whistling Tune"

KING CREOLE
(RCA EPA-4319)
July 1958. Two songs from each side of Elvis's *King Creole* soundtrack LP were featured in this EP. The cover photograph was the same as that on the LP except that it was reversed (Elvis faced left instead of right). *King Creole* entered *Billboard*'s EP chart at number one and stayed there for 29 weeks (23 of them consecutive)—a record for an Elvis EP. The total of 54 weeks on the chart was also an Elvis high. Sales of *King Creole* easily exceeded one million units, making it the second most successful of all of Elvis's extended-play albums (just behind *Jailhouse Rock*).

Side 1: "King Creole," "New Orleans"
Side 2: "As Long as I Have You," "Lover Doll"

KING CREOLE
(RCA EPA-5122)
November 1959. Gold Standard Series reissue of RCA EPA-4319.

KING CREOLE, VOLUME 2
(RCA EPA-4321)
August 1958. As with the first volume, *King Creole, Volume 2* featured two songs from each side of the movie soundtrack LP. It had a one-week stay at number one on *Billboard*'s EP chart, but was #2 for 17 weeks. In all, it stayed on the chart for 22 weeks.

Side 1: "Trouble," "Young Dreams"
Side 2: "Crawfish," "Dixieland Rock"

LOVE ME TENDER
(RCA EPA-4006)
November 1956. All four songs from Elvis's first movie

were included in this EP. *Love Me Tender* reached #22 on *Billboard*'s Best-Selling Pop Albums chart and #9 on the EP chart. One of these songs on this EP—"Poor Boy"—reached #35 on the singles chart. Two covers were issued, both using the same still from the film. One had a song-title strip at the top that contained the EP's number; the second pressing eliminated the strip.

Side 1: "Love Me Tender," "Let Me"
Side 2: "Poor Boy," "We're Gonna Move"

LOVING YOU, VOLUME 1
(RCA EPA 1-1515)
June 1957. *Loving You Volume 1* featured four tracks from the *Loving You* LP and that album's cover photo. When *Billboard*'s extended-play chart premiered (for the week ending September 28, 1957), *Loving You, Volume 1* was its first number one record.[1] It remained at the top of the chart for five weeks. Two versions of the cover were issued: one with a strip at the top listing the songs and record number, and one without the strip.

Side 1: "Loving You," "(Let's Have a) Party"
Side 2: "(Let Me Be Your) Teddy Bear," "True Love"

LOVING YOU, VOLUME 2
(RCA EPA 2-1515)
June 1957. Four tracks from the *Loving You* LP were included in *Loving You, Volume 2*. The cover photo was the same as that used on the LP and the *Loving You, Volume 1* EP. *Loving You, Volume 2* reached #4 on *Billboard*'s EP chart. As with many of the other EPs, two covers were issued: one with a strip at the top containing the song titles and record number, and one without.

(Photo courtesy Don Fink)

Side 1: "Lonesome Cowboy," "Hot Dog"
Side 2: "Mean Woman Blues," "Got a Lot o' Livin' to Do"

PEACE IN THE VALLEY
(RCA EPA-4054)
March 22, 1957. *Peace in the Valley* was Elvis's first religious release and the best-selling gospel EP of all time, selling a reported one million copies. It reached #3 on *Billboard*'s EP chart, #3 on the LP chart, and the title song peaked at #39 on the Top 100 singles chart. *Peace in the Valley* was the first RCA EP release in Great Britain that was identical to the American version.

Side 1: "(There'll Be) Peace in the Valley (for Me)," "It Is No Secret (What God Can Do)"
Side 2: "I Believe," "Take My Hand, Precious Lord"

PEACE IN THE VALLEY
(RCA EPA-5121)
November 1959. Gold Standard Series reissue of RCA EPA-4054, using the same cover photo.

PERFECT FOR PARTIES
(RCA SPA-7-37)
October 25, 1956. The six selections on this special EP were taken from six RCA LPs. Elvis introduced all the songs, including his own "Love Me." The *Perfect for Parties* Highlight Album was advertised in seventeen national magazines, among them *Life, Seventeen, HiFi, Schwann, Country Song, High Fidelity,* and *Forty-Five.* Spots appeared on radio's "The Bob and Ray Show," and on October 27, 1956, a 90-second color commercial aired on NBC-TV. To obtain *Perfect for Parties,* one simply had to clip a coupon from a print ad and send it, along with 25 cents, to: Dept. 776, RCA Victor, Philadelphia, 5, Pennsylvania. One could also buy twenty 7"-by-7" full-color album-cover reprints for an additional dollar. These albums were featured in the advertisement. The offer expired on December 31, 1956. Two label variations exist for this special EP. On one, "Not for Sale" appeared on the right side of the label; on the other, it appeared on the left side.

Side 1: "Love Me" (Elvis Presley), "Anchors Aweigh" (Tony Cabot and His Orchestra), "That's a Puente" (Tito Puente and His Orchestra)
Side 2: "Rock Me but Don't Roll Me" (Tony Scott and His Orchestra), "Happy Face Baby" (The Three Suns), "Prom to Prom" (Dave Pell Octet)

PROMOTION DISC
(RCA PRO-12)
December 1956. RCA promotion EP that featured Elvis's "Old Shep." The record was sent to radio stations.

Side 1: "Old Shep" (Elvis Presley), "I'm Movin' On"[2] (Hank Snow)
Side 2: "The Cattle Call" (Eddy Arnold with Hugo Winterhalter Orchestra and Chorus), "Four Walls" (Jim Reeves)

---

[1] Elvis's EPs occupied 4 of the top 10 positions that week: *Loving You, Volume 1* (#1), *Just for You* (#3), *Peace in the Valley* (#9), and *Loving You, Volume 2* (#10).
[2] The label incorrectly listed the title of the song as "I'm Moving On."

RCA FAMILY RECORD CENTER
(RCA PR-121)
February 1962. This odd record was a "Compact 33" promotional EP. It had a small spindle hole and played at 33⅓ RPM. Eight songs were included, one of which was Elvis's "Good Luck Charm." RCA released this EP for use only in record stores. None of the songs was complete, as an announcer on the disc frequently interrupted, hawking new RCA records.

Side 1: "Good Luck Charm" (Elvis Presley), "The Way You Look Tonight" (Peter Nero), "Younger Than Springtime" (Paul Anka), "Frenesi" (Living Strings)
Side 2: "Twistin' the Night Away" (Sam Cooke), "Easy Street" (Al Hirt), "Make Someone Happy" (Perry Como), "Moon River" (Henry Mancini)

THE REAL ELVIS
(RCA EPA-940)
September 1956. Both sides of Elvis's second and third original RCA singles were featured on this EP. Two years after its release, *The Real Elvis* spent five weeks on *Billboard*'s EP chart, peaking at #5.

Side 1: "Don't Be Cruel," "I Want You, I Need You, I Love You"
Side 2: "Hound Dog," "My Baby Left Me"

THE REAL ELVIS
(RCA EPA-5120)
November 1959. Gold Standard Series reissue of RCA EPA-940.

SAVE-ON RECORDS (BULLETIN FOR JUNE 1956)
(RCA SPA-7-27)
June 1956. Buyers who had RCA Victor Save-On Records Coupon Books received this special EP that featured one selection from each of ten current RCA albums. If the buyer decided to purchase any of the albums, he simply went to his local RCA dealer and presented the appropriate coupons. The LPs, which normally cost $3.98, sold for $2.98 with a coupon and were mailed from the RCA factory to the buyer's home, postage-free. This June 1956 bulletin contained Elvis's "I'm Gonna Sit Right Down and Cry (over You)." (Note: The record label left off the word *I'm* in the song's title.)

Side 1: "Intermezzo" (Frankie Carle), "Moonlight Cocktail" (Al Nevins), "I'm Gonna Sit Right Down and Cry (over You)" (Elvis Presley), "Adventure in Time" (Sauter-Finegan Orchestra), "Great Gettin' Up Morning" (Harry Belafonte)
Side 2: "Liebestraum" (Artur Rubenstein), "Voi Che Sapete" (Rise Stevens), "Beethoven: Symphony No. 9" (Arturo Toscanini), "Jalousie" (Arthur Fiedler and Boston Pops), "Symphonie Fantastique" (Boston Symphony Orchestra)

SEE THE USA, THE ELVIS WAY
(EPA-4386)
1964. *See the USA, the Elvis Way* was issued in New Zealand in both mono and stereo versions. The stereo release (RCA EPAS-4386) contained the true stereo version of "Viva Las Vegas," which so far has been unavailable in the United States.

Side 1: "Memphis, Tennessee," "Blue Moon of Kentucky"
Side 2: "New Orleans," "Viva Las Vegas"

THE SOUND OF LEADERSHIP
(RCA SPD-19)
June 1956. RCA Victor held its annual distributor meeting in Miami in June 1956. Distributors were given this eight-EP boxed set as a souvenir. All 32 songs in the set were RCA million-sellers and ranged from 1907's "Vesti La Giubba" by Enrico Caruso to 1956's "Heartbreak Hotel" by Elvis.

Side 1: "Vesti La Giubba" (1907; Enrico Caruso), "O Sole Mio" (1916; Enrico Caruso)
Side 2: "Ramona" (1928; Gene Austin), "Marie" (1937; Tommy Dorsey)
Side 3: "Boogie Woogie" (1938; Tommy Dorsey), "Jalousie" (1938; Boston Pops Orchestra)
Side 4: "Beer Barrel Polka" (1938; Will Glahe), "Begin the Beguine" (1938; Artie Shaw)
Side 5: "In the Mood" (1939; Glenn Miller), "Sunrise Serenade" (1939; Glenn Miller)
Side 6: "Blue Danube Waltz" (1939; Leopold Stokowksi), "Tuxedo Junction" (1940; Glenn Miller)
Side 7: "Stardust" (1940; Artie Shaw), "Tchaikovsky Piano Concerto" (1941; Freddy Martin)
Side 8: "Chattanooga Choo Choo" (1941; Glenn Miller), "Racing with the Moon" (1941; Vaughn Monroe)
Side 9: "Prisoner of Love" (1946; Perry Como), "Ballerina" (1947; Vaughn Monroe)
Side 10: "The Whiffenpoof Song" (1947; Robert Merrill), "Bouquet of Roses" (1948; Eddy Arnold)
Side 11: "Be My Love" (1950; Mario Lanza), "Anytime" (1951; Eddie Fisher)
Side 12: "The Loveliest Night of the Year" (1951; Mario Lanza), "Slow Poke" (1951; Pee Wee King)
Side 13: "Don't Let the Stars Get in Your Eyes" (1952; Perry Como), "You, You, You" (1953; The Ames Brothers)
Side 14: "I Need You Now" (1954; Eddie Fisher), "Cherry Pink and Apple Blossom White" (1954; Perez Prado)
Side 15: "Naughty Lady of Shady Lane" (1954; The Ames Brothers), "Rock and Roll Waltz" (1955; Kay Starr)
Side 16: "Hot Diggity" (1956; Perry Como), "Heartbreak Hotel" (1956; Elvis Presley)

STAY AWAY
(MTR-243)
1968. This EP is a rare promotional record featuring both sides of the single release, RCA 47-9465, on side 1 and the A sides of two other singles on side 2.

Side 1: "Stay Away," "U.S. Male"
Side 2: "Guitar Man," "Big Boss Man"

STRICTLY ELVIS
(RCA EPA-994)
January 1957. Technically, *Strictly Elvis* should be titled *Elvis, Volume 3*, since it was actually a continuation of EPA-992 and EPA-993. The remaining two cuts on each side of the *Elvis* LP are featured here. Two covers were issued for *Strictly Elvis*—the original with the song-title strip and record number at the top of the cover, and the second pressing without the strip. The cover photograph was taken at the same session as the one that appeared on the cover of the *Elvis* LP, but this time Elvis was facing the front. *Strictly Elvis* did not chart.

Side 1: "Long Tall Sally," "First in Line"
Side 2: "How Do You Think I Feel," "How's the World Treating You"

TICKLE ME
(RCA EPA-4383)

June 1965. *Tickle Me* featured five songs from the 1965 Allied Artists film of the same title. It reached #70 on *Billboard*'s Hot 100 chart—the last Elvis EP to appear on any of *Billboard*'s charts. Three covers were issued with the *Tickle Me* EP, all with the same cover photograph. One cover had "Coming Soon! Special Elvis Anniversary LP Album" along the bottom; another had "Ask for Special Elvis Anniversary LP Album"; and the third had no advertisement at all. (The LP referred to was *Elvis for Everyone*)

Side 1: "I Feel That I've Known You Forever," "Slowly but Surely"
Side 2: "Night Rider," "Put the Blame on Me," "Dirty, Dirty Feeling"

A TOUCH OF GOLD, VOLUME 1
(RCA EPA-5088)

April 1959. *A Touch of Gold, Volume 1* contained three of Elvis's top 10 RCA hits, along with an original Sun Records release. The cover had a shot of Elvis wearing his gold lamé suit. This was the same photo that later

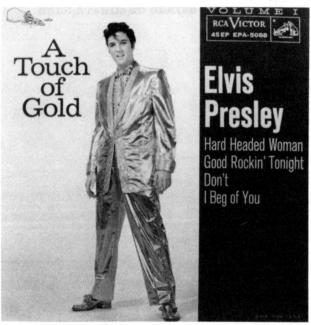

(Photo courtesy Don Fink)

appeared on the LP *50,000,000 Elvis Fans Can't Be Wrong—Elvis' Gold Records, Volume 2.* A fan club card from Elvis was enclosed with the EP. A few copies had a paper insert that read, "Thank you for buying this and other RCA records." *A Touch of Gold, Volume 1,* which was a Gold Standard Series original release, did not chart.

Side 1: "Hard Headed Woman," "Good Rockin' Tonight"
Side 2: "Don't," "I Beg of You"

A TOUCH OF GOLD, VOLUME 2
(RCA EPA-5101)

September 1959. As with Volume 1 of the series, Volume 2 featured three RCA hits along with a Sun Rec-

ords original. This time the cover had *two* shots of Elvis in his gold lamé suit. A few copies had a paper insert that read, "Thank you for buying this and other RCA records." An original Gold Standard Series release, *A Touch of Gold, Volume 2* did not chart.

Side 1: "Wear My Ring Around Your Neck," "Treat Me Nice"
Side 2: "One Night," "That's All Right (Mama)"

A TOUCH OF GOLD, VOLUME 3
(RCA EPA-5141)

January 1960. Continuing with the three-volume series, *A Touch of Gold, Volume 3* had three RCA hits along with a Sun Records original. *Three* shots of Elvis wearing his gold lamé suit graced the cover. A few copies had a paper insert that read, "Thank you for buying this and other RCA records." *A Touch of Gold, Volume 3* was a Gold Standard Series original. It did not chart.

Side 1: "All Shook Up," "Don't Ask Me Why"
Side 2: "Too Much," "Blue Moon of Kentucky"

TUPPERWARE'S HIT PARADE
(Tupperware THP-11973)

January 1973. A portion of Elvis's "All Shook Up" appeared on this 33⅓ promotional EP from the Tupperware Company.

TV GUIDE PRESENTS ELVIS PRESLEY
(RCA GB-MW-8705)

September 1956. An extremely rare record, this one-sided promotional EP was sent to radio stations. It consisted of recorded excerpts from an August 6, 1956, interview with Elvis by writer Paul Wilder at a Lakewood, Florida, performance. Wilder was there interviewing Elvis for a three-part series for *TV Guide* magazine. (The articles appeared in the September 8–14, September 22–28, and September 29–October 5 issues of the magazine.) *TV Guide Presents Elvis Presley* contained four bands of interview excerpts and two paper inserts. One insert (green) featured a photo of the September 8–14 cover of *TV Guide* and related how the interview came to be. The other insert (pink) contained suggested continuity, so that a disc jockey could conduct an "interview" of Elvis by asking the questions on the sheet and then playing the correct band on the record. Both the dialogue for the disc jockey and Elvis's transcribed answers were printed on the insert.

Band 1: "Pelvis" Nickname (:19)
Band 2: Adults' Reaction (:34)
Band 3: First Public Appearance (:54)
Band 4: How "Rockin' Motion" Started (:44)

VIVA LAS VEGAS
(RCA EPA-4382)

June 1964. Four songs from Elvis's 1964 film *Viva Las Vegas* were featured on this EP. A still photograph from the movie graced the cover. *Viva Las Vegas* reached #92 on *Billboard*'s Hot 100 chart, staying on the chart just one week. Oddly, the song "Viva Las Vegas" was not on this EP.

Side 1: "If You Think I Don't Need You," "I Need Somebody to Lean On"
Side 2: "C'mon Everybody," "Today, Tomorrow and Forever"

(NO TITLE)
(RCA DJ-7)

October 1956. Both sides of Elvis's RCA 47-6643 single and two cuts by Jean Chapel appeared on this special disc jockey promotional EP.

Side 1: "Love Me Tender," "Any Way You Want Me (That's How I Will Be)" (both by Elvis)
Side 2: "Welcome to the Club," "I Won't be Rockin' Tonight" (both by Jean Chapel)

(NO TITLE)
(RCA DJ-56)

January 1957. This disc jockey promotional EP featured both sides of Elvis's single RCA 47-6800, and two tracks by Dinah Shore.

Side 1: "Too Much," "Playing for Keeps" (both by Elvis)
Side 2: "Chantez Chantez," "Honky Tonk Heart" (both by Dinah Shore)

(NO TITLE)
(RCA SPD-15)

January 1956. This was a 10-EP promotional boxed set that featured one EP by Elvis (599-9089). Four of Elvis's Sun recordings were included on that EP, the seventh in the box: "That's All Right (Mama)" and "Baby, Let's Play House" on side 7, and "I Forgot to Remember to Forget" and "Mystery Train" on side 14. Over the years, this boxed set has grown in value to become the most collectible of all Elvis Presley releases. A complete set of the 10 EPs with black RCA Victor labels, the box, paper inserts, and sleeves is now (1988) worth about $3,000. Gray label EPs are worth $200–$300 less. The Elvis record itself may bring about $750.

Long-Playing Albums
Standard Releases

All Standard RCA, RCA Camden, Pickwick, and Pairs Records releases are included in this section. We've also included, because of their popularity and availability, three albums by the Music Works, *Singer Presents Elvis Singing Flaming Star and Others, Having Fun with Elvis on Stage, Elvis—A Canadian Tribute,* and two TV mail-order LPs, *Elvis* (RCA DPL2-0056 [e]) and *Elvis in Hollywood.* All songs on the albums in this section are cross-referenced in the Songs section. We've used a cutoff date of August 1, 1988.

Disc jockey promotional releases, RCA Record Club albums, Candelite Music LPs, and all other albums are listed in the next section, Long-Playing Albums—Miscellaneous Releases.

ALMOST IN LOVE
(RCA Camden CAS-2440)
November 1970. Songs from six of Elvis's films and two single cuts were featured on this LP. When initially released, *Almost in Love* contained an alternate take of "Stay Away, Joe" that was not included in the film of the same title. In that take Elvis messed up the lyrics. Apparently someone at RCA noticed that two consecutive Camden LPs, *Let's Be Friends* and *Almost in Love,* contained "Stay Away, Joe." In March 1973, RCA corrected the problem by reissuing *Almost in Love* with a mono version of "Stay Away," another tune from *Stay Away, Joe.* This was the first appearance of "Stay Away" on an album. The first pressing, although not particularly rare or valuable, is nonetheless sought by collectors. *Almost in Love,* which peaked at #65 on *Billboard*'s Top LPs chart and remained on the chart for 18 weeks, is the only album on which "My Little Friend" can be found.

Side 1: "Almost in Love," "Long Legged Girl (with the Short Dress On)," "Edge of Reality," "My Little Friend," and "A Little Less Conversation"
Side 2: "Rubberneckin'," "Clean Up Your Own Backyard," "U.S. Male," "Charro," and "Stay Away, Joe" ["Stay Away" in the 1973 reissue]

ALMOST IN LOVE
(Pickwick CAS-2440)
December 1975. Reissue of the 1973 version of RCA Camden CAS-2440. The song selections were identical and the same cover photo was used, but this time the photo had a circular border.

ALOHA FROM HAWAII VIA SATELLITE
(RCA VPSX-6089)
February 1973. This two-record set was the soundtrack to Elvis's January 14, 1973, world TV special, "Elvis: Aloha from Hawaii," and RCA's first Quadradisc album. Within a few days of release, the LP achieved over $1 million in sales, making it the first Quadradisc

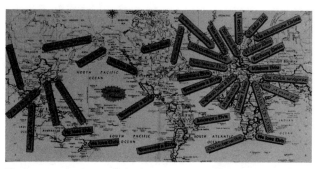

The inner jacket of *Aloha from Hawaii via Satellite.* (Photo courtesy Don Fink)

in the industry to go gold. (The Gold Record was certified by the RIAA on February 13, 1973.) The cover photograph was taken by the Apollo 15 astronauts (David R. Scott, Alfred M. Worden, and James B. Irwin) during their moon mission (July 26 to August 7, 1971). A depiction of Intelsat IV, the communications satellite that was used to broadcast the TV special to the world, also appeared on the cover. The album opened up to reveal the phrase "We Love Elvis," written in several different languages. Although it was issued in Quadraphonic, first pressings of *Aloha from Hawaii via Satellite* had "stereo" printed on the cover. In addition, no song titles were listed. To correct the problem, RCA attached two gold stickers: one that had the album's contents and one that said, "Quadradisc." Later pressings listed the song titles on a drawing of the planet Saturn and had "Quadradisc" printed on the jacket. A few promotional copies of *Aloha from Hawaii via Satellite* were sent to radio stations. Those copies, which were first pressings, had song titles and times listed on a white sticker.

The Stokely Van Camp Company, which sponsored the April 4, 1973, NBC-TV telecast of the special, took about four or five dozen of the RCA LPs and attached its own "Sneak Preview" sticker to the front cover and an advertisement to the back cover, then distributed them to some of its employees. The Sneak Preview sticker read: "Sneak Preview. Chicken of the Sea Sponsors Elvis Presley's Greatest TV Performance. 'Elvis, Aloha from Hawaii.' April 4/NBC/90 minutes. 8:30-10:00 EST."

Aloha from Hawaii via Satellite reached number one (for one week) on *Billboard*'s Top LPs chart and remained on the chart for 52 weeks. It was Elvis's last number one album.

Side 1: Introduction, "Also Sprach Zarathustra" (by Joe Guercio Orchestra), "See See Rider," "Burning Love," "Something," "You Gave Me a Mountain," and "Steamroller Blues"
Side 2: "My Way," "Love Me," "Johnny B. Goode," "It's Over," "Blue Suede Shoes," "I'm So Lonesome I Could Cry," "I Can't Stop Loving

You," and "Hound Dog"
Side 3: "What Now, My Love," "Fever," "Welcome To My World," "Suspicious Minds," and Introductions by Elvis
Side 4: "I'll Remember You," "Long Tall Sally"/"Whole Lotta Shakin' Goin' On," "An American Trilogy," "A Big Hunk o' Love," and "Can't Help Falling in Love"

ALOHA FROM HAWAII VIA SATELLITE
(RCA CPD2-2642)
1977. New Number assigned to RCA VPSX-6089.

THE ALTERNATE ALOHA
(RCA 6985-1-R)
May 1988. All songs from the January 12, 1973, re-hearsal concert for the TV special "Elvis: Aloha from Hawaii" were included on this album, with the exception of "Hound Dog." For some unexplained reason, RCA replaced "Hound Dog" with a bonus tune, "Blue Hawaii," which was recorded after the audience had left the building following the January 14 telecast. The complete program can be heard on the CD version of this album.

Side 1: "Also Sprach Zarathustra" (Joe Guercio Orchestra), "See See Rider," "Burning Love," "Something," "You Gave Me A Mountain," "Steamroller Blues," "My Way," "Love Me," "It's Over," "Blue Suede Shoes," and "I'm So Lonesome I Could Cry"
Side 2: "What Now, My Love," "Fever," "Welcome To My World," "Suspicious Minds," Introductions by Elvis, "I'll Remember You," "An American Trilogy," "A Big Hunk O' Love," "Can't Help Falling In Love," and "Blue Hawaii" (bonus)

ALWAYS ON MY MIND
(RCA AFL1-5430)
May 1985. Pressed on purple vinyl, *Always on My Mind* came with a special gold "50th" anniversary label in celebration of the 50th anniversary of Elvis's birth. *Always on My Mind* did not chart.

Side 1: "Separate Ways," "Don't Cry, Daddy," "My Boy," "Solitaire," "Bitter They Are, Harder They Fall," "Hurt," and "Pieces of My Life"
Side 2: "I Miss You," "It's Midnight," "I've Lost You," "You Gave Me a Mountain," "Unchained Melody," and "Always on My Mind"

BACK IN MEMPHIS
(RCA LSP-4429)
November 1970. *Back in Memphis* consisted of sides 3 and 4 of the two-record album set *From Memphis to Vegas/From Vegas to Memphis*. Except for the bottom song-title strip and the album title, the covers were identical. All songs on this LP were recorded at American Sound Studios in Memphis (January 13–23, 1969, and February 17–22, 1969). The original release of *Back in Memphis* was pressed on nonflexible vinyl. All later pressings used flexible vinyl.

Back in Memphis peaked at #183 on *Billboard*'s Top LPs chart and remained on the chart for only three weeks. This was the worst performance by any Elvis Presley album that reached the charts.

Side 1: "Inherit the Wind," "This Is the Story," "Stranger in My Own Home Town," "A Little Bit of Green," and "And the Grass Won't Pay No Mind"
Side 2: "Do You Know Who I Am," "From a Jack to a King," "The Fair Is Moving On," "You'll Think of Me," and "Without Love (There Is Nothing)"

BACK IN MEMPHIS
(RCA AFL1-4429)
1977. New number assigned to RCA LSP-4429.

BLUE HAWAII
(RCA LPM-2426)
October 1961. Soundtrack to Elvis's 1961 movie *Blue Hawaii*. A total of 14 songs were featured on the album, more than on any other Presley movie soundtrack LP. A red sticker advertising the single "Can't Help Falling in Love"/"Rock-a-Hula-Baby," appeared on the cover of some of the early pressings. *Blue Hawaii* quickly sold over a million copies, earning Elvis a Gold Disc award from the RIAA. Certification was made on December 21, 1961. The album eventually exceeded sales of over five million copies. *Blue Hawaii* was the first RCA album to use the new miracle surface process 317X. When polled by *Billboard* magazine, the nation's disc jockeys chose the album as their second most favorite LP of 1961.

Blue Hawaii took eight weeks to reach number one on *Billboard*'s Top LPs chart, but once in the top position, it remained there for 20 consecutive weeks. That set the record for a rock performer or group until Fleetwood Mac's *Rumors* LP in 1977. The soundtrack to *West Side Story* finally replaced *Blue Hawaii* at number one. After a stay of 79 weeks, *Blue Hawaii* left the charts.

Side 1: "Blue Hawaii," "Almost Always True," "Aloha Oe," "No More," "Can't Help Falling in Love," "Rock-a-Hula Baby," and "Moonlight Swim"
Side 2: "Ku-u-i-po," "Ito Eats," "Slicin' Sand," "Hawaiian Sunset," "Beach Boy Blues," "Island of Love (Kauai)," and "Hawaiian Wedding Song"

BLUE HAWAII
(RCA LSP-2426)
October 1961. Stereo vision of RCA LPM-2426. In January 1962 *Blue Hawaii* was the first Elvis stereo LP to reach number one on *Billboard*'s new stereo album chart, remaining there for four weeks. It spent a total of 12 weeks at the #2 position.

BLUE HAWAII
(RCA AFL1-2426)
September 1977. New number assigned to RCA LSP-2426.

BLUE HAWAII
(RCA AYL1-3683)
May 1980. New number assigned to RCA AFL1-2426.

BURNING LOVE AND HITS FROM HIS MOVIES, VOLUME 2
(RCA Camden CAS-2595)
November 1972. A follow-up to *Elvis Sings Hits from His Movies, Volume 1*, this album contained both sides of Elvis's hit single "Burning Love"/"It's a Matter of

Time," in addition to eight film songs. It achieved sales of over $1 million, qualifying it for a Gold Record—the first ever on the Camden imprint. A 7"-by-9" color bonus photo was included inside the album jacket. The first pressings of the jacket had a cover blurb that read, "Limited Offer—Special Bonus Photo Inside." Later pressings (1973 and later) deleted the blurb.

Burning Love and Hits from His Movies, Volume 2 had a 25-week stay on *Billboard*'s Top LPs chart, peaking at #22.

Side 1: "Burning Love," "Tender Feeling," "Am I Ready," "Tonight Is So Right for Love," and "Guadalajara"
Side 2: "It's a Matter of Time," "No More," "Santa Lucia," "We'll Be Together," and "I Love Only One Girl"

BURNING LOVE AND HITS FROM HIS MOVIES, VOLUME 2
(Pickwick CAS-2595)
December 1975. Reissue of RCA Camden CAS-2595. The song selections and cover photo were identical to the Camden release.

CLAMBAKE
(RCA LPM-3893)
November 19, 1967. *Clambake* featured all seven songs from the movie of the same title, plus five bonus tunes. A 12"-by-12" bonus color photo of Elvis and Priscilla's wedding was included inside the jacket. On the cover was a blurb that read, "Special Bonus Full Color Photo Inside This Album of Elvis and Priscilla Specially Autographed. This Offer for a Limited Time Only."

Clambake had a 14-week stay on *Billboard*'s Top LPs chart, peaking at #40.

Side 1: "Guitar Man" (bonus), "Clambake," "Who Needs Money," "A House That Has Everything," "Confidence," and "Hey, Hey, Hey"
Side 2: "You Don't Know Me," "The Girl I Never Loved," "How Can you Lose What You Never Had" (bonus), "Big Boss Man" (bonus), "Singing Tree" (bonus), and "Just Call Me Lonesome" (bonus)

CLAMBAKE
(RCA LSP-3893)
November 19, 1967. Stereo release.

CLAMBAKE
(RCA AFL1-2565)
September 1977. New number assigned to RCA LSP-3893. *Clambake* has now been deleted from RCA's catalog.

C'MON EVERYBODY
(RCA Camden CAL-2518)
Songs from four of Elvis's movies were featured: *Follow That Dream, Kid Galahad, Viva Las Vegas,* and *Easy Come, Easy Go.* For Elvis's opening night at the Sahara Tahoe Hotel on July 20, 1971, fans were given preview copies of *C'mon Everybody,* along with various other souvenir items.

C'mon Everybody reached #70 on *Billboard*'s Top LPs chart and remained on the chart for 11 weeks.

Side 1: "C'mon Everybody," "Angel," "Easy Come, Easy Go," "A Whistling Tune," and "Follow That Dream"
Side 2: "King of the Whole Wide World," "I'll Take Love," "Today, Tomorrow and Forever," "I'm Not the Marrying Kind," and "This Is Living"

C'MON EVERYBODY
(Pickwick CAS-2518)
December 1975. Reissue of RCA Camden CAL-2518. The song selections and cover photo were identical to the Camden release. Although the Pickwick number used a stereo prefix and the cover had a "Stereo" label, this reissue was in monaural.

THE COMPLETE SUN SESSIONS
(RCA 6414-1-R)
June 1987. This is the definitive Sun sessions set. Included on the two records were 16 Sun master recordings, 5 alternate takes of "I Love You Because," 7 alternate takes of "I'm Left, You're Right, She's Gone," and outtakes of 6 other tunes. Extensive liner notes by Peter Guralnick relating Elvis's months at Sun Records and background information on the songs was a nice touch. *The Complete Sun Sessions* is one of a half-dozen LPs that are musts for the Elvis aficionado.

Side A: The Master Takes—"That's All Right (Mama)," "Blue Moon of Kentucky," "Good Rockin' Tonight," "I Don't Care If the Sun Don't Shine," "Milkcow Blues Boogie," "You're a Heartbreaker," "Baby, Let's Play House," and "I'm Left, You're Right, She's Gone"
Side B: The Master Takes—"Mystery Train," "I Forgot to Remember to Forget," "I Love You Because," "Blue Moon," "Tomorrow Night," "I'll Never Let You Go (Little Darlin')," "Just Because," and "Tryin' to Get to You"
Side C: The Outtakes—"Harbor Lights," "I Love You Because" (takes #1 and #2), "That's All Right (Mama)," "Blue Moon of Kentucky," "I Don't Care If the Sun Don't Shine," "I'm Left, You're Right, She's Gone" ("My Baby's Gone," take #9), "I'll Never Let You Go (Little Darlin')," and "When It Rains, It Really Pours"
Side D: The Alternate Takes—"I Love You Because" (take #3), "I Love You Because" (take #4), "I Love You Because" (take #5), "I'm Left, You're Right, She's Gone" ("My Baby's Gone," take #7), "I'm Left, You're Right, She's Gone" ("My Baby's Gone," take #8), "I'm Left, You're Right, She's Gone" ("My Baby's Gone," take #10), "I'm Left, You're Right, She's Gone" ("My Baby's Gone," take #11), "I'm Left, You're Right, She's Gone" ("My Baby's Gone," take #13), and "I'm Left, You're Right, She's Gone" ("My Baby's Gone," take #12)

A DATE WITH ELVIS
(RCA LPM-2011)
September 1959. *A Date with Elvis* had a double cover. A photo of Elvis in an Army uniform sitting in a car adorned the front. The song titles were listed on a red sticker. The album opened up, to reveal a telegram from Elvis and photos of his departure from the United States for West Germany. The back cover originally featured a 1960 calendar with Elvis's discharge date (March 24) circled. Elvis, however, was actually discharged on March 5. Later pressings (1965) had advertisements for the first three volumes of *Elvis' Golden Records* instead of the calendar. Some of the early LPs came with a foil wraparound strip that read, "New Golden Age Sound Album."

A Date with Elvis spent only eight weeks on *Billboard*'s Best Selling LPs chart, peaking at #32.

Side 1: "Blue Moon of Kentucky," "Young and Beautiful," "(You're So Square) Baby, I Don't Care," "Milkcow Blues Boogie," and "Baby, Let's Play House"
Side 2: "Good Rockin' Tonight," "Is It So Strange," "We're Gonna Move," "I Want to Be Free," and "I Forgot to Remember to Forget"

A DATE WITH ELVIS
(RCA LSP-2011 [e])

January 1965. Electronically reprocessed stereo release.

A DATE WITH ELVIS
(RCA AFL1-2011 [e])

1977. New number assigned to RCA LSP-2011 (e).

DOUBLE DYNAMITE
(Pickwick DL2-5001)

December 1975. *Double Dynamite* was a two-record original Pickwick release featuring selections from nine of the ten previous RCA Camden LPs. (Only *Elvis' Christmas Album* was not represented.) It was released through special arrangement with RCA Camden. On the cover, the Pickwick logo appeared in the lower-right corner, while the upper-left corner featured the RCA Camden logo.

Side 1: "Burning Love," "I'll Be There (If Ever You Want Me)," "Fools Fall in Love," "Follow That Dream," and "You'll Never Walk Alone"
Side 2: "Flaming Star," "The Yellow Rose of Texas"/"The Eyes of Texas," "Old Shep," and "Mama"
Side 3: "Rubberneckin'," "U.S. Male," "Frankie and Johnny," "If You Think I Don't Need You," and "Easy Come, Easy Go"
Side 4: "Separate Ways," "Peace in the Valley," "Big Boss Man," and "It's a Matter of Time"

DOUBLE DYNAMITE
(RCA PDL2-1010)

1982. Reissue of the double LP Pickwick DL2-5001 from RCA Special Products on its Pair label. The song selections were identical except that "You'll Never Walk Alone" and "If you Think I Don't Need You" were omitted. A different cover photo was used.

DOUBLE TROUBLE
(RCA LPM-3787)

June 1967. All eight songs from the movie *Double Trouble* were featured in this album. The original pressings of *Double Trouble* had an announcement on the cover that read: "Special Bonus. Full Color Photo of Elvis Inside This Album. This Offer for a Limited Time Only." (The photo was 7"-by-9".) Later pressings eliminated the bonus photo announcement and replaced it with the words "Double Trouble." Reverse profiles of Elvis were on the cover. At the bottom, all 12 songs titles were printed in suitcases.

Double Trouble peaked at #47 on *Billboard*'s Top LPs chart, remaining on the chart for 20 weeks.

Side 1: "Double Trouble," "Baby, If You'll Give Me All of Your Love," "Could I Fall in Love," "Long Legged Girl (with the Short Dress On)," "City by Night," and "Old MacDonald"
Side 2: "I Love Only One Girl," "There Is So Much World to See," "It Won't Be Long" (bonus), "Never Ending" (bonus), "Blue River" (bonus), and "What Now, What Next, Where To" (bonus)

DOUBLE TROUBLE
(RCA LSP-3787)

June 1967. Stereo release.

DOUBLE TROUBLE
(RCA AFL1-2564)

September 1977. New number assigned to RCA LSP-3787.

ELVIS
(RCA LPM-1382)

October 19, 1956. Elvis's second album release. All songs except "So Glad You're Mine" were recorded at Radio Recorders, September 1–3, 1956. "So Glad You're Mine" was recorded on January 30, 1956, at RCA's New York City studios. The front cover photo of *Elvis* was taken by David B. Hecht. Eleven different back covers are known to exist; all versions include an article on Elvis, but the advertisements for other RCA albums vary. A few copies of *Elvis* have labels that read, "Band 1," "Band 2," etc., instead of just the numerals. Reportedly, an alternate take of "Old Shep" appeared on a few rare releases that had "17S" after the matrix number on the label. *Elvis* sold over three million copies, easily qualifying for a Gold Record. RIAA certification was made on February 17, 1960.

Elvis entered *Billboard*'s Best-Selling Pop Albums chart at the #7 position—the second highest chart entry of any Elvis LP. (*G. I. Blues* entered at #6.) Four weeks later, it was number one and stayed there for five straight weeks. *Elvis* was #2 for 11 weeks, 10 of them consecutive. The album spent a total of 32 weeks on the chart.

Side 1: "Rip It Up," "Love Me," "When My Blue Moon Turns to Gold Again," "Long Tall Sally," "First in Line," and "Paralyzed"
Side 2: "So Glad You're Mine," "Old Shep," "Ready Teddy," "Anyplace Is Paradise," "How's the World Treating You," and "How Do You Think I Feel"

ELVIS
(RCA LSP-1382 [e])

February 1962. Electronically reprocessed stereo release.

ELVIS
(RCA AFL1-1382 [e])

1977. New number assigned to RCA LSP-1382 (e).

ELVIS
(RCA AFM1-5199)

1985. To celebrate the 50th anniversary of Elvis's birthday, *Elvis* was rereleased with the songs digitally remastered in mono. The record was pressed on heavy virgin vinyl and had a special "50th" anniversary label. A gold paper band was wrapped around the album's jacket.

ELVIS
(RCA APL1-0283)

July 1973. Except for "It's Impossible," which was a live recording from a February 16, 1972, concert at the Las Vegas Hilton, all tracks were recorded at the RCA studios in Nashville (March and May 1971) and Hollywood (March 1972).

Elvis, sometimes referred to as the "Fool Album," reached #52 on *Billboard*'s Top LPs chart, remaining on the chart for 13 weeks.

Side 1: "Fool," "Where Do I Go from Here," "Love Me, Love the Life I Lead," "It's Still Here," and "It's Impossible"

Side 2: "For Lovin' Me," "Padre," "I'll Take you Home Again, Kathleen," "I Will Be True," and "Don't Think Twice, It's All Right"

ELVIS
(RCA DPL2-0056 [e])

August 1973. This single-pocket, two-record set contained 20 of Elvis's biggest hits and was sold exclusively on television. It was not available in stores. When *Elvis* was first released, "Brookville Records" was printed on the cover; the label was mustard brown in color and said "RCA Victor." A month later, in September 1973, the label was changed to a blue color and mentioned "RCA Special Products"; there was no mention of Brookville Records on the cover. *Elvis* was marketed by Brookville Marketing Corporation of New York through a licensing agreement with RCA. The record sold well over three million copies.

Side 1: "Hound Dog," "I Want You, I Need You, I Love You," "All Shook Up," "Don't," and "I Beg of You"

Side 2: "A Big Hunk o' Love," "Love Me," "Stuck on You," "Good Luck Charm," and "Return to Sender"

Side 3: "Don't Be Cruel," "Loving You," "Jailhouse Rock," "Can't Help Falling in Love," and "I Got Stung"

Side 4: "Teddy Bear," "Love Me Tender," "Hard Headed Woman," "It's Now or Never," and "Surrender"

ELVIS—A CANADIAN TRIBUTE
(RCA KKL1-7065)

October 1978. Originally issued in Canada, *Elvis—A Canadian Tribute* was later distributed and produced in the United States. Most songs on the album were written by Canadian composers. Early editions had a gold sticker on the front jacket that read, "Gold Collectors Edition Serial No. _____." Each one was individually numbered. Pressed on gold vinyl, it has been called the "Gold Album." U.S. copies of *Elvis—A Canadian Tribute* had a special inner sleeve, and Elvis's photo was printed on the record label. Sales exceeded 500,000 copies, qualifying it for a Gold Record.

Elvis—A Canadian Tribute had a seven-week stay on *Billboard*'s Top LPs chart, peaking at #86. It fared much better on the Hot Country LPs chart—#7, and an 18-week stay.

Side 1: Introduction, "Jailhouse Rock," Introduction, "Teddy Bear," "Loving You," "Until It's Time for You to Go," "Early Morning Rain," and Vancouver Press Conference (1957)

Side 2: "I'm Movin' On," "Snowbird," "For Lovin' Me," "Put Your Hand in the Hand," "Little Darlin'," and "My Way"

ELVIS—A LEGENDARY PERFORMER, VOLUME 1
(RCA CPL1-0341)

January 1974. The previously unreleased "Tonight's All Right for Love" and an alternate take of "I Love You Because" were featured on *Elvis—A Legendary Performer, Volume 1*. Until this album, "Tonight's All Right for Love" had been available only in non-English speaking countries. Also included were unreleased versions of "Love Me," "Tryin' to Get to You," and "Are You Lonesome Tonight?" from the 1968 TV special "Elvis"; two excerpts from the *Elvis Sails* EP; and seven previously released recordings. *Elvis—A Legendary Performer, Volume 1* came with a 16-page booklet, "The Early Years." The album jacket had a die-cut window that allowed the photo on the cardboard innersleeve to be seen. Later pressings had the standard cover. In 1978 RCA released an experimental picture disc using the contents of this LP.

Sales for *Elvis—A Legendary Performer, Volume 1* exceeded $1 million and a Gold Record was certified by the RIAA on January 8, 1975. The album had a 14-week stay on *Billboard*'s Top LPs chart, peaking at #43. After Elvis's death, the album recharted for another 14 weeks, this time reaching #62.

Side 1: "That's All Right (Mama)," "I Love You Because," "Heartbreak Hotel," "Don't Be Cruel," "Love Me," and "Trying to Get to You"

Side 2: "Love Me Tender," "Peace in the Valley," "A Fool Such as I," "Tonight's All Right for Love," "Are You Lonesome Tonight?," and "Can't Help Falling in Love"

ELVIS—A LEGENDARY PERFORMER, VOLUME 2
(RCA CPL1-1349)

January 1976. Featured on Volume 2 of the *Legendary Performer* series was an alternate take of "I Want You, I Need You, I Love You" in which Elvis reversed the lyrics; unreleased live versions of "Blue Suede Shoes" and "Baby What You Want Me to Do" from the "Elvis" TV special; an unreleased version of "Blue Hawaii" from the NBC telecast of the special "Elvis: Aloha from Hawaii"; two songs—"Harbor Lights" and "Cane and a High Starched Collar"—never released commercially by RCA; and six previously released songs, including "Such a Night" with two false starts. Also included was a radio interview of Elvis by Jay Thompson in Wichita Falls, Texas (April 10, 1956),[1] and a press conference held on March 25, 1961, for the USS *Arizona* Memorial benefit concert. *Elvis—A Legendary Performer, Volume 2* was originally released with a 16-page bonus booklet, "The Early Years Continued." A few records were pressed without the false starts on "Cane and a High Starched Collar" and "Such a Night." The album had a die-cut window allowing the photo on the innersleeve to be seen. Later pressings had the standard cover.

Sales for *Elvis—A Legendary Performer, Volume 2* exceeded $1 million and a Gold Record was certified

---

[1] RCA gave the date as April 10, 1956, but it was probably April 13.

by the RIAA on October 25, 1977. The album had a 17-week stay on *Billboard*'s Top LPs chart, peaking at #46.

Side 1: "Harbor Lights," Jay Thompson Interviews Elvis, "I Want You, I Need You, I Love You," "Blue Suede Shoes," "Blue Christmas," "Jailhouse Rock," and "It's Now or Never"
Side 2: "Cane and a High Starched Collar," Presentation of Awards to Elvis, "Blue Hawaii," "Such a Night," "Baby What You Want Me to Do," "How Great Thou Art," and "If I Can Dream"

ELVIS—A LEGENDARY PERFORMER, VOLUME 3 (RCA CPL1-3082)

December 1978. Two previously unreleased songs— "Danny" and "Britches"—were highlighted on this third edition of the *Legendary Performer* series. The album also contained unreleased alternate takes of "Fame and Fortune," "Frankfort Special," and "Guadalajara," as well as unreleased versions of "It Hurts Me" and "Let Yourself Go" from the "Elvis" TV special, and an unreleased live version of "Let it Be Me" from February 1970 at the International Hotel in Las Vegas. Four commercial recordings and an excerpt from the 1956 *TV Guide* interview completed the album. *Elvis— A Legendary Performer, Volume 3* was originally issued with a 16-page booklet, "Yesterdays." The LP jacket had a die-cut window allowing the photo on the innersleeve to be seen.

Picture disc version of *Elvis—A Legendary Performer, Volume 3*. (Photo courtesy Don Fink)

Sales for *Elvis—A Legendary Performer, Volume 3* exceeded $1 million and a Gold Record was certified by the RIAA on December 18, 1978. The album stayed on *Billboard*'s Top LPs chart for 11 weeks, peaking at #113. A 15-week stay and a #10 position were achieved on the Hot Country LPs chart.

Side 1: "Hound Dog," TV Guide Interview, "Danny," "Fame and For-

tune," "Frankfort Special," "Britches," and "Crying in the Chapel"
Side 2: "Surrender," "Guadalajara," "It Hurts Me," "Let Yourself Go," "In the Ghetto," and "Let It Be Me"

ELVIS—A LEGENDARY PERFORMER, VOLUME 3 (RCA CPL1-3078)

December 1978. This limited-edition picture disc included the same selections as RCA CPL1-3082.

ELVIS—A LEGENDARY PERFORMER, VOLUME 4 (RCA CPL1-4848)

November 1983. Finally, after 20 years, RCA released the Elvis–Ann-Margret duet, "The Lady Loves Me." The tune had previously appeared only on bootleg LPs. "Plantation Rock" also was officially released for the first time. "I'm Beginning to Forget You" and "Mona Lisa" were newly discovered at Graceland. Alternate and unreleased versions of eight other songs and Elvis interviews with Ray and Norma Pillow completed the album.

Elvis—A Legendary Performer, Volume 4 did not chart.

Side 1: "When It Rains, It Really Pours," Interviews by Ray and Norma Pillow, "One Night," "I'm Beginning to Forget You," "Mona Lisa," "Plantation Rock," and "Swing Down, Sweet Chariot"
Side 2: "The Lady Loves Me," "Wooden Heart," "That's All Right (Mama)," "Are You Lonesome Tonight?," "Reconsider Baby," and "I'll Remember You"

ELVIS ARON PRESLEY (RCA CPL8-3699)

July 1980. To commemorate the 25th anniversary of Elvis's signing with RCA Records, the company issued this eight-LP boxed set. Each record sleeve had a beautiful color photo on one side and recording information on the other. The 87 performances represented 78 different songs. Sixty-five of the performances were previously unreleased by RCA. One song—"Beyond the Reef"—had never been issued in any form. A highlight for most fans was the four songs from Elvis's last appearance (May 6, 1956) at the New Frontier Hotel in Las Vegas. The first pressing of 250,000 copies quickly sold out. *Elvis Aron Presley* had a 14-week stay on *Billboard*'s Top LPs chart, peaking at #27. On the Hot Country LPs chart, the boxed set reached #8.

Record 1: AN EARLY LIVE PERFORMANCE: "Heartbreak Hotel," "Long Tall Sally," "Blue Suede Shoes," "Money Honey," and an Elvis monologue
Record 2: AN EARLY BENEFIT PERFORMANCE: "Heartbreak Hotel," "All Shook Up," "(Now and Then There's) a Fool Such as I," "I Got a Woman," "Love Me," Introductions, "Such a Night," "Reconsider Baby," "I Need Your Love Tonight," "That's All Right (Mama)," "Don't Be Cruel," "One Night," "Are You Lonesome Tonight?," "It's Now or Never," "Swing Down, Sweet Chariot," and "Hound Dog"
Record 3: COLLECTORS' GOLD FROM THE MOVIE YEARS: "They Remind Me Too Much of You," "Tonight Is So Right for Love," "Follow That Dream," "Wild in the Country," "Datin'," "Shoppin' Around," "Can't Help Falling in Love," "A Dog's Life," "I'm Falling in Love Tonight," and "Thanks to the Rolling Sea"
Record 4: THE TV SPECIALS—"ELVIS: ALOHA FROM HAWAII," ELVIS IN CONCERT": "Jailhouse Rock," "Suspicious Minds," "Lawdy Miss Clawdy"/"Baby What You Want Me to Do," "Blue Christmas," "You

Gave Me a Mountain," "Welcome to My World," "Tryin' to Get to You," "I'll Remember You," and "My Way"

Record 5: THE LAS VEGAS YEARS: "Polk Salad Annie," "You've Lost That Lovin' Feelin'," "Sweet Caroline," "Kentucky Rain," "Are You Lonesome Tonight?," "My Babe," "In the Ghetto," "An American Trilogy," "Little Sister"/"Get Back," and "Yesterday"

Record 6: LOST SINGLES: "I'm Leavin'," "The First Time Ever I Saw Your Face," "High Heel Sneakers," "Softly, As I Leave You," "Unchained Melody," "Fool," "Rags to Riches," "It's Only Love," and "America, the Beautiful"

Record 7: ELVIS AT THE PIANO: "It's Still Here," "I'll Take You Home Again, Kathleen," "Beyond the Reef," and "I Will Be True." THE CONCERT YEARS, PART 1: "Also Sprach Zarathustra" (Joe Guercio Orchestra), "See See Rider," "I Got a Woman"/"Amen"/"I Got a Woman," "Love Me," "If You Love Me (Let Me Know)," "Love Me Tender," "All Shook Up," and "Teddy Bear"/"Don't Be Cruel"

Record 8: THE CONCERT YEARS, CONCLUDED: "Hound Dog," "The Wonder of You," "Burning Love," Dialogue/Introductions/ "Johnny B. Goode," Introductions/"Long Live Rock and Roll," "T-R-O-U-B-L-E," "Why Me Lord," "How Great Thou Art," "Let Me Be There," "An American Trilogy," "Funny How Time Slips Away," "Little Darlin'," "Mystery Train"/"Tiger Man," and "Can't Help Falling in Love"

ELVIS ARON PRESLEY—FOREVER
(RCA PDL2-1185)

March 1988. No new material was issued on this two-record release on RCA's Pairs label. As a matter of fact, eight of the ten songs on the LP *Elvis Today*, were included on this album. The studio version of "Blueberry Hill" hadn't been released since 1957. Three songs had been released just two months earlier on the *Essential Elvis—The First Movies* LP—"Mean Woman Blues," "Loving You," and "Got a Lot o' Livin' to Do." Granted, the first two songs were alternate takes of those on the earlier LP. But one would have thought that RCA could have been a little more creative with *Elvis Aron Presley—Forever*. (Note: Three titles have been used when referring to this album: *Forever, Forever—Elvis Aron Presley,* and *Elvis Aron Presley—Forever*. RCA has used the last title and we've chosen to do the same.)

Side 1: "Blue Hawaii," "Hawaiian Wedding Song," "No More," and "Early Morning Rain"

Side 2: "Pieces of My Life," "I Can Help," "Bringing It Back," and "Green, Green Grass of Home"

Side 3: "Mean Woman Blues," "Loving You," "Got a Lot o' Livin' to Do," and "Blueberry Hill"

Side 4: "T-R-O-U-B-L-E," "And I Love You So," "Woman Without Love," and "Shake a Hand"

ELVIS AS RECORDED AT MADISON SQUARE GARDEN
(RCA LSP-4776)

June 1972. All tracks on this album were recorded at Elvis's June 10, 1972, evening concert at Madison Square Garden. Sales of $1 million were quickly achieved and certification for a Gold Record was made by the RIAA on August 4, 1972. Special promotional copies were sent to radio stations with a white sticker on the front that read, "Promotional Album—Not For Sale."

Elvis as Recorded at Madison Square Garden stayed on *Billboard*'s Top LPs chart for 34 weeks, peaking at #11.

Side 1: "Also Sprach Zarathustra" (Joe Guercio Orchestra), "That's All Right (Mama)," "Proud Mary," "Never Been to Spain," "You Don't Have to Say You Love Me," "You've Lost That Lovin' Feelin'," "Polk Salad Annie," "Love Me," "All Shook Up," "Heartbreak Hotel," "Teddy Bear"/"Don't Be Cruel," and "Love Me Tender"

Side 2: "The Impossible Dream," Introductions by Elvis, "Hound Dog," "Suspicious Minds," "For the Good Times," "An American Trilogy," "Funny How Time Slips Away," "I Can't Stop Loving You," and "Can't Help Falling in Love"

ELVIS AS RECORDED AT MADISON SQUARE GARDEN
(RCA AQL1-4776)

1979. New number assigned to RCA LSP-4776.

ELVIS' CHRISTMAS ALBUM
(RCA LOC-1035)

November 1957. *Elvis' Christmas Album* featured eight Christmas songs recorded at Hollywood's Radio Recorders, September 5–7, 1957, and the four spiritual songs that appeared on the *Peace in the Valley* EP. The LP had a booklike cover that opened up to reveal a 10-page album of color photos of Elvis. Original issues had a gold gift sticker attached to the plastic bag that contained the album. The sticker had "From _____, To _____" on it, as well as "Elvis Sings" and listing of the 13 songs. *Elvis' Christmas Album* eventually achieved sales of over $1 million and a Gold Record was certified by the RIAA on August 13, 1963.

Elvis' Christmas Album went to number one on *Billboard*'s Best-Selling LPs chart in December 1957, succeeding the *Around the World in 80 Days* soundtrack. It remained in the top spot for three weeks and then fell

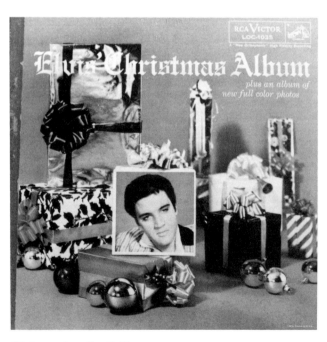

(Photo courtesy Don Fink)

to #2 when Bing Crosby's *Merry Christmas* album rose to number one. *Elvis' Christmas Album* regained the top spot one week later and then left the chart the next week. Ricky Nelson's *Ricky* LP was the nation's new number one album. In all, *Elvis' Christmas Album* was number one for four weeks and on the chart for a total of seven weeks.

Side 1: "Santa Claus Is Back in Town," "White Christmas," "Here Comes Santa Claus," "I'll Be Home for Christmas," "Blue Christmas," and "Santa, Bring My Baby Back (to Me)"
Side 2: "Oh Little Town of Bethlehem," "Silent Night," "Peace in the Valley," "I Believe," "Take My Hand, Precious Lord," and "It Is No Secret"

ELVIS' CHRISTMAS ALBUM
(RCA LPM-1951)

November 1958. New number assigned to RCA LOC-1035. The song selections were the same, but the front cover photo was changed, and the back featured four color photos of Elvis in the Army. This release of *Elvis' Christmas Album* reached *Billboard*'s Top LPs chart on three different occasions: January 1961 (#33); January 1962 (#120); and December 1962 (#59).

ELVIS' CHRISTMAS ALBUM
(RCA LSP-1951 [e])

November 1964. Electronically reprocessed stereo reissue of RCA LPM-1951.

ELVIS'S CHRISTMAS ALBUM
(RCA AFM1-5486)

September 1985. Digitally remastered monaural reissue of RCA LPM-1951. It was pressed on green vinyl and released in its original jacket. *Elvis' Christmas Album* peaked at #178 on *Billboard*'s Top LPs chart during its two weeks on the chart.

ELVIS' CHRISTMAS ALBUM
(RCA Camden CAL-2428)

November 1970. Although the same title was used, this is actually a different album than RCA LPM-1951. Eight Christmas songs were lifted from the earlier LP and "If Every Day Was Like Christmas" and "Mama Liked the Roses" were added. Different front and back covers were used. The front cover proclaimed, "By Request—'Mama Liked the Roses.'"

Side 1: "Blue Christmas," "Silent Night," "White Christmas," "Santa Claus Is Back In Town," and "I'll Be Home For Christmas"
Side 2: "If Every Day Was Like Christmas," "Here Comes Santa Claus," "Oh Little Town of Bethlehem," "Santa, Bring My Baby Back (To Me)," and "Mama Liked the Roses"

ELVIS' CHRISTMAS ALBUM
(Pickwick CAS-2428)

December 1975. Reissue of RCA Camden CAL-2428. A different front cover and two different back covers were used. Although a stereo prefix was used in the Pickwick number, all tracks were in monaural.

ELVIS COUNTRY
(RCA LSP-4460)

January 1971. All songs on this album were recorded at RCA's Nashville studios—"Snowbird" and "Whole Lotta Shakin' Goin' On" on September 22, 1970, and the other 10 cuts, June 4–8, 1970. The song "I Was Born About Ten Thousand Years Ago" was briefly sung at the end of each song. A tinted bonus photo of Elvis at the age of two was included with the album. The same photo appeared on the front cover. Original pressings of the record were on nonflexible vinyl; all pressings after 1971 were on flexible vinyl. Sales of *Elvis Country* exceeded $1 million. A Gold Record was certified by the RIAA on December 1, 1977.

Elvis Country had a 21-week stay on *Billboard*'s Top LPs chart, peaking at #12. It reached #6 on the Hot Country LPs chart and had a stay of 26 weeks. The eight-track version of *Elvis Country* peaked at #12 on the Best-Selling Cartridges chart.

Side 1: "Snowbird," "Tomorrow Never Comes," "Little Cabin on the Hill," "Whole Lotta Shakin' Goin' On," "Funny How Time Slips Away," and "I Really Don't Want to Know"
Side 2: "There Goes My Everything," "It's Your Baby, You Rock It," "The Fool," "Faded Love," "I Washed My Hands in Muddy Water," and "Make the World Go Away"

ELVIS COUNTRY
(RCA AFL1-4460)

1977. New number assigned to RCA LSP-4460.

ELVIS COUNTRY
(RCA AYM1-3956)

May 1981. New number assigned to RCA AFL1-4460. It is now one of the LPs in RCA's "Best Buy" series.

ELVIS FOR EVERYONE
(RCA LPM-3450)

July 1965. *Elvis For Everyone* was originally going to be called *Elvis' Anniversary Album* to commemorate Elvis's tenth year with RCA. Tracks on the album were primarily unreleased songs from recording sessions dating back as far as February 24, 1957. The cover featured Elvis behind a sales counter with the following five LP's displayed: *Elvis Presley*, *Elvis*, *Elvis' Golden Records*, *G. I. Blues*, and *Blue Hawaii*.

Elvis For Everyone reached #10 on *Billboard*'s Top LPs chart. It had a 27-week stay on the chart.

Side 1: "Your Cheatin' Heart," "Summer Kisses, Winter Tears," "Finders Keepers, Losers Weepers," "In My Way," "Tomorrow Night," and "Memphis, Tennessee"
Side 2: "For the Millionth and Last Time," "Forget Me Never," "Sound Advice," "Santa Lucia," "I Met Here Today," and "When It Rains, It Really Pours"

ELVIS FOR EVERYONE
(RCA LSP-3450)

July 1965. Stereo release.

ELVIS FOR EVERYONE
(RCA AFL1-3450)

1977. New number assigned to RCA LSP-3450.

ELVIS FOR EVERYONE
(RCA AYM1-4332)
February 1982. New number assigned to RCA AFL1-3450. This is one of RCA's "Best Buy" series of LPs.

ELVIS' GOLD RECORDS, VOLUME 4
(RCA LPM-3921)
February 1968. Yet another compilation of Elvis million-sellers, *Elvis' Gold Records, Volume 4* was the last of Elvis's monaural albums, except for those featuring early material or live cuts. This monaural release is quite rare. A 7″-by-9″ color photo of Elvis was included as a bonus. The "Ain't That Loving You, Baby" cut was rechanneled.

Elvis' Gold Records, Volume 4 had a 22-week stay on *Billboard*'s Top LPs chart, peaking at #33.

Side 1: "Love Letters," "Witchcraft," "It Hurts Me," "What'd I Say," "Please Don't Drag That String Around," and "Indescribably Blue"
Side 2: "(You're the Devil) In Disguise," "Lonely Man," "A Mess of Blues," "Ask Me," "Ain't That Loving You, Baby," and "Just Tell Her Jim Said Hello"

ELVIS' GOLD RECORDS, VOLUME 4
(RCA LSP-3921)
February 1968. Stereo release.

ELVIS' GOLD RECORDS, VOLUME 4
(RCA AFL1-3921)
1977. New number assigned to RCA LSP-3921.

ELVIS' GOLD RECORDS, VOLUME 5
(RCA AFL1-4941)
March 1984. Ten more worldwide million-sellers from RCA. *Elvis' Gold Records, Volume 5* did not chart.

Side 1: "Suspicious Minds," "Kentucky Rain," "In the Ghetto," "Clean Up Your Own Back Yard," and "If I Can Dream"
Side 2: "Burning Love," "If You Talk in Your Sleep," "For the Heart," "Moody Blue," and "Way Down"

ELVIS' GOLDEN RECORDS
(RCA LPM-1707)
April 1958. Fourteen million-selling singles were included on this LP. Originally, the title letters of *Elvis' Golden Records* were in light blue and no songs were listed on the front cover. Later pressings (from November 1963) of the jacket had white letters and all 14 songs listed. The album came with a special flyer advertising an Elvis photo book that could be purchased by sending in the coupon and 25 cents. Liner notes to *Elvis' Golden Records* contained mistakes. It was written that "Heartbreak Hotel" was given to Elvis by Mae Boren Axton while Elvis was appearing in Florida. Actually, she gave him the song at the Andrew Jackson Hotel in Nashville. The album also listed the recording date for "Heartbreak Hotel" as February 10, 1956. The correct date was *January* 10. The liner notes said that "I Want You, I Need You, I Love You" was recorded at the first session where a vocal backing group was used. In reality, Elvis had vocal backing at his first RCA session on January 10, 1956. Contrary to the liner notes, Elvis and Vera Matson did not write the musical

score for *Love Me Tender*. Ken Darby wrote the four songs used in the film. *Elvis' Golden Records* achieved sales of over $1 million. Gold Record certification was made by the RIAA on October 17, 1961. The British release of this album (RCA RB-16069) was the only Elvis record to be released on the Red Seal label.

Elvis' Golden Records entered *Billboard*'s Best-Selling Pop Albums chart at #9, but never got higher than #3. It had a 40-week stay on the chart. After Elvis's death, the album recharted, reaching #63 during its 23-week stay.

Side 1: "Hound Dog," "Loving You," "All Shook Up," "Heartbreak Hotel," "Jailhouse Rock," "Love Me," and "Too Much"
Side 2: "Don't Be Cruel," "That's When Your Heartaches Begin," "Teddy Bear," "Love Me Tender," "Treat Me Nice," "Any Way You Want Me," and "I Want You, I Need You, I Love You"

ELVIS' GOLDEN RECORDS
(RCA LSP-1707 [e])
February 1962. Electronically reprocessed stereo release.

ELVIS' GOLDEN RECORDS
(RCA AFL1-1707 [e])
1977. New number assigned to RCA LSP-1707 (e).

ELVIS' GOLDEN RECORDS
(RCA AQL1-1707 [e])
1979. New number assigned to RCA AFL1-1707 (e).

ELVIS' GOLDEN RECORDS
(RCA AFM1-5196)
1985. Special release in which all tracks were digitally remastered and restored to their original monaural sound. The album, which was pressed on heavy virgin vinyl with a special gold "50th" anniversary label, came packaged with a gold paper-band wraparound.

ELVIS' GOLDEN RECORDS, VOLUME 3
(RCA LPM-2765)
September 1963. This third in the series of million-seller compilations came with an 8″-by-10″ color photo booklet. *Elvis' Golden Records, Volume 3* was certified as a Gold Record by the RIAA on November 1, 1966.

Elvis' Golden Records, Volume 3 peaked at #3 on *Billboard*'s Top LPs chart, remaining on the chart for 40 weeks. After Elvis's death in 1977, the record recharted, reaching #64.

Side 1: "It's Now or Never," "Stuck on You," "Fame and Fortune," "I Gotta Know," "Surrender," and "I Feel So Bad"
Side 2: "Are You Lonesome Tonight?," "(Marie's the Name) His Latest Flame," "Little Sister," "Good Luck Charm," "Anything That's Part of You," and "She's Not You"

ELVIS' GOLDEN RECORDS, VOLUME 3
(RCA LSP-2765)
September 1963. Stereo release.

ELVIS' GOLDEN RECORDS, VOLUME 3
(RCA AFL1-2765)
1977. New number assigned to RCA LSP-2765.

ELVIS IN CONCERT
(RCA APL2-2587)

October 1977. All songs on *Elvis in Concert* were recorded live in Omaha, Nebraska (June 19, 1977), and Rapid City, South Dakota (June 21, 1977). Originally, RCA was there to record the shows for the CBS-TV special "Elvis in Concert." But after Elvis's death, it was decided to quickly release this two-record set. Sides A and B, plus "Early Morning Rain," were actually used in the TV special. An advertisement for current RCA LPs was included with each *Elvis in Concert* album. The album sold over one million copies within days of its release and received a Platinum certification from the RIAA on October 14, 1977.

Elvis in Concert peaked at #5 on *Billboard*'s Top LPs chart during its 17-week stay on the chart. To date, it has been Elvis's last top-10 album on the Top LPs chart.

Side A: Elvis' Fans' Comments/Opening Riff, "Also Sprach Zarathustra"/Opening Riff (reprise), "See See Rider," "That's All Right (Mama)," "Are You Lonesome Tonight?," "Teddy Bear"/"Don't Be Cruel," Elvis' Fans' Comments, "You Gave Me a Mountain," and "Jailhouse Rock"
Side B: Elvis' Fans' Comments, "How Great Thou Art," Elvis' Fans' Comments, "I Really Don't Want to Know," Elvis Introduces His Father, "Hurt," "Hound Dog," "My Way," "Can't Help Falling in Love," Closing Riff, and Special Message from Elvis's Father, Vernon Presley
Side C: "I Got a Woman"/"Amen," "Elvis Talks," "Love Me," "O Sole Mio" (Sherrill Nielsen)/"It's Now or Never" (Elvis), and "Tryin' to Get to You"
Side D: "Hawaiian Wedding Song," "Fairytale," "Little Sister," "Early Morning Rain," "What'd I Say," "Johnny B. Goode," and "And I Love You So"

ELVIS IN CONCERT
(RCA CPL2-2587)

1982. New number assigned to RCA APL2-2587.

ELVIS IN HOLLYWOOD
(RCA DPL2-0168)

January 1976. This two-record set, merchandised in a single-pocket jacket, was sold exclusively on television. The title and concept were based on Paul Lichter's 1975 book, *Elvis in Hollywood*. *Elvis in Hollywood* was marketed by the Brookville Marketing Corporation of New York City. Except for "Rock-a-Hula Baby," "Bossa Nova Baby," and "They Remind Me Too Much of You," all songs in the album were title tunes from Elvis's movies. The album came with a twenty-page bonus photo book.

Side 1: "Jailhouse Rock," "Rock-a-Hula Baby," "G. I. Blues," "Kissin' Cousins," and "Wild in the Country"
Side 2: "King Creole," "Blue Hawaii," "Fun in Acapulco," "Follow That Dream," and "Girls! Girls! Girls!"
Side 3: "Viva Las Vegas," "Bossa Nova Baby," "Flaming Star," "Girl Happy," and "Frankie and Johnny"
Side 4: "Roustabout," "Spinout," "Double Trouble," "Charro," and "They Remind Me Too Much of You"

ELVIS IN PERSON AT THE
INTERNATIONAL HOTEL, LAS VEGAS, NEVADA
(RCA LSP-4428)

November 1970. This album consisted of sides 1 and 2 of the double LP *From Memphis to Vegas/From Vegas to Memphis*. All songs on *Elvis in Person* were recorded live at the International Hotel from August 22 to 26, 1969. The original pressing was on nonflexible vinyl. Subsequent pressings were on flexible vinyl.

Elvis in Person did not chart.

Side 1: "Blue Suede Shoes," "Johnny B. Goode," "All Shook Up," "Are You Lonesome Tonight?," "Hound Dog," "I Can't Stop Loving You," and "My Babe"
Side 2: "Mystery Train"/"Tiger Man," "Words," "In the Ghetto," "Suspicious Minds," and "Can't Help Falling in Love"

ELVIS IN PERSON AT THE
INTERNATIONAL HOTEL, LAS VEGAS, NEVADA
(RCA AFL1-4428)

1977. New number assigned to RCA LSP-4428.

ELVIS IN PERSON AT THE
INTERNATIONAL HOTEL, LAS VEGAS, NEVADA
(RCA AYL1-3892)

February 1981. New number assigned to RCA AFL1-4428. This album is now one of RCA's "Best Buy" LPs.

ELVIS IS BACK
(RCA LPM-2231)

April 1960. Songs for this album were recorded at RCA's Nashville studios in March and April 1960. It's been reported that demonstration records for some of the songs were produced by Phil Spector. No song titles were listed on the original album jacket. Instead, the titles were printed on a yellow sticker that was affixed to the front cover. Later pressings had the titles printed directly on the jacket. *Elvis Is Back* opened up like a book. Bonus photos were contained inside. A few copies of this album had a civilian photo of Elvis on the front and an Army photo of Elvis on the back. According to RCA, sales of *Elvis Is Back* surpassed $1 million.

Elvis Is Back had a 56-week stay on *Billboard*'s Best-Selling LPs chart, peaking at #2 (for three weeks).

Side 1: "Make Me Know It," "Fever," "The Girl of My Best Friend," "I Will Be Home Again," "Dirty, Dirty Feeling," and "Thrill of Your Love"
Side 2: "Soldier Boy," "Such a Night," "It Feels So Right," "The Girl Next Door Went a' Walking," "Like a Baby," and "Reconsider Baby"

ELVIS IS BACK
(RCA LSP-2231)

April 1960. Stereo release—Elvis's first LP in true stereo. *Elvis Is Back* reached #9 on *Billboard*'s Best-Selling Stereophonic LPs chart and stayed on the chart for 14 weeks.

ELVIS IS BACK
(RCA AFL1-2231)

1977. New number assigned to RCA LSP-2231. *Elvis Is Back* has been deleted from RCA's catalog.

THE ELVIS MEDLEY
(RCA AHL1-4530)

November 1982. This LP was created around the single release "The Elvis Medley." In addition to the medley, full-length versions of the six songs in the medley appeared on the album, as well as three bonus tracks.

The Elvis Medley had a nine-week stay on *Billboard*'s Top LPs chart, peaking at #133. The album has now been deleted from RCA's catalog.

Side 1: "The Elvis Medley" ("Jailhouse Rock"/"Teddy Bear"/"Hound Dog"/"Don't Be Cruel"/"Burning Love"/"Suspicious Minds"), "Jailhouse Rock," "Teddy Bear," "Hound Dog," and "Don't Be Cruel"
Side 2: "Burning Love," "Suspicious Minds," "Always on My Mind," "Heartbreak Hotel," and "Hard Headed Woman"

ELVIS NOW
(RCA LSP-4671)

February 1972. Except for "Hey Jude," which was recorded at American Sound Studios in Memphis in January 1969, all songs on *Elvis Now* were recorded at RCA's Nashville studios on four different occasions in 1970 and 1971. "I Was Born About Ten Thousand Years Ago" had previously been heard only in excerpts on the 1971 LP *Elvis Country*. A few promotional copies of *Elvis Now* were released. The only difference from the commercial issue was a white sticker affixed to the front cover that had the songs and running times listed.

Elvis Now peaked at #43 on *Billboard*'s Top LPs chart during its 19-week stay.

Side 1: "Help Me Make It Through the Night," "Miracle of the Rosary," "Hey Jude," "Put Your Hand in the Hand," and "Until It's Time for You to Go"
Side 2: "We Can Make the Morning," "Early Morning Rain," "Sylvia," "Fools Rush In," and "I Was Born About Ten Thousand Years Ago"

ELVIS NOW
(RCA AFL1-4671)

1977. New number assigned to RCA LSP-4671. *Elvis Now* has been deleted from RCA's catalog.

ELVIS PRESLEY
(RCA LPM-1254)

March 13, 1956. *Elvis Presley*, Elvis's first album, consisted of five tracks recorded at Sun Records and seven recorded in January 1956 at the New York City and Nashville studios of RCA. The cover photo was credited to Popsie, a pseudonym of photographer William S. Randolph. Four photos of Elvis graced the back cover. First copies of the jacket had "Elvis" in light pink letters; in later pressings the letters were dark pink. *Elvis Presley* was the first album in history to sell one million copies. Certification as a million-seller was made by the RIAA on November 1, 1966. The album spawned a record five EPs.

Elvis Presley entered *Billboard*'s Best-Selling Pop Albums chart at #11. Within six weeks, it reached number one, remaining at the top for 10 consecutive weeks. The total stay on the chart was 49 weeks.

Side 1: "Blue Suede Shoes," "I'm Counting on You," "I Got a Woman," "One-Sided Love Affair," "I Love You Because," and "Just Because"

Side 2: "Tutti Frutti," "Tryin' to Get to You," "I'm Gonna Sit Right Down and Cry (Over You)," "I'll Never Let You Go (Little Darlin')," "Blue Moon," and "Money Honey"

ELVIS PRESLEY
(RCA LSP-1254 [e])

February 1962. Electronically reprocessed stereo release.

ELVIS PRESLEY
(RCA AFL1-1254 [e])

1977. New number assigned to RCA LSP-1254 (e).

ELVIS PRESLEY
(RCA AFM1-5198)

1985. To celebrate the 50th anniversary of Elvis's birth, *Elvis Presley* was released with the songs digitally remastered in monaural. The record was pressed on heavy virgin vinyl and had a special gold "50th" anniversary label. A gold paper band wrapped around the album's jacket.

ELVIS RECORDED LIVE ON STAGE IN MEMPHIS
(RCA CPL1-0606)

June 1974. This album was recorded at the Mid-South Coliseum in Memphis on March 20, 1974. Al Dvorin is the master of ceremonies heard on the LP. A credit on the album read, "Executive Producer—Elvis Presley."

Elvis Recorded Live on Stage in Memphis had a 13-week stay on *Billboard*'s Top LPs chart, peaking at #33.

Side 1: "See See Rider," "I Got a Woman," "Love Me," "Tryin' to Get to You," "Long Tall Sally"/"Whole Lotta Shakin' Goin' On"/"Your Mama Don't Dance"/"Flip, Flop and Fly," "Jailhouse Rock"/"Hound Dog," "Why Me Lord," and "How Great Thou Art"
Side 2: "Blueberry Hill"/"I Can't Stop Loving You," "Help Me," "An American Trilogy," "Let Me Be There," "My Baby Left Me," "Lawdy Miss Clawdy," and "Can't Stop Loving You"

ELVIS RECORDED LIVE ON STAGE IN MEMPHIS
(RCA APD1-0606)

June 1974. Quadradisc release.

ELVIS RECORDED LIVE ON STAGE IN MEMPHIS
(RCA AFL1-0606)

1977. New number assigned to RCA CPL1-0606.

ELVIS RECORDED LIVE ON STAGE IN MEMPHIS
(RCA AQL1-4776)

1979. New number assigned to RCA AFL1-0606.

ELVIS SINGS FLAMING STAR
(RCA Camden CAS 2304)

April 1969. *Elvis Sings Flaming Star*, which was originally issued as *Singer Presents Elvis Singing Flaming Star and Others*, was Elvis's first Camden release. All nine songs on the LP were listed on the front cover.

Elvis Sings Flaming Star had a 16-week stay on *Billboard*'s Top LP chart, peaking at #96.

Side 1: "Flaming Star," "Wonderful World," "Night Life," "All I Needed

Was the Rain," and "Too Much Monkey Business"
Side 2: "The Yellow Rose of Texas"/"The Eyes of Texas," "She's a Machine," "Do the Vega," and "Tiger Man"

ELVIS SINGS FLAMING STAR
(Pickwick CAS-2304)
December 1975. Pickwick reissue of RCA Camden CAS-2304.

ELVIS SINGS FOR CHILDREN AND GROWNUPS TOO!
(RCA CPL1-2901)
July 1978. Except for "Big Boots," all songs on *Elvis Sings for Children and Grownups Too!* had been previously released. "Big Boots" was an alternate take. A removable bonus greeting card was attached to the album's back cover.

Elvis Sings for Children and Grownups Too! reached #130 on *Billboard*'s Top LPs chart during its 11 weeks on the chart. It fared much better on the Country LPs chart—#5 and 16 weeks. *Elvis Sings for Children and Grownups Too!* has been deleted from RCA's catalog.

Side 1: "Teddy Bear," "Wooden Heart," "Five Sleepy Heads," "Puppet on a String," "Angel," and "Old MacDonald"
Side 2: "How Would You Like to Be," "Cotton Candy Land," "Old Shep," "Big Boots," and "Have a Happy"

ELVIS SINGS HITS FROM HIS MOVIES, VOLUME 1
(RCA Camden CAS-2567)
June 1972. Despite the album's title, two songs on *Elvis Sings Hits from His Movies, Volume 1* were never sung in his movies—"Guitar Man" and "Big Boss Man." Those two songs were from previously released singles.

Elvis Sings Hits from His Movies, Volume 1 had a 15-week stay on *Billboard*'s Top LPs chart, peaking at #87.

Side 1: "Down by the Riverside"/"When the Saints Go Marching In," "They Remind Me Too Much of You," "Confidence," "Frankie and Johnny," and "Guitar Man"
Side 2: "Long Legged Girl (with the Short Dress On)," "You Don't Know Me," "How Would You Like to Be," "Big Boss Man," and "Old MacDonald"

ELVIS SINGS HITS FROM HIS MOVIES, VOLUME 1
(Pickwick CAS-2567)
December 1975. Reissue of RCA Camden CAS-2567. The song selections and album cover were identical to the original release.

ELVIS SINGS THE WONDERFUL WORLD OF CHRISTMAS
(RCA LSP-4579)
October 1971. The eleven Christmas songs on this LP were recorded at RCA's Nashville studios on May 15 and 16, 1971. No photo of Elvis appeared on the front cover. Instead, there were drawn depictions of twelve seasonal items. A 5"-by-7" color bonus postcard was included inside the album jacket.

Side 1: "O Come, All Ye Faithful," "The First Noel," "On a Snowy Christmas Night," "Winter Wonderland," "The Wonderful World of Christmas," and "It Won't Seem Like Christmas (Without You)"
Side 2: "I'll Be Home on Christmas Day," "If I Get Home on Christmas Day," "Holly Leaves and Christmas Trees," "Merry Christmas, Baby," and "Silver Bells"

ELVIS SINGS THE WONDERFUL WORLD OF CHRISTMAS
(RCA ANL1-1936)
1973. New number assigned to RCA LSP-4579. This LP was released in the "Pure Gold" series. *Elvis Sings the Wonderful World of Christmas* sold over a million copies. The RIAA certified the album as a Gold Record on November 4, 1977. Twenty-seven days later (December 1), the album received a Platinum certification.

ELVIS: THE FIRST LIVE RECORDINGS
(Music Works PB-3601)
February 1984. Five recordings from Elvis's "Louisiana Hayride" appearances were featured on this release.

Elvis: The First Live Recordings had a four-week stay on *Billboard*'s Top LPs chart, peaking at #163.

Side 1: Introduction, Elvis with Horace Logan, "Baby, Let's Play House," "Maybellene," and "Tweedlee Dee"
Side 2: "That's All Right (Mama)," Recollections by Frank Page, and "Hound Dog"

ELVIS: THE HILLBILLY CAT
(Music Works PB-3602)
July 1984. This album marked the first official release of Elvis's first "Louisiana Hayride" appearance. Previously, "That's All Right (Mama)" and "Blue Moon of Kentucky" had been issued on numerous bootleg LPs. "Good Rockin' Tonight" and "I Got a Woman" were from a March 19, 1955, concert in Houston, at the Eagle's Hall.

Side 1: Introduction, Elvis with Horace Logan, "That's All Right (Mama)," and Elvis Talks with Horace Logan
Side 2: "Blue Moon of Kentucky," Recollections by Frank Page, "Good Rockin' Tonight," and "I Got a Woman"

ELVIS: THE OTHER SIDES— WORLDWIDE GOLD AWARD HITS, VOLUME 2
(RCA LPM-6402)
August 1971. Purporting to contain yet more million-sellers, *Elvis: The Other Sides—Worldwide Gold Award Hits, Volume 2* was an unusual four-record boxed set. It contained both sides of three singles, the A sides of two singles, and tracks from six EPs. Two bonuses came packaged with the album. The first was an envelope with a piece of Elvis's clothing inside (the white suit from *Clambake*), and the second was a large color photo of Elvis.

Elvis: The Other Sides—Worldwide Gold Award Hits, Volume 2 had a seven-week stay on *Billboard*'s Top LPs chart, peaking at #120.

Side 1: "Puppet on a String," "Witchcraft," "Trouble," "Poor Boy," "I Want to Be Free," "Doncha' Think It's Time," and "Young Dreams"

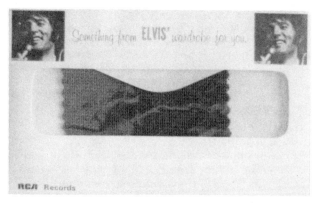

A piece of Elvis's clothing included as a bonus with *Elvis: The Other Sides—Worldwide Gold Award Hits, Volume 2*. (Photo courtesy Don Fink)

Side 2: "The Next Step Is Love," "You Don't Have to Say You Love Me," "Paralyzed," "My Wish Came True," "When My Blue Moon Turns to Gold Again," and "Lonesome Cowboy"

Side 3: "My Baby Left Me," "It Hurts Me," "I Need Your Love Tonight," "Tell Me Why," "Please Don't Drag That String Around," and "Young and Beautiful"

Side 4: "Hot Dog," "New Orleans," "We're Gonna Move," "Crawfish," "King Creole," "I Believe in the Man in the Sky," and "Dixieland Rock"

Side 5: "The Wonder of You," "They Remind Me Too Much of You," "Mean Woman Blues," "Lonely Man," "Any Day Now," and "Don't Ask Me Why"

Side 6: "(Marie's the Name) His Latest Flame," "I Really Don't Want to Know," "(You're So Square) Baby, I Don't Care," "I've Lost You," "Let Me," and "Love Me"

Side 7: "Got a Lot o' Livin' to Do," "Fame and Fortune," "Rip It Up," "There Goes My Everything," "Lover Doll," and "One Night"

Side 8: "Just Tell Her Jim Said Hello," "Ask Me," "Patch It Up," "As Long as I Have You," "You'll Think of Me," and "Wild in the Country"

ELVIS TODAY
(RCA APL1-1039)

May 1975. All songs on *Elvis Today* were recorded at RCA's Hollywood studios, March 10–13, 1975.

Elvis Today spent 13 weeks on *Billboard*'s Top LPs chart, peaking at #57.

Side 1: "T-R-O-U-B-L-E," "And I Love You So," "Susan When She Tried," "Woman Without Love," and "Shake a Hand"

Side 2: "Pieces of My Life," "Fairytale," "I Can Help," "Bringing It Back," and "Green, Green Grass of Home"

ELVIS TODAY
(RCA APD1-1039)

May 1975. Quadradisc release.

ELVIS TODAY
(RCA AFL1-1039)

1977. New Number assigned to RCA APL1-1039.

ELVIS—TV SPECIAL
(RCA LPM-4088)

November 25, 1968. All tracks on this soundtrack album of Elvis's 1968 TV special "Elvis," were recorded in June 1968 at Western Recorders in Hollywood and NBC-TV's Burbank studios. Although *Elvis—TV Spe-* cial was issued with a monaural prefix number, several of the cuts are in stereo. Original pressings of this album were on nonflexible vinyl; all pressings since 1971 have been on flexible vinyl. *Elvis—TV Special* achieved sales of over $1 million. Gold Record certification from the RIAA came on August 27, 1969.

Elvis—TV Special peaked at #8 on *Billboard*'s Top LPs chart during its 32-week stay.

Side 1: "Trouble"/"Guitar Man," "Lawdy Miss Clawdy"/"Baby What You Want Me To Do," Dialogue, "Heartbreak Hotel"/"Hound Dog"/ "All Shook Up"/"Can't Help Falling in Love"/"Jailhouse Rock," Dialogue, "Love Me Tender"

Side 2: Dialogue, "Where Could I Go but to the Lord"/"Up Above My Head"/"Saved," Dialogue, "Blue Christmas," Dialogue, "One Night," "Memories," "Nothingville"/Dialogue/"Big Boss Man"/"Guitar Man"/"Little Egypt"/"Trouble"/"Guitar Man," and "If I Can Dream"

ELVIS—TV SPECIAL
(RCA AFM1-4088)

1977. New number assigned to RCA LPM-4088.

ELVIS—TV SPECIAL
(RCA AYM1-3894)

February 1981. New number assigned to RCA AFM1-4088. This LP is one of RCA's "Best Buy" series of albums.

ELVIS: WORLDWIDE 50 GOLD AWARD HITS, VOLUME 1
(RCA LPM-6401)

August 1970. This was a four-record boxed set that included 50 songs that sold more than a million copies. As a bonus, a 20-page color photo booklet came with the box. Gold Record certification by the RIAA was made on February 13, 1973.

Elvis: Worldwide 50 Gold Award Hits, Volume 1 reached #45 on *Billboard*'s Top LPs chart, remaining on the chart for 22 weeks. On the Country LPs chart, it peaked at #25. After Elvis's death, the album re-charted, peaking at #83 (for 14 weeks) on the Top LPs chart.

Side 1: "Heartbreak Hotel," "I Was the One," "I Want You, I Need You, I Love You," "Don't Be Cruel," "Hound Dog," and "Love Me Tender"

Side 2: "Any Way You Want Me," "Too Much," "Playing for Keeps," "All Shook Up," "That's When Your Heartaches Begin," and "Loving You"

Side 3: "Teddy Bear," "Jailhouse Rock," "Treat Me Nice," "I Beg of You," "Don't," "Wear My Ring Around Your Neck," and "Hard Headed Woman"

Side 4: "I Got Stung," "(Now and Then There's) A Fool Such As I," "A Big Hunk o' Love," "Stuck on You," "A Mess of Blues," and "It's Now or Never"

Side 5: "I Gotta Know," "Are You Lonesome Tonight?," "Surrender," "I Feel So Bad," "Little Sister," and "Can't Help Falling in Love"

Side 6: "Rock-a-Hula Baby," "Anything That's Part of You," "Good Luck Charm," "She's Not You," "Return to Sender," "Where Do You Come From," and "One Broken Heart for Sale"

Side 7: "(You're the) Devil in Disguise," "Bossa Nova Baby," "Kissin' Cousins," "Viva Las Vegas," "Ain't That Loving You, Baby," and "Wooden Heart"

Side 8: "Crying in the Chapel," "If I Can Dream," "In the Ghetto," "Suspicious Minds," "Don't Cry, Daddy," "Kentucky Rain," and excerpts from *Elvis Sails*

ESSENTIAL ELVIS—THE FIRST MOVIES
(RCA 6738-1-R)
January 1988. All seventeen songs from Elvis's first three films appeared on this LP. Twelve of the 23 tracks had never been released by RCA.

Side 1: "Love Me Tender," "Let Me," "Poor Boy," "We're Gonna Move," "Loving You" (unreleased slow version, take #10), "Party" (unreleased version), "Hot Dog," "Teddy Bear," "Loving You" (unreleased fast version, takes #20 and #21), "Mean Woman Blues" (alternate film version), and "Got a Lot o' Livin' to Do" (unreleased version)

Side 2: "Loving You" (unreleased fast version, take #1), "Party," "Lonesome Cowboy," "Jailhouse Rock" (unreleased, with vocal overdub, take #6), "Treat Me Nice" (unreleased version, take #10), "Young and Beautiful" (unreleased version, take #12), "Don't Leave Me Now" (original version, take #12), "I Want to Be Free" (original version, take #11), "(You're So Square) Baby, I Don't Care" (original version, take #16; vocal overdub, take #6), "Jailhouse Rock" (unreleased version, take #5), "Got a Lot o' Livin' to Do," and "Love Me Tender" (unreleased version)

50,000,000 ELVIS FANS CAN'T BE WRONG—
ELVIS' GOLD RECORDS, VOLUME 2
(RCA LPM-2075)
December 1959. Both sides of five Elvis singles that sold over a million copies were featured on this album, the second in a series of "Gold Record" LPs. The cover photo was of Elvis in his gold lamé suit. "50,000,000 Elvis Fans Can't Be Wrong" was omitted from the label of some pressings. Although many sources refer to the title of this album as simply *Elvis' Gold Records, Volume 2,* the authors have chosen to use the full title, as that is how it appears in RCA's catalog. On November 1, 1966, *50,000,000 Elvis Fans Can't Be Wrong—Elvis' Gold Records, Volume 2* was certified by the RIAA as a Gold Record for sales exceeding $1 million.

50,000,000 Elvis Fans Can't Be Wrong—Elvis' Gold Records, Volume 2 reached #31 on *Billboard*'s Top LPs chart, remaining on the chart for six weeks.

Side 1: "I Need Your Love Tonight," "Don't," "Wear My Ring Around Your Neck," "My Wish Came True," and "I Got Stung"

Side 2: "One Night," "A Big Hunk o' Love," "I Beg of You," "A Fool Such as I," and "Doncha' Think It's Time"

50,000,000 ELVIS FANS CAN'T BE WRONG—
ELVIS' GOLD RECORDS, VOLUME 2
(RCA LSP-2075 [e])
February 1962. Electronically reprocessed stereo release.

50,000,000 ELVIS FANS CAN'T BE WRONG—
ELVIS' GOLD RECORDS, VOLUME 2
(RCA AFL1-2075 [e])
1977. New number assigned to RCA LSP-2075 (e).

50,000,000 ELVIS FANS CAN'T BE WRONG—
ELVIS' GOLD RECORDS, VOLUME 2
(RCA AFM1-5197)
1985. Special release in which all tracks were restored to original monaural and digitally remastered. The album, which was pressed on heavy virgin vinyl with a special gold "50th" anniversary label, came packaged with a gold paper band wraparound.

FOR LP FANS ONLY
(RCA LPM-1990)
February 9, 1959. *For LP Fans Only* was the first album in recording history to exclude the performer's name from the outside jacket. Even the LP's title was not prominent; it appeared in a box with the RCA logo. The back cover photo was of Private Presley in his Army dress uniform. A rare version had the same photo on the back as on the front.

For LP Fans Only reached #19 on *Billboard*'s Top LPs chart and had an eight-week stay on the chart.

Side 1: "That's All Right (Mama)," "Lawdy Miss Clawdy," "Mystery Train," "Playing for Keeps," and "Poor Boy"

Side 2: "My Baby Left Me," "I Was the One," "Shake, Rattle and Roll," "I'm Left, You're Right, She's Gone," and "You're a Heartbreaker"

FOR LP FANS ONLY
(RCA LSP-1990 [e])
January 1965. Electronically reprocessed stereo release.

FOR LP FANS ONLY
(RCA AFL1-1990 [e])
1977. New number assigned to RCA LSP-1990 (e).

FRANKIE AND JOHNNY
(RCA LPM-3553)
April 1966. Soundtrack album from Elvis's 1966 movie *Frankie and Johnny.* All twelve songs from the film were included in this album. Original issues of *Frankie and Johnny* came with a 12"-by-12" color photo. A cover sticker proclaimed, "Special Bonus! Full Color Portrait of Elvis Inside This Album. This Offer for a Limited Time Only."

Frankie and Johnny had a 19-week stay on *Billboard*'s Top LPs chart, peaking at #20. The album has now been deleted from RCA's catalog.

Side 1: "Frankie and Johnny," "Come Along," "Petunia, the Gardener's Daughter," "Chesay," "What Every Woman Lives For," and "Look Out, Broadway"

Side 2: "Beginner's Luck," "Down by the Riverside"/"When the Saints Go Marching In," "Shout It Out," "Hard Luck," "Please Don't Stop Loving Me," and "Everybody Come Aboard"

FRANKIE AND JOHNNY
(RCA LSP-3553)
April 1966. Stereo release. This album was deleted from RCA's catalog in 1968.

FRANKIE AND JOHNNY
(RCA APL1-2559)
September 1977. Reissue of RCA LSP-3553 after Elvis's death. This album has now been deleted from RCA's catalog.

FRANKIE & JOHNNY
(Pickwick ACL-7007)
November 1976. This album was not a reissue of RCA LSP-3553. Three songs—"Chesay," "Look Out, Broadway," and "Everybody Come Aboard"— were deleted, and the remaining nine tracks were in a different

order. Pickwick replaced both the front and back covers of *Frankie & Johnny*. The new front cover was the same as that used on *Elvis Now*. Some jackets had different borders. In addition, an ampersand replaced the *and* in the title.

Side 1: "Frankie and Johnny," "Come Along," "What Every Woman Lives For," "Hard Luck," and "Please Don't Stop Loving Me"
Side 2: "Down by the Riverside"/"When the Saints Go Marching In," "Petunia, the Gardener's Daughter," "Beginner's Luck," and "Shout It Out"

FROM ELVIS IN MEMPHIS
(RCA LSP-4155)

June 1969. All songs on *From Elvis in Memphis* were recorded at American Sound Studios in Memphis in January and February 1969. The original pressings were on nonflexible vinyl; later pressings were on flexible vinyl. An 8"-by-10" photo from Elvis's 1968 TV special was included as a bonus. Sales of the album exceeded $1 million and a Gold Record was certified by the RIAA on January 28, 1970.

From Elvis in Memphis had a 24-week stay on *Billboard*'s Top LPs chart, peaking at #13. On the Country LPs chart, the album reached #2 (for two weeks) and stayed on the chart for 34 weeks. The *Johnny Cash at San Quentin* album was number one for the two weeks that *From Elvis in Memphis* was #2. In England, the album reached number one. The eight-track cartridge release hit #14 on *Billboard*'s Best-Selling Cartridge chart.

Side 1: "Wearin' That Loved on Look," "Only the Strong Survive," "I'll Hold You in My Heart (Till I Can Hold You in My Arms)," "Long Black Limousine," "It Keeps Right on a-Hurtin'," and "I'm Movin' On"
Side 1: "Power of My Love," "Gentle on My Mind," "After Loving You," "True Love Travels on a Gravel Road," "Any Day Now," and "In the Ghetto"

FROM ELVIS IN MEMPHIS
(RCA AFL1-4155)

1977. New number assigned to RCA LSP-4155.

FROM ELVIS PRESLEY BOULEVARD, MEMPHIS, TENNESSEE
(RCA APL1-1506)

May 1976. All ten songs on this LP were recorded at Graceland, February 2–8, 1976. A Gold Record was certified by the RIAA on October 7, 1977, for sales exceeding 500,000 units.

From Elvis Presley Boulevard, Memphis, Tennessee had a 17-week stay on *Billboard*'s Top LPs chart, peaking at #41. The album reached number one on the Country LPs chart.

Side 1: "Hurt," "Never Again," "Blue Eyes Crying in the Rain," "Danny Boy," and "The Last Farewell"
Side 2: "For the Heart," "Bitter They Are, Harder They Fall," "Solitaire," "Love Coming Down," and "I'll Never Fall in Love Again"

FROM ELVIS PRESLEY BOULEVARD, MEMPHIS, TENNESSEE
(RCA APD1-1506)

May 1976. Quadradisc release.

FROM ELVIS PRESLEY BOULEVARD, MEMPHIS, TENNESSEE
(RCA AFL1-1506)

1977. New number assigned to RCA APL1-1506.

FROM MEMPHIS TO VEGAS/ FROM VEGAS TO MEMPHIS
(RCA LSP-6020)

November 16, 1969. This was the first double LP of Elvis's career. Sides 1 and 2 consisted of live recordings made at the International Hotel in Las Vegas in August 1969, and sides 3 and 4 were studio recordings from Elvis's two sessions at Memphis's American Sound Studios in January and February 1969. Two 8"-by-10" black-and-white photos from "Elvis," the 1968 TV special, came with the album. A total of four photos were available, but only two, in different combinations, were issued for each LP. The two-record set was originally pressed on nonflexible vinyl. From 1971 on, the pressings were on flexible vinyl. *From Memphis to Vegas/ From Vegas to Memphis* quickly reached sales of $1 million, qualifying it for a Gold Record. Certification was made by the RIAA on December 12, 1969. In November 1970, RCA released each record in this double LP individually. Sides 1 and 2 were titled *Elvis in Person at the International Hotel, Las Vegas, Nevada* and sides 3 and 4 were titled *Back in Memphis*.

From Memphis to Vegas/From Vegas to Memphis spent 24 weeks on *Billboard*'s Top LPs chart, reaching a high position of #12. It did slightly better on the Country LPs chart, peaking at #5.

Side 1: "Blue Suede Shoes," "Johnny B. Goode," "All Shook Up," "Are You Lonesome Tonight?," "Hound Dog," "I Can't Stop Loving You," and "My Babe"
Side 2: "Mystery Train"/"Tiger Man," "Words," "In the Ghetto," "Suspicious Minds," and "Can't Help Falling in Love"
Side 3: "Inherit the Wind," "This Is the Story," "Stranger in My Own Home Town," "A Little Bit of Green," and "And the Grass Won't Pay No Mind"
Side 4: "Do You Know Who I Am," "From a Jack to a King," "The Fair Is Moving On," "You'll Think of Me," and "Without Love (There Is Nothing)"

FUN IN ACAPULCO
(RCA LPM-2576)

December 1963. This was the soundtrack album to Elvis's 1963 film *Fun in Acapulco*. All eleven songs from the film were included, as well as two bonus songs. Sales of over $1 million are claimed for *Fun in Acapulco*, although it has never been officially certified.

A peak position of #3 on *Billboard*'s Top LPs chart was reached. The album remained on the chart for 24 weeks.

Side 1: "Fun in Acapulco," "Vino, Dinero y Amor," "Mexico," "El Toro," "Marguerita," "The Lady was a Bullfighter," and "(There's) No Room to Rhumba in a Sports Car"
Side 2: "I Think I'm Gonna Like It Here," "Bossa Nova Baby," "You Can't Say No in Acapulco," "Guadalajara," "Love Me Tonight" (bonus), and "Slowly but Surely" (bonus)

FUN IN ACAPULCO
(RCA LSP-2756)
December 1963. Stereo release.

FUN IN ACAPULCO
(RCA AFL1-2756)
1977. New number assigned to RCA LSP-2756. *Fun in Acapulco* has been deleted from RCA's catalog.

G. I. BLUES
(RCA LPM-2256)
October 1960. This was the soundtrack album to Elvis's 1960 film *G. I. Blues*. All eleven movie songs were included. The cover featured a photo of Elvis in his Army uniform. A special "Elvis Is Back!" innersleeve was provided. *G. I. Blues* sold over 3.5 million copies, easily qualifying for a Gold Record, which was certified by the RIAA on March 12, 1963.

G. I. Blues entered *Billboard*'s Top LPs chart in October 1960, at #6—the highest debut position for any Elvis LP. In six weeks it was the number one album in America. *G. I. Blues* remained number one for 10 weeks, although they were not consecutive. The total 111-week stay on the chart was the longest for any Elvis record.

Side 1: "Tonight Is So Right for Love," "What's She Really Like," "Frankfort Special," "Wooden Heart," and "G. I. Blues"
Side 2: "Pocketful of Rainbows," "Shoppin' Around," "Big Boots," "Didja' Ever," "Blue Suede Shoes," and "Doin' the Best I Can"

G. I. BLUES
(RCA LSP-2256)
October 1960. Stereo release. *G. I. Blues* reached #2 on *Billboard*'s Stereo LPs chart and remained on the chart for a total of 47 weeks.

G. I. BLUES
(RCA AFL1-2256)
1977. New number assigned to RCA LSP-2256.

G. I. BLUES
(RCA AYL1-3735)
1980. New number assigned to RCA AFL1-2256.

GIRL HAPPY
(RCA LPM-3338)
April 1965. All eleven songs from Elvis's 1965 film *Girl Happy* were included in this soundtrack album, as well as one bonus song, "You'll Be Gone," that had been recorded three years earlier. Sales of *Girl Happy* exceeded $1 million, but no Gold Record has been certified by the RIAA.

Girl Happy had a 31-week stay on *Billboard*'s Top LPs chart, reaching #8.

Side 1: "Girl Happy," "Spring Fever," "Fort Lauderdale Chamber of Commerce," "Startin' Tonight," "Wolf Call," and "Do Not Disturb"
Side 2: "Cross My Heart and Hope to Die," "The Meanest Girl in Town," "Do the Clam," "Puppet on a String," "I've Got to Find My Baby," and "You'll Be Gone" (bonus)

GIRL HAPPY
(RCA LSP-3338)
April 1965. Stereo release.

GIRL HAPPY
(RCA AFL1-3338)
1977. New number assigned to RCA LSP-3338.

GIRLS! GIRLS! GIRLS!
(RCA LPM-2621)
November 1962. This soundtrack LP from Elvis's 1962 movie *Girls! Girls! Girls!* contained thirteen of the songs from the film. The short "Dainty Little Moonbeams" was not included. Sales of *Girls! Girls! Girls!* exceeded $1 million, but no certification has been made by the RIAA.

Girls! Girls! Girls! had a 32-week stay on *Billboard*'s Top LPs chart, peaking at #3.

Side 1: "Girls! Girls! Girls!," "I Don't Wanna Be Tied," "Where Do You Come From," "I Don't Want To," "We'll Be Together," "A Boy Like Me, a Girl Like You," and "Earth Boy"
Side 2: "Return to Sender," "Because of Love," "Thanks to the Rolling Sea," "Song of the Shrimp," "The Walls Have Ears," and "We're Coming in Loaded"

GIRLS! GIRLS! GIRLS!
(RCA LSP-2621)
November 1962. Stereo release. *Girls! Girls! Girls!* reached #5 on *Billboard*'s Stereo LPs chart, and remained on the chart for 20 weeks.

GIRLS! GIRLS! GIRLS!
(RCA AFL1-2621)
1977. New number assigned to RCA LSP-2621. *Girls! Girls! Girls!* has been deleted from RCA's catalog.

A GOLDEN CELEBRATION
(RCA CPM6-5172)
October 1984. To celebrate the 50th anniversary of Elvis's birth, RCA released this fabulous six-record set. Included were Sun sessions outtakes; complete "Stage Show" appearances; complete Milton Berle and Steve Allen appearances; two performances at the Mississippi-Alabama Fair and Dairy Show on September 26, 1956; complete "Ed Sullivan Show" appearances; songs from the June 27, 1968, taping of the "Elvis" TV special; and nine newly discovered home recordings (five songs were never known to have been recorded by Elvis).

A Golden Celebration peaked at #80 on *Billboard*'s Top LPs chart, remaining on the chart for 19 weeks. On the Hot Country LPs chart, the boxed set reached #55 and had a seven-week stay.

Side 1: THE SUN SESSIONS OUTTAKES: "Harbor Lights," "That's All Right (Mama)," "Blue Moon of Kentucky," "I Don't Care If the Sun Don't Shine," "I'm Left, You're Right, She's Gone" (a.k.a. "My Baby's Gone"), "I'll Never Let You Go (Little Darlin')," and "When It Rains, It Really Pours"
Side 2: THE DORSEY BROTHERS' "STAGE SHOW": "Shake Rattle and Roll"/"Flip, Flop and Fly," "I Got a Woman," "Baby, Let's Play House," "Tutti Frutti," "Blue Suede Shoes," and "Heartbreak Hotel"

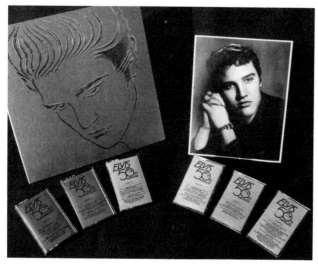

The cassette version of *A Golden Celebration*. (Photo courtesy Jeff Wheatcraft)

Side 3: THE DORSEY BROTHERS' "STAGE SHOW" (continued): "Tutti Frutti," "I Was the One," "Blue Suede Shoes," "Heartbreak Hotel," "Money Honey," and "Heartbreak Hotel"
Side 4: "THE MILTON BERLE SHOW": "Heartbreak Hotel," "Blue Suede Shoes," Dialogue, "Blue Suede Shoes," "Hound Dog," Dialogue, and "I Want You, I Need You, I Love You" "THE STEVE ALLEN SHOW": Dialogue, "I Want You, I Need You, I Love You," Introduction, and "Hound Dog"
Side 5: THE MISSISSIPPI-ALABAMA FAIR AND DAIRY SHOW: "Heartbreak Hotel," "Long Tall Sally," Introductions and Presentations, "I Was the One," "I Want You, I Need You, I Love You," and "I Got a Woman"
Side 6: THE MISSISSIPPI-ALABAMA FAIR AND DAIRY SHOW (continued): "Don't Be Cruel," "Ready Teddy," "Love Me Tender," "Hound Dog," Interviews (Vernon and Gladys Presley, Nick Adams, a Fan, and Elvis)
Side 7: THE MISSISSIPPI-ALABAMA FAIR AND DAIRY SHOW (continued): "Love Me Tender," "I Was the One," "I Got a Woman," "Don't Be Cruel," "Blue Suede Shoes," "Baby, Let's Play House," "Hound Dog," and Announcements
Side 8: "THE ED SULLIVAN SHOW": "Don't Be Cruel," "Love Me Tender," "Ready Teddy," "Hound Dog," "Don't Be Cruel," "Love Me Tender," "Love Me," and "Hound Dog"
Side 9: "THE ED SULLIVAN SHOW" (continued): "Hound Dog," "Love Me Tender," "Heartbreak Hotel," "Don't Be Cruel," "Too Much," "When My Blue Moon Turns to Gold Again," and "Peace in the Valley"
Side 10: ELVIS AT HOME: "Danny Boy," "Soldier Boy," "The Fool," "Earth Angel," and "He's Only a Prayer Away"
Side 11: COLLECTORS' TREASURES: Excerpt from an Interview for TV Guide, "My Heart Cries for You," "Dark Moon," "Write to Me from Naples," and "Suppose"
Side 12: ELVIS: "Blue Suede Shoes," "Tiger Man," "That's All Right (Mama)," "Lawdy Miss Clawdy," "Baby What You Want Me to Do," Monologue, "Love Me," "Are You Lonesome Tonight?," "Baby, What You Want Me to Do," Monologue, "Blue Christmas," Monologue, "One Night," and "Trying to Get to You"

GOOD TIMES
(RCA CPL1-0475)
March 1974. All songs were recorded at Stax Studios in Memphis in December 1973, except for "Take Good Care of Her" and "I've Got a Thing About You, Baby," which were recorded at Stax in July 1973.

Good Times spent eight weeks on *Billboard*'s Top LPs chart, peaking at #90.

Side 1: "Take Good Care of Her," "Lovin' Arms," "I Got a Feelin' in My Body," "If That Isn't Love," and "She Wears My Ring"
Side 2: "I've Got a Thing About You, Baby," "My Boy," "Spanish Eyes," "Talk About the Good Times," and "Good Time Charlie's Got the Blues"

GOOD TIMES
(RCA AFL1-0475)
1977. New number assigned to RCA CPL1-0475. *Good Times* has been deleted from RCA's catalog.

GREATEST HITS, VOLUME 1
(RCA AHL1-2347)
November 1981. While not too many would consider all the tracks on *Greatest Hits, Volume 1* as the "greatest," there were some cuts not previously released, making the album a must for Elvis collectors. "Suspicious Minds" and "The Sound of Your Cry" were released in stereo for the first time. Also appearing on an RCA release for the first time were live concert versions of "A Big Hunk o' Love," "What'd I Say," "Don't Cry, Daddy," and "Steamroller Blues,"

Side 1: "The Wonder of You," "A Big Hunk o' Love," "There Goes My Everything," "Suspicious Minds," and "What'd I Say"
Side 2: "Don't Cry, Daddy," "Steamroller Blues," "The Sound of Your Cry," "Burning Love," and "You'll Never Walk Alone"

GUITAR MAN
(RCA AAL1-3917)
January 1981. All songs on this album had been previously released. However, producer Felton Jarvis assembled a group of session musicians and vocalists at Young'un Sound in Nashville in October and November of 1980 to record new backing tracks for the ten songs on *Guitar Man*. This was done to give the songs a new modern sound. Five of the vocal tracks were alternate takes not previously released. A full-color flyer advertising the 1981 documentary *This Is Elvis* was included with the LP as an insert.

Guitar Man had a 12-week stay on *Billboard*'s Top LPs chart, peaking at #49. It fared much better on the Hot Country LPs chart, reaching #6 and staying for 31 weeks. *Guitar Man* has been deleted from RCA's catalog.

Side 1: "Guitar Man," "After Loving You" (alternate take), "Too Much Monkey Business," "Just Call Me Lonesome" (alternate take), and "Lovin' Arms" (alternate take)
Side 2: "You Asked Me To," "Clean Up Your Own Back Yard," "She Thinks I Still Care" (alternate take), "Faded Love," and "I'm Movin' On" (alternate take)

HARUM SCARUM
(RCA LPM-3468)
October 1965. This was the soundtrack LP of Elvis's 1965 film *Harum Scarum*. Two bonus songs were included with the nine songs from the movie. A 12"-by-12" color still from the film was a bonus item.

Harum Scarum reached #8 on *Billboard*'s Top LPs chart. Total time on the chart was 23 weeks.

Side 1: "Harem Holiday," "My Desert Serenade," "Go East, Young Man," "Mirage," "Kismet," and "Shake That Tambourine"

Side 2: "Hey, Little Girl," "Golden Coins," "So Close, Yet So Far (from Paradise)," "Animal Instinct" (bonus), and "Wisdom of the Ages" (bonus)

HARUM SCARUM
(RCA LSP-3468)

October 1965. Stereo release.

HARUM SCARUM
(RCA AFL1-2558)

September 1977. New number assigned to RCA LSP-3468. *Harum Scarum* has been deleted from RCA's catalog.

HAVING FUN WITH ELVIS ON STAGE
(Boxcar Records)

1974. *Having Fun with Elvis on Stage* was a talking album only. No songs were included. Basically, the album consisted of various comments made by Elvis in concert. The record label, instead of side 1 and side 2, read "Elvis 1" and "Elvis 2." Boxcar Records, based in Madison, Tennessee, was a label formed by Elvis and Colonel Tom Parker. Parker hawked the albums at souvenir stands in Las Vegas and other concert locations.

HAVING FUN WITH ELVIS ON STAGE
(RCA CPM1-0818)

October 1974. RCA reissue of the Boxcar Records original. Although no songs were contained on this album, it actually made *Billboard's* Top LPs chart for seven weeks, peaking at #130.

HAVING FUN WITH ELVIS ON STAGE
(RCA AFM1-0818)

1977. New number assigned to RCA CPM1-0818. *Having Fun with Elvis on Stage* has been deleted from RCA's catalog.

HE TOUCHED ME
(RCA LSP-4690)

April 1972. Elvis won his second Grammy Award (Best Inspirational Performance) for this collection of twelve gospel songs. Promotional copies sent to disc jockeys had a white sticker affixed to the front cover listing the song titles.

He Touched Me reached #79 on *Billboard's* Top LPs chart during its 10-week stay.

Side 1: "He Touched Me," "I've Got Confidence," "Amazing Grace," "Seeing Is Believing," "He Is My Everything," and "Bosom of Abraham"

Side 2: "An Evening Prayer," "Lead Me, Guide Me," "There Is No God but God," "A Thing Called Love," "I, John," and "Reach Out to Jesus"

HE TOUCHED ME
(RCA AFL1-4690)

1977. New number assigned to RCA LSP-4690.

HE WALKS BESIDE ME
(RCA AFL1-2772)

April 1978. Two of the eleven songs on this album were unreleased alternate takes: "The Impossible Dream" and "If I Can Dream." A 20-page booklet of color photos was included as a bonus.

He Walks Beside Me spent eight weeks on *Billboard's* Top LPs chart, reaching #113. It fared much better on the Country LPs chart, reaching #6 and staying on the chart for 20 weeks.

Side 1: "He Is My Everything," "Miracle of the Rosary," "Where Did They Go, Lord," "Somebody Bigger Than You and I," "An Evening Prayer," and "The Impossible Dream"

Side 2: "If I Can Dream," "Padre," "Known Only to Him," "Who Am I," and "How Great Thou Art"

HIS HAND IN MINE
(RCA LPM-2328)

December 1960. *His Hand in Mine* was Elvis's first gospel album. It did quite well, achieving sales of over $1 million. A Gold Record was certified by the RIAA on April 9, 1969. RCA claims that over 500,000 units have been sold. The front cover of *His Hand in Mine* featured a photo of Elvis sitting at a piano. On Mother's Day, May 9, 1965, the album received considerable airplay on radio stations across the country.

His Hand in Mine had a 20-week stay on *Billboard's* Top LPs chart, reaching a high of #13.

Side 1: "His Hand in Mine," "I'm Gonna Walk Dem Golden Stairs," "In My Father's House," "Milky White Way," "Known Only to Him," and "I Believe in the Man in the Sky"

Side 2: "Joshua Fit the Battle," "He Knows Just What I Need," "Swing Down, Sweet Chariot," "Mansion Over the Hilltop," "If We Never Meet Again," and "Working on the Building"

HIS HAND IN MINE
(RCA LSP-2328)

December 1960. Living stereo release.

HIS HAND IN MINE
(RCA ANL1-1319)

March 1976. Pure Gold series reissue of RCA LSP-2328. The songs were the same, but a new front cover was used. After Elvis's death, this new release of *His Hand in Mine* sold quite well. A second Gold Record was certified by the RIAA on December 1, 1977.

HIS HAND IN MINE
(RCA AYM1-3935)

May 1981. New number assigned to RCA ANL1-1319. *His Hand in Mine* is now one of RCA's "Best Buy" LPs.

HOW GREAT THOU ART
(RCA LPM-3758)

March 8, 1967. Elvis was awarded the first Grammy of his career for this album in the category Best Sacred Performance. The cover photo pictured Elvis in front of a country church. Sales for *How Great Thou Art* exceeded $1 million, and a Gold Record was certified by the RIAA on February 16, 1968.

How Great Thou Art made the Top LPs chart, reach-

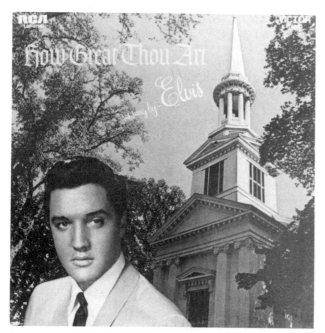

Elvis won his first Grammy award for *How Great Thou Art*. (Photo courtesy Don Fink)

ing as high as #18. It remained on the chart for 29 weeks.

Side 1: "How Great Thou Art," "In the Garden," "Somebody Bigger Than You and I," "Farther Along," "Stand By Me," and "Without Him"
Side 2: "So High," "Where Could I Go but to the Lord," "By and By," "If the Lord Wasn't Walking by My Side," "Run On," "Where No One Stands Alone," and "Crying in the Chapel"

HOW GREAT THOU ART
(RCA LSP-3758)
March 1967. Stereo release.

HOW GREAT THOU ART
(RCA AFL1-3758)
1977. New number assigned to RCA LSP-3758.

HOW GREAT THOU ART
(RCA AQL1-3758)
1979. New number assigned to RCA AFL1-3758.

I GOT LUCKY
(RCA Camden CAL-2533)
October, 1971. "Fools Fall in Love" and nine movie songs were featured on this album. *I Got Lucky* wasn't lucky when it came to chart activity. It peaked at #104 and had an eight-week stay on *Billboard*'s Top LPs chart.

Side 1: "I Got Lucky," "What a Wonderful Life," "I Need Somebody to Lean On," "Yoga Is as Yoga Does," and "Riding the Rainbow"
Side 2: "Fools Fall in Love," "The Love Machine," "Home Is Where the Heart Is," "You Gotta Stop," and "If You Think I Don't Need You"

I GOT LUCKY
(Pickwick CAS-2533)
December 1975. Pickwick reissue of RCA Camden CAL-2533. Although a stereo prefix was used in the Pickwick number, this release was in monaural. The same cover photo was used for both the Camden and Pickwick releases, but the title, *I Got Lucky*, was written in script on the Pickwick reissue instead of the block letters used on the Camden original. Song selections were identical.

I WAS THE ONE
(RCA AHL1-4678)
May 1983. Just as with the *Guitar Man* LP, the tracks on *I Was the One* were overdubbed in the early 1980s. All songs were from the 1950s except for "Little Sister," which was from 1961. *I Was the One* had a six-week stay on *Billboard*'s Top LPs chart, peaking at #103. On the Hot Country LPs chart, it reached #35 and had a stay of nine weeks.

Side 1: "My Baby Left Me," "(You're So Square) Baby, I Don't Care," "Little Sister," "Don't," "Wear My Ring Around Your Neck," and "Paralyzed"
Side 2: "Baby, Let's Play House," "I Was the One," "Rip It Up," "Young and Beautiful," and "Ready Teddy"

IT HAPPENED AT THE WORLD'S FAIR
(RCA LPM-2697)
April 1963. All ten songs from Elvis's 1963 movie *It Happened at the World's Fair* appeared on this soundtrack album.

It Happened at the World's Fair reached #4 on *Billboard*'s Top LPs chart, staying on the chart for 26 weeks. On the stereo LPs chart, it had a 17-week stay, peaking at #15.

Side 1: "Beyond the Bend," "Relax," "Take Me to the Fair," "They Remind Me Too Much of You," and "One Broken Heart for Sale"
Side 2: "I'm Falling in Love Tonight," "Cotton Candy Land," "A World of Our Own," "How Would You Like to Be," and "Happy Ending"

IT HAPPENED AT THE WORLD'S FAIR
(RCA LSP-2697)
April 1963. Stereo release.

IT HAPPENED AT THE WORLD'S FAIR
(RCA AFL1-2568)
September 1977. New number assigned to RCA LSP-2697. *It Happened at the World's Fair* has been deleted from RCA's catalog and is no longer available.

KING CREOLE
(RCA LPM-1884)
August 1958. All eleven of Elvis's songs in *King Creole* were featured on this soundtrack LP. An 8"-by-10" black-and-white photo of Elvis in his Army uniform was included as a bonus. RCA has claimed that *King Creole* was a million-seller.

King Creole entered *Billboard*'s Top LPs chart at #11, but was only able to reach #2 during its 15-week stay on the chart. Mitch Miller's *Sing Along with Mitch* album prevented *King Creole* from reaching the top spot.

Side 1: "King Creole," "As Long as I Have You," "Hard Headed

Woman," "Trouble," and "Dixieland Rock"
Side 2: "Don't Ask Me Why," "Lover Doll," "Crawfish," "Young Dreams," "Steadfast, Loyal and True," and "New Orleans"

KING CREOLE
(RCA LSP-1884 [e])
February 1982. Electronically reprocessed stereo release.

KING CREOLE
(RCA AFL1-1884 [e])
1977. New number assigned to RCA LSP-1884 (e).

KING CREOLE
(RCA AYL1-3733 [e])
November 1980. New number assigned to RCA AFL1-1884 (e). *King Creole* was one of the albums in RCA's "Best Buy" series.

KISSIN' COUSINS
(RCA LPM-2894)
March 1964. This was the soundtrack album of Elvis's 1964 film *Kissin' Cousins*. All nine songs from the movie were included, as well as three bonus songs. The original issue contained a family photograph of the Kwimper family (from the movie) in a movie frame in the lower right-hand corner of the cover. Some sources have indicated that *Kissin' Cousins* had sales exceeding $1 million, which would qualify it for a Gold Record.

Kissin' Cousins peaked at #6 on *Billboard*'s Top LPs chart during its 30-week stay.

Side 1: "Kissin' Cousins (No. 2)," "Smokey Mountain Boy" (bonus), "There's Gold in the Mountains," "One Boy, Two Little Girls," "Catchin' on Fast," and "Tender Feeling"
Side 2: "Anyone (Could Fall in Love with You)," "Barefoot Ballad," "Once is Enough," "Kissin' Cousins," "Echoes of Love" (bonus) and "(It's a) Long Lonely Highway" (bonus)

KISSIN' COUSINS
(RCA LSP-2894)
March 1964. Stereo release.

KISSIN' COUSINS
(RCA AFL1-2894)
1977. New number assigned to RCA LSP-2894.

KISSIN' COUSINS
(RCA AYM1-4115)
September 1981. New number assigned to RCA AFL1-2894. This album was one of RCA's "Best Buy" series. *Kissin' Cousins* has now been deleted from RCA's catalog.

LET'S BE FRIENDS
(RCA Camden CAS-2408)
April 1970. This album contains an interesting combination of songs. Two of them—"If I'm a Fool (for Loving You)" and "I'll Be There (If Ever You Want Me)"—were recorded at American Sound Studios in Memphis in 1969; three—"Stay Away, Joe," "Change of Habit," and "Have a Happy"—were taken from movie soundtracks; and three—"Let's Be Friends," "Let's Forget About the Stars," and "Mama"—were cut from the final releases of films. "Mama" was the only song on this stereo album in monaural. The version of "Almost" on this album is *not* the one that was used in *The Trouble with Girls*; it is an alternate take.

Let's Be Friends stayed on *Billboard*'s Top LPs chart for 11 weeks, peaking at #105.

Side 1: "Stay Away, Joe," "If I'm a Fool (for Loving You)," "Let's Be Friends," "Let's Forget About the Stars," and "Mama"
Side 2: "I'll Be There (If Ever You Want Me)," "Almost," "Change of Habit," and "Have a Happy"

LET'S BE FRIENDS
(Pickwick CAS-2408)
December 1975. Reissue of RCA Camden CAS-2408. It had the same cover photo, but a dark border was used along with different title lettering. Song selections were identical to the RCA Camden release.

LOVE LETTERS FROM ELVIS
(RCA LSP-4530)
May 1971. The original album jacket of *Love Letters from Elvis* had the words "Love Letters From" on one line and "Elvis" on the line below. The reissue had "Love Letters" on the top line and "From Elvis" on the bottom line. All songs on the LP were recorded at RCA's Nashville studios, June 4–8, 1970. The version of "Love Letters" on this LP is a different take than the one on the single release. It's more upbeat and Elvis adds a few moans and groans.

Love Letters from Elvis reached a peak position of #33 on the Top LPs chart and had a stay of 15 weeks. On the Country LPs chart, the album reached #12 and stayed on the chart for 12 weeks.

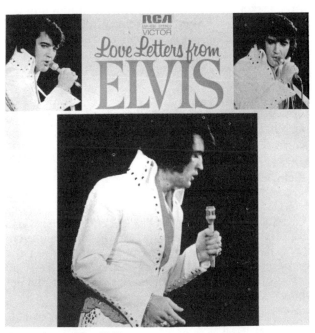

(Photo courtesy Don Fink)

Side 1: "Love Letters," "When I'm over You," "If I Were You," "Got My Mojo Working," and "Heart of Rome"
Side 2: "Only Believe," "This Is Our Dance," "Cindy, Cindy," "I'll Never Know," "It Ain't No Big Thing," and "Life"

LOVE LETTERS FROM ELVIS
(RCA AFL1-4530)
1977. New number assigned to RCA LSP-4530. *Love Letters from Elvis* has been deleted from RCA's catalog.

LOVING YOU
(RCA LPM-1515)
July 1957. All seven songs from Elvis's second film, *Loving You,* were on side one of this LP. Side 2 consisted of five non-movie songs that were recorded in January and February 1957 at Radio Recorders. The *Loving You* front cover was originally released with no song titles. Later pressings read, " 'Loving You,' '(Let Me Be Your) Teddy Bear,' 'Mean Woman Blues,' and others.' " The RIAA certified *Loving You* as a Gold Record on April 9, 1968.

Loving You first entered *Billboard'*s Top LPs chart at #11. The second week it was number one, remaining in the top spot for 10 straight weeks. This was the quickest rise to number one of any Elvis LP. The album remained on the chart for 29 weeks.

Side 1: "Mean Woman Blues," "(Let Me Be Your) Teddy Bear," "Loving You," "Got a Lot o' Livin' to Do," "Lonesome Cowboy," "Hot Dog," and "Party"
Side 2: "Blueberry Hill," "True Love," "Don't Leave Me Now," "Have I Told You Lately That I Love You," and "I Need You So"

LOVING YOU
(RCA LSP-1515[e])
February 1962. Electronically reprocessed stereo release. The front cover was identical to the monaural release except that a black strip was placed at the top of the jacket on which was printed the album number and the words "Stereo Electronically Reprocessed." The photo of Elvis was moved down to compensate for the strip.

LOVING YOU
(RCA AFL1-1515[e])
1977. New number assigned to RCA LSP-1515(e). *Loving You* has been deleted from RCA's catalog.

MAHALO FROM ELVIS
(Pickwick ACL-7064)
September 1978. All songs on side 1 of this Pickwick original release were recorded on January 14, 1973, for the NBC-TV version of Elvis's special "Elvis: Aloha from Hawaii." "No More," however, was not included in the broadcast. None of the songs appeared on the soundtrack LP. The five songs on side 2 were from various movie soundtracks. *Mahalo from Elvis* did not chart.

Side 1: "Blue Hawaii," "Early Morning Rain," "Hawaiian Wedding Song," "Ku-u-i-po," and "No More"
Side 2: "Relax," "Baby, If You'll Give Me All of Your Love," "One Broken Heart for Sale," "So Close, Yet So Far (from Paradise)," and "Happy Ending"

MEMORIES OF CHRISTMAS
(RCA CPL1-4395)
August 1982. *Memories of Christmas* was a repackaging of previously released Christmas songs. "Merry Christmas Baby," however, was the original master without James Burton's guitar solo overdubbed. A 7"-by-9" 1982–1983 calendar was included as a bonus. *Memories of Christmas* did not chart.

Side 1: "O Come, All Ye Faithful," "Silver Bells," "I'll Be Home for Christmas," and "Blue Christmas"
Side 2: "Santa Claus Is Back in Town," "Merry Christmas Baby," "If Every Day Was Like Christmas," and "Silent Night"

THE MEMPHIS RECORD
(RCA 6221-1-R)
June 1987. Twenty-three of the 29 successfully recorded songs from the two sessions of the American Sound Studios in January and February 1969, were included on this two-record set. The cover of *The Memphis Record* used a newspaper motif, printed with highlights from the year 1969. Extensive liner notes by Peter Guralnick were included.

Side A: "Stranger in My Own Home Town," "Power of My Love," "Only the Strong Survive," "Any Day Now," and "Suspicious Minds"
Side B: "Long Black Limousine," "Wearin' That Loved on Look," "I'll Hold You in My Heart," "After Loving You," "Rubberneckin'," and "I'm Movin' On"
Side C: "Gentle on My Mind," "True Love Travels on a Gravel Road," "It Keeps Right on a-Hurtin'," "You'll Think of Me," "Mama Liked the Roses," and "Don't Cry, Daddy"
Side D: "In the Ghetto," "The Fair is Moving On," "Inherit the Wind," "Kentucky Rain," "Without Love," and "Who Am I"

MOODY BLUE
(RCA AFL1-2428)
July 1977. "He'll Have to Go" and all songs on side 2 were recorded at Graceland in 1976. The rest of the tracks were live concert cuts. The original pressing (200,000 copies) was on blue translucent vinyl. As a result, the LP has been nicknamed the "Blue Album." Other colors of vinyl, such as white, green, red, and gold, were experimented with. After the first pressing, RCA switched to black vinyl, but after Elvis's sudden death, they went back to the blue. During the pressing of *Moody Blue,* RCA stamped its two-billionth record. *Moody Blue* quickly sold over one million copies and received a Platinum certification by the RIAA on September 12, 1977.

Moody Blue reached #3 on *Billboard'*s Top LPs chart, remaining on the chart for 31 weeks. It reached number one on the Country LPs chart.

Side 1: "Unchained Melody," "If You Love Me (Let Me Know)," "Little Darlin'," "He'll Have to Go," and "Let Me Be There"
Side 2: "Way Down," "Pledging My Love," "Moody Blue," "She Thinks I Still Care," and "It's Easy for You"

MOODY BLUE
(RCA AQL1-2428)
August 1977. New number assigned to RCA AFL1-2428.

THE NUMBER ONE HITS
(RCA 6382-1-R)

June 1987. All eighteen Elvis songs that reached number one on the various *Billboard* charts were included in this album, in chronological order. Chart information on the songs was printed on the back cover. The record came with a commemorative innersleeve and poster.

The Number One Hits had a nine-week stay on *Billboard*'s Top LPs chart, peaking at #143.

Side A: "Heartbreak Hotel," "I Want You, I Need You, I Love You," "Hound Dog," "Don't Be Cruel," "Love Me Tender," "Too Much," "All Shook Up," "Teddy Bear," and "Jailhouse Rock"

Side B: "Don't," "Hard Headed Woman," "A Big Hunk o' Love," "Stuck on You," "It's Now or Never," "Are You Lonesome Tonight?," "Surrender," "Good Luck Charm," and "Suspicious Minds"

ON STAGE—FEBRUARY, 1970
(RCA LSP-4362)

June 1970. All songs on this album were recorded at the International Hotel in Las Vegas, February 17–19, 1970, with the exception of "Runaway" and "Yesterday," which were recorded at the same hotel on August 22 and August 25, 1969, respectively. *On Stage—February, 1970* was originally pressed on nonflexible vinyl; that was changed to flexible vinyl in 1971. The jacket didn't have Elvis's name on the front or back—the second LP so distinguished (*For LP Fans Only* was the first.) Sales of *On Stage—February, 1970* exceeded $1 million and a Gold Record was certified by the RIAA on February 23, 1971.

On Stage—February, 1970 spent a total of 20 weeks on *Billboard*'s Top LPs chart, peaking at #13. It also peaked at #13 on the Country LPs chart.

Side 1: "See See Rider," "Release Me," "Sweet, Caroline," "Runaway," and "The Wonder of You"

Side 2: "Polk Salad Annie," "Yesterday," "Proud Mary," "Walk a Mile in My Shoes," and "Let It Be Me"

ON STAGE—FEBRUARY, 1970
(RCA AFL1-4362)

1977. New number assigned to RCA LSP-4362.

ON STAGE—FEBRUARY, 1970
(RCA AQL1-4362)

February 1983. New number assigned to RCA AFL1-4362.

OUR MEMORIES OF ELVIS
(RCA AQL1-3279)

February 1979. *Our Memories of Elvis* was an unusual album in that all the songs were presented without overdubbing by RCA—Elvis is heard just as he sounded in the recording studio. "Are You Sincere" was a previously unreleased alternate take. The catalog number and RCA logo appear nowhere on the front or back of the album jacket—just on the spine. A photograph of Vernon Presley and Colonel Parker in front of Graceland was featured on the cover.

Our Memories of Elvis lasted seven weeks on *Billboard*'s Top LPs chart, hitting a high of #132. It fared much better on the Country LPs chart, peaking at #6.

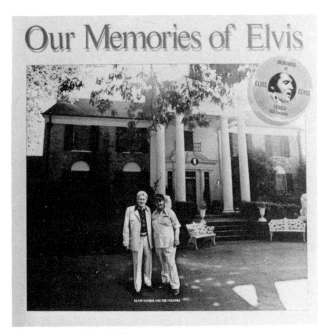

(Photo courtesy Don Fink)

RCA has deleted *Our Memories of Elvis* from its catalog.

Side 1: "Are You Sincere," "It's Midnight," "My Boy," "Girl of Mine," "Take Good Care of Her," and "I'll Never Fall in Love Again"

Side 2: "Your Love's Been a Long Time Coming," "Spanish Eyes," "Never Again," "She Thinks I Still Care," and "Solitaire"

OUR MEMORIES OF ELVIS, VOLUME 2
(RCA AQL1-3448)

August 1979. As with the first volume, *Our Memories of Elvis, Volume 2* featured Elvis in the recording studio without overdubbing by RCA. "Don't Think Twice, It's All Right" was a previously unreleased 8½-minute studio jam session. (The jam session actually lasted about 15 minutes; the total session has yet to be released.)

A five-week stay on *Billboard*'s Top LPs chart is all that *Our Memories of Elvis, Volume 2* could muster, peaking at #157. On the Country LPs chart, the album reached #12.

Our Memories of Elvis, Volume 2 has been deleted from RCA's catalog.

Side 1: "I Got A Feelin' In My Body," "Green, Green Grass of Home," "For the Heart," "She Wears My Ring," and "I Can Help"

Side 2: "Way Down," "There's A Honky Tonk Angel (Who Will Take Me Back In)," "Find Out What's Happening," "Thinking About You," and "Don't Think Twice, It's All Right"

PARADISE, HAWAIIAN STYLE
(RCA LPM-3643)

June 1966. This was the soundtrack album to Elvis's 1966 film *Paradise, Hawaiian Style*. All nine songs from the film were included, as well as "Sand Castles," which was cut. It's been reported that *Paradise, Hawaiian Style* achieved sales of over $1 million, but it's never been certified as a Gold Record by the RIAA.

Paradise, Hawaiian Style had a 19-week stay on *Billboard*'s Top LPs chart, peaking at #15.

Side 1: "Paradise, Hawaiian Style," "Queenie Wahine's Papaya," "Scratch My Back (Then I'll Scratch Yours)," "Drums of the Islands," and "Datin' "
Side 2: "A Dog's Life," "A House of Sand," "Stop Where You Are," "This Is My Heaven," and "Sand Castles" (bonus)

PARADISE, HAWAIIAN STYLE
(RCA LSP-3643)
June 1966. Stereo release.

PARADISE, HAWAIIAN STYLE
(RCA AFL1-3643)
1977. New number assigned to RCA LSP-3643. *Paradise, Hawaiian Style* has been deleted from RCA's catalog.

PICKWICK PACK
(Pickwick)
November 1978. For Christmas 1978, Pickwick offered this special seven-LP boxed set. The albums in the package were *Burning Love and Hits from His Movies, Volume 2*; *Elvis' Christmas Album*; *Elvis Sings Hits from His Movies, Volume 1*; *I Got Lucky*; *Mahalo from Elvis*; *Separate Ways*; and *You'll Never Walk Alone*. In February 1972, Pickwick replaced *Elvis' Christmas Album* with *Frankie and Johnny*.

POT LUCK
(RCA LPM-2523)
June 1962. Eight of the songs on *Pot Luck* were recorded in Nashville on March 18 and 19, 1962. The other four were recorded the previous year. "Steppin' Out of Line" was originally slated for *Blue Hawaii*, but was cut from the film. Sales of over $1 million were achieved, but the RIAA has never certified *Pot Luck* for a Gold Record.

Pot Luck reached #4 on *Billboard*'s Top LPs chart. It remained on the chart for a total of 31 weeks.

Side 1: "Kiss Me Quick," "Just for Old Time Sake," "Gonna Get Back Home Somehow," "(Such an) Easy Question," "Steppin' Out of Line," and "I'm Yours"
Side 2: "Something Blue," "Suspicion," "I Feel That I've Known You Forever," "Night Rider," "Fountain of Love," and "That's Someone You Never Forget"

POT LUCK
(RCA LSP-2523)
June 1962. Stereo release. This stereo version of *Pot Luck* peaked at #8 on *Billboard*'s stereo LPs chart and remained on the chart for 17 weeks.

POT LUCK
(RCA AFL1-2523)
1977. New number assigned to RCA LSP-2523. *Pot Luck* has now been deleted from RCA's catalog.

PROMISED LAND
(RCA-APL1-0873)
January 1975. All songs on *Promised Land* were recorded at Stax Studios in Memphis in December 1973.

Sales of more than half a million copies are claimed for this LP, qualifying it for a Gold Record. The RIAA has never certified it as a Gold Record, however.

Promised Land had a 12-week stay on *Billboard*'s Top LPs chart, peaking at #47.

Side 1: "Promised Land," "There's a Honky Tonk Angel (Who Will Take Me Back In)," "Help Me," "Mr. Songman," and "Love Song of the Year"
Side 2: "It's Midnight," "Your Love's Been a Long Time Coming," "If You Talk in Your Sleep," "Thinking About You," and "You Asked Me To"

PROMISED LAND
(RCA APD1-0873)
January 1975. Quadradisc release.

PROMISED LAND
(RCA AFL1-0873)
1977. New number assigned to RCA APD1-0873.

PURE ELVIS
(See *Our Memories of Elvis, Volume 2* in the Long-Playing Albums—Miscellaneous releases section)

PURE GOLD
(RCA ANL1-0971[e])
June 1975. This compilation of hits was released by RCA's budget line, the Pure Gold Series. *Pure Gold* achieved sales of over half a million copies, but the RIAA has never certified the album as Gold. In 1979 *Pure Gold* became the first licensed Elvis album to be released in Eastern-block countries. It's release number was Opus 91130625.

Side 1: "Kentucky Rain," "Fever," "It's Impossible," "Jailhouse Rock," and "Don't Be Cruel"
Side 2: "I Got a Woman," "All Shook Up," "Loving You," "In the Ghetto," and "Love Me Tender"

PURE GOLD
(RCA AYL1-3732)
November 1980. New number assigned to RCA ANL1-0971[e]. *Pure Gold* has now been deleted from RCA's catalog.

RAISED ON ROCK/FOR OL' TIMES SAKE
(RCA APL1-0388)
November 1973. All songs, except for two, were recorded at Stax Studios in Memphis, July 21–25, 1973. The two exceptions were "Are You Sincere" and "I Miss You," both of which were recorded at Elvis's Palm Springs home on September 24, 1973. *Raised on Rock/For Ol' Times Sake* was pressed on flexible vinyl. It is not currently available from RCA's catalog.

Raised on Rock/For Ol' Times Sake reached #50 on *Billboard*'s Top LPs chart during its 13-week stay.

Side 1: "Raised on Rock," "Are You Sincere," "Find Out What's Happening," "I Miss You," and "Girl of Mine"
Side 2: "For Ol' Times Sake," "If You Don't Come Back," "Just a Little Bit," "Sweet Angeline," and "Three Corn Patches"

RECONSIDER BABY
(RCA AFL1-5418)
April 1985. All tracks were rhythm & blues standards. Two songs—"One Night" and "Ain't That Loving You Baby"—were alternate takes. "Stranger In My Own Home Town" was an alternate mix, and "Merry Christmas Baby" was an alternate edit. "Tomorrow Night" was the original 1955 Sun Records version.

Reconsider Baby did not chart.

Side 1: "Reconsider Baby," "Tomorrow Night," "So Glad You're Mine," "One Night," "When It Rains, It Really Pours," "My Baby Left Me," and "Ain't That Loving You Baby"
Side 2: "I Feel So Bad," "Down in the Alley," "High Heel Sneakers," "Stranger in My Own Home Town," and "Merry Christmas Baby"

REMEMBERING ELVIS
(RCA PDL2-1037)
1983. This compilation of previously released tracks was issued on RCA Special Products' Pairs label.

Side 1: "Blue Moon of Kentucky," "Young and Beautiful," "Milkcow Blues Boogie," and "Baby, Let's Play House"
Side 2: "Good Rockin' Tonight," "We're Gonna Move," "I Want to Be Free," and "I Forgot to Remember to Forget"
Side 3: "Kiss Me Quick," "Just for Old Time Sake," "Gonna Get Back Somehow," and "(Such an) Easy Question"
Side 4: "Suspicion," "I Feel That I've Known You Forever," "Night Rider," and "Fountain of Love"

RETURN OF THE ROCKER
(RCA 5600-1-R)
1986. Just as the *Rocker* LP contained hits from the 1950s, this sequel included twelve Elvis hits from the period 1960–63.

Side 1: "King of the Whole Wide World," "(Marie's the Name) His Latest Flame," "Little Sister," "A Mess of Blues," "Like a Baby," and "I Want You with Me"
Side 2: "Stuck on You," "Return to Sender," "Make Me Know It," "Witchcraft," "I'm Comin' Home," and "Follow That Dream"

ROCKER
(RCA AFM1-5182)
October 1984. *Rocker* contained previously released material. It was pressed on blue vinyl and had a special gold "50th" anniversary label to commemorate the 50th anniversary of Elvis's birth. *Rocker* featured photos by Alfred Wertheimer on both the front and back covers of Elvis sitting on his Harley-Davidson motorcycle.

Rocker peaked at #154 on *Billboard*'s Top LPs chart.

Side 1: "Jailhouse Rock," "Blue Suede Shoes," "Tutti Frutti," "Lawdy Miss Clawdy," "I Got a Woman," and "Money Honey"

Side 2: "Ready Teddy," "Rip It Up," "Shake, Rattle and Roll," "Long Tall Sally," "(You're So Square) Baby, I Don't Care," and "Hound Dog"

ROUSTABOUT
(RCA LPM-2999)
October 1964. All eleven songs from Elvis's 1964 film *Roustabout* were included on this soundtrack album. The cover of *Roustabout* featured a still photo of Elvis in the foreground and a carnival scene in the background. A banner hanging on the side of a tent proclaimed, "The Original Soundtrack Album from the Paramount Picture Roustabout." Sales of the album exceeded $1 million, but the RIAA has not certified it as a Gold Record.

In January 1965, *Roustabout* succeeded *The Beach Boys Concert* LP as the nation's number one album. After a week at the top, it was replaced by *Beatles '65* (Capitol 2228). *Roustabout* spent a total of 27 weeks on *Billboard*'s Top LPs chart. It would be eight years before Elvis would have another number one LP.

Side 1: "Roustabout," "Little Egypt," "Poison Ivy League," "Hard Knocks," "It's a Wonderful World," and "Big Love, Big Heartache"
Side 2: "One Track Heart," "It's Carnival Time," "Carny Town," "There's a Brand New Day on the Horizon," and "Wheels on My Heels"

ROUSTABOUT
(RCA LSP-2999)
October 1964. Stereo release.

ROUSTABOUT
(RCA AFL1-2999)
1977. New number assigned to RCA LSP-2999. *Roustabout* has now been deleted from RCA's catalog.

SEPARATE WAYS
(RCA Camden CAS 2611)
January 1973. *Separate Ways* was a compilation of studio recordings and movie songs. Five of the ten tracks had previously appeared on the *Elvis for Everyone* LP. A 3"-by-5" color greeting card from Elvis was included as a bonus.

Separate Ways spent a total of 18 weeks on *Billboard*'s Top LPs chart, peaking at #46.

Side 1: "Separate Ways," "Sentimental Me," "In My Way," "I Met Her Today," and "What Now, What Next, Where To"
Side 2: "Always on My Mind," "I Slipped, I Stumbled, I Fell," "Is It So Strange," "Forget Me Never," and "Old Shep"

SEPARATE WAYS
(Pickwick CAS-2611)
December 1975. Pickwick reissue of RCA Camden CAS-2611.

SINGER PRESENTS ELVIS SINGING FLAMING STAR AND OTHERS
(RCA PRS-279)
November 1968. This album, which contained eight movie songs and two studio tracks, was available only at Singer Sewing Centers in conjunction with the December 3, 1968, NBC-TV special "Elvis." A bonus color photo from the TV special was included with the LP. The back of the photo had a list of Elvis's albums and tapes. Other than "Flaming Star," no other song titles were listed on the LP's cover. Although *Singer Presents Elvis Singing Flaming Star and Others* was released in stereo, "Tiger Man" was presented in monaural. RCA reissued this LP in 1969 as *Elvis Sings Flaming Star*.

Side 1: "Flaming Star," "Wonderful World," "Night Life," "All I Needed Was the Rain," and "Too Much Monkey Business"

Side 2: "The Yellow Rose of Texas"/"The Eyes of Texas," "She's a Machine," "Do the Vega," and "Tiger Man"

SOMETHING FOR EVERYBODY
(RCA LPM-2370)

June 1961. All songs on *Something for Everybody* except "I Slipped, I Stumbled, I Fell" were recorded at RCA's Nashville studios on March 12 and 13, 1961. Originally, the back cover had a photograph from the movie *Wild in the Country*, as well as advertisements for the EP *Elvis by Request* and the Compact 33 single "Wild in the Country"/"I Feel So Bad." Throughout the years, advertisements for other records have appeared. For example, the second pressing contained an ad for the *Viva Las Vegas* EP and the third pressing advertised two gospel LPs and the "Elvis" TV special.

Something for Everybody reached number one on *Billboard*'s Top LPs chart, displacing *Stars for a Summer Night*, a various-artists album. After three weeks at the top spot, *Something for Everybody* was replaced by Judy Garland's LP *Judy at Carnegie Hall*. *Something for Everybody* was on the chart for a total of 25 weeks.

Side 1: "There's Always Me," "Give Me the Right," "It's a Sin," "Sentimental Me," "Starting Today," and "Gently"

Side 2: "I'm Comin' Home," "In Your Arms," "Put the Blame on Me," "Judy," "I Want You with Me," and "I Slipped, I Stumbled, I Fell"

SOMETHING FOR EVERYBODY
(RCA LSP-2370)

July 1971. Stereo release. *Something for Everybody* had a 17-week stay on the stereo LPs chart, peaking at #14.

SOMETHING FOR EVERYBODY
(RCA AFL1-2370)

1977. New number assigned to RCA LSP-2370.

SOMETHING FOR EVERYBODY
(RCA AYM1-4116)

September 1981. New number assigned to RCA AFL1-2370. *Something for Everybody* was one of the albums in RCA's "Best Buy" series. It has now been deleted from RCA's catalog.

SPEEDWAY
(RCA LPM-3989)

June 1968. Side 1 of *Speedway* contained all six Elvis songs from his 1968 movie of the same title. Also included was his duet with Nancy Sinatra on "There Ain't Nothing Like a Song." Sinatra's solo effort, "Your Groovy Self," kicked off side 2, followed by five bonus songs. *Speedway* was the last Elvis LP to be released in both mono and stereo, and the only regular RCA Elvis album to contain a solo by another artist. An 8"-by-10" color photo was included as a bonus. Very few of the monaural albums were issued, making them extremely rare.

Speedway reached #82 on *Billboard*'s Top LPs chart during its 13-week stay on the chart.

(Photo courtesy Don Fink)

Side 1: "Speedway," "There Ain't Nothing Like a Song," "Your Time Hasn't Come Yet, Baby," "Who Are You (Who Am I)," "He's Your Uncle, Not Your Dad," and "Let Yourself Go"

Side 2: "Your Groovy Self" (Nancy Sinatra solo), "Five Sleepy Heads" (bonus), "Western Union" (bonus), "Mine" (bonus), "Goin' Home" (bonus), and "Suppose" (bonus)

SPEEDWAY
(RCA LSP-3989)

June 1968. Stereo release.

SPEEDWAY
(RCA AFL1-3989)

1977. New number assigned to RCA LSP-3989. *Speedway* has been deleted from RCA's catalog.

SPINOUT
(RCA LPM-3702)

October 1966. All nine songs from Elvis's 1966 movie *Spinout* were included in this soundtrack LP, along with three bonus songs. A special 12"-by-12" color photo was offered as a bonus.

A peak position of #18 was reached by *Spinout* on *Billboard*'s Top LPs chart, and it stayed on the chart for 32 weeks.

Side 1: "Stop, Look and Listen," "Adam and Evil," "All That I Am," "Never Say Yes," "Am I Ready," and "Beach Shack"

Side 2: "Spinout," "Smorgasbord," "I'll Be Back," "Tomorrow Is a Long Time" (bonus), "Down in the Alley" (bonus), and "I'll Remember You" (bonus)

SPINOUT
(RCA LSP-3702)

October 1966. Stereo release.

SPINOUT
(RCA AFL1-2560)
September 1977. New number assigned to RCA LSP-3702.

SPINOUT
(RCA AYL1-3684)
May 1980. New number assigned to RCA AFL1-2560. *Spinout* has been deleted from RCA's catalog.

STANDING ROOM ONLY
(RCA LSP-4672)
This projected long-playing album was never released. *Standing Room Only* was to have included songs from Elvis's live performances at the Hilton Hotel in Las Vegas (February 14–17, 1972) and studio tracks from Hollywood (March 27–29, 1972).

THE SUN SESSIONS
(RCA APM1-1675)
March 1975. Prompted by the wide distribution of the English import *The Sun Collection* (RCA Starcall HY-1001), RCA issued this album of 15 Sun recordings and an alternate take of "I Love You Because."

The Sun Sessions reached #76 on *Billboard*'s Top LPs chart during its 11 weeks on the chart.

Side 1: "That's All Right (Mama)," "Blue Moon of Kentucky," "I Don't Care if the Sun Don't Shine," "Good Rockin' Tonight," "Milkcow Blues Boogie," "You're a Heartbreaker," "I'm Left, You're Right, She's Gone," and "Baby, Let's Play House"
Side 2: "Mystery Train," "I Forgot to Remember to Forget," "I'll Never Let You Go (Little Darlin')," "I Love You Because," "Tryin' to Get to You," "Blue Moon," "Just Because," and "I Love You Because" (take #2)

THAT'S THE WAY IT IS
(RCA LSP-4445)
December 1970. Contrary to popular opinion, *That's the Way It Is* is not the soundtrack from the 1970 documentary. Only two of the twelve songs—"You Don't Have to Say You Love Me" and "The Next Step Is Love"—were lifted directly from the movie's soundtrack. Of the remaining ten songs, six were recorded at RCA's Nashville studios (June 4–6, 1970) and four were recorded live at the International Hotel in Las Vegas (August 13–14, 1970), but are not the tracks seen in the film. *That's the Way It Is* was originally pressed on nonflexible vinyl, but later pressings were on flexible vinyl. Sales exceeded $1 million and a Gold Record was certified by the RIAA on June 28, 1973.

That's the Way It Is spent 23 weeks on *Billboard*'s Top LPs chart, peaking at #21. On the Country LPs chart, the album reached #8 and had a 17-week stay.

The eight-track cartridge version of *That's the Way It Is* stayed on the Best-Selling Cartridges chart for seven weeks, peaking at #21.

Side 1: "I Just Can't Help Believin'," "Twenty Days and Twenty Nights," "How the Web Was Woven," "Patch It Up," "Mary in the Morning," and "You Don't Have to Say You Love Me"
Side 2: "You've Lost That Lovin' Feelin'," "I've Lost You," "Just Pretend," "Stranger in the Crowd," "The Next Step Is Love," and "Bridge over Troubled Water"

THAT'S THE WAY IT IS
(RCA AFL1-4445)
1977. New number assigned to RCA LSP-4445.

THAT'S THE WAY IT IS
(RCA AYM1-4114)
September 1981. New number assigned to RCA AFL1-4445. This album is now one of RCA's "Best Buy" series of LPs.

THIS IS ELVIS
(RCA CPL2-4031)
March 1981. This two-record set was the soundtrack to the 1981 documentary *This Is Elvis*. Both records came with special innersleeves. In addition to standard releases, the album contained a remix of "That's All Right (Mama)," a shorter version of "Merry Christmas Baby" with added strings, the film version of "Mean Woman Blues," alternate takes of "Too Much Monkey Business" and "Always on My Mind," a 1972 live version of "An American Trilogy," and a spliced version of "Blue Suede Shoes" from the "Elvis" TV special.

This Is Elvis had a 10-week stay on *Billboard*'s Top LPs chart, peaking at #115.

Side A: "(Marie's the Name) His Latest Flame," "Moody Blue," "That's All Right (Mama)," "Shake, Rattle and Roll"/"Flip, Flop and Fly," "Heartbreak Hotel," "Hound Dog," Excerpt from Hy Gardner Interview, and "My Baby Left Me"
Side B: "Merry Christmas Baby," "Mean Woman Blues," "Don't Be Cruel," "Teddy Bear," "Jailhouse Rock," Army Swearing In, "G. I. Blues," Excerpt from Departure for Germany Press Conference, and Excerpt from Home from Germany Press Conference
Side C: "Too Much Monkey Business," "Love Me Tender," "I've Got a Thing About You, Baby," "I Need Your Love Tonight," "Blue Suede Shoes," "Viva Las Vegas," and "Suspicious Minds"
Side D: Excerpt from Jaycees' award to Elvis, "Promised Land," Excerpt from Madison Square Garden Press Conference, "Always on My Mind," "Are You Lonesome Tonight?," "My Way," "An American Trilogy," and "Memories"

THE TOP TEN HITS
(RCA 6383-1-R)
June 1987. All 38 of Elvis's top 10 hits were included in this two-record set. Chart information on all of the songs was printed on the back cover. The album came with special commemorative innersleeves and a rare poster.

The Top Ten Hits had an eight-week stay on *Billboard*'s Top LPs chart, reaching a high of #117.

Side A: "Heartbreak Hotel," "I Want You, I Need You, I Love You," "Hound Dog," "Don't Be Cruel," "Love Me Tender," "Love Me," "Too Much," "All Shook Up," "Teddy Bear," and "Jailhouse Rock"
Side B: "Don't," "I Beg of You," "Wear My Ring Around Your Neck," "Hard Headed Woman," "One Night," "I Got Stung," "(Now and Then There's) A Fool Such As I," "I Need Your Love Tonight," and "A Big Hunk o' Love"
Side C: "Stuck on You," "It's Now or Never," "Are You Lonesome Tonight?," "Surrender," "I Feel So Bad," "Little Sister," "(Marie's the Name) His Latest Flame," "Can't Help Falling in Love," "Good Luck Charm," and "She's Not You"
Side D: "Return to Sender," "(You're the) Devil in Disguise," "Bossa Nova Baby," "Crying in the Chapel," "In the Ghetto," "Suspicious

Minds," "Don't Cry, Daddy," "The Wonder of You," and "Burning Love"

A VALENTINE GIFT FOR YOU
(RCA AFL1-5353)

January 1985. To kick off the year-long celebration of the 50th anniversary of Elvis's birth, RCA released this compilation of previously issued songs. The album was pressed on red vinyl with a special "50th" anniversary label. *A Valentine Gift for You* spent just three weeks on *Billboard's* Top LPs chart, peaking at #154.

Side 1: "Are You Lonesome Tonight?," "I Need Somebody to Lean On," "Young and Beautiful," "Playing for Keeps," "Tell Me Why," "Give Me the Right," and "It Feels So Right"

Side 2: "I Was the One," "Fever," "Tomorrow Is a Long Time," "Love Letters," "Fame and Fortune," and "Can't Help Falling in Love"

WELCOME TO MY WORLD
(RCA APL1-2274)

March 1977. *Welcome to My World* was a compilation of country tunes, all of which had been previously released except for "I Can't Stop Loving You." That song was from Elvis's June 10, 1972, afternoon concert at Madison Square Garden. Sales of over 500,000 copies resulted in certification as a Gold Record by the RIAA on September 30, 1977. The front cover of *Welcome to My World* featured a painting of Elvis instead of the usual photographic still.

Welcome to My World peaked at #44 on *Billboard's* Top LPs chart during its 25-week stay. On the Country LPs chart, it had an 11-week stay, but reached #4.

Side 1: "Welcome to My World," "Help Me Make It Through the Night," "Release Me," "I Really Don't Want to Know," and "For the Good Times"

Side 2: "Make the World Go Away," "Gentle on My Mind," "I'm So Lonesome I Could Cry," "Your Cheatin' Heart," and "I Can't Stop Loving You"

WELCOME TO MY WORLD
(RCA AFL1-2274)

1977. New number assigned to RCA APL1-2274.

WELCOME TO MY WORLD
(RCA AQL1-2274)

1977. New number assigned to RCA AFL1-2274.

YOU'LL NEVER WALK ALONE
(RCA Camden CALX-2472)

March 5, 1971. Four of the songs on *You'll Never Walk Alone* were in true stereo: "You'll Never Walk Alone," "Who Am I," "Let Us Pray," and "We Call on Him." All other cuts were in monaural. The front cover of this LP contained no mention of the album's title; "Elvis" is the only word that appeared.

You'll Never Walk Alone spent a total of 12 weeks on *Billboard's* Top LPs chart, peaking at #69.

Side 1: "You'll Never Walk Alone," "Who Am I," "Let Us Pray," "Peace in the Valley," and "We Call on Him"

Side 2: "I Believe," "It Is No Secret," "Sing You Children," and "Take My Hand, Precious Lord"

YOU'LL NEVER WALK ALONE
(Pickwick CAS-2472)

December 1975. Reissue of RCA Camden CALX-2472. The song selections and cover photo were identical to the Camden release.

Long-Playing Albums
Miscellaneous Releases

[Note: None of the songs on the albums in this section are cross-referenced in the SONGS section.]

THE AGE OF ROCK
(EMR Enterprises EMR RH-8)
1969. To promote the book *The Age of Rock: Sounds of the American Cultural Revolution*, by William James, Random House and Vintage Books had this promotional album prepared. The LP contained three Elvis selections: "Tutti Frutti," "Love Me Tender," and "Blue Suede Shoes."

ALL-TIME CHRISTMAS FAVORITES
(Collectors Edition CE-505)
November 1978. Ten singers were featured on this five-LP set of Christmas classics, with one singer and five selections to a side. It's possible that this release was a bootleg. The five Elvis songs on record four, side B, were "O Come, All Ye Faithful," "The First Noel," "I'll Be Home for Christmas," "Silver Bells," and "Winter Wonderland."

ALOHA FROM HAWAII VIA SATELLITE
(RCA R-213736)
February 1973. RCA Record Club release that was issued in stereo, not Quadraphonic, sound. It included the same selections as the standard RCA release.

AN AUDIO SELF-PORTRAIT
(RCA DJM1-0835)
1985. This disc jockey promotional release consisted entirely of interviews with Elvis. The record came with a special "50th" anniversary label.

Side A: THE 1956 INTERVIEWS: *TV Guide* interview excerpts and Mississippi-Alabama Fair and Dairy Show excerpts (September 26, 1956)
Side B: THE 1960-61 INTERVIEWS: Image Change Since Discharge from the Army—By Accident or Design?; Elvis Talks About His Mother; How Does Elvis View Himself?; Does He Enjoy His Work?; How Does He Relax?; Does He Read? If So, What Does He Read?; Does He Like Himself?: Does He Like to Work?; If He Were Starting Out Again, Would He Do Anything Differently?; Does He Have Any Specific Goals for the Future?; Does He Think He Has Changed Much as a Person?; How Does He View the Criticism That Has Been Leveled at Some of the People Surrounding Him?; If He Were a Father and Could Only Give One Piece of Advice, What Would It Be?

AVON VALENTINE FAVORITES
(RCA DPL1-0751)
1987. This LP was a special release by RCA and Avon and included love songs by various artists. Elvis's "Can't Help Falling in Love" was one of the tracks.

Side 1: "Lady" (Kenny Rogers), "My Funny Valentine" (Tony Bennett), "Feels So Right" (Alabama), "Theme from Love Story" (Henry Mancini), and "It's Impossible" (Perry Como)

Side 2: "Tonight, I Celebrate My Love" (Peabo Bryson and Roberta Flack), "Chances Are" (Johnny Mathis), "Can't Help Falling in Love" (Elvis Presley), "And I Love Her" (Jose Feliciano), and "Crazy" (Kenny Rogers)

THE BEGINNING YEARS
(Louisiana Hayride LH-3601)
1985. A twenty-page photo booklet, *D. J. Fontana Remembers Elvis*, was included as a bonus with this LP. In addition to the "Louisiana Hayride" performances by Elvis, various snippets of dialogue were included, including comments by Frank Page and a Horace Logan interview of Elvis.

Side 1: "That's All Right (Mama)," "Blue Moon of Kentucky," "Good Rockin' Tonight," and "I Got a Woman"
Side 2: "Tweedlee Dee," "Baby, Let's Play House," "Maybellene," "That's All Right (Mama)," and "Hound Dog"

BILLBOARD'S 1979 YEARBOOK
(Billboard Magazine)
December 1979. This five-record boxed set featured the five-hour radio special that reviewed the music of 1979. Dick Clark's successful TV movie *Elvis* was mentioned and "Hound Dog" was heard. A script of the program was included in the box.

THE BRIGHTEST STARS OF CHRISTMAS
(RCA DPL1-0086)
November 1974. This album consisted of eleven Christmas songs by eleven different RCA artists and was sold exclusively in J. C. Penney's stores during the Christmas season of 1974. It was not available at any other time. The Elvis tune in the album was "Here Comes Santa Claus."

Side 1: "We Wish You a Merry Christmas" (Eugene Normandy and the Philadelphia Orchestra), "Here Comes Santa Claus" (Elvis Presley), "Winter Wonderland" (Danny Davis and the Nashville Brass), "Home for the Holidays" (Perry Como), and "It Came upon a Midnight Clear"/"The First Noel"/"Away in a Manger" (Henry Mancini Orchestra and Chorus)
Side 2: "Jingle Bells" (Julie Andrews), "Joy to the World" (Ed Ames), "Sleigh Ride" (Arthur Fiedler and the Boston Pops), "Christmas in My Home Town" (Charley Pride), "Hark! The Herald Angels Sing" (Robert Shaw Chorale), and "Silent Night" (Sergio Franchi)

A CHRONOLOGY OF AMERICAN MUSIC
(More Music Production MM-333-72)
December 1972. Twenty-one records comprising 325 number one songs of the rock era were featured in this monumental boxed set. Of course, all of Elvis's number one records were included.

COUNTRY CLASSICS
(RCA R-233299[e])
1980. Special double-LP RCA Record Club release.

Side 1: "Faded Love," "Guitar Man," "Blue Moon of Kentucky," "Crying in the Chapel," and "Tomorrow Night"
Side 2: "I'm Comin' Home," "(Now and Then There's) A Fool Such As I," "From a Jack to a King," "I Really Don't Want to Know," and "It's a Sin"
Side 3: "That's All Right (Mama)," "Have I Told You Lately That I Love You," "He Touched Me," "I Love You Because," and "Just Call Me Lonesome"
Side 4: "Tomorrow Never Comes," "I'm Left, You're Right, She's Gone," "Peace in the Valley," and "There Goes My Everything"

COUNTRY MEMORIES
(RCA R-244069)
1978. Special double-LP RCA Record Club release. All song selections were previously issued on other albums.

Side 1: "I'll Hold You in My Heart," "Welcome to My World," "It Keeps Right on a-Hurtin'," "Release Me," and "Make the World Go Away"
Side 2: "Snowbird," "Early Morning Rain," "I'm So Lonesome I Could Cry," "Funny How Time Slips Away," and "I'm Movin' On"
Side 3: "Help Me Make It Through the Night," "You Don't Know Me," "How Great Thou Art," "I Washed My Hands in Muddy Water," and "I Forgot to Remember to Forget"
Side 4: "Your Cheatin' Heart," "Baby, Let's Play House," "Whole Lotta Shakin' Going' On," "Gentle on My Mind," and "For the Good Times"

COUNTRY MUSIC
(Time-Life STW-106)
1981. *Country Music* was sold exclusively in grocery stores. All songs on side 1, except for "Are You Lonesome Tonight?," were electronically rechanneled to simulate stereo.

Side 1: "Blue Moon of Kentucky," "Old Shep," "When My Blue Moon Turns to Gold Again," "Are You Lonesome Tonight?," and "Your Cheatin' Heart"
Side 2: "Wooden Heart," "Suspicious Minds," "Little Cabin on the Hill," and "U.S. Male"

COUNTRY MUSIC IN THE MODERN ERA
(New World Records NW-207)
1976. One Elvis selection—"Mystery Train"—appeared on this compilation of all-time great country tunes. A six-page booklet was bound in the fold of the booklike jacket.

Side 1: "Bouquet of Roses" (Eddy Arnold), "Never No More Blues" (Lefty Frizzell), "Much Too Young to Die" (Ray Price), "Squid Jiggin' Ground" (Hank Snow), "There's Poison in Your Heart" (Kitty Wells), "Try Me One More Time" (Ernest Tubb), "Love Letters in the Sand" (Patsy Cline), "Jean's Song" (Chet Atkins), and "Mystery Train" (Elvis Presley)
Side 2: "Little Ole You" (Jim Reeves), "Jimmy Martinez" (Marty Robbins), "I'm a Honky-Tonk Girl" (Loretta Lynn), "Lorena" (Johnny Cash), "Don't Let Her Know" (Buck Owens), "All I Love Is You" (Roger Miller), "Sing a Sad Song" (Merle Haggard), "Coat of Many Colors" (Dolly Parton)," and "Help Me Make It Through the Night" (Kris Kristofferson)

CURRENT AUDIO MAGAZINE
(Buddah CM Vol. 1, No. 1)
August–September 1972. This album was an attempt to have up-to-date news events available on record. After sixty days on the market, the album was deleted. Elvis

appeared on the first cut of side 2—his June 9, 1972, press conference at Madison Square Garden. The press conference actually took place in the Mercury Ballroom of the New York Hilton. Buddah Records, which released *Current Audio Magazine*, was sued by RCA in August 1972. The court ruled in favor of Buddah, stating that a press conference is in the public domain. This accounts for the various legitimate record labels that release Elvis interviews.

Side 1: Mick Jagger Speaks; Manson Will Escape; Robert Klein; Teddy Kennedy; Angela Davis; and Monty Python's Flying Circus—"Spam"
Side 2: Elvis: His First and Only Press Conference; The Killer Was a Narc; Bella Abzug Loses; Scoop's Column; Nader Group Hits Vega; Crime Watch; and Sensuous You

DINER
(Elektra EL-60107E)
1982. Elvis's "Don't Be Cruel" was heard in the 1982 Barry Levinson–directed film *Diner* and in this, the soundtrack album.

Side 1: "Whole Lotta' Shakin' Goin' On" (by Jerry Lee Lewis); "A Teenager in Love" (by Dion and the Belmonts); "A Thousand Miles Away" (by the Heartbeats); "Somethin' Else" (by Eddie Cochran); and "I Wonder Why" (by Dion and the Belmonts).
Side 2: "Honey Don't" (by Carl Perkins); "Mr. Blue" (by the Fleetwoods); "Reconsider Baby" (by Lowell Fulson); "Ain't Got No Home" (by Clarence Henry); and "Come Go With Me" (by the Del Vikings).
Side 3: "Beyond The Sea" (by Bobby Darin); "Theme From A Summer Place" (movie soundtrack); "Fascination" (by Jane Morgan); "Where or When" (by Dick Haynes) and "It's All In The Game" (by Tommy Edwards).
Side 4: "Whole Lot of Loving" (Fats Domino); "Take Out Some Insurance" (Jimmy Reed); "Dream Lover" (Bobby Darin); "Don't Be Cruel" (Elvis); and "Goodbye Baby" (Jack Scott).

EARTH NEWS
(EN 8-22-77)
August 1977. Radio stations that subscribed to the Earth News Network's programs aired this series of five-minutes segments twice a day for one week (August 22–29, 1977) after Elvis's death. Fourteen segments were featured.

Side 1: 1956 Elvis Interview; "Blue Suede Shoes" [from "Stage Show"]; "Don't Be Cruel" [from "The Ed Sullivan Show"]; "Heartbreak Hotel" [from "Stage Show"]; 1956 Elvis Interview; Jay Thompson's Elvis Interview; *Elvis Sails* Interview; Dick Clark/Elvis Phone Call [from "American Bandstand"]; and The Truth About Me
Side 2: 1956 Elvis Interview; 1961 Elvis Interview; Red West Interview; The Truth About Me; "Hound Dog"; Willie Mae Thornton Interview; The Truth About Me; "In the Ghetto"; Steve Binder Interview; and "Hey, Mr. Presley"/"I Dreamed I Was Elvis"/"My Baby's Crazy About Elvis"/"Elvis Presley for President"

ELVIS—A COLLECTORS EDITION
(RCA TB-1)
1976. This special boxed set manufactured in Canada was sold over American television. *Elvis—A Collectors Edition* consisted entirely of three previously marketed LPs: *Elvis* (RCA DPL2-0056[e]), *Elvis Forever*, and *Elvis in Hollywood*. A twenty-page booklet was included as a bonus.

ELVIS ARON PRESLEY
(RCA DJL8-3729)
July 1980. Single-record promotional disc sent to retail outlets that featured excerpts from RCA CPL8-3699).

ELVIS ARON PRESLEY
(RCA DJL8-3781)
July 1980. Single-record promotional disc sent to radio stations that featured excerpts from RCA CPL8-3699.

ELVIS ARON PRESLEY
(RCA NS [box number])
July 1980. This eight-LP boxed set was identical to RCA CPL8-3699, except each box was individually numbered and sent to media record reviewers.

ELVIS AS RECORDED AT
MADISON SQUARE GARDEN
(RCA SPS-33-571)
June 1972. This special disc jockey two-album set came with white labels and a white, double-pocket jacket. Song selections were listed on a white sticker. The records themselves were specially banded with extra space between the cuts so that disc jockeys could easily find a particular song. Because of the banding, it took two records to contain the songs that appeared on the single-record commercial release.

Side 1: Introduction, "Also Sprach Zarathustra" (Joe Guercio Orchestra), "That's All Right (Mama)," "Proud Mary," "Never Been to Spain," "You Don't Have to Say You Love Me," and "You've Lost That Lovin' Feelin' "
Side 2: "Polk Salad Annie," "Love Me," "All Shook Up," "Heartbreak Hotel," "Teddy Bear"/"Don't Be Cruel," and "Love Me Tender"
Side 3: "The Impossible Dream," Introductions by Elvis, "Hound Dog," "Suspicious Minds," and "For the Good Times"
Side 4: "An American Trilogy," "Funny How Time Slips Away," "I Can't Stop Loving You," "Can't Help Falling in Love," and Exit Music

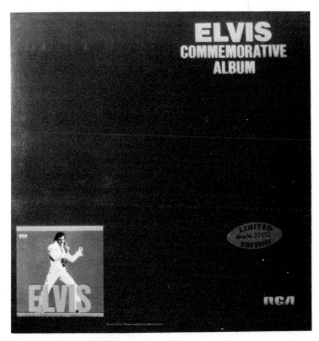

(Photo courtesy Don Fink)

ELVIS COMMEMORATIVE ALBUM
(RCA DPL2-0056[e])
1978. The *Elvis Commemorative Album* was a limited edition reissue of Brookville Marketing's 1973 LP *Elvis.* It even used the same catalog number. As with the earlier album, this one was sold on television. Instead of a single-pocket jacket, the *Elvis Commemorative Album* had two pockets with a gold-numbered sticker on the cover. Inside was a registered "Certificate of Ownership." Pressed on gold vinyl, the *Elvis Commemorative Album* had a black label that read "RCA Special Products." Brookville Marketing was not mentioned on the album jacket or record label.

ELVIS COUNTRY
(RCA DPL1-0647)
1984. RCA Mann featured this LP for the Dominion Music Corporation, which released it in discount stores on its own label, ERA Records (BU 3930).

Side A: "Are Your Lonesome Tonight?," "Suspicion," "Your Cheatin' Heart," "Blue Moon of Kentucky," "Don't," "I Forgot to Remember to Forget," and "Help Me Make It Through the Night"
Side B: "Kentucky Rain," "I Really Don't Want to Know," "Hurt," "There's A Honky Tonk Angel (Who Will Take Me Back In)," "Always On My Mind," and "Green, Green Grass of Home"

ELVIS FOREVER
(RCA KSL2-7031)
1974. Although a Canadian release, *Elvis Forever* was sold exclusively in the United States via television advertisements. It was a two-record, single-pocket compilation of some of Elvis's greatest hits.

Side 1: "Treat Me Nice," "I Need Your Love Tonight," "That's When Your Heartaches Begin," "G. I. Blues," "Blue Hawaii," and "Easy Come, Easy Go"
Side 2: "Suspicion," "Puppet on a String," "Heartbreak Hotel," "One Night," "Memories," and "Blue Suede Shoes"
Side 3: "Are You Lonesome Tonight?," "High Heel Sneakers," "Old Shep," "Rip It Up," "Such a Night," and "A Fool Such as I"
Side 4: "Tutti Frutti," "In the Ghetto," "Wear My Ring Around Your Neck," "Wooden Heart," "Crying in the Chapel," and "Don't Cry, Daddy"

ELVIS! HIS GREATEST HITS
(RCA RDA-0101A)
1979. This seven-LP boxed set from *Reader's Digest* came with a booklet of liner notes. All pre-1960 recordings were issued in electronically reprocessed stereo. The highlight of *Elvis! His Greatest Hits* was the alternate take of "Your Cheatin' Heart." In this take, the instrumental backing is different and Elvis's voice seems to have more power. A special bonus LP, *Elvis Sings Inspirational Favorites,* came with this boxed set.

Side 1: "Heartbreak Hotel," "Don't Be Cruel," "I Want You, I Need You, I Love You," "Blue Suede Shoes," "Any Way You Want Me," and "Hound Dog"
Side 2: "Love Me Tender," "Too Much," "Love Me," "I Was the One," "Playing for Keeps," and "Teddy Bear"
Side 3: "All Shook Up," "Loving You," "Treat Me Nice," "Blue Christmas," "That's When Your Heartaches Begin," and "Jailhouse Rock"
Side 4: "Don't," "I Beg of You," "Wear My Ring Around Your Neck," "One Night," "King Creole," and "Hard Headed Woman"

Side 5: "I Got Stung," "A Fool Such as I," "I Need Your Love Tonight," "My Wish Came True," "Doncha' Think It's Time," and "A Big Hunk o' Love"

Side 6: "Are You Lonesome Tonight?," "Stuck on You," "I Gotta Know," "Fame and Fortune," "A Mess of Blues," and "It's Now or Never"

Side 7: "Can't Help Falling in Love," "Surrender," "Little Sister," "Flaming Star," "I Feel So Bad," and "(Marie's the Name) His Latest Flame"

Side 8: "Return to Sender," "Good Luck Charm," "Follow That Dream," "Wooden Heart," "She's Not You," and "Rock-a-Hula Baby"

Side 9: "Blue Hawaii," "(You're the) Devil in Disguise," "One Broken Heart for Sale," "Bossa Nova Baby," "Such a Night," and "King of the Whole Wide World"

Side 10: "Kissin' Cousins," "Ask Me," "Ain't That Loving You Baby," "Viva Las Vegas," "Kiss Me Quick," and "What'd I Say"

Side 11: "Suspicious Minds," "In the Ghetto," "(Such an) Easy Question," "Don't Cry, Daddy," "If I Can Dream," and "Puppet on a String"

Side 12: "You Don't Have to Say You Love Me," "Burning Love," "The Wonder of You," "Steamroller Blues," "Kentucky Rain," and "My Way"

Side 13: "Mystery Train," "I'm Left, You're Right, She's Gone," "I Forgot to Remember to Forget," "Baby, Let's Play House," "That's All Right (Mama)," and "You're a Heartbreaker"

Side 14: "Your Cheatin' Heart," "I Really Don't Want to Know," "When My Blue Moon Turns to Gold Again," "There Goes My Everything," "Have I Told You Lately That I Love You," and "I Can't Stop Loving You"

ELVIS: HIS SONGS OF INSPIRATION
(RCA DML1-0264)

1977. Candlelite Music supplied this album to those who bought their five-LP boxed set *The Elvis Presley Story*.

Side 1: "Crying in the Chapel," "Put Your Hand in the Hand," "I Believe," "How Great Thou Art," and "If I Can Dream"

Side 2: "Peace in the Valley," "Amazing Grace," "An American Trilogy," "Follow That Dream," and "You'll Never Walk Alone"

ELVIS IN DEMAND
(RCA PL42003)

1977. To celebrate the twenty-first anniversary of the founding of the Official Elvis Presley Fan Club of Great Britain, RCA polled the club's membership as to the songs they'd like to see on an album. The results are on this LP.

Side 1: "Suspicion," "High Heel Sneakers," "Got a Lot o' Livin' To Do," "Have I Told You Lately That I Love You," "Please Don't Drag That String Around," "It's Only Love," "The Sound of Your Cry," and "Viva Las Vegas"

Side 2: "Do Not Disturb," "Tomorrow Is a Long Time," "(It's a) Long Lonely Highway," "Puppet on a String," "The First Time Ever I Saw Your Face," "Summer Kisses, Winter Tears," "It Hurts Me," and "Let It Be Me"

ELVIS LOVE SONGS
(K-Tel NU-9900)

October 1981. This album is one of many that the K-Tel company has sold via television and in the stores over the years. *Elvis Love Songs* was first available on television and then sold in record stores.

Side 1: "Suspicious Minds," "She's Not You," "The Wonder of You," "Love Letters," "Wooden Heart," "I Want You, I Need You, I Love You," "Memories," and "Kentucky Rain"

Side 2: "Love Me Tender," "It's Now or Never," "Are You Lonesome Tonight?," "You Don't Have to Say You Love Me," "I Just Can't Help Believin'," "Can't Help Falling in Love," "Surrender," and "Loving You"

ELVIS: MEMORIES
(ABC Radio ASP-1003)

December 1978. This three-LP boxed set was produced by ABC Radio for airing on its affiliate stations on January 7, 1979. The three-hour program was a retrospective of Elvis's career. The same program had aired on August 13, 1978.

Side 1: "Memories," "Elvis Memories" (Jingle/Logo), "That's All Right (Mama)," "Good Rockin' Tonight," "Mystery Train," "I Want You, I Need You, I Love You," and "Heartbreak Hotel"

Side 2: "Burning Love," "Rip It Up," "Follow That Dream" "Loving You," "Love Me Tender," "Hound Dog," "Don't Be Cruel," "Way Down," "Moody Blue," "(You're the) Devil in Disguise," and "Suspicion"

Side 3: "Elvis Memories" (Jingle/Logo), "(Marie's the Name) His Latest Flame," "All Shook Up," "Teddy Bear," "Jailhouse Rock," "It's Now or Never," "Elvis Memories" (Jingle/Logo), "I Got Stung," "One Night," "Wear My Ring Around Your Neck," and "Stuck on You"

Side 4: "Elvis Memories" (Jingle/Logo), "My Wish Came True," "Good Luck Charm," "The Grass Won't Pay No Mind," "Fame and Fortune," "Kentucky Rain," and "In the Ghetto"

Side 5: "Viva Las Vegas," "Don't Cry, Daddy," "Separate Ways," "You Don't Have to Say You Love Me," "Elvis Memories" (Jingle/Logo), "Blue Christmas," "Are You Lonesome Tonight?," and "Can't Help Falling in Love"

Side 6: "Elvis Memories" (Jingle/Logo), "My Way," "How Great Thou Art," "Crying in the Chapel," "If I Can Dream," "The Wonder of You," and "Memories"

THE ELVIS PRESLEY COLLECTION, VOLUME 1
(RCA Camden PDA-009)

1976. This double-LP English import contained the entire contents of two U.S. Camden releases: *You'll Never Walk Alone* and *Elvis Sings Hits from His Movies, Volume 1*.

Side 1: "You'll Never Walk Alone," "Who Am I," "Let Us Pray," "Peace in the Valley," and "We Call on Him"

Side 2: "I Believe," "It Is No Secret," "Sing You Children," "Take My Hand, Precious Lord," and "Swing Down, Sweet Chariot"

Side 3: "Down by the Riverside"/"When the Saints Go Marching In," "They Remind Me Too Much of You," "Confidence," "Frankie and Johnny," and "Guitar Man"

Side 4: "Long Legged Girl (with the Short Dress On)," "You Don't Know Me," "How Would You Like To Be," "Big Boss Man," and "Old MacDonald"

THE ELVIS PRESLEY COLLECTION, VOLUME 2
(RCA Camden PDA-042)

1979. Another double-LP English import containing previously released Camden material. In this set, sides 1 and 2 consist of the entire contents on the U.S. Camden release *Separate Ways*. Sides 3 and 4 are a mixture of various Camden LPs.

Side 1: "Separate Ways," "Sentimental Me," "In My Way," "I Met Her Today," and "What Now, What Next, Where To"

Side 2: "Always on My Mind," "I Slipped, I Stumbled, I Fell," "Is It So Strange," "Forget Me Never," and "Old Shep"

Side 3: "C'mon Everybody," "A Whistling Tune," "I'll Be There," "I Love

Only One Girl," "Easy Come, Easy Go," and "Santa Lucia"
Side 4: "Tonight Is So Right for Love," "Guadalajara," "Angel," "A Little Less Conversation," "Follow That Dream," and "Long Legged Girl (with the Short Dress On)"

THE ELVIS PRESLEY STORY
(RCA DML5-0263)
July 1977. Special five-LP boxed set sold by Candlelite Music on television and in print advertisements.

Side 1: "It's Now or Never," "Treat Me Nice," "For the Good Times," "I Got Stung," "Ask Me," and "Return to Sender"
Side 2: "The Wonder of You," "Hound Dog," "Make the World Go Away," "(Marie's the Name) His Latest Flame," and "Loving You"
Side 3: "One Night," "You Don't Know Me," "Blue Christmas," "Good Luck Charm," "Blue Suede Shoes," and "Surrender"
Side 4: "In the Ghetto," "Too Much," "Help Me Make It Through the Night," "I Was the One," "Love Me," and "Little Sister"
Side 5: "Can't Help Falling in Love," "Trouble," "Memories," "Wear My Ring Around Your Neck," "Blue Hawaii," and "Burning Love"
Side 6: "Love Me Tender," "Stuck on You," "Funny How Time Slips Away," "All Shook Up," "Puppet on a String," and "Jailhouse Rock"
Side 7: "Heartbreak Hotel," "I Just Can't Help Believin'," "I Beg of You," "Don't Cry, Daddy," "Hard Headed Woman," and "Are You Lonesome Tonight?"
Side 8: "Teddy Bear," "Hawaiian Wedding Song," "A Big Hunk o' Love," "I'm Yours," "(Now and Then There's) A Fool Such As I," and "Don't"
Side 9: "I Want You, I Need You, I Love You," "Kissin' Cousins," "I Can't Stop Loving You," "(You're the) Devil in Disguise," "Suspicion," and "Don't Be Cruel"
Side 10: "She's Not You," "From a Jack to a King," "I Need Your Love Tonight," "Wooden Heart," "Have I Told You Lately That I Love You," and "You Don't Have to Say You Love Me"

THE ELVIS PRESLEY STORY
(Watermark EPS 1A-13B)
1975. *The Elvis Presley Story* aired in 1970 as a 12-hour radio special. In 1975 it was issued with an additional hour on 13 LPs. The special, which consisted of interviews and several Elvis songs, was produced by Watermark, Inc., of Studio City, California. The letters of the title on the box were in pink.

Side 1: Introduction, Medley of Elvis Hits, "Old Shep," and "Jesus Knows What I Need" (comparison of versions by the Statesmen Quartet and Elvis)
Side 2: "That's All Right (Mama)" (Arthur Crudup), "Hound Dog" (Willie Mae Thornton), Early Fifties Medley: "Harbor Lights" (Sammy Kaye)/"Rag Mop" (Ames Brothers)/"The Tennessee Waltz" (Patti Page)/"The Cry of the Wild Goose" (Frankie Laine)/"You Belong to Me" (Jo Stafford)/"My Heart Cries for You" (Guy Mitchell)/"Come on-a My House" (Rosemary Clooney)/"Cry" (Johnnie Ray)/"Working on the Building" (comparison of versions by the Blackwood Brothers and Elvis)
Side 3: "That's All Right (Mama)," "Blue Moon of Kentucky," "Good Rockin' Tonight," "You're a Heartbreaker," and "Just Because"
Side 4: "Milkcow Blues Boogie," The Truth About Me, "Baby, Let's Play House," "I'm Left, You're Right, She's Gone," "Blue Moon," "I Forgot to Remember to Forget," and "Mystery Train"
Side 5: "Heartbreak Hotel," "I Was the One," "Heartbreak Hotel"(Stan Freberg), "Ready Teddy"/"Blueberry Hill"/"Money Honey"/"Rip It Up"/"I Got a Woman"/"Lawdy Miss Clawdy"/"Long Tall Sally"/"Shake, Rattle and Roll"/"Tutti Frutti," "Blue Suede Shoes," "I Want You, I Need You, I Love You"
Side 6: "Hound Dog," "Don't Be Cruel," "Love Me," "Love Me Tender,"

"One-Sided Love Affair," and "Too Much"
Side 7: "All Shook Up," "Loving You," "Teddy Bear," "Got a Lot o' Livin' to Do," and "Peace in the Valley"
Side 8: Medley of Songs About Elvis, "Party," "Jailhouse Rock," "(You're So Square) Baby, I Don't Care," "Oh Little Town Of Bethlehem," "Blue Christmas," and "Don't "
Side 9: "King Creole," "Dear 53310761" (Threeteens), "Wear My Ring Around Your Neck," "Hard Headed Woman," "If We Never Meet Again," and *Elvis Sails* Interview
Side 10: "Trouble," "I Got Stung," "(Now and Then There's) A Fool Such As I," "My Wish Came True," "A Big Hunk o' Love," and "I Will Be Home Again"
Side 11: "I'm Hanging Up My Rifle" (Bobby Bare), "Dirty, Dirty Feeling," "Stuck on You," "It's Now or Never," "Fever," and "G. I. Blues"
Side 12: "Wooden Heart," "Flaming Star," "Are You Lonesome Tonight?," "I Slipped, I Stumbled, I Fell," "His Hand in Mine," "Surrender," and "I'm Comin' Home"
Side 13: Medley of Elvis's Film Songs, "Blue Hawaii," "I Feel So Bad," "Can't Help Falling in Love," "Good Luck Charm," and "Return to Sender"
Side 14: "One Broken Heart for Sale," Medley of Elvis's Film Songs, "Bossa Nova Baby," "Happy Ending," "Memphis, Tennessee," and "Fun in Acapulco"
Side 15: "(You're the Devil) in Disguise," "Santa Lucia," "What'd I Say," "Crying in the Chapel," "Ain't That Loving You Baby," and "Your Cheatin' Heart"
Side 16: "Little Egypt," Medley of Silly Elvis Film Songs, "Down by the Riverside"/"When the Saints Go Marching In," "Puppet on a String," "Do the Clam," and "When It Rains, It Really Pours"
Side 17: "Old MacDonald," "(It's a) Long Lonely Highway," "Down in the Alley," "Tomorrow Is a Long Time," and "Paradise, Hawaiian Style"
Side 18: "If Everyday Was Like Christmas," "There Ain't Nothing Like a Song," "He's Your Uncle, Not your Dad," "Big Boss Man," and "How Great Thou Art"
Side 19: "Guitar Man," "U.S. Male," "A Little Less Conversation," "Memories," "The Yellow Rose of Texas"/"The Eyes of Texas," and "If I Can Dream"
Side 20: Songs from the NBC-TV Special, "Only the Strong Survive," "Gentle on My Mind," and "In the Ghetto"
Side 21: Songs from the *Elvis in Person at the International Hotel, Las Vegas, Nevada* LP, "Don't Cry, Daddy," and "Kentucky Rain"
Side 22: Songs from the *On Stage—February, 1970* LP, "You've Lost That Lovin' Feelin'," "The Wonder of You," and "The Next Step Is Love"
Side 23: "Patch It Up," "Bridge over Troubled Water," "Rags to Riches," "There Goes My Everything," "Whole Lotta Shakin' Goin' On," and "I'm Leavin' "
Side 24: "Help Me Make It Through the Night," "An American Trilogy," "Don't Think Twice, It's All Right," "Also Sprach Zarathustra" (Joe Guercio Orchestra)/"See See Rider," "Hound Dog," "Burning Love," and "It's a Matter of Time"
Side 25: "Separate Ways," "My Way," "I'm So Lonesome I Could Cry," "Raised on Rock," "Talk About the Good Times," and "Steamroller Blues"
Side 26: Medley of Elvis Hits, "I've Got a Thing About You, Baby," "Help Me," and "Promised Land"

THE ELVIS PRESLEY STORY
(Watermark EPS 1A-13B)
1977. This 13-LP boxed set was identical to the 1975 version of *The Elvis Presley Story* except for changes made on sides 1 and 26 due to Elvis's death. The letters in the title on the box were blue.

Side 1: Introduction (a different introduction was produced), Medley of Elvis Hits, "Old Shep," and "Jesus Knows What I Need" (comparison of versions by the Statesmen Quartet and Elvis)

Sides 2–25: Identical to the 1975 release

Side 26: Medley of Elvis Hits, "I've Got a Thing About You, Baby," and Medley of Elvis Hits Through 1977.

ELVIS RECORDED LIVE ON STAGE IN MEMPHIS
(RCA DJL1-0606)

June 1974. This was a special banded disc jockey release for radio stations. The bands between selections allowed the disc jockey to more easily find the song he wanted to play. The album jacket was identical to the commercial release, but a white sticker listing the song titles was affixed to the front cover.

ELVIS REMEMBERED
(Creative Radio CRS 1A-3B)

1978. Creative Radio Shows of Berkeley, California, produced this three-LP retrospective of Elvis's career. *Elvis Remembered* contained live versions of "I Can't Stop Loving You," "I Got a Woman"/"Amen," "See See Rider," and "Hurt" that hadn't previously been released. Cue sheets were included with the set.

Side 1:"Heartbreak Hotel," "Your Cheatin' Heart"/"When the Saints Go Marching In"/"Wear My Ring Around Your Neck," "Hound Dog"/ "King Creole"/"Don't Be Cruel"/"Blue Suede Shoes"/"Reconsider Baby"/"Hard Headed Woman"/"Loving You," "All Shook Up," "That's All Right (Mama)," "I Really Don't Want to Know," "Hound Dog," and "Make the World Go Away"
Side 2: "Jailhouse Rock," "I Forgot to Remember to Forget" "Money Honey," "Are You Sincere," "You Gave Me a Mountain," "Such a Night," and "Fame and Fortune"
Side 3: "I Got Stung"/"A Big Hunk o' Love"/"One Broken Heart for Sale"/"Return to Sender"/"Surrender"/"Down by the Riverside," "How Great Thou Art," "Treat Me Nice," "I Can't Stop Loving You"/"I Got a Woman"/"Amen," and "I Want You, I Need You, I Love You"
Side 4: "In The Ghetto," "It's Now or Never," "I Beg of You," "She Wears My Ring," "Wear My Ring Around Your Neck," and "Where Did They Go, Lord"
Side 5: "Love Me Tender," "I Can Help," "(Now and Then There's) A Fool Such as I," "Crying in the Chapel," "If I Can Dream," and "Suspicious Minds"
Side 6: "See See Rider," "Hurt," "There Goes My Everything," "Green, Green Grass of Home," "There's a Honky Tonk Angel (Who Will Take Me Back In)," "Memories," and "My Way"

ELVIS SINGS COUNTRY FAVORITES
(?)

1985. *Elvis Sings Country Favorites* was a bonus album with the *Reader's Digest* boxed set *The Great Country Entertainers.* Selections were unavailable at press time.

ELVIS SINGS INSPIRATIONAL FAVORITES
(Reader's Digest RDA-181D)

1979. This LP was included as a bonus with the seven-LP boxed set *Elvis! His Greatest Hits.*

Side 1: "How Great Thou Art," "Somebody Bigger Than You and I," "In the Garden," "It Is No Secret," "His Hand in Mine," and "Take My Hand, Precious Lord"
Side 2: "Crying in the Chapel," "Peace in the Valley," "Put Your Hand in the Hand," "Where Did They Go, Lord," "I Believe," and "You'll Never Walk Alone"

ELVIS SPEAKS TO YOU
(Green Valley Record Store GV-2001/2003)

April 1978. Sides 1 and 2 of this two-LP set had been previously released on the *Exclusive Live Press Conference* and *The King Speaks* LPs. Two songs by the Jordanaires were featured on sides 3 and 4, as well as an insightful conversation by the Jordanaires about Elvis's personal life. A Houston interview of Elvis was also included.

Side 1: 1961 Press Conference, Memphis, Tennessee (February 25, 1961)
Side 2: 1961 Press Conference, Memphis, Tennessee (continued)
Side 3: "How Great Thou Art" (by the Jordanaires) and Elvis Interview (Houston; February 27, 1970)
Side 4: Jordanaires Conversation and "From Graceland to the Promised Land" (by the Jordanaires)

ELVIS TALKS!—THE ELVIS PRESLEY INTERVIEW RECORD
(RCA 6313-1-R)

June 1987. Material contained on the 1985 disc jockey promotional record, *An Audio Self-Portrait,* was reissued on this LP. *Elvis Talks!* could be purchased only by mail order by sending $12.48 ($9.98 plus $2.50 postage and handling) to USA Fulfillment, P.O. Box 1065, Church Hill, Maryland 21690. A toll-free number was also provided (1-800-872-0728, ext. 722). A flyer advertising *Elvis Talks!* was included with Elvis LP releases in 1987. (For contents, see *An Audio Self-Portrait*)

ELVIS TALKS BACK
(Flashback Records)

1979. The Vancouver press conference and Peter Noone interview had appeared on other LPs. What was new on this album was the telephone conversation between Colonel Tom Parker and Canadian disc jockey Red Robinson, and a series of interviews on location of the movie *Charro!* with producer-director Charles Warren, actress Ina Balin, and actress Barbara Werle. The *Charro!* interviews were first heard on the radio program "Dick Strouth Reporting from Hollywood."

Side 1: Vancouver's Official Press Conference (August 31, 1957)
Side 2: Elvis and Peter Noone (August 19, 1965), Canadian DJ Talks to Colonel Parker (August 1965), and *Charro!* (August 1968)

THE ELVIS TAPES
(Great Northwest Music Co. GNW-4005)

December 1977. *The Elvis Tapes* consisted of Elvis's press conference in Vancouver, British Columbia, on August 31, 1957. Canadian disc jockey Red Robinson recorded the press conference, which took place at the Empire Stadium just before Elvis's performance. *The Elvis Tapes* was also released on Polydor Records (Polydor 2912 021)

EPIC OF THE 70's
(Century 21 Productions 1A-6B)

1976. This six-LP set featured highlights of events from the first half of the 1970s. Elvis's "Burning Love" was heard during the three-hour program, as was an interview excerpt.

EXCLUSIVE LIVE PRESS CONFERENCE
(Green Valley Record Store GV-2001)
October 1977. Elvis's February 25, 1961, press conference at the Claridge Hotel in Memphis was featured in this album. The press conference took place at 1:45 P.M. in the Empire Room. February 25 was Elvis Presley Day in Tennessee. Later that day Elvis gave two performances at Ellis Auditorium to raise money for the Elvis Presley Youth Center.

E-Z COUNTRY PROGRAMMING (NO. 2)
(RCA G70L-0108/9)
November 1955. Ten-inch sampler containing twelve country tunes from RCA artists.

Side 1: "When You Said Goodbye" (Eddy Arnold), "Hi De Ank Tum" (Nick, Rita, and Ruby), "Mystery Train" (Elvis Presley), "Honey" (Chet Atkins), "These Hands" (Hank Snow), and "The Last Frontier" (Sons of the Pioneers)
Side 2: "I Forgot to Remember to Forget" (Elvis Presley), "I Wore Dark Glasses" (Anita Carter), "Rock-a-Bye" (Skeeter Bonn), "Love and Marriage" (Homer and Jethro), "Love or Spite" (Hank Locklin), and "Handful of Sunshine" (Stuart Hamblen)

E-Z COUNTRY PROGRAMMING (NO. 3)
(RCA G8OL-0199/200)
February 1956. Ten-inch sampler containing twelve country tunes from RCA artists.

Side 1: "Heartbreak Hotel" (Elvis Presley), "I'm Movin' On" (Hank Snow), "If It Ain't on the Menu" (Hawkshaw Hawkins), "The Poor People of Paris" (Chet Atkins), "I Want to Be Loved" (Johnny and Jack and Ruby Wells), and "That's a Sad Affair" (Jim Reeves)
Side 2: "Do You Know Where God Lives" (Eddy Arnold), "If You Were

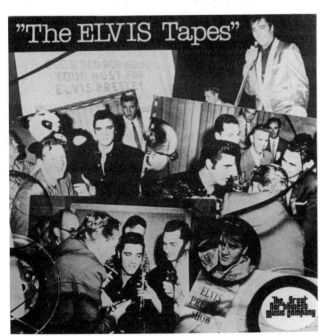

(Photo courtesy Don Fink)

Mine" (Jim Reeves), "The Little White Duck" (Dorothy Olsen), "Borrowing" (Hawkshaw Hawkins), "What Would You Do?" (Porter Wagoner), and "I Was the One" (Elvis Presley)

E-Z POP PROGRAMMING (NO. 5)
(RCA F70P-9681/2)
November 1955. Twelve-inch sampler of sixteen popular songs by RCA artists. This was the first twelve-inch sampler released by RCA.

Side 1: "Dungaree Doll" (Eddie Fisher), "Stolen Love" (Dinah Shore), "Take My Hand (Show Me the Way)" (Rhythmettes), "Not One Goodbye" (Jaye P. Morgan), "Don't Go to Strangers" (Vaughn Monroe), "The Rock and Roll Waltz" (Kay Starr), "I Forgot to Remember to Forget" (Elvis Presley), and "The Little Laplander" (Henri Rene)
Side 2: "The Large Large House" (Mike Pedicin), "All at Once You Love Her" (Perry Como), "When You Said Goodbye" (Eddy Arnold), "My Bewildered Heart" (Jaye P. Morgan), "Mystery Train" (Elvis Presley), "That's All There Is to That" (Dinah Shore), "Jean's Song" (Chet Atkins), and "Everybody's Got a Home but Me" (Eddie Fisher)

E-Z POP PROGRAMMING (NO. 6)
(RCA G70L-0197/8)
February 1956. Ten-inch sampler of twelve popular songs by RCA artists.

Side 1: "Lipstick and Candy and Rubbersole Shoes" (Julius LaRosa), "Mr. Wonderful" (Teddi King), "The Bitter with the Sweet" (Billy Eckstine), "Forever Darling" (Ames Brothers), "Sweet Lips" (Jaye P. Morgan), and "Do You Know Where God Lives" (Eddy Arnold)
Side 2: "Grapevine" (Billy Eckstine), "The Poor People of Paris" (Chet Atkins), "Juke Box Baby" (Perry Como), "The Little White Duck" (Dorothy Olsen), "I Was the One" (Elvis Presley), and "Hot Dog Rock and Roll" (The Singing Dogs)

FIFTY YEARS, FIFTY HITS
(RCA SVL3-0710)
1985. This three-LP set was first available via television advertisements. Later, it was sold through magazine ads.

Side A: "Heartbreak Hotel," "Don't Be Cruel," "I Want You, I Need You, I Love You," "(You're the) Devil in Disguise," "I Need Your Love Tonight," "Too Much," "Viva Las Vegas," "Hound Dog," and "Old Shep"
Side B: "The Wonder of You," "Loving You," "Kissin' Cousins," "Suspicion," "All Shook Up," "Love Me Tender," "What'd I Say," and "Don't"
Side C: "One Broken Heart for Sale," "Danny Boy," "Teddy Bear," "Good Luck Charm," "Suspicious Minds," "Treat Me Nice," "Return to Sender," and "If I Can Dream"
Side D: "A Big Hunk o' Love," "One Night," "Such a Night," "Love Me," "Don't Cry, Daddy," "Wear My Ring Around Your Neck," "It's Now or Never," and "My Wish Came True"
Side E: "I Got Stung," "(Now and Then There's) A Fool Such As I," "Blue Hawaii," "Kentucky Rain," "Can't Help Falling in Love," "Stuck on You," "(Such an) Easy Question," "Hard Headed Woman," and "I Beg of You"
Side F: "You Don't Have to Say You Love Me," "Crying in the Chapel," "She's Not You," "Puppet on a String," "Moody Blue," "Surrender," "In the Ghetto," and "Memories"

THE FRANTIC FIFTIES
(Mutual Broadcasting System RW-4082-L80P)

December 1959. A portion of Elvis's "Hound Dog" appeared on this retrospective of the 1950s issued by the Mutual Broadcasting System.

FROM ELVIS IN MEMPHIS
(MFSL 1-059)
1982. This was a special release by Mobile Fidelity Sound Laboratories. MFSL leased the original master recording tapes from RCA and pressed the album on quality vinyl in Japan. The album was mastered at half speed, giving it a sound that is amazingly clear, with little echo. Song selection was identical to the RCA commercial release of *From Elvis in Memphis*.

FROM ELVIS WITH LOVE
(RCA R-234340)
1978. RCA Record Club release that featured twenty songs with the word *love* in the title. *From Elvis with Love* was a single-pocket, two-record LP. A previously unreleased version of "Faded Love" is on side 3.

Side 1: "Love Me Tender," "Can't Help Falling in Love," "The Next Step Is Love," "I Need Your Love Tonight," and "I Can't Stop Loving You"
Side 2: "I Want You, I Need You, I Love You," "I Love You Because," "Love Letters," "A Thing Called Love," and "A Big Hunk o' Love"
Side 3: "Love Me," "Without Love (There is Nothing)," "Faded Love," "Loving You," and "You've Lost That Lovin' Feelin'"
Side 4: "Have I Told You Lately That I Love You," "You Don't Have to Say You Love Me," "True Love," "Ain't That Loving You Baby," and "Please Don't Stop Loving Me"

GOOD ROCKIN' TONIGHT
(RCA 130.252)
1956. This extremely rare French 10-inch LP contained both sides of Elvis's first four Sun Records releases. *Good Rockin' Tonight* is significant because it didn't have the echo that RCA added to all of the Sun material. What you have here is the basic Sun sound in all its glory.

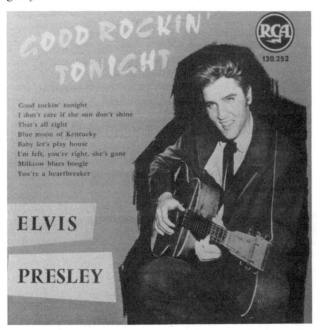

(Photo courtesy Don Fink)

Side 1: "Good Rockin' Tonight," "I Don't Care If the Sun Don't Shine," "That's All Right (Mama)," and "Blue Moon of Kentucky"
Side 2: "Baby, Let's Play House," "I'm Left, You're Right, She's Gone," "Milkcow Blues Boogie," and "You're a Heartbreaker"

GREATEST MOMENTS IN MUSIC
(RCA DML1-0413)
November 1979. *Greatest Moments in Music* was a bonus LP given to buyers of Candlelite Music's six-album boxed set *The Legendary Recordings of Elvis Presley*.

Side 1: "True Love," "Sweet Caroline," "Harbor Lights," "Rags to Riches," and "Let It Be Me"
Side 2: "Your Cheatin' Heart,.." "Yesterday," "Blueberry Hill," "Words," and "Bridge over Troubled Water"

THE GREATEST SHOW ON EARTH
(RCA DML1-0348)
1978. Candlelite Music included this LP as a bonus for those who bought its five-LP boxed set *Memories of Elvis*.

Side 1: "I'll Remember You," "Without Love (There Is Nothing)," "Gentle on My Mind," "It's Impossible," and "What Now My Love"
Side 2: "Until It's Time for You to Go," "Early Morning Rain," "Something," "The First Time Ever I Saw Your Face," and "The Impossible Dream"

IN THE BEGINNING
(ATV VMI)
1974. Elvis's "Lawdy Miss Clawdy" was included on this LP.

INTERNATIONAL HOTEL, LAS VEGAS, NEVADA, PRESENTS ELVIS—AUGUST, 1969
August 1969. RCA prepared this limited-edition boxed set for special guests at Elvis's opening at the International Hotel in Las Vegas. The set contained these items: *From Elvis in Memphis* LP, *Elvis—TV Special* LP, RCA's tape and record catalog of Elvis's releases, a 1969 Elvis pocket calendar, a nine-page letter from RCA and Colonel Tom Parker, one 8"-by-10" Elvis photo, and two 8"-by-10" black-and-white Elvis photos. The cover photo on the box was the same as that on the LP *Elvis in Person at the International Hotel, Las Vegas, Nevada*.

INTERNATIONAL HOTEL, LAS VEGAS, NEVADA, PRESENTS ELVIS—1970
February 1970. Another limited-edition boxed set prepared by RCA for an Elvis opening at the International Hotel. This set contained these items: *From Memphis to Vegas/From Vegas to Memphis* LP, "Kentucky Rain"/ "My Little Friend" single with picture sleeve, RCA's tape and record catalog of Elvis's releases, a 1970 Elvis pocket calendar, a souvenir photo album, one 8"-by-10" black-and-white photo of Elvis, an International Hotel menu, and a note from Elvis and Colonel Tom Parker.

INTERVIEWS WITH ELVIS
(Starday SD-995)
1978. Reissue of *The Elvis Tapes*.

JANIS MARTIN AND ELVIS PRESLEY
(RCA T-31-077)

1958. Ten-inch LP released in South Africa by that country's Teal Records Company. This album is one much sought by Elvis collectors.

Side 1: "Ooby Dooby" (Janis Martin), "I'm Left, You're Right, She's Gone" (Elvis Presley), "One More Year to Go" (Janis Martin), "You're a Heartbreaker" (Elvis Presley), and "I Forgot to Remember to Forget" (Elvis Presley)

Side 2: "My Boy Elvis" (Janis Martin), "All Right, Baby," (Janis Martin), "Mystery Train" (Elvis Presley), "Will You, Will Yum" (Janis Martin), and "Baby, Let's Play House" (Elvis Presley)

THE KING SPEAKS
(Great Northwest Music Co. GNW-4006)

December 1977. Reissue of *Exclusive Live Press Conference*, with the addition of opening and closing remarks by Canadian disc jockey Red Robinson.

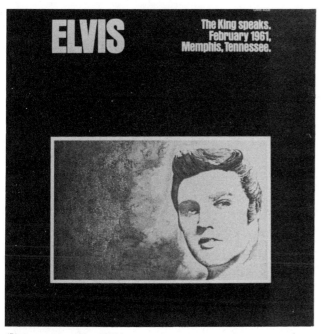

(Photo courtesy Don Fink)

LE DISQUE D'OR
(RCA 6886 807)

1978. This French import was sold widely in the United States in the later 1970s.

Side 1: "C'mon Everybody," "A Whistling Tune," "I'll Be There (If Ever You Want Me)," "I Love Only One Girl," "Easy Come, Easy Go," and "Santa Lucia"

Side 2: "Tonight Is So Right for Love," "Guadalajara," "Angel," "A Little Less Conversation," "Follow That Dream," and "Long Legged Girl (with the Short Dress On)"

THE LEGEND OF A KING
(ABI-1001)

1980. The three-hour radio special "The Legend of a King" was released minus the songs by Associated Broadcasting, Inc., on this LP. The record featured a 1970 photo of Elvis on both sides, and was called the first Elvis "disc-u-mentary."

LEGENDARY CONCERT PERFORMANCES
(RCA R-244047)

1978. Concert tracks from the Las Vegas Hilton, the International Hotel, and the "Elvis: Aloha from Hawaii" TV special were featured on this RCA Record Club two-LP release.

Side 1: "Blue Suede Shoes," "Sweet Caroline," "Burning Love," "Runaway," and "My Babe"

Side 2: "Johnny B. Goode," "Yesterday," "Mystery Train"/"Tiger Man," "You Gave Me a Mountain," and "Never Been to Spain"

Side 3: "See See Rider," "Words," "Proud Mary," "Walk a Mile in My Shoes," and "Steamroller Blues"

Side 4: "Polk Salad Annie," "Something," "Let It Be Me," "The Impossible Dream," and "My Way"

THE LEGENDARY MAGIC OF ELVIS PRESLEY
(RCA DVL1-0461)

September 1980. Candlelite Music included this album as a bonus to those who bought its six-LP boxed set *The Legendary Recordings of Elvis Presley.*

Side 1: "The Wonder of You," "(You're So Square) Baby, I Don't Care," "My Wish Came True," "Suspicious Minds," "I Want You, I Need You, I Love You," "Little Sister," "It's Now or Never," "Too Much," and "Are You Lonesome Tonight?"

Side 2: "Burning Love," "(Now and Then There's) A Fool Such As I," "Hard Headed Woman," "In the Ghetto," "When My Blue Moon Turns to Gold Again," "Don't Cry, Daddy," "Jailhouse Rock," "(Marie's the Name) His Latest Flame," and "One Night"

THE LEGENDARY RECORDINGS
OF ELVIS PRESLEY
(RCA DML6-0412)

November 1979. Candlelite Music sold this six-LP boxed set exclusively on television during the Christmas season in 1979.

Side 1: "Take My Hand, Precious Lord," "Where Could I Go but to the Lord," "In the Garden," "It Is No Secret," and "Stand by Me"

Side 2: "Mama Liked the Roses," "Padre," "All That I Am," "I'm Leavin'," and "Forget Me Never"

Side 3: "Frankie and Johnny," "Down by the Riverside"/"When the Saints Go Marching In," "Girl Happy," "Do the Clam," and "G. I. Blues"

Side 4: "Also Sprach Zarathustra"/"See See Rider," "Johnny B. Goode," "Lawdy Miss Clawdy"/"Baby What You Want Me To Do," "Whole Lotta Shakin' Goin' On"/"Long Tall Sally," and "It's Over"

Side 5: "Snowbird," "I Love You Because," "Just Because," "Release Me," and "Mystery Train"

Side 6: "Blue Moon of Kentucky," "It Keeps Right on a-Hurtin'," "I Don't Care If the Sun Don't Shine," "I'm Movin' On," and "Baby, Let's Play House"

Side 7: "Shake, Rattle and Roll," "I Slipped, I Stumbled, I Fell," "Tutti Frutti," and "Ain't That Loving You Baby"

Side 8: "(Let's Have a) Party," "Tiger Man," "Paralyzed," "High Heel Sneakers," and "I Got a Woman"

Side 9: "Any Day Now," "How's the World Treating You," "Only the Strong Survive," "Just for Old Times Sake," and "You've Lost That Lovin' Feelin' "

Side 10: "They Remind Me Too Much of You," "Danny," "Indescribably Blue," "It Feels So Right," and "Tell Me Why"

Side 11: "Fools Rush In," "Please Don't Stop Loving Me," "Proud Mary," "Never Been to Spain," and "Don't Think Twice, It's All Right"

Side 12: "Fools Fall in Love," "Walk a Mile in My Shoes," "Blue Moon," "Witchcraft," and "Runaway"

LOUISIANA HAYRIDE
(Louisiana Hayride NR-8454)
1976. Elvis's "Tweedlee Dee" was included in this "Louisiana Hayride" program.

LOUISIANA HAYRIDE
(Louisiana Hayride NR-8973)
1983. In addition to several interviews and the song "Fancy Pants" by Floyd Cramer and Jimmy Day, this album featured Elvis's "That's All Right (Mama)" and "Blue Moon of Kentucky" from his first "Louisiana Hayride" appearance (October 16, 1954) and "Tweedlee Dee" from a December 18, 1954, Gladewater, Texas, "Hayride" remote broadcast. The latter song featured Elvis, Scotty Moore, Bill Black, D. J. Fontana, Floyd Cramer (piano), and Jimmy Day (steel guitar). Side 2 included additional interviews and "Baby, Let's Play House," "Maybellene," and "That's All Right (Mama)" from an August 1955 "Hayride" appearance, and "I Was the One," "Love Me Tender," and "Hound Dog" from Elvis's last "Hayride" appearance on December 16, 1956.

LOUISIANA HAYRIDE SATURDAY NITE
(Louisiana Hayride LP 973)
January 1985. Elvis's "Tweedlee Dee" from a December 18, 1954, "Louisiana Hayride" appearance was included on this album. The broadcast was a remote from Gladewater, Texas.

MARCH OF DIMES GALAXY OF STARS
(GM-8M-0653/4)
December 1956. This 16-inch record was a radio promotional campaign presented by the National Foundation for Infantile Paralysis. Side 1 began with instructions by Howard Miller on how to use the record for maximum benefit. The remaining tracks on side 1 and all of side 2 were statements by several entertainers (including Elvis) soliciting contributions for the March of Dimes. The record was accompanied by 16 pages of announcements. All tracks were to be aired between January 2 and 31, 1957.

Side 1: Howard Miller (instructions), Eddie Fisher, Julie London, Denise Lor, Jim Lowe, Mills Brothers, Guy Mitchell, Vaughn Monroe, Elvis Presley, and Gale Robbins
Side 2: Pat Boone, Sammy Davis Jr., Gogi Grant, Bill Hayes, Eartha Kitt, Ray Price, Johnnie Ray, Henri Rene, Dinah Shore, Margaret Whiting, and Andy Williams

MARCH OF DIMES GALAXY OF STARS
(GM-8M-0657/8)
December 1956. To promote the 1957 March of Dimes campaign, the National Foundation for Infantile Paralysis issued this 16-inch promotional record to radio stations. Songs by six entertainers were featured, along with open-ended interviews with each. Disc jockeys were provided with a script so that they could conduct the "interviews." This record was to be played only between January 2 and 31, 1957.

Side 1: "I Love My Baby" (Jill Corey), "Love Me Tender" (Elvis Presley), and "Baby Doll" (Andy Williams)

Side 2: "Your Love Is My Love" (Alan Dale), "Paper Doll" (Mills Brothers), and "Singing the Blues" (Guy Mitchell)

MEMORIES OF ELVIS
(RCA DML5-0347)
1978. Candlelite Music released this five-LP boxed set. The cover of the box presented three illustrations by Robert Charles Howe of Elvis at early, midpoint, and later stages of his career. *Memories of Elvis* was subtitled *A Lasting Tribute to the King of Rock 'n' Roll*. A bonus album, *The Greatest Show on Earth*, was included with the boxed set, as was *Musical History's Finest Hour*, a 16-page booklet, and a loose bonus photo.

Side 1: "One Broken Heart for Sale," "Young and Beautiful," "A Mess of Blues," "The Next Step is Love," "I Gotta Know," and "Love Letters"
Side 2: "When My Blue Moon Turns to Gold Again," "If Every Day Was Like Christmas," "Steamroller Blues," "Any Way You Want Me," "(Such an) Easy Question," and "That's When Your Heartaches Begin"
Side 3: "Kentucky Rain," "Money Honey," "My Way," "Girls! Girls! Girls!," "Lonely Man," and "U.S. Male"
Side 4: "My Wish Came True," "Kiss Me Quick," "As Long as I Have You," "Bossa Nova Baby," "I Forgot to Remember to Forget," and "Such a Night"
Side 5: "I Really Don't Want to Know," "Doncha' Think It's Time," "His Hand in Mine," "That's All Right (Mama)," "Nothingville," and "(You're So Square) Baby, I Don't Care"
Side 6: "Playing for Keeps," "King of the Whole Wide World," "Don't Ask Me Why," "Flaming Star," "I'm Left, You're Right, She's Gone," and "What'd I Say"
Side 7: "There Goes My Everything," "Patch It Up," "Reconsider Baby," "Good Rockin' Tonight," "You Gave Me a Mountain," and "Rock-a-Hula Baby"
Side 8: "Mean Woman Blues," "It Hurts Me," "Fever," "I Want to Be Free," "Viva Las Vegas," and "Old Shep"
Side 9: "Anything That's Part of You," "My Baby Left Me," "Wild in the Country," "Memphis, Tennessee," "Don't Leave Me Now," and "I Feel So Bad"
Side 10: "Separate Ways," "Polk Salad Annie," "Fame and Fortune," "Tryin' to Get to You," "I've Lost You," and "King Creole"

MICHELOB PRESENTS
HIGHLIGHTS OF ELVIS MEMORIES
(ABC OCC810)
December 1978. A preview of the radio special "Elvis: Memories . . ." was on this LP. Michelob, which sponsored the broadcast, gave the album to its executives.

Side 1: "Memories," "Heartbreak Hotel," "Love Me Tender," "Hound Dog," "Don't Be Cruel," "Jailhouse Rock," and "It's Now or Never"
Side 2: "Viva Las Vegas," "Separate Ways," "You Don't Have to Say You Love Me," "Are You Lonesome Tonight?," "Can't Help Falling in Love," and "If I Can Dream"

MUSIC YOU CAN'T FORGET
(GSS CC-#167)
1979. This special LP was made for the Social Security Administration. Actress-singer Carol Channing was featured as the narrator of the program. Four Elvis tracks were included on the album: "Love Me Tender," "Spanish Eyes," "That's All Right (Mama)," and "Don't Be Cruel."

THE 1950'S ROCK 'N' ROLL MUSIC COLLECTION—THE ELVIS PRESLEY COLLECTION
(RCA DML3-0632)
1983. This three-LP set was produced and released by Candlelite Music.

Side A: "Don't Be Cruel," "Loving You," "Trouble," "I Was the One," and "When My Blue Moon Turns to Gold Again"
Side B: "Are You Lonesome Tonight?," "Hard Headed Woman," "Don't," and "Little Sister"
Side C: "One Night," "A Big Hunk o' Love," "(Marie's the Name) His Latest Flame," "I Got Stung," and "I Want You, I Need You, I Love You"
Side D: "Jailhouse Rock," "The Wonder of You," "Too Much," and "Love Me"
Side E: "All Shook Up," "Heartbreak Hotel," "Crying in the Chapel," "Teddy Bear," and "Can't Help Falling in Love"
Side F: "Hound Dog," "Love Me Tender," "Return to Sender," and "It's Now or Never"

ON THE RECORD—EVENTS OF 1977
(Caedmon TC-1572)
January 1978. Recap of the year 1977 by United Press International. A photo of Elvis appeared on the album cover, along with those of Bing Crosby, Muhammad Ali, Charlie Chaplin, Anwar Sadat, and Menachem Begin, among others. "Hound Dog" and a live version of "All Shook Up" were heard on the soundtrack.

ONE NIGHT WITH YOU
(RCA DVM1-0704)
January 1985. Home Box Office released this album in conjunction with its cable television special "One Night with You." The selections were identical to the 1968 album *Elvis—TV Special* (RCA LPM-4088).

OUR MEMORIES OF ELVIS, VOLUME 2
(RCA DJL1-3455)
August 1979. Only about 400 copies of this odd promotional album were sent to radio stations. Side A featured four songs as they were originally released to the public by RCA. Side B had the same four songs, but this time without the vocal and instrumental overdubbing, just as they appeared on the LP *Our Memories of Elvis, Volume 2*. The record came in a black-and-white jacket with the title *Pure Elvis* on both the front and back covers. The record label, however, used the title *Our Memories of Elvis, Volume 2*.

Side 1: "I Got a Feeling in My Body," "For the Heart," "She Wears My Ring," and "Find Out What's Happening"
Side 2: "I Got a Feeling in My Body," "For the Heart," "She Wears My Ring," and "Find Out What's Happening"

PERSONALLY ELVIS
(Silhouette Music 1001/2)
1979. In addition to the two records, this set came with a T-shirt silhouette transfer. None of the dates given for the four interviews was correct, with the possible exception of the Warwick Hotel interview. Listed are what we believe to be the correct dates.

Side 1: Interview in Memphis (by Bob Neal at WMPS, week of August 28, 1955); Interview in San Antonio, Texas (by Charlie Walker, April 15 or 22, 1956)
Side 2: Interview at New York City's Warwick Hotel (March 24, 1956)
Side 3: Interview at New York City's Warwick Hotel (continued)
Side 4: Interview in San Antonio, Texas (October 13, 1956); Interview in Honolulu (by Peter Noone on August 19, 1965)

PURE ELVIS
(See *Our Memories of Elvis, Volume 2*)

RADIO'S 1,000,000 PERFORMANCE SONGS
(CBS Songs SNGS-101)
1984. This promotional compilation album contained songs that have been performed at least one million times on the radio. Elvis's "Don't Be Cruel" was included.

ROCK 'N' ROLL FOREVER
(RCA DML1-0437)
August 1981. Candlelite gave this album of Elvis hits as a bonus to those who bought its five-LP boxed set *Top 100 Rock 'n' Roll Hits of All Time* (RCA DML5-0436).

Side 1: "One Night," "Teddy Bear," "Love Me Tender," "Don't Be Cruel," and "I Want You, I Need You, I Love You"
Side 2: "Jailhouse Rock," "Heartbreak Hotel," "Blue Suede Shoes," "Hound Dog," and "All Shook Up"

ROCK & ROLL—THE EARLY DAYS
(RCA AFM1-5463)
1985. Interestingly, none of the twelve songs on this compilation album were originally issued by RCA.

Side 1: "Good Rockin' Tonight" (Wynonie Harris), "Hound Dog" (Willie Mae Thornton), "(I'm Your) Hoochie Coochie Man" (Muddy Waters), "Shake, Rattle and Roll" (Joe Hunter), and "(We're Gonna) Rock Around the Clock" (Bill Haley and His Comets)
Side 2: "That's All Right (Mama)" (Elvis Presley), "Blue Suede Shoes" (Carl Perkins), "Maybellene" (Chuck Berry), "Bo Diddley" (Bo Diddley), "Tutti Frutti" (Little Richard), and "Great Balls of Fire" (Jerry Lee Lewis)

ROCK, ROCK, ROCK
(Original Sound Recordings OSR-11)
February 1972. This compilation album was also known as *All Star Rock, Volume 11*.

Side 1: "American Pie" (Don McLean), "Brand New Key" (Melanie), "Let's Stay Together" (Al Green), "Day After Day" (Badfinger), "Never Been to Spain" (Three Dog Night), "Until It's Time for You to Go" (Elvis Presley), and "Country Wine" (Paul Revere and the Raiders)
Side 2: "The Way of Love" (Cher), "Hurting Each Other" (the Carpenters), "Joy" (Apollo 100), "My World" (the Bee Gees), "Everything I Own" (Bread), "Feeling Alright" (Joe Cocker), and "Down by the Lazy River" (The Osmonds)

ROCK, ROLL & REMEMBER
(Dick Clark Productions DPE-402)
1977. Two Elvis songs were included on this six-LP retrospective: "I Want You, I Need You, I Love You" and "Wear My Ring Around Your Neck." Also included on the three-hour radio transcription was Dick Clark's 1959 transatlantic telephone conversation with Elvis on "American Bandstand." The box came with a script.

SHELBY SINGLETON PRESENTS SONGS FOR THE SEVENTIES
(Shelby Singleton #1)

December 1969. Elvis's "Such a Night" was part of this two-LP promotional set. A 66-page songbook was also included.

60 YEARS OF COUNTRY MUSIC
(RCA CPL2-4351)

June 1982. Country music hits from the 1920s to the 1980s, including Elvis's "Heartbreak Hotel," made up this two-LP set.

SOCIAL SECURITY PRESENTS DONNA FARGO
(Dept. of HEW HEW-77-10762)

January 1977. The Department of Health, Education, and Welfare presented this series of five-minute radio programs. One of the twelve programs on the two records featured "Moody Blue."

SOUND OF '77
(*Billboard* Publications)

December 1977. *Sound of '77* was a five-LP boxed set that featured a five-hour radio program reviewing the year 1977. One segment was devoted to Elvis. Songs heard on the soundtrack were "Moody Blue," "That's All Right (Mama)," "Baby, Let's Play House," "Mystery Train," "I Forgot to Remember to Forget," "Just Because," "Heartbreak Hotel," and "My Way." A script of the program was included in the box.

SPECIAL CHRISTMAS PROGRAMMING
(RCA UNRM-5697)

November 1967. This album was a promotional release for the December 3, 1967, radio special "Seasons Greetings from Elvis," and its December 10 rebroadcast. Script and programming information was included.

SPECIAL PALM SUNDAY PROGRAMMING
(RCA SP-33-461)

March 1967. RCA sent this special disc jockey promotional LP to about 300 radio stations. Disc jockeys were to play *Special Palm Sunday Programming* on Palm Sunday, March 19, 1967.

Side 1: "How Great Thou Art," "In the Garden," "Somebody Bigger Than You and I," and "Stand by Me"
Side 2: "Without Him," "Where Could I Go but to the Lord," "Where No One Stands Alone," "Crying in the Chapel," and "How Great Thou Art" (excerpt)

THE SUN COLLECTION
(RCA Starcall HY-1001)

August 1975. Fifteen songs recorded by Elvis at Sun Records in 1954 and 1955, as well as an alternate take of "I Love You Because," were included in this English import. In 1976 the album gained wide distribution in the United States, prompting RCA to release *The Sun Sessions*. (For songs, see *The Sun Sessions* entry)

THE SUN STORY
(Rhino Records RNDA 71103)

August 1986. A four-page booklet giving bios of the artists was included in this two-LP set from Rhino Records.

Side 1: "Good Rockin' Tonight" (Elvis Presley), "Rocket 88" (Jackie Brenston), "Blue Suede Shoes" (Carl Perkins), "Mystery Train" (Junior Parker), "Folsom Prison Blues" (Johnny Cash), "Sitting by My Window" (Five Tinos), and "Ooby Dooby" (Roy Orbison)
Side 2: "Get Rhythm" (Johnny Cash), "Devil Doll" (Roy Orbison), "Just Walking in the Rain" (Prisonaires), "Straight A's in Love" (Johnny Cash), "Ubangi Stomp" (Warren Smith), "Bearcat" (Rufus Thomas), and "That's All Right (Mama)" (Elvis Presley)
Side 3: "Whole Lotta Shakin' Goin' On" (Jerry Lee Lewis), "Match Box" (Carl Perkins), "Lonely Weekends" (Charlie Rich), "Mona Lisa" (Carl Mann), "My Bucket's Got a Hole in It" (Sonny Burgess), "Flyin' Saucers Rock 'n' Roll" (Billy Lee Riley) and "Great Balls of Fire" (Jerry Lee Lewis)
Side 4: "Honey Don't" (Carl Perkins), "High School Confidential" (Jerry Lee Lewis), "Red Hot" (Billy Lee Riley), "I Walk the Line" (Johnny Cash), "Who Will the Next Fool Be" (Charlie Rich), "Raunchy" (Bill Justis), and "Breathless" (Jerry Lee Lewis)

THE TIME-LIFE TREASURY OF CHRISTMAS
(Time-Life STL-107)

1986. This three-LP boxed set included two Elvis selections: "Here Comes Santa Claus" and "If Every Day Was Like Christmas."

Side 1: "White Christmas" (Bing Crosby), "Winter Wonderland"/ "Sleigh Ride" (Dolly Parton), "The Little Drummer Boy" (Harry Simeone Chorale), "Oh Little Town of Bethlehem" (Andre Previn), "The Twelve Days of Christmas" (Roger Whittaker), "Hark, the Herald Angels Sing" (Nat King Cole), and "O Holy Night" (Perry Como)
Side 2: "The Christmas Song" (Carpenters), "Carole of the Bells"/ "Deck the Halls with Boughs of Holly" (Robert Shaw Chorale), " 'Twas the Night Before Christmas" (Fred Waring and His Pennsylvanians), "Here Comes Santa Claus" (Elvis Presley), "Santa's Beard" (Beach Boys), "Christmas in My Home Town" (Charley Pride), "Away in a Manger" (Ed Ames), and "Silent Night" (Jim Reeves)
Side 3: "Home for the Holidays" (Perry Como), "Rudolph, the Red-Nosed Reindeer" (Gene Autry), "Feliz Navidad" (Jose Feliciano), "Good King Wenceslas" (Morton Gould and the RCA Symphony Orchestra), "Jingle Bell Rock" (Bobby Helms), "Here We Come a-Caroling"/"O Tannenbaum"/"I Saw Three Ships" (Arthur Fiedler and the Boston Pops), and "Ave Maria" (Leontyne Price with the Choir of St. Thomas Episcopal Church, New York City)
Side 4: "Ding Dong Merrily on High" (Roger Whittaker), "If Every Day Was Like Christmas" (Elvis Presley), "Rockin' Around the Christmas Tree" (Brenda Lee), "Santa Claus Is Coming to Town" (Perry Como), "Jingle Bells" (Jim Reeves), "What Child Is This" (Andre Previn), and "Adeste Fideles" (Luciano Pavarotti with the National Philharmonic, Kurt Herbert Adler, Conductor)
Side 5: "I'll Be Home for Christmas" (Perry Como), "God Rest Ye Merry Gentlemen" (Julie Andrews), "Christmas in Dixie" (Alabama), "Do You Hear What I Hear" (Bing Crosby), "Joy to the World"/"Angels We Have Heard on High" (Robert Shaw Chorale), "Blue Christmas" (Glen Campbell), "It Came Upon a Midnight Clear" (Philadelphia Orchestra and Chorus, Robert Page, Conductor), and "Have Yourself a Merry Little Christmas" (Judy Garland)
Side 6: "Mary's Boy Child" (Harry Belafonte), "Rockin' " (Roger Whittaker), "Let It Snow, Let It Snow, Let It Snow" (Lena Horne), "The First Noel" (Sergio Franchi), "Silver Bells" (Kate Smith), "Holly Jolly

Christmas" (Burl Ives), "It's Beginning to Look a Lot Like Christmas" (Perry Como and the Fontane Sisters), and "We Wish You a Merry Christmas" (Philadelphia Orchestra and Chorus, Eugene Ormandy, Conductor)

THE WORLD IN SOUND—1977
(Associated Press AP-1977)
January 1978. This news LP contained a retrospective on 1977. The death of Elvis was one of the many items covered. Photos of Elvis, Bing Crosby, and Jimmy Carter's inauguration were among the nine featured on the album's cover. An excerpt from a live version of "Hound Dog" was heard on the soundtrack.

WORLDWIDE GOLD AWARD HITS, PARTS 1 & 2
(RCA R-213690)
1974. The first four sides of *Elvis: Worldwide 50 Gold Award Hits, Volume 1* were featured on this special RCA Record Club two-LP release.

(Photo courtesy Don Fink)

WORLDWIDE GOLD AWARD HITS, PARTS 3 & 4
(RCA R-214657)
1978. Sides 5 through 8 of *Elvis: Worldwide 50 Gold Award Hits, Volume 1* were featured on this special RCA Record Club two-LP release.

WRCA PLAYS THE HITS FOR YOUR CUSTOMERS
(RCA DJL1-1785)
April 1976. RCA sent this promotional LP to selected dealers nationwide. The album was in the form of a make-believe radio program, with a disc jockey playing past hits of RCA artists. Elvis's "That's All Right (Mama)" was one of the tracks.

Note: In 1974 Economic Consultants and Omega Records began selling compilation albums by mail order, some of which included songs by Elvis. After RCA got a court order, the albums were discontinued. The following LPs are those known to have Elvis tracks on them.

COUNTRY & WESTERN CLASSICS—1955
(Economic Consultants)
Elvis songs: "Mystery Train" and "I Forgot to Remember to Forget."

COUNTRY & WESTERN CLASSICS—1956
(Economic Consultants)
Elvis songs: "Heartbreak Hotel," "I Was the One," "Love Me Tender," "Hound Dog," "I Want You, I Need You, I Love You," and "My Baby Left Me."

COUNTRY & WESTERN CLASSICS—1957
(Economic Consultants)
Elvis songs: "Teddy Bear," "Too Much," "Jailhouse Rock," and "All Shook Up."

COUNTRY & WESTERN CLASSICS—1958
(Economic Consultants)
Elvis song: "Don't."

COUNTRY SUPER SOUNDS—1956
(Omega Sales)
Elvis songs: "I Want You, I Need You, I Love You," "Hound Dog," "Heartbreak Hotel," and "Don't Be Cruel."

COUNTRY SUPER SOUNDS—1957
(Omega Sales)
Elvis songs: "Loving You," "Too Much," "Jailhouse Rock," and "All Shook Up."

COUNTRY SUPER SOUNDS—1958
(Omega Sales)
Elvis song: "Wear My Ring Around Your Neck."

JOURNEY INTO YESTERDAY—1956
(Economic Consultants)
Elvis songs: "Blue Suede Shoes" and "Tutti Frutti."

JOURNEY INTO YESTERDAY—1969
(Economic Consultants)
Elvis songs: "Suspicious Minds" and "In the Ghetto."

OLD & HEAVY GOLD—1956
(Economic Consultants)
Elvis songs: "Heartbreak Hotel," "I Want You, I Need You, I Love You," "Hound Dog," "Don't Be Cruel," and "Love Me Tender."

OLD & HEAVY GOLD—1957
(Economic Consultants)
Elvis songs: "Loving You," "Teddy Bear," "All Shook Up," and "That's When Your Heartaches Begin."

OLD & HEAVY GOLD—1958
(Economic Consultants)
Elvis song: "Don't."

OLD & HEAVY GOLD—1960
(Economic Consultants)
Elvis songs: "It's Now or Never" and "Stuck on You."

OLD & HEAVY GOLD—1961
(Economic Consultants)
Elvis song: "Surrender."

OLD & HEAVY GOLD—1962
(Economic Consultants)
Elvis songs: "Return to Sender" and "Good Luck Charm."

In the 1950s and early 1960s, RCA Records issued sampler albums. These samplers featured tracks from several of the current RCA LP releases. The following samplers are those known to contain Elvis tracks. They are listed in chronological order.

JULY 1956 SAMPLER
(RCA SP-33-4)
Elvis song: "Don't Be Cruel."

AUGUST 1958 SAMPLER
(RCA SP-33-10P)
Elvis song: "King Creole."

AUGUST 1959 SAMPLER
(RCA SPS-33-27)
Elvis song: "Blue Moon of Kentucky."

OCTOBER CHRISTMAS SAMPLER (1959)
(RCA SPS-33-54)
Elvis song: "Blue Christmas."

CHRISTMAS PROGRAMMING FROM RCA
(NOVEMBER 1959)
(RCA SP-33-66)
Elvis song: "I'll Be Home for Christmas."

OCTOBER 1960 POPULAR STEREO SAMPLER
(RCA SPS-33-96)
Elvis song: "Tonight Is So Right for Love."

OCTOBER '61 POP SAMPLER
(RCA SPS-33-141)
Elvis song: "Blue Hawaii."

(NO TITLE) (1962)
(RCA SPS-33-191)
Elvis songs: "I Don't Wanna Be Tied" and "Where Do You Come From."

OCTOBER '63 POP SAMPLER
(RCA SPS-33-219)
Elvis song: "Are You Lonesome Tonight?"

DECEMBER '63 POP SAMPLER
(RCA SPS-33-247)
Elvis song: "Fun in Acapulco."

OCTOBER '64 POP SAMPLER
(RCA SPS-33-272)
Elvis song: "Kissin' Cousins (No. 2)."

APRIL '65 POP SAMPLER
(RCA SPS-33-331)
Elvis song: "The Meanest Girl in Town."

AUGUST '65 POP SAMPLER
(RCA SPS-33-347)
Elvis song: "Your Cheatin' Heart."

APRIL '66 POP SAMPLER
(RCA SPS-33-403)
Elvis song: "Frankie and Johnny."

Compact Discs

THE ALTERNATE ALOHA
(RCA 6985-2-R)
May 1988. *The Alternate Aloha* was the first Elvis CD picture disc. The complete January 12, 1973, rehearsal concert for the "Elvis: Aloha from Hawaii" TV special was included, as well as three bonus songs that were recorded after the audience left the building following the January 14 telecast. This CD is the only official RCA version of the rehearsal concert, as the LP and cassette releases omitted "Hound Dog."

Contents
"Also Sprach Zarathustra" (Joe Guercio Orchestra), "See See Rider," "Burning Love," "Something," "You Gave Me A Mountain," "Steamroller Blues," "My Way," "Love Me," "It's Over," "Blue Suede Shoes," "I'm So Lonesome I Could Cry," "Hound Dog," "What Now, My Love," "Fever," "Welcome To My World," "Suspicious Minds," Introductions by Elvis, "I'll Remember You," "An American Trilogy," "A Big Hunk O' Love," "Can't Help Falling In Love," Closing Vamp, "Blue Hawaii" (bonus), "Hawaii Wedding Song" (bonus), and "Ku-u-i-po" (bonus)

ALWAYS ON MY MIND
(RCA PCD1-5430)
March 1985. Same selections as RCA AFL1-5430.

BLUE HAWAII
(RCA 3683-2-R)
May 1988. Same selections as RCA LSP-2426.

BURNING LOVE AND HITS FROM HIS MOVIES, VOLUME 2
(RCA Camden CAD1-2595)
1986. Same selections as RCA Camden CAS-2595.

DOUBLE DYNAMITE
(RCA PCD2-1010)
1986. Same selections as the double-LP set released by Pair Records, RCA PDL2-1010.

ELVIS
(RCA PCD1-5199)
November 1984. Same selections as RCA LPM-1382, digitally remastered and restored to monaural sound.

ELVIS ARON PRESLEY—FOREVER
(RCA PCD2-1185)
March 1988. Same selections as the double-LP set released by Pair Records, PDL2-1185.

ELVIS' CHRISTMAS ALBUM
(RCA PCD1-5486)
November 1985. Same selections as RCA LPM-1951, digitally remastered and restored to monaural sound.

ELVIS' CHRISTMAS ALBUM
(RCA Camden CAD1-2428)
1986. Same selections as RCA Camden CAL-2428.

ELVIS COUNTRY
(RCA 6330-2-R)
March 1988. While this compact disc had the same cover photograph and title as the 1971 LP *Elvis Country* (RCA LSP-4460), only two of the eight songs appeared on the earlier LP.

Contents
"Whole Lotta Shakin' Goin' On," "Funny How Time Slips Away," "Baby, Let's Play House," "Rip It Up," "Lovin' Arms," "You Asked Me To," "She Thinks I Still Care," and "Paralyzed"

ELVIS' GOLD RECORDS, VOLUME 5
(RCA PCD1-4941)
March 1984. Same selections as RCA AFL1-4941.

ELVIS' GOLDEN RECORDS
(RCA PCD1-1707)
January 1984. Same selections as RCA LPM-1707, digitally remastered and restored to monaural sound.

ELVIS' GOLDEN RECORDS
(RCA PCD1-5196)
November 1984. New number assigned to RCA PCD1-1707.

ELVIS PRESLEY
(RCA PCD1-1254)
January 1984. Same selections as RCA LPM-1254, digitally remastered and restored to monaural sound.

ELVIS PRESLEY
(RCA PCD1-5198)
November 1984. New number assigned to RCA PCD1-1254.

ELVIS SINGS THE WONDERFUL WORLD OF CHRISTMAS
(RCA 4579-2-R)
August 1988. Same selections as RCA LSP-4579.

ELVIS: WORLDWIDE 50 GOLD AWARD HITS, PART 1
(RCA 6401-2-R)
August 1988. The contents include sides 1 and 2 of the boxed set, RCA LPM-6401, as well as "I Gotta Know."

ELVIS: WORLDWIDE 50 GOLD AWARD HITS, PART 2
(RCA 6402-2-R)
August 1988. The contents include sides 3 and 4 of the boxed set, RCA LPM-6401, minus "I Gotta Know."

ESSENTIAL ELVIS—THE FIRST MOVIES
(RCA 6738-2-R)
January 1988. Same selections as RCA 6738-1-R, with the addition of four tracks: "Mean Woman Blues,"

"Loving You" (unreleased fast version, take #8), "Treat Me Nice," and "Love Me Tender" (unreleased version).

50,000,000 ELVIS FANS CAN'T BE WRONG—ELVIS' GOLD RECORDS, VOLUME 2
(RCA PCD1-5197)

November 1984. Same selections as RCA LPM-2075, digitally remastered and restored to monaural sound.

FROM ELVIS PRESLEY BOULEVARD, MEMPHIS, TENNESSEE
(RCA 1506-2-R)

June 1988. Same selections as RCA APL1-1506.

G. I. BLUES
(RCA 3735-2-R)

May 1988. Same selections as RCA LSP-2256, with the addition of one bonus track—an alternate take of "Tonight Is So Right for Love." The cover box of this compact disc incorrectly lists "What's She Really Like" as "She's All Mine." The disc itself has the correct title.

HIS HAND IN MINE
(RCA 1319-2-R)

August 1988. Same selections as RCA ANL1-1319.

HOW GREAT THOU ART
(RCA 3758-2-R)

August 1988. Same selections as RCA LSP-3758.

KING CREOLE
(RCA 3733-2-R)

May 1988. Same selections as RCA LPM-1884, digitally remastered and restored to monaural sound.

LOVING YOU
(RCA 1515-2-R)

May 1988. Same selections as RCA LPM-1515, digitally remastered and restored to monaural sound.

MEMORIES OF CHRISTMAS
(RCA 6221-2-R)

November 1986. Same selections as RCA CPL1-4395.

THE MEMPHIS RECORD
(RCA 6221-2-R)

June 1987. Same selections as RCA 6221-1-R.

MERRY CHRISTMAS
(RCA PCD1-5301)

November 1984. This compact disc was a new release, not based on a previously issued LP.

Contents

"I'll Be Home for Christmas," "White Christmas," "Blue Christmas," "Santa Claus Is Back in Town," "Merry Christmas Baby," "O Come, All Ye Faithful," "The First Noel," "Oh Little Town of Bethlehem," "Silent Night," and "Peace in the Valley"

MOODY BLUE
(RCA 2428-2-R)

June 1988. Same selections as RCA AFL1-2428. This CD was blue in color.

THE NUMBER ONE HITS
(RCA 6382-2-R)

June 1987. Same selections as RCA 6382-1-R.

POT LUCK
(RCA 2523-2-R)

May 1988. Same selections as RCA LSP-2523.

RECONSIDER BABY
(RCA PCD1-5418)

April 1985. Same selections as RCA AFL1-5418.

REMEMBERING ELVIS
(RCA PDC2-1037)

1988. Released on the Pair Records label, with the same selections as RCA PDL2-1037.

RETURN OF THE ROCKER
(RCA 5600-2-R)

December 1986. Same selections as RCA 5600-1-R.

ROCKER
(RCA PCD1-5182)

November 1984. Same selections as RCA AFM1-5182.

THE SUN SESSIONS
(RCA 6414-2-R)

June 1987. Although this compact disc is titled *The Sun Sessions*, it is actually the two-LP set *The Complete Sun Sessions* minus six tracks. Those six tracks are the outtake "I Love You Because" (take #1) and the alternate takes "I Love You Because" (take #4), "I'm Left, You're Right, She's Gone" ("My Baby's Gone") (takes #8, #10, #11, and #12).

THE TOP TEN HITS
(RCA 6383-2-R)

June 1987. Same selections as the two-LP set (RCA 6383-1-R) on two compact discs.

A VALENTINE GIFT FOR YOU
(RCA PCD1-5353)

January 1985. Same selections as RCA AFL1-5353.

YOU'LL NEVER WALK ALONE
(RCA Camden CAD1-2472)

1986. Same selections as RCA Camden CALX-2472.

Bootleg Albums

Certainly, not every bootleg LP ever released is listed in this section. To do so would take a book in itself. Rather, we decided to list about seventy representative bootlegs based on four criteria.

Of primary concern was that the LP contained songs or performances not available elsewhere. Failing that qualification, the record had to have a good variety of performances. The quality of the recording and popularity with the fans were the other two criteria used.

Every Elvis song on every bootleg in this section is cross-referenced in the Songs section, and alternate takes and recording information are usually listed there.

ALOHA REHEARSAL SHOW— KUI LEE CANCER BENEFIT
(Amiga Records 5 73 210)

1980. This bootleg was recorded directly from the January 12, 1973, videotaped rehearsal show for the "Elvis: Aloha from Hawaii" TV special. Front and back covers featured color photos of Elvis in concert at the January 14, 1973, broadcast.

Side 1: "Also Sprach Zarathustra" (by Joe Guercio Orchestra), "See See Rider," "Burning Love," "Something," "You Gave Me a Mountain," "Steamroller Blues," "My Way," "Love Me," "It's Over," "Blue Suede Shoes," "I'm So Lonesome I Could Cry," and "Hound Dog"

Side 2: "What Now, My Love," "Fever," "Welcome to My World," "Suspicious Minds," Introductions, "I'll Remember You," "An American Trilogy," "A Big Hunk o' Love," and "Can't Help Falling in Love"

AMERICA'S OWN
(Geneva 2LP 2001)

1979. The entire July 19, 1975, matinee concert at the Nassau Coliseum in Uniondale, New York, comprised this two-record bootleg. Black-and-white photos taken at the concert served as the cover. Although the album suggested that *America's Own* was a Japanese product, it was actually released in the United States. It's the only American-issued bootleg to feature "You Better Run."

Side 1: "Also Sprach Zarathustra" (by Joe Guercio Orchestra), "See See Rider," "I Got a Woman"/"Amen," "Big Boss Man," and "Love Me"

Side 2: "If You Love Me (Let Me Know)," "Love Me Tender," "All Shook Up," "Teddy Bear," "Don't Be Cruel," "Hound Dog," "The Wonder of You," "Tryin' to Get to You," and "Burning Love"

Side 3: Introductions, "Johnny B. Goode" (by James Burton), "Chickin' Pickin" (by James Burton), Drum Solo (by Ronnie Tutt), Bass Solo (by Jerry Scheff), Piano Solo (by Glenn Hardin), "School Day" (by Joe Guercio Orchestra), "T-R-O-U-B-L-E," "Heartbreak Hotel," and "Killing Me Softly" (by Voice)

Side 4: "Let Me Be There," "Bosom of Abraham," "You Better Run," "You Gave Me a Mountain," "Little Darlin'," "Mystery Train"/"Tiger Man," "Can't Help Falling in Love," and Closing Vamp

BEHIND CLOSED DOORS
(Audifon Records AFNS 66072-4)

1979. Four-record boxed set. The front cover features a color photo of Elvis taken in 1968 or 1969, while the back cover is a still from *Girl Happy*. Records 1 and 2 include various studio outtakes from *Wild in the Country, Blue Hawaii, Kid Galahad,* and *Paradise, Hawaiian Style.* Record 3, side 1 features studio outtakes from *The Trouble with Girls,* as well as alternate versions of "Gentle on My Mind" and "Faded Love." Five songs recorded live in concert in Las Vegas appear on side 2 of record 3. Record 4 features alternate versions of six songs with the highlight being a 10-minute, 42-second jam of "Don't Think Twice, It's All Right."

Side 1: "Lonely Man," "I Slipped, I Stumbled, I Fell," "I Slipped, I Stumbled, I Fell," "I Slipped, I Stumbled, I Fell," "Wild in the Country," "Wild in the Country," "In My Way," "Forget Me Never," and "Forget Me Never"

Side 2: "Hawaiian Wedding Song," "Island of Love," "Island of Love," "Steppin' Out of Line," "Steppin' Out of Line," "Almost Always True," "Almost Always True," "Moonlight Swim," and "Moonlight Swim"

Side 3: "Can't Help Falling in Love," "Can't Help Falling in Love," "Can't Help Falling in Love," "Can't Help Falling in Love," "Beach Boy Blues," "Beach Boy Blues," "King of the Whole Wide World," "This is Living," and "Home Is Where the Heart Is"

Side 4: "I Got Lucky," "A Whistling Tune," "A Whistling Tune," "A Whistling Tune," "Drums of the Islands," and "This Is My Heaven"

Side 5: "Swing Down, Sweet Chariot," "Almost," "Sign of the Zodiac," "The Whiffenpoof Song"/"Violet (Flower of NYU)", "Gentle on My Mind," and "Faded Love"

Side 6: "I Got a Woman," "Suspicious Minds," "Don't Cry, Daddy," "Kentucky Rain," and "Polk Salad Annie"

Side 7: "It's Your Baby, You Rock It," "Tomorrow Never Comes," "Funny How Time Slips Away," "I Washed My Hands in Muddy Water," and "The First Time Ever I Saw Your Face"

Side 8: "Don't Think Twice, It's All Right"

BIG BOSS MAN

All songs on the album were recorded live at the Las Vegas Hilton on August 19, 1974

Side 1: "Big Boss Man," "Proud Mary," "Down in the Alley," "Good Time Charlie's Got the Blues," "Never Been to Spain," "It's Midnight," "If You Talk in Your Sleep," and "Let Me Be There"

Side 2: "If You Love Me (Let Me Know)," Band and Group Intros, "Promised Land," Elvis Introduces Telly Savalas, "My Baby Left Me," "Bridge over Troubled Water," "Fever," "Hound Dog," and "Can't Help Falling in Love."

THE BLUE HAWAII BOX
(Laurel BPM-501-A)

1981. A total of 110 takes of all fourteen songs from *Blue Hawaii* were featured on this three-record boxed set, along with "Steppin' Out of Line," which was cut from the film. The set came with the free bonus picture booklet, "A New Era."

Side A: "No More" and "Slicin' Sand"

Side B: "Hawaiian Sunset," "Aloha Oe," and "Ku-u-i-po"
Side C: "Blue Hawaii," "Ito Eats," and "Hawaiian Wedding Song"
Side D: "Island of Love" and "Steppin' Out of Line"
Side E: "Steppin' Out of Line," "Almost Always True," and "Moonlight Swim"
Side F: "Moonlight Swim," "Can't Help Falling in Love," "Beach Boy Blues," and "Rock-a-Hula Baby"

THE BLUE HAWAII SESSIONS
(Laurel LPM LPM-2427)
1987. Alternate takes from seven of the fourteen songs from *Blue Hawaii* were featured on this album, as well as "Steppin' Out of Line," which was cut from the film.

Side 1: "Blue Hawaii," "Steppin' Out of Line," "Almost Always True," "Rock-a-Hula Baby," and "Ku-u-i-po"
Side 2: "Blue Hawaii," "Steppin' Out of Line," "No More," "Ito Eats," and "Slicin' Sand"

(Photo courtesy John Dawson)

THE BURBANK SESSIONS, VOLUME 1
(Audifon Records AFNS 62768)
1979. A two-record set that features the two June 27, 1968, studio performances for the "Elvis" TV special at NBC in Burbank, California. Record 1 contains the entire 6:00 P.M. show, while the 8:00 P.M. performance fills out record two. Both front and back covers feature color shots of Elvis in the black leather suit he wore in the "pit" session during the TV special.

Side 1: Dialogue, "That's All Right (Mama)," "Heartbreak Hotel," "Love Me," "Baby What You Want Me to Do," Dialogue, "Blue Suede Shoes," "Baby What You Want Me to Do," Dialogue, and "Lawdy Miss Clawdy"
Side 2: "Are You Lonesome Tonight?," "When My Blue Moon Turns to Gold Again," "Blue Christmas," "Tryin' to Get to You," "One Night," "Baby What You Want Me to Do," Dialogue, "One Night," and "Memories"
Side 3: Dialogue, "Heartbreak Hotel," "Baby What You Want Me to Do," Dialogue, "That's All Right (Mama)," "Are You Lonesome Tonight?," "Baby What You Want Me to Do," "Blue Suede Shoes,"

"One Night," and "MacArthur Park"
Side 4: "Love Me," Dialogue, "Tryin' to Get to You," "Lawdy Miss Clawdy," Dialogue, "Santa Claus Is Back in Town," "Blue Christmas," "Tiger Man," "When My Blue Moon Turns to Gold Again," and "Memories"

THE BURBANK SESSIONS, VOLUME 2
(Audifon Records AFNS 62 968)
A two-record set that features the two June 29, 1968, studio performances for the "Elvis" TV special. The 6:00 P.M. show is contained on record 1, while the 8:00 P.M. show is featured on record 2. As with *The Burbank Sessions, Volume 1*, this album features front and back cover shots of Elvis taken during the TV special.

Side 1: Introduction and Dialogue, "Heartbreak Hotel"/"One Night," "Heartbreak Hotel"/"Hound Dog"/"All Shook Up," "Can't Help Falling in Love," "Jailhouse Rock," "Don't Be Cruel," and "Blue Suede Shoes"
de 2: "Love Me Tender," Dialogue, "Trouble," Dialogue, "Baby What You Want Me to Do," and "If I Can Dream"
Side 3: Introduction and Dialogue, "Heartbreak Hotel"/"Hound Dog"/ "All Shook Up," "Can't Help Falling in Love," "Jailhouse Rock," "Don't Be Cruel," "Blue Suede Shoes," and "Love Me Tender"
Side 4: Dialogue, "Trouble," Dialogue, "Trouble"/"Guitar Man," Dialogue, "Trouble"/"Guitar Man," Dialogue; "Tip-Toe Through the Tulips"/"MacArthur Park," and "If I Can Dream"

CADILLAC ELVIS
(TCB Records 1-8-35)
1979. This album contains a conglomeration of cuts from *Elvis—That's the Way It Is*, live concerts, studio sessions, the "Elvis" TV special, "The Steve Allen Show," and *Elvis on Tour*. Interspersed among the tracks are interviews with Elvis, Peter Noone, and Colonel Tom Parker; and spoken tributes by various celebrities including Sammy Davis Jr., Ann-Margret, Pat Boone, Jerry Lewis, Steve Allen, Fats Domino, and Murray the K.

Side 1: "Polk Salad Annie," "Heartbreak Hotel," "Rags to Riches," "The Lady Loves Me," "That's All Right (Mama)," "Blue Suede Shoes," and "All Shook Up"
Side 2: "Shake a Hand," "Young and Beautiful"/"Happy Birthday"/ "The Mickey Mouse Club March," "I Want You, I Need You, I Love You," "Hound Dog," "Blueberry Hill," and "Lawdy Miss Clawdy"

COMMAND PERFORMANCE
(ECP 101)
1977. Sixteen concert tracks from 1970 to 1974 make up this album. All were recorded at the Las Vegas Hilton except for "Reconsider Baby," which was from a concert at Madison Square Garden in New York City, and "Oh Happy Day," which was from a performance at the International Hotel in Las Vegas. *Command Performance* is the only U.S.-issued album (RCA or bootleg) to feature a live version of "It's Midnight."

Side 1: "Also Sprach Zarathustra" (by Joe Guercio Orchestra), "See See Rider," "Mystery Train"/"Tiger Man," "Little Sister"/"Get Back," "My Babe," "Reconsider Baby," "Trouble," "My Boy," and "Spanish Eyes"
Side 2: "Oh Happy Day," "The First Time Ever I Saw Your Face," "Big Boss Man," "It's Midnight," "If You Talk in Your Sleep," "Hawaiian Wedding Song," "Softly, As I Leave You," and "It's Now or Never"

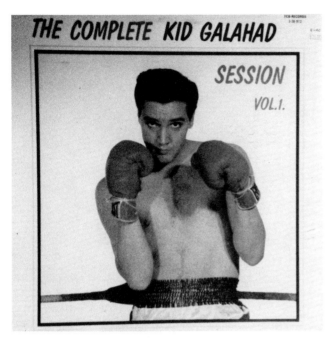

(Photo courtesy John Dawson)

THE COMPLETE KID GALAHAD SESSION, VOLUME 1
(TCB Records 3-30-973)
1987. Alternate takes of three songs from *Kid Galahad* were featured. A publicity still from the movie adorned the album cover.

Side 1: "King of the Whole Wide World"
Side 2: "A Whistling Tune" and "Home Is Where The Heart Is"

THE COMPLETE KID GALAHAD SESSION, VOLUME 2
(TCB Records 3-30-974)
1987. More alternate takes from the movie *Kid Galahad*.

Side 1: "Home Is Where the Heart Is"
Side 2: "Riding the Rainbow"

THE COMPLETE KID GALAHAD SESSION, VOLUME 3
(TCB Records 3-30-975)
1987. Side 1 consisted of more alternate takes from the movie *Kid Galahad*, while "King of the Whole Wide World" was the only song on side 2 that was from the movie.

Side 1: "I Got Lucky" and "This Is Living"
Side 2: "King of the Whole Wide World," "Wolf Call," "There Is So Much World to See," "In the Ghetto," and "Suspicious Minds"

THE COMPLETE WILD IN THE COUNTRY SESSIONS
(Laurel LPM-502-D)
February 1988. Reportedly, all takes of all five songs recorded for the 1961 movie *Wild in the Country* were represented on this two-record bootleg set. The recording session took place at Radio Recorders in Holly-

wood on November 7 and 8, 1960. A photograph of the Radio Recorders "tape legend" appeared on the cover.

Side 1: "In My Way"
Side 2: "Lonely Man" and "Forget Me Never"
Side 3: "Wild in the Country"
Side 4: "I Slipped, I Stumbled, I Fell"

A DOG'S LIFE
(Audifon Records 67361)
1980. This album contains alternate studio versions of movie songs from *Paradise, Hawaiian Style, Blue Hawaii*, and *Kid Galahad*, as well as songs from the "Elvis: Aloha from Hawaii" rehearsal and alternate takes of "There Goes My Everything" and "If I Were You." A photograph of Elvis and RCA's dog Nipper adorns the front cover, while the back cover features a still from the movie *Paradise, Hawaiian Style*

Side 1: "A Dog's Life," "Rock-a-Hula Baby," "It's Over," "There Goes My Everything," "Home Is Where the Heart Is," and "My Way"
Side 2: "Ridin' the Rainbow," "If I Were You," "An American Trilogy," "Hawaii USA" (actually "Paradise, Hawaiian Style"), "Scratch My Back," and "Can't Help Falling in Love"

DORSEY SHOWS
(Golden Archives Records 56-GA-100)
1976. All six of Elvis's appearances on TV's "Stage Show" from January 28 to March 24, 1956, are featured on this album.

Side 1: "Blue Suede Shoes," "Heartbreak Hotel," "Tutti Frutti," "I Was the One," "Shake, Rattle and Roll"/"Flip, Flop and Fly," and "I Got a Woman"
Side 2: "Baby, Let's Play House," "Tutti Frutti," "Blue Suede Shoes," "Heartbreak Hotel," "Money Honey," and "Heartbreak Hotel"

ELVIS
(Neuphone Records)
1974. "Shake, Rattle and Roll" is from Elvis's "Stage Show" appearance on January 28, 1956. All other cuts on side 1 are movie soundtrack recordings. "Kiss Me Quick" and "Suspicion" are both sides of RCA 447-0639. *Love Me Tender* soundtrack recordings of "Let Me" and "Love Me Tender" complete the songs on side 2 of this German-produced bootleg.

Side 1: "Change of Habit," "Rubberneckin'," "Spring Fever," "Girl Happy," "Shake, Rattle and Roll," "Party," and "Happy Ending"
Side 2: "Kiss Me Quick," "Suspicion," "Let Me," Departure from the U.S.A., Arrival in Germany, 1958; Arrival in the U.S.A., 1960; and "Love Me Tender"

ELVIS ON TOUR
(Amiga Records 2 72 020)
1980. This album was lifted from the soundtrack of the 1972 documentary of the same title. The cover photo was taken from the film. Although this is a soundtrack LP, not all of the songs in the film were included.

Side 1: Dialogue, "Johnny B. Goode," Dialogue, "See See Rider," "Polk Salad Annie," "Separate Ways," "Proud Mary," "Never Been to Spain," "Burning Love," and "You Gave Me a Mountain"
Side 2: "Lighthouse"/"Lead Me, Guide Me"/"Bosom of Abraham," "Love Me Tender," "I, John," "Bridge over Troubled Water," "Funny

How Time Slips Away," "An American Trilogy," Interview, "I Got a Woman," "A Big Hunk o' Love," and "Lawdy Miss Clawdy"

ELVIS' 1961 HAWAII BENEFIT CONCERT
(Golden Archives Records GA 200)
1978. All tracks on this album were recorded in concert on March 25, 1961, at the Bloch Arena in Pearl Harbor, Hawaii. The ticket proceeds went to the construction of a memorial to the USS *Arizona*, which the Japanese sank during the attack on December 7, 1941. The Pacific War Memorial Commission sponsored the show.

Side 1: "Heartbreak Hotel," "All Shook Up," "A Fool Such as I," "I Got a Woman," "Love Me," "Such a Night," "Reconsider Baby," and "I Need Your Love Tonight"
Side 2: "That's All Right (Mama)," "Don't Be Cruel," "One Night," "Are You Lonesome Tonight?," "It's Now or Never," "Swing Down, Sweet Chariot," and "Hound Dog"

ELVIS PRESLEY IS ALIVE AND WELL AND SINGING IN LAS VEGAS, VOLUME 1
(No Record Label)
1975. All of the songs on side 1, except "Amen" and "How Great Thou Art," were recorded in August 1974 at the Las Vegas Hilton. Those two songs and all of side 2 were also recorded at the Hilton, but in August 1975. This bootleg LP was a French release.

Side 1: "Big Boss Man," "If You Love Me (Let Me Know)," "Until It's Time for You to Go," "If You Talk in Your Sleep," "Hawaiian Wedding Song," "Early Morning Rain," "Softly As I Leave You," "Amen," and "How Great Thou Art,"
Side 2: "T-R-O-U-B-L-E," "And I Love You So," "Green, Green Grass of Home," "Fairytale," "Happy Birthday" (to James Burton), Glenn Hardin Solo, Joe Guercio Orchestra Solo, "Young and Beautiful," "It's Now or Never," and "Burning Love"

ELVIS ROCKS AND THE GIRLS ROLL
(Pink and Black LPM-1510)
1986. Dressing room rehearsals for the 1968 TV special "Elvis" were featured on side 1. Those songs were recorded in mid-June 1968. Side 2 consists of unreleased studio recordings, most of them for the film *Girls! Girls! Girls!* A highlight was "You're the Boss," an unreleased duet by Elvis and Ann-Margret from the *Viva Las Vegas* session.

Side 1: "I Got a Woman," "Blue Moon"/"Young Love"/"Oh Happy Day," "Guitar Boogie" (instrumental), "When It Rains, It Really Pours," "Blue Christmas," "Are You Lonesome Tonight?"/"That's My Desire"/"That's When Your Heartaches Begin," "Baby, What's Wrong"/"Peter Gunn"/"Guitar Boogie" (instrumentals), "Love Me," "When My Blue Moon Turns to Gold Again," and "Blue Christmas"/"Santa Claus Is Back in Town"
Side 2: "Mama," "Earth Boy," "I Don't Want to Be Tied," "Dainty Little Moonbeams"/"Girls! Girls! Girls!," "True Love Travels on a Gravel Road," "Night Life," and "You're the Boss"

ELVIS SINGS SONGS FROM TICKLE ME
(Audition Supertone US/53310761)
1987. Alternate tracks from all nine songs in the movie *Tickle Me* were featured, along with two songs from *Spinout.*

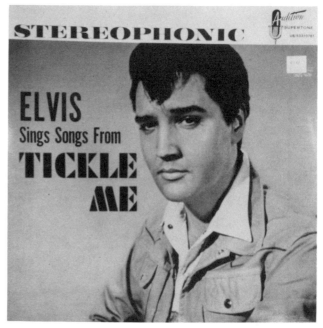

(Photo courtesy John Dawson)

Side 1: "It Feels So Right," "Put the Blame on Me," "(Such an) Easy Question," "Night Rider," "I'm Yours," "Smorgasbord"
Side 2: "Dirty, Dirty Feeling," "(It's a) Long Lonely Highway," "(It's a) Long Lonely Highway," "Slowly but Surely," "I Feel That I've Known You Forever," and "I'll Be Back"

THE ENTERTAINER
(Rooster Record Company R LP 501)
1978. Side 1 of this album focuses on Elvis's early years (1954–1956). Three of the cuts are "Louisiana Hayride" performances. "Flip, Flop and Fly" is from "Stage Show," while the final five tracks are taken from a January 29, 1955, concert at the Eagle's Hall in Houston. Side 2 consists of 1970s Las Vegas appearances, two studio jam sessions ("It's Your Baby, You Rock It" and "Don't Think Twice, it's All Right"), and one concert recording from the Sahara Tahoe Hotel ("Return to Sender").

Side 1: "That's All Right (Mama)," "Blue Moon of Kentucky," "Tweedlee Dee," "Flip, Flop and Fly," "Good Rockin' Tonight," "Baby, Let's Play House," "I Got a Woman," "Blue Moon of Kentucky," and "That's All Right (Mama)"
Side 2: "Polk Salad Annie," "Kentucky Rain," "I Got a Woman," "Don't Cry, Daddy," "It's Your Baby, You Rock It," "Don't Think Twice, It's All Right," "Wooden Heart"/"Young and Beautiful," "What Now My Love," "Folsom Prison Blues"/"I Walk the Line," and "Return to Sender"

ETERNAL ELVIS
(No Record Label)
1978. Brief celebrity tributes are interspersed among the songs on this bootleg. Studio alternate takes are featured on "Old Shep," "It Hurts Me," and "I'll Be Home for Christmas." The songs "Fame and Fortune" and "Stuck on You" were lifted from "The Frank Sinatra–Timex Special," and "Jambalaya" is a concert track. "If I Can Dream" comes from the "Elvis" TV

special. All other cuts are movie soundtrack recordings.

Side 1: Glen Campbell's Memories of Elvis, "Old Shep," Sammy Davis Jr.'s Statements, "You Don't Know Me," The Jordanaires Recollections, "Sign of the Zodiac"/"Violet (Flower of NYU)," James Blackwood's Reflections, "Swing Down, Sweet Chariot," Ray Walker's and Gordon Stoker's Comments, "The Lady Loves Me," Elvis Speaks, "C'mon Everybody," Bob Neal's Memories, "Love Me Tender," Mac Davis's Debt to Elvis, Fabian's Feelings, and "Dainty Little Moonbeams"

Side 2: Promotional interview of Elvis, Bill Black, Scotty Moore, and Bob Neal; "Fame and Fortune," "Stuck on You," Wolfman Jack's Memories, "The Next Step Is Love," Carl Perkins's Explanations, "One Broken Heart for Sale," James Brown's Statement, "Jambalaya," Floyd Cramer's Descriptions, "It Hurts Me," David Cramer's and Jody Miller's Recollections, Debbie Mann's Comparisons, "(Let's Have a) Party," "Husky Dusky Day," Bones Howe's Introduction, "If I Can Dream," Elvis's Greeting to You, and "I'll Be Home for Christmas"

ETERNAL ELVIS, VOLUME 2
(Eagle Records LPS 685)

1979. "And I Love You So," "Lawdy Miss Clawdy," and "Don't Be Cruel" are electronic duets with Shirley Bassey, Lloyd Price, and Jerry Lee Lewis, respectively. "That's All Right (Mama)" is followed by an interview with Sam Phillips; "Heartbreak Hotel" is followed by an interview with Chet Atkins. The second version of "Heartbreak Hotel" is from the "Elvis" TV special. Two concert cuts ("The Impossible Dream" and "It's Now or Never"), a song from "The Steve Allen Show" ("Hound Dog"), a standard release ("Tomorrow Night"), and five studio alternate takes complete the album.

Side 1: "And I Love You So," "That's All Right (Mama)," "Heartbreak Hotel," Hal Wallis Interview, "Heartbreak Hotel," "The Impossible Dream," Elvis Talks About Cars, "Hound Dog," and "It's Now or Never."

Side 2: "Lawdy Miss Clawdy," "Don't Be Cruel," "If You Think I Don't Need You," "Lonely Man," "I Slipped, I Stumbled, I Fell," "Forget Me Never," "Gonna Get Back Home Somehow," "Tomorrow Night," and Elvis Talks About Getting into Fights

THE FIRST YEAR—RECORDED LIVE
(Black Belt Records LP2)

1979. Side 1 includes five songs from Elvis's January 29, 1955, concert at the Eagle's Hall in Houston. Side 2 begins with a 1956 interview with disc jockey Jay Thompson in Wichita Falls, Texas, followed by three "Louisiana Hayride" appearances. The final cut is a 1955 interview with Bob Neal at WMPS radio in Memphis promoting a Texarkana, Arkansas, appearance.

Side 1: "Good Rockin' Tonight," "Baby, Let's Play House," "Blue Moon of Kentucky," "I Got a Woman," and "That's All Right (Mama)"

Side 2: Interview with Elvis After His Final Appearance on the Louisiana Hayride, "Tweedlee Dee," "That's All Right (Mama)," "Blue Moon of Kentucky," and the Texarkana Interview.

THE FIRST YEARS
(HALW 00001)

1979. Side 1 features interview segments with Scotty Moore. The often bootlegged concert at the Eagle's

Hall in Houston (January 29, 1955) is on side 2. A great publicity still of Elvis, Scotty, and Bill adorns the front cover, while the back has a copy of Elvis's managerial contract with Scotty Moore and early photographs and advertisements for Elvis's appearances.

Side 1: Interview with Scotty Moore: First Meeting; Discovery of Elvis by Sam Phillips; the First Recording Session; the Second Recording Session; Shows with the Starlite Wranglers; On Their Own; Stranded in Shreveport, Louisiana; and Grand Ole Opry Appearance

Side 2: "Good Rockin' Tonight," "Baby, Let's Play House," "Blue Moon of Kentucky," "I Got a Woman," and "That's All Right (Mama)"

FOREVER YOUNG, FOREVER BEAUTIFUL
(Memphis Flash Records JL 92447)

1978. This album was recorded at Eddie Fadal's Waco, Texas, house during the summer of 1958. Elvis was stationed at nearby Fort Hood at the time. Girlfriend Anita Wood (who sings "I Can't Help It" and "Who's Sorry Now") accompanied Elvis on the visit. Fadal simply turned on his tape recorder and the result was this home recording. On most of the songs on this album, Elvis sings along with phonograph records that were playing in the background. He accompanied himself on piano while singing "Just a Closer Walk with Thee."

Side 1: Dialogue, "I Understand"/Dialogue, "Happy, Happy Birthday Baby"/Dialogue, "I Can't Help It (If I'm Still in Love with You)" (by Anita Wood)/Dialogue, "Who's Sorry Now" (by Anita Wood)/Dialogue, "Who's Sorry Now" (by Anita Wood)/Dialogue, and "Happy, Happy Birthday Baby"

Side 2: "Happy, Happy Birthday Baby"/Dialogue, "Happy, Happy Birthday Baby"/Dialogue, "Happy, Happy Birthday Baby"/Dialogue, "Happy, Happy Birthday Baby"/Dialogue, "Tumbling Tumbleweeds," "Don't You Know"/Dialogue, "Tomorrow Night"/Dialogue, "Little Darlin' "/Dialogue, and "Just a Closer Walk with Thee"

FRANK SINATRA—WELCOME HOME, ELVIS
(S Records S-4)

1987. This bootleg album contains the complete musical soundtrack to the 1960 Frank Sinatra–Timex TV special "Welcome Home, Elvis," which was taped at the Fountainebleau Hotel in Miami Beach on March 26, 1960.

Side 1: "It's Nice to Go Traveling" (Elvis, Frank Sinatra, Nancy Sinatra, Joey Bishop, Sammy Davis Jr.), "Witchcraft" (Frank Sinatra), "There's a Boat That's Leavin' Soon for New York" (Sammy Davis Jr.), "Gone with the Wind" (Frank Sinatra), and "All the Way" (Sammy Davis Jr.)

Side 2: "Fame and Fortune" (Elvis), "Stuck on You" (Elvis), "Love Me Tender"/"Witchcraft" (Frank Sinatra and Elvis), "You Make Me Feel So Young" (Frank and Nancy Sinatra), "Shall We Dance" (Peter Lawford and Sammy Davis Jr.), and "It's Nice to Go Traveling" (Frank Sinatra)

FROM HOLLYWOOD TO VEGAS
(Brookville Records BRLP 301)

1974. This album consists of several movie soundtrack recordings and Las Vegas concerts. The only exception is the November 20, 1972, Honolulu press conference that announced the upcoming "Elvis: Aloha from Hawaii" television special that opens side 2. The cover features two photos—a still from *Follow That Dream* and one from the "Elvis: Aloha from Hawaii" TV special. Three different album covers are known to exist, each listing the contents in a different order and with different titles. The following listings are the tracks as they are actually heard on the album, not as they are listed on the various LP covers.

Side 1: "Loving You," "Husky Dusky Day," "On Top of Old Smokey," "Dainty Little Moonbeams," "Girls! Girls! Girls!," "Sign of the Zodiac"/"Violet (of NYU)," "Aura Lee," "Folsom Prison Blues," "I Walk the Line," "Oh Happy Day," "Reconsider Baby," "I Need Your Loving (Every Day)," "I Got a Woman"/"Amen," "Crying Time," and "Lovely Mamie"

Side 2: Press Interview for "Elvis: Aloha from Hawaii," "Whole Lotta Shakin' Goin' On"/"Your Mama Don't Dance"/"Flip, Flop and Fly"/ "Hound Dog," "My Boy," "When the Snow is on the Roses," and "All Right Baby" (unknown singer)

FROM LAS VEGAS . . . TO NIAGARA FALLS
(Live Productions LVLP 1897-98)
1974. Two 1970s concerts are chronicled in this two-record set. The dinner show of September 3, 1973, at the Las Vegas Hilton is featured on the first record, while the second record contains the evening show of June 24, 1974, at the Niagara Falls Convention Center.

Side 1: "See See Rider," "I Got a Woman"/"Amen," "Love Me," "Steamroller Blues," "You Gave Me a Mountain," "Trouble," Rock Medley: "Long Tall Sally"/"Whole Lotta Shakin' Goin' On"/"Your Mama Don't Dance"/"Flip, Flop and Fly"/"Hound Dog," and "Love Me Tender"

Side 2: "Fever," "Suspicious Minds," "My Boy," "I Can't Stop Loving You," "Teddy Bear"/"Don't Be Cruel," "The First Time Ever I Saw Your Face," and "Can't Help Falling in Love"

Side 3: "See See Rider," "I Got a Woman," "Love Me," "Tryin' to Get to You," "All Shook Up," "Love Me Tender," "Hound Dog," "Fever," "Polk Salad Annie," and "Why Me Lord" (with J. D. Sumner and the Stamps)

Side 4: "Suspicious Minds," "I Can't Stop Loving You," "Help Me," "An American Trilogy," "Let Me Be There," "Funny How Time Slips Away," "Big Boss Man," "Teddy Bear"/"Don't Be Cruel," and "Can't Help Falling in Love"

FROM THE BEACH TO THE BAYOU
(Graceland Records GL 1001)
1978. Several studio alternate takes from the *Blue Hawaii*, *King Creole*, and *Wild in the Country* sessions are featured here. The front cover includes two black-and-white photographs, one from *Blue Hawaii* and the other from *King Creole*.

Side 1: "Can't Help Falling in Love," "Beach Boy Blues," "Beach Boy Blues," and "Beach Boy Blues"

Side 2: "King Creole," "King Creole," "Crawfish," "Steadfast, Loyal and True," "As Long as I Have You," "As Long as I Have You," "Lover Doll," "King Creole," "King Creole" (instrumental), "Muskrat Ramble" (instrumental), and "Wild in the Country"

FROM THE WAIST UP
(Golden Archives 56-57 GA 150)
1976. All three of Elvis's "Ed Sullivan Show" appearances are on this bootleg, complete and in chronological order.

Side 1: "Don't Be Cruel," "Love Me Tender," "Ready Teddy," "Hound Dog," "Don't Be Cruel," "Love Me Tender," "Love Me," and "Hound Dog"

Side 2: "Hound Dog," "Love Me Tender," "Heartbreak Hotel," "Don't Be Cruel," "Peace in the Valley," "Too Much," and "When My Blue Moon Turns to Gold Again"

GOOD ROCKING TONIGHT
(Bopcat Records LP 100)
1974. Included on side 1 are the released versions of "Good Rockin' Tonight," "Mystery Train," and "I Forgot to Remember to Forget," as well as alternate takes of the other three cuts. Elvis is not found on side 2,

(Photo courtesy Don Fink)

which features other Sun recording artists. The highlight of the record, however, has to be the studio discussion between Sam Phillips and Jerry Lee Lewis about religion. Lewis argues that rock & roll is not Christian and doesn't promote the Lord's work. Phillips eventually persuades Lewis to record a rousing rendition of "Great Balls of Fire."

Side 1: "Good Rockin' Tonight," "My Baby Is Gone," "I Don't Care If the Sun Don't Shine," "Blue Moon of Kentucky," "I'll Never Let You Go (Little Darlin')," "Mystery Train," and "I Forgot to Remember to Forget"

Side 2: "The Return of Jerry Lee" (cut-in record by George Klein), "Savin' It All for You" (by Warren Smith), "Milkshake Mademoiselle" (by Jerry Lee Lewis), Studio Discussion, "Great Balls of Fire" (by Jerry Lee Lewis), "Rock with Me Baby" (by Billy Lee Riley), and "Trouble Bound" (by Billy Lee Riley)

GOT A LOT O' LIVIN' TO DO!
(Pirate Records PR 101)
1976. Soundtrack recordings from *Jailhouse Rock* are featured on side 1. Two Dick Clark television interviews from "American Bandstand" finish out the side. The first 10 cuts on side 2 are soundtrack recordings from *Loving You*. The final four songs are from Elvis's Sep-

tember 1, 1957, appearance in Vancouver, British Columbia. A commentary on Elvis's concert by Red Robinson is interspersed through the four songs.

Side 1: "Young and Beautiful," "I Want to Be Free," "Young and Beautiful," "Don't Leave Me Now," "Treat Me Nice," "Jailhouse Rock," "(You're So Square) Baby, I Don't Care," "Young and Beautiful," and Dick Clark Interviews
Side 2: "Loving You" (fast version), "Got a Lot o' Livin' to Do," "Party," "Party"/"Teddy Bear"/"Got a Lot o' Livin' to Do"/"Hot Dog," "Lonesome Cowboy," "Hot Dog," "Mean Woman Blues," "Teddy Bear," "Loving You" (slow version), "Got a Lot o' Livin' to Do," "Heartbreak Hotel," "I Was the One," "I Got a Woman," and "That's When Your Heartaches Begin"

HAWAII USA
(Laurel LPM-8665)
1987. Twenty-five unreleased takes from eight songs recorded during the *Paradise, Hawaiian Style* sessions of July and August 1965 are featured on this album.

Side 1: "Hawaii USA" (actually "Paradise, Hawaiian Style"), "Stop Where You Are," "Stop Where You Are" (second version), "Sand Castles " (instrumental track), "Queenie Wahine's Papaya" (instrumental track with Neal Matthews vocal), "Queenie Wahine's Papaya" (Elvis vocal), "Queenie Wahine's Papaya" (Elvis vocal, second version), "This Is My Heaven," and "Scratch My Back"
Side 2: "A Dog's Life," "Drums of the Islands," "Sand Castles" (instrumental track), and "Sand Castles" (Elvis vocal)

THE HILLBILLY CAT "LIVE"
(Spring Fever Record Club SFLP-301)
1970. All songs on this two-record bootleg were recorded in concert in August 1970 at the International Hotel in Las Vegas.

Side 1: "That's All Right (Mama)," "I Got a Woman," "Tiger Man," Dialogue, "Love Me Tender," "I've Lost You," and "I Just Can't Help Believin' "
Side 2: "You've Lost That Lovin' Feelin'," "Polk Salad Annie," Introductions, "Johnny B. Goode," Introductions, "The Wonder of You," "Heartbreak Hotel," and "One Night"
Side 3: "All Shook Up," "Blue Suede Shoes"/"Whole Lot of Shakin' Goin' On," "Hound Dog," "Bridge over Troubled Water," "Suspicious Minds," "Release Me," and "Can't Help Falling in Love"
Side 4: "I Got a Woman"/"Ave Maria," "Polk Salad Annie," "Heartbreak Hotel," "One Night," "Hound Dog," and "When the Snow Is on the Roses" (solo with piano)

THE HILLBILLY CAT, 1954-1974, VOLUME 1
(Brookville Records BRLP 311)
1974. Side 1 contains Elvis's first two appearances on "The Ed Sullivan Show." Previously released RCA singles make up side 2.

Side 1: "Don't Be Cruel," "Love Me Tender," "Ready Teddy," "Hound Dog," "Don't Be Cruel," "Love Me Tender," "Love Me," and "Hound Dog"
Side 2: "Rags to Riches," "The First Time Ever I Saw Your Face," "It's Only Love," "The Sound of Your Cry," "Come What May," "Where Did They Go, Lord," and "I'm Leavin' "

THE KING: FROM THE DARK TO THE LIGHT
(Tiger Records TR 101)
1974. Side 1 features soundtrack recordings from the

Elvis on Tour documentary, while side 2 consists of *Elvis—That's the Way It Is* soundtrack recordings.

Side 1: Theme, "Burning Love," "Lead Me, Guide Me," "Bosom of Abraham," "I, John," "I Got a Woman"/"Amen," "Big Hunk o' Love," "Lawdy Miss Clawdy," and Closing Vamp
Side 2: "The Next Step Is Love," "That's All Right (Mama)," "Words," "Little Sister," "What'd I Say," "Stranger in the Crowd," "How the Web Was Woven," "I Just Can't Help Believin'," "You Don't Have to Say You Love Me," "Bridge over Troubled Water," "Polk Salad Annie," and "One Night"

THE KING GOES WILD
(Wilde Productions PRP 207)
1975. As with *From the Waist Up*, all three Ed Sullivan show appearances were included on this record. However, the comments by Charles Laughton and Ed Sullivan were deleted.

Side 1: "Don't Be Cruel," "Love Me Tender," "Ready Teddy," "Hound Dog," "Don't Be Cruel," "Love Me Tender," and "Love Me"
Side 2: "Hound Dog," "Hound Dog," "Love Me Tender," "Heartbreak Hotel," "Don't Be Cruel," "Too Much," "When My Blue Moon Turns to Gold Again," and "Peace in the Valley"

KING OF LAS VEGAS LIVE
(Hazbin/Wizardo Records 351)
1973. Fourteen songs from the *Elvis—That's the Way It Is* soundtrack are included on this album.

Side 1: "That's All Right (Mama)," "I've Lost You," "Patch It Up," "Love Me Tender," "You've Lost That Lovin' Feelin'," and "Sweet Caroline"
Side 2: "I Just Can't Help Believin'," "Tiger Man," "Bridge over Troubled Water," "Heartbreak Hotel"/"One Night"/"Blue Suede Shoes"/"All Shook Up," and "Polk Salad Annie"

THE LAST FAREWELL
(E.P. Records PRP 781)
1977. Elvis's last concert performance is recorded on this two-record set. The concert took place at the Market Square Arena in Indianapolis at 8:30 P.M. on June 26, 1977. Some of the songs were instrumentals performed by the Joe Guercio Orchestra.

Side 1: "Also Sprach Zarathustra" (Joe Guercio Orchestra), "See See Rider," "I Got a Woman," "Amen," "Love Me," and "Fairytale"
Side 2: "You Gave Me a Mountain," "Jailhouse Rock," "O Sole Mio" (by Sherrill Nielsen), "It's Now or Never," "Little Sister," "Teddy Bear," "Don't Be Cruel," "Release Me," and "I Can't Stop Lovin' You"
Side 3: "Bridge over Troubled Water," Introductions of the Backing Vocalists, "Early Morning Rain," "What'd I Say," "Johnny B. Goode," TCB Band Theme, "Blues a la Scheff" (by Jerry Scheff), and "Two Miles Pike" (by Tony Brown)
Side 4: "I Really Don't Want to Know," "Bobby's Choice" (by Bobby Ogdin), "Jazzing in Vegas" (Joe Guercio Orchestra), "Hurt," "Hound Dog," "Can't Help Falling in Love," and Closing Vamp

LEAVIN' IT UP TO YOU
(Audifon Records AFNS 66173)
1980. "I'm Leavin' It Up to You" is from a Las Vegas rehearsal. "Fever," "Burning Love," and "You Gave Me a Mountain" were recorded during the "Elvis: Aloha from Hawaii" TV rehearsal concert on January 12, 1973. Studio alternate takes of "Patch It Up," "Mary in

the Morning," and six movie soundtrack songs complete the album.

Side 1: "I'm Leavin' It Up to You," "Stop Where You Are," "Fever," "Aloha Oe," "Sand Castles," and "Burning Love"
Side 2: "Patch It Up," "King of the Whole Wide World," "You Gave Me a Mountain," "I Slipped, I Stumbled, I Fell," "Queenie Wahine's Papaya," and "Mary in the Morning"

THE LEGEND LIVES ON
(Presley Collection Series PCS 1001)
1976. All songs, except one, are from Las Vegas shows in 1969 and 1972. The lone exception is "Bridge over Troubled Water," which is a studio outtake from February 5, 1970.

Side 1: Elvis Talks About His Career, "Yesterday"/"Hey Jude," Introductions of the Band and "Happy Birthday" to James Burton, "In the Ghetto," and "Suspicious Minds"
Side 2: "What'd I Say," "Can't Help Falling in Love," "It's Over," "A Big Hunk o' Love," "It's Impossible," "The Impossible Dream," and "Bridge over Troubled Water"

LONG LOST SONGS
(Vault Records EAP 1020)
1985. This bootleg consists entirely of Las Vegas concert recordings, except for "Where No One Stands Alone," which is from a February 19, 1977, performance in Johnson City, Tennessee.

Side 1: "Just Pretend" (December 1975), "It's a Matter of Time" (August 25, 1973), "Tiger Man" (1975), "Down in the Alley" (August 19, 1974), "Such a Night" (December 12, 1976), "Loving You" (August 1975), "Crying in the Chapel"/"Rip It Up" (August 1975), and "Roses Are Red"/"I'll Be There"/"You're the Reason I'm Living" (March 22, 1975)
Side 2: "Crying Time" (1970), "San Antonio Rose" (September 1, 1970), "Where No One Stands Alone" (February 19, 1977), "God Calls Me Home" (unknown), Bathroom Conversation, "Blue Suede Shoes" (1975), "Young and Beautiful" (1975), "Are You Lonesome Tonight?" (1975), "If You Love Me (Let Me Know)" (1975), and "Folsom Prison Blues"/"I Walk the Line" (August 14, 1970)

LOVING YOU
(Gold Suit Productions GSR 10001)
1975. All of side 1 and the first cut on side 2 are from the *Loving You* soundtrack. The rest of side 2 consists of soundtrack recordings from *King Creole*, *Love Me Tender*, and *Jailhouse Rock*, as well as two songs from "The Ed Sullivan Show" and "Love Me" from the *Perfect for Parties* EP. A special "March of Dimes" message and an alternate take of "Blue Moon of Kentucky" round out the side.

Side 1: "Loving You," "Got a Lot o' Livin' to Do," "Party," "Party"/"Teddy Bear"/"Got a Lot o' Livin' to Do"/"Hot Dog," "Lonesome Cowboy," "Hot Dog"/"Hot Dog," "Mean Woman Blues," and "Loving You"
Side 2: "Loving You"/"Got a Lot o' Livin' to Do," "Crawfish," "Love Me Tender," "I Want to Be Free," "Ready Teddy"/"Love Me Tender," Introductions and "Love Me," March of Dimes Message, and "Blue Moon of Kentucky"

LOVING YOU RECORDING SESSIONS
(Vik EPP 254)
1982. This British-produced bootleg contains several

takes of "Loving You," two 1956 interviews given in New Orleans, and alternate takes of "Jailhouse Rock" and "Treat Me Nice."

Side 1: "Loving You" (rockin' version)
Side 2: "Loving You" (ballad version), 1956 New Orleans Interviews, "Jailhouse Rock," and "Treat Me Nice"

LOVING YOU SESSIONS
(Laurel LPM-8557)
1985. A total of 33 takes of "Loving You" are featured on this bootleg.

Side 1: "Loving You" (rockin' version)
Side 2: "Loving You" (rockin' version) and "Loving You" (ballad version)

THE MILLION DOLLAR QUARTET
(Million Dollar Records OMD 001)
1980. All seventeen tracks were recorded on December 4, 1956, at the famous Million-Dollar Quartet session at Sun Records, with Elvis, Jerry Lee Lewis, Carl Perkins, and Johnny Cash. For further information on that session see the special article elsewhere in this book.

Side 1: "Just a Little Talk with Jesus," "That Lonesome Valley," "I Shall Not Be Moved," and "Peace in the Valley"
Side 2: "Down by the Riverside," "I'm with the Crowd (but Oh So Lonesome)," "Farther Along," "Jesus Hold My Hand," "On the Jericho Road," "I Just Can't Make It by Myself," "Little Cabin on the Hill," "Summertime Has Passed and Gone," "I Hear a Sweet Voice Calling," "Sweetheart You Done Me Wrong," "Keeper of the Key," "Crazy Arms," and "Don't Forbid Me"

THE MONOLOGUE L.P.
(Bullet Records)
1973. All songs were recorded at the International Hotel in Las Vegas on July 31, 1969, Elvis's first live concert appearance in eight years. (Note: It's possible that "I'm Leavin'" and other songs may actually be from a 1971 or 1972 Las Vegas appearance.

Side 1: The King Talks About His Career, "Jailhouse Rock"/"Don't Be Cruel," "Memories," "Lawdy Miss Clawdy," "Until It's Time for You to Go," "Oh Happy Day," "Sweet Inspiration," and "More"
Side 2: "Hey Jude," "What Now My Love," "Are You Laughing Tonight?," "I, John," "Baby What You Want Me to Do," "I'm Leavin'," and "What'd I Say"

THE ONE MILLION DOLLAR QUARTET
(S Records S-5001)
1987. Finally, after years of waiting, the entire Million-Dollar Quartet session was released on this two-record bootleg set. A picture disc version of the set was also available. After this release, Charly Records of Great Britain had its package of the session on sale in many record stores throughout the United States. For complete information on the Million-Dollar Quartet session, see the article elsewhere in this book.

Side 1: "You Belong to Me," "When God Dips His Love in my Heart," "Just a Little Talk with Jesus," "That Lonesome Valley," "I Shall Not Be Moved," "Peace in the Valley," and "Down by the Riverside"
Side 2: "I'm With the Crowd (but Oh So Lonesome)," "Farther Along," "Jesus Hold My Hand," "On the Jericho Road," "I Just Can't Make It by Myself," "Little Cabin on the Hill," "Summertime Has Passed and

(Photo courtesy John Dawson)

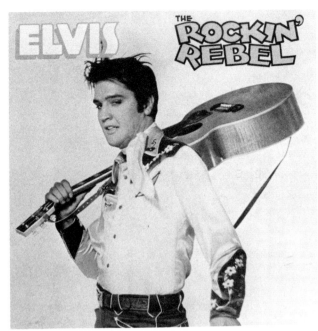

(Photo courtesy Don Fink)

Gone," "I Hear a Sweet Voice Calling," "Sweetheart You Done Me Wrong," "Keeper of the Key," "Crazy Arms," "Don't Forbid Me," "Brown-Eyed Handsome Man," "Out of Sight, Out of Mind," and "Brown-Eyed Handsome Man"

Side 3: "Don't Be Cruel," "Don't Be Cruel," "Paralyzed," "Don't Be Cruel," "Home, Sweet Home," "When the Saints Go Marching In," and "Softly and Tenderly"

Side 4: "Is It So Strange," "That's When Your Heartaches Begin," "Brown-Eyed Handsome Man," "Rip It Up," "I'm Gonna Bid My Blues Goodbye," "Crazy Arms," "That's My Desire," "End of the Road," "Jerry's Boogie," "You're the Only Star in My Blue Heaven," and Elvis Farewell

PLANTATION ROCK
(Audifon Records AFNS 67360)

1979. "Plantation Rock" was an unreleased song from the movie *Girls! Girls! Girls!* "I'll Remember You," "I'm So Lonesome I Could Cry," and "Something" are from the "Elvis: Aloha from Hawaii" rehearsal show. All other songs are alternate takes from *Blue Hawaii*.

Side 1: "Plantation Rock," "I'll Remember You," "Hawaiian Sunset," "No More," "Ku-u-i-po," and "Can't Help Falling in Love"

Side 2: "Sylvia," "I'm So Lonesome I Could Cry," "Slicin' Sand," "Only Believe," "Steppin' Out of Line," and "Something"

PLEASE RELEASE ME
(1st Records 161)

1970. The first two songs are from The Frank Sinatra–Timex Special "Welcome Home, Elvis" and "Baby What You Want Me to Do" is from the "Elvis" TV special. All other songs are from film soundtracks.

Side 1: "Fame and Fortune," "Stuck on You," "Teddy Bear," "Got a Lot o' Livin' to Do," "Treat Me Nice," "Jailhouse Rock," and "Cane and a High Starched Collar"

Side 2: "The Lady Loves Me," "C'Mon Everybody," "Dominick," "Baby What You Want Me to Do," and Tribute Program by Red Robinson

THE ROCKIN' REBEL
(Golden Archives Records GA 250)

1978. The first four cuts on side 1 are from "The Milton Berle Show" (June 5, 1956). A May 14, 1956, radio interview from La Crosse, Wisconsin, completes the side. Side 2 consists of alternate takes from the Sun Records sessions and the film *King Creole*. A color still from *Loving You* is featured on the front foldout cover.

Side 1: "Hound Dog," Elvis Meets Debra Paget, "I Want You, I Need You, I Love You," Presentation of *Billboard* Award, and Interview

Side 2: "My Baby's Gone," "I Don't Care If the Sun Don't Shine," "Blue Moon of Kentucky," "I'll Never Let You Go (Little Darlin')," "King Creole," and "As Long as I Have You"

THE ROCKIN' REBEL, VOLUME II
(Golden Archives Records GA 300)

1979. Songs on side 1 are from the famous January 29, 1955, concert at the Eagle's Hall in Houston. Side 2 contains five songs from "Louisiana Hayride" appearances.

Side 1: "Good Rockin' Tonight," "Baby, Let's Play House," "Blue Moon of Kentucky," "I Got a Woman," and "That's All Right (Mama)"

Side 2: "That's All Right (Mama)" and "Blue Moon of Kentucky" (both October 16, 1954), "Tweedlee Dee" (December 18, 1954), "I Was the One" and "Love Me Tender" (both December 16, 1956)

THE ROCKIN' REBEL, VOLUME III
(Golden Archives Records GA 350)

1979. Two versions of "Loving You," an alternate take of "Old Shep," and the two songs and skit presented on "The Steve Allen Show" make up side 1 of this bootleg. Side 2 begins with yet another take of "Loving You," followed by four songs sung on the first "Ed Sullivan Show" appearance. This album is the only bootleg to feature the entire introduction by actor Charles Laughton. The March of Dimes interview with "Love

Me Tender" and an Ed Ripley interview of Elvis from the summer of 1956 round out the side.

Side 1: "Loving You," "Old Shep," "Loving You," "I Want You, I Need You, I Love You," "Hound Dog," and Comedy Skit
Side 2: "Loving You," "Don't Be Cruel," "Love Me Tender," "Ready Teddy," "Hound Dog," March of Dimes Interview/"Love Me Tender," and Ed Ripley Interview.

ROCKIN' WITH ELVIS APRIL FOOL'S DAY
(Live Stage Productions 72722)
1980. With the exception of "Can't Help Falling In Love," which was taken directly from RCA's *Elvis as Recorded Live on Stage in Memphis*, all songs were recorded during the nine o'clock dinner show at the Las Vegas Hilton on April 1, 1975.

Side 1: "See See Rider," Dialogue, "I Got a Woman"/"Amen," Dialogue, "Love Me," "If You Love Me (Let Me Know)," "And I Love You So," "Big Boss Man," "The Wonder of You," "Burning Love," and Band Introductions
Side 2: Band Introductions, Introduction of Roy Clark, "My Boy," "I'll Remember You," "Let Me Be There," Introduction of Hugh O'Brian, "How Great Thou Art," "Hound Dog," "Fairytale," "Can't Help Falling in Love," and Closing Vamp (Joe Guercio Orchestra)

ROCKIN' WITH ELVIS NEW YEAR'S EVE PITTSBURGH, PA., DEC. 31, 1976
(Spirit of America Records HNY 7677)
1977. This entire two-record bootleg was recorded at Elvis's December 31, 1976, concert in Pittsburgh.

Side 1: "Also Sprach Zarathustra" (Joe Guercio Orchestra), "See See Rider," "I Got a Woman," "Amen," "Big Boss Man," "Love Me," and "Fairytale"
Side 2: "You Gave Me a Mountain," "Jailhouse Rock," Presentation of Liberty Bell, "O Sole Mio" (by Sherrill Nielsen), "It's Now or Never," "My Way," "Funny How Time Slips Away," "Auld Lang Syne," Introduction of Vernon and Lisa Marie Presley, "Blue Suede Shoes," and "Tryin' to Get to You"
Side 3: "Polk Salad Annie," Introduction of the Band, "Early Morning Rain" (by John Wilkinson), "What'd I Say" (by James Burton), "Johnny B. Goode" (by James Burton), Ronnie Tutt Drum Solo, Jerry Scheff Solo, Sonny Brown Solo, "Love Letters," "School Day" (Joe Guercio Orchestra), "Fever," and "Hurt"
Side 4: "Hound Dog," "Are You Lonesome Tonight?," "Reconsider Baby," "Little Sister," "Unchained Melody," "Rags to Riches," "Can't Help Falling in Love," and Closing Vamp (Joe Guercio Orchestra)

THE '68 COMEBACK
(Memphis Records MKS 101)
1976. Featured are prerecorded vocals for the December 3, 1968, TV special "Elvis." The vocals were recorded on June 28 and 30, 1968, at NBC-TV's Burbank studios.

Side 1: "Nothingville"/"Guitar Man"/"Let Yourself Go"/"Guitar Man"/ "Big Boss Man," "If I Can Dream" (instrumental), "Memories," and "Let Yourself Go" (instrumental)
Side 2: "It Hurts Me," "Trouble"/"Guitar Man," "Sometimes I Feel Like a Motherless Child"/"Where Could I Go but to the Lord"/"Up Above My Head"/"Saved," and "A Little Less Conversation" (instrumental)

THE '68 COMEBACK, VOLUME 2
(Amiga Records MKS 192)
1978. More prerecorded vocals from the "Elvis" TV special. As with *The '68 Comeback* album, the vocals were recorded on June 28 and 30, 1968.

Side 1: "Little Egypt"/"Trouble," "Guitar Man," "It Hurts Me," "Trouble," "If I Can Dream," and "Trouble,"
Side 2: "If I Can Dream," "Guitar Man," "Uh-Huh-Huh," "Trouble," "Let Yourself Go," "Trouble," and "Little Egypt"/"Trouble"

SOLD OUT
(E.P. Records PRP 251)
1974. "Burning Love," "Lawdy Miss Clawdy," and "Sweet Sweet Spirit" were lifted from the soundtrack of *Elvis on Tour*, while "I'm Leavin'," the rock medley, and "Help Me Make It Through the Night" were performed in Nashville on July 1, 1973. An Anaheim, California, concert provided the setting for "Steamroller Blues." "Reconsider Baby" was recorded from a performance in New York City, and "I, John" from one at the Sahara Tahoe Hotel. All other tracks on this bootleg came from Las Vegas shows in the 1970s.

Side 1: "Burning Love," "Lawdy Miss Clawdy," "Trouble," "I'm Leavin'," "When the Snow Is on the Roses," "I Need Your Loving (Every Day)," "Little Sister"/"Get Back," "Steamroller Blues," "Long Tall Sally"/"Whole Lotta Shakin' Goin' On"/"Your Mama Don't Dance"/ "Shake, Rattle and Roll"/"Jailhouse Rock"/"Whole Lotta Shakin' Goin' On," "Walk That Lonesome Road" (by J. D. Sumner), and "Help Me Make It Through the Night"/"Faded Love"
Side 2: "Heartbreak Hotel," "One Night," "Reconsider Baby," "Mystery Train"/"Tiger Man," "Jailhouse Rock," "Teddy Bear"/"Don't Be Cruel," "I, John," "Softly, As I Leave You," "It's Now or Never," "My Babe," "Sweet Sweet Spirit" (by the Stamps), "I'm Leaving It Up to You," "I Got a Woman," and "What'd I Say"

SPECIAL DELIVERY FROM ELVIS PRESLEY
(Flaming Star Records Co. FSR 3)
1979. "Love Me Tender" is an electronic duet with Linda Ronstadt. The rest of the album consists of various movie soundtrack recordings, studio alternate takes, and concert recordings.

Side 1: "Love Me Tender," "Love Me Tender," "In My Dreams," "Spring Fever," "Portrait of My Love," "Hawaiian Wedding Song," "King Creole," "Faded Love," "Wild in the Country," and "Can't Help Falling in Love"
Side 2: "When the Snow Is on the Roses," "Trouble"/"Guitar Man"/ "Little Egypt," "Tomorrow Never Comes," "Separate Ways," "The Next Step Is Love," "That's All Right (Mama)," "Words," "Rags to Riches," "The Sound of Your Cry," and "Party"

STANDING ROOM ONLY, VOLUME 2
(Eagle Records Corp. NOTN 3003)
1979. Although Volume 2 is indicated, this album is actually the first of a two-volume set. RCA Records had planned to release an LP in 1972 titled *Standing Room Only*, but eventually dropped the project. The bootleggers chose to begin this series with Volume 2. The songs on this album are in chronological order, ranging from 1955's "Tweedlee Dee" sung on the "Louisiana Hayride" to the last song Elvis ever sang in concert (June 26, 1977), "Can't Help Falling in Love." The rest

of the songs are from concert appearances, with the exception of "I Want You, I Need You, I Love You" ("The Steve Allen Show") and "Tiger Man" ("Elvis" TV special).

Side 1: "Tweedlee Dee," "Baby, Let's Play House," "I Want You, I Need You, I Love You," "Reconsider Baby," "Tiger Man," "My Babe," and "Kentucky Rain"

Side 2: "Little Sister"/"Get Back," "Proud Mary," "My Baby Left Me," "It's Now or Never," "Funny How Time Slips Away," "Are You Lonesome Tonight?," and "Can't Help Falling in Love"

STANDING ROOM ONLY, VOLUME 3
(Eagle Records Corp. NOTN 3004)

1980. As with Volume 2, the songs on this album are in chronological order, ranging from "Blue Moon of Kentucky" from Elvis's first "Louisiana Hayride" appearance (October 16, 1954) to 1977's "And I Love You So." All songs are concert cuts except for "Ready Teddy" ("The Ed Sullivan Show"), "Stuck on You" ("Welcome Home, Elvis"), "Santa Claus Is Back in Town"/"Blue Christmas" ("Elvis" TV special), and "Are You Lonesome Tonight?" ("Elvis" TV special).

Side 1: "Blue Moon of Kentucky," "I Got a Woman," "Ready Teddy," "Peace in the Valley," "Stuck on You," "A Fool Such as I," "Santa Claus Is Back in Town"/"Blue Christmas," and "Are You Lonesome Tonight?"

Side 2: "Release Me," "It's Now or Never," "That's All Right (Mama)," "I'll Remember You," "Help Me," "Big Boss Man," and "And I Love You So"

THE SUN YEARS
(Sun International Corp. Sun 1001)

1977. No song on this album is sung in its entirety. In some cases, the edited version only lasts 15 or 20 seconds. Standard Sun releases and alternate takes make up side 1, except for "Heartbreak Hotel," which is from Elvis's third appearance on TV's "Stage Show" (February 11, 1956). Actual recording sessions with the voices of Sam Phillips and Elvis can be heard. Side 2 features two more songs from "Stage Show"—"Shake, Rattle and Roll" (January 28, 1956) and "Blue Suede Shoes" (February 11, 1956) and three from Elvis's first "Ed Sullivan Show" appearance. Interviews with Jay Thompson in Wichita Falls and Charlie Walker in San Antonio, Texas, can also be heard. Shortly after the release of this album, RCA took legal action to have the Shelby Singleton–produced album removed from distribution. Later copies of the album were distributed by Charly Records of London, England. Gilbert Blasingame Jr. narrated *The Sun Years*.

Side 1: "I Love You Because," "That's All Right (Mama)," "That's All Right (Mama)," "Blue Moon of Kentucky," "Blue Moon of Kentucky," "Blue Moon of Kentucky," "I Don't Care If the Sun Don't Shine," "Good Rockin' Tonight," "I Don't Care If the Sun Don't Shine," "Milkcow Blues Boogie," "You're a Heartbreaker," "My Baby's Gone," "I'm Left, You're Right, She's Gone," "Baby, Let's Play House," "Mystery Train," "I Forgot to Remember to Forget," "Mystery Train," and "Heartbreak Hotel"

Side 2: Jay Thompson Interview, "Shake, Rattle and Roll," "Don't Be Cruel," "Love Me Tender," "Hound Dog," Charlie Walker Interview, "Blue Suede Shoes," and Radio Announcements

SUPERSTAR OUTTAKES
(E.P. Records PRP 254)

1976. The first three tracks are from "The Steve Allen Show." "Let Yourself Go" and "It Hurts Me" were recorded for the "Elvis" TV special. All cuts on side 2 except "Bridge over Troubled Water" (which is a studio alternate take recorded June 5, 1970) were recorded at the International Hotel in Las Vegas during August 1972.

Side 1: "I Want You, I Need You, I Love You," "Hound Dog," Comedy Skit, "Let Yourself Go," and "It Hurts Me"

Side 2: "Yesterday"/"Hey Jude," Elvis Talks, Introduction of the Band, "Happy Birthday, James Burton," "In the Ghetto," "Suspicious Minds," "What'd I Say," "Can't Help Falling in Love," and "Bridge over Troubled Water"

SUPERSTAR OUTTAKES, VOLUME 2
(E.P. Records PRP 258)

1977. All of the "Stage Show" appearances are featured on side 1. "Rags to Riches" and "The Sound of Your Cry" are studio outtakes, while the rest of the songs on side 2 were recorded at the Las Vegas Hilton in 1972.

Side 1: "Blue Suede Shoes," "Heartbreak Hotel," "Tutti Frutti," "I Was the One," "Shake, Rattle and Roll," "Flip, Flop and Fly," "I Got a Woman," "Baby, Let's Play House," "Tutti Frutti," "Blue Suede Shoes," "Heartbreak Hotel," "Money Honey," and "Heartbreak Hotel"

Side 2: "Rags to Riches," "The Sound of Your Cry," "An American Trilogy," "Never Been to Spain," "You Gave Me a Mountain," "A Big Hunk o' Love," "It's Impossible," "The Impossible Dream," and "It's Over"

SUSIE Q
(Astra AST-103)

1985. Except for "You Don't Know Me," which was a studio outtake, all songs were recorded in Las Vegas.

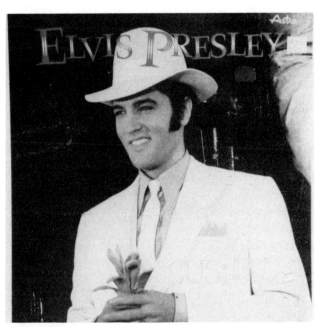

(Photo courtesy John Dawson)

The songs on side 1 were recorded at the International Hotel without an audience. Side 2 was recorded on stage with an audience.

Side 1: "True Love Travels on a Gravel Road," "True Love Travels on a Gravel Road," "Portrait of My Love," "You Don't Have to Say You Love Me," "Any Day Now," "My Way," and "You Don't Know Me"

Side 2: "Faded Love," "Good Time Charlie's Got the Blues," "Turn Around, Look at Me," "When My Blue Moon Turns to Gold Again," "You Can Have Her," "Blue Christmas," "Suzie Q," and "Blueberry Hill"

THAT'S THE WAY IT IS
(Amiga Records 2 71 190)
1980. All songs are from the soundtrack of the 1970 documentary *Elvis—That's the Way It Is.*

Side 1: "Mystery Train"/"Tiger Man," "The Next Step Is Love," "Crying Time," "Little Sister"/"What'd I Say"/"Stranger in the Crowd"/ "How the Web Was Woven," "You Don't Have to Say You Love Me," "Mary in the Morning," "Polk Salad Annie," "That's All Right (Mama)," "I've Lost You," "Patch It Up," and "You've Lost That Lovin' Feelin' "

Side 2: "Sweet Caroline," "I Just Can't Help Believin'," "Bridge over Troubled Water," "Heartbreak Hotel"/"One Night"/"Blue Suede Shoes"/"All Shook Up," "Suspicious Minds," and "Can't Help Falling in Love"

TO KNOW HIM IS TO LOVE HIM
(Black Belt Records LP1)
1978. All songs were recorded at the International Hotel in Las Vegas in 1969 and 1970.

Side 1: "Trouble," "Raised on Rock," "Steamroller Blues," "Sweet Inspiration," "Help Me Make It Through the Night," "More"/"Suspicious Minds," "Release Me," and "I, John"

Side 2: "Folsom Prison Blues"/"I Walk the Line," "Until It's Time for You to Go," "Fever," "I'm Leavin'," "Memphis, Tennessee," Elvis Introduces Bobby Darin, and "Can't Help Falling in Love"

UNFINISHED BUSINESS
(Reel to Reel Record Company 380)
1980. All songs are alternate takes. Eleven of the cuts are from soundtrack sessions.

Side 1: "My Baby's Gone," "I Want You, I Need You, I Love You," "King of the Whole Wide World," "It Hurts Me," "Can't Help Falling in Love," "Frankfort Special," "Forget Me Never," and "Gentle on My Mind"

Side 2: "King Creole," "Loving You," "Patch It Up," "Rock-a-Hula Baby," "I Slipped, I Stumbled, I Fell," "Almost Always True," "Steppin' Out of Line," "It's Your Baby, You Rock It," "A Dog's Life," and "I Washed My Hands in Muddy Water"

THE VEGAS YEARS, 1972–1975
(TAKRL 24913)
1976. A two-record set. "Hound Dog" is from "The Ed Sullivan Show" (October 28, 1956). The rest of side 1 and all of side 2 were recorded at the Las Vegas Hilton in 1972. The songs on side 3 are from a Las Vegas Hilton concert in 1974. Concert performances at the Hilton in 1975 are on side 4.

Side 1: "Hound Dog," "See See Rider," "Proud Mary," "Never Been to Spain," "Never Been to Spain," "You Gave Me a Mountain," "Until It's Time for You to Go," "Polk Salad Annie," and "Love Me"

Side 2: "All Shook Up," "Teddy Bear," "Don't Be Cruel," "Hound Dog," "A Big Hunk o' Love," "Bridge over Troubled Water," "An American Trilogy," and "Can't Help Falling in Love"

Side 3: "Big Boss Man," "If You Love Me (Let Me Know)," "Until It's Time for You to Go," "If You Talk in Your Sleep," "Hawaiian Wedding Song," "Early Morning Rain," and "Softly, As I Leave You"

Side 4: "Amen," "How Great Thou Art," "T-R-O-U-B-L-E," "And I Love You So," "Green, Green Grass of Home," "Fairytale," "Young and Beautiful," "It's Now Or Never," and "Burning Love"

VIVA LAS VEGAS!
(Lucky Records LR 711)
1979. All songs on this bootleg were lifted directly from the soundtrack of Elvis's 1964 movie *Viva Las Vegas,* except for "If You Think I Don't Need You." Three studio takes of that song are included. Ann-Margret sings solo on "Appreciation" and "My Rival" and in duet with Elvis on "The Lady Loves Me" and on the first rendition of "Viva Las Vegas"on side 2.

Side 1: Radio Spot No. 1, "Viva Las Vegas," "The Yellow Rose of Texas"/"The Eyes of Texas," "The Lady Loves Me," "C'mon Everybody," "Today, Tomorrow and Forever," "Cheek to Cheek" (instrumental), "What'd I Say," "Santa Lucia," and "If You Think I Don't Need You"

Side 2: Radio Spot No. 2, "Appreciation," "Viva Las Vegas," "I Need Somebody to Lean On," "My Rival," "Viva Las Vegas," "If You Think I Don't Need You," "If You Think I Don't Need You," and "If You Think I Don't Need You"

Novelty Records

ALL ABOUT ELVIS (PART I)/
ALL ABOUT ELVIS (PART 2)
(Pelvis 169)
1957. Recorded by Milt Oskins.

THE ALL AMERICAN BOY
(Fraternity 835)
1958. Recorded by Bill Parsons (Bobby Bare). Shortly after being drafted into the Army, Bobby Bare stopped by a recording studio to cut a few demo records. Also present was a singer by the name of Bill Parsons. When Fraternity Records released the record they put Bill Parsons's name on the label, and it wasn't until Bare was in his Army barracks that he first heard his song being played over the radio, but credited to Parsons. Bare had sold his rights to the song, composed by Orville Lunsford, for only $50. "All American Boy" is the most successful Elvis novelty record, having peaked at #2 on *Billboard*'s Hot 100 chart in February 1959.

ALRIGHT PRIVATE
(Crystalette 722)
1958. Recorded by Mo Klein and the Sargents.

ARE YOU LONESOME TONIGHT?
(RCA 47-7852)
1961. Recorded by Homer and Jethro.

ARE YOU LONESOME TONIGHT?
(Triodex 105)
1961. Recorded by Lenny Stone.

AROUND THE WORLD WITH ELWOOD
PRETZEL (PART 1)/AROUND THE WORLD
WITH ELWOOD PRETZEL (PART 2)
(Flair-X FI-3007)
1956. Recorded by Lee Tully with Milt Moss.

BYE BYE ELVIS
(ABC Paramount 9900)
1958. Recorded by Genee Harris. "Hound Dog" and "Don't Be Cruel" are mentioned in the lyrics.

CHANSON POUR ELVIS
(Kebec Disc KD-10104)
1975. Recorded by Diane Dufresne. Recorded in French, produced in Canada.

THE CLASS
(Parkway 804)
1959. Recorded by Chubby Checker. Checker imitated Elvis singing "Mary Had a Little Lamb." This was Checker's first record.

DEAR 53310761
(Rev 45-3516)
1958. Recorded by the Threeteens. Duane Eddy and Al Casey played guitar on the record. Trinity Music gave away 50,000 novelty Elvis Army dog tags to help promote the record.

THE DEATH OF ROCK & ROLL
(Columbia 21559)
1956. Recorded by the Maddox Brothers and Rose. The song featured a parody of Elvis singing "I Got a Woman."

DON'T BE MAD/LITTLE RED WEBB
(Capitol 4966)
1963. Recorded by Simon Crum (Ferlin Husky). The A side features a parody of "Don't Be Cruel," and the flip side mentions Elvis.

DON'T BLAME IT ON ELVIS
(Verve V-10029)
1956. Recorded by the Fabulous McClevertys.

DON'T KNOCK ELVIS
(Viva 1001)
1959. Recorded by Felton Jarvis, who would in 1969 become Elvis's record producer.

ELVIS
(Deluxe 45-6111)
1957. Recorded by Julie Lang.

(Photo courtesy Don Fink)

577

ELVIS AND ME
(RCA Victor EPA-4188)
1957. Recorded by the Kids. This song was from an extended-play album.

THE ELVIS BLUES
(RCA Victor 47-6585)
1956. Recorded by Otto Bash. A reference was made to both Elvis and to his recording of "Baby, Let's Play House."

ELVIS IN THE ARMY
(Trepur 1011-45)
1959. Recorded by Jaybee Wasden.

ELVIS IS ROCKING AGAIN
(Fortune Records 210)
1960. Recorded by Roy Hall and His Boys with the Hunt Sisters and Mark.

ELVIS IS THE KING/ELVIS IS THE KING
(Instrumental)
(WB Sound 1621)
Recorded by Memphis Mill. This is a Belgian release.

ELVIS IS THE KING
(Emerald 1001)
1977. Recorded by Louie Fontaine.

ELVIS LEAVES SORRENTO (Instrumental)
(Campus 125)
1961. Recorded by the Twisters.

ELVIS PEREZ
(L & M 1001)
1956. Recorded by Lalo Guerrero. References were made to Elvis's songs "Love Me Tender," "Hound Dog," and "Don't Be Cruel."

ELVIS PRESLEY BLUES
(Dream 1300)
1958. Recorded by Anita Ray and the Nature Boys.

ELVIS PRESLEY BLUES
(G & G 110)
1956. Recorded by Ivan Gregory and the Blue Notes. (The record label credited Arlin and Earl.)

ELVIS PRESLEY FOR PRESIDENT
(RCA Victor 47-6704)
1956. Recorded by Lou Monte.

ELVIS PRESLEY MEDLEY
(Scepter SDJ-12375)
1973. Recorded by Wheelie and the Hubcaps. The flip side featured the "Chuck Berry Medley."

(I WANNA BE) ELVIS PRESLEY'S SERGEANT
(Key 573)
1958. Recorded by the Bobolinks.

ELVIS STOLE MY BABY
(Rock-It LH-17077)
1978. Recorded by Huey Long. Although released after Elvis's death, the song had been recorded before his death in 1977.

THE E.P. EXPRESS
(Mercury 73690)
1975. Recorded by Carl Perkins. The song consists of a number of Elvis's song titles.

GO'WAY HOUND DOG
(Columbia 4-40865)
1957. Recorded by Cliff Johnson.

GONNA GET EVEN (WITH ELVIS PRESLEY'S SERGEANT)
(Key 576)
1958. Recorded by Janie Davids and the Four Lettermen.

HART BRAKE MOTEL/TWO-TONE SHOES
(RCA Victor 47-6542)
1956. Recorded by Homer and Jethro as a double-sided novelty takeoff on Elvis's "Heartbreak Hotel" and "Blue Suede Shoes."

HE ATE TOO MANY JELLY DONUTS
(RSO 870)
1976. Recorded by Rick Dees and His Cast of Idiots. Upon Elvis's death, this tasteless song by Los Angeles disc jockey Dees was quickly deleted from radio station airplay and the record's release was terminated.

HEARTBREAK HOTEL
(Capitol 3480)
1956. Recorded by Stan Freberg as a parody of Elvis's recordings.

HEARTBREAK STATION
(Wey-Vee 800)
1956. Recorded by Cozzia Bill Hamby.

HEY! MR. PRESLEY
(Fortune 200)
1958. Recorded by Peter DeBree and the Wanderers.

HOUND DOG MAN (PLAY IT AGAIN)
(Big Tree BT 16062)
1976. Recorded by Lenny LeBlanc.

HOUN' DAWG
(RCA Victor 47-6706)
1956. Recorded by Homer and Jethro.

I DON'T WANT BRACELETS OR DIAMONDS, I WANT ELVIS INSTEAD
(Warner Bros. Records)
Recorded by Mary Kaye.

I DREAMED I WAS ELVIS
(Rollin' Rock 45-001A)
Recorded by Sonny Cole and the Rhythm Roamers.

I HAVE RETURNED
(Autograph A-60-206)
1960. Recorded by the Unknown. The Unknown was a pseudonym used by singer Jimmy Fields. The song referred to Elvis's discharge from the Army.

I SAW ELVIS PRESLEY LAST NIGHT
(Liberty 56144)
1969. Recorded by Gary Lewis and the Playboys. Gary Lewis is the son of actor/comedian Jerry Lewis.

I WANNA SPEND CHRISTMAS WITH ELVIS
(Regent 45-7506-A)
1956. Recorded by Marlene Paula. The song was composed by Don Kirshner and Bobby Darin.

I WANNA SPEND X-MAS WITH ELVIS
(Atco 45-6082)
1956. Recorded by "Little Lambsie" Penn.

I WANT ELVIS FOR CHRISTMAS
(Liberty 55048)
1957. Recorded by the Holly Twins, featuring Eddie Cochran on guitar. The song was composed by Bobby Darin and Don Kirshner.

I'LL WAIT FOREVER
(Sun 361)
1961. Recorded by Anita Wood. The song was recorded by Elvis's former girlfriend, who after Elvis was inducted into the Army didn't wait forever—not even two years.

(Photo courtesy Don Fink)

I'M HANGIN' UP MY RIFLE
(Fraternity 861)
1959. Recorded by Bobby Bare as a follow-up to his miscredited hit "All American Boy." "I'm Hangin' Up My Rifle" was sung to the melody of "All American Boy."

I'M IN LOVE WITH ELVIS PRESLEY
(Melba 107)
1956. Recorded by Virginia Lowe.

IN LOVE WITH ELVIS
(Cinema CR-7516A)
1975. Recorded by the Real Pros.

THE KING (DON'T BE CRUEL)
(Epic 7645)
1971. Recorded by the Berries, a British group.

THE KING IS COMING BACK
(Top Rank RA-2017)
1959. Recorded by Billy and Eddie, and pertaining to Elvis's Army discharge.

THE KING IS COMING HOME
(McDowell 685)
1960. Recorded by Tony Senn.

KING OF ROCK & ROLL
(Ace 3011)
1975. Recorded by Mack Allen Smith.

LEAVE MY SIDEBURNS BE
(Mercury 70999)
1956. Recorded by Steve Schickel, a disc jockey at Chicago radio station WGN. The song was sung as a parody of "Blue Suede Shoes," in response to a report that Elvis was to be drafted.

LONELY THIS CHRISTMAS
(RAK 187)
1974. Recorded by Mud, a British group. The song, in which Elvis is wished a "Merry Christmas," went to number one in the U.K. for four weeks.

MARCHIN' ELVIS
(Ebb 145)
1958. Recorded by the Greats.

MEMORIES OF YOU
(Santo S-9008)
1961. Recorded by Anita Wood, Elvis's former girlfriend.

MEMPHIS MIRACLE
(Claridge 406 BS)
1975. Recorded by Sky Keegan.

MY BABY'S CRAZY ABOUT ELVIS
(Capitol 72071)
Recorded by Mike Sarne. This was a Canadian release.

MY BABY'S CRAZY 'BOUT ELVIS
(Decca F-11503)
1962. Recorded by Billy Boyle. This was a British release.

MY BOY ELVIS
(RCA 47-6652)
1956. Recorded by Janis Martin, who was billed by RCA as "The Female Elvis."

OH ELVIS!
(Pyramid PY-4012B)
Recorded by Reed Harper and the 3 Notes.

OH! IT WAS ELVIS
(Nancy 1004)
1961. Recorded by Carmela Rosella.

POUND DOG
(L&M 1000)
1956. Recorded by Lalo Guerrero.

PRESLEY ON HER MIND
(Reserve 118)
1957. Recorded by Don Hart.

RETURN OF THE ALL AMERICAN BOY
(Nau-Voo 805)
1959. Recorded by Billy Adams. This record is unique in that it is an answer record to an Elvis novelty record.

THE ROCK ERA (A TRIBUTE TO THE KING), PART 1/THE ROCK ERA (A TRIBUTE TO THE KING), PART 2
(Patti 10000)
1973. Recorded by the Phantom of Rock, which was a pseudonym of singer Wayne Stierle.

ROCK 'N' ROLL ABC'S
(MCA 40269)
1974. Recorded by Freddy Cannon.

THE ROOTS OF ELVIS: /"THE BILLY GOAT SONG"/"SWINGIN' IN THE ORCHARD"/ "WHO'S KICKIN' MY DOG AROUND"
(Legacy Park PK-2000)
1958. Recorded by Grandpa Jessie Presley, Elvis's paternal grandfather.

THE STORY OF ELVIS
(Drumfire DF-2)
1960. Recorded by Jim Ford.

TENNESSEE HERO (ELVIS)
(Pye 7N-45460)
1975. Recorded by Johnny Wakelin. This was a British release.

TUPELO, MISSISSIPPI FLASH
(RCA Victor 47-9334)
1967. Recorded by Jerry Reed, a friend of Elvis's.

TUPELO, MISSISSIPPI FLASH
(Parrot 40048)
1970. Recorded by Tom Jones, a friend of Elvis's. This was the flip side to "Daughter of Darkness."

(Photo courtesy Don Fink)

WHEN ELVIS MARCHES HOME AGAIN
(Viva 61)
1960. Recorded by the Sophisticates.

WHEN THE SERGEANT COMES MARCHING HOME
(Glover 202)
1960. Recorded by Titus Turner.

WHERE'S ELVIS
(Planet 1001)
1958. Recorded by Anonymous.

Tribute Records

AL WEET JE NIET WIE PRESLEY
(RKM 4B006-99551)
1977. Recorded by Joe Harris. Belgian release.

AMICO ELVIS/TO ELVIS
(CGD 10040)
1977. Recorded by the Magical Music Circus. Side 1 was recorded in Italian and side 2 in English.

ANGEL FROM HEAVEN
(Magic Touch MT-9009)
1978. Recorded by Rick Ardesano.

AUGUST 16 (ELVIS PRESLEY DAY)/
KING ELVIS, THE GREATEST
(Gur 3378)
1978. Recorded by Jimmy Busby.

AUGUST 16, 1977 (ELVIS)
(Universal A-1002)
????. Recorded by Ray Smith.

THE BALLAD OF ELVIS PRESLEY
(Larupin 100)
1977. Recorded by Rita Bevis and the California Gold.

BIG AS MEMPHIS (THE KING 35-77)/ROCK 'N'
ROLL HALL OF FAME
(Hot Rock HR45-005)
1980. Recorded by the Memphis Tenor C's. This was a British release.

BLUE CHRISTMAS/BLUE CHRISTMAS
(INSTRUMENTAL)
(Concorde CCD-23)
1977. Recorded by Johnny Farago. This was a Canadian release.

BLUE CHRISTMAS (WITHOUT ELVIS)
(Appaloosa AP 112)
1977. Recorded by Leigh Grady.

BLUE SUEDE SHOES (TRIBUTE TO ELVIS)/
READY TEDDY
(Mark 003)
1977. Recorded by Danny Fisher and released in Belgium.

BLUEST CHRISTMAS EVER/
ELVIS, GOD'S READY FOR A SONG
(Phono P-2658)
1977. Recorded by Chris Marshon.

THE BOY FROM TUPELO
(Noble NR 3130)
1979. Recorded by the Blue Ridge Mountain Girls.

(Photo courtesy Don Fink)

CANDY BARS FOR ELVIS/
CANDY BARS FOR ELVIS
(Tiffin International TI-300)
1977. Recorded by Barry Tiffan.

CAPRICORN KINGS
(Prairie Dust PD 7628)
1978. Recorded by Lee Wright.

A CHRISTMAS LETTER TO DADDY
(RTF 101)
1977. Recorded by Wilguis J. C. Raynor and Donna Jo.

A CHRISTMAS TRIBUTE TO ELVIS AND BING
(Polydor PD 14444)
1977. Recorded by Bob Luman, as a tribute to Elvis and Bing Crosby, both of whom died in 1977.

CHRISTMAS WITHOUT ELVIS/
CHRISTMAS CARD FOR ELVIS
(Delta 1151)
1978. Recorded by Patsy Sexton.

THE COLONEL AND THE KING
(Gusto GT4-9009)
1978. Recorded by Billy Joe Burnette.

CRY, CRY A FEW TEARS FOR ELVIS
(Allied Artists 008)
1977. Recorded by Leda Ray.

CRYING 'BOUT ELVIS
(Adam's Rib 1112)
1977. Recorded by the Songwriters.

**DARK CLOUD OVER MEMPHIS/
DARK CLOUD OVER MEMPHIS**
(Klub KL-5515)
1977. Recorded by Johnny Tollison.

THE DAY THE BEAT STOPPED
(Thunder TD-7801)
1978. Recorded by Ral Donner.

**DEAR ELVIS/ I DON'T KNOW WHERE
I'M GOING (GOODBYE TO THE KING)**
(Sagitario JS 500B)
1977. Recorded by Jimmy Staggs.

DEAR ELVIS/MEMORIES
(Rome RF 10309)
1980. Recorded by Dell Green and Jim Burlison. "Dear Elvis" used the same arrangement as Elvis's "An American Trilogy."

DEAR ELVIS PRESLEY, GOODBYE
(Command Performance 390)
1979. Recorded by the Tune Timers.

DEDICATED TO A KING
(MCM 007533)
1977. Recorded by Terry Turner.

**DISCO TO THE KING (PART 1)/
DISCO TO THE KING (PART 2)**
(Smash Disco SS 9706)
1977. Recorded by Douglas Roy and released on a 12-inch single.

D.O.A.
(Sun 1136)
1977. Recorded by Misty (actually, Tanya Tucker). The flip side featured "That's All Right (Mama)"/"Blue Moon of Kentucky" by Jimmy Ellis.

DO YOU REMEMBER
(Polydor 2121341)
1977. Recorded by Long Tall Ernie and the Shakers. This was a British release.

**DO YOU REMEMBER THE KING/
DO YOU REMEMBER THE KING (Instrumental)**
(Vandor BFI 13)
1977. Recorded by Polidori.

DR. PLEASE
(Gusto GT 4-9025)
1979. Recorded by Joe Scaife.

DON'T CRY LISA
(Heartsong IRDA-458)
1977. Recorded by Pamela Nichols.

A DREAM ABOUT ELVIS
(Dream Enterprises DESS-81280)
1980. Recorded by Roy Boren.

(ELVIS PRESLEY) EL REY DEL ROCK 'N' ROLL
(Teardrop TD 3397)
1977. Recorded by Juan Ramos.

ELVIS/ELVIS
(Westbound WB 55405)
1977. Recorded by Tom Durden. This song was sung to the tune of "Love Me Tender."

ELVIS/ELVIS
(Memory 38655)
1977. Recorded by Eddie Karr. This song was sung to the tune of "You'll Never Walk Alone."

ELVIS
(Disques Motors 2097226 EA)
1977. Recorded by Romain. This was a French release sung to the tune of "Love Me Tender."

ELVIS, A LEGENDARY ANGEL/FORGET ME NEVER
(Starr SF 9277)
1977. Recorded by Melody Lloyd.

ELVIS AND MARILYN
(Paradise PDS 8667)
1978. Recorded by Leon Russell. "Marilyn" was Marilyn Monroe.

ELVIS, CHRISTMAS WON'T BE CHRISTMAS WITHOUT YOU
(Country Jubilee CJ 0101)
1977. Recorded by Paul White.

ELVIS/DADDY'S GONE BYE BYE
(Blue Candle 1525)
1977. Recorded by Jenny Nicholas.

**ELVIS DREAMED AND IT CAME TRUE/
I DREAMED ELVIS SANG MY SONG**
(Dale IRDA-437)
1977. Recorded by Don Todd.

ELVIS FOREVER
(Philips 6021)
1977. Recorded by Jimmy Frey.

ELVIS: FROM US TO YOU
(Independent Sound LSPD-101)
1978. Recorded by Rufus Bill Whitehouse. This was sung to the tune of "Don't Be Cruel."

ELVIS, GONE BUT NOT FORGOTTEN
(Fleetwood 45-7711-1A)
1978. Recorded by Terry Nunley.

ELVIS GOODBYE/IMPRESSIONS
(Kimray KF-81677)
1977. Recorded by Bobby Freeman. "Elvis Goodbye" was sung to the tune of "Are You Lonesome Tonight?," while the flip side featured impressions of Elvis ("In the Ghetto"), Little Richard ("Lucille"), Neil Diamond ("Sweet Caroline"), the Big Bopper ("Chantilly Lace"), Buddy Holly ("Peggy Sue"), and Jerry Lee Lewis ("You Win Again").

ELVIS'S GREATEST SHOW
(Fox Fire 110)
1979. Recorded by Johnny Rystl.

ELVIS'S GREATEST SHOW
(K.E.Y. K 8666)
1978. Recorded by Ken Scott.

ELVIS HAD TWO ANGELS/ELVIS DREAMED AND IT CAME TRUE/SHE PLACED A ROSE ON ELVIS PRESLEY'S GRAVE/HE LEFT BEHIND SO MANY MEMORIES
(Dale NR 9950)
1978. Recorded by Sheila Norton (cuts 1 and 3) and by Al Ragsdale (cuts 2 and 4).

ELVIS HAS LEFT THE BUILDING
(QCA 461)
1977. Recorded by J. D. Sumner.

ELVIS, HOW COULD I RESIST/
ELVIS, HOW COULD I RESIST (Instrumental)
(Amour AM 8425)
1977. Recorded by Birds of a Feather.

ELVIS IN HEAVEN/ELVIS IN HEAVEN
(BI 5043)
1978. Recorded by Johnny Murrell.

ELVIS IN HEAVEN
(Texas Tornado DM 4845)
1978. Recorded by Norman Schilt.

ELVIS IN HEAVEN
(Born Again 358)
1978. Recorded by Jesse King.

ELVIS IN MEMORIAM/ELVIS IN MEMORIAM
(International 104AF)
1978. Recorded by Ben Wages.

ELVIS IS A LEGEND
(DeeBee DEB 20)
1977. Recorded by B. F. Snow.

ELVIS IS GONE (BUT HIS SPIRIT LIVES ON)
(Lil' Elvis World 114-62)
1977. Recorded by Bob (Lil' Elvis) Harrison.

ELVIS IS GONE (BUT NOT FORGOTTEN)
(QCA 463)
1977. Recorded by Con Archer. Although recorded in Canada, it was released only in the United States.

ELVIS IT'S TRUE SAD AND BLUE
(Mansion MA-4515)
1977. Recorded by the Country Dreamers.

ELVIS, KING OF ROCK AND ROLL
(MSR Records 2611-EK0)
1978. Recorded by Dick Kent.

ELVIS MAGIC
(Bonny T.S.S. 3253)
1978. Recorded by Bonnie Angelo.

ELVIS, OUR KING
(Command Performance 404)
1979. Recorded by the Tune Timers.

ELVIS PRESLEY BOOGIE
(Showland SL 2202)
1978. Recorded by Bennie Hess.

ELVIS SERENADE/
ELVIS SERENADE (Instrumental)
(Best Seller 4B006-60122)
1977. Recorded by Valery Pascale and the Soul Affair Orchestra. This was a Belgian release.

ELVIS THE KING
(Music Emporium VMRFP 1176)
1977. Recorded by Jim Matthews ("The Singing Surgeon").

ELVIS, THE MAN FROM TUPELO/
ELVIS, THE MAN FROM TUPELO
(Bar-Tone BR 77169)
1977. Recorded by George Pickard.

ELVIS, WE LOVE YOU/ELVIS, WE LOVE YOU
(Gusto-Starday SD 166)
1977. Recorded by Terry Tigre (real name: Terry Cobb).

ELVIS, WE MISS YOU
(Seaside SSB 050/010)
1981. Recorded by Danny Stanley.

ELVIS, WE MISS YOU
(Emery NR 8809)
1978. Recorded by Bill Yates.

ELVIS WE MISS YOU/MOODY BLUE
(Triple J069A)
1980. Recorded by Johnny Lawson.

ELVIS, WE MISS YOU TONIGHT
(American Sound AS 3090)

(Photo courtesy Don Fink)

1977. Recorded by Ron McKee and sung to the tune of "Are You Lonesome Tonight?"

**ELVIS, WE'RE SORRY WE FENCED YOU IN/
ELVIS, WE'RE SORRY WE FENCED YOU IN
(Instrumental)
(Shane 7101-12A)**
1977. Recorded by Jack Brand.

**ELVIS WON'T BE HERE FOR CHRISTMAS
(Great Northwest Music Co.)**
1979. Recorded by Linda Hughes. This was a Canadian release.

**ET LA VOIX D'ELVIS
(Barclay 620.373)**
1977. Recorded in France by Eddy Mitchell.

**FOR ELVIS
(Texas CR-1004)**
1977. Recorded by Frankie Rich and the Nashville East.

**FOR ELVIS, THE WORLD CRIES
(Perfection Sound Studios 665)**
1977. Recorded by Beth Peterson.

**A FRIEND I NEVER KNEW
(Sonic 3030)**
1977. Recorded by Phil Orsi and sung to the tune of "Love Me Tender."

**FROM GRACELAND TO THE PROMISED LAND/
ARE YOU LONESOME TONIGHT?
(MCA 40804)**
1977. Recorded by Merle Haggard. Both songs were

excerpted from Haggard's tribute album *From Graceland to the Promised Land*, on which the Jordanaires sang backup. On the A side Haggard incorrectly referred to both Elvis and his mother dying at the same age.

**FROM GRACELAND TO THE PROMISED LAND
(Tank BSS-304)**
1977. Recorded by Pete Nelson.

**(MERRY CHRISTMAS) FROM LISA MARIE
(Rock-It RI 501)**
1979. Recorded by Jana Sampson.

**THE GATE
(Worldwide Memorial Fan Club 2001)**
1977. Recorded by George Owens.

**GOD BROUGHT THE CURTAIN DOWN
(Shane S-001)**
1977. Recorded by Shilo.

**GOD CALLED ELVIS HOME/
ELVIS FOR JUST AN HOUR OR TWO
(Nif 1001 and Phono 2657)**
1977. Recorded by Chris Marshon.

**GOODBYE BING, ELVIS AND GUY
(Little Gem LG 1022)**
1977. Recorded by Diana Williams. Tribute record to Bing Crosby, Elvis, and Guy Lombardo.

**GOODBYE ELVIS/
GOODBYE ELVIS (Instrumental)
(Formule I 49-307)**
1977. Recorded by Ringo to the tune of "Such a Night." Released in France.

**GOODBYE ELVIS
(Lew Breyer Productions 77-178)**
1977. Recorded by Jim Whittington.

**GOODBYE ELVIS
(Arti Beno 1062)**
1977. Recorded by Ron Scott and released in Belgium.

**GOODBYE ELVIS
(Topkapi 2130 127A) Flemish version
(Topkapi 2133 128A) English version
(Tonpress R 0838) Polish version**
1977. Recorded by Will Tura.

**GOODBYE ELVIS
(Xclusive 2536A-S)**
1978. Recorded by A Tint of Darkness.

**GOODBYE KING OF ROCK 'N' ROLL
(True T-107)**
1977. Recorded by Leon Everette. Excerpted from his album *Goodbye King of Rock 'n' Roll*.

GOODBYE PRISCILLA (BYE BYE BLUE BABY)
(Teardrop TD-3405)
1977. Recorded by Gene Summers. The labels were misprinted. The correct title is "Goodbye Priscilla (Bye Bye Baby Blue)."

GOODNIGHT ELVIS/HEY GINGERBREAD
(Laurie LR 3660)
1977. Recorded by the Teardrops. Elvis's nickname for Ginger Alden was "Gingerbread."

THE GRACELAND KING OF ROCK
(Sweetland SW-001)
1978. Recorded by Mack Fishburn. Sung to the tune of "Love Me Tender."

THE GREATEST STAR OF THEM ALL
(Alaska ALA-2010)
1977. Recorded by Skip Jackson. This was a British release.

HAPPY BIRTHDAY ELVIS/
I NEED YOUR LOVE TONIGHT
(Page PR 1001)
1978. Recorded by Cliff Stout to the tune of "Are You Lonesome Tonight?"

HAPPY BIRTHDAY ELVIS (WE WISH YOU WERE HERE)/HAPPY BIRTHDAY ELVIS (WE WISH YOU WERE HERE) (Instrumental)
(Jet Sounds SO 16004/5)
1978. Recorded by Perry White.

HE LIVES (A TRIBUTE TO ELVIS)
(Chapman D-1118A)
1977. Recorded by Tarry Westley.

HERE'S TO THE KING
(Fable FB 310)
1977. Recorded by Josh Morgan. This was an Australian import.

HEROES AND IDOLS
(MDJ DS 1004)
1979. Recorded by David Smith.

HIS LEGEND LIVES ON
(Marshall NR 8735)
????. Recorded by Sheriff Dave and the Road Gang.

(ELVIS) HIS LEGEND'S STILL ALIVE
(IT'S GREAT TO HAVE AN IDOL) PART 1/
(ELVIS) HIS LEGEND'S STILL ALIVE
(IT'S GREAT TO HAVE AN IDOL) PART 2
(Encore VIP-1775)
1977. Recorded by Ray Hebel.

HIS MISSION/HE MUST BE SINGIN'
(Geri Mac B)
1979. Recorded by Gerri McQueen.

HOUND DOG MAN
(October 1013)
1977. Recorded by the Rubberband with Tommy Stuart.

HOUND DOG MAN
(Capitol P-4769)
1979. Recorded by Glen Campbell.

HOUND DOG MAN'S GONE HOME
(Music Mill MM 1012)
1977. Recorded by Arthur Alexander.

HOUND DOG MAN'S GONE HOME
(Music Mill MM 1011)
1977. Recorded by Lee and Lowe.

(Photo courtesy Don Fink)

I JUST WANTED YOU TO KNOW
(Scorpion SC 0553)
1978. Recorded as an open letter to Elvis by Ronnie McDowell and the Jordanaires.

I REMEMBER ELVIS
(WB Country Sound WB-7700)
1977. Recorded by Roy Williams.

I REMEMBER ELVIS PRESLEY
(Tonpress R 0797)
1978. Recorded in Poland by Danny Mirror.

I REMEMBER ELVIS
(Opus 91 43 0438)
1978. Recorded by Gustav Offerman. Czechoslovakian import.

I REMEMBER ELVIS PRESLEY/I REMEMBER ELVIS PRESLEY (Instrumental)
(Poker POS 15023)
1977. Recorded by Danny Mirror in Belgium. Includes the songs "Are You Lonesome Tonight?" and "Can't Help Falling In Love."

I REMEMBER ELVIS PRESLEY
(Tonpress S-259)
1979. Recorded in Poland by Mario Hribersek.

I SING THIS SONG FOR ELVIS
(Mercury 6198 171)
1977. Recorded by Terry Lee. This was a Dutch release.

IF IT WASN'T FOR ELVIS
(Paul, Dale, Tom & Ray 001)
1977. Recorded by Deke Rivers and the Hansen Brothers.

IL NE CHANTERA PLUS JAMAIS/
55m DE GAULOIS
(CBS 5896)
1977. Recorded by Petula Clark. Produced in France.

I'M NOT TRYING TO BE LIKE ELVIS
(Boblo BO 536)
1978. Recorded by Jimmy Ellis.

IS THE KING DEAD?
(Brand BX-00)
1978. Recorded by Arkey Tunstall.

IT'S BEEN A YEAR ELVIS
(E Records 77203)
1978. Recorded by Elgin Mann. This was a Canadian release.

JUST A COUNTRY BOY
(Rockfield UP 36337)
1977. Recorded by Frankie Allen and produced in Great Britain.

JUST FOR YOU DAD/JUST FOR YOU DAD
(Thor 20928)
1979. Recorded by Eldorado.

JUST SMILE AND SAY
HE SINGS FOR THE MASTER TODAY
(Shields 333)
1981. Recorded by Spring.

THE KING IS DEAD/THE KING IS DEAD
(The Scene SPO 1487)
1977. Recorded by Ronnie Kaye.

THE KING IS FREE (LOVE ME)
(LeCam LC 7277AAA)
1977. Recorded by Bruce Channel and Major Bill Smith.

THE KING IS GONE
(Scorpion GRT 135)
1977. Recorded by Ronnie McDowell. Upon learning of Elvis's death, Ronnie McDowell and Lee Morgan sat down that very evening and wrote this song, which became the fastest-selling single of 1977, reaching the million sales mark only five days after release.

THE KING IS GONE
(Concorde CCD 18)
1977. Recorded by Johnny Farago. Released in Canada.

THE KING IS GONE
(Release 900)
1977. Recorded by Charlie Murphy.

THE KING IS GONE
(CMM 001)
1977. Recorded by Ricky Tightrope.

THE KING OF BLUE SUEDE SOUL (IN MEMORY OF ELVIS)/JAILHOUSE ROCK
(Eclipse 1732)
1977. Recorded by Rick Saucedo, an Elvis imitator.

THE KING OF ROCK (HAS MET THE KING)
(Aspire 334)
1977. Recorded by Denny Reed.

KING OF ROCK & ROLL
(Dover D 1001)
1977. Recorded by Gary Edwards.

KING OF ROCK AND ROLL
(Polydor 2054-201)
1978. Recorded in West Germany by Olson.

THE KING OF ROCK 'N' ROLL
(WHY MUST A YOUNG MAN DIE)
(CBS 5713)
1977. Recorded by Drafti in West Germany.

KING OF ROCK & ROLL SONG
(CMA 001)
1978. Recorded by Chris Smith.

KING UPON THE THRONE
(Quest QI 45)
1977. Recorded by Neil Arthurs and released in Canada.

THE KING'S LAST CONCERT
(Gusto-Starday SD 180)
1978. Recorded by Red Sovine.

THE LAST ENCORE
(Webcore W 101)
1977. Recorded by Jim Fagen.

**LE KING N'EST PLUS/
DONNE MOI UN PEU DE TENDRESSE
(Concorde CCD 17)**
1977. Recorded by Johnny Farago. French versions of his tribute release "The King Is Gone"/"Surrender."

**THE LEGEND LIVES
(Canovan CV45-001A)**
1980. Recorded by Jim Van Hollebeke, author of the column "For Elvis Fans Only" in *Goldmine* magazine.

**THE LEGEND LIVES ON/
HOW GREAT THOU ART
(Fraternity 3416)**
1978. Recorded by Rick Saucedo, with vocal backup by the Jordanaires, and D. J. Fontana on drums.

**THE LEGEND OF A KING
(Paper Dragon 438)**
1977. Recorded by Warren Jacks.

**THE LEGEND OF ELVIS PRESLEY
(Professional Artists PAS 774588)**
1977. Recorded by Dub Crouch.

**LET THE KING REST
(DNO 0048)**
1979. Recorded by Doug Roberts.

**LET'S LET ELVIS GET SOME SLEEP
(Showcase SC 1023)**
1979. Recorded by Pat Minter.

**THE LETTER FROM ELVIS
(Eastern EST 01)**
1978. Recorded by Bill Tolson and the Jordanaires.

(Photo courtesy Don Fink)

**A LETTER TO ELVIS
(Little Gem LG 1020A)**
1977. Recorded by Odie Palmer.

**A LETTER TO ELVIS
(Magic Carpet 506)**
1979. Recorded by Michelle Prehle before Elvis's death and released afterward.

**THE LIFE OF ELVIS
(Moon M 1003)**
1977. Recorded by Pam Cassidy.

**LISA/I WAS THE ONE
(Mimi MR 2-26-78)**
1978. Recorded by Doug Demarche.

**LISA DADDY LOVES YOU/
THE BALLAD OF A KING
(Sly Fox JA2879)**
1979. Recorded by Bob Haley.

**LITTLE LISA
(Columbia 2324)**
1979. Recorded by Billy Gibson.

**A LONELY CHRISTMAS (WITHOUT ELVIS
PRESLEY)/A LONELY CHRISTMAS (WITHOUT
ELVIS PRESLEY) (Instrumental)
(Monopole 618)**
1977. Recorded by Buzz Jefferson in Belgium.

**THE LONELY KING OF ROCK & ROLL
(Via 81677)**
1977. Recorded by P. Sterling Radcliffe and His Sterling Sounds.

**LOVE HIM TENDER, SWEET JESUS
(Rice RR 5075)**
1977. Recorded by David Price.

**THE MAN CALLED ELVIS
(LAC UR-1362)**
1978. Recorded by Shela Horton to the tune of "How Great Thou Art" with narration by Bob Bowen.

**MEMORIES OF THE KING/MEMORIES OF THE
KING
(Memory 244)**
1977. Recorded by Elvis Wade (Cummins), an Elvis imitator.

**THE MEMORY OF ELVIS PRESLEY
(Cinema CR 7836)**
1978. Recorded by the Real Pros.

**MEMPHIS COWBOY/MEMPHIS COWBOY
(Honey Bee HB 2007)**
1977. Recorded by Danny Roberts.

MERCI ELVIS/MERCI ELVIS
(DJ DJS-002)
1980. Recorded by Pontiac in France.

MERRY CHRISTMAS ELVIS
(Safari SA 601)
1978. Recorded by Michele Cody.

MERRY CHRISTMAS ELVIS/
I'M SO LONESOME I COULD CRY
(Spin Chek SO-16021)
1978. Recorded by Paul White.

A MESSAGE FROM ELVIS
(Rich Tone 8109-1)
1981. Recorded by Jimmy Teasley.

A MESSAGE TO ELVIS FANS AND MY FRIENDS/
A MESSAGE TO ELVIS FANS AND MY FRIENDS
(Ves Pres WIM REC-1)
1979. Recorded by Vester Presley, Elvis's uncle.

MY DARLING GINGER
(LeCam LC 512)
1978. Recorded by Jimmy Luke and Bruce Channel and sung to the tune "Since I Met You, Baby." The title referred to Ginger Alden.

MY FATHER WATCHES OVER ME
(Age of Woman AOW 7144B)
1978. Recorded by Kathy Westmoreland, who sang the song at Elvis's funeral on August 18, 1977, as well as at the dedication in Tupelo of the Elvis Presley Memorial Chapel on August 17, 1979.

MY FRIEND ELVIS
(AAA-Aron 001)
1977. Recorded by the Hansen Brothers.

MY HEART'S CONTENT
(GOODBYE FROM THE KING)
(RTF 100)
1977. Recorded by Wilguis J. C. Raynor.

MY HERO
(Rubber ADUB-14)
1977. Recorded by Jackie Lyston. British release.

MY LITTLE GIRL'S PRAYER (FOR ELVIS)
(King's International KM 5099)
1977. Recorded by Kelly Leroux and Little Stacy King.

1935, BIRTH OF A LEGEND
(T.H.E. Records)
1977. Recorded by Jimmy Carr.

NEVER AGAIN (WILL THERE BE
ANOTHER KING OF ROCK & ROLL)
(Little Gem LG 1042)
1977. Recorded by Gene Jones.

NEW ANGEL TONIGHT
(A TRIBUTE TO ELVIS' MOTHER)
(Marathon RRD 502)
1958. Recorded by Red River Dave (Dave McEmery) as a tribute record to Gladys Presley, who had just died.

A NEW BEGINNING/OH YES HE'S GONE
(Hillside HS 77-08A)
1977. Recorded by Tom Holbrook.

A NEW STAR IN HEAVEN
(Dove 100)
1977. Recorded by Wally Fowler. The song also appears on his album *A Tribute to Elvis* (Dove 1000).

A NEW STAR IN HEAVEN
(Century 44836)
1977. Recorded by Banny Bannister.

OUR ELVIS
(MCM AA007531A)
1977. Recorded by Sherry King.

THE PASSING OF A KING
(Arco A 104)
1977. Recorded by Tony Copeland.

A PRAYER FOR ELVIS/
A MESSAGE FROM HAROLD
(Modern Age Enterprises)
1979. Recorded by Harold Lloyd, Elvis's uncle.

PRECIOUS MEMORIES OF ELVIS
(A BEDTIME STORY)
(Bejay 11079)
1977. Recorded by Don Barnes and Christi.

PRECIOUS MEMORIES OF ELVIS
(Miracle 7777)
1977. Recorded by Betty Hamar.

A PRESLEY MEDLEY
(LeCam LC 1117)
1978. Recorded by Bruce Channel with Bill, Larry, and Gene.

PRESLEY, THE KING (CADILLAC MAN)/
PRESLEY, THE KING (CADILLAC MAN)
(High Country SG-108)
1977. Recorded by Angelmaye North.

PRISCILLA/HE'LL NEVER BE LONELY AGAIN
(Dove DRI 2177)
1977. Recorded by Wally Fowler.

REFLECTIONS OF A MAN (ELVIS)
(Tap TR 5378)
1979. Recorded by Terry Hutchinson.

REQUIEM FOR ELVIS
(LeCam LC-12802)
1980. Recorded by Major Bill Smith.

REQUIEM FOR ELVIS
(Raintree RT-2206)
1977. Recorded by Jackie Kahane.

REQUIEM FOR ELVIS/
REQUIEM FOR ELVIS (Instrumental)
(Philips 6202.006)
1977. Recorded in West Germany by Regina.

ROCK & ROLL HEAVEN
(Aquarius Records)
1978. Recorded by Oliver Klaus.

ROCK & ROLL KING/ROCK & ROLL KING
(Instrumental)
(C.J. Records 675A)
1977. Recorded by Carl Jones.

ROCK ELVIS ROCK
(MCM 007527)
1977. Recorded by Clifford Clay.

ROCK ON AND ON AND ON
(Chart Action CA 114)
1977. Recorded by Doug Koempel.

ROCKIN' & ROLLIN' MAN
(LVG 336H)
1978. Recorded by L. Guardine.

(Photo courtesy Don Fink)

SALUTE TO ELVIS
(TSC 305)
1979. Recorded by Dorothy Carlson and Ray Jones.

THE SKY'S OVER GRACELAND
(Deltron DRP-3562)
1979. Recorded by Johnny Mac.

SOMEWHERE ELVIS IS SMILING/SOMEWHERE
ELVIS IS SMILING
(Nu-Sound 77N-422)
1977. Recorded by Keith Bradford.

A SONG ABOUT ELVIS
(Eagle VMR 1286)
1979. Recorded by Tommy Holly.

SOUL SALUTE TO ELVIS
(Fraternity 3406)
1977. Recorded by Larry and Vicky to the tune of "Jailhouse Rock."

SPEAKING TO ELVIS IN HEAVEN
(Timey 79 x 04)
1977. Recorded by P. M. Smith.

STATUE OF ELVIS
(Compass C-009)
1977. Recorded by Roger McDowell.

SWINGING DOWN IN MEMPHIS TOWN
(WHERE ELVIS WAS THE KING)
(Alpha AR 285)
1980. Recorded by Barry Dea.

THANK YOU, ELVIS
(Hawk HASP 411)
1977. Recorded by Brendon (Big Eight) Boyer in Ireland.

THERE'LL NEVER BE ANOTHER PRESLEY
(Dolphin D-212)
1977. Recorded by Gil Thomas.

THERE'S A BRAND NEW STAR
(Owl 197712)
1977. Recorded by Paul Adkins. Sung to the tune of "Are You Lonesome Tonight?"

TITLES OF THE KING
(Show Me Music 10921)
1977. Recorded by Gene Tucker.

TO ELVIS/TRIBUTE (Instrumental)
(Treehouse TH-12510)
1979. Recorded by Brenda Joyce.

TO ELVIS IN HEAVEN
(American Sound AS-3096)
1977. Recorded by Vicki Knight.

TO ELVIS, LOVE
(Music City MR-NO-102878)
1978. Recorded by Nell Owens.

TO THE MEMORY OF ELVIS/LISA MY LOVE
(Brougham BRM 0009)
1977. "To the Memory of Elvis" was recorded by Ann Haywood, and "Lisa My Love" was recorded by Dorris Haywood.

TOO MANY KINGS
(Encore VIP 178S-A)
1977. Recorded by the Bush Band.

A TRIBUTE TO A KING
(Okie NR 5597)
1977. Recorded by Bobby Wallace.

TRIBUTE TO A KING/
GIRL OF MY BEST FRIEND
(Honey 007)
1977. Recorded by Billy Joe Ward.

TRIBUTE TO ELVIS
(SCR-1347)
1977. Recorded by Tom Kelly.

A TRIBUTE TO ELVIS
(T.C.B. 9317)
1977. Recorded by Gary Walker.

A TRIBUTE TO ELVIS/A TRIBUTE TO HANK WILLIAMS
(Artist 781117)
1977. Recorded by Wink West and the 49ers.

A TRIBUTE TO ELVIS
(Riverside 047)
1977. Recorded by Chip Canterbury.

A TRIBUTE TO ELVIS
(Demo NR 8695-1)
1977. Recorded by Billy Crain.

A TRIBUTE TO ELVIS
(Tink TK 736)
1977. Recorded by Tink Grimmett.

A TRIBUTE TO ELVIS (PART 1)/
A TRIBUTE TO ELVIS (PART 2)
(Barclay 620.386)
1977. Recorded by the Rock Odyssey.

A TRIBUTE TO ELVIS
(A MEMORY—WE DIDN'T GET ENOUGH OF YOU)
(Pickin' Post NR 8830-1)
1977. Recorded by Nancy Jewell.

A TRIBUTE TO ELVIS: MEMORIES OF YOU/
A TRIBUTE TO ELVIS: MEMORIES OF YOU
(American Sound AS-3102)
1977. Recorded by Connie Lynne.

A TRIBUTE TO THE KING/
A TRIBUTE TO THE KING
(Tribute TR 001)
1977. Recorded by H. Fillingane using the same arrangement as "An American Trilogy."

A TRIBUTE TO THE KING OF R & R (FROM THE KING OF THE GOLDEN OLDIES)/
A TRIBUTE TO THE KING OF R & R (FROM THE KING OF THE GOLDEN OLDIES)
(No label or number)
1977. Recorded by Jim Camilli, the "King of Golden Oldies."

THE TROUBADOUR FROM MEMPHIS
(Lighthouse CD-3000)
1977. Recorded by Jean Sampson.

TUPELO, MISSISSIPPI, SON/
TUPELO, MISSISSIPPI, SON
(Moon Pie NO 1980)
1977. Recorded by John Moseley.

WE LOVED HIM TENDER
(Artist 780529)
1978. Recorded by Vernon Himes.

WELCOME HOME ELVIS
(Bertram International 45-1835)
1977. Recorded by Daddy Bob.

WELCOME HOME ELVIS
(Gusto-Starday SD 167)
1977. Recorded by Billy Joe Burnette, the son of Dorsey Burnette. This song also appears on his album *Welcome Home Elvis*.

(Photo courtesy Don Fink)

WE'LL HAVE A BLUE CHRISTMAS, ELVIS
(Music Emporium VMMP-7029)
1977. Recorded by Jim Matthews ("The Singing Surgeon").

WE'LL REMEMBER YOU
(El-Vee UMRP-1355)
1978. Recorded by Andy Michaels.

WE'RE SURE GONNA MISS YOU, OLD FRIEND
(Constellation CR 001)
1977. Recorded by Jack Hickox.

WHAT WILL WE DO WITHOUT YOU?
(Mark 004)
1978. Recorded by Bobby Fisher.

WHO WOULD DARE TRY/GRACELAND
(Delta A1152)
1977. Recorded by Patsy Sexton.

WHOLE WORLD MISSES YOU (ELVIS WE LOVE YOU)
(Jet 117)
1978. Recorded by Carl Perkins. This was a British release.

WHO'S GONNA SING
(Cosmopolitan 1006)
1977. Recorded by Trolly.

THE WORLD LOVES YOU ELVIS
(Rome RF 1017)
1977. Recorded by Wesley Gillespie.

YOU WERE THE MUSIC
(Age of Woman 5789A)
1978. Recorded by Kathy Westmoreland.

YOUR MEMORY IN MY MIND/
MY FRIEND ELVIS/IF IT WASN'T FOR ELVIS
(Starfire S 102)
1978. Recorded by the Hansen Brothers.

Novelty and Tribute Albums

ALAN PRESENTS THE ELVIS PRESLEY STORY
(Worldwide Presentation)
1974. Recorded by Alan Meyer.

BALLADS OF THE KING
(Liberty LRP 3198)
1961. Recorded by the Johnny Mann Singers.

THE BEST OF PER "ELVIS" GRANBERG
(Phillips 6478 031)
1974. Recorded by Per (Elvis) Granberg. Released in Norway.

BIG EL SHOW "IN CONCERT"
(Castle NS-1007)
1977. Recorded by Larry Seth.

BOBBY HACHEY SINGS ELVIS
(London SDS 5113)
1972. Recorded by Bobby Hachey. This LP was first released in Canada.

BY REQUEST, ELLIS SINGS ELVIS
(Boblo NI 78-829)
1978. Recorded by Jimmy Ellis.

CANADA'S OWN ELVIS
(G.C. Records G-2001)
1977. Recorded by Bobby Fisher. Released in Canada.

THE CASTAWAY STRINGS PLAY
THE ELVIS PRESLEY SONG BOOK
(Vee Jay VJ 1113)
1964. Recorded by the Castaway Strings.

THE CHARTBUSTERS SALUTE
THE HITS OF ELVIS PRESLEY
(Pye PSL 8004)
1973. Recorded by the Chartbusters and released in Canada.

A CHILD'S INTRODUCTION TO ELVIS PRESLEY
(Kidstuff KSB-1002)
1978. Recorded by the Wild Honey Singers.

CHRISTMAS TO ELVIS
(Classic CCR 1935)
1978. Recorded by the Jordanaires.

DAVE NELSON SINGS THE BEST OF ELVIS
(Stereo-Gold Award MER 388)
1975. Recorded by Dave Nelson. This was an English release.

DEDICATED TO THE KING
(Wand ADS-680)
1966. Recorded by Chuck Jackson.

DISCO TO THE KING
(Smash Disco SS-8888)
1977. Recorded by Douglas Roy. This Canadian release was actually a 12-inch single.

DUTY FREE
(EMI 3C 064-18315)
1978. Recorded by Duty Free. Released in Italy.

EDDIE BRANDON PRESENTS
A TRIBUTE TO THE KING OF ROCK AND ROLL
(Artco LPR-1147)
1977. Recorded by Eddie Brandon, live in concert.

ELVIS: A TRIBUTE TO THE KING
(Springboard 6015)
1978. Recorded by Bucky Dee James and the Nashville Explosion.

ELVIS CONNECTION
(RCA INTS 5078)
1981. A various artists LP released in England. The album contained novelties as well as original recordings of songs later covered by Elvis.

ELVIS' FAVORITE GOSPEL SONGS
(QCA 362)
1977. Recorded by J. D. Sumner and the Stamps.

ELVIS ON MY MIND
(Delta 1002)
1978. Recorded by Patsy Sexton.

ELVIS ON MY MIND—THE LEGEND LIVES ON
(States of America 231)
1978. Recorded by Vince Everett.

ELVIS PRESLEY'S GOLDEN HITS
(Pickwick SPC 3292)
1972. Recorded by Big Ross and the Memphis Sound.

(Photo courtesy Don Fink)

ELVIS, WE LOVE YOU
(Gusto-Starday SD-993X)
1977. Recorded by Terry Tigre.

THE FLYING SAUCER STORY
(Buchanan and Goodman 716)
1956. Recorded by Buchanan and Goodman. This LP contains several cut-in songs.

FOR ELVIS THE WORLD CRIES
(Sound Studios PLP-5230)
????. Recorded by Beth Peterson.

GOLDEN MEMORIES
(Belle Meade BM SLP 1002)
1977. Recorded by Paul Dragon, backed by Scotty Moore, Bob Moore, D. J. Fontana and vocal backup by the Jordanaires.

THE GOLDEN RING TRIBUTE TO ELVIS
(Arc AS-823)
????. Recorded by the Golden Ring in Canada.

GOODBYE KING OF ROCK 'N' ROLL
(True T-1002 LSP)
1977. Recorded by Leon Everette. This LP contains the title song "The World's Greatest Star Has Gone Home."

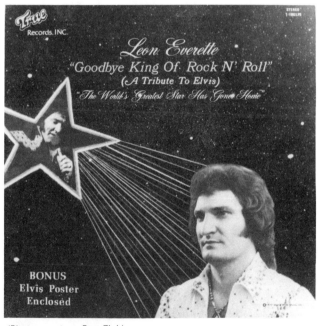

(Photo courtesy Don Fink)

THE GUITAR THAT CHANGED THE WORLD
(Epic LN 24103)
1964. Recorded by Scotty Moore.

GUNFIGHT AT CARNEGIE HALL
(A&M SP-9010)
1974. Recorded by Phil Ochs. This was a Canadian release.

THE HITS OF ELVIS PRESLEY
(Windmill WND-125)
1972. Recorded by Eden Perry and the Nashville Pops Orchestra. This LP was first released in Canada.

THE HITS OF ELVIS PRESLEY, VOLUME 1
(SpringBoard 4080)
????. Recorded by Bucky Dee James and the Nashville Explosion.

THE HITS OF ELVIS PRESLEY, VOL. 2
(Springboard 4081)
????. Recorded by Bucky Dee James and the Nashville Explosion.

HITS OF ELVIS PRESLEY & HITS OF JIM REEVES
(Mountain Dew 7029)
????. Recorded by the Nashville Country Singers.

THE HOLLYRIDGE STRINGS PLAY INSTRUMENTAL VERSIONS OF HITS BY ELVIS PRESLEY
(Capitol T-2221)
1965. Recorded by the Hollyridge Strings.

I CAN'T STOP LOVING YOU
(Philips 9114 017)
1977. Recorded by Per (Elvis) Granberg. Released in Norway.

I'VE BEEN AWAY FOR AWHILE NOW
(Mid-Eagle ME 2M7902)
1979. Recorded by Ral Donner on a double album. The album, which included 47 songs, also featured Scotty Moore, D. J. Fontana, and vocal backup by the Jordanaires.

JERRY KENNEDY'S DANCING GUITARS ROCK THE HITS OF THE KING
(Smash MGS 27004)
1961. Recorded by Jerry Kennedy.

JUST LIKE ELVIS
(Olympus ORS-1004)
1977. Recorded by Randy Schaeffer.

THE KING AND I
(Roc-co NI 77673)
1978. Recorded by Danny Chavis.

KING DOES THE KING'S THINGS
(Stax STS 2015)
1969. Recorded by Albert King.

THE KING IN BLACK DISCO
(Delphine GT-64501)
1977. Recorded by Black Paul. Released in Belgium.

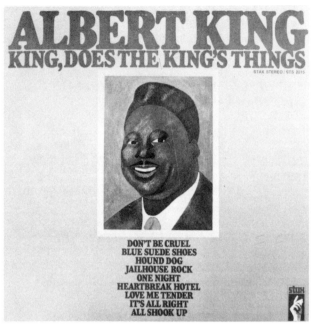

(Photo courtesy Don Fink)

THE KING'S MUSIC
(Thunderbird Productions CH34234)
1977. Recorded by the Thunderbird Singers.

LIL' ELVIS
(Lil' Elvis World Records)
1977. Recorded by Bob (Lil' Elvis) Harrison, an Elvis imitator.

THE MANY HEADS OF DICKIE GOODMAN
(Rori 3301)
????. Recorded by Dickie Goodman. Excerpts from Elvis's records appear on several tracks of this cut-in album.

MEMORIES OF OUR FRIEND ELVIS
(Blue Mark BMD 373)
1978. Recorded by J. D. Sumner and the Stamps.

MY FAREWELL TO ELVIS
(MCA 2314)
1977. Recorded by Merle Haggard. This album contained Haggard's "From Graceland to the Promised Land."

MYSTERY TRAIN
(BRB LPM-1956)
1978. Recorded by Bob and Rod. Canadian release.

101 STRINGS PLAY A TRIBUTE TO ELVIS PRESLEY
(Alshire S-5348)
1977. Recorded by the 101 Strings.

THE ORIGINAL FLYING SAUCERS
(IX Chains 9000)
1972. Recorded by Buchanan and Goodman. Excerpts from Elvis's songs appear on several tracks.

PAT BOONE SINGS . . . GUESS WHO?
(Dot 25501)
1964. Recorded by Pat Boone.

POUR LES AMATEURS D' ELVIS
(K-Tel KF 131)
1977. Recorded by Johnny Farago. Produced in Canada.

POUR LES AMATEURS D' ELVIS, VOLUME 2
(K-Tel KF 136)
1978. Recorded by Johnny Farago. Produced in Canada.

POUR LES FANS D' ELVIS SEULEMENT (FOR ELVIS FANS ONLY)
(Nobel NBL 508-9)
1977. Recorded by Johnny Farago in French. Produced in Canada.

THE PRESLEY STYLE OF RAL DONNER
(Gypsy TRG LP 1000)
1979. Recorded by Ral Donner. Although there are no Elvis songs on the album, the songs are sung in an Elvis style.

RAL DONNER'S ELVIS SCRAPBOOK
(Gone 5033)
????. Recorded by Ral Donner.

THE REAL HISTORY OF ROCK 'N' ROLL (TWO DECADES WITH THE KING)
(Candlelite 1002)
1972. Recorded by Wayne Stierle.

RICK PRESLEY LIVE
(Elvis II 1002)
1976. Recorded by Rick Presley, an Elvis imitator.

(Photo courtesy Don Fink)

RICK SAUCEDO LIVE
(Reality DG PRS 555)
1978. Recorded by Rick Saucedo.

ROCKABYE, ROLLABYE
(Philips 6478013)
????. Recorded by Per (Elvis) Granberg and the New Jordal Singers. Released in Norway.

SALUTE TO ELVIS
(CBS 9221)
1977. Recorded by Cahir O'Doherty. Produced in Ireland.

SCOTTY MOORE PLAYS THE BIG ELVIS PRESLEY HITS
(Epic EPC 53343)
????. Recorded by Scotty Moore.

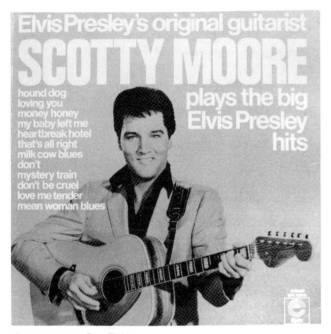

(Photo courtesy Don Fink)

SMASH HITS, PRESLEY STYLE
(MFP-5114)
1970. Recorded by Emi & Hamlyn Group in France.

THE SONGS I SANG FOR ELVIS
(Adonda SNAD 28076)
1981. Recorded by Sean (Sherrill) Nielsen.

SUSPICION
(Crusader CLP 1001)
1964. Recorded by Terry Stafford. The album features four songs made famous by Elvis, and the rest sung in an Elvis style.

THESE ARE MY SONGS
(Inner City 1032)
1977. Recorded by Otis Blackwell. Contains a few Blackwell songs recorded by Elvis.

TO ELVIS: LOVE STILL BURNING
(Fotoplay PSP-1000)
1978. Eleven tribute songs by various artists were included on this album. A portion of the proceeds went to the Elvis Presley Memorial Foundation in Memphis. The oil painting on this picture disc was painted by Marge Nichols.

TONY CANTA ELVIS
(RCA PL 31406)
1978. Recorded by Little Tony. Released in Italy.

TRIALS AND TRIBUTES
(Sunbird 949)
????. Recorded by Douglas Roy.

A TRIBUTE TO ELVIS
(Comstock Productions)
1977. Recorded by Johnny Rusk.

TRIBUTE TO ELVIS
(International KRIS 2004)
1978. Recorded by Little Tony. Released in Italy.

A TRIBUTE TO ELVIS PRESLEY
(Arrow LPM 1024)
????. Recorded by England Cover's Band and released in Argentina.

TRIBUTE TO ELVIS PRESLEY
(National NAT 16 200)
1978. Recorded by Burt Blanca and the King Creoles. This was a French release.

A TRIBUTE TO ELVIS PRESLEY'S GREATEST HITS
(Avenue 162)
1971. Recorded by Alan Caddy. Released in Great Britain.

A TRIBUTE TO THE KING, IN MEMORY
(Scorpion SCS-0015)
1979. Recorded by Ronnie McDowell with the Jordanaires.

VINCE EAGER PAYS TRIBUTE TO ELVIS PRESLEY
(Avenue AVE 093)
1972. Recorded by Vince Eager. Released in Great Britain.

WALLY FOWLER SINGS A TRIBUTE TO ELVIS
(Dove DRLP 1000)
1977. Recorded by Wally Fowler.

WERNER MULLER PLAYS ELVIS PRESLEY'S GREATEST HITS
(London SP 44217)
1974. Recorded by Werner Muller conducting the London Festival Orchestra. Released in Canada.

——— Songs That Mention Elvis in the Lyrics ———

ALL THE MONKEYS AIN'T IN THE ZOO
(Capitol 3655)
1957. Recorded by Tommy Collins.

AMERICAN PIE PART 1/AMERICAN PIE PART 2
(United Artists 50856)
1971. Recorded by Don McLean. Elvis is referred to as the King. The song went to number one on the *Billboard* Hot 100 chart.

AMERIKAN MUSIC
(Entrance ZS 7-7507)
1972. Recorded by Steve Alaimo.

ARE THE GOOD TIMES REALLY OVER
(Epic 14-02894)
1981. Recorded by Merle Haggard.

ARE YOU MY BABY
(Orbit R536X45-B)
1959. Recorded by Sammy Jackson.

BORN TO BOOGIE
(Warner Bros. 7-28369)
1987. Recorded by Hank Williams Jr.

BROOKLYN BRIDGE
(Fraternity 890)
1962. Recorded by Bobby Bare. This song was sung to the tune of "All American Boy."

CELEBRITY PARTY
(N.Y. Skyline 501)
1960. Recorded by the Scott Brothers.

A CHILD OF THE FIFTIES
(Mercury 76184)
1982. Recorded by the Statlers.

CHRISTMAS IN DIXIE
(RCA PB-13358)
1982. Recorded by Alabama.

THE COVER OF "ROLLING STONE"
(Columbia 45732)
1973. Recorded by Dr. Hook.

CRAZY WITH YOU
(Aladdin 45-3443)
1957. Recorded by Jeanette Baker.

THE CROSSING GAME
(Current C-111)
1966. Recorded by the Emperor's Friends (actually, Bob Hudson).

DO YOU REMEMBER?
(Capitol 2110)
1964. Recorded by the Beach Boys, on their album *All Summer Long*.

DREAM OF A CHILD/DREAM OF A CHILD
(Arista AS 0214)
1976. Recorded by David Forman.

EVERYBODY'S ROCKIN' BUT ME
(Columbia 4-21539)
1956. Recorded by Bobby Lord.

EVERYONE WAS THERE
(Carlton 482)
1958. Recorded by Bob Kayli (real name: Robert Gordy).

EV'RYBODY'S CRYIN'
(May MY 112)
1961. Recorded by Jimmy Beaumont.

GOT A GIRL
(Capitol 4362)
1960. Recorded by the Four Preps.

HEY FONZIE
(Casablanca NB 855)
1976. Recorded by Steve Sawyer.

HI HON!
(Crystalette 725X)
1959. Recorded by the Blockbusters.

HOLLYWOOD PARTY
(Era 45-1067)
1958. Recorded by Dick Bush.

HOOKED ON MUSIC
(Casablanca NB-2327)
1981. Recorded by Mac Davis.

I WILL ROCK AND ROLL WITH YOU
(Columbia 3-10888)
1978. Recorded by Johnny Cash. He also mentions other Sun artists—Jerry Lee Lewis, Billy Riley, Charlie Rich, Carl Perkins, Roy Orbison, and producers Sam Phillips and Jack Clement.

IF YOU DON'T KNOW
(ABC-Paramount 9765)
1956. Recorded by George Hamilton IV. Flip side of the hit "A Rose and a Baby Ruth."

I'M A SURVIVOR
(RCA PB-10319)
1975. Recorded by Barry Mann.

I'M LONESOME FOR YOU
(Roulette R 4352)
1961. Recorded by Paul Randal. Sung to the tune of "Are You Lonesome Tonight?"

IN MY WAY
(Decca F12073)
1965. Recorded by David Kaye. This was a British release.

IT WON'T HAPPEN WITH ME
(Sun 364)
1961. Recorded by Jerry Lee Lewis, who also mentions Ricky Nelson, Jackie Wilson, and Fabian.

(Photo courtesy Don Fink)

IT WON'T HAPPEN WITH ME
(Imperial 66032)
1964. Recorded by Johnny Rivers.

JINGLE BELL IMITATIONS
(Cameo 205)
1961. Recorded by Chubby Checker and Bobby Rydell.

JOHNNY BYE BYE
(Columbia 38-04772)
1985. Recorded by Bruce Springsteen.

JUDY
(Sun 290)
1958. Recorded by Rudy Grayzell and produced by Roy Orbison.

JUKE BOX SATURDAY NIGHT
(Madison 166)
1961. Recorded by Nino and the Ebb Tides.

THE KING OF ROCK AND ROLL
(Reprise 6462)
1971. Recorded by Little Richard, on his album *The King of Rock and Roll*. Although Elvis is mentioned in the lyrics, Little Richard refers to himself as the King of Rock and Roll.

THE LAND OF ROCK AND ROLL
(Melba 105)
1956. Recorded by Bobby Shields.

LEONARD
(MCA 51048)
1981. Recorded by Merle Haggard.

LET'S SING OUT AMERICA
(Memory 701)
????. Recorded by Ron South.

LEWIS BOOGIE
(Sun 301)
1958. Recorded by Jerry Lee Lewis.

LITTLE GIRL FEELING
(Columbia 3-10047)
1974. Recorded by Barbara Fairchild.

LITTLE JUKEBOX
(George 7778)
1961. Recorded by Wayne Newton with the Newton Brothers.

MAIN ATTRACTION
(Nabir NR 134)
????. Recorded by Jimmy DeHoney with Carson Smith's Roadrangers.

MEMORABILIA/MEMORABILIA
(Warner Bros. WBS 8462)
1977. Recorded by the Bellamy Brothers.

MIDNIGHT STAR
(Rock N' Roll ZS4 05606)
1985. Recorded by Weird Al Yankovic.

MIDTOWN AMERICAN MAIN STREET GANG/
MIDTOWN AMERICAN MAIN STREET GANG
(Lifesong ZS8-1770-5)
1978. Recorded by Dion.

THE MILLIONAIRE
(Capitol 4104)
1975. Recorded by Dr. Hook.

1959
(Warner Bros. WBS 49582)
1980. Recorded by John Anderson.

THE NAME GAME
(Epic 5-9393)
1959. Recorded by Joey Carter and Friends.

NEW FAD
(Dore 524)
1959. Recorded by Deane Hawley.

OH JOHNNY/THE DECISION
(Titanic 5006)
????. Recorded by Johnny and Donna. Both songs mention Elvis in the lyrics.

THE OLD PAYOLA ROLL BLUES (BEGINNING)/
THE OLD PAYOLA ROLL BLUES (END)
(Capitol 4329)
1960. Recorded by Stan Freberg.

PANCHO CLAUS
(L & M 1000)
1957. Recorded by Lalo Guerrero.

PROUD TO BE AN AMERICAN
(A&M 1826-S)
1976. Recorded by the Tubes.

PUT A LITTLE LOVIN' ON ME
(RCA PB-10718)
1976. Recorded by Bobby Bare.

THE REAL BUDDY HOLLY STORY
(Elecktra E-46616)
1980. Recorded by Sonny Curtis, a former member of the Crickets.

THE REAL THING (I WANT)
(Capitol 4246)
1976. Recorded by Stoney Edwards.

ROCK & ROLL HEAVEN (PART 1)/
ROCK & ROLL HEAVEN (PART 2)
(Press 45-2800)
1962. Recorded by the Flares.

ROCK AND ROLL
(Clark CLA 003)
1975. Recorded by Alan Clark and Wildfire.

ROCK AND ROLL HEAVEN
(Haven 7002)
1974. Recorded by the Righteous Brothers. This song reached #3 on *Billboard*'s Hot 100 chart.

ROCKABILLY PARTY
(Roulette R 4012)
1957. Recorded by Hugo Peretti & Luigi Creatore, two men who have composed songs that Elvis recorded.

ROCKIN' AT THE DRIVE-IN
(Capitol 3956)
1958. Recorded by the Beavers.

SHE CAN'T FIND HER KEYS
(Colpix 620)
1962. Recorded by Paul Peterson.

(Photo courtesy Don Fink)

SHORT FAT FANNY
(Specialty 608)
1957. Recorded by Larry Williams.

THE SOCK
(Iona 1003)
????. Recorded by the Valentines.

SON OF THE SOUTH
(Southern Tracks 1021)
1983. Recorded by Bill Anderson.

STAR OF A ROCK AND ROLL BAND
(Tara TRA 104)
1974. Recorded by Lee Dallon.

STORY OF THE ROCKERS
(Forever FR 6001)
1968. Recorded by Gene Vincent.

TEENAGE HEAVEN
(Kapp 524)
1963. Recorded by Johnny Cymbal.

TEENAGE WEDDING
(Vin 1004)
1958. Recorded by Johnny Angel.

TELE-VEE-SHUN
(Capitol 3687)
1957. Recorded by Stan Freberg.

THEY GAVE US ROCK AND ROLL
(Original Sound 108)
1973. Recorded by L. A. Walker.

TOP FORTY, NEWS, WEATHER AND SPORTS
(MGM K 12980)
1961. Recorded by Mark Dinning.

TRANSISTOR SISTER
(Swan 4078)
1961. Recorded by Freddy Cannon.

WENT TO SEE THE GYPSY
(Columbia 30290)
1970. Recorded by Bob Dylan from his album *New Morning*.

WHAT DID THEY DO BEFORE ROCK AND ROLL
(Colpix 631)
1962. Recorded by Shelly Fabares and Paul Peterson.

WHITE CHRISTMAS (PART 1)/
WHITE CHRISTMAS (PART 2)
(Thunderbird THE 102)
1975. Recorded by Freddie Starr. This was a British release.

WHO'S GONNA FILL THEIR SHOES
(Epic 34-05439)
1985. Recorded by George Jones.

WON'T Y' COME OUT, MARYANN
(Swan 4023)
1958. Recorded by the Quaker City Boys.

YOUNG COUNTRY
(Warner/Curb 7-28120)
1988. Recorded by Hank Williams Jr.

YOU'RE MY FAVORITE STAR
(Curb-WBS 49815)
1981. Recorded by the Bellamy Brothers.

YOU'RE THE TOP
(Warner Bros. 5047)
1959. Recorded by Edward Byrnes. Flip side of the hit recording of "Kookie, Kookie (Lend Me Your Comb)," with Connie Stevens.

Elvis Cut-In Records

(Records that include excerpts of Elvis's songs)

THE ANSWER TO THE FLYING SAUCER U.F.O.
(Cosmic 1001)
1956. Recorded by Syd Lawrence & Friends.

BUCHANAN & ANCELL MEET THE CREATURE/
THE CREATURE
(Flying Saucer XX-1232)
1960. Recorded by Bill Buchanan and Bob Ancell.

BUCHANAN AND GOODMAN ON TRIAL/CRAZY
(Luniverse 102)
1956. Recorded by Bill Buchanan and Dickie Goodman. There was a short excerpt from Elvis's "Hound Dog."

CHAOS (PART 1)/CHAOS (PART 2)
(Liberty 55197)
1959. Recorded by Abrogast and Ross.

THE COUNTRY SIDE OF '76/
THE COUNTRY SIDE OF '76
(Jellyroll 10676)
1976. Recorded by Jerry Osborne and Bruce Hamilton.

DEAR ELVIS (PART 1)/DEAR ELVIS WITH LOVE
FROM AUDREY (PART 2)
(Plus 104)
1956. Recorded by Audrey. Excerpts from Elvis's "I Don't Care If the Sun Don't Shine" and "Baby, Let's Play House" are played.

(Photo courtesy Don Fink)

DR. BEN CASEY
(Tuba U-11636)
1962. Recorded by Mickey Shorr and the Cutups. An excerpt from Elvis's "Good Luck Charm" is played.

ELVIS AND THE UNMENTIONABLES
(Town 2004 and Fun-E-Bone 816)
1961 and 1976. Recorded by Dave Harris.

ELVIS FOR X-MAS
(Million MS 20018 A45)
1957. Recorded by Mad Milo. Excerpts from Elvis's "Don't Be Cruel" and "Love Me" are played.

ELVIS ON TRIAL/A DATE WITH ELVIS
(Combo 131)
1957. Recorded by Mad Milo. Mad Milo was actually Roy Tan and the Combo.

FAREWELL TO THE KING
(Seatbelts Fastened EP 60)
1977. Recorded by Jimmy Jenkins.

THE FLIGHT/THE CHARIOT RACE
(Mark X 8007)
1960. "The Flight" was recorded by Aaron Plane. "The Chariot Race" was recorded by Ben Blur.

THE FLYING SAUCER (PART 1)/
THE FLYING SAUCER (PART 2)
(Luniverse 101)
1956. Recorded by (Bill) Buchanan and (Dickie) Goodman. This was the original cut-in record, featuring excerpts from fifteen songs, including Elvis's "Heartbreak Hotel." The song, which was originally titled "Back to Earth," has been credited to Mae Boren Axton as the composer, but this seems unlikely.

FLYING SAUCER (PART 1)/
FLYING SAUCER (PART 2)
(Aladdin 3331)
1956. Recorded by Sid Noel.

FLYING SAUCER THE 2ND
(Luniverse 105)
1957. Recorded by Buchanan and Goodman. An excerpt from Elvis's "All Shook Up" is heard.

FLYING SAUCER GOES WEST
(Luniverse 108)
1958. Recorded by Buchanan and Goodman.

FRANKENSTEIN OF '59 (PART 1)/
FRANKENSTEIN RETURNS (PART 2)
(Novelty 301)
1959. Recorded by Bill Buchanan and Dickie Good-

man. Excerpts from Elvis's "One Night" and "I Got Stung" were played.

THE GREAT DEBATE/THE GREAT DEBATE
(Trey 3013)
1960. Recorded by Ron Cameron Nazy. An excerpt from Elvis's "It's Now or Never" is heard.

HENRY GOES TO THE MOON (PART 1)/HENRY GOES TO THE MOON (PART 2)
(Cavalier 876A)
1958. Recorded by Ruff and Reddy.

INFLATION IN THE NATION
(Rainy Wednesday RW 209)
1974. Recorded by Dickie Goodman.

THE KING'S COUNTRY
(Quality 201)
1966. Recorded by Jerry Jay (Osborne).

MARTY ON PLANET MARS (PART 1)/
MARTY ON PLANET MARS (PART 2)
(Novelty 101)
1956. Recorded by Marty.

ON CAMPUS
(Cotique 158)
1969. Recorded by Dickie Goodman. An excerpt from Elvis's "In the Ghetto" is heard.

OUTER SPACE LOOTERS NO. 1/
OUTER SPACE LOOTERS NO. 2
(Satellite 6-33617-1)
1957. Recorded by the Mad Martians.

PLANE CRAZY/POLITICAL CIRCUS '72
(Jellyroll JR69 2)
1975. Recorded by Ratmore Slinky (Jerry Osborne).

PRESIDENTIAL PRESS CONFERENCE (PART 1)/
PRESIDENTIAL PRESS CONFERENCE (PART 2)
(Amy 824)
1961. Recorded by the Sicknics.

REPORT TO THE NATION (PART 1)/
REPORT TO THE NATION (PART 2)
(MK 101)
1960. Recorded by Winkley and Nutley (Jim Stag and Bob Mitchell). Excerpts from Elvis's "(Let's Have a) Party" and "Fame and Fortune" are heard.

ROCK 'N ROLL TRAGEDY
(Nightrain 906)
1957. Recorded by the Chestnuts. An excerpt from Elvis's "All Shook Up" was played.

SALUTE
(Warwick 533)
1960. Recorded by Jimmie Tennant (actually, Jimmy Velvet), who sang the Elvis sound-a-like cut-in songs.

SANTA AND THE SATELLITE (PART 1)/
SANTA AND THE SATELLITE (PART 2)
(Luniverse 107)
1957. Recorded by Buchanan and Goodman.

THE STORY OF ELVIS PRESLEY
(Drumfire DF-2)
1960. Recorded by Jim Ford.

THE TOUCHABLES
(Mark-X 8009)
1961. Recorded by Dickie Goodman.

THE TOUCHABLES IN BROOKLYN
(Mark-X 8010)
1961. Recorded by Dickie Goodman.

WAKE UP TO MUSIC
(RCA Victor 47-6712)
1956. Recorded by the Blenders.

WATERLOO '73
(Sunday 102)
1973. Recorded by the Conspirators. An excerpt of Elvis's "Steamroller Blues" is heard, along with fourteen other songs.

ARE YOU LONESOME TONIGHT?
(Shasta 146)
1960. Recorded by Linda Lee. Answer to "Are You Lonesome Tonight?"

BEAR CAT
(Sun 181)
1953. Recorded by Rufus Thomas. Answer to Willie (Big Mama) Thornton's "Hound Dog."

DON'T WANT YOUR LETTERS
(Big Top 45-3128)
1962. Recorded by Gerri Granger. Answer to "Return to Sender."

GO 'WAY HOUND DOG
(Columbia 4-40865)
1957. Recorded by Cliff Johnson. Answer to "Hound Dog."

HEY MEMPHIS
(Atlantic 2119)
1961. Recorded by LaVern Baker. Answer to "Little Sister."

(Photo courtesy Don Fink)

I DON'T WANT TO BE
ANOTHER GOOD LUCK CHARM
(Capitol 4745)
1962. Recorded by Jo Stafford. Answer to "Good Luck Charm."

I WON'T BE ROCKIN' TONIGHT
(Sun 244)
1956. Recorded by Jean Chapel. Answer to "Good Rockin' Tonight."

JUST TELL HIM JANE SAID HELLO
(Big Top 45-3150)
1963. Recorded by Gerri Granger. Answer to "Just Tell Her Jim Said Hello."

OH, HOW I MISS YOU TONIGHT
(Capitol 4492)
1961. Recorded by Jeanne Black. Answer to "Are You Lonesome Tonight?"

RETURN TO SANDRA
(Sabor 106)
1962. Recorded by Al Chaney. Answer to "Return to Sender."

WHO'S LONESOME TONIGHT, ACT III
(Del-Fi 4152)
1961. Recorded by Redd Dogg. Answer to "Are You Lonesome Tonight?"

YES, I'M LONESOME TONIGHT
(Coral 62241)
1961. Recorded by Thelma Carpenter. Answer to "Are You Lonesome Tonight?"

YES, I'M LONESOME TONIGHT
(Dot 16167)
1961. Recorded by Dodie Stevens. Answer to "Are You Lonesome Tonight?"

YES, I'M LONESOME TONIGHT
(Rendezvous R-139-A)
1961. Recorded by Ricky Page. Answer to "Are You Lonesome Tonight?"

YES, I'M LONESOME TONIGHT
(Glad A-1006)
1961. Recorded by Jo-Ann Perry. Answer to "Are You Lonesome Tonight?"

YOU DON'T HAVE A WOODEN HEART
(Coral 62285)
1961. Recorded by Bobbi Martin. Answer to "Wooden Heart."

YOU'RE A DOITY DOG
(Capitol 3607)
1957. Recorded by Mickey Katz. Answer to "Hound Dog."

Studio Recording Sessions

The following is a complete list of Elvis's studio recording sessions. Not included are live concert tapings, TV show tapings, and dates when vocal overdubbing may have been done.

For the Sun recording sessions, all songs known to have been recorded are listed. Obviously, to do so for the RCA sessions would take a book in itself. Next to some of the RCA sessions is the primary result of those sessions, i.e., film soundtracks and LPs.

1953

August or September	Memphis Recording Service	"My Happiness," "That's When Your Heartaches Begin"

1954

January 4	Memphis Recording Service	"I'll Never Stand in Your Way," "Casual Love Affair"
June	Sun Records	"Without You"
July 5	Sun Records	"Harbor Lights," "I Love You Because," "That's All Right (Mama)"
July 6	Sun Records	"Blue Moon of Kentucky," "Blue Moon"
September 10	Sun Records	"Tomorrow Night," "I'll Never Let You Go (Little Darlin')," "Satisfied," "Just Because," "Good Rockin' Tonight," "I Don't Care If the Sun Don't Shine"
December 10	Sun Records	"Milkcow Blues Boogie," "You're a Heartbreaker," "I'm Left, You're Right, She's Gone"

1955

February 5	Sun Records	"Baby, Let's Play House," "I Got a Woman," "Tryin' to Get to You"
July 11	Sun Records	"I Forgot to Remember to Forget," "Mystery Train," Tryin' to Get to You," "When It Rains, It Really Pours"

1956

January 10–11	RCA Studios (Nashville)	
January 30–31	RCA Studios (New York City)	
February 3	RCA Studios (New York City)	
April 11	RCA Studios (Nashville)	
July 2	RCA Studios (New York City)	
August 2 or September 24	Radio Recorders (Hollywood)	*Love Me Tender*
September 1–3	Radio Recorders (Hollywood)	*Elvis* LP

1957

January 12–13	Radio Recorders (Hollywood)	
January 19	Radio Recorders (Hollywood)	
January 24	Radio Recorders (Hollywood)	*Loving You*

February	Radio Recorders (Hollywood)	*Loving You*
February 23–24	Radio Recorders (Hollywood)	
April 30	Radio Recorders (Hollywood)	*Jailhouse Rock*
September 5–7	Radio Recorders (Hollywood)	*Elvis' Christmas Album*

1958

January 15–16	Radio Recorders (Hollywood)	*King Creole*
January 23	Radio Recorders (Hollywood)	*King Creole*
February 1	Radio Recorders (Hollywood)	
June 10–11	RCA Studios (Nashville)	

1960

March 20–21	RCA Studios (Nashville)	
April 3–4	RCA Studios (Nashville)	*Elvis Is Back* LP
April 27–28	RCA Studios (Nashville)	*G.I.Blues*
May 6	Radio Recorders (Hollywood)	*G.I. Blues*
Early August	Radio Recorders (Hollywood)	*Flaming Star*
October 30–31	RCA Studios (Nashville)	*His Hand in Mine* LP
November 7–8	Radio Recorders (Hollywood)	*Wild in the Country*

1961

March 12–13	RCA Studios (Nashville)	*Something for Everybody* LP
March 21–23	Radio Recorders (Hollywood)	*Blue Hawaii*
June 25–26	RCA Studios (Nashville)	
July 5	RCA Studios (Nashville)	*Follow That Dream*
October 15–16	RCA Studios (Nashville)	
October 26–27	Radio Recorders (Hollywood)	*Kid Galahad*

1962

March 18–19	RCA Studios (Nashville)	*Pot Luck* LP
Late March	Radio Recorders (Hollywood)	*Girls! Girls! Girls!*
Late September	Radio Recorders (Hollywood)	*It Happened at the World's Fair*

1963

January 22–23	Radio Recorders (Hollywood)	*Fun in Acapulco*
February 27	Radio Recorders (Hollywood)	*Fun In Acapulco*
May 26–27	RCA Studios (Nashville)	
July 9–11	Radio Recorders (Hollywood)	*Viva Las Vegas*
Early October	RCA Studios (Nashville)	*Kissin' Cousins*

1964

January 12	RCA Studios (Nashville)	
February 24–28	Radio Recorders (Hollywood)	*Roustabout*
March 2–6	Radio Recorders (Hollywood)	*Roustabout*
June–July	Radio Recorders (Hollywood)	*Girl Happy*

1965

February	RCA Studios (Nashville)	*Harum Scarum*
May	Radio Recorders (Hollywood)	*Frankie and Johnny*
August 2–4	Radio Recorders (Hollywood)	*Paradise, Hawaiian Style*

1966

February 15–17	Radio Recorders (Hollywood)	*Spinout*
May 25–28	RCA Studios (Nashville)	*How Great Thou Art* LP
June 10	RCA Studios (Nashville)	
Late June	Radio Recorders (Hollywood)	*Double Trouble*
September 28–29	Radio Recorders (Hollywood)	*Easy Come, Easy Go*

1967

February 21–22	RCA Studios (Nashville)	*Clambake*
March 20	RCA Studios (Nashville)	
June 20–21	MGM Studios (Culver City)	*Speedway*
June 26	MGM Studios (Culver City)	*Speedway*
September 10–12	RCA Studios (Nashville)	
October 2	RCA Studios (Nashville)	*Stay Away Joe*

1968

March 7	Western Recorders (Hollywood)	*Live a Little, Love a Little*
August 23	United Recorders (Los Angeles)	*The Trouble with Girls*
October 15	Samuel Goldwyn Studios (Los Angeles)	*Charro!*

1969

January 13–23	American Sound Studios (Memphis)	*From Memphis to Vegas/From Vegas to Memphis* LP
February 17–22	American Sound Studios (Memphis)	*From Memphis to Vegas/From Vegas to Memphis* LP
March 5–6	Decca Recording Studios (Universal City)	*Change of Habit*

1970

June 4–8	RCA Studios (Nashville)	
September 22	RCA Studios (Nashville)	

1971

March 15	RCA Studios (Nashville)	
May 15–21	RCA Studios (Nashville)	
June 8–9	RCA Studios (Nashville)	

1972

March 27–29	RCA Studios (Hollywood)	

1973

July 21–25	Stax Studios (Memphis)	*Raised on Rock/For Ol' Times Sake* LP
September 24	Elvis' Palm Springs home	
December 10–16	Stax Studios (Memphis)	*Promised Land* LP, *Good Times* LP

1975

| March 10–13 | RCA Studios (Hollywood) | *Elvis Today* LP |

1976

| February 2–8 | Graceland | *From Elvis Presley Boulevard, Memphis, Tennessee* LP |
| October 29–November 1 | Graceland | |

The Million-Dollar-Quartet Session

By December 4, 1956, little Sun Records, at 706 Union Avenue in Memphis, had launched the careers of Elvis Presley, Carl Perkins, Johnny Cash, and several black artists. Three days earlier, Jerry Lee Lewis's first record, "Crazy Arms"/"End of the Road," was released. On December 4, Carl Perkins had a recording session—the one that produced "Matchbox" and "Your True Love." Backing him was his trio, consisting of J. B. Perkins on rhythm guitar, Clayton Perkins on bass, and W. S. (Fluke) Holland on drums. Jerry Lee Lewis was in the studio playing piano at Jack Clement's request, earning fifteen dollars for his work. Perkins had asked Johnny Cash to drop by as his guest, and sit in the control room. Little did they realize the importance to Elvis fans this day would have several years later.

Elvis entered the studio in the afternoon arm-in-arm with nineteen-year-old Marilyn Evans, a dancer he had met while performing at the New Frontier Hotel in Las Vegas earlier in the year. He often stopped by the studio to see Sam Phillips, Jack Clement, and the various Sun artists. After exchanging a few pleasantries, Elvis sat down at the piano and began playing and singing "Blueberry Hill." Perkins, Lewis, and Cash soon joined him. Thus began the famed Million-Dollar-Quartet session.

Engineer Clement soon inserted a new tape and recorded the remainder of the session, which he later estimated to be two or three hours in length. Recognizing the publicity possibilities, Sam Phillips called Robert Johnson of the Memphis *Press-Scimitar*, who wrote a popular newspaper column called "TV News and Views." With staff photographer George Pierce, Johnson raced over to the Sun studios. Johnson's column of December 5, 1956, read:

> I never had a better time than yesterday when I dropped in at Sam Phillips' Sun Record bedlam on Union and Marshall. It was what one might call a barrelhouse of fun. Carl Perkins was in a recording session, and he has one that's going to hit as hard as "Blue Suede Shoes." We're trying to arrange an advance audition for you Memphis fans before the song is released in January. Johnny Cash dropped in. Jerry Lee Lewis was there, too, and then Elvis stopped by.
>
> Elvis headed for the piano and started in on "Blueberry Hill." The joint was really rocking before they got thru.
>
> Elvis is high on Jerry Lee Lewis. "That boy can go," he said. "I think he has a great future ahead of him. He has a different style, and the way he plays piano just gets inside me."
>
> I never saw Elvis more likeable than he was just fooling around with these other fellows who have the same interests as he does.
>
> If Sam Phillips had been on his toes, he'd have turned on the recorder when that very unrehearsed but talented bunch got to cutting up on "Blueberry Hill" and a lot of other songs. That quartet could sell a million.

Within the week, Sam Phillips mailed to disc jockeys a 7"-by-12" press release that reproduced Johnson's newspaper column and Pierce's photograph. He included the following handwritten message:

> Our Only Regret!
> That each and everyone of you wonderful D.J.'s who are responsible for these boys being among the best known and best liked in show business could not be there too! We thought however that you might like to read first hand about our little shindig—it was a dilly!
> Sincerely grateful,
> Sam Phillips

Soon after George Pierce took his famous photograph, Johnny Cash left the studio with wife June Carter to go shopping.

In 1969 Shelby Singleton bought Sam Phillips's Sun catalog of more than 10,000 hours of tape. After Elvis died, Singleton began a systematic search of his inventory and finally located the tape of the Million-Dollar-Quartet session. When plans were announced to release a five-volume set of the session, beginning with Volume 1 on December 15, 1977, RCA hit Singleton with a court injunction. Carl Perkins and Johnny Cash followed suit, although their primary objection was the rumor that additional instrumentation was going to be overdubbed.

The Million-Dollar-Quartet session was finally released in November 1980 as a bootleg album that sold for $16.95 at many retailers. The album *The Million Dollar Quartet* (One Million Dollar Records OMD 001), contained only seventeen of the reported dozens of songs sung during the session. The same material was issued in 1981 in England by Charly Records on the Sun label (Sun 1006). Many stores in America carried that import for a brief time.

In 1987 a bootleg titled *The One Million Dollar Quartet* (S Records S-5001) claimed to contain the entire session. Twenty-two more tracks from the session were added to the seventeen originally released. Again, a few months after the bootleg's release, the material was repackaged and imported to the United States from England by Charly Records.

In addition to the songs on *The One Million Dollar Quartet* bootleg, it's been reported that Jerry Lee Lewis sang "Strange Things Happen." As previously mentioned, "Blueberry Hill" began the session. Other songs reported to have been sung but that have not yet appeared on tape include "Vacation in Heaven," "Tutti Frutti," "Will the Circle Be Unbroken," "This Train," "The Old Rugged Cross," "My Isle of Golden Dreams," and "I Was There When It Happened." It may be that the material on *The One Million Dollar Quartet* bootleg is all that now exists from that historic day. It's possible, however, that more gems from that sessions will surface in the future. Let's hope so!

For a listing of the thirty-seven tracks released to date, see the entry on *The One Million Dollar Quartet* in the Bootleg section of this book. Each song is covered in its own entry in the Songs section.

Is That Really Elvis on That Record?

There have been many Elvis sound-alikes over the years—Vince Everett, Ral Donner, Terry Stafford, and Ronnie McDowell, to name just a few. But in almost all of these cases, the performer was clearly credited on the label and there was no attempt to deceive the public. In a few instances, however, out-and-out deception caused many Elvis fans to part with their hard-earned bucks, thinking they were buying an Elvis record.

The following is a short list of songs, singles, and LPs that have sown much confusion among Elvis fans. You'll note that Jimmy Ellis has figured prominently in most of these releases. Because of Ellis's uncanny vocal similarity to Elvis, Shelby Singleton of Sun International took full advantage and for several years packaged Ellis as the mysterious singer Orion. An Orion discography is also included in this section. Lest there still be doubters, Orion is *not* Elvis! He is Jimmy Ellis; he's told us so.

SONGS AND SINGLES
"Be-Bop-a-Lula"/"Breakup"
(Sun 1151)
1979. Both of these cuts were from the *Trio +* album. Jerry Lee Lewis and "Friend" were featured on "Be-Bop-a-Lula," while Charlie Rich and "Friend" performed "Breakup." On both songs, the "Friend" was Jimmy Ellis.

"Cold, Cold Heart"/"Hello, Josephine"
(Sun 1141)
1978. Singing duet with Jerry Lee Lewis on these two songs from the *Duets* album was "Friend" Jimmy Ellis.

"Don't Cry for Christmas"/"Dr. X-Mas"
(Sun ?)
197?. A question mark appeared on the label of this novelty record instead of the artist's name. Again, it's Jimmy Ellis singing, not Elvis, as Shelby Singleton would have you believe.

"Greenback Dollar, Watch and Chain"/
"Foolish Heart"
(Sun 272)
1957. For many years it was thought that Elvis played piano on both songs of this Sun release. However, research has discovered that Charlie Rich was the piano player. For the record, the rest of the personnel included Ray Harris on vocal and guitar, Wayne Cogswell on guitar, Red Hensley on guitar, and Joe Reisenberg on drums. The vocal backing was provided by Roy Orbison, Cogswell, and Hensley.

"I Can't Make It Without You"
A few private recordings of Elvis's concert appearances have turned up in recent years with this song as one of those alleged to be sung by Elvis. It is actually Charlie Hodge singing "I Can't Make It Without You." He is also the song's composer.

"In My Dreams"
A lot of controversy was created when this song was released in 1979 on the bootleg LP *Special Delivery from Elvis Presley*. It was thought by some to be an unreleased acetate recording from one of Elvis's RCA studio sessions. Still others believed the singer was Ral Donner, but Donner has denied any knowledge of "In My Dreams." It's the opinion of this book's authors that the recording is a demo made by another artist for Elvis's consideration.

"Save the Last Dance for Me"/
"Am I to Be the One"
(Sun 1139)
1978. In November 1978 disc jockeys suddenly began playing "Save the Last Dance for Me" and asking their audience to listen to the other voice singing with Jerry Lee Lewis. The voice supposedly belonged to Elvis, who had recorded the song while he and Lewis were both at Sun Records. It was further speculated that Elvis's name couldn't be mentioned because of a conflict of ownership between Sun and RCA. The truth is that Elvis left Sun Records before Jerry Lee Lewis began to record for the label. Furthermore, "Save the Last Dance for Me" was composed by Doc Pomus and Mort Shuman for the Drifters in 1960—five years after Elvis left Sun Records. Lewis recorded the song in 1963. It was released by Sun (Sun 367) that same year. Jimmy Ellis overdubbed his voice on the song for the *Duets* album in 1978.

"Am I to Be the One" also received much airplay in late 1978. Yet another cut from the *Duets* album, it was recorded by Jerry Lee Lewis in the late 1950s and first surfaced on Lewis's 1970 LP *A Taste of Honey* (Sun 114). Years later, Charlie Rich added his vocal overdub to the track. When first released, "Am I to Be the One" was reported by many uninformed music writers to be a duet by Lewis and Elvis. The song was written by Otis Blackwell and R. Stevenson.

"Tell Me Pretty Baby"/"Tell Me Pretty Baby"
(Elvis Classic EC 5478)
1978. When "Tell Me Pretty Baby" was first released in 1978, it was claimed that the song was from Elvis's first commercial recording session—predating his days at Sun Records. Supposedly, "Tell Me Pretty Baby" was recorded at Audio Recorders in Phoenix in early 1954. In an affidavit signed by Pete Falco on July 6, 1978, he stated that he paid Elvis fifteen dollars to record the song with his group, the Red Dots. "Tell Me Pretty Baby" was written by Andrew Lee Jackson and published by the Golgatha Publishing Company. The playing time was 2 minutes, 12 seconds.

In late 1978 Vernon Presley and RCA Records filed a suit in Dallas contesting the song's authenticity. During the four-day hearing before Judge Snowden Leftwich, Vernon Presley testified that Elvis was never in Phoe-

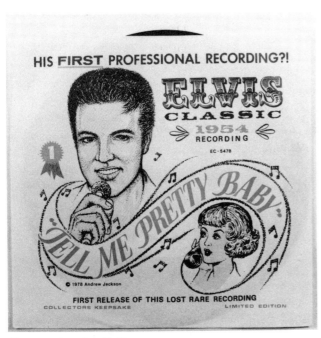

(Photo courtesy Don Fink)

nix in 1954. One of the exhibits at the hearing was the "original master tape from 1954." However, testimony from the tape manufacturer revealed that the tape used was not manufactured before 1957 or 1958. Singer Michael Conley came forward and admitted he made the fake recording at the request of his manager, Hal Freeman. Freeman said Conley was lying. On December 8, 1978, the court ordered the distributor of "Tell Me Pretty Baby" to cease production of the record.

"That's All Right (Mama)"/ "Blue Moon of Kentucky" (Sun 1129)

1972. This Sun single was originally released without artist credit, causing Elvis fans to believe that it consisted of outtakes from 1954. After RCA Records filed suit, Shelby Singleton was forced to list the real singer, Jimmy Ellis. It was Ellis's first record.

"That's All Right (Mama)"/ "Blue Moon of Kentucky"/"D.O.A." (Sun 1136)

1977. After Elvis's death, Shelby Singleton reissued Sun 1129 with the addition of the Elvis tribute "D.O.A.," by Misty (actually, Tanya Tucker).

LONG-PLAYING ALBUMS
Duets
(Sun 1011)

1978. The jacket of this album listed the artists as Jerry Lee Lewis and Friends. Although the "Friends" were not identified, the aim was apparently to deceive Elvis fans into believing that it was, or might be, Elvis singing duet with Jerry Lee Lewis. In actuality, Charlie Rich and Jimmy Ellis overdubbed their voices on the eleven tracks.

Side 1: "Save the Last Dance for Me" (with Jimmy Ellis), "Sweet Little Sixteen" (with Jimmy Ellis), "I Love You Because" (with Jimmy Ellis), "C.C. Rider" (with Jimmy Ellis). "Am I to Be the One" (with Charlie Rich), and "Sail Away" (with Charlie Rich)

Side 2: "Cold, Cold Heart" (with Jimmy Ellis), "Hello, Josephine" (with Jimmy Ellis), "It Won't Happen with Me" (with Jimmy Ellis), "What'd I Say" (with Jimmy Ellis), and "Good Golly, Miss Molly" (with Jimmy Ellis)

TRIO +
(Sun 1018)

1979. Still another fabricated-duets album from the fertile imagination of Shelby Singleton. This time the Elvis sound-alike sings with Jerry Lee Lewis, Charlie Rich, and Carl Perkins. All ten tracks were overdubbed by the talented Jimmy Ellis.

Side 1: "Be-Bop-a-Lula" (with Jerry Lee Lewis), "On My Knees" (with Charlie Rich), "Dixie Fried" (with Carl Perkins), "Gentle as a Lamb" (with Charlie Rich), and "Money" (with Jerry Lee Lewis)

Side 2: "Breakup" (with Charlie Rich), "Matchbox" (with Carl Perkins), "Good Rockin' Tonight" (with Jerry Lee Lewis), "Gone, Gone, Gone" (with Carl Perkins), and "Sittin' and Thinkin' " (with Charlie Rich)

ORION SINGLES
1979
- "Honey"/"Ebony Eyes" (Sun 1142)
- "Washing Machine"/"Before the Next Teardrop Falls" (Sun 1147)
- "Remember Bethlehem"/"Silent Night" (Sun 1148)
- "Stranger in My Place"/"It Ain't No Mystery" (Sun 1152)

1980
- "Faded Love"/Texas Tea" (Sun 1153)
- "Am I That Easy to Forget"/"Crazy Arms" (Sun 1156)

(Photo courtesy Don Fink)

- "Rockabilly Rebel"/"Memphis Sun"
  (Sun 1159)
- "Crazy Little Thing Called Love"/"Matchbox"
  (Sun 1162)

1981
- "Born"/"If I Can't Have You"
  (Sun 1165)
- "Some You Win, Some You Lose"
  (Sun 1170)

1982
- "Feelings"/"Baby, Please Say Yes"
  (Sun 1172)
- "Honky Tonk Heaven"/"Morning, Noon and Night"
  (Sun 1175)
- "Listen to Daddy"/"Remember Bethlehem"
  (Sun 1177)
- "I'm Saving Up My Pennies"/"I'm Saving Up My Pennies"
  (Kristal International Records KS-2292) (disc jockey promo)

ORION LONG-PLAYING ALBUMS
1979
- REBORN
  (Sun 1012)
- SUNRISE
  (Sun 1017)

1980
- COUNTRY
  (Sun 1019)
- ROCKABILLY
  (Sun 1021)
- GLORY
  (Sun 1025)

1981
- FRESH
  (Sun 1028)
- FEELINGS
  (Sun 144)

1982
- ORION—20 ALL-TIME FAVORITES
  (Suffolk Marketing SMI 1-27K) (sold on TV)
- SURPRISE
  (Sun 1029)

(Photo courtesy Jeff Wheatcraft)

Music Miscellanea

ALBUMS THAT REACHED THE TOP TEN

1. *Blue Hawaii* (#1 for 20 weeks)
2. *Elvis Presley* (#1 for 10 weeks)
3. *Loving You* (#1 for 10 weeks)
4. *G. I. Blues* (#1 for 10 weeks)
5. *Elvis* (#1 for 5 weeks)
6. *Elvis' Christmas Album* (#1 for 4 weeks)
7. *Something for Everybody* (#1 for 3 weeks)
8. *Roustabout* (#1 for 1 week)
9. *Aloha from Hawaii via Satellite* (#1 for 1 week)
10. *King Creole* (#2)
11. *Elvis Is Back* (#2)
12. *Elvis' Golden Records* (#3)
13. *Girls! Girls! Girls!* (#3)
14. *Elvis' Golden Records, Volume 3* (#3)
15. *Fun in Acapulco* (#3)
16. *Peace in the Valley* (EP) (#3)
17. *Moody Blue* (#3)
18. *Pot Luck* (#4)
19. *It Happened at the World's Fair* (#4)
20. *Elvis in Concert* (#5)
21. *Kissin' Cousins* (#6)
22. *Girl Happy* (#8)
23. *Harum Scarum* (#8)
24. *Elvis—TV Special* (#8)
25. *Elvis for Everyone* (#10)

ALBUMS THAT WERE ON THE CHARTS FOR ONE YEAR OR MORE

1. *G. I. Blues* (111 weeks)
2. *Blue Hawaii* (79 weeks)
3. *Elvis Is Back* (56 weeks)
4. *Aloha from Hawaii via Satellite* (52 weeks)

Elvis was the second white solo performer to have a #1 record on *Billboard*'s rhythm & blues chart. The first five:

1. Johnnie Ray ("Cry," 1952)
2. Elvis (Don't Be Cruel"/"Hound Dog," 1956)
3. Jerry Lee Lewis ("Whole Lotta Shakin' Goin' On," 1957)
4. Paul Anka ("Diana," 1957)
5. Jimmie Rodgers ("Honeycomb," 1957)

Although Elvis won only three Grammy Awards, he was nominated several other times. The following is a complete list of Elvis's Grammy nominations.

1959

1. Record of the Year—"A Fool Such as I" (lost to Bobby Darin's "Mack the Knife")
2. Best Performance by a "Top 40" Artist—"A Big Hunk o' Love" (lost to "Midnight Flyer" by Nat King Cole")
3. Best Rhythm and Blues Performance—"A Big Hunk o' Love" (lost to Dinah Washington's "What a Difference a Day Makes")
4. Best Album Cover—*For LP Fans Only* [this was an art director's award and Colonel Parker was nominated!] (lost to *Shostakovich: Symphony No. 5*)

1960

5. Record of the Year—"Are You Lonesome Tonight?" (lost to Percy Faith's "Theme from 'A Summer Place' ")
6. Best Vocal Performance, Male—"Are You Lonesome Tonight?" (lost to "Georgia on My Mind" by Ray Charles)
7. Best Performance by a Pop Singles Artist—"Are You Lonesome Tonight?" (lost to "Georgia on My Mind" by Ray Charles)
8. Best Vocal Performance, Male, Album—*G. I. Blues* (lost to *Genius of Ray Charles*)
9. Best Soundtrack Album or Recording of Original Cast from a Motion Picture or Television—*G. I. Blues* (lost to *Can-Can*)

1961

10. Best Soundtrack Album or Recording of Original Cast from a Motion Picture or Television—*Blue Hawaii* (lost to *West Side Story*)

1967

11. Best Sacred Performance—*How Great Thou Art* album (won)

1968

12. Best Sacred Performance—*You'll Never Walk Alone* album (lost to Jake Hess's album *Beautiful Isle of Somewhere*)

1972

13. Best Inspirational Performance—*He Touched Me* album (won)

1974

14. Best Inspirational Performance—"How Great Thou Art" [this was a track from the LP *Elvis Recorded Live on Stage in Memphis*] (won)

1978

15. Best Country Vocal Performance, Male—"Softly, as I Leave You" (lost to Willie Nelson's "Georgia on My Mind")

1980

16. Best Album Notes—*Elvis Aron Presley* [Lorene Lortic was nominated] (lost to Frank Sinatra's *Trilogy: Past, Present, and Future*)

From September 28, 1957, to January 10, 1959, Elvis was number one on *Billboard*'s extended-play album chart 60 of the 68 weeks. His number one EPs:

1. *King Creole, Volume 1* (#1 for 29 weeks)
2. *Jailhouse Rock* (#1 for 28 weeks)
3. *Loving You, Volume 1* (#1 for 5 weeks)
4. *Elvis, Volume 1* (#1 for 2 weeks)
5. *Elvis Sings Christmas Songs* (#1 for 2 weeks)
6. *King Creole, Volume 2* (#1 for 1 week)

"Long Legged Girl (with the Short Dress On)" had the shortest playing time of any Elvis single to reach *Billboard*'s Hot 100 chart—1 minute, 26 seconds. The three shortest to make the chart:

1. "Long Legged Girl (with the Short Dress on)" (1:26)
2. "One Broken Heart for Sale" (1:34)
3. "Follow That Dream" (1:34)

The shortest Elvis single to reach number one was "Teddy Bear" at 1 minute, 43 seconds. "Suspicious Minds" was the longest at 4 minutes, 22 seconds.

TOP 100/HOT 100 NUMBER ONE RECORDS
1. "All Shook Up" (8 weeks)
2. "Heartbreak Hotel" (7 weeks)
3. "Don't Be Cruel" (7 weeks)
4. "Teddy Bear" (7 weeks)
5. "Jailhouse Rock" (6 weeks)
6. "Are You Lonesome Tonight?" (6 weeks)
7. "It's Now or Never" (5 weeks)
8. "Love Me Tender" (4 weeks)
9. "Stuck on You" (4 weeks)
10. "A Big Hunk o' Love" (2 weeks)
11. "Good Luck Charm" (2 weeks)
12. "Surrender" (2 weeks)
13. "Don't" (1 week)
14. "Suspicious Minds" (1 week)

In addition to the above 14 songs, "I Want You, I Need You, I Love You" reached number one on the Best Sellers chart (but only #3 on the Top 100 chart), "Hound Dog" reached number one on the Juke Box and Best Sellers charts (but only #2 on the Top 100 chart), "Too Much" reached #1 on the Juke Box and Best Sellers charts (but only #2 on the Top 100 chart), and "Hard Headed Woman" reached #1 on the Juke Box and Best Sellers charts (but only #2 on the Top 100 chart).

NUMBER ONE RECORDS ON THE COUNTRY CHART
1. "Heartbreak Hotel" (17 weeks)
2. "I Was the One" (17 weeks)
3. "Don't Be Cruel" (5 weeks)
4. "Hound Dog" (5 weeks)
5. "I Forgot to Remember to Forget" (2 weeks)
6. "Mystery Train" (1 week)
7. "Teddy Bear" (1 week)
8. "Loving You" (1 week)
9. "Jailhouse Rock" (1 week)
10. "Treat Me Nice" (1 week)
11. "Moody Blue" (1 week)

12. "She Thinks I Still Care" (1 week)
13. "Way Down" (1 week)
14. "Pledging My Love" (1 week)
15. "Guitar Man" (1 week)

NUMBER ONE RHYTHM & BLUES RECORDS
1. "Jailhouse Rock" (5 weeks)
2. "Treat Me Nice" (5 weeks)
3. "All Shook Up" (4 weeks)
4. "Don't Be Cruel" (1 week)
5. "Hound Dog" (1 week)
6. "Teddy Bear" (1 week)
7. "Loving You" (1 week)

NUMBER ONE EASY-LISTENING RECORDS
1. "Crying in the Chapel" (7 weeks)
2. "Can't Help Falling in Love" (6 weeks)
3. "I'm Yours" (3 weeks)
4. "(Such an) Easy Question" (2 weeks)
5. "The Wonder of You" (1 week)
6. "You Don't Have to Say You Love Me" (1 week)
7. "My Boy" (1 week)

BRITISH NUMBER ONE RECORDS
1. "It's Now or Never" (8 weeks)
2. "All Shook Up" (7 weeks)
3. "Wooden Heart" (6 weeks)
4. "The Wonder of You" (6 weeks)
5. "A Fool Such as I" (5 weeks)
6. "I Need Your Love Tonight" (5 weeks)
7. "Good Luck Charm" (5 weeks)
8. "Way Down" (5 weeks)
9. "Are You Lonesome Tonight?" (4 weeks)
10. "Surrender" (4 weeks)
11. "(Marie's the Name) His Latest Flame" (4 weeks)
12. "Little Sister" (4 weeks)
13. "Can't Help Falling in Love" (4 weeks)
14. "Rock-a-Hula Baby" (4 weeks)
15. "Jailhouse Rock" (3 weeks)
16. "One Night" (3 weeks)
17. "I Got Stung" (3 weeks)
18. "She's Not You" (3 weeks)
19. "Return to Sender" (3 weeks)
20. "Crying in the Chapel" (2 weeks)
21. "(You're the) Devil in Disguise" (1 week)

"All Shook Up" spent 30 weeks on the Top 100 chart—the most of any Presley record. "I Forgot to Remember to Forget"/"Mystery Train" was on the country chart for 40 weeks. The Elvis best for the rhythm & blues chart was 18 weeks by "Don't Be Cruel"/"Hound Dog." The following is a list of all Elvis songs to stay on the Top 100/Hot 100 chart for more than 20 weeks.

1. "All Shook Up" (30 weeks)
2. "Hound Dog" (28 weeks)
3. "Don't Be Cruel" (27 weeks)
4. "Heartbreak Hotel" (27 weeks)
5. "Jailhouse Rock" (27 weeks)
6. "Teddy Bear" (25 weeks)

7. "I Want You, I Need You, I Love You" (24 weeks)
8. "Love Me Tender" (23 weeks)
9. "Loving You" (22 weeks)
10. "Way Down" (21 weeks)
11. "Don't" (20 weeks)
12. "It's Now or Never" (20 weeks)

VOCAL GROUPS THAT BACKED ELVIS

1. The Jordanaires
2. The Ken Darby Trio
3. The Surfers
4. The Amigos
5. The Mello Men
6. The Jubilee Four
7. The Anita Kerr Singers
8. The Carole Lombard Quartet
9. The Carole Lombard Trio
10. The Imperials
11. The Blossoms
12. The Sweet Inspirations
13. The Nashville Edition
14. J. D. Sumner and the Stamps Quartet
15. Voice
16. Lea Jane Berineti Singers

"Heartbreak Hotel" took longer to reach number one on the Top 100/Hot 100 chart than any Elvis song—10 weeks. "All Shook Up" and "Are You Lonesome Tonight?" took the shortest time to reach number one—three weeks.

The record for the highest position an Elvis song entered *Billboard*'s Top 100/Hot 100 chart is held by "Wear My Ring Around Your Neck." It entered the chart at #7 on April 12, 1958, but never reached number one during its 15 weeks on the chart.

The biggest one-week leap to number one by any Presley song was five positions. Both "All Shook Up" and "Stuck on You" went from #6 one week to number one the next week.

The biggest one-week leap of any record by any performer within the Top 40 is 33 positions. Elvis's "Are You Lonesome Tonight?" jumped from #35 one week to #2 the following week.

MOVIE DUETS

[Note: This list does not include songs in which someone sang a word or two or in which more than two people sang with Elvis.]

1. "Crawfish" (with Kitty White; *King Creole*)
2. "Husky Dusky Day" (with Hope Lange; *Wild in the Country*)
3. "Earth Boy" (with Ginny and Elizabeth Tiu; *Girls! Girls! Girls!*)
4. "How Would You Like to Be" (with Vicki Tiu; *It Happened at the World's Fair*)
5. "Happy Ending" (with Joan O'Brien; *It Happened at the World's Fair*)

6. "Mexico" (with Larry Domasin; *Fun in Acapulco*)
7. "The Lady Loves Me" (with Ann-Margret; *Viva Las Vegas*)
8. "Petunia, the Gardener's Daughter" (with Donna Douglas [actually dubbed by Eileen Wilson]; *Frankie and Johnny*)
9. "Queenie Wahine's Papaya" (with Donna Butterworth; *Paradise, Hawaiian Style*)
10. "Scratch My Back (Then I'll Scratch Yours)" (with Marianna Hill; *Paradise, Hawaiian Style*)
11. "Datin' " (with Donna Butterworth; *Paradise, Hawaiian Style*)
12. "Yoga Is as Yoga Does" (with Elsa Lanchester; *Easy Come, Easy Go*)
13. "Who Needs Money" (with Will Hutchins [actually dubbed by Ray Walker]; *Clambake*)
14. "There Ain't Nothing Like a Song" (with Nancy Sinatra; *Speedway*)
15. "Signs of the Zodiac" (with Marlyn Mason; *The Trouble with Girls*)

GOLD RECORDS

The following is a list of all of Elvis Presley's reported worldwide Gold Records according to the Recording Industry Association of America, RCA Records, and independent sources. To qualify for a Gold Record, singles releases and extended-play albums must sell over a million units. Long-playing albums must have had over $1 million in sales through December 31, 1974. On January 1, 1975, the criteria for Gold LPs changed. From that date to the present, an album must sell over 500,000 units. Sadly, RCA has not submitted several records to the RIAA for official certification. The following records are listed according to the year they were released, not the year they achieved Gold Record status.

1956
Singles: "Heartbreak Hotel," "I Was the One," "I Want You, I Need You, I Love You," "Don't Be Cruel," "Hound Dog," "Love Me Tender," "Any Way You Want Me"
LPs: *Elvis Presley, Elvis*

1957
Singles: "Too Much," "Playing for Keeps," "All Shook Up," "That's When Your Heartaches Begin," "Teddy Bear," "Loving You," "Jailhouse Rock," "Treat Me Nice," "Don't," "I Beg of You"
EPs: *Peace in the Valley, Jailhouse Rock*
LPs: *Loving You, Elvis' Christmas Album*

1958
Singles: "Wear My Ring Around Your Neck," "Hard Headed Woman," "I Got Stung," "One Night"
EPs: *King Creole, Volume 1*
LPs: *Elvis' Golden Records, King Creole*

1959
Singles: "(Now and Then There's) A Fool Such as I," "I Need Your Love Tonight," "A Big Hunk o' Love"
LPs: *50,000,000 Elvis Fans Can't Be Wrong—Elvis' Gold Records, Volume 2*

1960
Singles: "Stuck on You," "It's Now or Never," "A Mess of Blues," "Are

You Lonesome Tonight?," "I Gotta Know," "Wooden Heart" (in Europe)
LPs: *Elvis Is Back, G. I. Blues, His Hand in Mine*

1961
Singles: "Surrender," "I Feel So Bad," "Little Sister," "(Marie's the Name) His Latest Flame," "Can't Help Falling in Love," "Rock-a-Hula Baby"
EPs: *Elvis by Request*
LPs: *Something for Everybody, Blue Hawaii*

1962
Singles: "Good Luck Charm," "Anything That's Part of You," "She's Not You," "Return to Sender," "Where Do You Come From"
EPs: *Follow That Dream*
LPs: *Pot Luck, Girls! Girls! Girls!*

1963
Singles: "One Broken Heart for Sale," "(You're the) Devil in Disguise," "Bossa Nova Baby"
LPs: *Elvis' Golden Records, Volume 3, Fun in Acapulco, It Happened at the World's Fair*

1964
Singles: "Kissin' Cousins," "Viva Las Vegas," "Ain't That Loving You Baby," "Blue Christmas"
LPs: *Kissin' Cousins, Roustabout*

1965
Singles: "Crying in the Chapel," "I'm Yours," "Puppet on a String"
LPs: *Girl Happy, Elvis for Everyone, Harum Scarum*

1966
Singles: "Tell Me Why," "Frankie and Johnny," "Love Letters," "Spinout," "All That I Am," "If Every Day Was Like Christmas"
LPs: *Paradise, Hawaiian Style*

1967
Singles: "Indescribably Blue," "Big Boss Man"
LPs: *How Great Thou Art*

1968
Singles: "Guitar Man," "Stay Away," "We Call on Him," "Let Yourself Go," "Almost in Love," "If I Can Dream"
LPs: *Elvis—TV Special*

1969
Singles: "Charro," "His Hand in Mine," "In the Ghetto," "Clean Up Your Own Back Yard," "Suspicious Minds," "Don't Cry, Daddy"
LPs: *Elvis Sings Flaming Star, From Elvis in Memphis, From Memphis to Vegas/From Vegas to Memphis*

1970
Singles: "Kentucky Rain," "The Wonder of You," "Mama Liked the Roses," "I've Lost You," "You Don't Have to Say You Love Me," "Patch It Up," "I Really Don't Want to Know"
LPs: *On Stage—February, 1970; Elvis: Worldwide 50 Gold Award Hits, Volume 1; That's the Way It Is*

1971
Singles: "Where Did They Go, Lord," "Only Believe," "I'm Leavin'," "It's Only Love"
LPs: *Elvis Country, Elvis Sings the Wonderful World of Christmas*

1972
Singles: "An American Trilogy," "Burning Love," "Separate Ways"
LPs: *Elvis as Recorded at Madison Square Garden*

1973
Singles: "Raised on Rock"
LPs: *Aloha from Hawaii via Satellite, Elvis (RCA DPL2-0056[e])*

1974
Singles: "Take Good Care of Her," "It's Midnight"
LPs: *Elvis—A Legendary Performer, Volume 1*

1975
Singles: "My Boy," "T-R-O-U-B-L-E"
LPs: *Promised Land, Pure Gold*

1976
Singles: "Hurt"
LPs: *Elvis—A Legendary Performer, Volume 2; From Elvis Presley Boulevard, Memphis, Tennessee*

1977
Singles: "Way Down," "My Way"
LPs: *Welcome to My World, Moody Blue, Elvis in Concert*

1978
LPs: *Elvis—A Legendary Performer, Volume 3*

Fan Club Index

Elvis Presley Fan Club of Florida
John Beach
2202 Jammes Road
Jacksonville, Florida 32210

Elvis Presley Foundation
Box 1352
Norfolk, Virginia 23501

Elvis Lives On
270 Bronson Way NE
Renton, Washington 98056

Elvis World
Box 388
Bound Brook, New Jersey 08805

Elvis Dixieland Fan Club
1306 Rosedale Drive
Demopolis, Alabama 36732

Elvis the King Fan Club
4714 Dundee Drive
Jacksonville, Florida 32210

Elvis Love's Burning
Box 7462
Shreveport, Louisiana 71107

Elvis Friendship Circle
2908 Juen Lane
Bossier City, Louisiana 71112

Elvis Echoes of Love
5930 Montibello
Imperial, Missouri 63052

Elvis and Friends
333 W. State
Trenton, New Jersey 08618

Elvis Country
Box 9113
Austin, Texas 78766

Elvis Fan Club
Box 4537
Corpus Christi, Texas 78469

Elvis Chicago Style
Mike Keating
Box 388554
Chicago, Illinois 60638

Elvis Worldwide Fan Club
Box 53
Romulus, Michigan 48174

Elvis Fans United
110 Graston Avenue
Syracuse, New York 13219

Eternally Elvis TCB, Inc.
2251 N.W. 93rd Avenue
Pembroke Pines, Florida 33024

For the Heart Fan Club
5004 Lyngail Drive
Huntsville, Alabama 35810

Graceland Express
Box 16508
Memphis, Tennessee 38186

Graceland News
Beth Pease, Josh Cooke
Box 161431
Memphis, Tennessee

Having Fun with Elvis
Judy Dial
5310 Binz-Engleman Road
San Antonio, Texas 78219

It's Only Love Elvis Presley Fan Club
Jack Myers
266 Harmony Grove Road
Lilburn, Georgia 30247

King of Our Hearts Elvis Presley Fan Club
Irene Maleti
2445 Fernwood Avenue
San Jose, California 95128

Love 4 Elvis Fan Club
Fran Colvin
Box 2271
Clifton, New Jersey

Memories of Elvis Express
Betty Roloson
302 Whitman Court
Glen Burnie, Maryland 21061

Mile High on Elvis Fan Club
Box 2332
Arvada, Colorado 80001

The New Jersey State Association for Elvis
Robert Job
304 Carlton Avenue
Piscataway, New Jersey 08854

The Presley-ites Fan Club
Kathy Ferguson
1708 18th Street North
Zephyrhills, Florida 34248

The Press'ley Press
Box 15230
Milwaukee, Wisconsin 53215

Oklahoma Fans for Elvis
Keith Mitchell
302 S. 11th Street
Frederick, Oklahoma 73542

Reflections of Elvis
14210 Schwartz Road
Grabill, Indiana 46741

Remembering Elvis with TLC in Alabama
Linda Harrelson
725 Cherokee Trail
Anniston, Alabama 36206

Return to Sender
2501 Barclay Avenue
Portsmouth, Virginia 23702

Return to Sender Fan Club
3446 Dandelion Crescent
Virginia Beach, Virginia 23456

Suspicious Minds Fan Club
Julie Banhart
4610 Owen
Memphis, Tennessee 38122

TCB for Elvis Fans
Box 2655
Gastonia, North Carolina 28053

TCB Elvis Presley Fan Club of Virginia
Box 1158
Glen Allen, Virginia 23060

Then Now & Forever
Box 161130
Memphis, Tennessee 38116

TCB
Box 1925
Pittsfield, Massachusetts 01202

TCB Fan Club
2103 West 50th Street
Chicago, Illinois 60609

TCB in South Georgia
1220 N. Hutchinson Avenue
Adel, Georgia 31620

True Fans for Elvis Fan Club
Carole Brocher
Box 681
Saco, Maine 04072

We Remember Elvis Fan Club
Priscilla Parker
1215 Tennessee Avenue
Pittsburgh, Pennsylvania 15216

Welcome to Our Elvis World
Karen Oberender
5708 Van Dyke Road
Baltimore, Maryland 21206

FOREIGN FAN CLUBS
Elvis Till We Meet Again Fan Club
Doreen Oldroyd
124 Rankin Road
Sault Ste. Marie
Ontario, Canada P6A 4R8

Elvis in Canada
Fran Roberts
Box 6065
Station F
Hamilton
Ontario, Canada L9C 5S2

Elvis Presley King "O" Mania Fan Club
Mario Grenier
552 Croteau Quest
Thetford Mines, PQ
Canada G6G 6W7

Official Elvis Presley Fan Club
Todd Slaughter
P.O. Box 4
Leicester,
England

Elvisly Yours
Sid Shaw
P.O. Box 315
London NW10
England

The Elvis Collector
Earl Shilton
P.O. Box 10
Leicester LE9 7FD
England

Elvis—Today, Tomorrow & Forever Fan Club
Diana & Ray Hill
P.O. Box 41
Gloucester GL1 2LN
England

Elvis Is King Fan Club
David Trotter
59 Cambridge Road
New Silksworth
Sunderland SR3 2DQ
England

Elvis Presley Fan Club of Tasmania
Elaine Green
P.O. Box 165
Sorrell 7172
Tasmania, Australia

The Elvis Presley Fan Club of Queensland
Katrina Searle
P.O. Box 151
Chermside
Queensland 4032
Australia

Elvis Presley Fan Club of Victoria
Wayne Hawthorne
P.O. Box 82
Elsternwick
Victoria 3185
Australia